STATE PROFILES

STATE PROFILES

THE POPULATION AND ECONOMY OF EACH U.S. STATE

11th Edition
2019

Edited by Hannah Anderson Krog

Lanham, Maryland

Published in the United States of America
by Bernan Press, a wholly owned subsidiary of
The Rowman & Littlefield Publishing Group, Inc.
4501 Forbes Boulevard, Suite 200
Lanham, Maryland 20706

Bernan Press
800-462-6420
www.rowman.com/bernanpress

ISBN 13: 978-1-64143-380-8
E-ISBN: 978-1-64143-381-5

∞™ The paper used in this publication meets the minimum requirements of
American National Standard for Information Sciences—Permanence of
Paper for Printed Library Materials, ANSI/NISO Z39.48-1992.
Manufactured in the United States of America.

CONTENTS

LIST OF TABLES

The following tables are included for each state and the District of Columbia:

PREFACE

Bernan Press is pleased to present the eleventh edition of *State Profiles*, a publication that provides a state-by-state view of the United States. Topics covered include population composition by age, sex, race, and ethnicity; marital status; migration, origin, and language; households and housing; income and poverty; health insurance; employment; educational indicators; voting; crime; and other important aspects of the economy.

The publication's primary focus is on the 50 states and the District of Columbia, each of which possesses considerable differences in economic structure and demographics and has experienced various changes over time. Changes at the national level, including the diminished importance of agriculture and manufacturing and the growing influence of global trade, have resulted in today's information-based, service-providing economy. While national trends have laid the broad framework for change, each state has been affected differently. Cyclical fluctuations have also affected states in various ways during the nationwide recessions and the subsequent recovery periods. Recessions and recoveries spread unevenly among regions and states. Migration patterns have also reflected these changes, as states have experienced different influxes of workers from within the country and new residents from abroad.

Beyond the market forces, local and national government policies and expenditures on items such as education, health care, energy production and conservation, national defense, and homeland security have influenced economic circumstances.

The information provided in *State Profiles* aims to illuminate these trends. As such, the analysis and statistics are of interest not only to researchers and policy analysts but also to businesses seeking a broad basis for investments and expansion or relocation plans. The volume also profiles recent voting patterns, which will be of interest to political scientists.

DATA SELECTION

This edition of *State Profiles* generally continues the broad selection of information from previous editions. Most, but not all, of the data items have been updated through 2016, 2017, and even 2018, as demographic estimates from the U.S. Census Bureau became available.

As in the past, space constraints have influenced the amount of data presented for each state. The most meaningful and relevant data have thus been selected, analyzed, and highlighted. This edition expands upon the available information to include more detailed data on the demographics of each state, especially in regard to diversity of spoken languages and the foreign-born population. For most of the subjects addressed in this edition, further data are generally available from the source government agencies. Locations of sources of information are listed in notes and definitions at the end of the volume.

Although the editor has taken care to present accurate data, all statistical data are subject to a degree of error, resulting from sampling variability, erroneous reporting, and other causes. Many of the data are subject to subsequent revision.

The data in this book meet the publication standards of the federal agencies from which they were obtained. The responsibilities of the editor and publisher of this volume are limited to reasonable care in the reproduction and presentation of the data from the established sources.

Hannah Anderson Krog has edited the past five editions of *State Profiles*. She previously worked as an assistant editor for Bernan Press and is now a freelance writer and editor for several reference titles. She has a B.A. in journalism from the University of Maryland.

STATE PROFILES 2019 PROVIDES:

- Rankings of states for key demographic, economic, and social indicators
- A chapter for each state, complete with tables and figures that summarize and illustrate demographic, economic, and social characteristics
- Notes and definitions to assist with interpreting the information contained in this volume and to locate related data if desired

THE U.S. OVERVIEW. This short introduction to the demographics of the United States provides commentary on overall trends within the country.

THE STATE RANKINGS. The ranking tables that follow the national overview give state rankings by 33 characteristics, including population, demographic and age composition, income, per capita gross domestic product, homeownership, poverty, health indicators, education, and crime rates. These rankings provide the user with a quick analysis of the performance of each state in relation to the other states.

THE STATE CHAPTERS. The state chapters are the focus of this book. Each chapter follows a standard format and contains text highlighting the key features shown in the tables and figures. Some of these tables and figures contain references to the U.S. averages for the same characteristics.

Each of the state chapters is organized as follows:

Population. This table provides data on the state's total population and average annual population growth in comparison with the national average. It also shows the major population groups by sex, age, race, and ethnicity.

Marital status. The table shows the marital status for all men and women age 15 years and over.

Housing. This table showcases data pertaining to housing, such as number of households, types of households, housing characteristics, and median gross rent, mortgage, and monthly owner cost amounts.

Migration, origin, and language. This table provides statistics on residence one year ago, year of entry, place of origin, language spoken at home, and the native-born and foreign-born populations.

Income and poverty. Median household and family income and poverty rates by sex and age are contained in this table.

Health insurance coverage. This table provides information on health insurance, by type and coverage.

Employment. These tables illustrate each state's particular economic configuration. They exhibit employment status by detailed demographic group, labor force, participation rates, employment, unemployment, average wages and salaries by industry, and employment by family type.

Education. These tables provide the user with details on educational attainment, elementary and secondary school enrollment, student/teacher ratios, per student expenditures, and higher education enrollments.

Voter participation. Information is given on voter registration and voter participation in the 2018 mid-term election, categorized by sex and race/ethnicity.

Crime. This table include the number and rates of violent and property crime.

Government finance. These tables provide data on revenues and expenditures by source for each state and the District of Columbia. In addition, tax information for each state/district is included.

NOTES AND DEFINITIONS. Each chapter relies on the same standard set of federal data sources. Since the basic data sources are common to all chapters, the main body of the volume contains few footnotes. Basic data and corresponding definitions and sources are identified in the notes and definition section at the end of the volume. It provides brief descriptions, methodologies, data availability, information on calculations made by the editors, and references to additional sources of information.

Introduction

During the early 2000s, the United States experienced several economic fluctuations that had a great impact on the strength, size, and performance of its economy. The recession that began in March 2001 was concluded in a few months; however, the longer-lasting recession that began in December 2007 left a more serious impact on the country. The data in this book track the impact of that recession and subsequent recovery on the United States' economy over the past decade.

This edition of *State Profiles: The Population and Economy of Each U.S. State* creates a snapshot of the people and economy in each state and the District of Columbia. Each chapter (one per state/district) includes information on topics such as population, employment, marital status, crime, government finance, housing, education, and language.

Summary

The U.S. population grew 6.0 percent between 2010 and 2018. The District of Columbia experienced the largest population growth in the nation at 16.7 percent. The states with the largest population growth included Utah (14.4 percent), Texas (14.1 percent), Florida (13.3 percent), Colorado (13.2 percent), North Dakota (13.0 percent), Nevada (12.4 percent), Arizona (12.2 percent), Washington (12.1 percent), Idaho (11.9 percent), and South Carolina (9.9 percent). Two states' populations declined during that time period: Illinois (-0.7 percent) and West Virginia (-2.5 percent), and Connecticut's population increased marginally, with its percent change rounding to zero.

Utah had the highest percentage of population younger than 18 years old in 2018, with 29.5 percent of its population in this age group, followed by Texas at 25.8 percent. The District of Columbia had the smallest percent of minors, at 18.1 percent, followed by Vermont at 18.5 percent. Maine passed Florida to become the state with the highest percentage of people 65 years and older (20.6 percent and 20.5 percent of those states' populations are

in this age group, respectively). At 11.1 percent, Utah had the lowest percentage of senior residents, followed by Alaska at 11.8 percent and the District of Columbia at 12.1 percent.

In 2017, the median household income in the United States was $60,336. The District of Columbia had the highest median household income ($82,372), followed by Maryland ($80,776), New Jersey ($80,088), Hawaii ($77,765), and Massachusetts ($77,385). The states with the lowest median household incomes were West Virginia ($43,469), Mississippi ($43,529), Arkansas ($45,869), Louisiana ($46,145), and New Mexico ($46,744). Some correlation to the percentage of residents with a bachelor's degree or more can be inferred, as the District of Columbia, Massachusetts, Maryland, and New Jersey rank in the top five states in this category. Mississippi, West Virginia, Arkansas, and Louisiana rank in the bottom five states in this category. The unemployment rate for the United States was 3.9 percent in 2018, which was down from 4.4 percent in 2017. Alaska had the highest percentage of unemployed residents in 2018 (6.6 percent), followed by the District of Columbia (5.6 percent) and West Virginia (5.3 percent). Hawaii (2.4 percent), New Hampshire (2.5 percent), and Iowa (2.5 percent) had the lowest percentage of unemployed residents.

In the United States in 2017, 13.4 percent of the population lived below the poverty level. Mississippi, which had the second lowest median household income, had the highest poverty rate, with 19.8 percent of its residents below the poverty level. New Hampshire had the lowest poverty rate (7.7 percent). Louisiana had the highest rate of persons younger than 18 years of age below the poverty level (28.0 percent), followed by New Mexico (27.2 percent), Mississippi (26.9 percent), West Virginia (25.9 percent), and the District of Columbia (25.6 percent). The states with the fewest residents under 18 years of age below the poverty level included New Hampshire (10.3 percent), Utah (10.7 percent), North Dakota (10.9 percent), Hawaii (11.5 percent), and Minnesota (11.8 percent).

UNITED STATES RANKINGS

Population, 2018

Rank	State	Population
	United States......................	327,167,434
1	California....................	39,557,045
2	Texas..........................	28,701,845
3	Florida........................	21,299,325
4	New York.....................	19,542,209
5	Pennsylvania................	12,807,060
6	Illinois.........................	12,741,080
7	Ohio............................	11,689,442
8	Georgia........................	10,519,475
9	North Carolina..............	10,383,620
10	Michigan	9,995,915
11	New Jersey	8,908,520
12	Virginia........................	8,517,685
13	Washington	7,535,591
14	Arizona........................	7,171,646
15	Massachusetts	6,902,149
16	Tennessee	6,770,010
17	Indiana	6,691,878
18	Missouri	6,126,452
19	Maryland	6,042,718
20	Wisconsin	5,813,568
21	Colorado	5,695,564
22	Minnesota	5,611,179
23	South Carolina	5,084,127
24	Alabama	4,887,871
25	Louisiana	4,659,978
26	Kentucky	4,468,402
27	Oregon	4,190,713
28	Oklahoma	3,943,079
29	Connecticut	3,572,665
30	Utah	3,161,105
31	Iowa	3,156,145
32	Nevada	3,034,392
33	Arkansas	3,013,825
34	Mississippi	2,986,530
35	Kansas	2,911,505
36	New Mexico	2,095,428
37	Nebraska......................	1,929,268
38	West Virginia.................	1,805,832
39	Idaho...........................	1,754,208
40	Hawaii	1,420,491
41	New Hampshire..............	1,356,458
42	Maine	1,338,404
43	Montana	1,062,305
44	Rhode Island.................	1,057,315
45	Delaware	967,171
46	South Dakota	882,235
47	North Dakota.................	760,077
48	Alaska	737,438
49	District of Columbia	702,455
50	Vermont	626,299
51	Wyoming	577,737

Population, Percent Change, 2010–2018

Rank	State	Percent
	United States......................	6.0
1	District of Columbia	16.7
2	Utah	14.4
3	Texas...........................	14.1
4	Florida	13.3
5	Colorado	13.2
6	North Dakota	13.0
7	Nevada	12.4
8	Arizona	12.2
9	Washington	12.1
10	Idaho...........................	11.9
11	South Carolina	9.9
12	Oregon	9.4
13	North Carolina...............	8.9
14	Georgia	8.6
15	South Dakota	8.4
16	Delaware	7.7
17	Montana	7.4
18	Tennessee	6.7
19	Virginia	6.5
20	California......................	6.2
21	Minnesota	5.8
22	Nebraska	5.6
23	Massachusetts	5.4
24	Oklahoma	5.1
25	Maryland	4.7
26	Hawaii	4.4
27	Alaska	3.8
28	Iowa	3.6
29	Arkansas	3.4
30	Indiana	3.2
31	New Hampshire..............	3.0
31	Kentucky	3.0
33	Louisiana	2.8
34	Wyoming	2.5
35	Missouri	2.3
35	Alabama	2.3
37	Wisconsin	2.2
38	Kansas	2.0
39	New Mexico	1.8
40	New Jersey	1.3
40	Ohio	1.3
42	Michigan	1.1
43	New York......................	0.8
43	Pennsylvania.................	0.8
43	Maine	0.8
46	Mississippi....................	0.6
47	Rhode Island.................	0.5
48	Vermont	0.1
49	Connecticut	Z
50	Illinois	-0.7
51	West Virginia.................	-2.5

Z = Value greater than zero but less than half of the unit shown.

Percent Population Under 18 Years Old, 2018

Rank	State	Percent
	United States......................	22.4
1	Utah	29.5
2	Texas...........................	25.8
3	Idaho...........................	25.5
4	Alaska	24.9
5	Nebraska	24.7
5	South Dakota	24.7
7	Oklahoma	24.3
8	Kansas	24.2
9	Georgia	23.8
10	Mississippi	23.6
11	Louisiana	23.5
11	North Dakota.................	23.5
13	Indiana	23.4
14	Arkansas	23.3
14	Wyoming	23.3
16	Minnesota	23.2
16	Iowa	23.2
18	New Mexico	23.0
19	Arizona	22.9
20	California......................	22.7
20	Nevada	22.7
22	Kentucky	22.6
23	Missouri	22.5
24	Illinois	22.4
25	Alabama	22.3
26	Tennessee	22.2
26	Colorado	22.2
26	Ohio	22.2
26	Maryland	22.2
26	North Carolina...............	22.2
31	Washington	22.1
32	Virginia	22.0
32	Wisconsin	22.0
34	New Jersey	21.9
35	South Carolina	21.8
36	Michigan	21.7
37	Montana	21.6
38	Hawaii	21.4
39	Delaware	21.1
40	Oregon	20.8
40	New York......................	20.8
42	Pennsylvania.................	20.7
43	Connecticut	20.6
44	West Virginia.................	20.2
45	Florida	19.9
46	Massachusetts	19.8
47	Rhode Island.................	19.4
48	New Hampshire..............	19.0
49	Maine	18.7
50	Vermont	18.5
51	District of Columbia	18.1

Percent Population 65 Years and Over, 2018

Rank	State	Percent
	United States	16.0
1	Maine	20.6
2	Florida	20.5
3	West Virginia	19.9
4	Vermont	19.4
5	Montana	18.7
5	Delaware	18.7
7	Hawaii	18.4
8	Pennsylvania	18.2
9	New Hampshire	18.1
10	South Carolina	17.7
11	Oregon	17.6
12	Arizona	17.5
12	New Mexico	17.5
14	Rhode Island	17.2
14	Connecticut	17.2
14	Michigan	17.2
17	Iowa	17.1
17	Ohio	17.1
19	Arkansas	17.0
19	Wisconsin	17.0
21	Alabama	16.9
21	Missouri	16.9
23	South Dakota	16.6
24	Wyoming	16.5
24	Massachusetts	16.5
26	New York	16.4
26	Tennessee	16.4
26	Kentucky	16.4
29	North Carolina	16.3
30	New Jersey	16.1
31	Mississippi	15.9
31	Kansas	15.9
31	Idaho	15.9
31	Minnesota	15.9
35	Indiana	15.8
36	Nebraska	15.7
36	Oklahoma	15.7
36	Nevada	15.7
39	Illinois	15.6
40	Washington	15.4
40	Virginia	15.4
40	Louisiana	15.4
40	Maryland	15.4
44	North Dakota	15.3
44	California	14.3
46	Colorado	14.2
47	Georgia	13.9
48	Texas	12.6
49	District of Columbia	12.1
50	Alaska	11.8
51	Utah	11.1

Percent White Alone, 2018

Rank	State	Percent
	United States	76.5
1	Maine	94.6
2	Vermont	94.2
3	West Virginia	93.5
4	New Hampshire	93.2
5	Idaho	93.0
6	Wyoming	92.6
7	Iowa	90.7
7	Utah	90.7
9	Montana	89.0
10	Nebraska	88.3
11	Kentucky	87.6
12	Wisconsin	87.1
12	Colorado	87.1
14	North Dakota	87.0
15	Oregon	86.8
16	Kansas	86.4
17	Indiana	85.1
18	South Dakota	84.4
19	Minnesota	84.1
20	Rhode Island	83.9
21	Missouri	83.0
22	Arizona	82.8
23	New Mexico	82.0
24	Ohio	81.9
25	Pennsylvania	81.8
26	Massachusetts	80.8
27	Connecticut	80.0
28	Michigan	79.3
29	Arkansas	79.1
30	Washington	78.9
31	Texas	78.8
32	Tennessee	78.5
33	Florida	77.3
34	Illinois	76.9
35	Nevada	74.3
36	Oklahoma	74.2
37	California	72.1
38	New Jersey	72.0
39	North Carolina	70.6
40	New York	69.7
41	Virginia	69.5
41	Delaware	69.5
43	Alabama	69.1
44	South Carolina	68.5
45	Alaska	65.3
46	Louisiana	62.9
47	Georgia	60.5
48	Mississippi	59.1
49	Maryland	58.8
50	District of Columbia	45.6
51	Hawaii	25.6

Percent Black or African American Alone, 2018

Rank	State	Percent
	United States	13.4
1	District of Columbia	46.4
2	Mississippi	37.8
3	Louisiana	32.7
4	Georgia	32.4
5	Maryland	30.9
6	South Carolina	27.1
7	Alabama	26.8
8	Delaware	23.0
9	North Carolina	22.2
10	Virginia	19.9
11	New York	17.6
12	Tennessee	17.1
13	Florida	16.9
14	Arkansas	15.7
15	New Jersey	15.0
16	Illinois	14.6
17	Michigan	14.1
18	Ohio	13.0
19	Texas	12.8
20	Connecticut	12.0
20	Pennsylvania	12.0
22	Missouri	11.8
23	Nevada	10.1
24	Indiana	9.8
25	Massachusetts	8.9
26	Kentucky	8.4
26	Rhode Island	8.4
28	Oklahoma	7.8
29	Minnesota	6.8
30	Wisconsin	6.7
31	California	6.5
32	Kansas	6.1
33	Nebraska	5.1
33	Arizona	5.1
35	Colorado	4.6
36	Washington	4.3
37	Iowa	4.0
38	Alaska	3.8
39	West Virginia	3.6
40	North Dakota	3.4
41	New Mexico	2.6
42	South Dakota	2.4
43	Oregon	2.2
43	Hawaii	2.2
45	New Hampshire	1.7
46	Maine	1.6
47	Utah	1.4
47	Vermont	1.4
49	Wyoming	1.3
50	Idaho	0.9
51	Montana	0.6

Percent American Indian and Alaska Native Alone, 2018

Rank	State	Percent
	United States......................	1.3
1	Alaska	15.4
2	New Mexico	10.9
3	Oklahoma	9.3
4	South Dakota	9.0
5	Montana	6.6
6	North Dakota	5.5
7	Arizona.............................	5.3
8	Wyoming	2.7
9	Washington	1.9
10	Oregon	1.8
11	Idaho................................	1.7
11	Nevada	1.7
13	California	1.6
13	Colorado	1.6
13	North Carolina	1.6
16	Utah	1.5
16	Nebraska	1.5
18	Minnesota	1.4
19	Kansas	1.2
19	Wisconsin	1.2
21	Rhode Island.....................	1.1
22	Texas	1.0
22	Arkansas	1.0
22	New York	1.0
25	Louisiana	0.8
26	Michigan	0.7
26	Maine	0.7
26	Alabama	0.7
26	Delaware	0.7
30	Mississippi	0.6
30	New Jersey	0.6
30	District of Columbia	0.6
30	Maryland	0.6
30	Illinois	0.6
30	Missouri............................	0.6
30	Connecticut.......................	0.6
37	Virginia	0.5
37	South Carolina	0.5
37	Iowa	0.5
37	Georgia	0.5
37	Florida	0.5
37	Massachusetts	0.5
37	Tennessee	0.5
44	Indiana	0.4
44	Hawaii	0.4
44	Vermont	0.4
44	Pennsylvania	0.4
48	New Hampshire..................	0.3
48	Kentucky	0.3
48	Ohio	0.3
48	West Virginia.....................	0.3

Percent Asian Alone, 2018

Rank	State	Percent
	United States......................	5.9
1	Hawaii	37.6
2	California..........................	15.3
3	New Jersey	10.0
4	Washington.......................	9.3
5	New York	9.0
6	Nevada	8.7
7	Massachusetts	7.1
8	Virginia.............................	6.9
9	Maryland...........................	6.7
10	Alaska	6.6
11	Illinois	5.9
12	Texas	5.2
13	Minnesota	5.1
14	Connecticut.......................	4.9
15	Oregon	4.8
16	District of Columbia	4.4
17	Georgia	4.3
18	Delaware	4.1
19	Pennsylvania	3.7
19	Arizona.............................	3.7
21	Rhode Island.....................	3.6
22	Colorado	3.5
23	Michigan	3.4
24	North Carolina	3.2
25	Kansas	3.1
26	Wisconsin	3.0
26	New Hampshire..................	3.0
26	Florida	3.0
29	Iowa	2.7
29	Nebraska	2.7
29	Utah	2.7
32	Indiana	2.5
32	Ohio	2.5
34	Oklahoma	2.3
35	Missouri............................	2.1
36	Vermont	2.0
37	Tennessee	1.9
38	Louisiana	1.8
38	New Mexico	1.8
38	South Carolina	1.8
38	North Dakota.....................	1.8
42	South Dakota	1.7
42	Arkansas	1.7
44	Kentucky	1.6
44	Idaho................................	1.6
46	Alabama	1.5
47	Maine	1.2
48	Mississippi	1.1
48	Wyoming	1.1
50	Montana	0.9
51	West Virginia.....................	0.8

Percent Native Hawaiian and Other Pacific Islander Alone, 2018

Rank	State	Percent
	United States......................	0.2
1	Hawaii	10.2
2	Alaska	1.4
3	Utah	1.1
4	Nevada	0.8
4	Washington.......................	0.8
6	California	0.5
6	Oregon	0.5
8	Arkansas	0.4
9	Arizona.............................	0.3
10	Idaho................................	0.2
10	Rhode Island.....................	0.2
10	Colorado	0.2
10	Oklahoma	0.2
10	New Mexico	0.2
10	Missouri............................	0.2
16	Texas	0.1
16	District of Columbia	0.1
16	New York	0.1
16	Iowa	0.1
16	North Carolina	0.1
16	Kansas	0.1
16	Nebraska	0.1
16	Georgia	0.1
16	Virginia.............................	0.1
16	Florida	0.1
16	New Jersey	0.1
16	Maryland...........................	0.1
16	Delaware	0.1
16	Connecticut.......................	0.1
16	Massachusetts	0.1
16	Alabama	0.1
16	South Carolina	0.1
16	Wyoming	0.1
16	Tennessee	0.1
16	Kentucky	0.1
16	South Dakota	0.1
16	Montana	0.1
16	Pennsylvania	0.1
16	North Dakota.....................	0.1
16	Minnesota	0.1
16	Indiana	0.1
16	Illinois	0.1
16	Louisiana	0.1
16	Mississippi	0.1
16	Ohio	0.1
16	Wisconsin	0.1
47	New Hampshire..................	Z
47	Michigan	Z
47	Vermont	Z
47	Maine	Z
47	West Virginia.....................	Z

Z = Value greater than zero but less than half of the unit shown.

Percent Two or More Races, 2018

Rank	State	Percent
	United States	2.7
1	Hawaii	24.0
2	Alaska	7.4
3	Oklahoma	6.2
4	Washington	4.8
5	Nevada	4.5
6	California	3.9
7	Oregon	3.9
8	Colorado	3.1
8	Virginia	3.1
10	Kansas	3.0
11	Maryland	2.9
11	Arizona	2.9
13	Rhode Island	2.8
13	District of Columbia	2.8
13	Montana	2.8
16	Delaware	2.7
17	Utah	2.6
17	New York	2.6
17	New Mexico	2.6
20	Minnesota	2.5
20	Massachusetts	2.5
20	Idaho	2.5
20	Michigan	2.5
24	Connecticut	2.4
24	South Dakota	2.4
26	Missouri	2.3
26	Ohio	2.3
26	North Carolina	2.3
26	Nebraska	2.3
26	New Jersey	2.3
31	North Dakota	2.2
31	Wyoming	2.2
31	Florida	2.2
31	Georgia	2.2
31	Arkansas	2.2
36	Indiana	2.1
36	Pennsylvania	2.1
38	Texas	2.0
38	Illinois	2.0
38	Kentucky	2.0
38	Wisconsin	2.0
38	Vermont	2.0
38	Tennessee	2.0
44	South Carolina	1.9
44	Iowa	1.9
46	Maine	1.8
46	West Virginia	1.8
46	New Hampshire	1.8
49	Alabama	1.7
49	Louisiana	1.7
51	Mississippi	1.3

Percent Hispanic or Latino,[1] 2018

Rank	State	Percent
	United States	18.3
1	New Mexico	49.1
2	Texas	39.6
3	California	39.3
4	Arizona	31.6
5	Nevada	29.0
6	Florida	26.1
7	Colorado	21.7
8	New Jersey	20.6
9	New York	19.2
10	Illinois	17.4
11	Connecticut	16.5
12	Rhode Island	15.9
13	Utah	14.2
14	Oregon	13.3
15	Washington	12.9
16	Idaho	12.7
17	Massachusetts	12.3
18	Kansas	12.1
19	District of Columbia	11.3
20	Nebraska	11.2
21	Oklahoma	10.9
22	Hawaii	10.7
23	Maryland	10.4
24	Wyoming	10.1
25	Georgia	9.8
26	Virginia	9.6
26	North Carolina	9.6
28	Delaware	9.5
29	Arkansas	7.7
30	Pennsylvania	7.6
31	Alaska	7.2
32	Indiana	7.1
33	Wisconsin	6.9
34	Iowa	6.2
35	South Carolina	5.8
36	Tennessee	5.6
37	Minnesota	5.5
38	Louisiana	5.2
38	Michigan	5.2
40	Alabama	4.4
41	Missouri	4.3
42	South Dakota	4.1
43	Montana	4.0
44	Ohio	3.9
44	North Dakota	3.9
44	New Hampshire	3.9
47	Kentucky	3.8
48	Mississippi	3.4
49	Vermont	2.0
50	Maine	1.7
50	West Virginia	1.7

[1] May be of any race.

Percent White Alone, Not Hispanic or Latino, 2018

Rank	State	Percent
	United States	60.4
1	Maine	93.1
2	Vermont	92.5
3	West Virginia	92.1
4	New Hampshire	90.0
5	Montana	85.9
6	Iowa	85.3
7	Kentucky	84.3
8	North Dakota	84.0
9	Wyoming	83.8
10	Idaho	81.7
11	South Dakota	81.4
12	Wisconsin	81.1
13	Minnesota	79.5
14	Missouri	79.3
15	Indiana	78.9
16	Ohio	78.7
17	Nebraska	78.6
18	Utah	78.0
19	Pennsylvania	76.1
20	Kansas	75.7
21	Oregon	75.3
22	Michigan	74.9
23	Tennessee	73.7
24	Arkansas	72.2
25	Rhode Island	72.0
26	Massachusetts	71.4
27	Washington	68.0
28	Colorado	67.9
29	Connecticut	66.5
30	Alabama	65.4
31	Oklahoma	65.3
32	South Carolina	63.7
33	North Carolina	62.8
34	Delaware	61.9
35	Virginia	61.5
36	Illinois	61.0
37	Alaska	60.3
38	Louisiana	58.6
39	Mississippi	56.5
40	New York	55.4
41	New Jersey	54.9
42	Arizona	54.4
43	Florida	53.5
44	Georgia	52.4
45	Maryland	50.5
46	Nevada	48.7
47	Texas	41.5
48	New Mexico	37.1
48	District of Columbia	37.1
50	California	36.8
51	Hawaii	21.8

Birth Rate, 2017

Rank	State	Rate per 1,000 population
	United States	11.8
1	Utah	15.7
2	North Dakota	14.2
3	Alaska	14.1
4	South Dakota	14.0
5	District of Columbia	13.8
6	Texas	13.5
7	Nebraska	13.4
8	Louisiana	13.0
9	Idaho	12.9
10	Oklahoma	12.8
11	Arkansas	12.5
11	Kansas	12.5
11	Mississippi	12.5
14	Georgia	12.4
15	Hawaii	12.3
15	Indiana	12.3
15	Kentucky	12.3
15	Minnesota	12.3
19	Iowa	12.2
20	Alabama	12.1
20	Tennessee	12.1
22	California	11.9
22	Missouri	11.9
22	Nevada	11.9
22	Virginia	11.9
22	Wyoming	11.9
27	Maryland	11.8
27	Washington	11.8
29	Arizona	11.7
29	Illinois	11.7
29	North Carolina	11.7
29	Ohio	11.7
33	New York	11.6
34	Colorado	11.5
35	New Mexico	11.4
35	South Carolina	11.4
37	Delaware	11.3
38	Michigan	11.2
38	Montana	11.2
38	New Jersey	11.2
38	Wisconsin	11.2
42	Pennsylvania	10.8
43	Florida	10.7
44	Oregon	10.5
45	Massachusetts	10.3
45	West Virginia	10.3
47	Rhode Island	10.0
48	Connecticut	9.8
49	Maine	9.2
50	Vermont	9.1
51	New Hampshire	9.0

Drug Overdose Death Rate, 2017

Rank	State	Age-adjusted rate per 100,000 population
	United States	21.7
1	West Virginia	57.8
2	Ohio	46.3
3	Pennsylvania	44.3
4	District of Columbia	44.0
5	Kentucky	37.2
6	Delaware	37.0
6	New Hampshire	37.0
8	Maryland	36.3
9	Maine	34.4
10	Massachusetts	31.8
11	Rhode Island	31.0
12	Connecticut	30.9
13	New Jersey	30.0
14	Indiana	29.4
15	Michigan	27.8
16	Tennessee	26.6
17	Florida	25.1
18	New Mexico	24.8
19	Louisiana	24.5
20	North Carolina	24.1
21	Missouri	23.4
22	Vermont	23.2
23	Utah	22.3
24	Arizona	22.2
25	Illinois	21.6
25	Nevada	21.6
27	Wisconsin	21.2
28	South Carolina	20.5
29	Alaska	20.2
30	Oklahoma	20.1
31	New York	19.4
32	Alabama	18.0
33	Virginia	17.9
34	Colorado	17.6
35	Arkansas	15.5
36	Washington	15.2
37	Georgia	14.7
38	Idaho	14.4
39	Hawaii	13.8
40	Minnesota	13.3
41	Oregon	12.4
42	Mississippi	12.2
42	Wyoming	12.2
44	Kansas	11.8
45	California	11.7
45	Montana	11.7
47	Iowa	11.5
48	Texas	10.5
49	North Dakota	9.2
50	South Dakota	8.5
51	Nebraska	8.1

Voter Turnout, November 2018

Rank	State	Percent voted, total population
	United States	49.0
1	Maine	64.5
2	Montana	63.0
3	Wisconsin	62.6
4	North Dakota	59.8
5	Minnesota	59.5
6	Oregon	58.2
7	Michigan	57.7
8	Iowa	56.2
9	Washington	56.0
10	District of Columbia	55.2
11	Vermont	54.2
12	Utah	54.0
13	Colorado	53.8
13	Mississippi	53.8
15	Missouri	53.7
16	Kansas	53.6
17	New Hampshire	53.3
18	Arizona	52.2
19	Pennsylvania	52.1
20	Georgia	52.0
20	Virginia	52.0
22	Kentucky	51.8
23	Wyoming	51.2
24	Ohio	51.1
25	South Dakota	51.0
26	Alaska	50.2
27	Massachusetts	50.0
28	Maryland	49.7
29	North Carolina	49.3
30	Alabama	48.8
30	Delaware	48.8
32	Illinois	48.7
32	Rhode Island	48.7
34	Connecticut	48.3
34	New Jersey	48.3
36	Louisiana	47.9
37	Tennessee	47.8
38	Nebraska	47.3
39	Indiana	47.2
40	Oklahoma	47.1
41	Florida	47.0
42	South Carolina	46.9
43	New Mexico	45.3
44	Idaho	45.2
45	California	43.8
45	New York	43.8
47	West Virginia	43.4
48	Nevada	43.3
49	Texas	42.2
50	Arkansas	40.6
51	Hawaii	40.4

Percent of Persons 25 Years and Over with a Bachelor's Degree or More, 2017

Rank	State	Percent
	United States	32.0
1	District of Columbia	57.3
2	Massachusetts	43.4
3	Colorado	41.2
4	Maryland	39.7
4	New Jersey	39.7
6	Connecticut	38.7
6	Virginia	38.7
8	Vermont	38.3
9	New Hampshire	36.9
10	Minnesota	36.1
11	New York	36.0
12	Washington	35.5
13	Utah	34.6
14	Illinois	34.4
15	Kansas	33.7
15	Oregon	33.7
17	California	33.6
18	Rhode Island	33.5
19	Hawaii	32.9
20	Montana	32.3
21	Maine	32.1
22	Nebraska	31.7
23	Delaware	31.5
24	Pennsylvania	31.4
25	North Carolina	31.3
26	Georgia	30.9
27	North Dakota	30.7
28	Wisconsin	30.4
29	Florida	29.7
30	Texas	29.6
31	Arizona	29.4
32	Michigan	29.1
32	Missouri	29.1
34	Iowa	28.9
35	Alaska	28.8
36	South Dakota	28.1
37	Ohio	28.0
37	South Carolina	28.0
39	Wyoming	27.6
40	Tennessee	27.3
41	New Mexico	27.1
42	Idaho	26.8
42	Indiana	26.8
44	Alabama	25.5
44	Oklahoma	25.5
46	Nevada	24.9
47	Kentucky	24.0
48	Louisiana	23.8
49	Arkansas	23.4
50	Mississippi	21.9
51	West Virginia	20.2

Violent Crime, 2017

Rank	State	Rate per 100,000 population
	United States	394.0
1	District of Columbia[1]	1,004.9
2	Alaska	829.0
3	New Mexico	783.5
4	Tennessee	651.5
5	Louisiana	557.0
6	Nevada	555.9
7	Arkansas	554.9
8	Missouri	530.3
9	Alabama	524.2
10	Arizona	508.0
11	South Carolina	506.2
12	Maryland	500.2
13	Oklahoma	456.2
14	Delaware	453.4
15	Michigan	450.0
16	California	449.3
17	Texas	438.9
18	Illinois	438.8
19	South Dakota	433.6
20	Kansas	413.0
21	Florida	408.0
22	Indiana	399.0
23	Montana	377.1
24	Colorado	368.1
25	North Carolina	363.7
26	Massachusetts	358.0
27	Georgia	357.2
28	New York	356.7
29	West Virginia	350.7
30	Wisconsin	319.9
31	Pennsylvania	313.3
32	Nebraska	305.9
33	Washington	304.5
34	Ohio	297.5
35	Iowa	293.4
36	Mississippi	285.7
37	Oregon	281.8
38	North Dakota	281.3
39	Hawaii	250.6
40	Utah	238.9
41	Minnesota	238.3
42	Wyoming	237.5
43	Rhode Island	232.2
44	New Jersey	228.8
45	Connecticut	228.0
46	Idaho	226.4
47	Kentucky	225.8
48	Virginia	208.2
49	New Hampshire	198.7
50	Vermont	165.8
51	Maine	121.0

[1] Includes offenses reported by the Metro Transit Police and the District of Columbia Fire and Emergency Medical Services: Arson

Property Crime, 2017

Rank	State	Rate per 100,000 population
	United States	2,362.2
1	District of Columbia	4,283.9
2	New Mexico	3,941.7
3	Alaska	3,542.1
4	Louisiana	3,366.8
5	South Carolina	3,195.9
6	Washington	3,173.6
7	Arkansas	3,078.6
8	Oregon	2,986.5
9	Alabama	2,957.3
10	Tennessee	2,940.6
11	Arizona	2,914.9
12	Oklahoma	2,876.4
13	Georgia	2,860.2
14	Missouri	2,833.9
15	Hawaii	2,829.5
16	Kansas	2,800.9
17	Utah	2,780.2
18	Mississippi	2,733.9
19	Colorado	2,701.6
20	Nevada	2,612.4
21	Montana	2,591.6
22	Texas	2,562.6
23	North Carolina	2,545.3
24	Florida	2,512.4
25	California	2,496.7
26	Delaware	2,440.6
27	Ohio	2,419.1
28	Indiana	2,416.9
29	Nebraska	2,274.0
30	Maryland	2,222.3
31	North Dakota	2,197.8
32	Minnesota	2,191.5
33	Kentucky	2,129.1
34	Iowa	2,125.3
35	Illinois	2,011.4
36	South Dakota	1,876.2
37	West Virginia	1,852.0
38	Wyoming	1,830.4
39	Wisconsin	1,808.3
40	Michigan	1,800.0
41	Virginia	1,792.9
42	Connecticut	1,769.9
43	Rhode Island	1,751.6
44	Pennsylvania	1,649.4
45	Idaho	1,635.4
46	New Jersey	1,555.5
47	New York	1,514.2
48	Maine	1,507.1
49	Massachusetts	1,437.0
50	Vermont	1,436.7
51	New Hampshire	1,381.8

State & Local Government Employment, 2018
(Full-time equivalent employees)

Rank	State	State & local employees per 1,000 residents
	United States......................	50.9
1	Wyoming	86.8
2	District of Columbia	72.8
3	Alaska	70.3
4	Kansas	69.5
5	Vermont	63.3
6	Nebraska	63.2
7	Mississippi	62.6
8	North Dakota	61.9
9	New York	61.7
10	New Mexico	59.4
11	Iowa	59.0
12	Alabama	58.1
13	West Virginia	56.6
14	Arkansas	56.2
15	Louisiana	55.4
16	North Carolina	55.0
17	Kentucky	54.6
18	South Dakota	54.5
19	Minnesota	53.9
20	Montana	53.8
21	South Carolina	53.2
21	New Jersey	53.2
23	Virginia	53.1
24	Oklahoma	52.9
25	Hawaii	52.8
26	Texas	52.6
26	Colorado	52.6
28	Maine	52.0
28	Missouri	52.0
30	Connecticut	51.7
31	New Hampshire....................	51.6
32	Delaware	51.0
33	Washington........................	50.5
34	Ohio	50.4
35	Maryland	50.3
36	Georgia	49.7
37	Tennessee	49.6
38	Indiana	49.5
39	Massachusetts	49.4
40	Oregon	49.3
41	Utah	49.2
42	Wisconsin	48.9
43	Idaho.............................	48.8
44	Illinois............................	48.4
45	California..........................	47.3
46	Rhode Island......................	45.3
47	Pennsylvania......................	43.7
47	Michigan	43.7
49	Florida	42.2
50	Arizona	38.9
51	Nevada	38.3

Unemployment Rate, 2018

Rank	State	Unemployment rate
	United States......................	3.9
1	Alaska	6.6
2	District of Columbia	5.6
3	West Virginia......................	5.3
4	Louisiana	4.9
4	New Mexico	4.9
6	Arizona	4.8
6	Mississippi	4.8
8	Nevada	4.6
8	Ohio	4.6
10	Washington	4.5
11	Illinois............................	4.3
11	Kentucky	4.3
11	Pennsylvania......................	4.3
14	California..........................	4.2
14	Oregon	4.2
16	Connecticut	4.1
16	Michigan	4.1
16	New Jersey	4.1
16	New York..........................	4.1
16	Rhode Island......................	4.1
16	Wyoming	4.1
22	Alabama	3.9
22	Georgia	3.9
22	Maryland	3.9
22	North Carolina.....................	3.9
22	Texas	3.9
27	Delaware	3.8
28	Arkansas	3.7
28	Montana	3.7
30	Florida	3.6
31	Tennessee	3.5
32	Indiana	3.4
32	Kansas	3.4
32	Maine	3.4
32	Oklahoma	3.4
32	South Carolina	3.4
37	Colorado	3.3
37	Massachusetts	3.3
39	Missouri...........................	3.2
40	Utah	3.1
41	South Dakota	3.0
41	Virginia	3.0
41	Wisconsin	3.0
44	Minnesota	2.9
45	Idaho..............................	2.8
45	Nebraska	2.8
47	Vermont	2.7
48	North Dakota	2.6
49	Iowa	2.5
49	New Hampshire....................	2.5
51	Hawaii	2.4

Employees on Nonfarm Payrolls, Percent Change, 2017–2018

Rank	State	Percent
	United States......................	1.5
1	Nevada	3.4
2	Utah	3.2
3	Idaho.............................	3.1
4	Arizona	2.8
5	Washington........................	2.6
6	Florida	2.4
6	Colorado	2.4
6	South Carolina	2.4
9	Texas	2.3
10	California..........................	2.0
11	Georgia	1.9
12	Oregon	1.8
13	North Carolina.....................	1.7
14	Tennessee	1.6
15	Oklahoma	1.5
15	West Virginia......................	1.5
17	New Mexico	1.3
18	Alabama	1.2
19	New York..........................	1.1
19	Michigan	1.1
19	Virginia............................	1.1
19	Montana	1.1
19	Pennsylvania......................	1.1
19	South Dakota	1.1
19	Arkansas	1.1
26	Delaware	1.0
26	Indiana	1.0
26	District of Columbia	1.0
29	New Jersey	0.9
29	Illinois............................	0.9
29	Kansas	0.9
29	Massachusetts	0.9
33	Wisconsin	0.8
33	New Hampshire....................	0.8
33	Minnesota	0.8
36	Iowa	0.7
36	Maine	0.7
36	Maryland	0.7
36	Wyoming	0.7
40	Ohio	0.6
40	North Dakota	0.6
42	Rhode Island......................	0.5
42	Kentucky	0.5
42	Hawaii	0.5
42	Missouri...........................	0.5
42	Louisiana	0.5
47	Nebraska	0.4
48	Mississippi	0.3
49	Vermont	0.2
50	Connecticut	0.1
51	Alaska	-0.6

- = Zero or rounds to zero.

Per Capita Personal Income, 2018 (2018 Dollars)			Real Gross Domestic Product in Chained (2012) Dollars, 2018			Real Gross Domestic Product in Chained (2012) Dollars, Percent Change, 2017–2018		
Rank	State	Dollars	Rank	State	Dollars (millions)	Rank	State	Percent
	United States	53,712		United States	18,566,442		United States	2.9
1	District of Columbia	81,882	1	California	2,677,939	1	Washington	5.7
2	Connecticut	74,561	2	Texas	1,676,679	2	Utah	4.3
3	Massachusetts	70,073	3	New York	1,436,957	3	Idaho	4.1
4	New York	68,667	4	Florida	916,975	4	Arizona	4.0
5	New Jersey	67,609	5	Illinois	764,212	5	California	3.5
6	Maryland	62,914	6	Pennsylvania	712,101	5	Colorado	3.5
7	California	62,586	7	Ohio	601,496	5	Florida	3.5
8	New Hampshire	61,405	8	New Jersey	554,672	8	Oregon	3.4
9	Washington	60,781	9	Georgia	522,424	9	Nevada	3.2
10	Wyoming	60,095	10	Washington	506,706	9	Texas	3.2
11	Alaska	59,687	11	Massachusetts	501,337	11	Tennessee	3.0
12	Virginia	56,952	12	North Carolina	496,110	12	North Carolina	2.9
13	Illinois	56,933	13	Virginia	476,388	13	Virginia	2.8
14	Colorado	56,846	14	Michigan	468,387	14	Massachusetts	2.7
15	Minnesota	56,374	15	Maryland	367,915	14	Michigan	2.7
16	Pennsylvania	55,349	16	Colorado	336,365	16	Georgia	2.6
17	Hawaii	54,565	17	Minnesota	331,377	17	North Dakota	2.5
18	Rhode Island	54,523	18	Indiana	326,148	17	Wisconsin	2.5
19	North Dakota	54,306	19	Tennessee	322,898	19	West Virginia	2.4
20	Vermont	53,598	20	Arizona	309,067	20	Missouri	2.3
21	Nebraska	52,110	21	Wisconsin	299,835	21	Minnesota	2.2
22	Delaware	51,449	22	Missouri	282,208	21	New Hampshire	2.2
23	Wisconsin	50,756	23	Connecticut	242,171	23	District of Columbia	2.1
24	Kansas	50,155	24	Louisiana	231,161	23	Illinois	2.1
25	South Dakota	50,141	25	Oregon	213,708	23	New York	2.1
26	Oregon	49,908	26	South Carolina	202,771	23	Pennsylvania	2.1
27	Florida	49,417	27	Alabama	196,876	26	Alabama	2.0
28	Texas	49,161	28	Oklahoma	193,030	26	New Jersey	2.0
29	Iowa	48,823	29	Kentucky	186,148	29	Indiana	1.9
30	Ohio	48,242	30	Iowa	170,749	29	Kansas	1.9
31	Maine	48,241	31	Utah	157,233	29	Maine	1.9
32	Nevada	48,225	32	Kansas	152,262	32	New Mexico	1.8
33	Michigan	47,582	33	Nevada	146,225	32	Ohio	1.8
34	Tennessee	47,179	34	District of Columbia	124,007	32	Oklahoma	1.8
35	Montana	47,120	35	Arkansas	115,933	35	Maryland	1.6
36	Indiana	46,646	36	Nebraska	112,170	35	South Carolina	1.6
37	Missouri	46,635	37	Mississippi	101,630	37	Nebraska	1.5
38	Oklahoma	46,128	38	New Mexico	92,591	38	Iowa	1.4
39	North Carolina	45,834	39	Hawaii	80,798	38	Kentucky	1.4
40	Georgia	45,745	40	New Hampshire	75,615	40	South Dakota	1.3
41	Louisiana	45,542	41	West Virginia	71,321	41	Vermont	1.2
42	Utah	45,340	42	Idaho	69,892	42	Louisiana	1.1
43	Arizona	43,650	43	Delaware	63,855	43	Connecticut	1.0
44	Idaho	43,155	44	Maine	56,689	43	Hawaii	1.0
45	South Carolina	42,736	45	Rhode Island	53,741	43	Mississippi	1.0
46	Arkansas	42,566	46	Alaska	52,311	46	Arkansas	0.9
47	Alabama	42,334	47	North Dakota	51,160	46	Montana	0.9
48	Kentucky	41,779	48	South Dakota	45,874	48	Rhode Island	0.6
49	New Mexico	41,198	49	Montana	44,801	49	Delaware	0.3
50	West Virginia	40,578	50	Wyoming	38,369	49	Wyoming	0.3
51	Mississippi	37,994	51	Vermont	30,013	51	Alaska	-0.3

Median Household Income, 2017

Rank	State	Dollars
	United States......................	60,336
1	District of Columbia	82,372
2	Maryland............................	80,776
3	New Jersey	80,088
4	Hawaii	77,765
5	Massachusetts.....................	77,385
6	Connecticut.........................	74,168
7	New Hampshire....................	73,381
8	Alaska	73,181
9	California............................	71,805
10	Virginia..............................	71,535
11	Washington.........................	70,979
12	Colorado............................	69,117
13	Minnesota...........................	68,388
14	Utah..................................	68,358
15	New York............................	64,894
16	Rhode Island.......................	63,870
17	Illinois...............................	62,992
18	Delaware............................	62,852
19	North Dakota.......................	61,843
20	Wyoming............................	60,434
21	Oregon...............................	60,212
22	Nebraska............................	59,970
23	Wisconsin...........................	59,305
24	Texas.................................	59,206
25	Pennsylvania.......................	59,195
26	Iowa..................................	58,570
27	Nevada...............................	58,003
28	Vermont.............................	57,513
29	Arizona..............................	56,581
30	South Dakota	56,521
31	Kansas...............................	56,422
32	Maine................................	56,277
33	Georgia..............................	56,183
34	Michigan............................	54,909
35	Indiana...............................	54,181
36	Ohio..................................	54,021
37	Missouri..............................	53,578
38	Montana.............................	53,386
39	North Carolina.....................	52,752
40	Florida...............................	52,594
41	Idaho.................................	52,225
42	Tennessee..........................	51,340
43	South Carolina	50,570
44	Oklahoma...........................	50,051
45	Kentucky............................	48,375
46	Alabama.............................	48,123
47	New Mexico	46,744
48	Louisiana	46,145
49	Arkansas............................	45,869
50	Mississippi..........................	43,529
51	West Virginia.......................	43,469

Median Family Income, 2017

Rank	State	Dollars
	United States......................	73,891
1	District of Columbia	106,528
2	Massachusetts.....................	98,758
3	Maryland............................	98,393
4	New Jersey	97,300
5	Connecticut.........................	93,870
6	Hawaii	91,460
7	New Hampshire....................	91,029
8	Alaska	86,831
9	Minnesota...........................	86,416
10	Virginia..............................	86,279
11	Colorado............................	84,918
12	Washington.........................	84,594
13	Rhode Island.......................	84,557
14	California............................	82,009
15	North Dakota.......................	81,869
16	New York............................	80,114
17	Illinois...............................	79,168
18	Utah..................................	77,940
19	Delaware............................	77,082
20	Pennsylvania.......................	75,949
21	Wisconsin...........................	75,413
22	Nebraska............................	75,112
23	Iowa..................................	75,076
24	Wyoming............................	74,868
25	Vermont.............................	74,426
26	South Dakota	73,236
27	Oregon...............................	73,202
28	Maine................................	72,177
29	Kansas...............................	72,057
30	Texas.................................	70,136
31	Michigan............................	69,664
32	Ohio..................................	69,632
33	Montana.............................	68,994
34	Nevada...............................	68,276
35	Indiana...............................	68,085
36	Georgia..............................	67,983
37	Arizona..............................	67,886
38	Missouri..............................	67,317
39	North Carolina.....................	65,964
40	Idaho.................................	64,178
41	Florida...............................	64,003
42	Tennessee..........................	62,926
43	South Carolina	62,432
44	Kentucky............................	61,593
45	Alabama.............................	61,512
46	Oklahoma...........................	61,471
47	Louisiana	60,510
48	New Mexico	58,308
49	Arkansas............................	57,421
50	West Virginia.......................	56,086
51	Mississippi..........................	55,937

Persons Below Poverty Level, 2017

Rank	State	Percent
	United States......................	13.4
1	Mississippi..........................	19.8
2	Louisiana	19.7
2	New Mexico	19.7
4	West Virginia.......................	19.1
5	Kentucky............................	17.2
6	Alabama.............................	16.9
7	District of Columbia	16.6
8	Arkansas............................	16.4
9	Oklahoma...........................	15.8
10	South Carolina	15.4
11	Tennessee..........................	15.0
12	Arizona..............................	14.9
12	Georgia..............................	14.9
14	North Carolina.....................	14.7
14	Texas.................................	14.7
16	Michigan............................	14.2
17	New York............................	14.1
18	Florida...............................	14.0
18	Ohio..................................	14.0
20	Delaware............................	13.6
21	Indiana...............................	13.5
22	Missouri..............................	13.4
23	California............................	13.3
24	Oregon...............................	13.2
25	Nevada...............................	13.0
25	South Dakota	13.0
27	Idaho.................................	12.8
28	Illinois...............................	12.6
29	Montana.............................	12.5
29	Pennsylvania.......................	12.5
31	Kansas...............................	11.9
32	Rhode Island.......................	11.6
33	Vermont.............................	11.3
33	Wisconsin...........................	11.3
33	Wyoming............................	11.3
36	Alaska	11.1
36	Maine................................	11.1
38	Washington.........................	11.0
39	Nebraska............................	10.8
40	Iowa..................................	10.7
41	Virginia..............................	10.6
42	Massachusetts.....................	10.5
43	Colorado............................	10.3
43	North Dakota.......................	10.3
45	New Jersey	10.0
46	Utah..................................	9.7
47	Connecticut.........................	9.6
48	Hawaii	9.5
48	Minnesota...........................	9.5
50	Maryland............................	9.3
51	New Hampshire....................	7.7

Persons Under 18 Years Old Below Poverty Level, 2017

Rank	State	Percent
	United States	18.4
1	Louisiana	28.0
2	New Mexico	27.2
3	Mississippi	26.9
4	West Virginia	25.9
5	District of Columbia	25.6
6	Alabama	24.6
7	South Carolina	22.6
8	Arkansas	22.5
9	Kentucky	22.4
10	Oklahoma	21.5
11	North Carolina	21.2
11	Tennessee	21.2
13	Georgia	21.0
14	Texas	20.9
15	Arizona	20.8
16	Florida	20.3
17	Ohio	20.1
18	Michigan	19.7
18	New York	19.7
20	Missouri	18.6
21	Delaware	18.5
21	Nevada	18.5
23	Indiana	18.4
24	California	18.1
25	Illinois	17.0
25	Pennsylvania	17.0
27	Rhode Island	16.6
27	South Dakota	16.6
29	Oregon	16.5
30	Idaho	15.3
31	Alaska	14.9
32	Kansas	14.8
33	Montana	14.7
34	Wisconsin	14.5
35	Washington	14.3
36	Nebraska	14.1
37	Virginia	14.0
38	New Jersey	13.9
39	Vermont	13.8
40	Massachusetts	13.5
41	Wyoming	13.3
42	Maine	13.1
43	Connecticut	12.6
44	Iowa	12.3
45	Colorado	12.0
45	Maryland	12.0
47	Minnesota	11.8
48	Hawaii	11.5
49	North Dakota	10.9
50	Utah	10.7
51	New Hampshire	10.3

Energy Consumption Per Capita, 2017

Rank	State	Million Btu
	United States	300.2
1	Louisiana	959.5
2	Wyoming	884.8
3	North Dakota	835.8
4	Alaska	822.0
5	Iowa	495.9
6	Texas	471.9
7	Nebraska	456.8
8	South Dakota	440.7
9	Oklahoma	418.0
10	West Virginia	416.3
11	Indiana	405.5
12	Montana	399.4
13	Mississippi	393.5
14	Alabama	389.9
15	Kentucky	372.3
16	Kansas	368.7
17	Arkansas	352.2
18	Minnesota	329.1
19	South Carolina	327.3
20	New Mexico	326.5
21	Tennessee	322.9
22	Idaho	322.2
23	Ohio	312.4
24	Wisconsin	311.8
25	Illinois	302.8
26	Pennsylvania	297.7
27	Maine	293.6
28	Missouri	282.6
29	Washington	282.4
30	Delaware	281.9
31	Michigan	278.1
32	Virginia	272.0
33	Georgia	269.1
34	Utah	267.0
35	Colorado	260.5
36	Oregon	248.9
37	North Carolina	243.7
38	District of Columbia	240.9
39	New Jersey	240.2
40	Nevada	237.9
41	New Hampshire	235.2
42	Maryland	218.2
43	Vermont	215.8
44	Arizona	209.3
45	Massachusetts	207.5
46	Connecticut	203.2
47	Florida	200.6
48	California	200.0
49	Hawaii	199.0
50	New York	188.1
51	Rhode Island	174.0

Homeownership Rate, 2018

Rank	State	Percent
	United States	64.4
1	West Virginia	74.7
2	New Hampshire	73.4
3	Michigan	73.0
4	Mississippi	72.5
5	Utah	72.2
6	South Carolina	72.0
7	Vermont	71.4
8	Maine	71.2
9	Wyoming	71.1
10	Delaware	70.8
11	Alabama	70.3
12	Pennsylvania	69.9
13	Indiana	69.8
13	Kentucky	69.8
13	Minnesota	69.8
16	Missouri	69.7
17	Oklahoma	69.5
18	Idaho	69.2
19	South Dakota	69.1
20	Iowa	68.9
21	New Mexico	68.0
21	Tennessee	68.0
23	Wisconsin	67.9
24	Montana	67.4
25	Kansas	67.3
25	Ohio	67.3
27	Maryland	66.6
28	Nebraska	66.4
29	Illinois	66.0
29	Virginia	66.0
31	Arizona	65.7
31	Louisiana	65.7
33	Florida	65.5
34	Connecticut	65.3
35	North Carolina	65.2
36	New Jersey	65.0
37	Washington	64.9
38	Arkansas	64.7
39	Colorado	64.4
40	Georgia	63.8
41	Alaska	63.7
42	Texas	62.7
43	Oregon	62.0
44	North Dakota	61.9
45	Massachusetts	61.5
46	Rhode Island	60.7
47	Hawaii	59.5
48	Nevada	57.8
49	California	55.1
50	New York	51.0
51	District of Columbia	39.9

One-Unit Detached or Attached Housing Units, Percent of Total Housing Units, 2017

Rank	State	Percent
	United States	68.9
1	Iowa	79.5
2	Idaho	79.1
3	Kansas	79.0
4	Indiana	78.5
5	Nebraska	77.9
6	Michigan	77.5
7	Pennsylvania	76.6
8	Oklahoma	76.5
9	Utah	76.2
10	Missouri	75.8
11	Delaware	75.6
12	Ohio	75.0
13	Minnesota	74.6
14	Maryland	74.1
15	Virginia	73.8
15	West Virginia	73.8
17	Montana	73.7
18	Wyoming	73.3
19	Arkansas	73.0
20	Tennessee	72.8
21	Georgia	72.3
22	South Dakota	72.1
23	Alabama	71.8
24	Mississippi	71.6
25	Kentucky	71.5
26	Arizona	71.4
26	Colorado	71.4
28	Alaska	71.1
29	North Carolina	70.9
29	Wisconsin	70.9
31	Maine	70.8
32	Louisiana	70.3
33	Texas	69.3
34	New Mexico	68.7
34	Oregon	68.7
36	New Hampshire	68.6
37	South Carolina	68.4
38	Vermont	68.3
39	Washington	67.7
40	Nevada	66.8
41	Connecticut	66.5
41	Illinois	66.5
43	North Dakota	65.7
44	Hawaii	65.6
45	California	65.5
46	Florida	65.0
47	New Jersey	63.6
48	Rhode Island	59.6
49	Massachusetts	57.3
50	New York	47.1
51	District of Columbia	38.0

Percent of Population Not Covered by Private or Public Health Insurance, 2017

Rank	State	Percent
	United States	8.7
1	Texas	17.3
2	Oklahoma	14.2
3	Alaska	13.7
4	Georgia	13.4
5	Florida	12.9
6	Wyoming	12.3
7	Mississippi	12.0
8	Nevada	11.2
9	South Carolina	11.0
10	North Carolina	10.7
11	Arizona	10.1
11	Idaho	10.1
13	Tennessee	9.5
14	Alabama	9.4
15	Utah	9.2
16	Missouri	9.1
16	New Mexico	9.1
16	South Dakota	9.1
19	Virginia	8.8
20	Kansas	8.7
21	Montana	8.5
22	Louisiana	8.4
23	Nebraska	8.3
24	Indiana	8.2
25	Maine	8.1
26	Arkansas	7.9
27	New Jersey	7.7
28	Colorado	7.5
28	North Dakota	7.5
30	California	7.2
31	Illinois	6.8
31	Oregon	6.8
33	Maryland	6.1
33	Washington	6.1
33	West Virginia	6.1
36	Ohio	6.0
37	New Hampshire	5.8
38	New York	5.7
39	Connecticut	5.5
39	Pennsylvania	5.5
41	Delaware	5.4
41	Kentucky	5.4
41	Wisconsin	5.4
44	Michigan	5.2
45	Iowa	4.7
46	Rhode Island	4.6
46	Vermont	4.6
48	Minnesota	4.4
49	District of Columbia	3.8
49	Hawaii	3.8
51	Massachusetts	2.8

Traffic Fatalities Per 100 Million Vehicle Miles, 2017

Rank	State	Rate
	United States	1.16
1	South Carolina	1.80
2	Mississippi	1.67
3	Louisiana	1.58
4	Alaska	1.57
5	Kentucky	1.56
6	West Virginia	1.51
7	Arizona	1.47
8	Montana	1.46
9	Florida	1.44
10	Kansas	1.42
11	Arkansas	1.38
11	Idaho	1.38
11	South Dakota	1.38
11	Texas	1.38
15	Alabama	1.37
16	New Mexico	1.35
17	Oklahoma	1.33
18	Tennessee	1.30
18	Wyoming	1.30
20	Georgia	1.26
20	Missouri	1.26
22	Colorado	1.21
23	North Carolina	1.20
24	North Dakota	1.18
25	Delaware	1.16
25	Oregon	1.16
27	Indiana	1.14
27	Maine	1.14
29	Nevada	1.11
30	Nebraska	1.09
30	Pennsylvania	1.09
32	Rhode Island	1.04
33	California	1.02
33	Hawaii	1.02
33	Illinois	1.02
36	Ohio	1.01
37	Michigan	1.00
38	Virginia	0.98
39	Iowa	0.96
39	Wisconsin	0.96
41	Maryland	0.93
41	Vermont	0.93
43	Washington	0.92
44	Connecticut	0.87
44	District of Columbia	0.87
46	Utah	0.86
47	New Jersey	0.82
48	New York	0.77
49	New Hampshire	0.76
50	Minnesota	0.62
51	Massachusetts	0.58

ALABAMA

Facts and Figures

Location: Southeastern United States; bordered on the N by Tennessee, on the E by Georgia, on the S by Florida and the Gulf of Mexico, and on the W by Mississippi

Area: 52,420 sq. mi. (135,765 sq. km.); rank—30th

Population: 4,887,871 (2018 est.); rank—24th

Principal Cities: capital—Montgomery; largest—Birmingham

Statehood: December 14, 1819; 22nd state

U.S. Congress: 2 senators, 7 representatives

State Motto: *Audemus jura nostra defendere* ("We dare defend our rights")

State Song: "Alabama"

State Nicknames: The Yellowhammer State; The Heart of Dixie; The Cotton State

Abbreviations: AL; Ala.

State Symbols: flower—camellia; tree—Southern longleaf pine; bird—yellowhammer

At a Glance

- With an increase in population of 2.3 percent, Alabama ranked 35th among the states in growth from 2010 to 2018.

- Alabama's per capita personal income in 2018 was $42,334, ranking 47th in the nation.

- In 2018, Alabama had 58.1 full-time state and local government employees per 1,000 residents, a rate that ranked 12th in the nation.

- In 2017, 16.9 percent of Alabama residents lived below the poverty level, a percentage that ranked 6th in the nation.

- Alabama's violent crime rate in 2017 was 524.2 per 100,000 residents, compared to 394.0 for the entire nation.

- Alabama's median household income of $48,123 ranked 46th in the nation in 2017.

Table AL-1. Population by Age, Sex, Race, and Hispanic Origin

(Number, percent, except where noted.)

Sex, age, race, and Hispanic origin	2000	2010	2018[1]	Percent change, 2010–2018
Total Population................................	4,447,100	4,779,736	4,887,871	2.3
Percent of total U.S. population	1.6	1.5	1.5	X
Sex				
Male................................	2,146,504	2,320,188	2,364,115	1.9
Female	2,300,596	2,459,548	2,523,756	2.6
Age				
Under 5 years................................	295,992	304,957	293,203	-3.9
5 to 19 years................................	960,177	971,355	924,075	-4.9
20 to 64 years................................	2,611,133	2,845,632	2,843,699	-0.1
65 years and over................................	579,798	657,792	826,894	25.7
Median age (years)	35.8	37.9	39.2	3.4
Race and Hispanic Origin				
One race				
White................................	3,162,808	3,362,877	3,379,955	0.5
Black................................	1,155,930	1,259,224	1,310,802	4.1
American Indian and Alaska Native	22,430	32,903	34,375	4.5
Asian................................	31,346	55,240	73,167	32.5
Native Hawaiian or Other Pacific Islander	1,409	5,208	5,207	-
Two or more races	44,179	64,284	84,365	31.2
Hispanic (of any race)................................	75,830	192,498	217,181	12.8

X = Not applicable.
[1] Population figures for 2018 are July 1 estimates. The 2010 estimates are taken from the 2010 Census.
- = Zero or rounds to zero.

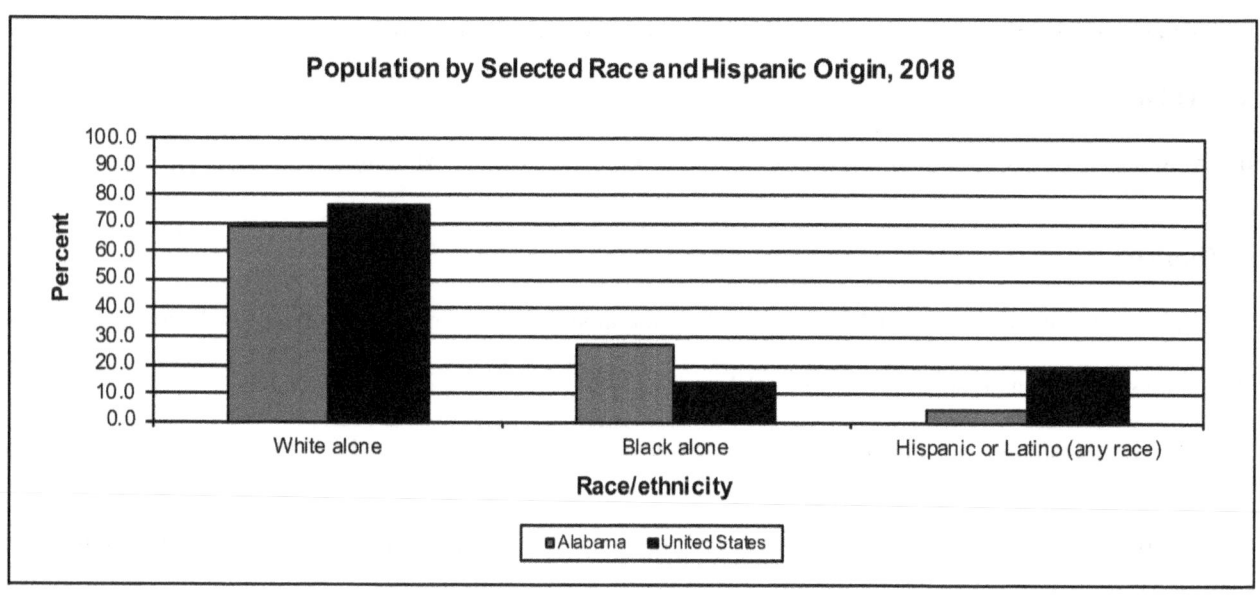

Table AL-2. Marital Status

(Number, percent distribution.)

Sex, age, and marital status	2000	2010	2017
Males, 15 Years and Over	1,666,798	1,844,661	1,895,814
Never married	26.7	32.5	34.7
Now married, except separated................................	59.0	50.6	48.8
Separated................................	1.8	2.5	1.8
Widowed................................	2.8	3.0	3.2
Divorced................................	9.8	11.4	11.6
Females, 15 Years and Over	1,847,401	2,004,450	2,076,310
Never married	21.4	26.1	29.4
Now married, except separated................................	52.5	45.9	44.7
Separated................................	2.5	3.1	2.7
Widowed................................	12.4	11.2	10.2
Divorced................................	11.2	13.6	13.0

Table AL-3. Households and Housing Characteristics

(Number, percent, dollars.)

Item	2000	2010	2017	Average annual percent change, 2010–2017
Total Households..	1,737,080	1,815,152	1,841,665	0.2
Family households	1,215,968	1,227,884	1,203,689	-0.3
Married-couple family	906,916	868,946	856,974	-0.2
Other family	309,052	358,938	346,715	-0.5
Male householder, no wife present................	62,586	79,308	77,556	-0.3
Female householder, no husband present.........	246,466	279,630	269,159	-0.5
Nonfamily households	521,112	587,268	637,976	1.2
Householder living alone.............................	453,898	511,708	551,345	1.1
Householder not living alone........................	67,214	75,560	86,631	2.1
Housing Characteristics				
Total housing units.......................................	1,963,711	2,174,428	2,258,669	0.6
Occupied housing units	1,737,080	1,815,152	1,841,665	0.2
Owner occupied	1,258,705	1,272,846	1,253,199	-0.2
Renter occupied	478,375	542,306	588,466	1.2
Average household size..................................	2.49	2.57	2.58	0.1
Financial Characteristics				
Median gross rent of renter-occupied housing	447	667	750	1.8
Median monthly owner costs for housing units with a mortgage	816	1,130	1,123	-0.1
Median value of owner-occupied housing units..........	85,100	123,900	141,300	2.0

- = Zero or rounds to zero.

Table AL-4. Migration, Origin, and Language

(Number, percent.)

Characteristic	State 2016	State 2017	Percent change	U.S. 2016	U.S. 2017	Percent change
Residence 1 Year Ago						
Population 1 year and over	4,810,126	4,819,343	0.2	319,361,956	321,994,428	0.8
Same house	86.1	86.3	X	85.4	85.7	X
Different house in the U.S............................	13.6	13.4	X	13.9	13.6	X
Same county	8.0	8.0	X	8.3	8.1	X
Different county	5.6	5.4	X	5.6	5.6	X
Same state	3.0	3.1	X	3.2	3.3	X
Different state	2.5	2.3	X	2.4	2.3	X
Abroad	0.3	0.3	X	0.7	0.7	X
Place of Birth						
Native born	4,699,671	4,705,681	0.1	279,388,170	281,193,323	0.6
Male	48.4	48.4	X	49.3	49.4	X
Female	51.6	51.6	X	50.7	50.6	X
Foreign born	163,629	169,066	3.3	43,739,345	44,525,855	1.8
Male	49.2	50	X	48.5	48.4	X
Female	50.8	50	X	51.5	51.6	X
Foreign born; naturalized U.S. citizen................	59,611	67,037	12.5	21,238,372	21,948,732	3.3
Male	45.9	44.6	X	45.9	45.9	X
Female	54.1	55.4	X	54.1	54.1	X
Foreign born; not a U.S. citizen.....................	104,018	102,029	-1.9	22,500,973	22,577,123	0.3
Male	51.1	53.5	X	51	50.8	X
Female	48.9	46.5	X	49	49.2	X
Entered 2010 or later	23.5	23.2	X	18.6	21.3	X
Entered 2000 to 2009	36.9	35.3	X	26.7	25.7	X
Entered before 2000................................	39.5	41.5	X	54.7	53.0	X
World Region of Birth, Foreign						
Foreign-born population, excluding population born at sea	163,629	169,066	3.3	43,738,901	44,525,458	1.8
Europe	10.2	11.2	X	10.9	10.8	X
Asia..	33.1	33.1	X	30.8	31.2	X
Africa	4.8	5.4	X	4.9	5.1	X
Oceania	0.4	0.7	X	0.6	0.6	X
Latin America	49.3	47.5	X	51	50.4	X
North America....................................	2.3	2.1	X	1.8	1.8	X
Language Spoken at Home and Ability to Speak English						
Population 5 years and over	4,576,657	4,585,850	0.2	303,328,961	305,924,019	0.9
English only	94.9	94.9	X	78.4	78.2	X
Language other than English........................	5.1	5.1	X	21.6	21.8	X
Speaks English less than "very well"................	2.1	1.9	X	8.6	8.5	X

NA = Not available.
X = Not applicable.
- = Zero or rounds to zero.

Table AL-5. Median Income and Poverty Status, 2017

(Number, percent, except as noted.)

Characteristic	State Number	State Percent	U.S. Number	U.S. Percent
Median Income				
Households (dollars)..	48,123	X	60,336	X
Families (dollars)	61,512	X	73,891	X
Below Poverty Level (All People)	802,656	16.9	42,583,651	13.4
Sex				
Male	347,538	15.2	19,004,547	12.2
Female	455,118	18.5	23,579,104	14.5
Age				
Under 18 years...	265,078	24.6	13,353,202	18.4
Related children under 18 years..	261,570	24.3	13,053,472	18.1
18 to 64 years..	459,701	15.9	24,648,677	12.6
65 years and over	77,877	9.9	4,581,772	9.3

X = Not applicable.

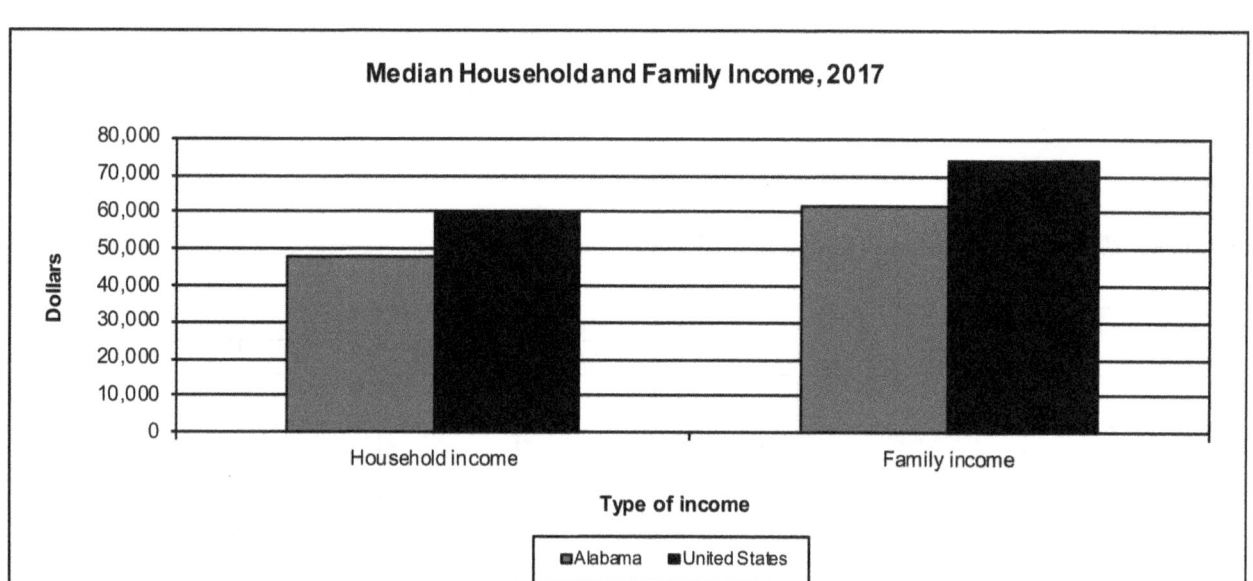

Table AL-6. Health Insurance Coverage Status for the Civilian Noninstitutionalized Population and Children Under 18 Years of Age

(Number; percent.)

Item	2009	2010	2011	2012	2013	2014	2015	2016	2017
Civilian Noninstitutionalized Population	4,616,028	4,702,769	4,720,067	4,741,698	4,755,381	4,767,383	4,781,070	4,782,529	4,793,512
Covered by Private or Public Insurance									
Number...	3,979,391	4,016,177	4,046,103	4,109,199	4,109,946	4,188,214	4,296,799	4,347,556	4,344,586
Percent..	86.2	85.4	85.7	86.7	86.4	87.9	89.9	90.9	90.6
Uninsured									
Number...	636,637	686,592	673,964	632,499	645,435	579,169	484,271	434,973	448,926
Percent..	13.8	14.6	14.3	13.3	13.6	12.1	10.1	9.1	9.4
Percent in the U.S. not covered..................................	15.1	15.5	15.1	14.8	14.5	11.7	9.4	8.6	8.7
Children Under 18 Years of Age[1]	1,124,227	1,133,638	1,122,125	1,123,000	1,107,844	1,106,847	1,106,716	1,098,052	1,169,489
Covered by Private or Public Insurance									
Number...	1,057,497	1,066,680	1,063,064	1,077,390	1,059,663	1,064,425	1,072,948	1,071,320	1,133,440
Percent..	94.1	94.1	94.7	95.9	95.7	96.2	96.9	97.6	96.9
Uninsured									
Number...	66,730	66,958	59,061	45,610	48,181	42,422	33,768	26,732	36,049
Percent..	5.9	5.9	5.3	4.1	4.3	3.8	3.1	2.4	3.1
Percent in the U.S. not covered..................................	8.6	8.0	7.5	7.2	7.1	6.0	4.8	4.5	5.0

[1] 2017 data is for individuals under 19 years of age.

Table AL-7. Employment Status by Demographic Group, 2018

(Numbers in thousands, percent.)

Characteristic	Civilian noninstitutional population	Civilian labor force		Employed		Unemployed	
		Number	Percent of population	Number	Percent of population	Number	Percent of population
Total....................................	3,847	2,208	57.4	2,121	55.1	87	3.9
Sex							
Male	1,820	1,180	64.9	1,135	62.4	45	3.8
Female	2,027	1,027	50.7	986	48.6	42	4.1
Race, Sex, and Hispanic Origin							
White	2,711	1,567	57.8	1,523	56.2	44	2.8
Male	1,310	880	67.2	857	65.4	23	2.6
Female	1,401	686	49.0	666	47.5	21	3.0
Black or African American..................	999	558	55.8	519	52.0	38	6.9
Male	443	254	57.4	235	53.1	19	7.4
Female	556	304	54.6	284	51.1	19	6.4
Hispanic or Latino ethnicity[1]	143	97	67.5	92	64.4	5	4.6
Male	75	66	87.4	64	85.1	2	2.6
Female	NA	NA	NA	NA	NA	NA	NA
Age							
16 to 19 years...............................	236	75	31.9	66	27.9	9	12.5
20 to 24 years...............................	333	228	68.5	212	63.8	16	6.8
25 to 34 years...............................	627	492	78.5	469	74.8	23	4.7
35 to 44 years...............................	578	451	78.0	433	75.0	18	3.9
45 to 54 years...............................	653	481	73.7	471	72.0	11	2.2
55 to 64 years...............................	666	353	53.0	347	52.1	6	1.7
65 years and over	753	127	16.9	123	16.3	5	3.6

NOTE: Data in Table 7 are from the Current Population Survey (CPS) and do not match the estimates in Table 8. See notes and definitions for further information.
[1] May be of any race.
NA = Not available.

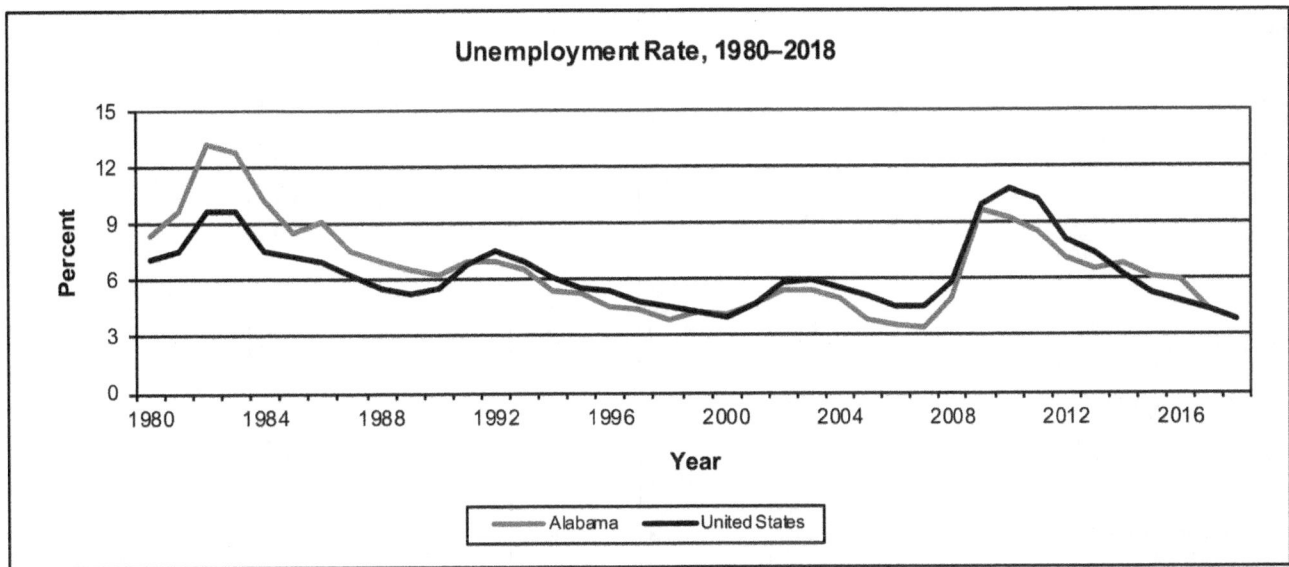

Table AL-8. Employment Status of the Civilian Noninstitutional Population Age 16 Years and Over

(Number, percent.)

Year	Civilian labor force	Civilian participation rate	Employed	Unemployed	Unemployment rate
2010..	2,196,042	59.5	1,964,559	231,483	10.5
2011..	2,202,670	59.1	1,990,413	212,257	9.6
2012..	2,176,337	58.1	2,003,290	173,047	8.0
2013..	2,174,000	57.8	2,017,043	156,957	7.2
2014..	2,161,618	57.2	2,015,087	146,531	6.8
2015..	2,157,376	56.8	2,025,949	131,427	6.1
2016..	2,173,175	57.0	2,045,624	127,551	5.9
2017..	2,168,444	56.6	2,073,106	95,338	4.4
2018..	2,198,837	57.2	2,112,347	86,490	3.9

Table AL-9. Employment and Average Wages by Industry

(Estimates are based on the 2012 *North American Industry Classification System* [NAICS].)

Industry	2011	2012	2013	2014	2015	2016	2017
	Number of Jobs						
Wage and Salary Employment by Industry......................	1,949,307	1,963,937	1,979,360	1,996,182	2,024,720	2,049,658	2,072,223
Farm Wage and Salary Employment...............................	8,188	7,349	7,713	5,318	7,451	7,213	9,217
Nonfarm Wage and Salary Employment...........................	1,941,119	1,956,588	1,971,647	1,990,864	2,017,269	2,042,445	2,063,006
Private wage and salary employment...........................	1,533,428	1,553,413	1,571,089	1,590,896	1,618,569	1,641,038	1,659,832
Forestry, fishing, and related activities..........................	8,468	8,568	8,780	8,875	8,938	8,925	8,785
Mining..	8,285	8,591	7,992	7,549	6,828	5,352	6,031
Utilities...	14,262	14,246	14,382	14,293	14,437	14,170	13,735
Construction	82,993	81,847	81,656	81,857	83,802	86,254	87,258
Manufacturing..	237,814	243,890	249,486	253,248	258,085	260,646	263,808
Durable goods manufacturing................................	148,024	154,396	159,691	165,133	169,191	170,054	171,555
Nondurable goods manufacturing...........................	89,790	89,494	89,795	88,115	88,894	90,592	92,253
Wholesale trade	72,261	72,882	73,366	73,150	73,926	74,025	73,890
Retail trade...	226,473	225,831	226,040	228,885	232,361	234,301	232,838
Transportation and warehousing..............................	53,771	55,515	57,208	59,202	59,792	59,991	60,738
Information	23,129	22,696	22,590	21,962	21,543	20,701	20,818
Finance and insurance..	71,743	72,114	73,202	74,309	74,795	75,063	76,392
Real estate and rental and leasing............................	21,545	21,722	22,228	22,039	22,338	22,845	23,258
Professional, scientific, and technical services	94,307	94,971	95,258	95,325	96,903	98,999	101,786
Management of companies and enterprises.................	15,986	16,874	15,935	15,130	15,432	16,467	16,116
Administrative and waste services............................	104,209	107,938	109,057	113,606	117,874	119,940	123,019
Educational services	28,603	28,790	29,535	29,599	29,691	30,392	30,294
Health care and social assistance............................	198,534	200,951	204,076	205,157	209,600	214,778	218,050
Arts, entertainment, and recreation..........................	16,397	16,098	16,360	16,990	16,906	19,019	20,062
Accommodation and food services............................	154,055	158,902	163,776	168,368	174,090	179,626	183,518
Other services, except public administration................	100,593	100,987	100,162	101,352	101,228	99,544	99,436
Government and government enterprises.....................	407,691	403,175	400,558	399,968	398,700	401,407	403,174
	Dollars						
Average Wages and Salaries by Industry	40,497	41,329	41,599	42,653	43,632	44,160	45,308
Average Farm Wages and Salaries	18,286	27,365	19,036	23,427	22,978	19,459	14,836
Average Nonfarm Wages and Salaries	40,591	41,381	41,687	42,704	43,708	44,248	45,445
Average private wages and salaries............................	39,709	40,715	41,063	42,068	43,140	43,659	44,867
Forestry, fishing, and related activities......................	32,464	33,393	33,914	35,336	36,652	38,235	38,957
Mining..	77,643	76,365	78,001	80,782	80,450	70,500	76,990
Utilities...	85,819	88,192	88,364	88,427	95,522	100,657	104,422
Construction	43,508	45,269	45,537	47,811	48,728	50,520	52,222
Manufacturing..	49,091	50,350	50,891	52,849	53,519	54,226	55,171
Durable goods manufacturing................................	51,716	52,919	53,246	55,057	55,744	56,609	57,567
Nondurable goods manufacturing...........................	44,763	45,919	46,704	48,709	49,283	49,755	50,717
Wholesale trade	56,129	56,945	57,873	59,953	62,110	62,828	64,485
Retail trade...	24,730	25,300	25,617	25,873	26,506	27,018	27,569
Transportation and warehousing..............................	43,095	44,308	44,321	46,116	47,341	47,458	48,986
Information	50,868	51,276	51,605	53,923	55,771	57,095	58,870
Finance and insurance..	62,077	64,336	65,033	67,934	71,769	71,115	73,915
Real estate and rental and leasing............................	36,634	38,777	38,489	40,047	41,559	42,222	43,817
Professional, scientific, and technical services	68,198	69,727	70,632	71,517	73,321	74,636	76,651
Management of companies and enterprises.................	78,600	80,786	83,524	85,374	87,533	91,142	102,206
Administrative and waste services............................	26,108	26,718	26,701	27,121	27,431	27,784	28,415
Educational services	24,540	25,207	25,272	26,112	26,888	27,323	27,378
Health care and social assistance............................	42,266	43,287	43,384	44,176	45,495	45,603	46,505
Arts, entertainment, and recreation..........................	18,764	19,794	20,198	20,329	21,420	20,572	20,394
Accommodation and food services............................	15,580	16,052	16,295	16,593	17,043	17,542	18,027
Other services, except public administration................	28,442	29,033	29,781	30,811	32,033	33,227	34,557
Government and government enterprises.....................	43,907	43,947	44,134	45,236	46,014	46,654	47,825

Table AL-10. Employment Characteristics by Family Type

(Number, percent.)

Family type and labor force status	2015		2016		2017	
	Total	Families with own children under 18 years	Total	Families with own children under 18 years	Total	Families with own children under 18 years
All Families..	1,213,540	486,977	1,208,362	473,593	1,203,689	470,337
FAMILY TYPE AND LABOR FORCE STATUS						
Married-Couple Families................................	863,674	306,591	864,330	304,039	856,974	295,425
Both husband and wife in labor force......................	45.6	64.0	46.2	64.6	44.8	64.9
Husband in labor force, wife not in labor force............	23.7	28.5	23.1	28.3	23.4	27.6
Wife in labor force, husband not in labor force............	8.0	4.2	8.4	4.3	8.6	4.6
Both husband and wife not in labor force..................	22.2	3.0	21.7	2.7	22.6	2.5
Other Families	349,866	180,386	344,032	169,554	346,715	174,912
Female householder, no husband present..................	77.6	80.8	76.4	79.2	77.6	82.0
In labor force	49.1	63.7	47.8	64.1	47.7	63.8
Not in labor force	28.5	17.1	28.6	15.1	29.9	18.1
Male householder, no wife present........................	22.4	19.2	23.6	20.8	22.4	18.0
In labor force	15.5	16.3	15.6	17.9	15.0	15.4
Not in labor force	6.8	2.9	7.9	2.9	7.4	2.6

Table AL-11. School Enrollment and Educational Attainment, 2017

(Number, percent.)

Item	State	U.S.
Enrollment		
Total population 3 years and over, enrolled in school	1,188,014	81,273,337
Enrolled in nursery school or preschool (percent)	5.3	6.0
Enrolled in kindergarten (percent)...........................	5.0	4.9
Enrolled in elementary school, grades 1-8 (percent)..........	41.9	40.6
Enrolled in high school, grades 9-12 (percent)	21.7	21.1
Enrolled in college or graduate school (percent).............	26.1	27.4
Attainment		
Total population 25 years and over	3,309,607	221,250,083
Less than ninth grade (percent)	4.2	5.1
9th to 12th grade, no diploma (percent)	9.4	6.9
High school graduate, including equivalency (percent)........	31.1	27.1
Some college, no degree (percent)	21.4	20.4
Associate's degree (percent)................................	8.4	8.5
Bachelor's degree (percent)	16.0	19.7
Graduate or professional degree (percent)...................	9.6	12.3
High school graduate or higher (percent)	86.5	88.0
Bachelor's degree or higher (percent).......................	25.5	32.0

Table AL-12. Public School Characteristics and Educational Indicators

(Number, percent; data derived from National Center of Education Statistics.)

Item	State	U.S.
Public Elementary and Secondary Schools		
Number of operational school districts, 2016-17	178	18,377
Number of operational schools, 2016-17.......................	1,513	98,330
Percent charter schools	0.1	7.1
Total public school enrollment, 2016-17.......................	744,930	50,587,859
Percent charter school enrollment...........................	NA	6.0
Student-teacher ratio, Fall 2015	18.2	16.0
Expenditures per student (dollars), 2015-16...................	9,258	11,841
Four-year adjusted cohort graduation rate (ACGR)[1]	89.3	84.6
Students eligible for free or reduced-price lunch (percent), 2015-16........	51.1	52.1
English language learners (percent), Fall 2016.................	2.8	9.6
Students age 3 to 21 served under IDEA, part B (percent), 2017-18	12.2	13.7

Public Schools by Type, 2016-17	Number	Percent of state public schools
Total number of schools..	1,513	100.0
Special education	34	2.2
Vocational education	68	4.5
Alternative education...	83	5.5

[1] Adjusted Cohort Graduation Rates (ACGR) differ from Averaged Freshmen Graduation Rates (AFGR).
NA = Not available.

Table AL-13. Reported Voting and Registration of the Voting-Age Population, November 2018

(Numbers in thousands, percent.)

Item	Total population	Total citizen population	Registered			Voted		
			Total registered	Percent registered (total population)	Percent registered (total citizen population)	Total voted	Percent voted (total population)	Percent voted (total citizen population)
U.S. Total	249,748	228,832	153,066	61.3	66.9	122,281	49.0	53.4
State Total	3,753	3,609	2,490	66.4	69.0	1,830	48.8	50.7
Sex								
Male	1,772	1,681	1,122	63.3	66.7	821	46.3	48.8
Female	1,982	1,927	1,368	69.0	71.0	1,010	50.9	52.4
Race								
White alone	2,610	2,534	1,774	68.0	70.0	1,309	50.1	51.6
White, non-Hispanic alone	2,494	2,470	1,760	70.6	71.3	1,298	52.1	52.6
Black alone	976	975	657	67.2	67.4	483	49.4	49.5
Asian alone	61	37	13	(B)	(B)	7	(B)	(B)
Hispanic (of any race)	169	77	26	15.6	34.3	22	13.2	29.1
White alone or in combination	2,636	2,561	1,796	68.1	70.1	1,322	50.2	51.6
Black alone or in combination	979	977	659	67.3	67.4	485	49.6	49.6
Asian alone or in combination	61	37	13	(B)	(B)	7	(B)	(B)
Age								
18 to 24 years	458	434	221	48.2	50.8	130	28.3	29.9
25 to 34 years	660	619	425	64.4	68.6	262	39.8	42.4
35 to 44 years	556	508	341	61.3	67.1	239	43.0	47.1
45 to 64 years	1,340	1,313	933	69.7	71.1	736	54.9	56.0
65 years and over	740	735	571	77.1	77.7	463	62.6	63.1

- = Zero or rounds to zero.
B = Base is less than 75,000 and therefore too small to show the derived measure.

Table AL-14. Crime

(Number, rate per 100,000. Data are derived from the FBI Uniform Crime Reports.)

Item	State			U.S.		
	2016	2017	Percent change	2016	2017	Percent change
TOTAL POPULATION[1]	4,860,545	4,874,747	0.3	323,405,935	325,719,178	0.7
VIOLENT CRIME						
Number	25,878	25,551	-1.3	1,285,606	1,283,220	-0.2
Rate	532.4	524.2	-1.6	397.5	394.0	-0.9
Murder and Nonnegligent Manslaughter						
Number	407	404	-0.7	17,413	17,284	-0.7
Rate	8.4	8.3		5.4	5.3	-1.4
Rape[2]						
Number	1,915	2,028	5.9	132,414	135,755	2.5
Rate	39.4	41.6	5.6	40.9	41.7	1.8
Robbery						
Number	4,687	4,217	-10.0	332,797	319,356	-4.0
Rate	96.4	86.5	-10.3	102.9	98.0	-4.7
Aggravated Assault						
Number	18,869	18,902	0.2	802,982	810,825	1.0
Rate	388.2	387.8	-0.1	248.3	248.9	0.3
PROPERTY CRIME						
Number	143,259	144,160	0.6	7,928,530	7,694,086	-3.0
Rate	2,947.4	2,957.3	0.3	2,451.6	2,362.2	-3.6
Burglary						
Number	34,045	31,477	-7.5	1,516,405	1,401,840	-7.6
Rate	700.4	645.7	-7.8	468.9	430.4	-8.2
Larceny-Theft						
Number	97,498	99,842	2.4	5,644,835	5,519,107	-2.2
Rate	2,005.9	2,048.1	2.1	1,745.4	1,694.4	-2.9
Motor Vehicle Theft						
Number	11,716	12,841	9.6	767,290	773,139	0.8
Rate	241.0	263.4	9.3	237.3	237.4	-

NOTE: Although arson data are included in the trend and clearance tables, sufficient data are not available to estimate totals for this offense. Therefore, no arson data are published in this table.
- = Zero or rounds to zero.
[1] Population figures are U.S. Census Bureau provisional estimates as of July 1, 2017.
[2] The figures shown in the rape (revised definition) column were estimated using the revised Uniform Crime Reporting (UCR) definition of rape.

Table AL-15. State Government Finances, 2017

(Dollar amounts in thousands, percent distribution.)

Item	Dollars	Percent distribution
Total Revenue	32,081,908	100.0
General revenue	26,772,097	83.4
Intergovernmental revenue	9,949,247	31.0
Taxes	10,418,152	32.5
General sales	2,654,883	8.3
Selective sales	2,592,411	8.1
License taxes	529,607	1.7
Individual income tax	3,624,543	11.3
Corporate income tax	520,113	1.6
Other taxes	496,595	1.5
Current charges	5,040,778	15.7
Miscellaneous general revenue	1,363,920	4.3
Utility revenue	0	-
Liquor stores revenue	325,393	1.0
Insurance trust revenue[1]	4,984,418	15.5
Total Expenditure	32,483,376	100.0
Intergovernmental expenditure	6,931,626	21.3
Direct expenditure	25,551,750	78.7
Current operation	17,672,634	54.4
Capital outlay	1,982,995	6.1
Insurance benefits and repayments	3,481,902	10.7
Assistance and subsidies	2,024,435	6.2
Interest on debt	389,784	1.2
Exhibit: Salaries and wages	4,922,514	15.2
Total Expenditure	32,483,376	100.0
General expenditure	28,680,131	88.3
Intergovernmental expenditure	6,931,626	21.3
Direct expenditure	21,748,505	67.0
General expenditure, by function:		
Education	11,471,899	35.3
Public welfare	8,547,055	26.3
Hospitals	2,875,275	8.9
Health	551,627	1.7
Highways	1,659,619	5.1
Police protection	171,607	0.5
Correction	553,944	1.7
Natural resources	295,316	0.9
Parks and recreation	22,814	0.1
Governmental administration	645,732	2.0
Interest on general debt	389,784	1.2
Other and unallocable	1,495,459	4.6
Utility expenditure	75	-
Liquor stores expenditure	321,268	1.0
Insurance trust expenditure	3,481,902	10.7
Debt at End of Fiscal Year	8,772,871	X
Cash and Security Holdings	46,184,255	X

X = Not applicable.
- = Zero or rounds to zero.
[1] Within insurance trust revenue, net earnings of state retirement systems is a calculated statistic (the item code in the data file is X08), and thus can be positive or negative. Net earnings is the sum of earnings on investments plus gains on investments minus losses on investments. The change made in 2002 for asset valuation from book to market value in accordance with Statement 34 of the Governmental Accounting Standards Board is reflected in the calculated statistics.

Table AL-16. State Government Tax Collections, 2018

(Dollars in thousands, percent.)

Item	Dollars	Percent distribution
Total Taxes	11,055,577	100.0
Property taxes	406,288	3.7
Sales and gross receipts	5,534,807	50.1
General sales and gross receipts	2,786,833	25.2
Selective sales and gross receipts	2,747,974	24.9
Alcoholic beverages	214,615	1.9
Amusements	0	-
Insurance premiums	376,766	3.4
Motor fuels	648,639	5.9
Pari-mutuels	1,146	-
Public utilities	747,657	6.8
Tobacco products	179,929	1.6
Other selective sales	579,222	5.2
Licenses	521,990	4.7
Alcoholic beverages	4,032	-
Amusements	X	-
Corporations in general	152,538	1.4
Hunting and fishing	21,451	0.2
Motor vehicle	220,483	2.0
Motor vehicle operators	33,425	0.3
Public utilities	14,146	0.1
Occupation and business, NEC	75,914	0.7
Other licenses	1	-
Income taxes	4,490,316	40.6
Individual income	3,912,800	35.4
Corporation net income	577,516	5.2
Other taxes	102,176	0.9
Death and gift	X	-
Documentary and stock transfer	46,014	0.4
Severance	56,162	0.5
Taxes, NEC	0	-

- = Zero or rounds to zero.
X = Not applicable.

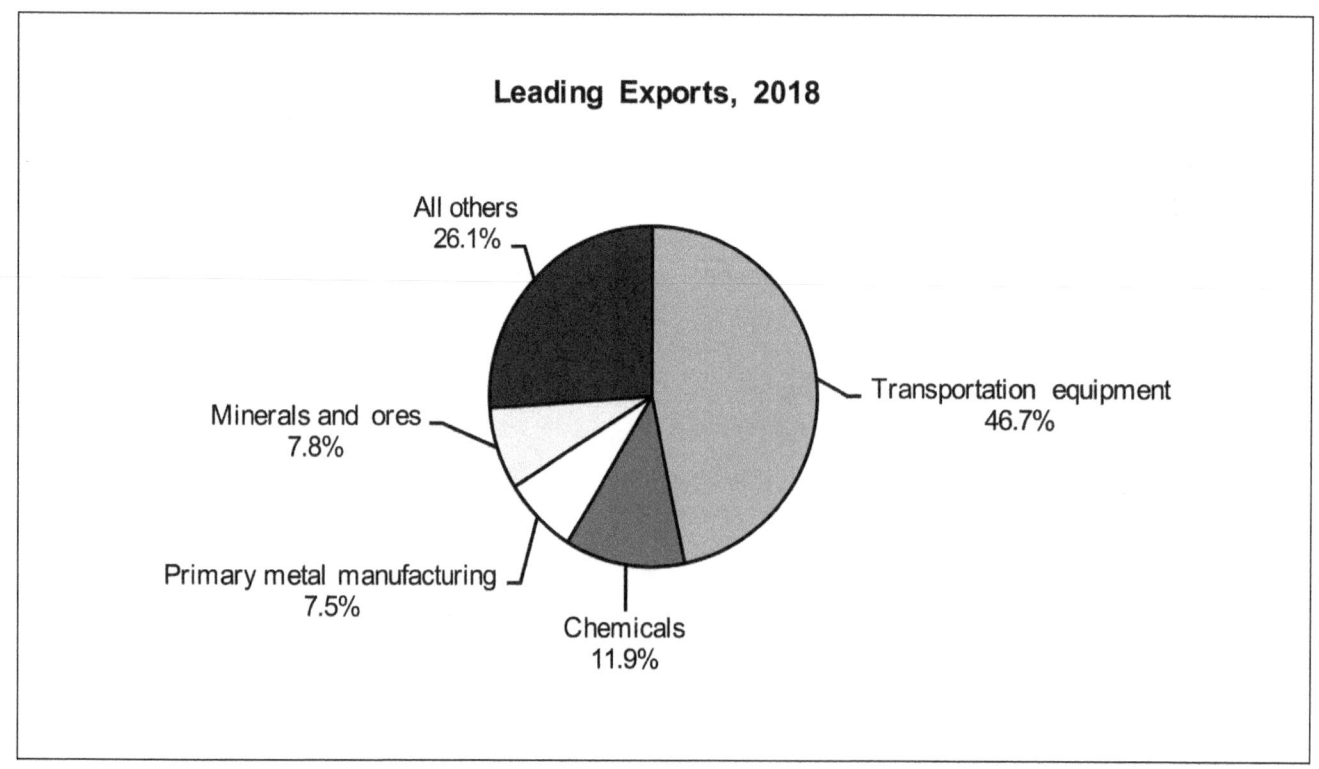

Leading Exports, 2018

All others 26.1%

Transportation equipment 46.7%

Minerals and ores 7.8%

Primary metal manufacturing 7.5%

Chemicals 11.9%

ALASKA

Facts and Figures

Location: Northwestern North America; bordered on the N by the Arctic Ocean, on the E by Canada, on the S by the Pacific Ocean and the Gulf of Alaska, and on the W by the Bering Sea

Area: 665,384 sq. mi. (1,717,854 sq. sq. km.); rank—1st

Population: 737,438 (2018 est.); rank—48th

Principal Cities: capital—Juneau; largest—Anchorage

Statehood: January 3, 1959; 49th state

U.S. Congress: 2 senators, 1 representative

State Motto: North to the Future

State Song: "Alaska's Flag"

State Nicknames: The Last Frontier; The Land of the Midnight Sun

Abbreviations: AK

State Symbols: flower—forget-me-not; tree—Sitka spruce; bird—willow ptarmigan

At a Glance

- With an increase in population of 3.8 percent, Alaska ranked 27th among the states for growth from 2010 to 2018.

- Alaska's 2017 violent crime rate ranked 2nd in the nation at 829.0 per 100,000 population, and the property crime rate (3,542.1 per 100,000 population) ranked 3rd.

- Alaska was the state with the 3rd highest birth rate in 2017, at 14.1 births per 1,000 population.

- In 2017, 11.1 percent of Alaskans lived below the poverty level, a percent that ranked 36th in the nation.

- Of all the states, Alaska had the 4th highest percentage of residents under 18 years old (24.9 percent) and the second lowest percentage of residents age 65 and over (11.8 percent) in 2018.

Table AK-1. Population by Age, Sex, Race, and Hispanic Origin

(Number, percent, except where noted.)

Sex, age, race, and Hispanic origin	2000	2010	2018[1]	Percent change, 2010–2018
Total Population..	626,932	710,231	737,438	3.8
Percent of total U.S. population	0.2	0.2	0.2	X
Sex				
Male..	324,112	369,628	384,573	4.0
Female..	302,820	340,603	352,865	3.6
Age				
Under 5 years..	47,591	53,996	53,115	-1.6
5 to 19 years..	160,526	153,844	148,078	-3.7
20 to 64 years..	383,116	447,453	449,234	0.4
65 years and over..	35,699	54,938	87,011	58.4
Median age (years)..	32.4	33.8	34.6	2.4
Race and Hispanic Origin				
One race				
White...	434,534	483,873	481,879	-0.4
Black..	21,787	24,441	27,942	14.3
American Indian and Alaska Native	98,043	106,268	113,516	6.8
Asian..	25,116	38,882	49,025	26.1
Native Hawaiian or Other Pacific Islander	3,309	7,622	10,221	34.1
Two or more races	34,146	49,105	54,855	11.7
Hispanic (of any race)..	25,852	44,490	53,288	19.8

X = Not applicable.
[1] Population figures for 2018 are July 1 estimates. The 2010 estimates are taken from the 2010 Census.
- = Zero or rounds to zero.

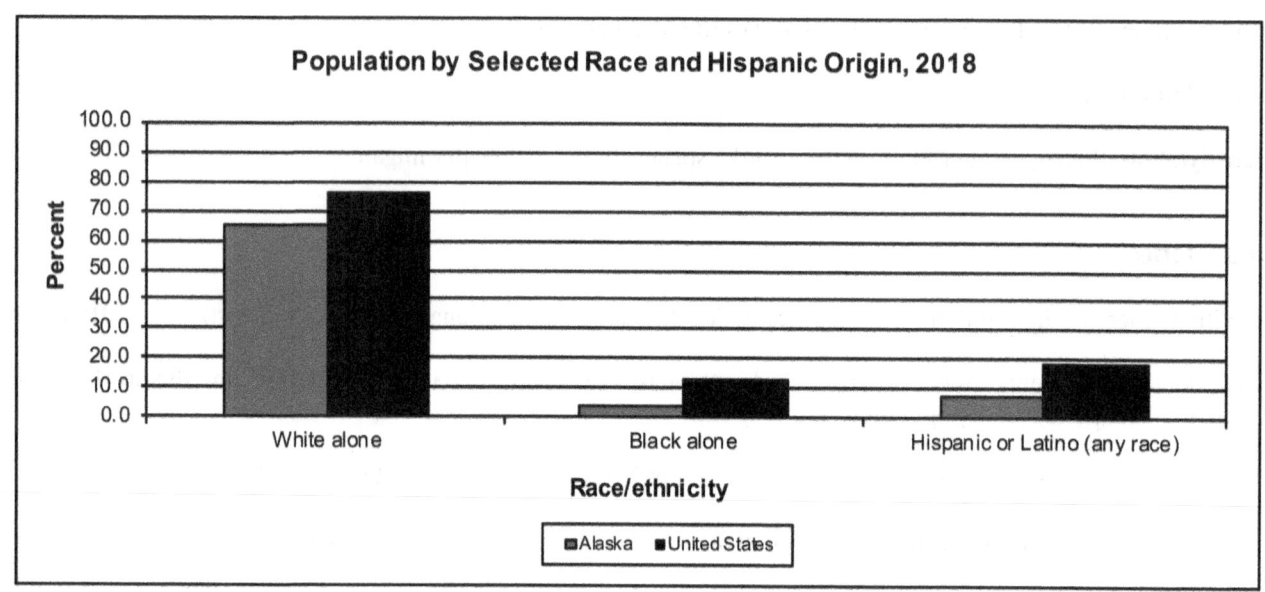

Population by Selected Race and Hispanic Origin, 2018

Table AK-2. Marital Status

(Number, percent distribution.)

Sex, age, and marital status	2000	2010	2017
Males, 15 Years and Over	243,024	290,598	307,088
Never married	32.5	35.5	38.2
Now married, except separated..	53.6	49.7	47.0
Separated..	1.7	1.7	1.4
Widowed..	1.4	1.8	2.1
Divorced..	10.8	11.4	11.4
Females, 15 Years and Over	225,837	267,563	276,551
Never married	24.1	27.3	29.4
Now married, except separated..	55.6	50.2	49.6
Separated..	2.3	2.6	2.2
Widowed..	5.6	6.1	5.5
Divorced..	12.5	13.7	13.2

Table AK-3. Households and Housing Characteristics

(Number, percent, dollars.)

Item	2000	2010	2017	Average annual percent change, 2010–2017
Total Households...	221,600	254,610	250,741	-0.2
Family households	152,337	170,859	167,401	-0.3
Married-couple family	116,318	127,969	123,825	-0.5
Other family	36,019	42,890	43,576	0.2
Male householder, no wife present....................................	12,082	14,211	15,002	0.8
Female householder, no husband present...........................	23,937	28,679	28,574	-0.1
Nonfamily households	69,263	83,751	83,340	-0.1
Householder living alone	52,060	63,698	63,504	-0.0
Householder not living alone...	17,203	20,053	19,836	-0.2
Housing Characteristics				
Total housing units..	260,978	307,065	316,968	0.5
Occupied housing units	221,600	254,610	250,741	-0.2
Owner occupied	138,509	162,785	159,344	-0.3
Renter occupied	83,091	91,825	91,397	-0.1
Average household size..	2.74	2.70	2.84	0.7
Financial Characteristics				
Median gross rent of renter-occupied housing	720	981	1,201	3.2
Median monthly owner costs for housing units with a mortgage	1,315	1,772	1,844	0.6
Median value of owner-occupied housing units	144,200	241,400	273,100	1.9

Table AK-4. Migration, Origin, and Language

(Number, percent.)

Characteristic	State			U.S.		
	2016	2017	Percent change	2016	2017	Percent change
Residence 1 Year Ago						
Population 1 year and over	731,760	730,874	-0.1	319,361,956	321,994,428	0.8
Same house	81.2	81.5	X	85.4	85.7	X
Different house in the U.S.	17.9	17.6	X	13.9	13.6	X
Same county	10.8	11.1	X	8.3	8.1	X
Different county	7.2	6.4	X	5.6	5.6	X
Same state	2.9	2.3	X	3.2	3.3	X
Different state	4.3	4.1	X	2.4	2.3	X
Abroad	0.9	0.9	X	0.7	0.7	X
Place of Birth						
Native born	684,530	681,608	-0.4	279,388,170	281,193,323	0.6
Male	53.0	52.8	X	49.3	49.4	X
Female	47.0	47.2	X	50.7	50.6	X
Foreign born	57,364	58,187	1.4	43,739,345	44,525,855	1.8
Male	48.1	44.3	X	48.5	48.4	X
Female	51.9	55.7	X	51.5	51.6	X
Foreign born; naturalized U.S. citizen.................................	32,772	31,164	-4.9	21,238,372	21,948,732	3.3
Male	49.8	44.1	X	45.9	45.9	X
Female	50.2	55.9	X	54.1	54.1	X
Foreign born; not a U.S. citizen	24,592	27,023	9.9	22,500,973	22,577,123	0.3
Male	45.9	44.6	X	51	50.8	X
Female	54.1	55.4	X	49	49.2	X
Entered 2010 or later	24.1	25.6	X	18.6	21.3	X
Entered 2000 to 2009	24.8	23.8	X	26.7	25.7	X
Entered before 2000..	51.1	50.6	X	54.7	53.0	X
World Region of Birth, Foreign						
Foreign-born population, excluding population born at sea	57,364	58,187	1.4	43,738,901	44,525,458	1.8
Europe	13.4	12.6	X	10.9	10.8	X
Asia..	57.8	57.5	X	30.8	31.2	X
Africa	2.6	6.6	X	4.9	5.1	X
Oceania	2.3	4	X	0.6	0.6	X
Latin America..	19.8	14.9	X	51	50.4	X
North America...	4.0	4.3	X	1.8	1.8	X
Language Spoken at Home and Ability to Speak English						
Population 5 years and over...	689,399	686,876	-0.4	303,328,961	305,924,019	0.9
English only	83.5	84.1	X	78.4	78.2	X
Language other than English...	16.5	15.9	X	21.6	21.8	X
Speaks English less than "very well"...............................	5.3	4.9	X	8.6	8.5	X

NA = Not available.
X = Not applicable.
- = Zero or rounds to zero.

Table AK-5. Median Income and Poverty Status, 2017

(Number, percent, except as noted.)

Characteristic	State		U.S.	
	Number	Percent	Number	Percent
Median Income				
Households (dollars)..	73,181	X	60,336	X
Families (dollars)	86,831	X	73,891	X
Below Poverty Level (All People)	80,012	11.1	42,583,651	13.4
Sex				
Male	40,894	11.0	19,004,547	12.2
Female	39,118	11.2	23,579,104	14.5
Age				
Under 18 years..	26,865	14.9	13,353,202	18.4
Related children under 18 years...	25,595	14.3	13,053,472	18.1
18 to 64 years...	47,104	10.3	24,648,677	12.6
65 years and over	6,043	7.4	4,581,772	9.3

X = Not applicable.

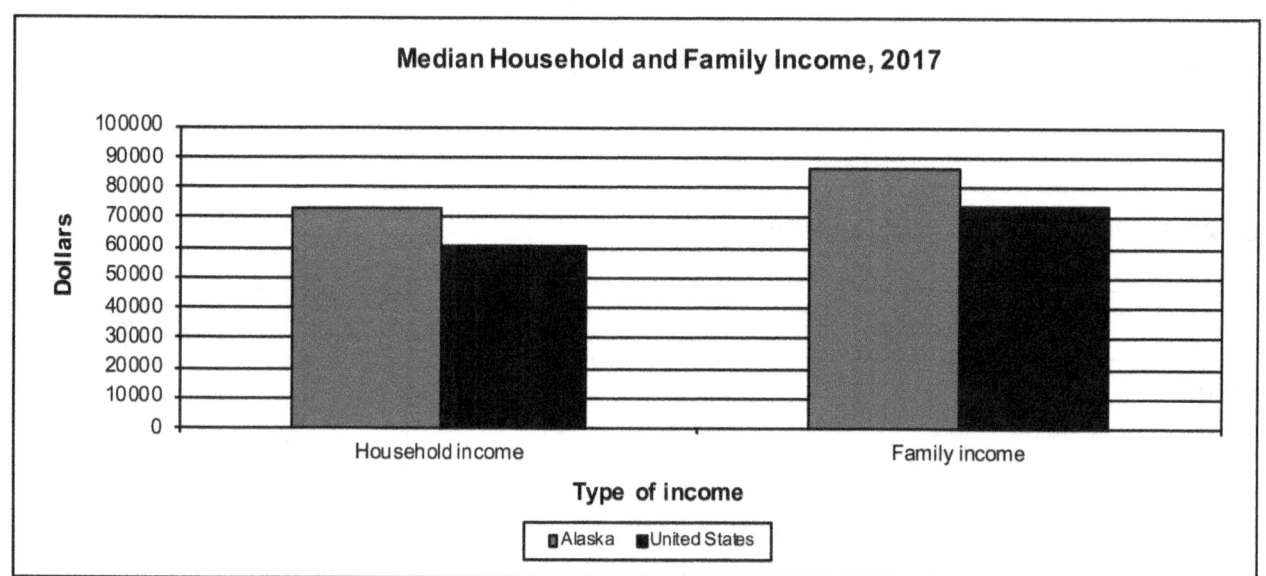

Table AK-6. Health Insurance Coverage Status for the Civilian Noninstitutionalized Population and Children Under 18 Years of Age

(Number; percent.)

Item	2009	2010	2011	2012	2013	2014	2015	2016	2017
Civilian Noninstitutionalized Population	678081	689249	699272	708946	712,248	711,541	713,082	718,419	716,178
Covered by Private or Public Insurance									
Number..	535,078	552,409	558,612	563,658	580,262	589,105	607,116	617,791	618,382
Percent..	78.9	80.1	79.9	79.5	81.5	82.8	85.1	86.0	86.3
Uninsured									
Number..	143,003	136,840	140,660	145,288	131,986	122,436	105,966	100,628	97,796
Percent..	21.1	19.9	20.1	20.5	18.5	17.2	14.9	14.0	13.7
Percent in the U.S. not covered..	15.1	15.5	15.1	14.8	14.5	11.7	9.4	8.6	8.7
Children Under 18 Years of Age[1]	183,261	187,984	187,708	187,072	187,885	186,245	185,917	186,839	194,383
Covered by Private or Public Insurance									
Number..	158,268	165,141	165,599	161,115	166,043	164,993	166,252	168,245	175,661
Percent..	86.4	87.8	88.2	86.1	88.4	88.6	89.4	90.0	90.4
Uninsured									
Number..	24,993	22,843	22,109	25,957	21,842	21,252	19,665	18,594	18,722
Percent..	13.6	12.2	11.8	13.9	11.6	11.4	10.6	10.0	9.6
Percent in the U.S. not covered..	8.6	8.0	7.5	7.2	7.1	6.0	4.8	4.5	5.0

[1] 2017 data is for individuals under 19 years of age.

Table AK-7. Employment Status by Demographic Group, 2018

(Numbers in thousands, percent.)

Characteristic	Civilian noninstitutional population	Civilian labor force		Employed		Unemployed	
		Number	Percent of population	Number	Percent of population	Number	Percent of population
Total..	546	355	65.0	332	60.7	23	6.6
Sex							
Male..	278	191	68.7	176	63.1	16	8.2
Female...	268	164	61.1	156	58.2	8	4.7
Race, Sex, and Hispanic Origin							
White...	351	233	66.3	224	63.6	10	4.1
Male...	182	127	70.0	121	66.4	7	5.1
Female.....................................	169	106	62.4	103	60.6	3	2.9
Black or African American..................	NA	NA	NA	NA	NA	NA	NA
Male...	NA	NA	NA	NA	NA	NA	NA
Female.....................................	NA	NA	NA	NA	NA	NA	NA
Hispanic or Latino ethnicity[1]...........	32	22	68.4	21	65.2	1	4.3
Male...	18	13	69.5	12	65.9	1	5.0
Female.....................................	NA	NA	NA	NA	NA	NA	NA
Age							
16 to 19 years...............................	38	13	35.3	11	28.2	3	20.0
20 to 24 years...............................	49	36	73.8	32	65.3	4	11.8
25 to 34 years...............................	108	86	79.8	80	73.8	7	7.6
35 to 44 years...............................	83	67	80.8	64	76.8	3	4.9
45 to 54 years...............................	82	66	80.9	63	77.0	3	4.8
55 to 64 years...............................	97	62	64.2	60	61.5	3	4.2
65 years and over...........................	89	23	26.0	22	24.9	1	4.3

NOTE: Data in Table 7 are from the Current Population Survey (CPS) and do not match the estimates in Table 8. See notes and definitions for further information.
[1] May be of any race.
NA = Not available.

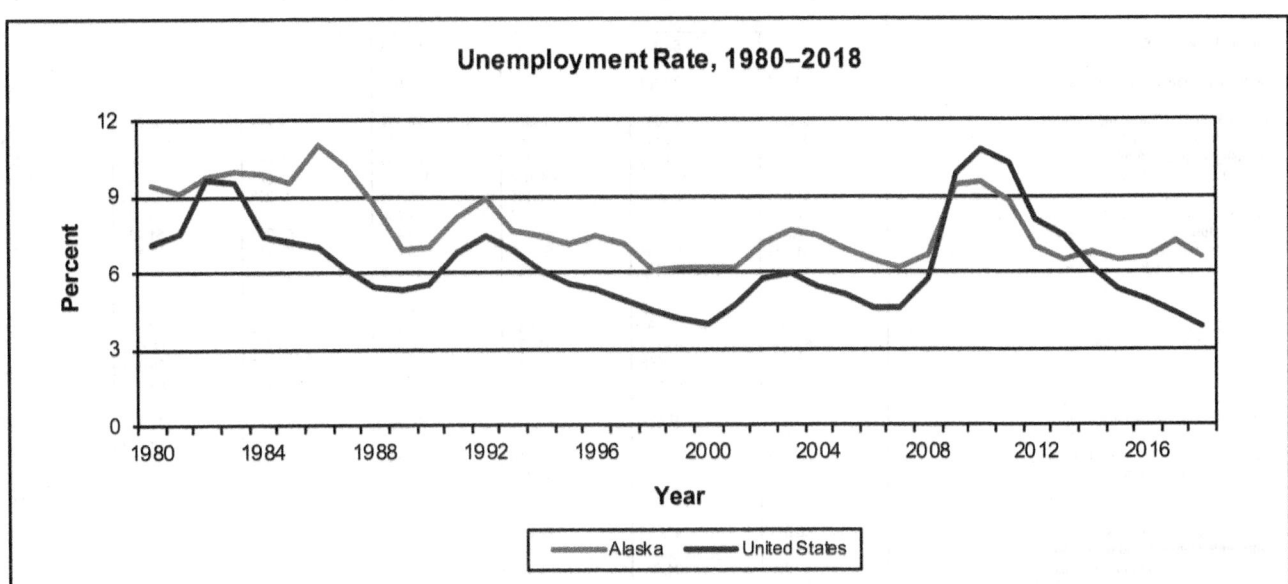

Table AK-8. Employment Status of the Civilian Noninstitutional Population Age 16 Years and Over

(Number, percent.)

Year	Civilian labor force	Civilian participation rate	Employed	Unemployed	Unemployment rate
2010..	361,913	69.8	333,416	28,497	7.9
2011..	365,913	69.2	338,161	27,752	7.6
2012..	365,519	68.3	339,474	26,045	7.1
2013..	365,292	67.9	339,801	25,491	7.0
2014..	365704	67.7	340585	25119	6.9
2015..	363,872	67.0	340,132	23,740	6.5
2016..	363,047	66.4	337,947	25,100	6.9
2017..	362,783	66.4	336,806	25,977	7.2
2018..	356,886	65.2	333,375	23,511	6.6

Table AK-9. Employment and Average Wages by Industry

(Estimates are based on the 2012 *North American Industry Classification System* [NAICS].)

Industry	2011	2012	2013	2014	2015	2016	2017
	Number of Jobs						
Wage and Salary Employment by Industry	358,363	364,972	365,773	366,038	367,546	361,040	356,627
Farm Wage and Salary Employment	602	421	426	509	465	435	434
Nonfarm Wage and Salary Employment	357,761	364,551	365,347	365,529	367,081	360,605	356,193
Private wage and salary employment	248,907	255,612	258,297	260,470	262,338	256,968	253,093
Forestry, fishing, and related activities	862	656	659	672	703	651	583
Mining	15,574	16,596	17,014	17,602	17,041	14,190	12,790
Utilities	2,106	2,117	2,135	2,112	2,138	2,122	2,118
Construction	16,232	16,688	16,840	17,546	18,154	16,682	15,550
Manufacturing	13,705	14,109	14,463	14,436	14,083	13,609	13,236
Durable goods manufacturing	1,862	2,203	2,254	2,074	2,143	2,014	1,900
Nondurable goods manufacturing	11,843	11,906	12,209	12,362	11,940	11,595	11,336
Wholesale trade	6,346	6,305	6,645	6,534	6,570	6,460	6,383
Retail trade	36,060	36,166	36,168	37,029	37,684	37,332	36,628
Transportation and warehousing	19,348	19,891	19,619	19,596	19,855	19,899	19,852
Information	6,326	6,210	6,156	6,250	6,320	6,289	5,974
Finance and insurance	7,382	7,392	7,411	7,323	7,357	7,388	7,312
Real estate and rental and leasing	5,020	4,950	4,957	4,927	4,920	4,827	4,786
Professional, scientific, and technical services	14,533	14,998	15,208	14,915	14,774	13,631	13,321
Management of companies and enterprises	2,773	3,007	3,058	3,002	3,139	2,914	2,866
Administrative and waste services	11,602	12,120	12,159	12,287	12,320	12,144	11,870
Educational services	3,212	3,207	3,304	3,306	3,345	3,313	3,408
Health care and social assistance	41,876	43,857	44,636	44,203	44,637	46,076	47,029
Arts, entertainment, and recreation	4,795	4,897	4,908	4,956	4,816	5,016	5,178
Accommodation and food services	27,888	28,580	29,005	29,518	30,357	30,546	30,472
Other services, except public administration	13,267	13,866	13,952	14,256	14,125	13,879	13,737
Government and government enterprises	108,854	108,939	107,050	105,059	104,743	103,637	103,100
	Dollars						
Average Wages and Salaries by Industry	52,383	53,670	54,540	56,348	57,716	56,711	57,052
Average Farm Wages and Salaries	24,176	39,081	38,577	32,921	33,882	38,538	38,265
Average Nonfarm Wages and Salaries	52,431	53,687	54,558	56,381	57,746	56,733	57,074
Average private wages and salaries	50,886	52,310	53,463	55,541	57,074	55,369	55,545
Forestry, fishing, and related activities	53,212	58,123	63,178	63,138	60,889	60,724	65,909
Mining	124,671	128,118	130,678	137,379	141,022	136,045	136,274
Utilities	81,393	85,966	88,145	88,411	93,208	91,065	92,863
Construction	72,577	74,450	77,234	81,766	83,982	80,225	77,491
Manufacturing	41,320	43,407	45,120	45,479	50,904	51,400	53,008
Durable goods manufacturing	51,396	56,167	58,428	59,770	63,117	59,193	60,685
Nondurable goods manufacturing	39,736	41,046	42,663	43,082	48,711	50,047	51,722
Wholesale trade	55,488	56,172	56,181	57,680	60,033	59,921	60,143
Retail trade	30,580	31,397	31,633	32,446	32,980	32,953	33,527
Transportation and warehousing	62,629	63,159	64,335	65,986	66,491	66,503	68,266
Information	61,585	62,058	63,542	65,864	68,366	66,399	67,627
Finance and insurance	60,078	62,611	63,365	65,869	68,484	69,305	71,567
Real estate and rental and leasing	40,723	41,827	42,502	44,035	45,346	46,528	46,369
Professional, scientific, and technical services	70,914	72,422	74,261	77,040	77,669	74,230	73,807
Management of companies and enterprises	85,026	84,471	81,416	87,345	87,860	88,688	91,782
Administrative and waste services	43,605	44,456	44,403	46,328	47,849	48,012	48,361
Educational services	28,366	29,396	29,697	29,120	29,303	29,840	30,899
Health care and social assistance	46,821	47,696	48,887	50,405	52,809	53,355	54,841
Arts, entertainment, and recreation	21,865	22,504	23,471	24,264	25,258	25,513	25,739
Accommodation and food services	23,939	24,696	25,329	26,737	27,572	27,767	28,255
Other services, except public administration	34,822	35,165	36,105	37,296	38,423	39,303	40,625
Government and government enterprises	55,964	56,918	57,200	58,463	59,431	60,116	60,829

Table AK-10. Employment Characteristics by Family Type

(Number, percent.)

Family type and labor force status	2015		2016		2017	
	Total	Families with own children under 18 years	Total	Families with own children under 18 years	Total	Families with own children under 18 years
All Families...	163,800	77,964	164,102	76,055	167,401	80,172
FAMILY TYPE AND LABOR FORCE STATUS						
Married-Couple Families.....................................	120,348	50,683	122,168	52,831	123,825	55,423
Both husband and wife in labor force................	56.4	64.3	55.9	66.6	51.8	60.7
Husband in labor force, wife not in labor force	24.2	30.4	21.5	24.8	22.9	30.2
Wife in labor force, husband not in labor force	6.5	3.5	9.0	6.5	10.1	6.3
Both husband and wife not in labor force................	12.4	1.5	12.7	2.0	14.5	2.3
Other Families	43,452	27,281	41,934	23,224	43,576	24,749
Female householder, no husband present................	65.2	66.7	65.7	65.7	65.6	67.1
In labor force..	50	58.8	48.5	55.5	49.7	57.9
Not in labor force	15.2	7.9	17.1	10.2	15.9	9.2
Male householder, no wife present..................	34.8	33.3	34.3	34.3	34.4	32.9
In labor force..	27.9	28.4	27.3	30.7	26.0	30.2
Not in labor force	6.9	4.9	7.1	3.6	8.4	2.8

Table AK-11. School Enrollment and Educational Attainment, 2017

(Number, percent.)

Item	State	U.S.
Enrollment		
Total population 3 years and over, enrolled in school	186,461	81,273,337
Enrolled in nursery school or preschool (percent)...	5.0	6.0
Enrolled in kindergarten (percent)...	6.2	4.9
Enrolled in elementary school, grades 1-8 (percent)..	43.2	40.6
Enrolled in high school, grades 9-12 (percent)..	21.7	21.1
Enrolled in college or graduate school (percent)...	23.8	27.4
Attainment		
Total population 25 years and over	481,561	221,250,083
Less than ninth grade (percent)	3	5.1
9th to 12th grade, no diploma (percent)	5.4	6.9
High school graduate, including equivalency (percent)..	27.6	27.1
Some college, no degree (percent)...	26.4	20.4
Associate's degree (percent)	8.9	8.5
Bachelor's degree (percent)	18.0	19.7
Graduate or professional degree (percent)..	10.8	12.3
High school graduate or higher (percent)	91.7	88
Bachelor's degree or higher (percent)..	28.8	32

Table AK-12. Public School Characteristics and Educational Indicators

(Number, percent; data derived from National Center of Education Statistics.)

Item	State	U.S.
Public Elementary and Secondary Schools		
Number of operational school districts, 2016-17	54	18,377
Number of operational schools, 2016-17...	507	98,330
Percent charter schools	5.5	7.1
Total public school enrollment, 2016-17..	132,737	50,587,859
Percent charter school enrollment	5.0	6.0
Student-teacher ratio, Fall 2015	16.9	16.0
Expenditures per student (dollars), 2015-16..	17,510	11,841
Four-year adjusted cohort graduation rate (ACGR)[1]	78.2	84.6
Students eligible for free or reduced-price lunch (percent), 2015-16................	42.7	52.1
English language learners (percent), Fall 2016	11.0	9.6
Students age 3 to 21 served under IDEA, part B (percent), 2017-18	14.3	13.7

Public Schools by Type, 2016-17		Percent of state public schools
Total number of schools..	507	100.0
Special education..	3	0.6
Vocational education...	3	0.6
Alternative education..	23	4.5

[1] Adjusted Cohort Graduation Rates (ACGR) differ from Averaged Freshmen Graduation Rates (AFGR).

Table AK-13. Reported Voting and Registration of the Voting-Age Population, November 2018

(Numbers in thousands, percent.)

Item	Total population	Total citizen population	Registered			Voted		
			Total registered	Percent registered (total population)	Percent registered (total citizen population)	Total voted	Percent voted (total population)	Percent voted (total citizen population)
U.S. Total	249,748	228,832	153,066	61.3	66.9	122,281	49.0	53.4
State Total	523	497	337	64.4	67.7	263	50.2	52.8
Sex								
Male	265	255	175	65.9	68.4	133	50.2	52.1
Female	258	242	162	62.9	67.1	130	50.2	53.6
Race								
White alone	330	324	236	71.6	73.0	193	58.6	59.7
White, non-Hispanic alone	314	310	229	73.0	73.9	187	59.5	60.3
Black alone	16	15	9	(B)	(B)	8	(B)	(B)
Asian alone	55	37	23	(B)	(B)	15	(B)	(B)
Hispanic (of any race)	20	18	10	(B)	(B)	8	(B)	(B)
White alone or in combination	356	350	255	71.6	72.9	210	59.0	60.1
Black alone or in combination	18	17	11	(B)	(B)	9	(B)	(B)
Asian alone or in combination	60	42	25	(B)	(B)	18	(B)	(B)
Age								
18 to 24 years	76	69	36	48.3	(B)	27	35.5	(B)
25 to 34 years	104	99	57	55.1	58.0	39	37.5	39.6
35 to 44 years	76	72	52	68.1	(B)	39	51.4	(B)
45 to 64 years	173	167	121	69.8	72.7	98	56.8	59.1
65 years and over	94	91	70	74.7	77.0	59	63.0	65.0

B = Base is less than 75,000 and therefore too small to show the derived measure.

Table AK-14. Crime

(Number, rate per 100,000. Data are derived from the FBI Uniform Crime Reports.)

Item	State			U.S.		
	2016	2017	Percent change	2016	2017	Percent change
TOTAL POPULATION[1]	741,522	739,795	-0.2	323,405,935	325,719,178	0.7
VIOLENT CRIME						
Number	5,966	6,133	2.8	1,285,606	1,283,220	-0.2
Rate	804.6	829.0	3.0	397.5	394.0	-0.9
Murder and Nonnegligent Manslaughter						
Number	52	62	19.2	17,413	17,284	-0.7
Rate	7.0	8.4	19.5	5.4	5.3	-1.4
Rape[2]						
Number	1,053	863	-18.0	132,414	135,755	2.5
Rate	142.0	116.7	-17.9	40.9	41.7	1.8
Robbery						
Number	850	951	11.9	332,797	319,356	-4.0
Rate	114.6	128.5	12.1	102.9	98.0	-4.7
Aggravated Assault						
Number	4,011	4,257	6.1	802,982	810,825	1.0
Rate	540.9	575.4	6.4	248.3	248.9	0.3
PROPERTY CRIME						
Number	24,876	26,204	5.3	7,928,530	7,694,086	-3.0
Rate	3,354.7	3,542.1	5.6	2,451.6	2,362.2	-3.6
Burglary						
Number	4,053	4,171	2.9	1,516,405	1,401,840	-7.6
Rate	546.6	563.8	3.2	468.9	430.4	-8.2
Larceny-Theft						
Number	17,766	17,775	0.1	5,644,835	5,519,107	-2.2
Rate	2,395.9	2,402.7	0.3	1,745.4	1,694.4	-2.9
Motor Vehicle Theft						
Number	3,057	4,258	39.3	767,290	773,139	0.8
Rate	412.3	575.6	39.6	237.3	237.4	-

NOTE: Although arson data are included in the trend and clearance tables, sufficient data are not available to estimate totals for this offense. Therefore, no arson data are published in this table.
- = Zero or rounds to zero.
[1] Population figures are U.S. Census Bureau provisional estimates as of July 1, 2017.
[2] The figures shown in the rape (revised definition) column were estimated using the revised Uniform Crime Reporting (UCR) definition of rape.

Table AK-15. State Government Finances, 2017

(Dollar amounts in thousands, percent distribution.)

Item	Dollars	Percent distribution
Total Revenue	10,561,638	100.0
General revenue	8,345,313	79.0
Intergovernmental revenue	3,286,785	31.1
Taxes	1,189,786	11.3
General sales	0	-
Selective sales	263,120	2.5
License taxes	134,928	1.3
Individual income tax	0	-
Corporate income tax	87,775	0.8
Other taxes	703,963	6.7
Current charges	748,504	7.1
Miscellaneous general revenue	3,120,238	29.5
Utility revenue	18,690	0.2
Liquor stores revenue	0	-
Insurance trust revenue[1]	2,197,635	20.8
Total Expenditure	11,290,460	100.0
Intergovernmental expenditure	1,829,640	16.2
Direct expenditure	9,460,820	83.8
Current operation	6,557,649	58.1
Capital outlay	1,175,802	10.4
Insurance benefits and repayments	1,367,744	12.1
Assistance and subsidies	158,721	1.4
Interest on debt	200,904	1.8
Exhibit: Salaries and wages	1,705,821	15.1
Total Expenditure	11,290,460	100.0
General expenditure	9,778,966	86.6
Intergovernmental expenditure	1,829,640	16.2
Direct expenditure	7,949,326	70.4
General expenditure, by function:		
Education	2,524,056	22.4
Public welfare	2,724,651	24.1
Hospitals	28,963	0.3
Health	229,041	2.0
Highways	1,143,967	10.1
Police protection	142,360	1.3
Correction	316,353	2.8
Natural resources	405,104	3.6
Parks and recreation	15,374	0.1
Governmental administration	665,074	5.9
Interest on general debt	198,252	1.8
Other and unallocable	1,385,771	12.3
Utility expenditure	143,750	1.4
Liquor stores expenditure	0	-
Insurance trust expenditure	1,367,744	12.1
Debt at End of Fiscal Year	5,921,713	X
Cash and Security Holdings	82,980,365	X

X = Not applicable.
- = Zero or rounds to zero.
[1] Within insurance trust revenue, net earnings of state retirement systems is a calculated statistic (the item code in the data file is X08), and thus can be positive or negative. Net earnings is the sum of earnings on investments plus gains on investments minus losses on investments. The change made in 2002 for asset valuation from book to market value in accordance with Statement 34 of the Governmental Accounting Standards Board is reflected in the calculated statistics.

Table AK-16. State Government Tax Collections, 2018

(Dollars in thousands, percent.)

Item	Dollars	Percent distribution
Total Taxes	1,641,733	100.0
Property taxes	121,563	7.4
Sales and gross receipts	252,974	15.4
General sales and gross receipts	X	-
Selective sales and gross receipts	252,974	15.4
Alcoholic beverages	39,217	2.4
Amusements	11,006	0.7
Insurance premiums	62,429	3.8
Motor fuels	47,149	2.9
Pari-mutuels	X	-
Public utilities	4,819	0.3
Tobacco products	55,500	3.4
Other selective sales	32,854	2.0
Licenses	139,691	8.5
Alcoholic beverages	1,433	0.1
Amusements	0	-
Corporations in general	X	-
Hunting and fishing	35,608	2.2
Motor vehicle	36,258	2.2
Motor vehicle operators	X	-
Public utilities	10,671	0.6
Occupation and business, NEC	51,608	3.1
Other licenses	4,113	0.3
Income taxes	196,321	12.0
Individual income	X	-
Corporation net income	196,321	12.0
Other taxes	931,184	56.7
Death and gift	X	-
Documentary and stock transfer	X	-
Severance	931,184	56.7
Taxes, NEC	0	-

X = Not applicable.
- = Zero or rounds to zero.

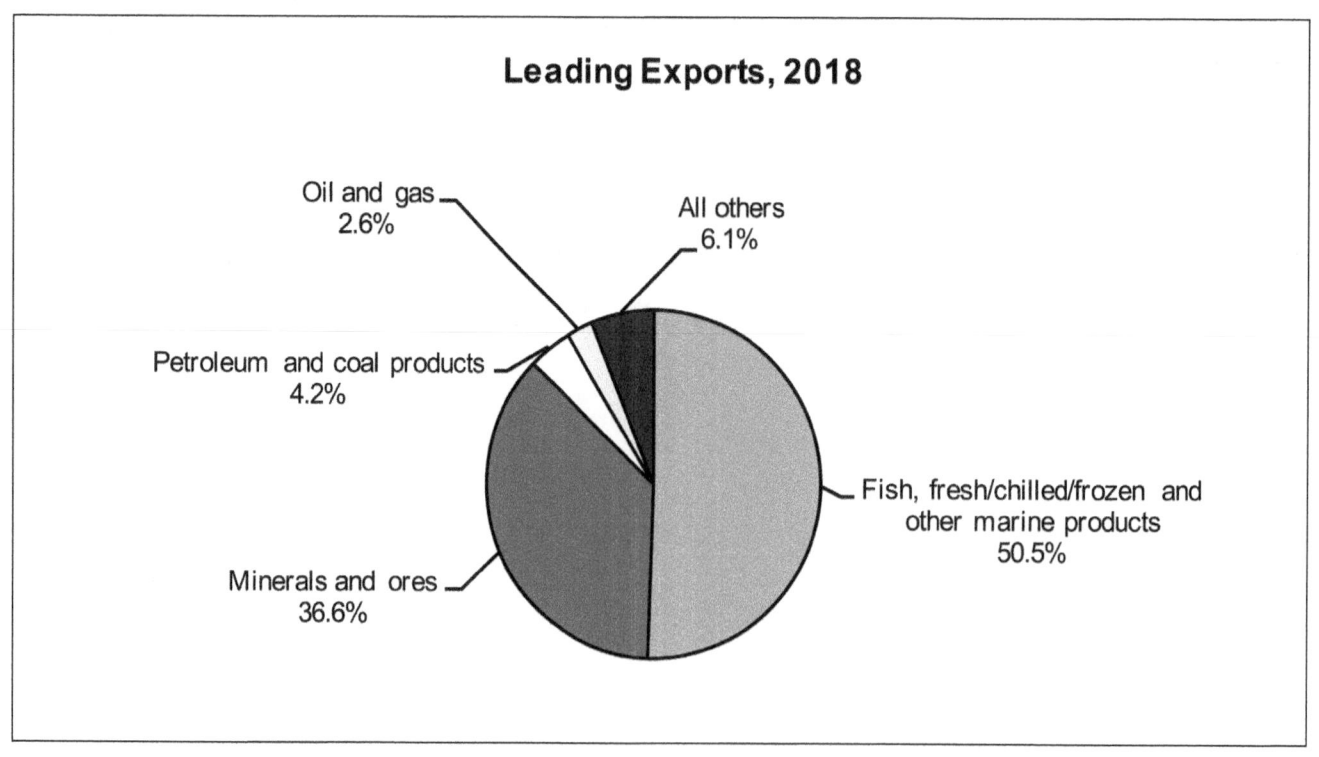

Leading Exports, 2018

Oil and gas 2.6%
All others 6.1%
Petroleum and coal products 4.2%
Fish, fresh/chilled/frozen and other marine products 50.5%
Minerals and ores 36.6%

ARIZONA

Facts and Figures

Location: Southwestern United States; bordered on the North by Utah, on the East by New Mexico, on the South by Mexico, and on the West by Nevada and California; Arizona is one of the Four Corner states—at its NE corner it touches Colorado, New Mexico, and Utah

Area: 113,990 sq, mi. (295,254 sq. km.); rank—6th

Population: 7,171,646 (2018 est.); rank—14th

Principal Cities: capital—Phoenix; largest—Phoenix

Statehood: February 14, 1912; 48th state

U.S. Congress: 2 senators, 9 representatives

State Motto: *Ditat Deus* ("God enriches")

State Song: "Arizona"

State Nickname: The Grand Canyon State

Abbreviations: AZ; Ariz.

State Symbols: flower—saguaro cactus blossom; tree—paloverde; bird—cactus wren

At a Glance

- With an increase in population of 12.2 percent, Arizona ranked 8th among the states in growth from 2010 to 2018.

- In 2018, 17.5 percent of Arizonans were age 65 and older, the 12th highest percent in the nation.

- Arizona's median household income in 2017 was $56,581, compared to the national median household income of $60,336.

- In 2017, 14.9 percent of Arizonans lived below the poverty level, a percentage that ranked 12th in the country.

- Arizona's violent crime rate in 2017 was 508.7 per 100,000 population, ranking 10th in the nation.

Table AZ-1. Population by Age, Sex, Race, and Hispanic Origin

(Number, percent, except where noted.)

Sex, age, race, and Hispanic origin	2000	2010	2018[1]	Percent change, 2010–2018
Total Population.......................	5,130,632	6,392,017	7,171,646	12.2
Percent of total U.S. population	1.8	2.1	2.2	X
Sex				
Male........................	2,561,057	3,175,823	3,565,339	12.3
Female	2,569,575	3,216,814	3,606,307	12.1
Age				
Under 5 years........................	382,386	455,715	435,936	-4.3
5 to 19 years......................	1,135,802	1,363,926	1,401,941	2.8
20 to 64 years......................	2,944,605	3,690,545	4,075,519	10.4
65 years and over	667,839	881,831	1,258,250	42.7
Median age (years)	34.2	35.9	37.9	5.6
Race and Hispanic Origin				
One race				
White	3,873,611	5,418,483	5,937,806	9.6
Black	158,873	280,905	364,280	29.7
American Indian and Alaska Native	255,879	335,278	380,160	13.4
Asian	92,236	188,456	263,696	39.9
Native Hawaiian or Other Pacific Islander	6,733	16,112	19,789	22.8
Two or more races	146,526	152,783	205,915	34.8
Hispanic (of any race).......................	1,295,617	1,943,466	2,266,343	16.6

X = Not applicable.
[1] Population figures for 2018 are July 1 estimates. The 2010 estimates are taken from the 2010 Census.

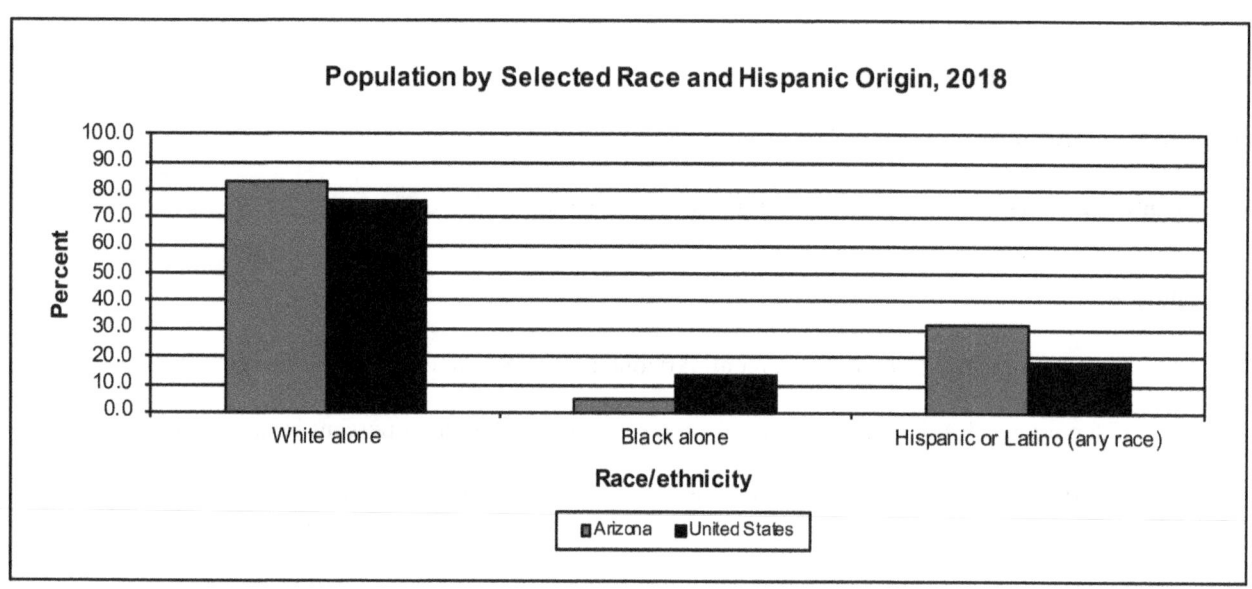

Table AZ-2. Marital Status

(Number, percent distribution.)

Sex, age, race, and Hispanic origin	2000	2010	2017
Males, 15 Years and Over	1,966,032	2,492,590	2,797,660
Never married	29.6	35.3	37.1
Now married, except separated.......................	56.4	50.1	47.9
Separated.......................	1.6	1.4	1.5
Widowed.......................	2.6	2.5	2.6
Divorced.......................	9.8	10.7	11.0
Females, 15 Years and Over	2,013,304	2,559,409	2,865,568
Never married	22.5	28.0	30.0
Now married, except separated.......................	53.6	48.0	45.9
Separated.......................	2.1	2.2	2.2
Widowed.......................	9.4	8.3	8.1
Divorced.......................	12.3	13.5	13.8

Table AZ-3. Households and Housing Characteristics

(Number, percent, dollars.)

Item	2000	2010	2017	Average annual percent change, 2010–2017
Total Households..	1,901,327	2,334,050	2,552,972	1.3
Family households	1,287,367	1,548,428	1,652,325	1.0
Married-couple family	986,303	1,134,229	1,206,518	0.9
Other family	310,064	414,199	445,807	1.1
Male householder, no wife present................	90,283	123,772	138,074	1.7
Female householder, no husband present.........	210,781	290,427	307,733	0.9
Nonfamily households	613,960	785,622	900,647	2.1
Householder living alone..........................	472,006	621,291	710,620	2.1
Householder not living alone......................	141,954	164,331	190,027	2.2
Housing Characteristics				
Total housing units	2,189,189	2,846,738	2,999,185	0.8
Occupied housing units	1,901,327	2,334,050	2,552,972	1.3
Owner occupied	1,293,556	1,522,938	1,652,321	1.2
Renter occupied	607,771	811,112	900,651	1.6
Average household size..............................	2.64	2.69	2.69	-
Financial Characteristics				
Median gross rent of renter-occupied housing	619	844	1020	3.0
Median monthly owner costs for housing units with a mortgage	1,039	1,442	1,365	-0.8
Median value of owner-occupied housing units.........	121,300	168,800	223,400	4.6

- = Zero or rounds to zero.

Table AZ-4. Migration, Origin, and Language

(Number, percent.)

Characteristic	State			U.S.		
	2016	2017	Percent change	2016	2017	Percent change
Residence 1 Year Ago						
Population 1 year and over	6,851,836	6,935,358	1.2	319,361,956	321,994,428	0.8
Same house	81.5	82.4	X	85.4	85.7	X
Different house in the U.S.	17.7	16.9	X	13.9	13.6	X
Same county	11.8	11.3	X	8.3	8.1	X
Different county	5.8	5.6	X	5.6	5.6	X
Same state	1.8	1.9	X	3.2	3.3	X
Different state	4.0	3.8	X	2.4	2.3	X
Abroad	0.8	0.7	X	0.7	0.7	X
Place of Birth						
Native born	5,996,188	6,091,370	1.6	279,388,170	281,193,323	0.6
Male	49.9	50.0	X	49.3	49.4	X
Female	50.1	50.0	X	50.7	50.6	X
Foreign born	934,883	924,900	-1.1	43,739,345	44,525,855	1.8
Male	48.7	47.6	X	48.5	48.4	X
Female	51.3	52.4	X	51.5	51.6	X
Foreign born; naturalized U.S. citizen................	399,036	401,048	0.5	21,238,372	21,948,732	3.3
Male	45.5	44.9	X	45.9	45.9	X
Female	54.5	55.1	X	54.1	54.1	X
Foreign born; not a U.S. citizen.....................	535,847	523,852	-2.2	22,500,973	22,577,123	0.3
Male	51.1	49.7	X	51	50.8	X
Female	48.9	50.3	X	49	49.2	X
Entered 2010 or later	16.5	18.8	X	18.6	21.3	X
Entered 2000 to 2009	24.7	24.5	X	26.7	25.7	X
Entered before 2000.................................	58.8	56.7	X	54.7	53.0	X
World Region of Birth, Foreign						
Foreign-born population, excluding population born at sea	934,770	924,900	-1.1	43,738,901	44,525,458	1.8
Europe	9.2	9.2	X	10.9	10.8	X
Asia...	20.5	20.9	X	30.8	31.2	X
Africa	3.3	3.2	X	4.9	5.1	X
Oceania	0.6	0.7	X	0.6	0.6	X
Latin America	61.6	61.6	X	51	50.4	X
North America	4.8	4.4	X	1.8	1.8	X
Language Spoken at Home and Ability to Speak English						
Population 5 years and over..........................	6,494,749	6,581,229	1.3	303,328,961	305,924,019	0.9
English only	72.9	72.6	X	78.4	78.2	X
Language other than English.........................	27.1	27.4	X	21.6	21.8	X
Speaks English less than "very well"................	8.8	8.7	X	8.6	8.5	X

NA = Not available.
X = Not applicable.
- = Zero or rounds to zero.

Table AZ-5. Median Income and Poverty Status, 2017

(Number, percent, except as noted.)

Characteristic	State		U.S.	
	Number	Percent	Number	Percent
Median Income				
Households (dollars)...	56,581	X	60,336	X
Families (dollars)	67,886	X	73,891	X
Below Poverty Level (All People)	1,018,935	14.9	42,583,651	13.4
Sex				
Male	468,950	13.9	19,004,547	12.2
Female	549,985	15.8	23,579,104	14.5
Age				
Under 18 years..	332,299	20.8	13,353,202	18.4
Related children under 18 years........................	325,717	20.4	13,053,472	18.1
18 to 64 years...	579,113	14.2	24,648,677	12.6
65 years and over..	107,523	9.0	4,581,772	9.3

X = Not applicable.

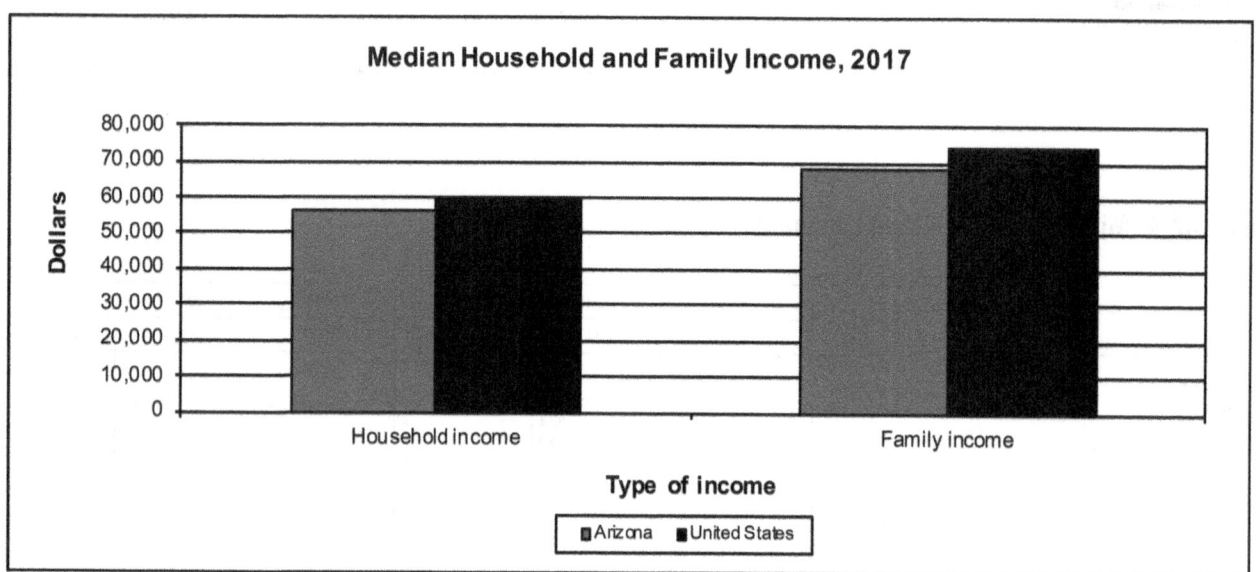

Table AZ-6. Health Insurance Coverage Status for the Civilian Noninstitutionalized Population and Children Under 18 Years of Age

(Number, percent.)

Item	2009	2010	2011	2012	2013	2014	2015	2016	2017
Civilian Noninstitutionalized Population	6,501,531	6,310,174	6,378,280	6,443,654	6,521,226	6,623,074	6,719,354	6,824,645	6,908,121
Covered by Private or Public Insurance									
Number..	5,375,026	5,245,042	5,283,270	5,312,695	5,403,040	5,719,746	5,991,378	6,143,407	6,213,331
Percent..	82.7	83.1	82.8	82.4	82.9	86.4	89.2	90.0	89.9
Uninsured									
Number..	1,126,505	1,065,132	1,095,010	1,130,959	1,118,186	903,328	727,976	681,238	694,790
Percent..	17.3	16.9	17.2	17.6	17.1	13.6	10.8	10.0	10.1
Percent in the U.S. not covered..............................	15.1	15.5	15.1	14.8	14.5	11.7	9.4	8.6	8.7
Children Under 18 Years of Age[1]	1,729,814	1,629,931	1,621,830	1,617,380	1,613,505	1,620,576	1,619,393	1,629,040	1,729,440
Covered by Private or Public Insurance									
Number..	1,521,961	1,421,964	1,413,411	1,403,418	1,421,745	1,458,722	1,485,146	1,509,594	1,596,296
Percent..	88.0	87.2	87.1	86.8	88.1	90.0	91.7	92.7	92.3
Uninsured									
Number..	207,853	207,967	208,419	213,962	191,760	161,854	134,247	119,446	133,144
Percent..	12.0	12.8	12.9	13.2	11.9	10.0	8.3	7.3	7.7
Percent in the U.S. not covered..............................	8.6	8.0	7.5	7.2	7.1	6.0	4.8	4.5	5.0

[1] 2017 data is for individuals under 19 years of age.

Table AZ-7. Employment Status by Demographic Group, 2018

(Numbers in thousands, percent.)

Characteristic	Civilian noninstitutional population	Civilian labor force		Employed		Unemployed	
		Number	Percent of population	Number	Percent of population	Number	Percent of population
Total....................................	5,568	3,409	61.2	3,250	58.4	159	4.7
Sex							
Male..	2,716	1,829	67.3	1,740	64.1	89	4.9
Female.....................................	2,852	1,580	55.4	1,510	52.9	70	4.4
Race, Sex, and Hispanic Origin							
White.......................................	4,776	2,879	60.3	2,755	57.7	125	4.3
Male......................................	2,328	1,554	66.7	1,482	63.7	72	4.6
Female...................................	2,448	1,326	54.2	1,273	52.0	53	4.0
Black or African American...........	240	173	72.1	158	66.0	15	8.4
Male......................................	NA	NA	NA	NA	NA	NA	NA
Female...................................	NA	NA	NA	NA	NA	NA	NA
Hispanic or Latino ethnicity[1].......	1,747	1,134	64.9	1,070	61.2	64	5.7
Male......................................	857	635	74.0	601	70.1	34	5.3
Female...................................	890	499	56.1	469	52.7	31	6.1
Age							
16 to 19 years..........................	416	143	34.3	118	28.4	25	17.3
20 to 24 years..........................	483	374	77.3	345	71.3	29	7.8
25 to 34 years..........................	894	725	81.0	688	77.0	36	5.0
35 to 44 years..........................	839	681	81.1	663	79.0	18	2.6
45 to 54 years..........................	910	719	79.0	702	77.2	17	2.3
55 to 64 years..........................	899	566	63.0	543	60.4	23	4.1
65 years and over......................	1,127	203	18.0	191	17.0	12	5.8

NOTE: Data in Table 7 are from the Current Population Survey (CPS) and do not match the estimates in Table 8. See notes and definitions for further information.
[1]May be of any race.
NA = Not available.

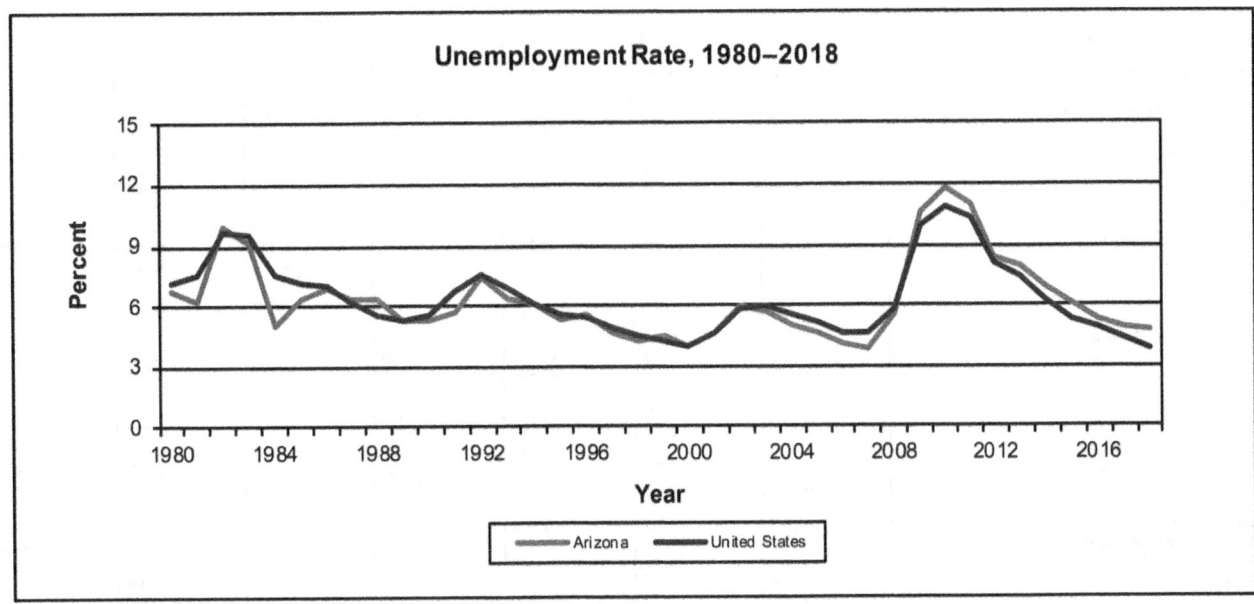

Table AZ-8. Employment Status of the Civilian Noninstitutional Population Age 16 Years and Over

(Number, percent.)

Year	Civilian labor force	Civilian participation rate	Employed	Unemployed	Unemployment rate
2010....................................	3,089,705	63.1	2,769,454	320,251	10.4
2011....................................	3,037,017	61.7	2,748,470	288,547	9.5
2012....................................	3,028,878	60.6	2,776,349	252,529	8.3
2013....................................	3,029,425	59.7	2,794,697	234,728	7.7
2014....................................	3,087,942	59.9	2,878,611	209,331	6.8
2015....................................	3,153,040	60.0	2,962,245	190,795	6.1
2016....................................	3,225,703	60.2	3,052,788	172,915	5.4
2017....................................	3,312,720	60.6	3,151,405	161,315	4.9
2018....................................	3,439,755	61.4	3,273,550	166,205	4.8

Table AZ-9. Employment and Average Wages by Industry

(Estimates are based on the 2012 *North American Industry Classification System* [NAICS].)

Industry	2011	2012	2013	2014	2015	2016	2017
				Number of Jobs			
Wage and Salary Employment by Industry........................	2,499,245	2,558,410	2,617,500	2,669,755	2,745,697	2,816,903	2,881,141
Farm Wage and Salary Employment................................	11,523	12,626	13,949	12,360	13,584	15,203	13,219
Nonfarm Wage and Salary Employment...........................	2,487,722	2,545,784	2,603,551	2,657,395	2,732,113	2,801,700	2,867,922
Private wage and salary employment.............................	2,045,870	2,102,624	2,159,150	2,212,261	2,287,470	2,355,879	2,419,272
Forestry, fishing, and related activities..........................	12,389	12,091	11,957	12,121	13,224	12,882	12,039
Mining..	10,917	11,924	12,616	12,303	11,732	11,298	11,723
Utilities..	11,971	12,290	11,934	11,952	12,086	12,369	12,263
Construction	113,952	119,422	126,937	128,148	130,978	138,537	149,183
Manufacturing..	148,211	153,559	153,985	155,073	156,499	158,462	162,538
Durable goods manufacturing..................................	117,558	121,627	121,335	121,607	121,099	121,163	123,367
Nondurable goods manufacturing............................	30,653	31,932	32,650	33,466	35,400	37,299	39,171
Wholesale trade	98,134	98,855	99,388	95,608	95,529	96,386	97,539
Retail trade..	297,189	300,017	301,687	314,829	324,208	330,485	334,074
Transportation and warehousing..................................	70,107	72,467	73,148	75,613	79,808	82,963	86,701
Information	36,751	38,239	41,815	43,379	45,202	45,360	45,378
Finance and insurance	124,879	129,216	135,835	140,603	149,899	156,893	166,474
Real estate and rental and leasing.............................	45,761	46,962	48,084	48,500	49,184	50,665	51,882
Professional, scientific, and technical services	124,864	124,885	128,475	131,733	134,738	142,187	146,242
Management of companies and enterprises...................	25,216	26,594	28,756	29,699	31,356	31,768	31,486
Administrative and waste services...............................	200,168	208,298	220,661	225,827	235,195	242,520	245,555
Educational services	54,218	57,055	56,136	57,639	59,936	60,523	61,316
Health care and social assistance................................	302,994	312,255	319,520	325,901	340,468	355,341	368,137
Arts, entertainment, and recreation..............................	33,287	34,868	35,646	38,940	40,121	41,359	43,786
Accommodation and food services...............................	227,149	233,348	241,506	249,539	260,870	269,978	278,135
Other services, except public administration.................	107,713	110,279	111,064	114,854	116,437	115,903	114,821
Government and government enterprises......................	441,852	443,160	444,401	445,134	444,643	445,821	448,650
				Dollars			
Average Wages and Salaries by Industry	45,412	46,493	46,838	47,847	48,814	49,431	51,157
Average Farm Wages and Salaries	33,151	35,086	35,429	38,593	29,719	30,742	35,559
Average Nonfarm Wages and Salaries	45,469	46,550	46,899	47,890	48,909	49,533	51,229
Average private wages and salaries.............................	45,294	46,544	46,909	47,957	48,946	49,567	51,329
Forestry, fishing, and related activities........................	23,221	23,693	24,102	25,956	25,729	28,279	30,220
Mining..	78,686	80,890	78,991	79,193	81,501	77,261	80,503
Utilities..	95,396	95,575	97,516	102,398	101,069	104,607	108,747
Construction	45,984	47,920	48,410	49,560	50,311	51,698	54,383
Manufacturing..	70,154	70,721	70,908	72,639	74,039	74,250	75,498
Durable goods manufacturing..................................	77,292	77,921	78,198	80,185	82,147	82,699	84,259
Nondurable goods manufacturing............................	42,777	43,298	43,818	45,218	46,300	46,804	47,907
Wholesale trade	67,066	71,461	68,749	72,278	74,866	76,105	78,597
Retail trade..	30,903	30,879	30,349	31,166	31,982	32,412	33,484
Transportation and warehousing..................................	49,567	50,253	50,494	50,818	52,807	53,029	54,720
Information	59,865	61,675	63,180	66,659	67,826	71,256	73,319
Finance and insurance	63,809	67,165	69,575	71,053	73,097	74,341	75,933
Real estate and rental and leasing.............................	44,646	46,793	46,637	48,586	50,253	51,405	52,749
Professional, scientific, and technical services	69,995	73,492	74,380	74,841	76,601	76,313	77,800
Management of companies and enterprises...................	77,280	82,771	85,738	92,256	89,998	88,594	95,516
Administrative and waste services...............................	33,596	33,994	34,833	35,935	37,106	37,722	39,262
Educational services	39,910	40,674	40,992	41,316	41,513	41,371	41,939
Health care and social assistance................................	48,743	49,217	49,494	50,265	51,047	51,300	52,877
Arts, entertainment, and recreation..............................	36,887	38,216	38,419	39,381	39,069	40,522	41,770
Accommodation and food services...............................	20,342	20,995	21,326	21,953	22,624	22,957	24,399
Other services, except public administration.................	28,708	29,666	30,719	31,995	32,893	34,053	36,335
Government and government enterprises......................	46,283	46,575	46,850	47,557	48,721	49,354	50,694

Table AZ-10. Employment Characteristics by Family Type

(Number, percent.)

Family type and labor force status	2015		2016		2017	
	Total	Families with own children under 18 years	Total	Families with own children under 18 years	Total	Families with own children under 18 years
All Families.................................	1,598,414	665,587	1,648,739	671,482	1,652,325	662,656
FAMILY TYPE AND LABOR FORCE STATUS						
Married-Couple Families......................	1,153,542	426,411	1,194,185	440,131	1,206,518	434,955
Both husband and wife in labor force..........	42.7	59.1	42.7	59.4	43.3	60.9
Husband in labor force, wife not in labor force..........	23.4	34.2	23.9	34.4	23.3	32.9
Wife in labor force, husband not in labor force..........	8	4.5	7.6	3.9	7.4	3.8
Both husband and wife not in labor force..........	25.2	2.0	24.9	1.8	25.0	1.8
Other Families	444,872	239,176	454,554	231,351	445,807	227,701
Female householder, no husband present..........	69.2	71.5	69.7	73.3	69.0	71.6
In labor force..........	48.5	59.3	49.3	60.3	49.0	60.0
Not in labor force..........	20.6	12.3	20.4	13.0	20.0	11.5
Male householder, no wife present..........	30.8	28.5	30.3	26.7	31.0	28.4
In labor force..........	24.5	25.4	23.8	23.9	24.3	26.1
Not in labor force..........	6.4	3.1	6.5	2.8	6.7	2.4

Table AZ-11. School Enrollment and Educational Attainment, 2017

(Number, percent.)

Item	State	U.S.
Enrollment		
Total population 3 years and over, enrolled in school	1,757,544	81,273,337
Enrolled in nursery school or preschool (percent)..........	5.0	6.0
Enrolled in kindergarten (percent)..........	4.6	4.9
Enrolled in elementary school, grades 1-8 (percent)..........	42.0	40.6
Enrolled in high school, grades 9-12 (percent)..........	21.8	21.1
Enrolled in college or graduate school (percent)..........	26.5	27.4
Attainment		
Total population 25 years and over	4,711,362	221,250,083
Less than ninth grade (percent)..........	5.4	5.1
9th to 12th grade, no diploma (percent)..........	7.4	6.9
High school graduate, including equivalency (percent)..........	24.1	27.1
Some college, no degree (percent)	25.0	20.4
Associate's degree (percent)..........	8.7	8.5
Bachelor's degree (percent)..........	18.3	19.7
Graduate or professional degree (percent)..........	11.0	12.3
High school graduate or higher (percent)..........	87.2	88.0
Bachelor's degree or higher (percent)..........	29.4	32.0

Table AZ-12. Public School Characteristics and Educational Indicators

(Number, percent; data derived from National Center of Education Statistics.)

Item	State	U.S.
Public Elementary and Secondary Schools		
Number of operational school districts, 2016-17..........	698	18,377
Number of operational schools, 2016-17..........	2,308	98,330
Percent charter schools	23.8	7.1
Total public school enrollment, 2016-17..........	1,123,137	50,587,859
Percent charter school enrollment..........	16.6	6.0
Student-teacher ratio, Fall 2015	23.1	16.0
Expenditures per student (dollars), 2015-16..........	7,772	11,841
Four-year adjusted cohort graduation rate (ACGR)[1]..........	78.0	84.6
Students eligible for free or reduced-price lunch (percent), 2015-16..........	50.2	52.1
English language learners (percent), Fall 2016	6.3	9.6
Students age 3 to 21 served under IDEA, part B (percent), 2017-18	12.5	13.7

Public Schools by Type, 2016-17		Percent of state public schools
Total number of schools..........	2,308	100.0
Special education..........	20	0.9
Vocational education..........	246	10.7
Alternative education..........	59	2.6

[1]Adjusted Cohort Graduation Rates (ACGR) differ from Averaged Freshmen Graduation Rates (AFGR).

Table AZ-13. Reported Voting and Registration of the Voting-Age Population, November 2018

(Numbers in thousands, percent.)

Item	Total population	Total citizen population	Registered			Voted		
			Total registered	Percent registered (total population)	Percent registered (total citizen population)	Total voted	Percent voted (total population)	Percent voted (total citizen population)
U.S. Total	249,748	228,832	153,066	61.3	66.9	122,281	49.0	53.4
State Total..............................	5,361	4,757	3,262	60.8	68.6	2,800	52.2	58.9
Sex								
Male	2,606	2,259	1,539	59.0	68.1	1,288	49.4	57.0
Female	2,755	2,497	1,723	62.5	69.0	1,512	54.9	60.6
Race								
White alone..............................	4,635	4,168	2,968	64.0	71.2	2,535	54.7	60.8
White, non-Hispanic alone	3,128	3,065	2,272	72.6	74.1	2,000	63.9	65.3
Black alone..............................	257	222	114	44.4	51.5	104	40.6	47.0
Asian alone	198	106	63	32.0	59.8	59	30.0	56.1
Hispanic (of any race)..............	1,624	1,205	757	46.6	62.8	588	36.2	48.8
White alone or in combination	4,688	4,216	2,996	63.9	71.1	2,563	54.7	60.8
Black alone or in combination..........	280	239	132	47.0	55.0	122	43.5	50.9
Asian alone or in combination............	209	117	71	34.0	60.8	67	32.1	57.4
Age								
18 to 24 years..............................	652	619	302	46.3	48.8	217	33.3	35.0
25 to 34 years..............................	876	729	360	41.1	49.4	287	32.8	39.4
35 to 44 years..............................	873	714	541	62.0	75.8	407	46.6	57.0
45 to 64 years..............................	1,834	1,637	1,229	67.0	75.0	1,090	59.4	66.6
65 years and over	1,126	1,057	830	73.7	78.5	799	71.0	75.6

Table AZ-14. Crime

(Number, rate per 100,000. Data are derived from the FBI Uniform Crime Reports.)

Item	State			U.S.		
	2016	2017	Percent change	2016	2017	Percent change
TOTAL POPULATION[1]	6,908,642	7,016,270	1.6	323,405,935	325,719,178	0.7
VIOLENT CRIME						
Number...	32,542	35,644	9.5	1,285,606	1,283,220	-0.2
Rate	471.0	508.0	7.9	397.5	394.0	-0.9
Murder and Nonnegligent Manslaughter						
Number...	389	416	6.9	17,413	17,284	-0.7
Rate	5.6	5.9	5.3	5.4	5.3	-1.4
Rape[2]						
Number...	3,304	3,581	8.4	132,414	135,755	2.5
Rate	47.8	51.0	6.7	40.9	41.7	1.8
Robbery						
Number...	7,045	7,440	5.6	332,797	319,356	-4.0
Rate	102.0	106.0	4.0	102.9	98.0	-4.7
Aggravated Assault						
Number...	21,804	24,207	11.0	802,982	810,825	1.0
Rate	315.6	345.0	9.3	248.3	248.9	0.3
PROPERTY CRIME						
Number...	207,317	204,515	-1.4	7,928,530	7,694,086	-3.0
Rate	3,000.8	2,914.9	-2.9	2,451.6	2,362.2	-3.6
Burglary						
Number...	38,216	37,627	-1.5	1,516,405	1,401,840	-7.6
Rate	553.2	536.3	-3.1	468.9	430.4	-8.2
Larceny-Theft						
Number...	150,618	147,830	-1.9	5,644,835	5,519,107	-2.2
Rate	2,180.1	2,107.0	-3.4	1,745.4	1,694.4	-2.9
Motor Vehicle Theft						
Number...	18,483	19,058	3.1	767,290	773,139	0.8
Rate	267.5	271.6	1.5	237.3	237.4	-

NOTE: Although arson data are included in the trend and clearance tables, sufficient data are not available to estimate totals for this offense. Therefore, no arson data are published in this table.
- = Zero or rounds to zero.
[1]Population figures are U.S. Census Bureau provisional estimates as of July 1, 2017.
[2]The figures shown in the rape (revised definition) column were estimated using the revised Uniform Crime Reporting (UCR) definition of rape.

Table AZ-15. State Government Finances, 2017

(Dollar amounts in thousands, percent distribution.)

Item	Dollars	Percent distribution
Total Revenue	43,761,432	100.0
General revenue	34,730,545	79.4
Intergovernmental revenue	15,247,776	34.8
Taxes	13,888,611	31.7
General sales	6,566,503	15.0
Selective sales	1,973,223	4.5
License taxes	505,494	1.2
Individual income tax	3,445,650	7.9
Corporate income tax	368,136	0.8
Other taxes	1,029,605	2.4
Current charges	3,095,542	7.1
Miscellaneous general revenue	2,498,616	5.7
Utility revenue	29,450	0.1
Liquor stores revenue	0	-
Insurance trust revenue[1]	9,001,437	20.6
Total Expenditure	39,231,708	100.0
Intergovernmental expenditure	8,094,626	20.6
Direct expenditure	31,137,082	79.4
Current operation	22,164,389	56.5
Capital outlay	1,623,355	4.1
Insurance benefits and repayments	4,314,875	11.0
Assistance and subsidies	2,499,568	6.4
Interest on debt	534,895	1.4
Exhibit: Salaries and wages	4,090,546	10.4
Total Expenditure	39,231,708	100.0
General expenditure	34,887,948	88.9
Intergovernmental expenditure	8,094,626	20.6
Direct expenditure	26,793,322	68.3
General expenditure, by function:		
Education	11,825,297	30.1
Public welfare	14,685,574	37.4
Hospitals	7,459	-
Health	583,978	1.5
Highways	2,217,232	5.7
Police protection	280,662	0.7
Correction	1,080,923	2.8
Natural resources	306,838	0.8
Parks and recreation	82,845	0.2
Governmental administration	770,064	2.0
Interest on general debt	533,062	1.4
Other and unallocable	2,514,014	6.4
Utility expenditure	28,885	0.1
Liquor stores expenditure	0	-
Insurance trust expenditure	4,314,875	11.0
Debt at End of Fiscal Year	14,291,349	X
Cash and Security Holdings	62,715,526	X

X = Not applicable.
- = Zero or rounds to zero.
[1] Within insurance trust revenue, net earnings of state retirement systems is a calculated statistic (the item code in the data file is X08), and thus can be positive or negative. Net earnings is the sum of earnings on investments plus gains on investments minus losses on investments. The change made in 2002 for asset valuation from book to market value in accordance with Statement 34 of the Governmental Accounting Standards Board is reflected in the calculated statistics.

Table AZ-16. State Government Tax Collections, 2018

(Dollars in thousands, percent.)

Item	Dollars	Percent distribution
Total Taxes	16,293,917	100.0
Property taxes	1,047,254	6.4
Sales and gross receipts	9,708,694	59.6
General sales and gross receipts	7,687,992	47.2
Selective sales and gross receipts	2,020,702	12.4
Alcoholic beverages	76,378	0.5
Amusements	3,621	-
Insurance premiums	550,438	3.4
Motor fuels	869,183	5.3
Pari-mutuels	183	-
Public utilities	21,805	0.1
Tobacco products	312,808	1.9
Other selective sales	186,286	1.1
Licenses	495,034	3.0
Alcoholic beverages	8,592	0.1
Amusements	X	-
Corporations in general	14,493	0.1
Hunting and fishing	37,005	0.2
Motor vehicle	230,095	1.4
Motor vehicle operators	29,922	0.2
Public utilities	20	-
Occupation and business, NEC	173,274	1.1
Other licenses	1,633	-
Income taxes	4,918,318	30.2
Individual income	4,545,242	27.9
Corporation net income	373,076	2.3
Other taxes	124,617	0.8
Death and gift	X	-
Documentary and stock transfer	18,263	0.1
Severance	24,562	0.2
Taxes, NEC	81,792	0.5

- = Zero or rounds to zero.
X = Not applicable.

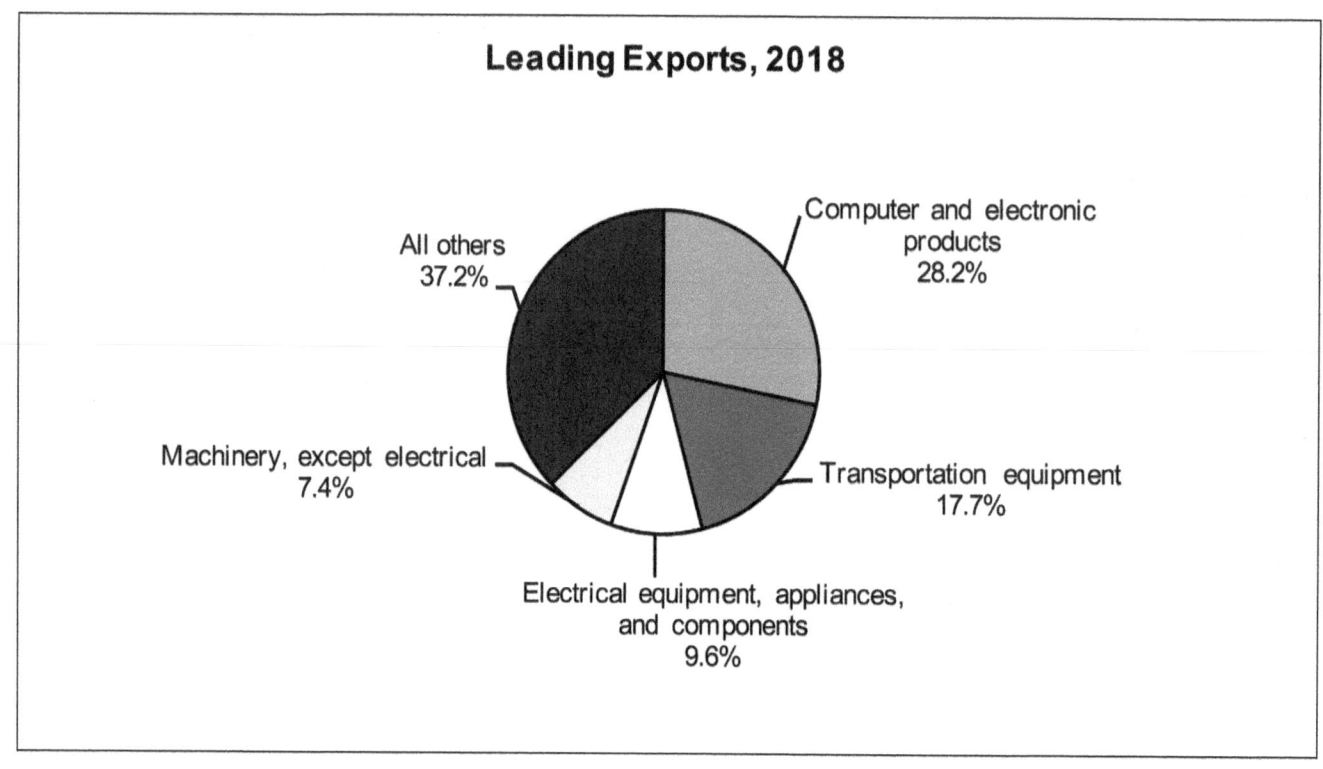

Leading Exports, 2018

Computer and electronic products 28.2%

All others 37.2%

Machinery, except electrical 7.4%

Electrical equipment, appliances, and components 9.6%

Transportation equipment 17.7%

ARKANSAS

Facts and Figures

Location: South central United States; bordered on the N by Missouri, on the E by Tennessee and Mississippi, on the S by Louisiana, and on the W by Oklahoma and Texas

Area: 53,178 sq. mi. (137,733 sq. km.); rank—29th

Population: 3,013,825 (2018 est.); rank—33rd

Principal Cities: capital—Little Rock; largest—Little Rock

Statehood: June 15, 1836; 25th state

U.S. Congress: 2 senators, 4 representatives

State Motto: *Regnat populus* ("The people rule")

State Song: "Arkansas"

State Nicknames: The Natural State; The Land of Opportunity

Abbreviations: AR; Ark.

State Symbols: flower—apple blossom; tree—pine; bird—mockingbird

At a Glance

- With an increase in population of 3.4 percent, Arkansas ranked 29th among the states in growth from 2010 to 2018.

- In 2017, 23.4 percent of Arkansas residents had a bachelor's degree or higher, the 3rd lowest percent in the nation.

- Arkansas's median household income in 2017 was $45,869, and 16.4 percent of the population lived below the poverty level.

- In 2017, 7.9 percent of Arkansans did not have health insurance, which the same as the previous year.

- Arkansas' property crime rate in 2017 was 3,078.6 per 100,000 population, which ranked 7th in the nation.

Table AR-1. Population by Age, Sex, Race, and Hispanic Origin

(Number, percent, except where noted.)

Sex, age, race, and Hispanic origin	2000	2010	2018[1]	Percent change, 2010–2018
Total Population...	2,673,400	2,915,918	3,013,825	3.4
Percent of total U.S. population	0.9	0.9	0.9	X
Sex				
Male..	1,304,693	1,431,637	1,480,143	3.4
Female	1,368,707	1,484,281	1,533,682	3.3
Age				
Under 5 years..	181,585	197,689	190,343	-3.7
5 to 19 years...	578,924	598,241	591,777	-1.1
20 to 64 years...	1,538,872	1,700,007	1,719,878	1.2
65 years and over	374,019	419,981	511,827	21.9
Median age (years)	36.0	37.4	38.3	2.4
Race and Hispanic Origin				
One race				
White	2,138,598	2,342,403	2,385,213	1.8
Black	418,950	454,021	472,287	4.0
American Indian and Alaska Native	17,808	26,134	30,225	15.7
Asian..	20,220	37,537	50,301	34.0
Native Hawaiian or Other Pacific Islander	1,668	6,685	10,881	62.8
Two or more races	35,744	49,138	64,918	32.1
Hispanic (of any race)	86,866	191,535	233,187	21.7

X = Not applicable.
[1] Population figures for 2018 are July 1 estimates. The 2010 estimates are taken from the 2010 Census.

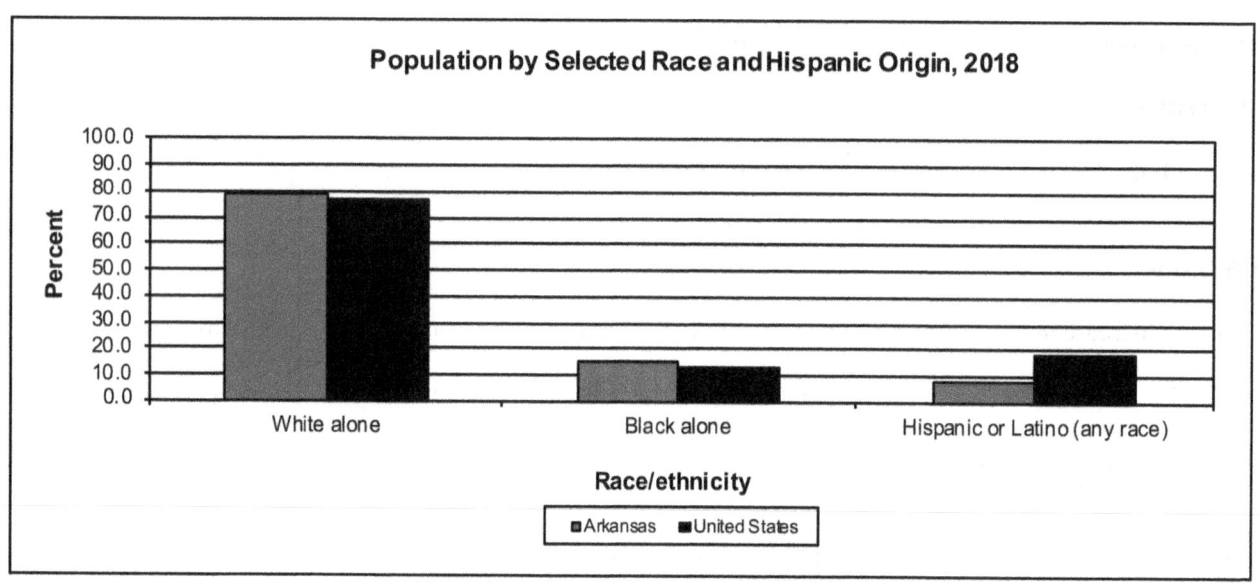

Population by Selected Race and Hispanic Origin, 2018

Race/ethnicity

☐ Arkansas ■ United States

Table AR-2. Marital Status

(Number, percent distribution.)

Sex, age, race, and Hispanic origin	2000	2010	2017
Males, 15 Years and Over...	1,015,594	1,128,804	1,179,013
Never married	24.2	29.5	31.3
Now married, except separated..	61.0	53.3	50.5
Separated...	1.6	2.2	2.1
Widowed...	2.7	3.1	3.4
Divorced...	10.4	12.0	12.7
Females, 15 Years and Over...	1,096,069	1,200,974	1,239,036
Never married	18.4	23.5	24.6
Now married, except separated..	55.7	48.8	48.0
Separated...	2.2	2.9	2.9
Widowed...	12.2	11.2	10.1
Divorced...	11.6	13.6	14.5

Table AR-3. Households and Housing Characteristics

(Number, percent, dollars.)

Item	2000	2010	2017	Average annual percent change, 2010–2017
Total Households..	1,042,696	1,114,902	1,153,082	0.5
Family households..	732,261	761,361	754,699	-0.1
Married-couple family..........................	566,401	554,946	552,852	-0.1
Other family..	165,860	206,415	201,847	-0.3
Male householder, no wife present............	39,299	51,620	53,801	0.6
Female householder, no husband present....	126,561	154,795	148,046	-0.6
Nonfamily households.........................	310,435	353,541	398,383	1.8
Householder living alone.....................	266,585	302,127	336,052	1.6
Householder not living alone.................	43,850	51,414	62,331	3.0
Housing Characteristics				
Total housing units............................	1,173,043	1,317,818	1,370,109	0.6
Occupied housing units	1,042,696	1,114,902	1,153,082	0.5
Owner occupied..............................	723,535	751,568	752,399	0.0
Renter occupied.............................	319,161	363,334	400,683	1.5
Average household size......................	2.49	2.55	2.53	-0.1
Financial Characteristics				
Median gross rent of renter-occupied housing	453	638	711	1.6
Median monthly owner costs for housing units with a mortgage	737	987	1025	0.6
Median value of owner-occupied housing units.........	72,800	106,300	128,500	3.0

Table AR-4. Migration, Origin, and Language

(Number, percent.)

Characteristic	State			U.S.		
	2016	2017	Percent change	2016	2017	Percent change
Residence 1 Year Ago						
Population 1 year and over	2,949,650	2,968,395	0.6	319,361,956	321,994,428	0.8
Same house	84.2	84.5	X	85.4	85.7	X
Different house in the U.S.	15.5	15.2	X	13.9	13.6	X
Same county	9.4	8.6	X	8.3	8.1	X
Different county	6.1	6.6	X	5.6	5.6	X
Same state	3.7	3.9	X	3.2	3.3	X
Different state	2.4	2.7	X	2.4	2.3	X
Abroad	0.3	0.3	X	0.7	0.7	X
Place of Birth						
Native born	2,849,656	2,864,201	0.5	279,388,170	281,193,323	0.6
Male	49.1	49.1	X	49.3	49.4	X
Female	50.9	50.9	X	50.7	50.6	X
Foreign born	138,592	140,078	1.1	43,739,345	44,525,855	1.8
Male	49.4	51.5	X	48.5	48.4	X
Female	50.6	48.5	X	51.5	51.6	X
Foreign born; naturalized U.S. citizen.........	44,284	45,139	1.9	21,238,372	21,948,732	3.3
Male	50.6	44.5	X	45.9	45.9	X
Female	49.4	55.5	X	54.1	54.1	X
Foreign born; not a U.S. citizen.........	94,308	94,939	0.7	22,500,973	22,577,123	0.3
Male	48.8	54.8	X	51	50.8	X
Female	51.2	45.2	X	49	49.2	X
Entered 2010 or later	22	23.4	X	18.6	21.3	X
Entered 2000 to 2009	28.6	28.1	X	26.7	25.7	X
Entered before 2000.........	49.4	48.5	X	54.7	53.0	X
World Region of Birth, Foreign						
Foreign-born population, excluding population born at sea	138,592	140,078	1.1	43,738,901	44,525,458	1.8
Europe	7.9	5.9	X	10.9	10.8	X
Asia.........	23.7	25.5	X	30.8	31.2	X
Africa	3.7	2.1	X	4.9	5.1	X
Oceania	4.5	4.5	X	0.6	0.6	X
Latin America.........	58.9	59.9	X	51	50.4	X
North America.........	1.3	2.0	X	1.8	1.8	X
Language Spoken at Home and Ability to Speak English						
Population 5 years and over.........	2,799,532	2,817,639	0.6	303,328,961	305,924,019	0.9
English only	92.7	92.5	X	78.4	78.2	X
Language other than English.........	7.3	7.5	X	21.6	21.8	X
Speaks English less than "very well".........	3.1	3.1	X	8.6	8.5	X

NA = Not available.
X = Not applicable.
- = Zero or rounds to zero.

Table AR-5. Median Income and Poverty Status, 2017

(Number, percent, except as noted.)

Characteristic	State Number	State Percent	U.S. Number	U.S. Percent
Median Income				
Households (dollars)	45,869	X	60,336	X
Families (dollars)	57,421	X	73,891	X
Below Poverty Level (All People)	478,365	16.4	42,583,651	13.4
Sex				
Male	216,159	15.1	19,004,547	12.2
Female	262,206	17.6	23,579,104	14.5
Age				
Under 18 years	156,427	22.5	13,353,202	18.4
Related children under 18 years	153,384	22.1	13,053,472	18.1
18 to 64 years	273,126	15.7	24,648,677	12.6
65 years and over	48,812	10.2	4,581,772	9.3

X = Not applicable.

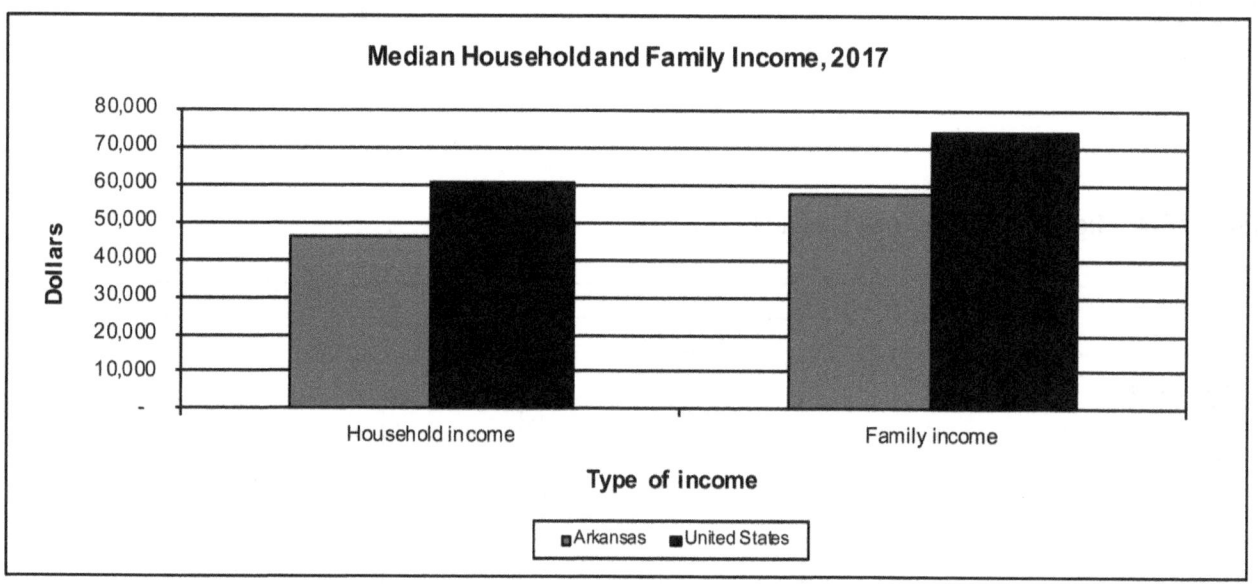

Table AR-6. Health Insurance Coverage Status for the Civilian Noninstitutionalized Population and Children Under 18 Years of Age

(Number, percent.)

Item	2009	2010	2011	2012	2013	2014	2015	2016	2017
Civilian Noninstitutionalized Population	2,833,391	2,867,611	2,885,212	2,896,297	2,907,014	2,914,376	2,924,307	2,934,272	2,949,305
Covered by Private or Public Insurance									
Number	2,350,818	2,366,998	2,392,902	2,419,987	2,442,064	2,571,205	2,646,760	2,702,497	2,717,503
Percent	83.0	82.5	82.9	83.6	84.0	88.2	90.5	92.1	92.1
Uninsured									
Number	482,573	500,613	492,310	476,310	464,950	343,171	277,547	231,775	231,802
Percent	17.0	17.5	17.1	16.4	16.0	11.8	9.5	7.9	7.9
Percent in the U.S. not covered	15.1	15.5	15.1	14.8	14.5	11.7	9.4	8.6	8.7
Children Under 18 Years of Age[1]	706,684	709,374	708,888	709,407	709,125	703,811	703,701	705,155	751,794
Covered by Private or Public Insurance									
Number	662,623	662,879	668,938	667,257	669,866	669,732	669,147	679,612	718,394
Percent	93.8	93.4	94.4	94.1	94.5	95.2	95.1	96.4	95.6
Uninsured									
Number	44,061	46,495	39,950	42,150	39,259	34,079	34,554	25,543	33,400
Percent	6.2	6.6	5.6	5.9	5.5	4.8	4.9	3.6	4.4
Percent in the U.S. not covered	8.6	8.0	7.5	7.2	7.1	6.0	4.8	4.5	5.0

[1] 2017 data is for individuals under 19 years of age.

Table AR-7. Employment Status by Demographic Group, 2018

(Numbers in thousands, percent.)

Characteristic	Civilian noninstitutional population	Civilian labor force		Employed		Unemployed	
		Number	Percent of population	Number	Percent of population	Number	Percent of population
Total....................................	2,341	1,342	57.3	1,291	55.2	50	3.8
Sex							
Male....................................	1,126	707	62.8	680	60.4	28	3.9
Female.................................	1,215	634	52.2	611	50.3	23	3.6
Race, Sex, and Hispanic Origin							
White...................................	1,887	1,080	57.2	1,047	55.5	33	3.0
Male....................................	916	583	63.6	565	61.7	18	3.0
Female.................................	971	497	51.2	482	49.6	15	3.1
Black or African American.............	344	200	57.9	186	54.0	13	6.7
Male....................................	155	89	57.7	82	52.8	8	8.6
Female.................................	190	110	58.1	105	55.1	6	5.2
Hispanic or Latino ethnicity[1]........	168	115	68.8	111	66.2	4	3.7
Male....................................	87	66	76.3	63	73.0	3	4.4
Female.................................	81	49	60.8	48	59.0	1	2.8
Age							
16 to 19 years........................	157	51	32.2	46	29.3	5	9.1
20 to 24 years........................	217	149	68.7	138	63.3	12	7.8
25 to 34 years........................	398	307	77.1	295	74.0	12	4.0
35 to 44 years........................	328	262	80.0	255	77.8	7	2.8
45 to 54 years........................	368	279	75.9	272	74.0	7	2.4
55 to 64 years........................	380	216	56.9	210	55.2	6	2.8
65 years and over.....................	493	77	15.7	76	15.4	2	2.1

NOTE: Data in Table 7 are from the Current Population Survey (CPS) and do not match the estimates in Table 8. See notes and definitions for further information.
[1] May be of any race.

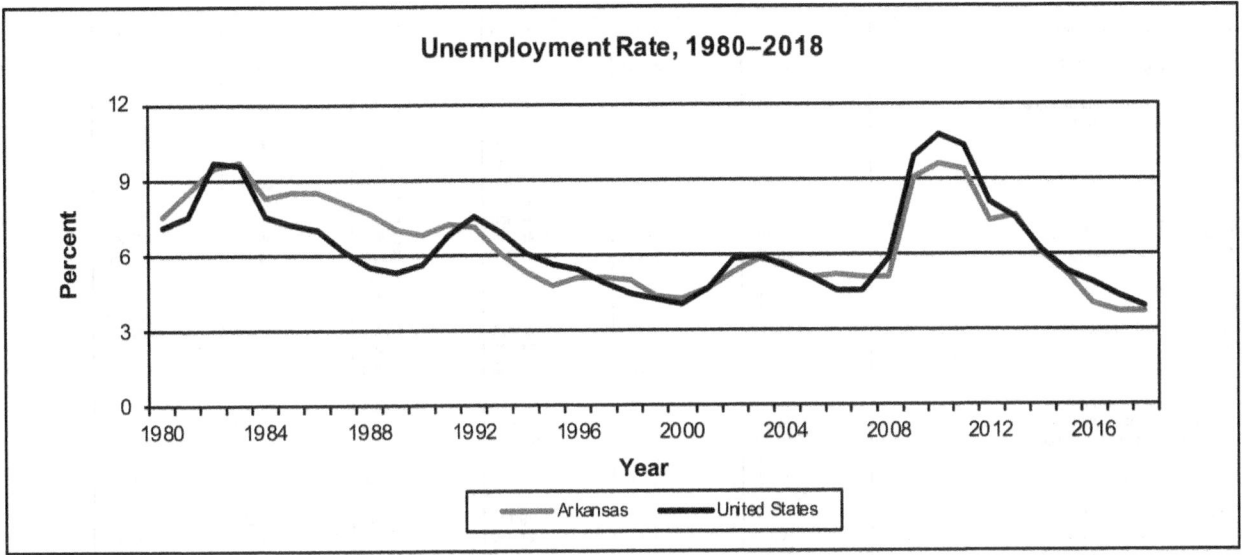

Unemployment Rate, 1980–2018

Table AR-8. Employment Status of the Civilian Noninstitutional Population Age 16 Years and Over

(Number, percent.)

Year	Civilian labor force	Civilian participation rate	Employed	Unemployed	Unemployment rate
2010....................................	1,353,338	60.6	1,242,496	110,842	8.2
2011....................................	1,362,682	60.5	1,249,514	113,168	8.3
2012....................................	1,342,753	59.3	1,241,127	101,626	7.6
2013....................................	1,322,576	58.2	1,226,859	95,717	7.2
2014....................................	1,316,595	57.6	1,237,316	79,279	6.0
2015....................................	1,332,255	58.0	1,265,166	67,089	5.0
2016....................................	1,342,561	58.1	1,289,549	53,012	3.9
2017....................................	1,354,265	58.2	1,304,434	49,831	3.7
2018....................................	1,351,496	57.9	1,301,459	50,037	3.7

Table AR-9. Employment and Average Wages by Industry

(Estimates are based on the 2012 *North American Industry Classification System* [NAICS].)

Industry	2011	2012	2013	2014	2015	2016	2017
	Number of Jobs						
Wage and Salary Employment by Industry........................	1,223,928	1,229,574	1,231,398	1,243,481	1,264,491	1,279,315	1,286,301
Farm Wage and Salary Employment.............................	12,021	9,006	11,167	11,319	12,578	15,485	15,067
Nonfarm Wage and Salary Employment..........................	1,211,907	1,220,568	1,220,231	1,232,162	1,251,913	1,263,830	1,271,234
Private wage and salary employment...........................	977,260	985,006	986,315	999,839	1,021,012	1,035,525	1,044,980
Forestry, fishing, and related activities......................	7,910	8,082	8,079	8,138	8,120	8,195	8,196
Mining..	8,975	8,650	7,537	6,714	5,858	4,135	3,789
Utilities...	7,169	7,705	8,089	7,903	7,950	7,706	7,707
Construction	48,572	48,752	46,679	47,269	50,481	51,554	52,333
Manufacturing..	157,418	154,586	152,137	153,246	155,035	154,876	157,462
Durable goods manufacturing...............................	77,724	76,799	75,364	76,254	75,951	74,259	74,645
Nondurable goods manufacturing...........................	79,694	77,787	76,773	76,992	79,084	80,617	82,817
Wholesale trade	46,806	47,421	46,484	46,707	47,396	46,424	47,076
Retail trade..	132,249	133,491	133,986	136,980	141,322	143,065	141,373
Transportation and warehousing.............................	53,548	54,325	53,905	54,971	56,785	56,652	56,385
Information..	16,105	15,592	15,365	14,848	13,342	13,244	12,778
Finance and insurance	37,217	36,772	37,086	37,058	37,458	38,441	38,804
Real estate and rental and leasing...........................	13,498	13,492	13,436	13,133	13,346	13,520	13,616
Professional, scientific, and technical services	39,443	39,118	40,199	40,942	41,710	42,877	43,163
Management of companies and enterprises..................	26,907	30,898	31,441	32,432	33,440	35,078	35,131
Administrative and waste services............................	55,513	54,544	57,965	61,160	64,396	65,246	66,703
Educational services	15,649	15,678	16,431	16,627	16,465	16,776	16,946
Health care and social assistance............................	156,338	159,845	160,095	160,455	163,297	169,383	174,015
Arts, entertainment, and recreation..........................	9,714	9,777	10,109	10,772	10,774	11,237	11,418
Accommodation and food services...........................	90,941	93,543	95,373	97,670	101,521	104,760	106,011
Other services, except public administration................	53,288	52,735	51,919	52,814	52,316	52,356	52,074
Government and government enterprises....................	234,647	235,562	233,916	232,323	230,901	228,305	226,254
	Dollars						
Average Wages and Salaries by Industry	37,820	38,940	39,629	40,580	41,444	42,102	43,490
Average Farm Wages and Salaries	17,328	29,341	25,708	21,544	22,574	19,813	16,662
Average Nonfarm Wages and Salaries	38,024	39,011	39,756	40,755	41,634	42,375	43,807
Average private wages and salaries...........................	37,890	39,091	39,858	40,952	41,856	42,561	44,064
Forestry, fishing, and related activities......................	31,497	32,480	33,106	34,564	36,158	38,048	38,546
Mining..	67,734	67,770	69,133	71,749	70,983	66,626	65,906
Utilities...	74,937	76,777	79,100	82,651	83,731	86,407	89,436
Construction	40,831	42,241	41,657	43,247	45,023	46,673	48,195
Manufacturing..	42,274	43,537	44,366	45,927	46,431	47,187	48,695
Durable goods manufacturing...............................	44,401	45,646	46,744	48,254	48,503	49,290	51,779
Nondurable goods manufacturing...........................	40,199	41,455	42,032	43,622	44,441	45,251	45,915
Wholesale trade	58,142	59,862	62,357	63,998	66,635	67,785	69,617
Retail trade..	24,344	24,927	25,296	25,794	26,288	27,250	28,023
Transportation and warehousing.............................	44,129	45,333	46,273	47,698	48,328	47,359	49,090
Information..	50,155	49,644	51,181	53,498	55,713	56,971	58,904
Finance and insurance	54,883	57,775	57,838	59,968	61,981	63,509	64,980
Real estate and rental and leasing...........................	32,900	34,299	34,677	35,968	37,085	37,755	39,084
Professional, scientific, and technical services	56,492	55,015	57,064	58,294	59,877	60,534	62,596
Management of companies and enterprises..................	89,559	96,029	103,322	105,737	107,812	106,958	117,489
Administrative and waste services............................	26,984	27,160	26,920	27,610	28,070	29,188	30,142
Educational services	26,730	26,716	27,383	27,896	28,608	29,578	29,619
Health care and social assistance............................	37,540	38,501	39,143	40,340	41,522	42,367	43,305
Arts, entertainment, and recreation..........................	20,405	20,782	21,049	21,391	22,325	22,977	23,611
Accommodation and food services...........................	15,050	15,617	15,844	16,294	16,769	17,406	18,145
Other services, except public administration................	26,411	27,430	28,252	29,357	30,718	31,793	32,971
Government and government enterprises....................	38,581	38,678	39,328	39,907	40,652	41,533	42,625

Table AR-10. Employment Characteristics by Family Type

(Number, percent.)

Family type and labor force status	2015		2016		2017	
	Total	Families with own children under 18 years	Total	Families with own children under 18 years	Total	Families with own children under 18 years
All Families....................................	761,494	311,436	747,917	305,770	754,699	312,050
FAMILY TYPE AND LABOR FORCE STATUS						
Married-Couple Families....................................	561,297	205,898	549,997	199,797	552,852	203,599
Both husband and wife in labor force....................	47	62.4	46.4	64.7	47.3	65.9
Husband in labor force, wife not in labor force..............	21.7	29.2	21.9	26.9	21.1	26.6
Wife in labor force, husband not in labor force..............	9	5.0	10.1	6.1	8.9	4.7
Both husband and wife not in labor force................	21.8	3.1	21.2	2.2	22.0	2.5
Other Families	200,197	105,538	197,920	105,973	201,847	108,451
Female householder, no husband present......................	75	74.9	76.1	77.7	73.3	75.0
In labor force....................................	48	59.3	50.3	62.6	49.3	61.1
Not in labor force	26.9	15.5	25.9	15.2	24.1	14.0
Male householder, no wife present......................	25.0	25.1	23.9	22.3	26.7	25.0
In labor force	18.3	21.5	17.4	19.7	19.2	21.6
Not in labor force	6.8	3.6	6.5	2.5	7.4	3.3

Table AR-11. School Enrollment and Educational Attainment, 2017

(Number, percent.)

Item	State	U.S.
Enrollment		
Total population 3 years and over, enrolled in school	743,696	81,273,337
Enrolled in nursery school or preschool (percent)	6.4	6.0
Enrolled in kindergarten (percent)................	5.5	4.9
Enrolled in elementary school, grades 1-8 (percent)................	42.7	40.6
Enrolled in high school, grades 9-12 (percent)	21.7	21.1
Enrolled in college or graduate school (percent)................	23.7	27.4
Attainment		
Total population 25 years and over	2,008,398	221,250,083
Less than ninth grade (percent)................	4.6	5.1
9th to 12th grade, no diploma (percent)	8.7	6.9
High school graduate, including equivalency (percent)................	34.0	27.1
Some college, no degree (percent)................	22.1	20.4
Associate's degree (percent)................	7.1	8.5
Bachelor's degree (percent)	15.0	19.7
Graduate or professional degree (percent)	8.4	12.3
High school graduate or higher (percent)	86.7	88.0
Bachelor's degree or higher (percent)................	23.4	32.0

Table AR-12. Public School Characteristics and Educational Indicators

(Number, percent; data derived from National Center of Education Statistics.)

Item	State	U.S.
Public Elementary and Secondary Schools		
Number of operational school districts, 2016-17	292	18,377
Number of operational schools, 2016-17................	1,090	98,330
Percent charter schools	6.9	7.1
Total public school enrollment, 2016-17................	493,447	50,587,859
Percent charter school enrollment	5.7	6.0
Student-teacher ratio, Fall 2015	13.7	16.0
Expenditures per student (dollars), 2015-16................	9,900	11,841
Four-year adjusted cohort graduation rate (ACGR)[1]	88.0	84.6
Students eligible for free or reduced-price lunch (percent), 2015-16................	63.6	52.1
English language learners (percent), Fall 2016	8.4	9.6
Students age 3 to 21 served under IDEA, part B (percent), 2017-18	14.8	13.7

Public Schools by Type, 2016-17		Percent of state public schools
Total number of schools................	1,089	100.0
Special education................	4	0.4
Vocational education................	24	2.2
Alternative education................	5	0.5

[1] Adjusted Cohort Graduation Rates (ACGR) differ from Averaged Freshmen Graduation Rates (AFGR).

Table AR-13. Reported Voting and Registration of the Voting-Age Population, November 2018

(Numbers in thousands, percent.)

Item	Total population	Total citizen population	Registered			Voted		
			Total registered	Percent registered (total population)	Percent registered (total citizen population)	Total voted	Percent voted (total population)	Percent voted (total citizen population)
U.S. Total	249,748	228,832	153,066	61.3	66.9	122,281	49.0	53.4
State Total..........................	2,261	2,158	1,262	55.8	58.5	919	40.6	42.6
Sex								
Male	1,093	1,034	602	55.1	58.3	431	39.4	41.7
Female	1,169	1,125	660	56.5	58.7	488	41.8	43.4
Race								
White alone............................	1,833	1,765	1,031	56.2	58.4	756	41.3	42.8
White, non-Hispanic alone............	1,678	1,676	995	59.3	59.3	737	43.9	44.0
Black alone............................	327	317	178	54.5	56.1	132	40.3	41.6
Asian alone	37	19	9	(B)	(B)	6	(B)	(B)
Hispanic (of any race)................	172	102	43	25.2	42.3	21	12.3	20.8
White alone or in combination	1,878	1,805	1,061	56.5	58.7	771	41.1	42.7
Black alone or in combination...........	336	325	184	54.7	56.6	135	40.2	41.6
Asian alone or in combination...........	53	31	18	(B)	(B)	7	(B)	(B)
Age								
18 to 24 years......................	281	258	119	42.4	46.3	61	21.9	23.9
25 to 34 years......................	433	395	204	47.2	51.8	122	28.0	30.8
35 to 44 years......................	302	278	154	50.9	55.3	100	33.2	36.1
45 to 64 years......................	737	723	433	58.8	59.9	341	46.2	47.1
65 years and over	508	505	352	69.3	69.7	295	58.0	58.4

B = Base is less than 75,000 and therefore too small to show the derived measure.

Table AR-14. Crime

(Number, rate per 100,000. Data are derived from the FBI Uniform Crime Reports.)

Item	State			U.S.		
	2016	2017	Percent change	2016	2017	Percent change
TOTAL POPULATION[1]	2,988,231	3,004,279	0.5	323,405,935	325,719,178	0.7
VIOLENT CRIME						
Number..	16,563	16,671	0.7	1,285,606	1,283,220	-0.2
Rate..	554.3	554.9	0.1	397.5	394.0	-0.9
Murder and Nonnegligent Manslaughter						
Number..	217	258	18.9	17,413	17,284	-0.7
Rate..	7.3	8.6	18.3	5.4	5.3	-1.4
Rape[2]						
Number..	2,214	2,053	-7.3	132,414	135,755	2.5
Rate..	74.1	68.3	-7.8	40.9	41.7	1.8
Robbery						
Number..	2,125	1,935	-8.9	332,797	319,356	-4.0
Rate..	71.1	64.4	-9.4	102.9	98.0	-4.7
Aggravated Assault						
Number..	12,007	12,425	3.5	802,982	810,825	1.0
Rate..	401.8	413.6	2.9	248.3	248.9	0.3
PROPERTY CRIME						
Number..	98,092	92,489	-5.7	7,928,530	7,694,086	-3.0
Rate..	3,282.6	3,078.6	-6.2	2,451.6	2,362.2	-3.6
Burglary						
Number..	23,814	21,862	-8.2	1,516,405	1,401,840	-7.6
Rate..	796.9	727.7	-8.7	468.9	430.4	-8.2
Larceny-Theft						
Number..	67,091	63,374	-5.5	5,644,835	5,519,107	-2.2
Rate..	2,245.2	2,109.5	-6.0	1,745.4	1,694.4	-2.9
Motor Vehicle Theft						
Number..	7,187	7,253	0.9	767,290	773,139	0.8
Rate..	240.5	241.4	0.4	237.3	237.4	-

NOTE: Although arson data are included in the trend and clearance tables, sufficient data are not available to estimate totals for this offense. Therefore, no arson data are published in this table.
- = Zero or rounds to zero.
[1] Population figures are U.S. Census Bureau provisional estimates as of July 1, 2017.
[2] The figures shown in the rape (revised definition) column were estimated using the revised Uniform Crime Reporting (UCR) definition of rape.

Table AR-15. State Government Finances, 2017

(Dollar amounts in thousands, percent distribution.)

Item	Dollars	Percent distribution
Total Revenue	25,946,351	100.0
General revenue	21,149,036	81.5
Intergovernmental revenue	7,916,365	30.5
Taxes	9,516,281	36.7
General sales	3,384,394	13.0
Selective sales	1,317,474	5.1
License taxes	384,559	1.5
Individual income tax	2,767,767	10.7
Corporate income tax	396,989	1.5
Other taxes	1,265,098	4.9
Current charges	2,563,526	9.9
Miscellaneous general revenue	1,152,864	4.4
Utility revenue	0	-
Liquor stores revenue	0	-
Insurance trust revenue[1]	4,797,315	18.5
Total Expenditure	23,058,497	100.0
Intergovernmental expenditure	5,373,102	23.3
Direct expenditure	17,685,395	76.7
Current operation	13,700,779	59.4
Capital outlay	1,368,534	5.9
Insurance benefits and repayments	1,979,698	8.6
Assistance and subsidies	484,283	2.1
Interest on debt	152,101	0.7
Exhibit: Salaries and wages	3,021,356	13.1
Total Expenditure	23,058,497	100.0
General expenditure	21,078,799	91.4
Intergovernmental expenditure	5,373,102	23.3
Direct expenditure	15,705,697	68.1
General expenditure, by function:		
Education	7,843,665	34.0
Public welfare	7,482,277	32.4
Hospitals	1,159,401	5.0
Health	245,899	1.1
Highways	1,743,755	7.6
Police protection	125,399	0.5
Correction	420,114	1.8
Natural resources	283,602	1.2
Parks and recreation	68,072	0.3
Governmental administration	627,664	2.7
Interest on general debt	152,101	0.7
Other and unallocable	926,850	4.0
Utility expenditure	0	-
Liquor stores expenditure	0	-
Insurance trust expenditure	1,979,698	8.6
Debt at End of Fiscal Year	4,801,939	X
Cash and Security Holdings	35,053,849	X

X = Not applicable.
- = Zero or rounds to zero.
[1] Within insurance trust revenue, net earnings of state retirement systems is a calculated statistic (the item code in the data file is X08), and thus can be positive or negative. Net earnings is the sum of earnings on investments plus gains on investments minus losses on investments. The change made in 2002 for asset valuation from book to market value in accordance with Statement 34 of the Governmental Accounting Standards Board is reflected in the calculated statistics.

Table AR-16. State Government Tax Collections, 2018

(Dollars in thousands, percent.)

Item	Dollars	Percent distribution
Total Taxes	9,843,173	100.0
Property taxes	1,212,794	12.3
Sales and gross receipts	4,834,983	49.1
General sales and gross receipts	3,498,073	35.5
Selective sales and gross receipts	1,336,910	13.6
Alcoholic beverages	58,036	0.6
Amusements	64,580	0.7
Insurance premiums	223,362	2.3
Motor fuels	492,945	5.0
Pari-mutuels	2,335	-
Public utilities	X	-
Tobacco products	226,728	2.3
Other selective sales	268,924	2.7
Licenses	409,856	4.2
Alcoholic beverages	6,128	0.1
Amusements	488	-
Corporations in general	29,673	0.3
Hunting and fishing	26,672	0.3
Motor vehicle	164,617	1.7
Motor vehicle operators	22,631	0.2
Public utilities	8,346	0.1
Occupation and business, NEC	149,452	1.5
Other licenses	1,849	-
Income taxes	3,256,931	33.1
Individual income	2,866,175	29.1
Corporation net income	390,756	4.0
Other taxes	128,609	1.3
Death and gift	0	-
Documentary and stock transfer	44,892	0.5
Severance	54,655	0.6
Taxes, NEC	29,062	0.3

- = Zero or rounds to zero.
X = Not applicable.

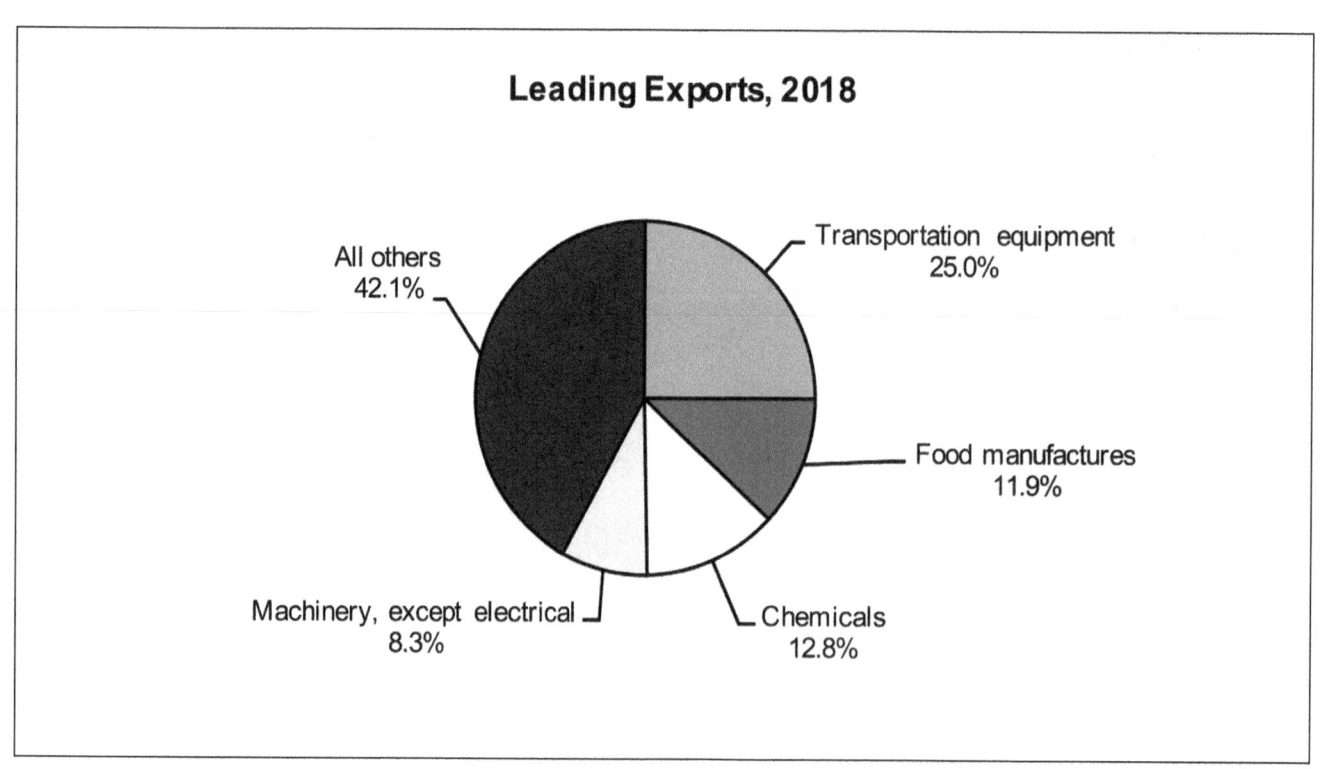

Leading Exports, 2018

All others 42.1%

Transportation equipment 25.0%

Food manufactures 11.9%

Chemicals 12.8%

Machinery, except electrical 8.3%

CALIFORNIA

Facts and Figures

Location: Western United States; bordered on the N by Oregon, on the E by Nevada and Arizona, on the S by Mexico, and on the W by the Pacific Ocean

Area: 163,694 sq. mi. (423,970 sq. km.); rank—3rd

Population: 39,557,045 (2018 est.); rank—1st

Principal Cities: capital—Sacramento; largest—Los Angeles

Statehood: September 9, 1850; 31st state

U.S. Congress: 2 senators, 53 representatives

State Motto: *Eureka* ("I have found it")

State Song: "I Love You, California"

State Nickname: The Golden State

Abbreviations: CA; Calif.

State Symbols: flower—California poppy; tree—redwood; bird—California valley quail

At a Glance

- With an increase in population of 6.2 percent, California ranked 20th among the states in growth from 2010 to 2018.

- In 2017, California's median household income was $71,805, and 13.3 percent of the population lived below the poverty level.

- California's violent crime rate in 2017 was 449.3 per 100,000 population, compared to 394.0 for the entire nation.

- In 2018, California's unemployment rate of 4.2 percent ranked 14th in the nation.

- Approximately 15.3 percent of Californians self-identified their race as "Asian Alone" in 2018, which was the 2nd highest percent in the country.

Table CA-1. Population by Age, Sex, Race, and Hispanic Origin

(Number, percent, except where noted.)

Sex, age, race, and Hispanic origin	2000	2010	2018 [1]	Percent change, 2010–2018
Total population..	33,871,648	37,253,956	39,557,045	6.2
Percent of total U.S. population	12.0	12.1	12.1	X
Sex				
Male..	16,874,892	18,517,830	19,663,577	6.2
Female..	16,996,756	18,736,126	19,893,468	6.2
Age				
Under 5 years...	2,486,981	2,531,333	2,441,300	-3.6
5 to 19 years..	7,747,590	7,920,709	7,582,250	-4.3
20 to 64 years...	20,041,419	22,555,400	23,864,470	5.8
65 years and over	3,595,658	4,246,514	5,669,025	33.5
Median age (years)	33.3	35.2	36.8	4.5
Race and Hispanic origin				
One race				
White	20,170,059	27,636,403	28,531,740	3.2
Black..	2,263,882	2,486,549	2,556,000	2.8
American Indian and Alaska Native	333,346	622,107	651,076	4.7
Asian..	3,697,513	5,038,123	6,063,600	20.4
Native Hawaiian or Other Pacific Islander	116,961	181,431	199,872	10.2
Two or more races	1,607,646	1,289,343	1,554,757	20.6
Hispanic (of any race)..	10,966,556	14,440,187	15,540,142	7.6

X = Not applicable.

[1] Population figures for 2018 are July 1 estimates. The 2010 estimates are taken from the 2010 Census.

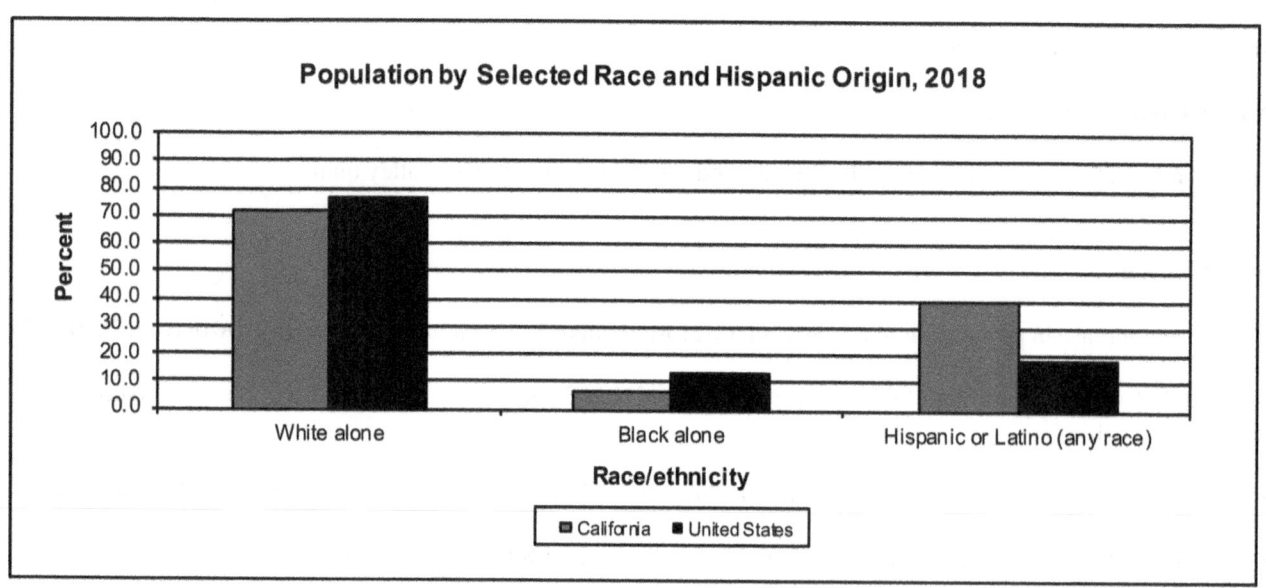

Table CA-2. Marital Status

(Number, percent distribution.)

Sex, age, race, and Hispanic origin	2000	2010	2017
Males, 15 Years and Over	12,844,669	14,662,335	15,802,609
Never married	33.8	39.8	40.9
Now married, except separated.....................................	54.1	48.2	47.8
Separated..	2.0	1.9	1.6
Widowed..	2.2	2.1	2.1
Divorced..	7.9	8.0	7.7
Females, 15 Years and Over	13,231,494	15,043,190	16,207,248
Never married	26.5	32.3	33.6
Now married, except separated.....................................	50.7	45.7	45.4
Separated..	2.9	2.7	2.4
Widowed..	8.9	8.1	7.6
Divorced..	11.0	11.2	10.9

Table CA-3. Households and Housing Characteristics

(Number, percent, dollars.)

Item	2000	2010	2017	Average annual percent change, 2010–2017
Total Households..	11,502,870	12,406,475	13,005,097	0.7
Family households	7,920,049	8,507,856	8,910,617	0.7
Married-couple family	5,877,084	6,082,566	6,446,965	0.9
Other family	2,042,965	2,425,290	2,463,652	0.2
Male householder, no wife present..	594,455	736,626	773,212	0.7
Female householder, no husband present	1,448,510	1,688,664	1,690,440	-
Nonfamily households	3,582,821	3,898,619	4,094,480	0.7
Householder living alone...	2,708,308	3,001,307	3,125,424	0.6
Householder not living alone..	874,513	897,312	969,056	1.1
Housing Characteristics				
Total housing units..	12,214,549	13,682,976	14,177,270	0.5
Occupied housing units	11,502,870	12,406,475	13,005,097	0.7
Owner occupied	6,546,334	6,903,175	7,125,090	0.5
Renter occupied	4,956,536	5,503,300	5,880,007	1.0
Average household size...	2.87	2.94	2.98	0.2
Financial Characteristics				
Median gross rent of renter-occupied housing	747	1,163	1,447	3.5
Median monthly owner costs for housing units with a mortgage	1,478	2,242	2,269	0.2
Median value of owner-occupied housing units	211,500	370,900	509,400	5.3

Table CA-4. Migration, Origin, and Language

(Number, percent.)

Characteristic	State 2016	State 2017	State Percent change	U.S. 2016	U.S. 2017	U.S. Percent change
Residence 1 Year Ago						
Population 1 year and over	38,783,436	39,085,984	0.8	319,361,956	321,994,428	0.8
Same house	86.6	87.0	X	85.4	85.7	X
Different house in the U.S...	12.5	12.2	X	13.9	13.6	X
Same county	8.4	8.1	X	8.3	8.1	X
Different county	4.1	4.1	X	5.6	5.6	X
Same state	2.8	2.8	X	3.2	3.3	X
Different state	1.3	1.3	X	2.4	2.3	X
Abroad	0.9	0.8	X	0.7	0.7	X
Place of Birth						
Native born	28,572,354	28,883,239	1.1	279,388,170	281,193,323	0.6
Male	50.2	50.3	X	49.3	49.4	X
Female	49.8	49.7	X	50.7	50.6	X
Foreign born	10,677,663	10,653,414	-0.2	43,739,345	44,525,855	1.8
Male	48.3	48	X	48.5	48.4	X
Female	51.7	52	X	51.5	51.6	X
Foreign born; naturalized U.S. citizen............................	5,369,508	5,500,685	2.4	21,238,372	21,948,732	3.3
Male	45.8	45.9	X	45.9	45.9	X
Female	54.2	54.1	X	54.1	54.1	X
Foreign born; not a U.S. citizen	5,308,155	5,152,729	-2.9	22,500,973	22,577,123	0.3
Male	50.8	50.3	X	51	50.8	X
Female	49.2	49.7	X	49	49.2	X
Entered 2010 or later	13.6	15.4	X	18.6	21.3	X
Entered 2000 to 2009	23	22.2	X	26.7	25.7	X
Entered before 2000..	63.4	62.4	X	54.7	53.0	X
World Region of Birth, Foreign						
Foreign-born population, excluding population born at sea	10,677,502	10,653,414	-0.2	43,738,901	44,525,458	1.8
Europe	6.3	6.4	X	10.9	10.8	X
Asia..	38.9	39.7	X	30.8	31.2	X
Africa	1.8	1.7	X	4.9	5.1	X
Oceania	0.8	0.9	X	0.6	0.6	X
Latin America..	51.1	50	X	51	50.4	X
North America	1.1	1.2	X	1.8	1.8	X
Language Spoken at Home and Ability to Speak English						
Population 5 years and over...	36,767,595	37,076,228	0.8	303,328,961	305,924,019	0.9
English only	55.4	55.6	X	78.4	78.2	X
Language other than English...	44.6	44.4	X	21.6	21.8	X
Speaks English less than "very well"..........................	18.6	17.9	X	8.6	8.5	X

NA = Not available.
X = Not applicable.
- = Zero or rounds to zero.

Table CA-5. Median Income and Poverty Status, 2017

(Number, percent, except as noted.)

Characteristic	State		U.S.	
	Number	Percent	Number	Percent
Median Income				
Households (dollars)..	71,805	X	60,336	X
Families (dollars)	82,009	X	73,891	X
Below Poverty Level (All People)	5,160,208	13.3	42,583,651	13.4
Sex				
Male	2,340,073	12.2	19,004,547	12.2
Female	2,820,135	14.4	23,579,104	14.5
Age				
Under 18 years..	1,618,889	18.1	13,353,202	18.4
Related children under 18 years...................	1,580,002	17.8	13,053,472	18.1
18 to 64 years...	2,990,445	12.2	24,648,677	12.6
65 years and over	550,874	10.2	4,581,772	9.3

X = Not applicable.

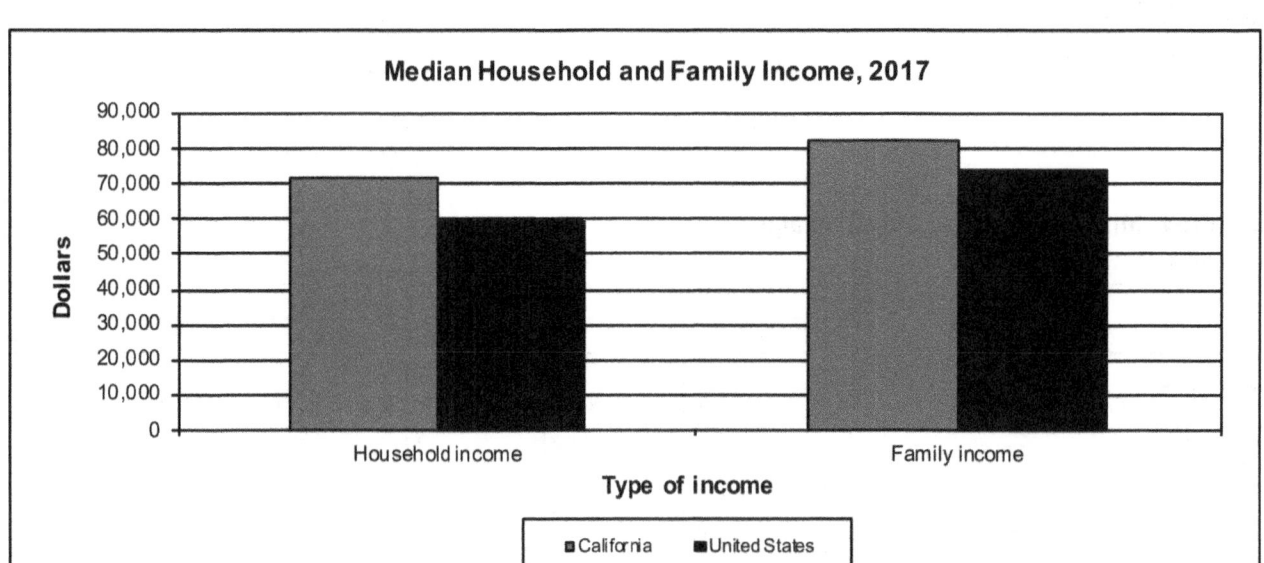

Table CA-6. Health Insurance Coverage Status for the Civilian Noninstitutionalized Population and Children Under 18 Years of Age

(Number, percent.)

Item	2009	2010	2011	2012	2013	2014	2015	2016	2017
Civilian Noninstitutionalized Population	36,376,938	36,815,569	37,161,789	37,524,274	37,831,553	38,297,457	38,649,621	38,763,815	39,046,835
Covered by Private or Public Insurance									
Number..	29,817,590	29,990,656	30,436,185	30,814,688	31,331,374	33,530,746	35,332,356	35,919,912	36,250,246
Percent..	82.0	81.5	81.9	82.1	82.8	87.6	91.4	92.7	92.8
Uninsured									
Number..	6,559,348	6,824,913	6,725,604	6,709,586	6,500,179	4,766,711	3,317,265	2,843,903	2,796,589
Percent..	18.0	18.5	18.1	17.9	17.2	12.4	8.6	7.3	7.2
Percent in the U.S. not covered....................	15.1	15.5	15.1	14.8	14.5	11.7	9.4	8.6	8.7
Children Under 18 Years of Age[1]	9,422,686	9,288,691	9,252,466	9,223,488	9,157,955	9,135,133	9,103,139	9,079,778	9,567,473
Covered by Private or Public Insurance									
Number..	8,531,688	8,455,939	8,507,669	8,493,396	8,484,747	8,638,043	8,800,771	8,811,963	9,266,841
Percent..	90.5	91.0	92.0	92.1	92.6	94.6	96.7	97.1	96.9
Uninsured									
Number..	890,998	832,752	744,797	730,092	673,208	497,090	302,368	267,815	300,632
Percent..	9.5	9.0	8.0	7.9	7.4	5.4	3.3	2.9	3.1
Percent in the U.S. not covered....................	8.6	8.0	7.5	7.2	7.1	6.0	4.8	4.5	5.0

[1] 2017 data is for individuals under 19 years of age.

Table CA-7. Employment Status by Demographic Group, 2018

(Numbers in thousands, percent.)

Characteristic	Civilian noninstitutional population	Civilian labor force		Employed		Unemployed	
		Number	Percent of population	Number	Percent of population	Number	Percent of population
Total...	31,238	19,479	62.4	18,666	59.8	813	4.2
Sex							
Male..	15,270	10,631	69.6	10,218	66.9	413	3.9
Female....................................	15,968	8,848	55.4	8,448	52.9	400	4.5
Race, Sex, and Hispanic Origin							
White......................................	22,638	14,094	62.3	13,511	59.7	583	4.1
Male.....................................	11,201	7,829	69.9	7,534	67.3	295	3.8
Female.................................	11,437	6,265	54.8	5,977	52.3	288	4.6
Black or African American............	1,962	1,207	61.5	1,128	57.5	79	6.5
Male.....................................	932	612	65.7	574	61.5	39	6.3
Female.................................	1,029	595	57.8	555	53.9	40	6.7
Hispanic or Latino ethnicity[1]	11,231	7,366	65.6	6,992	62.3	374	5.1
Male.....................................	5,578	4,142	74.2	3,951	70.8	191	4.6
Female.................................	5,653	3,224	57.0	3,041	53.8	183	5.7
Age							
16 to 19 years...........................	2,014	545	27.1	457	22.7	88	16.2
20 to 24 years...........................	2,633	1,731	65.8	1,609	61.1	123	7.1
25 to 34 years...........................	5,790	4,683	80.9	4,477	77.3	207	4.4
35 to 44 years...........................	5,363	4,339	80.9	4,203	78.4	137	3.1
45 to 54 years...........................	5,084	4,043	79.5	3,914	77.0	129	3.2
55 to 64 years...........................	4,721	3,029	64.1	2,928	62.0	100	3.3
65 years and over	5,633	1,108	19.7	1,079	19.1	29	2.6

NOTE: Data in Table 7 are from the Current Population Survey (CPS) and do not match the estimates in Table 8. See notes and definitions for further information.
[1] May be of any race.

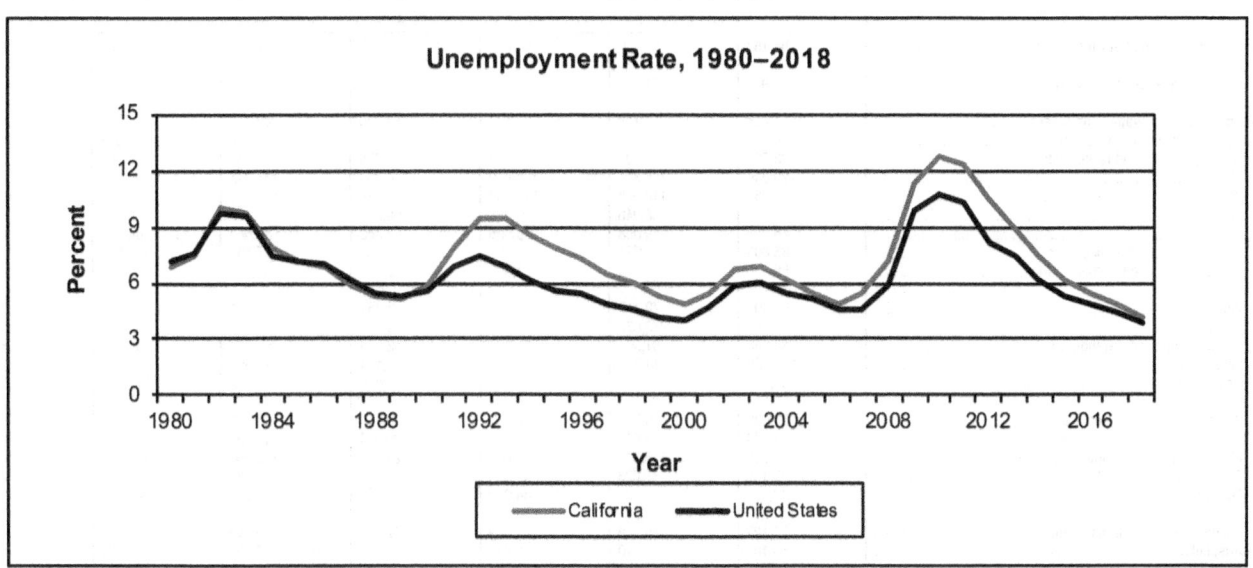

Table CA-8. Employment Status of the Civilian Noninstitutional Population Age 16 Years and Over

(Number, percent.)

Year	Civilian labor force	Civilian participation rate	Employed	Unemployed	Unemployment rate
2010...	18,336,271	64.2	16,091,945	2,244,326	12.2
2011...	18,415,100	63.5	16,258,133	2,156,967	11.7
2012...	18,523,793	63.1	16,602,672	1,921,121	10.4
2013...	18,624,992	62.7	16,958,403	1,666,589	8.9
2014...	18,758,399	62.4	17,351,318	1,407,081	7.5
2015...	18,896,477	62.1	17,724,799	1,171,678	6.2
2016...	19,093,658	62.2	18,048,827	1,044,831	5.5
2017...	19,311,958	62.3	18,393,077	918,881	4.8
2018...	19,398,212	62.4	18,582,802	815,410	4.2

Table CA-9. Employment and Average Wages by Industry

(Estimates are based on the 2012 *North American Industry Classification System* [NAICS].)

Industry	2011	2012	2013	2014	2015	2016	2017
	Number of Jobs						
Wage and Salary Employment by Industry.........................	15,091,751	15,713,601	16,212,158	16,693,308	17,184,799	17,601,469	17,908,517
Farm Wage and Salary Employment.................................	163,479	158,788	165,674	180,221	179,440	176,653	172,128
Nonfarm Wage and Salary Employment...........................	14,928,272	15,554,813	16,046,484	16,513,087	17,005,359	17,424,816	17,736,389
Private wage and salary employment...............................	12,311,710	12,963,186	13,445,494	13,874,518	14,311,872	14,675,233	14,955,488
Forestry, fishing, and related activities...........................	194,107	202,464	212,185	216,078	221,675	227,847	229,704
Mining..	26,268	28,029	27,880	28,616	26,194	22,024	19,497
Utilities..	58,292	59,386	58,934	57,870	57,551	58,632	58,396
Construction	575,807	605,845	653,646	689,301	749,682	794,232	828,950
Manufacturing..	1,246,275	1,252,180	1,252,668	1,271,835	1,294,100	1,304,558	1,313,515
Durable goods manufacturing....................................	777,531	781,013	779,778	793,945	811,294	817,927	824,782
Nondurable goods manufacturing..............................	468,744	471,167	472,890	477,890	482,806	486,631	488,733
Wholesale trade	661,306	678,616	701,188	714,838	722,323	723,793	726,800
Retail trade..	1,547,731	1,581,339	1,612,398	1,640,400	1,672,856	1,689,860	1,701,741
Transportation and warehousing...................................	417,126	428,246	445,100	466,636	499,896	531,662	572,178
Information	430,480	434,346	446,949	460,552	488,581	523,574	530,963
Finance and insurance	541,389	553,000	552,430	556,165	566,857	580,509	587,953
Real estate and rental and leasing...............................	254,549	257,827	265,164	269,110	277,188	283,083	289,013
Professional, scientific, and technical services	1,066,332	1,115,325	1,151,705	1,184,133	1,217,060	1,229,180	1,239,785
Management of companies and enterprises...................	199,316	203,653	219,138	221,154	225,551	227,375	232,202
Administrative and waste services...............................	887,252	940,725	988,951	1,033,800	1,066,852	1,094,415	1,110,782
Educational services	347,199	361,723	368,637	382,035	389,083	396,083	404,030
Health care and social assistance................................	1,524,903	1,843,149	1,982,932	2,043,669	2,128,175	2,216,053	2,294,651
Arts, entertainment, and recreation..............................	250,981	259,975	271,186	286,999	292,053	304,940	312,929
Accommodation and food services...............................	1,291,797	1,345,526	1,412,324	1,484,742	1,546,596	1,605,211	1,648,514
Other services, except public administration................	790,600	811,832	822,079	866,585	869,599	862,202	853,885
Government and government enterprises......................	2,616,562	2,591,627	2,600,990	2,638,569	2,693,487	2,749,583	2,780,901
	Dollars						
Average Wages and Salaries by Industry	56,157	57,479	57,605	59,412	62,099	63,389	66,308
Average Farm Wages and Salaries	25,977	31,152	33,195	28,480	28,742	28,763	36,215
Average Nonfarm Wages and Salaries	56,488	57,748	57,857	59,750	62,451	63,740	66,600
Average private wages and salaries.............................	56,281	57,618	57,663	59,607	62,447	63,668	66,744
Forestry, fishing, and related activities........................	23,594	24,709	25,739	26,635	28,554	30,769	31,560
Mining...	129,646	135,371	135,880	138,799	138,043	135,635	123,937
Utilities..	108,051	110,928	117,333	118,239	127,775	127,185	134,138
Construction	57,237	58,946	59,058	60,303	63,126	65,313	68,477
Manufacturing..	76,506	79,008	79,505	83,083	85,683	88,883	94,066
Durable goods manufacturing....................................	88,803	90,621	90,367	95,085	97,536	102,554	109,955
Nondurable goods manufacturing..............................	56,108	59,758	61,593	63,144	65,766	65,906	67,253
Wholesale trade	68,407	70,047	70,517	73,481	77,371	77,302	80,533
Retail trade..	32,560	33,622	33,511	34,297	35,809	35,632	36,627
Transportation and warehousing...................................	49,862	51,303	51,889	52,784	54,206	56,792	58,508
Information	107,963	114,747	134,254	138,154	147,503	149,199	170,295
Finance and insurance	97,212	102,721	103,204	109,870	114,562	117,344	124,158
Real estate and rental and leasing...............................	53,095	55,976	57,127	60,432	63,881	65,138	68,984
Professional, scientific, and technical services	94,944	103,643	98,970	105,281	113,039	113,017	118,157
Management of companies and enterprises...................	103,626	108,414	113,055	121,048	126,291	130,292	131,384
Administrative and waste services...............................	39,139	40,623	40,034	40,736	42,688	43,755	46,016
Educational services	42,327	43,183	44,049	45,536	46,688	47,300	47,979
Health care and social assistance................................	54,722	49,346	47,359	47,956	49,614	50,456	51,587
Arts, entertainment, and recreation..............................	55,105	56,770	55,940	57,359	58,589	59,729	61,765
Accommodation and food services...............................	21,967	22,651	22,907	23,712	24,922	26,344	27,335
Other services, except public administration................	30,735	31,330	31,859	32,521	34,052	35,424	37,965
Government and government enterprises......................	57,461	58,400	58,856	60,498	62,471	64,124	65,824

Table CA-10. Employment Characteristics by Family Type

(Number, percent.)

Family type and labor force status	2015 Total	2015 Families with own children under 18 years	2016 Total	2016 Families with own children under 18 years	2017 Total	2017 Families with own children under 18 years
All Families...	8,835,906	3,973,103	8,887,761	3,938,382	8,910,617	3,879,831
FAMILY TYPE AND LABOR FORCE STATUS						
Married-Couple Families..............................	6,342,293	2,783,907	6,406,893	2,779,534	6,446,965	2,743,414
Both husband and wife in labor force............................	49.0	59.7	49.2	60.0	49.5	61.0
Husband in labor force, wife not in labor force	26.2	33.9	25.7	33.7	25.5	32.8
Wife in labor force, husband not in labor force	7.5	3.9	7.5	4.0	7.5	3.9
Both husband and wife not in labor force.........................	16.2	2.0	16.4	1.9	16.2	1.8
Other Families	2,493,613	1,189,196	2,480,868	1,158,848	2,463,652	1,136,417
Female householder, no husband present.................................	68.9	71.3	68.7	70.7	68.6	70.5
In labor force...	47.0	56.0	46.9	56.4	47.7	57.3
Not in labor force	21.8	15.2	21.7	14.2	20.9	13.3
Male householder, no wife present...........................	31.1	28.7	31.3	29.3	31.4	29.5
In labor force..	25.0	26.3	25.1	27.0	25.1	27.0
Not in labor force	6.1	2.5	6.2	2.4	6.3	2.4

Table CA-11. School Enrollment and Educational Attainment, 2017

(Number, percent.)

Item	State	U.S.
Enrollment		
Total population 3 years and over, enrolled in school	10,455,915	81,273,337
Enrolled in nursery school or preschool (percent)...........................	5.7	6.0
Enrolled in kindergarten (percent)...........................	5.0	4.9
Enrolled in elementary school, grades 1-8 (percent)...........................	38.0	40.6
Enrolled in high school, grades 9-12 (percent)...........................	20.4	21.1
Enrolled in college or graduate school (percent)...........................	30.9	27.4
Attainment		
Total population 25 years and over	26,679,273	221,250,083
Less than ninth grade (percent)...........................	9.2	5.1
9th to 12th grade, no diploma (percent)...........................	7.5	6.9
High school graduate, including equivalency (percent)...........................	20.8	27.1
Some college, no degree (percent)...........................	21.1	20.4
Associate's degree (percent)...........................	7.8	8.5
Bachelor's degree (percent)...........................	21.1	19.7
Graduate or professional degree (percent)...........................	12.6	12.3
High school graduate or higher (percent)...........................	83.3	88.0
Bachelor's degree or higher (percent)...........................	33.6	32.0

Table CA-12. Public School Characteristics and Educational Indicators

(Number, percent; data derived from National Center of Education Statistics.)

Item	State	U.S.
Public Elementary and Secondary Schools		
Number of operational school districts, 2016-17	1,159	18,377
Number of operational schools, 2016-17...............................	10,291	98,330
Percent charter schools	12.1	7.1
Total public school enrollment, 2016-17...............................	6,309,138	50,587,859
Percent charter school enrollment	9.7	6.0
Student-teacher ratio, Fall 2015...............................	23.9	16.0
Expenditures per student (dollars), 2015-16...............................	11,420	11,841
Four-year adjusted cohort graduation rate (ACGR)[1]	82.7	84.6
Students eligible for free or reduced-price lunch (percent), 2015-16.............	58.9	52.1
English language learners (percent), Fall 2016	20.2	9.6
Students age 3 to 21 served under IDEA, part B (percent), 2017-18	12.2	13.7

Public Schools by Type, 2016-17		Percent of state public schools
Total number of schools...................................	10,286	100.0
Special education...................................	150	1.5
Vocational education...................................	68	0.7
Alternative education...................................	1,103	10.7

[1] Adjusted Cohort Graduation Rates (ACGR) differ from Averaged Freshmen Graduation Rates (AFGR).

Table CA-13. Reported Voting and Registration of the Voting-Age Population, November 2018

(Numbers in thousands, percent.)

Item	Total population	Total citizen population	Registered			Voted		
			Total registered	Percent registered (total population)	Percent registered (total citizen population)	Total voted	Percent voted (total population)	Percent voted (total citizen population)
U.S. Total	249,748	228,832	153,066	61.3	66.9	122,281	49.0	53.4
State Total...........................	30,243	25,525	15,690	51.9	61.5	13,240	43.8	51.9
Sex								
Male	14,767	12,449	7,372	49.9	59.2	6,205	42.0	49.8
Female	15,476	13,076	8,318	53.8	63.6	7,035	45.5	53.8
Race								
White alone...........................	21,467	18,311	11,711	54.6	64.0	10,005	46.6	54.6
White, non-Hispanic alone	11,986	11,587	8,005	66.8	69.1	7,116	59.4	61.4
Black alone............................	1,912	1,845	1,061	55.5	57.5	933	48.8	50.6
Asian alone	5,222	3,983	2,061	39.5	51.7	1,620	31.0	40.7
Hispanic (of any race)	10,595	7,613	4,211	39.7	55.3	3,300	31.1	43.3
White alone or in combination	22,303	19,010	12,125	54.4	63.8	10,332	46.3	54.3
Black alone or in combination...........	2,094	1,999	1,154	55.1	57.7	998	47.6	49.9
Asian alone or in combination...........	5,571	4,320	2,278	40.9	52.7	1,795	32.2	41.5
Age								
18 to 24 years	3,385	3,100	1,407	41.6	45.4	1,096	32.4	35.3
25 to 34 years	5,861	4,734	2,706	46.2	57.2	2,045	34.9	43.2
35 to 44 years	5,487	4,187	2,444	44.5	58.4	2,058	37.5	49.2
45 to 64 years	9,975	8,415	5,554	55.7	66.0	4,792	48.0	56.9
65 years and over	5,535	5,089	3,580	64.7	70.3	3,248	58.7	63.8

Table CA-14. Crime

(Number, rate per 100,000. Data are derived from the FBI Uniform Crime Reports.)

Item	State			U.S.		
	2016	2017	Percent change	2016	2017	Percent change
TOTAL POPULATION[1]	39,296,476	39,536,653	0.6	323,405,935	325,719,178	0.7
VIOLENT CRIME						
Number	174,796	177,627	1.6	1,285,606	1,283,220	-0.2
Rate	444.8	449.3	1.0	397.5	394.0	-0.9
Murder and Nonnegligent Manslaughter						
Number..................................	1,930	1,830	-5.2	17,413	17,284	-0.7
Rate	4.9	4.6	-5.8	5.4	5.3	-1.4
Rape[2]						
Number..................................	13,702	14,721	7.4	132,414	135,755	2.5
Rate	34.9	37.2	6.8	40.9	41.7	1.8
Robbery						
Number..................................	54,789	56,622	3.3	332,797	319,356	-4.0
Rate	139.4	143.2	2.7	102.9	98.0	-4.7
Aggravated Assault						
Number..................................	104,375	104,454	0.1	802,982	810,825	1.0
Rate	265.6	264.2	-0.5	248.3	248.9	0.3
PROPERTY CRIME						
Number..................................	1,002,070	987,114	-1.5	7,928,530	7,694,086	-3.0
Rate	2,550.0	2,496.7	-2.1	2,451.6	2,362.2	-3.6
Burglary						
Number..................................	188,304	176,690	-6.2	1,516,405	1,401,840	-7.6
Rate	479.2	446.9	-6.7	468.9	430.4	-8.2
Larceny-Theft						
Number..................................	637,010	642,033	0.8	5,644,835	5,519,107	-2.2
Rate	1,621.0	1,623.9	0.2	1,745.4	1,694.4	-2.9
Motor Vehicle Theft						
Number..................................	176,756	168,391	-4.7	767,290	773,139	0.8
Rate	449.8	425.9	-5.3	237.3	237.4	-

NOTE: Although arson data are included in the trend and clearance tables, sufficient data are not available to estimate totals for this offense. Therefore, no arson data are published in this table.
- = Zero or rounds to zero.
[1] Population figures are U.S. Census Bureau provisional estimates as of July 1, 2017.
[2] The figures shown in the rape (revised definition) column were estimated using the revised Uniform Crime Reporting (UCR) definition of rape.

Table CA-15. State Government Finances, 2017

(Dollar amounts in thousands, percent distribution.)

Item	Dollars	Percent distribution
Total Revenue	398,622,040	100.0
General revenue	288,583,711	72.4
Intergovernmental revenue	93,013,830	23.3
Taxes	155,632,088	39.0
General sales	35,357,699	8.9
Selective sales	12,582,663	3.2
License taxes	10,525,972	2.6
Individual income tax	84,196,751	21.1
Corporate income tax	10,112,520	2.5
Other taxes	2,856,483	0.7
Current charges	30,603,893	7.7
Miscellaneous general revenue	9,333,900	2.3
Utility revenue	1,004,089	0.3
Liquor stores revenue	0	-
Insurance trust revenue[1]	109,034,240	27.4
Total Expenditure	350,012,165	100.0
Intergovernmental expenditure	107,877,299	30.8
Direct expenditure	242,134,866	69.2
Current operation	169,982,770	48.6
Capital outlay	8,776,504	2.5
Insurance benefits and repayments	50,990,054	14.6
Assistance and subsidies	5,316,416	1.5
Interest on debt	7,069,122	2.0
Exhibit: Salaries and wages	35,729,577	10.2
Total Expenditure	350,012,165	100.0
General expenditure	296,779,736	84.8
Intergovernmental expenditure	107,877,299	30.8
Direct expenditure	188,902,437	54.0
General expenditure, by function:		
Education	97,240,115	27.8
Public welfare	124,082,248	35.5
Hospitals	13,426,724	3.8
Health	7,503,590	2.1
Highways	10,825,735	3.1
Police protection	1,907,378	0.5
Correction	8,528,075	2.4
Natural resources	5,747,925	1.6
Parks and recreation	613,467	0.2
Governmental administration	8,662,176	2.5
Interest on general debt	6,899,122	2.0
Other and unallocable	11,343,181	3.2
Utility expenditure	2,242,375	0.6
Liquor stores expenditure	0	-
Insurance trust expenditure	50,990,054	14.6
Debt at End of Fiscal Year	152,772,292	X
Cash and Security Holdings	720,855,259	X

X = Not applicable.
- = Zero or rounds to zero.
[1] Within insurance trust revenue, net earnings of state retirement systems is a calculated statistic (the item code in the data file is X08), and thus can be positive or negative. Net earnings is the sum of earnings on investments plus gains on investments minus losses on investments. The change made in 2002 for asset valuation from book to market value in accordance with Statement 34 of the Governmental Accounting Standards Board is reflected in the calculated statistics.

Table CA-16. State Government Tax Collections, 2018

(Dollars in thousands, percent.)

Item	Dollars	Percent distribution
Total Taxes	175,016,884	100.0
Property taxes	2,837,386	1.6
Sales and gross receipts	53,846,346	30.8
General sales and gross receipts	36,188,907	20.7
Selective sales and gross receipts	17,657,439	10.1
Alcoholic beverages	376,735	0.2
Amusements	X	-
Insurance premiums	2,569,271	1.5
Motor fuels	6,351,756	3.6
Pari-mutuels	15,871	-
Public utilities	688,489	0.4
Tobacco products	2,428,121	1.4
Other selective sales	5,227,196	3.0
Licenses	10,504,521	6.0
Alcoholic beverages	60,519	-
Amusements	20,583	-
Corporations in general	80,029	-
Hunting and fishing	112,138	0.1
Motor vehicle	4,635,040	2.6
Motor vehicle operators	281,045	0.2
Public utilities	752,340	0.4
Occupation and business, NEC	4,535,825	2.6
Other licenses	27,002	-
Income taxes	107,640,534	61.5
Individual income	95,152,230	54.4
Corporation net income	12,488,304	7.1
Other taxes	188,097	0.1
Death and gift	577	-
Documentary and stock transfer	X	-
Severance	108,912	0.1
Taxes, NEC	78,608	0.0

- = Zero or rounds to zero.
X = Not applicable.

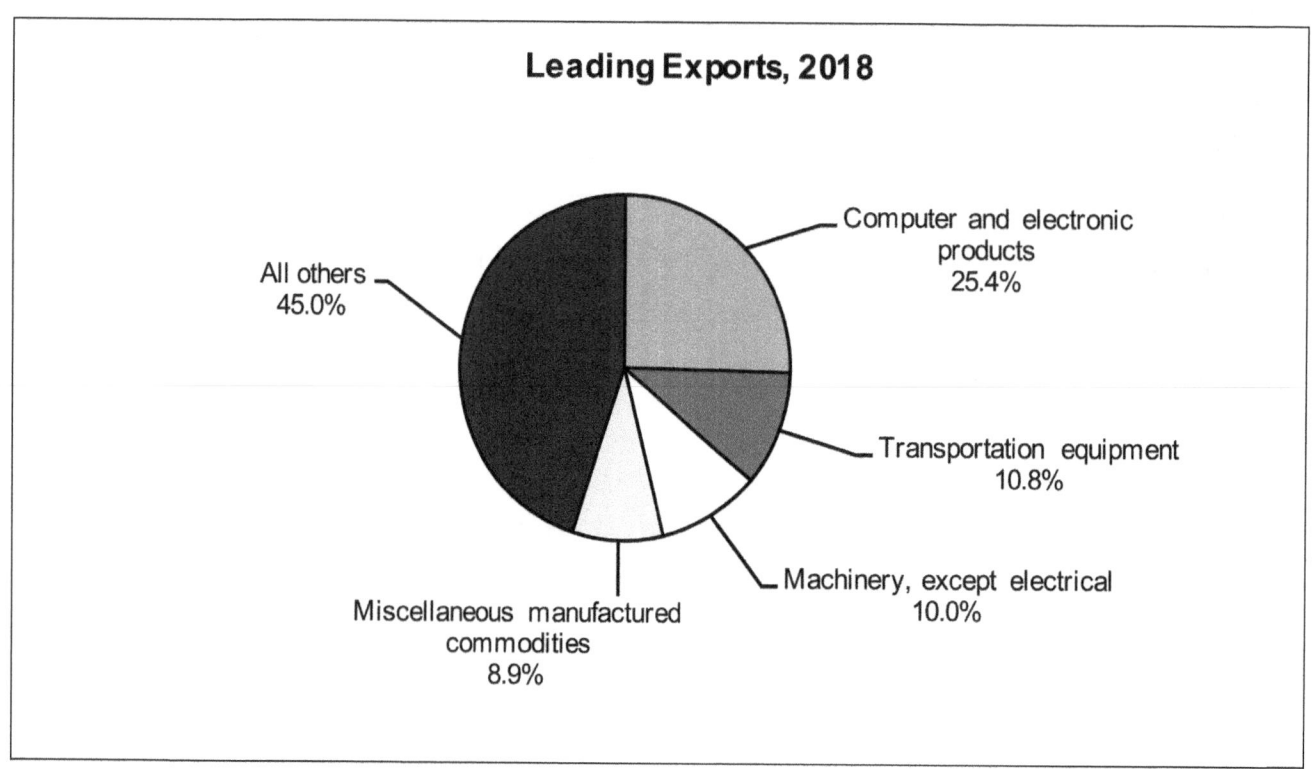

Leading Exports, 2018

- All others 45.0%
- Computer and electronic products 25.4%
- Transportation equipment 10.8%
- Machinery, except electrical 10.0%
- Miscellaneous manufactured commodities 8.9%

COLORADO

Facts and Figures

Location: Western United States; bordered on the N by Wyoming and Nebraska, on the E by Nebraska and Kansas, on the S by Oklahoma and New Mexico, and on the W by Utah; Colorado is one of the Four Corner states—at its SW corner it touches Arizona, New Mexico, and Utah

Area: 104,093 sq. mi. (269,601 sq. km.); rank—8th

Population: 5,695,564 (2018 est.); rank—21st

Principal Cities: capital—Denver; largest—Denver

Statehood: August 1, 1876; 38th state

U.S. Congress: 2 senators, 7 representatives

State Motto: *Nil sine numine* ("Nothing without providence")

State Songs: "Where the Columbines Grow"; "Rocky Mountain High"

State Nicknames: The Centennial State; Colorful Colorado

Abbreviations: CO; Colo.

State Symbols: flower—Rocky Mountain columbine; tree—Colorado blue spruce; bird—lark bunting

At a Glance

- With an increase in population of 13.2 percent, Colorado ranked 5th among the states in growth from 2010 to 2018.

- In 2017, 7.5 percent of Coloradans did not have health insurance, compared to 8.7 percent of the total U.S. population.

- At a rate of 17.6 per 100,000 residents, the 2017 drug overdose death rate in Colorado was lower than the national average of 21.7 deaths per 100,000 population.

- In Colorado, 10.3 percent of the total population and 12.0 percent of persons under 18 years old lived below the poverty level in 2017, compared to nationwide poverty levels of 13.4 percent and 18.4 percent, respectively.

Table CO-1. Population by Age, Sex, Race, and Hispanic Origin

(Number, percent, except where noted.)

Sex, age, race, and Hispanic origin	2000	2010	2018[1]	Percent change, 2010–2018
Total Population..	4,301,261	5,029,196	5,695,564	13.2
Percent of total U.S. population	1.5	1.6	1.7	X
Sex				
Male...	2,165,983	2,520,662	2,867,868	13.8
Female	2,135,278	2,508,534	2,827,696	12.7
Age				
Under 5 years...	297,505	343,960	336,854	-2.1
5 to 19 years...	927,163	1,020,732	1,076,695	5.5
20 to 64 years..	2,660,520	3,114,879	3,473,786	11.5
65 years and over	416,073	549,625	808,229	47.1
Median age (years)	34.3	36.1	36.9	2.2
Race and Hispanic Origin				
One race				
White	3,560,005	4,450,623	4,959,310	11.4
Black	165,063	214,919	259,711	20.8
American Indian and Alaska Native	44,241	78,144	91,120	16.6
Asian	95,213	144,819	197,634	36.5
Native Hawaiian or Other Pacific Islander	4,621	8,420	10,933	29.8
Two or more races	122,187	132,271	176,856	33.7
Hispanic (of any race)...................................	735,601	1,078,225	1,235,117	14.6

X = Not applicable.
[1] Population figures for 2018 are July 1 estimates. The 2010 estimates are taken from the 2010 Census.

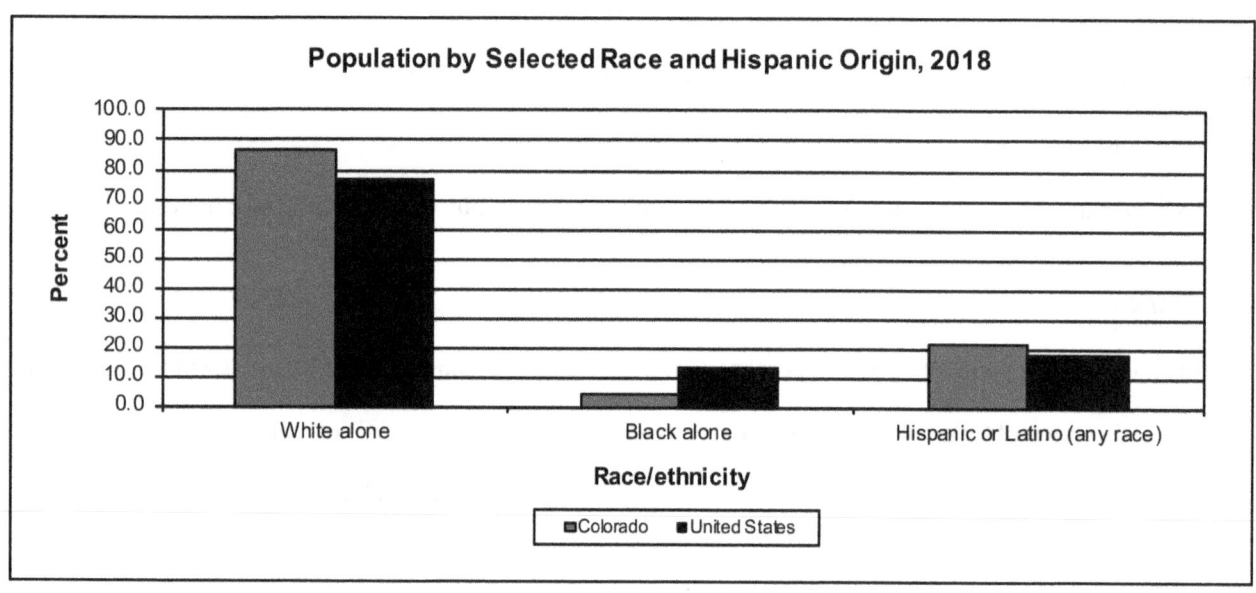

Table CO-2. Marital Status

(Number, percent distribution.)

Sex, age, race, and Hispanic origin	2000	2010	2017
Males, 15 Years and Over...................................	1,694,635	2,004,303	2,281,955
Never married	30.5	34.4	35.9
Now married, except separated.............................	56.6	51.7	50.4
Separated..	1.4	1.6	1.2
Widowed...	1.9	2.0	2.1
Divorced...	9.6	10.3	10.4
Females, 15 Years and Over.................................	1,690,734	2,017,425	2,276,620
Never married	23.4	26.9	28.5
Now married, except separated.............................	54.7	50.8	49.9
Separated..	1.8	2.0	1.5
Widowed...	7.6	7.0	6.6
Divorced...	12.5	13.3	13.4

Table CO-3. Households and Housing Characteristics

(Number, percent, dollars.)

Item	2000	2010	2017	Average annual percent change, 2010–2017
Total Households..	1,658,238	1,960,585	2,139,207	1.3
Family households	1,084,461	1,258,885	1,366,807	1.2
Married-couple family	858,671	959,624	1,062,314	1.5
Other family	225,790	299,261	304,493	0.2
Male householder, no wife present	66,811	90,518	100,541	1.6
Female householder, no husband present ..	158,979	208,743	203,952	-0.3
Nonfamily households	573,777	701,700	772,400	1.4
Householder living alone............................	435,778	555,080	578,735	0.6
Householder not living alone......................	137,999	146,620	193,665	4.6
Housing Characteristics				
Total housing units......................................	1,808,037	2,214,262	2,385,495	1.1
Occupied housing units	1,658,238	1,960,585	2,139,207	1.3
Owner occupied	1,116,173	1,292,792	1,394,824	1.1
Renter occupied	542,101	667,793	744,383	1.6
Average household size................................	2.53	2.52	2.57	0.3
Financial Characteristics				
Median gross rent of renter-occupied housing	671	863	1240	6.2
Median monthly owner costs for housing units with a mortgage	1,197	1,590	1,681	0.8
Median value of owner-occupied housing units........	166,600	236,600	348,900	6.8

Table CO-4. Migration, Origin, and Language

(Number, percent.)

Characteristic	State 2016	State 2017	State Percent change	U.S. 2016	U.S. 2017	U.S. Percent change
Residence 1 Year Ago						
Population 1 year and over	5,476,928	5,542,282	1.2	319,361,956	321,994,428	0.8
Same house	81.5	82.0	X	85.4	85.7	X
Different house in the U.S...................................	17.9	17.3	X	13.9	13.6	X
Same county	8.7	8.2	X	8.3	8.1	X
Different county	9.1	9.1	X	5.6	5.6	X
Same state	5	5	X	3.2	3.3	X
Different state	4.1	4.1	X	2.4	2.3	X
Abroad	0.6	0.6	X	0.7	0.7	X
Place of Birth						
Native born	4,995,812	5,056,386	1.2	279,388,170	281,193,323	0.6
Male	50.6	50.4	X	49.3	49.4	X
Female	49.4	49.6	X	50.7	50.6	X
Foreign born	544,733	550,768	1.1	43,739,345	44,525,855	1.8
Male	48.3	49.7	X	48.5	48.4	X
Female	51.7	50.3	X	51.5	51.6	X
Foreign born; naturalized U.S. citizen...................	215,995	234,274	8.5	21,238,372	21,948,732	3.3
Male	44.6	46.4	X	45.9	45.9	X
Female	55.4	53.6	X	54.1	54.1	X
Foreign born; not a U.S. citizen...........................	328,738	316,494	-3.7	22,500,973	22,577,123	0.3
Male	50.7	52.1	X	51	50.8	X
Female	49.3	47.9	X	49	49.2	X
Entered 2010 or later	19	21.3	X	18.6	21.3	X
Entered 2000 to 2009	29	28	X	26.7	25.7	X
Entered before 2000...	51.9	50.7	X	54.7	53.0	X
World Region of Birth, Foreign						
Foreign-born population, excluding population born at sea	544,733	550,768	1.1	43,738,901	44,525,458	1.8
Europe	13.1	12.7	X	10.9	10.8	X
Asia..	24.7	25.8	X	30.8	31.2	X
Africa	5.8	7.5	X	4.9	5.1	X
Oceania	1.4	0.9	X	0.6	0.6	X
Latin America..	52.3	50.5	X	51	50.4	X
North America..	2.7	2.6	X	1.8	1.8	X
Language Spoken at Home and Ability to Speak English						
Population 5 years and over......................................	5,205,474	5,274,561	1.3	303,328,961	305,924,019	0.9
English only	82.9	83.1	X	78.4	78.2	X
Language other than English................................	17.1	16.9	X	21.6	21.8	X
Speaks English less than "very well"...................	6.1	5.5	X	8.6	8.5	X

NA = Not available.
X = Not applicable.
- = Zero or rounds to zero.

Table CO-5. Median Income and Poverty Status, 2017

(Number, percent, except as noted.)

Characteristic	State Number	State Percent	U.S. Number	U.S. Percent
Median Income				
Households (dollars)...	69,117	X	60,336	X
Families (dollars)	84,918	X	73,891	X
Below Poverty Level (All People)	564,312	10.3	42,583,651	13.4
Sex				
Male	257,815	9.4	19,004,547	12.2
Female	306,497	11.2	23,579,104	14.5
Age				
Under 18 years...	149,043	12.0	13,353,202	18.4
Related children under 18 years..	145,060	11.7	13,053,472	18.1
18 to 64 years..	356,341	10.2	24,648,677	12.6
65 years and over	58,928	7.8	4,581,772	9.3

X = Not applicable.

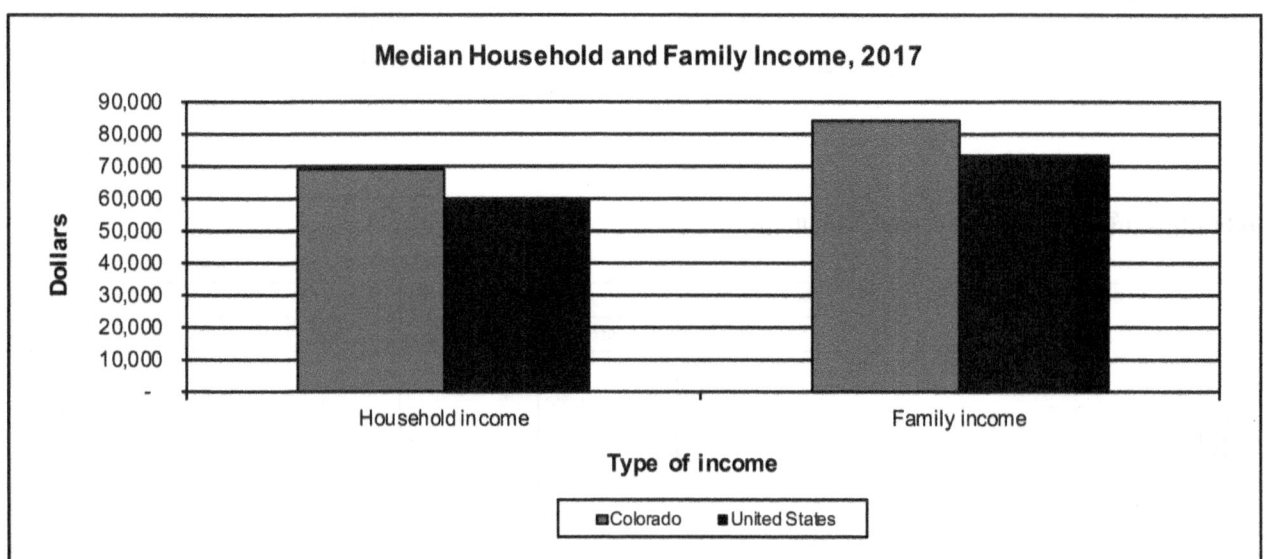

Median Household and Family Income, 2017

Table CO-6. Health Insurance Coverage Status for the Civilian Noninstitutionalized Population and Children Under 18 Years of Age

(Number, percent.)

Item	2009	2010	2011	2012	2013	2014	2015	2016	2017
Civilian Noninstitutionalized Population	4,930,142	4,956,873	5,024,885	5,094,766	5,173,272	5,266,022	5,367,335	5,447,760	5,514,070
Covered by Private or Public Insurance									
Number..	4,152,348	4,167,764	4,265,266	4,343,522	4,444,084	4,723,411	4,934,713	5,038,017	5,099,993
Percent..	84.2	84.1	84.9	85.3	85.9	89.7	91.9	92.5	92.5
Uninsured									
Number..	777,794	789,109	759,619	751,244	729,188	542,611	432,622	409,743	414,077
Percent..	15.8	15.9	15.1	14.7	14.1	10.3	8.1	7.5	7.5
Percent in the U.S. not covered................................	15.1	15.5	15.1	14.8	14.5	11.7	9.4	8.6	8.7
Children Under 18 Years of Age[1]	1,225,211	1,226,208	1,226,828	1,229,008	1,239,191	1,245,432	1,254,800	1,258,167	1,334,235
Covered by Private or Public Insurance									
Number..	1,100,845	1,102,080	1,111,102	1,120,313	1,137,042	1,175,348	1,202,377	1,207,518	1,276,752
Percent..	89.8	89.9	90.6	91.2	91.8	94.4	95.8	96.0	95.7
Uninsured									
Number..	124,366	124,128	115,726	108,695	102,149	70,084	52,423	50,649	57,483
Percent..	10.2	10.1	9.4	8.8	8.2	5.6	4.2	4.0	4.3
Percent in the U.S. not covered................................	8.6	8.0	7.5	7.2	7.1	6.0	4.8	4.5	5.0

[1] 2017 data is for individuals under 19 years of age.

Table CO-7. Employment Status by Demographic Group, 2018

(Numbers in thousands, percent.)

Characteristic	Civilian noninstitutional population	Civilian labor force		Employed		Unemployed	
		Number	Percent of population	Number	Percent of population	Number	Percent of population
Total...............................	4,468	3,091	69.2	2,988	66.9	103	3.3
Sex							
Male..............................	2,215	1,677	75.7	1,610	72.7	68	4.0
Female	2,253	1,414	62.7	1,379	61.2	35	2.5
Race, Sex, and Hispanic Origin							
White	3,932	2,729	69.4	2,642	67.2	87	3.2
Male..............................	1,947	1,471	75.6	1,416	72.7	55	3.8
Female	1,986	1,258	63.3	1,226	61.8	31	2.5
Black or African American...........	NA	NA	NA	NA	NA	NA	NA
Male..............................	NA	NA	NA	NA	NA	NA	NA
Female	NA	NA	NA	NA	NA	NA	NA
Hispanic or Latino ethnicity[1]	860	601	69.9	581	67.5	21	3.4
Male..............................	425	324	76.2	314	73.9	10	3.1
Female	435	277	63.8	267	61.4	11	3.8
Age							
16 to 19 years	NA	NA	NA	NA	NA	NA	NA
20 to 24 years	357	273	76.5	262	73.4	11	4.1
25 to 34 years	868	764	88.0	739	85.1	25	3.3
35 to 44 years	773	663	85.8	648	83.8	15	2.3
45 to 54 years	705	591	83.9	580	82.2	12	2.0
55 to 64 years	706	499	70.7	480	67.9	19	3.8
65 years and over	795	191	24.0	186	23.4	5	2.4

NOTE: Data in Table 7 are from the Current Population Survey (CPS) and do not match the estimates in Table 8. See notes and definitions for further information.
[1] May be of any race.
NA = Not available.

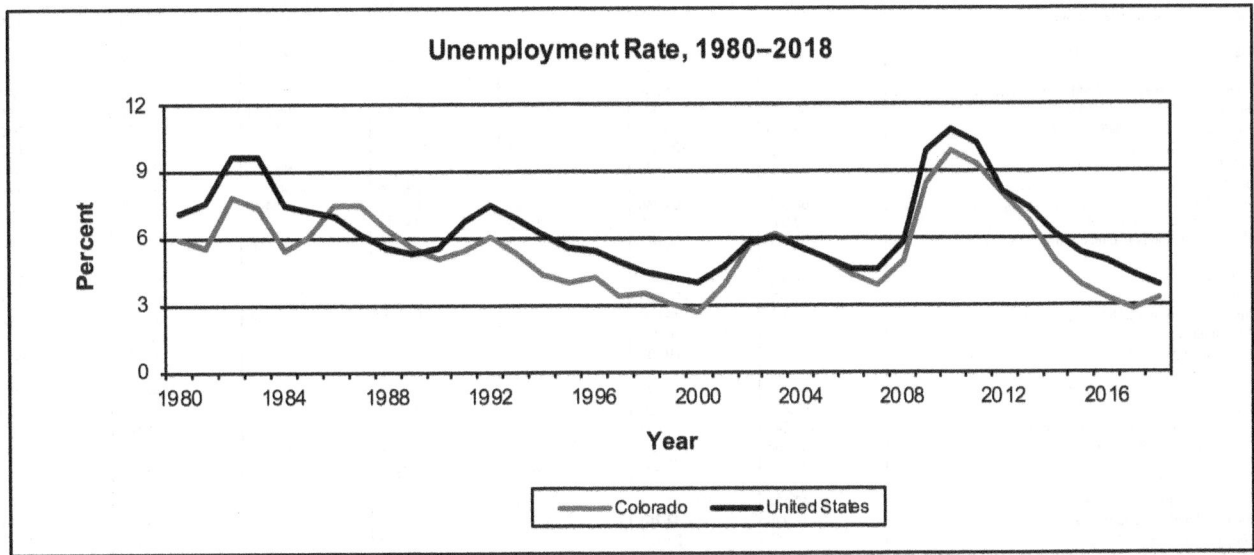

Unemployment Rate, 1980–2018

Table CO-8. Employment Status of the Civilian Noninstitutional Population Age 16 Years and Over

(Number, percent.)

Year	Civilian labor force	Civilian participation rate	Employed	Unemployed	Unemployment rate
2010..	2,724,417	70.4	2,486,404	238,013	8.7
2011..	2,736,079	69.7	2,507,265	228,814	8.4
2012..	2,757,222	69.1	2,539,941	217,281	7.9
2013..	2,767,153	68.2	2,577,556	189,597	6.9
2014..	2,799,491	67.7	2,659,474	140,017	5.0
2015..	2,824,759	66.8	2,715,059	109,700	3.9
2016..	2,893,268	67.0	2,798,928	94,340	3.3
2017..	2,992,307	68.1	2,907,468	84,839	2.8
2018..	3,096,358	69.2	2,994,752	101,606	3.3

Table CO-9. Employment and Average Wages by Industry

(Estimates are based on the 2012 *North American Industry Classification System* [NAICS].)

Industry	2011	2012	2013	2014	2015	2016	2017
	Number of Jobs						
Wage and Salary Employment by Industry.......................	2,383,753	2,437,001	2,507,504	2,593,887	2,670,453	2,726,685	2,784,085
Farm Wage and Salary Employment................................	11,877	11,957	12,747	11,976	11,633	12,285	14,783
Nonfarm Wage and Salary Employment.........................	2,371,876	2,425,044	2,494,757	2,581,911	2,658,820	2,714,400	2,769,302
Private wage and salary employment.............................	1,916,436	1,968,170	2,029,421	2,111,086	2,180,679	2,227,860	2,276,555
Forestry, fishing, and related activities......................	5,800	6,108	6,374	6,409	6,495	6,562	6,819
Mining..	27,576	30,044	30,308	33,706	30,394	23,467	25,450
Utilities..	8,138	8,045	7,842	8,148	8,209	8,235	8,078
Construction..	115,256	119,066	131,178	145,844	152,503	159,077	167,337
Manufacturing..	129,309	132,146	132,880	136,558	141,021	142,505	144,217
Durable goods manufacturing................................	84,024	86,423	86,041	88,226	90,250	89,998	90,372
Nondurable goods manufacturing..........................	45,285	45,723	46,839	48,332	50,771	52,507	53,845
Wholesale trade...	92,104	94,555	97,108	100,328	103,721	105,320	107,159
Retail trade..	241,787	245,704	251,142	256,824	264,890	270,865	272,508
Transportation and warehousing................................	61,632	63,818	66,343	69,499	71,547	71,747	76,057
Information...	72,463	69,954	69,965	70,263	70,896	71,819	71,692
Finance and insurance	102,442	104,547	107,600	108,816	111,546	114,229	117,228
Real estate and rental and leasing............................	42,210	42,821	43,882	45,165	47,843	49,637	51,414
Professional, scientific, and technical services	173,334	179,766	190,421	198,200	206,260	211,670	217,294
Management of companies and enterprises................	29,920	31,795	34,657	35,483	36,532	36,902	39,048
Administrative and waste services.............................	138,636	146,695	149,934	155,233	158,618	159,784	159,123
Educational services..	42,191	44,095	45,384	47,937	49,513	51,541	52,255
Health care and social assistance.............................	242,995	250,396	254,277	264,876	278,667	290,427	296,680
Arts, entertainment, and recreation...........................	46,135	47,327	47,882	50,692	51,295	53,627	56,534
Accommodation and food services.............................	226,823	234,043	243,327	252,399	263,057	272,071	278,945
Other services, except public administration..............	117,685	117,245	118,917	124,706	127,672	128,375	128,717
Government and government enterprises	455,440	456,874	465,336	470,825	478,141	486,540	492,747
	Dollars						
Average Wages and Salaries by Industry	49,675	51,271	51,654	53,428	54,855	55,370	57,603
Average Farm Wages and Salaries	33,019	37,999	39,764	40,852	35,594	39,020	32,613
Average Nonfarm Wages and Salaries	49,759	51,336	51,714	53,486	54,939	55,444	57,736
Average private wages and salaries............................	50,214	52,051	52,348	54,236	55,709	56,096	58,590
Forestry, fishing, and related activities......................	24,710	25,262	26,161	27,564	29,364	30,278	31,656
Mining..	105,931	105,002	109,884	113,727	115,767	115,853	118,670
Utilities..	91,735	100,644	90,929	93,431	96,785	99,390	103,508
Construction..	49,861	51,114	51,968	54,558	56,260	58,235	60,346
Manufacturing..	63,371	64,045	64,234	67,036	68,409	68,151	71,315
Durable goods manufacturing................................	69,997	70,910	71,178	73,717	76,079	76,279	81,167
Nondurable goods manufacturing..........................	51,077	51,071	51,478	54,841	54,776	54,218	54,778
Wholesale trade...	72,920	75,103	75,681	78,930	80,926	81,393	84,954
Retail trade..	28,108	28,931	29,322	30,248	31,248	31,739	32,732
Transportation and warehousing................................	47,524	49,628	52,144	54,509	55,752	56,478	59,225
Information...	85,854	90,244	92,101	97,812	96,212	97,571	102,935
Finance and insurance	76,358	79,751	81,359	84,937	89,862	91,805	94,354
Real estate and rental and leasing............................	45,197	48,327	50,535	51,946	54,434	56,279	58,544
Professional, scientific, and technical services	82,875	85,538	86,365	88,599	90,251	91,729	94,929
Management of companies and enterprises................	133,541	155,621	127,658	136,932	145,522	131,163	151,767
Administrative and waste services.............................	36,062	36,853	35,887	37,137	38,891	40,050	42,401
Educational services..	34,476	35,047	35,715	35,525	36,042	36,304	36,687
Health care and social assistance.............................	46,174	47,124	47,365	48,225	49,540	50,098	51,116
Arts, entertainment, and recreation...........................	34,325	34,761	35,788	36,906	39,520	40,065	40,151
Accommodation and food services.............................	20,453	21,121	21,678	22,479	23,385	24,106	25,429
Other services, except public administration..............	32,543	34,254	35,168	35,861	37,392	38,704	40,419
Government and government enterprises	47,843	48,257	48,949	50,124	51,429	52,460	53,795

Table CO-10. Employment Characteristics by Family Type

(Number, percent.)

Family type and labor force status	2015		2016		2017	
	Total	Families with own children under 18 years	Total	Families with own children under 18 years	Total	Families with own children under 18 years
All Families..........	1,331,861	597,501	1,347,936	595,865	1,366,807	588,760
FAMILY TYPE AND LABOR FORCE STATUS						
Married-Couple Families..........	1,038,040	435,028	1,051,388	437,459	1,062,314	428,750
Both husband and wife in labor force..........	54.3	65.4	53.9	65.9	53.8	65.6
Husband in labor force, wife not in labor force	22.0	28.5	22.5	29.0	22.2	28.9
Wife in labor force, husband not in labor force	7.2	3.9	7.3	3.4	6.8	3.5
Both husband and wife not in labor force..........	15.5	1.7	15.4	1.1	16.1	1.4
Other Families	293,821	162,473	296,548	158,406	304,493	160,010
Female householder, no husband present..........	68.3	69.9	66.7	71.9	67.0	67.5
In labor force..........	50.1	57.9	50.6	61.8	49.4	58.0
Not in labor force	18.2	11.9	16.1	10.1	17.5	9.4
Male householder, no wife present..........	31.7	30.1	33.3	28.1	33.0	32.5
In labor force..........	26.4	28.6	27.4	26.4	27.4	30.3
Not in labor force	5.3	1.5	5.9	1.7	5.6	2.2

Table CO-11. School Enrollment and Educational Attainment, 2017

(Number, percent.)

Item	State	U.S.
Enrollment		
Total population 3 years and over, enrolled in school	1,394,563	81,273,337
Enrolled in nursery school or preschool (percent)	6.0	6.0
Enrolled in kindergarten (percent)..........	5.0	4.9
Enrolled in elementary school, grades 1-8 (percent)..........	40.9	40.6
Enrolled in high school, grades 9-12 (percent)..........	21.0	21.1
Enrolled in college or graduate school (percent)..........	27.1	27.4
Attainment		
Total population 25 years and over	3,822,068	221,250,083
Less than ninth grade (percent)..........	3.4	5.1
9th to 12th grade, no diploma (percent)..........	5.0	6.9
High school graduate, including equivalency (percent)..........	21.3	27.1
Some college, no degree (percent)	20.9	20.4
Associate's degree (percent)..........	8.2	8.5
Bachelor's degree (percent)..........	26.0	19.7
Graduate or professional degree (percent)..........	15.2	12.3
High school graduate or higher (percent)	91.6	88.0
Bachelor's degree or higher (percent)..........	41.2	32.0

Table CO-12. Public School Characteristics and Educational Indicators

(Number, percent; data derived from National Center of Education Statistics.)

Item	State	U.S.
Public Elementary and Secondary Schools		
Number of operational school districts, 2016-17	267	18,377
Number of operational schools, 2016-17..........	1,888	98,330
Percent charter schools	12.6	7.1
Total public school enrollment, 2016-17..........	905,019	50,587,859
Percent charter school enrollment	12.7	6.0
Student-teacher ratio, Fall 2015	17.4	16.0
Expenditures per student (dollars), 2015-16..........	9,619	11,841
Four-year adjusted cohort graduation rate (ACGR)[1]	79.1	84.6
Students eligible for free or reduced-price lunch (percent), 2015-16..........	41.8	52.1
English language learners (percent), Fall 2016	11.7	9.6
Students age 3 to 21 served under IDEA, part B (percent), 2017-18	11.2	13.7

Public Schools by Type, 2016-17		Percent of state public schools
Total number of schools..........	1,888	100.0
Special education..........	7	0.4
Vocational education..........	8	0.4
Alternative education..........	98	5.2

[1] Adjusted Cohort Graduation Rates (ACGR) differ from Averaged Freshmen Graduation Rates (AFGR).

Table CO-13. Reported Voting and Registration of the Voting-Age Population, November 2018

(Numbers in thousands, percent.)

Item	Total population	Total citizen population	Registered			Voted		
			Total registered	Percent registered (total population)	Percent registered (total citizen population)	Total voted	Percent voted (total population)	Percent voted (total citizen population)
U.S. Total	249,748	228,832	153,066	61.3	66.9	122,281	49.0	53.4
State Total..........................	4,353	4,029	2,645	60.8	65.6	2,342	53.8	58.1
Sex								
Male	2,171	2,004	1,315	60.6	65.6	1,144	52.7	57.1
Female	2,182	2,025	1,330	61.0	65.7	1,198	54.9	59.2
Race								
White alone..............................	3,911	3,666	2,439	62.4	66.5	2,185	55.9	59.6
White, non-Hispanic alone	3,136	3,107	2,141	68.3	68.9	1,945	62.0	62.6
Black alone..............................	185	170	73	39.6	43.1	51	27.8	30.3
Asian alone	156	93	75	47.7	80.6	66	42.3	71.5
Hispanic (of any race).................	806	590	323	40.1	54.8	259	32.1	43.9
White alone or in combination	3,998	3,753	2,486	62.2	66.2	2,213	55.4	59.0
Black alone or in combination........	219	204	88	40.3	43.3	63	28.8	31.0
Asian alone or in combination.......	185	121	89	48.3	73.8	73	39.2	60.0
Age								
18 to 24 years..........................	437	404	228	52.2	56.4	166	38.0	41.1
25 to 34 years..........................	859	751	433	50.4	57.7	367	42.7	48.8
35 to 44 years..........................	841	763	509	60.5	66.7	432	51.3	56.6
45 to 64 years..........................	1,389	1,312	876	63.1	66.8	797	57.4	60.8
65 years and over	827	798	598	72.3	75.0	580	70.1	72.7

Table CO-14. Crime

(Number, rate per 100,000. Data are derived from the FBI Uniform Crime Reports.)

Item	State			U.S.		
	2016	2017	Percent change	2016	2017	Percent change
TOTAL POPULATION[1]	5,530,105	5,607,154	1.4	323,405,935	325,719,178	0.7
VIOLENT CRIME						
Number..	19,030	20,638	8.4	1,285,606	1,283,220	-0.2
Rate..	344.1	368.1	7.0	397.5	394.0	-0.9
Murder and Nonnegligent Manslaughter						
Number..	189	221	16.9	17,413	17,284	-0.7
Rate..	3.4	3.9	15.3	5.4	5.3	-1.4
Rape[2]						
Number..	3,635	3,858	6.1	132,414	135,755	2.5
Rate..	65.7	68.8	4.7	40.9	41.7	1.8
Robbery						
Number..	3,525	3,838	8.9	332,797	319,356	-4.0
Rate..	63.7	68.4	7.4	102.9	98.0	-4.7
Aggravated Assault						
Number..	11,681	12,721	8.9	802,982	810,825	1.0
Rate..	211.2	226.9	7.4	248.3	248.9	0.3
PROPERTY CRIME						
Number..	152,146	151,483	-0.4	7,928,530	7,694,086	-3.0
Rate..	2,751.2	2,701.6	-1.8	2,451.6	2,362.2	-3.6
Burglary						
Number..	23,825	22,813	-4.2	1,516,405	1,401,840	-7.6
Rate..	430.8	406.9	-5.6	468.9	430.4	-8.2
Larceny-Theft						
Number..	108,680	106,809	-1.7	5,644,835	5,519,107	-2.2
Rate..	1,965.2	1,904.9	-3.1	1,745.4	1,694.4	-2.9
Motor Vehicle Theft						
Number..	19,641	21,861	11.3	767,290	773,139	0.8
Rate..	355.2	389.9	9.8	237.3	237.4	-

NOTE: Although arson data are included in the trend and clearance tables, sufficient data are not available to estimate totals for this offense. Therefore, no arson data are published in this table.
- = Zero or rounds to zero.
[1] Population figures are U.S. Census Bureau provisional estimates as of July 1, 2017.
[2] The figures shown in the rape (revised definition) column were estimated using the revised Uniform Crime Reporting (UCR) definition of rape.

Table CO-15. State Government Finances, 2017

(Dollar amounts in thousands, percent distribution.)

Item	Dollars	Percent distribution
Total Revenue	34,758,620	100.0
General revenue	27,870,020	80.2
Intergovernmental revenue	8,463,350	24.3
Taxes	13,197,606	38.0
General sales	2,978,382	8.6
Selective sales	2,150,470	6.2
License taxes	748,284	2.2
Individual income tax	6,791,929	19.5
Corporate income tax	528,541	1.5
Other taxes	0	0.0
Current charges	4,144,982	11.9
Miscellaneous general revenue	2,064,082	5.9
Utility revenue	0	-
Liquor stores revenue	0	-
Insurance trust revenue[1]	6,888,600	19.8
Total Expenditure	34,949,835	100.0
Intergovernmental expenditure	7,604,250	21.8
Direct expenditure	27,345,585	78.2
Current operation	18,708,930	53.5
Capital outlay	1,802,663	5.2
Insurance benefits and repayments	5,602,527	16.0
Assistance and subsidies	506,663	1.4
Interest on debt	724,802	2.1
Exhibit: Salaries and wages	5,509,418	15.8
Total Expenditure	34,949,835	100.0
General expenditure	29,332,236	83.9
Intergovernmental expenditure	7,604,250	21.8
Direct expenditure	21,727,986	62.2
General expenditure, by function:		
Education	12,011,319	34.4
Public welfare	8,465,159	24.2
Hospitals	1,024,929	2.9
Health	573,255	1.6
Highways	1,990,230	5.7
Police protection	235,845	0.7
Correction	1,035,100	3.0
Natural resources	416,303	1.2
Parks and recreation	102,706	0.3
Governmental administration	984,755	2.8
Interest on general debt	712,314	2.0
Other and unallocable	1,780,321	5.1
Utility expenditure	15,072	-
Liquor stores expenditure	0	-
Insurance trust expenditure	5,602,527	16.0
Debt at End of Fiscal Year	16,980,689	X
Cash and Security Holdings	73,633,548	X

X = Not applicable.
- = Zero or rounds to zero.
[1] Within insurance trust revenue, net earnings of state retirement systems is a calculated statistic (the item code in the data file is X08), and thus can be positive or negative. Net earnings is the sum of earnings on investments plus gains on investments minus losses on investments. The change made in 2002 for asset valuation from book to market value in accordance with Statement 34 of the Governmental Accounting Standards Board is reflected in the calculated statistics.

Table CO-16. State Government Tax Collections, 2018

(Dollars in thousands, percent.)

Item	Dollars	Percent distribution
Total Taxes	14,802,263	100.0
Property taxes	X	-
Sales and gross receipts	5,712,243	38.6
General sales and gross receipts	3,211,909	21.7
Selective sales and gross receipts	2,500,334	16.9
Alcoholic beverages	46,989	0.3
Amusements	124,714	0.8
Insurance premiums	262,411	1.8
Motor fuels	675,962	4.6
Pari-mutuels	525	-
Public utilities	X	-
Tobacco products	193,881	1.3
Other selective sales	1,195,852	8.1
Licenses	816,832	5.5
Alcoholic beverages	9,102	0.1
Amusements	728	-
Corporations in general	21,265	0.1
Hunting and fishing	76,251	0.5
Motor vehicle	597,097	4.0
Motor vehicle operators	41,794	0.3
Public utilities	13,742	0.1
Occupation and business, NEC	56,774	0.4
Other licenses	79	-
Income taxes	8,170,466	55.2
Individual income	7,510,366	50.7
Corporation net income	660,100	4.5
Other taxes	102,722	-
Death and gift	X	-
Documentary and stock transfer	X	-
Severance	102,722	-
Taxes, NEC	0	-

X = Not applicable.
- = Zero or rounds to zero.

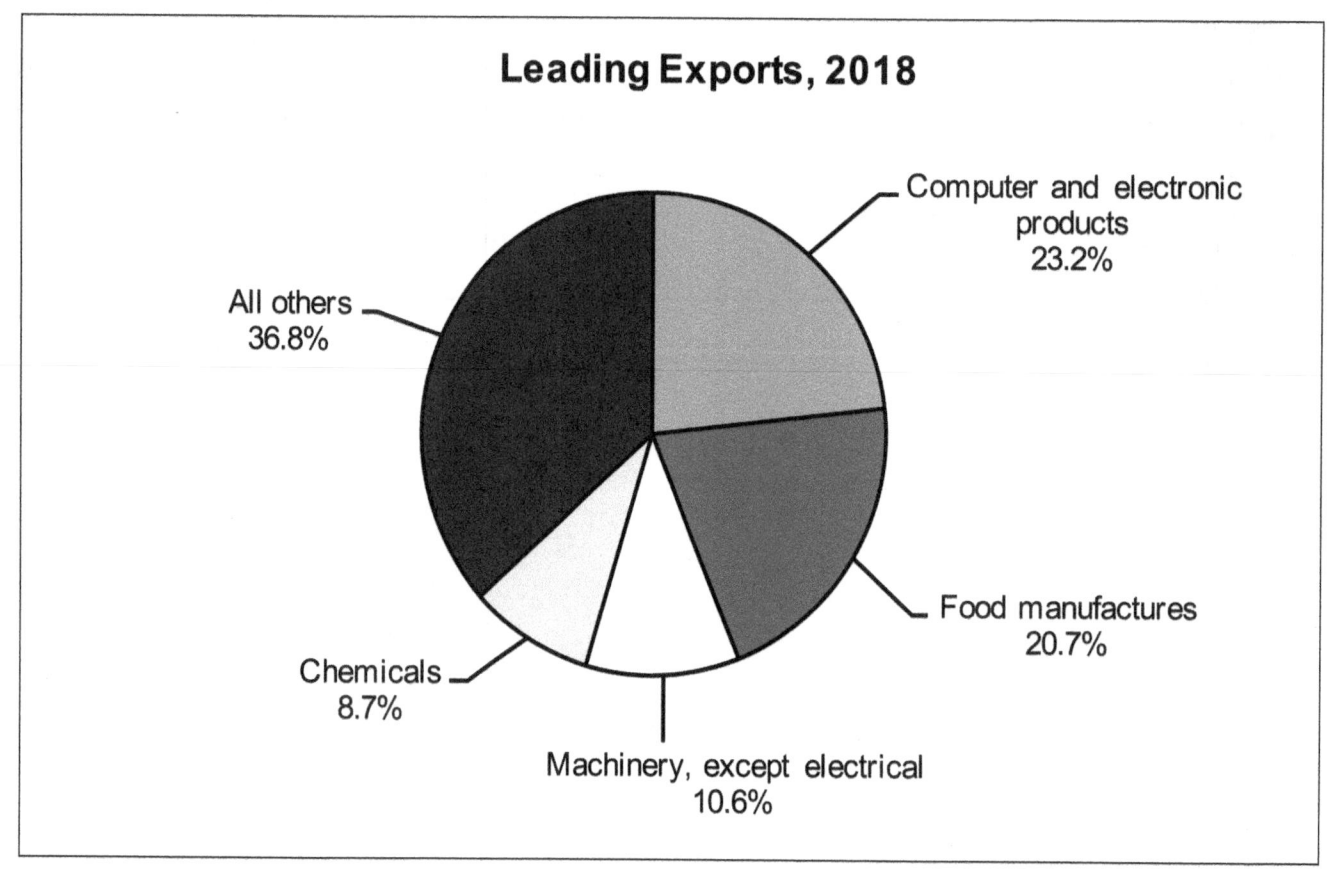

Leading Exports, 2018

Computer and electronic products 23.2%

All others 36.8%

Food manufactures 20.7%

Machinery, except electrical 10.6%

Chemicals 8.7%

CONNECTICUT

Facts and Figures

Location: Northeastern United States; bordered on the N by Massachusetts, on the E by Rhode Island, on the S by Long Island Sound, and on the W by New York

Area: 5,543 sq. mi. (14,357); rank—48th

Population: 3,572,665 (2018 est.); rank—29th

Principal Cities: capital—Hartford; largest—Bridgeport

Statehood: January 9, 1788; 5th state

U.S. Congress: 2 senators, 5 representatives

State Motto: *Qui transtulit sustinet* ("He who transplanted still sustains")

State Song: "Yankee Doodle"

State Nicknames: The Constitution State; The Nutmeg State

Abbreviations: CT; Conn.

State Symbols: flower—mountain laurel; tree—white oak; bird—American robin

At a Glance

- Connecticut experienced a small decrease in population between 2010 and 2018. It was one of only three states where the population decreased over this time period.

- Connecticut's median household income in 2017 was $74,168, compared to the national median household income of $60,336.

- In 2017, 38.7 percent of Connecticut residents age 25 and older had a bachelor's degree or higher, which was the 6th highest percent in the country.

- Connecticut's per capita personal income in 2018 was $74,561, ranking 2nd in the nation.

- The violent and property crime rates in Connecticut in 2017 were below the national average, at 228.0 and 1,769.9 incidences per 100,000 population respectively.

Table CT-1. Population by Age, Sex, Race, and Hispanic Origin

(Number, percent, except where noted.)

Sex, age, race, and Hispanic origin	2000	2010	2018[1]	Percent change, 2010–2018
Total Population...	3,405,565	3,574,097	3,572,665	-
Percent of total U.S. population	1.2	1.2	1.1	X
Sex				
Male...	1,649,319	1,739,614	1,743,395	0.2
Female..	1,756,246	1,834,483	1,829,270	-0.3
Age				
Under 5 years..	233,344	202,106	183,134	-9.4
5 to 19 years..	702,358	713,670	655,812	-8.1
20 to 64 years...	2,009,680	2,151,762	2,118,598	-1.5
65 years and over...	470,183	506,559	615,121	21.4
Median age (years)	37.4	40.0	41.0	2.5
Race and Hispanic Origin				
One race				
White	2,780,355	2,950,820	2,859,280	-3.1
Black	309,843	392,131	429,298	9.5
American Indian and Alaska Native	9,639	16,734	19,943	19.2
Asian	82,313	140,516	173,799	23.7
Native Hawaiian or Other Pacific Islander	1,366	3,491	3,840	10.0
Two or more races...	74,848	70,405	86,505	22.9
Hispanic (of any race)..	320,323	498,638	589,809	18.3

X = Not applicable.
[1] Population figures for 2018 are July 1 estimates. The 2010 estimates are taken from the 2010 Census.
- = Zero or rounds to zero.

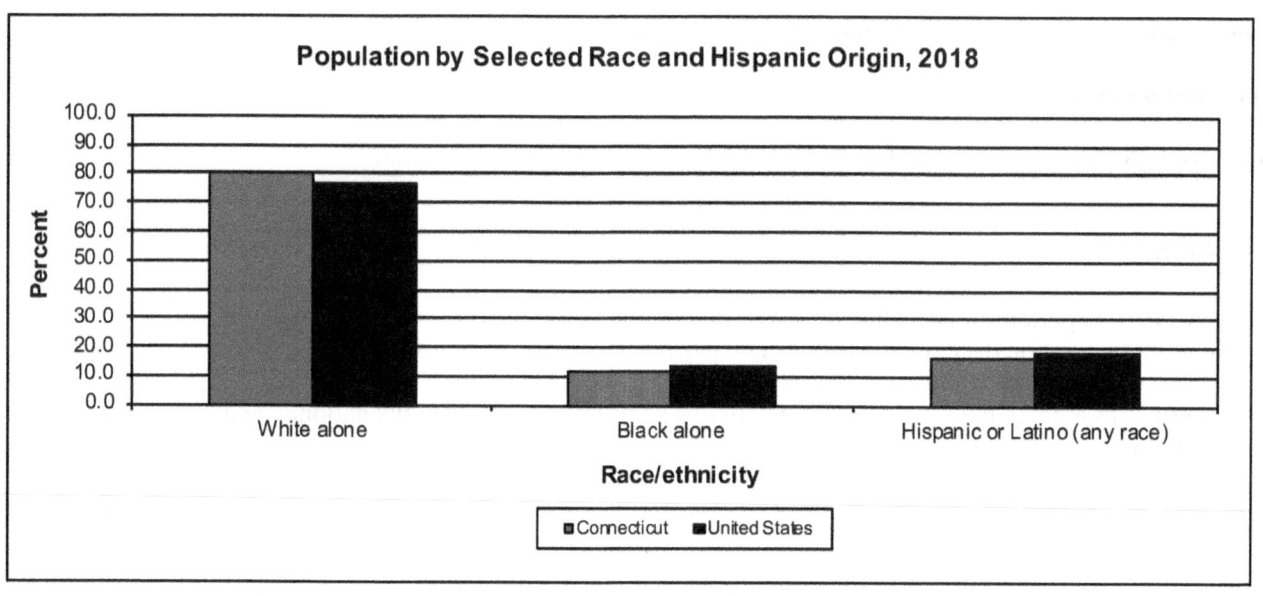

Table CT-2. Marital Status

(Number, percent distribution.)

Sex, age, race, and Hispanic origin	2000	2010	2017
Males, 15 Years and Over	1,284,881	1,399,329	1,442,504
Never married	30.0	36.3	38.1
Now married, except separated..	58.0	50.6	48.9
Separated..	1.3	1.1	1.2
Widowed..	2.7	2.7	2.6
Divorced..	7.9	9.3	9.1
Females, 15 Years and Over	1,411,369	1,512,492	1,544,333
Never married	24.5	29.9	32.2
Now married, except separated..	52.3	46.5	45.0
Separated..	1.8	1.8	1.4
Widowed..	10.8	9.3	8.8
Divorced..	10.5	12.5	12.6

Table CT-3. Households and Housing Characteristics

(Number, percent, dollars.)

Item	2000	2010	2017	Average annual percent change, 2010–2017
Total Households...	1,301,670	1,358,809	1,356,762	-
Family households	881,170	890,770	877,293	-0.2
Married-couple family	676,467	656,629	649,561	-0.2
Other family	204,703	234,141	227,732	-0.4
Male householder, no wife present........................	47,292	58,325	61,317	0.7
Female householder, no husband present.............	157,411	175,816	166,415	-0.8
Nonfamily households	420,500	468,039	479,469	0.3
Householder living alone	334,224	384,382	393,209	0.3
Householder not living alone..................................	76,276	83,657	86,260	0.4
Housing Characteristics				
Total housing units...	1,385,975	1,488,215	1,517,495	0.3
Occupied housing units...	1,301,670	1,358,809	1,356,762	-
Owner occupied	869,729	923,617	898,234	-0.4
Renter occupied	431,941	435,192	458,528	0.8
Average household size...	2.53	2.55	2.56	0.1
Financial Characteristics				
Median gross rent of renter-occupied housing	681	992	1,125	1.9
Median monthly owner costs for housing units with a mortgage	1,426	2,068	1,976	-0.6
Median value of owner-occupied housing units.........	166,900	288,800	273,100	-0.8

- = Zero or rounds to zero

Table CT-4. Migration, Origin, and Language

(Number, percent.)

Characteristic	State			U.S.		
	2016	2017	Percent change	2016	2017	Percent change
Residence 1 Year Ago						
Population 1 year and over	3,541,758	3,556,297	0.4	319,361,956	321,994,428	0.8
Same house	88.0	88.2	X	85.4	85.7	X
Different house in the U.S...	11.3	11.1	X	13.9	13.6	X
Same county	7.2	6.8	X	8.3	8.1	X
Different county	4	4.3	X	5.6	5.6	X
Same state	1.9	1.9	X	3.2	3.3	X
Different state	2.1	2.3	X	2.4	2.3	X
Abroad	0.7	0.7	X	0.7	0.7	X
Place of Birth						
Native born	3,062,402	3,057,939	-0.1	279,388,170	281,193,323	0.6
Male	49.1	49	X	49.3	49.4	X
Female	50.9	51	X	50.7	50.6	X
Foreign born	514,050	530,245	3.2	43,739,345	44,525,855	1.8
Male	47.1	47.6	X	48.5	48.4	X
Female	52.9	52.4	X	51.5	51.6	X
Foreign born; naturalized U.S. citizen........................	270,273	272,795	0.9	21,238,372	21,948,732	3.3
Male	43.9	45.1	X	45.9	45.9	X
Female	56.1	54.9	X	54.1	54.1	X
Foreign born; not a U.S. citizen..................................	243,777	257,450	5.6	22,500,973	22,577,123	0.3
Male	50.8	50.2	X	51	50.8	X
Female	49.2	49.8	X	49	49.2	X
Entered 2010 or later	19.2	20.8	X	18.6	21.3	X
Entered 2000 to 2009	26	27	X	26.7	25.7	X
Entered before 2000...	54.8	52.2	X	54.7	53.0	X
World Region of Birth, Foreign						
Foreign-born population, excluding population born at sea	514,050	530,245	3.2	43,738,901	44,525,458	1.8
Europe	24.2	23.6	X	10.9	10.8	X
Asia	25.1	24.2	X	30.8	31.2	X
Africa	5	4.6	X	4.9	5.1	X
Oceania	0.4	0.2	X	0.6	0.6	X
Latin America	42.7	45.1	X	51	50.4	X
North America...	2.6	2.3	X	1.8	1.8	X
Language Spoken at Home and Ability to Speak English						
Population 5 years and over	3,391,423	3,405,990	0.4	303,328,961	305,924,019	0.9
English only	77.3	77.6	X	78.4	78.2	X
Language other than English....................................	22.7	22.4	X	21.6	21.8	X
Speaks English less than "very well".....................	7.9	8.6	X	8.6	8.5	X

NA = Not available.
X = Not applicable.
- = Zero or rounds to zero.

Table CT-5. Median Income and Poverty Status, 2017

(Number, percent, except as noted.)

Characteristic	State		U.S.	
	Number	Percent	Number	Percent
Median Income				
Households (dollars)...	74,168	X	60,336	X
Families (dollars)	93,870	X	73,891	X
Below Poverty Level (All People)	334,128	9.6	42,583,651	13.4
Sex				
Male	145,395	8.6	19,004,547	12.2
Female	188,733	10.6	23,579,104	14.5
Age				
Under 18 years..	92,583	12.6	13,353,202	18.4
Related children under 18 years...	90,557	12.4	13,053,472	18.1
18 to 64 years...	200,502	9.2	24,648,677	12.6
65 years and over	41,043	7.1	4,581,772	9.3

X = Not applicable.

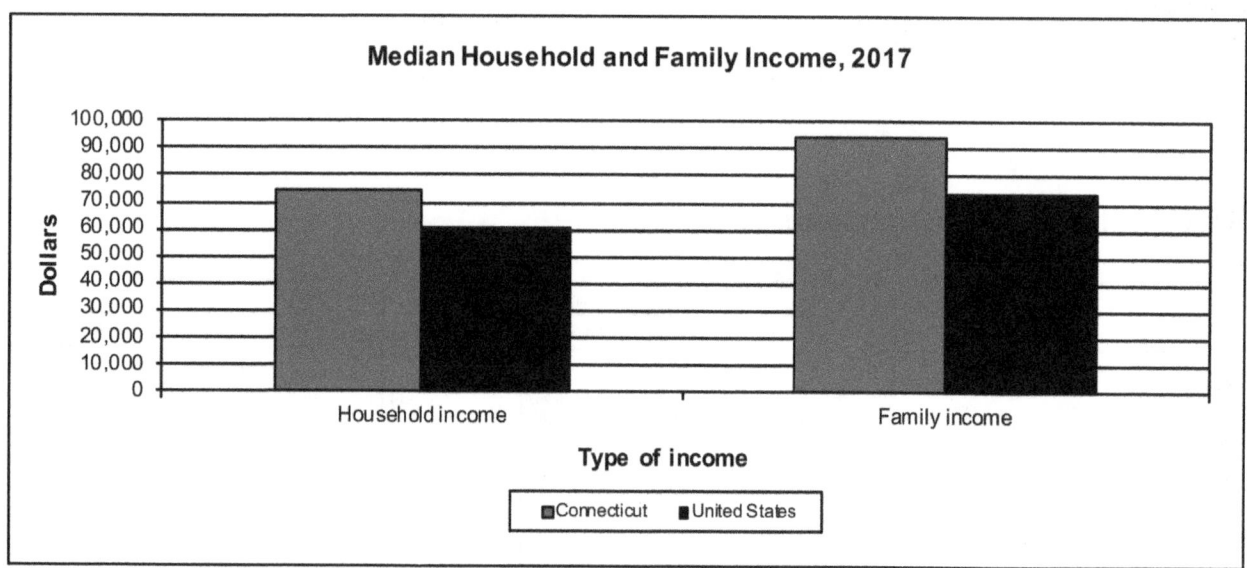

Table CT-6. Health Insurance Coverage Status for the Civilian Noninstitutionalized Population and Children Under 18 Years of Age

(Number, percent.)

Item	2009	2010	2011	2012	2013	2014	2015	2016	2017
Civilian Noninstitutionalized Population	3,456,856	3,519,913	3,522,709	3,534,619	3,541,409	3,541,282	3,537,983	3,525,154	3,536,522
Covered by Private or Public Insurance									
Number...	3,151,646	3,199,780	3,213,764	3,212,647	3,208,906	3,295,883	3,327,461	3,352,940	3,342,726
Percent..	91.2	90.9	91.2	90.9	90.6	93.1	94.0	95.1	94.5
Uninsured									
Number...	305,210	320,133	308,945	321,972	332,503	245,399	210,522	172,214	193,796
Percent..	8.8	9.1	8.8	9.1	9.4	6.9	6.0	4.9	5.5
Percent in the U.S. not covered...........................	15.1	15.5	15.1	14.8	14.5	11.7	9.4	8.6	8.7
Children Under 18 Years of Age[1]	806,799	815,010	802,350	791,825	784,159	774,021	761,921	751,459	792,881
Covered by Private or Public Insurance									
Number...	776,366	790,896	778,973	761,897	750,504	745,151	736,821	730,592	768,525
Percent..	96.2	97.0	97.1	96.2	95.7	96.3	96.7	97.2	96.9
Uninsured									
Number...	30,433	24,114	23,377	29,928	33,655	28,870	25,100	20,867	24,356
Percent..	3.8	3.0	2.9	3.8	4.3	3.7	3.3	2.8	3.1
Percent in the U.S. not covered...........................	8.6	8.0	7.5	7.2	7.1	6.0	4.8	4.5	5.0

[1] 2017 data is for individuals under 19 years of age.

Table CT-7. Employment Status by Demographic Group, 2018

(Numbers in thousands, percent.)

Characteristic	Civilian noninstitutional population	Civilian labor force		Employed		Unemployed	
		Number	Percent of population	Number	Percent of population	Number	Percent of population
Total..	2,897	1,907	65.8	1,828	63.1	79	4.1
Sex							
Male...	1,395	987	70.8	942	67.5	46	4.6
Female..	1,502	920	61.3	887	59.0	33	3.6
Race, Sex, and Hispanic Origin							
White...	2,390	1,576	65.9	1,521	63.6	55	3.5
Male..	1,170	828	70.8	795	67.9	34	4.1
Female...	1,220	748	61.3	726	59.5	21	2.9
Black or African American........................	324	209	64.5	190	58.8	19	8.9
Male..	149	96	64.3	84	56.6	11	12.0
Female...	175	113	64.7	106	60.6	7	6.3
Hispanic or Latino ethnicity[1]...................	428	271	63.4	252	59.0	19	6.9
Male..	206	141	68.5	130	63.3	11	7.6
Female...	222	130	58.6	122	55.0	8	6.1
Age							
16 to 19 years..	NA	NA	NA	NA	NA	NA	NA
20 to 24 years..	185	125	67.5	112	60.5	13	10.4
25 to 34 years..	503	434	86.3	419	83.3	15	3.4
35 to 44 years..	432	356	82.5	345	80.0	11	3.0
45 to 54 years..	466	408	87.6	392	84.1	16	4.0
55 to 64 years..	539	383	71.0	373	69.2	10	2.5
65 years and over....................................	598	139	23.3	135	22.5	4	3.0

NOTE: Data in Table 7 are from the Current Population Survey (CPS) and do not match the estimates in Table 8. See notes and definitions for further information.
[1] May be of any race.

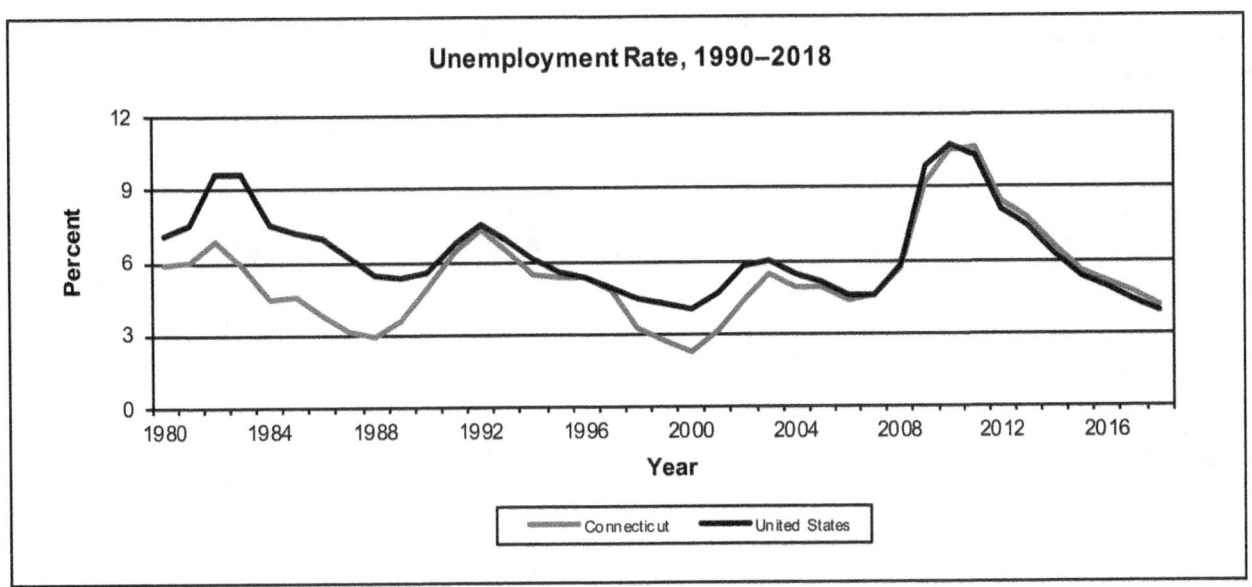

Table CT-8. Employment Status of the Civilian Noninstitutional Population Age 16 Years and Over

(Number, percent.)

Year	Civilian labor force	Civilian participation rate	Employed	Unemployed	Unemployment rate
2010..	1,911,712	68.3	1,737,449	174,263	9.1
2011..	1,914,775	67.6	1,745,967	168,808	8.8
2012..	1,887,419	66.3	1,729,838	157,581	8.3
2013..	1,863,337	65.1	1,717,764	145,573	7.8
2014..	1,892,451	65.9	1,767,282	125,169	6.6
2015..	1,895,832	65.9	1,787,434	108,398	5.7
2016..	1,904,556	66.1	1,806,575	97,981	5.1
2017..	1,918,576	66.4	1,828,858	89,718	4.7
2018..	1,905,312	66.1	1,827,070	78,242	4.1

Table CT-9. Employment and Average Wages by Industry

(Estimates are based on the 2012 *North American Industry Classification System* [NAICS].)

Industry	2011	2012	2013	2014	2015	2016	2017
	Number of Jobs						
Wage and Salary Employment by Industry.........................	1,685,883	1,704,885	1,717,324	1,730,733	1,740,318	1,744,009	1,745,197
Farm Wage and Salary Employment..............................	4,806	4,775	5,456	5,478	5,457	5,093	5,082
Nonfarm Wage and Salary Employment...........................	1,681,077	1,700,110	1,711,868	1,725,255	1,734,861	1,738,916	1,740,115
Private wage and salary employment.............................	1,420,068	1,438,397	1,450,184	1,464,155	1,474,568	1,480,847	1,485,960
Forestry, fishing, and related activities.........................	678	659	677	701	699	665	640
Mining..	542	554	543	547	553	556	539
Utilities...	6,172	5,935	6,042	5,943	5,613	5,624	5,333
Construction..	52,872	53,036	55,067	57,247	59,404	60,582	59,702
Manufacturing..	166,402	165,374	164,028	159,808	159,090	156,561	158,977
Durable goods manufacturing..............................	128,541	128,713	127,615	124,431	123,740	122,910	124,503
Nondurable goods manufacturing.........................	37,861	36,661	36,413	35,377	35,350	33,651	34,474
Wholesale trade	63,646	63,477	63,406	63,318	62,765	62,774	62,813
Retail trade..	181,644	183,737	185,017	186,160	186,038	185,905	184,782
Transportation and warehousing...............................	40,932	41,741	42,425	43,729	45,324	46,057	47,477
Information	31,493	31,332	32,093	32,073	32,462	32,412	31,604
Finance and insurance	117,939	116,421	114,260	111,566	112,247	111,681	110,578
Real estate and rental and leasing.............................	19,358	19,381	19,468	19,550	20,255	20,355	20,197
Professional, scientific, and technical services	88,562	90,230	91,038	95,986	96,505	97,601	97,079
Management of companies and enterprises..................	28,621	30,593	30,693	31,893	32,936	32,956	32,344
Administrative and waste services.............................	81,479	84,676	85,619	86,270	88,780	88,997	90,347
Educational services	65,968	67,065	67,406	69,227	69,664	70,996	72,567
Health care and social assistance.............................	254,173	258,189	261,725	263,880	265,909	268,872	270,919
Arts, entertainment, and recreation...........................	24,268	25,135	26,156	27,197	27,025	27,802	28,861
Accommodation and food services............................	113,851	118,349	122,065	124,573	125,095	127,212	128,884
Other services, except public administration................	81,468	82,513	82,456	84,487	84,204	83,239	82,317
Government and government enterprises	261,009	261,713	261,684	261,100	260,293	258,069	254,155
	Dollars						
Average Wages and Salaries by Industry	60,205	61,139	61,406	62,975	64,569	64,903	65,748
Average Farm Wages and Salaries	20,317	30,594	27,295	28,804	23,619	29,043	26,415
Average Nonfarm Wages and Salaries	60,319	61,225	61,515	63,084	64,698	65,008	65,863
Average private wages and salaries.............................	61,431	62,580	62,768	64,319	65,835	66,145	66,938
Forestry, fishing, and related activities.........................	24,184	25,434	25,866	26,502	28,070	30,146	29,830
Mining..	68,862	64,532	64,799	70,247	71,329	71,847	76,534
Utilities...	111,542	109,727	110,980	111,297	116,881	112,092	124,289
Construction..	58,329	59,259	59,402	61,080	64,270	66,586	68,656
Manufacturing..	77,205	78,936	81,583	81,393	80,712	79,460	81,880
Durable goods manufacturing..............................	76,328	78,616	81,638	82,095	81,069	81,468	83,623
Nondurable goods manufacturing.........................	80,183	80,058	81,387	78,927	79,465	72,127	75,585
Wholesale trade	83,396	85,394	85,972	87,743	92,686	93,605	94,572
Retail trade..	31,160	31,505	31,555	32,092	33,016	33,264	33,529
Transportation and warehousing...............................	47,352	47,947	47,007	47,790	48,688	48,832	48,587
Information	78,930	82,320	89,129	92,966	99,237	102,355	103,193
Finance and insurance	152,296	153,299	150,126	159,068	163,498	163,344	166,847
Real estate and rental and leasing.............................	59,736	64,694	64,018	65,776	69,524	70,679	66,303
Professional, scientific, and technical services	89,721	91,739	92,642	95,867	99,005	101,154	103,410
Management of companies and enterprises..................	139,181	156,209	161,131	163,472	162,487	163,349	154,205
Administrative and waste services.............................	40,827	41,264	40,821	43,014	44,072	44,064	45,640
Educational services	46,912	48,754	51,044	52,516	53,340	52,998	54,359
Health care and social assistance.............................	47,569	48,446	48,564	49,835	50,277	50,890	51,493
Arts, entertainment, and recreation...........................	29,038	29,258	29,226	30,081	31,216	31,386	31,777
Accommodation and food services............................	20,617	21,236	21,382	22,063	23,102	23,922	24,574
Other services, except public administration................	31,428	32,081	32,806	33,578	34,657	35,312	36,517
Government and government enterprises.............................	54,267	53,774	54,569	56,160	58,257	58,482	59,577

Table CT-10. Employment Characteristics by Family Type

(Number, percent.)

Family type and labor force status	2015		2016		2017	
	Total	Families with own children under 18 years	Total	Families with own children under 18 years	Total	Families with own children under 18 years
All Families..	876,188	365,594	880,600	359,819	877,293	361,083
FAMILY TYPE AND LABOR FORCE STATUS						
Married-Couple Families..	647,589	248,839	648,449	246,535	649,561	248,324
Both husband and wife in labor force.............................	57.3	71.1	56.8	71.4	55.9	71.7
Husband in labor force, wife not in labor force...............	19.8	24.3	19.3	23.5	19.1	22.9
Wife in labor force, husband not in labor force..............	7.4	2.9	7.5	3.4	8.0	4.0
Both husband and wife not in labor force.......................	14.6	1.2	15.7	1.1	15.9	0.8
Other Families	228,599	116,755	232,151	113,284	227,732	112,759
Female householder, no husband present........................	74.6	78.9	74.4	79.3	73.1	75.2
In labor force..	55.3	69.0	54.4	68.0	53.8	64.3
Not in labor force...	19.4	9.8	19.9	11.3	19.2	10.9
Male householder, no wife present................................	25.4	21.1	25.6	20.7	26.9	24.8
In labor force..	20.9	19.8	20.2	19.1	21.0	22.6
Not in labor force...	4.5	1.4	5.4	1.6	6.0	2.2

Table CT-11. School Enrollment and Educational Attainment, 2017

(Number, percent.)

Item	State	U.S.
Enrollment		
Total population 3 years and over, enrolled in school	898,609	81,273,337
Enrolled in nursery school or preschool (percent)..	5.9	6.0
Enrolled in kindergarten (percent)..	3.9	4.9
Enrolled in elementary school, grades 1-8 (percent)..	37.7	40.6
Enrolled in high school, grades 9-12 (percent)..	21.8	21.1
Enrolled in college or graduate school (percent)...	30.6	27.4
Attainment		
Total population 25 years and over	2,493,854	221,250,083
Less than ninth grade (percent)...	4.1	5.1
9th to 12th grade, no diploma (percent)..	5.5	6.9
High school graduate, including equivalency (percent)...	27.1	27.1
Some college, no degree (percent)..	16.5	20.4
Associate's degree (percent)..	8.1	8.5
Bachelor's degree (percent)..	21.4	19.7
Graduate or professional degree (percent)..	17.3	12.3
High school graduate or higher (percent)..	90.4	88.0
Bachelor's degree or higher (percent)...	38.7	32.0

Table CT-12. Public School Characteristics and Educational Indicators

(Number, percent; data derived from National Center of Education Statistics.)

Item	State	U.S.
Public Elementary and Secondary Schools		
Number of operational school districts, 2016-17..	205	18,377
Number of operational schools, 2016-17..	1,250	98,330
Percent charter schools	1.9	7.1
Total public school enrollment, 2016-17..	535,118	50,587,859
Percent charter school enrollment..	1.8	6.0
Student-teacher ratio, Fall 2015..	12.3	16.0
Expenditures per student (dollars), 2015-16...	19,615	11,841
Four-year adjusted cohort graduation rate (ACGR)[1]	87.9	84.6
Students eligible for free or reduced-price lunch (percent), 2015-16......................................	37.9	52.1
English language learners (percent), Fall 2016..	6.8	9.6
Students age 3 to 21 served under IDEA, part B (percent), 2017-18	15.1	13.7
Public Schools by Type, 2016-17		Percent of state public schools
Total number of schools...	1,250	100.0
Special education..	156	12.5
Vocational education...	17	1.4
Alternative education..	21	1.7

[1] Adjusted Cohort Graduation Rates (ACGR) differ from Averaged Freshmen Graduation Rates (AFGR).

Table CT-13. Reported Voting and Registration of the Voting-Age Population, November 2018

(Numbers in thousands, percent.)

Item	Total population	Total citizen population	Registered			Voted		
			Total registered	Percent registered (total population)	Percent registered (total citizen population)	Total voted	Percent voted (total population)	Percent voted (total citizen population)
U.S. Total	249,748	228,832	153,066	61.3	66.9	122,281	49.0	53.4
State Total................................	2,834	2,539	1,726	60.9	68.0	1,370	48.3	54.0
Sex								
Male	1,365	1,222	804	58.9	65.8	662	48.5	54.2
Female	1,469	1,316	921	62.7	70.0	708	48.2	53.8
Race								
White alone.............................	2,326	2,141	1,483	63.8	69.3	1,193	51.3	55.7
White, non-Hispanic alone	1,934	1,888	1,347	69.7	71.3	1,090	56.4	57.7
Black alone..............................	319	258	158	49.6	61.3	124	39.0	48.2
Asian alone	142	100	51	36.1	51.4	38	26.5	37.7
Hispanic (of any race)	464	293	164	35.3	55.9	120	25.9	41.1
White alone or in combination	2,356	2,171	1,506	63.9	69.4	1,201	51.0	55.3
Black alone or in combination	335	274	174	51.9	63.5	132	39.5	48.3
Asian alone or in combination.............	154	112	59	38.4	52.9	38	24.5	33.7
Age								
18 to 24 years	235	219	112	47.8	51.2	77	32.7	35.1
25 to 34 years	551	481	261	47.4	54.2	177	32.1	36.7
35 to 44 years	446	356	251	56.3	70.5	196	43.9	54.9
45 to 64 years	1,020	917	642	63.0	70.1	539	52.8	58.8
65 years and over	583	565	459	78.8	81.3	382	65.5	67.5

Table CT-14. Crime

(Number, rate per 100,000. Data are derived from the FBI Uniform Crime Reports.)

Item	State			U.S.		
	2016	2017	Percent change	2016	2017	Percent change
TOTAL POPULATION[1]	3,587,685	3,588,184	-	323,405,935	325,719,178	0.7
VIOLENT CRIME						
Number...........................	8,169	8,180	0.1	1,285,606	1,283,220	-0.2
Rate	227.7	228.0	0.1	397.5	394.0	-0.9
Murder and Nonnegligent Manslaughter						
Number...........................	79	102	29.1	17,413	17,284	-0.7
Rate	2.2	2.8	29.1	5.4	5.3	-1.4
Rape[2]						
Number...........................	791	837	5.8	132,414	135,755	2.5
Rate	22.0	23.3	5.8	40.9	41.7	1.8
Robbery						
Number...........................	2,711	2,813	3.8	332,797	319,356	-4.0
Rate	75.6	78.4	3.7	102.9	98.0	-4.7
Aggravated Assault						
Number...........................	4,588	4,428	-3.5	802,982	810,825	1.0
Rate	127.9	123.4	-3.5	248.3	248.9	0.3
PROPERTY CRIME						
Number...........................	64,875	63,509	-2.1	7,928,530	7,694,086	-3.0
Rate	1,808.3	1,769.9	-2.1	2,451.6	2,362.2	-3.6
Burglary						
Number...........................	10,107	8,890	-12.0	1,516,405	1,401,840	-7.6
Rate	281.7	247.8	-12.1	468.9	430.4	-8.2
Larceny-Theft						
Number...........................	47,642	47,310	-0.7	5,644,835	5,519,107	-2.2
Rate	1,327.9	1,318.5	-0.7	1,745.4	1,694.4	-2.9
Motor Vehicle Theft						
Number...........................	7,126	7,309	2.6	767,290	773,139	0.8
Rate	198.6	203.7	2.6	237.3	237.4	-

NOTE: Although arson data are included in the trend and clearance tables, sufficient data are not available to estimate totals for this offense. Therefore, no arson data are published in this table.
- = Zero or rounds to zero.
[1] Population figures are U.S. Census Bureau provisional estimates as of July 1, 2017.
[2] The figures shown in the rape (revised definition) column were estimated using the revised Uniform Crime Reporting (UCR) definition of rape.

Table CT-15. State Government Finances, 2017

(Dollar amounts in thousands, percent distribution.)

Item	Dollars	Percent distribution
Total Revenue	34,641,196	100.0
General revenue	27,797,919	80.2
Intergovernmental revenue	7,535,049	21.8
Taxes	16,345,525	47.2
General sales	4,236,619	12.2
Selective sales	2,413,089	7.0
License taxes	442,290	1.3
Individual income tax	7,959,492	23.0
Corporate income tax	897,247	2.6
Other taxes	396,788	1.1
Current charges	2,359,724	6.8
Miscellaneous general revenue	1,557,621	4.5
Utility revenue	35,981	0.1
Liquor stores revenue	0	-
Insurance trust revenue[1]	6,807,296	19.7
Total Expenditure	31,485,082	100.0
Intergovernmental expenditure	9,190,177	29.2
Direct expenditure	22,294,905	70.8
Current operation	13,315,998	42.3
Capital outlay	2,187,546	6.9
Insurance benefits and repayments	4,753,225	15.1
Assistance and subsidies	498,407	1.6
Interest on debt	1,539,729	4.9
Exhibit: Salaries and wages	4,535,378	14.4
Total Expenditure	31,485,082	100.0
General expenditure	26,217,073	83.3
Intergovernmental expenditure	9,190,177	29.2
Direct expenditure	17,026,896	54.1
General expenditure, by function:		
Education	11,397,615	36.2
Public welfare	4,261,286	13.5
Hospitals	1,458,785	4.6
Health	1,041,145	3.3
Highways	1,694,567	5.4
Police protection	251,026	0.8
Correction	622,024	2.0
Natural resources	237,327	0.8
Parks and recreation	36,408	0.1
Governmental administration	1,520,386	4.8
Interest on general debt	1,539,729	4.9
Other and unallocable	2,156,775	6.9
Utility expenditure	514,784	1.5
Liquor stores expenditure	0	-
Insurance trust expenditure	4,753,225	15.1
Debt at End of Fiscal Year	38,756,156	X
Cash and Security Holdings	48,089,603	X

X = Not applicable.
- = Zero or rounds to zero.
[1] Within insurance trust revenue, net earnings of state retirement systems is a calculated statistic (the item code in the data file is X08), and thus can be positive or negative. Net earnings is the sum of earnings on investments plus gains on investments minus losses on investments. The change made in 2002 for asset valuation from book to market value in accordance with Statement 34 of the Governmental Accounting Standards Board is reflected in the calculated statistics.

Table CT-16. State Government Tax Collections, 2018

(Dollars in thousands, percent.)

Item	Dollars	Percent distribution
Total Taxes	19,081,475	100.0
Property taxes	X	-
Sales and gross receipts	7,699,557	40.4
General sales and gross receipts	4,530,509	23.7
Selective sales and gross receipts	3,169,048	16.6
Alcoholic beverages	63,211	0.3
Amusements	275,266	1.4
Insurance premiums	209,026	1.1
Motor fuels	487,327	2.6
Pari-mutuels	3,937	-
Public utilities	261,184	1.4
Tobacco products	376,814	2.0
Other selective sales	1,492,283	7.8
Licenses	476,434	2.5
Alcoholic beverages	13,968	0.1
Amusements	230	-
Corporations in general	30,705	0.2
Hunting and fishing	5,754	-
Motor vehicle	238,351	1.2
Motor vehicle operators	42,816	0.2
Public utilities	X	-
Occupation and business, NEC	141,008	0.7
Other licenses	3,602	-
Income taxes	10,511,490	55.1
Individual income	9,733,258	51.0
Corporation net income	778,232	4.1
Other taxes	393,994	2.1
Death and gift	223,789	1.2
Documentary and stock transfer	169,695	0.9
Severance	X	-
Taxes, NEC	510	-

- = Zero or rounds to zero.
X = Not applicable.

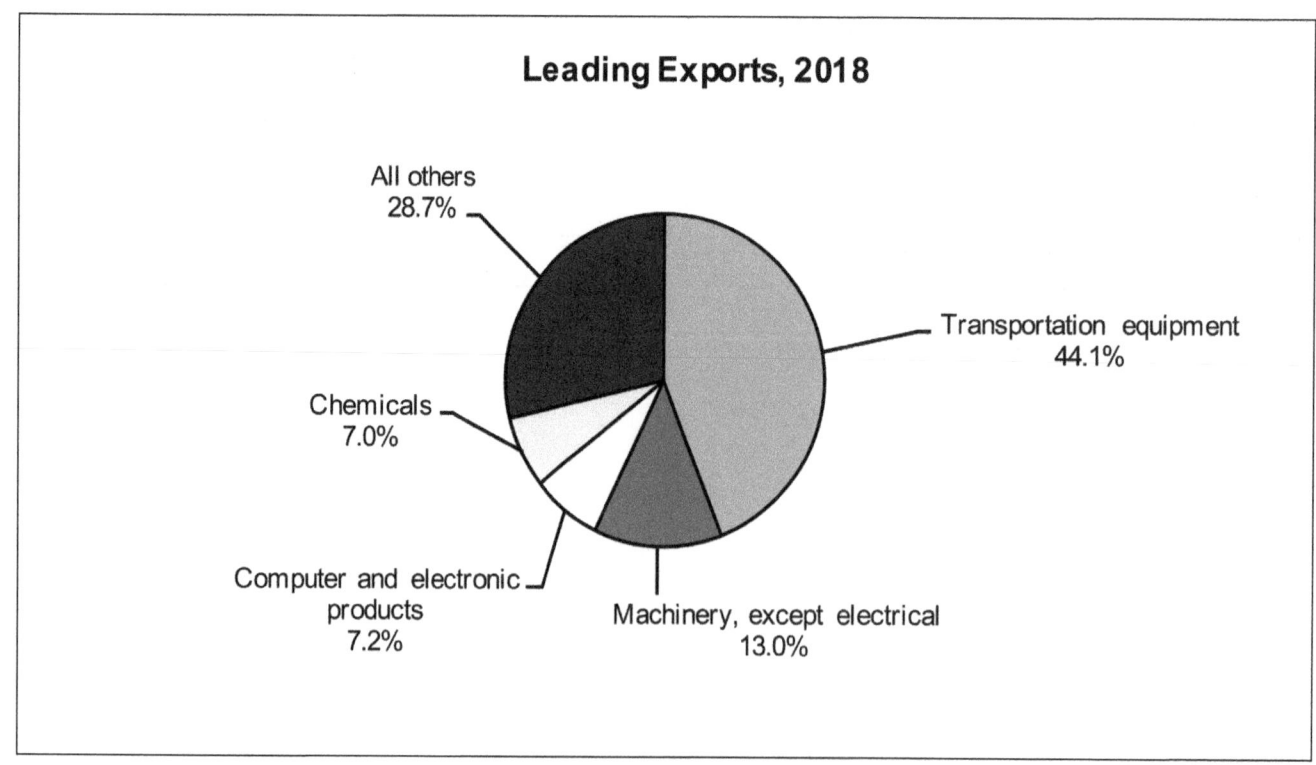

Leading Exports, 2018

All others 28.7%
Transportation equipment 44.1%
Chemicals 7.0%
Computer and electronic products 7.2%
Machinery, except electrical 13.0%

DELAWARE

Facts and Figures

Location: Northeastern United States; bordered on the N by Pennsylvania, on the E by New Jersey, and on the S and W by Maryland

Area: 2,488 sq. mi. (6,447 sq. km.); rank—49th

Population: 967,171 (2018 est.); rank—45th

Principal Cities: capital—Dover; largest—Wilmington

Statehood: December 7, 1787; 1st state

U.S. Congress: 2 senators, 1 representative

State Motto: Liberty and Independence

State Song: "Our Delaware"

State Nickname: The First State

Abbreviations: DE; Del.

State Symbols: flower—peach blossom; tree—American holly; bird—blue hen chicken

At a Glance

- With an increase in population of 7.7 percent, Delaware ranked 16th among the states in growth from 2010 to 2018.

- In 2017, 5.4 percent of Delawareans did not have health insurance, compared to 8.7 percent of the total U.S. population.

- Delaware's violent crime rate in 2017 was 453.4 per 100,000 population, compared to 394.0 for the entire nation.

- Delaware's homeownership rate ranked 10th in the nation in 2018, with 70.8 percent of the population owning homes.

- In 2017, 13.6 percent of Delawareans lived below the poverty level, compared to 13.4 percent of the total U.S. population.

Table DE-1. Population by Age, Sex, Race, and Hispanic Origin

(Number, percent, except where noted.)

Sex, age, race, and Hispanic origin	2000	2010	2018 [1]	Percent change, 2010–2018
Total Population..	783,600	897,934	967,171	7.7
Percent of total U.S. population	0.3	0.3	0.3	X
Sex				
Male..	380,541	434,939	467,927	7.6
Female..	403,059	462,995	499,244	7.8
Age				
Under 5 years..	51,531	55,886	54,811	-1.9
5 to 19 years...	166,719	177,917	174,264	-2.1
20 to 64 years...	463,624	648,387	557,010	-14.1
65 years and over..	101,726	129,277	181,086	40.1
Median age (years)	36.0	38.8	40.7	4.9
Race and Hispanic Origin				
One race				
White..	584,773	645,770	672,019	4.1
Black...	150,666	196,281	222,070	13.1
American Indian and Alaska Native	2,731	5,929	6,458	8.9
Asian...	16,259	29,342	39,584	34.9
Native Hawaiian or Other Pacific Islander	283	690	1,049	52.0
Two or more races..	13,033	19,922	25,991	30.5
Hispanic (of any race)...	37,277	76,137	91,974	20.8

X = Not applicable.
[1] Population figures for 2018 are July 1 estimates. The 2010 estimates are taken from the 2010 Census.
- = Zero or rounds to zero.

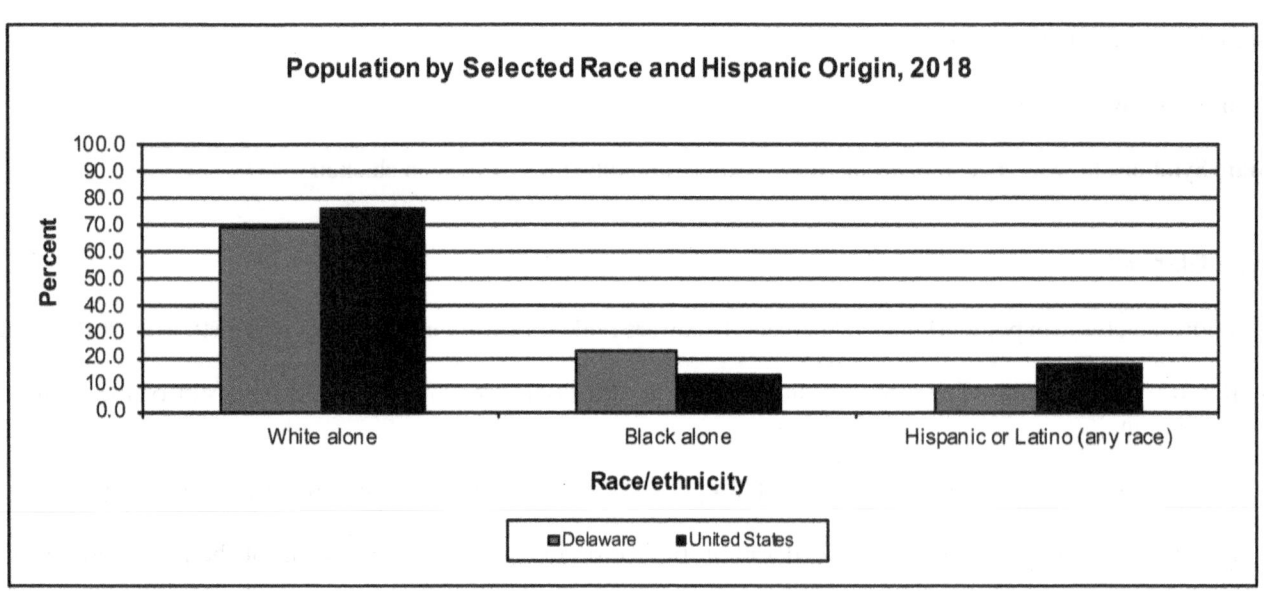

Table DE-2. Marital Status

(Number, percent distribution.)

Sex, age, race, and Hispanic origin	2000	2010	2017
Males, 15 Years and Over..	296,619	350,025	379,153
Never married	29.4	35.3	35.8
Now married, except separated..	57.4	50.4	50.4
Separated..	1.8	1.9	1.5
Widowed..	2.8	2.9	2.8
Divorced..	8.7	9.4	9.5
Females, 15 Years and Over..	324,042	380,618	413,358
Never married	25.3	30.8	32.3
Now married, except separated..	50.9	45.3	44.6
Separated..	2.2	2.0	2.0
Widowed..	10.7	9.8	9.1
Divorced..	10.9	12.1	12.1

Table DE-3. Households and Housing Characteristics

(Number, percent, dollars.)

Item	2000	2010	2017	Average annual percent change, 2010–2017
Total Households..	298,736	328,765	357,937	1.3
Family households..	204,590	221,233	235,795	0.9
Married-couple family..	153,136	161,575	176,947	1.4
Other family...	51,454	59,658	58,848	-0.2
Male householder, no wife present.....................	12,468	14,124	16,516	2.4
Female householder, no husband present............	38,986	45,534	42,332	-1.0
Nonfamily households...	94,146	107,532	122,142	1.9
Householder living alone......................................	74,639	86,990	99,176	2.0
Householder not living alone................................	19,507	20,542	22,966	1.7
Housing Characteristics				
Total housing units..	343,072	406,489	432,853	0.9
Occupied housing units	298,736	328,765	357,937	1.3
Owner occupied..	216,038	239,884	253,948	0.8
Renter occupied...	86,698	88,881	103,989	2.4
Average household size...	2.54	2.66	2.62	-0.2
Financial Characteristics				
Median gross rent of renter-occupied housing	639	952	1086	2.0
Median monthly owner costs for housing units with a mortgage	1,101	1,569	1,507	-0.6
Median value of owner-occupied housing units.......	130,400	243,600	252,800	0.5

- = Zero or rounds to zero.

Table DE-4. Migration, Origin, and Language

(Number, percent.)

Characteristic	State			U.S.		
	2016	2017	Percent change	2016	2017	Percent change
Residence 1 Year Ago						
Population 1 year and over	942,073	952,449	1.1	319,361,956	321,994,428	0.8
Same house	86.8	87.2	X	85.4	85.7	X
Different house in the U.S.	12.6	12.3	X	13.9	13.6	X
Same county	8.1	7.2	X	8.3	8.1	X
Different county	4.4	5.1	X	5.6	5.6	X
Same state	0.9	1.1	X	3.2	3.3	X
Different state	3.5	4	X	2.4	2.3	X
Abroad	0.6	0.4	X	0.7	0.7	X
Place of Birth						
Native born	862,674	863,446	0.1	279,388,170	281,193,323	0.6
Male	48.2	48.5	X	49.3	49.4	X
Female	51.8	51.5	X	50.7	50.6	X
Foreign born	89,391	98,493	10.2	43,739,345	44,525,855	1.8
Male	50	47.5	X	48.5	48.4	X
Female	50	52.5	X	51.5	51.6	X
Foreign born; naturalized U.S. citizen....................	44,083	45,984	4.3	21,238,372	21,948,732	3.3
Male	47.9	45.4	X	45.9	45.9	X
Female	52.1	54.6	· X	54.1	54.1	X
Foreign born; not a U.S. citizen	45,308	52,509	15.9	22,500,973	22,577,123	0.3
Male	51.9	49.3	X	51	50.8	X
Female	48.1	50.7	X	49	49.2	X
Entered 2010 or later	22.3	25.6	X	18.6	21.3	X
Entered 2000 to 2009	31.8	32.8	X	26.7	25.7	X
Entered before 2000..	46.0	41.6	X	54.7	53.0	X
World Region of Birth, Foreign						
Foreign-born population, excluding population born at sea	89,391	98,493	10.2	43,738,901	44,525,458	1.8
Europe	10.9	9.7	X	10.9	10.8	X
Asia..	33	34.5	X	30.8	31.2	X
Africa	11.6	8.2	X	4.9	5.1	X
Oceania	0.2	0.4	X	0.6	0.6	X
Latin America..	43	45.6	X	51	50.4	X
North America...	1.3	1.5	X	1.8	1.8	X
Language Spoken at Home and Ability to Speak English						
Population 5 years and over.....................................	896,824	907,032	1.1	303,328,961	305,924,019	0.9
English only	87.1	86.1	X	78.4	78.2	X
Language other than English.................................	12.9	13.9	X	21.6	21.8	X
Speaks English less than "very well".....................	4.6	4.4	X	8.6	8.5	X

NA = Not available.
X = Not applicable.
- = Zero or rounds to zero.

Table DE-5. Median Income and Poverty Status, 2017

(Number, percent, except as noted.)

Characteristic	State		U.S.	
	Number	Percent	Number	Percent
Median Income				
Households (dollars)..	62,852	X	60,336	X
Families (dollars)	77,082	X	73,891	X
Below Poverty Level (All People)	126,986	13.6	42,583,651	13.4
Sex				
Male	54,069	12.0	19,004,547	12.2
Female	72,917	15.1	23,579,104	14.5
Age				
Under 18 years..	36,755	18.5	13,353,202	18.4
Related children under 18 years..	36,282	18.3	13,053,472	18.1
18 to 64 years	75,873	13.4	24,648,677	12.6
65 years and over	14,358	8.5	4,581,772	9.3

X = Not applicable.

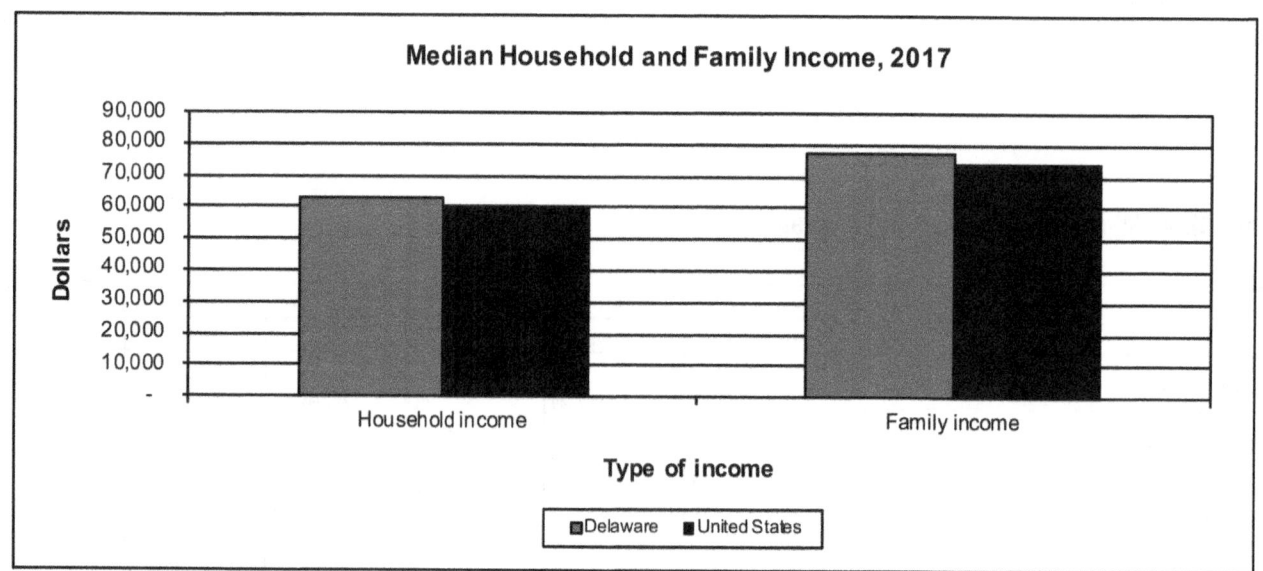

Table DE-6. Health Insurance Coverage Status for the Civilian Noninstitutionalized Population and Children Under 18 Years of Age

(Number, percent.)

Item	2009	2010	2011	2012	2013	2014	2015	2016	2017
Civilian Noninstitutionalized Population	869,483	885,232	892132	902,915	911,502	920,930	931,203	937,935	947,259
Covered by Private or Public Insurance									
Number..	780,384	799,431	808,137	823,021	828,218	849,333	876,705	884,796	896,016
Percent..	89.8	90.3	90.6	91.2	90.9	92.2	94.1	94.3	94.6
Uninsured									
Number..	89,099	85,801	83,995	79,894	83,284	71,597	54,498	53,139	51,243
Percent..	10.2	9.7	9.4	8.8	9.1	7.8	5.9	5.7	5.4
Percent in the U.S. not covered................................	15.1	15.5	15.1	14.8	14.5	11.7	9.4	8.6	8.7
Children Under 18 Years of Age[1]	206,764	206,046	204,295	204,494	203,339	203,414	203,771	203,704	218,473
Covered by Private or Public Insurance									
Number..	195,454	195,034	194,916	197,329	194,251	191,762	197,686	197,461	210,828
Percent..	94.5	94.7	95.4	96.5	95.5	94.3	97.0	96.9	96.5
Uninsured									
Number..	11,310	11,012	9,379	7,165	9,088	11,652	6,085	6,243	7,645
Percent..	5.5	5.3	4.6	3.5	4.5	5.7	3.0	3.1	3.5
Percent in the U.S. not covered................................	8.6	8.0	7.5	7.2	7.1	6.0	4.8	4.5	5.0

[1] 2017 data is for individuals under 19 years of age.

Table DE-7. Employment Status by Demographic Group, 2018

(Numbers in thousands, percent.)

Characteristic	Civilian noninstitutional population	Civilian labor force		Employed		Unemployed	
		Number	Percent of population	Number	Percent of population	Number	Percent of population
Total..............................	775	488	62.9	469	60.5	19	3.8
Sex							
Male...........................	368	250	68.0	241	65.5	9	3.7
Female........................	408	238	58.3	228	56.0	9	3.9
Race, Sex, and Hispanic Origin							
White...........................	552	339	61.4	329	59.6	10	3.0
Male........................	268	180	67.1	174	64.9	6	3.1
Female.....................	284	159	56.0	155	54.5	4	2.8
Black or African American...................	167	112	67.0	105	62.8	7	6.2
Male........................	75	52	68.9	49	64.8	3	6.0
Female.....................	92	60	65.4	56	61.2	4	6.3
Hispanic or Latino ethnicity[1]	62	45	72.4	43	69.6	2	3.8
Male........................	29	25	87.9	24	85.3	1	3.0
Female.....................	33	20	59.1	19	56.2	1	5.0
Age							
16 to 19 years.................	42	18	42	15	37	2	13
20 to 24 years.................	64	47	73.1	43	66.8	4	8.6
25 to 34 years.................	127	110	86.3	106	83.3	4	3.6
35 to 44 years.................	108	91	83.9	89	82.0	2	2.1
45 to 54 years.................	115	96	83.3	93	80.9	3	2.8
55 to 64 years.................	143	95	66.3	92	64.2	3	3.3
65 years and over	177	33	18.4	32	18.0	1	2.1

NOTE: Data in Table 7 are from the Current Population Survey (CPS) and do not match the estimates in Table 8. See notes and definitions for further information.
[1] May be of any race.
NA = Not Available

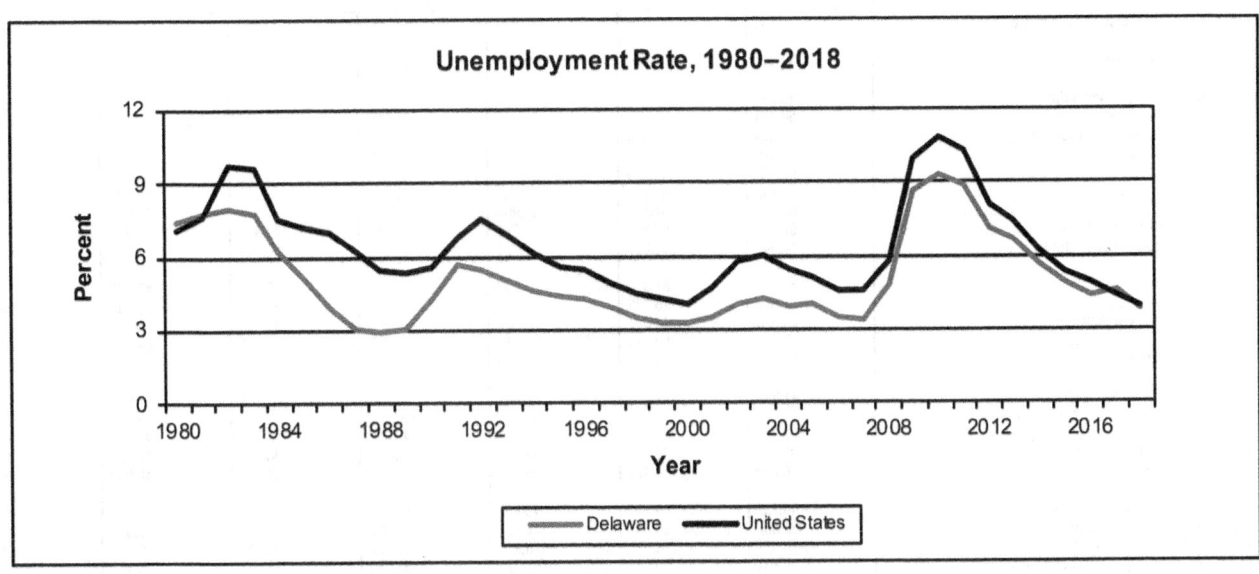

Table DE-8. Employment Status of the Civilian Noninstitutional Population Age 16 Years and Over

(Number, percent.)

Year	Civilian labor force	Civilian participation rate	Employed	Unemployed	Unemployment rate
2010..............................	434,419	62.0	397,869	36,550	8.4
2011..............................	443,346	62.3	410,086	33,260	7.5
2012..............................	445,572	61.9	413,457	32,115	7.2
2013..............................	442,728	60.8	413,119	29,609	6.7
2014..............................	453,312	61.4	427,386	25,926	5.7
2015..............................	467,110	62.5	444,404	22,706	4.9
2016..............................	473,881	62.6	452,434	21,447	4.5
2017..............................	477,349	62.3	455,427	21,922	4.6
2018..............................	482,465	62.5	464,337	18,128	3.8

Table DE-9. Employment and Average Wages by Industry

(Estimates are based on the 2012 *North American Industry Classification System* [NAICS].)

Industry	2011	2012	2013	2014	2015	2016	2017
	Number of Jobs						
Wage and Salary Employment by Industry.........................	429,319	433,059	441,311	450,681	459,075	464,150	466,853
Farm Wage and Salary Employment................................	1,144	1,813	1,672	1,797	1,740	2,100	2,022
Nonfarm Wage and Salary Employment...........................	428,175	431,246	439,639	448,884	457,335	462,050	464,831
Private wage and salary employment...................................	355,381	357,457	365,494	374,768	384,132	388,238	390,629
Forestry, fishing, and related activities..........................	(D)	(D)	(D)	(D)	(D)	(D)	(D)
Mining..	(D)	(D)	(D)	(D)	(D)	(D)	(D)
Utilities..	1,961	2,017	2,086	2,148	2,158	2,156	2,194
Construction	19,798	19,054	20,104	20,893	21,283	21,484	22,274
Manufacturing..	25,693	25,781	25,379	25,713	27,070	25,749	25,777
Durable goods manufacturing..............................	9,693	9,638	9,428	9,198	9,370	9,325	9,321
Nondurable goods manufacturing.........................	16,000	16,143	15,951	16,515	17,700	16,424	16,456
Wholesale trade...	12,535	12,521	12,254	12,028	11,850	11,915	10,901
Retail trade..	50,968	51,073	51,840	52,732	53,335	54,029	53,774
Transportation and warehousing..................................	10,088	10,439	11,680	12,910	14,433	14,703	14,371
Information	5,663	5,457	5,259	4,893	4,724	4,614	4,557
Finance and insurance	37,732	37,981	39,224	40,628	42,034	42,412	43,259
Real estate and rental and leasing...............................	5,639	5,547	5,619	5,359	5,455	5,581	5,552
Professional, scientific, and technical services	26,120	27,421	28,704	29,138	28,700	25,828	25,930
Management of companies and enterprises.....................	8,050	7,535	5,968	5,498	4,888	8,654	8,305
Administrative and waste services................................	22,046	22,018	23,886	25,469	26,699	27,155	28,027
Educational services	6,722	6,690	6,734	6,951	6,807	6,814	6,850
Health care and social assistance..............................	58,516	59,867	61,952	64,096	66,848	68,691	69,809
Arts, entertainment, and recreation.............................	8,913	8,682	9,730	10,261	10,202	10,020	10,247
Accommodation and food services...............................	34,499	35,293	36,328	37,252	38,776	39,780	40,191
Other services, except public administration...................	19,861	19,487	18,082	18,132	18,171	17,968	17,987
Government and government enterprises.....................	72,794	73,789	74,145	74,116	73,203	73,812	74,202
	Dollars						
Average Wages and Salaries by Industry	49,684	50,882	51,204	52,400	53,319	53,090	55,134
Average Farm Wages and Salaries	22,014	22,896	25,308	24,949	21,048	20,014	18,864
Average Nonfarm Wages and Salaries	49,758	50,999	51,302	52,510	53,442	53,241	55,292
Average private wages and salaries............................	50,354	51,673	51,925	53,225	54,024	53,664	55,837
Forestry, fishing, and related activities.............................	(D)	(D)	(D)	(D)	(D)	(D)	(D)
Mining..	(D)	(D)	(D)	(D)	(D)	(D)	(D)
Utilities..	96,243	95,649	98,745	104,323	106,632	108,019	112,877
Construction	52,482	51,044	53,046	53,826	55,137	56,708	59,142
Manufacturing..	56,133	57,103	57,904	59,590	64,072	59,925	62,019
Durable goods manufacturing..............................	67,993	67,300	68,272	70,859	71,350	69,125	71,670
Nondurable goods manufacturing.........................	48,948	51,015	51,775	53,313	60,219	54,702	56,552
Wholesale trade...	82,538	81,340	79,102	83,268	79,874	80,225	72,552
Retail trade..	25,989	26,182	26,439	27,181	28,290	28,453	28,844
Transportation and warehousing..................................	43,920	46,067	45,486	46,350	46,374	45,770	47,972
Information	57,323	59,143	61,110	62,356	63,640	64,959	64,658
Finance and insurance	84,276	86,424	89,500	91,004	91,800	92,870	97,349
Real estate and rental and leasing...............................	41,523	42,022	42,687	44,534	46,197	47,648	49,847
Professional, scientific, and technical services	89,500	97,522	94,591	100,162	107,091	93,242	101,410
Management of companies and enterprises.....................	127,279	129,314	143,251	143,788	115,525	128,572	154,953
Administrative and waste services................................	32,719	33,683	33,748	35,343	36,623	37,228	39,067
Educational services	36,263	38,471	39,156	41,294	41,321	40,943	40,990
Health care and social assistance..............................	48,737	49,752	49,862	50,998	51,986	52,299	53,505
Arts, entertainment, and recreation.............................	31,382	30,868	27,721	27,057	27,177	27,852	27,891
Accommodation and food services...............................	18,471	18,732	18,917	19,488	20,220	20,872	21,212
Other services, except public administration...................	28,854	30,148	32,571	33,288	34,261	35,257	35,979
Government and government enterprises.....................	46,848	47,738	48,233	48,890	50,389	51,015	52,421

D = Not shown to avoid disclosure of confidential information, but the estimates for this item are included in the total.
L = Less than 10 jobs, but the estimates for this item are included in the total.

Table DE-10. Employment Characteristics by Family Type

(Number, percent.)

Family type and labor force status	2015		2016		2017	
	Total	Families with own children under 18 years	Total	Families with own children under 18 years	Total	Families with own children under 18 years
All Families...	235,385	90,959	232,433	86,100	235,795	87,784
FAMILY TYPE AND LABOR FORCE STATUS						
Married-Couple Families.....................................	170,416	57,755	167,306	54,769	176,947	58,059
Both husband and wife in labor force..................	50.1	69.4	49.9	73.0	45.2	61.0
Husband in labor force, wife not in labor force	18.9	24.8	18.9	23.0	21.4	31.3
Wife in labor force, husband not in labor force	8.6	4.8	8.0	2.5	8.9	5.1
Both husband and wife not in labor force.............	21.1	0.5	21.9	1.3	23.5	2.2
Other Families	64,969	33,204	65,127	31,331	58,848	29,725
Female householder, no husband present..........................	75.1	77.9	78.6	80.9	71.9	73.1
In labor force..	54.9	66.7	57.5	72.3	51.2	63.4
Not in labor force	20.2	11.2	21.1	8.6	20.8	9.7
Male householder, no wife present....................	24.9	22.1	21.4	19.1	28.1	26.9
In labor force..	19.1	19.2	15.9	17.8	22.1	25.3
Not in labor force	5.8	2.9	5.5	1.3	6.0	1.6

Table DE-11. School Enrollment and Educational Attainment, 2017

(Number, percent.)

Item	State	U.S.
Enrollment		
Total population 3 years and over, enrolled in school	233,046	81,273,337
Enrolled in nursery school or preschool (percent)...	5.8	6.0
Enrolled in kindergarten (percent)...	5.3	4.9
Enrolled in elementary school, grades 1-8 (percent)..	40.0	40.6
Enrolled in high school, grades 9-12 (percent)..	19.4	21.1
Enrolled in college or graduate school (percent)...	29.6	27.4
Attainment		
Total population 25 years and over	673,686	221,250,083
Less than ninth grade (percent)...	3.5	5.1
9th to 12th grade, no diploma (percent)...	6.0	6.9
High school graduate, including equivalency (percent)...	32.4	27.1
Some college, no degree (percent)...	19.0	20.4
Associate's degree (percent)..	7.7	8.5
Bachelor's degree (percent)...	18.0	19.7
Graduate or professional degree (percent)...	13.5	12.3
High school graduate or higher (percent)...	90.6	88.0
Bachelor's degree or higher (percent)...	31.5	32.0

Table DE-12. Public School Characteristics and Educational Indicators

(Number, percent; data derived from National Center of Education Statistics.)

Item	State	U.S.
Public Elementary and Secondary Schools		
Number of operational school districts, 2016-17	49	18,377
Number of operational schools, 2016-17..	228	98,330
Percent charter schools	11.8	7.1
Total public school enrollment, 2016-17..	136,264	50,587,859
Percent charter school enrollment	10.8	6.0
Student-teacher ratio, Fall 2015..	15.0	16.0
Expenditures per student (dollars), 2015-16...	14,397	11,841
Four-year adjusted cohort graduation rate (ACGR)[1] -------------------------------------	86.9	84.6
Students eligible for free or reduced-price lunch (percent), 2015-16................................	37.7	52.1
English language learners (percent), Fall 2016	7.9	9.6
Students age 3 to 21 served under IDEA, part B (percent), 2017-18	16.9	13.7

Public Schools by Type, 2016-17		Percent of state public schools
Total number of schools..	228	100.0
Special education...	18	7.9
Vocational education..	6	2.6
Alternative education...	6	2.6

[1] Adjusted Cohort Graduation Rates (ACGR) differ from Averaged Freshmen Graduation Rates (AFGR).

Table DE-13. Reported Voting and Registration of the Voting-Age Population, November 2018

(Numbers in thousands, percent.)

Item	Total population	Total citizen population	Registered			Voted		
			Total registered	Percent registered (total population)	Percent registered (total citizen population)	Total voted	Percent voted (total population)	Percent voted (total citizen population)
U.S. Total	249,748	228,832	153,066	61.3	66.9	122,281	49.0	53.4
State Total.................................	756	713	472	62.4	66.3	369	48.8	51.8
Sex								
Male	359	334	215	59.8	64.3	167	46.4	49.9
Female	397	379	258	64.8	68.0	202	50.9	53.4
Race								
White alone....................................	540	513	340	62.9	66.2	264	48.8	51.4
White, non-Hispanic alone..............	477	468	316	66.3	67.6	247	51.7	52.7
Black alone....................................	163	159	109	66.5	68.2	90	54.8	56.2
Asian alone	41	28	15	(B)	(B)	11	(B)	(B)
Hispanic (of any race)......................	73	52	27	(B)	(B)	20	(B)	(B)
White alone or in combination	548	521	346	63.2	66.5	266	48.6	51.1
Black alone or in combination............	173	168	116	67.3	68.9	93	53.8	55.2
Asian alone or in combination...........	43	31	15	(B)	(B)	11	(B)	(B)
Age								
18 to 24 years................................	76	74	32	42.3	(B)	23	29.8	(B)
25 to 34 years................................	133	112	68	50.9	60.3	42	31.7	37.5
35 to 44 years................................	110	99	69	62.2	69.0	47	42.7	47.4
45 to 64 years................................	269	261	183	67.8	69.9	154	57.3	59.1
65 years and over	168	166	121	72.3	73.1	103	61.2	61.9

B = Base is less than 75,000 and therefore too small to show the derived measure.

Table DE-14. Crime

(Number, rate per 100,000. Data are derived from the FBI Uniform Crime Reports.)

Item	State			U.S.		
	2016	2017	Percent change	2016	2017	Percent change
TOTAL POPULATION[1]	952,698	961,939	1.0	323,405,935	325,719,178	0.7
VIOLENT CRIME						
Number...	4,859	4,361	-10.2	1,285,606	1,283,220	-0.2
Rate	510.0	453.4	-11.1	397.5	394.0	-0.9
Murder and Nonnegligent Manslaughter						
Number...	58	54	-6.9	17,413	17,284	-0.7
Rate	6.1	5.6	-7.8	5.4	5.3	-1.4
Rape[2]						
Number...	311	334	7.4	132,414	135,755	2.5
Rate	32.6	34.7	6.4	40.9	41.7	1.8
Robbery						
Number...	1,359	1,082	-20.4	332,797	319,356	-4.0
Rate	142.6	112.5	-21.1	102.9	98.0	-4.7
Aggravated Assault						
Number...	3,131	2,891	-7.7	802,982	810,825	1.0
Rate	328.6	300.5	-8.6	248.3	248.9	0.3
PROPERTY CRIME						
Number...	26,370	23,477	-11.0	7,928,530	7,694,086	-3.0
Rate	2,767.9	2,440.6	-11.8	2,451.6	2,362.2	-3.6
Burglary						
Number...	5,028	3,970	-21.0	1,516,405	1,401,840	-7.6
Rate	527.8	412.7	-21.8	468.9	430.4	-8.2
Larceny-Theft						
Number...	19,812	18,138	-8.4	5,644,835	5,519,107	-2.2
Rate	2,079.6	1,885.6	-9.3	1,745.4	1,694.4	-2.9
Motor Vehicle Theft						
Number...	1,530	1,369	-10.5	767,290	773,139	0.8
Rate	160.6	142.3	-11.4	237.3	237.4	-

NOTE: Although arson data are included in the trend and clearance tables, sufficient data are not available to estimate totals for this offense. Therefore, no arson data are published in this table.
- = Zero or rounds to zero.
[1] Population figures are U.S. Census Bureau provisional estimates as of July 1, 2017.
[2] The figures shown in the rape (revised definition) column were estimated using the revised Uniform Crime Reporting (UCR) definition of rape.

Table DE-15. State Government Finances, 2017

(Dollar amounts in thousands, percent distribution.)

Item	Dollars	Percent distribution
Total Revenue	9,552,088	100.0
General revenue	8,340,428	87.3
Intergovernmental revenue	2,415,919	25.3
Taxes	3,588,905	37.6
General sales	0	-
Selective sales	556,490	5.8
License taxes	1,503,083	15.7
Individual income tax	1,180,975	12.4
Corporate income tax	246,175	2.6
Other taxes	102,182	1.1
Current charges	1,067,920	11.2
Miscellaneous general revenue	1,267,684	13.3
Utility revenue	22,485	0.2
Liquor stores revenue	0	-
Insurance trust revenue[1]	1,189,175	12.4
Total Expenditure	10,029,991	100.0
Intergovernmental expenditure	1,583,343	15.8
Direct expenditure	8,446,648	84.2
Current operation	6,296,600	62.8
Capital outlay	903,515	9.0
Insurance benefits and repayments	725,011	7.2
Assistance and subsidies	335,566	3.3
Interest on debt	185,956	1.9
Exhibit: Salaries and wages	1,424,947	14.2
Total Expenditure	10,029,991	100.0
General expenditure	9,158,993	91.3
Intergovernmental expenditure	1,583,343	15.8
Direct expenditure	7,575,650	75.5
General expenditure, by function:		
Education	3,315,487	33.1
Public welfare	2,551,364	25.4
Hospitals	47,256	0.5
Health	410,368	4.1
Highways	832,628	8.3
Police protection	148,671	1.5
Correction	324,144	3.2
Natural resources	113,363	1.1
Parks and recreation	49,457	0.5
Governmental administration	503,657	5.0
Interest on general debt	185,956	1.9
Other and unallocable	676,642	6.7
Utility expenditure	145,987	1.5
Liquor stores expenditure	0	-
Insurance trust expenditure	725,011	7.2
Debt at End of Fiscal Year	4,561,576	X
Cash and Security Holdings	12,510,776	X

X = Not applicable.
- = Zero or rounds to zero.
[1] Within insurance trust revenue, net earnings of state retirement systems is a calculated statistic (the item code in the data file is X08), and thus can be positive or negative. Net earnings is the sum of earnings on investments plus gains on investments minus losses on investments. The change made in 2002 for asset valuation from book to market value in accordance with Statement 34 of the Governmental Accounting Standards Board is reflected in the calculated statistics.

Table DE-16. State Government Tax Collections, 2018

(Dollars in thousands, percent.)

Item	Dollars	Percent distribution
Total Taxes	4,219,706	100.0
Property taxes	X	-
Sales and gross receipts	585,645	13.9
General sales and gross receipts	X	-
Selective sales and gross receipts	585,645	13.9
Alcoholic beverages	26,556	0.6
Amusements	X	-
Insurance premiums	110,292	2.6
Motor fuels	131,864	3.1
Pari-mutuels	67	-
Public utilities	53,228	1.3
Tobacco products	123,026	2.9
Other selective sales	140,612	3.3
Licenses	1,574,576	37.3
Alcoholic beverages	1,816	0.0
Amusements	321	-
Corporations in general	1,378,003	32.7
Hunting and fishing	3,759	0.1
Motor vehicle	58,969	1.4
Motor vehicle operators	5,838	0.1
Public utilities	134	-
Occupation and business, NEC	117,494	2.8
Other licenses	8,242	0.2
Income taxes	1,907,137	45.2
Individual income	1,652,335	39.2
Corporation net income	254,802	6.0
Other taxes	152,348	3.6
Death and gift	4,425	0.1
Documentary and stock transfer	146,774	3.5
Severance	X	-
Taxes, NEC	1,149	-

X = Not applicable.
- = Zero or rounds to zero.

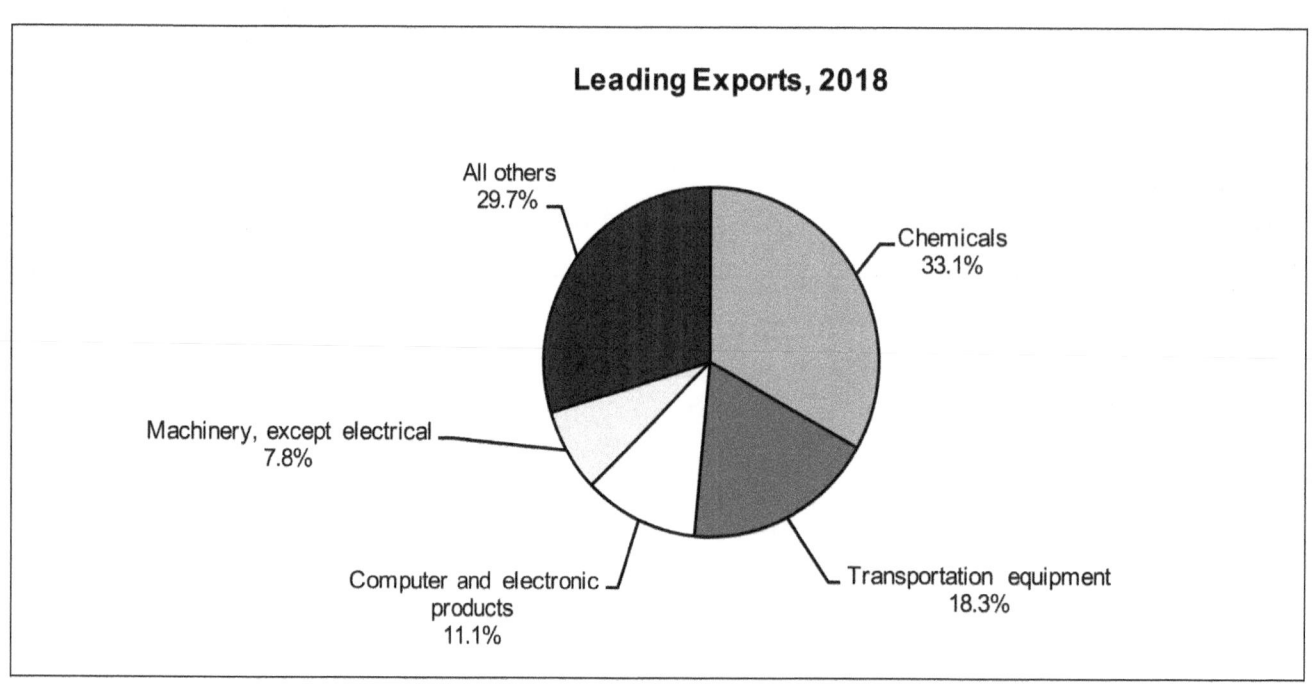

Leading Exports, 2018

All others 29.7%
Chemicals 33.1%
Machinery, except electrical 7.8%
Computer and electronic products 11.1%
Transportation equipment 18.3%

DISTRICT OF COLUMBIA

Facts and Figures:

Location: South Atlantic United States; bordered on the SE, NE, and NW by Maryland and on the SW by Virginia

Area: 68 sq. mi.

Population: 702,455 (2018 est.); rank—49th

Official Motto: Justitia omnibus ("Justice for All")

U.S. Congress: 1 delegate

Abbreviation: D.C.

Symbols: flower—American beauty rose; tree—scarlet oak; bird—wood thrush

At a Glance

- From 2010 to 2018, the population of the District of Columbia rose 16.7 percent, the highest increase in the country.

- The violent crime rate in the District of Columbia was 1,004.9 per 100,000 population in 2017, more than twice the national rate of 394.0 per 100,000.

- In 2017, The District of Columbia also had the highest property crime rate in the country (4,283.9 per 100,000 population).

- Compared to the 50 states, the District of Columbia had the lowest percentage of people under 18 years of age (18.1 percent), and the 3rd lowest percentage of people 65 years and older (12.1 percent) in 2018.

- The District of Columbia had the highest median family income in the United States ($82,372) and the 7th highest percent of residents below the poverty level (16.6 percent) in 2017. It had the 5th highest percent of children under 18 years of age in poverty (25.6 percent).

Table DC-1. Population by Age, Sex, Race, and Hispanic Origin

(Number, percent, except where noted.)

Sex, age, race, and Hispanic origin	2000	2010	2018 [1]	Percent change, 2010–2018
Total Population..	572,059	601,723	702,455	16.7
Percent of total U.S. population	0.2	0.2	0.2	X
Sex				
Male...	269,366	284,222	333,307	17.3
Female..	302,693	317,501	369,148	16.3
Age				
Under 5 years..	32,536	32,613	45,617	39.9
5 to 19 years...	103,270	91,107	103,095	13.2
20 to 64 years...	366,355	409,194	468,440	14.5
65 years and over..	69,898	68,809	85,303	24.0
Median age (years)	34.8	33.8	34.0	0.6
Race and Hispanic Origin				
One race				
White	176,101	251,265	320,374	27.5
Black...	343,312	310,379	326,181	5.1
American Indian and Alaska Native	1,713	3,264	4,296	31.6
Asian...	15,189	21,705	31,025	42.9
Native Hawaiian or Other Pacific Islander	348	770	975	26.6
Two or more races...	13,446	14,340	19,604	36.7
Hispanic (of any race).......................................	44,953	57,833	79,249	37.0

X = Not applicable.
- = Zero or rounds to zero.
[1] Population figures for 2018 are July 1 estimates. The 2010 estimates are taken from the 2010 Census.

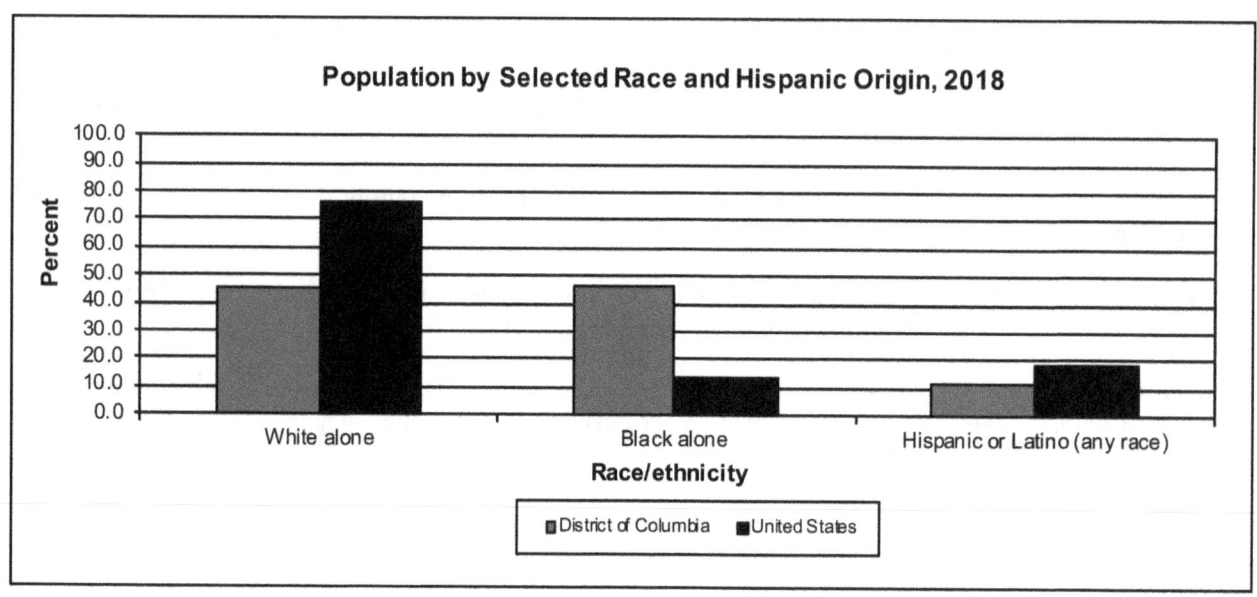

Table DC-2. Marital Status

(Number, percent distribution.)

Sex, age, race, and Hispanic origin	2000	2010	2017
Males, 15 Years and Over	219,706	243,152	274,333
Never married	51.2	58.9	59.0
Now married, except separated...	32.8	28.2	30.1
Separated..	3.9	2.4	2.1
Widowed..	3.4	2.1	1.4
Divorced..	8.7	8.4	7.4
Females, 15 Years and Over	254,711	277,203	310,828
Never married	46.0	55.8	55.6
Now married, except separated...	27.5	22.8	26.3
Separated..	4.4	3.1	2.1
Widowed..	11.6	7.5	6.8
Divorced..	10.6	10.8	9.1

Table DC-3. Households and Housing Characteristics

(Number, percent, dollars.)

Item	2000	2010	2017	Average annual percent change, 2010–2017
Total Households.................................	248,338	252,388	281,475	1.6
Family households	114,166	101,519	119,357	2.5
Married-couple family	56,631	57,275	70,576	3.3
Other family	57,535	44,244	48,781	1.5
Male householder, no wife present...........	10,503	8,740	9,991	2.0
Female householder, no husband present......	47,032	35,504	38,790	1.3
Nonfamily households	134,172	150,869	162,118	1.1
Householder living alone......................	108,744	121,036	127,144	0.7
Householder not living alone.................	25,428	29,833	34,974	2.5
Housing Characteristics				
Total housing units.............................	274,845	296,836	314,843	0.9
Occupied housing units	248,338	252,388	281,475	1.6
Owner occupied	101,214	107,193	118,805	1.5
Renter occupied	147,124	145,195	162,670	1.7
Average household size........................	2.16	2.24	2.32	0.5
Financial Characteristics				
Median gross rent of renter-occupied housing	618	1,198	1,499	3.6
Median monthly owner costs for housing units with a mortgage	1,291	2,297	2,432	0.8
Median value of owner-occupied housing units......	157,200	426,900	607,200	6.0

Table DC-4. Migration, Origin, and Language

(Number, percent.)

Characteristic	State 2016	State 2017	State Percent change	U.S. 2016	U.S. 2017	U.S. Percent change
Residence 1 Year Ago						
Population 1 year and over	672,022	684,810	1.9	319,361,956	321,994,428	0.8
Same house	80.1	80.9	X	85.4	85.7	X
Different house in the U.S....................	18.2	17.6	X	13.9	13.6	X
Same county	9.5	9.3	X	8.3	8.1	X
Different county	8.7	8.2	X	5.6	5.6	X
Same state	0.0	0.0	X	3.2	3.3	X
Different state	8.7	8.2	X	2.4	2.3	X
Abroad	1.7	1.5	X	0.7	0.7	X
Place of Birth						
Native born	590,539	592,112	0.3	279,388,170	281,193,323	0.6
Male	47.3	47.1	X	49.3	49.4	X
Female	52.7	52.9	X	50.7	50.6	X
Foreign born	90,631	101,860	12.4	43,739,345	44,525,855	1.8
Male	48.7	49.3	X	48.5	48.4	X
Female	51.3	50.7	X	51.5	51.6	X
Foreign born; naturalized U.S. citizen........	40,003	38,891	-2.8	21,238,372	21,948,732	3.3
Male	45.1	47.2	X	45.9	45.9	X
Female	54.9	52.8	X	54.1	54.1	X
Foreign born; not a U.S. citizen	50,628	62,969	24.4	22,500,973	22,577,123	0.3
Male	51.5	50.6	X	51	50.8	X
Female	48.5	49.4	X	49	49.2	X
Entered 2010 or later	25.6	35.4	X	18.6	21.3	X
Entered 2000 to 2009	31.5	29.2	X	26.7	25.7	X
Entered before 2000.........................	43	35.4	X	54.7	53.0	X
World Region of Birth, Foreign						
Foreign-born population, excluding population born at sea	90,631	101,860	12.4	43,738,901	44,525,458	1.8
Europe	17.1	17.9	X	10.9	10.8	X
Asia......................................	19.3	21.7	X	30.8	31.2	X
Africa....................................	15.4	15.1	X	4.9	5.1	X
Oceania	0.8	0.6	X	0.6	0.6	X
Latin America.............................	45.1	42.8	X	51	50.4	X
North America.............................	2.3	1.9	X	1.8	1.8	X
Language Spoken at Home and Ability to Speak English						
Population 5 years and over......................	637,624	648,907	1.8	303,328,961	305,924,019	0.9
English only	82.9	82.4	X	78.4	78.2	X
Language other than English.................	17.1	17.6	X	21.6	21.8	X
Speaks English less than "very well"........	6.1	6.3	X	8.6	8.5	X

NA = Not available.
X = Not applicable.
- = Zero or rounds to zero.

Table DC-5. Median Income and Poverty Status, 2017

(Number, percent, except as noted.)

Characteristic	State		U.S.	
	Number	Percent	Number	Percent
Median Income				
Households (dollars)...	82,372	X	60,336	X
Families (dollars)	106,528	X	73,891	X
Below Poverty Level (All People)	109,920	16.6	42,583,651	13.4
Sex				
Male	45,030	14.4	19,004,547	12.2
Female	64,890	18.7	23,579,104	14.5
Age				
Under 18 years..	31,618	25.6	13,353,202	18.4
Related children under 18 years...........................	31,538	25.6	13,053,472	18.1
18 to 64 years...	66,743	14.6	24,648,677	12.6
65 years and over..	11,559	14.2	4,581,772	9.3

X = Not applicable.

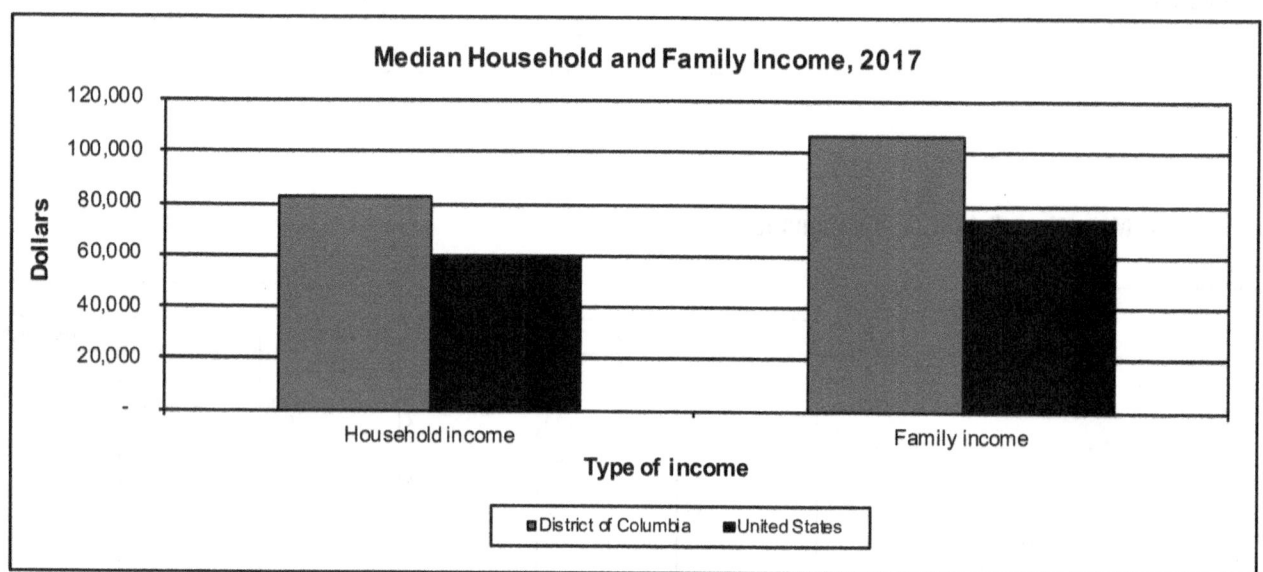

Table DC-6. Health Insurance Coverage Status for the Civilian Noninstitutionalized Population and Children Under 18 Years of Age

(Number, percent.)

Item	2009	2010	2011	2012	2013	2014	2015	2016	2017
Civilian Noninstitutionalized Population	589,408	594,282	608,165	621,380	635,833	647,966	660,682	670,985	683,808
Covered by Private or Public Insurance									
Number..	548,016	549,118	566,158	584,526	593,538	613,778	635,702	644,639	657,797
Percent..	93.0	92.4	93.1	94.1	93.3	94.7	96.2	96.1	96.2
Uninsured									
Number..	41,392	45,164	42,007	36,854	42,295	34,188	24,980	26,346	26,011
Percent..	7.0	7.6	6.9	5.9	6.7	5.3	3.8	3.9	3.8
Percent in the U.S. not covered...............................	15.1	15.5	15.1	14.8	14.5	11.7	9.4	8.6	8.7
Children Under 18 Years of Age[1]	113,710	100,990	105,312	109,182	111,287	114,834	117,415	120,313	133,635
Covered by Private or Public Insurance									
Number..	110,512	98,681	101,179	107,312	108,657	112,449	115,609	116,572	132,060
Percent..	97.2	97.7	96.1	98.3	97.6	97.9	98.5	96.9	98.8
Uninsured									
Number..	3,198	2,309	4,133	1,870	2,630	2,385	1,806	3,741	1,575
Percent..	2.8	2.3	3.9	1.7	2.4	2.1	1.5	3.1	1.2
Percent in the U.S. not covered...............................	8.6	8.0	7.5	7.2	7.1	6.0	4.8	4.5	5.0

[1] 2017 data is for individuals under 19 years of age.

Table DC-7. Employment Status by Demographic Group, 2018

(Numbers in thousands, percent.)

Characteristic	Civilian noninstitutional population	Civilian labor force		Employed		Unemployed	
		Number	Percent of population	Number	Percent of population	Number	Percent of population
Total..	576	406	70.4	383	66.5	23	5.6
Sex							
Male...	268	200	74.7	189	70.5	11	5.6
Female...	308	206	66.8	194	63.0	12	5.6
Race, Sex, and Hispanic Origin							
White..	271	226	83.2	221	81.4	5	2.1
Male...	135	115	85.0	112	83.1	3	2.3
Female...	137	111	81.4	109	79.7	2	2.0
Black or African American...................	258	145	56.1	128	49.4	17	11.9
Male...	113	70	61.9	62	54.6	8	11.8
Female...	145	75	51.6	66	45.3	9	12.1
Hispanic or Latino ethnicity[1]	54	42	78.1	40	75.2	2	3.7
Male...	26	22	82.8	21	79.9	1	3.1
Female...	27	20	73.5	19	70.3	1	4.3
Age							
16 to 19 years................................	NA	NA	NA	NA	NA	NA	NA
20 to 24 years................................	52	38	73.8	34	66.0	4	10.7
25 to 34 years................................	175	156	89.0	148	84.3	8	5.3
35 to 44 years................................	102	90	88.0	86	84.5	4	4.0
45 to 54 years................................	71	56	78.7	54	75.2	3	4.5
55 to 64 years................................	63	39	62.5	38	59.8	2	4.3
65 years and over............................	92	22	24.2	21	22.8	1	5.8

NOTE: Data in Table 7 are from the Current Population Survey (CPS) and do not match the estimates in Table 8. See notes and definitions for further information.
[1] May be of any race.
NA = Not available.

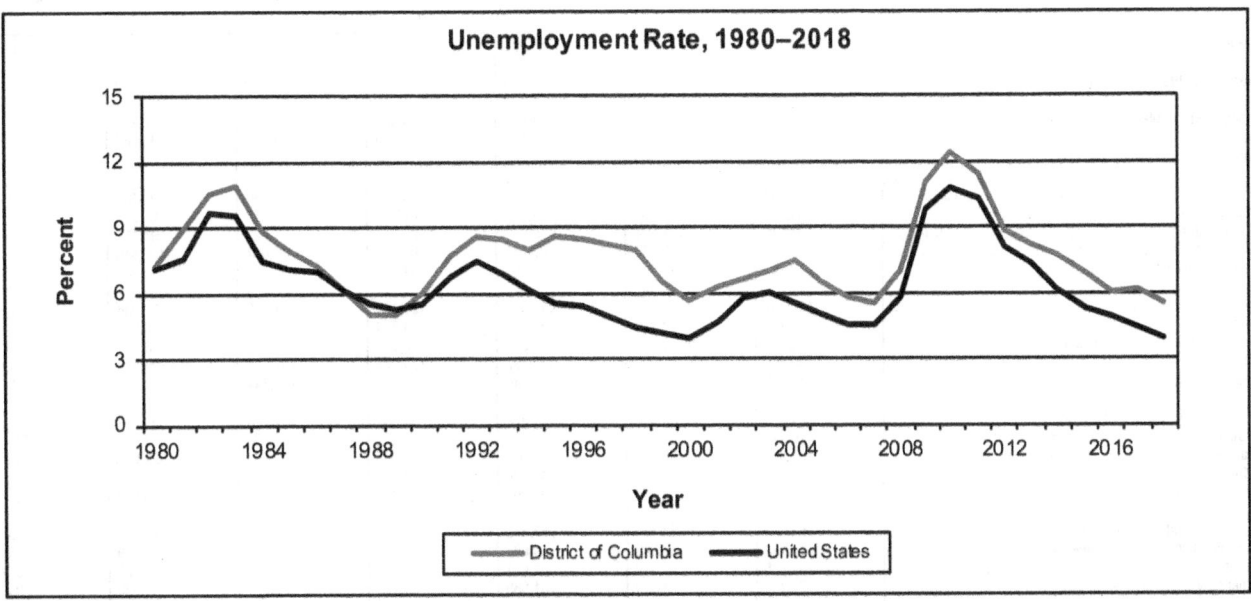

Unemployment Rate, 1980–2018

Table DC-8. Employment Status of the Civilian Noninstitutional Population Age 16 Years and Over

(Number, percent.)

Year	Civilian labor force	Civilian participation rate	Employed	Unemployed	Unemployment rate
2010..	346,065	68.8	313,508	32,557	9.4
2011..	350,778	67.9	315,171	35,607	10.2
2012..	364,989	69.1	331,984	33,005	9.0
2013..	374,126	69.6	342,351	31,775	8.5
2014..	378,380	69.3	348,981	29,399	7.8
2015..	388,057	70.0	361,324	26,733	6.9
2016..	394,586	70.1	370,521	24,065	6.1
2017..	400,894	70.4	376,633	24,261	6.1
2018..	404,610	70.4	382,140	22,470	5.6

Table DC-9. Employment and Average Wages by Industry

(Estimates are based on the 2012 *North American Industry Classification System* [NAICS].)

Industry	2011	2012	2013	2014	2015	2016	2017
				Number of Jobs			
Wage and Salary Employment by Industry......................	742,832	749,247	758,641	767,130	775,658	788,013	793,524
Farm Wage and Salary Employment.................................	0	0	0	0	0	0	0
Nonfarm Wage and Salary Employment...........................	742,832	749,247	758,641	767,130	775,658	788,013	793,524
Private wage and salary employment................................	481,618	492,831	505,628	515,390	527,234	537,330	543,372
Forestry, fishing, and related activities	0	0	0	0	0	0	0
Mining..	0	0	0	0	0	0	0
Utilities..	1,830	1,850	1,891	1,920	2,004	1,998	2,028
Construction	12,476	14,020	14,450	14,679	15,019	15,762	(D)
Manufacturing...	1,043	973	1,008	1,031	1,104	1,218	(D)
Durable goods manufacturing...	424	423	441	418	456	542	(D)
Nondurable goods manufacturing....................................	619	550	567	613	648	676	(D)
Wholesale trade	4,643	4,973	4,868	4,934	4,874	5,035	4,948
Retail trade..	18,862	19,172	20,212	21,465	22,636	23,084	23,489
Transportation and warehousing......................................	4,184	4,138	3,780	3,938	4,435	4,397	4,643
Information	18,710	17,524	17,059	17,245	17,190	17,058	17,853
Finance and insurance	14,918	14,939	14,818	15,137	15,157	14,986	15,142
Real estate and rental and leasing..................................	10,447	11,033	11,057	11,988	12,280	12,609	12,708
Professional, scientific, and technical services	103,505	107,364	108,658	109,564	113,169	115,828	117,328
Management of companies and enterprises.......................	2,018	2,011	2,046	2,157	2,148	2,434	2,770
Administrative and waste services...................................	45,404	45,916	46,399	46,928	48,013	48,184	47,528
Educational services	50,541	50,231	55,898	56,763	56,811	57,552	56,729
Health care and social assistance....................................	61,562	62,712	64,578	65,113	66,150	68,204	68,973
Arts, entertainment, and recreation.................................	7,008	7,108	6,994	7,501	7,757	8,397	9,156
Accommodation and food services...................................	55,790	58,617	61,256	62,993	65,735	66,657	68,005
Other services, except public administration....................	68,677	70,250	70,656	72,034	72,752	73,927	75,133
Government and government enterprises	261,214	256,416	253,013	251,740	248,424	250,683	250,152
				Dollars			
Average Wages and Salaries by Industry	80,485	81,631	81,981	84,301	87,230	88,771	91,720
Average Farm Wages and Salaries	0	0	0	0	0	0	0
Average Nonfarm Wages and Salaries	80,485	81,631	81,981	84,301	87,230	88,771	91,720
Average private wages and salaries..................................	73,873	75,604	76,130	78,350	81,005	82,164	85,094
Forestry, fishing, and related activities.............................	0	0	0	0	0	0	0
Mining..	0	0	0	0	0	0	0
Utilities..	91,284	91,637	98,332	98,384	103,130	107,138	112,671
Construction	63,422	63,606	62,917	65,118	63,558	63,956	(D)
Manufacturing...	104,670	107,621	109,943	95,381	95,827	93,412	(D)
Durable goods manufacturing...	83,321	83,154	83,778	82,557	91,037	96,915	(D)
Nondurable goods manufacturing....................................	119,294	126,438	130,295	104,126	99,198	90,604	(D)
Wholesale trade	107,681	114,079	116,530	120,472	121,059	117,984	123,920
Retail trade..	32,237	34,279	33,264	33,259	33,784	35,894	36,001
Transportation and warehousing......................................	70,687	74,295	73,687	76,131	75,677	78,164	75,769
Information	106,855	111,999	122,427	120,673	121,514	126,473	131,082
Finance and insurance	137,723	142,871	148,745	156,450	167,244	171,256	179,061
Real estate and rental and leasing...................................	74,973	77,647	80,027	94,266	94,226	94,846	104,188
Professional, scientific, and technical services	120,110	122,651	122,637	126,655	128,788	131,857	135,788
Management of companies and enterprises........................	201,885	235,286	219,007	232,866	297,382	222,637	215,427
Administrative and waste services...................................	45,886	46,982	48,390	49,074	51,283	50,649	52,521
Educational services	45,674	47,274	47,291	48,006	50,042	50,840	52,272
Health care and social assistance....................................	57,534	58,183	57,758	60,404	62,661	62,653	63,999
Arts, entertainment, and recreation.................................	55,120	50,292	54,688	57,353	82,527	76,579	86,288
Accommodation and food services...................................	32,338	32,519	33,531	34,457	35,685	36,833	37,848
Other services, except public administration....................	77,267	78,610	81,565	83,422	86,877	88,936	90,897
Government and government enterprises..........................	92,678	93,217	93,673	96,486	100,441	102,932	106,114

Table DC-10. Employment Characteristics by Family Type

(Number, percent.)

Family type and labor force status	2015		2016		2017	
	Total	Families with own children under 18 years	Total	Families with own children under 18 years	Total	Families with own children under 18 years
All Families...	125,178	54,494	122,732	52,056	119,357	48,098
FAMILY TYPE AND LABOR FORCE STATUS						
Married-Couple Families.................................	71,857	27,840	71,204	27,175	70,576	27,000
Both husband and wife in labor force............................	65.0	76.8	62.5	76.3	61.8	75.5
Husband in labor force, wife not in labor force	14.1	18.8	15.1	19.6	15.1	18.9
Wife in labor force, husband not in labor force	5.2	0.8	7.4	2.7	7.2	2.7
Both husband and wife not in labor force.........................	12.2	2.5	9.7	0.3	9.5	0.6
Other Families	53,321	26,654	51,528	24,881	48,781	21,098
Female householder, no husband present...........................	79.7	82.6	82.1	86.0	79.5	81.6
In labor force..	52.3	65.1	54.0	69.5	46.7	58.5
Not in labor force	27.4	17.5	28.1	16.5	32.8	23.1
Male householder, no wife present...............................	20.3	17.4	17.9	14.0	20.5	18.4
In labor force..	15.6	16.2	14.2	12.8	15.1	16.3
Not in labor force	4.7	1.2	3.8	1.2	5.4	2.1

Table DC-11. School Enrollment and Educational Attainment, 2017

(Number, percent.)

Item	District	U.S.
Enrollment		
Total population 3 years and over, enrolled in school	167,649	81,273,337
Enrolled in nursery school or preschool (percent)..	7.8	6.0
Enrolled in kindergarten (percent)...	5.7	4.9
Enrolled in elementary school, grades 1-8 (percent)..	29.0	40.6
Enrolled in high school, grades 9-12 (percent)	13.3	21.1
Enrolled in college or graduate school (percent)...	44.3	27.4
Attainment		
Total population 25 years and over	494,614	221,250,083
Less than ninth grade (percent)..	4.3	5.1
9th to 12th grade, no diploma (percent)	5.5	6.9
High school graduate, including equivalency (percent)..	17.2	27.1
Some college, no degree (percent)	12.5	20.4
Associate's degree (percent)..	3.2	8.5
Bachelor's degree (percent)...	23.9	19.7
Graduate or professional degree (percent)..	33.4	12.3
High school graduate or higher (percent)	90.2	88.0
Bachelor's degree or higher (percent)...	57.3	32.0

Table DC-12. Public School Characteristics and Educational Indicators

(Number, percent; data derived from National Center of Education Statistics.)

Item	State	U.S.
Public Elementary and Secondary Schools		
Number of operational school districts, 2016-17...	67	18,377
Number of operational schools, 2016-17..	223	98,330
Percent charter schools	49.3	7.1
Total public school enrollment, 2016-17..	85,850	50,587,859
Percent charter school enrollment	43.7	6.0
Student-teacher ratio, Fall 2015..	12.4	16.0
Expenditures per student (dollars), 2015-16...	21,135	11,841
Four-year adjusted cohort graduation rate (ACGR)[1]	73.2	84.6
Students eligible for free or reduced-price lunch (percent), 2015-16...............................	76.4	52.1
English language learners (percent), Fall 2016...	7.7	9.6
Students age 3 to 21 served under IDEA, part B (percent), 2017-18................................	15.5	13.7

Public Schools by Type, 2016-17		Percent of district public schools
Total number of schools..	223	100.0
Special education...	2	0.9
Vocational education..	0	-
Alternative education...	4	1.8

[1] Adjusted Cohort Graduation Rates (ACGR) differ from Averaged Freshmen Graduation Rates (AFGR).
- = Zero or rounds to zero.

Table DC-13. Reported Voting and Registration of the Voting-Age Population, November 2018

(Numbers in thousands, percent.)

Item	Total population	Total citizen population	Registered			Voted		
			Total registered	Percent registered (total population)	Percent registered (total citizen population)	Total voted	Percent voted (total population)	Percent voted (total citizen population)
U.S. Total	249,748	228,832	153,066	61.3	66.9	122,281	49.0	53.4
State Total.................................	567	512	397	70.0	77.6	313	55.2	61.1
Sex								
Male	264	235	179	68.1	76.3	141	53.3	59.8
Female	304	277	218	71.7	78.6	172	56.7	62.3
Race								
White alone...............................	270	247	207	76.5	83.5	168	62.1	67.8
White, non-Hispanic alone	235	223	191	81.3	85.8	155	65.9	69.5
Black alone.................................	251	228	163	65.2	71.7	123	48.9	53.7
Asian alone	30	22	16	(B)	(B)	13	(B)	(B)
Hispanic (of any race)	53	35	24	(B)	(B)	20	(B)	(B)
White alone or in combination	281	257	214	76.3	83.4	174	62.0	67.8
Black alone or in combination............	258	234	169	65.5	72.1	128	49.5	54.5
Asian alone or in combination............	33	25	17	(B)	(B)	14	(B)	(B)
Age								
18 to 24 years	61	54	38	(B)	(B)	29	(B)	(B)
25 to 34 years	173	156	117	67.6	75.1	93	53.6	59.5
35 to 44 years	105	90	76	72.1	84.2	61	57.9	67.7
45 to 64 years	133	121	91	68.8	75.6	69	52.3	57.5
65 years and over	95	91	75	79.1	82.9	60	63.7	66.7

B = Base is less than 75,000 and therefore too small to show the derived measure.

Table DC-14. Crime

(Number, rate per 100,000. Data are derived from the FBI Uniform Crime Reports.)

Item	District [1]			U.S.		
	2016	2017	Percent change	2016	2017	Percent change
TOTAL POPULATION[2]	684,336	693,972	1.4	323,405,935	325,719,178	0.7
VIOLENT CRIME						
Number..	8,236	6,974	-15.3	1,285,606	1,283,220	-0.2
Rate	1,203.5	1,004.9	-16.5	397.5	394.0	-0.9
Murder and Nonnegligent Manslaughter						
Number..	136	116	-14.7	17,413	17,284	-0.7
Rate	19.9	16.7	-15.9	5.4	5.3	-1.4
Rape[3]						
Number..	533	444	-16.7	132,414	135,755	2.5
Rate	77.9	64.0	-17.9	40.9	41.7	1.8
Robbery						
Number..	3,500	2,623	-25.1	332,797	319,356	-4.0
Rate	511.4	378.0	-26.1	102.9	98.0	-4.7
Aggravated Assault						
Number..	4,067	3,791	-6.8	802,982	810,825	1.0
Rate	594.3	546.3	-8.1	248.3	248.9	0.3
PROPERTY CRIME						
Number..	32,377	29,729	-8.2	7,928,530	7,694,086	-3.0
Rate	4,731.2	4,283.9	-9.5	2,451.6	2,362.2	-3.6
Burglary						
Number..	2,361	1,809	-23.4	1,516,405	1,401,840	-7.6
Rate	345.0	260.7	-24.4	468.9	430.4	-8.2
Larceny-Theft						
Number..	27,089	25,333	-6.5	5,644,835	5,519,107	-2.2
Rate	3,958.4	3,650.4	-7.8	1,745.4	1,694.4	-2.9
Motor Vehicle Theft						
Number..	2,927	2,587	-11.6	767,290	773,139	0.8
Rate	427.7	372.8	-12.8	237.3	237.4	-

NOTE: Although arson data are included in the trend and clearance tables, sufficient data are not available to estimate totals for this offense. Therefore, no arson data are published in this table.
- = Zero or rounds to zero.
[1] Includes offenses reported by the Metro Transit Police and the District of Columbia Fire and Emergency Medical Services: Arson
[2] Population figures are U.S. Census Bureau provisional estimates as of July 1, 2017.
[3] The figures shown in the rape (revised definition) column were estimated using the revised Uniform Crime Reporting (UCR) definition of rape.

Table DC-15. Local Government Finances, 2016

(Dollar amounts in thousands, percent distribution.)

Item	Dollars	Percent distribution
Total Revenue	14,629,174	100.0
General revenue	13,613,748	93.1
Intergovernmental revenue	4,483,920	30.7
Taxes	7,418,679	50.7
Property	2,418,896	16.5
Sales and gross receipts	1,783,982	12.2
Individual income tax	1,907,862	13.0
Corporate income tax	556,468	3.8
Motor vehicle license	36,751	0.3
Other taxes	714,720	4.9
Current charges	800,212	5.5
Miscellaneous general revenue	910,937	6.2
Utility revenue	1,033,925	7.1
Liquor stores revenue	0	-
Insurance trust revenue[1]	-18,499	-0.1
Total Expenditure	16,593,661	100.0
Intergovernmental expenditure	0	-
Direct expenditure	16,593,661	100.0
Current operation	12,578,563	75.8
Capital outlay	2,778,170	16.7
Insurance benefits and repayments	508,838	3.1
Assistance and subsidies	152,274	0.9
Interest on debt	575,816	3.5
Exhibit: Salaries and wages	3,889,036	23.4
Direct Expenditure	16,593,661	100.0
Direct expenditure by function:		
Direct general expenditure	12,770,520	77.0
Education	2,765,772	16.7
Public welfare	3,785,463	22.8
Hospitals	269,888	1.6
Health	455,573	2.7
Highways	354,822	2.1
Police protection	593,345	3.6
Correction	144,915	0.9
Natural resources	67,548	0.4
Parks and recreation	328,468	2.0
Governmental administration	698,676	4.2
Interest on general debt	561,678	3.4
Other and unallocable	824,792	5.0
Utility expenditure	3,314,303	20.0
Liquor stores expenditure	0	-
Insurance trust expenditure	508,838	3.1
Debt at End of Fiscal Year	14,520,507	X
Cash and Security Holdings	15,454,008	X

Note: At the time of publication, the Census Bureau had not yet released 2015 finance data for the District of Columbia.

X = Not applicable.

- = Zero or rounds to zero.

[1] Within insurance trust revenue, net earnings of state retirement systems is a calculated statistic (the item code in the data file is X08), and thus can be positive or negative. Net earnings is the sum of earnings on investments plus gains on investments minus losses on investments. The change made in 2002 for asset valuation from book to market value in accordance with Statement 34 of the Governmental Accounting Standards Board is reflected in the calculated statistics.

Table DC-16. District Government Tax Collections, 2018

(Dollars in thousands, percent.)

Item	Dollars	Percent distribution
Total Taxes	7,959,386	100.0
Property taxes	2,621,626	32.9
Sales and gross receipts	1,930,168	24.3
General sales and gross receipts	1,493,101	18.8
Selective sales and gross receipts	437,067	5.5
Alcoholic beverages	6,560	0.1
Amusements	X	-
Insurance premiums	115,290	1.4
Motor fuels	26,268	0.3
Pari-mutuels	X	-
Public utilities	179,065	2.2
Tobacco products	27,956	0.4
Other selective sales	81,928	1.0
Licenses	198,930	2.5
Alcoholic beverages	5,691	0.1
Amusements	X	-
Corporations in general	36,217	0.5
Hunting and fishing	81	-
Motor vehicle	39,514	0.5
Motor vehicle operators	6,074	0.1
Public utilities	X	-
Occupation and business, NEC	58,429	0.7
Other licenses	52,924	0.7
Income taxes	2,641,587	33.2
Individual income	2,066,842	26.0
Corporation net income	574,745	7.2
Other taxes	567,075	7.1
Death and gift	35,708	0.4
Documentary and stock transfer	472,444	5.9
Severance	X	-
Taxes, NEC	58,923	0.7

X = Not applicable.
- = Zero or rounds to zero.

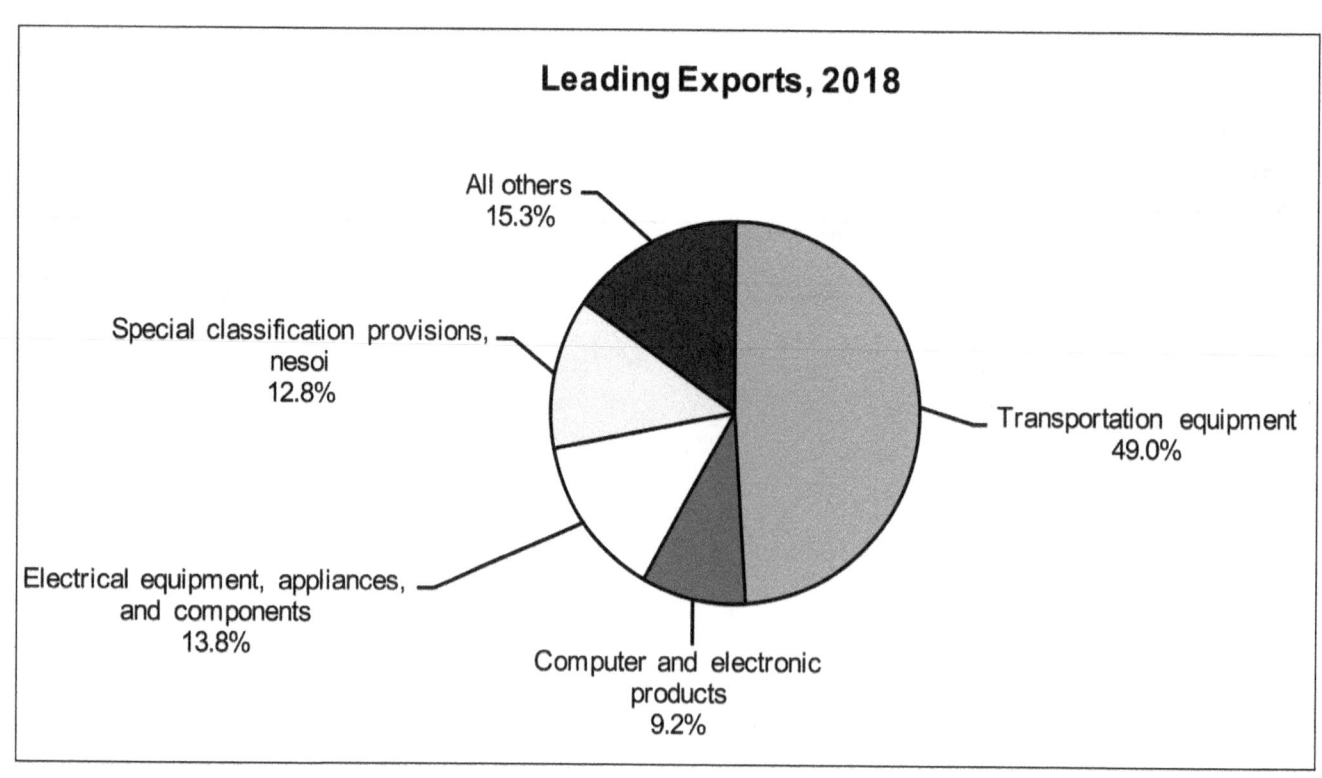

Leading Exports, 2018

- All others 15.3%
- Special classification provisions, nesoi 12.8%
- Electrical equipment, appliances, and components 13.8%
- Computer and electronic products 9.2%
- Transportation equipment 49.0%

FLORIDA

Facts and Figures

Location: Southeastern United States; bordered on the N by Georgia and Alabama, on the E by the Atlantic Ocean, on the S by the Straits of Florida, and on the W by Alabama and the Gulf of Mexico

Area: 65,757 sq. mi. (170,304 sq. km.); rank—22nd

Population: 21,299,325 (2018 est.); rank—3rd

Principal Cities: capital—Tallahassee; largest—Jacksonville

Statehood: March 3, 1845; 27th state

U.S. Congress: 2 senators, 27 representatives

State Motto: In God We Trust

State Song: "The Swanee River (Old Folks at Home)"

State Nickname: The Sunshine State

Abbreviations: FL; Fla.

State Symbols: flower—orange blossom; tree—Sabal palm (cabbage palm); bird—mockingbird

At a Glance

- With an increase in population of 13.3 percent, Florida ranked 4th among the states in growth from 2010 to 2018.

- Florida's violent crime rate in 2017 was 408.0 incidences per 100,000 population, compared to 394.0 for the entire nation.

- In 2018, Florida was the state with the second largest percentage of its population in the 65 and older age group (20.5 percent).

- Florida ranked 6th among the states for the highest percent of Hispanic or Latino residents (26.1 percent) in 2018. Hispanic or Latino residents may be of any race.

- In 2017, 12.9 percent of all Florida residents were uninsured, compared to the national average of 8.7 percent.

Table FL-1. Population by Age, Sex, Race, and Hispanic Origin

(Number, percent, except where noted.)

Sex, age, race, and Hispanic origin	2000	2010	2018 [1]	Percent change, 2010–2018
Total Population..	15,982,378	18,801,310	21,299,325	13.3
Percent of total U.S. population	5.7	6.1	6.5	X
Sex				
Male..	7,797,715	9,189,355	10,411,777	13.3
Female	8,184,663	9,611,955	10,887,548	13.3
Age				
Under 5 years...	945,823	1,073,506	1,143,183	6.5
5 to 19 years...	3,102,809	3,439,484	3,570,256	3.8
20 to 64 years...	9,126,149	11,034,718	12,227,815	10.8
65 years and over..	2,807,597	3,259,602	4,358,071	33.7
Median age (years)	38.7	40.7	42.2	3.7
Race and Hispanic Origin				
One race				
White	12,465,029	14,808,867	16,472,125	11.2
Black	2,335,505	3,078,067	3,600,121	17.0
American Indian and Alaska Native	53,541	89,119	106,984	20.0
Asian	266,256	474,199	631,737	33.2
Native Hawaiian or Other Pacific Islander	8,625	18,790	24,353	29.6
Two or more races	376,315	332,268	464,005	39.6
Hispanic (of any race)..	2,682,715	4,301,853	5,562,417	29.3

X = Not applicable.

[1] Population figures for 2018 are July 1 estimates. The 2010 estimates are taken from the 2010 Census.

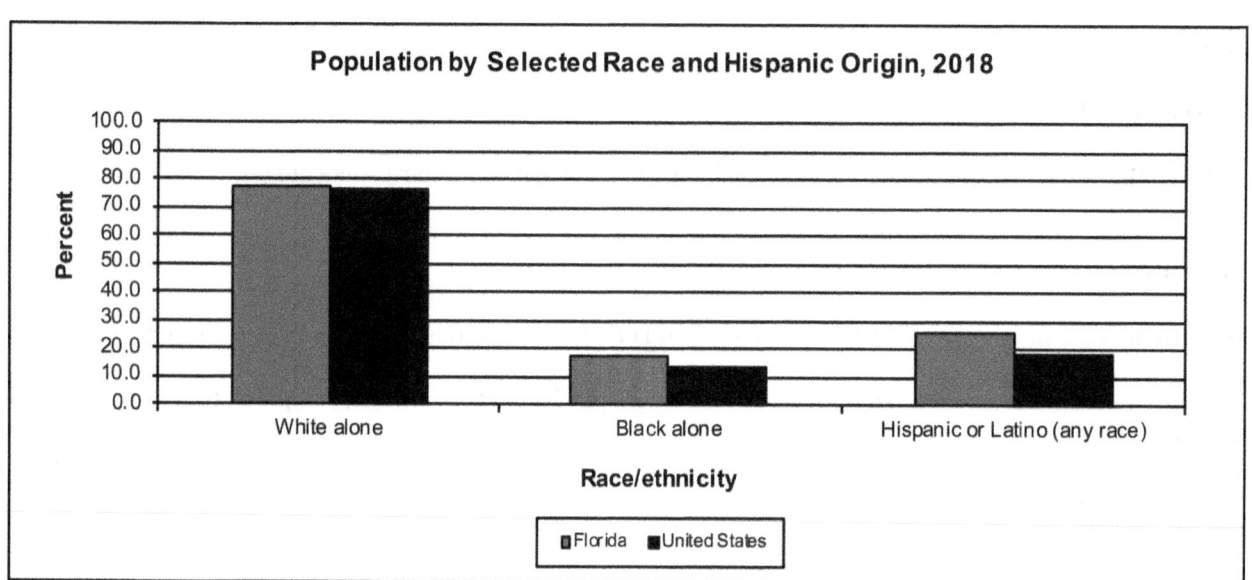

Population by Selected Race and Hispanic Origin, 2018

(Legend: Florida, United States)

Table FL-2. Marital Status

(Number, percent distribution.)

Sex, age, race, and Hispanic origin	2000	2010	2017
Males, 15 Years and Over..	6,232,987	7,534,535	8,482,987
Never married	27.3	33.9	35.2
Now married, except separated....................................	56.9	49.3	48.3
Separated..	2.1	2.2	1.9
Widowed..	3.2	3.2	3.2
Divorced..	10.5	11.5	11.4
Females, 15 Years and Over...	6,714,003	8,021,290	9,031,211
Never married	20.5	26.6	28.5
Now married, except separated....................................	51.9	45.1	44.1
Separated..	2.7	3.0	2.5
Widowed..	12.3	10.8	10.3
Divorced..	12.7	14.5	14.6

Table FL-3. Households and Housing Characteristics

(Number, percent, dollars.)

Item	2000	2010	2017	Average annual percent change, 2010–2017
Total Households..	6,337,929	7,035,068	7,689,964	1.3
Family households	4,210,760	4,556,930	4,943,506	1.2
Married-couple family	3,192,266	3,307,884	3,588,295	1.2
Other family	1,018,494	1,249,046	1,355,211	1.2
Male householder, no wife present...........	259,924	313,305	377,628	2.9
Female householder, no husband present......	759,000	935,741	977,583	0.6
Nonfamily households	2,127,169	2,478,138	2,746,458	1.5
Householder living alone...........................	1,687,303	2,013,028	2,217,993	1.5
Householder not living alone......................	439,886	465,110	528,465	1.9
Housing Characteristics				
Total housing units......................................	7,302,947	8,994,091	9,441,585	0.7
Occupied housing units	6,337,929	7,035,068	7,689,964	1.3
Owner occupied	4,441,799	4,794,130	5,010,187	0.6
Renter occupied	1,896,130	2,240,938	2,679,777	2.8
Average household size................................	2.46	2.62	2.67	0.3
Financial Characteristics				
Median gross rent of renter-occupied housing	641	947	1128	2.7
Median monthly owner costs for housing units with a mortgage	1,004	1,505	1,423	-0.8
Median value of owner-occupied housing units	105,500	164,200	214,000	4.3

Table FL-4. Migration, Origin, and Language

(Number, percent.)

Characteristic	State 2016	State 2017	State Percent change	U.S. 2016	U.S. 2017	U.S. Percent change
Residence 1 Year Ago						
Population 1 year and over	20,401,575	20,772,371	1.8	319,361,956	321,994,428	0.8
Same house	84.2	84.5	X	85.4	85.7	X
Different house in the U.S.	14.7	14.3	X	13.9	13.6	X
Same county.......................................	8.7	8.4	X	8.3	8.1	X
Different county	6.0	5.9	X	5.6	5.6	X
Same state	3.0	3.2	X	3.2	3.3	X
Different state	3.0	2.7	X	2.4	2.3	X
Abroad	1.1	1.2	X	0.7	0.7	X
Place of Birth						
Native born	16,375,928	16,605,059	1.4	279,388,170	281,193,323	0.6
Male	49.4	49.4	X	49.3	49.4	X
Female	50.6	50.6	X	50.7	50.6	X
Foreign born	4,236,511	4,379,341	3.4	43,739,345	44,525,855	1.8
Male	46.9	46.8	X	48.5	48.4	X
Female	53.1	53.2	X	51.5	51.6	X
Foreign born; naturalized U.S. citizen............	2,334,825	2,418,826	3.6	21,238,372	21,948,732	3.3
Male	43.9	44.1	X	45.9	45.9	X
Female	56.1	55.9	X	54.1	54.1	X
Foreign born; not a U.S. citizen....................	1,901,686	1,960,515	3.1	22,500,973	22,577,123	0.3
Male	50.6	50.1	X	51	50.8	X
Female	49.4	49.9	X	49	49.2	X
Entered 2010 or later	20.7	23.6	X	18.6	21.3	X
Entered 2000 to 2009	26.5	25.3	X	26.7	25.7	X
Entered before 2000................................	52.8	51.1	X	54.7	53.0	X
World Region of Birth, Foreign						
Foreign-born population, excluding population born at sea	4,236,511	4,379,341	3.4	43,738,901	44,525,458	1.8
Europe	9.7	9.2	X	10.9	10.8	X
Asia	10.8	10.6	X	30.8	31.2	X
Africa	1.8	1.8	X	4.9	5.1	X
Oceania	0.2	0.2	X	0.6	0.6	X
Latin America	74.9	75.6	X	51	50.4	X
North America......................................	2.6	2.6	X	1.8	1.8	X
Language Spoken at Home and Ability to Speak English						
Population 5 years and over......................	19,494,972	19,855,078	1.8	303,328,961	305,924,019	0.9
English only	71.2	70.3	X	78.4	78.2	X
Language other than English......................	28.8	29.7	X	21.6	21.8	X
Speaks English less than "very well".........	12.0	12.2	X	8.6	8.5	X

NA = Not available.
X = Not applicable.
- = Zero or rounds to zero.

Table FL-5. Median Income and Poverty Status, 2017

(Number, percent, except as noted.)

Characteristic	State		U.S.	
	Number	Percent	Number	Percent
Median Income				
Households (dollars)...	52,594	X	60,336	X
Families (dollars)	64,003	X	73,891	X
Below Poverty Level (All People)	2,889,506	14.0	42,583,651	13.4
Sex				
Male	1,300,570	13.0	19,004,547	12.2
Female	1,588,936	15.0	23,579,104	14.5
Age				
Under 18 years..	840,179	20.3	13,353,202	18.4
Related children under 18 years..	822,648	20.0	13,053,472	18.1
18 to 64 years...	1,625,804	13.2	24,648,677	12.6
65 years and over	423,523	10.2	4,581,772	9.3

X = Not applicable.

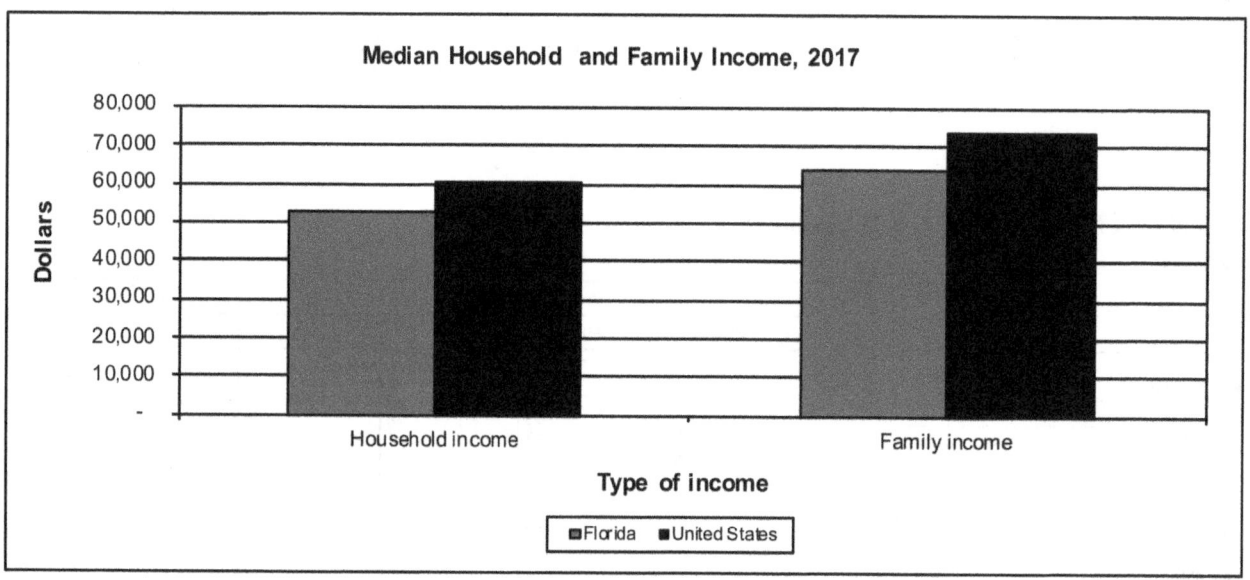

Table FL-6. Health Insurance Coverage Status for the Civilian Noninstitutionalized Population and Children Under 18 Years of Age

(Number, percent.)

Item	2009	2010	2011	2012	2013	2014	2015	2016	2017
Civilian Noninstitutionalized Population	18,192,784	18,534,081	18,752,294	19,011,070	19,245,127	19,583,357	19,960,169	20,294,479	20,678,704
Covered by Private or Public Insurance									
Number...	14,397,455	14,593,021	14,840,913	15,195,230	15,392,164	16,338,196	17,298,620	17,750,232	18,002,557
Percent..	79.1	78.7	79.1	79.9	80.0	83.4	86.7	87.5	87.1
Uninsured									
Number...	3,795,329	3,941,060	3,911,381	3,815,840	3,852,963	3,245,161	2,661,549	2,544,247	2,676,147
Percent..	20.9	21.3	20.9	20.1	20.0	16.6	13.3	12.5	12.9
Percent in the U.S. not covered................................	15.1	15.5	15.1	14.8	14.5	11.7	9.4	8.6	8.7
Children Under 18 Years of Age[1]	4,050,661	3,990,247	3,986,946	3,991,143	4,019,835	4,046,150	4,093,401	4,136,345	4,450,443
Covered by Private or Public Insurance									
Number...	3,450,124	3,483,313	3,511,834	3,554,977	3,574,800	3,668,163	3,809,595	3,879,598	4,125,583
Percent..	85.2	87.3	88.1	89.1	88.9	90.7	93.1	93.8	92.7
Uninsured									
Number...	600,537	506,934	475,112	436,166	445,035	377,987	283,806	256,747	324,860
Percent..	14.8	12.7	11.9	10.9	11.1	9.3	6.9	6.2	7.3
Percent in the U.S. not covered................................	8.6	8.0	7.5	7.2	7.1	6.0	4.8	4.5	5.0

[1] 2017 data is for individuals under 19 years of age.

Table FL-7. Employment Status by Demographic Group, 2018

(Numbers in thousands, percent.)

Characteristic	Civilian noninstitutional population	Civilian labor force		Employed		Unemployed	
		Number	Percent of population	Number	Percent of population	Number	Percent of population
Total...	17,246	10,248	59.4	9,879	57.3	369	3.6
Sex							
Male..	8,263	5,380	65.1	5,200	62.9	179	3.3
Female	8,984	4,868	54.2	4,679	52.1	190	3.9
Race, Sex, and Hispanic Origin							
White..	13,769	8,011	58.2	7,773	56.5	239	3.0
Male...	6,678	4,302	64.4	4,176	62.5	126	2.9
Female...	7,091	3,709	52.3	3,597	50.7	112	3.0
Black or African American............................	2,691	1,727	64.2	1,619	60.2	108	6.2
Male...	1,235	824	66.7	781	63.2	43	5.2
Female...	1,456	903	62.0	839	57.6	65	7.2
Hispanic or Latino ethnicity[1]	4,309	2,756	64.0	2,659	61.7	98	3.5
Male...	2,079	1,525	73.4	1,475	70.9	50	3.3
Female...	2,230	1,232	55.2	1,184	53.1	48	3.9
Age							
16 to 19 years..	985	306	31.1	266	27.0	41	13.2
20 to 24 years..	1,267	874	69.0	815	64.3	59	6.8
25 to 34 years..	2,613	2,106	80.6	2,028	77.6	78	3.7
35 to 44 years..	2,520	2,084	82.7	2,039	80.9	46	2.2
45 to 54 years..	2,859	2,288	80.0	2,219	77.6	69	3.0
55 to 64 years..	2,852	1,806	63.3	1,753	61.5	53	2.9
65 years and over	4,151	784	18.9	760	18.3	24	3.1

NOTE: Data in Table 7 are from the Current Population Survey (CPS) and do not match the estimates in Table 8. See notes and definitions for further information.
[1] May be of any race.

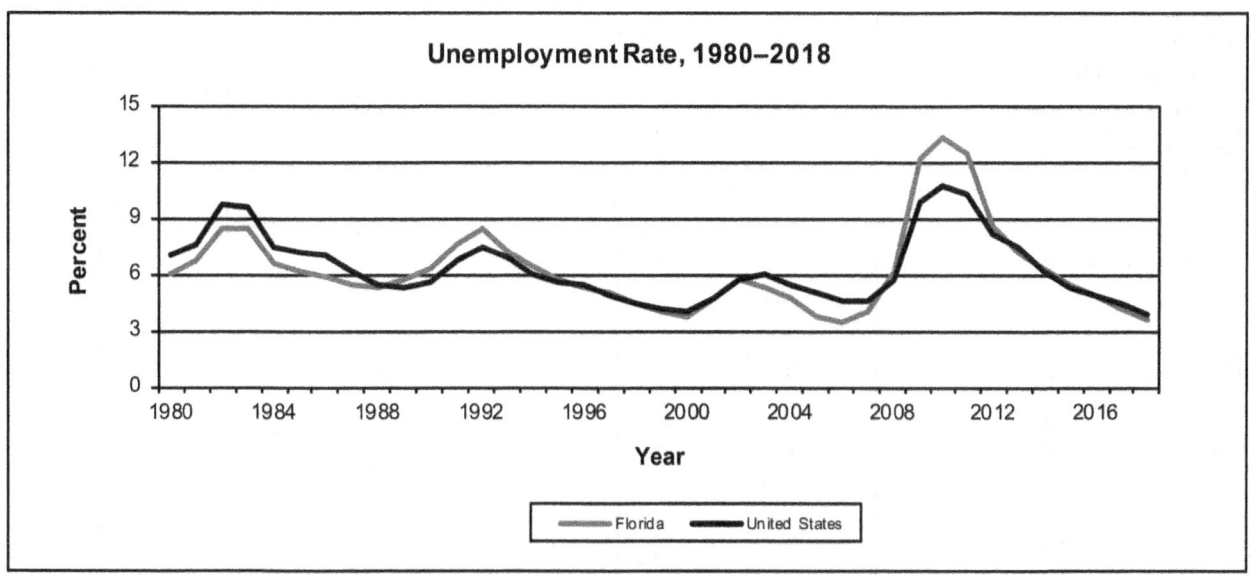

Table FL-8. Employment Status of the Civilian Noninstitutional Population Age 16 Years and Over

(Number, percent.)

Year	Civilian labor force	Civilian participation rate	Employed	Unemployed	Unemployment rate
2010..	9,212,066	61.6	8,193,659	1,018,407	11.1
2011..	9,300,542	61.0	8,371,638	928,904	10.0
2012..	9,382,993	60.6	8,588,669	794,324	8.5
2013..	9,453,747	60.2	8,770,084	683,663	7.2
2014..	9,581,083	59.9	8,979,399	601,684	6.3
2015..	9,629,632	59.0	9,104,357	525,275	5.5
2016..	9,846,000	59.1	9,373,059	472,941	4.8
2017..	10,100,266	59.6	9,680,820	419,446	4.2
2018..	10,234,770	59.4	9,869,673	365,097	3.6

Table FL-9. Employment and Average Wages by Industry

(Estimates are based on the 2012 *North American Industry Classification System* [NAICS].)

Industry	2011	2012	2013	2014	2015	2016	2017
	Number of Jobs						
Wage and Salary Employment by Industry.......................	7,601,048	7,760,916	7,935,168	8,192,310	8,472,417	8,736,178	8,917,106
Farm Wage and Salary Employment.............................	44,307	47,948	44,639	48,772	42,091	40,153	41,185
Nonfarm Wage and Salary Employment..........................	7,556,741	7,712,968	7,890,529	8,143,538	8,430,326	8,696,025	8,875,921
Private wage and salary employment..............................	6,375,012	6,547,323	6,727,155	6,985,325	7,264,806	7,518,605	7,689,525
Forestry, fishing, and related activities..........................	43,000	42,231	44,342	45,168	45,084	44,502	44,302
Mining...	3,871	3,949	3,958	4,101	4,086	4,168	4,072
Utilities...	22,433	22,656	22,301	21,994	22,482	22,870	23,027
Construction...	343,275	352,138	375,700	406,888	442,777	486,257	516,274
Manufacturing...	311,633	317,158	322,368	331,796	342,989	355,287	363,807
Durable goods manufacturing..................................	205,625	209,441	214,950	222,982	233,236	240,649	246,969
Nondurable goods manufacturing.............................	106,008	107,717	107,418	108,814	109,753	114,638	116,838
Wholesale trade	309,349	318,467	323,244	329,238	336,379	341,302	345,243
Retail trade..	963,199	988,240	1,012,294	1,048,918	1,089,637	1,109,347	1,122,391
Transportation and warehousing..................................	213,024	220,419	227,419	236,636	247,659	258,231	267,916
Information..	134,621	134,183	134,306	136,999	136,522	137,186	138,289
Finance and insurance	338,920	349,953	355,260	362,719	373,924	382,421	398,315
Real estate and rental and leasing...............................	155,343	164,673	169,643	173,664	181,370	184,489	186,498
Professional, scientific, and technical services	448,063	455,250	472,286	490,220	512,240	533,897	550,970
Management of companies and enterprises.....................	81,039	83,653	91,063	94,208	96,989	100,512	103,655
Administrative and waste services...............................	532,777	545,726	562,736	589,521	623,558	659,953	678,097
Educational services..	149,945	149,735	150,980	157,364	160,664	163,712	168,159
Health care and social assistance................................	950,667	971,872	989,336	1,012,894	1,050,710	1,089,556	1,113,358
Arts, entertainment, and recreation..............................	191,373	197,534	199,627	214,735	218,786	226,725	232,269
Accommodation and food services...............................	768,771	806,872	843,316	880,179	921,201	955,848	975,798
Other services, except public administration....................	413,709	422,614	426,976	448,083	457,749	462,342	457,085
Government and government enterprises	1,181,729	1,165,645	1,163,374	1,158,213	1,165,520	1,177,420	1,186,396
	Dollars						
Average Wages and Salaries by Industry	43,686	44,593	45,143	46,225	47,674	48,463	49,906
Average Farm Wages and Salaries	23,233	21,189	27,609	23,125	23,223	28,468	25,060
Average Nonfarm Wages and Salaries	43,806	44,738	45,242	46,363	47,796	48,555	50,021
Average private wages and salaries...............................	42,992	44,099	44,622	45,764	47,262	48,007	49,506
Forestry, fishing, and related activities..........................	23,080	24,260	24,570	25,086	26,977	28,353	29,273
Mining...	60,938	68,100	64,248	66,302	67,422	68,235	71,827
Utilities...	84,352	86,090	88,022	92,404	95,342	100,224	104,623
Construction...	42,075	42,633	43,177	44,725	46,835	48,240	50,231
Manufacturing...	54,493	55,385	56,251	57,716	59,611	59,927	61,537
Durable goods manufacturing..................................	57,537	58,609	59,406	60,813	62,234	62,727	65,002
Nondurable goods manufacturing.............................	48,587	49,118	49,938	51,370	54,036	54,050	54,214
Wholesale trade	65,048	67,187	68,366	70,252	72,746	73,188	75,809
Retail trade..	28,290	28,779	29,157	29,809	30,765	31,067	31,819
Transportation and warehousing..................................	48,123	49,244	50,619	52,104	53,956	54,211	55,791
Information..	66,554	68,861	70,725	72,998	76,092	79,632	82,763
Finance and insurance	71,150	73,596	75,465	79,152	81,777	83,081	86,374
Real estate and rental and leasing...............................	41,860	43,128	44,274	46,655	48,658	49,090	50,948
Professional, scientific, and technical services	67,045	69,493	69,649	71,547	73,655	75,571	77,110
Management of companies and enterprises.....................	95,596	106,313	101,672	104,365	107,054	106,511	114,612
Administrative and waste services...............................	34,067	34,696	34,654	35,356	36,550	37,422	38,271
Educational services..	37,706	37,574	37,951	38,711	39,170	39,757	39,045
Health care and social assistance................................	46,902	47,763	48,221	49,229	50,874	51,147	52,237
Arts, entertainment, and recreation..............................	37,240	38,376	38,147	38,860	40,840	41,769	42,900
Accommodation and food services...............................	21,689	22,384	22,984	23,595	24,264	24,726	25,245
Other services, except public administration....................	29,843	30,688	31,585	32,436	33,747	34,762	36,175
Government and government enterprises............................	48,197	48,328	48,826	49,977	51,123	52,059	53,362

Table FL-10. Employment Characteristics by Family Type

(Number, percent.)

Family type and labor force status	2015		2016		2017	
	Total	Families with own children under 18 years	Total	Families with own children under 18 years	Total	Families with own children under 18 years
All Families..	4,806,611	1,781,366	4,864,461	1,787,004	4,943,506	1,801,318
FAMILY TYPE AND LABOR FORCE STATUS						
Married-Couple Families........................	3,444,776	1,117,422	3,513,794	1,133,704	3,588,295	1,163,791
Both husband and wife in labor force............	44.3	64.9	43.8	65.0	44.1	64.5
Husband in labor force, wife not in labor force	20.2	27.7	20.1	27.4	20.6	28.0
Wife in labor force, husband not in labor force	8.4	4.9	8.3	4.7	8.1	4.6
Both husband and wife not in labor force...........	26.3	2.2	26.7	2.4	26.0	2.3
Other Families	1,361,835	663,944	1,350,667	653,300	1,355,211	637,527
Female householder, no husband present..............	73.6	75.7	73.0	75.9	72.1	73.7
In labor force............................	51.4	63.3	51.0	64.2	49.8	61.3
Not in labor force	22.2	12.4	22.0	11.6	22.3	12.3
Male householder, no wife present..............	26.4	24.3	27.0	24.1	27.9	26.3
In labor force............................	20.3	22.3	20.5	22.2	21.0	23.3
Not in labor force	6.1	2.0	6.5	2.0	6.8	3.0

Table FL-11. School Enrollment and Educational Attainment, 2017

(Number, percent.)

Item	State	U.S.
Enrollment		
Total population 3 years and over, enrolled in school	4,770,596	81,273,337
Enrolled in nursery school or preschool (percent)	6.1	6.0
Enrolled in kindergarten (percent)...	4.8	4.9
Enrolled in elementary school, grades 1-8 (percent)..	39.6	40.6
Enrolled in high school, grades 9-12 (percent)	20.8	21.1
Enrolled in college or graduate school (percent)...	28.8	27.4
Attainment		
Total population 25 years and over	15,020,177	221,250,083
Less than ninth grade (percent)	4.7	5.1
9th to 12th grade, no diploma (percent)	6.9	6.9
High school graduate, including equivalency (percent)..	28.8	27.1
Some college, no degree (percent)	19.9	20.4
Associate's degree (percent)	10.0	8.5
Bachelor's degree (percent)	18.9	19.7
Graduate or professional degree (percent)..	10.8	12.3
High school graduate or higher (percent)	88.4	88.0
Bachelor's degree or higher (percent)..	29.7	32.0

Table FL-12. Public School Characteristics and Educational Indicators

(Number, percent; data derived from National Center of Education Statistics.)

Item	State	U.S.
Public Elementary and Secondary Schools		
Number of operational school districts, 2016-17	77	18,377
Number of operational schools, 2016-17..	4,336	98,330
Percent charter schools	15.1	7.1
Total public school enrollment, 2016-17..	2,816,791	50,587,859
Percent charter school enrollment	10.1	6.0
Student-teacher ratio, Fall 2015	15.3	16.0
Expenditures per student (dollars), 2015-16..	9,176	11,841
Four-year adjusted cohort graduation rate (ACGR)[1]	82.3	84.6
Students eligible for free or reduced-price lunch (percent), 2015-16...........................	58.8	52.1
English language learners (percent), Fall 2016	10.3	9.6
Students age 3 to 21 served under IDEA, part B (percent), 2017-18	13.7	13.7

Public Schools by Type, 2016-17		Percent of state public schools
Total number of schools..	4,178	100.0
Special education	171	4.1
Vocational education	35	0.8
Alternative education	392	9.4

[1] Adjusted Cohort Graduation Rates (ACGR) differ from Averaged Freshmen Graduation Rates (AFGR).

Table FL-13. Reported Voting and Registration of the Voting-Age Population, November 2018

(Numbers in thousands, percent.)

Item	Total population	Total citizen population	Registered			Voted		
			Total registered	Percent registered (total population)	Percent registered (total citizen population)	Total voted	Percent voted (total population)	Percent voted (total citizen population)
U.S. Total	249,748	228,832	153,066	61.3	66.9	122,281	49.0	53.4
State Total......................................	16,845	15,047	9,435	56.0	62.7	7,918	47.0	52.6
Sex								
Male	8,035	7,145	4,383	54.6	61.4	3,648	45.4	51.1
Female	8,810	7,902	5,052	57.3	63.9	4,270	48.5	54.0
Race								
White alone......................................	13,425	12,154	7,798	58.1	64.2	6,579	49.0	54.1
White, non-Hispanic alone......................	9,592	9,332	6,211	64.8	66.6	5,315	55.4	57.0
Black alone......................................	2,644	2,317	1,340	50.7	57.9	1,094	41.4	47.2
Asian alone	454	330	159	35.0	48.2	134	29.4	40.5
Hispanic (of any race)	4,288	3,146	1,723	40.2	54.8	1,393	32.5	44.3
White alone or in combination	13,676	12,353	7,899	57.8	63.9	6,666	48.7	54.0
Black alone or in combination..................	2,842	2,463	1,418	49.9	57.6	1,167	41.1	47.4
Asian alone or in combination..................	458	334	159	34.8	47.7	134	29.2	40.1
Age								
18 to 24 years....................................	1,656	1,511	655	39.6	43.4	449	27.1	29.7
25 to 34 years....................................	2,561	2,128	1,160	45.3	54.5	852	33.3	40.0
35 to 44 years....................................	2,689	2,223	1,272	47.3	57.2	977	36.3	44.0
45 to 64 years....................................	5,697	5,166	3,472	60.9	67.2	2,993	52.5	57.9
65 years and over	4,241	4,018	2,877	67.8	71.6	2,647	62.4	65.9

Table FL-14. Crime

(Number, rate per 100,000. Data are derived from the FBI Uniform Crime Reports.)

Item	State			U.S.		
	2016	2017	Percent change	2016	2017	Percent change
TOTAL POPULATION[1]	20,656,589	20,984,400	1.6	323,405,935	325,719,178	0.7
VIOLENT CRIME						
Number..	88,700	85,625	-3.5	1,285,606	1,283,220	-0.2
Rate..	429.4	408.0	-5.0	397.5	394.0	-0.9
Murder and Nonnegligent Manslaughter						
Number..	1,111	1,057	-4.9	17,413	17,284	-0.7
Rate..	5.4	5.0	-6.3	5.4	5.3	-1.4
Rape[2]						
Number..	7,598	7,940	4.5	132,414	135,755	2.5
Rate..	36.8	37.8	2.9	40.9	41.7	1.8
Robbery						
Number..	20,175	18,597	-7.8	332,797	319,356	-4.0
Rate..	97.7	88.6	-9.3	102.9	98.0	-4.7
Aggravated Assault						
Number..	59,816	58,031	-3.0	802,982	810,825	1.0
Rate..	289.6	276.5	-4.5	248.3	248.9	0.3
PROPERTY CRIME						
Number..	553,812	527,220	-4.8	7,928,530	7,694,086	-3.0
Rate..	2,681.0	2,512.4	-6.3	2,451.6	2,362.2	-3.6
Burglary						
Number..	100,325	88,853	-11.4	1,516,405	1,401,840	-7.6
Rate..	485.7	423.4	-12.8	468.9	430.4	-8.2
Larceny-Theft						
Number..	410,352	395,453	-3.6	5,644,835	5,519,107	-2.2
Rate..	1,986.5	1,884.5	-5.1	1,745.4	1,694.4	-2.9
Motor Vehicle Theft						
Number..	43,135	42,914	-0.5	767,290	773,139	0.8
Rate..	208.8	204.5	-2.1	237.3	237.4	-

NOTE: Although arson data are included in the trend and clearance tables, sufficient data are not available to estimate totals for this offense. Therefore, no arson data are published in this table.
- = Zero or rounds to zero.
[1] Population figures are U.S. Census Bureau provisional estimates as of July 1, 2017.
[2] The figures shown in the rape (revised definition) column were estimated using the revised Uniform Crime Reporting (UCR) definition of rape.

Table FL-15. State Government Finances, 2017

(Dollar amounts in thousands, percent distribution.)

Item	Dollars	Percent distribution
Total Revenue	107,476,847	100.0
General revenue	84,010,368	78.2
Intergovernmental revenue	27,852,122	25.9
Taxes	40,218,365	37.4
General sales	25,346,166	23.6
Selective sales	7,993,390	7.4
License taxes	2,032,331	1.9
Individual income tax	0	-
Corporate income tax	2,383,783	2.2
Other taxes	2,462,695	2.3
Current charges	8,372,808	7.8
Miscellaneous general revenue	7,567,073	7.0
Utility revenue	24,652	-
Liquor stores revenue	0	-
Insurance trust revenue[1]	23,441,827	21.8
Total Expenditure	92,696,645	100.0
Intergovernmental expenditure	21,484,868	23.2
Direct expenditure	71,211,777	76.8
Current operation	51,805,721	55.9
Capital outlay	7,272,080	7.8
Insurance benefits and repayments	9,314,690	10.0
Assistance and subsidies	1,902,844	2.1
Interest on debt	916,442	1.0
Exhibit: Salaries and wages	9,319,466	10.1
Total Expenditure	92,696,645	100.0
General expenditure	83,041,726	89.6
Intergovernmental expenditure	21,484,868	23.2
Direct expenditure	61,556,858	66.4
General expenditure, by function:		
Education	27,071,608	29.2
Public welfare	27,111,988	29.2
Hospitals	1,210,889	1.3
Health	3,957,991	4.3
Highways	8,747,688	9.4
Police protection	577,197	0.6
Correction	2,385,256	2.6
Natural resources	1,485,972	1.6
Parks and recreation	168,872	0.2
Governmental administration	2,478,109	2.7
Interest on general debt	916,442	1.0
Other and unallocable	6,929,714	7.5
Utility expenditure	340,229	0.3
Liquor stores expenditure	0	-
Insurance trust expenditure	9,314,690	10.0
Debt at End of Fiscal Year	28,823,847	X
Cash and Security Holdings	224,703,818	X

X = Not applicable.
- = Zero or rounds to zero.
[1] Within insurance trust revenue, net earnings of state retirement systems is a calculated statistic (the item code in the data file is X08), and thus can be positive or negative. Net earnings is the sum of earnings on investments plus gains on investments minus losses on investments. The change made in 2002 for asset valuation from book to market value in accordance with Statement 34 of the Governmental Accounting Standards Board is reflected in the calculated statistics.

Table FL-16. State Government Tax Collections, 2018

(Dollars in thousands, percent.)

Item	Dollars	Percent distribution
Total Taxes	45,961,204	100.0
Property taxes	X	-
Sales and gross receipts	38,456,615	83.7
General sales and gross receipts	29,562,900	64.3
Selective sales and gross receipts	8,893,715	19.4
Alcoholic beverages	293,098	0.6
Amusements	207,460	0.5
Insurance premiums	1,084,872	2.4
Motor fuels	2,799,610	6.1
Pari-mutuels	8,352	-
Public utilities	2,387,900	5.2
Tobacco products	1,172,492	2.6
Other selective sales	939,931	2.0
Licenses	2,123,462	4.6
Alcoholic beverages	6,418	-
Amusements	16,000	-
Corporations in general	263,623	0.6
Hunting and fishing	16,629	-
Motor vehicle	1,449,604	3.2
Motor vehicle operators	165,332	0.4
Public utilities	24,424	0.1
Occupation and business, NEC	171,749	0.4
Other licenses	9,683	-
Income taxes	2,426,900	5.3
Individual income	X	-
Corporation net income	2,426,900	5.3
Other taxes	2,954,227	6.4
Death and gift	1,927	-
Documentary and stock transfer	2,916,100	6.3
Severance	36,200	0.1
Taxes, NEC	0	-

X = Not applicable.
- = Zero or rounds to zero.

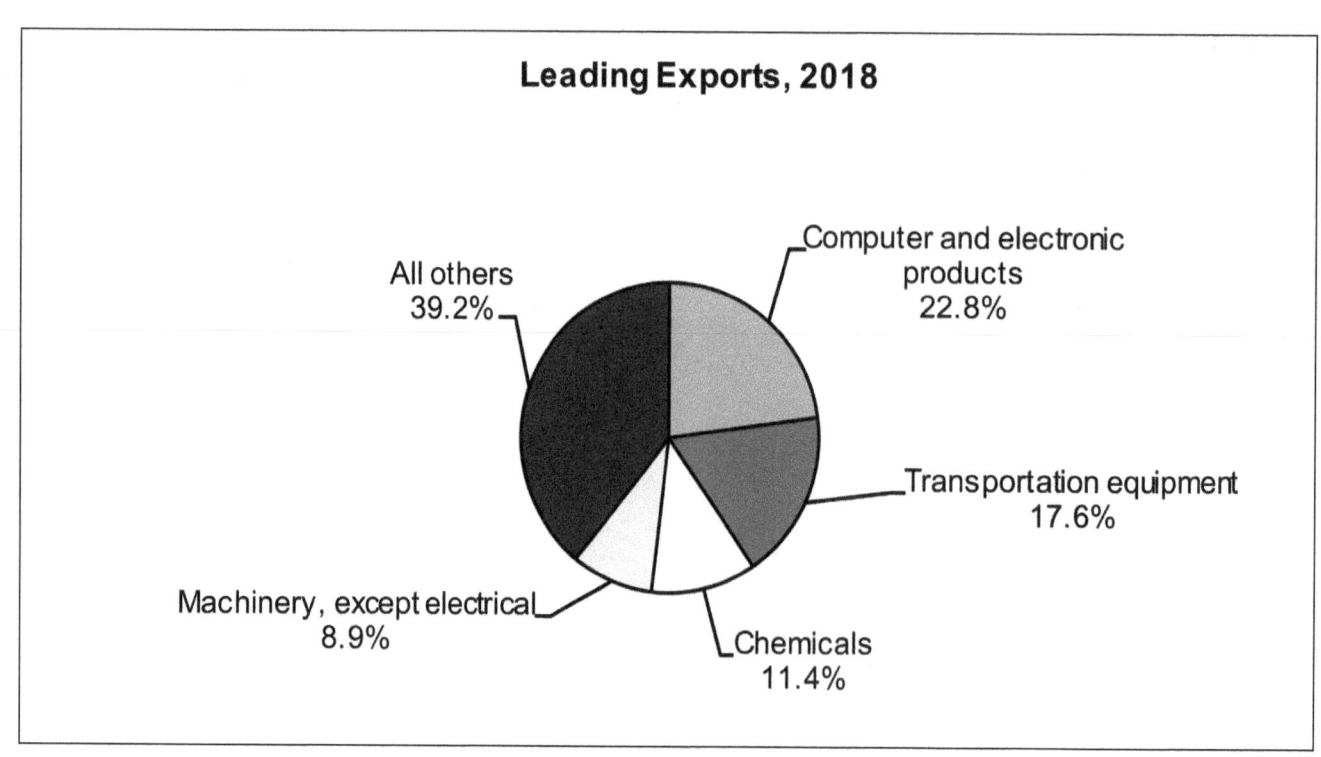

Leading Exports, 2018

- All others 39.2%
- Computer and electronic products 22.8%
- Transportation equipment 17.6%
- Chemicals 11.4%
- Machinery, except electrical 8.9%

GEORGIA

Facts and Figures

Location: Southeastern United States; bordered on the N by Tennessee and North Carolina, on the E by South Carolina and the Atlantic Ocean, on the S by Florida, and on the W by Florida and Alabama

Area: 59,425 sq. mi. (153,909 sq. km.); rank—21st

Population: 10,519,475 (2018 est.); rank—8th

Principal Cities: capital—Atlanta; largest—Atlanta

Statehood: January 2, 1788; 4th state

U.S. Congress: 2 senators, 14 representatives

State Motto: Wisdom, Justice, and Moderation

State Song: "Georgia on My Mind"

State Nicknames: The Empire State of the South; The Peach State

Abbreviations: GA; Ga.

State Symbols: flower—Cherokee rose; tree—live oak; bird—brown thrasher

At a Glance

- With an increase in population of 8.6 percent, Georgia ranked 14th among the states in growth from 2010 to 2018.

- Georgia's median household income in 2017 was $56,183, and 14.9 percent of the state's population lived below the poverty level.

- In 2017, 13.4 percent of Georgians did not have health insurance, which was the 4th highest percent among the states.

- Georgia's violent crime rate was 357.2 per 100,000 population, compared to 394.0 for the U.S. as a whole in 2017.

- The property crime rate in Georgia in 2017 was 2,860.2 per 100,000 population, a rate that ranked 13th among the states.

Table GA-1. Population by Age, Sex, Race, and Hispanic Origin

(Number, percent, except where noted.)

Sex, age, race, and Hispanic origin	2000	2010	2018 [1]	Percent change, 2010–2018
Total Population.........	8,186,453	9,687,653	10,519,475	8.6
Percent of total U.S. population	2.9	3.1	3.2	X
Sex				
Male.........	4,027,113	4,729,171	5,115,416	8.2
Female	4,159,340	4,958,482	5,404,059	9.0
Age				
Under 5 years.........	595,150	686,785	657,414	-4.3
5 to 19 years.........	1,819,620	2,094,844	2,142,032	2.3
20 to 64 years.........	4,986,408	5,873,989	6,259,620	6.6
65 years and over	785,275	1,032,035	1,460,409	41.5
Median age (years)	33.4	35.3	36.9	4.5
Race and Hispanic Origin				
One race				
White	5,327,281	6,144,931	6,360,528	3.5
Black.........	2,349,542	2,993,927	3,411,145	13.9
American Indian and Alaska Native	21,737	48,599	54,882	12.9
Asian.........	173,170	323,459	453,488	40.2
Native Hawaiian or Other Pacific Islander	4,246	10,454	12,432	18.9
Two or more races	114,188	166,283	227,000	36.5
Hispanic (of any race).........	435,227	911,863	1,026,737	12.6

X = Not applicable.
[1] Population figures for 2018 are July 1 estimates. The 2010 estimates are taken from the 2010 Census.

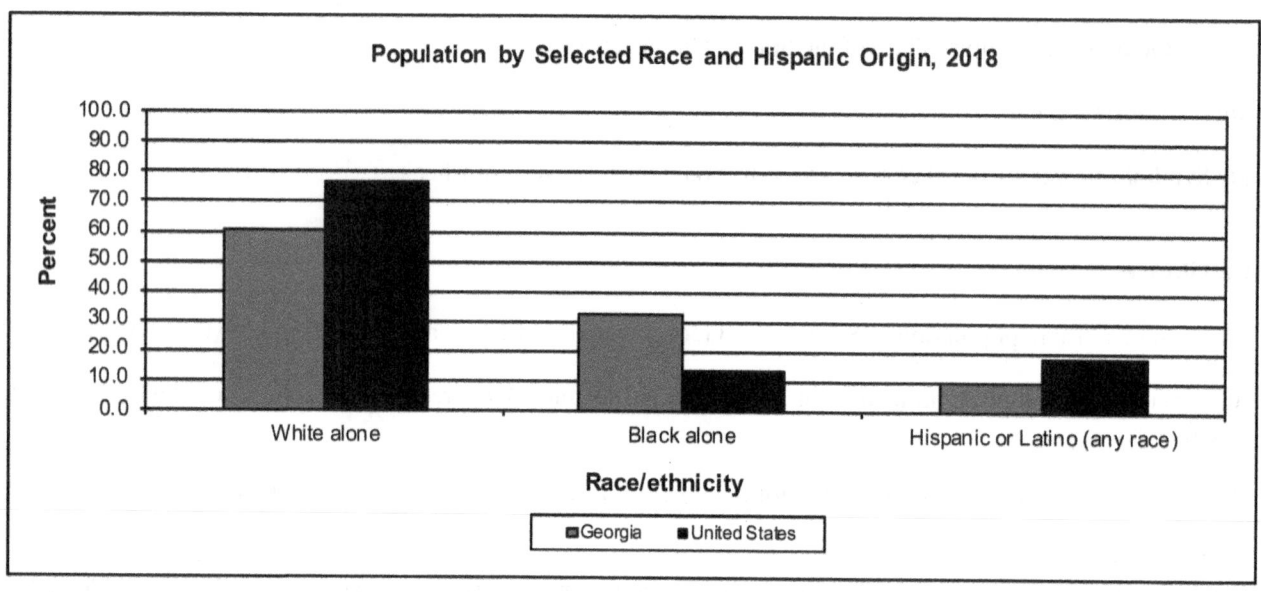

Table GA-2. Marital Status

(Number, percent distribution.)

Sex, age, race, and Hispanic origin	2000	2010	2017
Males, 15 Years and Over	3,092,736	3,683,258	4,009,958
Never married	30.4	35.4	37.2
Now married, except separated.........	56.5	50.5	48.9
Separated.........	2.0	2.1	1.8
Widowed.........	2.1	2.2	2.2
Divorced.........	9.0	9.9	9.9
Females, 15 Years and Over	3,273,889	3,954,542	4,339,766
Never married	24.4	29.7	31.8
Now married, except separated.........	51.5	46.1	44.7
Separated.........	2.7	2.9	2.6
Widowed.........	9.8	8.6	8.3
Divorced.........	11.6	12.7	12.5

Table GA-3. Households and Housing Characteristics

(Number, percent, dollars.)

Item	2000	2010	2017	Average annual percent change, 2010–2017
Total Households..	3,006,369	3,482,420	3,745,074	1.1
Family households..	2,111,647	2,385,969	2,525,783	0.8
Married-couple family..	1,548,800	1,688,896	1,788,755	0.8
Other family	562,847	697,073	737,028	0.8
Male householder, no wife present.......................	127,437	161,001	177,791	1.5
Female householder, no husband present...............	435,410	536,072	559,237	0.6
Nonfamily households	894,722	1,096,451	1,219,291	1.6
Householder living alone......................................	710,523	921,005	1,000,794	1.2
Householder not living alone.................................	184,199	175,446	218,497	3.5
Housing Characteristics				
Total housing units...	3,281,737	4,091,482	4,282,254	0.7
Occupied housing units	3,006,369	3,482,420	3,745,074	1.1
Owner occupied	2,029,154	2,304,165	2,354,922	0.3
Renter occupied	977,215	1,178,255	1,390,152	2.6
Average household size...	2.65	2.72	2.72	-
Financial Characteristics				
Median gross rent of renter-occupied housing	613	819	958	2.4
Median monthly owner costs for housing units with a mortgage	1,039	1,390	1,341	-0.5
Median value of owner-occupied housing units	111,200	156,200	173,700	1.6

Table GA-4. Migration, Origin, and Language

(Number, percent.)

Characteristic	State			U.S.		
	2016	2017	Percent change	2016	2017	Percent change
Residence 1 Year Ago						
Population 1 year and over	10,179,860	10,299,497	1.2	319,361,956	321,994,428	0.8
Same house	83.6	85.1	X	85.4	85.7	X
Different house in the U.S.	15.7	14.4	X	13.9	13.6	X
Same county	7.8	7.0	X	8.3	8.1	X
Different county	7.9	7.4	X	5.6	5.6	X
Same state	4.9	4.7	X	3.2	3.3	X
Different state	3	2.7	X	2.4	2.3	X
Abroad	0.7	0.6	X	0.7	0.7	X
Place of Birth						
Native born	9,272,059	9,363,411	1.0	279,388,170	281,193,323	0.6
Male	48.5	48.4	X	49.3	49.4	X
Female	51.5	51.6	X	50.7	50.6	X
Foreign born	1,038,312	1,065,968	2.7	43,739,345	44,525,855	1.8
Male	50.1	50.2	X	48.5	48.4	X
Female	49.9	49.8	X	51.5	51.6	X
Foreign born; naturalized U.S. citizen......................	427,092	464,394	8.7	21,238,372	21,948,732	3.3
Male	47	47.4	X	45.9	45.9	X
Female	53	52.6	X	54.1	54.1	X
Foreign born; not a U.S. citizen..............................	611,220	601,574	-1.6	22,500,973	22,577,123	0.3
Male	52.3	52.3	X	51	50.8	X
Female	47.7	47.7	X	49	49.2	X
Entered 2010 or later	20.8	22.9	X	18.6	21.3	X
Entered 2000 to 2009	32.4	31.5	X	26.7	25.7	X
Entered before 2000..	46.8	45.7	X	54.7	53.0	X
World Region of Birth, Foreign						
Foreign-born population, excluding population born at sea	1,038,312	1,065,968	2.7	43,738,901	44,525,458	1.8
Europe	8.7	9.3	X	10.9	10.8	X
Asia	30.1	31	X	30.8	31.2	X
Africa	10.2	9.3	X	4.9	5.1	X
Oceania	0.3	0.5	X	0.6	0.6	X
Latin America	49.1	48.1	X	51	50.4	X
North America	1.6	1.7	X	1.8	1.8	X
Language Spoken at Home and Ability to Speak English						
Population 5 years and over.......................................	9,655,493	9,774,156	1.2	303,328,961	305,924,019	0.9
English only	86	85.9	X	78.4	78.2	X
Language other than English..................................	14	14.1	X	21.6	21.8	X
Speaks English less than "very well".....................	5.7	5.5	X	8.6	8.5	X

NA = Not available.
X = Not applicable.
- = Zero or rounds to zero.

Table GA-5. Median Income and Poverty Status, 2017

(Number, percent, except as noted.)

Characteristic	State Number	State Percent	U.S. Number	U.S. Percent
Median Income				
Households (dollars)..	56,183	X	60,336	X
Families (dollars)	67,983	X	73,891	X
Below Poverty Level (All People)	1,517,702	14.9	42,583,651	13.4
Sex				
Male	669,833	13.7	19,004,547	12.2
Female	847,869	16.1	23,579,104	14.5
Age				
Under 18 years..	519,099	21.0	13,353,202	18.4
Related children under 18 years.........................	510,534	20.7	13,053,472	18.1
18 to 64 years..	859,783	13.6	24,648,677	12.6
65 years and over	138,820	10.1	4,581,772	9.3

X = Not applicable.

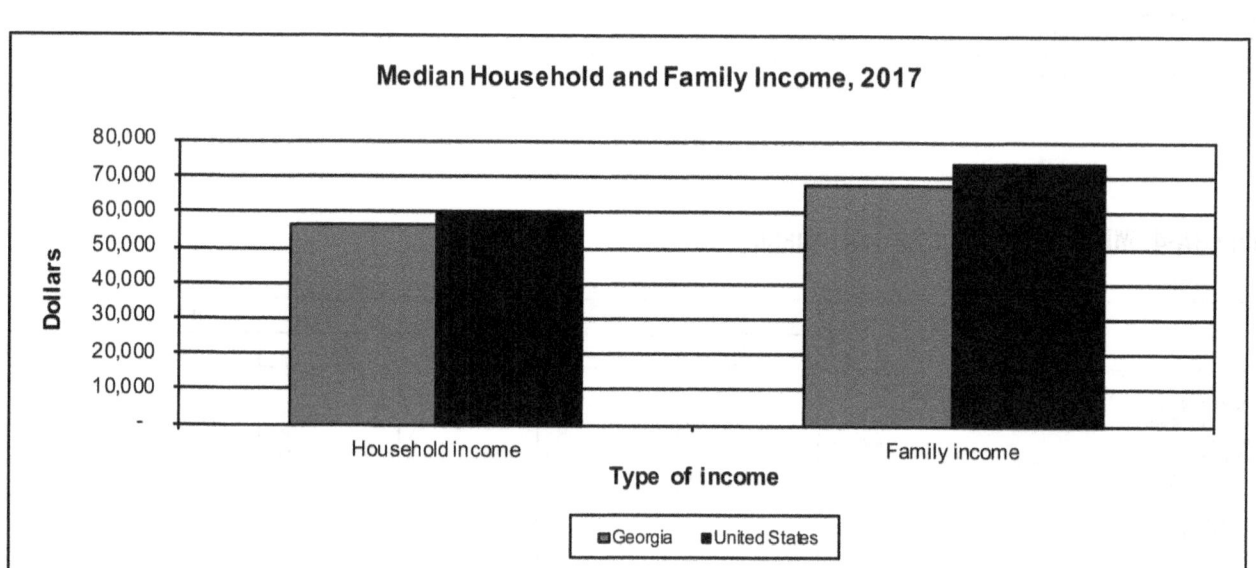

Table GA-6. Health Insurance Coverage Status for the Civilian Noninstitutionalized Population and Children Under 18 Years of Age

(Number, percent.)

Item	2009	2010	2011	2012	2013	2014	2015	2016	2017
Civilian Noninstitutionalized Population	9,594,277	9,519,836	9,619,740	9,719,411	9,800,887	9,906,878	10,024,056	10,120,788	10,241,594
Covered by Private or Public Insurance									
Number..	7,757,931	7,644,270	7,736,982	7,927,092	7,954,582	8,338,497	8,635,656	8,811,215	8,866,418
Percent..	80.9	80.3	80.4	81.6	81.2	84.2	86.1	87.1	86.6
Uninsured									
Number..	1,836,346	1,875,566	1,882,758	1,792,319	1,846,305	1,568,381	1,388,400	1,309,573	1,375,176
Percent..	19.1	19.7	19.6	18.4	18.8	15.8	13.9	12.9	13.4
Percent in the U.S. not covered..................................	15.1	15.5	15.1	14.8	14.5	11.7	9.4	8.6	8.7
Children Under 18 Years of Age[1]	2,575,689	2,492,281	2,484,715	2,492,161	2,487,079	2,488,247	2,499,334	2,506,326	2,670,877
Covered by Private or Public Insurance									
Number..	2,294,545	2,248,277	2,248,147	2,272,200	2,249,028	2,299,212	2,333,101	2,343,554	2,471,248
Percent..	89.1	90.2	90.5	91.2	90.4	92.4	93.3	93.5	92.5
Uninsured									
Number..	281,144	244,004	236,568	219,961	238,051	189,035	166,233	162,772	199,629
Percent..	10.9	9.8	9.5	8.8	9.6	7.6	6.7	6.5	7.5
Percent in the U.S. not covered..................................	8.6	8.0	7.5	7.2	7.1	6.0	4.8	4.5	5.0

[1] 2017 data is for individuals under 19 years of age.

Table GA-7. Employment Status by Demographic Group, 2018

(Numbers in thousands, percent.)

Characteristic	Civilian noninstitutional population	Civilian labor force		Employed		Unemployed	
		Number	Percent of population	Number	Percent of population	Number	Percent of population
Total..	8,117	5,125	63.1	4,927	60.7	198	3.9
Sex							
Male..	3,840	2,672	69.6	2,574	67.0	97	3.6
Female	4,278	2,453	57.3	2,352	55.0	101	4.1
Race, Sex, and Hispanic Origin							
White	5,028	3,155	62.7	3,066	61.0	89	2.8
Male...	2,464	1,740	70.6	1,692	68.7	48	2.8
Female......................................	2,564	1,415	55.2	1,375	53.6	41	2.9
Black or African American...................	2,562	1,627	63.5	1,528	59.7	98	6.0
Male...	1,137	752	66.1	705	62.0	47	6.2
Female......................................	1,425	875	61.4	823	57.8	51	5.9
Hispanic or Latino ethnicity[1]	639	456	71.4	440	68.9	16	3.4
Male...	334	276	82.5	269	80.7	6	2.2
Female......................................	305	180	59.2	171	56.1	10	5.3
Age							
16 to 19 years................................	583	182	31.2	155	26.6	27	14.8
20 to 24 years................................	676	478	70.8	443	65.5	36	7.4
25 to 34 years................................	1,424	1,162	81.6	1,114	78.3	47	4.1
35 to 44 years................................	1,335	1,107	82.9	1,077	80.6	30	2.7
45 to 54 years................................	1,423	1,148	80.6	1,118	78.6	29	2.6
55 to 64 years................................	1,254	783	62.4	763	60.8	20	2.6
65 years and over	1,423	266	18.7	258	18.1	8	3.1

NOTE: Data in Table 7 are from the Current Population Survey (CPS) and do not match the estimates in Table 8. See notes and definitions for further information.
[1] May be of any race.

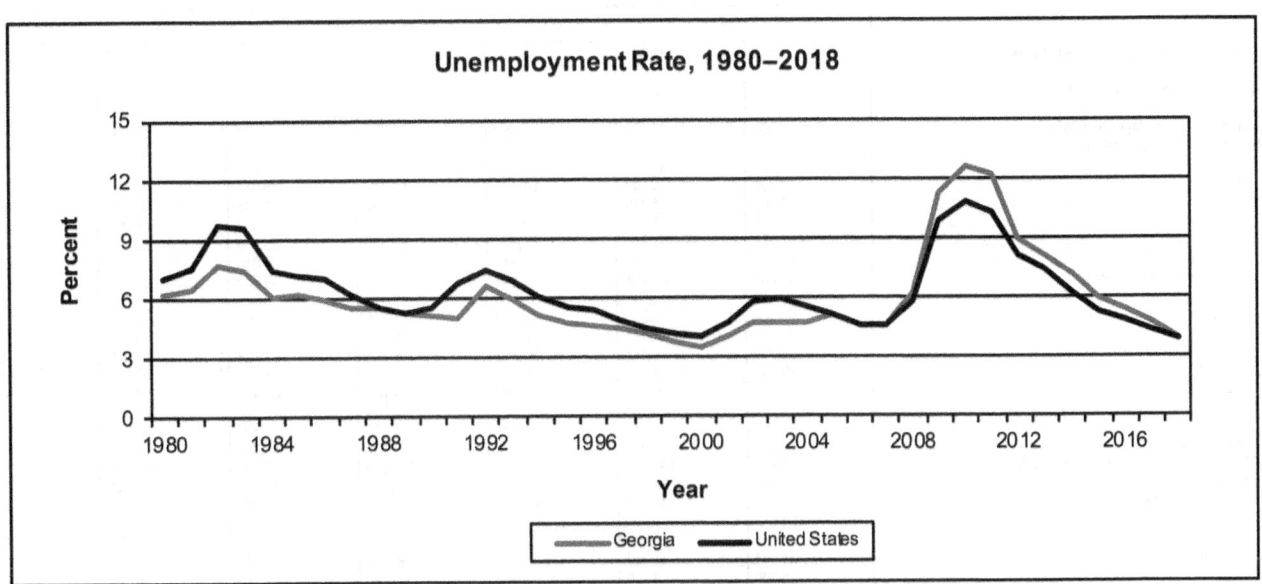

Table GA-8. Employment Status of the Civilian Noninstitutional Population Age 16 Years and Over

(Number, percent.)

Year	Civilian labor force	Civilian participation rate	Employed	Unemployed	Unemployment rate
2010..	4,696,676	64.1	4,202,052	494,624	10.5
2011..	4,748,754	64.3	4,263,305	485,449	10.2
2012..	4,787,367	64.0	4,348,083	439,284	9.2
2013..	4,756,157	62.9	4,366,374	389,783	8.2
2014..	4,752,639	62.0	4,416,145	336,494	7.1
2015..	4,788,858	61.6	4,503,150	285,708	6.0
2016..	4,926,945	62.4	4,662,849	264,096	5.4
2017..	5,061,399	63.2	4,821,622	239,777	4.7
2018..	5,107,656	63.1	4,906,411	201,245	3.9

Table GA-9. Employment and Average Wages by Industry

(Estimates are based on the 2012 *North American Industry Classification System* [NAICS].)

Industry	2011	2012	2013	2014	2015	2016	2017
	Number of Jobs						
Wage and Salary Employment by Industry...............	4,066,303	4,123,085	4,199,911	4,319,374	4,438,480	4,551,906	4,641,076
Farm Wage and Salary Employment...............	14,838	16,206	15,251	16,194	15,830	19,165	22,342
Nonfarm Wage and Salary Employment...............	4,051,465	4,106,879	4,184,660	4,303,180	4,422,650	4,532,741	4,618,734
Private wage and salary employment...............	3,267,962	3,328,951	3,413,979	3,538,369	3,655,461	3,762,412	3,842,545
Forestry, fishing, and related activities...............	14,568	14,627	15,075	15,296	15,945	16,024	15,497
Mining...............	4,805	4,668	4,728	4,851	4,839	5,056	5,175
Utilities...............	19,997	19,852	19,862	19,784	20,081	20,117	19,628
Construction...............	149,821	145,455	149,968	160,672	170,197	181,116	187,242
Manufacturing...............	351,589	355,136	358,221	367,979	377,861	388,287	398,346
Durable goods manufacturing...............	161,856	167,070	171,753	177,266	182,689	187,999	193,741
Nondurable goods manufacturing...............	189,733	188,066	186,468	190,713	195,172	200,288	204,605
Wholesale trade...............	198,155	202,263	205,696	211,049	218,267	220,140	221,978
Retail trade...............	445,228	448,450	456,754	470,363	487,904	495,594	500,521
Transportation and warehousing...............	165,404	168,952	170,113	177,721	186,180	195,626	204,878
Information...............	98,723	99,994	102,998	107,159	106,459	111,825	116,656
Finance and insurance...............	158,842	163,235	166,267	171,889	175,162	178,824	182,621
Real estate and rental and leasing...............	57,359	57,495	58,430	60,375	63,838	65,293	67,025
Professional, scientific, and technical services...............	225,501	233,847	240,337	253,845	262,918	263,526	272,074
Management of companies and enterprises...............	54,025	57,375	59,654	62,511	66,017	68,431	68,370
Administrative and waste services...............	268,045	275,132	290,869	306,243	314,679	326,336	334,688
Educational services...............	80,358	80,907	82,140	83,138	83,652	86,476	88,034
Health care and social assistance...............	406,881	416,605	429,181	436,674	452,427	470,611	478,321
Arts, entertainment, and recreation...............	40,485	41,590	43,002	45,308	47,015	50,133	52,343
Accommodation and food services...............	343,391	354,749	370,739	386,845	402,836	418,930	428,991
Other services, except public administration...............	184,785	188,619	189,945	196,667	199,184	200,067	200,157
Government and government enterprises...............	783,503	777,928	770,681	764,811	767,189	770,329	776,189
	Dollars						
Average Wages and Salaries by Industry...............	46,136	47,376	47,794	49,111	50,474	51,557	53,035
Average Farm Wages and Salaries...............	18,357	26,128	20,665	23,633	22,913	19,254	14,500
Average Nonfarm Wages and Salaries...............	46,237	47,460	47,892	49,207	50,572	51,694	53,221
Average private wages and salaries...............	46,730	48,217	48,777	50,085	51,472	52,661	54,193
Forestry, fishing, and related activities...............	31,566	32,708	33,463	34,282	35,229	37,054	37,234
Mining...............	57,388	59,302	61,195	63,247	66,017	70,118	71,195
Utilities...............	84,500	84,893	85,496	86,958	92,943	98,948	100,514
Construction...............	47,173	48,781	49,807	51,770	53,933	56,808	59,240
Manufacturing...............	53,749	54,916	55,955	57,070	57,906	58,598	59,861
Durable goods manufacturing...............	57,132	57,236	58,519	59,990	60,915	61,134	62,112
Nondurable goods manufacturing...............	50,863	52,855	53,593	54,356	55,089	56,217	57,729
Wholesale trade...............	69,927	71,359	72,490	73,984	75,963	77,316	78,791
Retail trade...............	27,365	27,823	28,274	28,843	30,268	30,699	31,407
Transportation and warehousing...............	52,796	54,252	56,416	58,889	59,733	62,536	62,881
Information...............	79,932	85,033	85,827	89,003	88,600	92,509	98,349
Finance and insurance...............	76,803	79,979	81,700	84,165	87,955	89,532	93,267
Real estate and rental and leasing...............	48,994	51,103	51,897	53,684	55,099	57,553	58,964
Professional, scientific, and technical services...............	74,502	77,932	77,425	79,297	82,387	85,929	86,474
Management of companies and enterprises...............	94,492	100,310	99,236	106,149	110,283	107,215	115,838
Administrative and waste services...............	34,976	35,597	35,734	36,367	37,775	38,479	39,730
Educational services...............	41,384	42,628	43,326	44,515	45,027	45,784	46,431
Health care and social assistance...............	45,731	47,025	47,593	48,411	49,960	50,823	51,945
Arts, entertainment, and recreation...............	35,654	34,980	35,605	36,602	36,978	36,253	38,858
Accommodation and food services...............	18,880	19,516	19,682	20,197	19,876	20,332	21,041
Other services, except public administration...............	29,814	30,279	31,088	31,744	33,016	34,093	35,444
Government and government enterprises...............	44,181	44,220	43,974	45,143	46,287	46,969	48,411

Table GA-10. Employment Characteristics by Family Type

(Number, percent.)

Family type and labor force status	2015		2016		2017	
	Total	Families with own children under 18 years	Total	Families with own children under 18 years	Total	Families with own children under 18 years
All Families...............	2,466,415	1,097,585	2,479,003	1,103,858	2,525,783	1,104,801
FAMILY TYPE AND LABOR FORCE STATUS						
Married-Couple Families...........................	1,750,409	714,312	1,748,096	716,617	1,788,755	725,048
Both husband and wife in labor force.....................	50.3	63.8	50.8	65.6	50.6	65.3
Husband in labor force, wife not in labor force	24.0	30.3	23.6	28.6	23.2	29.0
Wife in labor force, husband not in labor force	7.9	3.9	7.9	4.0	7.9	3.7
Both husband and wife not in labor force..................	17.3	1.7	17.0	1.4	17.4	1.5
Other Families	716,006	383,273	730,907	387,241	737,028	379,753
Female householder, no husband present.....................	76.6	78.6	76.1	78.8	75.9	80.5
In labor force.............................	53.6	65.7	53.8	66.8	53.4	68.0
Not in labor force	23.0	12.8	22.3	12.0	22.5	12.4
Male householder, no wife present...........................	23.4	21.4	23.9	21.2	24.1	19.5
In labor force.............................	17.7	18.8	18.0	19.2	18.8	18.0
Not in labor force	5.7	2.6	6.0	2.0	5.3	1.6

Table GA-11. School Enrollment and Educational Attainment, 2017

(Number, percent.)

Item	State	U.S.
Enrollment		
Total population 3 years and over, enrolled in school	2,748,599	81,273,337
Enrolled in nursery school or preschool (percent)	6.4	6.0
Enrolled in kindergarten (percent).........................	4.9	4.9
Enrolled in elementary school, grades 1-8 (percent)	41.8	40.6
Enrolled in high school, grades 9-12 (percent)	21.7	21.1
Enrolled in college or graduate school (percent)	25.2	27.4
Attainment		
Total population 25 years and over	6,896,026	221,250,083
Less than ninth grade (percent)	4.5	5.1
9th to 12th grade, no diploma (percent)	8.4	6.9
High school graduate, including equivalency (percent)	28.1	27.1
Some college, no degree (percent)	20.2	20.4
Associate's degree (percent)...............................	7.8	8.5
Bachelor's degree (percent)	19.0	19.7
Graduate or professional degree (percent)..................	11.9	12.3
High school graduate or higher (percent)	87.0	88.0
Bachelor's degree or higher (percent)......................	30.9	32.0

Table GA-12. Public School Characteristics and Educational Indicators

(Number, percent; data derived from National Center of Education Statistics.)

Item	State	U.S.
Public Elementary and Secondary Schools		
Number of operational school districts, 2016-17...............	226	18,377
Number of operational schools, 2016-17......................	2,300	98,330
Percent charter schools	3.7	7.1
Total public school enrollment, 2016-17.....................	1,764,346	50,587,859
Percent charter school enrollment	3.8	6.0
Student-teacher ratio, Fall 2015	15.5	16.0
Expenditures per student (dollars), 2015-16.................	9,835	11,841
Four-year adjusted cohort graduation rate (ACGR)[1]	80.6	84.6
Students eligible for free or reduced-price lunch (percent), 2015-16...	62.4	52.1
English language learners (percent), Fall 2016	6.5	9.6
Students age 3 to 21 served under IDEA, part B (percent), 2017-18 ...	12.1	13.7

Public Schools by Type, 2016-17		Percent of state public schools
Total number of schools....................................	2,300	100.0
Special education	19	0.8
Vocational education	0	-
Alternative education	41	1.8

[1] Adjusted Cohort Graduation Rates (ACGR) differ from Averaged Freshmen Graduation Rates (AFGR).
- = Zero or rounds to zero.

Table GA-13. Reported Voting and Registration of the Voting-Age Population, November 2018

(Numbers in thousands, percent.)

Item	Total population	Total citizen population	Registered			Voted		
			Total registered	Percent registered (total population)	Percent registered (total citizen population)	Total voted	Percent voted (total population)	Percent voted (total citizen population)
U.S. Total	249,748	228,832	153,066	61.3	66.9	122,281	49.0	53.4
State Total.................................	7,850	7,311	4,840	61.7	66.2	4,084	52.0	55.9
Sex								
Male	3,700	3,417	2,189	59.2	64.0	1,814	49.0	53.1
Female	4,150	3,893	2,651	63.9	68.1	2,270	54.7	58.3
Race								
White alone..............................	4,949	4,686	3,093	62.5	66.0	2,581	52.2	55.1
White, non-Hispanic alone	4,491	4,454	2,973	66.2	66.8	2,496	55.6	56.1
Black alone..............................	2,439	2,305	1,577	64.7	68.4	1,374	56.3	59.6
Asian alone..............................	318	191	108	33.9	56.4	84	26.3	43.8
Hispanic (of any race)................	525	264	135	25.7	51.2	101	19.2	38.2
White alone or in combination	5,043	4,780	3,135	62.2	65.6	2,609	51.7	54.6
Black alone or in combination	2,495	2,361	1,600	64.1	67.8	1,382	55.4	58.5
Asian alone or in combination.............	327	200	108	33.0	53.9	84	25.6	41.9
Age								
18 to 24 years...........................	1,037	978	516	49.8	52.8	359	34.6	36.7
25 to 34 years...........................	1,322	1,232	746	56.4	60.5	576	43.6	46.8
35 to 44 years...........................	1,357	1,207	801	59.0	66.3	685	50.5	56.7
45 to 64 years...........................	2,589	2,398	1,694	65.4	70.6	1,489	57.5	62.1
65 years and over	1,545	1,496	1,084	70.2	72.5	976	63.2	65.2

Table GA-14. Crime

(Number, rate per 100,000. Data are derived from the FBI Uniform Crime Reports.)

Item	State			U.S.		
	2016	2017	Percent change	2016	2017	Percent change
TOTAL POPULATION[1]	10,313,620	10,429,379	1.1	323,405,935	325,719,178	0.7
VIOLENT CRIME						
Number..............	40,268	37,258	-7.5	1,285,606	1,283,220	-0.2
Rate	390.4	357.2	-8.5	397.5	394.0	-0.9
Murder and Nonnegligent Manslaughter						
Number..............	682	703	3.1	17,413	17,284	-0.7
Rate	6.6	6.7	1.9	5.4	5.3	-1.4
Rape[2]						
Number..............	3,381	2,718	-19.6	132,414	135,755	2.5
Rate	32.8	26.1	-20.5	40.9	41.7	1.8
Robbery						
Number..............	12,114	10,044	-17.1	332,797	319,356	-4.0
Rate	117.5	96.3	-18.0	102.9	98.0	-4.7
Aggravated Assault						
Number..............	24,091	23,793	-1.2	802,982	810,825	1.0
Rate	233.6	228.1	-2.3	248.3	248.9	0.3
PROPERTY CRIME						
Number..............	307,305	298,298	-2.9	7,928,530	7,694,086	-3.0
Rate	2,979.6	2,860.2	-4.0	2,451.6	2,362.2	-3.6
Burglary						
Number..............	62,715	55,374	-11.7	1,516,405	1,401,840	-7.6
Rate	608.1	530.9	-12.7	468.9	430.4	-8.2
Larceny-Theft						
Number..............	218,127	216,661	-0.7	5,644,835	5,519,107	-2.2
Rate	2,114.9	2,077.4	-1.8	1,745.4	1,694.4	-2.9
Motor Vehicle Theft						
Number..............	26,463	26,263	-0.8	767,290	773,139	0.8
Rate	256.6	251.8	-1.9	237.3	237.4	-

NOTE: Although arson data are included in the trend and clearance tables, sufficient data are not available to estimate totals for this offense. Therefore, no arson data are published in this table.
- = Zero or rounds to zero.
[1] Population figures are U.S. Census Bureau provisional estimates as of July 1, 2017.
[2] The figures shown in the rape (revised definition) column were estimated using the revised Uniform Crime Reporting (UCR) definition of rape.

Table GA-15. State Government Finances, 2017

(Dollar amounts in thousands, percent distribution.)

Item	Dollars	Percent distribution
Total Revenue	56,851,799	100.0
General revenue	44,066,051	77.5
Intergovernmental revenue	15,183,797	26.7
Taxes	22,419,440	39.4
General sales	5,729,916	10.1
Selective sales	3,078,034	5.4
License taxes	672,897	1.2
Individual income tax	10,977,693	19.3
Corporate income tax	971,898	1.7
Other taxes	989,002	1.7
Current charges	3,732,054	6.6
Miscellaneous general revenue	2,730,760	4.8
Utility revenue	9,949	-
Liquor stores revenue	0	-
Insurance trust revenue[1]	12,775,799	22.5
Total Expenditure	49,539,792	100.0
Intergovernmental expenditure	12,325,151	24.9
Direct expenditure	37,214,641	75.1
Current operation	25,548,965	51.6
Capital outlay	3,272,796	6.6
Insurance benefits and repayments	6,543,985	13.2
Assistance and subsidies	1,256,042	2.5
Interest on debt	592,853	1.2
Exhibit: Salaries and wages	6,680,415	13.5
Total Expenditure	49,539,792	100.0
General expenditure	42,923,904	86.6
Intergovernmental expenditure	12,325,151	24.9
Direct expenditure	30,598,753	61.8
General expenditure, by function:		
Education	18,962,098	38.3
Public welfare	12,475,750	25.2
Hospitals	1,360,471	2.7
Health	1,487,054	3.0
Highways	2,969,100	6.0
Police protection	516,693	1.0
Correction	1,326,803	2.7
Natural resources	539,800	1.1
Parks and recreation	263,359	0.5
Governmental administration	927,268	1.9
Interest on general debt	592,853	1.2
Other and unallocable	1,502,655	3.0
Utility expenditure	71,903	0.1
Liquor stores expenditure	0	-
Insurance trust expenditure	6,543,985	13.2
Debt at End of Fiscal Year	13,050,862	X
Cash and Security Holdings	101,104,433	X

X = Not applicable.
- = Zero or rounds to zero.
[1] Within insurance trust revenue, net earnings of state retirement systems is a calculated statistic (the item code in the data file is X08), and thus can be positive or negative. Net earnings is the sum of earnings on investments plus gains on investments minus losses on investments. The change made in 2002 for asset valuation from book to market value in accordance with Statement 34 of the Governmental Accounting Standards Board is reflected in the calculated statistics.

Table GA-16. State Government Tax Collections, 2018

(Dollars in thousands, percent.)

Item	Dollars	Percent distribution
Total Taxes	23,602,510	100.0
Property taxes	927,590	3.9
Sales and gross receipts	9,132,965	38.7
General sales and gross receipts	5,938,448	25.2
Selective sales and gross receipts	3,194,517	13.5
Alcoholic beverages	195,696	0.8
Amusements	X	-
Insurance premiums	505,054	2.1
Motor fuels	1,801,798	7.6
Pari-mutuels	X	-
Public utilities	X	-
Tobacco products	224,910	1.0
Other selective sales	467,059	2.0
Licenses	719,422	3.0
Alcoholic beverages	4,103	-
Amusements	X	-
Corporations in general	59,608	0.3
Hunting and fishing	35,418	0.2
Motor vehicle	395,140	1.7
Motor vehicle operators	114,915	0.5
Public utilities	X	-
Occupation and business, NEC	81,296	0.3
Other licenses	28,942	0.1
Income taxes	12,648,079	53.6
Individual income	11,643,781	49.3
Corporation net income	1,004,298	4.3
Other taxes	174,454	0.7
Death and gift	0	-
Documentary and stock transfer	0	-
Severance	X	-
Taxes, NEC	174,454	0.7

X = Not applicable.
- = Zero or rounds to zero.

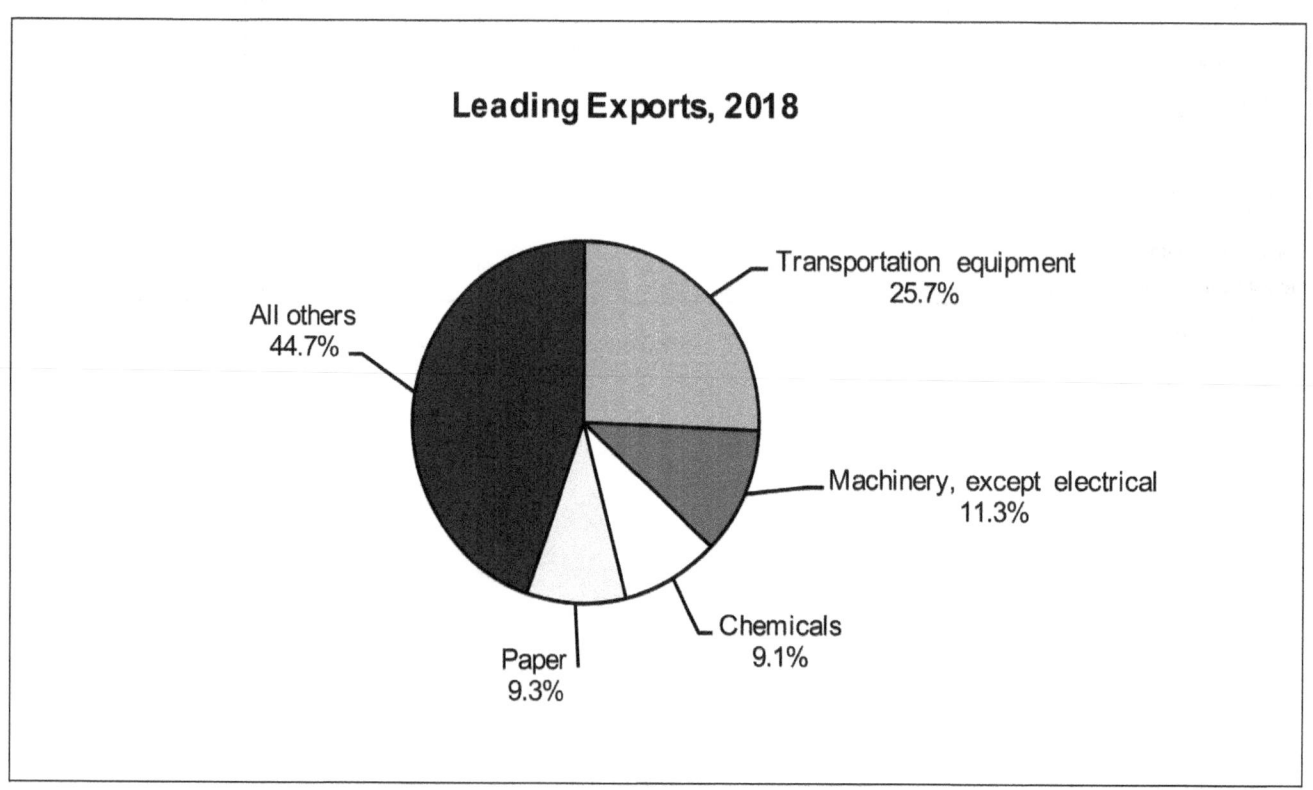

Leading Exports, 2018

Transportation equipment 25.7%

All others 44.7%

Machinery, except electrical 11.3%

Chemicals 9.1%

Paper 9.3%

HAWAII

Location: North Pacific Ocean

Area: 10,931 sq. mi. (28,311 sq. km.); rank—43rd

Population: 1,420,491 (2018 est.); rank—40th

Principal Cities: capital—Honolulu; largest—Honolulu

Statehood: August 21, 1959; 50th state

U.S. Congress: 2 senators, 2 representatives

State Motto: *Ua mau ke ea o ka'ina i ka pono* ("The life of the land is perpetuated in righteousness")

State Song: "Hawai'i Pono' (Hawaii's Own)"

State Nickname: The Aloha State

Abbreviations: HI

State Symbols: flower—native yellow hibiscus; tree—kukui (candlenut tree); bird—nene (Hawaiian goose)

At a Glance

- With an increase in population of 4.4 percent, Hawaii ranked 26th among the states in growth from 2010 to 2018.

- In 2017, 3.8 percent of Hawaiians did not have health insurance, compared to 8.7 percent of the total U.S. population, a rate that was the 2nd lowest in the country.

- Hawaii had the 15th highest property crime rate in the country in 2017, with 2,829.5 incidents per 100,000 population.

- Hawaii had the highest proportion of state government employees to total residents in 2018, with 52.8 state and local employees per 1,000 residents, compared to the national average of 50.9 employees per 1,000 residents.

- Hawaii had the largest percent of Asian Alone residents in 2018, with 37.6 percent of its residents self-identifying as Asian.

Table HI-1. Population by Age, Sex, Race, and Hispanic Origin

(Number, percent, except where noted.)

Sex, age, race, and Hispanic origin	2000	2010	2018 [1]	Percent change, 2010–2018
Total Population...	1,211,537	1,360,301	1,420,491	4.4
Percent of total U.S. population	0.4	0.4	0.4	X
Sex				
Male...	563,891	681,243	711,002	4.4
Female...	544,338	679,058	709,489	4.5
Age				
Under 5 years....................................	78,163	87,407	87,704	0.3
5 to 19 years.....................................	249,088	250,894	246,002	-1.9
20 to 64 years....................................	723,685	826,868	825,818	-0.1
65 years and over................................	160,601	195,138	260,967	33.7
Median age (years)	36.2	38.6	39.2	1.6
Race and Hispanic Origin				
One race				
White	294,102	349,051	363,549	4.2
Black...	22,003	22,473	31,138	38.6
American Indian and Alaska Native	3,535	4,960	5,629	13.5
Asian...	503,868	531,633	534,651	0.6
Native Hawaiian or Other Pacific Islander	113,539	138,292	144,806	4.7
Two or more races	259,343	313,892	340,718	8.5
Hispanic (of any race)............................	87,699	133,342	151,357	13.5

X = Not applicable.
[1] Population figures for 2018 are July 1 estimates. The 2010 estimates are taken from the 2010 Census.

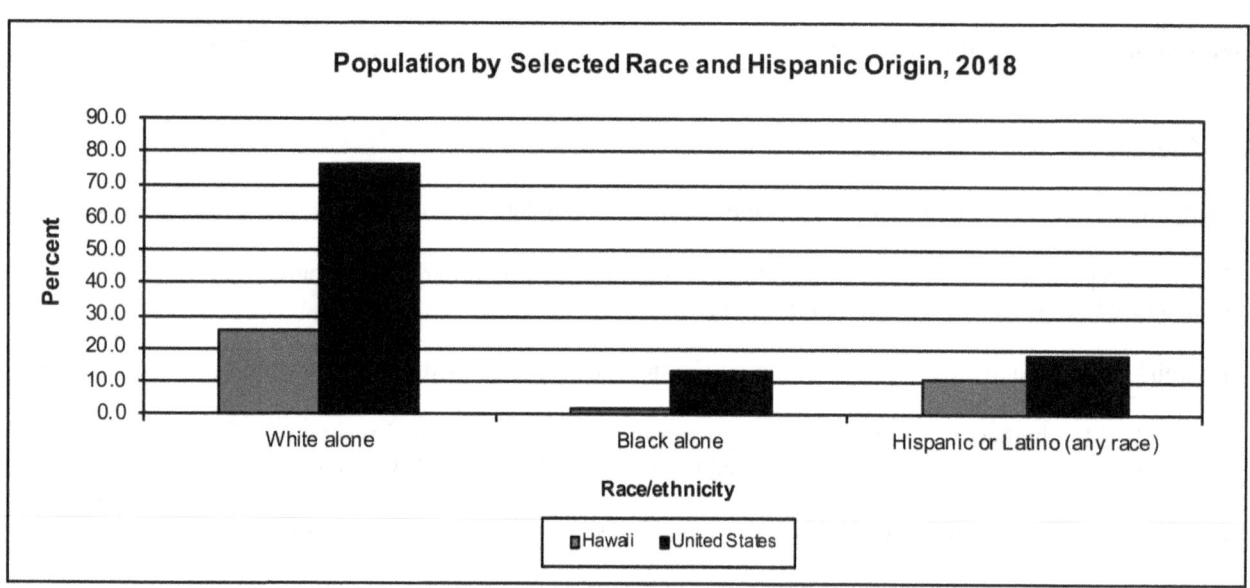

Table HI-2. Marital Status

(Number, percent distribution.)

Sex, age, race, and Hispanic origin	2000	2010	2017
Males, 15 Years and Over............................	481,768	554,154	582,993
Never married.....................................	34.6	37.8	38.5
Now married, except separated........................	53.7	49.1	49.7
Separated...	1.4	1.2	1.0
Widowed...	2.2	2.7	2.5
Divorced...	8.1	9.2	8.3
Females, 15 Years and Over..........................	484,107	556,915	584,827
Never married.....................................	25.9	28.7	28.7
Now married, except separated........................	52.5	48.5	49.0
Separated...	1.7	1.8	1.3
Widowed...	9.8	10.1	10.1
Divorced...	10.0	11.0	11.0

Table HI-3. Households and Housing Characteristics

(Number, percent, dollars.)

Item	2000	2010	2017	Average annual percent change, 2010–2017
Total Households...	403,240	445,812	458,078	0.4
Family households	287,068	303,075	320,336	0.8
Married-couple family	216,077	224,402	233,373	0.6
Other family	70,991	78,673	86,963	1.5
Male householder, no wife present	21,068	24,247	28,521	2.5
Female householder, no husband present	49,923	54,426	58,442	1.1
Nonfamily households	116,172	142,737	137,742	-0.5
Householder living alone	88,153	108,872	111,773	0.4
Householder not living alone	28,019	33,865	25,969	-3.3
Housing Characteristics				
Total housing units...	460,542	519,992	542,955	0.6
Occupied housing units	403,240	445,812	458,078	0.4
Owner occupied	227,888	258,533	268,078	0.5
Renter occupied	175,352	187,279	190,000	0.2
Average household size...	2.92	2.96	3.02	0.3
Financial Characteristics				
Median gross rent of renter-occupied housing	779	1,291	1,573	3.1
Median monthly owner costs for housing units with a mortgage	1,636	2,240	2,337	0.6
Median value of owner-occupied housing units	272,700	525,400	617,400	2.5

Table HI-4. Migration, Origin, and Language

(Number, percent.)

Characteristic	State 2016	State 2017	State Percent change	U.S. 2016	U.S. 2017	U.S. Percent change
Residence 1 Year Ago						
Population 1 year and over	1,410,258	1,410,750	-	319,361,956	321,994,428	0.8
Same house	86.3	87.3	X	85.4	85.7	X
Different house in the U.S.	12.4	11.5	X	13.9	13.6	X
Same county	7.8	7.7	X	8.3	8.1	X
Different county	4.6	3.8	X	5.6	5.6	X
Same state	0.6	0.5	X	3.2	3.3	X
Different state	4.1	3.3	X	2.4	2.3	X
Abroad	1.2	1.2	X	0.7	0.7	X
Place of Birth						
Native born	1,166,072	1,161,973	-0.4	279,388,170	281,193,323	0.6
Male	52.3	52.3	X	49.3	49.4	X
Female	47.7	47.7	X	50.7	50.6	X
Foreign born	262,485	265,565	1.2	43,739,345	44,525,855	1.8
Male	41.4	41.1	X	48.5	48.4	X
Female	58.6	58.9	X	51.5	51.6	X
Foreign born; naturalized U.S. citizen....................	149,397	161,063	7.8	21,238,372	21,948,732	3.3
Male	41.8	40.6	X	45.9	45.9	X
Female	58.2	59.4	X	54.1	54.1	X
Foreign born; not a U.S. citizen...........................	113,088	104,502	-7.6	22,500,973	22,577,123	0.3
Male	40.9	41.8	X	51	50.8	X
Female	59.1	58.2	X	49	49.2	X
Entered 2010 or later	18.6	19.7	X	18.6	21.3	X
Entered 2000 to 2009	22.9	20.6	X	26.7	25.7	X
Entered before 2000...	58.5	59.7	X	54.7	53.0	X
World Region of Birth, Foreign						
Foreign-born population, excluding population born at sea	262,485	265,565	1.2	43,738,901	44,525,458	1.8
Europe	3.7	4.2	X	10.9	10.8	X
Asia	78.8	80	X	30.8	31.2	X
Africa	0.4	0.6	X	4.9	5.1	X
Oceania	10.9	8.6	X	0.6	0.6	X
Latin America	4.6	4.5	X	51	50.4	X
North America	1.7	2.1	X	1.8	1.8	X
Language Spoken at Home and Ability to Speak English						
Population 5 years and over...................................	1,337,835	1,337,965	-	303,328,961	305,924,019	0.9
English only	73.5	74.2	X	78.4	78.2	X
Language other than English................................	26.5	25.8	X	21.6	21.8	X
Speaks English less than "very well"....................	12.2	11.4	X	8.6	8.5	X

NA = Not available.
X = Not applicable.
- = Zero or rounds to zero.

Table HI-5. Median Income and Poverty Status, 2017

(Number, percent, except as noted.)

Characteristic	State		U.S.	
	Number	Percent	Number	Percent
Median Income				
Households (dollars)...	77,765	X	60,336	X
Families (dollars)	91,460	X	73,891	X
Below Poverty Level (All People)	132,549	9.5	42,583,651	13.4
Sex				
Male	59,326	8.6	19,004,547	12.2
Female	73,223	10.5	23,579,104	14.5
Age				
Under 18 years..	34,441	11.5	13,353,202	18.4
Related children under 18 years..............................	32,754	11.0	13,053,472	18.1
18 to 64 years...	75,032	8.9	24,648,677	12.6
65 years and over	23,076	9.3	4,581,772	9.3

X = Not applicable.

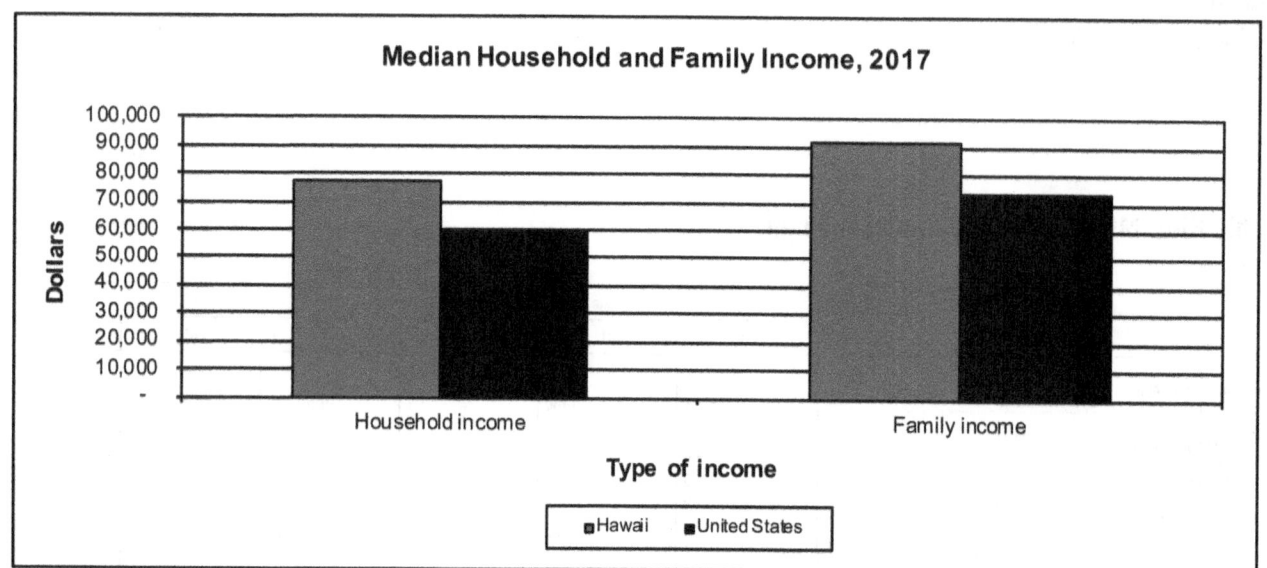

Table HI-6. Health Insurance Coverage Status for the Civilian Noninstitutionalized Population and Children Under 18 Years of Age

(Number, percent.)

Item	2009	2010	2011	2012	2013	2014	2015	2016	2017
Civilian Noninstitutionalized Population	1,231,549	1,315,677	1,326,065	1,341,708	1,345,168	1,367,770	1,375,062	1,378,730	1,373,202
Covered by Private or Public Insurance									
Number..	1,145,658	1,211,913	1,231,666	1,249,370	1,254,413	1,295,659	1,320,531	1,330,057	1,320,375
Percent..	93.0	92.1	92.9	93.1	93.3	94.7	96.0	96.5	96.2
Uninsured									
Number..	85,891	103,764	94,399	92,338	90,755	72,111	54,531	48,673	52,827
Percent..	7.0	7.9	7.1	6.9	6.7	5.3	4.0	3.5	3.8
Percent in the U.S. not covered...............................	15.1	15.5	15.1	14.8	14.5	11.7	9.4	8.6	8.7
Children Under 18 Years of Age[1]	287,944	303,661	304,077	302,565	306,848	308,018	310,995	307,561	320,949
Covered by Private or Public Insurance									
Number..	280,878	292,545	293,097	292,102	297,513	298,466	305,950	300,664	313,911
Percent..	97.5	96.3	96.4	96.5	97.0	96.9	98.4	97.8	97.8
Uninsured									
Number..	7,066	11,116	10,980	10,463	9,335	9,552	5,045	6,897	7,038
Percent..	2.5	3.7	3.6	3.5	3.0	3.1	1.6	2.2	2.2
Percent in the U.S. not covered...............................	8.6	8.0	7.5	7.2	7.1	6.0	4.8	4.5	5.0

[1] 2017 data is for individuals under 19 years of age.

Table HI-7. Employment Status by Demographic Group, 2018

(Numbers in thousands, percent.)

Characteristic	Civilian noninstitutional population	Civilian labor force		Employed		Unemployed	
		Number	Percent of population	Number	Percent of population	Number	Percent of population
Total..	1,095	680	62.1	663	60.5	18	2.6
Sex							
Male..	529	351	66.3	340	64.4	10	3.0
Female	567	330	58.2	322	56.9	7	2.2
Race, Sex, and Hispanic Origin							
White	265	163	61.6	159	60.2	4	2.3
Male..	132	90	67.8	87	66.2	2	2.3
Female	133	74	55.5	72	54.3	2	2.2
Black or African American....................	NA	NA	NA	NA	NA	NA	NA
Male..	NA	NA	NA	NA	NA	NA	NA
Female	NA	NA	NA	NA	NA	NA	NA
Hispanic or Latino ethnicity[1]	95	61	63.9	58	61.5	2	3.9
Male..	NA	NA	NA	NA	NA	NA	NA
Female	NA	NA	NA	NA	NA	NA	NA
Age							
16 to 19 years	NA	NA	NA	NA	NA	NA	NA
20 to 24 years	78	56	71.2	54	68.8	2	3.4
25 to 34 years	164	133	80.8	129	78.8	3	2.5
35 to 44 years	181	149	82.4	145	80.4	4	2.5
45 to 54 years	175	140	80.2	137	78.3	3	2.4
55 to 64 years	178	126	70.6	124	69.7	2	1.2
65 years and over	251	55	21.9	54	21.3	1	2.5

NOTE: Data in Table 7 are from the Current Population Survey (CPS) and do not match the estimates in Table 8. See notes and definitions for further information.
[1] May be of any race.
NA = Not available.

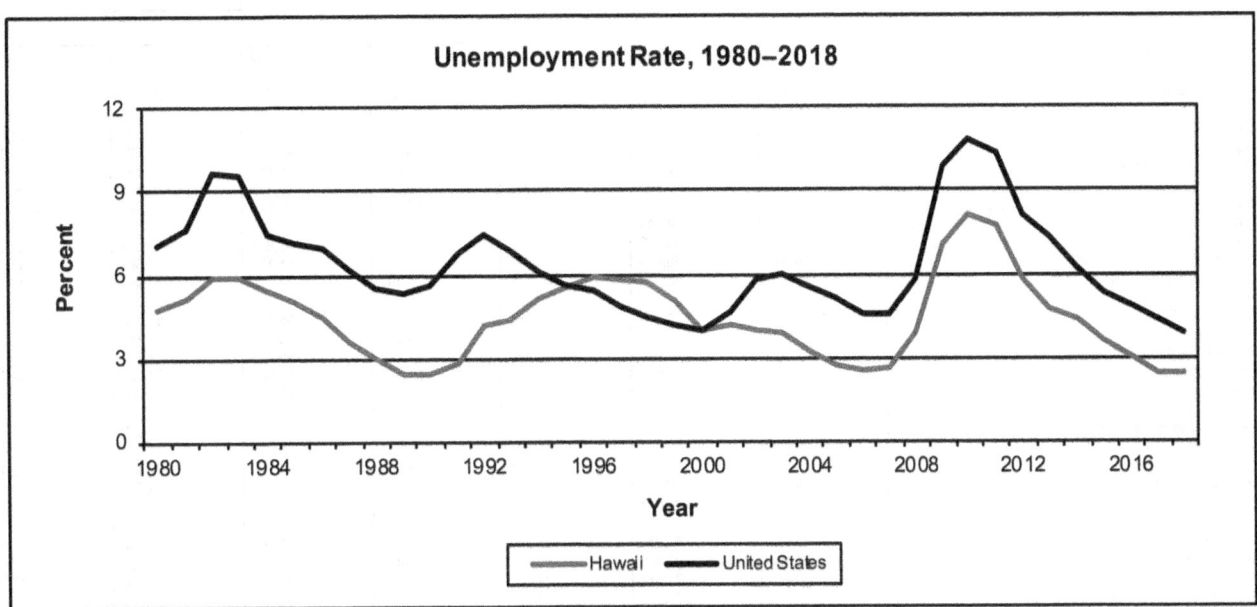

Unemployment Rate, 1980–2018

Table HI-8. Employment Status of the Civilian Noninstitutional Population Age 16 Years and Over

(Number, percent.)

Year	Civilian labor force	Civilian participation rate	Employed	Unemployed	Unemployment rate
2010..	647,249	62.8	602,282	44,967	6.9
2011..	660,253	62.6	615,319	44,934	6.8
2012..	647,185	60.8	608,302	38,883	6.0
2013..	651,557	60.7	619,691	31,866	4.9
2014..	666,674	61.6	637,661	29,013	4.4
2015..	675,506	62.0	651,459	24,047	3.6
2016..	684,167	62.5	664,032	20,135	2.9
2017..	685,418	62.6	669,241	16,177	2.4
2018..	678,734	62.1	662,128	16,606	2.4

Table HI-9. Employment and Average Wages by Industry

(Estimates are based on the 2012 *North American Industry Classification System* [NAICS].)

Industry	2011	2012	2013	2014	2015	2016	2017
				Number of Jobs			
Wage and Salary Employment by Industry............................	668,971	680,842	693,539	702,977	715,201	722,186	727,610
Farm Wage and Salary Employment................................	6,528	6,099	6,168	7,376	6,734	6,294	6,281
Nonfarm Wage and Salary Employment............................	662,443	674,743	687,371	695,601	708,467	715,892	721,329
Private wage and salary employment................................	480,350	491,653	504,592	512,575	522,855	532,367	538,955
Forestry, fishing, and related activities..........................	1,411	1,471	1,518	1,532	1,574	1,534	1,517
Mining..	332	298	255	252	279	232	237
Utilities..	3,328	3,567	3,771	3,808	3,827	3,772	3,785
Construction..	29,143	30,006	31,569	32,592	35,572	38,592	36,747
Manufacturing..	13,185	13,348	13,588	13,934	14,097	14,130	14,281
Durable goods manufacturing..............................	3,884	3,619	3,632	3,600	3,699	3,728	3,853
Nondurable goods manufacturing.........................	9,301	9,729	9,956	10,334	10,398	10,402	10,428
Wholesale trade..	17,514	17,737	17,819	17,778	18,085	17,902	18,001
Retail trade...	67,652	69,401	70,183	70,323	71,285	71,115	71,669
Transportation and warehousing...............................	23,939	25,096	25,967	26,659	27,442	28,075	29,333
Information..	8,530	8,459	8,792	8,482	8,724	8,829	9,039
Finance and insurance	15,977	16,031	15,762	15,671	15,962	16,168	16,344
Real estate and rental and leasing............................	11,602	11,779	12,031	12,197	12,213	12,542	12,691
Professional, scientific, and technical services	24,471	24,584	24,584	24,554	24,763	24,638	24,549
Management of companies and enterprises..................	6,925	7,508	8,255	8,377	8,507	8,720	8,886
Administrative and waste services............................	44,303	45,533	47,612	49,794	50,888	50,865	49,380
Educational services...	15,846	16,284	16,101	15,805	15,566	15,791	16,051
Health care and social assistance.............................	62,142	62,804	64,960	65,709	67,839	69,307	70,974
Arts, entertainment, and recreation..........................	10,697	11,436	12,097	12,398	11,860	12,243	12,882
Accommodation and food services............................	92,975	96,442	99,657	101,678	103,306	106,668	110,982
Other services, except public administration................	30,378	29,869	30,071	31,032	31,066	31,244	31,607
Government and government enterprises.....................	182,093	183,090	182,779	183,026	185,612	183,525	182,374
				Dollars			
Average Wages and Salaries by Industry	44,025	45,043	45,440	46,681	48,332	49,584	50,968
Average Farm Wages and Salaries	24,174	39,050	38,569	32,882	33,869	38,552	38,271
Average Nonfarm Wages and Salaries	44,220	45,097	45,501	46,828	48,470	49,681	51,078
Average private wages and salaries............................	40,562	41,670	42,376	43,490	45,347	46,621	48,169
Forestry, fishing, and related activities......................	22,470	23,039	24,211	24,690	26,890	29,399	29,452
Mining..	77,337	82,822	88,325	93,694	96,878	94,345	86,181
Utilities..	88,468	90,380	92,306	94,486	99,620	97,875	102,023
Construction..	63,605	64,744	65,056	66,496	70,603	72,552	73,834
Manufacturing..	40,339	40,053	40,692	41,272	42,871	44,634	45,428
Durable goods manufacturing..............................	50,960	49,973	50,854	53,247	55,157	57,387	57,994
Nondurable goods manufacturing.........................	35,903	36,363	36,986	37,101	38,500	40,064	40,785
Wholesale trade..	49,758	51,350	52,573	54,246	55,790	57,552	60,247
Retail trade...	28,179	28,371	28,805	29,668	30,302	31,310	32,202
Transportation and warehousing...............................	43,547	44,754	46,390	48,239	50,711	52,924	56,569
Information..	57,632	58,686	58,677	61,975	63,566	62,027	62,255
Finance and insurance	60,308	63,162	64,472	65,693	69,119	71,270	74,809
Real estate and rental and leasing............................	42,511	44,022	46,221	46,937	49,914	51,520	55,526
Professional, scientific, and technical services	63,579	65,873	66,764	68,333	69,889	71,154	74,432
Management of companies and enterprises..................	79,843	83,753	82,657	84,358	86,738	87,986	88,437
Administrative and waste services............................	29,705	30,837	31,048	31,586	32,928	34,415	35,500
Educational services...	33,637	34,027	34,625	34,911	35,627	35,237	36,045
Health care and social assistance.............................	46,672	47,933	48,295	49,759	51,504	52,256	54,016
Arts, entertainment, and recreation..........................	27,193	27,555	28,622	30,001	30,141	29,660	32,452
Accommodation and food services............................	30,472	31,811	32,598	33,759	35,234	36,416	37,749
Other services, except public administration................	32,786	33,438	34,110	34,818	36,223	37,368	38,602
Government and government enterprises.....................	53,871	54,300	54,129	56,176	57,266	58,557	59,676

Table HI-10. Employment Characteristics by Family Type

(Number, percent.)

Family type and labor force status	2015		2016		2017	
	Total	Families with own children under 18 years	Total	Families with own children under 18 years	Total	Families with own children under 18 years
All Families..	309,386	115,039	315,505	115,996	320,336	119,273
FAMILY TYPE AND LABOR FORCE STATUS						
Married-Couple Families..................................	232,451	87,488	236,236	85,855	233,373	87,101
Both husband and wife in labor force.........................	51.2	64.8	52.4	65.3	50.6	67.2
Husband in labor force, wife not in labor force	22.0	29.6	19.3	27.0	19.1	25.8
Wife in labor force, husband not in labor force	8.3	4.1	10.3	5.5	9.3	4.4
Both husband and wife not in labor force....................	17.6	1.3	16.9	1.9	19.5	1.9
Other Families	76,935	27,551	79,269	30,141	86,963	32,172
Female householder, no husband present......................	67.7	68.8	67.2	66.7	67.2	69.7
In labor force	41.6	56.8	40.9	54.5	41.1	55.5
Not in labor force	26.1	12.0	26.3	12.2	26.1	14.1
Male householder, no wife present...........................	32.3	31.2	32.8	33.3	32.8	30.3
In labor force	23.1	27.7	24.6	30.7	23.6	27.0
Not in labor force	9.2	3.5	8.2	2.6	9.2	3.4

Table HI-11. School Enrollment and Educational Attainment, 2017

(Number, percent.)

Item	State	U.S.
Enrollment		
Total population 3 years and over, enrolled in school	324,608	81,273,337
Enrolled in nursery school or preschool (percent)	7.2	6.0
Enrolled in kindergarten (percent)	5.2	4.9
Enrolled in elementary school, grades 1-8 (percent)..	40.0	40.6
Enrolled in high school, grades 9-12 (percent)	19.0	21.1
Enrolled in college or graduate school (percent)...	28.5	27.4
Attainment		
Total population 25 years and over	997,744	221,250,083
Less than ninth grade (percent)	3.5	5.1
9th to 12th grade, no diploma (percent)...	4.3	6.9
High school graduate, including equivalency (percent)...	28.1	27.1
Some college, no degree (percent)...	20.5	20.4
Associate's degree (percent)..	10.7	8.5
Bachelor's degree (percent)...	21.7	19.7
Graduate or professional degree (percent)..	11.2	12.3
High school graduate or higher (percent)	92.3	88.0
Bachelor's degree or higher (percent)	32.9	32.0

Table HI-12. Public School Characteristics and Educational Indicators

(Number, percent; data derived from National Center of Education Statistics.)

Item	State	U.S.
Public Elementary and Secondary Schools		
Number of operational school districts, 2016-17..	1	18,377
Number of operational schools, 2016-17..	290	98,330
Percent charter schools	11.7	7.1
Total public school enrollment, 2016-17..	181,550	50,587,859
Percent charter school enrollment	5.9	6.0
Student-teacher ratio, Fall 2015..	15.5	16.0
Expenditures per student (dollars), 2015-16..	13,748	11,841
Four-year adjusted cohort graduation rate (ACGR)[1]..	82.7	84.6
Students eligible for free or reduced-price lunch (percent), 2015-16...	49.6	52.1
English language learners (percent), Fall 2016	7.0	9.6
Students age 3 to 21 served under IDEA, part B (percent), 2017-18	10.6	13.7
Public Schools by Type, 2016-17		Percent of state public schools
Total number of schools..	290	100.0
Special education..	1	0.3
Vocational education...	0	-
Alternative education..	1	0.3

[1] Adjusted Cohort Graduation Rates (ACGR) differ from Averaged Freshmen Graduation Rates (AFGR).
- = Zero or rounds to zero.

Table HI-13. Reported Voting and Registration of the Voting-Age Population, November 2018

(Numbers in thousands, percent.)

Item	Total population	Total citizen population	Registered			Voted		
			Total registered	Percent registered (total population)	Percent registered (total citizen population)	Total voted	Percent voted (total population)	Percent voted (total citizen population)
U.S. Total	249,748	228,832	153,066	61.3	66.9	122,281	49.0	53.4
State Total...	1,057	971	523	49.5	53.9	427	40.4	44.0
Sex								
Male	504	462	237	46.9	51.2	193	38.3	41.7
Female	553	509	287	51.9	56.4	234	42.4	46.1
Race								
White alone..	237	231	137	57.9	59.3	111	46.8	47.9
White, non-Hispanic alone.....................	211	206	125	59.3	60.7	104	49.3	50.4
Black alone..	22	21	10	(B)	(B)	4	(B)	(B)
Asian alone	480	417	218	45.4	52.2	186	38.7	44.6
Hispanic (of any race)...........................	82	79	34	41.3	42.9	25	29.7	30.9
White alone or in combination	351	346	211	60.0	61.0	171	48.6	49.3
Black alone or in combination	28	27	15	(B)	(B)	8	(B)	(B)
Asian alone or in combination................	590	527	285	48.2	54.0	241	40.9	45.7
Age								
18 to 24 years	134	121	36	26.8	29.5	29	21.7	23.9
25 to 34 years	152	132	64	42.4	48.7	50	32.7	37.5
35 to 44 years	165	150	73	44.1	48.5	49	29.4	32.3
45 to 64 years	346	317	192	55.4	60.5	159	45.9	50.0
65 years and over	261	251	159	60.9	63.4	141	54.3	56.5

B = Base is less than 75,000 and therefore too small to show the derived measure.

Table HI-14. Crime

(Number, rate per 100,000. Data are derived from the FBI Uniform Crime Reports.)

Item	State			U.S.		
	2016	2017	Percent change	2016	2017	Percent change
TOTAL POPULATION[1]	1,428,683	1,427,538	-0.1	323,405,935	325,719,178	0.7
VIOLENT CRIME						
Number...	3,452	3,577	3.6	1,285,606	1,283,220	-0.2
Rate	241.6	250.6	3.7	397.5	394.0	-0.9
Murder and Nonnegligent Manslaughter						
Number...	35	39	11.4	17,413	17,284	-0.7
Rate	2.4	2.7	11.5	5.4	5.3	-1.4
Rape[2]						
Number...	601	567	-5.7	132,414	135,755	2.5
Rate	42.1	39.7	-5.6	40.9	41.7	1.8
Robbery						
Number...	985	1,077	9.3	332,797	319,356	-4.0
Rate	68.9	75.4	9.4	102.9	98.0	-4.7
Aggravated Assault						
Number...	1,831	1,894	3.4	802,982	810,825	1.0
Rate	128.2	132.7	3.5	248.3	248.9	0.3
PROPERTY CRIME						
Number...	42,353	40,392	-4.6	7,928,530	7,694,086	-3.0
Rate	2,964.5	2,829.5	-4.6	2,451.6	2,362.2	-3.6
Burglary						
Number...	5,983	5,549	-7.3	1,516,405	1,401,840	-7.6
Rate	418.8	388.7	-7.2	468.9	430.4	-8.2
Larceny-Theft						
Number...	30,871	29,574	-4.2	5,644,835	5,519,107	-2.2
Rate	2,160.8	2,071.7	-4.1	1,745.4	1,694.4	-2.9
Motor Vehicle Theft						
Number...	5,499	5,269	-4.2	767,290	773,139	0.8
Rate	384.9	369.1	-4.1	237.3	237.4	-

NOTE: Although arson data are included in the trend and clearance tables, sufficient data are not available to estimate totals for this offense. Therefore, no arson data are published in this table.
- = Zero or rounds to zero.
[1] Population figures are U.S. Census Bureau provisional estimates as of July 1, 2017.
[2] The figures shown in the rape (revised definition) column were estimated using the revised Uniform Crime Reporting (UCR) definition of rape.

Table HI-15. State Government Finances, 2017

(Dollar amounts in thousands, percent distribution.)

Item	Dollars	Percent distribution
Total Revenue	16,136,298	100.0
General revenue	13,451,636	83.4
Intergovernmental revenue	2,787,412	17.3
Taxes	7,029,026	43.6
General sales	3,239,225	20.1
Selective sales	1,126,631	7.0
License taxes	269,224	1.7
Individual income tax	2,095,601	13.0
Corporate income tax	184,840	1.1
Other taxes	113,505	0.7
Current charges	1,896,868	11.8
Miscellaneous general revenue	1,738,330	10.8
Utility revenue	0	-
Liquor stores revenue	0	-
Insurance trust revenue[1]	2,684,662	16.6
Total Expenditure	12,680,681	100.0
Intergovernmental expenditure	328,020	2.6
Direct expenditure	12,352,661	97.4
Current operation	9,715,969	76.6
Capital outlay	914,929	7.2
Insurance benefits and repayments	1,488,946	11.7
Assistance and subsidies	118,899	0.9
Interest on debt	113,918	0.9
Exhibit: Salaries and wages	3,353,048	26.4
Total Expenditure	12,680,681	100.0
General expenditure	11,191,735	88.3
Intergovernmental expenditure	328,020	2.6
Direct expenditure	10,863,715	85.7
General expenditure, by function:		
Education	3,409,731	26.9
Public welfare	2,984,204	23.5
Hospitals	619,245	4.9
Health	550,157	4.3
Highways	318,005	2.5
Police protection	44,877	0.4
Correction	228,646	1.8
Natural resources	161,860	1.3
Parks and recreation	84,206	0.7
Governmental administration	595,200	4.7
Interest on general debt	113,918	0.9
Other and unallocable	2,081,686	16.4
Utility expenditure	0	-
Liquor stores expenditure	0	-
Insurance trust expenditure	1,488,946	11.7
Debt at End of Fiscal Year	9,656,278	X
Cash and Security Holdings	24,623,403	X

X = Not applicable.
- = Zero or rounds to zero.
[1] Within insurance trust revenue, net earnings of state retirement systems is a calculated statistic (the item code in the data file is X08), and thus can be positive or negative. Net earnings is the sum of earnings on investments plus gains on investments minus losses on investments. The change made in 2002 for asset valuation from book to market value in accordance with Statement 34 of the Governmental Accounting Standards Board is reflected in the calculated statistics.

Table HI-16. State Government Tax Collections, 2018

(Dollars in thousands, percent.)

Item	Dollars	Percent distribution
Total Taxes	**7,714,451**	**100.0**
Property taxes	X	-
Sales and gross receipts	4,732,032	61.3
General sales and gross receipts	3,529,065	45.7
Selective sales and gross receipts	1,202,967	15.6
Alcoholic beverages	51,383	0.7
Amusements	X	-
Insurance premiums	165,602	2.1
Motor fuels	88,377	1.1
Pari-mutuels	X	-
Public utilities	117,641	1.5
Tobacco products	120,386	1.6
Other selective sales	659,578	8.5
Licenses	275,600	3.6
Alcoholic beverages	X	-
Amusements	X	-
Corporations in general	1,818	-
Hunting and fishing	665	-
Motor vehicle	191,757	2.5
Motor vehicle operators	306	-
Public utilities	15,001	0.2
Occupation and business, NEC	53,544	0.7
Other licenses	12,509	0.2
Income taxes	2,576,863	33.4
Individual income	2,430,032	31.5
Corporation net income	146,831	1.9
Other taxes	129,956	1.7
Death and gift	29,351	0.4
Documentary and stock transfer	100,605	1.3
Severance	X	-
Taxes, NEC	0	-

X = Not applicable.
- = Zero or rounds to zero.

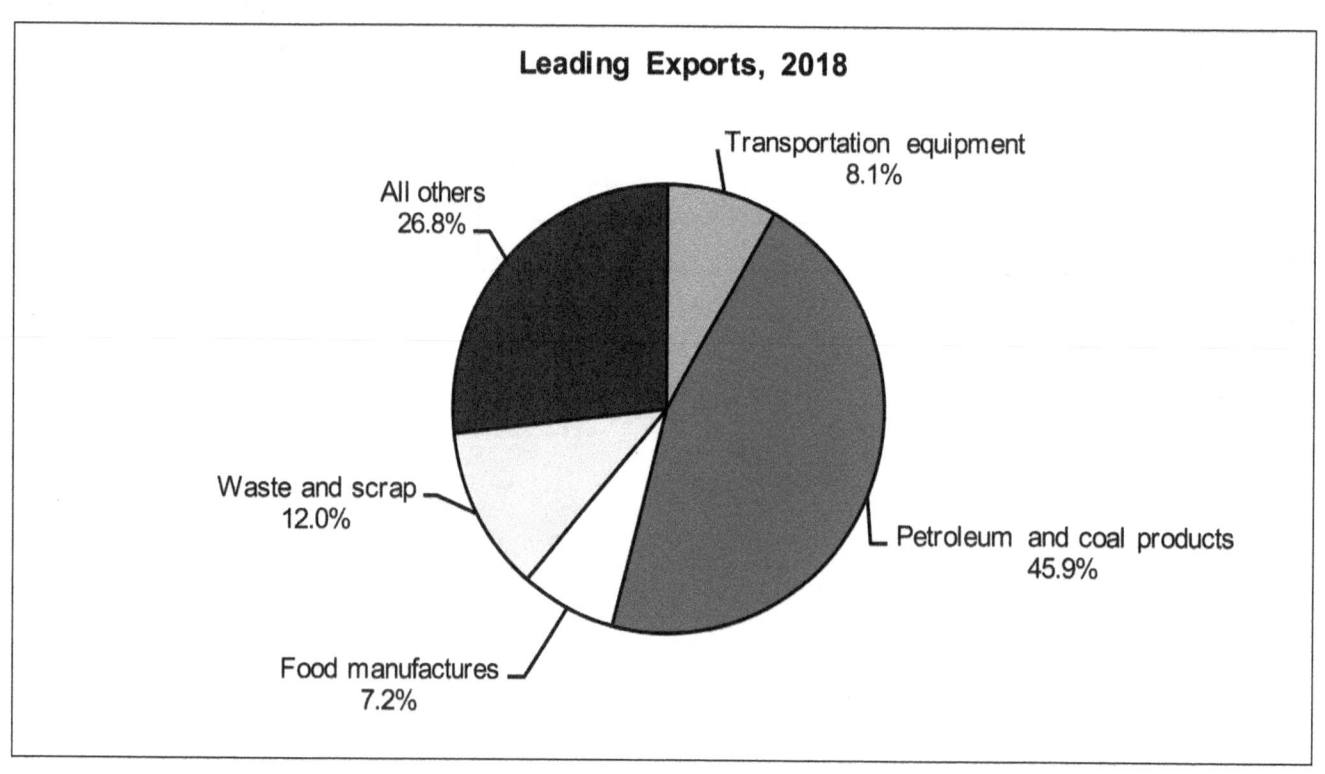

Leading Exports, 2018

- Transportation equipment 8.1%
- Petroleum and coal products 45.9%
- Food manufactures 7.2%
- Waste and scrap 12.0%
- All others 26.8%

Facts and Figures

Location: Northwestern United States; bordered on the N by Canada, on the E by Montana and Wyoming, on the S by Nevada and Utah, and on the W by Washington and Oregon

Area: 83,568 sq. mi. (216,446 sq. km.); rank—14th

Population: 1,754,208 (2018 est.); rank—39th

Principal Cities: capital—Boise; largest—Boise

Statehood: July 3, 1890; 43rd state

U.S. Congress: 2 senators, 2 representatives

State Motto: *Esto perpetua* ("Let it be perpetual")

State Song: "Here We Have Idaho"

State Nickname: The Gem State

Abbreviations: ID

State Symbols: flower—syringa (mock orange); tree—Western white pine; bird—mountain bluebird

At a Glance

- With an increase in population of 11.9 percent, Idaho ranked 10th among the states in growth from 2010 to 2018.

- With 1,635.4 incidences per 100,000 population, Idaho had the 7th lowest property crime rate in the country in 2017.

- Idaho's violent crime rate in 2017 was 226.4 per 100,000 population, compared to 394.0 for the entire nation.

- With 25.5 percent of its population under age 18, Idaho ranked 3rd among the states for the highest percent children in 2018.

- Idaho's unemployment rate ranked 45th in the nation in 2018, with 2.8 percent of the population unemployed, compared to 3.9 of the entire country.

Table ID-1. Population by Age, Sex, Race, and Hispanic Origin

(Number, percent, except where noted.)

Sex, age, race, and Hispanic origin	2000	2010	2018[1]	Percent change, 2010–2018
Total Population..	1,293,953	1,567,582	1,754,208	11.9
Percent of total U.S. population	0.5	0.5	0.5	X
Sex				
Male..	648,660	785,324	879,077	11.9
Female..	645,293	782,258	875,131	11.9
Age				
Under 5 years...	97,643	121,772	116,339	-4.5
5 to 19 years...	316,222	353,509	378,507	7.1
20 to 64 years..	734,172	897,633	981,080	9.3
65 years and over...	145,916	194,668	278,282	43.0
Median age (years)	33.2	34.6	36.6	5.8
Race and Hispanic Origin				
One race				
White..	1,177,304	1,476,097	1,632,188	10.6
Black..	5,456	10,950	15,775	44.1
American Indian and Alaska Native	17,645	25,782	30,449	18.1
Asian..	11,889	20,034	27,819	38.9
Native Hawaiian or Other Pacific Islander	1,308	2,786	3,883	39.4
Two or more races..	25,609	31,933	44,094	38.1
Hispanic (of any race)...	101,690	182,424	222,908	22.2

X = Not applicable.

[1] Population figures for 2018 are July 1 estimates. The 2010 estimates are taken from the 2010 Census.

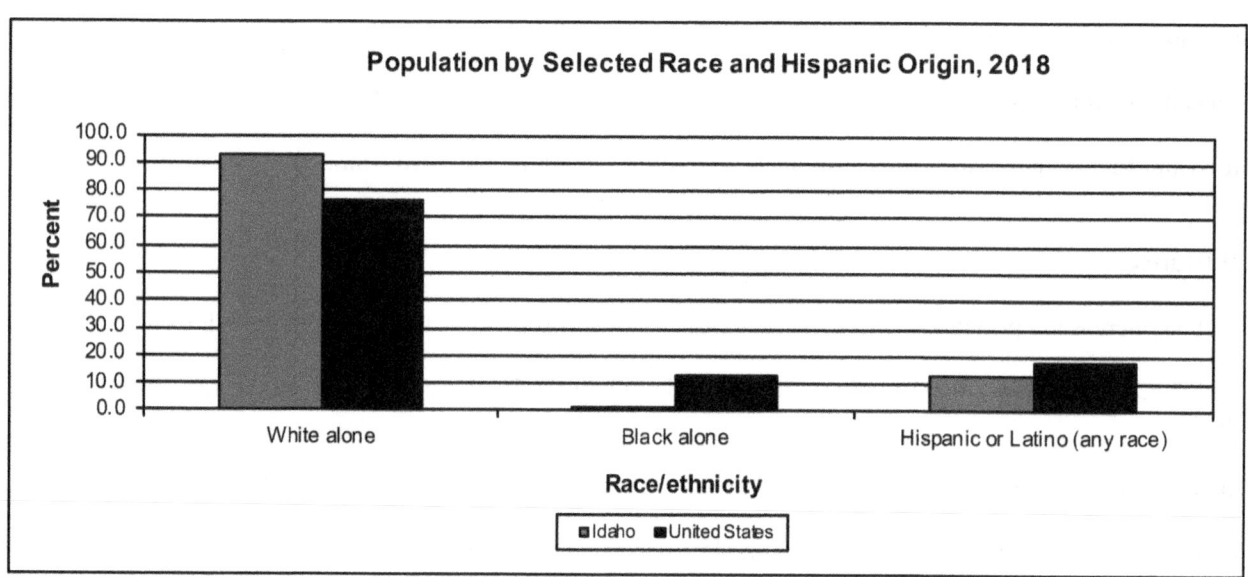

Population by Selected Race and Hispanic Origin, 2018

Table ID-2. Marital Status

(Number, percent distribution.)

Sex, age, race, and Hispanic origin	2000	2010	2017
Males, 15 Years and Over..	493,045	602,308	673,450
Never married..	26.1	28.3	31.2
Now married, except separated..	61.0	57.0	53.4
Separated..	1.0	1.4	0.9
Widowed..	2.1	2.4	2.9
Divorced...	9.9	10.9	11.7
Females, 15 Years and Over..	498,579	608,900	675,999
Never married..	19.6	22.4	24.4
Now married, except separated..	59.0	55.3	53.6
Separated..	1.3	1.6	1.1
Widowed..	8.6	7.6	8.2
Divorced...	11.4	13.1	12.7

Table ID-3. Households and Housing Characteristics

(Number, percent, dollars.)

Item	2000	2010	2017	Average annual percent change, 2010–2017
Total Households..	469,645	576,709	625,135	1.2
Family households	333,588	401,806	419,774	0.6
Married-couple family	276,511	322,129	338,425	0.7
Other family	59,077	79,677	81,349	0.3
Male householder, no wife present........................	18,228	23,583	26,933	2.0
Female householder, no husband present...............	40,849	56,094	54,416	-0.4
Nonfamily households	134,057	174,903	205,361	2.5
Householder living alone.......................................	105,175	139,909	171,683	3.2
Householder not living alone.................................	28,882	34,994	33,678	-0.5
Housing Characteristics				
Total housing units...	527,824	668,634	721,818	1.1
Occupied housing units	469,645	576,709	625,135	1.2
Owner occupied	339,960	401,532	435,493	1.2
Renter occupied	129,685	175,177	189,642	1.2
Average household size..	2.69	2.67	2.70	0.2
Financial Characteristics				
Median gross rent of renter-occupied housing	515	683	822	2.9
Median monthly owner costs for housing units with a mortgage	887	1,187	1,213	0.3
Median value of owner-occupied housing units.........	106,300	165,100	207,100	3.6

- = Zero or rounds to zero

Table ID-4. Migration, Origin, and Language

(Number, percent.)

Characteristic	State			U.S.		
	2016	2017	Percent change	2016	2017	Percent change
Residence 1 Year Ago						
Population 1 year and over	1,663,756	1,694,182	1.8	319,361,956	321,994,428	0.8
Same house	82.3	83.0	X	85.4	85.7	X
Different house in the U.S.	17.2	16.7	X	13.9	13.6	X
Same county	9.4	9.2	X	8.3	8.1	X
Different county	7.8	7.4	X	5.6	5.6	X
Same state	3.5	3.2	X	3.2	3.3	X
Different state	4.3	4.2	X	2.4	2.3	X
Abroad	0.5	0.4	X	0.7	0.7	X
Place of Birth						
Native born	1,585,187	1,615,803	1.9	279,388,170	281,193,323	0.6
Male	50.1	50.4	X	49.3	49.4	X
Female	49.9	49.6	X	50.7	50.6	X
Foreign born	97,953	101,140	3.3	43,739,345	44,525,855	1.8
Male	48.4	48.5	X	48.5	48.4	X
Female	51.6	51.5	X	51.5	51.6	X
Foreign born; naturalized U.S. citizen.........................	37,899	40,197	6.1	21,238,372	21,948,732	3.3
Male	46.4	44.7	X	45.9	45.9	X
Female	53.6	55.3	X	54.1	54.1	X
Foreign born; not a U.S. citizen	60,054	60,943	1.5	22,500,973	22,577,123	0.3
Male	49.6	51.0	X	51	50.8	X
Female	50.4	49.0	X	49	49.2	X
Entered 2010 or later	19.4	22.9	X	18.6	21.3	X
Entered 2000 to 2009	29.9	26.6	X	26.7	25.7	X
Entered before 2000...	50.8	50.4	X	54.7	53.0	X
World Region of Birth, Foreign						
Foreign-born population, excluding population born at sea	97,953	101,140	3.3	43,738,901	44,525,458	1.8
Europe	13.9	14.2	X	10.9	10.8	X
Asia	21.1	18.6	X	30.8	31.2	X
Africa	1.9	3.7	X	4.9	5.1	X
Oceania	0.9	0.9	X	0.6	0.6	X
Latin America...	58.1	57.4	X	51	50.4	X
North America	4.0	5.2	X	1.8	1.8	X
Language Spoken at Home and Ability to Speak English						
Population 5 years and over.......................................	1,568,997	1,600,717	2.0	303,328,961	305,924,019	0.9
English only	89.2	89.4	X	78.4	78.2	X
Language other than English....................................	10.8	10.6	X	21.6	21.8	X
Speaks English less than "very well"......................	4.2	3.7	X	8.6	8.5	X

NA = Not available.
X = Not applicable.
- = Zero or rounds to zero.

Table ID-5. Median Income and Poverty Status, 2017

(Number, percent, except as noted.)

Characteristic	State		U.S.	
	Number	Percent	Number	Percent
Median Income				
Households (dollars)..	52,225	X	60,336	X
Families (dollars)	64,178	X	73,891	X
Below Poverty Level (All People)	216,309	12.8	42,583,651	13.4
Sex				
Male	97,165	11.5	19,004,547	12.2
Female	119,144	14.1	23,579,104	14.5
Age				
Under 18 years..	67,147	15.3	13,353,202	18.4
Related children under 18 years..	65,555	15.0	13,053,472	18.1
18 to 64 years...	128,263	13.0	24,648,677	12.6
65 years and over	20,899	8.1	4,581,772	9.3

X = Not applicable.

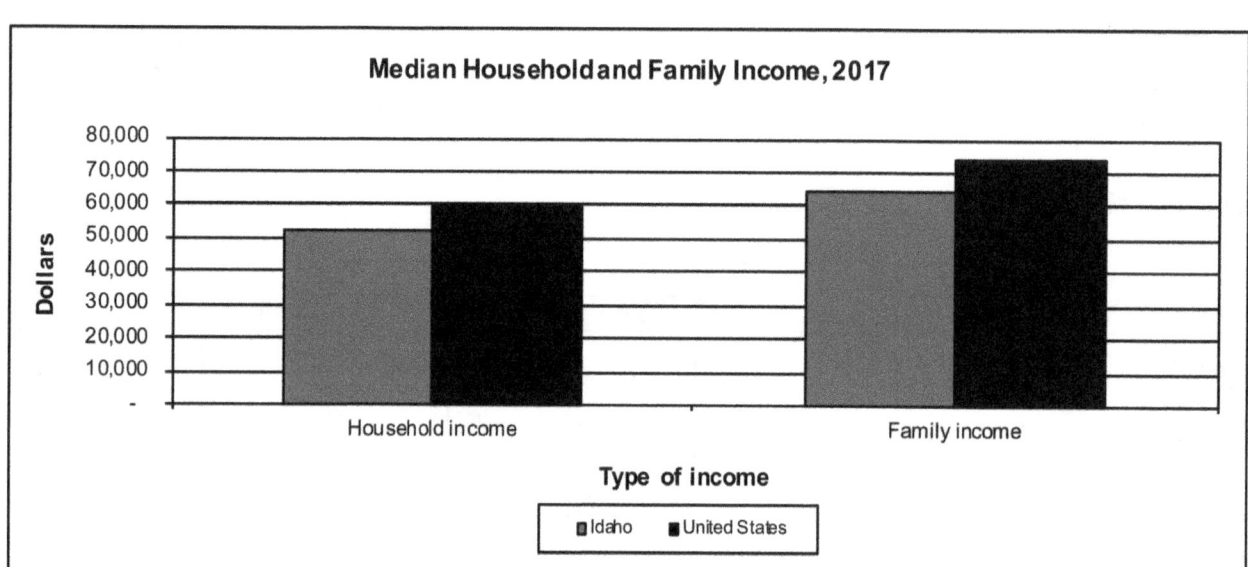

Table ID-6. Health Insurance Coverage Status for the Civilian Noninstitutionalized Population and Children Under 18 Years of Age

(Number, percent.)

Item	2009	2010	2011	2012	2013	2014	2015	2016	2017
Civilian Noninstitutionalized Population	1,520,563	1,551,635	1,565,645	1,575,682	1,592,172	1,612,889	1,632,247	1,662,867	1,695,273
Covered by Private or Public Insurance									
Number..	1,256,279	1,276,231	1,306,551	1,320,939	1,334,697	1,394,182	1,451,902	1,494,757	1,523,260
Percent...	82.6	82.3	83.5	83.8	83.8	86.4	89.0	89.9	89.9
Uninsured									
Number..	264,284	275,404	259,094	254,743	257,475	218,707	180,345	168,110	172,013
Percent...	17.4	17.7	16.5	16.2	16.2	13.6	11.0	10.1	10.1
Percent in the U.S. not covered	15.1	15.5	15.1	14.8	14.5	11.7	9.4	8.6	8.7
Children Under 18 Years of Age[1]	418,172	428,296	427,064	423,926	425,948	430,662	431,339	435,630	471,739
Covered by Private or Public Insurance									
Number..	371,201	383,292	388,096	387,897	387,931	396,885	406,497	415,147	450,102
Percent...	88.8	89.5	90.9	91.5	91.1	92.2	94.2	95.3	95.4
Uninsured									
Number..	46,971	45,004	38,968	36,029	38,017	33,777	24,842	20,483	21,637
Percent...	11.2	10.5	9.1	8.5	8.9	7.8	5.8	4.7	4.6
Percent in the U.S. not covered................................	8.6	8.0	7.5	7.2	7.1	6.0	4.8	4.5	5.0

[1] 2017 data is for individuals under 19 years of age.

Table ID-7. Employment Status by Demographic Group, 2018

(Numbers in thousands, percent.)

Characteristic	Civilian noninstitutional population	Civilian labor force		Employed		Unemployed	
		Number	Percent of population	Number	Percent of population	Number	Percent of population
Total..	1,335	857	64.2	831	62.3	26	3.0
Sex							
Male..	662	473	71.4	459	69.4	13	2.8
Female.......................................	673	384	57.1	372	55.2	13	3.3
Race, Sex, and Hispanic Origin							
White...	1,259	808	64.2	784	62.3	24	3.0
Male.......................................	625	444	71.1	432	69.1	12	2.7
Female....................................	634	364	57.4	352	55.5	12	3.3
Black or African American...............	NA	NA	NA	NA	NA	NA	NA
Male.......................................	NA	NA	NA	NA	NA	NA	NA
Female....................................	NA	NA	NA	NA	NA	NA	NA
Hispanic or Latino ethnicity[1]	174	124	71.0	118	67.6	6	4.7
Male.......................................	90	74	82.3	72	79.4	3	3.5
Female....................................	84	49	58.7	46	55.0	3	6.4
Age							
16 to 19 years..............................	94	41	43.1	36	38.1	5	11.5
20 to 24 years..............................	112	88	79.2	85	76.4	3	3.5
25 to 34 years..............................	231	189	81.9	185	80.3	4	2.0
35 to 44 years..............................	214	181	84.5	175	82.0	5	3.0
45 to 54 years..............................	198	163	82.5	159	80.3	4	2.6
55 to 64 years..............................	222	151	67.9	147	66.4	4	2.3
65 years and over	265	44	16.6	43	16.1	1	3.0

NOTE: Data in Table 7 are from the Current Population Survey (CPS) and do not match the estimates in Table 8. See notes and definitions for further information.
[1] May be of any race.
NA = Not available.

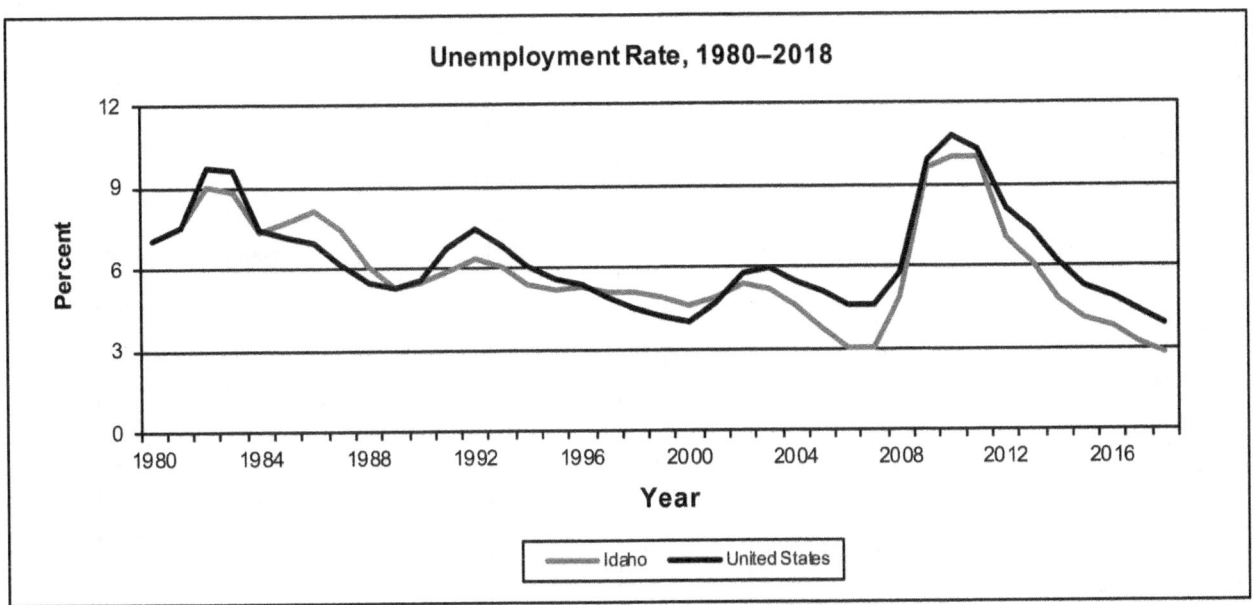

Table ID-8. Employment Status of the Civilian Noninstitutional Population Age 16 Years and Over

(Number, percent.)

Year	Civilian labor force	Civilian participation rate	Employed	Unemployed	Unemployment rate
2010..	761,056	65.3	692,826	68,230	9.0
2011..	765,178	64.9	701,466	63,712	8.3
2012..	769,256	64.5	713,704	55,552	7.2
2013..	770,833	63.8	723,636	47,197	6.1
2014..	779,631	63.6	741,525	38,106	4.9
2015..	794,675	63.9	761,009	33,666	4.2
2016..	812,856	64.0	782,279	30,577	3.8
2017..	833,462	64.0	807,163	26,299	3.2
2018..	857,049	64.1	832,732	24,317	2.8

Table ID-9. Employment and Average Wages by Industry

(Estimates are based on the 2012 North American Industry Classification System [NAICS].)

Industry	2011	2012	2013	2014	2015	2016	2017
	Number of Jobs						
Wage and Salary Employment by Industry	646,362	652,207	667,781	685,278	703,568	726,463	748,265
Farm Wage and Salary Employment	16,704	16,505	16,382	17,623	17,001	17,215	19,927
Nonfarm Wage and Salary Employment	629,658	635,702	651,399	667,655	686,567	709,248	728,338
Private wage and salary employment	502,838	509,174	524,718	540,229	557,474	578,017	595,200
Forestry, fishing, and related activities	7,700	7,836	8,168	8,381	8,669	8,502	8,412
Mining	2,565	2,672	2,548	2,417	2,322	2,364	2,178
Utilities	2,797	2,826	2,806	2,912	3,013	3,010	2,983
Construction	30,296	30,380	32,611	34,682	37,071	40,444	43,723
Manufacturing	54,586	56,592	59,236	59,928	61,656	63,840	66,166
Durable goods manufacturing	31,289	32,650	34,027	34,482	35,615	36,847	37,811
Nondurable goods manufacturing	23,297	23,942	25,209	25,446	26,041	26,993	28,355
Wholesale trade	26,273	26,981	28,270	28,721	28,728	28,476	28,783
Retail trade	75,525	77,029	78,526	80,215	83,374	85,021	86,158
Transportation and warehousing	18,372	18,685	18,744	19,520	20,481	20,570	21,109
Information	9,432	9,301	9,236	9,221	9,187	9,001	8,960
Finance and insurance	21,317	21,341	21,748	22,246	22,870	23,766	24,698
Real estate and rental and leasing	6,808	6,688	6,830	6,925	7,281	7,390	7,819
Professional, scientific, and technical services	32,491	31,627	31,241	32,732	34,369	35,433	36,228
Management of companies and enterprises	5,874	5,915	5,435	5,479	5,538	5,302	5,832
Administrative and waste services	36,882	37,323	39,807	40,258	39,886	44,552	46,743
Educational services	10,717	11,059	11,201	11,482	11,994	12,077	12,150
Health care and social assistance	77,120	77,844	80,845	83,485	86,519	89,123	90,422
Arts, entertainment, and recreation	8,549	9,048	9,336	9,990	9,684	10,373	11,113
Accommodation and food services	50,805	51,994	53,652	56,054	58,519	61,884	64,414
Other services, except public administration	24,729	24,033	24,478	25,581	26,313	26,889	27,309
Government and government enterprises	126,820	126,528	126,681	127,426	129,093	131,231	133,138
	Dollars						
Average Wages and Salaries by Industry	36,297	37,030	37,817	38,886	39,610	40,488	42,022
Average Farm Wages and Salaries	30,022	34,588	38,875	36,986	30,600	34,986	30,398
Average Nonfarm Wages and Salaries	36,463	37,093	37,791	38,936	39,833	40,621	42,341
Average private wages and salaries	36,548	37,128	37,973	39,248	40,072	40,897	42,708
Forestry, fishing, and related activities	28,289	27,866	29,061	30,530	31,918	33,602	34,944
Mining	69,025	71,441	76,004	76,496	71,394	72,985	72,739
Utilities	74,956	76,798	78,927	81,030	83,034	83,414	87,769
Construction	39,368	39,972	39,813	40,059	40,859	42,485	43,691
Manufacturing	51,714	52,016	54,776	60,062	57,217	56,983	63,310
Durable goods manufacturing	58,200	57,972	62,222	69,867	63,801	63,429	73,275
Nondurable goods manufacturing	43,004	43,893	44,725	46,776	48,214	48,184	50,023
Wholesale trade	48,830	49,686	50,886	53,289	56,868	58,131	60,051
Retail trade	26,158	26,860	27,644	28,755	29,828	30,673	31,508
Transportation and warehousing	38,919	40,658	41,186	42,278	43,129	43,367	45,122
Information	44,336	46,946	46,882	48,206	48,946	51,110	53,068
Finance and insurance	49,427	52,471	53,870	55,761	58,075	60,895	62,298
Real estate and rental and leasing	28,686	30,188	31,973	33,981	34,640	34,647	36,383
Professional, scientific, and technical services	58,086	57,132	59,102	59,336	61,457	60,824	63,902
Management of companies and enterprises	86,645	89,677	87,249	78,953	78,142	81,546	85,748
Administrative and waste services	26,984	27,044	27,074	27,832	29,584	32,197	34,791
Educational services	26,741	26,851	27,204	27,426	28,293	27,745	28,234
Health care and social assistance	37,442	37,583	38,617	39,640	41,028	42,382	42,486
Arts, entertainment, and recreation	18,919	18,822	19,479	19,864	20,702	21,393	21,799
Accommodation and food services	15,287	15,875	16,026	16,618	17,175	17,809	18,494
Other services, except public administration	24,785	26,126	26,896	27,565	28,517	29,643	31,227
Government and government enterprises	36,129	36,953	37,037	37,617	38,804	39,407	40,696

Table ID-10. Employment Characteristics by Family Type

(Number, percent.)

Family type and labor force status	2015		2016		2017	
	Total	Families with own children under 18 years	Total	Families with own children under 18 years	Total	Families with own children under 18 years
All Families..	400,347	175,338	411,617	176,108	419,774	185,978
FAMILY TYPE AND LABOR FORCE STATUS						
Married-Couple Families............................	320,853	126,719	328,906	128,484	338,425	138,998
Both husband and wife in labor force..........	48.4	62.7	47.4	59.3	48.5	60.5
Husband in labor force, wife not in labor force.......	23.1	31.9	25.2	35.2	23.6	33.7
Wife in labor force, husband not in labor force........	7.2	3.2	7.0	3.6	7.2	3.0
Both husband and wife not in labor force..........	20.9	2.1	19.9	1.7	20.3	2.3
Other Families	79,494	48,619	82,711	47,624	81,349	46,980
Female householder, no husband present..........	70.7	70.7	66.9	68.5	66.9	70.0
In labor force..........	49.7	57.6	46.1	54.6	48.8	58.4
Not in labor force..........	21.0	13.1	20.8	13.9	18.1	11.6
Male householder, no wife present	29.3	29.3	33.1	31.5	33.1	30.0
In labor force..........	23.7	26.6	25.6	28.0	26.4	27.3
Not in labor force..........	5.7	2.7	7.6	3.4	6.7	2.8

Table ID-11. School Enrollment and Educational Attainment, 2017

(Number, percent.)

Item	State	U.S.
Enrollment		
Total population 3 years and over, enrolled in school	454,019	81,273,337
Enrolled in nursery school or preschool (percent)	5.6	6.0
Enrolled in kindergarten (percent)..........	4.6	4.9
Enrolled in elementary school, grades 1-8 (percent)..........	44.5	40.6
Enrolled in high school, grades 9-12 (percent)..........	22.5	21.1
Enrolled in college or graduate school (percent)..........	22.8	27.4
Attainment		
Total population 25 years and over	1,111,788	221,250,083
Less than ninth grade (percent)..........	3.3	5.1
9th to 12th grade, no diploma (percent)..........	5.9	6.9
High school graduate, including equivalency (percent)..........	28.2	27.1
Some college, no degree (percent)	26.3	20.4
Associate's degree (percent)..........	9.7	8.5
Bachelor's degree (percent)..........	18.2	19.7
Graduate or professional degree (percent)..........	8.5	12.3
High school graduate or higher (percent)	90.8	88.0
Bachelor's degree or higher (percent)	26.8	32.0

Table ID-12. Public School Characteristics and Educational Indicators

(Number, percent; data derived from National Center of Education Statistics.)

Item	State	U.S.
Public Elementary and Secondary Schools		
Number of operational school districts, 2016-17	160	18,377
Number of operational schools, 2016-17..........	745	98,330
Percent charter schools	7.7	7.1
Total public school enrollment, 2016-17..........	297,200	50,587,859
Percent charter school enrollment	6.9	6.0
Student-teacher ratio, Fall 2015	18.7	16.0
Expenditures per student (dollars), 2015-16..........	7,178	11,841
Four-year adjusted cohort graduation rate (ACGR)[1]	79.7	84.6
Students eligible for free or reduced-price lunch (percent), 2015-16..........	46.9	52.1
English language learners (percent), Fall 2016	5.4	9.6
Students age 3 to 21 served under IDEA, part B (percent), 2017-18	11.0	13.7

Public Schools by Type, 2016-17		Percent of state public schools
Total number of schools..........	745	100.0
Special education..........	11	1.5
Vocational education..........	14	1.9
Alternative education..........	74	9.9

[1] Adjusted Cohort Graduation Rates (ACGR) differ from Averaged Freshmen Graduation Rates (AFGR).

Table ID-13. Reported Voting and Registration of the Voting-Age Population, November 2018

(Numbers in thousands, percent.)

Item	Total population	Total citizen population	Registered			Voted		
			Total registered	Percent registered (total population)	Percent registered (total citizen population)	Total voted	Percent voted (total population)	Percent voted (total citizen population)
U.S. Total	249,748	228,832	153,066	61.3	66.9	122,281	49.0	53.4
State Total....................................	1,299	1,226	743	57.2	60.6	587	45.2	47.9
Sex								
Male	645	608	362	56.1	59.5	286	44.3	47.0
Female	654	618	381	58.2	61.6	301	46.0	48.7
Race								
White alone..................................	1,214	1,163	708	58.3	60.9	555	45.7	47.7
White, non-Hispanic alone	1,048	1,044	664	63.3	63.6	531	50.6	50.9
Black alone..................................	8	8	8	(B)	(B)	6	(B)	(B)
Asian alone	33	22	9	(B)	(B)	8	(B)	(B)
Hispanic (of any race).....................	182	126	51	27.7	40.0	30	16.5	23.8
White alone or in combination	1,232	1,178	715	58.0	60.7	562	45.6	47.7
Black alone or in combination...........	12	12	11	(B)	(B)	9	(B)	(B)
Asian alone or in combination..........	33	22	9	(B)	(B)	8	(B)	(B)
Age								
18 to 24 years	177	165	53	30.2	32.4	35	19.9	21.4
25 to 34 years	202	176	96	47.3	54.2	62	30.9	35.3
35 to 44 years	228	206	133	58.4	64.4	100	43.8	48.3
45 to 64 years	437	428	284	64.9	66.2	232	53.0	54.1
65 years and over	256	250	177	69.2	70.7	158	61.7	63.1

B = Base is less than 75,000 and therefore too small to show the derived measure.

Table ID-14. Crime

(Number, rate per 100,000. Data are derived from the FBI Uniform Crime Reports.)

Item	State			U.S.		
	2016	2017	Percent change	2016	2017	Percent change
TOTAL POPULATION[1]	1,680,026	1,716,943	2.2	323,405,935	325,719,178	0.7
VIOLENT CRIME						
Number..	3,876	3,888	0.3	1,285,606	1,283,220	-0.2
Rate	230.7	226.4	-1.8	397.5	394.0	-0.9
Murder and Nonnegligent Manslaughter						
Number..	49	32	-34.7	17,413	17,284	-0.7
Rate	2.9	1.9	-36.1	5.4	5.3	-1.4
Rape[2]						
Number..	719	707	-1.7	132,414	135,755	2.5
Rate	42.8	41.2	-3.8	40.9	41.7	1.8
Robbery						
Number..	213	196	-8.0	332,797	319,356	-4.0
Rate	12.7	11.4	-10.0	102.9	98.0	-4.7
Aggravated Assault						
Number..	2,895	2,953	2.0	802,982	810,825	1.0
Rate	172.3	172.0	-0.2	248.3	248.9	0.3
PROPERTY CRIME						
Number..	29,357	28,079	-4.4	7,928,530	7,694,086	-3.0
Rate	1,747.4	1,635.4	-6.4	2,451.6	2,362.2	-3.6
Burglary						
Number..	6,318	5,655	-10.5	1,516,405	1,401,840	-7.6
Rate	376.1	329.4	-12.4	468.9	430.4	-8.2
Larceny-Theft						
Number..	20,962	20,278	-3.3	5,644,835	5,519,107	-2.2
Rate	1,247.7	1,181.1	-5.3	1,745.4	1,694.4	-2.9
Motor Vehicle Theft						
Number..	2,077	2,146	3.3	767,290	773,139	0.8
Rate	123.6	125.0	1.1	237.3	237.4	-

NOTE: Although arson data are included in the trend and clearance tables, sufficient data are not available to estimate totals for this offense. Therefore, no arson data are published in this table.
- = Zero or rounds to zero.
[1] Population figures are U.S. Census Bureau provisional estimates as of July 1, 2017.
[2] The figures shown in the rape (revised definition) column were estimated using the revised Uniform Crime Reporting (UCR) definition of rape.

Table ID-15. State Government Finances, 2017

(Dollar amounts in thousands, percent distribution.)

Item	Dollars	Percent distribution
Total Revenue	11,761,129	100.0
General revenue	8,476,653	72.1
Intergovernmental revenue	2,622,679	22.3
Taxes	4,511,208	38.4
General sales	1,650,498	14.0
Selective sales	594,858	5.1
License taxes	383,702	3.3
Individual income tax	1,660,248	14.1
Corporate income tax	216,641	1.8
Other taxes	5,261	0.0
Current charges	866,572	7.4
Miscellaneous general revenue	476,194	4.0
Utility revenue	0	-
Liquor stores revenue	164,153	1.4
Insurance trust revenue[1]	3,120,323	26.5
Total Expenditure	9,571,879	100.0
Intergovernmental expenditure	2,408,604	25.2
Direct expenditure	7,163,275	74.8
Current operation	5,257,363	54.9
Capital outlay	457,908	4.8
Insurance benefits and repayments	1,146,546	12.0
Assistance and subsidies	159,842	1.7
Interest on debt	141,616	1.5
Exhibit: Salaries and wages	1,470,850	15.4
Total Expenditure	9,571,879	100.0
General expenditure	8,298,096	86.7
Intergovernmental expenditure	2,408,604	25.2
Direct expenditure	5,889,492	61.5
General expenditure, by function:		
Education	3,115,269	32.5
Public welfare	2,495,878	26.1
Hospitals	52,251	0.5
Health	151,848	1.6
Highways	704,780	7.4
Police protection	65,099	0.7
Correction	280,588	2.9
Natural resources	242,630	2.5
Parks and recreation	39,105	0.4
Governmental administration	393,536	4.1
Interest on general debt	141,616	1.5
Other and unallocable	615,496	6.4
Utility expenditure	0	-
Liquor stores expenditure	127,237	1.3
Insurance trust expenditure	1,146,546	12.0
Debt at End of Fiscal Year	3,369,178	X
Cash and Security Holdings	25,117,950	X

X = Not applicable.
- = Zero or rounds to zero.
[1] Within insurance trust revenue, net earnings of state retirement systems is a calculated statistic (the item code in the data file is X08), and thus can be positive or negative. Net earnings is the sum of earnings on investments plus gains on investments minus losses on investments. The change made in 2002 for asset valuation from book to market value in accordance with Statement 34 of the Governmental Accounting Standards Board is reflected in the calculated statistics.

Table ID-16. State Government Tax Collections, 2018

(Dollars in thousands, percent.)

Item	Dollars	Percent distribution
Total Taxes	4,848,359	100.0
Property taxes	X	-
Sales and gross receipts	2,396,117	49.4
General sales and gross receipts	1,790,830	36.9
Selective sales and gross receipts	605,287	12.5
Alcoholic beverages	9,710	0.2
Amusements	X	-
Insurance premiums	97,359	2.0
Motor fuels	362,234	7.5
Pari-mutuels	884	-
Public utilities	2,592	0.1
Tobacco products	51,141	1.1
Other selective sales	81,367	1.7
Licenses	367,178	7.6
Alcoholic beverages	1,721	-
Amusements	258	-
Corporations in general	2,962	0.1
Hunting and fishing	46,428	1.0
Motor vehicle	195,431	4.0
Motor vehicle operators	10,341	0.2
Public utilities	58,067	1.2
Occupation and business, NEC	47,431	1.0
Other licenses	4,539	0.1
Income taxes	2,076,673	42.8
Individual income	1,835,864	37.9
Corporation net income	240,809	5.0
Other taxes	8,391	0.2
Death and gift	X	-
Documentary and stock transfer	X	-
Severance	5,463	0.1
Taxes, NEC	2,928	-

X = Not applicable.
- = Zero or rounds to zero.

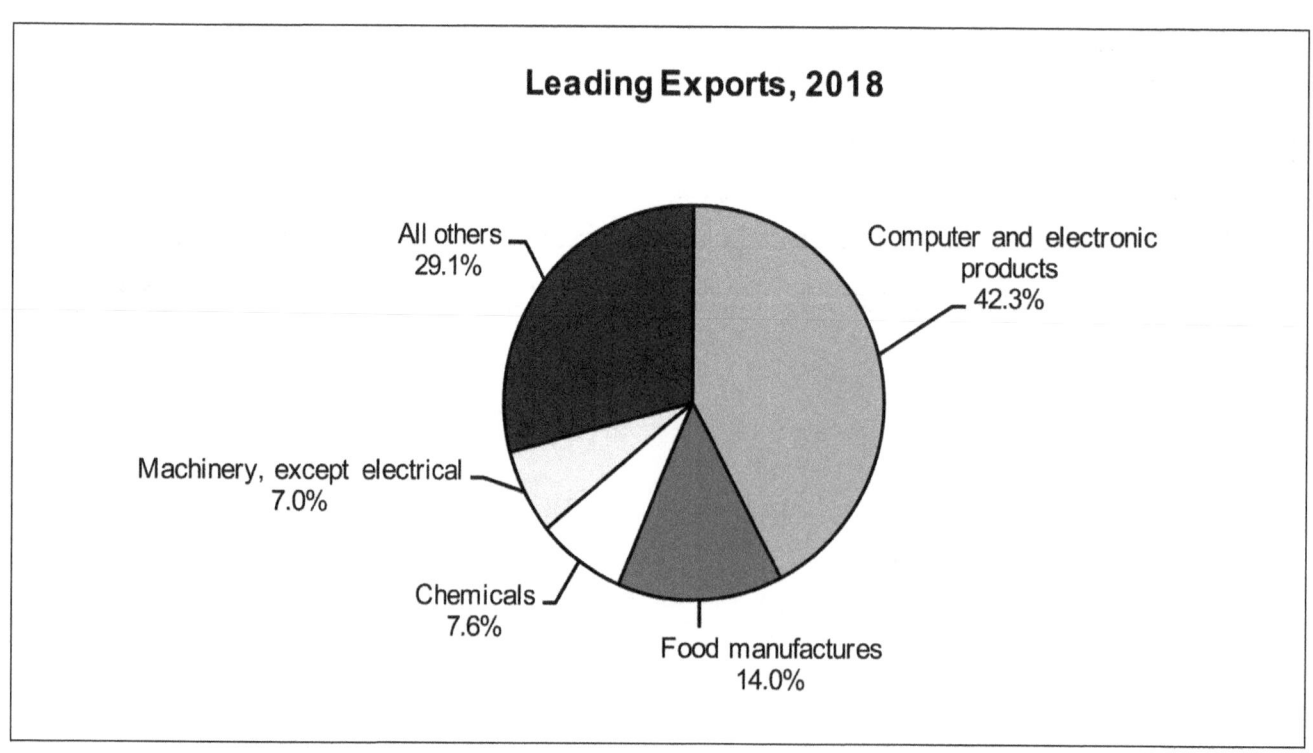

Leading Exports, 2018

All others 29.1%

Computer and electronic products 42.3%

Machinery, except electrical 7.0%

Chemicals 7.6%

Food manufactures 14.0%

Facts and Figures

Location: North central United States; bordered on the N by Wisconsin, on the E by Lake Michigan and Indiana, on the S by Kentucky, and on the W by Iowa and Missouri

Area: 57,913 sq. mi. (149,998 sq. km.); rank—25th

Population: 12,741,080 (2018 est.); rank—6th

Principal Cities: capital—Springfield; largest—Chicago

Statehood: December 3, 1818; 21st state

U.S. Congress: 2 senators, 18 representatives

State Motto: State Sovereignty, National Union

State Song: "Illinois"

State Nicknames: The Prairie State; The Land of Lincoln

Abbreviations: IL; Ill.

State Symbols: flower—native violet; tree—white oak; bird—cardinal

At a Glance

- Illinois was one of three states that experienced a population decline between 2010 and 2018, with a decrease in population of 0.7 percent.

- In 2018, Illinois employed 48.4 state and local government employees per 1,000 residents, which was the 8th lowest ratio in the country.

- The violent crime rate in Illinois was 438.8 per 100,000 residents in 2017, compared to the nationwide rate of 394.0 per 100,000 residents.

- Illinois ranked 17th for median household income in 2017, with an income of $62,992.

- In 2017, 6.8 percent of Illinois residents did not have health insurance, compared to 8.7 percent of the entire U.S. population.

Table IL-1. Population by Age, Sex, Race, and Hispanic Origin

(Number, percent, except where noted.)

Sex, age, race, and Hispanic origin	2000	2010	2018 [1]	Percent change, 2010–2018
Total Population...	12,419,293	12,830,632	12,741,080	-0.7
Percent of total U.S. population	4.4	4.2	3.9	X
Sex				
Male...	6,080,336	6,292,276	6,260,901	-0.5
Female..	6,338,957	6,538,356	6,480,179	-0.9
Age				
Under 5 years...	876,549	835,557	760,619	-9.0
5 to 19 years...	2,728,957	2,660,945	2,425,455	-8.8
20 to 64 years...	7,313,762	7,724,917	7,562,045	-2.1
65 years and over...	1,500,025	1,609,213	1,992,961	23.8
Median age (years)...	34.7	36.6	38.3	4.6
Race and Hispanic Origin				
One race				
White...	9,125,471	10,030,587	9,791,840	-2.4
Black..	1,878,875	1,903,458	1,860,190	-2.3
American Indian and Alaska Native	31,006	73,486	75,567	2.8
Asian..	423,603	604,399	748,722	23.9
Native Hawaiian or Other Pacific Islander	4,610	7,436	8,445	13.6
Two or more races	235,016	210,906	256,316	21.5
Hispanic (of any race)..	1,530,262	2,073,054	2,214,142	6.8

X = Not applicable.
[1] Population figures for 2018 are July 1 estimates. The 2010 estimates are taken from the 2010 Census.
- = Zero or rounds to zero.

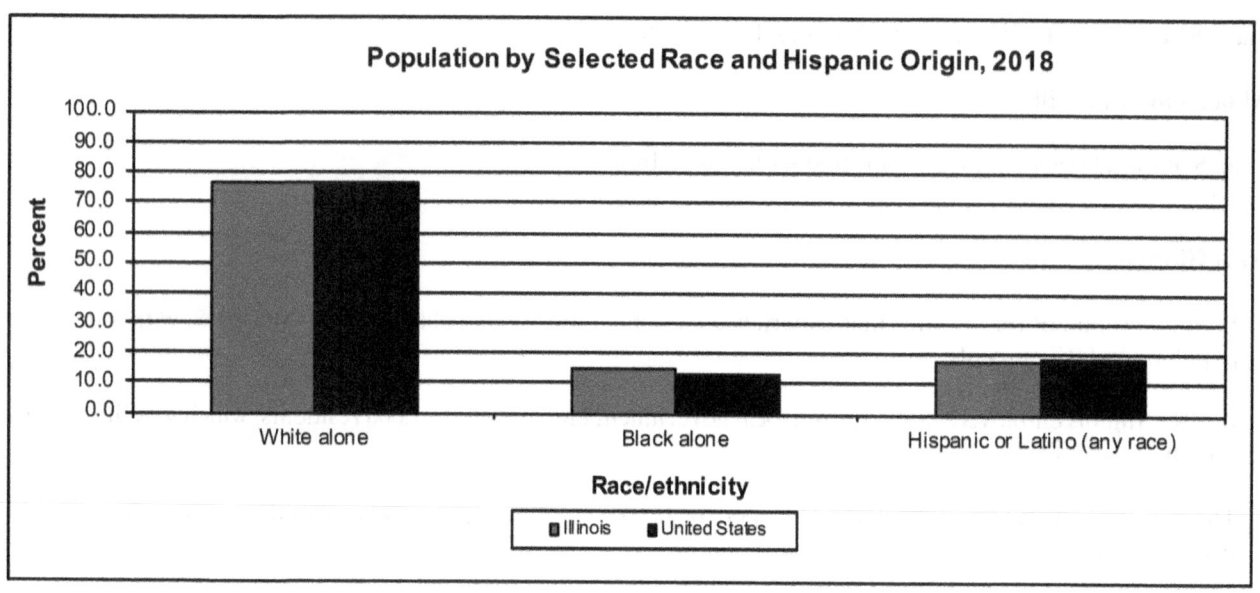

Table IL-2. Marital Status

(Number, percent distribution.)

Sex, age, race, and Hispanic origin	2000	2010	2017
Males, 15 Years and Over...	4,685,982	4,977,964	5,075,158
Never married	31.9	37.2	38.7
Now married, except separated..	56.1	50.0	48.8
Separated..	1.6	1.4	1.4
Widowed..	2.5	2.6	2.6
Divorced..	7.9	8.8	8.5
Females, 15 Years and Over...	5,021,855	5,289,803	5,337,919
Never married	26.1	31.1	32.7
Now married, except separated..	51.3	46.3	46.0
Separated..	2.0	2.1	1.7
Widowed..	10.7	9.5	8.9
Divorced..	9.9	11.0	10.7

Table IL-3. Households and Housing Characteristics

(Number, percent, dollars.)

Item	2000	2010	2017	Average annual percent change, 2010–2017
Total Households..	4,591,779	4,752,857	4,808,672	0.2
Family households..	3,105,513	3,133,813	3,083,543	-0.2
Married-couple family..............................	2,353,892	2,301,009	2,277,277	-0.1
Other family...	751,621	832,804	806,266	-0.5
Male householder, no wife present...........	187,903	220,197	223,035	0.2
Female householder, no husband present...	563,718	612,607	583,231	-0.7
Nonfamily households..................................	1,486,266	1,619,044	1,725,129	0.9
Householder living alone............................	1,229,807	1,340,394	1,426,454	0.9
Householder not living alone.......................	256,459	278,650	298,675	1.0
Housing Characteristics				
Total housing units......................................	4,885,615	5,297,077	5,359,416	0.2
Occupied housing units	4,591,779	4,752,857	4,808,672	0.2
Owner occupied.......................................	3,088,884	3,219,338	3,182,232	-0.2
Renter occupied.......................................	1,502,895	1,533,519	1,626,440	0.9
Average household size................................	2.63	2.64	2.60	-0.2
Financial Characteristics				
Median gross rent of renter-occupied housing	605	848	974	2.1
Median monthly owner costs for housing units with a mortgage	1,198	1,655	1,603	-0.4
Median value of owner-occupied housing units........	130,800	191,800	195,300	0.3

- = Zero or rounds to zero.

Table IL-4. Migration, Origin, and Language

(Number, percent.)

Characteristic	State			U.S.		
	2016	2017	Percent change	2016	2017	Percent change
Residence 1 Year Ago						
Population 1 year and over	12,654,142	12,659,328	-	319,361,956	321,994,428	0.8
Same house	86.9	87.1	X	85.4	85.7	X
Different house in the U.S.	12.6	12.3	X	13.9	13.6	X
Same county	8.3	8.1	X	8.3	8.1	X
Different county	4.2	4.2	X	5.6	5.6	X
Same state	2.6	2.6	X	3.2	3.3	X
Different state	1.6	1.5	X	2.4	2.3	X
Abroad	0.5	0.6	X	0.7	0.7	X
Place of Birth						
Native born	11,018,065	10,969,602	-0.4	279,388,170	281,193,323	0.6
Male	49.0	49.1	X	49.3	49.4	X
Female	51.0	50.9	X	50.7	50.6	X
Foreign born	1,783,474	1,832,421	2.7	43,739,345	44,525,855	1.8
Male	50.1	49.3	X	48.5	48.4	X
Female	49.9	50.7	X	51.5	51.6	X
Foreign born; naturalized U.S. citizen...........	883,621	921,225	4.3	21,238,372	21,948,732	3.3
Male	47.6	47.7	X	45.9	45.9	X
Female	52.4	52.3	X	54.1	54.1	X
Foreign born; not a U.S. citizen...............	899,853	911,196	1.3	22,500,973	22,577,123	0.3
Male	52.5	51.0	X	51	50.8	X
Female	47.5	49.0	X	49	49.2	X
Entered 2010 or later	15.4	17.9	X	18.6	21.3	X
Entered 2000 to 2009	25.7	24.6	X	26.7	25.7	X
Entered before 2000...........................	58.9	57.6	X	54.7	53.0	X
World Region of Birth, Foreign						
Foreign-born population, excluding population born at sea	1,783,474	1,832,421	2.7	43,738,901	44,525,458	1.8
Europe..	20.7	20.6	X	10.9	10.8	X
Asia..	30.0	30.0	X	30.8	31.2	X
Africa..	3.5	4.0	X	4.9	5.1	X
Oceania.......................................	0.3	0.2	X	0.6	0.6	X
Latin America.................................	44.6	44.2	X	51	50.4	X
North America.................................	0.9	1.0	X	1.8	1.8	X
Language Spoken at Home and Ability to Speak English						
Population 5 years and over.....................	12,032,049	12,034,675	-	303,328,961	305,924,019	0.9
English only	77.1	76.5	X	78.4	78.2	X
Language other than English....................	22.9	23.5	X	21.6	21.8	X
Speaks English less than "very well"..........	8.7	8.8	X	8.6	8.5	X

NA = Not available.
X = Not applicable.
- = Zero or rounds to zero.

Table IL-5. Median Income and Poverty Status, 2017

(Number, percent, except as noted.)

Characteristic	State		U.S.	
	Number	Percent	Number	Percent
Median Income				
Households (dollars)..	62,992	X	60,336	X
Families (dollars)	79,168	X	73,891	X
Below Poverty Level (All People)	1,569,753	12.6	42,583,651	13.4
Sex				
Male	696,068	11.4	19,004,547	12.2
Female	873,685	13.7	23,579,104	14.5
Age				
Under 18 years..	486,196	17.0	13,353,202	18.4
Related children under 18 years.......................................	477,202	16.8	13,053,472	18.1
18 to 64 years...	921,313	11.9	24,648,677	12.6
65 years and over	162,244	8.6	4,581,772	9.3

X = Not applicable.

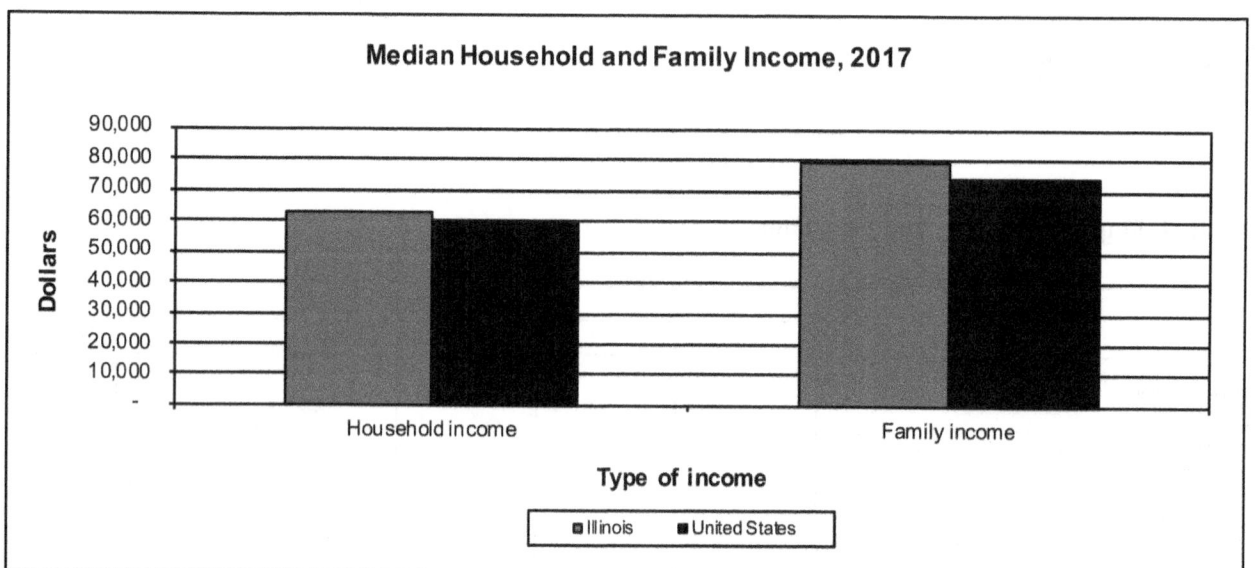

Median Household and Family Income, 2017

Table IL-6. Health Insurance Coverage Status for the Civilian Noninstitutionalized Population and Children Under 18 Years of Age

(Number, percent.)

Item	2009	2010	2011	2012	2013	2014	2015	2016	2017
Civilian Noninstitutionalized Population	12,719,575	12,673,245	12,688,006	12,698,371	12,704,616	12,702,393	12,679,860	12,620,388	12,620,126
Covered by Private or Public Insurance									
Number...	11,025,183	10,927,689	11,028,731	11,075,906	11,086,412	11,464,467	11,779,571	11,803,786	11,760,869
Percent..	86.7	86.2	86.9	87.2	87.3	90.3	92.9	93.5	93.2
Uninsured									
Number...	1,694,392	1,745,556	1,659,275	1,622,465	1,618,204	1,237,926	900,289	816,602	859,257
Percent..	13.3	13.8	13.1	12.8	12.7	9.7	7.1	6.5	6.8
Percent in the U.S. not covered............................	15.1	15.5	15.1	14.8	14.5	11.7	9.4	8.6	8.7
Children Under 18 Years of Age[1]	3,168,258	3,121,719	3,091,887	3,059,055	3,017,960	2,980,902	2,956,262	2,919,863	3,069,418
Covered by Private or Public Insurance									
Number...	3,025,989	2,981,614	2,978,576	2,957,589	2,892,609	2,881,400	2,880,990	2,848,544	2,980,069
Percent..	95.5	95.5	96.3	96.7	95.8	96.7	97.5	97.6	97.1
Uninsured									
Number...	142,269	140,105	113,311	101,466	125,351	99,502	75,272	71,319	89,349
Percent..	4.5	4.5	3.7	3.3	4.2	3.3	2.5	2.4	2.9
Percent in the U.S. not covered............................	8.6	8.0	7.5	7.2	7.1	6.0	4.8	4.5	5.0

[1] 2017 data is for individuals under 19 years of age.

Table IL-7. Employment Status by Demographic Group, 2018

(Numbers in thousands, percent.)

Characteristic	Civilian noninstitutional population	Civilian labor force		Employed		Unemployed	
		Number	Percent of population	Number	Percent of population	Number	Percent of population
Total................................	10,053	6,482	64.5	6,207	61.7	275	4.2
Sex							
Male..................................	4,869	3,412	70.1	3,257	66.9	155	4.6
Female...............................	5,184	3,070	59.2	2,950	56.9	120	3.9
Race, Sex, and Hispanic Origin							
White.................................	7,796	5,090	65.3	4,911	63.0	180	3.5
Male..............................	3,823	2,722	71.2	2,623	68.6	100	3.7
Female...........................	3,973	2,368	59.6	2,288	57.6	80	3.4
Black or African American...........	1,404	847	60.3	773	55.1	73	8.7
Male..............................	628	394	62.8	352	56.1	42	10.7
Female...........................	776	452	58.3	422	54.3	31	6.8
Hispanic or Latino ethnicity[1]......	1,576	1,082	68.7	1,037	65.8	45	4.2
Male..............................	788	601	76.3	577	73.2	24	4.0
Female...........................	788	482	61.1	461	58.4	21	4.3
Age							
16 to 19 years......................	684	239	34.9	204	29.8	35	14.5
20 to 24 years......................	843	606	71.9	557	66.0	50	8.2
25 to 34 years......................	1,694	1,423	84.0	1,364	80.5	58	4.1
35 to 44 years......................	1,618	1,337	82.6	1,294	80.0	43	3.2
45 to 54 years......................	1,714	1,398	81.6	1,359	79.3	39	2.8
55 to 64 years......................	1,617	1,111	68.7	1,072	66.3	39	3.5
65 years and over...................	1,884	369	19.6	357	19.0	12	3.2

NOTE: Data in Table 7 are from the Current Population Survey (CPS) and do not match the estimates in Table 8. See notes and definitions for further information.
[1] May be of any race.

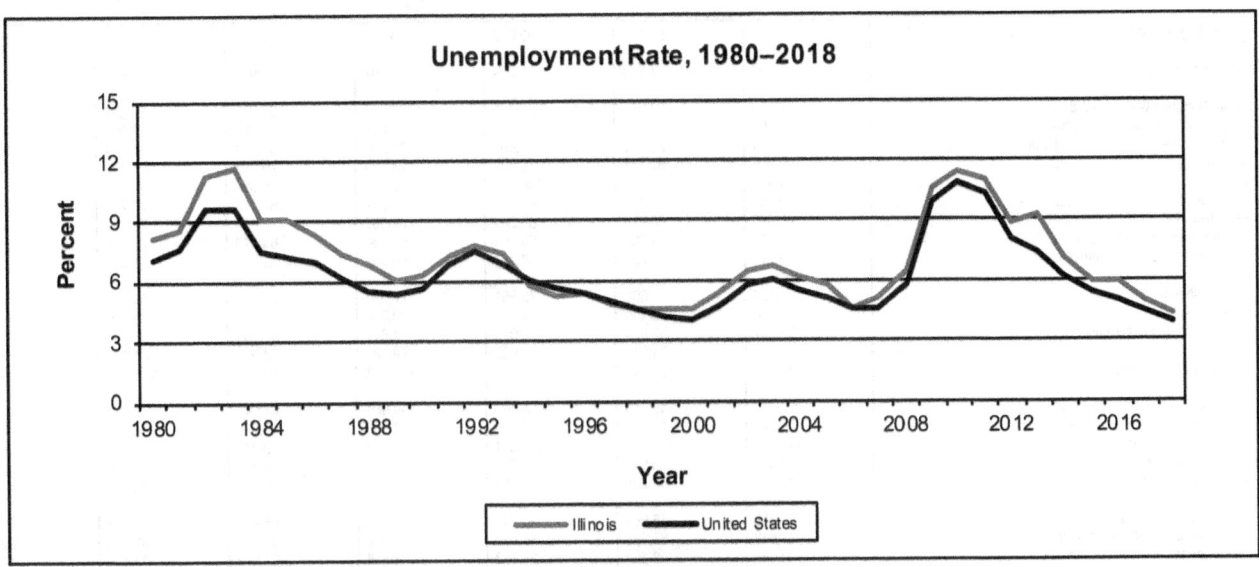

Unemployment Rate, 1980–2018

Table IL-8. Employment Status of the Civilian Noninstitutional Population Age 16 Years and Over

(Number, percent.)

Year	Civilian labor force	Civilian participation rate	Employed	Unemployed	Unemployment rate
2010..........................	6,625,321	66.9	5,937,047	688,274	10.4
2011..........................	6,586,893	66.2	5,948,366	638,527	9.7
2012..........................	6,581,867	65.9	5,990,644	591,223	9.0
2013..........................	6,549,473	65.3	5,956,749	592,724	9.0
2014..........................	6,508,356	64.8	6,047,243	461,113	7.1
2015..........................	6,507,228	64.7	6,119,271	387,957	6.0
2016..........................	6,549,991	65.1	6,169,560	380,431	5.8
2017..........................	6,492,578	64.5	6,170,676	321,902	5.0
2018..........................	6,469,668	64.5	6,191,319	278,349	4.3

Table IL-9. Employment and Average Wages by Industry

(Estimates are based on the 2012 *North American Industry Classification System* [NAICS].)

Industry	2011	2012	2013	2014	2015	2016	2017
				Number of Jobs			
Wage and Salary Employment by Industry......................	5,851,115	5,922,889	5,965,073	6,044,058	6,139,569	6,176,576	6,210,786
Farm Wage and Salary Employment...............................	16,969	15,801	12,653	11,710	14,743	14,215	13,744
Nonfarm Wage and Salary Employment...........................	5,834,146	5,907,088	5,952,420	6,032,348	6,124,826	6,162,361	6,197,042
Private wage and salary employment...............................	4,942,947	5,025,358	5,075,143	5,157,446	5,248,161	5,289,354	5,325,125
Forestry, fishing, and related activities...............................	4,257	4,623	4,798	5,916	5,539	5,506	5,545
Mining...	9,494	10,086	9,651	9,862	9,281	7,991	7,767
Utilities..	23,524	23,858	23,795	24,015	24,175	24,342	24,498
Construction...	201,222	194,654	196,717	206,988	219,298	224,264	225,044
Manufacturing..	574,618	583,660	580,224	580,285	581,803	575,079	577,022
Durable goods manufacturing..	343,514	354,425	350,844	349,987	348,363	338,173	337,375
Nondurable goods manufacturing.....................................	231,104	229,235	229,380	230,298	233,440	236,906	239,647
Wholesale trade	290,615	295,532	300,062	301,268	302,974	303,421	307,063
Retail trade..	600,310	601,923	603,470	608,907	619,278	621,993	616,295
Transportation and warehousing..	237,983	243,968	244,418	250,953	260,188	263,092	267,560
Information...	100,324	100,489	98,983	99,409	101,208	99,945	96,901
Finance and insurance	291,550	294,447	293,581	292,392	301,046	300,797	303,359
Real estate and rental and leasing....................................	73,237	73,565	75,399	76,273	78,867	80,978	83,064
Professional, scientific, and technical services..................	357,058	366,532	378,991	390,558	405,693	413,069	414,877
Management of companies and enterprises........................	98,255	102,739	103,688	103,279	94,810	94,766	97,166
Administrative and waste services.....................................	382,012	401,331	412,263	428,116	429,444	431,272	437,045
Educational services	161,953	165,379	167,053	167,562	167,399	171,459	172,250
Health care and social assistance......................................	708,459	720,347	730,629	739,200	756,950	767,222	773,274
Arts, entertainment, and recreation...................................	77,500	79,885	80,840	84,554	85,565	89,245	92,370
Accommodation and food services.....................................	447,835	459,660	469,073	477,469	495,937	511,854	521,878
Other services, except public administration......................	302,741	302,680	301,508	310,440	308,706	303,059	302,147
Government and government enterprises............................	891,199	881,730	877,277	874,902	876,665	873,007	871,917
				Dollars			
Average Wages and Salaries by Industry	51,736	53,140	53,662	55,135	57,019	57,568	59,191
Average Farm Wages and Salaries	31,092	27,573	30,784	35,797	31,985	33,559	28,697
Average Nonfarm Wages and Salaries	51,796	53,209	53,711	55,173	57,080	57,623	59,258
Average private wages and salaries....................................	52,202	53,625	54,054	55,691	57,765	58,368	60,081
Forestry, fishing, and related activities...............................	28,339	28,351	27,490	30,293	32,704	34,104	36,287
Mining...	66,425	67,946	70,867	74,133	75,785	77,109	76,964
Utilities..	104,533	107,861	106,958	112,947	115,566	119,109	121,534
Construction...	60,767	61,284	62,917	65,709	68,753	70,235	71,990
Manufacturing..	62,992	64,782	65,364	67,867	70,429	70,639	72,453
Durable goods manufacturing..	64,518	65,768	65,704	67,130	68,518	70,030	71,696
Nondurable goods manufacturing.....................................	60,723	63,257	64,844	68,987	73,281	71,508	73,518
Wholesale trade	73,186	75,602	75,651	77,996	80,382	80,954	82,827
Retail trade..	27,770	28,485	28,858	29,240	30,427	30,769	31,820
Transportation and warehousing..	50,564	52,094	52,970	54,647	56,069	56,608	58,339
Information...	72,821	74,844	77,539	79,721	82,940	84,910	87,456
Finance and insurance	97,230	101,087	99,778	105,553	110,729	112,954	117,580
Real estate and rental and leasing....................................	53,528	56,399	58,407	60,964	64,986	66,051	67,422
Professional, scientific, and technical services..................	86,246	88,928	89,210	91,935	95,726	96,237	98,477
Management of companies and enterprises........................	117,314	121,338	123,511	124,603	129,845	127,623	130,002
Administrative and waste services.....................................	34,897	35,550	35,253	36,660	38,853	39,585	41,630
Educational services	42,573	43,228	44,224	45,434	46,491	46,500	47,462
Health care and social assistance......................................	45,339	45,960	46,442	47,377	48,431	49,375	50,726
Arts, entertainment, and recreation...................................	35,613	37,036	36,956	36,316	38,594	39,220	39,405
Accommodation and food services.....................................	20,025	20,804	21,168	21,616	22,573	23,148	23,865
Other services, except public administration......................	34,541	35,070	35,984	37,582	38,926	40,012	41,637
Government and government enterprises............................	49,541	50,838	51,725	52,120	52,979	53,109	54,235

Table IL-10. Employment Characteristics by Family Type

(Number, percent.)

Family type and labor force status	2015 Total	2015 Families with own children under 18 years	2016 Total	2016 Families with own children under 18 years	2017 Total	2017 Families with own children under 18 years
All Families...	3,099,463	1,348,476	3,100,613	1,342,579	3,083,543	1,318,911
FAMILY TYPE AND LABOR FORCE STATUS						
Married-Couple Families...............................	2,285,540	929,523	2,266,786	911,333	2,277,277	909,579
Both husband and wife in labor force..........................	53.3	66.4	54.1	68.5	52.8	67.3
Husband in labor force, wife not in labor force	22.2	28.6	20.9	26.3	21.6	27.6
Wife in labor force, husband not in labor force	7.6	3.3	7.6	3.7	7.5	3.3
Both husband and wife not in labor force......................	16.2	1.4	16.6	1.1	17.2	1.3
Other Families	813,923	418,953	833,827	431,246	806,266	409,332
Female householder, no husband present.........................	73.7	77.0	73.1	75.5	72.3	75.0
In labor force...	53.1	65.5	53.0	64.5	52.6	65.0
Not in labor force...	20.6	11.5	20.2	11.0	19.7	10.0
Male householder, no wife present.............................	26.3	23.0	26.9	24.5	27.7	25.0
In labor force...	20.8	21.5	21.4	22.6	21.9	22.9
Not in labor force...	5.5	1.4	5.5	2.0	5.7	2.1

Table IL-11. School Enrollment and Educational Attainment, 2017

(Number, percent.)

Item	State	U.S.
Enrollment		
Total population 3 years and over, enrolled in school	3,216,701	81,273,337
Enrolled in nursery school or preschool (percent)................................	6.7	6.0
Enrolled in kindergarten (percent)..	4.6	4.9
Enrolled in elementary school, grades 1-8 (percent).............................	40.7	40.6
Enrolled in high school, grades 9-12 (percent)	21.5	21.1
Enrolled in college or graduate school (percent)...............................	26.6	27.4
Attainment		
Total population 25 years and over	8,707,057	221,250,083
Less than ninth grade (percent)..	4.9	5.1
9th to 12th grade, no diploma (percent)	6.0	6.9
High school graduate, including equivalency (percent)...........................	26.1	27.1
Some college, no degree (percent)...	20.6	20.4
Associate's degree (percent)...	8.0	8.5
Bachelor's degree (percent)..	21.0	19.7
Graduate or professional degree (percent).......................................	13.4	12.3
High school graduate or higher (percent)..	89.1	88.0
Bachelor's degree or higher (percent)...	34.4	32.0

Table IL-12. Public School Characteristics and Educational Indicators

(Number, percent; data derived from National Center of Education Statistics.)

Item	State	U.S.
Public Elementary and Secondary Schools		
Number of operational school districts, 2016-17...	1,057	18,377
Number of operational schools, 2016-17...	4,173	98,330
Percent charter schools	1.5	7.1
Total public school enrollment, 2016-17..	2,026,718	50,587,859
Percent charter school enrollment	3.2	6.0
Student-teacher ratio, Fall 2015...	15.7	16.0
Expenditures per student (dollars), 2015-16...	14,327	11,841
Four-year adjusted cohort graduation rate (ACGR)[1]	87.0	84.6
Students eligible for free or reduced-price lunch (percent), 2015-16......................	49.9	52.1
English language learners (percent), Fall 2016..	9.8	9.6
Students age 3 to 21 served under IDEA, part B (percent), 2017-18	14.6	13.7

Public Schools by Type, 2016-17		Percent of state public schools
Total number of schools..	4,173	100.0
Special education	110	2.6
Vocational education	0	-
Alternative education...	141	3.4

[1] Adjusted Cohort Graduation Rates (ACGR) differ from Averaged Freshmen Graduation Rates (AFGR).
- = Zero or rounds to zero.

Table IL-13. Reported Voting and Registration of the Voting-Age Population, November 2018

(Numbers in thousands, percent.)

Item	Total population	Total citizen population	Registered			Voted		
			Total registered	Percent registered (total population)	Percent registered (total citizen population)	Total voted	Percent voted (total population)	Percent voted (total citizen population)
U.S. Total	249,748	228,832	153,066	61.3	66.9	122,281	49.0	53.4
State Total..	9,732	8,947	6,068	62.4	67.8	4,740	48.7	53.0
Sex								
Male	4,711	4,316	2,794	59.3	64.7	2,183	46.3	50.6
Female	5,021	4,630	3,274	65.2	70.7	2,557	50.9	55.2
Race								
White alone..	7,564	7,078	4,892	64.7	69.1	3,802	50.3	53.7
White, non-Hispanic alone	6,248	6,120	4,436	71.0	72.5	3,494	55.9	57.1
Black alone..	1,334	1,274	861	64.5	67.6	723	54.2	56.8
Asian alone	673	455	205	30.5	45.1	150	22.4	33.1
Hispanic (of any race)........................	1,458	1,061	537	36.8	50.6	354	24.3	33.3
White alone or in combination	7,666	7,180	4,973	64.9	69.3	3,857	50.3	53.7
Black alone or in combination............	1,382	1,322	895	64.7	67.7	740	53.5	56.0
Asian alone or in combination............	688	470	214	31.2	45.6	160	23.2	34.0
Age								
18 to 24 years..	1,199	1,098	531	44.3	48.4	339	28.3	30.9
25 to 34 years..	1,721	1,514	955	55.5	63.1	650	37.8	42.9
35 to 44 years..	1,588	1,404	923	58.1	65.7	680	42.9	48.4
45 to 64 years..	3,407	3,152	2,317	68.0	73.5	1,920	56.3	60.9
65 years and over	1,817	1,778	1,343	73.9	75.5	1,151	63.3	64.7

Table IL-14. Crime

(Number, rate per 100,000. Data are derived from the FBI Uniform Crime Reports.)

Item	State			U.S.		
	2016	2017	Percent change	2016	2017	Percent change
TOTAL POPULATION[1]	12,835,726	12,802,023	-0.3	323,405,935	325,719,178	0.7
VIOLENT CRIME						
Number..	56,054	56,180	0.2	1,285,606	1,283,220	-0.2
Rate	436.7	438.8	0.5	397.5	394.0	-0.9
Murder and Nonnegligent Manslaughter						
Number..	1,061	997	-6.0	17,413	17,284	-0.7
Rate	8.3	7.8	-5.8	5.4	5.3	-1.4
Rape[2]						
Number..	5,003	5,556	11.1	132,414	135,755	2.5
Rate	39.0	43.4	11.3	40.9	41.7	1.8
Robbery						
Number..	17,829	17,567	-1.5	332,797	319,356	-4.0
Rate	138.9	137.2	-1.2	102.9	98.0	-4.7
Aggravated Assault						
Number..	32,161	32,060	-0.3	802,982	810,825	1.0
Rate	250.6	250.4	-0.1	248.3	248.9	0.3
PROPERTY CRIME						
Number..	263,256	257,497	-2.2	7,928,530	7,694,086	-3.0
Rate	2,051.0	2,011.4	-1.9	2,451.6	2,362.2	-3.6
Burglary						
Number..	48,193	43,459	-9.8	1,516,405	1,401,840	-7.6
Rate	375.5	339.5	-9.6	468.9	430.4	-8.2
Larceny-Theft						
Number..	195,196	193,157		5,644,835	5,519,107	-2.2
Rate	1,520.7	1,508.8	-0.8	1,745.4	1,694.4	-2.9
Motor Vehicle Theft						
Number..	19,867	20,881	5.1	767,290	773,139	0.8
Rate	154.8	163.1	5.4	237.3	237.4	-

NOTE: Although arson data are included in the trend and clearance tables, sufficient data are not available to estimate totals for this offense. Therefore, no arson data are published in this table.
- = Zero or rounds to zero.
[1] Population figures are U.S. Census Bureau provisional estimates as of July 1, 2017.
[2] The figures shown in the rape (revised definition) column were estimated using the revised Uniform Crime Reporting (UCR) definition of rape.

Table IL-15. State Government Finances, 2017

(Dollar amounts in thousands, percent distribution.)

Item	Dollars	Percent distribution
Total Revenue	87,942,021	100.0
General revenue	67,992,261	77.3
Intergovernmental revenue	19,736,635	22.4
Taxes	37,978,923	43.2
General sales	11,363,366	12.9
Selective sales	7,266,528	8.3
License taxes	2,793,983	3.2
Individual income tax	13,256,769	15.1
Corporate income tax	2,877,499	3.3
Other taxes	420,778	0.5
Current charges	5,360,979	6.1
Miscellaneous general revenue	4,915,724	5.6
Utility revenue	0	-
Liquor stores revenue	0	-
Insurance trust revenue[1]	19,949,760	22.7
Total Expenditure	85,515,251	100.0
Intergovernmental expenditure	19,192,558	22.4
Direct expenditure	66,322,693	77.6
Current operation	40,462,146	47.3
Capital outlay	5,544,884	6.5
Insurance benefits and repayments	15,292,921	17.9
Assistance and subsidies	1,529,313	1.8
Interest on debt	3,493,429	4.1
Exhibit: Salaries and wages	8,199,405	9.6
Total Expenditure	85,515,251	100.0
General expenditure	70,222,330	82.1
Intergovernmental expenditure	19,192,558	22.4
Direct expenditure	51,029,772	59.7
General expenditure, by function:		
Education	18,520,513	21.7
Public welfare	23,289,719	27.2
Hospitals	1,653,877	1.9
Health	1,989,331	2.3
Highways	6,762,593	7.9
Police protection	439,719	0.5
Correction	1,358,464	1.6
Natural resources	238,887	0.3
Parks and recreation	270,821	0.3
Governmental administration	1,442,772	1.7
Interest on general debt	3,493,429	4.1
Other and unallocable	10,762,205	12.6
Utility expenditure	0	-
Liquor stores expenditure	0	-
Insurance trust expenditure	15,292,921	17.9
Debt at End of Fiscal Year	61,821,319	X
Cash and Security Holdings	155,112,477	X

X = Not applicable.
- = Zero or rounds to zero.
[1] Within insurance trust revenue, net earnings of state retirement systems is a calculated statistic (the item code in the data file is X08), and thus can be positive or negative. Net earnings is the sum of earnings on investments plus gains on investments minus losses on investments. The change made in 2002 for asset valuation from book to market value in accordance with Statement 34 of the Governmental Accounting Standards Board is reflected in the calculated statistics.

Table IL-16. State Government Tax Collections, 2018

(Dollars in thousands, percent.)

Item	Dollars	Percent distribution
Total Taxes	39,857,069	100.0
Property taxes	59,589	0.1
Sales and gross receipts	18,699,777	46.9
General sales and gross receipts	11,336,866	28.4
Selective sales and gross receipts	7,362,911	18.5
Alcoholic beverages	296,162	0.7
Amusements	888,260	2.2
Insurance premiums	456,406	1.1
Motor fuels	1,367,939	3.4
Pari-mutuels	6,387	-
Public utilities	1,439,894	3.6
Tobacco products	764,296	1.9
Other selective sales	2,143,567	5.4
Licenses	2,751,479	6.9
Alcoholic beverages	18,160	-
Amusements	15,918	-
Corporations in general	342,729	0.9
Hunting and fishing	39,534	0.1
Motor vehicle	1,618,750	4.1
Motor vehicle operators	116,118	0.3
Public utilities	15,016	-
Occupation and business, NEC	552,696	1.4
Other licenses	32,558	0.1
Income taxes	17,883,834	44.9
Individual income	15,296,693	38.4
Corporation net income	2,587,141	6.5
Other taxes	462,390	1.2
Death and gift	382,081	1.0
Documentary and stock transfer	80,309	0.2
Severance	X	-
Taxes, NEC	0	-

X = Not applicable.
- = Zero or rounds to zero.

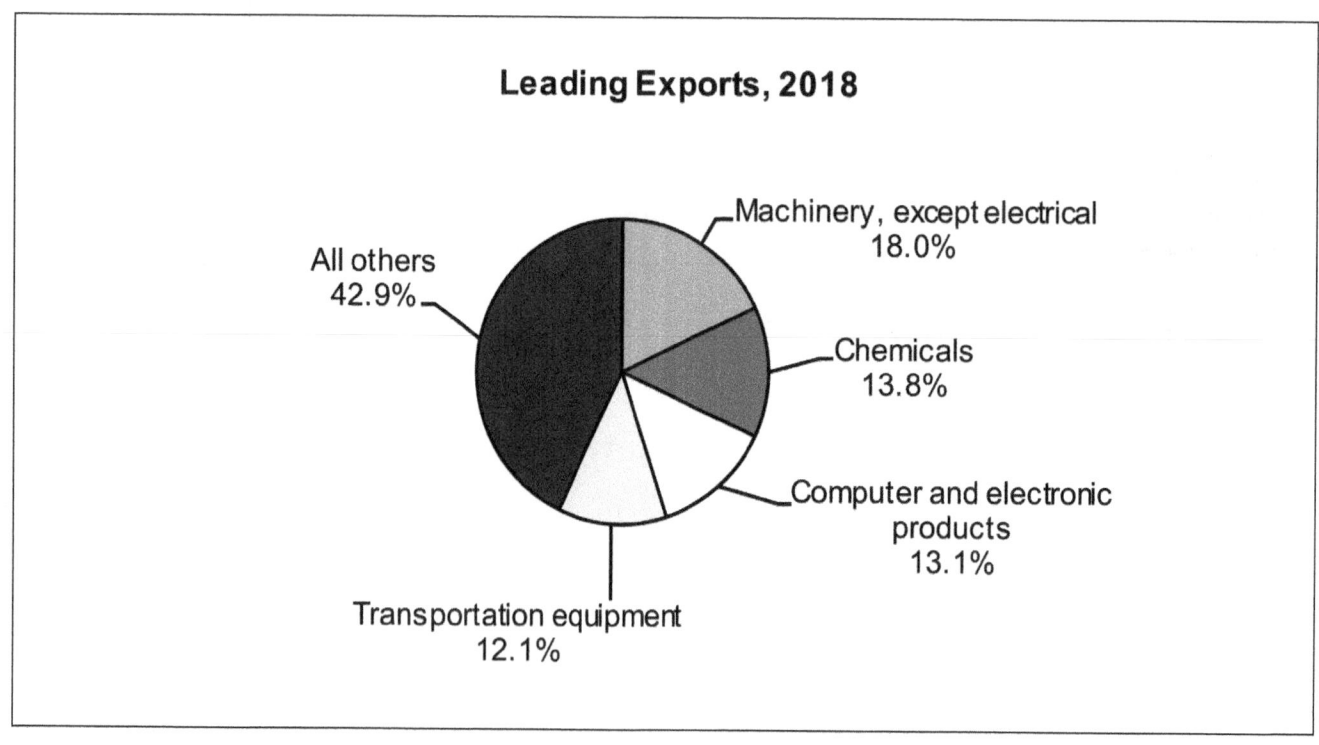

Leading Exports, 2018

Machinery, except electrical 18.0%

Chemicals 13.8%

Computer and electronic products 13.1%

Transportation equipment 12.1%

All others 42.9%

Facts and Figures

Location: East north central United States; bordered on the N by Michigan and Lake Michigan, on the E by Ohio, on the S by Kentucky, and on the W by Illinois

Area: 36,418 sq. mi. (94,321 sq. km.); rank—38th

Population: 6,691,878 (2018 est.); rank—17th

Principal Cities: capital—Indianapolis; largest—Indianapolis

Statehood: December 11, 1816; 19th state

U.S. Congress: 2 senators, 9 representatives

State Motto: The Crossroads of America

State Song: "On the Banks of the Wabash, Far Away"

State Nickname: The Hoosier State

Abbreviations: IN; Ind.

State Symbols: flower—peony; tree—tulip tree; bird—cardinal

At a Glance

- With an increase in population of 3.2 percent, Indiana ranked 30th among the states in growth from 2010 to 2018.

- Indiana's violent crime rate in 2017 was 399.0 per 100,000 population, compared to 394.0 for the entire nation.

- The property crime rate in Indiana in 2017 was 2,416.9 per 100,000 population, ranking 28th in the nation.

- The median household income in Indiana in 2017 was $54,181, compared to the nationwide median of $60,336.

- Approximately 13.5 percent of all Indianans and 18.4 percent of children under 18 years of age in Indiana lived in poverty in 2017.

Table IN-1. Population by Age, Sex, Race, and Hispanic Origin

(Number, percent, except where noted.)

Sex, age, race, and Hispanic origin	2000	2010	2018 [1]	Percent change, 2010–2018
Total Population...	6,080,485	6,483,802	6,691,878	3.2
Percent of total U.S. population	2.2	2.1	2.0	X
Sex				
Male...	2,982,474	3,189,737	3,300,302	3.5
Female...	3,098,011	3,294,065	3,391,576	3.0
Age				
Under 5 years..	423,215	434,075	418,544	-3.6
5 to 19 years..	1,340,171	1,372,507	1,334,349	-2.8
20 to 64 years..	3,564,268	3,836,112	3,883,964	1.2
65 years and over..	752,831	841,108	1,055,021	25.4
Median age (years)	35.2	37.0	37.9	2.4
Race and Hispanic Origin				
One race				
White	5,320,022	5,638,833	5,694,468	1.0
Black	510,034	603,797	658,729	9.1
American Indian and Alaska Native	15,815	24,487	27,740	13.3
Asian...	59,126	105,535	165,368	56.7
Native Hawaiian or Other Pacific Islander	2,005	3,532	4,542	28.6
Two or more races...	75,672	107,618	141,031	31.0
Hispanic (of any race)..	214,536	403,234	475,237	17.9

X = Not applicable.
[1] Population figures for 2018 are July 1 estimates. The 2010 estimates are taken from the 2010 Census.

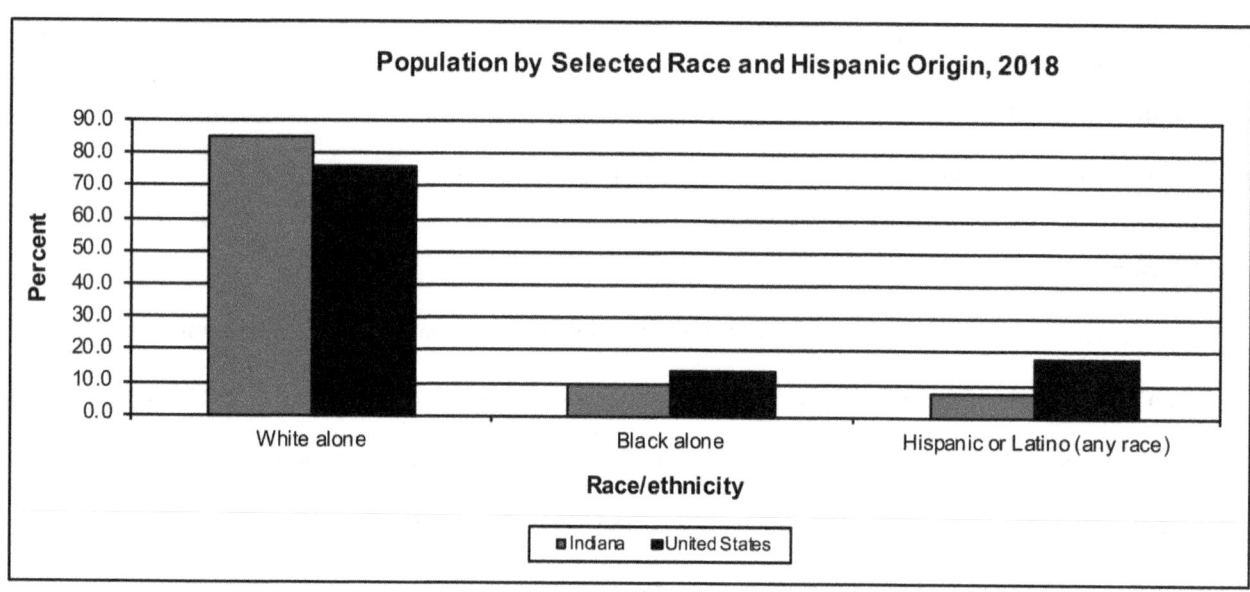

Table IN-2. Marital Status

(Number, percent distribution.)

Sex, age, race, and Hispanic origin	2000	2010	2017
Males, 15 Years and Over..	2,308,917	2,513,953	2,615,670
Never married	27.9	32.6	35.1
Now married, except separated...	58.5	52.3	49.9
Separated...	1.3	1.1	1.1
Widowed...	2.4	2.5	2.8
Divorced...	10.0	11.4	11.2
Females, 15 Years and Over..	2,462,123	2,644,068	2,748,941
Never married	22.0	26.7	28.0
Now married, except separated...	54.3	49.1	48.0
Separated...	1.5	1.8	1.5
Widowed...	10.6	9.2	9.0
Divorced...	11.6	13.2	13.5

Table IN-3. Households and Housing Characteristics

(Number, percent, dollars.)

Item	2000	2010	2017	Average annual percent change, 2010–2017
Total Households...	2,336,306	2,470,905	2,557,299	0.5
Family households..	1,602,501	1,656,386	1,660,102	-
Married-couple family	1,251,458	1,236,518	1,232,773	-
Other family	351,043	419,868	427,329	0.3
Male householder, no wife present......................................	91,671	110,663	125,983	2.0
Female householder, no husband present............................	259,372	309,205	301,346	-0.4
Nonfamily households	733,805	814,519	897,197	1.5
Householder living alone..	605,428	678,460	738,296	1.3
Householder not living alone..	128,377	136,059	158,901	2.4
Housing Characteristics				
Total housing units..	2,532,319	2,797,172	2,885,342	0.5
Occupied housing units	2,336,306	2,470,905	2,557,299	0.5
Owner occupied	1,669,192	1,736,751	1,765,500	0.2
Renter occupied	667,144	734,154	791,799	1.1
Average household size...	2.53	2.55	2.53	-0.1
Financial Characteristics				
Median gross rent of renter-occupied housing	521	683	793	2.3
Median monthly owner costs for housing units with a mortgage	869	1,090	1,089	-
Median value of owner-occupied housing units	94,300	123,300	141,100	2.1

Table IN-4. Migration, Origin, and Language

(Number, percent.)

Characteristic	State			U.S.		
	2016	2017	Percent change	2016	2017	Percent change
Residence 1 Year Ago						
Population 1 year and over	6,554,084	6,591,598	0.6	319,361,956	321,994,428	0.8
Same house	85.1	85.5	X	85.4	85.7	X
Different house in the U.S.	14.5	14.2	X	13.9	13.6	X
Same county	8.5	8.3	X	8.3	8.1	X
Different county	6.0	5.9	X	5.6	5.6	X
Same state	3.7	3.7	X	3.2	3.3	X
Different state	2.2	2.2	X	2.4	2.3	X
Abroad	0.4	0.4	X	0.7	0.7	X
Place of Birth						
Native born	6,283,884	6,315,585	0.5	279,388,170	281,193,323	0.6
Male	49.2	49.2	X	49.3	49.4	X
Female	50.8	50.8	X	50.7	50.6	X
Foreign born	349,169	351,233	0.6	43,739,345	44,525,855	1.8
Male	51.0	50.5	X	48.5	48.4	X
Female	49.0	49.5	X	51.5	51.6	X
Foreign born; naturalized U.S. citizen....................	139,428	135,045	-3.1	21,238,372	21,948,732	3.3
Male	46.6	48.9	X	45.9	45.9	X
Female	53.4	51.1	X	54.1	54.1	X
Foreign born; not a U.S. citizen..............................	209,741	216,188	3.1	22,500,973	22,577,123	0.3
Male	53.9	51.5	X	51	50.8	X
Female	46.1	48.5	X	49	49.2	X
Entered 2010 or later	27.6	32.2	X	18.6	21.3	X
Entered 2000 to 2009	29.9	29.3	X	26.7	25.7	X
Entered before 2000..	42.4	38.4	X	54.7	53.0	X
World Region of Birth, Foreign						
Foreign-born population, excluding population born at sea	349,169	351,233	0.6	43,738,901	44,525,458	1.8
Europe	12.4	11.2	X	10.9	10.8	X
Asia..	35.8	35.4	X	30.8	31.2	X
Africa..	7.0	8.8	X	4.9	5.1	X
Oceania	0.6	0.2	X	0.6	0.6	X
Latin America	42.5	42.6	X	51	50.4	X
North America	1.8	1.8	X	1.8	1.8	X
Language Spoken at Home and Ability to Speak English						
Population 5 years and over.......................................	6,212,686	6,247,266	0.6	303,328,961	305,924,019	0.9
English only	91.3	91.2	X	78.4	78.2	X
Language other than English....................................	8.7	8.8	X	21.6	21.8	X
Speaks English less than "very well"...................	3.3	3.2	X	8.6	8.5	X

NA = Not available.
X = Not applicable.
- = Zero or rounds to zero.

Table IN-5. Median Income and Poverty Status, 2017

(Number, percent, except as noted.)

Characteristic	State		U.S.	
	Number	Percent	Number	Percent
Median Income				
Households (dollars)...	54,181	X	60,336	X
Families (dollars)	68,085	X	73,891	X
Below Poverty Level (All People)	871,247	13.5	42,583,651	13.4
Sex				
Male	388,624	12.2	19,004,547	12.2
Female	482,623	14.7	23,579,104	14.5
Age				
Under 18 years..	282,390	18.4	13,353,202	18.4
Related children under 18 years........................	273,183	17.9	13,053,472	18.1
18 to 64 years...	513,055	13.0	24,648,677	12.6
65 years and over	75,802	7.7	4,581,772	9.3

X = Not applicable.

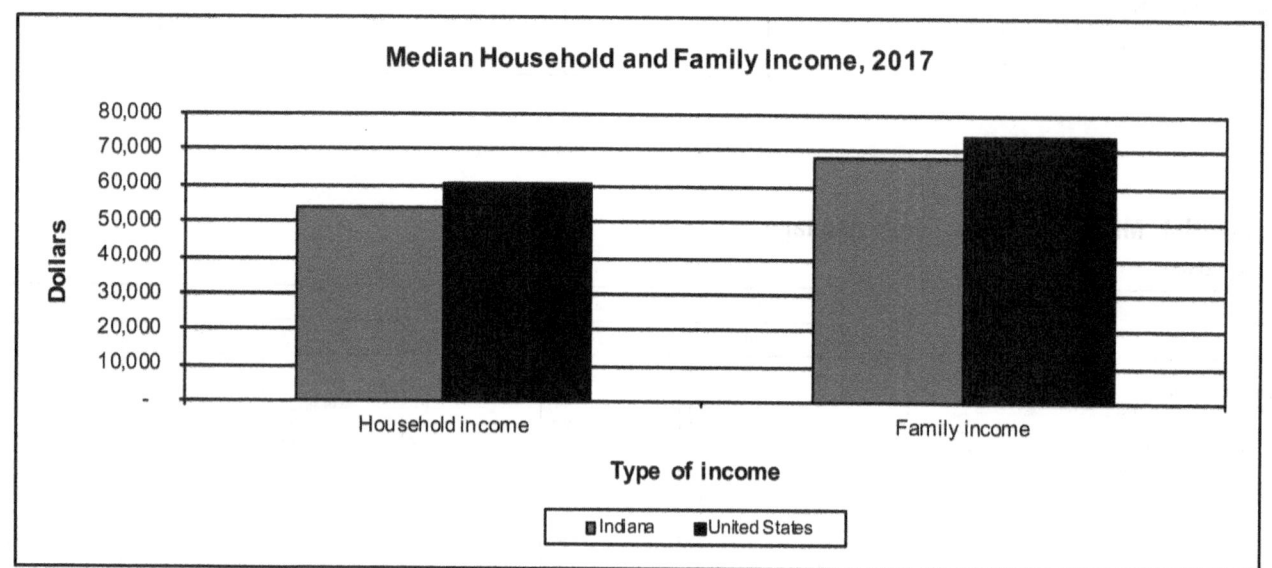

Median Household and Family Income, 2017

Table IN-6. Health Insurance Coverage Status for the Civilian Noninstitutionalized Population and Children Under 18 Years of Age

(Number, percent.)

Item	2009	2010	2011	2012	2013	2014	2015	2016	2017
Civilian Noninstitutionalized Population	6,316,260	6,391,470	6,417,644	6,437,142	6,471,551	6,498,029	6,520,267	6,534,914	6,568,434
Covered by Private or Public Insurance									
Number..	5,415,098	5,443,550	5,486,815	5,517,276	5,568,640	5,722,145	5,892,506	6,004,551	6,032,035
Percent..	85.7	85.2	85.5	85.7	86.0	88.1	90.4	91.9	91.8
Uninsured									
Number..	901,162	947,920	930,829	919,866	902,911	775,884	627,761	530,363	536,399
Percent..	14.3	14.8	14.5	14.3	14.0	11.9	9.6	8.1	8.2
Percent in the U.S. not covered........................	15.1	15.5	15.1	14.8	14.5	11.7	9.4	8.6	8.7
Children Under 18 Years of Age[1]	1,582,770	1,602,320	1,593,636	1,585,435	1,584,015	1,579,992	1,576,006	1,573,925	1,670,417
Covered by Private or Public Insurance									
Number..	1,442,759	1,459,648	1,464,911	1,451,515	1,454,011	1,466,497	1,469,681	1,481,775	1,564,632
Percent..	91.2	91.1	91.9	91.6	91.8	92.8	93.3	94.1	93.7
Uninsured									
Number..	140,011	142,672	128,725	133,920	130,004	113,495	106,325	92,150	105,785
Percent..	8.8	8.9	8.1	8.4	8.2	7.2	6.7	5.9	6.3
Percent in the U.S. not covered........................	8.6	8.0	7.5	7.2	7.1	6.0	4.8	4.5	5.0

[1] 2017 data is for individuals under 19 years of age.

Table IN-7. Employment Status by Demographic Group, 2018

(Numbers in thousands, percent.)

Characteristic	Civilian noninstitutional population	Civilian labor force		Employed		Unemployed	
		Number	Percent of population	Number	Percent of population	Number	Percent of population
Total..	5,215	3,412	65.4	3,293	63.1	119	3.5
Sex							
Male..	2,534	1,837	72.5	1,775	70.1	62	3.4
Female..	2,681	1,575	58.8	1,518	56.6	57	3.6
Race, Sex, and Hispanic Origin							
White..	4,502	2,939	65.3	2,848	63.3	92	3.1
Male..	2,204	1,601	72.6	1,553	70.4	48	3.0
Female..	2,298	1,338	58.2	1,295	56.4	43	3.2
Black or African American.................	492	321	65.2	301	61.3	20	6.1
Male..	225	157	69.9	149	66.2	8	5.2
Female..	267	163	61.3	152	57.1	11	6.9
Hispanic or Latino ethnicity[1]	338	252	74.6	244	72.2	8	3.2
Male..	185	160	86.3	155	83.7	5	3.0
Female..	NA	NA	NA	NA	NA	NA	NA
Age							
16 to 19 years................................	362	156	43.2	138	38.2	18	11.4
20 to 24 years................................	450	363	80.7	338	75.0	26	7.0
25 to 34 years................................	856	716	83.7	697	81.4	19	2.7
35 to 44 years................................	829	715	86.2	694	83.7	21	3.0
45 to 54 years................................	804	658	81.8	641	79.6	17	2.6
55 to 64 years................................	912	615	67.4	603	66.1	12	2.0
65 years and over	1,001	188	18.8	183	18.3	6	3.0

NOTE: Data in Table 7 are from the Current Population Survey (CPS) and do not match the estimates in Table 8. See notes and definitions for further information.
[1] May be of any race.

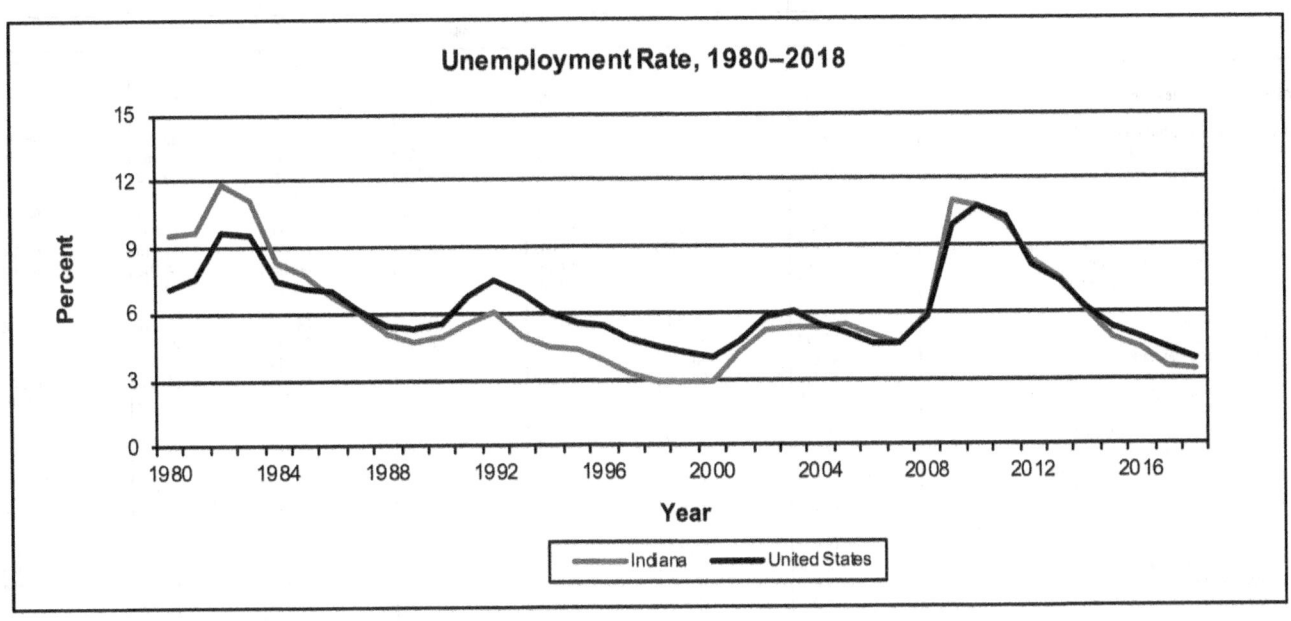

Unemployment Rate, 1980–2018

Table IN-8. Employment Status of the Civilian Noninstitutional Population Age 16 Years and Over

(Number, percent.)

Year	Civilian labor force	Civilian participation rate	Employed	Unemployed	Unemployment rate
2010..	3,175,192	64.0	2,845,608	329,584	10.4
2011..	3,181,991	63.6	2,891,945	290,046	9.1
2012..	3,169,835	63.0	2,905,549	264,286	8.3
2013..	3,188,406	63.0	2,944,275	244,131	7.7
2014..	3,224,871	63.3	3,032,693	192,178	6.0
2015..	3,267,121	63.8	3,109,362	157,759	4.8
2016..	3,327,139	64.6	3,180,104	147,035	4.4
2017..	3,320,409	64.1	3,203,351	117,058	3.5
2018..	3,381,713	64.9	3,265,580	116,133	3.4

Table IN-9. Employment and Average Wages by Industry

(Estimates are based on the 2012 *North American Industry Classification System* [NAICS].)

Industry	2011	2012	2013	2014	2015	2016	2017
	Number of jobs						
Wage and Salary Employment by Industry...................	2,916,485	2,976,626	3,009,962	3,054,388	3,104,469	3,150,896	3,185,079
Farm Wage and Salary Employment...........................	10,519	13,757	12,374	11,533	10,443	10,556	12,285
Nonfarm Wage and Salary Employment......................	2,905,966	2,962,869	2,997,588	3,042,855	3,094,026	3,140,340	3,172,794
Private wage and salary employment...........................	2,454,573	2,516,011	2,554,567	2,599,475	2,650,738	2,694,913	2,728,126
Forestry, fishing, and related activities	3,192	3,324	3,464	4,115	3,997	4,124	4,082
Mining..	6,574	6,737	6,686	6,876	6,511	5,900	5,749
Utilities..	14,726	14,349	14,176	14,131	13,984	13,782	13,796
Construction	123,292	128,533	126,643	126,078	130,349	135,007	141,283
Manufacturing..	464,374	482,653	492,421	507,857	519,217	522,988	534,745
Durable goods manufacturing...............................	330,432	346,391	352,175	363,607	373,274	375,482	384,838
Nondurable goods manufacturing..........................	133,942	136,262	140,246	144,250	145,943	147,506	149,907
Wholesale trade	115,443	116,494	117,483	118,184	119,785	118,612	119,705
Retail trade..	310,342	314,794	318,444	320,938	326,942	334,474	335,031
Transportation and warehousing.............................	114,398	117,796	120,990	124,819	125,909	129,155	129,575
Information	34,339	35,761	35,780	35,616	33,673	32,752	31,528
Finance and insurance	97,902	98,080	97,777	99,242	101,191	102,928	103,924
Real estate and rental and leasing..........................	32,721	33,017	33,231	33,324	33,986	35,123	35,450
Professional, scientific, and technical services	99,030	100,721	102,737	105,982	110,404	113,407	115,596
Management of companies and enterprises................	28,093	29,151	31,072	32,149	33,353	34,601	34,425
Administrative and waste services............................	163,780	171,556	175,934	185,014	188,620	187,984	189,081
Educational services	64,485	65,164	66,107	66,540	67,741	68,557	68,623
Health care and social assistance............................	359,268	366,660	374,683	374,814	383,901	397,702	406,602
Arts, entertainment, and recreation..........................	41,374	41,418	41,626	41,968	41,120	42,036	42,842
Accommodation and food services...........................	238,078	245,526	250,452	254,236	261,550	266,700	267,348
Other services, except public administration..............	143,162	144,277	144,861	147,592	148,505	149,081	148,741
Government and government enterprises......................	451,393	446,858	443,021	443,380	443,288	445,427	444,668
	Dollars						
Average Wages and Salaries by Industry	40,849	41,874	42,370	43,306	44,675	45,264	46,897
Average Farm Wages and Salaries	29,912	27,050	31,286	35,447	32,159	32,835	29,055
Average Nonfarm Wages and Salaries	40,889	41,942	42,416	43,336	44,717	45,306	46,966
Average private wages and salaries...........................	41,377	42,502	42,975	43,969	45,426	45,968	47,720
Forestry, fishing, and related activities	22,931	23,854	24,396	29,100	30,843	33,179	33,525
Mining..	65,065	65,181	68,309	70,368	69,950	68,931	72,557
Utilities..	82,392	84,756	88,376	90,448	94,778	94,861	96,836
Construction	52,415	54,948	54,396	53,371	54,650	55,692	57,983
Manufacturing..	57,060	57,987	58,049	59,489	60,997	61,016	63,016
Durable goods manufacturing...............................	56,709	57,959	57,395	58,775	60,495	60,308	62,335
Nondurable goods manufacturing..........................	57,926	58,056	59,693	61,289	62,282	62,817	64,763
Wholesale trade	56,961	58,567	59,601	62,019	64,345	65,951	67,765
Retail trade..	24,774	25,317	25,502	26,193	27,217	27,645	28,542
Transportation and warehousing.............................	42,806	43,741	44,013	45,507	47,211	47,009	48,645
Information	52,153	54,119	55,509	56,579	58,084	58,733	61,370
Finance and insurance	59,246	62,101	63,148	65,697	68,542	68,568	71,403
Real estate and rental and leasing..........................	36,677	38,008	39,005	41,596	42,902	43,488	45,251
Professional, scientific, and technical services	58,610	60,155	62,986	62,616	64,875	66,661	68,955
Management of companies and enterprises................	84,390	86,342	88,129	90,730	94,601	97,003	101,034
Administrative and waste services............................	28,418	28,728	29,162	29,571	30,392	31,466	33,129
Educational services	30,404	31,143	31,467	32,192	32,735	32,878	33,646
Health care and social assistance............................	42,037	43,404	43,893	44,893	46,549	47,232	49,008
Arts, entertainment, and recreation..........................	32,778	33,028	33,366	33,707	35,054	35,368	36,379
Accommodation and food services...........................	15,417	15,990	16,199	16,536	17,214	17,695	18,404
Other services, except public administration..............	28,068	28,990	29,674	30,655	31,865	32,698	33,895
Government and government enterprises......................	38,236	38,792	39,191	39,624	40,482	41,302	42,339

Table IN-10. Employment Characteristics by Family Type

(Number, percent.)

Family type and labor force status	2015		2016		2017	
	Total	Families with own children under 18 years	Total	Families with own children under 18 years	Total	Families with own children under 18 years
All Families..	1,633,695	702,854	1,645,758	700,451	1,660,102	708,126
FAMILY TYPE AND LABOR FORCE STATUS						
Married-Couple Families...........................	1,213,558	465,663	1,225,255	463,721	1,232,773	464,625
Both husband and wife in labor force...............	52.1	68.4	52.4	67.7	52.7	69.4
Husband in labor force, wife not in labor force	21.4	26.0	21.2	26.4	20.7	25.4
Wife in labor force, husband not in labor force	7.7	3.7	7.8	3.9	7.5	3.3
Both husband and wife not in labor force............	18.1	1.5	17.9	1.6	18.4	1.5
Other Families	420,137	237,191	420,503	236,730	427,329	243,501
Female householder, no husband present...........	71.8	73.2	71.1	73.0	70.5	72.9
In labor force....................................	50.9	60.9	50.9	62.0	49.9	60.1
Not in labor force	20.9	12.3	20.3	11.0	20.6	12.8
Male householder, no wife present.................	28.2	26.8	28.9	27.0	29.5	27.1
In labor force....................................	22.4	24.2	22.5	24.4	23.4	24.7
Not in labor force	5.8	2.5	6.3	2.7	6.1	2.4

Table IN-11. School Enrollment and Educational Attainment, 2017

(Number, percent.)

Item	State	U.S.
Enrollment		
Total population 3 years and over, enrolled in school	1,661,841	81,273,337
Enrolled in nursery school or preschool (percent)........................	6.1	6.0
Enrolled in kindergarten (percent)..	5.2	4.9
Enrolled in elementary school, grades 1-8 (percent)......................	42.0	40.6
Enrolled in high school, grades 9-12 (percent)..........................	21.5	21.1
Enrolled in college or graduate school (percent)........................	25.1	27.4
Attainment		
Total population 25 years and over	4,435,317	221,250,083
Less than ninth grade (percent)	3.6	5.1
9th to 12th grade, no diploma (percent)	7.7	6.9
High school graduate, including equivalency (percent)...................	32.7	27.1
Some college, no degree (percent)	20.2	20.4
Associate's degree (percent)	8.9	8.5
Bachelor's degree (percent)	17.0	19.7
Graduate or professional degree (percent)..............................	9.8	12.3
High school graduate or higher (percent)	88.6	88.0
Bachelor's degree or higher (percent)	26.8	32.0

Table IN-12. Public School Characteristics and Educational Indicators

(Number, percent; data derived from National Center of Education Statistics.)

Item	State	U.S.
Public Elementary and Secondary Schools		
Number of operational school districts, 2016-17..........................	423	18,377
Number of operational schools, 2016-17..................................	1,921	98,330
Percent charter schools	4.8	7.1
Total public school enrollment, 2016-17..................................	1,049,547	50,587,859
Percent charter school enrollment	4.1	6.0
Student-teacher ratio, Fall 2015..	18.1	16.0
Expenditures per student (dollars), 2015-16..............................	9,691	11,841
Four-year adjusted cohort graduation rate (ACGR)[1]......................	83.8	84.6
Students eligible for free or reduced-price lunch (percent), 2015-16......	48.3	52.1
English language learners (percent), Fall 2016	4.5	9.6
Students age 3 to 21 served under IDEA, part B (percent), 2017-18........	16.8	13.7

Public Schools by Type, 2016-17		Percent of state public schools
Total number of schools..	1,921	100.0
Special education	22	1.1
Vocational education	28	1.5
Alternative education..	8	0.4

[1] Adjusted Cohort Graduation Rates (ACGR) differ from Averaged Freshmen Graduation Rates (AFGR).

Table IN-13. Reported Voting and Registration of the Voting-Age Population, November 2018

(Numbers in thousands, percent.)

Item	Total population	Total citizen population	Registered			Voted		
			Total registered	Percent registered (total population)	Percent registered (total citizen population)	Total voted	Percent voted (total population)	Percent voted (total citizen population)
U.S. Total	249,748	228,832	153,066	61.3	66.9	122,281	49.0	53.4
State Total....................................	5,006	4,792	3,131	62.5	65.3	2,364	47.2	49.3
Sex								
Male	2,404	2,331	1,522	63.3	65.3	1,115	46.4	47.8
Female	2,602	2,461	1,609	61.8	65.4	1,249	48.0	50.7
Race								
White alone................................	4,260	4,125	2,723	63.9	66.0	2,066	48.5	50.1
White, non-Hispanic alone	3,937	3,921	2,634	66.9	67.2	1,996	50.7	50.9
Black alone................................	484	468	299	61.8	63.9	221	45.7	47.2
Asian alone	138	98	40	28.9	40.5	27	19.7	27.6
Hispanic (of any race)	337	212	96	28.4	45.2	77	22.9	36.5
White alone or in combination	4,342	4,197	2,775	63.9	66.1	2,099	48.3	50.0
Black alone or in combination	544	518	329	60.4	63.5	245	45.0	47.2
Asian alone or in combination	147	108	49	33.5	45.7	34	22.8	31.1
Age								
18 to 24 years..............................	652	583	288	44.2	49.4	181	27.8	31.1
25 to 34 years..............................	834	785	437	52.4	55.7	285	34.2	36.3
35 to 44 years..............................	792	756	515	65.0	68.1	358	45.2	47.3
45 to 64 years..............................	1,745	1,688	1,156	66.2	68.5	959	55.0	56.8
65 years and over	983	980	735	74.8	75.1	580	59.0	59.2

B = Base is less than 75,000 and therefore too small to show the derived measure.

Table IN-14. Crime

(Number, rate per 100,000. Data are derived from the FBI Uniform Crime Reports.)

Item	State			U.S.		
	2016	2017	Percent change	2016	2017	Percent change
TOTAL POPULATION[1]	6,634,007	6,666,818	0.5	323,405,935	325,719,178	0.7
VIOLENT CRIME						
Number..	26,516	26,598	0.3	1,285,606	1,283,220	-0.2
Rate	399.7	399.0	-0.2	397.5	394.0	-0.9
Murder and Nonnegligent Manslaughter						
Number..	431	397	-7.9	17,413	17,284	-0.7
Rate	6.5	6.0	-8.3	5.4	5.3	-1.4
Rape[2]						
Number..	2,449	2,625	7.2	132,414	135,755	2.5
Rate	36.9	39.4	6.7	40.9	41.7	1.8
Robbery						
Number..	7,291	6,600	-9.5	332,797	319,356	-4.0
Rate	109.9	99.0	-9.9	102.9	98.0	-4.7
Aggravated Assault						
Number..	16,345	16,976	3.9	802,982	810,825	1.0
Rate	246.4	254.6	3.3	248.3	248.9	0.3
PROPERTY CRIME						
Number..	168,460	161,132	-4.3	7,928,530	7,694,086	-3.0
Rate	2,539.3	2,416.9	-4.8	2,451.6	2,362.2	-3.6
Burglary						
Number..	33,567	30,140	-10.2	1,516,405	1,401,840	-7.6
Rate	506.0	452.1	-10.7	468.9	430.4	-8.2
Larceny-Theft						
Number..	120,454	115,591	-4.0	5,644,835	5,519,107	-2.2
Rate	1,815.7	1,733.8	-4.5	1,745.4	1,694.4	-2.9
Motor Vehicle Theft						
Number..	14,439	15,401	6.7	767,290	773,139	0.8
Rate	217.7	231.0	6.1	237.3	237.4	-

NOTE: Although arson data are included in the trend and clearance tables, sufficient data are not available to estimate totals for this offense. Therefore, no arson data are published in this table.
- = Zero or rounds to zero.
[1] Population figures are U.S. Census Bureau provisional estimates as of July 1, 2017.
[2] The figures shown in the rape (revised definition) column were estimated using the revised Uniform Crime Reporting (UCR) definition of rape.

Table IN-15. State Government Finances, 2017

(Dollar amounts in thousands, percent distribution.)

Item	Dollars	Percent distribution
Total Revenue	43,733,220	100.0
General revenue	38,491,515	88.0
Intergovernmental revenue	14,712,679	33.6
Taxes	18,051,598	41.3
General sales	7,556,326	17.3
Selective sales	3,338,102	7.6
License taxes	681,547	1.6
Individual income tax	5,435,292	12.4
Corporate income tax	1,025,498	2.3
Other taxes	14,833	0.0
Current charges	3,549,814	8.1
Miscellaneous general revenue	2,177,424	5.0
Utility revenue	0	-
Liquor stores revenue	0	-
Insurance trust revenue[1]	5,241,705	12.0
Total Expenditure	40,795,988	100.0
Intergovernmental expenditure	9,987,853	24.5
Direct expenditure	30,808,135	75.5
Current operation	23,417,533	57.4
Capital outlay	2,236,324	5.5
Insurance benefits and repayments	2,880,788	7.1
Assistance and subsidies	1,382,810	3.4
Interest on debt	890,680	2.2
Exhibit: Salaries and wages	4,578,985	11.2
Total Expenditure	40,795,988	100.0
General expenditure	37,915,156	92.9
Intergovernmental expenditure	9,987,853	24.5
Direct expenditure	27,927,303	68.5
General expenditure, by function:		
Education	15,742,709	38.6
Public welfare	13,967,124	34.2
Hospitals	140,733	0.3
Health	571,486	1.4
Highways	2,499,289	6.1
Police protection	267,728	0.7
Correction	708,261	1.7
Natural resources	380,565	0.9
Parks and recreation	51,922	0.1
Governmental administration	812,627	2.0
Interest on general debt	890,680	2.2
Other and unallocable	1,882,032	4.6
Utility expenditure	44	-
Liquor stores expenditure	0	-
Insurance trust expenditure	2,880,788	7.1
Debt at End of Fiscal Year	21,842,716	X
Cash and Security Holdings	51,894,819	X

X = Not applicable.
- = Zero or rounds to zero.
[1] Within insurance trust revenue, net earnings of state retirement systems is a calculated statistic (the item code in the data file is X08), and thus can be positive or negative. Net earnings is the sum of earnings on investments plus gains on investments minus losses on investments. The change made in 2002 for asset valuation from book to market value in accordance with Statement 34 of the Governmental Accounting Standards Board is reflected in the calculated statistics.

Table IN-16. State Government Tax Collections, 2018

(Dollars in thousands, percent.)

Item	Dollars	Percent distribution
Total Taxes	19,397,879	100.0
Property taxes	12,927	0.1
Sales and gross receipts	12,119,558	62.5
General sales and gross receipts	7,795,091	40.2
Selective sales and gross receipts	4,324,467	22.3
Alcoholic beverages	51,578	0.3
Amusements	602,410	3.1
Insurance premiums	236,175	1.2
Motor fuels	1,420,135	7.3
Pari-mutuels	1,760	-
Public utilities	202,149	1.0
Tobacco products	418,810	2.2
Other selective sales	1,391,450	7.2
Licenses	749,114	3.9
Alcoholic beverages	12,726	0.1
Amusements	5,792	-
Corporations in general	8,582	-
Hunting and fishing	19,495	0.1
Motor vehicle	321,055	1.7
Motor vehicle operators	252,033	1.3
Public utilities	X	-
Occupation and business, NEC	51,828	0.3
Other licenses	77,603	0.4
Income taxes	6,514,797	33.6
Individual income	5,816,072	30.0
Corporation net income	698,725	3.6
Other taxes	1,483	-
Death and gift	409	-
Documentary and stock transfer	X	-
Severance	1,074	-
Taxes, NEC	0	-

- = Zero or rounds to zero.
X = Not applicable.

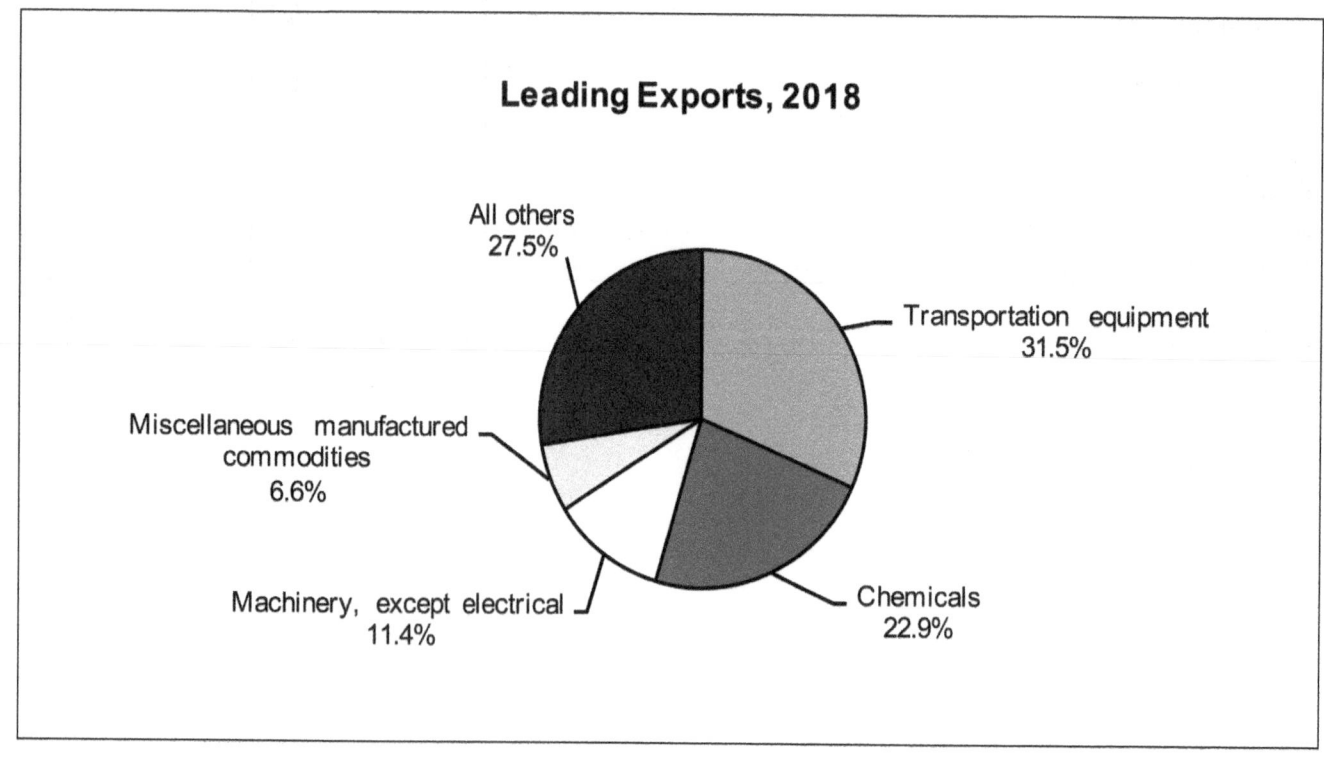

Leading Exports, 2018

All others 27.5%

Transportation equipment 31.5%

Miscellaneous manufactured commodities 6.6%

Machinery, except electrical 11.4%

Chemicals 22.9%

IOWA

Facts and Figures

Location: North central United States; bordered on the N by Minnesota, on the E by Wisconsin and Illinois, on the S by Missouri, and on the W by Nebraska and South Dakota

Area: 56,272 sq. mi. (145,743 sq. km.); rank—26th

Population: 3,156,145 (2018 est.); rank—31st

Principal Cities: capital—Des Moines; largest—Des Moines

Statehood: December 28, 1846; 29th state

U.S. Congress: 2 senators, 4 representatives

State Motto: Our Liberties We Prize and Our Rights We Will Maintain

State Song: "The Song of Iowa"

State Nickname: The Hawkeye State

Abbreviations: IA; Ia.

State Symbols: flower—wild prairie rose; tree—oak; bird—Eastern goldfinch

At a Glance

- With an increase in population of 3.6 percent, Iowa ranked 28th among the states in growth from 2010 to 2018.

- In 2017, Iowa's median household income was $58,570, and 10.7 percent of the population lived below the poverty level.

- Compared to 8.7 percent of the total U.S. population, 4.7 percent of Iowans did not have health insurance in 2017, which was the 6th lowest percent in the country.

- Iowa's violent crime rate in 2017 was 293.4 per 100,000 population, compared to the rate of 394.0 for the United States as a whole.

- Iowa had the highest percent of single-family homes in 2017, with 79.5 percent of housing units being one-unit attached or detached homes.

Table IA-1. Population by Age, Sex, Race, and Hispanic Origin

(Number, percent, except where noted.)

Sex, age, race, and Hispanic origin	2000	2010	2018 [1]	Percent change, 2010–2018
Total Population..	2,926,324	3,046,355	3,156,145	3.6
Percent of total U.S. population	1.0	1.0	1.0	X
Sex				
Male..	1,435,515	1,508,319	1,570,807	4.1
Female	1,490,809	1,538,036	1,585,338	3.1
Age				
Under 5 years...	188,413	202,123	198,218	-1.9
5 to 19 years..	639,570	618,387	623,801	0.9
20 to 64 years..	1,662,128	1,772,957	1,794,296	1.2
65 years and over......................................	436,213	452,888	539,830	19.2
Median age (years)	36.6	38.1	38.2	0.3
Race and Hispanic Origin				
One race				
White	2,748,640	2,839,615	2,864,126	0.9
Black	61,853	91,695	124,819	36.1
American Indian and Alaska Native	8,989	13,563	16,681	23.0
Asian	36,635	54,232	85,708	58.0
Native Hawaiian or Other Pacific Islander	1,009	2,419	4,232	74.9
Two or more races	31,778	44,831	60,579	35.1
Hispanic (of any race)	82,473	156,932	194,432	23.9

X = Not applicable.
- = Zero or rounds to zero.
[1] Population figures for 2018 are July 1 estimates. The 2010 estimates are taken from the 2010 Census.

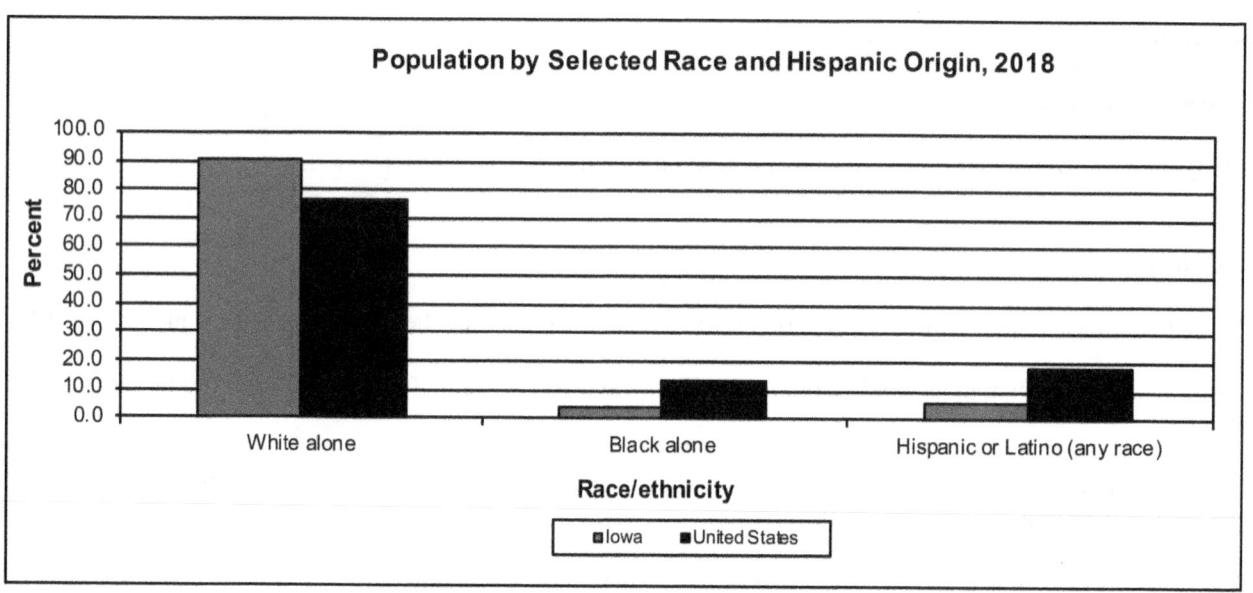

Table IA-2. Marital Status

(Number, percent distribution.)

Sex, age, race, and Hispanic origin	2000	2010	2017
Males, 15 Years and Over...	1,126,566	1,199,509	1,252,885
Never married..	28.2	31.3	33.6
Now married, except separated...	59.8	55.2	52.9
Separated...	0.9	1.1	1.0
Widowed...	2.5	2.6	2.6
Divorced...	8.5	9.7	9.9
Females, 15 Years and Over..	1,198,297	1,250,612	1,284,977
Never married..	21.8	24.7	26.3
Now married, except separated...	55.8	52.4	51.7
Separated...	1.1	1.5	1.3
Widowed...	11.6	10.2	9.2
Divorced...	9.6	11.2	11.5

Table IA-3. Households and Housing Characteristics

(Number, percent, dollars.)

Item	2000	2010	2017	Average annual percent change, 2010–2017
Total Households...	1,149,276	1,223,439	1,257,505	0.4
Family households...	769,684	793,768	794,614	-
Married-couple family	633,254	633,602	634,509	-
Other family	136,430	160,166	160,105	-
Male householder, no wife present.................	38,160	46,829	52,144	1.6
Female householder, no husband present........	98,270	113,337	107,961	-0.7
Nonfamily households	379,592	429,671	462,891	1.1
Householder living alone...................................	313,083	349,736	366,664	0.7
Householder not living alone.............................	66,509	79,935	96,227	2.9
Housing Characteristics				
Total housing units..	1,232,511	1,337,563	1,397,739	0.6
Occupied housing units	1,149,276	1,223,439	1,257,505	0.4
Owner occupied	831,419	885,284	900,362	0.2
Renter occupied	317,857	338,155	357,143	0.8
Average household size.......................................	2.46	2.41	2.42	0.1
Financial Characteristics				
Median gross rent of renter-occupied housing	470	629	760	3.0
Median monthly owner costs for housing units with a mortgage ...	829	1,140	1,205	0.8
Median value of owner-occupied housing units.......	82,500	123,400	149,100	3.0

- = Zero or rounds to zero.

Table IA-4. Migration, Origin, and Language

(Number, percent.)

Characteristic	State 2016	State 2017	State Percent change	U.S. 2016	U.S. 2017	U.S. Percent change
Residence 1 Year Ago						
Population 1 year and over	3,097,283	3,106,880	0.3	319,361,956	321,994,428	0.8
Same house	84.7	85.4	X	85.4	85.7	X
Different house in the U.S..................................	14.9	14.2	X	13.9	13.6	X
Same county	8.7	8.1	X	8.3	8.1	X
Different county	6.2	6.1	X	5.6	5.6	X
Same state	3.7	3.6	X	3.2	3.3	X
Different state	2.5	2.5	X	2.4	2.3	X
Abroad	0.4	0.4	X	0.7	0.7	X
Place of Birth						
Native born	2,974,504	2,978,983	0.2	279,388,170	281,193,323	0.6
Male	49.6	49.6	X	49.3	49.4	X
Female	50.4	50.4	X	50.7	50.6	X
Foreign born	160,189	166,728	4.1	43,739,345	44,525,855	1.8
Male	51.5	51.4	X	48.5	48.4	X
Female	48.5	48.6	X	51.5	51.6	X
Foreign born; naturalized U.S. citizen....................	62,016	65,654	5.9	21,238,372	21,948,732	3.3
Male	48.3	47.3	X	45.9	45.9	X
Female	51.7	52.7	X	54.1	54.1	X
Foreign born; not a U.S. citizen..........................	98,173	101,074	3.0	22,500,973	22,577,123	0.3
Male	53.4	54.0	X	51	50.8	X
Female	46.6	46.0	X	49	49.2	X
Entered 2010 or later	30.2	32.5	X	18.6	21.3	X
Entered 2000 to 2009	29.8	30.5	X	26.7	25.7	X
Entered before 2000...	40.0	37.0	X	54.7	53.0	X
World Region of Birth, Foreign						
Foreign-born population, excluding population born at sea	160,189	166,728	4.1	43,738,901	44,525,458	1.8
Europe...	12.4	11.2	X	10.9	10.8	X
Asia...	36.2	37.9	X	30.8	31.2	X
Africa..	10.4	11.3	X	4.9	5.1	X
Oceania...	1.0	1.3	X	0.6	0.6	X
Latin America...	38.2	37.3	X	51	50.4	X
North America..	1.9	1.0	X	1.8	1.8	X
Language Spoken at Home and Ability to Speak English						
Population 5 years and over.................................	2,937,206	2,947,088	0.3	303,328,961	305,924,019	0.9
English only	92.3	91.9	X	78.4	78.2	X
Language other than English..............................	7.7	8.1	X	21.6	21.8	X
Speaks English less than "very well".................	3.4	3.3	X	8.6	8.5	X

NA = Not available.
X = Not applicable.
- = Zero or rounds to zero.

Table IA-5. Median Income and Poverty Status, 2017

(Number, percent, except as noted.)

Characteristic	State		U.S.	
	Number	Percent	Number	Percent
Median Income				
Households (dollars)...	58,570	X	60,336	X
Families (dollars)	75,076	X	73,891	X
Below Poverty Level (All People)	326,636	10.7	42,583,651	13.4
Sex				
Male	147,345	9.8	19,004,547	12.2
Female	179,291	11.7	23,579,104	14.5
Age				
Under 18 years...	88,070	12.3	13,353,202	18.4
Related children under 18 years...	84,583	11.9	13,053,472	18.1
18 to 64 years...	205,563	11.2	24,648,677	12.6
65 years and over	33,003	6.6	4,581,772	9.3

X = Not applicable.

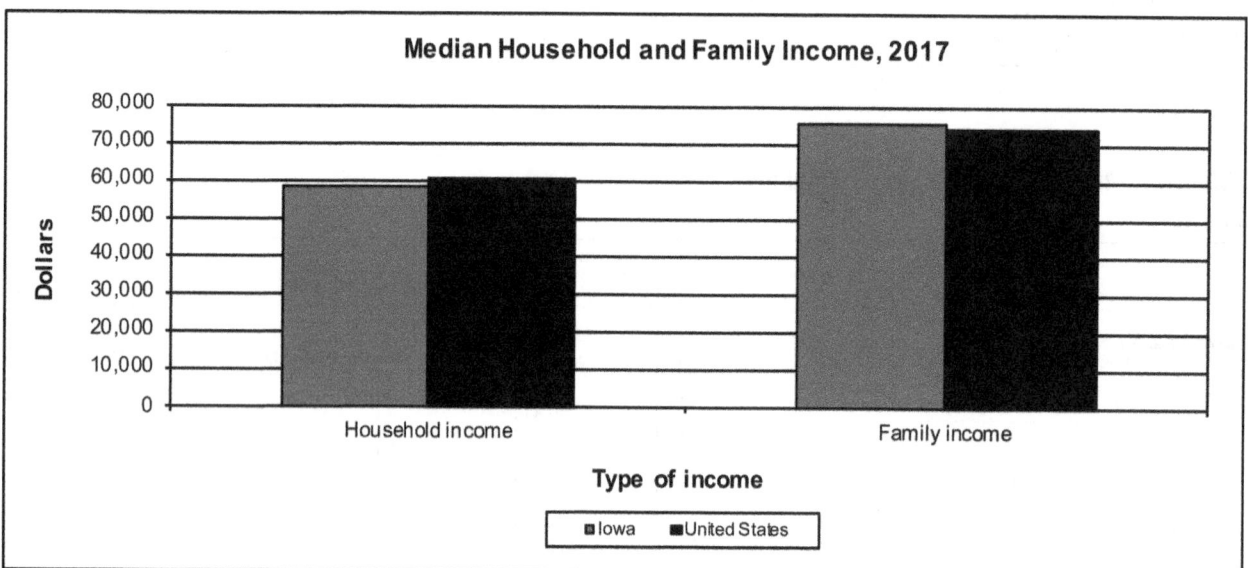

Table IA-6. Health Insurance Coverage Status for the Civilian Noninstitutionalized Population and Children Under 18 Years of Age

(Number, percent.)

Item	2009	2010	2011	2012	2013	2014	2015	2016	2017
Civilian Noninstitutionalized Population	2,956,722	3,004,885	3,017,465	3,028,864	3,045,284	3,062,900	3,080,411	3,091,437	3,102,179
Covered by Private or Public Insurance									
Number..	2,701,821	2,725,074	2,747,975	2,774,589	2,797,567	2,874,015	2,925,441	2,959,825	2,956,162
Percent..	91.4	90.7	91.1	91.6	91.9	93.8	95.0	95.7	95.3
Uninsured									
Number..	254,901	279,811	269,490	254,275	247,717	188,885	154,970	131,612	146,017
Percent..	8.6	9.3	8.9	8.4	8.1	6.2	5.0	4.3	4.7
Percent in the U.S. not covered.................................	15.1	15.5	15.1	14.8	14.5	11.7	9.4	8.6	8.7
Children Under 18 Years of Age[1]	706,873	721,762	721,561	720,427	721,264	723,351	726,495	724,997	775,929
Covered by Private or Public Insurance									
Number..	674,561	692,716	689,820	691,735	691,509	700,117	700,899	706,555	751,885
Percent..	95.4	96.0	95.6	96.0	95.9	96.8	96.5	97.5	96.9
Uninsured									
Number..	32,312	29,046	31,741	28,692	29,755	23,234	25,596	18,442	24,044
Percent..	4.6	4.0	4.4	4.0	4.1	3.2	3.5	2.5	3.1
Percent in the U.S. not covered.................................	8.6	8.0	7.5	7.2	7.1	6.0	4.8	4.5	5.0

[1] 2017 data is for individuals under 19 years of age.

Table IA-7. Employment Status by Demographic Group, 2018

(Numbers in thousands, percent.)

Characteristic	Civilian noninstitutional population	Civilian labor force		Employed		Unemployed	
		Number	Percent of population	Number	Percent of population	Number	Percent of population
Total..	2,468	1,691	68.5	1,649	66.8	43	2.5
Sex							
Male..	1,218	899	73.8	876	72.0	23	2.5
Female..	1,251	792	63.4	772	61.8	20	2.5
Race, Sex, and Hispanic Origin							
White...	2,266	1,551	68.5	1,516	66.9	35	2.2
Male..	1,109	820	73.9	801	72.2	19	2.3
Female..	1,156	732	63.3	715	61.9	16	2.2
Black or African American............................	NA	NA	NA	NA	NA	NA	NA
Male..	NA	NA	NA	NA	NA	NA	NA
Female..	NA	NA	NA	NA	NA	NA	NA
Hispanic or Latino ethnicity[1].......................	159	124	77.8	118	74.0	6	4.9
Male..	NA	NA	NA	NA	NA	NA	NA
Female..	NA	NA	NA	NA	NA	NA	NA
Age							
16 to 19 years.......................................	NA	NA	NA	NA	NA	NA	NA
20 to 24 years.......................................	217	170	78.5	162	74.6	9	5.0
25 to 34 years.......................................	419	368	87.8	362	86.5	6	1.5
35 to 44 years.......................................	362	317	87.4	310	85.5	7	2.1
45 to 54 years.......................................	372	333	89.7	325	87.5	8	2.4
55 to 64 years.......................................	396	292	73.7	285	72.1	6	2.2
65 years and over....................................	536	121	22.7	120	22.3	2	1.5

NOTE: Data in Table 7 are from the Current Population Survey (CPS) and do not match the estimates in Table 8. See notes and definitions for further information.
[1] May be of any race.
NA = Not available

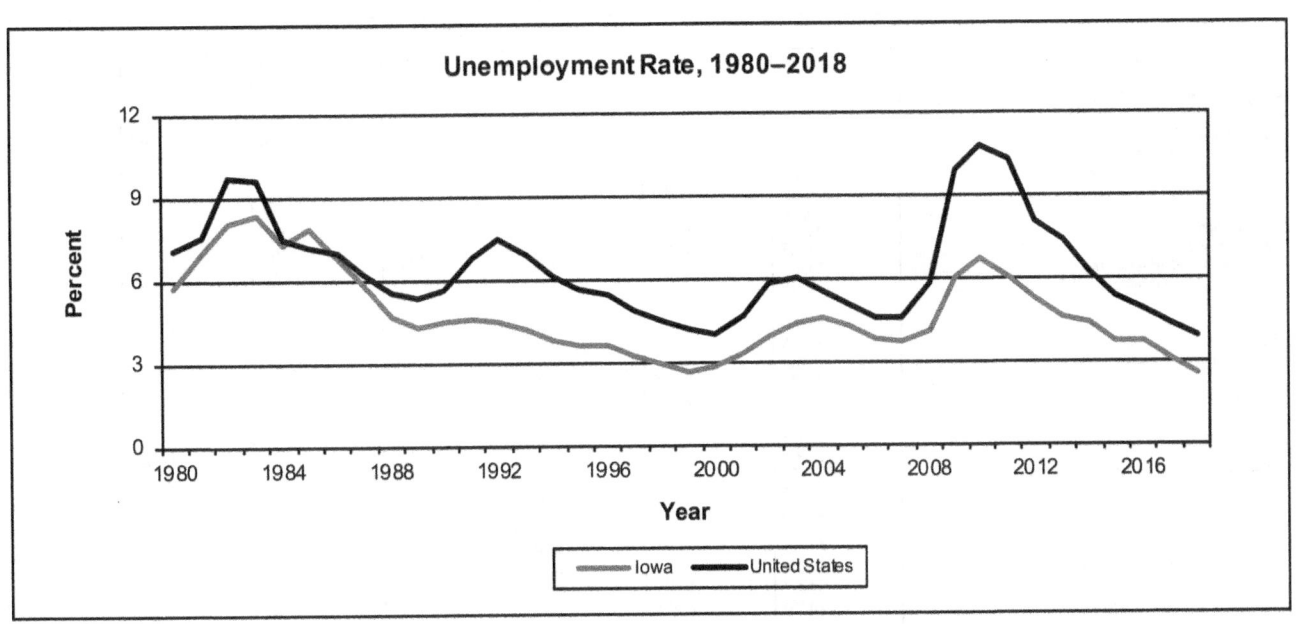

Table IA-8. Employment Status of the Civilian Noninstitutional Population Age 16 Years and Over

(Number, percent.)

Year	Civilian labor force	Civilian participation rate	Employed	Unemployed	Unemployment rate
2010...	1,678,281	71.2	1,577,447	100,834	6.0
2011...	1,662,376	70.0	1,570,177	92,199	5.5
2012...	1,653,141	69.2	1,569,879	83,262	5.0
2013...	1,674,190	69.7	1,594,891	79,299	4.7
2014...	1,700,756	70.4	1,628,505	72,251	4.2
2015...	1,701,317	70.1	1,637,118	64,199	3.8
2016...	1,696,113	69.5	1,634,964	61,149	3.6
2017...	1,678,549	68.4	1,626,036	52,513	3.1
2018...	1,686,840	68.4	1,644,280	42,560	2.5

Table IA-9. Employment and Average Wages by Industry

(Estimates are based on the 2012 *North American Industry Classification System* [NAICS].)

Industry	2011	2012	2013	2014	2015	2016	2017
				Number of jobs			
Wage and Salary Employment by Industry......................	1,551,027	1,570,535	1,592,602	1,607,246	1,626,375	1,632,862	1,630,848
Farm Wage and Salary Employment.............................	18,155	15,984	19,233	14,833	19,160	18,686	16,838
Nonfarm Wage and Salary Employment..........................	1,532,872	1,554,551	1,573,369	1,592,413	1,607,215	1,614,176	1,614,010
Private wage and salary employment............................	1,264,671	1,287,087	1,306,151	1,324,779	1,339,726	1,345,784	1,344,056
Forestry, fishing, and related activities........................	7,090	7,830	8,507	7,618	7,516	7,536	7,560
Mining...	2,173	2,198	2,228	2,166	2,218	2,185	2,319
Utilities..	6,606	6,499	6,456	6,483	6,576	6,467	6,424
Construction..	64,084	66,390	69,595	76,100	80,228	82,845	77,897
Manufacturing..	206,355	210,980	214,678	217,229	216,587	214,043	216,231
Durable goods manufacturing.................................	122,229	126,596	128,846	130,959	129,087	124,756	123,658
Nondurable goods manufacturing............................	84,126	84,384	85,832	86,270	87,500	89,287	92,573
Wholesale trade	67,130	68,924	69,595	69,307	67,995	67,051	66,789
Retail trade..	175,652	177,214	177,330	178,004	181,529	183,744	182,861
Transportation and warehousing................................	56,315	57,283	59,378	60,184	61,221	60,391	60,944
Information	28,231	27,019	26,152	25,715	24,997	22,635	21,916
Finance and insurance	92,051	92,975	94,033	94,402	95,725	98,235	99,336
Real estate and rental and leasing.............................	13,353	13,346	13,756	14,192	14,529	14,629	14,835
Professional, scientific, and technical services	43,560	45,125	46,939	48,713	49,874	52,159	52,940
Management of companies and enterprises....................	14,851	16,068	16,590	18,215	19,227	19,069	19,177
Administrative and waste services.............................	67,924	69,721	69,515	70,349	70,442	68,255	67,838
Educational services	39,977	40,430	40,730	40,632	40,515	41,968	42,206
Health care and social assistance..............................	179,782	182,688	185,875	187,465	189,647	192,604	193,817
Arts, entertainment, and recreation............................	20,417	19,773	18,683	19,168	18,999	20,958	20,780
Accommodation and food services.............................	111,967	115,159	118,582	119,711	121,618	122,631	123,249
Other services, except public administration..................	67,153	67,465	67,529	69,126	70,283	68,379	66,937
Government and government enterprises.......................	268,201	267,464	267,218	267,634	267,489	268,392	269,954
				Dollars			
Average Wages and Salaries by Industry	38,268	39,575	40,185	41,763	43,053	43,898	45,186
Average Farm Wages and Salaries	27,296	42,055	30,150	46,445	30,060	30,621	42,389
Average Nonfarm Wages and Salaries	38,398	39,550	40,308	41,720	43,208	44,052	45,215
Average private wages and salaries............................	38,262	39,506	40,235	41,730	43,269	44,086	45,292
Forestry, fishing, and related activities........................	25,390	26,979	26,895	29,698	30,753	31,868	32,863
Mining...	45,468	45,574	46,947	51,767	54,337	57,509	58,119
Utilities..	79,983	82,978	80,939	86,365	86,924	88,081	91,440
Construction	45,121	47,133	48,520	51,967	54,959	58,064	55,428
Manufacturing	51,117	52,117	52,891	54,389	55,915	56,038	58,605
Durable goods manufacturing.................................	54,515	55,183	55,992	57,375	58,761	58,312	61,859
Nondurable goods manufacturing............................	46,179	47,517	48,236	49,854	51,717	52,861	54,258
Wholesale trade	53,948	55,888	57,035	58,796	60,250	61,105	63,237
Retail trade..	23,208	23,781	23,903	24,595	25,212	25,820	26,526
Transportation and warehousing................................	40,818	42,105	42,306	44,646	45,973	45,679	47,242
Information	46,715	47,039	49,005	50,756	52,858	53,842	55,937
Finance and insurance	61,212	63,343	65,911	68,254	71,512	72,359	75,272
Real estate and rental and leasing.............................	39,329	41,087	41,119	42,772	44,782	44,589	45,680
Professional, scientific, and technical services	53,975	57,666	58,913	60,423	62,962	64,378	66,684
Management of companies and enterprises....................	71,651	76,997	75,656	77,926	81,841	82,341	83,123
Administrative and waste services.............................	26,248	27,276	27,730	28,546	29,634	30,970	32,308
Educational services	23,610	23,913	24,130	24,755	24,740	26,212	26,242
Health care and social assistance..............................	37,397	38,159	38,397	39,437	41,349	41,944	42,701
Arts, entertainment, and recreation............................	20,613	20,209	18,928	19,642	20,242	19,494	19,791
Accommodation and food services.............................	14,324	15,120	15,631	16,179	16,755	17,547	18,113
Other services, except public administration..................	26,465	27,640	28,516	29,461	30,625	32,619	33,421
Government and government enterprises.......................	39,036	39,762	40,663	41,667	42,903	43,878	44,830

Table IA-10. Employment Characteristics by Family Type

(Number, percent.)

Family type and labor force status	2015		2016		2017	
	Total	Families with own children under 18 years	Total	Families with own children under 18 years	Total	Families with own children under 18 years
All Families..	796,799	340,225	795,043	350,304	794,614	344,569
FAMILY TYPE AND LABOR FORCE STATUS						
Married-Couple Families...............................	628,004	235,322	630,993	243,407	634,509	243,177
Both husband and wife in labor force..............	58.4	77.5	58.0	76.6	57.8	77.3
Husband in labor force, wife not in labor force	16.8	18.4	17.6	19.3	17.1	18.5
Wife in labor force, husband not in labor force	7.1	2.6	7.1	2.7	7.4	3.1
Both husband and wife not in labor force................	17.1	1.2	16.6	1.0	17.2	0.8
Other Families	168,795	104,903	164,050	106,897	160,105	101,392
Female householder, no husband present..............	68.3	68.9	69.4	71.5	67.4	67.8
In labor force	53.0	61.1	53.4	61.3	52.5	59.1
Not in labor force	15.3	7.8	16.0	10.2	14.9	8.7
Male householder, no wife present......................	31.7	31.1	30.6	28.5	32.6	32.2
In labor force..	26.6	28.7	25.7	26.1	27.4	29.4
Not in labor force	5.1	2.5	4.9	2.4	5.2	2.8

Table IA-11. School Enrollment and Educational Attainment, 2017

(Number, percent.)

Item	State	U.S.
Enrollment		
Total population 3 years and over, enrolled in school	802,489	81,273,337
Enrolled in nursery school or preschool (percent)	6.5	6.0
Enrolled in kindergarten (percent)........................	5.2	4.9
Enrolled in elementary school, grades 1-8 (percent).......	40.7	40.6
Enrolled in high school, grades 9-12 (percent)...........	20.2	21.1
Enrolled in college or graduate school (percent)..........	27.3	27.4
Attainment		
Total population 25 years and over	2,093,909	221,250,083
Less than ninth grade (percent)	3.1	5.1
9th to 12th grade, no diploma (percent)	4.8	6.9
High school graduate, including equivalency (percent).....	30.5	27.1
Some college, no degree (percent)	21.0	20.4
Associate's degree (percent).............................	11.6	8.5
Bachelor's degree (percent)..............................	19.4	19.7
Graduate or professional degree (percent)................	9.5	12.3
High school graduate or higher (percent).................	92.1	88.0
Bachelor's degree or higher (percent)....................	28.9	32.0

Table IA-12. Public School Characteristics and Educational Indicators

(Number, percent; data derived from National Center of Education Statistics.)

Item	State	U.S.
Public Elementary and Secondary Schools		
Number of operational school districts, 2016-17.............	342	18,377
Number of operational schools, 2016-17....................	1,328	98,330
Percent charter schools	0.2	7.1
Total public school enrollment, 2016-17...................	509,831	50,587,859
Percent charter school enrollment	0.1	6.0
Student-teacher ratio, Fall 2015	14.2	16.0
Expenditures per student (dollars), 2015-16...............	11,148	11,841
Four-year adjusted cohort graduation rate (ACGR)[1]	91.0	84.6
Students eligible for free or reduced-price lunch (percent), 2015-16.........	41.4	52.1
English language learners (percent), Fall 2016	5.6	9.6
Students age 3 to 21 served under IDEA, part B (percent), 2017-18	12.9	13.7

Public Schools by Type, 2016-17		Percent of state public schools
Total number of schools...................................	1,328	100.0
Special education	3	0.2
Vocational education.....................................	0	-
Alternative education....................................	18	1.4

[1] Adjusted Cohort Graduation Rates (ACGR) differ from Averaged Freshmen Graduation Rates (AFGR).
- = Zero or rounds to zero.

Table IA-13. Reported Voting and Registration of the Voting-Age Population, November 2018

(Numbers in thousands, percent.)

Item	Total population	Total citizen population	Registered			Voted		
			Total registered	Percent registered (total population)	Percent registered (total citizen population)	Total voted	Percent voted (total population)	Percent voted (total citizen population)
U.S. Total	249,748	228,832	153,066	61.3	66.9	122,281	49.0	53.4
State Total..	2,376	2,239	1,658	69.8	74.0	1,335	56.2	59.6
Sex								
Male	1,176	1,105	833	70.8	75.4	660	56.1	59.7
Female	1,201	1,134	825	68.7	72.7	675	56.2	59.5
Race								
White alone..	2,192	2,119	1,580	72.1	74.5	1,270	57.9	59.9
White, non-Hispanic alone	2,007	1,983	1,499	74.7	75.6	1,206	60.1	60.8
Black alone...	89	76	47	52.6	61.3	41	46.4	54.1
Asian alone	62	22	14	(B)	(B)	12	(B)	(B)
Hispanic (of any race).........................	206	148	85	41.5	57.8	69	33.5	46.7
White alone or in combination	2,218	2,133	1,591	71.8	74.6	1,279	57.7	60.0
Black alone or in combination...............	100	80	49	48.9	60.6	41	41.4	51.3
Asian alone or in combination..............	72	26	19	(B)	(B)	16	(B)	(B)
Age								
18 to 24 years....................................	287	259	133	46.3	51.3	89	30.9	34.2
25 to 34 years....................................	445	402	273	61.4	68.1	192	43.2	47.9
35 to 44 years....................................	341	306	228	66.8	74.3	174	51.0	56.8
45 to 64 years....................................	764	732	557	72.9	76.0	462	60.5	63.1
65 years and over	539	539	467	86.5	86.5	418	77.4	77.4

B = Base is less than 75,000 and therefore too small to show the derived measure.

Table IA-14. Crime

(Number, rate per 100,000. Data are derived from the FBI Uniform Crime Reports.)

Item	State			U.S.		
	2016	2017	Percent change	2016	2017	Percent change
TOTAL POPULATION[1]	3,130,869	3,145,711	0.5	323,405,935	325,719,178	0.7
VIOLENT CRIME						
Number..	9,170	9,230	0.7	1,285,606	1,283,220	-0.2
Rate	292.9	293.4	0.2	397.5	394.0	-0.9
Murder and Nonnegligent Manslaughter						
Number..	73	104	42.5	17,413	17,284	-0.7
Rate	2.3	3.3	41.8	5.4	5.3	-1.4
Rape[2]						
Number..	1,278	1,234	-3.4	132,414	135,755	2.5
Rate	40.8	39.2	-3.9	40.9	41.7	1.8
Robbery						
Number..	1,150	1,253	9.0	332,797	319,356	-4.0
Rate	36.7	39.8	8.4	102.9	98.0	-4.7
Aggravated Assault						
Number..	6,669	6,639	-0.4	802,982	810,825	1.0
Rate	213.0	211.0	-0.9	248.3	248.9	0.3
PROPERTY CRIME						
Number..	65,888	66,855	1.5	7,928,530	7,694,086	-3.0
Rate	2,104.5	2,125.3	1.0	2,451.6	2,362.2	-3.6
Burglary						
Number..	15,306	15,078	-1.5	1,516,405	1,401,840	-7.6
Rate	488.9	479.3	-2.0	468.9	430.4	-8.2
Larceny-Theft						
Number..	45,580	46,198	1.4	5,644,835	5,519,107	-2.2
Rate	1,455.8	1,468.6	0.9	1,745.4	1,694.4	-2.9
Motor Vehicle Theft						
Number..	5,002	5,579	11.5	767,290	773,139	0.8
Rate	159.8	177.4	11.0	237.3	237.4	-

NOTE: Although arson data are included in the trend and clearance tables, sufficient data are not available to estimate totals for this offense. Therefore, no arson data are published in this table.
- = Zero or rounds to zero.
[1] Population figures are U.S. Census Bureau provisional estimates as of July 1, 2017.
[2] The figures shown in the rape (revised definition) column were estimated using the revised Uniform Crime Reporting (UCR) definition of rape.

Table IA-15. State Government Finances, 2017

(Dollar amounts in thousands, percent distribution.)

Item	Dollars	Percent distribution
Total Revenue	26,798,284	100.0
General revenue	21,134,343	78.9
Intergovernmental revenue	6,245,956	23.3
Taxes	9,755,430	36.4
General sales	3,205,997	12.0
Selective sales	1,407,088	5.3
License taxes	947,549	3.5
Individual income tax	3,655,462	13.6
Corporate income tax	432,020	1.6
Other taxes	107,314	0.4
Current charges	3,619,516	13.5
Miscellaneous general revenue	1,513,441	5.6
Utility revenue	0	-
Liquor stores revenue	306,174	1.1
Insurance trust revenue[1]	5,357,767	20.0
Total Expenditure	23,251,836	100.0
Intergovernmental expenditure	5,505,683	23.7
Direct expenditure	17,746,153	76.3
Current operation	12,246,043	52.7
Capital outlay	2,043,786	8.8
Insurance benefits and repayments	2,629,519	11.3
Assistance and subsidies	620,231	2.7
Interest on debt	206,574	0.9
Exhibit: Salaries and wages	3,573,499	15.4
Total Expenditure	23,251,836	100.0
General expenditure	20,409,385	87.8
Intergovernmental expenditure	5,505,683	23.7
Direct expenditure	14,903,702	64.1
General expenditure, by function:		
Education	7,282,938	31.3
Public welfare	6,010,233	25.8
Hospitals	1,887,069	8.1
Health	275,215	1.2
Highways	2,304,141	9.9
Police protection	104,622	0.4
Correction	288,880	1.2
Natural resources	294,582	1.3
Parks and recreation	31,175	0.1
Governmental administration	598,565	2.6
Interest on general debt	206,574	0.9
Other and unallocable	1,125,391	4.8
Utility expenditure	0	-
Liquor stores expenditure	212,932	0.9
Insurance trust expenditure	2,629,519	11.3
Debt at End of Fiscal Year	6,149,694	X
Cash and Security Holdings	44,122,139	X

X = Not applicable.
- = Zero or rounds to zero.
[1] Within insurance trust revenue, net earnings of state retirement systems is a calculated statistic (the item code in the data file is X08), and thus can be positive or negative. Net earnings is the sum of earnings on investments plus gains on investments minus losses on investments. The change made in 2002 for asset valuation from book to market value in accordance with Statement 34 of the Governmental Accounting Standards Board is reflected in the calculated statistics.

Table IA-16. State Government Tax Collections, 2018

(Dollars in thousands, percent.)

Item	Dollars	Percent distribution
Total Taxes	10,088,480	100.0
Property taxes	1,671	-
Sales and gross receipts	4,687,073	46.5
General sales and gross receipts	3,279,789	32.5
Selective sales and gross receipts	1,407,284	13.9
Alcoholic beverages	22,183	0.2
Amusements	303,374	3.0
Insurance premiums	114,363	1.1
Motor fuels	671,937	6.7
Pari-mutuels	3,818	-
Public utilities	39,039	0.4
Tobacco products	212,469	2.1
Other selective sales	40,101	0.4
Licenses	954,503	9.5
Alcoholic beverages	16,456	0.2
Amusements	30,314	0.3
Corporations in general	34,590	0.3
Hunting and fishing	28,200	0.3
Motor vehicle	664,178	6.6
Motor vehicle operators	21,833	0.2
Public utilities	9,865	0.1
Occupation and business, NEC	146,470	1.5
Other licenses	2,597	-
Income taxes	4,340,423	43.0
Individual income	3,897,236	38.6
Corporation net income	443,187	4.4
Other taxes	104,810	1.0
Death and gift	82,600	0.8
Documentary and stock transfer	22,210	0.2
Severance	X	-
Taxes, NEC	0	-

X = Not applicable.
- = Zero or rounds to zero.

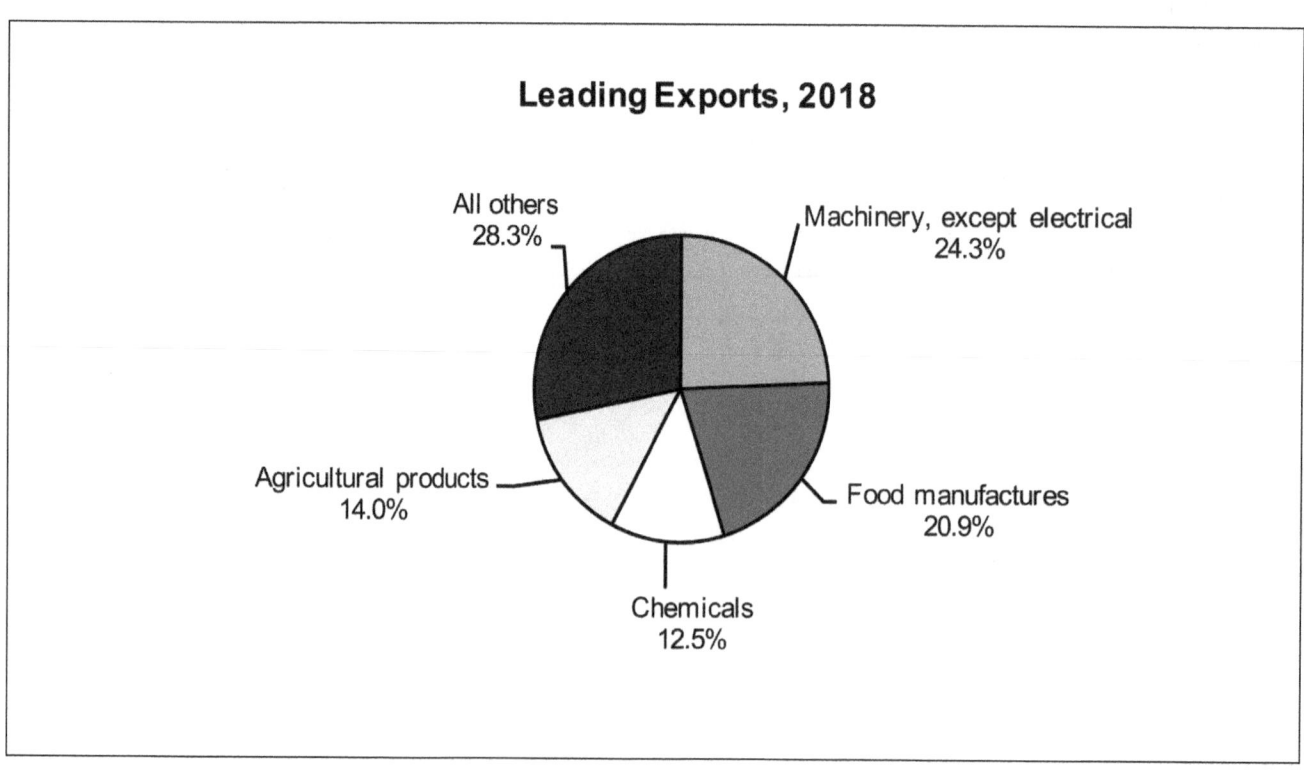

Leading Exports, 2018

All others 28.3%

Machinery, except electrical 24.3%

Agricultural products 14.0%

Food manufactures 20.9%

Chemicals 12.5%

KANSAS

Facts and Figures

Location: Central United States; bordered on the N by Nebraska, on the E by Missouri, on the S by Oklahoma, and on the W by Colorado

Area: 82,277 sq. mi. (213,096 sq. km.); rank—15th

Population: 2,911,505 (2018 est.); rank—35th

Principal Cities: capital—Topeka; largest—Wichita

Statehood: January 29, 1861; 34th state

U.S. Congress: 2 senators, 4 representatives

State Motto: *Ad astra per aspera* ("To the stars through difficulties")

State Song: "Home on the Range"

State Nicknames: The Sunflower State; The Jayhawk State

Abbreviations: KS; Kan.; Kans.

State Symbols: flower—wild native sunflower; tree—cottonwood; bird—Western meadowlark

At a Glance

- With an increase in population of 2.0 percent, Kansas ranked 38th among the states in growth from 2010 to 2018.

- In 2017, 8.7 percent of Kansans did not have health insurance, which was the same percent as the overall U.S. population.

- Approximately 24.2 percent of Kansans were under 18 years old in 2018, the 8th highest percentage in the United States.

- Kansas's unemployment rate was 3.4 percent in 2018, compared to the national rate of 3.9 percent.

- In Kansas, 11.9 percent of the total population and 14.8 percent of children under age 18 lived in poverty in 2017, compared to that national averages of 13.4 percent and 18.4 percent respectively.

Table KS-1. Population by Age, Sex, Race, and Hispanic Origin

(Number, percent, except where noted.)

Sex, age, race, and Hispanic origin	2000	2010	2018 [1]	Percent change, 2010–2018
Total Population...	2,688,418	2,853,118	2,911,505	2.0
Percent of total U.S. population	1.0	0.9	0.9	X
Sex				
Male..	1,328,474	1,415,408	1,450,406	2.5
Female..	1,359,944	1,437,710	1,461,099	1.6
Age				
Under 5 years...	188,708	205,492	189,335	-7.9
5 to 19 years...	609,710	605,152	598,341	-1.1
20 to 64 years...	1,533,771	1,666,358	1,661,588	-0.3
65 years and over	356,229	376,116	462,241	22.9
Median age (years)	35.2	36.0	36.9	2.5
Race and Hispanic Origin				
One race				
White	2,313,944	2,501,057	2,515,351	0.6
Black...	154,198	173,298	178,618	3.1
American Indian and Alaska Native	24,936	33,044	34,817	5.4
Asian...	46,806	69,628	91,229	31.0
Native Hawaiian or Other Pacific Islander	1,313	2,864	3,619	26.4
Two or more races	56,496	73,227	87,871	20.0
Hispanic (of any race)...	188,252	311,460	351,180	12.8

X = Not applicable.
- = Zero or rounds to zero.
[1] Population figures for 2018 are July 1 estimates. The 2010 estimates are taken from the 2010 Census.

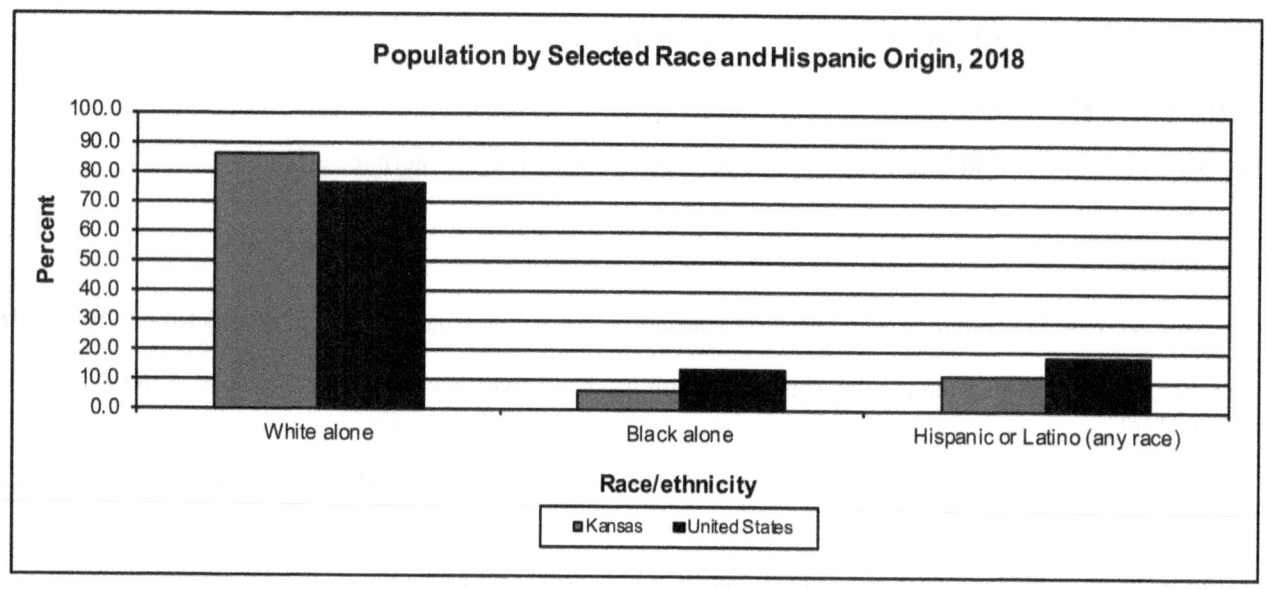

Table KS-2. Marital Status

(Number, percent distribution.)

Sex, age, race, and Hispanic origin	2000	2010	2017
Males, 15 Years and Over...	1,025,114	1,106,102	1,148,850
Never married	27.4	31.6	33.1
Now married, except separated...	59.9	53.9	52.8
Separated...	1.1	1.4	1.2
Widowed..	2.3	2.6	2.8
Divorced..	9.2	10.5	10.1
Females, 15 Years and Over...	1,075,542	1,145,453	1,169,771
Never married	20.8	25.1	25.4
Now married, except separated...	56.4	51.4	51.6
Separated...	1.3	1.7	1.5
Widowed..	10.6	9.2	8.8
Divorced..	10.9	12.6	12.6

Table KS-3. Households and Housing Characteristics

(Number, percent, dollars.)

Item	2000	2010	2017	Average annual percent change, 2010–2017
Total Households...	1,037,891	1,101,658	1,128,983	0.4
Family households	701,547	721,592	733,649	0.2
Married-couple family	567,924	559,199	572,393	0.3
Other family	133,623	162,393	161,256	-0.1
Male householder, no wife present.............................	36,962	46,692	49,987	1.0
Female householder, no husband present....................	96,661	115,701	111,269	-0.5
Nonfamily households	336,344	380,066	395,334	0.6
Householder living alone..	280,387	313,390	327,502	0.6
Householder not living alone.......................................	55,957	66,676	67,832	0.2
Housing Characteristics				
Total housing units..	1,131,200	1,234,037	1,273,776	0.5
Occupied housing units	1,037,891	1,101,658	1,128,983	0.4
Owner occupied	718,703	749,907	743,508	-0.1
Renter occupied	319,188	351,751	385,475	1.4
Average household size..	2.51	2.52	2.51	-0.1
Financial Characteristics				
Median gross rent of renter-occupied housing	498	682	815	2.8
Median monthly owner costs for housing units with a mortgage	888	1,239	1,314	0.9
Median value of owner-occupied housing units	83,500	127,300	150,600	2.6

Table KS-4. Migration, Origin, and Language

(Number, percent.)

Characteristic	State			U.S.		
	2016	2017	Percent change	2016	2017	Percent change
Residence 1 Year Ago						
Population 1 year and over	2,870,529	2,876,925	0.2	319,361,956	321,994,428	0.8
Same house	83.4	83.9	X	85.4	85.7	X
Different house in the U.S..	16.0	15.7	X	13.9	13.6	X
Same county	9.4	9.0	X	8.3	8.1	X
Different county	6.6	6.7	X	5.6	5.6	X
Same state	3.5	3.7	X	3.2	3.3	X
Different state	3.1	3.0	X	2.4	2.3	X
Abroad	0.6	0.4	X	0.7	0.7	X
Place of Birth						
Native born	2,701,767	2,712,566	0.4	279,388,170	281,193,323	0.6
Male	49.9	49.7	X	49.3	49.4	X
Female	50.1	50.3	X	50.7	50.6	X
Foreign born	205,522	200,557	-2.4	43,739,345	44,525,855	1.8
Male	49.5	51.4	X	48.5	48.4	X
Female	50.5	48.6	X	51.5	51.6	X
Foreign born; naturalized U.S. citizen................................	81,256	81,129	-0.2	21,238,372	21,948,732	3.3
Male	45.6	50.6	X	45.9	45.9	X
Female	54.4	49.4	X	54.1	54.1	X
Foreign born; not a U.S. citizen	124,266	119,428	-3.9	22,500,973	22,577,123	0.3
Male	52.0	52.0	X	51	50.8	X
Female	48.0	48.0	X	49	49.2	X
Entered 2010 or later	20.6	24.7	X	18.6	21.3	X
Entered 2000 to 2009	32.9	28.5	X	26.7	25.7	X
Entered before 2000...	46.5	46.9	X	54.7	53.0	X
World Region of Birth, Foreign						
Foreign-born population, excluding population born at sea	205,522	200,557	-2.4	43,738,901	44,525,458	1.8
Europe	7.0	6.8	X	10.9	10.8	X
Asia...	32.2	32.6	X	30.8	31.2	X
Africa	3.7	6.0	X	4.9	5.1	X
Oceania	0.5	0.9	X	0.6	0.6	X
Latin America	55.0	51.7	X	51	50.4	X
North America	1.6	2.1	X	1.8	1.8	X
Language Spoken at Home and Ability to Speak English						
Population 5 years and over...	2,709,883	2,720,074	0.4	303,328,961	305,924,019	0.9
English only	88.3	88.1	X	78.4	78.2	X
Language other than English...	11.7	11.9	X	21.6	21.8	X
Speaks English less than "very well"............................	4.6	4.5	X	8.6	8.5	X

NA = Not available.
X = Not applicable.
- = Zero or rounds to zero.

Table KS-5. Median Income and Poverty Status, 2017

(Number, percent, except as noted.)

Characteristic	State		U.S.	
	Number	Percent	Number	Percent
Median Income				
Households (dollars)..	56,422	X	60,336	X
Families (dollars)	72,057	X	73,891	X
Below Poverty Level (All People)	336,487	11.9	42,583,651	13.4
Sex				
Male	150,434	10.7	19,004,547	12.2
Female	186,053	13.1	23,579,104	14.5
Age				
Under 18 years...	103,689	14.8	13,353,202	18.4
Related children under 18 years......................................	99,801	14.4	13,053,472	18.1
18 to 64 years...	201,393	11.8	24,648,677	12.6
65 years and over	31,405	7.3	4,581,772	9.3

X = Not applicable.

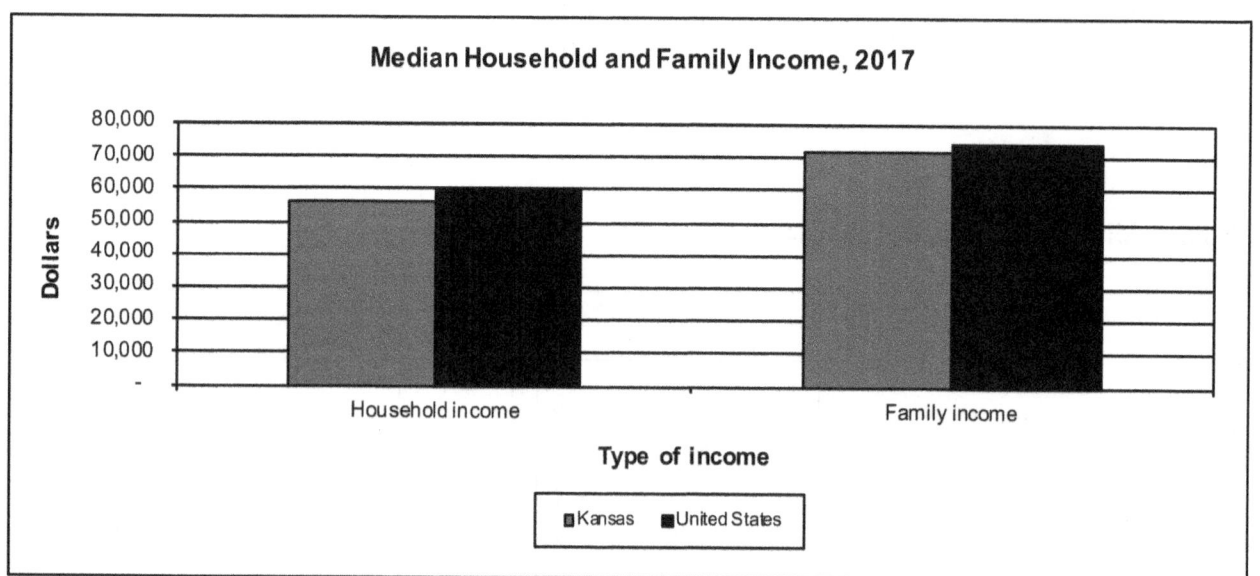

Table KS-6. Health Insurance Coverage Status for the Civilian Noninstitutionalized Population and Children Under 18 Years of Age

(Number, percent.)

Item	2009	2010	2011	2012	2013	2014	2015	2016	2017
Civilian Noninstitutionalized Population	2,756,827	2,804,461	2,813,530	2,825,416	2,836,733	2,845,414	2,850,159	2,850,862	2,855,454
Covered by Private or Public Insurance									
Number......................................	2,394,276	2,415,015	2,458,900	2,469,852	2,488,636	2,553,940	2,589,651	2,601,888	2,606,062
Percent.......................................	86.8	86.1	87.4	87.4	87.7	89.8	90.9	91.3	91.3
Uninsured									
Number......................................	362,551	389,446	354,630	355,564	348,097	291,474	260,508	248,974	249,392
Percent.......................................	13.2	13.9	12.6	12.6	12.3	10.2	9.1	8.7	8.7
Percent in the U.S. not covered.................................	15.1	15.5	15.1	14.8	14.5	11.7	9.4	8.6	8.7
Children Under 18 Years of Age[1]	700,794	725,437	721,211	719,917	718,934	720,908	718,994	713,102	755,441
Covered by Private or Public Insurance									
Number......................................	643,077	665,654	674,866	672,059	674,804	681,497	682,459	682,190	715,965
Percent.......................................	91.8	91.8	93.6	93.4	93.9	94.5	94.9	95.7	94.8
Uninsured									
Number......................................	57,717	59,783	46,345	47,858	44,130	39,411	36,535	30,912	39,476
Percent.......................................	8.2	8.2	6.4	6.6	6.1	5.5	5.1	4.3	5.2
Percent in the U.S. not covered.................................	8.6	8.0	7.5	7.2	7.1	6.0	4.8	4.5	5.0

[1] 2017 data is for individuals under 19 years of age.

Table KS-7. Employment Status by Demographic Group, 2018

(Numbers in thousands, percent.)

Characteristic	Civilian noninstitutional population	Civilian labor force		Employed		Unemployed	
		Number	Percent of population	Number	Percent of population	Number	Percent of population
Total..........................	2,227	1,485	66.7	1,434	64.4	51	3.4
Sex							
Male..........................	1,091	796	73.0	770	70.6	26	3.3
Female........................	1,136	689	60.6	664	58.5	25	3.6
Race, Sex, and Hispanic Origin							
White.........................	1,933	1,290	66.7	1,252	64.8	38	2.9
Male.......................	946	693	73.3	673	71.2	20	2.8
Female.....................	987	597	60.5	579	58.6	18	3.1
Black or African American..........	130	78	60.0	71	54.5	7	9.1
Male.......................	NA	NA	NA	NA	NA	NA	NA
Female.....................	NA	NA	NA	NA	NA	NA	NA
Hispanic or Latino ethnicity[1]........	235	174	73.9	167	71.0	7	3.9
Male.......................	124	102	82.1	99	79.7	3	2.9
Female.....................	111	72	64.8	68	61.2	4	5.4
Age							
16 to 19 years.................	148	70	47.7	65	44.0	5	7.7
20 to 24 years.................	196	153	78.0	144	73.4	9	5.9
25 to 34 years.................	373	322	86.3	311	83.3	11	3.4
35 to 44 years.................	362	301	83.3	290	80.2	11	3.7
45 to 54 years.................	327	275	84.1	270	82.7	5	1.7
55 to 64 years.................	364	254	69.8	248	68.0	7	2.6
65 years and over..............	458	110	24.0	107	23.3	3	2.7

NOTE: Data in Table 7 are from the Current Population Survey (CPS) and do not match the estimates in Table 8. See notes and definitions for further information.
[1] May be of any race.

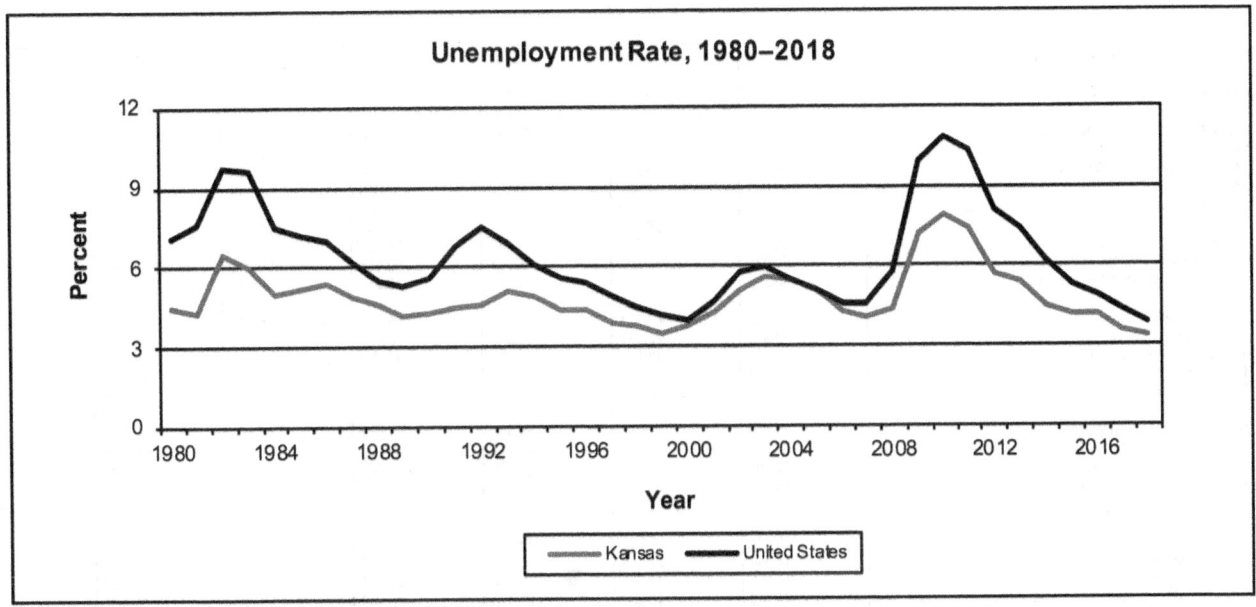

Table KS-8. Employment Status of the Civilian Noninstitutional Population Age 16 Years and Over

(Number, percent.)

Year	Civilian labor force	Civilian participation rate	Employed	Unemployed	Unemployment rate
2010..................................	1,500,764	69.8	1,394,958	105,806	7.1
2011..................................	1,491,087	69.0	1,394,082	97,005	6.5
2012..................................	1,485,220	68.3	1,400,122	85,098	5.7
2013..................................	1,485,917	68.1	1,407,217	78,700	5.3
2014..................................	1,491,710	68.0	1,424,016	67,694	4.5
2015..................................	1,489,829	67.7	1,427,731	62,098	4.2
2016..................................	1,485,336	67.2	1,425,413	59,923	4.0
2017..................................	1,478,783	66.6	1,425,216	53,567	3.6
2018..................................	1,482,220	66.7	1,432,387	49,833	3.4

Table KS-9. Employment and Average Wages by Industry

(Estimates are based on the 2012 *North American Industry Classification System* [NAICS].)

Industry	2011	2012	2013	2014	2015	2016	2017
	Number of jobs						
Wage and Salary Employment by Industry.........................	1,417,054	1,433,074	1,447,857	1,471,209	1,481,464	1,480,741	1,479,026
Farm Wage and Salary Employment................................	12,101	10,891	9,329	11,907	12,622	13,057	12,209
Nonfarm Wage and Salary Employment...........................	1,404,953	1,422,183	1,438,528	1,459,302	1,468,842	1,467,684	1,466,817
Private wage and salary employment.............................	1,105,001	1,124,115	1,140,839	1,162,817	1,173,655	1,176,547	1,176,479
Forestry, fishing, and related activities...........................	4,231	4,509	4,760	4,873	4,946	4,972	4,844
Mining..	9,032	9,906	10,397	10,397	8,453	6,803	6,703
Utilities...	8,047	7,978	7,752	7,779	6,751	6,677	6,557
Construction..	54,298	56,531	58,356	61,255	62,557	62,853	61,666
Manufacturing...	161,246	163,106	163,196	162,639	161,550	160,402	161,240
Durable goods manufacturing..	98,028	100,083	100,573	98,917	98,142	95,852	94,849
Nondurable goods manufacturing.....................................	63,218	63,023	62,623	63,722	63,408	64,550	66,391
Wholesale trade..	59,631	59,108	60,109	61,612	60,459	60,006	60,251
Retail trade..	142,893	143,782	145,275	147,386	149,623	151,142	148,429
Transportation and warehousing......................................	46,624	48,529	48,598	49,893	50,656	52,515	55,652
Information..	27,979	27,818	27,560	27,822	21,004	20,589	19,304
Finance and insurance	60,110	60,937	61,395	62,461	63,930	63,287	64,110
Real estate and rental and leasing..................................	14,907	14,081	14,233	14,708	15,414	15,638	15,578
Professional, scientific, and technical services	60,912	63,161	66,717	67,723	70,277	73,532	73,923
Management of companies and enterprises......................	13,982	13,633	15,197	18,627	27,605	24,459	25,001
Administrative and waste services...................................	75,086	78,046	81,323	83,957	82,181	81,524	79,596
Educational services	19,658	20,271	20,496	21,013	21,120	20,862	21,170
Health care and social assistance...................................	167,217	169,482	170,780	172,158	177,433	180,201	180,522
Arts, entertainment, and recreation.................................	13,842	15,613	16,038	16,638	16,432	17,015	17,241
Accommodation and food services..................................	101,778	104,514	105,974	107,159	110,080	111,220	112,067
Other services, except public administration....................	63,528	63,110	62,683	64,717	63,184	62,850	62,625
Government and government enterprises......................	299,952	298,068	297,689	296,485	295,187	291,137	290,338
	Dollars						
Average Wages and Salaries by Industry	41,004	42,298	42,734	43,805	45,013	45,361	46,413
Average Farm Wages and Salaries	34,657	43,052	40,813	40,727	35,122	39,385	36,632
Average Nonfarm Wages and Salaries	41,059	42,292	42,746	43,830	45,097	45,414	46,494
Average private wages and salaries.................................	41,621	43,067	43,570	44,747	46,113	46,215	47,413
Forestry, fishing, and related activities...........................	23,848	24,580	25,020	25,900	27,664	29,592	29,970
Mining..	54,889	57,542	56,352	59,869	56,546	56,131	55,936
Utilities...	88,094	85,020	88,168	89,266	91,013	93,697	95,824
Construction..	46,011	48,167	48,738	50,537	51,819	52,538	53,775
Manufacturing...	53,522	53,798	54,585	55,328	56,996	57,782	59,548
Durable goods manufacturing..	58,228	58,502	58,731	59,423	60,941	61,125	62,178
Nondurable goods manufacturing.....................................	46,226	46,328	47,927	48,971	50,890	52,817	55,791
Wholesale trade..	60,032	63,453	63,096	65,377	66,424	67,079	69,026
Retail trade..	24,813	25,531	25,643	26,073	27,013	27,461	27,880
Transportation and warehousing......................................	46,446	48,136	48,361	49,923	50,841	49,755	50,404
Information..	64,605	67,210	69,737	73,230	62,757	63,733	63,392
Finance and insurance	61,319	66,251	66,714	69,665	71,941	74,125	75,414
Real estate and rental and leasing..................................	35,352	36,216	36,996	38,449	40,661	41,516	42,101
Professional, scientific, and technical services	59,749	62,278	63,647	65,809	68,735	69,406	70,123
Management of companies and enterprises......................	87,706	95,088	93,022	94,652	105,172	99,034	103,795
Administrative and waste services...................................	35,552	36,764	37,320	36,741	36,928	37,215	38,426
Educational services	28,317	28,748	29,199	29,754	30,428	29,731	30,055
Health care and social assistance...................................	39,485	40,909	40,844	41,531	42,671	42,265	43,473
Arts, entertainment, and recreation.................................	18,344	20,544	20,977	20,862	21,623	21,620	21,948
Accommodation and food services..................................	15,080	15,698	16,084	16,695	17,271	17,783	18,388
Other services, except public administration....................	27,738	28,599	29,410	30,345	32,065	32,862	34,125
Government and government enterprises......................	38,988	39,371	39,588	40,232	41,060	42,181	42,771

Table KS-10. Employment Characteristics by Family Type

(Number, percent.)

Family type and labor force status	2015		2016		2017	
	Total	Families with own children under 18 years	Total	Families with own children under 18 years	Total	Families with own children under 18 years
All Families........................	720,780	324,072	716,005	315,508	733,649	326,685
FAMILY TYPE AND LABOR FORCE STATUS						
Married-Couple Families........................	560,633	228,023	555,970	219,403	572,393	229,995
Both husband and wife in labor force......................	55.5	69.3	55.7	69.3	55.9	71.3
Husband in labor force, wife not in labor force..........	21.2	25.3	20.7	26.2	20.6	24.3
Wife in labor force, husband not in labor force..........	7.1	3.6	7.1	3.2	7.1	2.7
Both husband and wife not in labor force....................	15.6	1.3	15.9	1.0	15.8	1.3
Other Families	160,147	96,049	160,035	96,105	161,256	96,690
Female householder, no husband present................	68.5	70.9	69.1	70.7	69.0	71.5
In labor force................................	51.2	59.8	53.4	62.7	51.8	60.9
Not in labor force	17.3	11.2	15.7	8.0	17.2	10.6
Male householder, no wife present........................	31.5	29.1	30.9	29.3	31.0	28.5
In labor force........................	25.5	26.4	25.9	26.7	26.4	27.2
Not in labor force	5.9	2.7	5.0	2.7	4.6	1.3

Table KS-11. School Enrollment and Educational Attainment, 2017

(Number, percent.)

Item	State	U.S.
Enrollment		
Total population 3 years and over, enrolled in school	777,271	81,273,337
Enrolled in nursery school or preschool (percent)....................	7.3	6.0
Enrolled in kindergarten (percent)....................	5.1	4.9
Enrolled in elementary school, grades 1-8 (percent)....................	40.6	40.6
Enrolled in high school, grades 9-12 (percent)....................	20.4	21.1
Enrolled in college or graduate school (percent)....................	26.6	27.4
Attainment		
Total population 25 years and over	1,904,528	221,250,083
Less than ninth grade (percent)....................	3.5	5.1
9th to 12th grade, no diploma (percent)....................	5.5	6.9
High school graduate, including equivalency (percent)....................	25.8	27.1
Some college, no degree (percent)....................	22.7	20.4
Associate's degree (percent)....................	8.8	8.5
Bachelor's degree (percent)....................	21.2	19.7
Graduate or professional degree (percent)....................	12.6	12.3
High school graduate or higher (percent)....................	91.0	88.0
Bachelor's degree or higher (percent)....................	33.7	32.0

Table KS-12. Public School Characteristics and Educational Indicators

(Number, percent; data derived from National Center of Education Statistics.)

Item	State	U.S.
Public Elementary and Secondary Schools		
Number of operational school districts, 2016-17	317	18,377
Number of operational schools, 2016-17....................	1,318	98,330
Percent charter schools	0.8	7.1
Total public school enrollment, 2016-17....................	494,347	50,587,859
Percent charter school enrollment	0.6	6.0
Student-teacher ratio, Fall 2015	12.4	16.0
Expenditures per student (dollars), 2015-16....................	10,216	11,841
Four-year adjusted cohort graduation rate (ACGR)[1]	86.5	84.6
Students eligible for free or reduced-price lunch (percent), 2015-16....................	49.2	52.1
English language learners (percent), Fall 2016	11.1	9.6
Students age 3 to 21 served under IDEA, part B (percent), 2017-18	14.9	13.7
Public Schools by Type, 2016-17		Percent of state public schools
Total number of schools....................	1,318	100.0
Special education	4	0.3
Vocational education	0	-
Alternative education....................	1	0.1

[1] Adjusted Cohort Graduation Rates (ACGR) differ from Averaged Freshmen Graduation Rates (AFGR).
- = Zero or rounds to zero.

Table KS-13. Reported Voting and Registration of the Voting-Age Population, November 2018

(Numbers in thousands, percent.)

Item	Total population	Total citizen population	Registered			Voted		
			Total registered	Percent registered (total population)	Percent registered (total citizen population)	Total voted	Percent voted (total population)	Percent voted (total citizen population)
U.S. Total	249,748	228,832	153,066	61.3	66.9	122,281	49.0	53.4
State Total.................................	2,149	2,026	1,449	67.4	71.5	1,152	53.6	56.9
Sex								
Male	1,049	980	692	66.0	70.6	554	52.8	56.5
Female	1,100	1,046	757	68.8	72.4	598	54.4	57.2
Race								
White alone................................	1,880	1,777	1,311	69.7	73.8	1,028	54.7	57.8
White, non-Hispanic alone................	1,667	1,662	1,249	74.9	75.2	982	58.9	59.1
Black alone................................	129	125	65	50.1	51.9	58	44.9	46.5
Asian alone................................	59	46	33	(B)	(B)	33	(B)	(B)
Hispanic (of any race).....................	231	134	71	30.8	53.3	55	23.9	41.4
White alone or in combination	1,934	1,831	1,338	69.2	73.1	1,050	54.3	57.3
Black alone or in combination	136	131	66	48.9	50.6	60	43.9	45.4
Asian alone or in combination..............	64	51	36	(B)	(B)	36	(B)	(B)
Age								
18 to 24 years............................	262	246	152	58.1	62.0	93	35.4	37.7
25 to 34 years............................	358	319	175	48.8	54.7	134	37.3	41.8
35 to 44 years............................	378	335	234	61.8	69.8	180	47.5	53.7
45 to 64 years............................	723	700	540	74.6	77.1	447	61.8	63.9
65 years and over	428	426	349	81.5	81.9	299	69.9	70.2

B = Base is less than 75,000 and therefore too small to show the derived measure.

Table KS-14. Crime

(Number, rate per 100,000. Data are derived from the FBI Uniform Crime Reports.)

Item	State			U.S.		
	2016	2017	Percent change	2016	2017	Percent change
TOTAL POPULATION[1]	2,907,731	2,913,123	0.2	323,405,935	325,719,178	0.7
VIOLENT CRIME						
Number....................................	11,665	12,030	3.1	1,285,606	1,283,220	-0.2
Rate	401.2	413.0	2.9	397.5	394.0	-0.9
Murder and Nonnegligent Manslaughter						
Number....................................	132	160	21.2	17,413	17,284	-0.7
Rate	4.5	5.5	21.0	5.4	5.3	-1.4
Rape[2]						
Number....................................	1,618	1,627	0.6	132,414	135,755	2.5
Rate	55.6	55.9	0.4	40.9	41.7	1.8
Robbery						
Number....................................	1,757	1,785	1.6	332,797	319,356	-4.0
Rate	60.4	61.3	1.4	102.9	98.0	-4.7
Aggravated Assault						
Number....................................	8,158	8,458	3.7	802,982	810,825	1.0
Rate	280.6	290.3	3.5	248.3	248.9	0.3
PROPERTY CRIME						
Number....................................	82,293	81,593	-0.9	7,928,530	7,694,086	-3.0
Rate	2,830.1	2,800.9		2,451.6	2,362.2	-3.6
Burglary						
Number....................................	14,759	13,931	-5.6	1,516,405	1,401,840	-7.6
Rate	507.6	478.2	-5.8	468.9	430.4	-8.2
Larceny-Theft						
Number....................................	60,119	59,816	-0.5	5,644,835	5,519,107	-2.2
Rate	2,067.6	2,053.3	-0.7	1,745.4	1,694.4	-2.9
Motor Vehicle Theft						
Number....................................	7,415	7,846	5.8	767,290	773,139	0.8
Rate	255.0	269.3	5.6	237.3	237.4	-

NOTE: Although arson data are included in the trend and clearance tables, sufficient data are not available to estimate totals for this offense. Therefore, no arson data are published in this table.
- = Zero or rounds to zero.
[1] Population figures are U.S. Census Bureau provisional estimates as of July 1, 2017.
[2] The figures shown in the rape (revised definition) column were estimated using the revised Uniform Crime Reporting (UCR) definition of rape.

Table KS-15. State Government Finances, 2017

(Dollar amounts in thousands, percent distribution.)

Item	Dollars	Percent distribution
Total Revenue	21,425,762	100.0
General revenue	17,685,552	82.5
Intergovernmental revenue	4,160,844	19.4
Taxes	8,173,821	38.1
General sales	3,209,506	15.0
Selective sales	1,092,059	5.1
License taxes	421,080	2.0
Individual income tax	2,327,652	10.9
Corporate income tax	386,966	1.8
Other taxes	736,558	3.4
Current charges	4,118,746	19.2
Miscellaneous general revenue	1,232,141	5.8
Utility revenue	0	-
Liquor stores revenue	0	-
Insurance trust revenue[1]	3,740,210	17.5
Total Expenditure	19,597,970	100.0
Intergovernmental expenditure	4,860,179	24.8
Direct expenditure	14,737,791	75.2
Current operation	10,931,043	55.8
Capital outlay	1,505,017	7.7
Insurance benefits and repayments	1,912,827	9.8
Assistance and subsidies	208,775	1.1
Interest on debt	180,129	0.9
Exhibit: Salaries and wages	2,951,778	15.1
Total Expenditure	19,597,970	100.0
General expenditure	17,685,143	90.2
Intergovernmental expenditure	4,860,179	24.8
Direct expenditure	12,824,964	65.4
General expenditure, by function:		
Education	7,402,958	37.8
Public welfare	4,101,965	20.9
Hospitals	2,681,576	13.7
Health	397,821	2.0
Highways	1,239,281	6.3
Police protection	111,385	0.6
Correction	350,931	1.8
Natural resources	224,912	1.1
Parks and recreation	38,835	0.2
Governmental administration	474,356	2.4
Interest on general debt	180,129	0.9
Other and unallocable	480,994	2.5
Utility expenditure	0	-
Liquor stores expenditure	0	-
Insurance trust expenditure	1,912,827	9.8
Debt at End of Fiscal Year	7,538,475	X
Cash and Security Holdings	24,083,668	X

X = Not applicable.
- = Zero or rounds to zero.
[1] Within insurance trust revenue, net earnings of state retirement systems is a calculated statistic (the item code in the data file is X08), and thus can be positive or negative. Net earnings is the sum of earnings on investments plus gains on investments minus losses on investments. The change made in 2002 for asset valuation from book to market value in accordance with Statement 34 of the Governmental Accounting Standards Board is reflected in the calculated statistics.

Table KS-16. State Government Tax Collections, 2018

(Dollars in thousands, percent.)

Item	Dollars	Percent distribution
Total Taxes	9,546,790	100.0
Property taxes	714,895	7.5
Sales and gross receipts	4,494,809	47.1
General sales and gross receipts	3,304,091	34.6
Selective sales and gross receipts	1,190,718	12.5
Alcoholic beverages	142,126	1.5
Amusements	304	-
Insurance premiums	408,321	4.3
Motor fuels	461,075	4.8
Pari-mutuels	X	-
Public utilities	373	-
Tobacco products	130,247	1.4
Other selective sales	48,272	0.5
Licenses	433,229	4.5
Alcoholic beverages	3,647	-
Amusements	6,993	0.1
Corporations in general	28,187	0.3
Hunting and fishing	32,780	0.3
Motor vehicle	222,978	2.3
Motor vehicle operators	31,881	0.3
Public utilities	5,857	0.1
Occupation and business, NEC	98,132	1.0
Other licenses	2,774	-
Income taxes	3,851,644	40.3
Individual income	3,413,677	35.8
Corporation net income	437,967	4.6
Other taxes	52,213	0.5
Death and gift	0	-
Documentary and stock transfer	X	-
Severance	52,213	0.5
Taxes, NEC	0	-

- = Zero or rounds to zero.

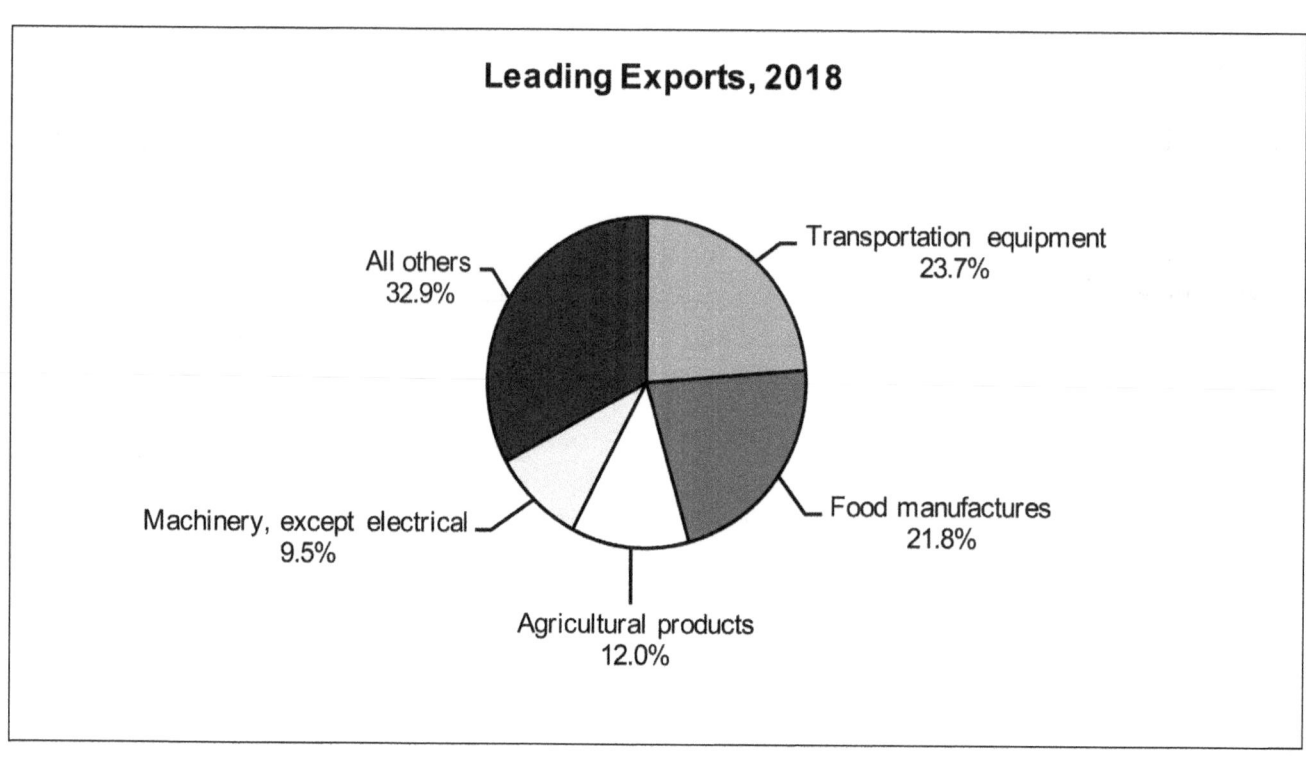

Leading Exports, 2018

Transportation equipment 23.7%

Food manufactures 21.8%

Agricultural products 12.0%

Machinery, except electrical 9.5%

All others 32.9%

KENTUCKY

Facts and Figures

Location: East central United States; bordered on the N by Illinois, Indiana, and Ohio, on the E by West Virginia and Virginia, on the S by Tennessee, and on the W by Missouri and Illinois

Area: 40,409 sq. mi. (104,659 sq. km.); rank—37th

Population: 4,468,402 (2018 est.); rank—26th

Principal Cities: capital—Frankfort; largest—Lexington

Statehood: June 1, 1792; 15th state

U.S. Congress: 2 senators, 6 representatives

State Motto: United We Stand, Divided We Fall

State Song: "My Old Kentucky Home"

State Nickname: The Bluegrass State

Abbreviations: KY; Ky.

State Symbols: flower—goldenrod; tree—tulip poplar; bird—cardinal

At a Glance

- With an increase in population of 3.0 percent, Kentucky ranked 31st among the states in growth from 2010 to 2018.

- Kentucky ranked 5th in the nation for the highest rate of drug overdose deaths in 2017, with 37.2 deaths per 100,000 population.

- In 2017, Kentucky's median household income was $48,375, the 7th lowest in the country. The state's poverty level was 17.2 percent, the 5th highest in the country.

- The property crime rate in Kentucky in 2017 was 2,129.1 per 100,000 population, compared to the U.S. rate of 2,362.2 per 100,000 population.

- In 2017, 5.4 percent of Kentucky residents did not have health insurance, compared to 8.7 percent of all U.S. residents.

Table KY-1. Population by Age, Sex, Race, and Hispanic Origin

(Number, percent, except where noted.)

Sex, age, race, and Hispanic origin	2000	2010	2018 [1]	Percent change, 2010–2018
Total Population...	4,041,769	4,339,367	4,468,402	3.0
Percent of total U.S. population	1.4	1.4	1.4	X
Sex				
Male..	1,975,368	2,134,952	2,201,511	3.1
Female...	2,066,401	2,204,425	2,266,891	2.8
Age				
Under 5 years...	265,901	282,367	275,412	-2.5
5 to 19 years..	847,743	863,837	849,619	-1.6
20 to 64 years..	2,423,332	2,614,936	2,612,745	-0.1
65 years and over..	504,793	578,227	730,626	26.4
Median age (years)	35.9	38.1	38.9	2.1
Race and Hispanic Origin				
One race				
White	3,640,889	3,864,193	3,913,936	1.3
Black..	295,994	342,804	375,972	9.7
American Indian and Alaska Native	8,616	12,105	13,412	10.8
Asian..	29,744	50,177	72,806	45.1
Native Hawaiian or Other Pacific Islander	1,460	3,199	4,058	26.9
Two or more races	42,443	66,889	88,218	31.9
Hispanic (of any race)....................................	59,939	138,618	171,933	24.0

X = Not applicable.
[1] Population figures for 2018 are July 1 estimates. The 2010 estimates are taken from the 2010 Census.
- = Zero or rounds to zero.

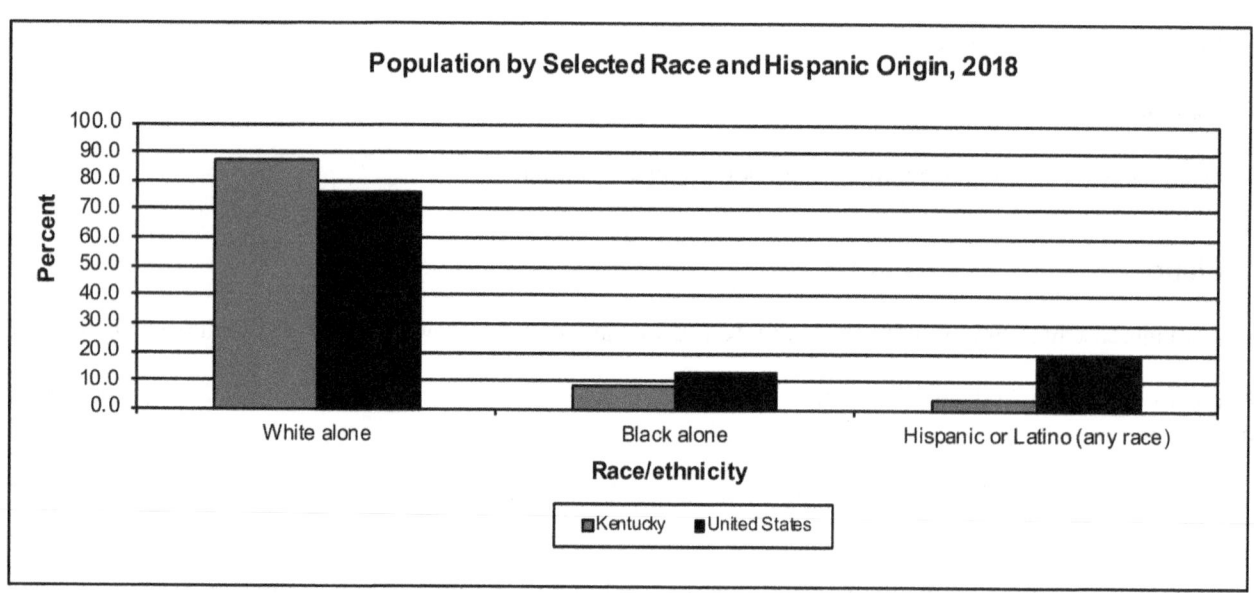

Population by Selected Race and Hispanic Origin, 2018

Table KY-2. Marital Status

(Number, percent distribution.)

Sex, age, race, and Hispanic origin	2000	2010	2017
Males, 15 Years and Over	1,551,174	1,702,020	1,761,269
Never married	25.9	30.8	32.2
Now married, except separated..	59.9	52.0	51.0
Separated...	1.5	2.1	1.9
Widowed..	2.6	2.8	3.1
Divorced..	10.2	12.3	11.8
Females, 15 Years and Over	1,665,993	1,794,164	1,851,260
Never married	19.7	24.2	25.5
Now married, except separated..	55.0	48.9	48.0
Separated...	2.1	2.6	2.3
Widowed..	11.5	10.6	9.8
Divorced..	11.8	13.7	14.4

Table KY-3. Households and Housing Characteristics

(Number, percent, dollars.)

Item	2000	2010	2017	Average annual percent change, 2010–2017
Total Households..	1,590,647	1,684,348	1,725,034	0.3
Family households	1,104,398	1,126,685	1,129,828	-
Married-couple family	857,944	833,872	837,553	0.1
Other family	246,454	292,813	292,275	-
Male householder, no wife present......................................	58,497	76,832	81,524	0.9
Female householder, no husband present............................	187,957	215,981	210,751	-0.3
Nonfamily households	486,249	557,663	595,206	1.0
Householder living alone..	414,095	470,103	492,850	0.7
Householder not living alone..	72,154	87,560	102,356	2.4
Housing Characteristics				
Total housing units...	1,750,927	1,928,617	1,984,235	0.4
Occupied housing units	1,590,647	1,684,348	1,725,034	0.3
Owner occupied	1,125,397	1,156,292	1,146,668	-0.1
Renter occupied	465,250	528,056	578,366	1.4
Average household size...	2.47	2.51	2.51	-
Financial Characteristics				
Median gross rent of renter-occupied housing	445	613	724	2.6
Median monthly owner costs for housing units with a mortgage	816	1,072	1,123	0.7
Median value of owner-occupied housing units	86,700	121,600	141,000	2.3

- = Zero or rounds to zero.

Table KY-4. Migration, Origin, and Language

(Number, percent.)

Characteristic	State			U.S.		
	2016	2017	Percent change	2016	2017	Percent change
Residence 1 Year Ago						
Population 1 year and over	4,385,213	4,404,279	0.4	319,361,956	321,994,428	0.8
Same house	84.3	84.5	X	85.4	85.7	X
Different house in the U.S...	15.2	15.2	X	13.9	13.6	X
Same county	8.9	8.9	X	8.3	8.1	X
Different county	6.3	6.3	X	5.6	5.6	X
Same state	3.7	3.9	X	3.2	3.3	X
Different state	2.6	2.4	X	2.4	2.3	X
Abroad	0.4	0.4	X	0.7	0.7	X
Place of Birth						
Native born	4,281,010	4,285,104	0.1	279,388,170	281,193,323	0.6
Male	49.0	49.2	X	49.3	49.4	X
Female	51.0	50.8	X	50.7	50.6	X
Foreign born	155,964	169,085	8.4	43,739,345	44,525,855	1.8
Male	52.1	51.2	X	48.5	48.4	X
Female	47.9	48.8	X	51.5	51.6	X
Foreign born; naturalized U.S. citizen...................................	60,913	69,967	14.9	21,238,372	21,948,732	3.3
Male	47.7	47.5	X	45.9	45.9	X
Female	52.3	52.5	X	54.1	54.1	X
Foreign born; not a U.S. citizen	95,051	99,118	4.3	22,500,973	22,577,123	0.3
Male	54.9	53.8	X	51	50.8	X
Female	45.1	46.2	X	49	49.2	X
Entered 2010 or later	29.8	36.3	X	18.6	21.3	X
Entered 2000 to 2009	35.3	31.4	X	26.7	25.7	X
Entered before 2000...	34.9	32.3	X	54.7	53.0	X
World Region of Birth, Foreign						
Foreign-born population, excluding population born at sea	155,964	169,085	8.4	43,738,901	44,525,458	1.8
Europe	12.8	14.9	X	10.9	10.8	X
Asia	36.7	32.9	X	30.8	31.2	X
Africa	11.2	13.2	X	4.9	5.1	X
Oceania	0.8	1.4	X	0.6	0.6	X
Latin America	36.2	35.3	X	51	50.4	X
North America..	2.2	2.2	X	1.8	1.8	X
Language Spoken at Home and Ability to Speak English						
Population 5 years and over..	4,164,025	4,177,833	0.3	303,328,961	305,924,019	0.9
English only	94.8	94.4	X	78.4	78.2	X
Language other than English...	5.2	5.6	X	21.6	21.8	X
Speaks English less than "very well"...................................	2.1	2.4	X	8.6	8.5	X

NA = Not available.
X = Not applicable.
- = Zero or rounds to zero.

Table KY-5. Median Income and Poverty Status, 2017

(Number, percent, except as noted.)

Characteristic	State		U.S.	
	Number	Percent	Number	Percent
Median Income				
Households (dollars)..................................	48,375	X	60,336	X
Families (dollars)	61,593	X	73,891	X
Below Poverty Level (All People)	744,239	17.2	42,583,651	13.4
Sex				
Male	335,410	15.8	19,004,547	12.2
Female	408,829	18.6	23,579,104	14.5
Age				
Under 18 years..	222,906	22.4	13,353,202	18.4
Related children under 18 years................	217,208	22.0	13,053,472	18.1
18 to 64 years...	450,475	17.1	24,648,677	12.6
65 years and over	70,858	10.3	4,581,772	9.3

X = Not applicable.

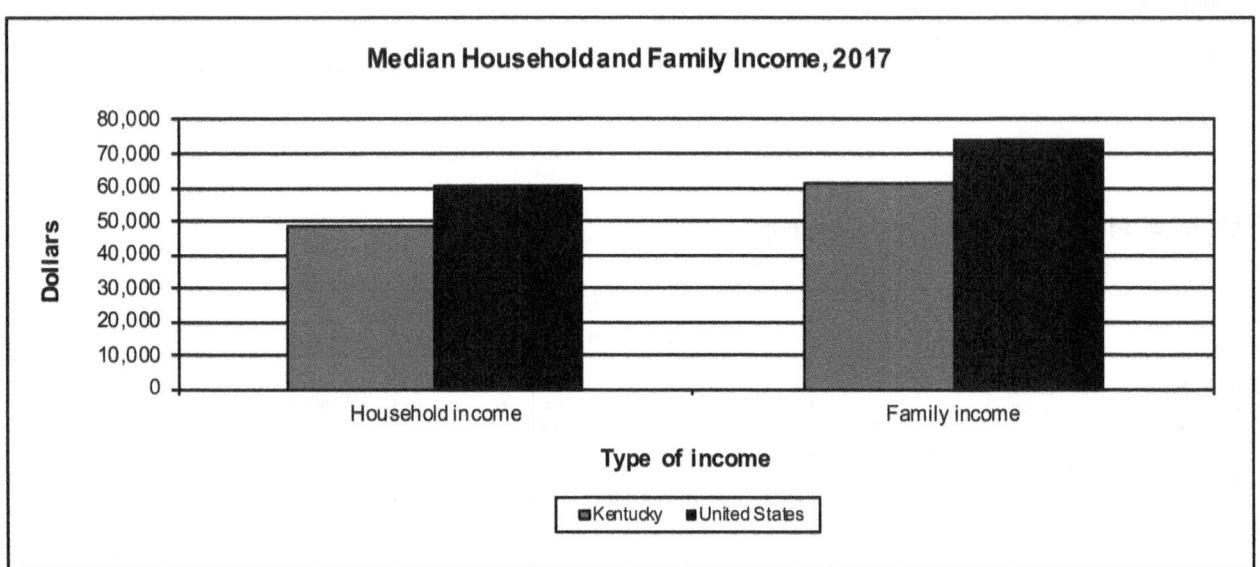

Table KY-6. Health Insurance Coverage Status for the Civilian Noninstitutionalized Population and Children Under 18 Years of Age

(Number, percent.)

Item	2009	2010	2011	2012	2013	2014	2015	2016	2017
Civilian Noninstitutionalized Population	4,225,355	4,242,714	4,284,357	4,292,718	4,312,100	4,328,524	4,342,711	4,354,380	4,370,940
Covered by Private or Public Insurance									
Number..	3,612,074	3,595,673	3,665,899	3,697,258	3,695,652	3,962,462	4,081,243	4,131,030	4,135,713
Percent..	85.5	84.7	85.6	86.1	85.7	91.5	94.0	94.9	94.6
Uninsured									
Number..	613,281	647,041	618,458	595,460	616,448	366,062	261,468	223,350	235,227
Percent..	14.5	15.3	14.4	13.9	14.3	8.5	6.0	5.1	5.4
Percent in the U.S. not covered...................	15.1	15.5	15.1	14.8	14.5	11.7	9.4	8.6	8.7
Children Under 18 Years of Age[1]	1,014,997	1,018,375	1,022,948	1,016,026	1,012,120	1,012,771	1,008,187	1,009,986	1,078,842
Covered by Private or Public Insurance									
Number..	950,590	957,195	960,504	959,668	952,590	969,473	965,380	977,991	1,037,936
Percent..	93.7	94.0	93.9	94.5	94.1	95.7	95.8	96.8	96.2
Uninsured									
Number..	64,407	61,180	62,444	56,358	59,530	43,298	42,807	31,995	40,906
Percent..	6.3	6.0	6.1	5.5	5.9	4.3	4.2	3.2	3.8
Percent in the U.S. not covered....................	8.6	8.0	7.5	7.2	7.1	6.0	4.8	4.5	5.0

[1] 2017 data is for individuals under 19 years of age.

Table KY-7. Employment Status by Demographic Group, 2018

(Numbers in thousands, percent.)

Characteristic	Civilian noninstitutional population	Civilian labor force		Employed		Unemployed	
		Number	Percent of population	Number	Percent of population	Number	Percent of population
Total...	3,493	2,067	59.2	1,977	56.6	90	4.4
Sex							
Male..	1,688	1,092	64.7	1,044	61.8	49	4.4
Female.....................................	1,805	974	54.0	933	51.7	42	4.3
Race, Sex, and Hispanic Origin							
White.......................................	3,147	1,834	58.3	1,759	55.9	75	4.1
Male....................................	1,524	979	64.3	939	61.6	41	4.1
Female.................................	1,623	855	52.6	821	50.6	34	4.0
Black or African American..............	263	176	66.9	164	62.5	11	6.5
Male....................................	124	84	67.9	78	63.1	6	7.1
Female.................................	139	92	65.9	86	62.0	6	6.0
Hispanic or Latino ethnicity[1]	122	88	71.9	83	68.0	5	5.5
Male....................................	NA	NA	NA	NA	NA	NA	NA
Female.................................	NA	NA	NA	NA	NA	NA	NA
Age							
16 to 19 years...........................	235	100	42.4	87	37.0	13	12.7
20 to 24 years...........................	289	218	75.7	197	68.4	21	9.6
25 to 34 years...........................	555	463	83.5	444	80.0	20	4.2
35 to 44 years...........................	544	433	79.5	418	76.9	14	3.3
45 to 54 years...........................	549	412	75.1	402	73.2	11	2.5
55 to 64 years...........................	580	331	57.2	322	55.6	9	2.7
65 years and over	742	110	14.8	106	14.3	4	3.3

NOTE: Data in Table 7 are from the Current Population Survey (CPS) and do not match the estimates in Table 8. See notes and definitions for further information.
[1] May be of any race.
NA = Not available.

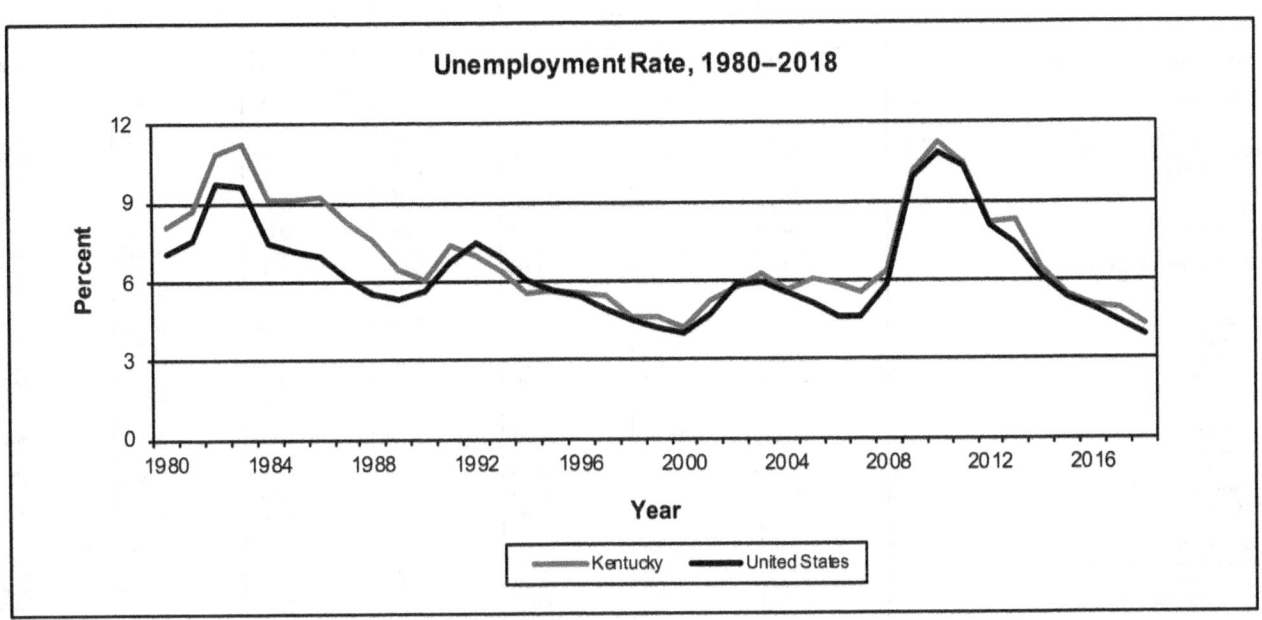

Unemployment Rate, 1980–2018

Table KY-8. Employment Status of the Civilian Noninstitutional Population Age 16 Years and Over

(Number, percent.)

Year	Civilian labor force	Civilian participation rate	Employed	Unemployed	Unemployment rate
2010....................	2,054,375	61.3	1,844,650	209,725	10.2
2011....................	2,056,410	61.0	1,862,928	193,482	9.4
2012....................	2,059,127	60.8	1,891,162	167,965	8.2
2013....................	2,055,442	60.4	1,890,879	164,563	8.0
2014....................	2,003,842	58.6	1,874,516	129,326	6.5
2015....................	1,976,967	57.5	1,872,326	104,641	5.3
2016....................	2,012,279	58.2	1,909,158	103,121	5.1
2017....................	2,052,368	59.0	1,952,066	100,302	4.9
2018....................	2,061,622	59.1	1,972,312	89,310	4.3

Table KY-9. Employment and Average Wages by Industry

(Estimates are based on the 2012 *North American Industry Classification System* [NAICS].)

Industry	2011	2012	2013	2014	2015	2016	2017
	Number of jobs						
Wage and Salary Employment by Industry	1,884,604	1,908,719	1,923,075	1,948,724	1,978,345	1,996,627	2,011,592
Farm Wage and Salary Employment	14,003	14,782	13,643	14,615	16,632	13,699	15,865
Nonfarm Wage and Salary Employment	1,870,601	1,893,937	1,909,432	1,934,109	1,961,713	1,982,928	1,995,727
Private wage and salary employment	1,490,022	1,522,575	1,542,028	1,571,828	1,604,398	1,629,710	1,642,284
Forestry, fishing, and related activities	7,271	7,259	7,399	7,494	7,642	7,676	7,522
Mining	22,617	20,291	17,194	16,239	13,697	10,269	9,970
Utilities	6,514	6,566	6,512	6,624	6,569	6,630	6,689
Construction	69,393	69,231	69,877	74,634	77,693	78,754	79,214
Manufacturing	212,924	223,358	229,642	235,105	241,530	247,875	250,363
Durable goods manufacturing	128,809	138,673	143,824	149,467	155,815	161,255	162,396
Nondurable goods manufacturing	84,115	84,685	85,818	85,638	85,715	86,620	87,967
Wholesale trade	72,481	73,052	74,302	74,692	74,963	76,045	76,620
Retail trade	202,569	204,433	204,656	206,292	211,056	215,557	216,755
Transportation and warehousing	85,609	87,281	86,629	91,110	96,076	100,709	103,806
Information	26,876	26,593	26,325	26,348	25,234	22,753	22,723
Finance and insurance	70,120	72,187	73,788	74,966	76,865	77,606	78,109
Real estate and rental and leasing	18,197	18,225	18,609	18,477	18,904	19,521	19,817
Professional, scientific, and technical services	69,286	68,005	69,913	72,136	73,925	75,209	74,403
Management of companies and enterprises	20,013	20,516	20,570	20,674	19,975	20,917	20,127
Administrative and waste services	99,149	105,394	111,610	119,005	122,984	122,011	120,656
Educational services	31,670	32,053	32,093	32,688	32,355	31,982	32,246
Health care and social assistance	225,816	232,874	233,506	231,575	236,804	242,165	246,350
Arts, entertainment, and recreation	18,513	19,819	20,232	20,657	21,259	22,144	23,239
Accommodation and food services	151,866	156,173	160,199	162,843	167,682	172,860	175,063
Other services, except public administration	79,138	79,265	78,972	80,269	79,185	79,027	78,612
Government and government enterprises	380,579	371,362	367,404	362,281	357,315	353,218	353,443
	Dollars						
Average Wages and Salaries by Industry	39,548	40,372	40,706	41,801	43,129	43,894	44,855
Average Farm Wages and Salaries	15,892	21,053	23,254	22,251	16,509	23,002	18,025
Average Nonfarm Wages and Salaries	39,725	40,523	40,830	41,948	43,355	44,038	45,068
Average private wages and salaries	39,125	40,132	40,487	41,710	43,154	43,888	44,971
Forestry, fishing, and related activities	26,386	26,904	27,654	28,264	29,557	31,139	32,106
Mining	69,630	66,789	68,374	68,621	68,432	66,123	70,065
Utilities	72,232	74,120	76,422	79,771	82,316	82,806	84,902
Construction	44,010	45,919	47,383	49,895	51,655	51,748	53,167
Manufacturing	51,283	52,623	53,287	55,076	56,727	57,098	58,153
Durable goods manufacturing	53,238	54,336	54,819	56,307	58,260	58,546	59,528
Nondurable goods manufacturing	48,289	49,819	50,720	52,927	53,940	54,404	55,615
Wholesale trade	53,673	54,849	55,076	57,413	60,114	60,932	62,489
Retail trade	24,111	24,672	24,817	25,140	26,006	26,702	27,199
Transportation and warehousing	47,809	49,004	49,502	50,633	52,110	51,977	53,637
Information	44,468	45,928	46,387	48,989	48,963	52,807	54,778
Finance and insurance	58,934	60,340	60,937	63,905	66,598	68,434	71,541
Real estate and rental and leasing	35,391	36,417	35,431	37,190	38,383	39,440	40,079
Professional, scientific, and technical services	52,945	55,164	56,276	57,921	60,464	61,523	62,967
Management of companies and enterprises	91,247	95,316	91,138	91,845	97,259	100,861	102,759
Administrative and waste services	25,695	26,558	26,771	27,252	28,340	29,978	31,059
Educational services	24,248	24,711	25,076	24,816	25,708	25,813	26,209
Health care and social assistance	41,999	42,901	43,444	44,570	46,584	47,347	48,077
Arts, entertainment, and recreation	21,842	22,095	22,471	23,848	23,492	23,118	23,447
Accommodation and food services	15,500	16,064	16,181	16,848	17,412	17,968	18,617
Other services, except public administration	27,750	29,405	30,094	30,997	32,279	33,146	34,407
Government and government enterprises	42,073	42,122	42,271	42,985	44,256	44,728	45,520

Table KY-10. Employment Characteristics by Family Type

(Number, percent.)

Family type and labor force status	2015		2016		2017	
	Total	Families with own children under 18 years	Total	Families with own children under 18 years	Total	Families with own children under 18 years
All Families..	1,131,839	455,703	1,121,404	463,090	1,129,828	458,500
FAMILY TYPE AND LABOR FORCE STATUS						
Married-Couple Families..............................	828,120	300,055	812,069	298,129	837,553	307,600
Both husband and wife in labor force.............	46.7	65.2	48.1	67.2	48.5	68.4
Husband in labor force, wife not in labor force	21.1	25.3	20.0	24.3	19.6	22.7
Wife in labor force, husband not in labor force	9.5	5.5	9.3	5.0	9.1	5.0
Both husband and wife not in labor force........	22.1	3.6	22.0	3.0	22.1	3.4
Other Families	303,719	155,648	309,335	164,961	292,275	150,900
Female householder, no husband present.....................	71.8	73.8	73.0	74.9	72.1	72.3
In labor force..	43.6	56.6	46.5	59.3	46.1	58.1
Not in labor force	28.1	17.2	26.5	15.6	26.0	14.2
Male householder, no wife present....................	28.2	26.2	27.0	25.1	27.9	27.7
In labor force..	19.4	21.1	18.2	20.8	21.1	24.6
Not in labor force	8.8	5.1	8.8	4.3	6.8	3.1

Table KY-11. School Enrollment and Educational Attainment, 2017

(Number, percent.)

Item	State	U.S.
Enrollment		
Total population 3 years and over, enrolled in school	1,051,294	81,273,337
Enrolled in nursery school or preschool (percent)	6.0	6.0
Enrolled in kindergarten (percent)............................	4.9	4.9
Enrolled in elementary school, grades 1-8 (percent)..................	42.7	40.6
Enrolled in high school, grades 9-12 (percent).....................	21.7	21.1
Enrolled in college or graduate school (percent).....................	24.8	27.4
Attainment		
Total population 25 years and over	3,018,953	221,250,083
Less than ninth grade (percent)	5.4	5.1
9th to 12th grade, no diploma (percent)	8.2	6.9
High school graduate, including equivalency (percent)............	33.0	27.1
Some college, no degree (percent)	21.3	20.4
Associate's degree (percent)	8.0	8.5
Bachelor's degree (percent)	14.0	19.7
Graduate or professional degree (percent)......................	9.9	12.3
High school graduate or higher (percent)	86.3	88.0
Bachelor's degree or higher (percent).............................	24.0	32.0

Table KY-12. Public School Characteristics and Educational Indicators

(Number, percent; data derived from National Center of Education Statistics.)

Item	State	U.S.
Public Elementary and Secondary Schools		
Number of operational school districts, 2016-17..................................	186	18,377
Number of operational schools, 2016-17..	1,539	98,330
Percent charter schools	-	7.1
Total public school enrollment, 2016-17..	684,017	50,587,859
Percent charter school enrollment	-	6.0
Student-teacher ratio, Fall 2015...	16.4	16.0
Expenditures per student (dollars), 2015-16...............................	9,831	11,841
Four-year adjusted cohort graduation rate (ACGR)[1]	89.7	84.6
Students eligible for free or reduced-price lunch (percent), 2015-16...........	59.4	52.1
English language learners (percent), Fall 2016	3.2	9.6
Students age 3 to 21 served under IDEA, part B (percent), 2017-18.............	15.3	13.7
Public Schools by Type, 2016-17		Percent of state public schools
Total number of schools..	1,539	100.0
Special education	8	0.5
Vocational education..	121	7.9
Alternative education..	184	12.0

[1] Adjusted Cohort Graduation Rates (ACGR) differ from Averaged Freshmen Graduation Rates (AFGR).
- = Zero or rounds to zero.

Table KY-13. Reported Voting and Registration of the Voting-Age Population, November 2018

(Numbers in thousands, percent.)

Item	Total population	Total citizen population	Registered			Voted		
			Total registered	Percent registered (total population)	Percent registered (total citizen population)	Total voted	Percent voted (total population)	Percent voted (total citizen population)
U.S. Total	249,748	228,832	153,066	61.3	66.9	122,281	49.0	53.4
State Total..................................	3,370	3,249	2,389	70.9	73.5	1,746	51.8	53.8
Sex								
Male	1,627	1,553	1,092	67.1	70.3	789	48.5	50.8
Female	1,743	1,696	1,297	74.5	76.5	958	55.0	56.5
Race								
White alone................................	3,014	2,954	2,194	72.8	74.3	1,587	52.7	53.7
White, non-Hispanic alone	2,928	2,921	2,183	74.5	74.7	1,579	53.9	54.1
Black alone.................................	248	233	164	66.2	70.7	131	52.8	56.4
Asian alone	82	37	14	17.4	(B)	12	14.1	(B)
Hispanic (of any race)	96	37	15	15.8	(B)	12	12.9	(B)
White alone or in combination	3,036	2,976	2,207	72.7	74.2	1,600	52.7	53.8
Black alone or in combination	264	248	171	64.8	68.9	138	52.2	55.5
Asian alone or in combination	82	37	14	17.4	(B)	12	14.1	(B)
Age								
18 to 24 years	436	413	228	52.2	55.2	100	22.9	24.2
25 to 34 years	539	507	332	61.6	65.6	236	43.7	46.5
35 to 44 years	518	484	344	66.4	71.1	242	46.8	50.1
45 to 64 years	1,079	1,048	836	77.5	79.8	662	61.3	63.1
65 years and over	798	798	649	81.4	81.4	507	63.5	63.5

B = Base is less than 75,000 and therefore too small to show the derived measure.

Table KY-14. Crime

(Number, rate per 100,000. Data are derived from the FBI Uniform Crime Reports.)

Item	State			U.S.		
	2016	2017	Percent change	2016	2017	Percent change
TOTAL POPULATION[1]	4,436,113	4,454,189	0.4	323,405,935	325,719,178	0.7
VIOLENT CRIME						
Number...	10,452	10,056	-3.8	1,285,606	1,283,220	-0.2
Rate	235.6	225.8	-4.2	397.5	394.0	-0.9
Murder and Nonnegligent Manslaughter						
Number...	265	263	-0.8	17,413	17,284	-0.7
Rate	6.0	5.9	-1.2	5.4	5.3	-1.4
Rape[2]						
Number...	1,748	1,661	-5.0	132,414	135,755	2.5
Rate	39.4	37.3	-5.4	40.9	41.7	1.8
Robbery						
Number...	3,371	2,958	-12.3	332,797	319,356	-4.0
Rate	76.0	66.4	-12.6	102.9	98.0	-4.7
Aggravated Assault						
Number...	5,068	5,174	2.1	802,982	810,825	1.0
Rate	114.2	116.2	1.7	248.3	248.9	0.3
PROPERTY CRIME						
Number...	97,713	94,833	-2.9	7,928,530	7,694,086	-3.0
Rate	2,202.7	2,129.1	-3.3	2,451.6	2,362.2	-3.6
Burglary						
Number...	20,932	20,195	-3.5	1,516,405	1,401,840	-7.6
Rate	471.9	453.4	-3.9	468.9	430.4	-8.2
Larceny-Theft						
Number...	66,833	64,394	-3.6	5,644,835	5,519,107	-2.2
Rate	1,506.6	1,445.7	-4.0	1,745.4	1,694.4	-2.9
Motor Vehicle Theft						
Number...	9,948	10,244	3.0	767,290	773,139	0.8
Rate	224.3	230.0	2.6	237.3	237.4	-

NOTE: Although arson data are included in the trend and clearance tables, sufficient data are not available to estimate totals for this offense. Therefore, no arson data are published in this table.
- = Zero or rounds to zero.
[1] Population figures are U.S. Census Bureau provisional estimates as of July 1, 2017.
[2] The figures shown in the rape (revised definition) column were estimated using the revised Uniform Crime Reporting (UCR) definition of rape.

Table KY-15. State Government Finances, 2017

(Dollar amounts in thousands, percent distribution.)

Item	Dollars	Percent distribution
Total Revenue	33,778,547	100.0
General revenue	27,713,601	82.0
Intergovernmental revenue	10,829,538	32.1
Taxes	11,907,759	35.3
General sales	3,490,639	10.3
Selective sales	2,159,069	6.4
License taxes	500,447	1.5
Individual income tax	4,394,185	13.0
Corporate income tax	458,650	1.4
Other taxes	904,769	2.7
Current charges	3,907,379	11.6
Miscellaneous general revenue	1,068,925	3.2
Utility revenue	0	-
Liquor stores revenue	0	-
Insurance trust revenue[1]	6,064,946	18.0
Total Expenditure	36,311,322	100.0
Intergovernmental expenditure	5,730,213	15.8
Direct expenditure	30,581,109	84.2
Current operation	22,105,249	60.9
Capital outlay	2,175,833	6.0
Insurance benefits and repayments	4,550,003	12.5
Assistance and subsidies	1,104,855	3.0
Interest on debt	645,169	1.8
Exhibit: Salaries and wages	4,373,700	12.0
Total Expenditure	36,311,322	100.0
General expenditure	31,724,376	87.4
Intergovernmental expenditure	5,730,213	15.8
Direct expenditure	25,994,163	71.6
General expenditure, by function:		
Education	11,263,480	31.0
Public welfare	11,508,013	31.7
Hospitals	1,894,482	5.2
Health	500,808	1.4
Highways	1,996,782	5.5
Police protection	274,012	0.8
Correction	666,606	1.8
Natural resources	396,106	1.1
Parks and recreation	128,387	0.4
Governmental administration	1,188,743	3.3
Interest on general debt	645,169	1.8
Other and unallocable	1,261,788	3.5
Utility expenditure	31,081	0.1
Liquor stores expenditure	5862	-
Insurance trust expenditure	4,550,003	12.5
Debt at End of Fiscal Year	14,403,514	X
Cash and Security Holdings	40,783,327	X

X = Not applicable.
- = Zero or rounds to zero.
[1] Within insurance trust revenue, net earnings of state retirement systems is a calculated statistic (the item code in the data file is X08), and thus can be positive or negative. Net earnings is the sum of earnings on investments plus gains on investments minus losses on investments. The change made in 2002 for asset valuation from book to market value in accordance with Statement 34 of the Governmental Accounting Standards Board is reflected in the calculated statistics.

Table KY-16. State Government Tax Collections, 2018

(Dollars in thousands, percent.)

Item	Dollars	Percent distribution
Total Taxes	12,059,970	100.0
Property taxes	660,902	5.5
Sales and gross receipts	5,714,427	47.4
General sales and gross receipts	3,600,598	29.9
Selective sales and gross receipts	2,113,829	17.5
Alcoholic beverages	145,648	1.2
Amusements	196	-
Insurance premiums	165,161	1.4
Motor fuels	702,651	5.8
Pari-mutuels	7,704	0.1
Public utilities	61,126	0.5
Tobacco products	228,749	1.9
Other selective sales	802,594	6.7
Licenses	499,502	4.1
Alcoholic beverages	6,801	0.1
Amusements	279	-
Corporations in general	115,618	1.0
Hunting and fishing	30,531	0.3
Motor vehicle	211,646	1.8
Motor vehicle operators	16,795	0.1
Public utilities	X	-
Occupation and business, NEC	112,292	0.9
Other licenses	5,540	-
Income taxes	5,010,439	41.5
Individual income	4,499,086	37.3
Corporation net income	511,353	4.2
Other taxes	174,700	1.4
Death and gift	48,248	0.4
Documentary and stock transfer	3,480	-
Severance	122,972	1.0
Taxes, NEC	0	-

- = Zero or rounds to zero.
X = Not applicable.

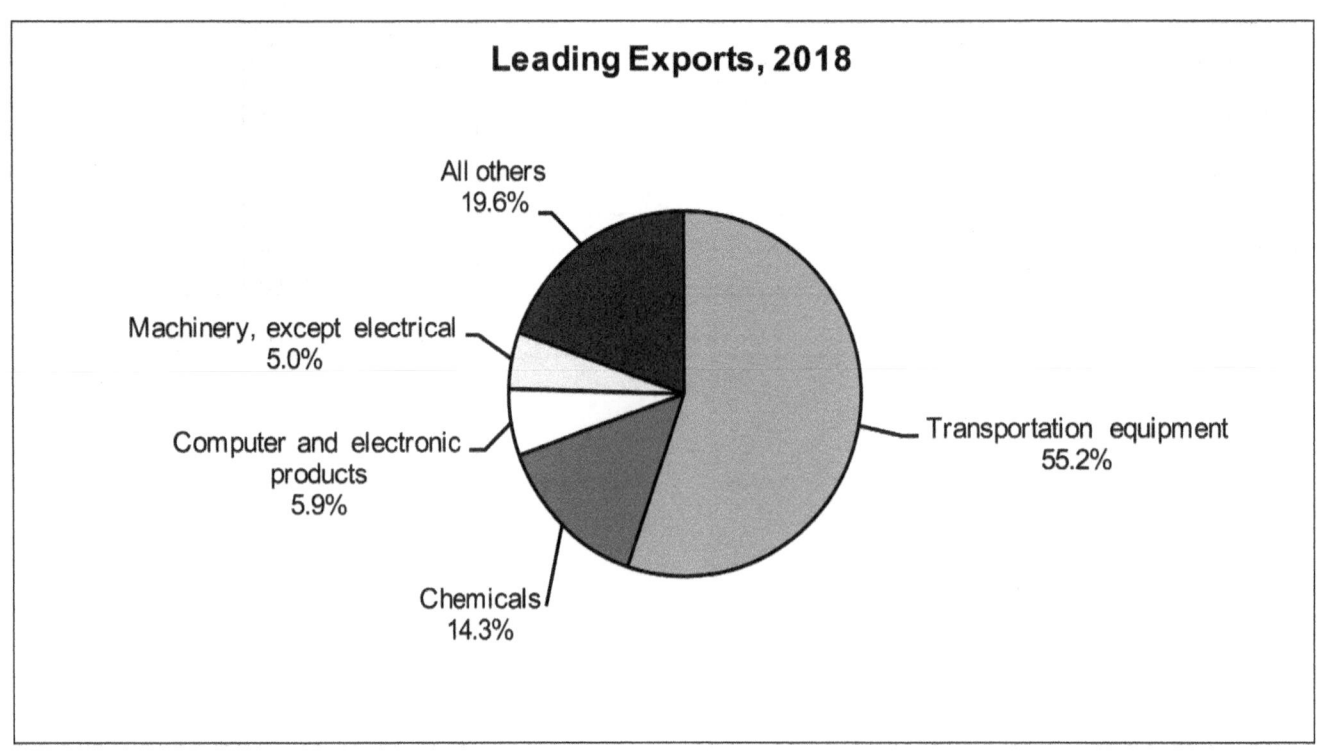

Leading Exports, 2018

All others 19.6%

Machinery, except electrical 5.0%

Computer and electronic products 5.9%

Chemicals 14.3%

Transportation equipment 55.2%

LOUISIANA

Location: South central United States; bordered on the N by Arkansas, on the E by Mississippi, on the S by the Gulf of Mexico, and on the W by Texas

Area: 51,840 sq. mi. (134,264 sq. km.); rank—31st

Population: 4,659,978 (2018 est.); rank—25th

Principal Cities: capital—Baton Rouge; largest—New Orleans

Statehood: April 30, 1812; 18th state

U.S. Congress: 2 senators, 6 representatives

State Motto: Union, Justice, Confidence

State Song: "Give Me Louisiana"

State Nicknames: The Pelican State; The Bayou State

Abbreviations: LA; La.

State Symbols: flower—magnolia; tree—bald cypress; bird—Eastern brown pelican

At a Glance

- With an increase in population of 2.8 percent, Louisiana ranked 33rd in population growth from 2010 to 2018.

- Louisiana's median household income in 2017 was $46,145, the 4th lowest in the country, and 19.7 percent of the population lived below the poverty level, which was the 2nd highest poverty rate among the states.

- In 2018, Louisiana had the 3rd highest percent of residents who self-identified as "Black or African-American Alone," with 32.7 percent of residents in this category.

- In 2017, 8.4 percent of Louisiana's population did not have health insurance, which was down from 10.3 percent the year before.

- Louisiana consumed the most energy per capita in 2017, using 959.5 million Btu per person, compared to the U.S. average of 300.2 million Btu per capita.

Table LA-1. Population by Age, Sex, Race, and Hispanic Origin

(Number, percent, except where noted.)

Sex, age, race, and Hispanic origin	2000	2010	2018 [1]	Percent change, 2010–2018
Total Population..	4,468,976	4,533,372	4,659,978	2.8
Percent of total U.S. population	1.6	1.5	1.4	X
Sex				
Male..	2,162,903	2,219,292	2,274,759	2.5
Female..	2,306,073	2,314,080	2,385,219	3.1
Age				
Under 5 years.......................................	317,392	314,260	307,019	-2.3
5 to 19 years..	1,050,637	939,977	904,938	-3.7
20 to 64 years.......................................	2,584,018	2,721,278	2,729,588	0.3
65 years and over....................................	516,929	557,857	718,433	28.8
Median age (years)	34.0	35.8	37.2	3.9
Race and Hispanic Origin				
One race				
White	2,856,161	2,902,875	2,930,432	0.9
Black	1,451,944	1,462,969	1,526,090	4.3
American Indian and Alaska Native	25,477	33,037	36,500	10.5
Asian	54,758	71,829	84,271	17.3
Native Hawaiian or Other Pacific Islander	1,240	2,588	2,889	11.6
Two or more races	48,265	60,074	79,796	32.8
Hispanic (of any race)	107,738	200,653	243,811	21.5

X = Not applicable.
[1] Population figures for 2018 are July 1 estimates. The 2010 estimates are taken from the 2010 Census.

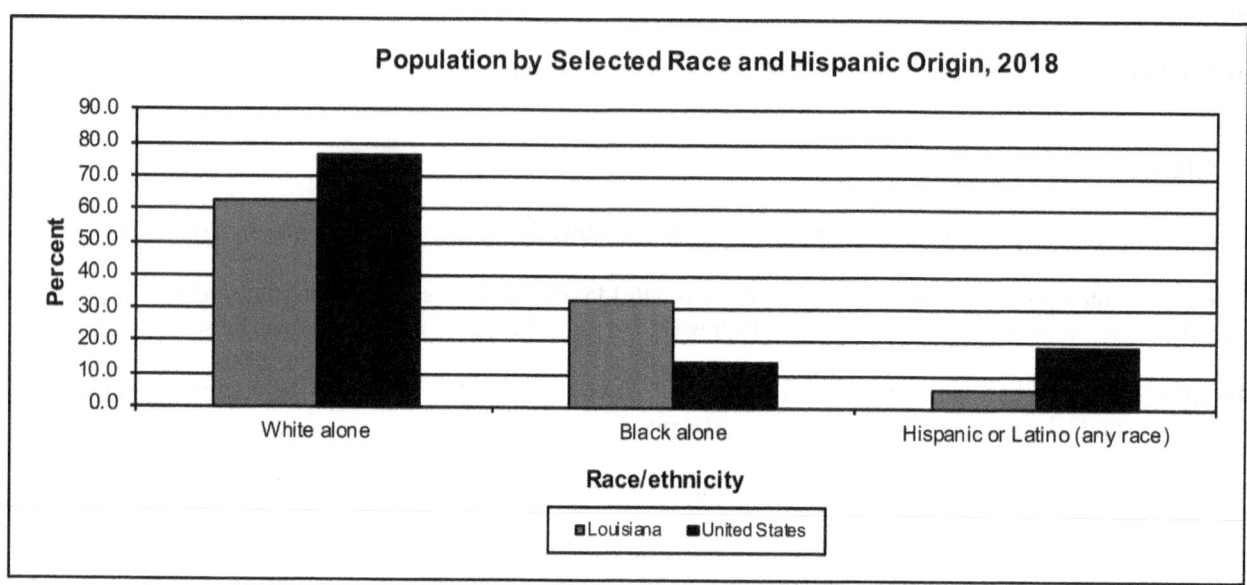

Table LA-2. Marital Status

(Number, percent distribution.)

Sex, age, race, and Hispanic origin	2000	2010	2017
Males, 15 Years and Over...............................	1,648,133	1,751,556	1,815,900
Never married	31.2	37.0	39.7
Now married, except separated.........................	54.5	47.2	44.5
Separated..	2.2	2.2	2.2
Widowed...	2.8	2.8	3.3
Divorced...	9.2	10.8	10.4
Females, 15 Years and Over.............................	1,828,247	1,861,490	1,944,494
Never married	26.3	30.8	33.7
Now married, except separated.........................	48.2	42.6	41.2
Separated..	2.9	3.2	2.7
Widowed...	11.5	10.1	9.7
Divorced...	11.1	13.3	12.7

Table LA-3. Households and Housing Characteristics

(Number, percent, dollars.)

Item	2000	2010	2017	Average annual percent change, 2010–2017
Total Households...	1,656,053	1,689,822	1,737,123	0.4
Family households..	1,156,438	1,129,117	1,107,245	-0.3
Married-couple family..	809,498	753,423	744,011	-0.2
Other family...	346,940	375,694	363,234	-0.5
Male householder, no wife present...................................	71,865	79,560	87,339	1.4
Female householder, no husband present..........................	275,075	296,134	275,895	-1.0
Nonfamily households	499,615	560,705	629,878	1.8
Householder living alone..	419,200	468,853	533,354	2.0
Householder not living alone..	80,415	91,852	96,524	0.7
Housing Characteristics				
Total housing units..	1,847,181	1,967,947	2,061,582	0.7
Occupied housing units	1,656,053	1,689,822	1,737,123	0.4
Owner occupied..	1,125,135	1,141,504	1,132,229	-0.1
Renter occupied...	530,918	548,318	604,894	1.5
Average household size...	2.62	2.61	2.62	0.1
Financial Characteristics				
Median gross rent of renter-occupied housing	466	736	836	1.9
Median monthly owner costs for housing units with a mortgage	816	1,163	1,233	0.9
Median value of owner-occupied housing units...........................	85,000	137,500	162,500	2.6

Table LA-4. Migration, Origin, and Language

(Number, percent.)

Characteristic	State 2016	State 2017	State Percent change	U.S. 2016	U.S. 2017	U.S. Percent change
Residence 1 Year Ago						
Population 1 year and over	4,622,042	4,629,962	0.2	319,361,956	321,994,428	0.8
Same house	86.4	87.1	X	85.4	85.7	X
Different house in the U.S.	13.2	12.7	X	13.9	13.6	X
Same county	8.1	7.5	X	8.3	8.1	X
Different county	5.1	5.1	X	5.6	5.6	X
Same state	3.2	3.5	X	3.2	3.3	X
Different state	1.8	1.6	X	2.4	2.3	X
Abroad	0.3	0.3	X	0.7	0.7	X
Place of Birth						
Native born	4,491,745	4,492,930	0.0	279,388,170	281,193,323	0.6
Male	48.8	48.7	X	49.3	49.4	X
Female	51.2	51.3	X	50.7	50.6	X
Foreign born	189,921	191,403	0.8	43,739,345	44,525,855	1.8
Male	52.0	52.5	X	48.5	48.4	X
Female	48.0	47.5	X	51.5	51.6	X
Foreign born; naturalized U.S. citizen...................................	79,688	74,233	-6.8	21,238,372	21,948,732	3.3
Male	48.0	46.5	X	45.9	45.9	X
Female	52.0	53.5	X	54.1	54.1	X
Foreign born; not a U.S. citizen	110,233	117,170	6.3	22,500,973	22,577,123	0.3
Male	55.0	56.2	X	51	50.8	X
Female	45.0	43.8	X	49	49.2	X
Entered 2010 or later	26.8	29.2	X	18.6	21.3	X
Entered 2000 to 2009	29.1	29.9	X	26.7	25.7	X
Entered before 2000...	44.1	40.9	X	54.7	53.0	X
World Region of Birth, Foreign						
Foreign-born population, excluding population born at sea	189,921	191,403	0.8	43,738,901	44,525,458	1.8
Europe	8.5	8.3	X	10.9	10.8	X
Asia..	31.2	30.3	X	30.8	31.2	X
Africa	4.2	4.6	X	4.9	5.1	X
Oceania	0.4	0.2	X	0.6	0.6	X
Latin America...	54.5	55.4	X	51	50.4	X
North America..	1.2	1.3	X	1.8	1.8	X
Language Spoken at Home and Ability to Speak English						
Population 5 years and over...	4,374,703	4,378,120	0.1	303,328,961	305,924,019	0.9
English only	91.9	91.9	X	78.4	78.2	X
Language other than English..	8.1	8.1	X	21.6	21.8	X
Speaks English less than "very well".................................	2.8	3.0	X	8.6	8.5	X

NA = Not available.
X = Not applicable.
- = Zero or rounds to zero.

Table LA-5. Median Income and Poverty Status, 2017

(Number, percent, except as noted.)

Characteristic	State		U.S.	
	Number	Percent	Number	Percent
Median Income				
Households (dollars)...	46,145	X	60,336	X
Families (dollars)	60,510	X	73,891	X
Below Poverty Level (All People)	899,039	19.7	42,583,651	13.4
Sex				
Male	390,074	17.7	19,004,547	12.2
Female	508,965	21.7	23,579,104	14.5
Age				
Under 18 years..	306,513	28.0	13,353,202	18.4
Related children under 18 years..	302,973	27.8	13,053,472	18.1
18 to 64 years...	511,707	18.4	24,648,677	12.6
65 years and over	80,819	12.0	4,581,772	9.3

X = Not applicable.

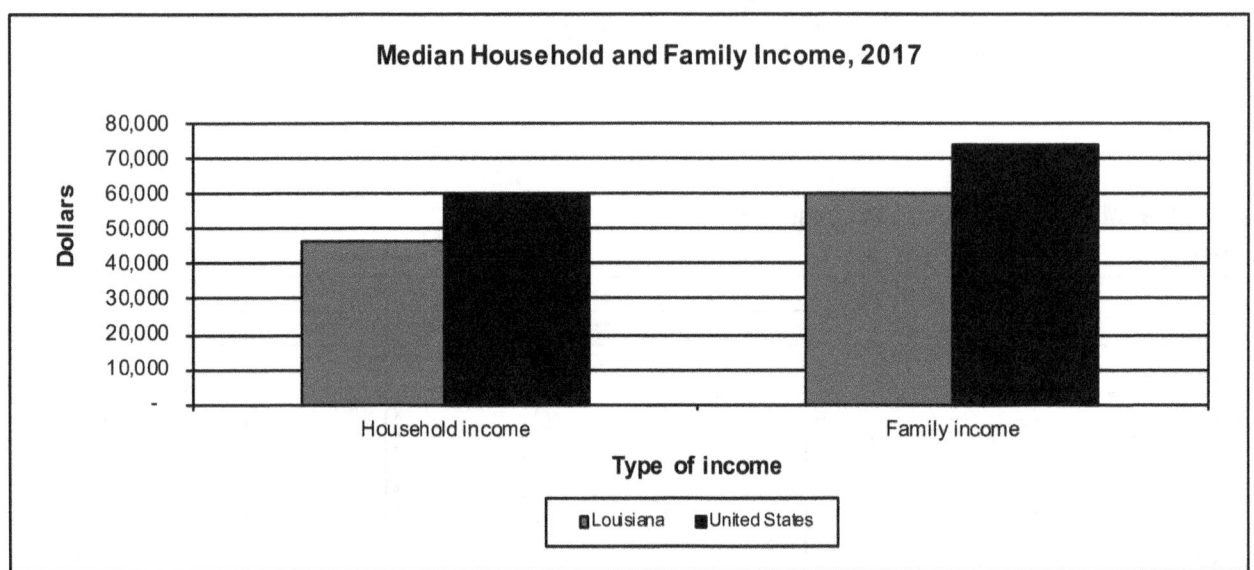

Median Household and Family Income, 2017

Louisiana   United States

Table LA-6. Health Insurance Coverage Status for the Civilian Noninstitutionalized Population and Children Under 18 Years of Age

(Number, percent.)

Item	2009	2010	2011	2012	2013	2014	2015	2016	2017
Civilian Noninstitutionalized Population	4,391,561	4,440,314	4,473,068	4,498,884	4,522,910	4,547,572	4,567,431	4,577,182	4,580,258
Covered by Private or Public Insurance									
Number..	3,629,320	3,649,327	3,689,053	3,739,257	3,771,587	3,875,819	4,021,800	4,107,350	4,197,609
Percent..	82.6	82.2	82.5	83.1	83.4	85.2	88.1	89.7	91.6
Uninsured									
Number..	762,241	790,987	784,015	759,627	751,323	671,753	545,631	469,832	382,649
Percent..	17.4	17.8	17.5	16.9	16.6	14.8	11.9	10.3	8.4
Percent in the U.S. not covered....................	15.1	15.5	15.1	14.8	14.5	11.7	9.4	8.6	8.7
Children Under 18 Years of Age[1]	1,120,435	1,113,329	1,117,293	1,117,427	1,110,977	1,112,618	1,114,678	1,115,457	1,175,200
Covered by Private or Public Insurance									
Number..	1,047,677	1,051,611	1,052,658	1,058,356	1,047,665	1,055,087	1,074,755	1,081,831	1,139,133
Percent..	93.5	94.5	94.2	94.7	94.3	94.8	96.4	97.0	96.9
Uninsured									
Number..	72,758	61,718	64,635	59,071	63,312	57,531	39,923	33,626	36,067
Percent..	6.5	5.5	5.8	5.3	5.7	5.2	3.6	3.0	3.1
Percent in the U.S. not covered....................	8.6	8.0	7.5	7.2	7.1	6.0	4.8	4.5	5.0

[1] 2017 data is for individuals under 19 years of age.

Table LA-7. Employment Status by Demographic Group, 2018

(Numbers in thousands, percent.)

Characteristic	Civilian noninstitutional population	Civilian labor force		Employed		Unemployed	
		Number	Percent of population	Number	Percent of population	Number	Percent of population
Total..	3,598	2,113	58.7	2,009	55.8	104	4.9
Sex							
Male...	1,707	1,100	64.4	1,049	61.5	50	4.6
Female..	1,891	1,013	53.6	960	50.7	54	5.3
Race, Sex, and Hispanic Origin							
White..	2,319	1,379	59.5	1,331	57.4	48	3.5
Male..	1,131	753	66.6	729	64.5	24	3.1
Female.....................................	1,188	626	52.7	602	50.7	25	3.9
Black or African American..................	1,118	638	57.0	589	52.6	49	7.7
Male..	498	294	58.9	271	54.3	23	7.9
Female.....................................	620	344	55.5	318	51.3	26	7.5
Hispanic or Latino ethnicity[1].............	214	143	66.8	136	63.6	7	4.8
Male..	112	90	80.6	86	77.4	4	3.9
Female.....................................	102	53	51.7	50	48.5	3	6.2
Age							
16 to 19 years...............................	248	71	28.6	59	23.7	12	17.1
20 to 24 years...............................	277	195	70.2	175	63.1	20	10.3
25 to 34 years...............................	641	506	79.0	482	75.2	24	4.8
35 to 44 years...............................	582	476	81.7	456	78.4	19	4.1
45 to 54 years...............................	554	420	75.8	407	73.5	13	3.0
55 to 64 years...............................	582	322	55.2	309	53.1	12	3.8
65 years and over	713	123	17.3	120	16.8	3	2.4

NOTE: Data in Table 7 are from the Current Population Survey (CPS) and do not match the estimates in Table 8. See notes and definitions for further information.
[1] May be of any race.

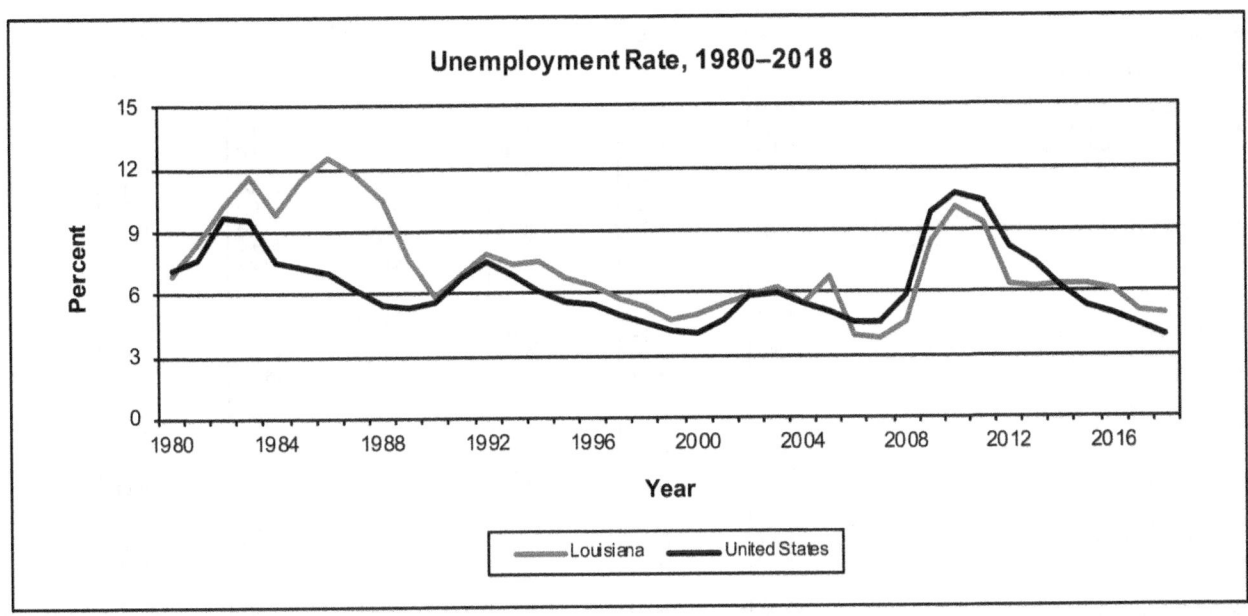

Table LA-8. Employment Status of the Civilian Noninstitutional Population Age 16 Years and Over

(Number, percent.)

Year	Civilian labor force	Civilian participation rate	Employed	Unemployed	Unemployment rate
2010..	2,086,076	60.7	1,919,852	166,224	8.0
2011..	2,073,217	59.6	1,911,021	162,196	7.8
2012..	2,080,280	59.4	1,933,137	147,143	7.1
2013..	2,101,416	59.6	1,960,539	140,877	6.7
2014..	2,153,613	60.7	2,016,083	137,530	6.4
2015..	2,162,410	60.5	2,025,661	136,749	6.3
2016..	2,125,934	59.2	1,997,358	128,576	6.0
2017..	2,112,320	58.8	2,004,003	108,317	5.1
2018..	2,103,495	58.7	2,000,791	102,704	4.9

Table LA-9. Employment and Average Wages by Industry

(Estimates are based on the 2012 *North American Industry Classification System* [NAICS].)

Industry	2011	2012	2013	2014	2015	2016	2017
	Number of jobs						
Wage and Salary Employment by Industry.........................	1,996,055	2,016,911	2,038,049	2,066,426	2,074,947	2,048,289	2,044,106
Farm Wage and Salary Employment...............................	8,286	7,181	6,545	6,186	8,839	7,889	8,873
Nonfarm Wage and Salary Employment..........................	1,987,769	2,009,730	2,031,504	2,060,240	2,066,108	2,040,400	2,035,233
Private wage and salary employment........................	1,590,146	1,622,059	1,653,425	1,694,081	1,703,916	1,680,979	1,677,702
Forestry, fishing, and related activities	6,976	7,088	7,169	7,301	7,323	7,371	7,079
Mining..	50,231	51,663	51,242	50,921	44,887	35,578	32,369
Utilities..	9,340	9,152	9,155	8,838	8,606	8,442	8,487
Construction...	125,155	129,980	134,785	142,781	144,369	143,671	150,707
Manufacturing..	139,621	141,978	144,069	147,286	143,922	135,936	134,813
Durable goods manufacturing...........................	71,142	73,087	74,639	77,252	73,206	65,135	63,599
Nondurable goods manufacturing.....................	68,479	68,891	69,430	70,034	70,716	70,801	71,214
Wholesale trade..	72,427	72,847	73,614	73,774	72,620	70,785	69,877
Retail trade...	222,502	224,260	225,750	228,572	234,486	236,483	233,064
Transportation and warehousing......................	71,971	74,577	77,132	80,813	80,318	74,609	73,039
Information..	23,746	24,909	26,672	26,099	26,756	23,668	22,917
Finance and insurance...................................	61,916	60,785	60,698	61,150	60,897	61,030	61,345
Real estate and rental and leasing....................	31,667	32,266	33,379	32,488	31,900	30,773	30,020
Professional, scientific, and technical services	81,696	85,426	87,145	89,156	89,874	87,375	87,347
Management of companies and enterprises.........	24,369	25,109	25,286	25,220	23,716	23,372	23,543
Administrative and waste services....................	92,048	94,708	96,677	100,015	101,498	100,804	100,190
Educational services......................................	39,214	40,441	42,757	43,269	44,070	44,700	44,975
Health care and social assistance....................	239,568	243,370	248,617	256,461	261,494	267,282	269,971
Arts, entertainment, and recreation..................	28,050	28,748	29,844	31,221	30,565	29,819	30,004
Accommodation and food services....................	173,945	179,416	184,631	191,715	199,015	203,324	204,593
Other services, except public administration.........	95,704	95,336	94,803	97,001	97,600	95,957	93,362
Government and government enterprises	397,623	387,671	378,079	366,159	362,192	359,421	357,531
	Dollars						
Average Wages and Salaries by Industry	43,120	44,127	44,852	46,186	46,833	46,684	47,645
Average Farm Wages and Salaries	16,656	29,145	24,975	20,814	21,564	19,807	17,157
Average Nonfarm Wages and Salaries	43,230	44,181	44,916	46,262	46,941	46,788	47,778
Average private wages and salaries........................	43,314	44,398	45,292	46,801	47,441	47,117	48,140
Forestry, fishing, and related activities	33,194	34,485	35,416	36,254	36,193	38,268	39,337
Mining..	85,282	88,612	90,699	95,698	95,943	94,793	93,516
Utilities..	76,678	78,370	80,347	84,563	87,825	88,130	91,684
Construction...	51,917	52,387	53,505	56,620	58,684	60,537	62,713
Manufacturing..	63,894	65,573	66,506	69,388	71,444	72,816	74,772
Durable goods manufacturing...........................	56,763	57,764	58,508	60,885	60,902	60,435	62,618
Nondurable goods manufacturing.....................	71,302	73,857	75,104	78,768	82,357	84,207	85,627
Wholesale trade..	57,333	59,794	61,105	63,252	64,206	63,641	65,421
Retail trade...	25,904	26,652	27,072	27,388	27,991	28,197	28,823
Transportation and warehousing......................	57,779	60,190	62,046	64,640	63,532	60,855	60,990
Information..	51,452	51,786	49,788	52,546	53,560	55,040	57,467
Finance and insurance	58,968	60,188	61,991	65,880	66,183	67,369	69,275
Real estate and rental and leasing....................	48,231	48,319	49,093	50,114	49,381	47,632	48,999
Professional, scientific, and technical services	62,925	64,437	66,830	68,199	69,956	68,919	70,296
Management of companies and enterprises.........	70,946	73,290	79,415	78,501	81,133	83,247	86,760
Administrative and waste services....................	34,347	35,018	35,421	36,807	38,452	37,464	38,200
Educational services......................................	34,316	34,570	34,687	34,902	35,099	36,045	36,065
Health care and social assistance....................	38,921	39,440	39,877	41,189	42,843	43,304	43,977
Arts, entertainment, and recreation..................	34,977	34,535	34,699	34,571	36,219	37,456	38,079
Accommodation and food services....................	18,992	19,513	19,868	20,380	20,944	21,063	21,532
Other services, except public administration.........	28,887	30,181	31,370	32,111	33,273	34,236	35,510
Government and government enterprises.............................	42,896	43,271	43,275	43,770	44,586	45,249	46,079

Table LA-10. Employment Characteristics by Family Type

(Number, percent.)

Family type and labor force status	2015		2016		2017	
	Total	Families with own children under 18 years	Total	Families with own children under 18 years	Total	Families with own children under 18 years
All Families.......................	1,108,586	471,898	1,097,712	463,602	1,107,245	458,621
FAMILY TYPE AND LABOR FORCE STATUS						
Married-Couple Families...............	746,504	278,801	735,458	271,349	744,011	272,793
Both husband and wife in labor force...............	48.0	65.2	47.4	67.4	47.7	66.0
Husband in labor force, wife not in labor force	24.8	28.3	23.8	26.2	22.8	26.8
Wife in labor force, husband not in labor force	8.2	4.5	8.4	3.9	8.8	4.4
Both husband and wife not in labor force............	18.4	1.7	19.8	2.3	20.1	2.6
Other Families	362,082	193,097	362,254	192,253	363,234	185,828
Female householder, no husband present............	76.3	78.7	76.1	78.1	76.0	77.8
In labor force............	50.8	64.2	50.3	63.0	49.5	62.1
Not in labor force	25.4	14.6	25.8	15.1	26.5	15.8
Male householder, no wife present............	23.7	21.3	23.9	21.9	24.0	22.2
In labor force............	17.4	19.4	16.4	18.3	17.3	18.6
Not in labor force	6.4	1.8	7.5	3.6	6.7	3.5

Table LA-11. School Enrollment and Educational Attainment, 2017

(Number, percent.)

Item	State	U.S.
Enrollment		
Total population 3 years and over, enrolled in school	1,176,248	81,273,337
Enrolled in nursery school or preschool (percent)	6.8	6.0
Enrolled in kindergarten (percent)...........................	4.9	4.9
Enrolled in elementary school, grades 1-8 (percent)...........................	43.0	40.6
Enrolled in high school, grades 9-12 (percent)...........................	21.7	21.1
Enrolled in college or graduate school (percent)...........................	23.7	27.4
Attainment		
Total population 25 years and over	3,120,277	221,250,083
Less than ninth grade (percent)...........................	4.9	5.1
9th to 12th grade, no diploma (percent)...........................	10.0	6.9
High school graduate, including equivalency (percent)...........................	34.0	27.1
Some college, no degree (percent)	21.4	20.4
Associate's degree (percent)...........................	5.9	8.5
Bachelor's degree (percent)...........................	15.5	19.7
Graduate or professional degree (percent)...........................	8.3	12.3
High school graduate or higher (percent)...........................	85.1	88.0
Bachelor's degree or higher (percent)...........................	23.8	32.0

Table LA-12. Public School Characteristics and Educational Indicators

(Number, percent; data derived from National Center of Education Statistics.)

Item	State	U.S.
Public Elementary and Secondary Schools		
Number of operational school districts, 2016-17...........................	185	18,377
Number of operational schools, 2016-17...........................	1,404	98,330
Percent charter schools	10.8	7.1
Total public school enrollment, 2016-17...........................	716,293	50,587,859
Percent charter school enrollment	11.0	6.0
Student-teacher ratio, Fall 2015	12.3	16.0
Expenditures per student (dollars), 2015-16...........................	11,169	11,841
Four-year adjusted cohort graduation rate (ACGR)[1]...........................	78.1	84.6
Students eligible for free or reduced-price lunch (percent), 2015-16...........................	61.3	52.1
English language learners (percent), Fall 2016	3.2	9.6
Students age 3 to 21 served under IDEA, part B (percent), 2017-18	11.8	13.7
Public Schools by Type, 2016-17		Percent of state public schools
Total number of schools...........................	1,404	100.0
Special education	32	2.3
Vocational education	12	0.9
Alternative education...........................	5	0.4

[1] Adjusted Cohort Graduation Rates (ACGR) differ from Averaged Freshmen Graduation Rates (AFGR).

Table LA-13. Reported Voting and Registration of the Voting-Age Population, November 2018

(Numbers in thousands, percent.)

Item	Total population	Total citizen population	Registered			Voted		
			Total registered	Percent registered (total population)	Percent registered (total citizen population)	Total voted	Percent voted (total population)	Percent voted (total citizen population)
U.S. Total	249,748	228,832	153,066	61.3	66.9	122,281	49.0	53.4
State Total.................................	3,458	3,326	2,263	65.4	68.0	1,656	47.9	49.8
Sex								
Male	1,635	1,557	1,032	63.1	66.3	774	47.3	49.7
Female	1,823	1,770	1,231	67.5	69.5	882	48.4	49.8
Race								
White alone................................	2,212	2,120	1,501	67.9	70.8	1,075	48.6	50.7
White, non-Hispanic alone..............	2,047	2,023	1,455	71.1	71.9	1,046	51.1	51.7
Black alone................................	1,076	1,072	688	63.9	64.1	531	49.4	49.5
Asian alone	60	34	17	(B)	(B)	9	(B)	(B)
Hispanic (of any race)...................	189	112	56	29.7	50.2	35	18.4	31.1
White alone or in combination	2,289	2,188	1,543	67.4	70.5	1,106	48.3	50.6
Black alone or in combination...........	1,133	1,125	712	62.9	63.4	552	48.7	49.1
Asian alone or in combination..........	70	42	23	(B)	(B)	12	(B)	(B)
Age								
18 to 24 years	409	390	202	49.3	51.7	98	24.0	25.2
25 to 34 years	587	549	335	57.2	61.1	217	37.0	39.5
35 to 44 years	607	573	376	61.9	65.5	257	42.2	44.8
45 to 64 years	1,144	1,112	791	69.1	71.1	633	55.3	56.9
65 years and over	711	702	560	78.7	79.7	452	63.5	64.3

B = Base is less than 75,000 and therefore too small to show the derived measure.

Table LA-14. Crime

(Number, rate per 100,000. Data are derived from the FBI Uniform Crime Reports.)

Item	State			U.S.		
	2016	2017	Percent change	2016	2017	Percent change
TOTAL POPULATION[1]	4,686,157	4,684,333	-	323,405,935	325,719,178	0.7
VIOLENT CRIME						
Number..	26,477	26,092	-1.5	1,285,606	1,283,220	-0.2
Rate...	565.0	557.0	-1.4	397.5	394.0	-0.9
Murder and Nonnegligent Manslaughter						
Number..	555	582	4.9	17,413	17,284	-0.7
Rate...	11.8	12.4	4.9	5.4	5.3	-1.4
Rape[2]						
Number..	1,819	1,867	2.6	132,414	135,755	2.5
Rate...	38.8	39.9	2.7	40.9	41.7	1.8
Robbery						
Number..	5,575	5,358	-3.9	332,797	319,356	-4.0
Rate...	119.0	114.4	-3.9	102.9	98.0	-4.7
Aggravated Assault						
Number..	18,528	18,285	-1.3	802,982	810,825	1.0
Rate...	395.4	390.3	-1.3	248.3	248.9	0.3
PROPERTY CRIME						
Number..	154,511	157,712	2.1	7,928,530	7,694,086	-3.0
Rate...	3,297.2	3,366.8	2.1	2,451.6	2,362.2	-3.6
Burglary						
Number..	34,689	34,265	-1.2	1,516,405	1,401,840	-7.6
Rate...	740.2	731.5	-1.2	468.9	430.4	-8.2
Larceny-Theft						
Number..	109,492	112,485	2.7	5,644,835	5,519,107	-2.2
Rate...	2,336.5	2,401.3	2.8	1,745.4	1,694.4	-2.9
Motor Vehicle Theft						
Number..	10,330	10,962	6.1	767,290	773,139	0.8
Rate...	220.4	234.0	6.2	237.3	237.4	-

NOTE: Although arson data are included in the trend and clearance tables, sufficient data are not available to estimate totals for this offense. Therefore, no arson data are published in this table.
- = Zero or rounds to zero.
[1] Population figures are U.S. Census Bureau provisional estimates as of July 1, 2017.
[2] The figures shown in the rape (revised definition) column were estimated using the revised Uniform Crime Reporting (UCR) definition of rape.

Table LA-15. State Government Finances, 2017

(Dollar amounts in thousands, percent distribution.)

Item	Dollars	Percent distribution
Total Revenue	36,527,447	100.0
General revenue	27,795,508	76.1
Intergovernmental revenue	12,636,842	34.6
Taxes	11,104,720	30.4
General sales	4,215,378	11.5
Selective sales	2,799,119	7.7
License taxes	368,318	1.0
Individual income tax	2,949,939	8.1
Corporate income tax	291,321	0.8
Other taxes	480,645	1.3
Current charges	2,067,797	5.7
Miscellaneous general revenue	1,986,149	5.4
Utility revenue	8,821	-
Liquor stores revenue	0	-
Insurance trust revenue[1]	8,723,118	23.9
Total Expenditure	33,813,850	100.0
Intergovernmental expenditure	6,415,070	19.0
Direct expenditure	27,398,780	81.0
Current operation	19,142,386	56.6
Capital outlay	2,143,229	6.3
Insurance benefits and repayments	4,662,324	13.8
Assistance and subsidies	636,171	1.9
Interest on debt	814,670	2.4
Exhibit: Salaries and wages	4,049,934	12.0
Total Expenditure	33,813,850	100.0
General expenditure	29,143,517	86.2
Intergovernmental expenditure	6,415,070	19.0
Direct expenditure	22,728,447	67.2
General expenditure, by function:		
Education	9,299,171	27.5
Public welfare	11,226,836	33.2
Hospitals	356,728	1.1
Health	421,737	1.2
Highways	1,493,443	4.4
Police protection	358,733	1.1
Correction	667,656	2.0
Natural resources	796,006	2.4
Parks and recreation	347,548	1.0
Governmental administration	954,369	2.8
Interest on general debt	814,670	2.4
Other and unallocable	2,406,620	7.1
Utility expenditure	8,009	-
Liquor stores expenditure	0	-
Insurance trust expenditure	4,662,324	13.8
Debt at End of Fiscal Year	18,092,508	X
Cash and Security Holdings	62,499,521	X

X = Not applicable.
- = Zero or rounds to zero.
[1] Within insurance trust revenue, net earnings of state retirement systems is a calculated statistic (the item code in the data file is X08), and thus can be positive or negative. Net earnings is the sum of earnings on investments plus gains on investments minus losses on investments. The change made in 2002 for asset valuation from book to market value in accordance with Statement 34 of the Governmental Accounting Standards Board is reflected in the calculated statistics.

Table LA-16. State Government Tax Collections, 2018

(Dollars in thousands, percent.)

Item	Dollars	Percent distribution
Total Taxes	11,357,686	100.0
Property taxes	60,172	0.5
Sales and gross receipts	6,864,723	60.4
General sales and gross receipts	4,252,693	37.4
Selective sales and gross receipts	2,612,030	23.0
Alcoholic beverages	75,774	0.7
Amusements	708,462	6.2
Insurance premiums	870,872	7.7
Motor fuels	631,641	5.6
Pari-mutuels	5,191	-
Public utilities	9,349	0.1
Tobacco products	163,770	1.4
Other selective sales	146,971	1.3
Licenses	393,129	3.5
Alcoholic beverages	X	-
Amusements	X	-
Corporations in general	148,116	1.3
Hunting and fishing	31,994	0.3
Motor vehicle	79,284	0.7
Motor vehicle operators	15,477	0.1
Public utilities	7,577	0.1
Occupation and business, NEC	106,475	0.9
Other licenses	4,206	-
Income taxes	3,604,434	31.7
Individual income	3,246,226	28.6
Corporation net income	358,208	3.2
Other taxes	435,228	3.8
Death and gift	X	-
Documentary and stock transfer	X	-
Severance	435,228	3.8
Taxes, NEC	0	-

- = Zero or rounds to zero.
X = Not applicable.

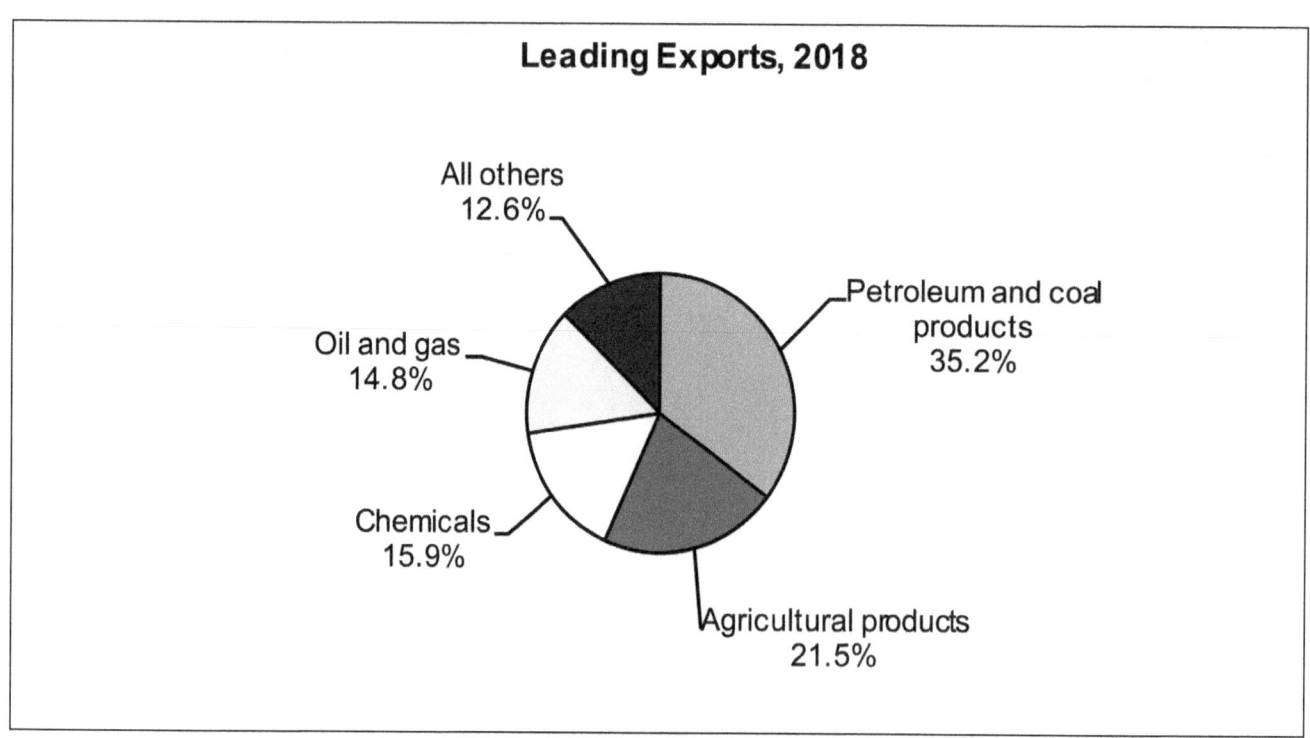

Leading Exports, 2018

All others 12.6%
Petroleum and coal products 35.2%
Oil and gas 14.8%
Chemicals 15.9%
Agricultural products 21.5%

MAINE

Facts and Figures

Location: Northeast corner of the United States; bordered on the N and E by New Brunswick, Canada; on the S by the Atlantic Ocean; on the W by New Hampshire; and on the NW by Quebec, Canada

Area: 35,385 sq. mi. (91,646 sq. km.); rank—39th

Population: 1,338,404 (2018 est.); rank—42nd

Principal Cities: capital—Augusta; largest—Portland

Statehood: March 15, 1820; 23rd state

U.S. Congress: 2 senators, 2 representatives

State Motto: *Dirigo* ("I lead")

State Song: "State of Maine Song"

State Nickname: The Pine Tree State

Abbreviations: ME; Me.

State Symbols: flower—white pinecone and tassel; tree—Eastern white pine; bird—chickadee

At a Glance

- With a population that grew 0.8 percent, Maine ranked 43rd among the states in growth from 2010 to 2018.

- Maine had the highest percent of residents who identified as "White alone" in 2018, with 94.6 percent of its residents in this category.

- Along with West Virginia, Maine had the lowest percent of its population who identified as "Hispanic or Latino" in 2018, with just 1.7 percent of residents in this category.

- With 20.6 percent of its population in the 65 and older age group, Maine passed Florida to become the state with the most people in this category in 2018.

- Maine's birth rate of 9.2 per 1,000 population was the 3rd lowest in the country in 2017.

Table ME-1. Population by Age, Sex, Race, and Hispanic Origin

(Number, percent, except where noted.)

Sex, age, race, and Hispanic origin	2000	2010	2018 [1]	Percent change, 2010–2018
Total Population...	1,274,923	1,328,361	1,338,404	0.8
Percent of total U.S. population	0.5	0.4	0.4	X
Sex				
Male...	620,309	650,056	655,373	0.8
Female..	654,614	678,305	683,031	0.7
Age				
Under 5 years..	70,726	69,520	64,282	-7.5
5 to 19 years..	264,729	241,439	218,222	-9.6
20 to 64 years...	756,036	806,322	779,901	-3.3
65 years and over	183,402	211,080	275,999	30.8
Median age (years)..	38.6	42.7	44.9	5.2
Race and Hispanic Origin				
One race				
White	1,236,014	1,269,764	1,265,648	-0.3
Black	6,760	16,269	21,877	34.5
American Indian and Alaska Native	7,098	8,771	9,657	10.1
Asian..	9,111	13,783	16,674	21.0
Native Hawaiian or Other Pacific Islander	382	377	455	20.7
Two or more races	12,647	19,397	24,093	24.2
Hispanic (of any race)...	9,360	18,261	22,850	25.1

X = Not applicable.
- = Zero or rounds to zero.
[1] Population figures for 2018 are July 1 estimates. The 2010 estimates are taken from the 2010 Census.

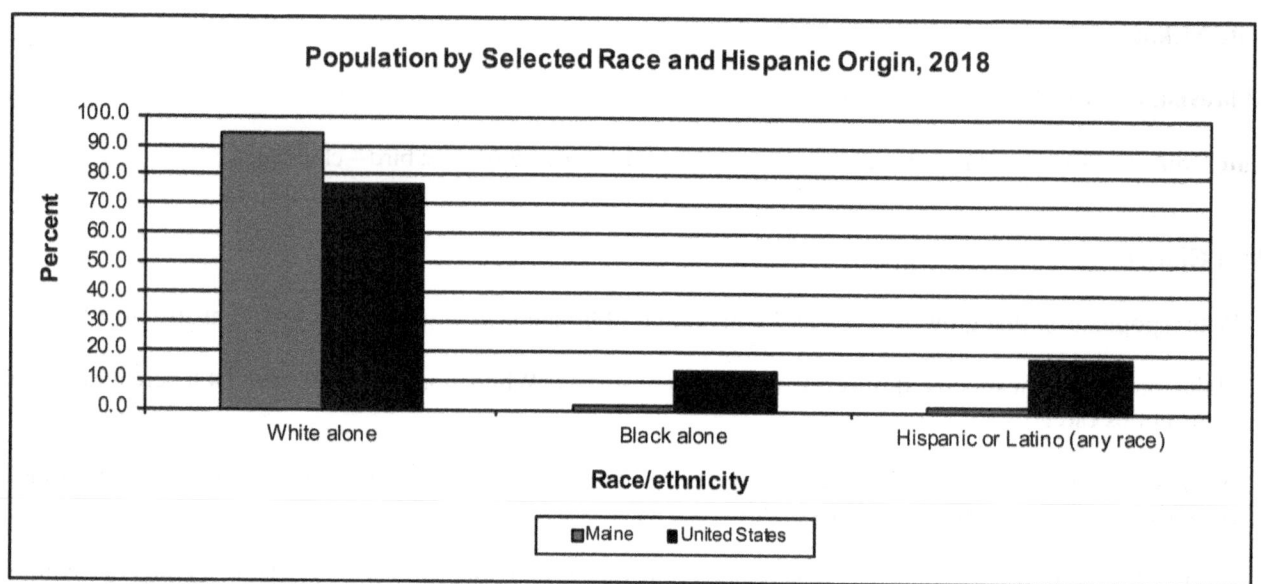

Population by Selected Race and Hispanic Origin, 2018

Table ME-2. Marital Status

(Number, percent distribution.)

Sex, age, race, and Hispanic origin	2000	2010	2017
Males, 15 Years and Over	494,217	534,474	548,428
Never married	26.8	31.0	32.6
Now married, except separated	58.8	52.5	50.4
Separated	1.1	1.2	0.6
Widowed..	2.8	2.9	3.0
Divorced..	10.5	12.5	13.3
Females, 15 Years and Over	534,606	570,281	579,869
Never married	21.2	24.2	25.6
Now married, except separated	54.1	49.3	48.4
Separated	1.3	1.6	1.0
Widowed..	11.0	9.9	9.2
Divorced..	12.4	15.0	15.8

Table ME-3. Households and Housing Characteristics

(Number, percent, dollars.)

Item	2000	2010	2017	Average annual percent change, 2010–2017
Total Households..	518,200	545,417	540,959	-0.1
Family households..	340,685	345,328	330,106	-0.6
Married-couple family...	272,152	266,670	263,878	-0.1
Other family...	68,533	78,658	66,228	-2.3
Male householder, no wife present...............................	19,511	23,620	21,476	-1.3
Female householder, no husband present......................	49,022	55,038	44,752	-2.7
Nonfamily households..	177,515	200,089	210,853	0.8
Householder living alone...	139,969	155,623	164,809	0.8
Householder not living alone...	37,546	44,466	46,044	0.5
Housing Characteristics				
Total housing units..	651,901	722,217	742,644	0.4
Occupied housing units	518,200	545,417	540,959	-0.1
Owner occupied...	370,905	396,395	395,809	-
Renter occupied...	147,295	149,022	145,150	-0.4
Average household size..	2.39	2.37	2.4	0.2
Financial Characteristics				
Median gross rent of renter-occupied housing	497	707	806	2.0
Median monthly owner costs for housing units with a mortgage	923	1,289	1,313	0.3
Median value of owner-occupied housing units.....................	98,700	179,100	191,200	1.0

Table ME-4. Migration, Origin, and Language

(Number, percent.)

Characteristic	State			U.S.		
	2016	2017	Percent change	2016	2017	Percent change
Residence 1 Year Ago						
Population 1 year and over	1,319,292	1,322,591	0.3	319,361,956	321,994,428	0.8
Same house...	86.9	86.2	X	85.4	85.7	X
Different house in the U.S..	12.8	13.5	X	13.9	13.6	X
Same county...	7.1	7.5	X	8.3	8.1	X
Different county..	5.7	6.0	X	5.6	5.6	X
Same state..	2.8	3.4	X	3.2	3.3	X
Different state...	2.9	2.6	X	2.4	2.3	X
Abroad..	0.3	0.3	X	0.7	0.7	X
Place of Birth						
Native born	1,280,711	1,290,474	0.8	279,388,170	281,193,323	0.6
Male	49.1	49.3	X	49.3	49.4	X
Female	50.9	50.7	X	50.7	50.6	X
Foreign born	50,768	45,433	-10.5	43,739,345	44,525,855	1.8
Male	42.2	40.9	X	48.5	48.4	X
Female	57.8	59.1	X	51.5	51.6	X
Foreign born; naturalized U.S. citizen...............................	28,046	26,227	-6.5	21,238,372	21,948,732	3.3
Male	42.7	36.1	X	45.9	45.9	X
Female	57.3	63.9	X	54.1	54.1	X
Foreign born; not a U.S. citizen..	22,722	19,206	-15.5	22,500,973	22,577,123	0.3
Male	41.5	47.3	X	51	50.8	X
Female	58.5	52.7	X	49	49.2	X
Entered 2010 or later	23.6	27.6	X	18.6	21.3	X
Entered 2000 to 2009	21.9	18.4	X	26.7	25.7	X
Entered before 2000...	54.5	54.1	X	54.7	53.0	X
World Region of Birth, Foreign						
Foreign-born population, excluding population born at sea	50,768	45,433	-10.5	43,738,901	44,525,458	1.8
Europe	20.5	24.6	X	10.9	10.8	X
Asia	30.8	28.4	X	30.8	31.2	X
Africa	16.2	15.2	X	4.9	5.1	X
Oceania	1.1	0.5	X	0.6	0.6	X
Latin America	9.7	11.5	X	51	50.4	X
North America...	21.7	19.6	X	1.8	1.8	X
Language Spoken at Home and Ability to Speak English						
Population 5 years and over..	1,267,538	1,271,517	0.3	303,328,961	305,924,019	0.9
English only	93.8	94.2	X	78.4	78.2	X
Language other than English...	6.2	5.8	X	21.6	21.8	X
Speaks English less than "very well"................................	1.7	1.4	X	8.6	8.5	X

NA = Not available.
X = Not applicable.
- = Zero or rounds to zero.

Table ME-5. Median Income and Poverty Status, 2017

(Number, percent, except as noted.)

Characteristic	State		U.S.	
	Number	Percent	Number	Percent
Median Income				
Households (dollars)..	56,277	X	60,336	X
Families (dollars)	72,177	X	73,891	X
Below Poverty Level (All People)	144,012	11.1	42,583,651	13.4
Sex				
Male	66,177	10.4	19,004,547	12.2
Female	77,835	11.7	23,579,104	14.5
Age				
Under 18 years..	32,567	13.1	13,353,202	18.4
Related children under 18 years..	30,678	12.4	13,053,472	18.1
18 to 64 years...	90,460	11.4	24,648,677	12.6
65 years and over	20,985	8.1	4,581,772	9.3

X = Not applicable.

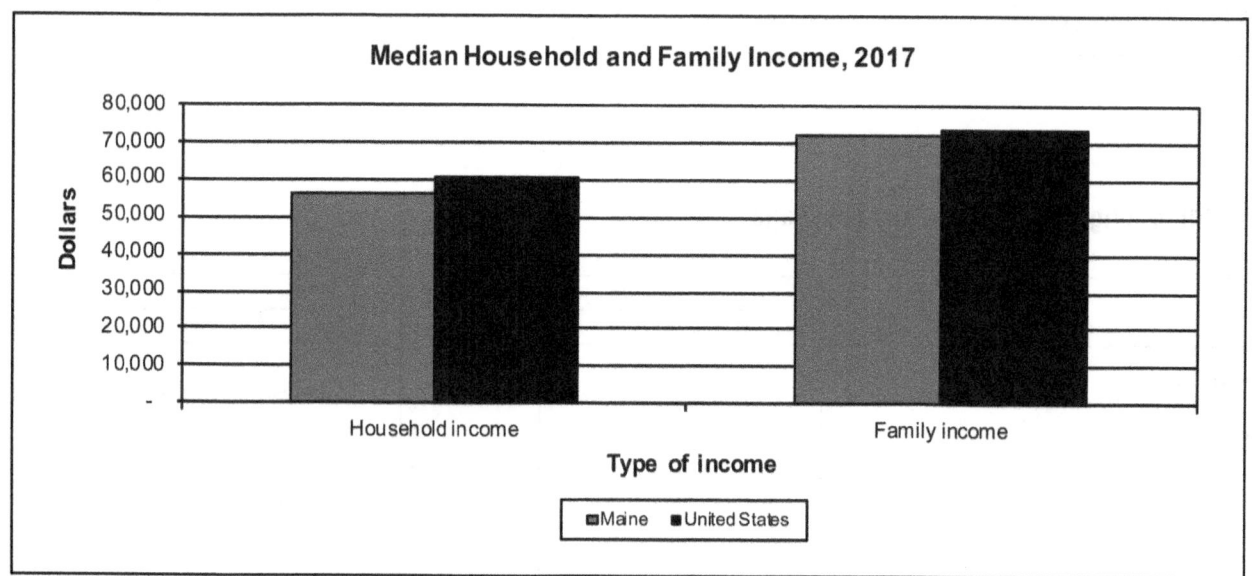

Table ME-6. Health Insurance Coverage Status for the Civilian Noninstitutionalized Population and Children Under 18 Years of Age

(Number, percent.)

Item	2009	2010	2011	2012	2013	2014	2015	2016	2017
Civilian Noninstitutionalized Population	1,300,904	1,313,037	1,314,121	1,315,703	1,314,191	1,315,996	1,314,849	1,317,148	1,321,649
Covered by Private or Public Insurance									
Number...	1,163,900	1,179,972	1,173,956	1,180,994	1,167,176	1,182,465	1,204,341	1,211,175	1,214,582
Percent..	89.5	89.9	89.3	89.8	88.8	89.9	91.6	92.0	91.9
Uninsured									
Number...	137,004	133,065	140,165	134,709	147,015	133,531	110,508	105,973	107,067
Percent..	10.5	10.1	10.7	10.2	11.2	10.1	8.4	8.0	8.1
Percent in the U.S. not covered...........................	15.1	15.5	15.1	14.8	14.5	11.7	9.4	8.6	8.7
Children Under 18 Years of Age[1]	270,440	273,098	269,901	265,495	259,827	257,390	255,319	254,723	271,746
Covered by Private or Public Insurance									
Number...	255,246	262,163	255,736	253,255	244,441	241,098	240,871	243,104	258,321
Percent..	94.4	96.0	94.8	95.4	94.1	93.7	94.3	95.4	95.1
Uninsured									
Number...	15,194	10,935	14,165	12,240	15,386	16,292	14,448	11,619	13,425
Percent..	5.6	4.0	5.2	4.6	5.9	6.3	5.7	4.6	4.9
Percent in the U.S. not covered...........................	8.6	8.0	7.5	7.2	7.1	6.0	4.8	4.5	5.0

[1] 2017 data is for individuals under 19 years of age.

Table ME-7. Employment Status by Demographic Group, 2018

(Numbers in thousands, percent.)

Characteristic	Civilian noninstitutional population	Civilian labor force		Employed		Unemployed	
		Number	Percent of population	Number	Percent of population	Number	Percent of population
Total...	1,107	698	63.1	674	60.9	25	3.5
Sex							
Male..	537	361	67.2	347	64.6	14	3.8
Female...	571	338	59.2	327	57.3	11	3.2
Race, Sex, and Hispanic Origin							
White...	1,048	661	63.1	640	61.1	21	3.2
Male..	506	341	67.5	329	65.0	12	3.6
Female...	542	320	59.1	311	57.4	9	2.8
Black or African American.....................	NA	NA	NA	NA	NA	NA	NA
Male..	NA	NA	NA	NA	NA	NA	NA
Female...	NA	NA	NA	NA	NA	NA	NA
Hispanic or Latino ethnicity[1]...............	NA	NA	NA	NA	NA	NA	NA
Male..	NA	NA	NA	NA	NA	NA	NA
Female...	NA	NA	NA	NA	NA	NA	NA
Age							
16 to 19 years.................................	NA	NA	NA	NA	NA	NA	NA
20 to 24 years.................................	78	59	76.3	55	70.6	4	7.4
25 to 34 years.................................	162	137	84.3	133	82.1	4	2.6
35 to 44 years.................................	144	123	85.6	120	83.7	3	2.3
45 to 54 years.................................	180	150	83.7	147	82.0	3	1.9
55 to 64 years.................................	214	149	69.9	146	68.5	3	2.0
65 years and over.............................	266	47	17.8	46	17.1	2	3.8

NOTE: Data in Table 7 are from the Current Population Survey (CPS) and do not match the estimates in Table 8. See notes and definitions for further information.
[1] May be of any race.
NA = Not available.

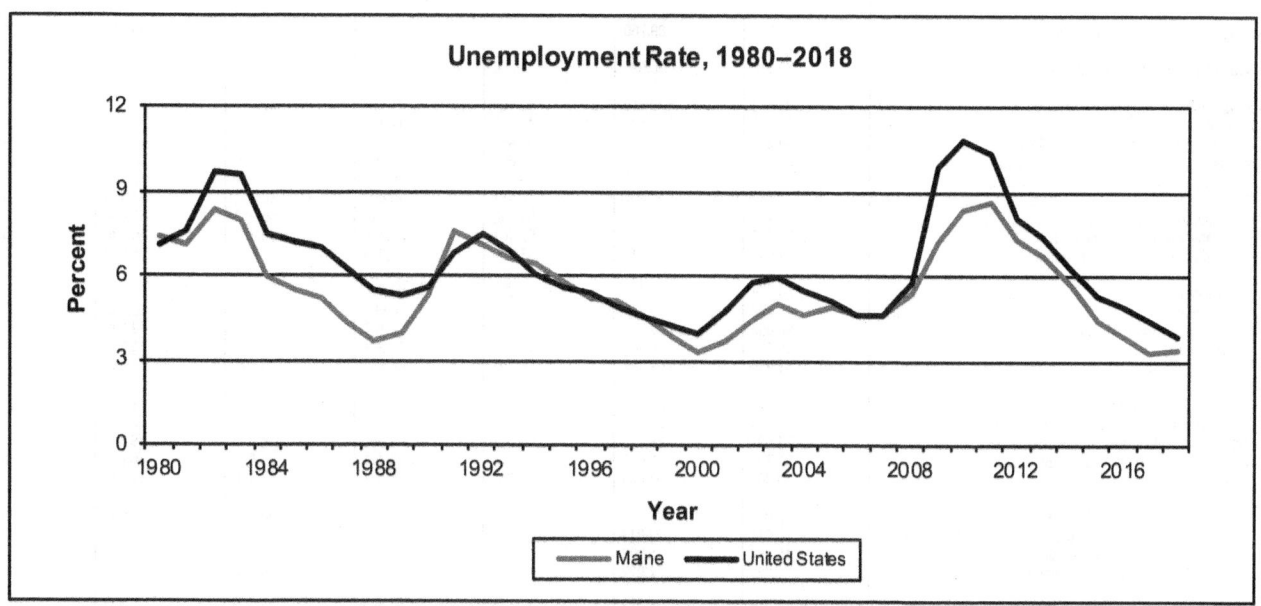

Table ME-8. Employment Status of the Civilian Noninstitutional Population Age 16 Years and Over

(Number, percent.)

Year	Civilian labor force	Civilian participation rate	Employed	Unemployed	Unemployment rate
2010...	695,182	64.8	638,630	56,552	8.1
2011...	699,281	64.8	644,085	55,196	7.9
2012...	702,636	64.9	650,117	52,519	7.5
2013...	705,417	65.0	658,522	46,895	6.6
2014...	696,298	64.0	657,066	39,232	5.6
2015...	683,369	62.7	653,330	30,039	4.4
2016...	692,154	63.3	665,911	26,243	3.8
2017...	700,099	63.6	677,141	22,958	3.3
2018...	698,745	63.3	675,221	23,524	3.4

Table ME-9. Employment and Average Wages by Industry

(Estimates are based on the 2012 *North American Industry Classification System* [NAICS].)

Industry	2011	2012	2013	2014	2015	2016	2017
	Number of jobs						
Wage and Salary Employment by Industry.........................	608,840	611,800	615,236	619,376	624,837	632,306	637,895
Farm Wage and Salary Employment................................	3,071	3,632	4,150	4,166	4,151	3,875	3,867
Nonfarm Wage and Salary Employment...........................	605,769	608,168	611,086	615,210	620,686	628,431	634,028
Private wage and salary employment...............................	497,037	500,034	504,103	508,479	514,553	521,322	526,706
Forestry, fishing, and related activities............................	4,009	(D)	4,098	4,150	4,240	4,080	4,173
Mining..	203	(D)	187	190	191	211	209
Utilities..	1,609	1,629	1,619	1,551	1,630	1,647	1,669
Construction..	25,899	26,301	26,227	26,613	27,220	28,095	28,994
Manufacturing..	50,822	50,768	50,423	50,253	50,700	50,744	51,059
Durable goods manufacturing...	27,176	27,105	27,255	27,769	28,159	28,490	28,695
Nondurable goods manufacturing...................................	23,646	23,663	23,168	22,484	22,541	22,254	22,364
Wholesale trade..	19,116	19,515	19,666	19,815	20,120	20,027	19,693
Retail trade..	81,786	81,946	81,883	82,192	82,224	82,522	82,039
Transportation and warehousing.....................................	15,736	15,648	16,031	16,578	16,584	16,987	17,579
Information...	8,302	7,913	7,641	7,453	7,595	7,710	7,366
Finance and insurance	25,226	24,954	24,993	23,683	23,984	24,024	24,270
Real estate and rental and leasing.................................	6,418	6,478	6,601	6,550	6,517	6,736	6,756
Professional, scientific, and technical services	23,651	23,949	24,814	25,004	25,341	25,527	26,019
Management of companies and enterprises.....................	7,141	7,563	7,428	9,091	9,124	9,984	10,484
Administrative and waste services..................................	27,057	27,124	28,301	29,666	30,492	30,824	30,685
Educational services...	14,350	14,709	15,043	15,339	15,703	16,406	16,750
Health care and social assistance..................................	100,880	101,942	102,287	102,230	103,776	104,899	106,554
Arts, entertainment, and recreation................................	8,143	8,813	8,879	8,594	8,747	9,148	9,384
Accommodation and food services.................................	52,373	53,192	54,182	55,013	55,712	56,993	58,499
Other services, except public administration..................	24,316	23,267	23,800	24,514	24,653	24,758	24,524
Government and government enterprises	108,732	108,134	106,983	106,731	106,133	107,109	107,322
	Dollars						
Average Wages and Salaries by Industry	39,078	39,760	40,466	41,622	42,896	43,715	45,053
Average Farm Wages and Salaries	20,316	30,596	27,296	28,810	23,619	29,036	26,405
Average Nonfarm Wages and Salaries	39,173	39,815	40,555	41,709	43,025	43,806	45,167
Average private wages and salaries................................	38,727	39,503	40,266	41,481	42,792	43,586	44,989
Forestry, fishing, and related activities............................	40,283	(D)	40,456	42,281	44,051	44,496	47,475
Mining..	53,207	(D)	55,807	58,853	59,550	58,867	61,407
Utilities..	75,636	77,633	79,952	87,721	82,707	83,565	91,798
Construction..	42,557	43,407	44,581	45,895	46,668	47,453	48,840
Manufacturing..	52,155	52,293	53,348	54,619	55,913	55,856	57,467
Durable goods manufacturing...	52,603	52,278	53,401	54,578	56,096	56,135	57,058
Nondurable goods manufacturing...................................	51,641	52,311	53,285	54,669	55,684	55,500	57,992
Wholesale trade..	54,774	55,863	56,996	59,646	62,620	63,598	65,400
Retail trade..	25,277	25,519	25,897	26,691	27,567	28,042	28,984
Transportation and warehousing.....................................	38,666	39,615	40,707	42,107	43,350	43,183	43,805
Information...	45,597	45,968	47,606	47,964	49,867	53,244	54,814
Finance and insurance	61,935	63,967	66,306	68,723	70,446	71,553	75,841
Real estate and rental and leasing.................................	35,568	37,013	37,690	39,041	40,832	41,897	43,063
Professional, scientific, and technical services	58,064	60,017	60,997	63,727	66,422	68,131	70,484
Management of companies and enterprises.....................	71,593	75,202	75,334	74,508	76,518	79,648	79,996
Administrative and waste services..................................	32,737	33,075	33,479	34,423	35,872	36,926	37,732
Educational services...	34,002	34,655	35,338	36,647	37,438	37,335	38,057
Health care and social assistance..................................	42,027	42,757	43,364	44,540	45,798	46,556	47,676
Arts, entertainment, and recreation................................	25,011	24,913	26,339	26,737	27,027	28,177	28,616
Accommodation and food services.................................	18,352	18,992	19,662	20,553	21,471	22,489	23,731
Other services, except public administration..................	26,608	27,922	28,690	29,414	30,528	31,576	32,844
Government and government enterprises............................	41,215	41,257	41,916	42,794	44,153	44,875	46,041

D = Not shown to avoid disclosure of confidential information, but the estimates for this item are included in the total.

Table ME-10. Employment Characteristics by Family Type

(Number, percent.)

Family type and labor force status	2015 Total	2015 Families with own children under 18 years	2016 Total	2016 Families with own children under 18 years	2017 Total	2017 Families with own children under 18 years
All Families	342,926	126,257	329,554	118,579	330,106	117,749
FAMILY TYPE AND LABOR FORCE STATUS						
Married-Couple Families	264,442	79,988	256,503	78,442	263,878	80,334
Both husband and wife in labor force	51.3	71.0	52.4	75.5	52.2	74.9
Husband in labor force, wife not in labor force	17.4	21.2	16.0	16.6	15.9	17.9
Wife in labor force, husband not in labor force	9.4	4.8	9.4	5.2	9.7	4.1
Both husband and wife not in labor force	20.7	2.2	21.3	2.4	21.1	2.2
Other Families	78,484	46,269	73,051	40,137	66,228	37,415
Female householder, no husband present	68.3	68.3	66.6	65.4	67.6	66.0
In labor force	47.8	53.0	46.9	53.4	48.1	54.2
Not in labor force	20.5	15.3	19.6	12.0	19.5	11.8
Male householder, no wife present	31.7	31.7	33.4	34.6	32.4	34.0
In labor force	24.4	28.0	25.2	30.0	24.4	29.3
Not in labor force	7.3	3.7	8.3	4.6	8.0	4.7

Table ME-11. School Enrollment and Educational Attainment, 2017

(Number, percent.)

Item	State	U.S.
Enrollment		
Total population 3 years and over, enrolled in school	289,898	81,273,337
Enrolled in nursery school or preschool (percent)	5.0	6.0
Enrolled in kindergarten (percent)	4.7	4.9
Enrolled in elementary school, grades 1-8 (percent)	39.9	40.6
Enrolled in high school, grades 9-12 (percent)	21.9	21.1
Enrolled in college or graduate school (percent)	28.5	27.4
Attainment		
Total population 25 years and over	971,740	221,250,083
Less than ninth grade (percent)	2.6	5.1
9th to 12th grade, no diploma (percent)	5.1	6.9
High school graduate, including equivalency (percent)	30.9	27.1
Some college, no degree (percent)	19.0	20.4
Associate's degree (percent)	10.3	8.5
Bachelor's degree (percent)	19.9	19.7
Graduate or professional degree (percent)	12.1	12.3
High school graduate or higher (percent)	92.3	88.0
Bachelor's degree or higher (percent)	32.1	32.0

Table ME-12. Public School Characteristics and Educational Indicators

(Number, percent; data derived from National Center of Education Statistics.)

Item	State	U.S.
Public Elementary and Secondary Schools		
Number of operational school districts, 2016-17	268	18,377
Number of operational schools, 2016-17	605	98,330
Percent charter schools	1.5	7.1
Total public school enrollment, 2016-17	180,512	50,587,859
Percent charter school enrollment	1.1	6.0
Student-teacher ratio, Fall 2015	12.2	16.0
Expenditures per student (dollars), 2015-16	14,202	11,841
Four-year adjusted cohort graduation rate (ACGR)[1]	86.9	84.6
Students eligible for free or reduced-price lunch (percent), 2015-16	46.0	52.1
English language learners (percent), Fall 2016	2.9	9.6
Students age 3 to 21 served under IDEA, part B (percent), 2017-18	18.4	13.7

Public Schools by Type, 2016-17		Percent of state public schools
Total number of schools	605	100.0
Special education	1	0.2
Vocational education	27	4.5
Alternative education	0	-

[1] Adjusted Cohort Graduation Rates (ACGR) differ from Averaged Freshmen Graduation Rates (AFGR).
- = Zero or rounds to zero.

Table ME-13. Reported Voting and Registration of the Voting-Age Population, November 2018

(Numbers in thousands, percent.)

Item	Total population	Total citizen population	Registered			Voted		
			Total registered	Percent registered (total population)	Percent registered (total citizen population)	Total voted	Percent voted (total population)	Percent voted (total citizen population)
U.S. Total	249,748	228,832	153,066	61.3	66.9	122,281	49.0	53.4
State Total	1,074	1,056	828	77.1	78.4	693	64.5	65.6
Sex								
Male	527	519	397	75.4	76.6	329	62.4	63.4
Female	546	537	431	78.8	80.1	364	66.6	67.7
Race								
White alone........................	1,011	1,002	796	78.7	79.4	669	66.2	66.8
White, non-Hispanic alone	1,001	994	788	78.7	79.2	666	66.5	67.0
Black alone........................	17	11	5	B	B	3	B	B
Asian alone	20	17	6	B	B	6	B	B
Hispanic (of any race).............	11	10	8	B	B	3	B	B
White alone or in combination	1,032	1,023	815	79.0	79.6	682	66.1	66.6
Black alone or in combination.......	20	14	7	B	B	5	B	B
Asian alone or in combination.......	20	17	6	B	B	6	B	B
Age								
18 to 24 years.....................	89	89	46	51.5	51.5	26	29.2	29.2
25 to 34 years.....................	174	171	108	61.9	63.2	88	50.3	51.3
35 to 44 years.....................	149	148	122	81.5	82.1	93	62.4	62.9
45 to 64 years.....................	385	378	317	82.5	83.9	273	70.9	72.1
65 years and over	276	270	235	85.3	87.1	213	77.3	78.9

B = Base is less than 75,000 and therefore too small to show the derived measure.

Table ME-14. Crime

(Number, rate per 100,000. Data are derived from the FBI Uniform Crime Reports.)

Item	State			U.S.		
	2016	2017	Percent change	2016	2017	Percent change
TOTAL POPULATION[1]	1,330,232	1,335,907	0.4	323,405,935	325,719,178	0.7
VIOLENT CRIME						
Number	1,649	1,617	-1.9	1,285,606	1,283,220	-0.2
Rate	124.0	121.0	-2.4	397.5	394.0	-0.9
Murder and Nonnegligent Manslaughter						
Number	20	23	15.0	17,413	17,284	-0.7
Rate	1.5	1.7	14.5	5.4	5.3	-1.4
Rape[2]						
Number	413	473	14.5	132,414	135,755	2.5
Rate	31.0	35.4	14.0	40.9	41.7	1.8
Robbery						
Number	268	249	-7.1	332,797	319,356	-4.0
Rate	20.1	18.6	-7.5	102.9	98.0	-4.7
Aggravated Assault						
Number	948	872	-8.0	802,982	810,825	1.0
Rate	71.3	65.3	-8.4	248.3	248.9	0.3
PROPERTY CRIME						
Number	21,908	20,133	-8.1	7,928,530	7,694,086	-3.0
Rate	1,646.9	1,507.1	-8.5	2,451.6	2,362.2	-3.6
Burglary						
Number	4,001	3,334	-16.7	1,516,405	1,401,840	-7.6
Rate	300.8	249.6	-17.0	468.9	430.4	-8.2
Larceny-Theft						
Number	17,131	16,006	-6.6	5,644,835	5,519,107	-2.2
Rate	1,287.8	1,198.1	-7.0	1,745.4	1,694.4	-2.9
Motor Vehicle Theft						
Number	776	793	2.2	767,290	773,139	0.8
Rate	58.3	59.4	1.8	237.3	237.4	-

NOTE: Although arson data are included in the trend and clearance tables, sufficient data are not available to estimate totals for this offense. Therefore, no arson data are published in this table.
- = Zero or rounds to zero.
[1] Population figures are U.S. Census Bureau provisional estimates as of July 1, 2017.
[2] The figures shown in the rape (revised definition) column were estimated using the revised Uniform Crime Reporting (UCR) definition of rape.

Table ME-15. State Government Finances, 2017

(Dollar amounts in thousands, percent distribution.)

Item	Dollars	Percent distribution
Total Revenue	10,630,716	100.0
General revenue	8,579,443	80.7
Intergovernmental revenue	3,020,597	28.4
Taxes	4,232,556	39.8
General sales	1,441,867	13.6
Selective sales	723,275	6.8
License taxes	274,760	2.6
Individual income tax	1,534,866	14.4
Corporate income tax	175,239	1.6
Other taxes	82,549	0.8
Current charges	859,687	8.1
Miscellaneous general revenue	466,603	4.4
Utility revenue	9,835	0.1
Liquor stores revenue	33	-
Insurance trust revenue[1]	2,041,405	19.2
Total Expenditure	10,145,529	100.0
Intergovernmental expenditure	2,428,618	23.9
Direct expenditure	7,716,911	76.1
Current operation	5,952,841	58.7
Capital outlay	399,970	3.9
Insurance benefits and repayments	1,028,113	10.1
Assistance and subsidies	167,960	1.7
Interest on debt	168,027	1.7
Exhibit: Salaries and wages	1,069,165	10.5
Total Expenditure	10,145,529	100.0
General expenditure	9,096,491	89.7
Intergovernmental expenditure	2,428,618	23.9
Direct expenditure	6,667,873	65.7
General expenditure, by function:		
Education	3,251,164	32.0
Public welfare	3,257,172	32.1
Hospitals	62,151	0.6
Health	147,214	1.5
Highways	777,991	7.7
Police protection	90,368	0.9
Correction	162,568	1.6
Natural resources	138,331	1.4
Parks and recreation	7,075	0.1
Governmental administration	374,233	3.7
Interest on general debt	168,027	1.7
Other and unallocable	660,197	6.5
Utility expenditure	20,925	0.2
Liquor stores expenditure	0	-
Insurance trust expenditure	1,028,113	10.1
Debt at End of Fiscal Year	4,750,384	X
Cash and Security Holdings	19,481,257	X

X = Not applicable.
- = Zero or rounds to zero.
[1] Within insurance trust revenue, net earnings of state retirement systems is a calculated statistic (the item code in the data file is X08), and thus can be positive or negative. Net earnings is the sum of earnings on investments plus gains on investments minus losses on investments. The change made in 2002 for asset valuation from book to market value in accordance with Statement 34 of the Governmental Accounting Standards Board is reflected in the calculated statistics.

Table ME-16. State Government Tax Collections, 2018

(Dollars in thousands, percent.)

Item	Dollars	Percent distribution
Total Taxes	4,410,632	100.0
Property taxes	39,308	0.9
Sales and gross receipts	2,250,293	51.0
General sales and gross receipts	1,529,113	34.7
Selective sales and gross receipts	721,180	16.4
Alcoholic beverages	19,647	0.4
Amusements	56,264	1.3
Insurance premiums	99,654	2.3
Motor fuels	250,468	5.7
Pari-mutuels	1,435	-
Public utilities	21,573	0.5
Tobacco products	132,950	3.0
Other selective sales	139,189	3.2
Licenses	281,155	6.4
Alcoholic beverages	6,237	0.1
Amusements	536	-
Corporations in general	11,095	0.3
Hunting and fishing	16,578	0.4
Motor vehicle	112,557	2.6
Motor vehicle operators	10,816	0.2
Public utilities	X	-
Occupation and business, NEC	113,492	2.6
Other licenses	9,844	0.2
Income taxes	1,790,833	40.6
Individual income	1,605,096	36.4
Corporation net income	185,737	4.2
Other taxes	49,043	1.1
Death and gift	13,801	0.3
Documentary and stock transfer	35,242	0.8
Severance	X	-
Taxes, NEC	0	-

X = Not applicable.
- = Zero or rounds to zero.

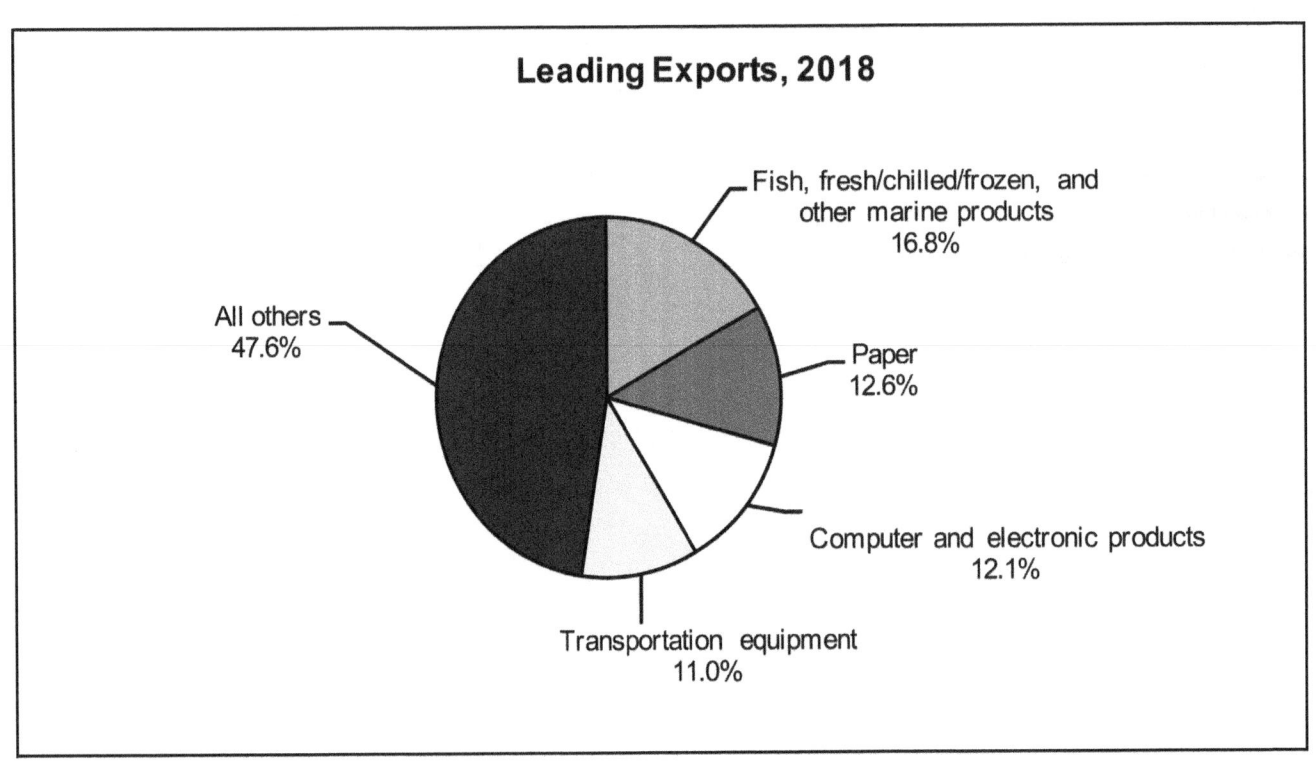

Leading Exports, 2018

Fish, fresh/chilled/frozen, and other marine products 16.8%

Paper 12.6%

Computer and electronic products 12.1%

Transportation equipment 11.0%

All others 47.6%

MARYLAND

Facts and Figures

Location: Eastern United States; bordered on the N by Pennsylvania, on the E by Delaware and the Atlantic Ocean, and on the S and W by Virginia and West Virginia

Area: 12,407 sq. mi. (32,133 sq. km.); rank—42nd

Population: 6,042,718 (2018 est.); rank—19th

Principal Cities: capital—Annapolis; largest—Baltimore

Statehood: April 28, 1788; 7th state

U.S. Congress: 2 senators, 8 representatives

State Motto: *Fatti maschii parole femine* ("Manly deeds, womanly words")

State Song: "Maryland, My Maryland"

State Nicknames: The Old Line State; The Free State

Abbreviations: MD; Md.

State Symbols: flower—black-eyed susan; tree—white oak; bird—Baltimore oriole

At a Glance

- With an increase in population of 4.7 percent, Maryland ranked 25th among the states in growth from 2010 to 2018.

- Maryland's 2017 median household income of $80,776 was the 2nd highest in the country, and its poverty rate of 9.3 percent was the 2nd lowest among the states.

- Maryland's violent crime rate in 2017 was 500.2 per 100,000 population, compared to 394.0 for the entire nation.

- In 2017, 6.1 percent of all Marylanders were uninsured, compared to the national average of 8.7 percent.

- Approximately 30.9 percent of Marylanders self-identified their race as "Black or African American alone" in 2018, which was the 5th highest percentage in the country.

Table MD-1. Population by Age, Sex, Race, and Hispanic Origin

(Number, percent, except where noted.)

Sex, age, race, and Hispanic origin	2000	2010	2018 [1]	Percent change, 2010–2018
Total Population....................................	5,296,486	5,773,552	6,042,718	4.7
Percent of total U.S. population	1.9	1.9	1.8	X
Sex				
Male..	2,557,794	2,791,762	2,928,921	4.9
Female	2,738,692	2,981,790	3,113,797	4.4
Age				
Under 5 years..................................	353,393	364,488	364,504	-
5 to 19 years..................................	1,139,572	1,152,138	1,130,454	-1.9
20 to 64 years.................................	3,204,214	3,549,284	3,616,624	1.9
65 years and over..............................	599,307	707,642	931,136	31.6
Median age (years)	36.0	38.0	38.8	2.1
Race and Hispanic Origin				
One race				
White	3,391,308	3,542,379	3,552,355	0.3
Black	1,477,411	1,731,513	1,867,592	7.9
American Indian and Alaska Native	15,423	30,885	36,188	17.2
Asian	210,929	326,655	405,682	24.2
Native Hawaiian or Other Pacific Islander	2,303	5,391	6,746	25.1
Two or more races	103,587	137,729	174,155	26.4
Hispanic (of any race)	227,916	493,811	628,433	27.3

X = Not applicable.
[1] Population figures for 2018 are July 1 estimates. The 2010 estimates are taken from the 2010 Census.
- = Zero or rounds to zero.

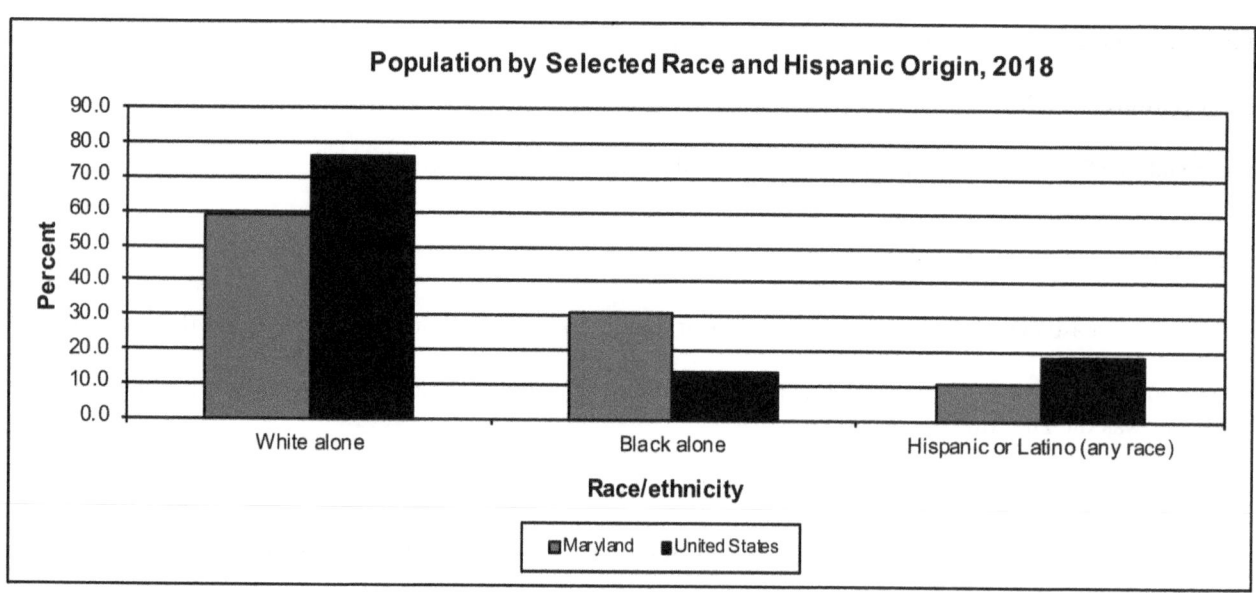

Table MD-2. Marital Status

(Number, percent distribution.)

Sex, age, race, and Hispanic origin	2000	2010	2017
Males, 15 Years and Over	1,972,921	2,232,162	2,365,357
Never married	31.0	36.8	37.8
Now married, except separated...	56.3	50.2	49.3
Separated...	2.8	2.3	2.0
Widowed..	2.5	2.7	2.5
Divorced..	7.4	8.0	8.4
Females, 15 Years and Over	2,186,715	2,442,021	2,571,187
Never married	26.8	32.2	33.0
Now married, except separated...	49.7	45.3	45.0
Separated...	3.4	2.9	2.1
Widowed..	10.1	9.0	8.6
Divorced..	10.1	10.7	11.3

Table MD-3. Households and Housing Characteristics

(Number, percent, dollars.)

Item	2000	2010	2017	Average annual percent change, 2010–2017
Total Households	1,980,859	2,127,439	2,207,343	0.5
Family households	1,359,318	1,431,958	1,469,830	0.4
Married-couple family	994,549	1,022,613	1,052,297	0.4
Other family	364,789	409,345	417,533	0.3
Male householder, no wife present	84,893	104,112	104,699	0.1
Female householder, no husband present	279,876	305,233	312,834	0.4
Nonfamily households	621,541	695,481	737,513	0.9
Householder living alone	495,459	570,388	605,688	0.9
Householder not living alone	126,082	125,093	131,825	0.8
Housing Characteristics				
Total housing units	2,145,283	2,380,605	2,449,123	0.4
Occupied housing units	1,980,859	2,127,439	2,207,343	0.5
Owner occupied	1,341,751	1,426,267	1,472,500	0.5
Renter occupied	639,108	701,172	734,843	0.7
Average household size	2.61	2.65	2.68	0.2
Financial Characteristics				
Median gross rent of renter-occupied housing	689	1,131	1,337	2.6
Median monthly owner costs for housing units with a mortgage	1,296	2,016	1,915	-0.7
Median value of owner-occupied housing units	146,000	301,400	312,500	0.5

Table MD-4. Migration, Origin, and Language

(Number, percent.)

Characteristic	State			U.S.		
	2016	2017	Percent change	2016	2017	Percent change
Residence 1 Year Ago						
Population 1 year and over	5,949,566	5,988,007	0.6	319,361,956	321,994,428	0.8
Same house	86.4	86.3	X	85.4	85.7	X
Different house in the U.S.	12.9	12.9	X	13.9	13.6	X
Same county	7.3	7.4	X	8.3	8.1	X
Different county	5.6	5.5	X	5.6	5.6	X
Same state	2.9	2.8	X	3.2	3.3	X
Different state	2.7	2.8	X	2.4	2.3	X
Abroad	0.7	0.8	X	0.7	0.7	X
Place of Birth						
Native born	5,094,577	5,124,241	0.6	279,388,170	281,193,323	0.6
Male	48.4	48.6	X	49.3	49.4	X
Female	51.6	51.4	X	50.7	50.6	X
Foreign born	921,870	927,936	0.7	43,739,345	44,525,855	1.8
Male	49.0	48.2	X	48.5	48.4	X
Female	51.0	51.8	X	51.5	51.6	X
Foreign born; naturalized U.S. citizen	467,964	487,180	3.4	21,238,372	21,948,732	3.3
Male	46.8	45.7	X	45.9	45.9	X
Female	53.2	54.3	X	54.1	54.1	X
Foreign born; not a U.S. citizen	453,906	440,756	-2.9	22,500,973	22,577,123	0.3
Male	51.2	50.9	X	51.0	50.8	X
Female	48.8	49.1	X	49.0	49.2	X
Entered 2010 or later	19.9	23.4	X	18.6	21.3	X
Entered 2000 to 2009	32.7	30.6	X	26.7	25.7	X
Entered before 2000	47.4	46.0	X	54.7	53.0	X
World Region of Birth, Foreign						
Foreign-born population, excluding population born at sea	921,870	927,936	0.7	43,738,901	44,525,458	1.8
Europe	9.3	9.2	X	10.9	10.8	X
Asia	32.8	32.7	X	30.8	31.2	X
Africa	17.3	17.5	X	4.9	5.1	X
Oceania	0.2	0.4	X	0.6	0.6	X
Latin America	39.5	39.3	X	51.0	50.4	X
North America	0.7	1.0	X	1.8	1.8	X
Language Spoken at Home and Ability to Speak English						
Population 5 years and over	5,653,552	5,688,864	0.6	303,328,961	305,924,019	0.9
English only	81.1	80.9	X	78.4	78.2	X
Language other than English	18.9	19.1	X	21.6	21.8	X
Speaks English less than "very well"	7.0	6.9	X	8.6	8.5	X

NA = Not available.
X = Not applicable.
- = Zero or rounds to zero.

Table MD-5. Median Income and Poverty Status, 2017

(Number, percent, except as noted.)

Characteristic	State		U.S.	
	Number	Percent	Number	Percent
Median Income				
Households (dollars)..	80,776	X	60,336	X
Families (dollars)	98,393	X	73,891	X
Below Poverty Level (All People)	549,171	9.3	42,583,651	13.4
Sex				
Male	239,742	8.4	19,004,547	12.2
Female	309,429	10.1	23,579,104	14.5
Age				
Under 18 years..	159,886	12.0	13,353,202	18.4
Related children under 18 years..	155,219	11.7	13,053,472	18.1
18 to 64 years...	319,477	8.6	24,648,677	12.6
65 years and over	69,808	7.9	4,581,772	9.3

X = Not applicable.

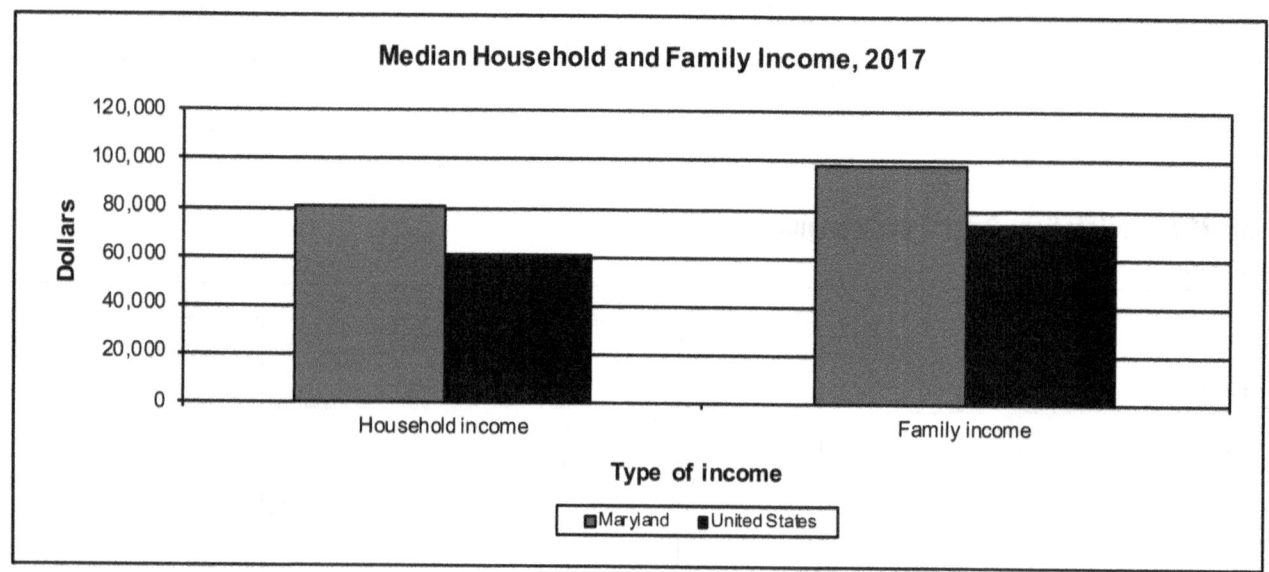

Table MD-6. Health Insurance Coverage Status for the Civilian Noninstitutionalized Population and Children Under 18 Years of Age

(Number, percent.)

Item	2009	2010	2011	2012	2013	2014	2015	2016	2017
Civilian Noninstitutionalized Population	5,589,768	5,687,998	5,736,588	5,788,196	5,834,039	5,885,847	5,908,522	5,918,535	5,957,871
Covered by Private or Public Insurance									
Number...	4,968,978	5,047,137	5,138,144	5,190,642	5,240,861	5,422,579	5,519,323	5,555,356	5,592,274
Percent...	88.9	88.7	89.6	89.7	89.8	92.1	93.4	93.9	93.9
Uninsured									
Number...	620,790	640,861	598,444	597,554	593,178	463,268	389,199	363,179	365,597
Percent...	11.1	11.3	10.4	10.3	10.2	7.9	6.6	6.1	6.1
Percent in the U.S. not covered.................................	15.1	15.5	15.1	14.8	14.5	11.7	9.4	8.6	8.7
Children Under 18 Years of Age[1]	1,348,039	1,350,011	1,344,498	1,341,118	1,343,118	1,349,767	1,346,154	1,344,588	1,419,540
Covered by Private or Public Insurance									
Number...	1,283,491	1,285,713	1,283,012	1,289,667	1,283,833	1,307,172	1,293,887	1,299,633	1,365,464
Percent...	95.2	95.2	95.4	96.2	95.6	96.8	96.1	96.7	96.2
Uninsured									
Number...	64,548	64,298	61,486	51,451	59,285	42,595	52,267	44,955	54,076
Percent...	4.8	4.8	4.6	3.8	4.4	3.2	3.9	3.3	3.8
Percent in the U.S. not covered.................................	8.6	8.0	7.5	7.2	7.1	6.0	4.8	4.5	5.0

[1] 2017 data is for individuals under 19 years of age.

Table MD-7. Employment Status by Demographic Group, 2018

(Numbers in thousands, percent.)

Characteristic	Civilian noninstitutional population	Civilian labor force		Employed		Unemployed	
		Number	Percent of population	Number	Percent of population	Number	Percent of population
Total..	4,790	3,207	66.9	3,074	64.2	133	4.2
Sex							
Male..	2,265	1,660	73.3	1,591	70.2	69	4.2
Female...	2,525	1,547	61.3	1,482	58.7	64	4.2
Race, Sex, and Hispanic Origin							
White...	2,883	1,940	67.3	1,880	65.2	60	3.1
Male...	1,404	1,043	74.3	1,012	72.1	31	3.0
Female...	1,480	897	60.6	868	58.6	29	3.2
Black or African American...........................	1,455	972	66.8	913	62.8	59	6.0
Male...	651	457	70.2	430	66.0	27	5.9
Female...	804	515	64.0	483	60.1	32	6.2
Hispanic or Latino ethnicity[1]	461	354	76.8	335	72.8	19	5.2
Male...	242	213	88.0	204	84.2	9	4.4
Female...	219	141	64.4	132	60.2	9	6.6
Age							
16 to 19 years...	NA	NA	NA	NA	NA	NA	NA
20 to 24 years...	396	272	68.8	251	63.4	22	7.9
25 to 34 years...	842	721	85.6	695	82.6	26	3.5
35 to 44 years...	712	625	87.8	601	84.5	24	3.8
45 to 54 years...	812	680	83.8	661	81.4	19	2.8
55 to 64 years...	810	583	72.0	567	70.0	16	2.7
65 years and over	920	223	24.2	212	23.0	11	4.9

NOTE: Data in Table 7 are from the Current Population Survey (CPS) and do not match the estimates in Table 8. See notes and definitions for further information.
[1] May be of any race.

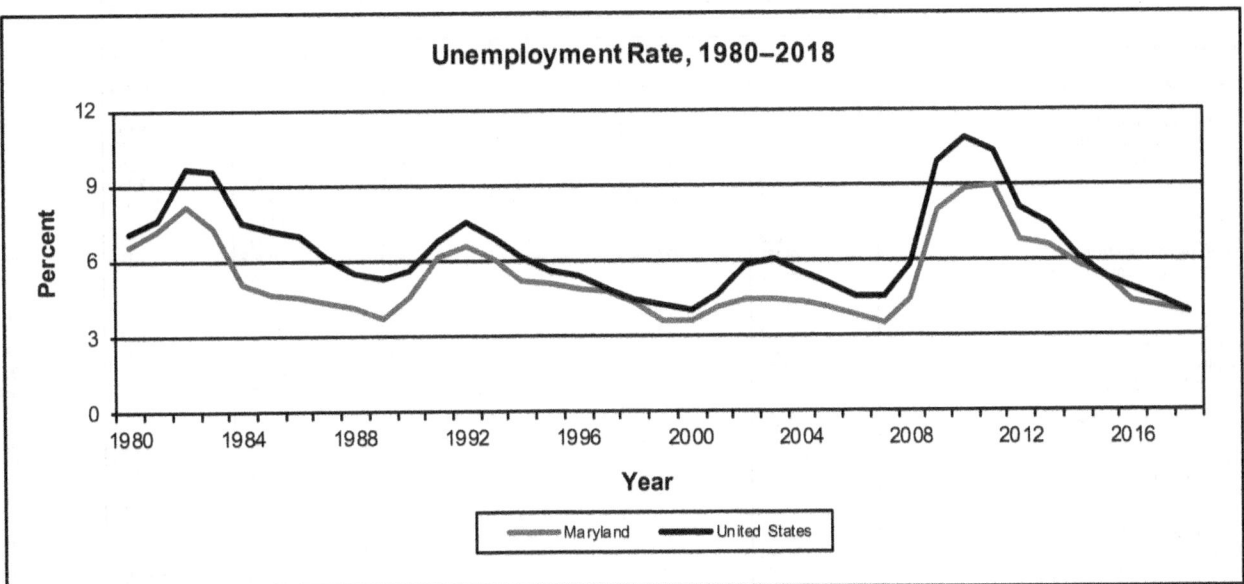

Unemployment Rate, 1980–2018

Table MD-8. Employment Status of the Civilian Noninstitutional Population Age 16 Years and Over

(Number, percent.)

Year	Civilian labor force	Civilian participation rate	Employed	Unemployed	Unemployment rate
2010..	3,073,826	68.5	2,838,492	235,334	7.7
2011..	3,096,561	68.0	2,872,084	224,477	7.2
2012..	3,119,647	67.8	2,902,307	217,340	7.0
2013..	3,129,352	67.4	2,923,498	205,854	6.6
2014..	3,129,933	66.9	2,947,943	181,990	5.8
2015..	3,151,142	66.9	2,990,942	160,200	5.1
2016..	3,178,646	67.1	3,037,763	140,883	4.4
2017..	3,219,455	67.6	3,086,246	133,209	4.1
2018..	3,197,137	67.2	3,071,652	125,485	3.9

Table MD-9. Employment and Average Wages by Industry

(Estimates are based on the 2012 North American Industry Classification System [NAICS].)

Industry	2011	2012	2013	2014	2015	2016	2017
				Number of jobs			
Wage and Salary Employment by Industry......................	2,647,062	2,683,738	2,702,351	2,727,672	2,767,425	2,804,311	2,828,811
Farm Wage and Salary Employment................................	4,744	6,475	5,973	6,416	6,214	7,499	7,224
Nonfarm Wage and Salary Employment...........................	2,642,318	2,677,263	2,696,378	2,721,256	2,761,211	2,796,812	2,821,587
Private wage and salary employment............................	2,074,739	2,107,842	2,127,875	2,154,238	2,194,027	2,229,746	2,252,674
Forestry, fishing, and related activities	1,994	1,972	2,012	2,049	2,148	2,180	2,143
Mining..	1,432	1,523	1,340	1,260	1,297	1,165	1,147
Utilities...	10,069	10,103	9,781	9,738	9,579	9,836	9,760
Construction	147,116	147,174	150,016	153,215	158,344	165,045	165,951
Manufacturing...	112,910	108,821	106,376	103,372	103,588	103,395	106,654
Durable goods manufacturing..............................	60,181	57,851	56,308	53,737	54,416	53,950	55,618
Nondurable goods manufacturing...........................	52,729	50,970	50,068	49,635	49,172	49,445	51,036
Wholesale trade	86,449	86,409	86,166	85,221	86,291	86,195	86,660
Retail trade..	282,639	286,190	286,362	288,620	291,328	291,889	289,803
Transportation and warehousing...............................	66,428	67,825	69,178	71,829	77,313	78,919	81,963
Information...	41,070	39,909	39,537	38,977	38,457	38,667	37,633
Finance and insurance	98,637	98,965	99,368	98,448	99,469	100,123	98,738
Real estate and rental and leasing...........................	42,950	43,619	44,037	44,236	45,492	45,800	48,103
Professional, scientific, and technical services	230,728	235,818	237,217	241,058	243,808	248,333	248,745
Management of companies and enterprises......................	22,267	24,713	25,906	25,570	25,198	26,278	26,043
Administrative and waste services	147,374	152,517	156,609	159,631	164,658	171,021	171,937
Educational services	71,459	72,587	71,879	73,895	74,754	77,105	79,593
Health care and social assistance............................	334,335	342,410	345,961	349,793	359,018	366,468	373,141
Arts, entertainment, and recreation..........................	36,568	38,170	42,270	45,412	45,917	46,235	47,084
Accommodation and food services	198,393	207,221	213,420	217,225	223,139	228,047	235,163
Other services, except public administration.................	141,921	141,896	140,440	144,689	144,229	143,045	142,413
Government and government enterprises	567,579	569,421	568,503	567,018	567,184	567,066	568,913
				Dollars			
Average Wages and Salaries by Industry	54,517	55,466	55,555	56,911	58,701	59,587	61,133
Average Farm Wages and Salaries	22,020	22,899	25,305	24,960	21,052	20,019	18,860
Average Nonfarm Wages and Salaries	54,576	55,545	55,622	56,987	58,786	59,693	61,242
Average private wages and salaries...........................	51,853	53,108	53,220	54,484	56,173	57,088	58,632
Forestry, fishing, and related activities	27,777	28,043	28,744	29,364	30,863	32,305	33,701
Mining..	61,110	61,372	60,106	62,669	61,487	68,482	71,257
Utilities...	110,154	118,938	115,067	114,555	122,170	123,671	129,820
Construction	56,026	56,902	57,115	59,213	61,090	63,514	66,103
Manufacturing...	68,822	70,367	70,972	72,408	75,452	75,788	79,280
Durable goods manufacturing..............................	76,136	77,469	78,362	78,132	80,302	82,117	84,914
Nondurable goods manufacturing...........................	60,473	62,307	62,661	66,210	70,084	68,883	73,140
Wholesale trade	72,955	74,448	75,204	77,533	79,704	79,625	80,876
Retail trade..	29,016	29,414	29,502	30,137	31,544	31,935	32,526
Transportation and warehousing...............................	50,351	50,747	50,614	53,256	54,576	54,904	54,494
Information...	78,552	80,336	83,111	85,334	86,578	90,327	90,499
Finance and insurance	85,557	93,587	93,248	96,713	100,457	103,524	106,609
Real estate and rental and leasing...........................	56,573	57,966	58,010	60,650	62,817	63,249	65,219
Professional, scientific, and technical services	88,597	91,181	90,280	92,647	94,261	95,588	97,803
Management of companies and enterprises......................	106,411	105,288	107,487	111,217	116,537	112,929	123,799
Administrative and waste services	38,796	39,137	39,506	40,229	42,003	42,838	44,869
Educational services	45,530	47,129	47,722	49,286	50,578	50,678	51,205
Health care and social assistance............................	48,974	49,647	49,977	51,012	52,786	53,166	54,291
Arts, entertainment, and recreation..........................	31,460	32,543	32,623	33,114	34,714	36,461	37,046
Accommodation and food services	20,485	20,953	21,283	21,879	22,668	23,458	24,789
Other services, except public administration.................	35,226	36,600	37,724	38,414	39,904	41,073	42,745
Government and government enterprises	64,527	64,565	64,615	66,494	68,891	69,937	71,575

Table MD-10. Employment Characteristics by Family Type

(Number, percent.)

Family type and labor force status	2015		2016		2017	
	Total	Families with own children under 18 years	Total	Families with own children under 18 years	Total	Families with own children under 18 years
All Families...	1,454,839	629,970	1,458,953	624,358	1,469,830	615,231
FAMILY TYPE AND LABOR FORCE STATUS						
Married-Couple Families.............................	1,042,467	429,625	1,039,902	419,478	1,052,297	423,110
Both husband and wife in labor force................	57.5	71.5	57.8	73.3	58.4	72.9
Husband in labor force, wife not in labor force	19.9	23.6	19.0	21.6	19.0	22.4
Wife in labor force, husband not in labor force	7.4	3.3	7.7	3.4	7.0	3.1
Both husband and wife not in labor force...........	14.2	1.0	14.4	1.1	14.6	0.8
Other Families	412,372	200,345	419,051	204,880	417,533	192,121
Female householder, no husband present............	73.7	75.4	73.4	74.2	74.9	76.6
In labor force	55.2	65.5	54.8	65.2	56.3	68.1
Not in labor force	18.6	9.9	18.6	9.0	18.6	8.5
Male householder, no wife present....................	26.3	24.6	26.6	25.8	25.1	23.4
In labor force	21.0	22.5	22.3	24.5	19.9	21.7
Not in labor force	5.3	2.2	4.3	1.4	5.2	1.7

Table MD-11. School Enrollment and Educational Attainment, 2017

(Number, percent.)

Item	State	U.S.
Enrollment		
Total population 3 years and over, enrolled in school	1,536,509	81,273,337
Enrolled in nursery school or preschool (percent).........................	6.4	6.0
Enrolled in kindergarten (percent).......................................	4.5	4.9
Enrolled in elementary school, grades 1-8 (percent)......................	39.1	40.6
Enrolled in high school, grades 9-12 (percent)...........................	20.5	21.1
Enrolled in college or graduate school (percent).........................	29.7	27.4
Attainment		
Total population 25 years and over	4,167,604	221,250,083
Less than ninth grade (percent)...	4.0	5.1
9th to 12th grade, no diploma (percent).................................	6.1	6.9
High school graduate, including equivalency (percent)....................	24.5	27.1
Some college, no degree (percent).......................................	18.9	20.4
Associate's degree (percent)..	6.8	8.5
Bachelor's degree (percent)...	21.3	19.7
Graduate or professional degree (percent)...............................	18.3	12.3
High school graduate or higher (percent)	89.9	88.0
Bachelor's degree or higher (percent)...................................	39.7	32.0

Table MD-12. Public School Characteristics and Educational Indicators

(Number, percent; data derived from National Center of Education Statistics.)

Item	State	U.S.
Public Elementary and Secondary Schools		
Number of operational school districts, 2016-17...........................	25	18,377
Number of operational schools, 2016-17....................................	1,424	98,330
Percent charter schools	3.4	7.1
Total public school enrollment, 2016-17...................................	886,221	50,587,859
Percent charter school enrollment	2.5	6.0
Student-teacher ratio, Fall 2015..	14.8	16.0
Expenditures per student (dollars), 2015-16...............................	14,523	11,841
Four-year adjusted cohort graduation rate (ACGR)[1].......................	87.7	84.6
Students eligible for free or reduced-price lunch (percent), 2015-16......	45.0	52.1
English language learners (percent), Fall 2016............................	7.8	9.6
Students age 3 to 21 served under IDEA, part B (percent), 2017-18	12.1	13.7
Public Schools by Type, 2016-17		Percent of state public schools
Total number of schools..	1,424	100.0
Special education..	37	2.6
Vocational education...	25	1.8
Alternative education..	44	3.1

[1] Adjusted Cohort Graduation Rates (ACGR) differ from Averaged Freshmen Graduation Rates (AFGR).

Table MD-13. Reported Voting and Registration of the Voting-Age Population, November 2018

(Numbers in thousands, percent.)

Item	Total population	Total citizen population	Registered			Voted		
			Total registered	Percent registered (total population)	Percent registered (total citizen population)	Total voted	Percent voted (total population)	Percent voted (total citizen population)
U.S. Total...............................	249,748	228,832	153,066	61.3	66.9	122,281	49.0	53.4
State Total..............................	4,666	4,281	3,095	66.3	72.3	2,320	49.7	54.2
Sex								
Male	2,217	2,047	1,457	65.7	71.2	1,107	49.9	54.1
Female	2,449	2,235	1,639	66.9	73.3	1,213	49.5	54.3
Race								
White alone............................	2,800	2,635	2,021	72.2	76.7	1,536	54.9	58.3
White, non-Hispanic alone	2,466	2,421	1,869	75.8	77.2	1,414	57.3	58.4
Black alone............................	1,414	1,293	856	60.5	66.2	630	44.5	48.7
Asian alone	315	217	142	44.9	65.1	94	29.9	43.4
Hispanic (of any race).............	500	328	195	39.0	59.5	158	31.7	48.3
White alone or in combination	2,874	2,708	2,064	71.8	76.2	1,572	54.7	58.1
Black alone or in combination.........	1,467	1,346	887	60.5	65.9	651	44.4	48.4
Asian alone or in combination.........	331	234	154	46.6	66.1	103	31.2	44.3
Age								
18 to 24 years..........................	653	584	354	54.2	60.6	220	33.7	37.7
25 to 34 years..........................	780	690	477	61.2	69.2	302	38.7	43.8
35 to 44 years..........................	689	616	444	64.5	72.1	340	49.3	55.2
45 to 64 years..........................	1,604	1,486	1,101	68.6	74.1	902	56.2	60.7
65 years and over......................	939	906	719	76.6	79.4	556	59.2	61.4

Table MD-14. Crime

(Number, rate per 100,000. Data are derived from the FBI Uniform Crime Reports.)

Item	State			U.S.		
	2016	2017	Percent change	2016	2017	Percent change
TOTAL POPULATION[1]	6,024,752	6,052,177	0.5	323,405,935	325,719,178	0.7
VIOLENT CRIME						
Number..................................	29,019	30,273	4.3	1,285,606	1,283,220	-0.2
Rate......................................	481.7	500.2	3.8	397.5	394.0	-0.9
Murder and Nonnegligent Manslaughter						
Number..................................	536	546	1.9	17,413	17,284	-0.7
Rate......................................	8.9	9.0	1.4	5.4	5.3	-1.4
Rape[2]						
Number..................................	1,827	1,691	-7.4	132,414	135,755	2.5
Rate......................................	30.3	27.9	-7.9	40.9	41.7	1.8
Robbery						
Number..................................	10,815	11,200	3.6	332,797	319,356	-4.0
Rate......................................	179.5	185.1	3.1	102.9	98.0	-4.7
Aggravated Assault						
Number..................................	15,841	16,836	6.3	802,982	810,825	1.0
Rate......................................	262.9	278.2	5.8	248.3	248.9	0.3
PROPERTY CRIME						
Number..................................	139,716	134,496	-3.7	7,928,530	7,694,086	-3.0
Rate......................................	2,319.0	2,222.3	-4.2	2,451.6	2,362.2	-3.6
Burglary						
Number..................................	24,832	23,508	-5.3	1,516,405	1,401,840	-7.6
Rate......................................	412.2	388.4	-5.8	468.9	430.4	-8.2
Larceny-Theft						
Number..................................	100,995	97,420	-3.5	5,644,835	5,519,107	-2.2
Rate......................................	1,676.3	1,609.7	-4.0	1,745.4	1,694.4	-2.9
Motor Vehicle Theft						
Number..................................	13,889	13,568	-2.3	767,290	773,139	0.8
Rate......................................	230.5	224.2	-2.8	237.3	237.4	-

NOTE: Although arson data are included in the trend and clearance tables, sufficient data are not available to estimate totals for this offense. Therefore, no arson data are published in this table.
- = Zero or rounds to zero.
[1] Population figures are U.S. Census Bureau provisional estimates as of July 1, 2017.
[2] The figures shown in the rape (revised definition) column were estimated using the revised Uniform Crime Reporting (UCR) definition of rape.

Table MD-15. State Government Finances, 2017

(Dollar amounts in thousands, percent distribution.)

Item	Dollars	Percent distribution
Total Revenue	47,556,977	100.0
General revenue	41,021,463	86.3
Intergovernmental revenue	13,203,944	27.8
Taxes	21,599,795	45.4
General sales	4,609,538	9.7
Selective sales	4,633,222	9.7
License taxes	866,391	1.8
Individual income tax	9,066,709	19.1
Corporate income tax	1,001,934	2.1
Other taxes	1,422,001	3.0
Current charges	3,810,875	8.0
Miscellaneous general revenue	2,406,849	5.1
Utility revenue	149,012	0.3
Liquor stores revenue	0	-
Insurance trust revenue[1]	6,386,502	13.4
Total Expenditure	45,313,681	100.0
Intergovernmental expenditure	9,631,764	21.3
Direct expenditure	35,681,917	78.7
Current operation	25,026,384	55.2
Capital outlay	3,329,842	7.3
Insurance benefits and repayments	4,367,219	9.6
Assistance and subsidies	1,761,798	3.9
Interest on debt	1,196,674	2.6
Exhibit: Salaries and wages	5,495,407	12.1
Total Expenditure	45,313,681	100.0
General expenditure	39,692,648	87.6
Intergovernmental expenditure	9,631,764	21.3
Direct expenditure	30,060,884	66.3
General expenditure, by function:		
Education	12,663,513	27.9
Public welfare	12,929,570	28.5
Hospitals	578,878	1.3
Health	2,190,864	4.8
Highways	2,556,791	5.6
Police protection	643,786	1.4
Correction	1,479,811	3.3
Natural resources	563,293	1.2
Parks and recreation	185,408	0.4
Governmental administration	1,495,436	3.3
Interest on general debt	1,196,674	2.6
Other and unallocable	3,208,624	7.1
Utility expenditure	1,253,814	2.6
Liquor stores expenditure	0	-
Insurance trust expenditure	4,367,219	9.6
Debt at End of Fiscal Year	28,027,363	X
Cash and Security Holdings	51,861,857	X

X = Not applicable.
- = Zero or rounds to zero.
[1] Within insurance trust revenue, net earnings of state retirement systems is a calculated statistic (the item code in the data file is X08), and thus can be positive or negative. Net earnings is the sum of earnings on investments plus gains on investments minus losses on investments. The change made in 2002 for asset valuation from book to market value in accordance with Statement 34 of the Governmental Accounting Standards Board is reflected in the calculated statistics.

Table MD-16. State Government Tax Collections, 2018

(Dollars in thousands, percent.)

Item	Dollars	Percent distribution
Total Taxes	22,427,037	100.0
Property taxes	808,763	3.6
Sales and gross receipts	9,567,244	42.7
General sales and gross receipts	4,716,179	21.0
Selective sales and gross receipts	4,851,065	21.6
Alcoholic beverages	31,682	0.1
Amusements	1,022,368	4.6
Insurance premiums	541,758	2.4
Motor fuels	1,084,195	4.8
Pari-mutuels	1,175	-
Public utilities	145,437	0.6
Tobacco products	372,724	1.7
Other selective sales	1,651,726	7.4
Licenses	850,913	3.8
Alcoholic beverages	1,524	-
Amusements	1,953	-
Corporations in general	119,084	0.5
Hunting and fishing	17,207	0.1
Motor vehicle	501,417	2.2
Motor vehicle operators	27,929	0.1
Public utilities	X	-
Occupation and business, NEC	179,997	0.8
Other licenses	1,802	-
Income taxes	10,540,951	47.0
Individual income	9,507,776	42.4
Corporation net income	1,033,175	4.6
Other taxes	659,166	2.9
Death and gift	214,378	1.0
Documentary and stock transfer	241,668	1.1
Severance	X	-
Taxes, NEC	203,120	0.9

X = Not applicable.
- = Zero or rounds to zero.

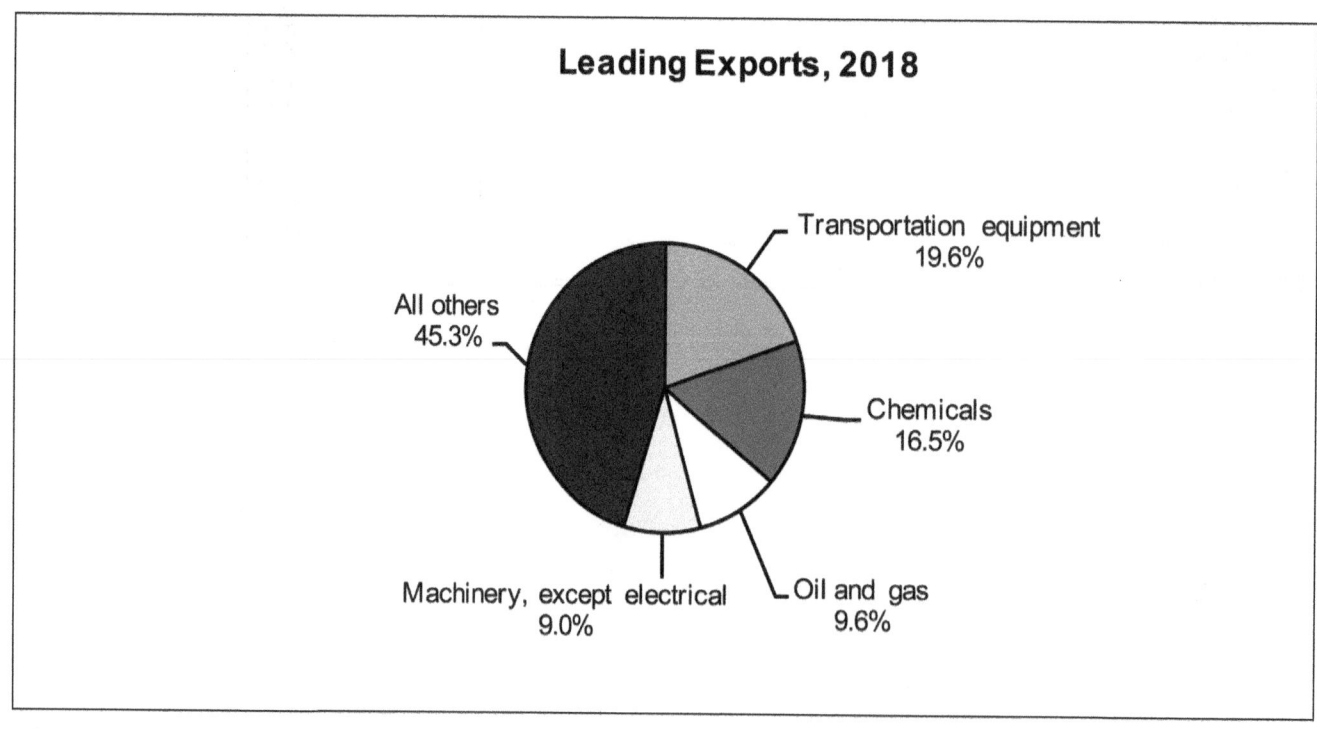

Leading Exports, 2018

Transportation equipment 19.6%
Chemicals 16.5%
Oil and gas 9.6%
Machinery, except electrical 9.0%
All others 45.3%

Facts and Figures

Location: Northeastern United States; bordered on the N by Vermont and New Hampshire, on the E by the Atlantic Ocean, on the S by Connecticut and Rhode Island, and on the W by New York

Area: 10,555 sq. mi. (27,336 sq. km.); rank—44th

Population: 6,902,149 (2018 est.); rank—15th

Principal Cities: capital—Boston; largest—Boston

Statehood: February 6, 1788; 6th state

U.S. Congress: 2 senators, 9 representatives

State Motto: *Ense petit placidam sub libertate quietem* ("By the sword we seek peace, but peace only under liberty")

State Song: "All Hail to Massachusetts"

State Nickname: The Bay State

Abbreviations: MA; Mass.

State Symbols: flower—mayflower; tree—American elm; bird—chickadee

At a Glance

- With an increase in population of 5.4 percent, Massachusetts ranked 23rd among the states in growth from 2010 to 2018.

- Massachusetts's median household income in 2017 was $77,385, the 5th highest in the country.

- Approximately 10.5 percent of Massachusetts' population lived below the poverty level in 2017, compared to 13.4 percent of the entire U.S. population.

- Massachusetts's violent crime rate in 2017 was 358.0 per 100,000 population, compared to 394.0 for the entire nation.

- Massachusetts's drug overdose death rate ranked 10th in the nation, with 31.8 deaths per 100,000 population.

Table MA-1. Population by Age, Sex, Race, and Hispanic Origin

(Number, percent, except where noted.)

Sex, age, race, and Hispanic origin	2000	2010	2018 [1]	Percent change, 2010–2018
Total Population...	6,349,097	6,547,629	6,902,149	5.4
Percent of total U.S. population	2.3	2.1	2.1	X
Sex				
Male..	3,058,816	3,166,628	3,350,528	5.8
Female...	3,290,281	3,381,001	3,551,621	5.0
Age				
Under 5 years..	397,268	367,087	360,161	-1.9
5 to 19 years...	1,277,845	1,254,056	1,214,558	-3.1
20 to 64 years...	3,813,822	4,023,762	4,188,330	4.1
65 years and over...	860,162	902,724	1,139,100	26.2
Median age (years)	36.5	39.1	39.4	0.8
Race and Hispanic Origin				
One race				
White	5,367,286	5,524,937	5,577,194	0.9
Black	343,454	504,365	617,097	22.4
American Indian and Alaska Native	15,015	29,944	34,112	13.9
Asian	238,124	359,673	492,508	36.9
Native Hawaiian or Other Pacific Islander	2,489	5,971	7,417	24.2
Two or more races	146,005	122,739	173,821	41.6
Hispanic (of any race)..	428,729	656,888	847,223	29.0

X = Not applicable.
[1] Population figures for 2018 are July 1 estimates. The 2010 estimates are taken from the 2010 Census.
- = Zero or rounds to zero.

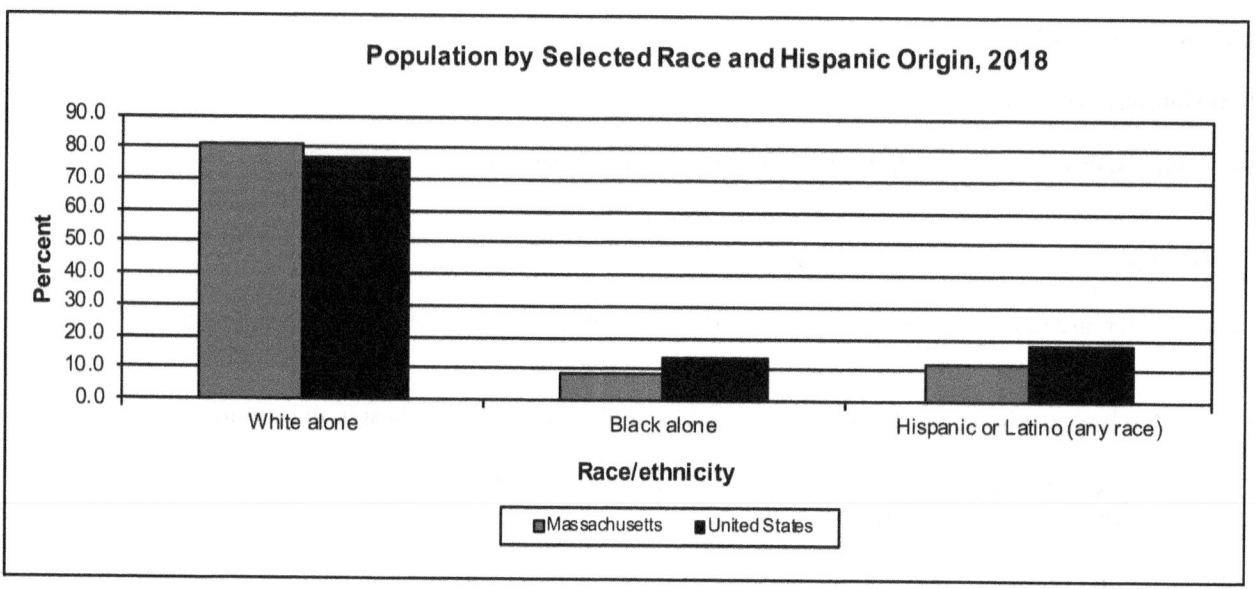

Population by Selected Race and Hispanic Origin, 2018

Table MA-2. Marital Status

(Number, percent distribution.)

Sex, age, race, and Hispanic origin	2000	2010	2017
Males, 15 Years and Over.....................................	2,412,349	2,579,221	2,758,162
Never married	33.9	38.7	39.7
Now married, except separated..............................	54.7	49.1	48.7
Separated...	1.6	1.6	1.3
Widowed...	2.7	2.7	2.4
Divorced...	7.0	8.0	7.8
Females, 15 Years and Over...................................	2,679,020	2,819,768	2,980,604
Never married	28.5	33.2	34.4
Now married, except separated..............................	48.9	44.1	44.1
Separated...	2.3	2.4	2.0
Widowed...	10.8	9.1	8.5
Divorced...	9.5	11.1	11.1

Table MA-3. Households and Housing Characteristics

(Number, percent, dollars.)

Item	2000	2010	2017	Average annual percent change, 2010–2017
Total Households...	2,443,580	2,520,419	2,604,954	0.5
Family households..	1,576,696	1,590,257	1,652,214	0.6
Married-couple family..	1,197,917	1,166,204	1,223,401	0.7
Other family...	378,779	424,053	428,813	0.2
Male householder, no wife present..	88,835	100,400	111,658	1.6
Female householder, no husband present..............................	289,944	323,653	317,155	-0.3
Nonfamily households	866,884	930,162	952,740	0.3
Householder living alone..	684,345	736,320	745,478	0.2
Householder not living alone...	182,539	193,842	207,262	1.0
Housing Characteristics				
Total housing units..	2,621,989	2,808,727	2,894,590	0.4
Occupied housing units	2,443,580	2,520,419	2,604,954	0.5
Owner occupied	1,508,052	1,568,382	1,623,515	0.5
Renter occupied	935,528	952,037	981,439	0.4
Average household size...	2.51	2.51	2.54	0.2
Financial Characteristics				
Median gross rent of renter-occupied housing	684	1,009	1,208	2.8
Median monthly owner costs for housing units with a mortgage	1,353	2,036	2,108	0.5
Median value of owner-occupied housing units..........................	185,700	334,100	385,400	2.2

Table MA-4. Migration, Origin, and Language

(Number, percent.)

Characteristic	State 2016	State 2017	State Percent change	U.S. 2016	U.S. 2017	U.S. Percent change
Residence 1 Year Ago						
Population 1 year and over	6,745,441	6,789,798	0.7	319,361,956	321,994,428	0.8
Same house	87.0	86.7	X	85.4	85.7	X
Different house in the U.S...	12.0	12.1	X	13.9	13.6	X
Same county	7.1	7.0	X	8.3	8.1	X
Different county	4.8	5.1	X	5.6	5.6	X
Same state	2.6	2.9	X	3.2	3.3	X
Different state	2.2	2.2	X	2.4	2.3	X
Abroad	1.1	1.1	X	0.7	0.7	X
Place of Birth						
Native born	5,687,897	5,703,347	0.3	279,388,170	281,193,323	0.6
Male	48.6	48.7	X	49.3	49.4	X
Female	51.4	51.3	X	50.7	50.6	X
Foreign born	1,123,882	1,156,472	2.9	43,739,345	44,525,855	1.8
Male	47.9	48.1	X	48.5	48.4	X
Female	52.1	51.9	X	51.5	51.6	X
Foreign born; naturalized U.S. citizen........................	592,761	606,490	2.3	21,238,372	21,948,732	3.3
Male	45.4	46.1	X	45.9	45.9	X
Female	54.6	53.9	X	54.1	54.1	X
Foreign born; not a U.S. citizen.................................	531,121	549,982	3.6	22,500,973	22,577,123	0.3
Male	50.8	50.4	X	51	50.8	X
Female	49.2	49.6	X	49	49.2	X
Entered 2010 or later	23.9	28.2	X	18.6	21.3	X
Entered 2000 to 2009	26.1	25.1	X	26.7	25.7	X
Entered before 2000...	50.0	46.8	X	54.7	53.0	X
World Region of Birth, Foreign						
Foreign-born population, excluding population born at sea	1,123,882	1,156,472	2.9	43,738,901	44,525,458	1.8
Europe	20.5	20.5	X	10.9	10.8	X
Asia	30.3	30.9	X	30.8	31.2	X
Africa	9.3	10.1	X	4.9	5.1	X
Oceania	0.4	0.4	X	0.6	0.6	X
Latin America...	37.0	35.7	X	51	50.4	X
North America..	2.5	2.4	X	1.8	1.8	X
Language Spoken at Home and Ability to Speak English						
Population 5 years and over.......................................	6,452,005	6,499,483	0.7	303,328,961	305,924,019	0.9
English only	76.3	76.0	X	78.4	78.2	X
Language other than English.....................................	23.7	24.0	X	21.6	21.8	X
Speaks English less than "very well"..........................	9.2	9.7	X	8.6	8.5	X

NA = Not available.
X = Not applicable.
- = Zero or rounds to zero.

Table MA-5. Median Income and Poverty Status, 2017

(Number, percent, except as noted.)

Characteristic	State		U.S.	
	Number	Percent	Number	Percent
Median Income				
Households (dollars)...	77,385	X	60,336	X
Families (dollars)	98,758	X	73,891	X
Below Poverty Level (All People)	692,201	10.5	42,583,651	13.4
Sex				
Male	297,373	9.2	19,004,547	12.2
Female	394,828	11.6	23,579,104	14.5
Age				
Under 18 years..	182,470	13.5	13,353,202	18.4
Related children under 18 years..	177,135	13.2	13,053,472	18.1
18 to 64 years	413,538	9.8	24,648,677	12.6
65 years and over	96,193	9.0	4,581,772	9.3

X = Not applicable.

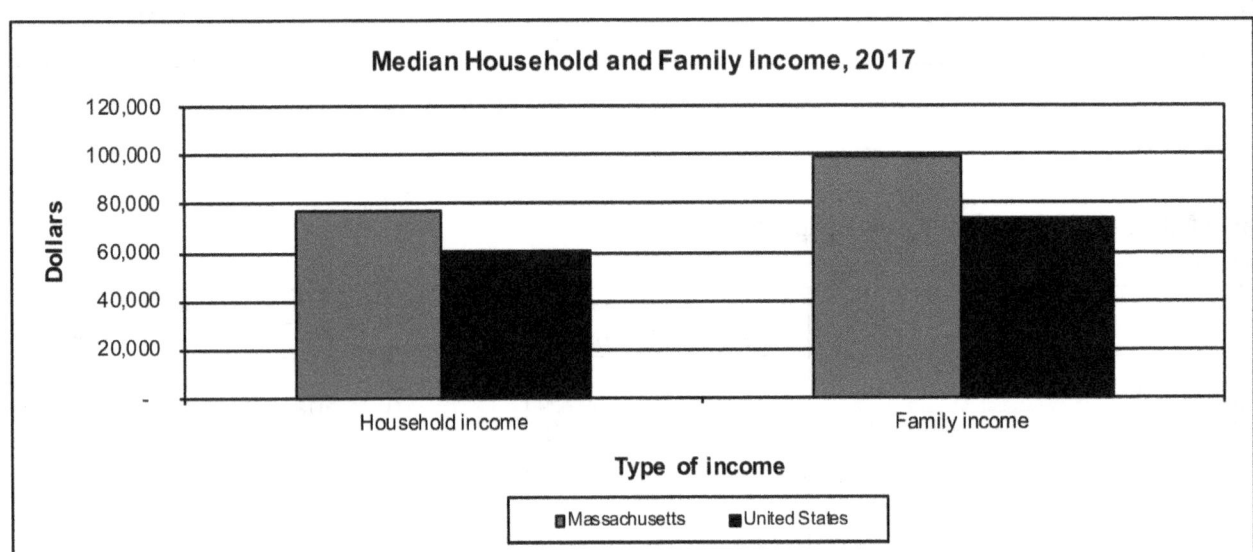

Table MA-6. Health Insurance Coverage Status for the Civilian Noninstitutionalized Population and Children Under 18 Years of Age

(Number, percent.)

Item	2009	2010	2011	2012	2013	2014	2015	2016	2017
Civilian Noninstitutionalized Population	6,495,905	6,478,067	6,507,596	6,566,851	6,613,654	6,668,348	6,718,090	6,736,017	6,785,622
Covered by Private or Public Insurance									
Number..	6,224,815	6,192,350	6,230,656	6,312,556	6,366,988	6,449,626	6,528,817	6,564,958	6,595,821
Percent..	95.8	95.6	95.7	96.1	96.3	96.7	97.2	97.5	97.2
Uninsured									
Number..	271,090	285,717	276,940	254,295	246,666	218,722	189,273	171,059	189,801
Percent..	4.2	4.4	4.3	3.9	3.7	3.3	2.8	2.5	2.8
Percent in the U.S. not covered..	15.1	15.5	15.1	14.8	14.5	11.7	9.4	8.6	8.7
Children Under 18 Years of Age[1]	1,430,695	1,414,746	1,401,873	1,397,972	1,389,165	1,387,398	1,383,924	1,375,244	1,478,961
Covered by Private or Public Insurance									
Number..	1,410,879	1,393,064	1,377,774	1,377,766	1,368,086	1,366,087	1,368,039	1,362,535	1,457,076
Percent..	98.6	98.5	98.3	98.6	98.5	98.5	98.9	99.1	98.5
Uninsured									
Number..	19,816	21,682	24,099	20,206	21,079	21,311	15,885	12,709	21,885
Percent..	1.4	1.5	1.7	1.4	1.5	1.5	1.1	0.9	1.5
Percent in the U.S. not covered..	8.6	8.0	7.5	7.2	7.1	6.0	4.8	4.5	5.0

[1] 2017 data is for individuals under 19 years of age.

Table MA-7. Employment Status by Demographic Group, 2018

(Numbers in thousands, percent.)

Characteristic	Civilian noninstitutional population	Civilian labor force		Employed		Unemployed	
		Number	Percent of population	Number	Percent of population	Number	Percent of population
Total...........................	5,624	3,819	67.9	3,689	65.6	130	3.4
Sex							
Male.............................	2,699	1,955	72.4	1,879	69.6	76	3.9
Female..........................	2,925	1,864	63.7	1,810	61.9	54	2.9
Race, Sex, and Hispanic Origin							
White...........................	4,584	3,109	67.8	3,010	65.7	99	3.2
Male.........................	2,185	1,595	73.0	1,534	70.2	62	3.9
Female.......................	2,399	1,514	63.1	1,476	61.5	38	2.5
Black or African American....	469	315	67.2	299	63.8	16	5.0
Male.........................	222	150	67.7	142	63.8	9	5.7
Female.......................	247	165	66.8	158	63.9	7	4.4
Hispanic or Latino ethnicity[1]	571	398	69.8	377	66.0	22	5.4
Male.........................	279	206	73.9	194	69.3	13	6.2
Female.......................	292	192	65.8	183	62.8	9	4.6
Age							
16 to 19 years................	313	110	35.1	96	30.6	14	12.7
20 to 24 years................	473	336	71.0	324	68.4	12	3.7
25 to 34 years................	1,052	903	85.9	874	83.1	29	3.2
35 to 44 years................	831	713	85.7	694	83.5	18	2.6
45 to 54 years................	947	797	84.2	774	81.7	23	2.9
55 to 64 years................	976	711	72.9	688	70.6	23	3.2
65 years and over.............	1,032	250	24.2	239	23.2	11	4.2

NOTE: Data in Table 7 are from the Current Population Survey (CPS) and do not match the estimates in Table 8. See notes and definitions for further information.
[1] May be of any race.

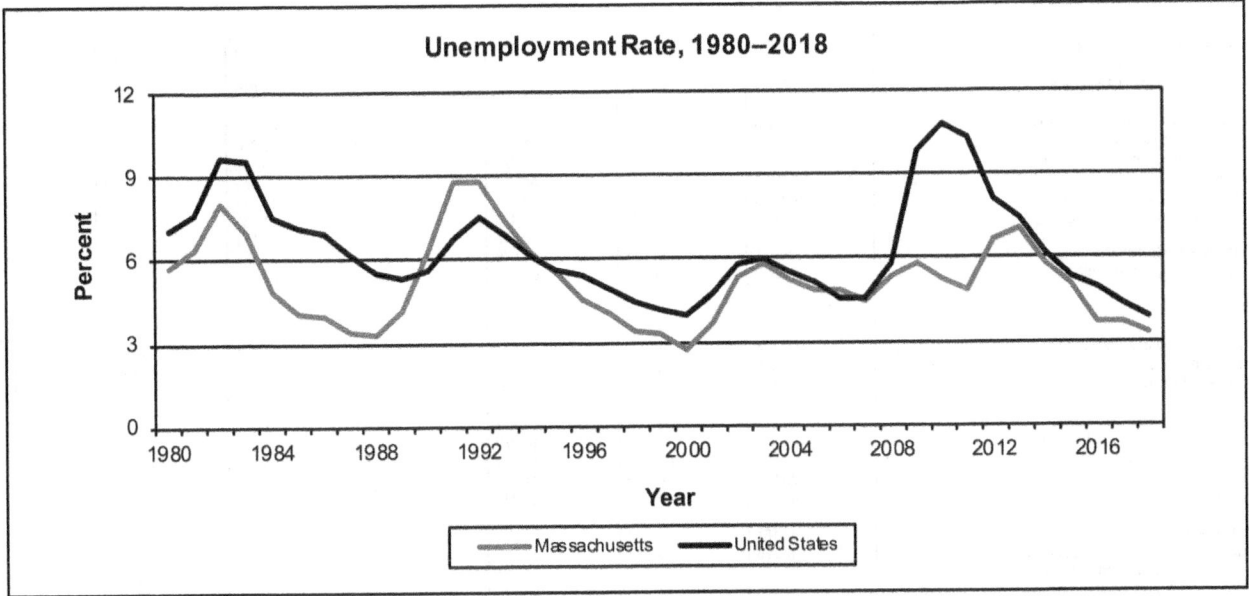

Table MA-8. Employment Status of the Civilian Noninstitutional Population Age 16 Years and Over

(Number, percent.)

Year	Civilian labor force	Civilian participation rate	Employed	Unemployed	Unemployment rate
2010..........	3,480,083	66.3	3,190,818	289,265	8.3
2011..........	3,469,308	65.5	3,217,754	251,554	7.3
2012..........	3,485,161	65.2	3,252,531	232,630	6.7
2013..........	3,512,827	65.0	3,276,792	236,035	6.7
2014..........	3,566,237	65.3	3,361,811	204,426	5.7
2015..........	3,588,241	65.2	3,415,874	172,367	4.8
2016..........	3,611,418	65.2	3,471,112	140,306	3.9
2017..........	3,657,173	65.5	3,521,482	135,691	3.7
2018..........	3,805,450	67.6	3,678,402	127,048	3.3

Table MA-9. Employment and Average Wages by Industry

(Estimates are based on the 2012 *North American Industry Classification System* [NAICS].)

Industry	2011	2012	2013	2014	2015	2016	2017
	Number of jobs						
Wage and Salary Employment by Industry.........................	3,338,324	3,420,747	3,474,851	3,541,525	3,610,422	3,674,544	3,719,842
Farm Wage and Salary Employment...............................	4,019	4,433	5,066	5,086	5,067	4,729	4,718
Nonfarm Wage and Salary Employment............................	3,334,305	3,416,314	3,469,785	3,536,439	3,605,355	3,669,815	3,715,124
Private wage and salary employment..............................	2,883,532	2,963,094	3,014,049	3,074,997	3,144,958	3,206,294	3,252,372
Forestry, fishing, and related activities........................	4,001	4,082	3,794	3,804	4,241	4,283	4,411
Mining..	1,002	866	886	931	984	995	998
Utilities..	10,451	10,267	10,056	10,683	10,478	10,750	11,345
Construction..	113,674	118,795	125,756	132,057	142,509	150,148	155,526
Manufacturing..	254,194	252,155	250,877	250,705	249,312	245,917	244,876
Durable goods manufacturing.................................	167,165	165,381	163,559	162,504	161,249	158,703	157,566
Nondurable goods manufacturing.............................	87,029	86,774	87,318	88,201	88,063	87,214	87,310
Wholesale trade	123,756	122,166	123,945	124,461	124,366	125,948	126,080
Retail trade..	345,877	348,519	349,842	351,989	355,737	357,947	357,605
Transportation and warehousing................................	74,052	75,478	77,461	80,756	83,769	86,032	89,712
Information	84,607	87,110	86,170	86,286	88,393	89,427	91,898
Finance and insurance	173,257	171,537	170,688	171,493	173,584	175,885	176,642
Real estate and rental and leasing.............................	41,127	42,007	42,976	43,688	44,862	46,241	47,264
Professional, scientific, and technical services	258,498	267,883	276,156	285,445	296,561	307,409	316,886
Management of companies and enterprises......................	58,632	63,320	64,315	63,553	65,262	65,663	67,545
Administrative and waste services..............................	163,166	165,090	169,291	173,016	178,042	181,947	184,767
Educational services	186,425	189,835	194,122	196,028	200,043	202,199	205,229
Health care and social assistance...............................	516,657	557,716	570,887	587,124	606,592	625,701	634,959
Arts, entertainment, and recreation............................	49,885	51,224	52,768	56,126	57,355	60,112	61,901
Accommodation and food services..............................	266,894	276,584	283,856	289,644	295,598	304,429	309,789
Other services, except public administration....................	157,377	158,460	160,203	167,208	167,270	165,261	164,939
Government and government enterprises	450,773	453,220	455,736	461,442	460,397	463,521	462,752
	Dollars						
Average Wages and Salaries by Industry	58,604	59,551	60,418	62,668	65,208	65,995	68,455
Average Farm Wages and Salaries	20,319	30,594	27,291	28,801	23,615	29,038	26,415
Average Nonfarm Wages and Salaries	58,650	59,589	60,467	62,717	65,267	66,043	68,508
Average private wages and salaries..............................	59,529	60,430	61,220	63,557	66,096	66,932	69,487
Forestry, fishing, and related activities........................	55,381	55,158	53,924	51,466	50,127	52,105	54,212
Mining..	57,109	57,637	58,369	62,006	65,063	68,340	68,096
Utilities..	109,938	107,855	107,734	110,017	111,654	111,359	125,368
Construction	63,252	65,167	66,425	68,657	71,081	72,698	75,377
Manufacturing	77,547	79,523	79,816	83,375	86,138	86,358	88,088
Durable goods manufacturing.................................	86,721	89,053	88,676	91,978	92,882	96,440	98,467
Nondurable goods manufacturing.............................	59,926	61,359	63,220	67,525	73,790	68,013	69,358
Wholesale trade	82,179	82,374	84,447	88,341	91,561	93,483	97,610
Retail trade..	27,906	28,321	28,920	30,072	31,369	32,368	33,531
Transportation and warehousing................................	45,484	46,529	46,717	48,371	50,048	50,924	51,593
Information	95,862	97,032	97,443	103,276	107,910	110,437	114,193
Finance and insurance	119,356	124,465	126,306	136,261	144,057	143,052	150,147
Real estate and rental and leasing.............................	63,202	66,484	69,829	72,759	73,244	74,656	76,834
Professional, scientific, and technical services	103,955	108,231	110,270	113,987	118,817	121,441	128,560
Management of companies and enterprises......................	123,026	115,721	118,770	126,648	140,155	130,775	131,718
Administrative and waste services..............................	39,804	41,049	41,119	42,262	44,277	45,426	47,122
Educational services	45,581	46,330	47,248	48,623	49,361	50,544	51,947
Health care and social assistance...............................	52,161	51,240	51,640	52,548	53,537	54,033	55,205
Arts, entertainment, and recreation............................	37,776	38,245	38,513	38,551	39,923	40,817	42,075
Accommodation and food services..............................	21,811	22,443	23,134	23,978	25,130	26,266	27,426
Other services, except public administration....................	31,840	32,846	33,343	34,127	35,356	36,731	37,845
Government and government enterprises	53,029	54,090	55,481	57,114	59,603	59,895	61,634

Table MA-10. Employment Characteristics by Family Type

(Number, percent.)

Family type and labor force status	2015		2016		2017	
	Total	Families with own children under 18 years	Total	Families with own children under 18 years	Total	Families with own children under 18 years
All Families...	1,613,404	684,676	1,633,661	683,699	1,652,214	673,731
FAMILY TYPE AND LABOR FORCE STATUS						
Married-Couple Families...................................	1,188,714	474,202	1,194,726	471,078	1,223,401	469,685
Both husband and wife in labor force.........................	57.7	72.5	58.6	74.9	57.5	73.4
Husband in labor force, wife not in labor force..........	18.1	22.0	17.3	20.1	17.9	20.7
Wife in labor force, husband not in labor force...........	7.7	3.4	7.7	3.3	7.7	3.6
Both husband and wife not in labor force....................	15.1	1.2	14.9	1.0	15.3	1.4
Other Families	424,690	210,474	438,935	212,621	428,813	204,046
Female householder, no husband present...................	75.2	80.4	73.6	76.5	74.0	79.0
In labor force...	53.7	66.2	52.1	62.2	51.8	64.3
Not in labor force..	21.5	14.3	21.6	14.3	22.2	14.7
Male householder, no wife present.............................	24.8	19.6	26.4	23.5	26.0	21.0
In labor force...	19.3	18.0	21.0	21.9	20.2	19.6
Not in labor force..	5.5	1.6	5.3	1.6	5.8	1.4

Table MA-11. School Enrollment and Educational Attainment, 2017

(Number, percent.)

Item	State	U.S.
Enrollment		
Total population 3 years and over, enrolled in school	1,714,245	81,273,337
Enrolled in nursery school or preschool (percent)	6.1	6.0
Enrolled in kindergarten (percent)...	4.4	4.9
Enrolled in elementary school, grades 1-8 (percent)...	35.4	40.6
Enrolled in high school, grades 9-12 (percent)	20.1	21.1
Enrolled in college or graduate school (percent)..	34.1	27.4
Attainment		
Total population 25 years and over	4,788,573	221,250,083
Less than ninth grade (percent)...	4.3	5.1
9th to 12th grade, no diploma (percent)..	4.9	6.9
High school graduate, including equivalency (percent)...	24.3	27.1
Some college, no degree (percent)...	15.5	20.4
Associate's degree (percent)..	7.5	8.5
Bachelor's degree (percent)	23.9	19.7
Graduate or professional degree (percent)..	19.5	12.3
High school graduate or higher (percent)	90.8	88.0
Bachelor's degree or higher (percent)	43.4	32.0

Table MA-12. Public School Characteristics and Educational Indicators

(Number, percent; data derived from National Center of Education Statistics.)

Item	State	U.S.
Public Elementary and Secondary Schools		
Number of operational school districts, 2016-17...	431	18,377
Number of operational schools, 2016-17..	1,856	98,330
Percent charter schools	4.2	7.1
Total public school enrollment, 2016-17..	964,514	50,587,859
Percent charter school enrollment	4.5	6.0
Student-teacher ratio, Fall 2015..	13.4	16.0
Expenditures per student (dollars), 2015-16...	16,986	11,841
Four-year adjusted cohort graduation rate (ACGR)[1]...	88.3	84.6
Students eligible for free or reduced-price lunch (percent), 2015-16...........................	39.9	52.1
English language learners (percent), Fall 2016..	9.0	9.6
Students age 3 to 21 served under IDEA, part B (percent), 2017-18	18.0	13.7
Public Schools by Type, 2016-17		Percent of state public schools
Total number of schools...	1,856	100.0
Special education	8	0.4
Vocational education	38	2.0
Alternative education...	21	1.1

[1] Adjusted Cohort Graduation Rates (ACGR) differ from Averaged Freshmen Graduation Rates (AFGR).

Table MA-13. Reported Voting and Registration of the Voting-Age Population, November 2018

(Numbers in thousands, percent.)

Item	Total population	Total citizen population	Registered			Voted		
			Total registered	Percent registered (total population)	Percent registered (total citizen population)	Total voted	Percent voted (total population)	Percent voted (total citizen population)
U.S. Total	249,748	228,832	153,066	61.3	66.9	122,281	49.0	53.4
State Total..	5,460	4,919	3,345	61.3	68.0	2,731	50.0	55.5
Sex								
Male	2,594	2,335	1,556	60.0	66.6	1,280	49.4	54.8
Female	2,866	2,583	1,789	62.4	69.3	1,451	50.6	56.2
Race								
White alone...................................	4,417	4,156	2,934	66.4	70.6	2,397	54.3	57.7
White, non-Hispanic alone..............................	4,006	3,858	2,737	68.3	70.9	2,266	56.6	58.7
Black alone..................................	454	413	240	52.8	58.0	194	42.7	47.0
Asian alone...................................	416	234	113	27.0	48.2	101	24.2	43.1
Hispanic (of any race).........................	565	414	249	44.1	60.2	177	31.3	42.7
White alone or in combination....................	4,584	4,266	2,993	65.3	70.2	2,437	53.2	57.1
Black alone or in combination....................	561	464	258	46.0	55.6	203	36.2	43.7
Asian alone or in combination....................	467	284	144	30.9	50.8	125	26.9	44.1
Age								
18 to 24 years................................	644	556	240	37.3	43.2	188	29.3	33.9
25 to 34 years................................	1,038	905	549	52.8	60.6	417	40.2	46.1
35 to 44 years................................	813	666	429	52.8	64.4	324	39.8	48.6
45 to 64 years................................	1,870	1,729	1,326	70.9	76.7	1,121	59.9	64.9
65 years and over.............................	1,095	1,063	801	73.2	75.4	681	62.2	64.1

Table MA-14. Crime

(Number, rate per 100,000. Data are derived from the FBI Uniform Crime Reports.)

Item	State			U.S.		
	2016	2017	Percent change	2016	2017	Percent change
TOTAL POPULATION[1]	6,823,721	6,859,819	0.5	323,405,935	325,719,178	0.7
VIOLENT CRIME						
Number..	25,975	24,560	-5.4	1,285,606	1,283,220	-0.2
Rate..	380.7	358.0	-5.9	397.5	394.0	-0.9
Murder and Nonnegligent Manslaughter						
Number..	135	173	28.1	17,413	17,284	-0.7
Rate..	2.0	2.5	27.5	5.4	5.3	-1.4
Rape[2]						
Number..	2,141	2,197	2.6	132,414	135,755	2.5
Rate..	31.4	32.0	2.1	40.9	41.7	1.8
Robbery						
Number..	5,365	4,871	-9.2	332,797	319,356	-4.0
Rate..	78.6	71.0	-9.7	102.9	98.0	-4.7
Aggravated Assault						
Number..	18,334	17,319	-5.5	802,982	810,825	1.0
Rate..	268.7	252.5	-6.0	248.3	248.9	0.3
PROPERTY CRIME						
Number..	106,430	98,575	-7.4	7,928,530	7,694,086	-3.0
Rate..	1,559.7	1,437.0	-7.9	2,451.6	2,362.2	-3.6
Burglary						
Number..	19,204	17,089	-11.0	1,516,405	1,401,840	-7.6
Rate..	281.4	249.1	-11.5	468.9	430.4	-8.2
Larceny-Theft						
Number..	79,155	73,946	-6.6	5,644,835	5,519,107	-2.2
Rate..	1,160.0	1,078.0	-7.1	1,745.4	1,694.4	-2.9
Motor Vehicle Theft						
Number..	8,071	7,540	-6.6	767,290	773,139	0.8
Rate..	118.3	109.9	-7.1	237.3	237.4	-

NOTE: Although arson data are included in the trend and clearance tables, sufficient data are not available to estimate totals for this offense. Therefore, no arson data are published in this table.
- = Zero or rounds to zero.
[1] Population figures are U.S. Census Bureau provisional estimates as of July 1, 2017.
[2] The figures shown in the rape (revised definition) column were estimated using the revised Uniform Crime Reporting (UCR) definition of rape.

Table MA-15. State Government Finances, 2017

(Dollar amounts in thousands, percent distribution.)

Item	Dollars	Percent distribution
Total Revenue	67,489,472	100.0
General revenue	54,786,749	81.2
Intergovernmental revenue	16,331,054	24.2
Taxes	27,518,360	40.8
General sales	6,240,822	9.2
Selective sales	2,577,525	3.8
License taxes	1,112,162	1.6
Individual income tax	14,724,277	21.8
Corporate income tax	2,196,474	3.3
Other taxes	667,100	1.0
Current charges	5,573,313	8.3
Miscellaneous general revenue	5,364,022	7.9
Utility revenue	926,211	1.4
Liquor stores revenue	0	-
Insurance trust revenue[1]	11,776,512	17.4
Total Expenditure	65,748,099	100.0
Intergovernmental expenditure	9,129,315	13.9
Direct expenditure	56,618,784	86.1
Current operation	40,678,206	61.9
Capital outlay	4,859,445	7.4
Insurance benefits and repayments	6,784,356	10.3
Assistance and subsidies	1,022,829	1.6
Interest on debt	3,273,948	5.0
Exhibit: Salaries and wages	7,084,206	10.8
Total Expenditure	65,748,099	100.0
General expenditure	55,701,753	84.7
Intergovernmental expenditure	9,129,315	13.9
Direct expenditure	46,572,438	70.8
General expenditure, by function:		
Education	13,179,277	20.0
Public welfare	22,403,061	34.1
Hospitals	718,405	1.1
Health	1,484,458	2.3
Highways	3,120,132	4.7
Police protection	922,066	1.4
Correction	954,978	1.5
Natural resources	257,190	0.4
Parks and recreation	202,643	0.3
Governmental administration	2,524,342	3.8
Interest on general debt	2,960,038	4.5
Other and unallocable	6,975,163	10.6
Utility expenditure	3,261,990	4.8
Liquor stores expenditure	0	-
Insurance trust expenditure	6,784,356	10.3
Debt at End of Fiscal Year	77,043,165	X
Cash and Security Holdings	105,140,487	X

X = Not applicable.
- = Zero or rounds to zero.
[1] Within insurance trust revenue, net earnings of state retirement systems is a calculated statistic (the item code in the data file is X08), and thus can be positive or negative. Net earnings is the sum of earnings on investments plus gains on investments minus losses on investments. The change made in 2002 for asset valuation from book to market value in accordance with Statement 34 of the Governmental Accounting Standards Board is reflected in the calculated statistics.

Table MA-16. State Government Tax Collections, 2018

(Dollars in thousands, percent.)

Item	Dollars	Percent distribution
Total Taxes	29,654,803	100.0
Property taxes	7,197	-
Sales and gross receipts	9,022,362	30.4
General sales and gross receipts	6,490,305	21.9
Selective sales and gross receipts	2,532,057	8.5
Alcoholic beverages	85,843	0.3
Amusements	70,467	0.2
Insurance premiums	406,251	1.4
Motor fuels	769,144	2.6
Pari-mutuels	887	-
Public utilities	X	-
Tobacco products	594,173	2.0
Other selective sales	605,292	-
Licenses	1,154,719	3.9
Alcoholic beverages	3,702	-
Amusements	15,767	0.1
Corporations in general	25,701	0.1
Hunting and fishing	5,637	-
Motor vehicle	444,827	1.5
Motor vehicle operators	101,432	0.3
Public utilities	X	-
Occupation and business, NEC	301,510	1.0
Other licenses	256,143	0.9
Income taxes	18,689,278	63.0
Individual income	16,280,331	54.9
Corporation net income	2,408,947	8.1
Other taxes	781,247	2.6
Death and gift	472,956	1.6
Documentary and stock transfer	308,291	1.0
Severance	X	-
Taxes, NEC	0	-

X = Not applicable.
- = Zero or rounds to zero.

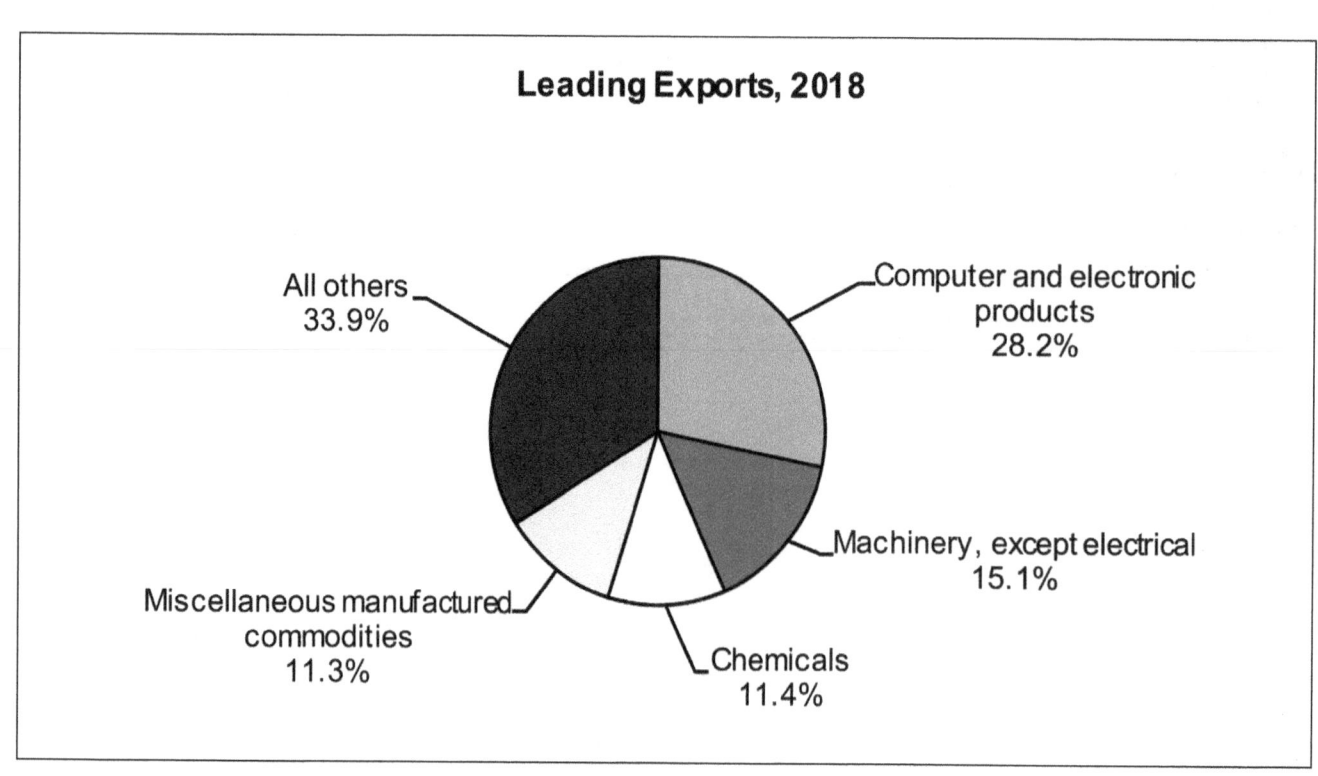

Leading Exports, 2018

All others 33.9%

Computer and electronic products 28.2%

Machinery, except electrical 15.1%

Chemicals 11.4%

Miscellaneous manufactured commodities 11.3%

MICHIGAN

Facts and Figures

Location: East north central United States; bordered on the N by Lake Superior, on the E by Ontario, Canada, and Lakes Huron and Erie, on the S by Indiana and Ohio, and on the W by Wisconsin and Lake Michigan

Area: 96,716 sq. mi. (250,494 sq. km.); rank—11th

Population: 9,995,915 (2018 est.); rank—10th

Principal Cities: capital—Lansing; largest—Detroit

Statehood: January 26, 1837; 26th state

U.S. Congress: 2 senators, 14 representatives

State Motto: *Si quaeris peninsulam amoenam, circumspice* ("If you seek a pleasant peninsula, look about you")

State Song: "Michigan, My Michigan"

State Nicknames: The Wolverine State; The Great Lakes State

Abbreviations: MI; Mich.

State Symbols: flower—apple blossom; tree—Eastern white pine; bird—robin

At a Glance

- With an increase in population of 1.1 percent, Michigan ranked 42nd among the states in growth from 2010 to 2018.

- In 2017, 5.2 percent of Michiganders did not have health insurance, compared to 8.7 percent of the total U.S. population.

- Michigan's violent crime rate in 2017 was 450.0 per 100,000 population, compared to the U.S. rate of 394.0 per 100,000 population.

- Approximately 14.2 percent of Michigan residents lived below the poverty level in 2017, compared to the national poverty rate of 13.4 percent.

- Michigan's unemployment rate of 4.1 percent ranked 16th in the nation in 2018.

Table MI-1. Population by Age, Sex, Race, and Hispanic Origin

(Number, percent, except where noted.)

Sex, age, race, and Hispanic origin	2000	2010	2018 [1]	Percent change, 2010–2018
Total Population...	9,938,444	9,883,640	9,995,915	1.1
Percent of total U.S. population	3.5	3.2	3.1	X
Sex				
Male...	4,873,095	4,848,114	4,922,143	1.5
Female	5,065,349	5,035,526	5,073,772	0.8
Age				
Under 5 years..	672,005	596,286	572,163	-4.0
5 to 19 years..	2,212,060	2,052,599	1,859,817	-9.4
20 to 64 years..	5,835,361	5,873,225	5,847,331	-0.4
65 years and over	1,219,018	1,361,530	1,716,604	26.1
Median age (years)	35.5	38.9	39.8	2.3
Race and Hispanic Origin				
One race				
White	7,966,053	7,949,497	7,923,927	-0.3
Black	1,412,742	1,416,067	1,408,392	-0.5
American Indian and Alaska Native	58,479	68,396	73,499	7.5
Asian..	176,510	243,062	337,336	38.8
Native Hawaiian or Other Pacific Islander	2,692	3,442	4,142	20.3
Two or more races	192,416	203,176	248,619	22.4
Hispanic (of any race)...	323,877	459,751	519,022	12.9

X = Not applicable.
- = Zero or rounds to zero.
[1] Population figures for 2018 are July 1 estimates. The 2010 estimates are taken from the 2010 Census.

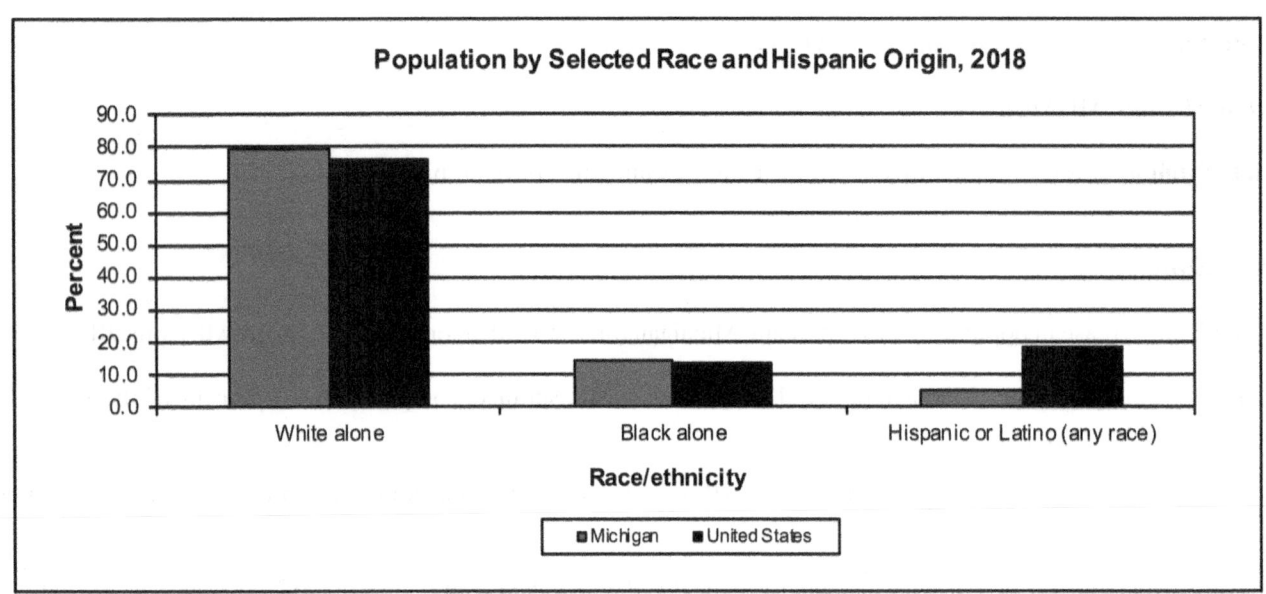

Table MI-2. Marital Status

(Number, percent distribution.)

Sex, age, race, and Hispanic origin	2000	2010	2017
Males, 15 Years and Over..	3,761,881	3,875,107	3,994,283
Never married	30.8	34.9	36.5
Now married, except separated...	56.1	50.5	49.2
Separated..	1.3	1.3	1.0
Widowed..	2.5	2.7	2.8
Divorced..	9.3	10.6	10.5
Females, 15 Years and Over..	4,013,722	4,099,384	4,186,302
Never married	25.0	29.0	30.5
Now married, except separated...	51.8	47.2	46.8
Separated..	1.6	1.6	1.4
Widowed..	10.4	9.7	8.8
Divorced..	11.2	12.5	12.5

Table MI-3. Households and Housing Characteristics

(Number, percent, dollars.)

Item	2000	2010	2017	Average annual percent change, 2010–2017
Total Households..	3,785,661	3,806,621	3,930,017	0.5
Family households..	2,575,699	2,508,780	2,518,003	0.1
Married-couple family.......................................	1,947,610	1,845,094	1,856,750	0.1
Other family...	627,989	663,686	661,253	-0.1
Male householder, no wife present...............	154,187	168,337	189,558	1.8
Female householder, no husband present.....	473,802	495,349	471,695	-0.7
Nonfamily households.......................................	1,209,962	1,297,841	1,412,014	1.3
Householder living alone.................................	993,607	1,090,126	1,162,080	0.9
Householder not living alone..........................	216,335	207,715	249,934	2.9
Housing Characteristics				
Total housing units...	4,234,279	4,531,231	4,595,274	0.2
Occupied housing units	3,785,661	3,806,621	3,930,017	0.5
Owner occupied..	2,793,124	2,769,474	2,803,372	0.2
Renter occupied..	992,537	1,037,147	1,126,645	1.2
Average household size....................................	2.56	2.53	2.48	-0.3
Financial Characteristics				
Median gross rent of renter-occupied housing	546	730	835	2.1
Median monthly owner costs for housing units with a mortgage	972	1,288	1,231	-0.6
Median value of owner-occupied housing units..........	115,600	123,300	155,700	3.8

Table MI-4. Migration, Origin, and Language

(Number, percent.)

Characteristic	State			U.S.		
	2016	2017	Percent change	2016	2017	Percent change
Residence 1 Year Ago						
Population 1 year and over	9,813,772	9,851,330	0.4	319,361,956	321,994,428	0.8
Same house	85.2	85.8	X	85.4	85.7	X
Different house in the U.S...............................	14.2	13.7	X	13.9	13.6	X
Same county	8.8	8.3	X	8.3	8.1	X
Different county	5.4	5.4	X	5.6	5.6	X
Same state	3.8	3.9	X	3.2	3.3	X
Different state	1.6	1.5	X	2.4	2.3	X
Abroad...	0.6	0.5	X	0.7	0.7	X
Place of Birth						
Native born	9,266,021	9,258,505	-0.1	279,388,170	281,193,323	0.6
Male	49.1	49.2	X	49.3	49.4	X
Female	50.9	50.8	X	50.7	50.6	X
Foreign born	662,279	703,806	6.3	43,739,345	44,525,855	1.8
Male	50.1	49.4	X	48.5	48.4	X
Female	49.9	50.6	X	51.5	51.6	X
Foreign born; naturalized U.S. citizen................	342,999	357,978	4.4	21,238,372	21,948,732	3.3
Male	48.5	47.4	X	45.9	45.9	X
Female	51.5	52.6	X	54.1	54.1	X
Foreign born; not a U.S. citizen.........................	319,280	345,828	8.3	22,500,973	22,577,123	0.3
Male	51.8	51.5	X	51	50.8	X
Female	48.2	48.5	X	49	49.2	X
Entered 2010 or later	26.0	30.1	X	18.6	21.3	X
Entered 2000 to 2009	25.0	24.5	X	26.7	25.7	X
Entered before 2000..	49.0	45.4	X	54.7	53.0	X
World Region of Birth, Foreign						
Foreign-born population, excluding population born at sea	662,202	703,806	6.3	43,738,901	44,525,458	1.8
Europe	20.2	19.1	X	10.9	10.8	X
Asia	51.0	51.6	X	30.8	31.2	X
Africa	4.1	5.3	X	4.9	5.1	X
Oceania	0.3	0.3	X	0.6	0.6	X
Latin America	19.1	18.5	X	51	50.4	X
North America	5.3	5.2	X	1.8	1.8	X
Language Spoken at Home and Ability to Speak English						
Population 5 years and over...................................	9,356,637	9,389,941	0.4	303,328,961	305,924,019	0.9
English only	90.5	90.1	X	78.4	78.2	X
Language other than English.............................	9.5	9.9	X	21.6	21.8	X
Speaks English less than "very well".................	3.5	3.4	X	8.6	8.5	X

NA = Not available.
X = Not applicable.
- = Zero or rounds to zero.

Table MI-5. Median Income and Poverty Status, 2017

(Number, percent, except as noted.)

Characteristic	State		U.S.	
	Number	Percent	Number	Percent
Median Income				
Households (dollars)...	54,909	X	60,336	X
Families (dollars)	69,664	X	73,891	X
Below Poverty Level (All People)	1,377,766	14.2	42,583,651	13.4
Sex				
Male	626,548	13.1	19,004,547	12.2
Female	751,218	15.1	23,579,104	14.5
Age				
Under 18 years..	419,449	19.7	13,353,202	18.4
Related children under 18 years...........................	408,553	19.3	13,053,472	18.1
18 to 64 years...	820,311	13.7	24,648,677	12.6
65 years and over	138,006	8.5	4,581,772	9.3

X = Not applicable.

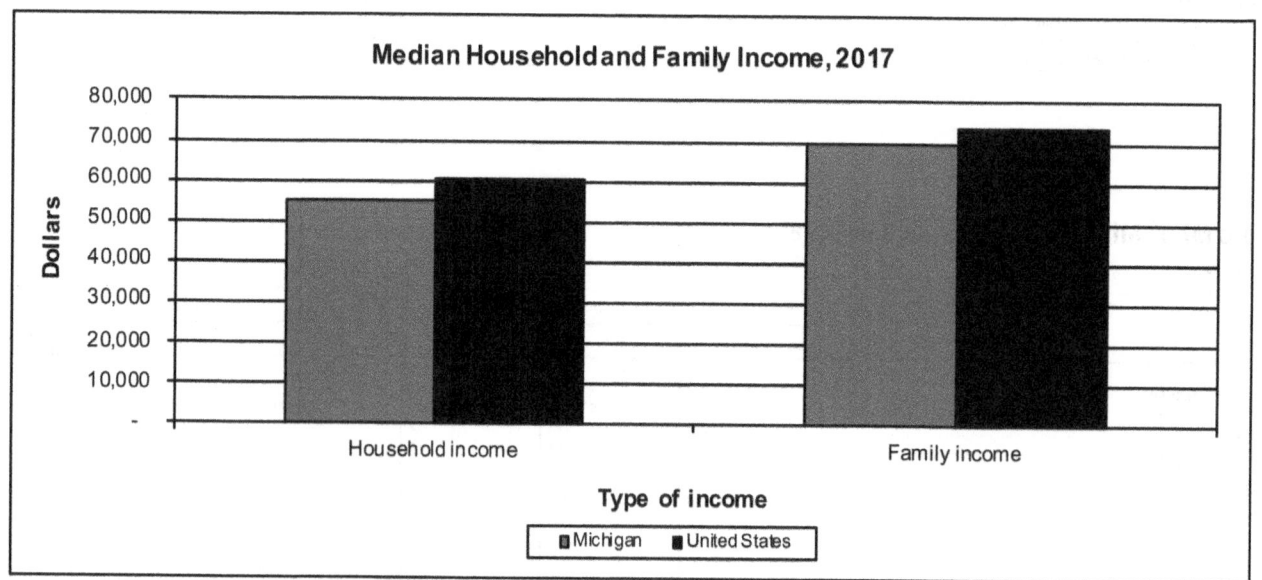

Table MI-6. Health Insurance Coverage Status for the Civilian Noninstitutionalized Population and Children Under 18 Years of Age

(Number, percent.)

Item	2009	2010	2011	2012	2013	2014	2015	2016	2017
Civilian Noninstitutionalized Population	9,834,865	9,763,683	9,762,306	9,772,550	9,784,451	9,798,621	9,810,800	9,818,099	9,853,156
Covered by Private or Public Insurance									
Number..	8,632,028	8,556,299	8,612,395	8,658,229	8,712,930	8,961,893	9,214,158	9,291,109	9,343,617
Percent..	87.8	87.6	88.2	88.6	89.0	91.5	93.9	94.6	94.8
Uninsured									
Number..	1,202,837	1,207,384	1,149,911	1,114,321	1,071,521	836,728	596,642	526,990	509,539
Percent..	12.2	12.4	11.8	11.4	11.0	8.5	6.1	5.4	5.2
Percent in the U.S. not covered...................................	15.1	15.5	15.1	14.8	14.5	11.7	9.4	8.6	8.7
Children Under 18 Years of Age[1]	2,342,793	2,331,475	2,289,531	2,263,671	2,240,003	2,219,940	2,204,443	2,187,554	2,312,692
Covered by Private or Public Insurance									
Number..	2,235,984	2,236,372	2,195,721	2,173,626	2,150,062	2,136,686	2,136,367	2,124,318	2,243,515
Percent..	95.4	95.9	95.9	96.0	96.0	96.2	96.9	97.1	97.0
Uninsured									
Number..	106,809	95,103	93,810	90,045	89,941	83,254	68,076	63,236	69,177
Percent..	4.6	4.1	4.1	4.0	4.0	3.8	3.1	2.9	3.0
Percent in the U.S. not covered...................................	8.6	8.0	7.5	7.2	7.1	6.0	4.8	4.5	5.0

[1] 2017 data is for individuals under 19 years of age.

Table MI-7. Employment Status by Demographic Group, 2018

(Numbers in thousands, percent.)

Characteristic	Civilian noninstitutional population	Civilian labor force		Employed		Unemployed	
		Number	Percent of population	Number	Percent of population	Number	Percent of population
Total...	7,981	4,903	61.4	4,699	58.9	203	4.1
Sex							
Male...	3,875	2,597	67.0	2,480	64.0	117	4.5
Female.....................................	4,106	2,306	56.2	2,219	54.1	87	3.8
Race, Sex, and Hispanic Origin							
White..	6,435	3,983	61.9	3,832	59.6	151	3.8
Male......................................	3,153	2,140	67.9	2,053	65.1	87	4.1
Female...................................	3,281	1,843	56.2	1,779	54.2	64	3.5
Black or African American............	1,062	609	57.4	571	53.7	39	6.4
Male......................................	479	287	59.9	266	55.5	21	7.5
Female...................................	583	322	55.3	305	52.3	17	5.4
Hispanic or Latino ethnicity[1].........	320	196	61.1	186	58.1	10	4.9
Male......................................	179	131	73.2	124	69.5	7	5.0
Female...................................	NA	NA	NA	NA	NA	NA	NA
Age							
16 to 19 years...........................	557	219	39.4	194	34.8	26	11.7
20 to 24 years...........................	635	481	75.8	443	69.7	38	8.0
25 to 34 years...........................	1,297	1,071	82.6	1,026	79.1	45	4.2
35 to 44 years...........................	1,139	927	81.4	900	79.0	27	2.9
45 to 54 years...........................	1,379	1,127	81.7	1,096	79.5	31	2.8
55 to 64 years...........................	1,331	801	60.2	776	58.3	25	3.2
65 years and over.......................	1,643	276	16.8	265	16.1	11	4.1

NOTE: Data in Table 7 are from the Current Population Survey (CPS) and do not match the estimates in Table 8. See notes and definitions for further information.
[1] May be of any race.

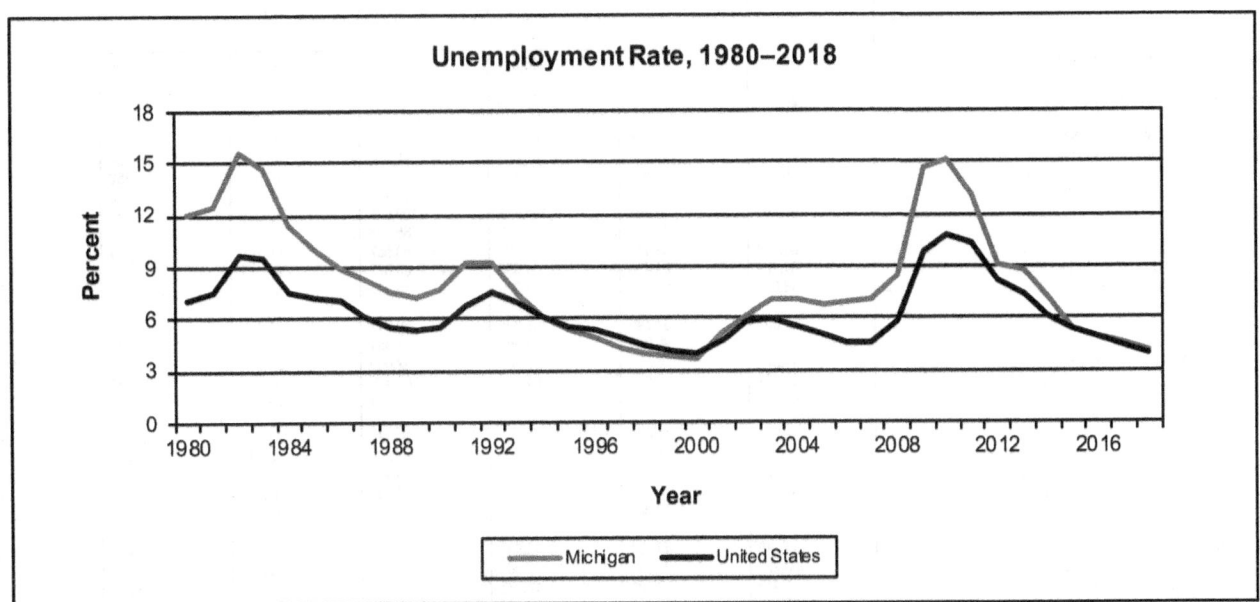

Unemployment Rate, 1980–2018

Table MI-8. Employment Status of the Civilian Noninstitutional Population Age 16 Years and Over

(Number, percent.)

Year	Civilian labor force	Civilian participation rate	Employed	Unemployed	Unemployment rate
2010..	4,798,954	62.0	4,194,041	604,913	12.6
2011..	4,685,164	60.5	4,198,349	486,815	10.4
2012..	4,672,695	60.0	4,246,658	426,037	9.1
2013..	4,723,945	60.4	4,308,030	415,915	8.8
2014..	4,753,626	60.6	4,409,394	344,232	7.2
2015..	4,751,234	60.4	4,493,447	257,787	5.4
2016..	4,840,281	61.2	4,599,266	241,015	5.0
2017..	4,883,815	61.5	4,657,272	226,543	4.6
2018..	4,902,069	61.4	4,698,845	203,224	4.1

Table MI-9. Employment and Average Wages by Industry

(Estimates are based on the 2012 *North American Industry Classification System* [NAICS].)

Industry	2011	2012	2013	2014	2015	2016	2017
	Number of jobs						
Wage and Salary Employment by Industry......................	4,026,177	4,101,235	4,179,314	4,254,464	4,326,978	4,403,195	4,450,757
Farm Wage and Salary Employment...............................	23,531	20,285	21,907	22,981	25,200	23,888	19,689
Nonfarm Wage and Salary Employment.......................	4,002,646	4,080,950	4,157,407	4,231,483	4,301,778	4,379,307	4,431,068
Private wage and salary employment...........................	3,371,314	3,461,164	3,546,556	3,625,384	3,697,754	3,770,111	3,817,777
Forestry, fishing, and related activities...............	7,561	7,885	8,019	8,841	8,733	8,844	8,774
Mining..	5,910	6,299	6,488	6,647	6,001	5,442	5,440
Utilities..	19,333	19,213	19,365	19,771	19,886	20,128	20,221
Construction	128,280	131,821	137,048	145,189	151,927	158,918	165,982
Manufacturing...	505,452	530,780	547,814	569,317	587,225	601,514	616,940
Durable goods manufacturing....................	375,328	398,359	412,355	429,988	444,244	453,043	465,504
Nondurable goods manufacturing..............	130,124	132,421	135,459	139,329	142,981	148,471	151,436
Wholesale trade	155,597	159,845	164,489	168,267	170,394	172,668	173,444
Retail trade..	451,579	452,893	458,347	463,520	470,246	475,776	477,144
Transportation and warehousing.....................	99,224	102,915	106,356	111,706	116,778	118,748	123,588
Information	55,937	56,177	57,915	60,548	59,398	59,691	56,720
Finance and insurance	139,208	143,731	147,348	148,015	149,836	153,793	157,815
Real estate and rental and leasing...................	51,340	49,205	50,570	51,416	52,223	53,548	55,161
Professional, scientific, and technical services	244,412	257,270	270,738	278,920	289,045	297,902	295,285
Management of companies and enterprises.........	50,856	52,109	54,692	55,222	56,447	58,820	66,206
Administrative and waste services..................	269,766	280,378	288,980	290,280	294,446	293,249	290,334
Educational services....................................	76,755	76,796	79,001	80,199	79,975	77,807	78,560
Health care and social assistance..................	546,186	557,068	561,965	564,568	575,466	590,800	597,455
Arts, entertainment, and recreation................	48,298	47,490	48,629	50,633	50,767	52,477	54,146
Accommodation and food services.................	332,349	343,664	351,819	358,738	364,933	375,190	380,854
Other services, except public administration.........	183,271	185,625	186,973	193,587	194,028	194,796	193,708
Government and government enterprises.....................	631,332	619,786	610,851	606,099	604,024	609,196	613,291
	Dollars						
Average Wages and Salaries by Industry	45,186	46,228	46,641	47,998	49,580	50,526	52,069
Average Farm Wages and Salaries	23,963	36,411	31,235	35,035	31,790	38,290	37,907
Average Nonfarm Wages and Salaries	45,311	46,276	46,723	48,069	49,684	50,592	52,132
Average private wages and salaries............................	45,221	46,211	46,688	48,099	49,830	50,794	52,421
Forestry, fishing, and related activities...............	25,076	25,802	27,178	27,683	29,663	31,352	32,479
Mining..	74,858	73,543	73,367	77,103	75,619	73,910	75,506
Utilities..	98,202	102,208	104,105	109,025	112,220	112,552	117,090
Construction	51,999	53,187	53,620	55,588	57,317	59,088	61,529
Manufacturing...	61,539	62,113	62,522	63,557	65,106	65,174	66,205
Durable goods manufacturing....................	64,484	64,479	64,898	65,872	67,441	67,389	68,333
Nondurable goods manufacturing..............	53,046	54,994	55,290	56,412	57,851	58,417	59,662
Wholesale trade	67,001	67,799	67,328	69,917	71,148	72,291	73,923
Retail trade..	26,026	26,398	26,508	27,351	28,511	29,225	30,108
Transportation and warehousing.....................	48,870	50,209	50,567	52,009	53,215	54,242	55,121
Information	62,031	62,077	64,329	65,440	67,887	69,531	70,832
Finance and insurance	63,953	66,388	68,194	70,864	73,988	75,787	77,812
Real estate and rental and leasing...................	36,009	37,630	38,258	39,689	42,286	43,734	45,355
Professional, scientific, and technical services	74,262	75,518	75,935	77,809	80,717	82,247	86,365
Management of companies and enterprises.........	113,268	116,214	110,684	119,947	122,438	124,357	132,243
Administrative and waste services..................	30,998	31,731	31,712	32,443	33,934	34,730	35,934
Educational services....................................	28,358	29,861	29,963	30,854	31,474	32,628	33,123
Health care and social assistance..................	44,415	44,951	45,527	46,451	48,168	48,775	49,479
Arts, entertainment, and recreation................	30,221	31,947	32,587	32,998	33,896	35,378	36,358
Accommodation and food services.................	16,412	16,835	17,073	17,584	18,576	19,244	20,117
Other services, except public administration.........	28,789	29,505	30,172	31,225	32,649	33,645	34,729
Government and government enterprises..................	45,792	46,640	46,924	47,887	48,791	49,343	50,335

Table MI-10. Employment Characteristics by Family Type

(Number, percent.)

Family type and labor force status	2015		2016		2017	
	Total	Families with own children under 18 years	Total	Families with own children under 18 years	Total	Families with own children under 18 years
All Families...	2,479,724	1,004,689	2,476,595	992,441	2,518,003	1,007,817
FAMILY TYPE AND LABOR FORCE STATUS						
Married-Couple Families...	1,821,803	658,920	1,819,434	652,348	1,856,750	667,073
Both husband and wife in labor force...	48.4	67.0	48.7	66.7	48.9	67.6
Husband in labor force, wife not in labor force	20.7	26.3	20.6	26.5	20.4	26.0
Wife in labor force, husband not in labor force	8.5	4.5	8.6	4.6	8.5	4.1
Both husband and wife not in labor force............................	22.1	2.0	21.6	1.9	21.6	1.8
Other Families	657,921	345,769	657,161	340,093	661,253	340,744
Female householder, no husband present............................	72.3	74.4	72.6	75.0	71.3	72.4
In labor force...	48.6	60.6	49.3	61.6	48.6	59.4
Not in labor force...	23.7	13.8	23.3	13.4	22.8	13.0
Male householder, no wife present............................	27.7	25.6	27.4	25.0	28.7	27.6
In labor force...	20.5	22.7	20.3	22.4	21.6	24.6
Not in labor force	7.2	2.9	7.1	2.7	7.1	3.1

Table MI-11. School Enrollment and Educational Attainment, 2017

(Number, percent.)

Item	State	U.S.
Enrollment		
Total population 3 years and over, enrolled in school	2,452,202	81,273,337
Enrolled in nursery school or preschool (percent)............................	5.8	6.0
Enrolled in kindergarten (percent)............................	4.9	4.9
Enrolled in elementary school, grades 1-8 (percent)............................	39.3	40.6
Enrolled in high school, grades 9-12 (percent)............................	21.9	21.1
Enrolled in college or graduate school (percent)............................	28.1	27.4
Attainment		
Total population 25 years and over	6,819,310	221,250,083
Less than ninth grade (percent)............................	2.8	5.1
9th to 12th grade, no diploma (percent)............................	6.3	6.9
High school graduate, including equivalency (percent)............................	28.9	27.1
Some college, no degree (percent)............................	23.4	20.4
Associate's degree (percent)............................	9.5	8.5
Bachelor's degree (percent)............................	17.6	19.7
Graduate or professional degree (percent)............................	11.5	12.3
High school graduate or higher (percent)............................	90.9	88.0
Bachelor's degree or higher (percent)............................	29.1	32.0

Table MI-12. Public School Characteristics and Educational Indicators

(Number, percent; data derived from National Center of Education Statistics.)

Item	State	U.S.
Public Elementary and Secondary Schools		
Number of operational school districts, 2016-17............................	899	18,377
Number of operational schools, 2016-17............................	3,458	98,330
Percent charter schools	10.9	7.1
Total public school enrollment, 2016-17............................	1,528,666	50,587,859
Percent charter school enrollment	10.0	6.0
Student-teacher ratio, Fall 2015	18.2	16.0
Expenditures per student (dollars), 2015-16............................	11,051	11,841
Four-year adjusted cohort graduation rate (ACGR)[1]............................	80.2	84.6
Students eligible for free or reduced-price lunch (percent), 2015-16............................	46.1	52.1
English language learners (percent), Fall 2016	6.2	9.6
Students age 3 to 21 served under IDEA, part B (percent), 2017-18	13.1	13.7

Public Schools by Type, 2016-17		Percent of state public schools
Total number of schools............................	3,458	100.0
Special education............................	180	5.2
Vocational education............................	4	0.1
Alternative education............................	323	9.3

[1] Adjusted Cohort Graduation Rates (ACGR) differ from Averaged Freshmen Graduation Rates (AFGR).

Table MI-13. Reported Voting and Registration of the Voting-Age Population, November 2018

(Numbers in thousands, percent.)

Item	Total population	Total citizen population	Registered			Voted		
			Total registered	Percent registered (total population)	Percent registered (total citizen population)	Total voted	Percent voted (total population)	Percent voted (total citizen population)
U.S. Total	249,748	228,832	153,066	61.3	66.9	122,281	49.0	53.4
State Total	7,657	7,430	5,453	71.2	73.4	4,418	57.7	59.5
Sex								
Male	3,688	3,564	2,563	69.5	71.9	2,072	56.2	58.1
Female	3,970	3,866	2,890	72.8	74.8	2,346	59.1	60.7
Race								
White alone	6,257	6,171	4,620	73.8	74.9	3,724	59.5	60.4
White, non-Hispanic alone	6,033	5,973	4,526	75.0	75.8	3,648	60.5	61.1
Black alone	1,027	1,003	670	65.2	66.8	557	54.2	55.5
Asian alone	242	134	91	37.5	67.9	72	29.9	54.1
Hispanic (of any race)	241	203	99	41.1	48.9	81	33.8	40.1
White alone or in combination	6,335	6,243	4,671	73.7	74.8	3,770	59.5	60.4
Black alone or in combination	1,078	1,048	690	63.9	65.8	571	53.0	54.5
Asian alone or in combination	265	157	114	43.0	72.7	96	36.1	61.0
Age								
18 to 24 years	841	825	455	54.1	55.1	279	33.2	33.9
25 to 34 years	1,300	1,249	823	63.3	65.9	589	45.3	47.2
35 to 44 years	1,152	1,077	793	68.8	73.6	625	54.3	58.1
45 to 64 years	2,733	2,673	2,071	75.8	77.5	1,733	63.4	64.8
65 years and over	1,631	1,605	1,311	80.4	81.7	1,190	73.0	74.1

Table MI-14. Crime

(Number, rate per 100,000. Data are derived from the FBI Uniform Crime Reports.)

Item	State			U.S.		
	2016	2017	Percent change	2016	2017	Percent change
TOTAL POPULATION[1]	9,933,445	9,962,311	0.3	323,405,935	325,719,178	0.7
VIOLENT CRIME						
Number	45,782	44,826	-2.1	1,285,606	1,283,220	-0.2
Rate	460.9	450.0	-2.4	397.5	394.0	-0.9
Murder and Nonnegligent Manslaughter						
Number	612	569	-7.0	17,413	17,284	-0.7
Rate	6.2	5.7	-7.3	5.4	5.3	-1.4
Rape[2]						
Number	7,268	7,031	-3.3	132,414	135,755	2.5
Rate	73.2	70.6	-3.5	40.9	41.7	1.8
Robbery						
Number	7,123	6,488	-8.9	332,797	319,356	-4.0
Rate	71.7	65.1	-9.2	102.9	98.0	-4.7
Aggravated Assault						
Number	30,779	30,738	-0.1	802,982	810,825	1.0
Rate	309.9	308.5	-0.4	248.3	248.9	0.3
PROPERTY CRIME						
Number	190,249	179,318	-5.7	7,928,530	7,694,086	-3.0
Rate	1,915.2	1,800.0	-6.0	2,451.6	2,362.2	-3.6
Burglary						
Number	39,738	35,641	-10.3	1,516,405	1,401,840	-7.6
Rate	400.0	357.8	-10.6	468.9	430.4	-8.2
Larceny-Theft						
Number	130,249	124,104	-4.7	5,644,835	5,519,107	-2.2
Rate	1,311.2	1,245.7	-5.0	1,745.4	1,694.4	-2.9
Motor Vehicle Theft						
Number	20,262	19,573	-3.4	767,290	773,139	0.8
Rate	204.0	196.5	-3.7	237.3	237.4	-

NOTE: Although arson data are included in the trend and clearance tables, sufficient data are not available to estimate totals for this offense. Therefore, no arson data are published in this table.
- = Zero or rounds to zero.
[1] Population figures are U.S. Census Bureau provisional estimates as of July 1, 2017.
[2] The figures shown in the rape (revised definition) column were estimated using the revised Uniform Crime Reporting (UCR) definition of rape.

Table MI-15. State Government Finances, 2017

(Dollar amounts in thousands, percent distribution.)

Item	Dollars	Percent distribution
Total Revenue	80,390,225	100.0
General revenue	63,998,679	79.6
Intergovernmental revenue	21,350,680	26.6
Taxes	28,628,517	35.6
General sales	9,223,737	11.5
Selective sales	4,473,004	5.6
License taxes	1,787,867	2.2
Individual income tax	9,485,325	11.8
Corporate income tax	1,195,399	1.5
Other taxes	2,463,185	3.1
Current charges	9,501,634	11.8
Miscellaneous general revenue	4,517,848	5.6
Utility revenue	0	-
Liquor stores revenue	1,082,256	1.3
Insurance trust revenue[1]	15,309,290	19.0
Total Expenditure	72,117,697	100.0
Intergovernmental expenditure	21,279,004	29.5
Direct expenditure	50,838,693	70.5
Current operation	37,254,365	51.7
Capital outlay	2,529,535	3.5
Insurance benefits and repayments	8,057,620	11.2
Assistance and subsidies	1,449,111	2.0
Interest on debt	1,548,062	2.1
Exhibit: Salaries and wages	9,900,659	13.7
Total Expenditure	72,117,697	100.0
General expenditure	63,187,306	87.6
Intergovernmental expenditure	21,279,004	29.5
Direct expenditure	41,908,302	58.1
General expenditure, by function:		
Education	25,890,299	35.9
Public welfare	18,791,853	26.1
Hospitals	4,385,477	6.1
Health	1,640,230	2.3
Highways	3,012,998	4.2
Police protection	501,930	0.7
Correction	1,894,849	2.6
Natural resources	369,721	0.5
Parks and recreation	154,384	0.2
Governmental administration	1,083,566	1.5
Interest on general debt	1,548,062	2.1
Other and unallocable	3,913,937	5.4
Utility expenditure	0	-
Liquor stores expenditure	872,771	1.2
Insurance trust expenditure	8,057,620	11.2
Debt at End of Fiscal Year	33,463,604	X
Cash and Security Holdings	90,783,251	X

X = Not applicable.
- = Zero or rounds to zero.
[1] Within insurance trust revenue, net earnings of state retirement systems is a calculated statistic (the item code in the data file is X08), and thus can be positive or negative. Net earnings is the sum of earnings on investments plus gains on investments minus losses on investments. The change made in 2002 for asset valuation from book to market value in accordance with Statement 34 of the Governmental Accounting Standards Board is reflected in the calculated statistics.

Table MI-16. State Government Tax Collections, 2018

(Dollars in thousands, percent.)

Item	Dollars	Percent distribution
Total Taxes	30,508,361	100.0
Property taxes	2,161,275	7.1
Sales and gross receipts	14,692,735	48.2
General sales and gross receipts	9,854,016	32.3
Selective sales and gross receipts	4,838,719	15.9
Alcoholic beverages	157,335	0.5
Amusements	124,677	0.4
Insurance premiums	395,999	1.3
Motor fuels	1,445,786	4.7
Pari-mutuels	2,903	-
Public utilities	42,471	0.1
Tobacco products	1,007,822	3.3
Other selective sales	1,661,726	5.4
Licenses	1,948,194	6.4
Alcoholic beverages	19,693	0.1
Amusements	X	-
Corporations in general	25,958	0.1
Hunting and fishing	48,618	0.2
Motor vehicle	1,322,630	4.3
Motor vehicle operators	58,228	0.2
Public utilities	34,678	0.1
Occupation and business, NEC	217,314	0.7
Other licenses	221,075	0.7
Income taxes	11,333,887	37.2
Individual income	10,238,864	33.6
Corporation net income	1,095,023	3.6
Other taxes	372,270	1.2
Death and gift	283	-
Documentary and stock transfer	340,570	1.1
Severance	31,417	0.1
Taxes, NEC	0	-

- = Zero or rounds to zero.
X = Not applicable.

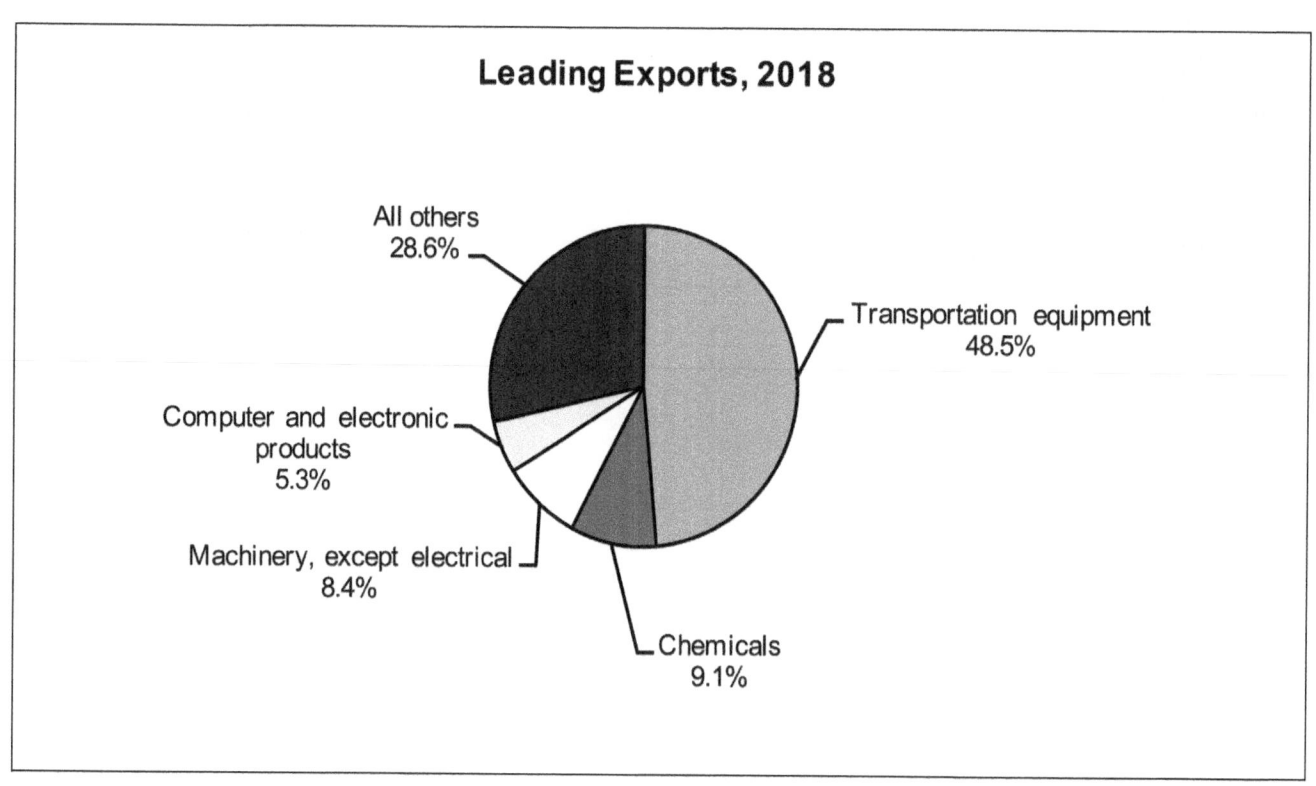

Leading Exports, 2018

All others 28.6%

Transportation equipment 48.5%

Computer and electronic products 5.3%

Machinery, except electrical 8.4%

Chemicals 9.1%

MINNESOTA

Facts and Figures

Location: North central United States; bordered on the N by Canada (Manitoba and Ontario), on the E by Lake Superior and Wisconsin, on the S by Iowa, and on the W by North Dakota and South Dakota

Area: 86,939 sq. mi. (225,171 sq. km.); rank—12th

Population: 5,611,179 (2018 est.); rank—22nd

Principal Cities: capital—St. Paul; largest—Minneapolis

Statehood: May 11, 1858; 32nd state

U.S. Congress: 2 senators, 8 representatives

State Motto: *L'Etoile du Nord* ("The Star of the North")

State Song: "Hail! Minnesota"

State Nicknames: The North Star State; The Land of 10,000 Lakes; The Gopher State

Abbreviations: MN; Minn.

State Symbols: flower—showy (pink and white) lady's slipper; tree—red (Norway) pine; bird—loon

At a Glance

- With an increase in population of 5.8 percent, Minnesota ranked 21st among the states in growth from 2010 to 2018.

- Minnesota's violent crime rate in 2017 was 238.3 per 100,000 population, compared to 394.0 for the entire nation.

- With a property crime rate of 2,191.5 per 100,000 population in 2017, Minnesota ranked 32nd in the nation.

- Minnesota's median household income was $68,388 in 2017, which ranked 13th among the states.

- In 2017, 9.5 percent of all Minnesotans and 11.8 percent of children in Minnesota lived below the poverty level, compared to 13.4 percent of the entire U.S. population and 18.4 percent of all U.S. children.

Table MN-1. Population by Age, Sex, Race, and Hispanic Origin

(Number, percent, except where noted.)

Sex, age, race, and Hispanic origin	2000	2010	2018 [1]	Percent change, 2010–2018
Total Population...	4,919,479	5,303,925	5,611,179	5.8
Percent of total U.S. population	1.7	1.7	1.7	X
Sex				
Male..	2,435,631	2,632,132	2,794,801	6.2
Female...	2,483,848	2,671,793	2,816,378	5.4
Age				
Under 5 years...	329,594	355,504	355,291	-0.1
5 to 19 years..	1,105,251	1,075,707	1,088,895	1.2
20 to 64 years...	2,890,368	3,189,593	3,277,191	2.7
65 years and over...	594,266	683,121	889,802	30.3
Median age (years)	35.4	37.4	38.1	1.9
Race and Hispanic Origin				
One race				
White	4,400,282	4,623,461	4,718,176	2.0
Black	171,731	280,949	380,414	35.4
American Indian and Alaska Native	54,967	67,325	76,616	13.8
Asian	141,968	217,792	288,975	32.7
Native Hawaiian or Other Pacific Islander	1,979	2,958	4,145	40.1
Two or more races	82,742	111,440	142,853	28.2
Hispanic (of any race)..	143,382	264,432	309,283	17.0

X = Not applicable.
- = Zero or rounds to zero.
[1] Population figures for 2018 are July 1 estimates. The 2010 estimates are taken from the 2010 Census.

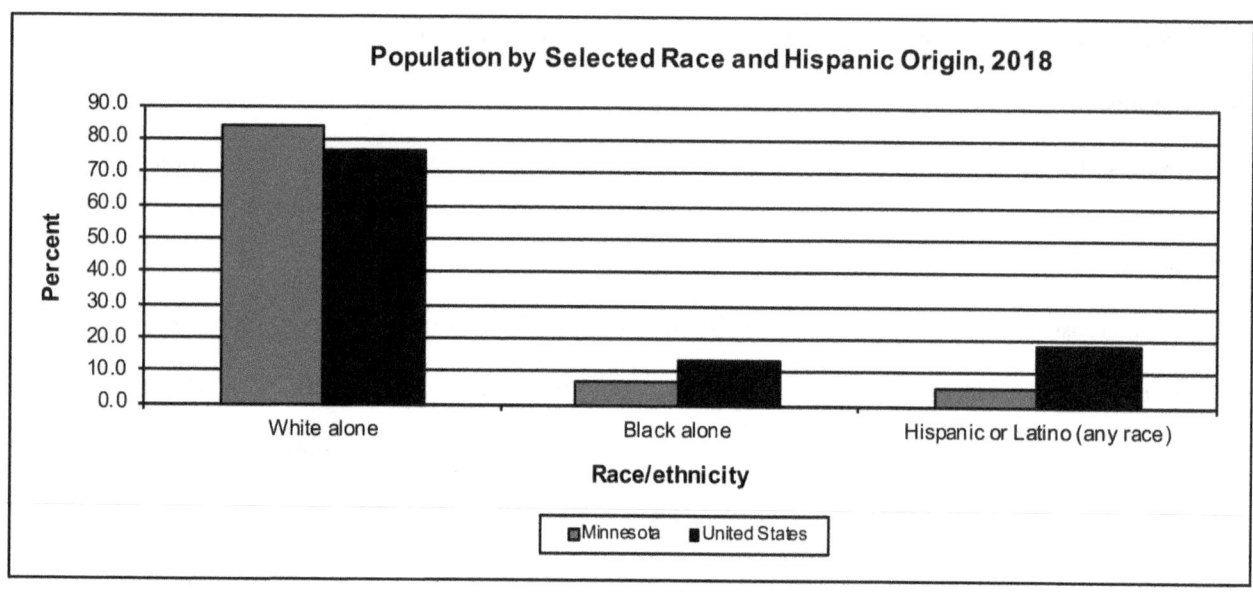

Population by Selected Race and Hispanic Origin, 2018

Table MN-2. Marital Status

(Number, percent distribution.)

Sex, age, race, and Hispanic origin	2000	2010	2017
Males, 15 Years and Over..	1,889,936	2,090,940	2,226,162
Never married	31.3	34.6	35.3
Now married, except separated...	57.7	53.5	52.6
Separated..	0.9	0.9	0.9
Widowed..	2.1	2.2	2.1
Divorced..	8.0	8.7	9.1
Females, 15 Years and Over...	1,967,819	2,155,042	2,267,124
Never married	25.0	28.2	29.0
Now married, except separated...	55.0	51.5	51.2
Separated..	1.2	1.2	1.0
Widowed..	9.4	8.4	7.6
Divorced..	9.5	10.7	11.2

Table MN-3. Households and Housing Characteristics

(Number, percent, dollars.)

Item	2000	2010	2017	Average annual percent change, 2010–2017
Total Households...	1,895,127	2,091,548	2,162,211	0.5
Family households	1,255,141	1,353,758	1,388,742	0.4
Married-couple family	1,018,245	1,069,000	1,106,647	0.5
Other family	236,986	284,758	282,095	-0.1
Male householder, no wife present	68,114	87,757	89,316	0.3
Female householder, no husband present	168,782	197,001	192,779	-0.3
Nonfamily households	639,986	737,790	773,469	0.7
Householder living alone	509,468	591,124	614,838	0.6
Householder not living alone	130,518	146,666	158,631	1.2
Housing Characteristics				
Total housing units...	2,065,946	2,348,242	2,437,726	0.5
Occupied housing units	1,895,127	2,091,548	2,162,211	0.5
Owner occupied	1,412,865	1,527,328	1,547,594	0.2
Renter occupied	482,262	564,220	614,617	1.3
Average household size...	2.52	2.47	2.52	0.3
Financial Characteristics				
Median gross rent of renter-occupied housing	566	764	939	3.3
Median monthly owner costs for housing units with a mortgage	1,044	1,503	1,500	-
Median value of owner-occupied housing units	122,400	194,300	224,000	2.2

- = Zero or rounds to zero.

Table MN-4. Migration, Origin, and Language

(Number, percent.)

Characteristic	State			U.S.		
	2016	2017	Percent change	2016	2017	Percent change
Residence 1 Year Ago						
Population 1 year and over	5,455,904	5,510,902	0.6	319,361,956	321,994,428	0.8
Same house	85.6	85.8	X	85.4	85.7	X
Different house in the U.S.	13.9	13.8	X	13.9	13.6	X
Same county	7.1	7.3	X	8.3	8.1	X
Different county	6.7	6.5	X	5.6	5.6	X
Same state	4.7	4.4	X	3.2	3.3	X
Different state	2.0	2.1	X	2.4	2.3	X
Abroad	0.6	0.4	X	0.7	0.7	X
Place of Birth						
Native born	5,067,516	5,090,363	0.2	279,388,170	281,193,323	0.6
Male	49.8	49.9	X	49.3	49.4	X
Female	50.2	50.1	X	50.7	50.6	X
Foreign born	452,436	486,243	6.1	43,739,345	44,525,855	1.8
Male	49.8	49.5	X	48.5	48.4	X
Female	50.2	50.5	X	51.5	51.6	X
Foreign born; naturalized U.S. citizen...............................	229,473	254,798	3.5	21,238,372	21,948,732	3.3
Male	47.9	46.8	X	45.9	45.9	X
Female	52.1	53.2	X	54.1	54.1	X
Foreign born; not a U.S. citizen	222,963	231,445	8.9	22,500,973	22,577,123	0.3
Male	51.8	52.4	X	51	50.8	X
Female	48.2	47.6	X	49	49.2	X
Entered 2010 or later	24.6	27.5	X	18.6	21.3	X
Entered 2000 to 2009	31.6	29.8	X	26.7	25.7	X
Entered before 2000..	43.7	42.7	X	54.7	53.0	X
World Region of Birth, Foreign						
Foreign-born population, excluding population born at sea	452,436	486,243	6.1	43,738,901	44,525,458	1.8
Europe	10.1	9.8	X	10.9	10.8	X
Asia..	37.4	37.2	X	30.8	31.2	X
Africa	23.8	27.7	X	4.9	5.1	X
Oceania	0.4	0.5	X	0.6	0.6	X
Latin America...	25.8	22.3	X	51	50.4	X
North America	2.4	2.5	X	1.8	1.8	X
Language Spoken at Home and Ability to Speak English						
Population 5 years and over	5,168,872	5,222,746	0.7	303,328,961	305,924,019	0.9
English only	88.4	88.1	X	78.4	78.2	X
Language other than English..	11.6	11.9	X	21.6	21.8	X
Speaks English less than "very well"...............................	4.6	4.7	X	8.6	8.5	X

NA = Not available.
X = Not applicable.
- = Zero or rounds to zero.

Table MN-5. Median Income and Poverty Status, 2017

(Number, percent, except as noted.)

Characteristic	State		U.S.	
	Number	Percent	Number	Percent
Median Income				
Households (dollars)..	68,388	X	60,336	X
Families (dollars)	86,416	X	73,891	X
Below Poverty Level (All People)	517,476	9.5	42,583,651	13.4
Sex				
Male	233,693	8.6	19,004,547	12.2
Female	283,783	10.4	23,579,104	14.5
Age				
Under 18 years..	149,926	11.8	13,353,202	18.4
Related children under 18 years...........................	143,559	11.3	13,053,472	18.1
18 to 64 years..	309,826	9.3	24,648,677	12.6
65 years and over	57,724	7.0	4,581,772	9.3

X = Not applicable.

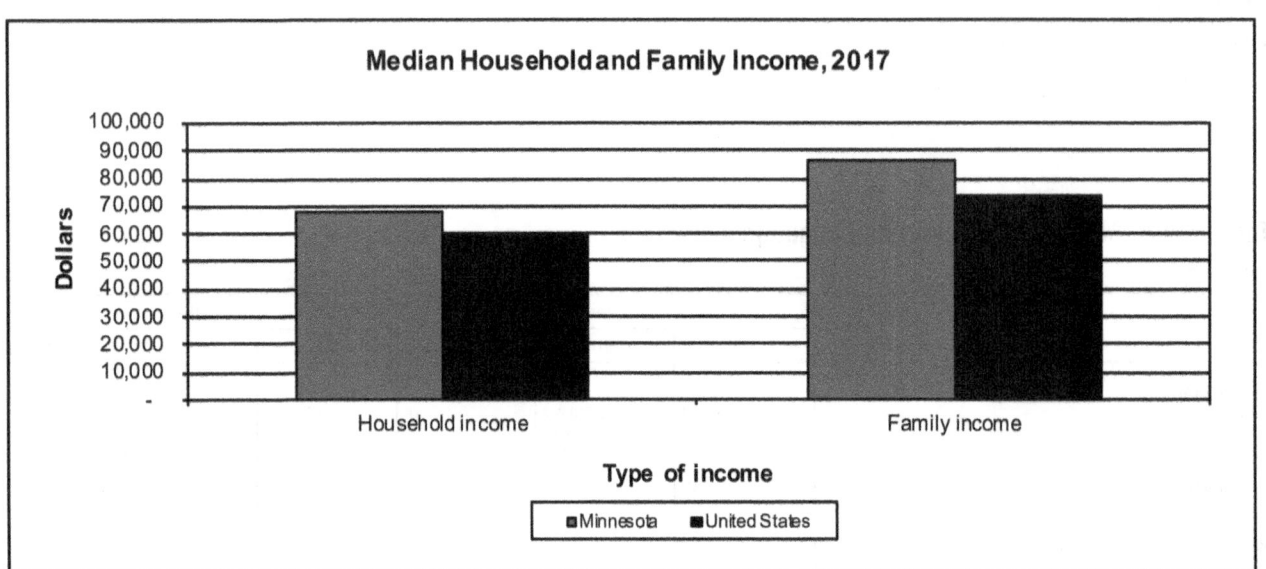

Table MN-6. Health Insurance Coverage Status for the Civilian Noninstitutionalized Population and Children Under 18 Years of Age

(Number, percent.)

Item	2009	2010	2011	2012	2013	2014	2015	2016	2017
Civilian Noninstitutionalized Population	5,196,720	5,252,092	5,286,728	5,319,783	5,362,681	5,398,211	5,431,894	5,462,438	5,519,199
Covered by Private or Public Insurance									
Number..	4,723,891	4,775,833	4,819,295	4,895,121	4,922,902	5,080,954	5,186,786	5,237,492	5,276,690
Percent..	90.9	90.9	91.2	92.0	91.8	94.1	95.5	95.9	95.6
Uninsured									
Number..	472,829	476,259	467,433	424,662	439,779	317,257	245,108	224,946	242,509
Percent..	9.1	9.1	8.8	8.0	8.2	5.9	4.5	4.1	4.4
Percent in the U.S. not covered...........................	15.1	15.5	15.1	14.8	14.5	11.7	9.4	8.6	8.7
Children Under 18 Years of Age[1]	1,255,596	1,281,022	1,276,035	1,275,509	1,280,236	1,280,791	1,280,978	1,286,323	1,372,988
Covered by Private or Public Insurance									
Number..	1,172,539	1,196,857	1,196,211	1,207,024	1,208,254	1,231,774	1,241,570	1,243,038	1,325,783
Percent..	93.4	93.4	93.7	94.6	94.4	96.2	96.9	96.6	96.6
Uninsured									
Number..	83,057	84,165	79,824	68,485	71,982	49,017	39,408	43,285	47,205
Percent..	6.6	6.6	6.3	5.4	5.6	3.8	3.1	3.4	3.4
Percent in the U.S. not covered...........................	8.6	8.0	7.5	7.2	7.1	6.0	4.8	4.5	5.0

[1] 2017 data is for individuals under 19 years of age.

Table MN-7. Employment Status by Demographic Group, 2018

(Numbers in thousands, percent.)

Characteristic	Civilian noninstitutional population	Civilian labor force		Employed		Unemployed	
		Number	Percent of population	Number	Percent of population	Number	Percent of population
Total..	4,410	3,073	69.7	2,986	67.7	88	2.8
Sex							
Male	2,179	1,594	73.2	1,540	70.7	55	3.4
Female	2,232	1,479	66.3	1,446	64.8	33	2.2
Race, Sex, and Hispanic Origin							
White	3,796	2,663	70.2	2,596	68.4	68	2.5
Male	1,880	1,386	73.7	1,343	71.4	43	3.1
Female	1,916	1,277	66.7	1,253	65.4	25	1.9
Black or African American..........	256	182	70.9	171	66.8	11	5.8
Male	NA	NA	NA	NA	NA	NA	NA
Female	NA	NA	NA	NA	NA	NA	NA
Hispanic or Latino ethnicity[1]	201	145	72.0	138	68.9	6	4.2
Male	NA	NA	NA	NA	NA	NA	NA
Female	NA	NA	NA	NA	NA	NA	NA
Age							
16 to 19 years	300	152	50.7	144	48.0	8	5.4
20 to 24 years	323	238	73.7	227	70.3	11	4.7
25 to 34 years	780	684	87.7	660	84.6	24	3.5
35 to 44 years	700	616	88.0	599	85.5	17	2.8
45 to 54 years	696	610	87.6	601	86.2	9	1.5
55 to 64 years	768	570	74.3	557	72.6	13	2.3
65 years and over	843	203	24.1	199	23.5	4	2.1

NOTE: Data in Table 7 are from the Current Population Survey (CPS) and do not match the estimates in Table 8. See notes and definitions for further information.
[1] May be of any race.
NA = Not available.

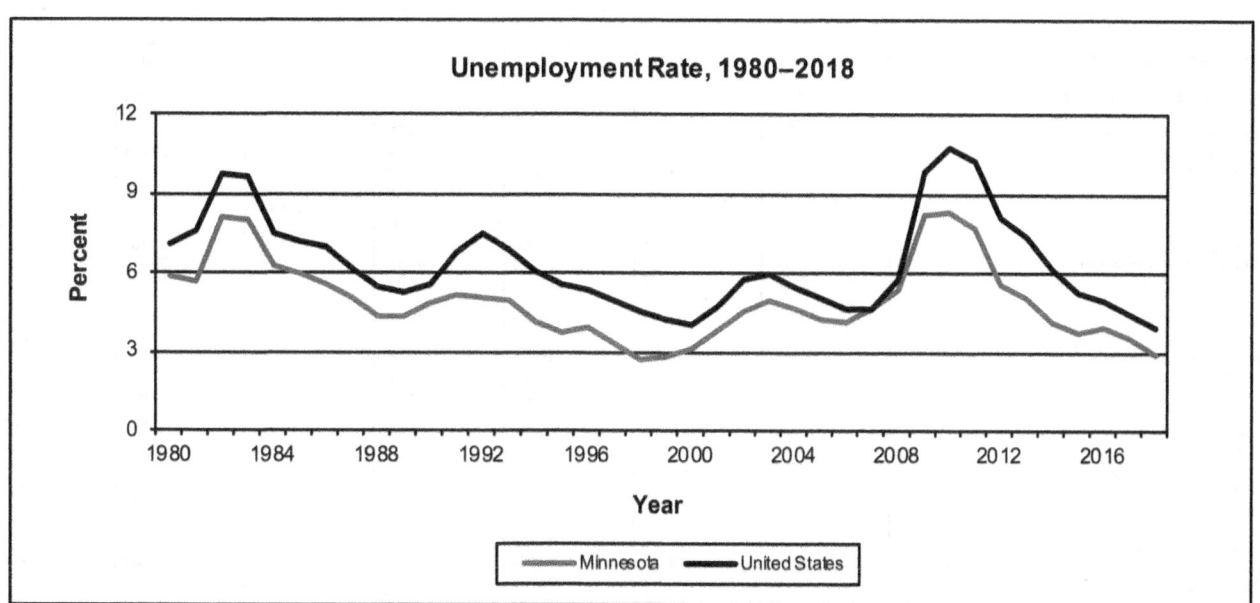

Unemployment Rate, 1980–2018

Table MN-8. Employment Status of the Civilian Noninstitutional Population Age 16 Years and Over

(Number, percent.)

Year	Civilian labor force	Civilian participation rate	Employed	Unemployed	Unemployment rate
2010..................................	2,938,795	71.4	2,721,194	217,601	7.4
2011..................................	2,946,279	71.0	2,755,264	191,015	6.5
2012..................................	2,946,356	70.4	2,781,141	165,215	5.6
2013..................................	2,958,596	70.1	2,811,762	146,834	5.0
2014..................................	2,973,073	69.9	2,849,017	124,056	4.2
2015..................................	2,998,352	70.0	2,887,683	110,669	3.7
2016..................................	3,036,278	70.3	2,919,097	117,181	3.9
2017..................................	3,063,604	70.2	2,957,838	105,766	3.5
2018..................................	3,070,224	69.9	2,980,885	89,339	2.9

Table MN-9. Employment and Average Wages by Industry

(Estimates are based on the 2012 *North American Industry Classification System* [NAICS].)

Industry	2011	2012	2013	2014	2015	2016	2017
	Number of jobs						
Wage and Salary Employment by Industry........................	2,747,346	2,789,630	2,833,384	2,873,671	2,923,387	2,956,259	2,993,016
Farm Wage and Salary Employment...............................	16,871	17,591	15,781	14,250	17,516	15,629	14,372
Nonfarm Wage and Salary Employment..........................	2,730,475	2,772,039	2,817,603	2,859,421	2,905,871	2,940,630	2,978,644
Private wage and salary employment..........................	2,315,281	2,355,209	2,400,023	2,439,900	2,484,119	2,517,643	2,549,805
Forestry, fishing, and related activities.......................	5,646	5,786	5,931	6,024	6,349	6,319	6,394
Mining...	5,810	6,247	6,219	6,370	6,164	5,364	5,735
Utilities...	12,804	12,707	13,012	12,863	12,787	12,506	12,365
Construction...	94,171	97,561	103,303	110,288	118,035	118,934	122,517
Manufacturing...	301,242	305,822	307,551	312,306	317,562	317,743	319,342
Durable goods manufacturing..............................	190,190	194,460	195,244	198,796	202,763	201,568	201,543
Nondurable goods manufacturing.........................	111,052	111,362	112,307	113,510	114,799	116,175	117,799
Wholesale trade	126,373	129,028	131,002	132,434	133,441	132,365	132,904
Retail trade	282,356	284,992	288,449	290,302	295,140	300,057	300,353
Transportation and warehousing...............................	79,679	79,915	81,017	84,145	86,677	89,201	93,829
Information	53,826	53,788	53,354	52,715	51,801	50,471	50,343
Finance and insurance..	141,298	141,737	144,250	142,018	145,230	144,212	148,179
Real estate and rental and leasing...........................	36,561	39,793	40,541	39,814	40,067	35,163	35,368
Professional, scientific, and technical services	128,816	131,487	136,866	142,057	146,753	159,537	160,647
Management of companies and enterprises..................	72,685	74,804	77,025	78,753	78,193	78,539	80,109
Administrative and waste services............................	130,202	132,747	133,859	134,589	135,137	136,995	134,942
Educational services	70,395	70,305	71,353	71,779	73,374	73,845	74,390
Health care and social assistance............................	398,122	408,255	421,144	428,762	437,733	451,246	462,523
Arts, entertainment, and recreation..........................	38,132	39,184	39,821	41,508	42,073	43,559	45,825
Accommodation and food services...........................	203,239	207,756	211,853	215,110	218,979	223,638	226,752
Other services, except public administration................	133,924	133,295	133,473	138,063	138,624	137,949	137,288
Government and government enterprises......................	415,194	416,830	417,580	419,521	421,752	422,987	428,839
	Dollars						
Average Wages and Salaries by Industry	46,948	48,513	49,258	50,759	52,611	53,460	55,310
Average Farm Wages and Salaries	24,614	38,798	31,962	35,874	32,212	39,843	38,819
Average Nonfarm Wages and Salaries	47,086	48,575	49,355	50,833	52,734	53,533	55,389
Average private wages and salaries...........................	47,673	49,361	50,105	51,602	53,601	54,303	56,365
Forestry, fishing, and related activities......................	26,869	28,575	28,965	29,394	30,746	32,471	33,376
Mining...	81,393	82,202	84,167	85,443	79,646	78,727	84,829
Utilities..	90,387	92,771	97,246	99,314	102,120	104,112	107,561
Construction	53,463	55,582	57,332	58,950	61,519	63,271	65,467
Manufacturing...	57,522	58,741	59,555	61,096	63,256	63,760	65,731
Durable goods manufacturing..............................	61,813	63,099	64,219	65,804	67,881	68,161	70,303
Nondurable goods manufacturing.........................	50,174	51,131	51,447	52,850	55,087	56,125	57,908
Wholesale trade	71,767	74,413	75,995	76,985	79,117	78,961	83,308
Retail trade...	24,869	25,382	25,970	27,215	28,235	28,815	29,513
Transportation and warehousing...............................	46,159	48,086	48,374	50,238	51,247	52,538	53,053
Information	66,100	65,012	66,769	69,447	72,050	72,019	75,483
Finance and insurance..	82,044	89,512	88,624	92,787	96,809	95,689	100,079
Real estate and rental and leasing...........................	46,890	51,846	53,617	55,046	58,217	50,221	51,800
Professional, scientific, and technical services	76,217	79,033	81,015	83,875	85,984	90,119	91,695
Management of companies and enterprises..................	109,610	112,152	112,836	115,301	120,493	119,059	125,055
Administrative and waste services............................	31,645	32,344	32,271	33,895	35,996	38,245	41,339
Educational services	29,380	30,190	30,140	30,746	30,931	31,215	31,695
Health care and social assistance............................	43,487	44,690	44,937	45,851	48,030	49,005	50,481
Arts, entertainment, and recreation..........................	31,619	31,456	32,284	32,425	34,035	34,692	35,635
Accommodation and food services...........................	16,550	17,104	17,493	18,240	19,426	20,382	21,342
Other services, except public administration................	27,932	28,936	29,991	30,973	32,240	33,063	34,938
Government and government enterprises......................	43,817	44,136	45,044	46,364	47,629	48,950	49,589

Table MN-10. Employment Characteristics by Family Type

(Number, percent.)

Family type and labor force status	2015		2016		2017	
	Total	Families with own children under 18 years	Total	Families with own children under 18 years	Total	Families with own children under 18 years
All Families...	1,383,950	613,580	1,367,104	608,671	1,388,742	610,127
FAMILY TYPE AND LABOR FORCE STATUS						
Married-Couple Families..............................	1,091,358	433,140	1,081,567	435,650	1,106,647	443,523
Both husband and wife in labor force.............................	60.1	77.3	60.6	77.8	59.0	76.8
Husband in labor force, wife not in labor force	15.9	18.2	15.1	17.3	16.1	18.2
Wife in labor force, husband not in labor force	7.2	3.2	6.9	3.3	7.4	3.6
Both husband and wife not in labor force...............................	16.1	0.9	16.6	1.2	16.6	0.9
Other Families	292,592	180,440	285,537	173,021	282,095	166,604
Female householder, no husband present........................	67.4	69.8	66.9	69.2	68.3	70.0
In labor force...	52.4	60.4	51.4	59.5	53.4	62.6
Not in labor force	15.1	9.4	15.5	9.7	14.9	7.5
Male householder, no wife present...........................	32.6	30.2	33.1	30.8	31.7	30.0
In labor force...	27.8	28.1	28.5	29.3	27.1	28.2
Not in labor force	4.7	2.1	4.6	1.5	4.6	1.8

Table MN-11. School Enrollment and Educational Attainment, 2017

(Number, percent.)

Item	State	U.S.
Enrollment		
Total population 3 years and over, enrolled in school	1,404,105	81,273,337
Enrolled in nursery school or preschool (percent)	6.8	6.0
Enrolled in kindergarten (percent)...	5.1	4.9
Enrolled in elementary school, grades 1-8 (percent).................................	41.2	40.6
Enrolled in high school, grades 9-12 (percent)....................................	21.2	21.1
Enrolled in college or graduate school (percent).................................	25.7	27.4
Attainment		
Total population 25 years and over	3,778,416	221,250,083
Less than ninth grade (percent)..	3.0	5.1
9th to 12th grade, no diploma (percent)....................................	3.9	6.9
High school graduate, including equivalency (percent).........................	24.8	27.1
Some college, no degree (percent)	20.9	20.4
Associate's degree (percent)..	11.3	8.5
Bachelor's degree (percent)...	23.5	19.7
Graduate or professional degree (percent)...................................	12.5	12.3
High school graduate or higher (percent).......................................	93.1	88.0
Bachelor's degree or higher (percent)...	36.1	32.0

Table MN-12. Public School Characteristics and Educational Indicators

(Number, percent; data derived from National Center of Education Statistics.)

Item	State	U.S.
Public Elementary and Secondary Schools		
Number of operational school districts, 2016-17	567	18,377
Number of operational schools, 2016-17...	2,513	98,330
Percent charter schools	8.8	7.1
Total public school enrollment, 2016-17..	875,021	50,587,859
Percent charter school enrollment	6.2	6.0
Student-teacher ratio, Fall 2015..	15.4	16.0
Expenditures per student (dollars), 2015-16.....................................	12,364	11,841
Four-year adjusted cohort graduation rate (ACGR)[1]	82.7	84.6
Students eligible for free or reduced-price lunch (percent), 2015-16.................	38.1	52.1
English language learners (percent), Fall 2016	8.2	9.6
Students age 3 to 21 served under IDEA, part B (percent), 2017-18	15.3	13.7

Public Schools by Type, 2016-17		Percent of state public schools
Total number of schools...	2,513	100.0
Special education..	306	12.2
Vocational education..	8	0.3
Alternative education...	500	19.9

[1] Adjusted Cohort Graduation Rates (ACGR) differ from Averaged Freshmen Graduation Rates (AFGR).

Table MN-13. Reported Voting and Registration of the Voting-Age Population, November 2018

(Numbers in thousands, percent.)

Item	Total population	Total citizen population	Registered			Voted		
			Total registered	Percent registered (total population)	Percent registered (total citizen population)	Total voted	Percent voted (total population)	Percent voted (total citizen population)
U.S. Total	249,748	228,832	153,066	61.3	66.9	122,281	49.0	53.4
State Total...................................	4,238	4,006	3,000	70.8	74.9	2,523	59.5	63.0
Sex								
Male	2,099	1,969	1,429	68.1	72.6	1,194	56.9	60.7
Female	2,139	2,037	1,570	73.4	77.1	1,329	62.1	65.2
Race								
White alone...................................	3,632	3,537	2,727	75.1	77.1	2,286	62.9	64.7
White, non-Hispanic alone.................	3,485	3,471	2,683	77.0	77.3	2,249	64.5	64.8
Black alone...................................	252	194	128	50.8	66.1	106	42.1	54.7
Asian alone...................................	225	157	78	34.6	49.7	68	30.2	43.3
Hispanic (of any race)......................	156	65	44	28.2	(B)	37	23.8	(B)
White alone or in combination..............	3,698	3,593	2,772	75.0	77.2	2,327	62.9	64.8
Black alone or in combination..............	287	219	153	53.5	70.0	127	44.5	58.2
Asian alone or in combination.............	241	172	93	38.7	54.1	83	34.5	48.2
Age								
18 to 24 years...............................	440	410	210	47.8	51.2	175	39.9	42.7
25 to 34 years...............................	795	696	434	54.7	62.4	330	41.5	47.4
35 to 44 years...............................	692	653	502	72.5	76.9	419	60.6	64.2
45 to 64 years...............................	1,519	1,461	1,155	76.0	79.0	981	64.6	67.1
65 years and over...........................	793	785	699	88.1	89.0	618	77.9	78.7

B = Base is less than 75,000 and therefore too small to show the derived measure.

Table MN-14. Crime

(Number, rate per 100,000. Data are derived from the FBI Uniform Crime Reports.)

Item	State [1]			U.S.		
	2016	2017	Percent change	2016	2017	Percent change
TOTAL POPULATION[1]	5,525,050	5,576,606	0.9	323,405,935	325,719,178	0.7
VIOLENT CRIME						
Number..	13,365	13,291	-0.6	1,285,606	1,283,220	-0.2
Rate	241.9	238.3	-1.5	397.5	394.0	-0.9
Murder and Nonnegligent Manslaughter						
Number..	101	113	11.9	17,413	17,284	-0.7
Rate	1.8	2.0	10.8	5.4	5.3	-1.4
Rape[2]						
Number..	2,349	2,385	1.5	132,414	135,755	2.5
Rate	42.5	42.8	0.6	40.9	41.7	1.8
Robbery						
Number..	3,730	3,621	-2.9	332,797	319,356	-4.0
Rate	67.5	64.9	-3.8	102.9	98.0	-4.7
Aggravated Assault						
Number..	7,185	7,172	-0.2	802,982	810,825	1.0
Rate	130.0	128.6	-1.1	248.3	248.9	0.3
PROPERTY CRIME						
Number..	117,723	122,212	3.8	7,928,530	7,694,086	-3.0
Rate	2,130.7	2,191.5	2.9	2,451.6	2,362.2	-3.6
Burglary						
Number..	18,582	18,787	1.1	1,516,405	1,401,840	-7.6
Rate	336.3	336.9	0.2	468.9	430.4	-8.2
Larceny-Theft						
Number..	90,421	93,446	3.3	5,644,835	5,519,107	-2.2
Rate	1,636.6	1,675.7	2.4	1,745.4	1,694.4	-2.9
Motor Vehicle Theft						
Number..	8,720	9,979	14.4	767,290	773,139	0.8
Rate	157.8	178.9	13.4	237.3	237.4	-

NOTE: Although arson data are included in the trend and clearance tables, sufficient data are not available to estimate totals for this offense. Therefore, no arson data are published in this table.
- = Zero or rounds to zero.
[1] Population figures are U.S. Census Bureau provisional estimates as of July 1, 2017.
[2] The figures shown in the rape (revised definition) column were estimated using the revised Uniform Crime Reporting (UCR) definition of rape.

Table MN-15. State Government Finances, 2017

(Dollar amounts in thousands, percent distribution.)

Item	Dollars	Percent distribution
Total Revenue	53,870,383	100.0
General revenue	41,353,995	76.8
Intergovernmental revenue	10,939,218	20.3
Taxes..	25,594,522	47.5
General sales..	5,888,795	10.9
Selective sales...	4,718,840	8.8
License taxes...	1,477,319	2.7
Individual income tax...	10,956,205	20.3
Corporate income tax...	1,227,028	2.3
Other taxes..	1,326,335	2.5
Current charges	2,704,967	5.0
Miscellaneous general revenue	2,115,288	3.9
Utility revenue...	104,120	0.2
Liquor stores revenue...	0	-
Insurance trust revenue[1]	12,412,268	23.0
Total Expenditure	47,309,258	100.0
Intergovernmental expenditure	13,546,867	28.6
Direct expenditure..	33,762,391	71.4
Current operation..	24,615,533	52.0
Capital outlay	1,847,895	3.9
Insurance benefits and repayments	5,534,021	11.7
Assistance and subsidies..	1,194,529	2.5
Interest on debt..	570,413	1.2
Exhibit: Salaries and wages..	5,679,113	12.0
Total Expenditure	47,309,258	100.0
General expenditure	41,303,514	87.3
Intergovernmental expenditure	13,546,867	28.6
Direct expenditure..	27,756,647	58.7
General expenditure, by function:		
Education	16,094,986	34.0
Public welfare	14,507,128	30.7
Hospitals..	325,095	0.7
Health...	515,239	1.1
Highways	2,789,319	5.9
Police protection...	486,835	1.0
Correction	635,229	1.3
Natural resources...	682,934	1.4
Parks and recreation...	291,717	0.6
Governmental administration...	1,141,228	2.4
Interest on general debt	570,370	1.2
Other and unallocable	3,263,434	6.9
Utility expenditure...	471,723	0.9
Liquor stores expenditure..	0	-
Insurance trust expenditure	5,534,021	11.7
Debt at End of Fiscal Year	16,363,418	X
Cash and Security Holdings	75,597,031	X

X = Not applicable.
- = Zero or rounds to zero.
[1] Within insurance trust revenue, net earnings of state retirement systems is a calculated statistic (the item code in the data file is X08), and thus can be positive or negative. Net earnings is the sum of earnings on investments plus gains on investments minus losses on investments. The change made in 2002 for asset valuation from book to market value in accordance with Statement 34 of the Governmental Accounting Standards Board is reflected in the calculated statistics.

Table MN-16. State Government Tax Collections, 2018

(Dollars in thousands, percent.)

Item	Dollars	Percent distribution
Total Taxes	26,697,469	100.0
Property taxes	818,513	3.1
Sales and gross receipts	10,614,808	39.8
General sales and gross receipts	5,830,256	21.8
Selective sales and gross receipts	4,784,552	17.9
Alcoholic beverages	91,745	0.3
Amusements	75,597	0.3
Insurance premiums	519,547	1.9
Motor fuels	936,893	3.5
Pari-mutuels	1,192	-
Public utilities	54	-
Tobacco products	593,410	2.2
Other selective sales	2,566,114	9.6
Licenses	1,476,228	5.5
Alcoholic beverages	2,765	-
Amusements	1,144	-
Corporations in general	9,045	-
Hunting and fishing	66,634	0.2
Motor vehicle	800,981	3.0
Motor vehicle operators	45,796	0.2
Public utilities	785	-
Occupation and business, NEC	484,398	1.8
Other licenses	64,680	0.2
Income taxes	13,239,334	49.6
Individual income	11,882,330	44.5
Corporation net income	1,357,004	5.1
Other taxes	548,586	2.1
Death and gift	214,698	0.8
Documentary and stock transfer	234,141	0.9
Severance	49,623	0.2
Taxes, NEC	50,124	0.2

- = Zero or rounds to zero.

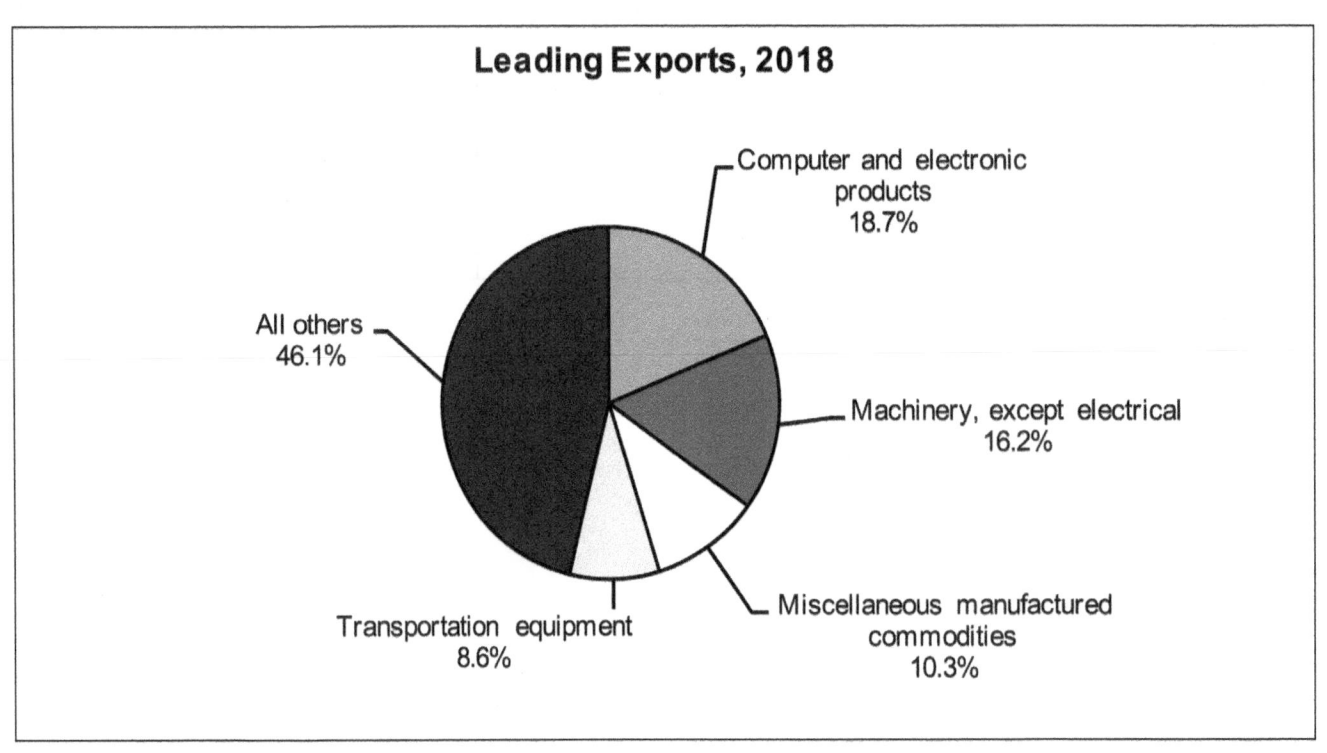

Leading Exports, 2018

Computer and electronic products 18.7%

All others 46.1%

Machinery, except electrical 16.2%

Transportation equipment 8.6%

Miscellaneous manufactured commodities 10.3%

Facts and Figures

Location: South central United States; bordered on the N by Tennessee, on the E by Alabama, on the S by Louisiana and the Gulf of Mexico, and on the W by Arkansas and Louisiana

Area: 48,430 sq. mi. (125,434 sq. km.); rank—32nd

Population: 2,986,530 (2018 est.); rank—34th

Principal Cities: capital—Jackson; largest—Jackson

Statehood: December 10, 1817; 20th state

U.S. Congress: 2 senators, 4 representatives

State Motto: *Virtute et armis* ("By valor and arms")

State Song: "Go, Mississippi"

State Nicknames: The Magnolia State; The Hospitality State

Abbreviations: MS; Miss.

State Symbols: flower—magnolia blossom; tree—Southern magnolia; bird—mockingbird

At a Glance

- With an increase in population of 0.6 percent, Mississippi ranked 46th among the states in growth from 2010 to 2018.

- In 2017, Mississippi had the 2nd lowest median household income in the country ($43,529) and the highest percent of population living the below the poverty level (19.8 percent).

- In 2017, 12.0 percent of Mississippians did not have health insurance, compared to 8.7 percent of the total U.S. population.

- Mississippi had the 2nd highest traffic fatality rate in 2017, with 1.67 deaths per 100 million vehicle miles.

- In 2017, 21.9 percent of Mississippians age 25 years and older had a bachelor's degree or higher, which was the 2nd lowest percentage among states.

Table MS-1. Population by Age, Sex, Race, and Hispanic Origin

(Number, percent, except where noted.)

Sex, age, race, and Hispanic origin	2000	2010	2018 [1]	Percent change, 2010–2018
Total Population..	2,844,658	2,967,297	2,986,530	0.6
Percent of total U.S. population	1.0	1.0	0.9	X
Sex				
Male..	1,373,554	1,441,240	1,447,735	0.5
Female	1,471,104	1,526,057	1,538,795	0.8
Age				
Under 5 years..	204,364	210,956	185,477	-12.1
5 to 19 years...	668,850	638,539	605,827	-5.1
20 to 64 years...	1,627,921	1,737,395	1,720,751	-1.0
65 years and over	343,523	380,407	474,475	24.7
Median age (years)	33.8	36.0	37.7	4.7
Race and Hispanic Origin				
One race				
White	1,746,099	1,789,391	1,766,301	-1.3
Black	1,033,809	1,103,101	1,128,912	2.3
American Indian and Alaska Native	11,652	16,837	18,423	9.4
Asian	18,626	26,477	32,152	21.4
Native Hawaiian or Other Pacific Islander	667	1,700	1,812	6.6
Two or more races	20,021	29,791	38,930	30.7
Hispanic (of any race)..	39,569	85,107	100,168	17.7

X = Not applicable.
- = Zero or rounds to zero.
[1] Population figures for 2018 are July 1 estimates. The 2010 estimates are taken from the 2010 Census.

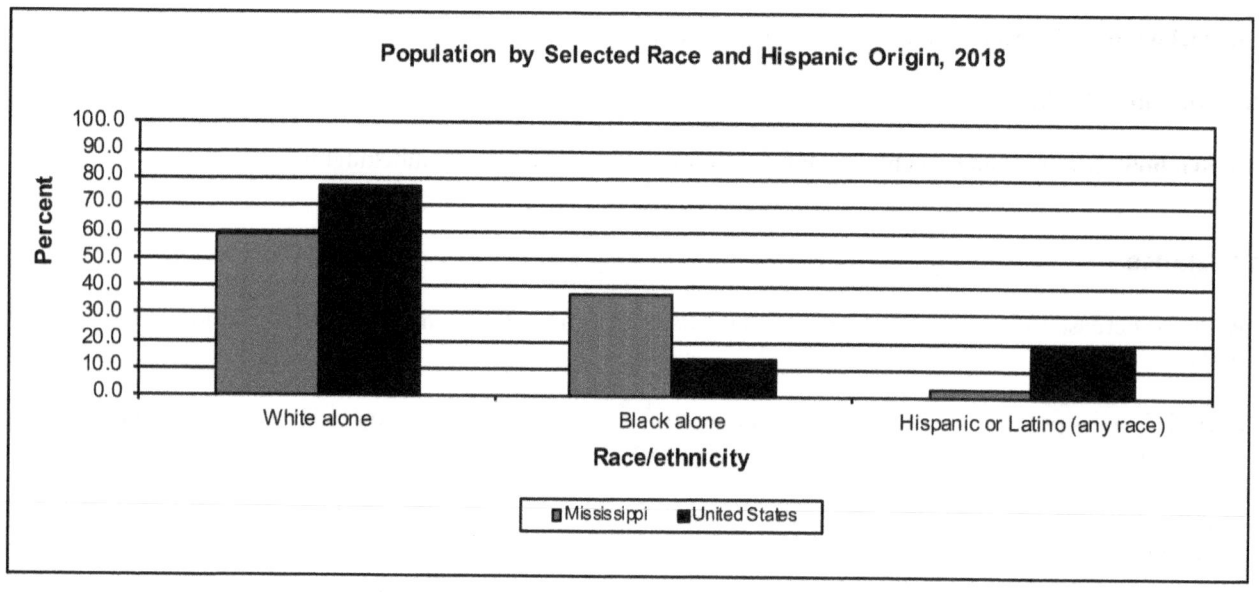

Table MS-2. Marital Status

(Number, percent distribution.)

Sex, age, race, and Hispanic origin	2000	2010	2017
Males, 15 Years and Over.................................	1,046,252	1,121,265	1,144,988
Never married	30.6	34.9	37.6
Now married, except separated............................	54.6	48.3	45.6
Separated...	2.4	2.5	2.6
Widowed..	2.9	2.7	3.1
Divorced..	9.5	11.7	11.1
Females, 15 Years and Over..............................	1,157,363	1,224,423	1,248,031
Never married	25.1	29.8	32.2
Now married, except separated............................	48.6	43.8	42.0
Separated...	3.2	3.4	3.2
Widowed..	12.5	10.8	10.5
Divorced..	10.6	12.3	12.2

Table MS-3. Households and Housing Characteristics

(Number, percent, dollars.)

Item	2000	2010	2017	Average annual percent change, 2010–2017
Total Households...	1,046,434	1,079,999	1,091,980	0.2
Family households	747,159	746,115	716,451	-0.6
Married-couple family	520,884	501,571	482,684	-0.5
Other family	226,315	244,544	233,767	-0.6
Male householder, no wife present	45,610	51,400	54,881	1.0
Female householder, no husband present	180,705	193,144	178,886	-1.1
Nonfamily households	299,275	333,884	375,529	1.8
Householder living alone..	257,708	293,185	327,330	1.7
Householder not living alone..................................	41,567	40,699	48,199	2.6
Housing Characteristics				
Total housing units...	1,161,953	1,276,441	1,323,754	0.5
Occupied housing units	1,046,434	1,079,999	1,091,980	0.2
Owner occupied	756,967	753,374	748,055	-0.1
Renter occupied	289,467	326,625	343,925	0.8
Average household size...	2.63	2.66	2.65	-0.1
Financial Characteristics				
Median gross rent of renter-occupied housing	439	672	742	1.5
Median monthly owner costs for housing units with a mortgage	762	1,043	1,090	0.6
Median value of owner-occupied housing units...............	71,400	100,100	120,200	2.9

Table MS-4. Migration, Origin, and Language

(Number, percent.)

Characteristic	State 2016	State 2017	State Percent change	U.S. 2016	U.S. 2017	U.S. Percent change
Residence 1 Year Ago						
Population 1 year and over	2,951,081	2,946,971	-0.1	319,361,956	321,994,428	0.8
Same house	86.6	86.6	X	85.4	85.7	X
Different house in the U.S.	13.2	13.1	X	13.9	13.6	X
Same county	7.6	6.8	X	8.3	8.1	X
Different county	5.6	6.3	X	5.6	5.6	X
Same state	3.4	3.8	X	3.2	3.3	X
Different state	2.2	2.5	X	2.4	2.3	X
Abroad	0.2	0.2	X	0.7	0.7	X
Place of Birth						
Native born	2,929,960	2,918,382	-0.4	279,388,170	281,193,323	0.6
Male	48.2	48.4	X	49.3	49.4	X
Female	51.8	51.6	X	50.7	50.6	X
Foreign born	58,766	65,718	11.8	43,739,345	44,525,855	1.8
Male	49.0	52.5	X	48.5	48.4	X
Female	51.0	47.5	X	51.5	51.6	X
Foreign born; naturalized U.S. citizen........................	23,466	28,028	19.4	21,238,372	21,948,732	3.3
Male	45.1	47.3	X	45.9	45.9	X
Female	54.9	52.7	X	54.1	54.1	X
Foreign born; not a U.S. citizen..............................	35,300	37,690	6.8	22,500,973	22,577,123	0.3
Male	51.6	56.4	X	51	50.8	X
Female	48.4	43.6	X	49	49.2	X
Entered 2010 or later	22.4	31.1	X	18.6	21.3	X
Entered 2000 to 2009	30.4	24.1	X	26.7	25.7	X
Entered before 2000..	47.2	44.8	X	54.7	53.0	X
World Region of Birth, Foreign						
Foreign-born population, excluding population born at sea	58,766	65,718	11.8	43,738,901	44,525,458	1.8
Europe	8.9	11.1	X	10.9	10.8	X
Asia	34.2	34.5	X	30.8	31.2	X
Africa	5.4	2.3	X	4.9	5.1	X
Oceania	0.5	0.8	X	0.6	0.6	X
Latin America	47.9	48.8	X	51	50.4	X
North America	3.1	2.5	X	1.8	1.8	X
Language Spoken at Home and Ability to Speak English						
Population 5 years and over...	2,801,896	2,801,633	-	303,328,961	305,924,019	0.9
English only	96.2	96.3	X	78.4	78.2	X
Language other than English.....................................	3.8	3.7	X	21.6	21.8	X
Speaks English less than "very well"....................	1.4	1.5	X	8.6	8.5	X

NA = Not available.
X = Not applicable.
- = Zero or rounds to zero.

Table MS-5. Median Income and Poverty Status, 2017

(Number, percent, except as noted.)

Characteristic	State		U.S.	
	Number	Percent	Number	Percent
Median Income				
Households (dollars)...	43,529	X	60,336	X
Families (dollars)	55,937	X	73,891	X
Below Poverty Level (All People)	571,219	19.8	42,583,651	13.4
Sex				
Male	242,722	17.5	19,004,547	12.2
Female	328,497	21.9	23,579,104	14.5
Age				
Under 18 years..	189,541	26.9	13,353,202	18.4
Related children under 18 years...	186,755	26.7	13,053,472	18.1
18 to 64 years...	319,768	18.4	24,648,677	12.6
65 years and over	61,910	13.7	4,581,772	9.3

X = Not applicable.

Median Household and Family Income, 2017

Table MS-6. Health Insurance Coverage Status for the Civilian Noninstitutionalized Population and Children Under 18 Years of Age

(Number, percent.)

Item	2009	2010	2011	2012	2013	2014	2015	2016	2017
Civilian Noninstitutionalized Population	2,879,805	2,902,907	2,911,811	2,918,405	2,925,211	2,927,088	2,927,568	2,924,168	2,920,808
Covered by Private or Public Insurance									
Number...	2,365,681	2,374,812	2,395,398	2,420,895	2,425,362	2,502,958	2,555,983	2,577,987	2,569,054
Percent...	82.1	81.8	82.3	83.0	82.9	85.5	87.3	88.2	88.0
Uninsured									
Number...	514,124	528,095	516,413	497,510	499,849	424,130	371,585	346,181	351,754
Percent...	17.9	18.2	17.7	17.0	17.1	14.5	12.7	11.8	12.0
Percent in the U.S. not covered..	15.1	15.5	15.1	14.8	14.5	11.7	9.4	8.6	8.7
Children Under 18 Years of Age[1]	764,182	751,985	749,572	745,603	734,075	729,802	725,664	721,108	763,456
Covered by Private or Public Insurance									
Number...	685,673	688,483	688,589	690,862	677,926	690,970	696,297	688,518	726,463
Percent...	89.7	91.6	91.9	92.7	92.4	94.7	96.0	95.5	95.2
Uninsured									
Number...	78,509	63,502	60,983	54,741	56,149	38,832	29,367	32,590	36,993
Percent...	10.3	8.4	8.1	7.3	7.6	5.3	4.0	4.5	4.8
Percent in the U.S. not covered	8.6	8.0	7.5	7.2	7.1	6.0	4.8	4.5	5.0

[1] 2017 data is for individuals under 19 years of age.

Table MS-7. Employment Status by Demographic Group, 2018

(Numbers in thousands, percent.)

Characteristic	Civilian noninstitutional population	Civilian labor force		Employed		Unemployed	
		Number	Percent of population	Number	Percent of population	Number	Percent of population
Total...	2,294	1,277	55.7	1,215	53.0	62	4.8
Sex							
Male..	1,078	658	61.0	627	58.1	31	4.7
Female...	1,215	620	51.0	589	48.4	31	5.0
Race, Sex, and Hispanic Origin							
White..	1,400	782	55.8	756	54.0	26	3.3
Male..	682	431	63.2	418	61.2	13	3.1
Female..	719	351	48.8	339	47.1	12	3.4
Black or African American......................	835	467	55.9	432	51.8	35	7.5
Male..	372	213	57.3	196	52.6	17	8.1
Female..	463	254	54.8	236	51.0	18	6.9
Hispanic or Latino ethnicity[1]	55	36	65.5	34	61.2	2	6.4
Male..	NA	NA	NA	NA	NA	NA	NA
Female..	NA	NA	NA	NA	NA	NA	NA
Age							
16 to 19 years......................................	178	45	25.4	36	20.3	9	20.1
20 to 24 years......................................	176	113	64.2	99	56.3	14	12.4
25 to 34 years......................................	371	299	80.6	281	75.8	18	5.9
35 to 44 years......................................	366	289	79.1	282	76.9	8	2.7
45 to 54 years......................................	349	261	74.6	256	73.4	4	1.7
55 to 64 years......................................	393	205	52.1	198	50.3	7	3.3
65 years and over.................................	460	65	14.2	63	13.7	2	3.5

NOTE: Data in Table 7 are from the Current Population Survey (CPS) and do not match the estimates in Table 8. See notes and definitions for further information.
[1] May be of any race.
NA = Not available.

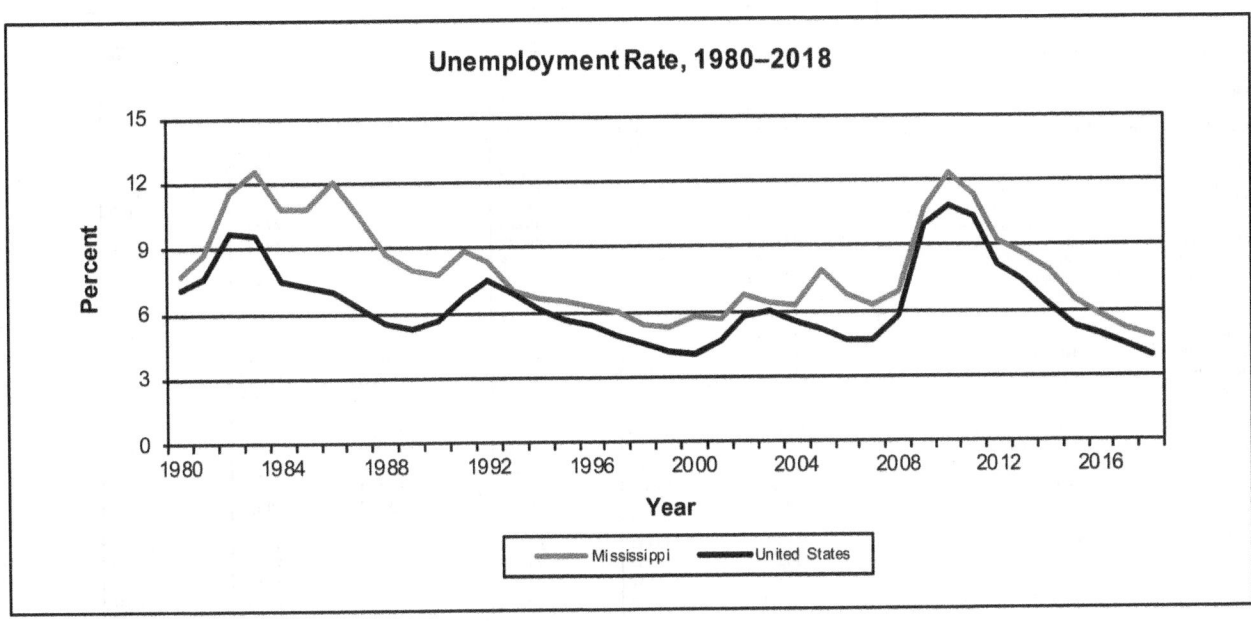

Unemployment Rate, 1980–2018

Table MS-8. Employment Status of the Civilian Noninstitutional Population Age 16 Years and Over

(Number, percent.)

Year	Civilian labor force	Civilian participation rate	Employed	Unemployed	Unemployment rate
2010..	1,306,608	58.6	1,170,879	135,729	10.4
2011..	1,342,808	59.8	1,208,747	134,061	10.0
2012..	1,316,536	58.4	1,198,196	118,340	9.0
2013..	1,272,477	56.2	1,163,752	108,725	8.5
2014..	1,248,014	55.0	1,154,058	93,956	7.5
2015..	1,263,925	55.5	1,182,779	81,146	6.4
2016..	1,278,960	56.0	1,204,481	74,479	5.8
2017..	1,280,071	55.9	1,215,115	64,956	5.1
2018..	1,275,721	55.6	1,214,992	60,729	4.8

Table MS-9. Employment and Average Wages by Industry

(Estimates are based on the 2012 *North American Industry Classification System* [NAICS].)

Industry	2011	2012	2013	2014	2015	2016	2017
	Number of jobs						
Wage and Salary Employment by Industry	1,166,461	1,174,648	1,179,070	1,194,211	1,202,135	1,209,425	1,214,455
Farm Wage and Salary Employment	9,231	8,188	6,941	12,119	9,375	8,367	9,411
Nonfarm Wage and Salary Employment	1,157,230	1,166,460	1,172,129	1,182,092	1,192,760	1,201,058	1,205,044
Private wage and salary employment	877,807	887,008	895,338	906,128	918,425	927,828	933,189
Forestry, fishing, and related activities	7,667	7,665	7,820	7,883	7,956	8,133	7,925
Mining	6,123	6,309	6,181	6,254	5,053	3,840	4,062
Utilities	7,732	7,727	7,870	7,826	7,870	7,942	8,058
Construction	50,095	49,682	52,593	50,321	47,193	45,577	44,493
Manufacturing	135,440	137,110	136,980	139,717	141,925	143,245	144,164
Durable goods manufacturing	88,048	90,779	90,651	93,638	94,756	94,960	95,211
Nondurable goods manufacturing	47,392	46,331	46,329	46,079	47,169	48,285	48,953
Wholesale trade	34,418	34,360	34,274	34,202	34,673	34,443	34,920
Retail trade	134,085	134,545	134,447	136,557	139,036	141,604	141,263
Transportation and warehousing	39,843	40,226	40,983	42,729	44,834	46,905	48,292
Information	11,898	12,586	12,806	13,246	13,622	12,143	11,579
Finance and insurance	34,043	34,145	33,492	33,162	33,233	33,380	33,517
Real estate and rental and leasing	11,609	11,688	11,734	11,679	11,756	11,781	11,823
Professional, scientific, and technical services	31,862	31,463	30,863	31,226	31,088	30,949	31,390
Management of companies and enterprises	10,141	10,217	10,777	10,658	10,611	11,055	11,017
Administrative and waste services	52,590	55,584	57,901	60,368	63,962	66,616	66,079
Educational services	19,401	19,893	19,868	19,651	19,368	18,769	19,094
Health care and social assistance	121,902	122,818	123,653	124,814	127,523	129,870	132,735
Arts, entertainment, and recreation	10,891	11,261	11,588	11,562	11,413	11,572	9,780
Accommodation and food services	108,917	111,047	113,061	115,149	118,393	122,156	125,560
Other services, except public administration	49,150	48,682	48,447	49,124	48,916	47,848	47,438
Government and government enterprises	279,423	279,452	276,791	275,964	274,335	273,230	271,855
	Dollars						
Average Wages and Salaries by Industry	35,931	36,935	37,468	37,993	38,553	39,118	39,825
Average Farm Wages and Salaries	16,657	29,000	24,977	20,815	21,563	19,807	17,156
Average Nonfarm Wages and Salaries	36,084	36,990	37,542	38,169	38,687	39,252	40,002
Average private wages and salaries	35,575	36,691	37,286	37,953	38,369	38,778	39,557
Forestry, fishing, and related activities	30,558	31,572	32,599	33,883	35,655	36,681	37,378
Mining	69,900	75,136	75,693	78,592	78,763	76,571	75,657
Utilities	68,272	71,127	71,797	73,931	77,768	79,649	81,758
Construction	42,506	44,735	46,684	47,288	47,198	48,655	49,772
Manufacturing	43,690	45,043	45,847	47,644	48,334	49,256	50,376
Durable goods manufacturing	45,286	46,432	47,286	49,077	49,515	50,790	52,063
Nondurable goods manufacturing	40,724	42,321	43,031	44,732	45,963	46,239	47,095
Wholesale trade	50,428	52,049	53,067	54,638	56,191	57,121	59,080
Retail trade	24,018	24,677	25,035	25,352	25,866	26,212	26,539
Transportation and warehousing	41,991	43,682	43,631	44,378	45,444	44,486	45,661
Information	44,092	44,868	46,406	47,748	46,180	49,525	50,490
Finance and insurance	50,222	52,506	54,719	55,916	57,529	58,760	60,371
Real estate and rental and leasing	31,885	33,464	33,502	34,837	35,615	35,607	36,758
Professional, scientific, and technical services	53,122	54,825	55,784	55,970	57,826	59,015	59,463
Management of companies and enterprises	77,951	81,480	80,302	82,985	84,889	83,167	87,488
Administrative and waste services	25,557	26,397	27,641	27,745	27,822	27,891	28,005
Educational services	26,660	27,711	28,563	28,893	28,131	29,306	29,244
Health care and social assistance	39,729	40,723	40,630	41,006	41,532	41,904	42,486
Arts, entertainment, and recreation	24,212	23,899	23,868	23,540	24,256	24,112	21,757
Accommodation and food services	18,414	18,617	18,787	18,920	18,869	19,190	19,671
Other services, except public administration	26,476	27,793	28,641	29,567	30,401	31,647	32,748
Government and government enterprises	37,683	37,940	38,370	38,877	39,748	40,862	41,532

Table MS-10. Employment Characteristics by Family Type

(Number, percent.)

Family type and labor force status	2015		2016		2017	
	Total	Families with own children under 18 years	Total	Families with own children under 18 years	Total	Families with own children under 18 years
All Families..................................	743,154	308,522	730,719	297,034	716,451	295,103
FAMILY TYPE AND LABOR FORCE STATUS						
Married-Couple Families.............................	485,198	175,460	489,734	175,322	482,684	174,760
Both husband and wife in labor force...............	47.3	67.5	48.2	67.9	47.3	66.3
Husband in labor force, wife not in labor force..........	21.4	24.0	22.1	25.0	21.8	25.7
Wife in labor force, husband not in labor force..........	9.4	5.4	8.8	4.7	9.5	5.4
Both husband and wife not in labor force...............	21.6	3.0	20.5	2.2	20.6	2.5
Other Families	257,956	133,062	240,985	121,712	233,767	120,343
Female householder, no husband present......................	78.1	80.1	80.3	83.1	76.5	79.8
In labor force................................	50.3	63.9	51.1	68.3	48.6	61.5
Not in labor force	27.8	16.2	29.2	14.8	27.9	18.3
Male householder, no wife present......................	21.9	19.9	19.7	16.9	23.5	20.2
In labor force................................	15.7	17.8	13.8	14.6	16.0	17.7
Not in labor force	6.2	2.1	5.8	2.3	7.4	2.5

Table MS-11. School Enrollment and Educational Attainment, 2017

(Number, percent.)

Item	State	U.S.
Enrollment		
Total population 3 years and over, enrolled in school	779,151	81,273,337
Enrolled in nursery school or preschool (percent)..	6.2	6.0
Enrolled in kindergarten (percent)..	5.2	4.9
Enrolled in elementary school, grades 1-8 (percent)..	42.3	40.6
Enrolled in high school, grades 9-12 (percent)..	21.4	21.1
Enrolled in college or graduate school (percent)..	24.9	27.4
Attainment		
Total population 25 years and over	1,959,341	221,250,083
Less than ninth grade (percent)..	4.8	5.1
9th to 12th grade, no diploma (percent)..	10.8	6.9
High school graduate, including equivalency (percent)..	30.4	27.1
Some college, no degree (percent)..	22.0	20.4
Associate's degree (percent)..	10.1	8.5
Bachelor's degree (percent)	13.5	19.7
Graduate or professional degree (percent)..	8.3	12.3
High school graduate or higher (percent)..	84.4	88.0
Bachelor's degree or higher (percent)..	21.9	32.0

Table MS-12. Public School Characteristics and Educational Indicators

(Number, percent; data derived from National Center of Education Statistics.)

Item	State	U.S.
Public Elementary and Secondary Schools		
Number of operational school districts, 2016-17..	158	18,377
Number of operational schools, 2016-17..	1,066	98,330
Percent charter schools..	0.3	7.1
Total public school enrollment, 2016-17..	483,150	50,587,859
Percent charter school enrollment..	0.1	6.0
Student-teacher ratio, Fall 2015..	15.1	16.0
Expenditures per student (dollars), 2015-16..	8,692	11,841
Four-year adjusted cohort graduation rate (ACGR)[1]..	83.0	84.6
Students eligible for free or reduced-price lunch (percent), 2015-16..	74.9	52.1
English language learners (percent), Fall 2016..	2.7	9.6
Students age 3 to 21 served under IDEA, part B (percent), 2017-18..	14.5	13.7
Public Schools by Type, 2016-17		Percent of state public schools
Total number of schools..	1,066	100.0
Special education..	1	0.1
Vocational education..	91	8.5
Alternative education..	66	6.2

[1] Adjusted Cohort Graduation Rates (ACGR) differ from Averaged Freshmen Graduation Rates (AFGR).

Table MS-13. Reported Voting and Registration of the Voting-Age Population, November 2018

(Numbers in thousands, percent.)

Item	Total population	Total citizen population	Registered			Voted		
			Total registered	Percent registered (total population)	Percent registered (total citizen population)	Total voted	Percent voted (total population)	Percent voted (total citizen population)
U.S. Total	249,748	228,832	153,066	61.3	66.9	122,281	49.0	53.4
State Total.................................	2,194	2,178	1,599	72.9	73.4	1,180	53.8	54.2
Sex								
Male	1,027	1,016	718	69.9	70.7	531	51.7	52.2
Female	1,167	1,162	881	75.5	75.8	650	55.7	55.9
Race								
White alone...............................	1,353	1,341	956	70.6	71.2	688	50.9	51.3
White, non-Hispanic alone..............	1,317	1,314	943	71.6	71.8	679	51.6	51.7
Black alone................................	798	796	621	77.8	78.1	476	59.6	59.8
Asian alone	16	14	3	(B)	(B)	-	(B)	(B)
Hispanic (of any race)...................	44	33	16	(B)	(B)	11	(B)	(B)
White alone or in combination	1,370	1,359	969	70.7	71.3	700	51.1	51.5
Black alone or in combination...........	812	809	630	77.7	77.9	484	59.6	59.8
Asian alone or in combination..........	19	17	5	(B)	(B)	-	(B)	(B)
Age								
18 to 24 years...........................	269	269	123	45.7	45.7	72	26.7	26.7
25 to 34 years...........................	365	354	253	69.5	71.5	133	36.5	37.6
35 to 44 years...........................	353	353	267	75.7	75.7	187	53.1	53.1
45 to 64 years...........................	727	722	571	78.5	79.1	472	64.9	65.4
65 years and over	481	481	385	80.1	80.1	316	65.8	65.8

B = Base is less than 75,000 and therefore too small to show the derived measure.
- = Zero or rounds to zero.

Table MS-14. Crime

(Number, rate per 100,000. Data are derived from the FBI Uniform Crime Reports.)

Item	State			U.S.		
	2016	2017	Percent change	2016	2017	Percent change
TOTAL POPULATION[1]	2,985,415	2,984,100	-0.0	323,405,935	325,719,178	0.7
VIOLENT CRIME						
Number...	8,411	8,526	1.4	1,285,606	1,283,220	-0.2
Rate	281.7	285.7	1.4	397.5	394.0	-0.9
Murder and Nonnegligent Manslaughter						
Number...	237	245	3.4	17,413	17,284	-0.7
Rate	7.9	8.2	3.4	5.4	5.3	-1.4
Rape[2]						
Number...	1,282	1,091	-14.9	132,414	135,755	2.5
Rate	42.9	36.6	-14.9	40.9	41.7	1.8
Robbery						
Number...	2,433	2,071	-14.9	332,797	319,356	-4.0
Rate	81.5	69.4	-14.8	102.9	98.0	-4.7
Aggravated Assault						
Number...	4,459	5,119	14.8	802,982	810,825	1.0
Rate	149.4	171.5	14.9	248.3	248.9	0.3
PROPERTY CRIME						
Number...	82,521	81,581	-1.1	7,928,530	7,694,086	-3.0
Rate	2,764.1	2,733.9	-1.1	2,451.6	2,362.2	-3.6
Burglary						
Number...	23,489	24,710	5.2	1,516,405	1,401,840	-7.6
Rate	786.8	828.1	5.2	468.9	430.4	-8.2
Larceny-Theft						
Number...	54,725	52,240	-4.5	5,644,835	5,519,107	-2.2
Rate	1,833.1	1,750.6	-4.5	1,745.4	1,694.4	-2.9
Motor Vehicle Theft						
Number...	4,307	4,631	7.5	767,290	773,139	0.8
Rate	144.3	155.2	7.6	237.3	237.4	-

NOTE: Although arson data are included in the trend and clearance tables, sufficient data are not available to estimate totals for this offense. Therefore, no arson data are published in this table.
- = Zero or rounds to zero.
[1] Population figures are U.S. Census Bureau provisional estimates as of July 1, 2017.
[2] The figures shown in the rape (revised definition) column were estimated using the revised Uniform Crime Reporting (UCR) definition of rape.

Table MS-15. State Government Finances, 2017

(Dollar amounts in thousands, percent distribution.)

Item	Dollars	Percent distribution
Total Revenue	24,026,565	100.0
General revenue	18,716,811	77.9
Intergovernmental revenue	8,211,496	34.2
Taxes	7,783,031	32.4
General sales	3,526,913	14.7
Selective sales	1,461,425	6.1
License taxes	480,741	2.0
Individual income tax	1,834,688	7.6
Corporate income tax	407,913	1.7
Other taxes	71,351	0.3
Current charges	2,241,068	9.3
Miscellaneous general revenue	481,216	2.0
Utility revenue	218	-
Liquor stores revenue	349,534	1.5
Insurance trust revenue[1]	4,960,002	20.6
Total Expenditure	21,631,786	100.0
Intergovernmental expenditure	4,527,299	20.9
Direct expenditure	17,104,487	79.1
Current operation	12,566,720	58.1
Capital outlay	1,077,250	5.0
Insurance benefits and repayments	2,745,997	12.7
Assistance and subsidies	398,739	1.8
Interest on debt	315,781	1.5
Exhibit: Salaries and wages	2,599,156	12.0
Total Expenditure	21,631,786	100.0
General expenditure	18,598,310	86.0
Intergovernmental expenditure	4,527,299	20.9
Direct expenditure	14,071,011	65.0
General expenditure, by function:		
Education	5,540,542	25.6
Public welfare	6,657,719	30.8
Hospitals	1,524,943	7.0
Health	414,397	1.9
Highways	1,164,028	5.4
Police protection	139,829	0.6
Correction	330,982	1.5
Natural resources	302,124	1.4
Parks and recreation	37,970	0.2
Governmental administration	454,374	2.1
Interest on general debt	315,781	1.5
Other and unallocable	1,715,621	7.9
Utility expenditure	0	-
Liquor stores expenditure	287,479	1.3
Insurance trust expenditure	2,745,997	12.7
Debt at End of Fiscal Year	7,470,178	X
Cash and Security Holdings	34,730,611	X

X = Not applicable.
= Zero or rounds to zero.
[1] Within insurance trust revenue, net earnings of state retirement systems is a calculated statistic (the item code in the data file is X08), and thus can be positive or negative. Net earnings is the sum of earnings on investments plus gains on investments minus losses on investments. The change made in 2002 for asset valuation from book to market value in accordance with Statement 34 of the Governmental Accounting Standards Board is reflected in the calculated statistics.

Table MS-16. State Government Tax Collections, 2018

(Dollars in thousands, percent.)

Item	Dollars	Percent distribution
Total Taxes	7,890,571	100.0
Property taxes	29,540	0.4
Sales and gross receipts	5,030,854	63.8
General sales and gross receipts	3,557,752	45.1
Selective sales and gross receipts	1,473,102	18.7
Alcoholic beverages	40,883	0.5
Amusements	129,880	1.6
Insurance premiums	338,576	4.3
Motor fuels	436,245	5.5
Pari-mutuels	X	-
Public utilities	1,496	-
Tobacco products	139,733	1.8
Other selective sales	386,289	4.9
Licenses	492,415	6.2
Alcoholic beverages	1,252	-
Amusements	26,515	0.3
Corporations in general	137,989	1.7
Hunting and fishing	2,703	-
Motor vehicle	158,283	2.0
Motor vehicle operators	14,362	0.2
Public utilities	6,583	0.1
Occupation and business, NEC	81,682	1.0
Other licenses	63,046	0.8
Income taxes	2,290,344	29.0
Individual income	1,852,937	23.5
Corporation net income	437,407	5.5
Other taxes	47,418	0.6
Death and gift	0	-
Documentary and stock transfer	X	-
Severance	47,418	0.6
Taxes, NEC	0	-

- = Zero or rounds to zero.
X = Not applicable.

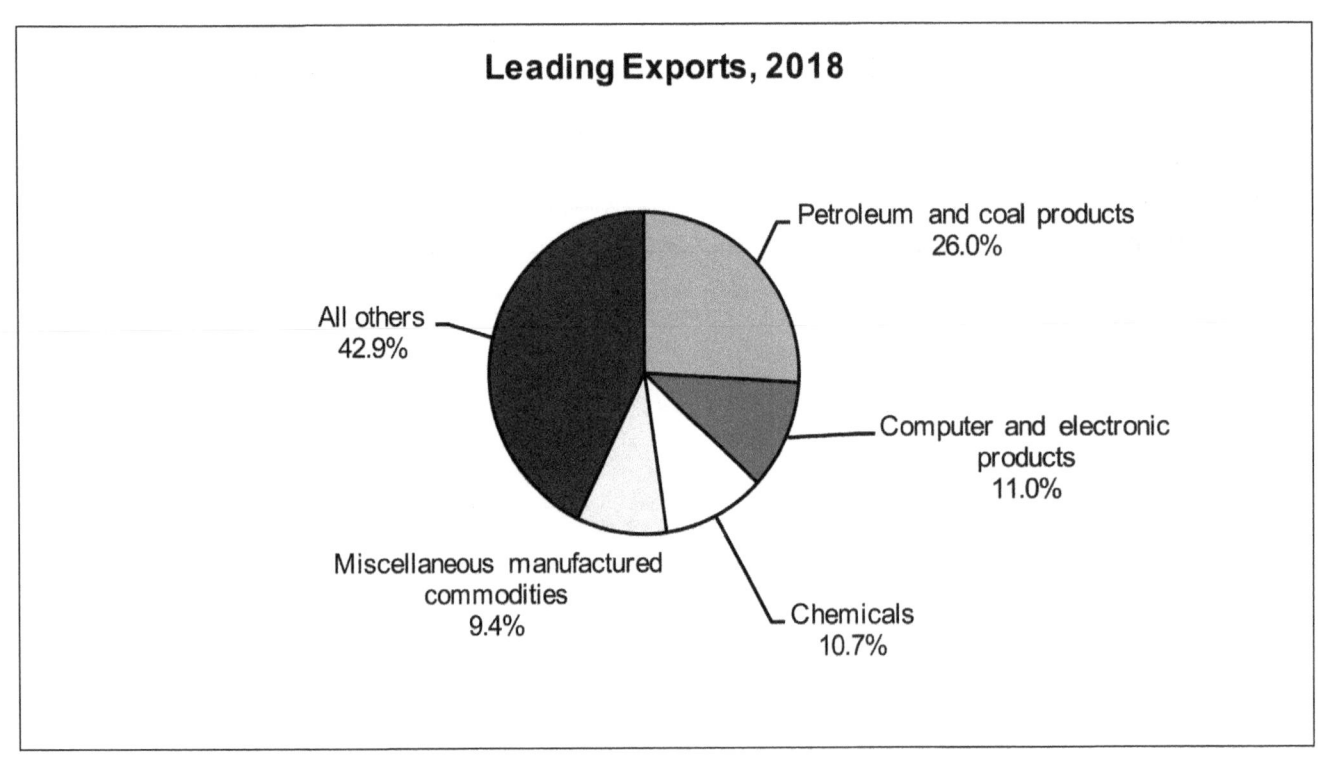

Leading Exports, 2018

Petroleum and coal products 26.0%

Computer and electronic products 11.0%

Chemicals 10.7%

Miscellaneous manufactured commodities 9.4%

All others 42.9%

Facts and Figures

Location: Central United States; bordered on the N by Iowa, on the E by Illinois, Kentucky, and Tennessee, on the S by Arkansas, and on the W by Oklahoma, Kansas, and Nebraska

Area: 69,704 sq. mi. (180,533 sq. km.); rank—21st

Population: 6,126,452 (2018 est.); rank—18th

Principal Cities: capital—Jefferson City; largest—Kansas City

Statehood: August 10, 1821; 24th state

U.S. Congress: 2 senators, 8 representatives

State Motto: *Salus populi suprema lex esto* ("The welfare of the people shall be the supreme law")

State Song: "Missouri Waltz"

State Nickname: The Show Me State

Abbreviations: MO; Mo

State Symbols: flower—hawthorn; tree—flowering dogwood; bird—Eastern bluebird

At a Glance

- With an increase in population of 2.3 percent, Missouri ranked 35th among the states in growth from 2010 to 2018.

- In 2017, 9.1 percent of Missourians did not have health insurance, compared to the national average of 8.7 percent.

- Missouri's violent crime rate was 530.3 per 100,000 population in 2017, compared to the U.S. rate of 394.0 per 100,000 population.

- Missouri's median household income of $53,578 ranked 37th in the country in 2017.

- In Missouri in 2017, 13.4 percent of residents lived below the poverty level, which was the same as the national average; 18.6 percent of Missouri children lived in poverty, which was slightly higher than the national average of 18.4 percent.

Table MO-1. Population by Age, Sex, Race, and Hispanic Origin

(Number, percent, except where noted.)

Sex, age, race, and Hispanic origin	2000	2010	2018 [1]	Percent change, 2010–2018
Total Population..	5,595,211	5,988,927	6,126,452	2.3
Percent of total U.S. population	2.0	1.9	1.9	X
Sex				
Male	2,720,177	2,933,477	3,007,563	2.5
Female	2,875,034	3,055,450	3,118,889	2.1
Age				
Under 5 years...	269,898	390,237	372,713	-4.5
5 to 19 years..	1,224,274	1,211,174	1,161,274	-4.1
20 to 64 years..	3,245,660	3,549,222	3,558,501	0.3
65 years and over	755,379	838,294	1,033,964	23.3
Median age (years)	36.1	37.9	38.7	2.1
Race and Hispanic Origin				
One race				
White	4,748,083	5,038,407	5,082,571	0.9
Black	629,391	700,178	724,529	3.5
American Indian and Alaska Native	25,076	30,595	35,019	14.5
Asian..	61,595	100,213	131,046	30.8
Native Hawaiian or Other Pacific Islander	3,178	7,178	9,585	33.5
Two or more races	82,061	112,356	143,702	27.9
Hispanic (of any race)..	118,592	223,421	263,265	17.8

X = Not applicable.
[1] Population figures for 2018 are July 1 estimates. The 2010 estimates are taken from the 2010 Census.
- = Zero or rounds to zero.

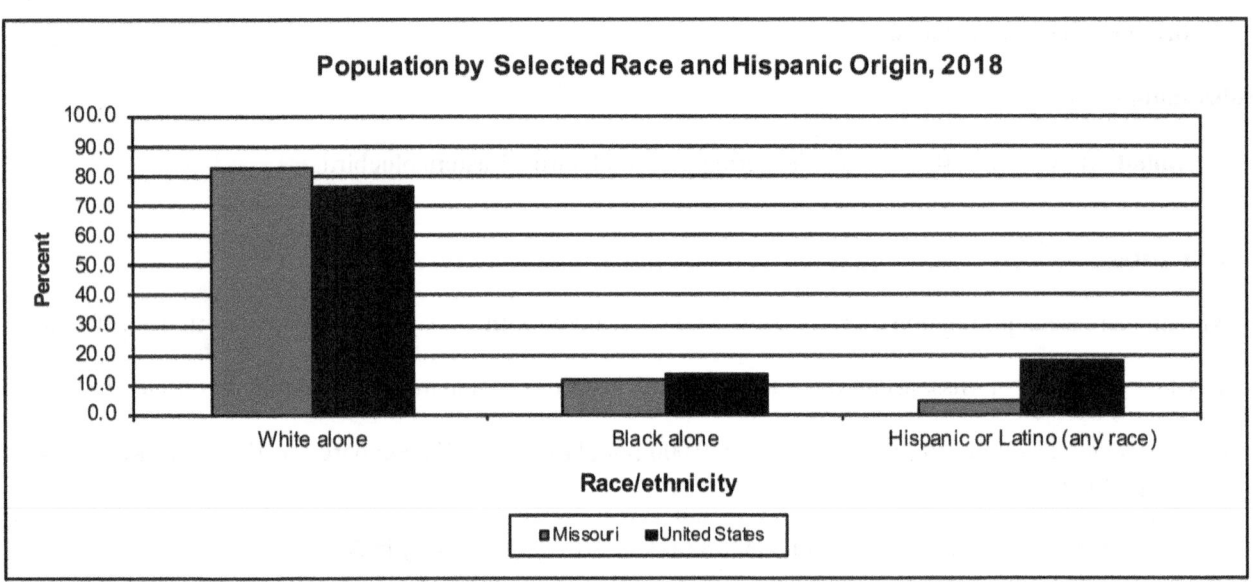

Table MO-2. Marital Status

(Number, percent distribution.)

Sex, age, race, and Hispanic origin	2000	2010	2017
Males, 15 Years and Over	2,114,280	2,332,888	2,414,301
Never married	27.8	32.1	34.0
Now married, except separated..	58.0	52.5	50.0
Separated...	1.6	1.7	1.6
Widowed...	2.6	2.6	2.8
Divorced...	10.0	11.0	11.6
Females, 15 Years and Over	2,300,111	2,492,198	2,549,283
Never married	22.1	26.8	27.6
Now married, except separated..	53.1	48.2	47.1
Separated...	2.0	2.2	2.0
Widowed...	11.3	10.0	9.7
Divorced...	11.5	12.8	13.6

Table MO-3. Households and Housing Characteristics

(Number, percent, dollars.)

Item	2000	2010	2017	Average annual percent change, 2010–2017
Total Households...	2,194,594	2,350,628	2,385,135	0.2
Family households	1,476,516	1,524,078	1,527,260	-
Married-couple family	1,140,866	1,146,501	1,138,262	-0.1
Other family	335,650	377,577	388,998	0.4
Male householder, no wife present	81,890	99,807	109,918	1.4
Female householder, no husband present.........	253,760	277,770	279,080	0.1
Nonfamily households	718,078	826,550	857,875	0.5
Householder living alone	599,808	689,361	702,802	0.3
Householder not living alone............................	118,270	137,189	155,073	1.9
Housing Characteristics				
Total housing units..	2,442,017	2,714,017	2,792,445	0.4
Occupied housing units	2,194,594	2,350,628	2,385,135	0.2
Owner occupied	1,542,149	1,621,371	1,596,870	-0.2
Renter occupied	652,445	729,257	788,265	1.2
Average household size......................................	2.48	2.48	2.49	0.1
Financial Characteristics				
Median gross rent of renter-occupied housing	484	682	800	2.5
Median monthly owner costs for housing units with a mortgage	861	1,182	1,207	0.3
Median value of owner-occupied housing units......	89,900	139,000	156,700	1.8

- = Zero or rounds to zero

Table MO-4. Migration, Origin, and Language

(Number, percent.)

Characteristic	State			U.S.		
	2016	2017	Percent change	2016	2017	Percent change
Residence 1 Year Ago						
Population 1 year and over	6,022,165	6,039,877	0.3	319,361,956	321,994,428	0.8
Same house	84.3	84.6	X	85.4	85.7	X
Different house in the U.S.	15.3	15.0	X	13.9	13.6	X
Same county	8.5	8.1	X	8.3	8.1	X
Different county	6.8	6.9	X	5.6	5.6	X
Same state	4.1	4.2	X	3.2	3.3	X
Different state	2.7	2.7	X	2.4	2.3	X
Abroad	0.4	0.4	X	0.7	0.7	X
Place of Birth						
Native born	5,843,798	5,856,430	-	279,388,170	281,193,323	0.6
Male	49.2	49.1	X	49.3	49.4	X
Female	50.8	50.9	X	50.7	50.6	X
Foreign born	249,202	257,102	3.2	43,739,345	44,525,855	1.8
Male	49.0	48.4	X	48.5	48.4	X
Female	51.0	51.6	X	51.5	51.6	X
Foreign born; naturalized U.S. citizen................	118,808	123,943	4.3	21,238,372	21,948,732	3.3
Male	46.6	46.0	X	45.9	45.9	X
Female	53.4	54.0	X	54.1	54.1	X
Foreign born; not a U.S. citizen......................	130,394	133,159	2.1	22,500,973	22,577,123	0.3
Male	51.1	50.6	X	51	50.8	X
Female	48.9	49.4	X	49	49.2	X
Entered 2010 or later	23.9	27.5	X	18.6	21.3	X
Entered 2000 to 2009	30.3	29.2	X	26.7	25.7	X
Entered before 2000......................................	45.7	43.2	X	54.7	53.0	X
World Region of Birth, Foreign						
Foreign-born population, excluding population born at sea	249,202	257,102	3.2	43,738,901	44,525,458	1.8
Europe	18.5	18.9	X	10.9	10.8	X
Asia	39.5	39.9	X	30.8	31.2	X
Africa	8.4	9.2	X	4.9	5.1	X
Oceania	1.5	1.1	X	0.6	0.6	X
Latin America	29.6	28.8	X	51	50.4	X
North America	2.5	2.1	X	1.8	1.8	X
Language Spoken at Home and Ability to Speak English						
Population 5 years and over..............................	5,721,468	5,739,531	0.3	303,328,961	305,924,019	0.9
English only	93.7	93.8	X	78.4	78.2	X
Language other than English............................	6.3	6.2	X	21.6	21.8	X
Speaks English less than "very well"..................	2.2	2.2	X	8.6	8.5	X

NA = Not available.
X = Not applicable.
- = Zero or rounds to zero.

Table MO-5. Median Income and Poverty Status, 2017

(Number, percent, except as noted.)

Characteristic	State		U.S.	
	Number	Percent	Number	Percent
Median Income				
Households (dollars)...	53,578	X	60,336	X
Families (dollars)	67,317	X	73,891	X
Below Poverty Level (All People)	795,732	13.4	42,583,651	13.4
Sex				
Male	349,592	12.1	19,004,547	12.2
Female	446,140	14.7	23,579,104	14.5
Age				
Under 18 years...	252,041	18.6	13,353,202	18.4
Related children under 18 years...	244,180	18.1	13,053,472	18.1
18 to 64 years..	459,363	12.8	24,648,677	12.6
65 years and over	84,328	8.7	4,581,772	9.3

X = Not applicable.

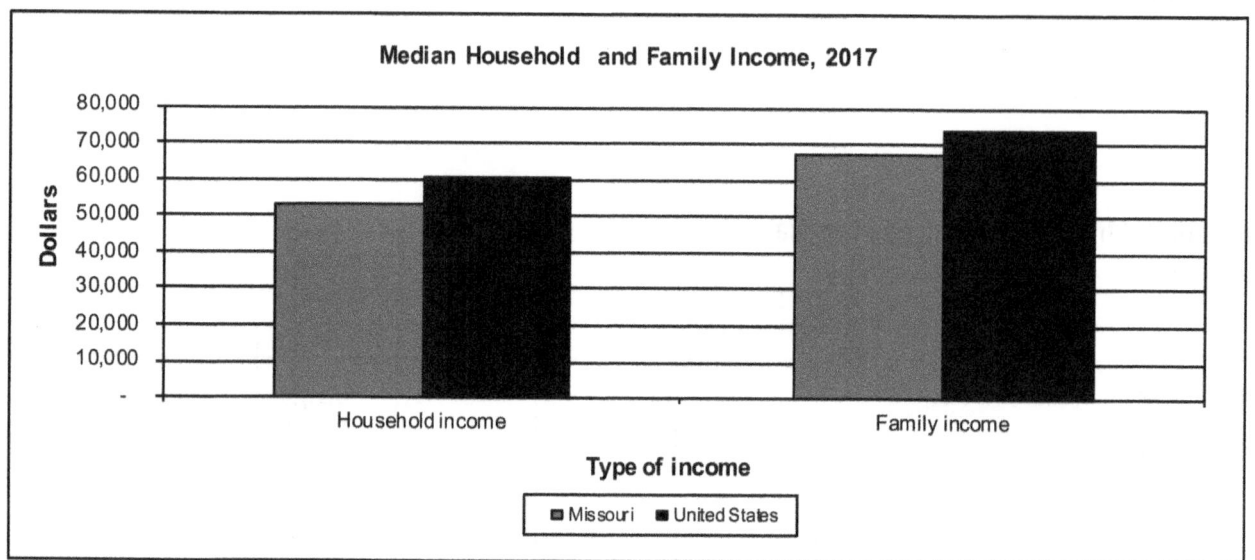

Table MO-6. Health Insurance Coverage Status for the Civilian Noninstitutionalized Population and Children Under 18 Years of Age

(Number, percent.)

Item	2009	2010	2011	2012	2013	2014	2015	2016	2017
Civilian Noninstitutionalized Population	5,871,474	5,879,864	5,898,968	5,908,769	5,930,677	5,950,606	5,969,392	5,977,199	6,000,326
Covered by Private or Public Insurance									
Number..	5,097,861	5,105,970	5,091,554	5,107,389	5,157,844	5,256,728	5,386,284	5,445,276	5,452,055
Percent...	86.8	86.8	86.3	86.4	87.0	88.3	90.2	91.1	90.9
Uninsured									
Number..	773,613	773,894	807,414	801,380	772,833	693,878	583,108	531,923	548,271
Percent...	13.2	13.2	13.7	13.6	13.0	11.7	9.8	8.9	9.1
Percent in the U.S. not covered.......................................	15.1	15.5	15.1	14.8	14.5	11.7	9.4	8.6	8.7
Children Under 18 Years of Age[1]	1,426,899	1,413,730	1,409,255	1,399,674	1,394,588	1,387,561	1,387,714	1,386,471	1,464,725
Covered by Private or Public Insurance									
Number..	1,328,434	1,325,585	1,314,321	1,301,641	1,297,042	1,287,589	1,308,016	1,324,598	1,390,219
Percent...	93.1	93.8	93.3	93.0	93.0	92.8	94.3	95.5	94.9
Uninsured									
Number..	98,465	88,145	94,934	98,033	97,546	99,972	79,698	61,873	74,506
Percent...	6.9	6.2	6.7	7.0	7.0	7.2	5.7	4.5	5.1
Percent in the U.S. not covered.......................................	8.6	8.0	7.5	7.2	7.1	6.0	4.8	4.5	5.0

[1] 2017 data is for individuals under 19 years of age.

Table MO-7. Employment Status by Demographic Group, 2018

(Numbers in thousands, percent.)

Characteristic	Civilian noninstitutional population	Civilian labor force		Employed		Unemployed	
		Number	Percent of population	Number	Percent of population	Number	Percent of population
Total..	4,806	3,066	63.8	2,966	61.7	99	3.2
Sex							
Male..	2,318	1,574	67.9	1,512	65.2	62	4.0
Female.......................................	2,488	1,491	60.0	1,455	58.5	37	2.5
Race, Sex, and Hispanic Origin							
White..	4,055	2,596	64.0	2,523	62.2	73	2.8
Male.......................................	1,971	1,348	68.4	1,305	66.2	43	3.2
Female....................................	2,083	1,248	59.9	1,218	58.5	30	2.4
Black or African American................	527	342	64.9	322	61.1	20	5.9
Male.......................................	237	158	66.7	144	60.5	15	9.3
Female....................................	290	184	63.5	179	61.6	5	2.9
Hispanic or Latino ethnicity[1]..........	190	139	73.0	131	68.9	8	5.6
Male.......................................	NA	NA	NA	NA	NA	NA	NA
Female....................................	NA	NA	NA	NA	NA	NA	NA
Age							
16 to 19 years.............................	312	117	37.6	107	34.2	11	9.2
20 to 24 years.............................	347	268	77.2	251	72.4	17	6.2
25 to 34 years.............................	796	680	85.5	657	82.6	23	3.4
35 to 44 years.............................	788	671	85.1	650	82.4	21	3.1
45 to 54 years.............................	684	562	82.3	551	80.6	11	2.0
55 to 64 years.............................	833	541	64.9	528	63.4	13	2.3
65 years and over.........................	1,047	226	21.6	223	21.3	4	1.7

NOTE: Data in Table 7 are from the Current Population Survey (CPS) and do not match the estimates in Table 8. See notes and definitions for further information.
[1] May be of any race.

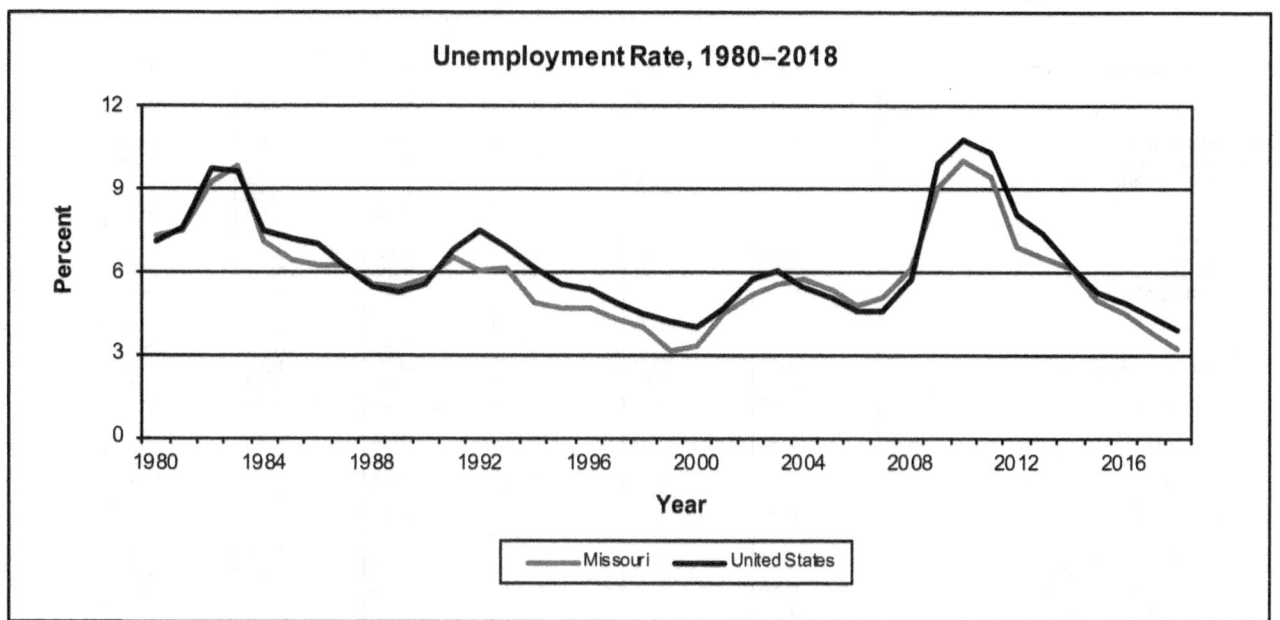

Unemployment Rate, 1980–2018

Table MO-8. Employment Status of the Civilian Noninstitutional Population Age 16 Years and Over

(Number, percent.)

Year	Civilian labor force	Civilian participation rate	Employed	Unemployed	Unemployment rate
2010..	3,056,484	66.0	2,763,535	292,949	9.6
2011..	3,047,786	65.6	2,789,224	258,562	8.5
2012..	3,025,309	64.8	2,815,275	210,034	6.9
2013..	3,020,202	64.4	2,817,435	202,767	6.7
2014..	3,048,576	64.7	2,861,721	186,855	6.1
2015..	3,077,535	65.0	2,923,107	154,428	5.0
2016..	3,079,559	64.8	2,939,309	140,250	4.6
2017..	3,050,713	63.8	2,936,126	114,587	3.8
2018..	3,052,386	63.6	2,954,808	97,578	3.2

Table MO-9. Employment and Average Wages by Industry

(Estimates are based on the 2012 *North American Industry Classification System* [NAICS].)

Industry	2011	2012	2013	2014	2015	2016	2017
	Number of jobs						
Wage and Salary Employment by Industry.........................	2,744,993	2,776,672	2,808,712	2,834,816	2,886,985	2,925,546	2,948,639
Farm Wage and Salary Employment..............................	8,837	9,093	8,666	7,131	9,971	10,251	7,000
Nonfarm Wage and Salary Employment..........................	2,736,156	2,767,579	2,800,046	2,827,685	2,877,014	2,915,295	2,941,639
Private wage and salary employment................................	2,255,008	2,291,158	2,324,189	2,355,073	2,406,070	2,444,246	2,470,258
Forestry, fishing, and related activities.............................	5,151	5,332	5,420	5,511	5,563	5,548	5,555
Mining..	4,017	3,977	3,947	3,896	3,924	3,874	4,045
Utilities..	12,342	12,178	12,119	11,960	11,859	11,696	11,721
Construction...	106,012	107,530	110,818	112,846	117,327	123,585	125,925
Manufacturing..	246,550	248,753	252,924	256,197	261,529	263,424	266,025
Durable goods manufacturing.......................................	143,205	144,051	147,852	152,374	157,248	158,166	158,627
Nondurable goods manufacturing.................................	103,345	104,702	105,072	103,823	104,281	105,258	107,398
Wholesale trade	116,576	117,880	119,023	121,339	120,887	120,876	121,688
Retail trade..	303,430	304,821	304,040	307,128	313,852	317,778	315,670
Transportation and warehousing....................................	86,300	88,366	91,333	93,645	97,436	97,739	99,446
Information	53,682	52,910	52,592	52,327	50,237	49,421	48,280
Finance and insurance	124,853	128,663	127,897	127,945	128,619	130,039	134,287
Real estate and rental and leasing.................................	35,755	35,520	35,063	35,433	36,487	37,286	37,875
Professional, scientific, and technical services.................	124,760	131,425	133,669	137,240	147,236	154,149	160,098
Management of companies and enterprises......................	63,490	60,588	63,607	66,114	65,571	65,139	65,320
Administrative and waste services..................................	147,054	147,449	151,796	155,217	159,788	161,260	158,683
Educational services	63,647	66,103	66,460	66,661	67,075	67,722	68,420
Health care and social assistance..................................	356,692	373,205	381,487	382,244	392,708	401,488	411,141
Arts, entertainment, and recreation................................	41,764	42,156	43,333	44,674	41,793	42,888	41,938
Accommodation and food services.................................	230,598	234,124	238,999	243,763	252,424	258,390	263,189
Other services, except public administration....................	132,335	130,178	129,662	130,933	131,755	131,944	130,952
Government and government enterprises..........................	481,148	476,421	475,857	472,612	470,944	471,049	471,381
	Dollars						
Average Wages and Salaries by Industry	42,434	43,692	44,066	45,342	46,609	47,193	48,525
Average Farm Wages and Salaries	28,851	42,770	30,512	48,171	28,872	30,824	41,151
Average Nonfarm Wages and Salaries	42,478	43,695	44,108	45,334	46,671	47,250	48,543
Average private wages and salaries................................	42,932	44,321	44,707	46,008	47,384	47,959	49,290
Forestry, fishing, and related activities.............................	25,287	26,092	26,656	27,280	28,299	30,393	32,143
Mining..	69,742	70,237	68,204	69,599	69,625	66,847	69,193
Utilities..	82,724	83,300	85,825	89,324	91,273	94,222	98,147
Construction	49,635	51,250	51,649	53,441	55,396	57,009	58,802
Manufacturing..	52,098	54,037	54,661	56,945	58,403	58,309	59,247
Durable goods manufacturing.......................................	54,380	55,525	57,330	59,918	60,666	60,625	61,818
Nondurable goods manufacturing.................................	48,936	51,991	50,905	52,580	54,990	54,828	55,450
Wholesale trade	60,363	62,216	62,175	64,575	66,392	67,400	69,105
Retail trade..	25,556	26,248	26,418	26,916	27,918	28,370	29,096
Transportation and warehousing....................................	44,467	45,694	47,024	48,232	49,109	49,582	50,545
Information	68,181	72,432	70,516	71,213	74,871	75,881	76,091
Finance and insurance	65,051	69,155	69,348	71,785	75,164	77,124	79,329
Real estate and rental and leasing.................................	36,569	38,759	39,113	40,598	42,984	43,107	44,272
Professional, scientific, and technical services	68,836	71,308	71,063	72,691	76,146	76,178	78,016
Management of companies and enterprises......................	90,859	96,072	97,530	102,956	101,218	100,100	104,518
Administrative and waste services..................................	31,851	32,329	32,893	33,927	34,429	35,530	37,246
Educational services	32,843	34,065	35,034	36,057	36,151	36,371	36,764
Health care and social assistance..................................	42,394	42,618	42,710	43,102	44,536	45,155	46,096
Arts, entertainment, and recreation................................	37,824	38,161	40,037	39,973	42,390	41,782	40,560
Accommodation and food services.................................	16,890	17,263	17,555	18,114	18,959	19,477	20,339
Other services, except public administration....................	28,929	30,077	30,700	31,653	32,865	33,987	35,224
Government and government enterprises.............................	40,351	40,684	41,185	41,980	43,028	43,572	44,626

Table MO-10. Employment Characteristics by Family Type

(Number, percent.)

Family type and labor force status	2015		2016		2017	
	Total	Families with own children under 18 years	Total	Families with own children under 18 years	Total	Families with own children under 18 years
All Families...	1,519,299	633,503	1,527,349	633,173	1,527,260	624,089
FAMILY TYPE AND LABOR FORCE STATUS						
Married-Couple Families..	1,137,014	423,324	1,139,135	422,248	1,138,262	414,861
Both husband and wife in labor force.................................	52.6	70.9	52.2	71.9	51.5	70.5
Husband in labor force, wife not in labor force	19.1	23.4	19.2	22.6	19.2	23.0
Wife in labor force, husband not in labor force	8.6	3.9	8.2	3.3	8.2	4.2
Both husband and wife not in labor force...............................	19.2	1.5	19.8	1.7	20.3	1.7
Other Families	382,285	210,179	388,214	210,925	388,998	209,228
Female householder, no husband present...............................	73.3	74.8	72.0	73.5	71.7	73.7
In labor force...	51.8	62.4	51.4	62.2	51.3	62.9
Not in labor force	21.5	12.4	20.6	11.3	20.4	10.9
Male householder, no wife present......................	26.7	25.2	28.0	26.5	28.3	26.3
In labor force...	20.3	22.6	21.3	24.1	21.9	23.3
Not in labor force	6.4	2.7	6.7	2.5	6.3	2.9

Table MO-11. School Enrollment and Educational Attainment, 2017

(Number, percent.)

Item	State	U.S.
Enrollment		
Total population 3 years and over, enrolled in school	1,484,234	81,273,337
Enrolled in nursery school or preschool (percent).............................	6.5	6.0
Enrolled in kindergarten (percent)...	4.6	4.9
Enrolled in elementary school, grades 1-8 (percent)...........................	42.0	40.6
Enrolled in high school, grades 9-12 (percent)................................	21.2	21.1
Enrolled in college or graduate school (percent).............................	25.7	27.4
Attainment		
Total population 25 years and over	4,150,275	221,250,083
Less than ninth grade (percent)...	3.1	5.1
9th to 12th grade, no diploma (percent)	7.2	6.9
High school graduate, including equivalency (percent)........................	30.8	27.1
Some college, no degree (percent)...	22.0	20.4
Associate's degree (percent)...	7.9	8.5
Bachelor's degree (percent)	17.9	19.7
Graduate or professional degree (percent)....................................	11.1	12.3
High school graduate or higher (percent).....................................	89.7	88.0
Bachelor's degree or higher (percent)..	29.1	32.0

Table MO-12. Public School Characteristics and Educational Indicators

(Number, percent; data derived from National Center of Education Statistics.)

Item	State	U.S.
Public Elementary and Secondary Schools		
Number of operational school districts, 2016-17	566	18,377
Number of operational schools, 2016-17..	2,424	98,330
Percent charter schools	3.0	7.1
Total public school enrollment, 2016-17.......................................	915,040	50,587,859
Percent charter school enrollment	2.5	6.0
Student-teacher ratio, Fall 2015..	13.6	16.0
Expenditures per student (dollars), 2015-16...................................	10,385	11,841
Four-year adjusted cohort graduation rate (ACGR)[1]	88.3	84.6
Students eligible for free or reduced-price lunch (percent), 2015-16...........	50.1	52.1
English language learners (percent), Fall 2016	3.4	9.6
Students age 3 to 21 served under IDEA, part B (percent), 2017-18	14.3	13.7
Public Schools by Type, 2016-17		Percent of state public schools
Total number of schools...	2,424	100.0
Special education...	53	2.2
Vocational education..	63	2.6
Alternative education...	59	2.4

[1] Adjusted Cohort Graduation Rates (ACGR) differ from Averaged Freshmen Graduation Rates (AFGR).

Table MO-13. Reported Voting and Registration of the Voting-Age Population, November 2018

(Numbers in thousands, percent.)

Item	Total population	Total citizen population	Registered			Voted		
			Total registered	Percent registered (total population)	Percent registered (total citizen population)	Total voted	Percent voted (total population)	Percent voted (total citizen population)
U.S. Total	249,748	228,832	153,066	61.3	66.9	122,281	49.0	53.4
State Total...........................	4,676	4,564	3,299	70.6	72.3	2,509	53.7	55.0
Sex								
Male	2,243	2,202	1,541	68.7	70.0	1,162	51.8	52.8
Female	2,433	2,361	1,758	72.3	74.5	1,346	55.3	57.0
Race								
White alone................................	4,006	3,944	2,887	72.1	73.2	2,227	55.6	56.5
White, non-Hispanic alone	3,874	3,856	2,839	73.3	73.6	2,185	56.4	56.7
Black alone................................	504	497	326	64.8	65.7	238	47.3	47.9
Asian alone................................	55	35	17	(B)	(B)	3	(B)	(B)
Hispanic (of any race).................	176	108	53	30.0	49.1	47	26.5	43.3
White alone or in combination	4,060	3,991	2,927	72.1	73.3	2,253	55.5	56.5
Black alone or in combination	531	519	340	64.0	65.5	245	46.1	47.2
Asian alone or in combination.......	55	35	17	(B)	(B)	3	(B)	(B)
Age								
18 to 24 years	522	488	307	58.8	62.9	202	38.7	41.4
25 to 34 years	805	774	544	67.6	70.2	373	46.3	48.1
35 to 44 years	780	759	517	66.3	68.2	386	49.5	50.9
45 to 64 years	1,462	1,450	1,064	72.8	73.4	832	56.9	57.4
65 years and over	1,107	1,093	867	78.3	79.3	716	64.7	65.6

B = Base is less than 75,000 and therefore too small to show the derived measure.

Table MO-14. Crime

(Number, rate per 100,000. Data are derived from the FBI Uniform Crime Reports.)

Item	State			U.S.		
	2016	2017	Percent change	2016	2017	Percent change
TOTAL POPULATION[1]	6,091,176	6,113,532	0.4	323,405,935	325,719,178	0.7
VIOLENT CRIME						
Number..	31,720	32,420	2.2	1,285,606	1,283,220	-0.2
Rate	520.8	530.3	1.8	397.5	394.0	-0.9
Murder and Nonnegligent Manslaughter						
Number..	538	600	11.5	17,413	17,284	-0.7
Rate	8.8	9.8	11.1	5.4	5.3	-1.4
Rape[2]						
Number..	2,557	2,729	6.7	132,414	135,755	2.5
Rate	42.0	44.6	6.3	40.9	41.7	1.8
Robbery						
Number..	6,576	6,351	-3.4	332,797	319,356	-4.0
Rate	108.0	103.9	-3.8	102.9	98.0	-4.7
Aggravated Assault						
Number..	22,049	22,740	3.1	802,982	810,825	1.0
Rate	362.0	372.0	2.8	248.3	248.9	0.3
PROPERTY CRIME						
Number..	170,661	173,253	1.5	7,928,530	7,694,086	-3.0
Rate	2,801.8	2,833.9	1.1	2,451.6	2,362.2	-3.6
Burglary						
Number..	31,716	30,081	-5.2	1,516,405	1,401,840	-7.6
Rate	520.7	492.0	-5.5	468.9	430.4	-8.2
Larceny-Theft						
Number..	120,649	123,251	2.2	5,644,835	5,519,107	-2.2
Rate	1,980.7	2,016.0	1.8	1,745.4	1,694.4	-2.9
Motor Vehicle Theft						
Number..	18,296	19,921	8.9	767,290	773,139	0.8
Rate	300.4	325.9	8.5	237.3	237.4	-

NOTE: Although arson data are included in the trend and clearance tables, sufficient data are not available to estimate totals for this offense. Therefore, no arson data are published in this table.
- = Zero or rounds to zero.
[1] Population figures are U.S. Census Bureau provisional estimates as of July 1, 2017.
[2] The figures shown in the rape (revised definition) column were estimated using the revised Uniform Crime Reporting (UCR) definition of rape.

Table MO-15. State Government Finances, 2017

(Dollar amounts in thousands, percent distribution.)

Item	Dollars	Percent distribution
Total Revenue	39,873,277	100.0
General revenue	29,530,314	74.1
Intergovernmental revenue	11,322,122	28.4
Taxes	12,495,505	31.3
General sales	3,604,570	9.0
Selective sales	1,799,366	4.5
License taxes	590,747	1.5
Individual income tax	6,149,468	15.4
Corporate income tax	307,443	0.8
Other taxes	43,911	0.1
Current charges	3,116,903	7.8
Miscellaneous general revenue	2,595,784	6.5
Utility revenue	0	-
Liquor stores revenue	0	-
Insurance trust revenue[1]	10,342,963	25.9
Total Expenditure	33,703,997	100.0
Intergovernmental expenditure	6,298,000	18.7
Direct expenditure	27,405,997	81.3
Current operation	20,005,078	59.4
Capital outlay	1,248,841	3.7
Insurance benefits and repayments	4,739,931	14.1
Assistance and subsidies	639,495	1.9
Interest on debt	772,652	2.3
Exhibit: Salaries and wages	4,027,051	11.9
Total Expenditure	33,703,997	100.0
General expenditure	28,964,066	85.9
Intergovernmental expenditure	6,298,000	18.7
Direct expenditure	22,666,066	67.3
General expenditure, by function:		
Education	9,976,109	29.6
Public welfare	8,995,674	26.7
Hospitals	2,212,142	6.6
Health	1,988,453	5.9
Highways	1,391,549	4.1
Police protection	235,665	0.7
Correction	827,462	2.5
Natural resources	370,717	1.1
Parks and recreation	69,035	0.2
Governmental administration	569,498	1.7
Interest on general debt	772,652	2.3
Other and unallocable	1,555,110	4.6
Utility expenditure	0	-
Liquor stores expenditure	0	-
Insurance trust expenditure	4,739,931	14.1
Debt at End of Fiscal Year	18,419,751	X
Cash and Security Holdings	73,595,342	X

X = Not applicable.
- = Zero or rounds to zero.
[1] Within insurance trust revenue, net earnings of state retirement systems is a calculated statistic (the item code in the data file is X08), and thus can be positive or negative. Net earnings is the sum of earnings on investments plus gains on investments minus losses on investments. The change made in 2002 for asset valuation from book to market value in accordance with Statement 34 of the Governmental Accounting Standards Board is reflected in the calculated statistics.

Table MO-16. State Government Tax Collections, 2018

(Dollars in thousands, percent.)

Item	Dollars	Percent distribution
Total Taxes	13,027,504	100.0
Property taxes	33,267	0.3
Sales and gross receipts	5,539,227	42.5
General sales and gross receipts	3,686,274	28.3
Selective sales and gross receipts	1,852,953	14.2
Alcoholic beverages	38,932	0.3
Amusements	369,410	2.8
Insurance premiums	464,418	3.6
Motor fuels	717,894	5.5
Pari-mutuels	X	-
Public utilities	X	-
Tobacco products	97,408	0.7
Other selective sales	164,891	1.3
Licenses	598,601	4.6
Alcoholic beverages	5,478	-
Amusements	2,462	-
Corporations in general	2,200	-
Hunting and fishing	33,692	0.3
Motor vehicle	296,849	2.3
Motor vehicle operators	17,596	0.1
Public utilities	19,628	0.2
Occupation and business, NEC	142,822	1.1
Other licenses	77,874	0.6
Income taxes	6,843,948	52.5
Individual income	6,510,224	50.0
Corporation net income	333,724	2.6
Other taxes	12,461	0.1
Death and gift	54	-
Documentary and stock transfer	12,331	0.1
Severance	2	-
Taxes, NEC	74	-

- = Zero or rounds to zero.
X = Not applicable.

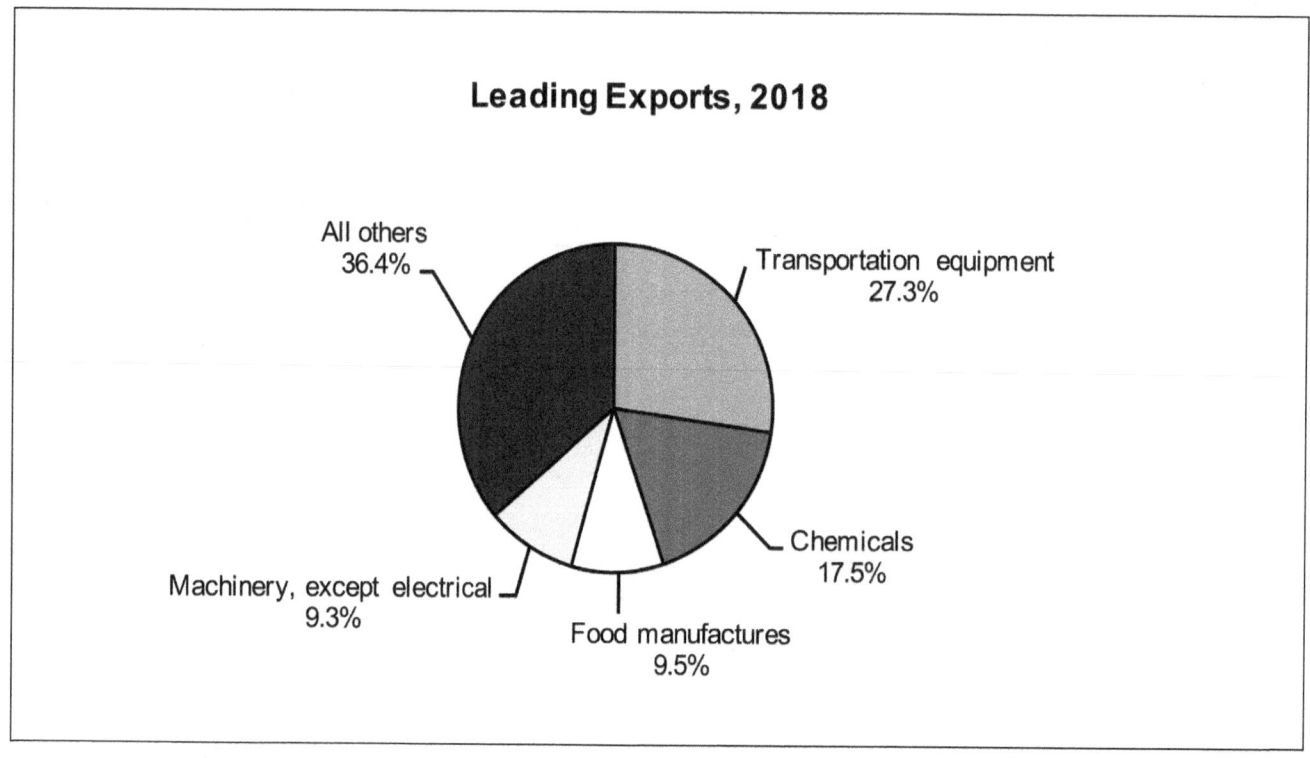

Leading Exports, 2018

All others 36.4%

Transportation equipment 27.3%

Chemicals 17.5%

Food manufactures 9.5%

Machinery, except electrical 9.3%

MONTANA

Facts and Figures

Location: Northwestern United States; bordered on the N by Canada (British Columbia, Alberta, and Saskatchewan), on the E by North Dakota and South Dakota, on the S by Idaho and Wyoming, and on the W by Idaho

Area: 147,042 sq. mi. (380,838 sq. km.); rank—4th

Population: 1,062,305 (2018 est.); rank—43rd

Principal Cities: capital—Helena; largest—Billings

Statehood: November 8, 1889; 41st state

U.S. Congress: 2 senators, 1 representative

State Motto: *Oro y plata* ("Gold and silver")

State Song: "Montana"

State Nicknames: The Treasure State; Big Sky Country

Abbreviations: MT; Mont.

State Symbols: flower—bitterroot; tree—ponderosa pine; bird—Western meadowlark

At a Glance

- With an increase in population of 7.4 percent, Montana ranked 17th among the states in growth from 2010 to 2018.

- The median household income in Montana in 2017 was $53,386 compared to the national median household income of $60,336.

- In 2018, 18.7 percent of Montana residents were in the 65 and older age group, a percentage that ranked 5th in the country.

- Approximately 0.6 percent of Montana residents self-identified as "Black or African-American alone" in 2018, which was the lowest percentage among all the states.

Table MT-1. Population by Age, Sex, Race, and Hispanic Origin

(Number, percent, except where noted.)

Sex, age, race, and Hispanic origin	2000	2010	2018 [1]	Percent change, 2010–2018
Total Population...	902,195	989,415	1,062,305	7.4
Percent of total U.S. population	0.3	0.3	0.3	X
Sex				
Male...	449,480	496,667	534,852	7.7
Female...	452,715	492,748	527,453	7.0
Age				
Under 5 years..	54,869	62,423	62,536	0.2
5 to 19 years...	202,571	188,613	192,830	2.2
20 to 64 years...	523,806	591,637	608,037	2.8
65 years and over..	120,949	146,742	198,902	35.5
Median age (years)	37.5	39.8	39.9	0.3
Race and Hispanic Origin				
One race				
White..	817,229	891,529	945,132	6.0
Black..	2,692	4,215	6,237	48.0
American Indian and Alaska Native	56,068	63,495	70,603	11.2
Asian..	4,691	6,379	9,852	54.4
Native Hawaiian or Other Pacific Islander	470	734	893	21.7
Two or more races	15,730	23,063	29,588	28.3
Hispanic (of any race)...	18,081	31,018	42,503	37.0

X = Not applicable.
[1] Population figures for 2018 are July 1 estimates. The 2010 estimates are taken from the 2010 Census.
- = Zero or rounds to zero.

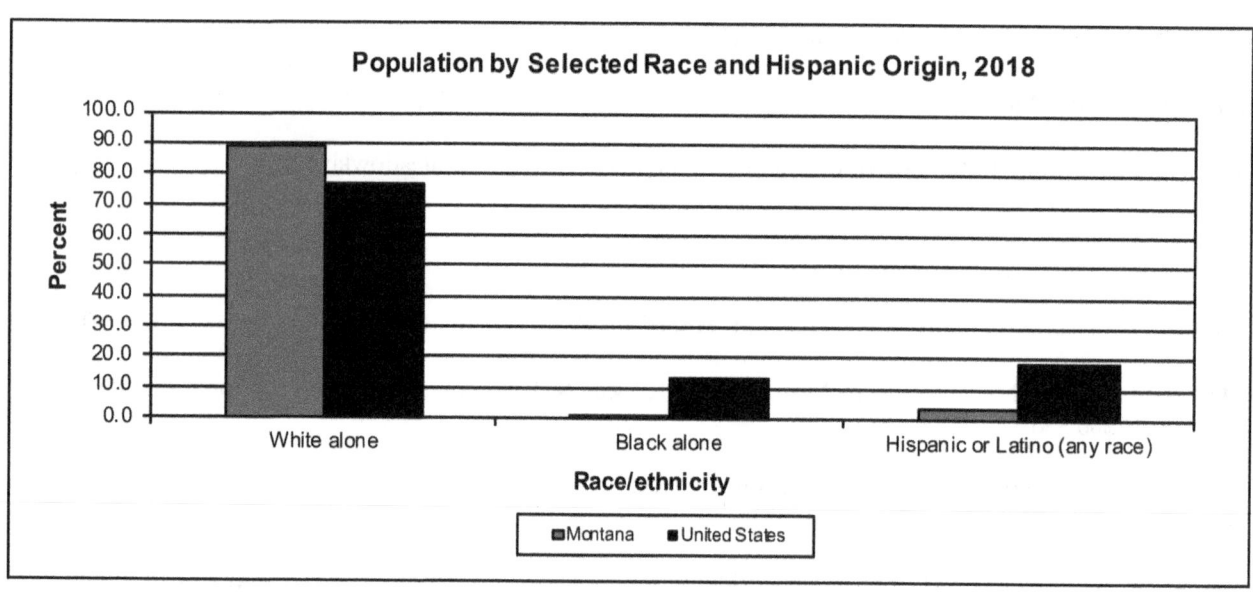

Population by Selected Race and Hispanic Origin, 2018

Table MT-2. Marital Status

(Number, percent distribution.)

Sex, age, race, and Hispanic origin	2000	2010	2017
Males, 15 Years and Over	353,801	404,179	428,973
Never married	27.7	30.5	32.4
Now married, except separated..	58.3	53.4	51.9
Separated..	1.2	1.5	1.0
Widowed..	2.6	2.3	2.7
Divorced..	10.2	12.4	12.0
Females, 15 Years and Over	362,114	403,766	430,355
Never married	20.4	23.5	25.0
Now married, except separated..	56.3	52.9	52.2
Separated..	1.3	1.6	1.3
Widowed..	10.4	9.7	8.4
Divorced..	11.6	12.3	13.1

Table MT-3. Households and Housing Characteristics

(Number, percent, dollars.)

Item	2000	2010	2017	Average annual percent change, 2010–2017
Total Households.....................................	358,667	402,747	423,091	0.7
Family households	237,407	255,199	262,726	0.4
Married-couple family	192,067	203,500	213,118	0.7
Other family	45,340	51,699	49,608	-0.6
Male householder, no wife present........................	13,324	16,926	17,119	0.2
Female householder, no husband present.............	32,016	34,773	32,489	-0.9
Nonfamily households	121,260	147,548	160,365	1.2
Householder living alone...................................	98,422	119,762	128,489	1.0
Householder not living alone............................	22,838	27,786	31,876	2.1
Housing Characteristics				
Total housing units...	412,633	483,006	510,408	0.8
Occupied housing units	358,667	402,747	423,091	0.7
Owner occupied	247,723	280,633	292,585	0.6
Renter occupied	110,944	122,114	130,506	1.0
Average household size.......................................	2.45	2.39	2.41	0.1
Financial Characteristics				
Median gross rent of renter-occupied housing	447	642	759	2.6
Median monthly owner costs for housing units with a mortgage	863	1,217	1,367	1.8
Median value of owner-occupied housing units	99,500	181,200	231,300	3.9

Table MT-4. Migration, Origin, and Language

(Number, percent.)

Characteristic	State			U.S.		
	2016	2017	Percent change	2016	2017	Percent change
Residence 1 Year Ago						
Population 1 year and over	1,032,794	1,039,170	0.6	319,361,956	321,994,428	0.8
Same house	83.6	85.0	X	85.4	85.7	X
Different house in the U.S.	16.1	14.6	X	13.9	13.6	X
Same county	8.9	8.1	X	8.3	8.1	X
Different county	7.2	6.6	X	5.6	5.6	X
Same state	3.5	3.1	X	3.2	3.3	X
Different state	3.7	3.4	X	2.4	2.3	X
Abroad	0.3	0.4	X	0.7	0.7	X
Place of Birth						
Native born	1,020,627	1,027,384	0.7	279,388,170	281,193,323	0.6
Male	50.7	50.3	X	49.3	49.4	X
Female	49.3	49.7	X	50.7	50.6	X
Foreign born	21,893	23,109	5.6	43,739,345	44,525,855	1.8
Male	39.1	42.9	X	48.5	48.4	X
Female	60.9	57.1	X	51.5	51.6	X
Foreign born; naturalized U.S. citizen.................	11,585	12,151	4.9	21,238,372	21,948,732	3.3
Male	28.8	43.0	X	45.9	45.9	X
Female	71.2	57.0	X	54.1	54.1	X
Foreign born; not a U.S. citizen..........................	10,308	10,958	6.3	22,500,973	22,577,123	0.3
Male	50.8	42.7	X	51	50.8	X
Female	49.2	57.3	X	49	49.2	X
Entered 2010 or later	24.1	27.9	X	18.6	21.3	X
Entered 2000 to 2009	16.7	17.2	X	26.7	25.7	X
Entered before 2000..	59.2	54.8	X	54.7	53.0	X
World Region of Birth, Foreign						
Foreign-born population, excluding population born at sea	21,893	23,109	5.6	43,738,901	44,525,458	1.8
Europe	33.9	33.2	X	10.9	10.8	X
Asia	34.0	24.7	X	30.8	31.2	X
Africa	2.9	3.6	X	4.9	5.1	X
Oceania	0.7	2.0	X	0.6	0.6	X
Latin America..	10.3	22.0	X	51	50.4	X
North America...	18.2	14.5	X	1.8	1.8	X
Language Spoken at Home and Ability to Speak English						
Population 5 years and over................................	981,377	989,088	0.8	303,328,961	305,924,019	0.9
English only	96.3	95.7	X	78.4	78.2	X
Language other than English..............................	3.7	4.3	X	21.6	21.8	X
Speaks English less than "very well".............	0.7	1.0	X	8.6	8.5	X

NA = Not available.
X = Not applicable.
- = Zero or rounds to zero.

Table MT-5. Median Income and Poverty Status, 2017

(Number, percent, except as noted.)

Characteristic	State Number	State Percent	U.S. Number	U.S. Percent
Median Income				
Households (dollars)..	53,386	X	60,336	X
Families (dollars)	68,994	X	73,891	X
Below Poverty Level (All People)	127,777	12.5	42,583,651	13.4
Sex				
Male	58,070	11.4	19,004,547	12.2
Female	69,707	13.6	23,579,104	14.5
Age				
Under 18 years...	32,857	14.7	13,353,202	18.4
Related children under 18 years...	31,962	14.4	13,053,472	18.1
18 to 64 years..	81,639	13.3	24,648,677	12.6
65 years and over	13,281	7.2	4,581,772	9.3

X = Not applicable.

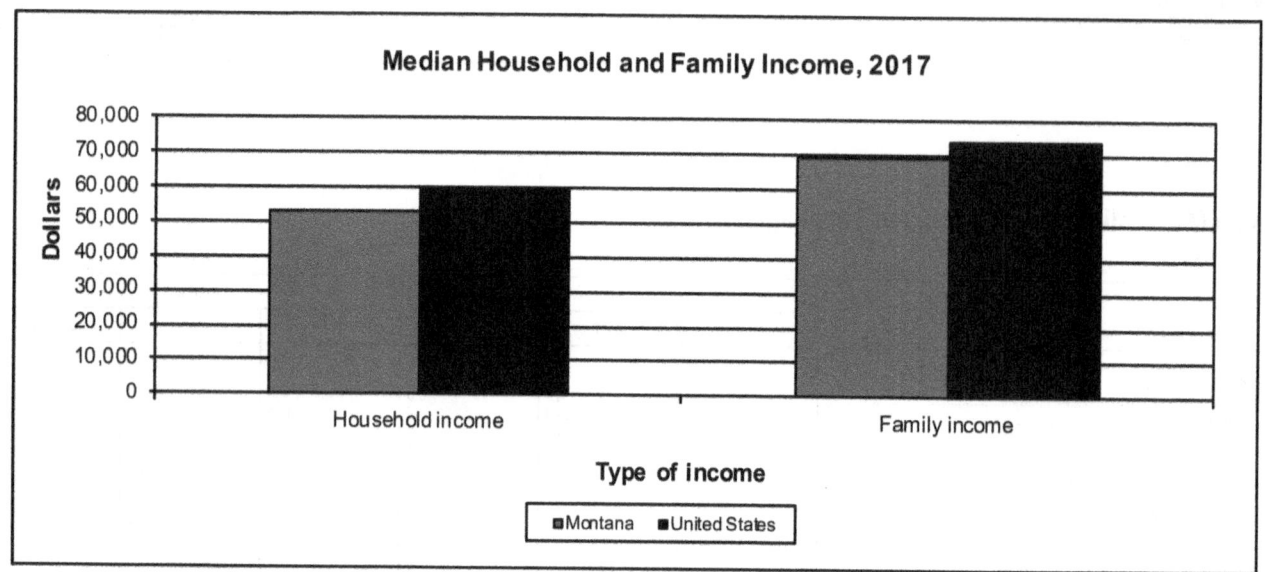

Median Household and Family Income, 2017

Table MT-6. Health Insurance Coverage Status for the Civilian Noninstitutionalized Population and Children Under 18 Years of Age

(Number, percent.)

Item	2009	2010	2011	2012	2013	2014	2015	2016	2017
Civilian Noninstitutionalized Population	957,586	975,562	983,214	989,823	999,390	1,008,116	1,017,458	1,027,510	1,036,245
Covered by Private or Public Insurance									
Number...	783,294	806,581	803,639	811,411	834,842	864,795	898,949	944,094	948,536
Percent..	81.8	82.7	81.7	82.0	83.5	85.8	88.4	91.9	91.5
Uninsured									
Number...	174,292	168,981	179,575	178,412	164,548	143,321	118,509	83,416	87,709
Percent..	18.2	17.3	18.3	18.0	16.5	14.2	11.6	8.1	8.5
Percent in the U.S. not covered..................................	15.1	15.5	15.1	14.8	14.5	11.7	9.4	8.6	8.7
Children Under 18 Years of Age[1]	220,411	221,455	222,102	219,198	223,043	224,051	225,169	227,631	240,764
Covered by Private or Public Insurance									
Number...	191,941	193,897	196,540	194,796	200,548	205,630	208,050	217,003	226,900
Percent..	87.1	87.6	88.5	88.9	89.9	91.8	92.4	95.3	94.2
Uninsured									
Number...	28,470	27,558	25,562	24,402	22,495	18,421	17,119	10,628	13,864
Percent..	12.9	12.4	11.5	11.1	10.1	8.2	7.6	4.7	5.8
Percent in the U.S. not covered	8.6	8.0	7.5	7.2	7.1	6.0	4.8	4.5	5.0

[1] 2017 data is for individuals under 19 years of age.

Table MT-7. Employment Status by Demographic Group, 2018

(Numbers in thousands, percent.)

Characteristic	Civilian noninstitutional population	Civilian labor force		Employed		Unemployed	
		Number	Percent of population	Number	Percent of population	Number	Percent of population
Total..	842	525	62.3	506	60.0	19	3.7
Sex							
Male..	420	280	66.7	268	63.8	12	4.4
Female..	423	245	58.0	238	56.3	7	2.9
Race, Sex, and Hispanic Origin							
White..	787	493	62.7	476	60.5	17	3.5
Male..	394	264	67.1	254	64.4	11	4.0
Female..	393	229	58.2	222	56.5	7	2.9
Black or African American................	NA	NA	NA	NA	NA	NA	NA
Male..	NA	NA	NA	NA	NA	NA	NA
Female..	NA	NA	NA	NA	NA	NA	NA
Hispanic or Latino ethnicity[1].........	24	19	80.2	18	76.3	1	4.9
Male..	NA	NA	NA	NA	NA	NA	NA
Female..	NA	NA	NA	NA	NA	NA	NA
Age							
16 to 19 years..................................	48	21	43.8	19	39.8	2	9.4
20 to 24 years..................................	66	51	77.6	48	73.3	3	5.5
25 to 34 years..................................	138	119	86.3	114	82.5	5	4.5
35 to 44 years..................................	127	105	82.5	102	80.4	3	2.6
45 to 54 years..................................	109	88	80.5	85	77.8	3	3.3
55 to 64 years..................................	153	101	65.9	99	64.3	3	2.5
65 years and over.............................	203	41	20.2	40	19.6	1	3.4

NOTE: Data in Table 7 are from the Current Population Survey (CPS) and do not match the estimates in Table 8. See notes and definitions for further information.
[1] May be of any race.
NA = Not available.

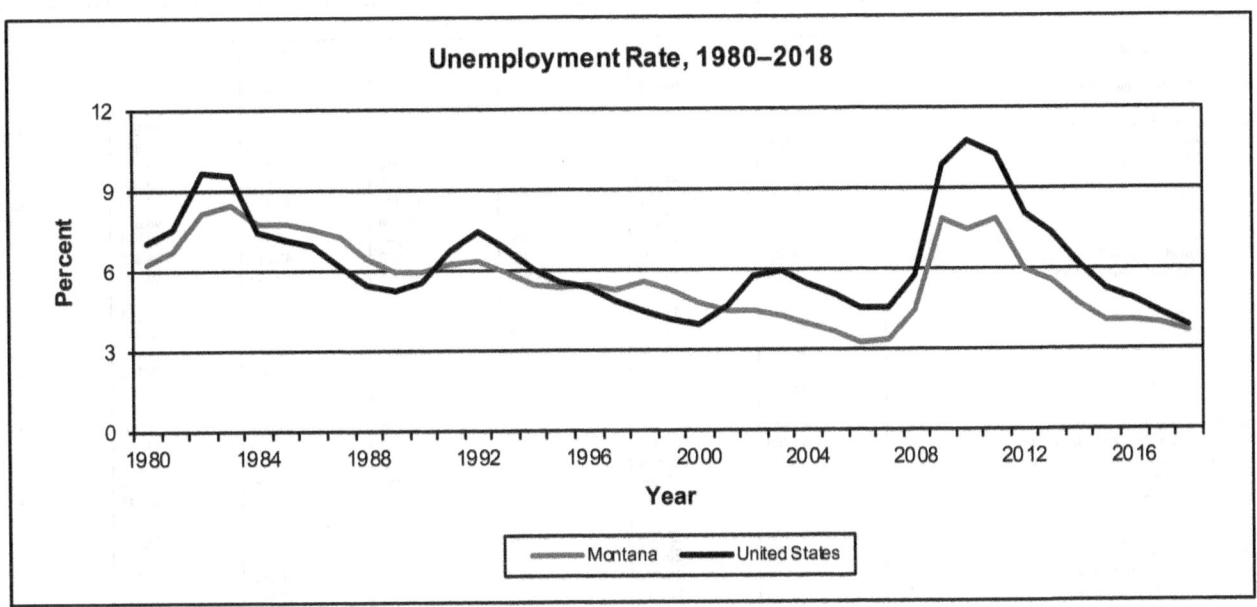

Unemployment Rate, 1980–2018

Table MT-8. Employment Status of the Civilian Noninstitutional Population Age 16 Years and Over

(Number, percent.)

Year	Civilian labor force	Civilian participation rate	Employed	Unemployed	Unemployment rate
2010..	500,525	64.4	463,998	36,527	7.3
2011..	501,225	63.9	466,403	34,822	6.9
2012..	506,485	64.1	476,174	30,311	6.0
2013..	510,781	64.0	483,071	27,710	5.4
2014..	511,501	63.5	487,629	23,872	4.7
2015..	516,845	63.6	495,298	21,547	4.2
2016..	521,628	63.5	499,990	21,638	4.1
2017..	525,453	63.2	504,279	21,174	4.0
2018..	528,244	62.7	508,588	19,656	3.7

Table MT-9. Employment and Average Wages by Industry

(Estimates are based on the 2012 *North American Industry Classification System* [NAICS].)

Industry	2011	2012	2013	2014	2015	2016	2017
	Number of jobs						
Wage and Salary Employment by Industry......................	451,230	460,264	466,811	470,408	479,194	484,003	489,276
Farm Wage and Salary Employment.................................	5,488	6,668	6,618	6,407	6,867	6,954	8,049
Nonfarm Wage and Salary Employment............................	445,742	453,596	460,193	464,001	472,327	477,049	481,227
Private wage and salary employment............................	349,707	358,437	365,084	368,689	376,987	380,970	385,073
Forestry, fishing, and related activities	3,185	3,464	3,573	3,663	3,809	3,850	3,882
Mining..	7,554	8,714	8,833	8,527	7,560	6,377	6,322
Utilities..	3,116	3,197	3,179	3,157	3,080	3,029	2,874
Construction..	23,305	23,703	24,728	25,585	27,160	27,736	28,405
Manufacturing...	16,848	17,575	18,355	18,909	19,131	19,513	19,921
Durable goods manufacturing.........................	9,742	10,620	11,115	11,567	11,714	11,778	11,925
Nondurable goods manufacturing....................	7,106	6,955	7,240	7,342	7,417	7,735	7,996
Wholesale trade	15,696	16,322	17,126	17,000	17,621	17,378	17,268
Retail trade..	55,173	55,733	56,388	57,657	59,101	59,697	59,453
Transportation and warehousing........................	13,737	14,519	15,111	15,491	15,610	15,252	15,218
Information...	7,226	6,942	6,907	6,420	6,377	6,334	6,408
Finance and insurance......................................	16,253	15,697	15,945	16,059	16,196	16,209	16,324
Real estate and rental and leasing....................	5,214	5,243	5,389	5,375	5,699	5,685	6,007
Professional, scientific, and technical services	19,164	19,679	20,203	20,296	21,004	21,774	22,127
Management of companies and enterprises.........	2,009	2,056	1,973	1,962	2,067	2,074	2,079
Administrative and waste services......................	19,219	19,690	17,732	17,304	17,545	16,943	17,124
Educational services	5,538	5,687	5,935	6,064	6,066	6,004	6,138
Health care and social assistance......................	59,915	62,064	63,365	63,958	65,115	67,420	69,089
Arts, entertainment, and recreation....................	10,829	10,851	11,280	11,535	11,596	11,876	11,941
Accommodation and food services.....................	45,901	47,409	49,009	49,326	51,399	52,932	53,548
Other services, except public administration........	19,825	19,892	20,053	20,401	20,851	20,887	20,945
Government and government enterprises.................	96,035	95,159	95,109	95,312	95,340	96,079	96,154
	Dollars						
Average Wages and Salaries by Industry	35,826	37,175	37,741	39,059	40,143	40,885	42,133
Average Farm Wages and Salaries	30,024	34,585	38,873	38,757	30,604	34,987	30,401
Average Nonfarm Wages and Salaries	35,897	37,213	37,725	39,063	40,282	40,971	42,329
Average private wages and salaries...................	35,020	36,520	37,106	38,558	39,768	40,303	41,712
Forestry, fishing, and related activities	27,103	28,511	29,412	31,018	33,383	35,761	37,654
Mining..	80,467	82,024	83,422	88,252	87,576	88,061	87,727
Utilities..	78,151	76,652	78,666	81,114	87,486	86,271	88,971
Construction..	42,751	43,856	44,794	46,108	47,823	48,673	50,355
Manufacturing...	42,591	43,491	43,690	45,742	47,243	47,751	48,811
Durable goods manufacturing.........................	39,943	41,801	42,902	44,078	45,719	46,455	47,771
Nondurable goods manufacturing....................	46,222	46,070	44,901	48,363	49,649	49,724	50,362
Wholesale trade	47,897	49,861	50,785	53,237	54,828	55,004	56,941
Retail trade..	24,683	25,341	25,851	26,867	27,695	28,327	29,254
Transportation and warehousing........................	47,005	48,506	49,651	51,891	51,640	51,166	52,802
Information...	41,894	43,033	44,055	45,667	48,405	50,183	51,874
Finance and insurance......................................	49,826	53,665	55,555	57,632	60,144	61,507	64,932
Real estate and rental and leasing....................	28,438	30,577	30,464	32,246	34,492	34,976	35,784
Professional, scientific, and technical services	51,799	57,597	54,412	57,893	59,350	59,324	61,327
Management of companies and enterprises.........	59,505	68,648	73,095	71,993	75,761	75,235	76,186
Administrative and waste services......................	27,846	29,306	28,766	30,153	32,095	33,560	34,415
Educational services	22,010	21,704	22,048	22,756	23,552	24,347	24,793
Health care and social assistance......................	39,160	39,969	41,061	42,133	44,380	45,445	47,345
Arts, entertainment, and recreation....................	20,233	20,309	21,069	22,631	23,280	23,988	25,163
Accommodation and food services.....................	16,046	16,790	17,300	18,179	18,862	19,437	20,211
Other services, except public administration........	25,408	26,337	26,994	27,976	28,968	30,204	31,470
Government and government enterprises.................	39,092	39,824	40,102	41,016	42,311	43,616	44,801

Table MT-10. Employment Characteristics by Family Type

(Number, percent.)

Family type and labor force status	2015		2016		2017	
	Total	Families with own children under 18 years	Total	Families with own children under 18 years	Total	Families with own children under 18 years
All Families...	253,101	99,864	257,449	101,061	262,726	98,444
FAMILY TYPE AND LABOR FORCE STATUS						
Married-Couple Families..	202,848	70,742	207,675	74,795	213,118	72,373
Both husband and wife in labor force	51.2	68.1	53.0	71.6	51.6	68.9
Husband in labor force, wife not in labor force	19.5	25.3	17.3	22.0	17.9	23.8
Wife in labor force, husband not in labor force	8.8	3.8	8.1	3.6	8.4	5.3
Both husband and wife not in labor force............................	20.2	2.6	21.1	2.6	21.2	1.1
Other Families	50,253	29,122	49,774	26,266	49,608	26,071
Female householder, no husband present...............................	69.0	68.5	66.3	67.2	65.5	64.9
In labor force..	46.4	53.0	46.0	57.3	45.7	54.0
Not in labor force	22.5	15.5	20.3	9.9	19.8	10.9
Male householder, no wife present.......................................	31.0	31.5	33.7	32.8	34.5	35.1
In labor force..	23.6	27.6	25.3	31.0	25.9	29.3
Not in labor force	7.4	3.9	8.3	1.9	8.6	5.8

Table MT-11. School Enrollment and Educational Attainment, 2017

(Number, percent.)

Item	State	U.S.
Enrollment		
Total population 3 years and over, enrolled in school	236,016	81,273,337
Enrolled in nursery school or preschool (percent)	6.3	6.0
Enrolled in kindergarten (percent)...	5.6	4.9
Enrolled in elementary school, grades 1-8 (percent)...	43.0	40.6
Enrolled in high school, grades 9-12 (percent)	21.0	21.1
Enrolled in college or graduate school (percent)...	24.1	27.4
Attainment		
Total population 25 years and over	723,666	221,250,083
Less than ninth grade (percent)	2.2	5.1
9th to 12th grade, no diploma (percent)	4.8	6.9
High school graduate, including equivalency (percent)...................................	28.1	27.1
Some college, no degree (percent)	23.5	20.4
Associate's degree (percent)...	9.1	8.5
Bachelor's degree (percent)	21.7	19.7
Graduate or professional degree (percent)...	10.6	12.3
High school graduate or higher (percent)	93.0	88.0
Bachelor's degree or higher (percent)...	32.3	32.0

Table MT-12. Public School Characteristics and Educational Indicators

(Number, percent; data derived from National Center of Education Statistics.)

Item	State	U.S.
Public Elementary and Secondary Schools		
Number of operational school districts, 2016-17..	487	18,377
Number of operational schools, 2016-17..	820	98,330
Percent charter schools	NA	7.1
Total public school enrollment, 2016-17...	146,375	50,587,859
Percent charter school enrollment	NA	6.0
Student-teacher ratio, Fall 2015...	14.0	16.0
Expenditures per student (dollars), 2015-16...	11,374	11,841
Four-year adjusted cohort graduation rate (ACGR)[1]	85.8	84.6
Students eligible for free or reduced-price lunch (percent), 2015-16........................	46.2	52.1
English language learners (percent), Fall 2016...	2.0	9.6
Students age 3 to 21 served under IDEA, part B (percent), 2017-18	12.8	13.7
Public Schools by Type, 2016-17		Percent of state public schools
Total number of schools..	820	100.0
Special education..	2	0.2
Vocational education..	0	-
Alternative education...	4	0.5

[1] Adjusted Cohort Graduation Rates (ACGR) differ from Averaged Freshmen Graduation Rates (AFGR).
NA = Not available.
- = Zero or rounds to zero.

Table MT-13. Reported Voting and Registration of the Voting-Age Population, November 2018

(Numbers in thousands, percent.)

Item	Total population	Total citizen population	Registered			Voted		
			Total registered	Percent registered (total population)	Percent registered (total citizen population)	Total voted	Percent voted (total population)	Percent voted (total citizen population)
U.S. Total	249,748	228,832	153,066	61.3	66.9	122,281	49.0	53.4
State Total................................	822	812	579	70.4	71.3	518	63.0	63.8
Sex								
Male	405	402	279	68.8	69.5	247	61.1	61.6
Female	417	411	300	71.9	73.0	271	64.9	66.0
Race								
White alone..............................	769	760	546	71.0	71.8	494	64.3	65.0
White, non-Hispanic alone	747	740	534	71.5	72.1	483	64.7	65.3
Black alone...............................	4	4	1	(B)	(B)	-	(B)	(B)
Asian alone	5	4	3	(B)	(B)	3	(B)	(B)
Hispanic (of any race)........................	22	20	11	(B)	(B)	11	(B)	(B)
White alone or in combination	784	775	557	71.0	71.8	504	64.3	65.0
Black alone or in combination................	7	7	3	(B)	(B)	1	(B)	(B)
Asian alone or in combination................	8	7	5	(B)	(B)	4	(B)	(B)
Age								
18 to 24 years	83	81	41	49.7	50.5	32	38.3	38.9
25 to 34 years	147	144	89	60.9	62.3	71	48.0	49.2
35 to 44 years	127	124	90	70.6	72.4	76	59.8	61.3
45 to 64 years	254	253	192	75.5	75.8	178	70.1	70.3
65 years and over	212	210	167	78.8	79.4	162	76.6	77.1

- = Zero or rounds to zero.
B = Base is less than 75,000 and therefore too small to show the derived measure.

Table MT-14. Crime

(Number, rate per 100,000. Data are derived from the FBI Uniform Crime Reports.)

Item	State			U.S.		
	2016	2017	Percent change	2016	2017	Percent change
TOTAL POPULATION¹	1,038,656	1,050,493	1.1	323,405,935	325,719,178	0.7
VIOLENT CRIME						
Number...	3,886	3,961	1.9	1,285,606	1,283,220	-0.2
Rate	374.1	377.1	0.8	397.5	394.0	-0.9
Murder and Nonnegligent Manslaughter						
Number...	37	41	10.8	17,413	17,284	-0.7
Rate	3.6	3.9	9.6	5.4	5.3	-1.4
Rape²						
Number...	598	613	2.5	132,414	135,755	2.5
Rate	57.6	58.4	1.4	40.9	41.7	1.8
Robbery						
Number...	268	295	10.1	332,797	319,356	-4.0
Rate	25.8	28.1	8.8	102.9	98.0	-4.7
Aggravated Assault						
Number...	2,983	3,012	1.0	802,982	810,825	1.0
Rate	287.2	286.7	-0.2	248.3	248.9	0.3
PROPERTY CRIME						
Number...	28,156	27,225	-3.3	7,928,530	7,694,086	-3.0
Rate	2,710.8	2,591.6	-4.4	2,451.6	2,362.2	-3.6
Burglary						
Number...	3,966	3,615	-8.9	1,516,405	1,401,840	-7.6
Rate	381.8	344.1	-9.9	468.9	430.4	-8.2
Larceny-Theft						
Number...	21,427	21,018	-1.9	5,644,835	5,519,107	-2.2
Rate	2,063.0	2,000.8	-3.0	1,745.4	1,694.4	-2.9
Motor Vehicle Theft						
Number...	2,763	2,592	-6.2	767,290	773,139	0.8
Rate	266.0	246.7	-7.2	237.3	237.4	

NOTE: Although arson data are included in the trend and clearance tables, sufficient data are not available to estimate totals for this offense. Therefore, no arson data are published in this table.
- = Zero or rounds to zero.
¹ Population figures are U.S. Census Bureau provisional estimates as of July 1, 2017.
² The figures shown in the rape (revised definition) column were estimated using the revised Uniform Crime Reporting (UCR) definition of rape.

Table MT-15. State Government Finances, 2017

(Dollar amounts in thousands, percent distribution.)

Item	Dollars	Percent distribution
Total Revenue	9,068,008	100.0
General revenue	6,618,079	73.0
Intergovernmental revenue	3,054,845	33.7
Taxes	2,654,444	29.3
General sales	0	-
Selective sales	576,214	6.4
License taxes	329,874	3.6
Individual income tax	1,177,958	13.0
Corporate income tax	125,003	1.4
Other taxes	445,395	4.9
Current charges	505,976	5.6
Miscellaneous general revenue	402,814	4.4
Utility revenue	0	-
Liquor stores revenue	96,514	1.1
Insurance trust revenue[1]	2,353,415	26.0
Total Expenditure	7,748,311	100.0
Intergovernmental expenditure	1,128,565	14.6
Direct expenditure	6,619,746	85.4
Current operation	4,932,982	63.7
Capital outlay	370,538	4.8
Insurance benefits and repayments	1,068,360	13.8
Assistance and subsidies	139,041	1.8
Interest on debt	108,825	1.4
Exhibit: Salaries and wages	1,149,813	14.8
Total Expenditure	7,748,311	100.0
General expenditure	6,581,311	84.9
Intergovernmental expenditure	1,128,565	14.6
Direct expenditure	5,452,746	70.4
General expenditure, by function:		
Education	1,917,495	24.7
Public welfare	2,169,871	28.0
Hospitals	65,323	0.8
Health	206,634	2.7
Highways	613,223	7.9
Police protection	39,216	0.5
Correction	212,280	2.7
Natural resources	284,876	3.7
Parks and recreation	17,017	0.2
Governmental administration	436,858	5.6
Interest on general debt	108,825	1.4
Other and unallocable	509,693	6.6
Utility expenditure	15,492	0.2
Liquor stores expenditure	83,148	1.1
Insurance trust expenditure	1,068,360	13.8
Debt at End of Fiscal Year	2,795,614	X
Cash and Security Holdings	19,403,925	X

X = Not applicable.
- = Zero or rounds to zero.
[1] Within insurance trust revenue, net earnings of state retirement systems is a calculated statistic (the item code in the data file is X08), and thus can be positive or negative. Net earnings is the sum of earnings on investments plus gains on investments minus losses on investments. The change made in 2002 for asset valuation from book to market value in accordance with Statement 34 of the Governmental Accounting Standards Board is reflected in the calculated statistics.

Table MT-16. State Government Tax Collections, 2018

(Dollars in thousands, percent.)

Item	Dollars	Percent distribution
Total Taxes	2,944,827	100.0
Property taxes	294,519	10.0
Sales and gross receipts	631,797	21.5
General sales and gross receipts	X	-
Selective sales and gross receipts	631,797	21.5
Alcoholic beverages	33,816	1.1
Amusements	46,655	1.6
Insurance premiums	110,827	3.8
Motor fuels	254,167	8.6
Pari-mutuels	51	-
Public utilities	41,718	1.4
Tobacco products	80,532	2.7
Other selective sales	64,031	2.2
Licenses	352,066	12.0
Alcoholic beverages	3,478	0.1
Amusements	8,231	0.3
Corporations in general	4,921	0.2
Hunting and fishing	38,414	1.3
Motor vehicle	154,528	5.2
Motor vehicle operators	9,276	0.3
Public utilities	18	-
Occupation and business, NEC	112,971	3.8
Other licenses	20,229	0.7
Income taxes	1,476,941	50.2
Individual income	1,300,809	44.2
Corporation net income	176,132	6.0
Other taxes	189,504	6.4
Death and gift	X	-
Documentary and stock transfer	X	-
Severance	185,823	6.3
Taxes, NEC	3,681	0.1

X = Not applicable.
- = Zero or rounds to zero.

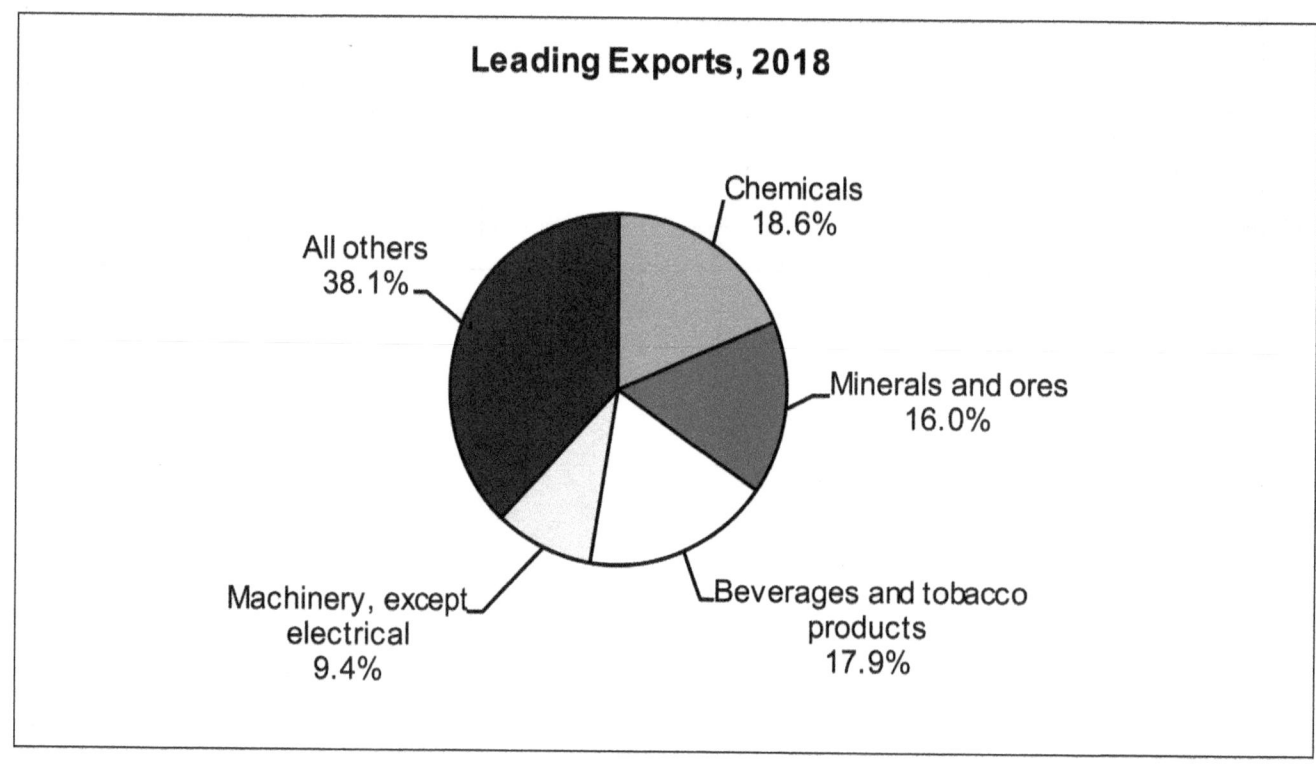

Leading Exports, 2018

Chemicals 18.6%

Minerals and ores 16.0%

Beverages and tobacco products 17.9%

Machinery, except electrical 9.4%

All others 38.1%

Facts and Figures

Location: Central United States; bordered on the N by South Dakota, on the E by Iowa and Missouri, on the S by Kansas and Colorado, and on the W by Wyoming

Area: 77,354 sq. mi. (200,345 sq. km.); rank—16th

Population: 1,929,268 (2018 est.); rank—37th

Principal Cities: capital—Lincoln; largest—Omaha

Statehood: March 1, 1867; 37th state

U.S. Congress: 2 senators, 3 representatives

State Motto: Equality Before the Law

State Song: "Beautiful Nebraska"

State Nickname: The Cornhusker State

Abbreviations: NE; Nebr.; Neb.

State Symbols: flower—goldenrod; tree—cottonwood; bird—Western meadowlark

At a Glance

- With an increase in population of 5.6 percent, Nebraska ranked 22nd among the states in growth from 2010 to 2018.

- In 2017, 8.3 percent of Nebraskans did not have health insurance, a percent slightly lower than the national average of 8.7 percent.

- The birth rate in Nebraska in 2017 was 13.4 births per 1,000 population, compared to the national average of 11.8 births per 1,000 population.

- Nebraska had the lowest rate of drug overdose deaths among the states in 2017, with 8.1 deaths per 100,000 population. That number was up from 6.4 deaths per 100,000 population in 2016.

- The state's violent crime rate in 2017 was 305.9 per 100,000 population, compared to the national rate of 394.0 per 100,000 population.

Table NE-1. Population by Age, Sex, Race, and Hispanic Origin

(Number, percent, except where noted.)

Sex, age, race, and Hispanic origin	2000	2010	2018 [1]	Percent change, 2010–2018
Total Population..	1,711,263	1,826,341	1,929,268	5.6
Percent of total U.S. population	0.6	0.6	0.6	X
Sex				
Male..	843,351	906,296	963,382	6.3
Female	867,912	920,045	965,886	5.0
Age				
Under 5 years..	117,048	131,908	132,968	0.8
5 to 19 years..	387,288	380,564	397,401	4.4
20 to 64 years..	974,732	1,067,192	1,095,233	2.6
65 years and over	232,195	246,677	303,666	23.1
Median age (years)	35.3	36.2	36.6	1.1
Race and Hispanic Origin				
One race				
White	1,533,261	1,649,264	1,703,446	3.3
Black	68,541	85,971	98,757	14.9
American Indian and Alaska Native	14,896	23,418	28,663	22.4
Asian	21,931	33,322	52,343	57.1
Native Hawaiian or Other Pacific Islander	836	2,061	2,338	13.4
Two or more races	23,953	32,305	43,721	35.3
Hispanic (of any race)...	94,425	173,058	215,872	24.7

X = Not applicable.
- = Zero or rounds to zero.
[1] Population figures for 2018 are July 1 estimates. The 2010 estimates are taken from the 2010 Census.

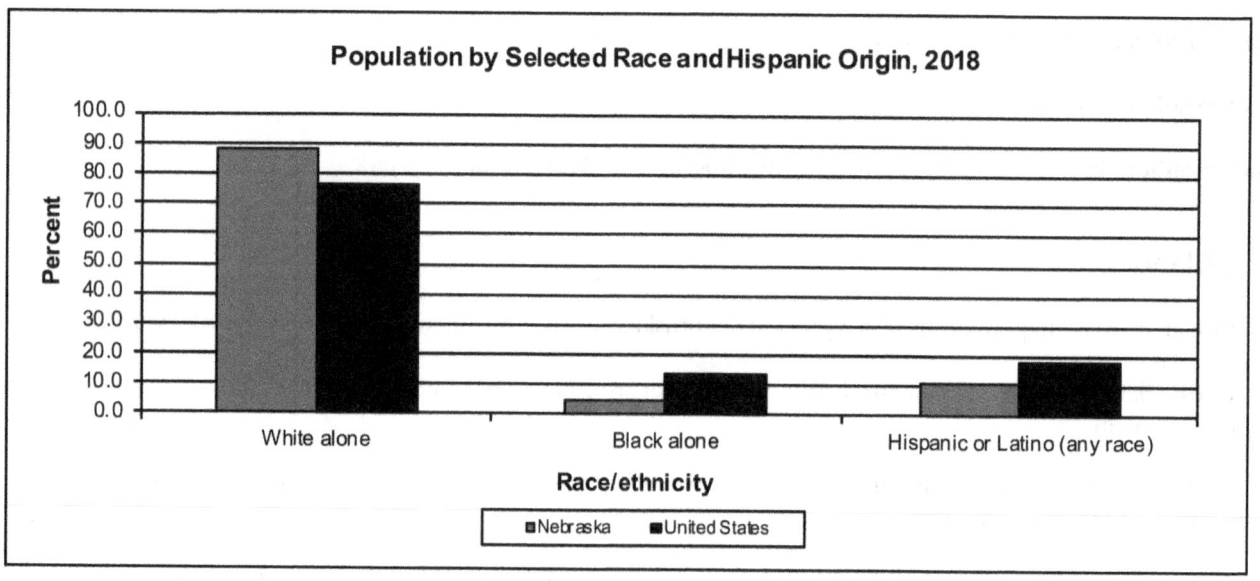

Table NE-2. Marital Status

(Number, percent distribution.)

Sex, age, race, and Hispanic origin	2000	2010	2017
Males, 15 Years and Over..	654,559	708,783	753,862
Never married	29.2	32.4	33.2
Now married, except separated..	59.1	54.0	53.8
Separated..	1.0	1.4	1.0
Widowed..	2.4	2.3	2.4
Divorced...	8.3	9.9	9.6
Females, 15 Years and Over..	687,863	735,744	767,383
Never married	22.5	25.3	27.2
Now married, except separated..	55.7	52.7	52.2
Separated..	1.3	1.5	1.3
Widowed..	10.8	9.5	8.3
Divorced...	9.7	10.9	11.0

Table NE-3. Households and Housing Characteristics

(Number, percent, dollars.)

Item	2000	2010	2017	Average annual percent change, 2010–2017
Total Households..............................	666,184	719,304	754,490	0.7
Family households.............................	443,411	468,407	484,989	0.5
Married-couple family......................	360,996	368,023	384,345	0.6
Other family.................................	82,415	100,384	100,644	-
Male householder, no wife present............	22,072	31,177	33,470	1.1
Female householder, no husband present.......	60,343	69,207	67,174	-0.4
Nonfamily households........................	222,773	250,897	269,501	1.1
Householder living alone....................	183,550	205,263	220,493	1.1
Householder not living alone................	39,223	45,634	49,008	1.1
Housing Characteristics				
Total housing units.........................	722,668	797,677	837,540	0.7
Occupied housing units......................	666,184	719,304	754,490	0.7
Owner occupied............................	449,317	484,649	500,086	0.5
Renter occupied...........................	216,867	234,655	254,404	1.2
Average household size......................	2.49	2.47	2.48	0.1
Financial Characteristics				
Median gross rent of renter-occupied housing	491	669	801	2.8
Median monthly owner costs for housing units with a mortgage	895	1,218	1,334	1.4
Median value of owner-occupied housing units........	88,000	127,600	155,800	3.2

Table NE-4. Migration, Origin, and Language

(Number, percent.)

Characteristic	State 2016	State 2017	State Percent change	U.S. 2016	U.S. 2017	U.S. Percent change
Residence 1 Year Ago						
Population 1 year and over	1,882,987	1,894,217	0.6	319,361,956	321,994,428	0.8
Same house........................	83.5	83.8	X	85.4	85.7	X
Different house in the U.S............	15.9	15.6	X	13.9	13.6	X
Same county.......................	9.4	9.2	X	8.3	8.1	X
Different county...................	6.5	6.4	X	5.6	5.6	X
Same state.......................	3.7	3.6	X	3.2	3.3	X
Different state...................	2.7	2.8	X	2.4	2.3	X
Abroad............................	0.5	0.6	X	0.7	0.7	X
Place of Birth						
Native born	1,772,979	1,776,745	0.2	279,388,170	281,193,323	0.6
Male..............................	49.7	49.8	X	49.3	49.4	X
Female............................	50.3	50.2	X	50.7	50.6	X
Foreign born	134,137	143,331	6.9	43,739,345	44,525,855	1.8
Male..............................	51.3	52.0	X	48.5	48.4	X
Female............................	48.7	48.0	X	51.5	51.6	X
Foreign born; naturalized U.S. citizen........	44,976	56,317	25.2	21,238,372	21,948,732	3.3
Male..............................	44.4	52.0	X	45.9	45.9	X
Female............................	55.6	48.0	X	54.1	54.1	X
Foreign born; not a U.S. citizen........	89,161	87,014	-2.4	22,500,973	22,577,123	0.3
Male..............................	54.9	52.1	X	51	50.8	X
Female............................	45.1	47.9	X	49	49.2	X
Entered 2010 or later	29.8	25.8	X	18.6	21.3	X
Entered 2000 to 2009	33.1	34.8	X	26.7	25.7	X
Entered before 2000................	37.2	39.4	X	54.7	53.0	X
World Region of Birth, Foreign						
Foreign-born population, excluding population born at sea	134,137	143,331	6.9	43,738,901	44,525,458	1.8
Europe	6.3	7.5	X	10.9	10.8	X
Asia..............................	29.7	27.9	X	30.8	31.2	X
Africa	8.4	9.1	X	4.9	5.1	X
Oceania	0.3	0.4	X	0.6	0.6	X
Latin America	54.6	53.8	X	51	50.4	X
North America	0.8	1.3	X	1.8	1.8	X
Language Spoken at Home and Ability to Speak English						
Population 5 years and over	1,774,959	1,788,397	0.8	303,328,961	305,924,019	0.9
English only	88.5	88.1	X	78.4	78.2	X
Language other than English........	11.5	11.9	X	21.6	21.8	X
Speaks English less than "very well"......	5.4	5.5	X	8.6	8.5	X

NA = Not available.
X = Not applicable.
- = Zero or rounds to zero.

Table NE-5. Median Income and Poverty Status, 2017

(Number, percent, except as noted.)

Characteristic	State		U.S.	
	Number	Percent	Number	Percent
Median Income				
Households (dollars)..	59,970	X	60,336	X
Families (dollars)	75,112	X	73,891	X
Below Poverty Level (All People)	200,909	10.8	42,583,651	13.4
Sex				
Male	88,353	9.5	19,004,547	12.2
Female	112,556	12.0	23,579,104	14.5
Age				
Under 18 years..	65,591	14.1	13,353,202	18.4
Related children under 18 years..	62,997	13.6	13,053,472	18.1
18 to 64 years...	115,127	10.3	24,648,677	12.6
65 years and over	20,191	7.2	4,581,772	9.3

X = Not applicable.

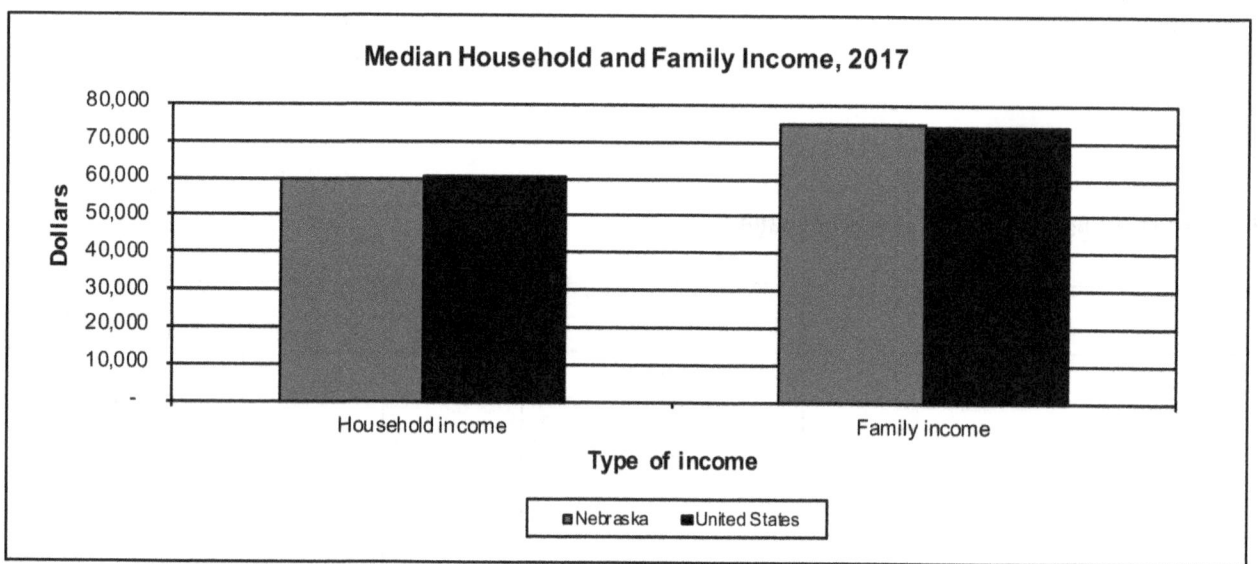

Table NE-6. Health Insurance Coverage Status for the Civilian Noninstitutionalized Population and Children Under 18 Years of Age

(Number, percent.)

Item	2009	2010	2011	2012	2013	2014	2015	2016	2017
Civilian Noninstitutionalized Population	1,762,977	1,802,049	1,814,388	1,826,832	1,840,659	1,853,684	1,866,488	1,877,654	1,891,453
Covered by Private or Public Insurance									
Number...	1,552,712	1,594,396	1,607,294	1,621,225	1,632,081	1,674,478	1,712,699	1,717,091	1,734,669
Percent...	88.1	88.5	88.6	88.7	88.7	90.3	91.8	91.4	91.7
Uninsured									
Number...	210,265	207,653	207,094	205,607	208,578	179,206	153,789	160,563	156,784
Percent...	11.9	11.5	11.4	11.3	11.3	9.7	8.2	8.6	8.3
Percent in the U.S. not covered.................................	15.1	15.5	15.1	14.8	14.5	11.7	9.4	8.6	8.7
Children Under 18 Years of Age[1]	444,973	458,869	459,191	461,309	462,637	466,590	469,243	472,689	500,004
Covered by Private or Public Insurance									
Number...	416,973	433,135	432,299	433,503	437,258	441,795	444,513	448,982	474,289
Percent...	93.7	94.4	94.1	94.0	94.5	94.7	94.7	95.0	94.9
Uninsured									
Number...	28,000	25,734	26,892	27,806	25,379	24,795	24,730	23,707	25,715
Percent...	6.3	5.6	5.9	6.0	5.5	5.3	5.3	5.0	5.1
Percent in the U.S. not covered.................................	8.6	8.0	7.5	7.2	7.1	6.0	4.8	4.5	5.0

[1] 2017 data is for individuals under 19 years of age.

Table NE-7. Employment Status by Demographic Group, 2018

(Numbers in thousands, percent.)

Characteristic	Civilian noninstitutional population	Civilian labor force		Employed		Unemployed	
		Number	Percent of population	Number	Percent of population	Number	Percent of population
Total...............................	1,478	1,032	69.8	1,003	67.9	29	2.8
Sex							
Male...............................	728	547	75.1	531	72.9	17	3.0
Female............................	749	485	64.7	472	63.0	13	2.6
Race, Sex, and Hispanic Origin							
White..............................	1,336	941	70.4	918	68.7	23	2.4
Male...............................	662	500	75.5	487	73.5	13	2.6
Female............................	674	442	65.5	432	64.1	10	2.2
Black or African American...............	NA	NA	NA	NA	NA	NA	NA
Male...............................	NA	NA	NA	NA	NA	NA	NA
Female............................	NA	NA	NA	NA	NA	NA	NA
Hispanic or Latino ethnicity[1]	168	126	74.8	119	70.5	7	5.7
Male...............................	90	75	83.3	71	78.8	4	5.4
Female............................	NA	NA	NA	NA	NA	NA	NA
Age							
16 to 19 years.....................	NA	NA	NA	NA	NA	NA	NA
20 to 24 years.....................	142	113	79.5	108	75.8	5	4.6
25 to 34 years.....................	255	226	88.7	219	85.7	8	3.4
35 to 44 years.....................	230	201	87.6	197	85.7	5	2.3
45 to 54 years.....................	217	190	87.5	187	86.2	3	1.5
55 to 64 years.....................	237	177	74.4	174	73.2	3	1.6
65 years and over..................	301	77	25.6	75	25.1	2	2.1

NOTE: Data in Table 7 are from the Current Population Survey (CPS) and do not match the estimates in Table 8. See notes and definitions for further information.
[1] May be of any race.
NA = Not available.

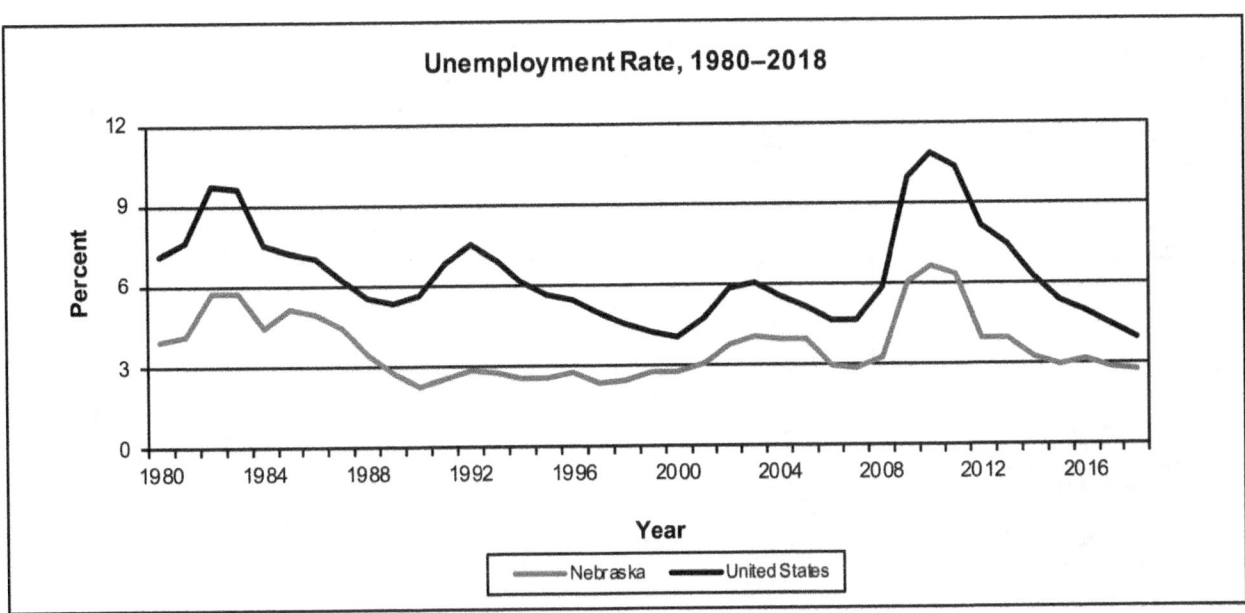

Unemployment Rate, 1980–2018

Table NE-8. Employment Status of the Civilian Noninstitutional Population Age 16 Years and Over

(Number, percent.)

Year	Civilian labor force	Civilian participation rate	Employed	Unemployed	Unemployment rate
2010...............................	993,398	71.6	947,360	46,038	4.6
2011...............................	1,003,256	71.6	959,059	44,197	4.4
2012...............................	1,014,980	71.9	974,428	40,552	4.0
2013...............................	1,018,294	71.6	979,937	38,357	3.8
2014...............................	1,011,564	70.6	978,377	33,187	3.3
2015...............................	1,007,585	69.9	977,279	30,306	3.0
2016...............................	1,008,715	69.4	977,622	31,093	3.1
2017...............................	1,007,011	68.7	977,444	29,567	2.9
2018...............................	1,020,197	69.2	991,688	28,509	2.8

Table NE-9. Employment and Average Wages by Industry

(Estimates are based on the 2012 *North American Industry Classification System* [NAICS].)

Industry	2011	2012	2013	2014	2015	2016	2017
	Number of jobs						
Wage and Salary Employment by Industry.........................	970,527	988,861	1,000,260	1,013,641	1,030,768	1,036,447	1,040,572
Farm Wage and Salary Employment...............................	13,693	12,116	12,277	12,168	16,089	14,485	15,416
Nonfarm Wage and Salary Employment.........................	956,834	976,745	987,983	1,001,473	1,014,679	1,021,962	1,025,156
Private wage and salary employment...........................	782,368	803,258	814,673	827,481	840,079	846,330	849,342
Forestry, fishing, and related activities............................	5,299	5,684	6,089	6,009	5,629	5,935	5,895
Mining..	1,024	1,126	1,042	1,133	1,066	982	1,044
Utilities..	1,627	1,605	1,290	1,264	1,081	1,072	1,090
Construction..	41,521	43,354	45,389	47,336	50,140	51,812	52,402
Manufacturing..	93,680	95,078	96,556	97,553	97,417	96,952	98,181
Durable goods manufacturing.............................	42,745	43,994	44,995	45,916	45,416	44,055	43,982
Nondurable goods manufacturing.......................	50,935	51,084	51,561	51,637	52,001	52,897	54,199
Wholesale trade..	40,989	41,515	42,126	43,089	42,490	42,021	41,258
Retail trade..	105,478	106,356	107,151	108,732	110,649	111,143	109,938
Transportation and warehousing..................................	51,174	52,037	52,199	52,871	53,998	51,282	50,974
Information	17,196	17,199	17,220	17,068	17,581	18,515	18,224
Finance and insurance	55,110	55,494	55,716	56,626	57,200	58,296	59,214
Real estate and rental and leasing.............................	9,151	9,039	9,208	9,269	9,605	9,828	10,059
Professional, scientific, and technical services............	43,484	45,086	44,382	44,353	44,885	44,306	45,234
Management of companies and enterprises..................	16,670	16,734	19,340	20,410	22,127	21,451	21,638
Administrative and waste services..............................	43,097	45,366	46,686	48,908	50,543	52,286	51,371
Educational services	18,517	18,555	18,192	18,393	18,736	18,806	18,916
Health care and social assistance..............................	112,993	120,575	122,094	122,955	123,890	127,301	128,331
Arts, entertainment, and recreation.............................	12,414	13,003	13,376	13,996	14,280	14,418	14,951
Accommodation and food services..............................	69,867	71,676	72,910	73,748	74,629	76,602	77,491
Other services, except public administration.................	43,077	43,776	43,727	43,768	44,133	43,322	43,131
Government and government enterprises	174,466	173,487	173,310	173,992	174,600	175,632	175,814
	Dollars						
Average Wages and Salaries by Industry	39,741	40,923	41,505	42,842	44,387	45,205	46,540
Average Farm Wages and Salaries	34,291	41,296	39,781	41,575	35,024	37,944	36,458
Average Nonfarm Wages and Salaries	39,819	40,918	41,527	42,857	44,535	45,308	46,692
Average private wages and salaries...........................	39,274	40,471	41,050	42,463	44,215	44,963	46,406
Forestry, fishing, and related activities	23,345	24,022	25,367	26,665	28,705	29,078	29,900
Mining...	47,736	51,673	52,361	53,190	54,466	56,775	55,635
Utilities..	90,708	91,395	86,069	111,415	108,917	97,390	100,708
Construction..	42,004	43,496	44,169	46,649	48,319	49,264	50,577
Manufacturing..	44,471	45,116	45,685	47,428	48,627	49,341	51,502
Durable goods manufacturing.............................	47,902	48,097	48,850	50,525	51,226	51,690	54,307
Nondurable goods manufacturing.......................	41,592	42,548	42,923	44,674	46,357	47,385	49,226
Wholesale trade..	52,709	55,204	56,263	58,760	60,528	61,600	63,149
Retail trade..	23,917	24,791	25,153	25,664	26,526	27,528	28,349
Transportation and warehousing..................................	50,582	53,426	52,183	55,065	56,732	56,582	58,875
Information	53,874	54,763	56,486	57,571	60,021	62,532	63,741
Finance and insurance	57,220	59,313	61,257	62,849	65,635	67,233	70,110
Real estate and rental and leasing.............................	34,039	35,805	37,370	39,145	40,540	42,149	42,300
Professional, scientific, and technical services	59,617	62,036	60,872	62,021	64,690	66,513	68,473
Management of companies and enterprises..................	80,414	90,239	92,162	95,500	100,137	96,435	97,150
Administrative and waste services..............................	29,927	31,163	32,392	34,211	36,077	37,227	39,015
Educational services	30,423	30,996	30,577	29,690	30,322	31,358	31,732
Health care and social assistance..............................	41,047	40,537	40,959	41,594	44,045	45,098	46,216
Arts, entertainment, and recreation.............................	18,022	18,368	18,863	19,227	19,496	20,154	20,578
Accommodation and food services..............................	14,439	15,151	15,506	16,169	17,072	17,899	18,437
Other services, except public administration.................	27,326	27,813	28,640	29,881	30,758	32,064	33,175
Government and government enterprises.....................	42,259	42,993	43,767	44,733	46,075	46,971	48,071

Table NE-10. Employment Characteristics by Family Type

(Number, percent.)

Family type and labor force status	2015		2016		2017	
	Total	Families with own children under 18 years	Total	Families with own children under 18 years	Total	Families with own children under 18 years
All Families..	469,797	214,069	476,436	216,690	484,989	221,744
FAMILY TYPE AND LABOR FORCE STATUS						
Married-Couple Families...................................	369,426	153,745	369,253	153,651	384,345	158,020
Both husband and wife in labor force........................	59.9	74.5	61.4	75.4	60.6	75.8
Husband in labor force, wife not in labor force	18.7	21.5	17.3	20.3	18.0	20.4
Wife in labor force, husband not in labor force...........	6.4	3.0	6.5	3.3	6.7	2.7
Both husband and wife not in labor force....................	14.5	0.8	14.3	0.8	14.2	0.8
Other Families	100,371	60,324	107,183	63,039	100,644	63,724
Female householder, no husband present...................	70.7	73.2	72.7	76.5	66.7	70.1
In labor force....................................	54.5	65.1	56.6	68.3	52.2	60.0
Not in labor force.................................	16.2	8.1	16.1	8.2	14.6	10.2
Male householder, no wife present...............	29.3	26.8	27.3	23.5	33.3	29.9
In labor force.......................................	24.5	25.0	22.5	22.0	28.0	27.5
Not in labor force.................................	4.8	1.8	4.8	1.5	5.2	2.3

Table NE-11. School Enrollment and Educational Attainment, 2017

(Number, percent.)

Item	State	U.S.
Enrollment		
Total population 3 years and over, enrolled in school	507,288	81,273,337
Enrolled in nursery school or preschool (percent).................................	7.1	6.0
Enrolled in kindergarten (percent).................................	5.2	4.9
Enrolled in elementary school, grades 1-8 (percent).................................	41.2	40.6
Enrolled in high school, grades 9-12 (percent)	20.0	21.1
Enrolled in college or graduate school (percent).................................	26.5	27.4
Attainment		
Total population 25 years and over	1,259,254	221,250,083
Less than ninth grade (percent).................................	3.9	5.1
9th to 12th grade, no diploma (percent).................................	4.8	6.9
High school graduate, including equivalency (percent).................................	26.3	27.1
Some college, no degree (percent).................................	23.1	20.4
Associate's degree (percent).................................	10.2	8.5
Bachelor's degree (percent).................................	20.9	19.7
Graduate or professional degree (percent).................................	10.8	12.3
High school graduate or higher (percent).................................	91.3	88.0
Bachelor's degree or higher (percent).................................	31.7	32.0

Table NE-12. Public School Characteristics and Educational Indicators

(Number, percent; data derived from National Center of Education Statistics.)

Item	State	U.S.
Public Elementary and Secondary Schools		
Number of operational school districts, 2016-17.................................	284	18,377
Number of operational schools, 2016-17.................................	1,095	98,330
Percent charter schools	NA	7.1
Total public school enrollment, 2016-17.................................	319,194	50,587,859
Percent charter school enrollment	NA	6.0
Student-teacher ratio, Fall 2015	13.6	16.0
Expenditures per student (dollars), 2015-16.................................	12,379	11,841
Four-year adjusted cohort graduation rate (ACGR)[1].................................	89.1	84.6
Students eligible for free or reduced-price lunch (percent), 2015-16.................	44.2	52.1
English language learners (percent), Fall 2016	7.1	9.6
Students age 3 to 21 served under IDEA, part B (percent), 2017-18	15.6	13.7
Public Schools by Type, 2016-17		Percent of state public schools
Total number of schools.................................	1,095	100.0
Special education	27	2.5
Vocational education	0	-
Alternative education.................................	49	4.5

[1] Adjusted Cohort Graduation Rates (ACGR) differ from Averaged Freshmen Graduation Rates (AFGR).
NA = Not available.
- = Zero or rounds to zero.

Table NE-13. Reported Voting and Registration of the Voting-Age Population, November 2018

(Numbers in thousands, percent.)

Item	Total population	Total citizen population	Registered			Voted		
			Total registered	Percent registered (total population)	Percent registered (total citizen population)	Total voted	Percent voted (total population)	Percent voted (total citizen population)
U.S. Total	249,748	228,832	153,066	61.3	66.9	122,281	49.0	53.4
State Total..................................	1,428	1,332	883	61.9	66.3	676	47.3	50.8
Sex								
Male	710	652	418	58.9	64.1	314	44.2	48.1
Female	718	680	466	64.8	68.5	362	50.5	53.3
Race								
White alone................................	1,277	1,203	822	64.4	68.4	633	49.6	52.6
White, non-Hispanic alone	1,113	1,108	782	70.2	70.5	606	54.5	54.7
Black alone................................	60	59	26	(B)	(B)	15	(B)	(B)
Asian alone	58	37	11	(B)	(B)	8	(B)	(B)
Hispanic (of any race).................	175	105	50	28.7	47.7	34	19.7	32.8
White alone or in combination	1,301	1,226	839	64.5	68.4	649	49.9	52.9
Black alone or in combination.......	66	65	29	(B)	(B)	18	(B)	(B)
Asian alone or in combination.......	60	40	11	(B)	(B)	8	(B)	(B)
Age								
18 to 24 years............................	172	157	69	40.1	43.9	50	29.2	32.0
25 to 34 years............................	286	268	165	57.6	61.4	112	39.1	41.7
35 to 44 years............................	215	181	113	52.6	62.5	81	37.9	45.0
45 to 64 years............................	467	439	311	66.5	70.7	244	52.2	55.5
65 years and over	288	286	226	78.5	79.0	189	65.5	66.0

B = Base is less than 75,000 and therefore too small to show the derived measure.
- = Zero or rounds to zero.

Table NE-14. Crime

(Number, rate per 100,000. Data are derived from the FBI Uniform Crime Reports.)

Item	State			U.S.		
	2016	2017	Percent change	2016	2017	Percent change
TOTAL POPULATION[1]	1,907,603	1,920,076	0.7	323,405,935	325,719,178	0.7
VIOLENT CRIME						
Number..................................	5,661	5,873	3.7	1,285,606	1,283,220	-0.2
Rate	296.8	305.9	3.1	397.5	394.0	-0.9
Murder and Nonnegligent Manslaughter						
Number..................................	49	43	-12.2	17,413	17,284	-0.7
Rate	2.6	2.2	-12.8	5.4	5.3	-1.4
Rape[2]						
Number..................................	1,108	1,191	7.5	132,414	135,755	2.5
Rate	58.1	62.0	6.8	40.9	41.7	1.8
Robbery						
Number..................................	946	968	2.3	332,797	319,356	-4.0
Rate	49.6	50.4	1.7	102.9	98.0	-4.7
Aggravated Assault						
Number..................................	3,558	3,671	3.2	802,982	810,825	1.0
Rate	186.5	191.2	2.5	248.3	248.9	0.3
PROPERTY CRIME						
Number..................................	43,197	43,663	1.1	7,928,530	7,694,086	-3.0
Rate	2,264.5	2,274.0	0.4	2,451.6	2,362.2	-3.6
Burglary						
Number..................................	6,459	6,472	0.2	1,516,405	1,401,840	-7.6
Rate	338.6	337.1	-0.4	468.9	430.4	-8.2
Larceny-Theft						
Number..................................	32,009	31,988	-0.1	5,644,835	5,519,107	-2.2
Rate	1,678.0	1,666.0	-0.7	1,745.4	1,694.4	-2.9
Motor Vehicle Theft						
Number..................................	4,729	5,203	10.0	767,290	773,139	0.8
Rate	247.9	271.0	9.3	237.3	237.4	-

NOTE: Although arson data are included in the trend and clearance tables, sufficient data are not available to estimate totals for this offense. Therefore, no arson data are published in this table.
- = Zero or rounds to zero.
[1] Population figures are U.S. Census Bureau provisional estimates as of July 1, 2017.
[2] The figures shown in the rape (revised definition) column were estimated using the revised Uniform Crime Reporting (UCR) definition of rape.

Table NE-15. State Government Finances, 2017

(Dollar amounts in thousands, percent distribution.)

Item	Dollars	Percent distribution
Total Revenue	12,173,777	100.0
General revenue	10,025,526	82.4
Intergovernmental revenue	3,179,745	26.1
Taxes	5,103,105	41.9
General sales	1,835,037	15.1
Selective sales	572,477	4.7
License taxes	182,791	1.5
Individual income tax	2,228,486	18.3
Corporate income tax	264,440	2.2
Other taxes	19,874	0.2
Current charges	996,662	8.2
Miscellaneous general revenue	746,014	6.1
Utility revenue	0	-
Liquor stores revenue	0	-
Insurance trust revenue[1]	2,148,251	17.6
Total Expenditure	10,618,168	100.0
Intergovernmental expenditure	2,457,060	23.1
Direct expenditure	8,161,108	76.9
Current operation	6,315,925	59.5
Capital outlay	816,316	7.7
Insurance benefits and repayments	761,279	7.2
Assistance and subsidies	209,343	2.0
Interest on debt	58,245	0.5
Exhibit: Salaries and wages	1,579,254	14.9
Total Expenditure	10,618,168	100.0
General expenditure	9,849,096	92.8
Intergovernmental expenditure	2,457,060	23.1
Direct expenditure	7,392,036	69.6
General expenditure, by function:		
Education	3,825,588	36.0
Public welfare	2,771,780	26.1
Hospitals	189,098	1.8
Health	306,760	2.9
Highways	824,452	7.8
Police protection	90,473	0.9
Correction	349,865	3.3
Natural resources	224,856	2.1
Parks and recreation	53,442	0.5
Governmental administration	295,374	2.8
Interest on general debt	58,245	0.5
Other and unallocable	859,163	8.1
Utility expenditure	7793	0.1
Liquor stores expenditure	0	-
Insurance trust expenditure	761,279	7.2
Debt at End of Fiscal Year	2,014,523	X
Cash and Security Holdings	20,996,903	X

X = Not applicable.
- = Zero or rounds to zero.
[1] Within insurance trust revenue, net earnings of state retirement systems is a calculated statistic (the item code in the data file is X08), and thus can be positive or negative. Net earnings is the sum of earnings on investments plus gains on investments minus losses on investments. The change made in 2002 for asset valuation from book to market value in accordance with Statement 34 of the Governmental Accounting Standards Board is reflected in the calculated statistics.

Table NE-16. State Government Tax Collections, 2018

(Dollars in thousands, percent.)

Item	Dollars	Percent distribution
Total Taxes	5,393,093	100.0
Property taxes	129	-
Sales and gross receipts	2,502,020	46.4
General sales and gross receipts	1,900,037	35.2
Selective sales and gross receipts	601,983	11.2
Alcoholic beverages	31,230	0.6
Amusements	5,815	0.1
Insurance premiums	62,662	1.2
Motor fuels	373,889	6.9
Pari-mutuels	138	-
Public utilities	44,942	0.8
Tobacco products	57,123	1.1
Other selective sales	26,184	0.5
Licenses	196,215	3.6
Alcoholic beverages	707	-
Amusements	710	-
Corporations in general	16,086	0.3
Hunting and fishing	15,906	0.3
Motor vehicle	113,733	2.1
Motor vehicle operators	11,538	0.2
Public utilities	X	-
Occupation and business, NEC	36,475	0.7
Other licenses	1,060	-
Income taxes	2,674,286	49.6
Individual income	2,360,596	43.8
Corporation net income	313,690	5.8
Other taxes	20,443	0.4
Death and gift	X	-
Documentary and stock transfer	17,207	0.3
Severance	3,236	0.1
Taxes, NEC	0	-

- = Zero or rounds to zero.
X = Not applicable.

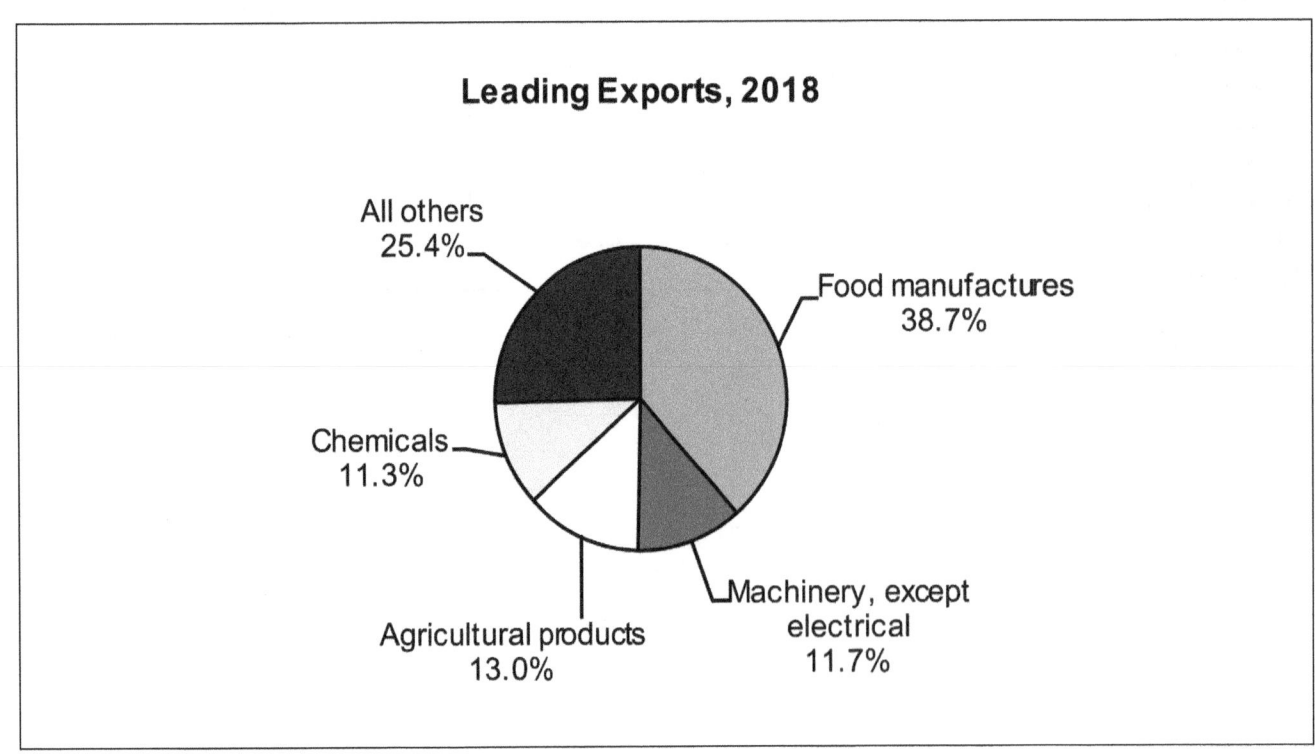

Leading Exports, 2018

All others 25.4%
Food manufactures 38.7%
Chemicals 11.3%
Agricultural products 13.0%
Machinery, except electrical 11.7%

NEVADA

Location: Western United States; bordered on the N by Oregon and Idaho, on the E by Utah and Arizona, on the S by Arizona and California, and on the W by California

Area: 110,561 sq. mi. (286,351 sq. km.); rank—7th

Population: 3,034,392 (2018 est.); rank—32nd

Principal Cities: capital—Carson City; largest—Las Vegas

Statehood: October 31, 1864; 36th state

U.S. Congress: 2 senators, 4 representatives

State Motto: All for Our Country

State Song: "Home Means Nevada"

State Nicknames: The Silver State; The Sagebrush State

Abbreviations: NV; Nev.

State Symbols: flower—sagebrush; tree—single-leaf piñon and bristlecone pine; bird—mountain bluebird

At a Glance

- With an increase in population of 12.4 percent, Nevada ranked 7th among the states in growth from 2010 to 2018.

- In 2018, 4.6 percent of Nevadans were unemployed, compared to 3.9 percent of the total U.S. population.

- Nevada's violent crime rate in 2017 was 555.9 per 100,000 population, which ranked 6th among the states. The national violent crime rate was 394.0 per 100,000 population.

- Approximately 29.0 percent of Nevadans self-identified their ethnicity as "Hispanic or Latino" in 2018, the 5th highest percentage in the country.

Table NV-1. Population by Age, Sex, Race, and Hispanic Origin

(Number, percent, except where noted.)

Sex, age, race, and Hispanic origin	2000	2010	2018 [1]	Percent change, 2010–2018
Total Population..	1,998,257	2,700,551	3,034,392	12.4
Percent of total U.S. population	0.7	0.9	0.9	X
Sex				
Male...	1,018,051	1,363,616	1,521,555	11.6
Female	980,206	1,336,935	1,512,837	13.2
Age				
Under 5 years..	145,817	187,478	185,995	-0.8
5 to 19 years..	415,684	548,850	569,727	3.8
20 to 64 years..	1,217,827	1,639,864	1,802,489	9.9
65 years and over	218,929	324,359	476,181	46.8
Median age (years)	35.0	36.3	38.1	5.0
Race and Hispanic Origin				
One race				
White	1,501,886	2,106,494	2,253,711	7.0
Black..	135,477	231,224	305,848	32.3
American Indian and Alaska Native	26,420	42,965	50,871	18.4
Asian..	90,266	203,478	264,411	29.9
Native Hawaiian or Other Pacific Islander	8,426	19,307	23,962	24.1
Two or more races..	76,428	97,083	135,589	39.7
Hispanic (of any race)..	393,970	741,200	881,148	18.9

X = Not applicable.

[1] Population figures for 2018 are July 1 estimates. The 2010 estimates are taken from the 2010 Census.

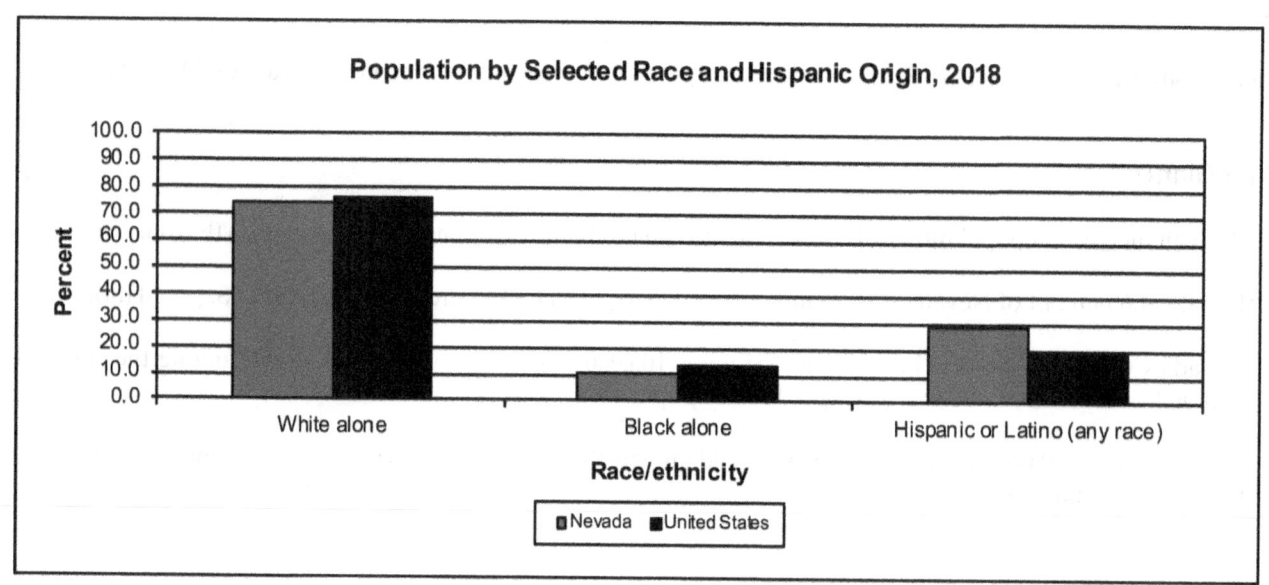

Population by Selected Race and Hispanic Origin, 2018

Table NV-2. Marital Status

(Number, percent distribution.)

Sex, age, race, and Hispanic origin	2000	2010	2017
Males, 15 Years and Over	792,317	1,081,514	1,214,411
Never married	28.8	35.0	37.0
Now married, except separated....................................	53.8	47.6	46.0
Separated...	2.0	2.0	1.8
Widowed...	2.5	2.9	2.5
Divorced...	12.9	12.5	12.7
Females, 15 Years and Over	771,263	1,069,123	1,215,389
Never married	20.9	27.2	29.5
Now married, except separated....................................	53.1	47.2	44.9
Separated...	2.7	2.8	2.7
Widowed...	8.6	8.0	7.8
Divorced...	14.7	14.8	15.1

Table NV-3. Households and Housing Characteristics

(Number, percent, dollars.)

Item	2000	2010	2017	Average annual percent change, 2010–2017
Total Households............................	751,165	989,811	1,094,613	1.5
Family households	498,333	639,686	700,449	1.4
Married-couple family	373,201	452,361	491,128	1.2
Other family	125,132	187,325	209,321	1.7
Male householder, no wife present........	41,650	63,327	66,875	0.8
Female householder, no husband present..	83,482	123,998	142,446	2.1
Nonfamily households	252,832	350,125	394,164	1.8
Householder living alone.....................	186,745	266,232	307,721	2.2
Householder not living alone................	66,087	83,893	86,443	0.4
Housing Characteristics				
Total housing units.............................	827,457	1,175,070	1,249,733	0.9
Occupied housing units	751,165	989,811	1,094,613	1.5
Owner occupied	457,247	565,869	619,309	1.3
Renter occupied	293,918	423,942	475,304	1.7
Average household size........................	2.62	2.70	2.70	-
Financial Characteristics				
Median gross rent of renter-occupied housing	699	952	1051	1.5
Median monthly owner costs for housing units with a mortgage	1,190	1,638	1,428	-1.8
Median value of owner-occupied housing units..........	142,000	174,800	258,200	6.8

- = Zero or rounds to zero.

Table NV-4. Migration, Origin, and Language

(Number, percent.)

Characteristic	State 2016	State 2017	State Percent change	U.S. 2016	U.S. 2017	U.S. Percent change
Residence 1 Year Ago						
Population 1 year and over	2,907,243	2,963,456	1.9	319,361,956	321,994,428	0.8
Same house	82.6	82.0	X	85.4	85.7	X
Different house in the U.S.	16.9	17.4	X	13.9	13.6	X
Same county	12.0	12.1	X	8.3	8.1	X
Different county	4.9	5.3	X	5.6	5.6	X
Same state	0.9	0.9	X	3.2	3.3	X
Different state	4.1	4.5	X	2.4	2.3	X
Abroad	0.5	0.6	X	0.7	0.7	X
Place of Birth						
Native born	2,353,259	2,402,020	2.1	279,388,170	281,193,323	0.6
Male	51.0	50.8	X	49.3	49.4	X
Female	49.0	49.2	X	50.7	50.6	X
Foreign born	586,799	596,019	1.6	43,739,345	44,525,855	1.8
Male	46.7	48.1	X	48.5	48.4	X
Female	53.3	51.9	X	51.5	51.6	X
Foreign born; naturalized U.S. citizen......	278,711	293,206	5.2	21,238,372	21,948,732	3.3
Male	45.2	45.4	X	45.9	45.9	X
Female	54.8	54.6	X	54.1	54.1	X
Foreign born; not a U.S. citizen............	308,088	302,813	-1.7	22,500,973	22,577,123	0.3
Male	48.1	50.6	X	51	50.8	X
Female	51.9	49.4	X	49	49.2	X
Entered 2010 or later	13.8	15.2	X	18.6	21.3	X
Entered 2000 to 2009	28.0	27.7	X	26.7	25.7	X
Entered before 2000..........................	58.2	57.0	X	54.7	53.0	X
World Region of Birth, Foreign						
Foreign-born population, excluding population born at sea	586,741	596,019	1.6	43,738,901	44,525,458	1.8
Europe	7.2	6.5	X	10.9	10.8	X
Asia	30.6	32.2	X	30.8	31.2	X
Africa	3.1	3.3	X	4.9	5.1	X
Oceania	0.7	0.4	X	0.6	0.6	X
Latin America	56.3	55.8	X	51	50.4	X
North America	2.1	1.8	X	1.8	1.8	X
Language Spoken at Home and Ability to Speak English						
Population 5 years and over..................	2,756,697	2,813,984	2.1	303,328,961	305,924,019	0.9
English only	69.3	68.9	X	78.4	78.2	X
Language other than English..................	30.7	31.1	X	21.6	21.8	X
Speaks English less than "very well"........	11.8	11.2	X	8.6	8.5	X

NA = Not available.
X = Not applicable.
- = Zero or rounds to zero.

Table NV-5. Median Income and Poverty Status, 2017

(Number, percent, except as noted.)

Characteristic	State Number	State Percent	U.S. Number	U.S. Percent
Median Income				
Households (dollars)........................	58,003	X	60,336	X
Families (dollars)	68,276	X	73,891	X
Below Poverty Level (All People)	384,120	13.0	42,583,651	13.4
Sex				
Male	182,121	12.3	19,004,547	12.2
Female	201,999	13.7	23,579,104	14.5
Age				
Under 18 years...........................	124,514	18.5	13,353,202	18.4
Related children under 18 years..........	121,417	18.2	13,053,472	18.1
18 to 64 years	221,017	12.1	24,648,677	12.6
65 years and over	38,589	8.5	4,581,772	9.3

X = Not applicable.

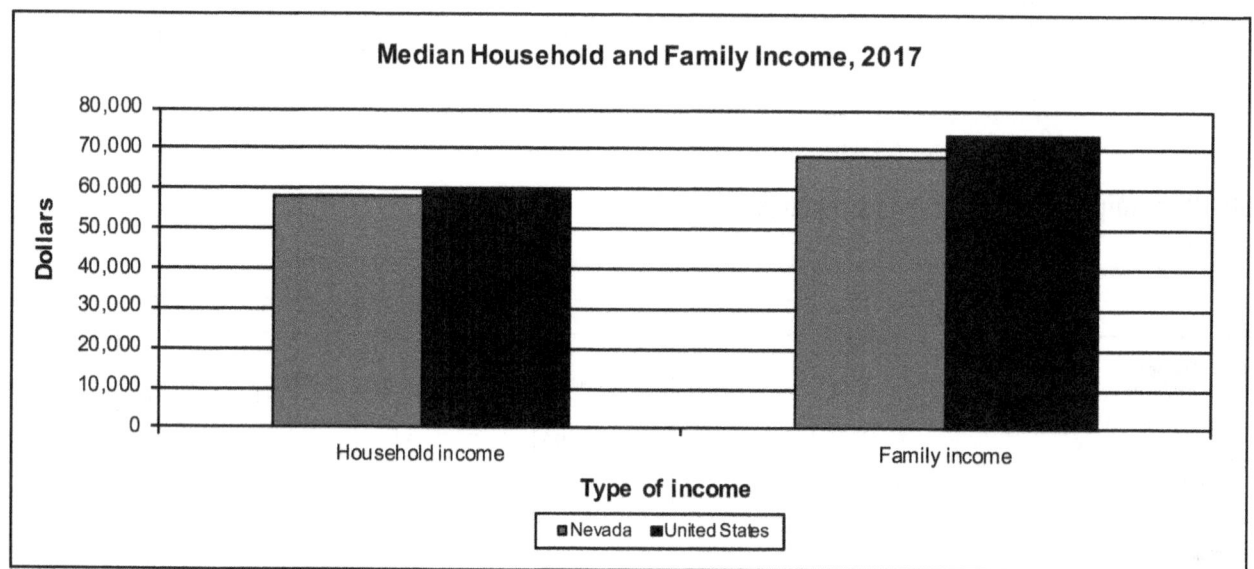

Table NV-6. Health Insurance Coverage Status for the Civilian Noninstitutionalized Population and Children Under 18 Years of Age

(Number, percent.)

Item	2009	2010	2011	2012	2013	2014	2015	2016	2017
Civilian Noninstitutionalized Population	2,610,041	2,668,966	2,686,989	2,723,965	2,757,207	2,805,532	2,855,974	2,905,767	2,962,236
Covered by Private or Public Insurance									
Number.................................	2,038,426	2,065,266	2,098,195	2,120,540	2,187,128	2,378,879	2,505,290	2,575,349	2,629,612
Percent.................................	78.1	77.4	78.1	77.8	79.3	84.8	87.7	88.6	88.8
Uninsured									
Number.................................	571,615	603,700	588,794	603,425	570,079	426,653	350,684	330,418	332,624
Percent.................................	21.9	22.6	21.9	22.2	20.7	15.2	12.3	11.4	11.2
Percent in the U.S. not covered	15.1	15.5	15.1	14.8	14.5	11.7	9.4	8.6	8.7
Children Under 18 Years of Age[1]	681,911	663,742	662,359	663,481	661,097	661,634	667,602	676,435	718,836
Covered by Private or Public Insurance									
Number.................................	560,525	548,403	554,955	553,334	562,588	597,902	617,152	630,576	661,283
Percent.................................	82.2	82.6	83.8	83.4	85.1	90.4	92.4	93.2	92.0
Uninsured									
Number.................................	121,386	115,339	107,404	110,147	98,509	63,732	50,450	45,859	57,553
Percent.................................	17.8	17.4	16.2	16.6	14.9	9.6	7.6	6.8	8.0
Percent in the U.S. not covered	8.6	8.0	7.5	7.2	7.1	6.0	4.8	4.5	5.0

[1] 2017 data is for individuals under 19 years of age.

Table NV-7. Employment Status by Demographic Group, 2018

(Numbers in thousands, percent.)

Characteristic	Civilian noninstitutional population	Civilian labor force		Employed		Unemployed	
		Number	Percent of population	Number	Percent of population	Number	Percent of population
Total.............................	2,402	1,523	63.4	1,454	60.5	69	4.5
Sex							
Male.............................	1,187	826	69.6	790	66.6	36	4.3
Female..........................	1,215	697	57.4	664	54.7	33	4.7
Race, Sex, and Hispanic Origin							
White...........................	1,763	1,087	61.6	1,040	59.0	47	4.3
Male.........................	888	603	67.9	576	64.8	28	4.6
Female......................	874	483	55.3	464	53.1	19	4.0
Black or African American..........	223	145	65.2	136	61.0	10	6.6
Male.........................	105	74	71.1	71	67.7	4	4.8
Female......................	118	71	60.1	65	55.1	6	8.4
Hispanic or Latino ethnicity[1].........	641	458	71.4	434	67.7	24	5.1
Male.........................	322	263	81.5	250	77.6	13	4.8
Female......................	319	195	61.2	184	57.8	11	5.6
Age							
16 to 19 years.................	149	50	33.6	41	27.7	9	17.5
20 to 24 years.................	189	146	77.4	138	73.0	8	5.5
25 to 34 years.................	419	352	84.0	333	79.7	18	5.1
35 to 44 years.................	401	333	83.2	323	80.6	10	3.1
45 to 54 years.................	390	312	79.8	300	76.9	11	3.7
55 to 64 years.................	380	232	60.9	223	58.7	8	3.6
65 years and over..............	474	99	20.8	95	20.0	4	4.0

NOTE: Data in Table 7 are from the Current Population Survey (CPS) and do not match the estimates in Table 8. See notes and definitions for further information.
[1] May be of any race.

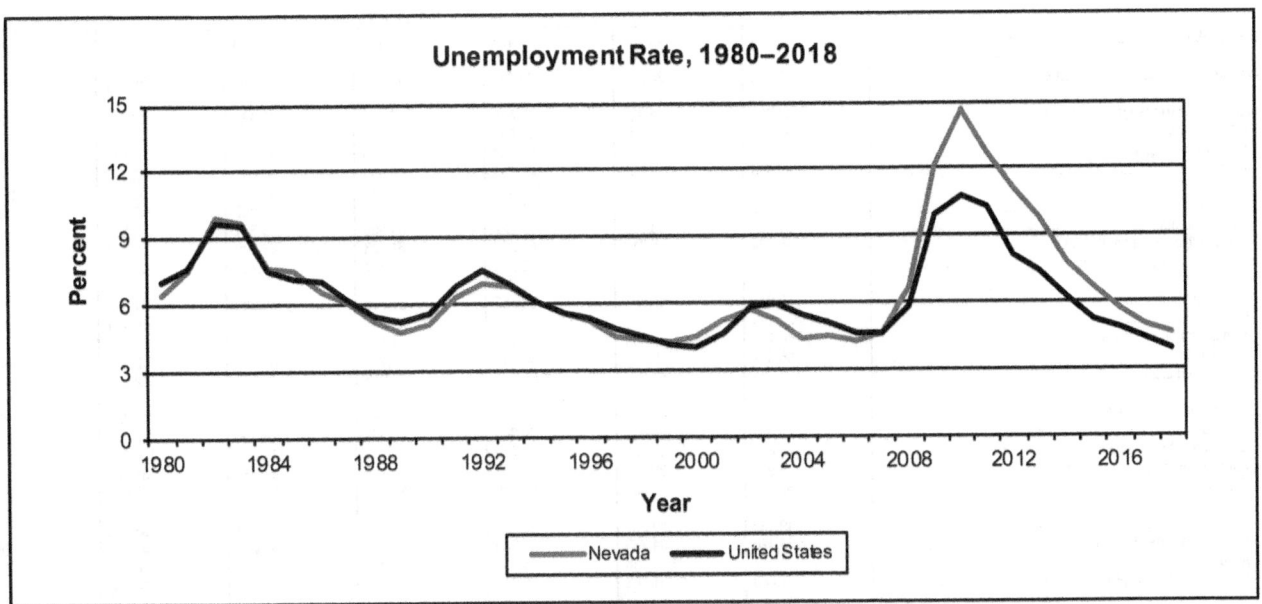

Unemployment Rate, 1980–2018

Table NV-8. Employment Status of the Civilian Noninstitutional Population Age 16 Years and Over

(Number, percent.)

Year	Civilian labor force	Civilian participation rate	Employed	Unemployed	Unemployment rate
2010...........................	1,358,578	65.9	1,174,774	183,804	13.5
2011...........................	1,373,115	65.5	1,194,264	178,851	13.0
2012...........................	1,376,381	64.6	1,222,710	153,671	11.2
2013...........................	1,381,157	63.8	1,248,122	133,035	9.6
2014...........................	1,394,758	63.3	1,284,292	110,466	7.9
2015...........................	1,413,739	62.9	1,318,024	95,715	6.8
2016...........................	1,430,344	62.3	1,348,265	82,079	5.7
2017...........................	1,462,955	62.3	1,389,372	73,583	5.0
2018...........................	1,500,377	63.0	1,431,959	68,418	4.6

Table NV-9. Employment and Average Wages by Industry

(Estimates are based on the 2012 *North American Industry Classification System* [NAICS].)

Industry	2011	2012	2013	2014	2015	2016	2017
	Number of jobs						
Wage and Salary Employment by Industry........................	1,161,009	1,179,620	1,207,788	1,251,274	1,292,456	1,329,421	1,371,359
Farm Wage and Salary Employment...............................	1,980	2,105	2,245	2,109	2,049	2,164	2,603
Nonfarm Wage and Salary Employment..........................	1,159,029	1,177,515	1,205,543	1,249,165	1,290,407	1,327,257	1,368,756
Private wage and salary employment.............................	992,490	1,012,194	1,038,884	1,081,124	1,121,731	1,156,181	1,193,494
Forestry, fishing, and related activities.....................	649	685	699	707	719	700	701
Mining..	13,881	15,419	15,314	14,382	14,174	13,681	14,208
Utilities...	4,187	4,037	3,967	3,884	3,962	4,068	4,094
Construction	53,499	53,325	58,397	64,752	71,996	77,697	85,110
Manufacturing...	38,243	39,281	40,618	41,555	42,157	43,570	47,829
Durable goods manufacturing...............................	24,679	25,117	25,653	25,800	26,121	26,827	30,175
Nondurable goods manufacturing...........................	13,564	14,164	14,965	15,755	16,036	16,743	17,654
Wholesale trade	32,886	32,774	33,087	34,105	34,600	34,727	36,305
Retail trade..	129,859	133,354	136,214	140,762	144,244	145,018	146,844
Transportation and warehousing...............................	47,581	49,694	50,543	53,705	57,727	60,242	63,774
Information	12,592	12,826	12,834	13,727	13,934	14,801	14,805
Finance and insurance	31,429	31,923	33,047	33,420	34,592	35,972	37,272
Real estate and rental and leasing...........................	22,174	22,280	23,195	23,939	25,681	26,386	26,800
Professional, scientific, and technical services	47,453	48,133	49,416	50,786	52,762	54,782	56,657
Management of companies and enterprises.......................	18,130	19,618	20,230	20,909	22,638	24,016	25,319
Administrative and waste services............................	75,541	78,567	81,323	85,369	92,745	98,446	101,020
Educational services	9,795	9,763	9,984	10,509	10,642	11,015	11,429
Health care and social assistance............................	95,653	97,871	100,435	104,345	109,657	115,611	120,868
Arts, entertainment, and recreation..........................	26,990	27,067	27,424	28,927	28,979	30,571	31,876
Accommodation and food services..............................	290,069	291,497	297,984	308,993	313,804	316,293	319,533
Other services, except public administration.................	41,879	44,080	44,173	46,348	46,718	48,585	49,050
Government and government enterprises.........................	166,539	165,321	166,659	168,041	168,676	171,076	175,262
	Dollars						
Average Wages and Salaries by Industry	44,364	44,969	45,473	46,109	47,113	48,331	49,316
Average Farm Wages and Salaries	33,026	38,014	39,763	40,856	35,590	39,012	32,620
Average Nonfarm Wages and Salaries	44,383	44,982	45,483	46,118	47,131	48,346	49,348
Average private wages and salaries...........................	43,227	43,992	44,581	45,206	46,204	47,459	48,439
Forestry, fishing, and related activities....................	33,673	34,578	34,887	35,950	34,978	34,819	35,665
Mining..	84,480	83,092	87,105	88,539	92,025	93,753	94,809
Utilities...	94,634	96,337	107,058	103,117	106,040	106,302	108,021
Construction	53,112	52,097	51,424	52,620	53,287	55,375	58,144
Manufacturing...	51,728	53,000	53,722	54,809	55,581	54,849	56,591
Durable goods manufacturing...............................	56,724	58,719	60,387	61,833	62,200	60,834	63,007
Nondurable goods manufacturing...........................	42,636	42,859	42,295	43,307	44,799	45,260	45,625
Wholesale trade	62,941	65,887	65,555	67,763	70,536	71,324	75,419
Retail trade..	28,195	28,741	29,158	29,575	29,951	30,484	31,317
Transportation and warehousing...............................	50,170	50,684	51,400	52,110	53,037	50,946	51,427
Information	56,817	58,218	58,537	59,454	61,440	62,446	65,834
Finance and insurance	59,723	62,575	65,330	67,013	71,723	72,278	74,901
Real estate and rental and leasing...........................	40,179	40,838	42,074	43,620	46,815	47,385	48,945
Professional, scientific, and technical services	68,378	69,910	70,305	71,397	72,256	73,481	74,571
Management of companies and enterprises.......................	110,895	116,733	121,210	120,702	114,037	130,468	123,383
Administrative and waste services............................	29,948	29,759	29,657	30,274	31,341	31,766	32,851
Educational services	35,504	36,054	37,472	37,533	38,453	39,003	39,420
Health care and social assistance............................	49,432	50,251	50,551	51,255	52,504	53,106	54,111
Arts, entertainment, and recreation..........................	34,426	34,239	34,269	35,955	37,027	50,390	38,694
Accommodation and food services..............................	34,612	35,136	35,497	35,906	36,402	36,775	37,563
Other services, except public administration.................	31,685	31,263	32,045	32,461	33,688	34,388	35,731
Government and government enterprises.........................	51,278	51,040	51,104	51,989	53,295	54,345	55,537

Table NV-10. Employment Characteristics by Family Type

(Number, percent.)

Family type and labor force status	2015		2016		2017	
	Total	Families with own children under 18 years	Total	Families with own children under 18 years	Total	Families with own children under 18 years
All Families..	659,355	282,664	670,968	282,717	700,449	295,792
FAMILY TYPE AND LABOR FORCE STATUS						
Married-Couple Families..............................	456,740	176,363	469,014	179,823	491,128	190,647
Both husband and wife in labor force......................	47.5	62.4	48.0	63.6	46.9	61.4
Husband in labor force, wife not in labor force	22.7	31.8	23.2	30.4	23.2	31.0
Wife in labor force, husband not in labor force	8.3	3.3	8.3	3.9	8.2	4.7
Both husband and wife not in labor force..................	20.6	2.1	19.3	1.4	20.5	2.4
Other Families	202,615	106,301	201,954	102,894	209,321	105,145
Female householder, no husband present	68.7	70.8	67.9	70.2	68.1	71.8
In labor force..	50.1	59.0	50.0	59.3	49.4	62.1
Not in labor force	18.6	11.8	17.9	11.0	18.6	9.7
Male householder, no wife present........................	31.3	29.2	32.1	29.8	31.9	28.2
In labor force..	25.8	27.6	25.9	27.4	25.4	25.8
Not in labor force	5.5	1.6	6.2	2.4	6.6	2.5

Table NV-11. School Enrollment and Educational Attainment, 2017

(Number, percent.)

Item	State	U.S.
Enrollment		
Total population 3 years and over, enrolled in school	697,092	81,273,337
Enrolled in nursery school or preschool (percent)...	4.9	6.0
Enrolled in kindergarten (percent)..	5.2	4.9
Enrolled in elementary school, grades 1-8 (percent)..	44.0	40.6
Enrolled in high school, grades 9-12 (percent)..	22.4	21.1
Enrolled in college or graduate school (percent)	23.5	27.4
Attainment		
Total population 25 years and over	2,063,180	221,250,083
Less than ninth grade (percent)...	5.2	5.1
9th to 12th grade, no diploma (percent)	8.0	6.9
High school graduate, including equivalency (percent)......................................	28.7	27.1
Some college, no degree (percent)	25.1	20.4
Associate's degree (percent)..	8.0	8.5
Bachelor's degree (percent)..	16.5	19.7
Graduate or professional degree (percent)...	8.4	12.3
High school graduate or higher (percent)...	86.8	88.0
Bachelor's degree or higher (percent)...	24.9	32.0

Table NV-12. Public School Characteristics and Educational Indicators

(Number, percent; data derived from National Center of Education Statistics.)

Item	State	U.S.
Public Elementary and Secondary Schools		
Number of operational school districts, 2016-17...	19	18,377
Number of operational schools, 2016-17	663	98,330
Percent charter schools	7.4	7.1
Total public school enrollment, 2016-17	473,744	50,587,859
Percent charter school enrollment	8.5	6.0
Student-teacher ratio, Fall 2015...	20.6	16.0
Expenditures per student (dollars), 2015-16...	8,753	11,841
Four-year adjusted cohort graduation rate (ACGR)[1]	80.9	84.6
Students eligible for free or reduced-price lunch (percent), 2015-16.......................	58.8	52.1
English language learners (percent), Fall 2016	15.9	9.6
Students age 3 to 21 served under IDEA, part B (percent), 2017-18	12.5	13.7
Public Schools by Type, 2016-17		Percent of state public schools
Total number of schools...	657	100.0
Special education	13	2.0
Vocational education..	0	-
Alternative education...	33	5.0

[1] Adjusted Cohort Graduation Rates (ACGR) differ from Averaged Freshmen Graduation Rates (AFGR).
- = Zero or rounds to zero.

Table NV-13. Reported Voting and Registration of the Voting-Age Population, November 2018

(Numbers in thousands, percent.)

Item	Total population	Total citizen population	Registered			Voted		
			Total registered	Percent registered (total population)	Percent registered (total citizen population)	Total voted	Percent voted (total population)	Percent voted (total citizen population)
U.S. Total	249,748	228,832	153,066	61.3	66.9	122,281	49.0	53.4
State Total....................................	2,324	2,067	1,277	55.0	61.8	1,006	43.3	48.7
Sex								
Male	1,145	1,043	616	53.8	59.0	497	43.4	47.7
Female	1,179	1,024	662	56.1	64.6	509	43.2	49.7
Race								
White alone...................................	1,731	1,573	1,009	58.3	64.2	818	47.2	52.0
White, non-Hispanic alone	1,261	1,239	850	67.4	68.6	701	55.6	56.6
Black alone...................................	197	178	108	55.0	60.9	65	33.3	36.8
Asian alone	230	177	69	30.2	39.2	49	21.4	27.8
Hispanic (of any race)......................	584	415	212	36.2	51.0	156	26.7	37.7
White alone or in combination	1,798	1,635	1,058	58.8	64.7	854	47.5	52.2
Black alone or in combination..............	205	185	114	55.7	61.5	69	33.7	37.1
Asian alone or in combination.............	248	195	78	31.5	40.1	58	23.4	29.7
Age								
18 to 24 years	260	238	119	45.7	49.9	77	29.7	32.4
25 to 34 years	433	373	192	44.3	51.5	115	26.6	30.9
35 to 44 years	373	323	191	51.3	59.3	141	37.8	43.7
45 to 64 years	791	687	452	57.2	65.8	372	47.0	54.2
65 years and over	467	447	323	69.1	72.3	301	64.5	67.4

Table NV-14. Crime

(Number, rate per 100,000. Data are derived from the FBI Uniform Crime Reports.)

Item	State			U.S.		
	2016	2017	Percent change	2016	2017	Percent change
TOTAL POPULATION[1]	2,939,254	2,998,039	2.0	323,405,935	325,719,178	0.7
VIOLENT CRIME						
Number...	19,924	16,667	-16.3	1,285,606	1,283,220	-0.2
Rate..	677.9	555.9	-18.0	397.5	394.0	-0.9
Murder and Nonnegligent Manslaughter						
Number...	228	274	20.2	17,413	17,284	-0.7
Rate..	7.8	9.1	17.8	5.4	5.3	-1.4
Rape[2]						
Number...	1,729	1,890	9.3	132,414	135,755	2.5
Rate..	58.8	63.0	7.2	40.9	41.7	1.8
Robbery						
Number...	6,338	4,841	-23.6	332,797	319,356	-4.0
Rate..	215.6	161.5	-25.1	102.9	98.0	-4.7
Aggravated Assault						
Number...	11,629	9,662	-16.9	802,982	810,825	1.0
Rate..	395.6	322.3	-18.5	248.3	248.9	0.3
PROPERTY CRIME						
Number...	75,922	78,322	3.2	7,928,530	7,694,086	-3.0
Rate..	2,583.0	2,612.4	1.1	2,451.6	2,362.2	-3.6
Burglary						
Number...	18,816	20,049	6.6	1,516,405	1,401,840	-7.6
Rate..	640.2	668.7	4.5	468.9	430.4	-8.2
Larceny-Theft						
Number...	43,949	45,461	3.4	5,644,835	5,519,107	-2.2
Rate..	1,495.2	1,516.4	1.4	1,745.4	1,694.4	-2.9
Motor Vehicle Theft						
Number...	13,157	12,812	-2.6	767,290	773,139	0.8
Rate..	447.6	427.3	-4.5	237.3	237.4	-

NOTE: Although arson data are included in the trend and clearance tables, sufficient data are not available to estimate totals for this offense. Therefore, no arson data are published in this table.
- = Zero or rounds to zero.
[1] Population figures are U.S. Census Bureau provisional estimates as of July 1, 2017.
[2] The figures shown in the rape (revised definition) column were estimated using the revised Uniform Crime Reporting (UCR) definition of rape.

Table NV-15. State Government Finances, 2017

(Dollar amounts in thousands, percent distribution.)

Item	Dollars	Percent distribution
Total Revenue	22,421,180	100.0
General revenue	15,342,157	68.4
Intergovernmental revenue	5,234,577	23.3
Taxes	8,624,618	38.5
General sales	4,756,243	21.2
Selective sales	2,167,041	9.7
License taxes	666,527	3.0
Individual income tax	0	-
Corporate income tax	0	-
Other taxes	1,034,807	4.6
Current charges	824,663	3.7
Miscellaneous general revenue	658,299	2.9
Utility revenue	43,332	0.2
Liquor stores revenue	0	-
Insurance trust revenue[1]	7,035,691	31.4
Total Expenditure	16,221,269	100.0
Intergovernmental expenditure	4,772,756	29.4
Direct expenditure	11,448,513	70.6
Current operation	7,313,033	45.1
Capital outlay	896,872	5.5
Insurance benefits and repayments	2,605,908	16.1
Assistance and subsidies	494,244	3.0
Interest on debt	138,456	0.9
Exhibit: Salaries and wages	1,737,065	10.7
Total Expenditure	16,221,269	100.0
General expenditure	13,571,159	83.7
Intergovernmental expenditure	4,772,756	29.4
Direct expenditure	8,798,403	54.2
General expenditure, by function:		
Education	5,150,123	31.7
Public welfare	3,892,730	24.0
Hospitals	269,434	1.7
Health	296,213	1.8
Highways	1,000,032	6.2
Police protection	95,406	0.6
Correction	312,785	1.9
Natural resources	140,690	0.9
Parks and recreation	22,795	0.1
Governmental administration	444,316	2.7
Interest on general debt	138,456	0.9
Other and unallocable	1,808,179	11.1
Utility expenditure	44,202	0.2
Liquor stores expenditure	0	-
Insurance trust expenditure	2,605,908	16.1
Debt at End of Fiscal Year	3,248,814	X
Cash and Security Holdings	42,075,637	X

X = Not applicable.
- = Zero or rounds to zero.
[1] Within insurance trust revenue, net earnings of state retirement systems is a calculated statistic (the item code in the data file is X08), and thus can be positive or negative. Net earnings is the sum of earnings on investments plus gains on investments minus losses on investments. The change made in 2002 for asset valuation from book to market value in accordance with Statement 34 of the Governmental Accounting Standards Board is reflected in the calculated statistics.

Table NV-16. State Government Tax Collections, 2018

(Dollars in thousands, percent.)

Item	Dollars	Percent distribution
Total Taxes	9,157,036	100.0
Property taxes	317,136	3.5
Sales and gross receipts	7,329,456	80.0
General sales and gross receipts	5,095,689	55.6
Selective sales and gross receipts	2,233,767	24.4
Alcoholic beverages	45,340	0.5
Amusements	915,531	10.0
Insurance premiums	395,701	4.3
Motor fuels	343,386	3.7
Pari-mutuels	3	-
Public utilities	46,300	0.5
Tobacco products	177,161	1.9
Other selective sales	310,345	3.4
Licenses	661,240	7.2
Alcoholic beverages	X	-
Amusements	82,640	0.9
Corporations in general	78,782	0.9
Hunting and fishing	12,144	0.1
Motor vehicle	198,263	2.2
Motor vehicle operators	28,099	0.3
Public utilities	X	-
Occupation and business, NEC	256,769	2.8
Other licenses	4,543	0.0
Income taxes	X	-
Individual income	X	-
Corporation net income	X	-
Other taxes	849,204	9.3
Death and gift	X	-
Documentary and stock transfer	111,422	1.2
Severance	155,938	1.7
Taxes, NEC	581,844	6.4

X = Not applicable.
- = Zero or rounds to zero.

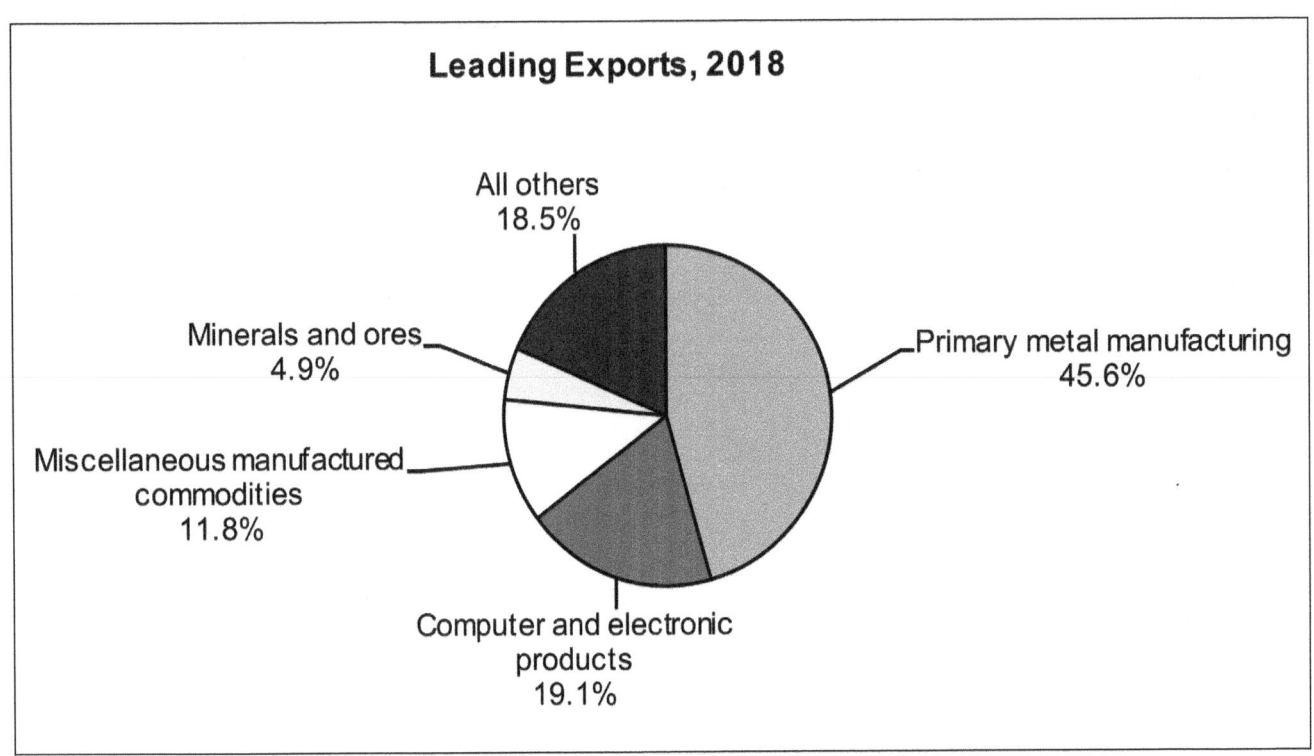

Leading Exports, 2018

- All others 18.5%
- Primary metal manufacturing 45.6%
- Computer and electronic products 19.1%
- Miscellaneous manufactured commodities 11.8%
- Minerals and ores 4.9%

Facts and Figures

Location: Northeastern United States; bordered on the N by Canada (Quebec), on the E by Maine, on the SE by the Atlantic Ocean, on the S by Massachusetts, and on the W by Vermont

Area: 9,350 sq. mi. (24,216 sq. km.); rank—46th

Population: 1,356,458 (2018 est.); rank—41st

Principal Cities: capital—Concord; largest—Manchester

Statehood: June 21, 1788; 9th state

U.S. Congress: 2 senators, 2 representatives

State Motto: Live Free or Die

State Song: "Old New Hampshire"

State Nickname: The Granite State

Abbreviations: NH; N.H.

State Symbols: flower—purple lilac; tree—white birch; bird—purple finch

At a Glance

- With an increase in population of 3.0 percent, New Hampshire ranked 31st among the states in growth from 2010 to 2018.

- New Hampshire's violent crime rate in 2017 was 198.7 per 100,000 population, the 3rd lowest in the country, compared to a rate of 394.0 for the entire nation.

- The state's property crime rate, 1,381.8 per 100,000 population, was the lowest in the country in 2017.

- New Hampshire had the 6th highest rate of drug overdose deaths in 2017, with 37.0 deaths per 100,000 population.

- New Hampshire had the lowest birth rate in the country in 2017, with 9.0 births per 1,000 population.

Table NH-1. Population by Age, Sex, Race, and Hispanic Origin

(Number, percent, except where noted.)

Sex, age, race, and Hispanic origin	2000	2010	2018 [1]	Percent change, 2010–2018
Total Population..	1,235,786	1,316,470	1,356,458	3.0
Percent of total U.S. population	0.4	0.4	0.4	X
Sex				
Male..	607,687	649,394	672,266	3.5
Female..	628,099	667,076	684,192	2.6
Age				
Under 5 years..	75,685	69,806	64,020	-8.3
5 to 19 years...	268,480	255,996	230,605	-9.9
20 to 64 years...	743,651	812,400	816,188	0.5
65 years and over..	147,970	178,268	245,645	37.8
Median age (years)	37.1	41.1	43.0	4.6
Race and Hispanic Origin				
One race				
White	1,186,851	1,248,321	1,264,217	1.3
Black	9,035	16,365	23,293	42.3
American Indian and Alaska Native	2,964	3,530	4,090	15.9
Asian	15,931	28,933	40,460	39.8
Native Hawaiian or Other Pacific Islander	371	532	637	19.7
Two or more races..	13,214	18,789	23,761	26.5
Hispanic (of any race)..	20,489	38,688	52,663	36.1

X = Not applicable.
- = Zero or rounds to zero.
[1] Population figures for 2018 are July 1 estimates. The 2010 estimates are taken from the 2010 Census.

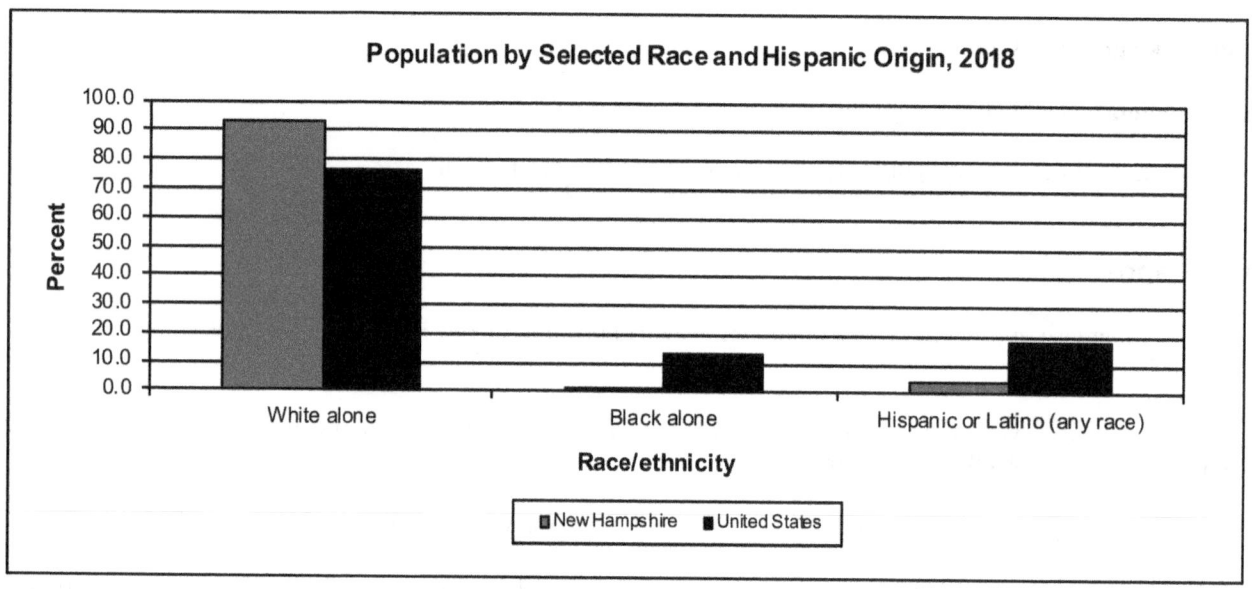

Table NH-2. Marital Status

(Number, percent distribution.)

Sex, age, race, and Hispanic origin	2000	2010	2017
Males, 15 Years and Over...	476,409	529,439	557,566
Never married	27.7	30.5	32.3
Now married, except separated..	59.1	54.7	52.8
Separated..	1.2	1.3	1.4
Widowed..	2.4	2.6	2.5
Divorced..	9.6	10.9	10.9
Females, 15 Years and Over...	502,232	555,698	576,178
Never married	22.3	25.4	26.9
Now married, except separated..	55.7	51.4	50.0
Separated..	1.5	1.3	1.2
Widowed..	9.2	8.6	8.1
Divorced..	11.3	13.4	13.7

Table NH-3. Households and Housing Characteristics

(Number, percent, dollars.)

Item	2000	2010	2017	Average annual percent change, 2010–2017
Total Households...	474,606	515,431	528,700	0.4
Family households	323,651	344,057	346,213	0.1
Married-couple family	262,438	274,195	275,525	0.1
Other family	61,213	69,862	70,688	0.2
Male householder, no wife present......................................	18,261	22,205	25,876	2.4
Female householder, no husband present...........................	42,952	47,657	44,812	-0.9
Nonfamily households	150,955	171,374	182,487	0.9
Householder living alone...	116,014	130,327	138,388	0.9
Householder not living alone...	34,941	41,047	44,099	1.1
Housing Characteristics				
Total housing units..	547,024	614,996	634,689	0.5
Occupied housing units	474,606	515,431	528,700	0.4
Owner occupied	330,700	369,448	369,037	-
Renter occupied	143,906	145,983	159,663	1.3
Average household size..	2.53	2.48	2.46	-0.1
Financial Characteristics				
Median gross rent of renter-occupied housing	646	951	1072	1.8
Median monthly owner costs for housing units with a mortgage	1,226	1,853	1,874	0.2
Median value of owner-occupied housing units......................	133,300	243,000	263,600	1.2

- = Zero or rounds to zero.

Table NH-4. Migration, Origin, and Language

(Number, percent.)

	State			U.S.		
Characteristic	2016	2017	Percent change	2016	2017	Percent change
Residence 1 Year Ago						
Population 1 year and over	1,322,101	1,330,742	0.7	319,361,956	321,994,428	0.8
Same house	84.9	85.2	X	85.4	85.7	X
Different house in the U.S.	14.6	14.3	X	13.9	13.6	X
Same county	8.0	7.6	X	8.3	8.1	X
Different county	6.6	6.7	X	5.6	5.6	X
Same state	2.6	2.7	X	3.2	3.3	X
Different state	4.0	4.0	X	2.4	2.3	X
Abroad	0.5	0.5	X	0.7	0.7	X
Place of Birth						
Native born	1,258,486	1,259,628	0.1	279,388,170	281,193,323	0.6
Male	49.8	49.7	X	49.3	49.4	X
Female	50.2	50.3	X	50.7	50.6	X
Foreign born	76,309	83,167	9.0	43,739,345	44,525,855	1.8
Male	49.8	47.2	X	48.5	48.4	X
Female	50.2	52.8	X	51.5	51.6	X
Foreign born; naturalized U.S. citizen......................	40,403	43,683	8.1	21,238,372	21,948,732	3.3
Male..	45.7	45.1	X	45.9	45.9	X
Female	54.3	54.9	X	54.1	54.1	X
Foreign born; not a U.S. citizen..............................	35,906	39,484	10.0	22,500,973	22,577,123	0.3
Male..	54.3	49.6	X	51	50.8	X
Female	45.7	50.4	X	49	49.2	X
Entered 2010 or later	26.0	28.8	X	18.6	21.3	X
Entered 2000 to 2009	22.6	19.9	X	26.7	25.7	X
Entered before 2000..	51.4	51.4	X	54.7	53.0	X
World Region of Birth, Foreign						
Foreign-born population, excluding population born at sea	76,309	83,167	9.0	43,738,901	44,525,458	1.8
Europe	22.7	24.4	X	10.9	10.8	X
Asia	37.9	39.8	X	30.8	31.2	X
Africa	8.2	5.7	X	4.9	5.1	X
Oceania	1.2	0.3	X	0.6	0.6	X
Latin America	19.5	19.3	X	51	50.4	X
North America..	10.5	10.4	X	1.8	1.8	X
Language Spoken at Home and Ability to Speak English						
Population 5 years and over...................................	1,270,317	1,279,272	0.7	303,328,961	305,924,019	0.9
English only	92.3	92.0	X	78.4	78.2	X
Language other than English..............................	7.7	8.0	X	21.6	21.8	X
Speaks English less than "very well"...................	2.5	2.5	X	8.6	8.5	X

NA = Not available.
X = Not applicable.
- = Zero or rounds to zero.

Table NH-5. Median Income and Poverty Status, 2017

(Number, percent, except as noted.)

Characteristic	State		U.S.	
	Number	Percent	Number	Percent
Median Income				
Households (dollars)...	73,381	X	60,336	X
Families (dollars)	91,029	X	73,891	X
Below Poverty Level (All People)	99,966	7.7	42,583,651	13.4
Sex				
Male	43,596	6.8	19,004,547	12.2
Female	56,370	8.6	23,579,104	14.5
Age				
Under 18 years...	25,909	10.3	13,353,202	18.4
Related children under 18 years......................................	24,632	9.8	13,053,472	18.1
18 to 64 years...	60,931	7.4	24,648,677	12.6
65 years and over	13,126	5.8	4,581,772	9.3

X = Not applicable.

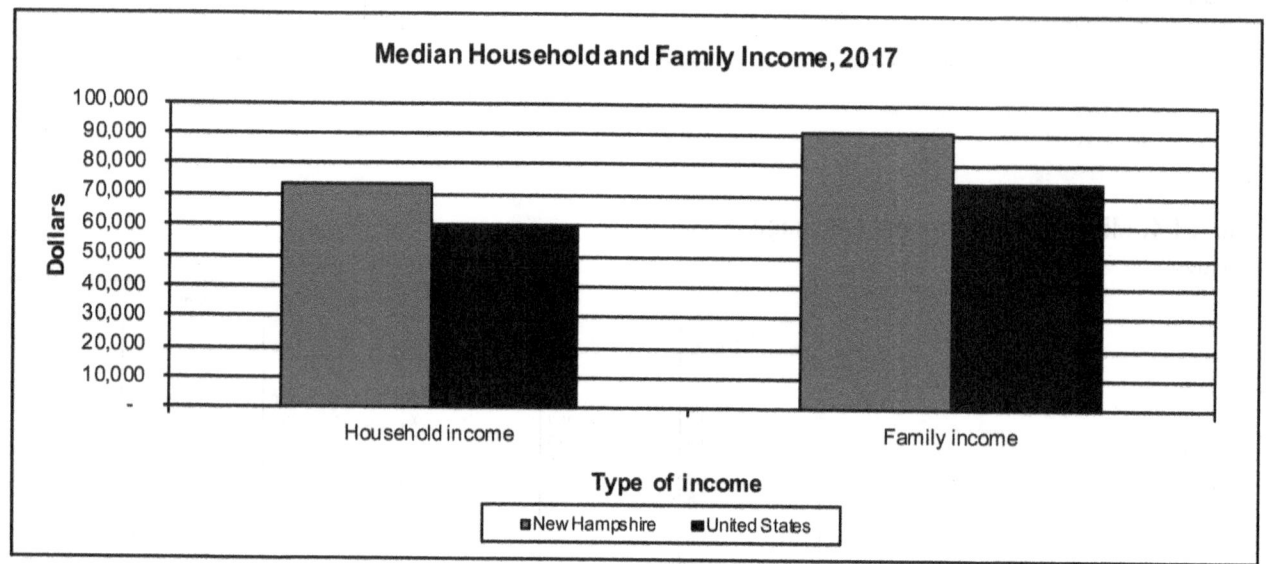

Table NH-6. Health Insurance Coverage Status for the Civilian Noninstitutionalized Population and Children Under 18 Years of Age

(Number, percent.)

Item	2009	2010	2011	2012	2013	2014	2015	2016	2017
Civilian Noninstitutionalized Population	1,308,729	1,302,639	1,303,868	1,306,026	1,308,658	1,311,921	1,314,249	1,316,467	1,325,016
Covered by Private or Public Insurance									
Number...	1,174,696	1,157,626	1,166,946	1,167,184	1,168,406	1,191,465	1,230,861	1,238,790	1,247,957
Percent...	89.8	88.9	89.5	89.4	89.3	90.8	93.7	94.1	94.2
Uninsured									
Number...	134,033	145,013	136,922	138,842	140,252	120,456	83,388	77,677	77,059
Percent...	10.2	11.1	10.5	10.6	10.7	9.2	6.3	5.9	5.8
Percent in the U.S. not covered..	15.1	15.5	15.1	14.8	14.5	11.7	9.4	8.6	8.7
Children Under 18 Years of Age[1]	288,780	285,730	279,210	274,563	270,642	266,833	262,932	259,410	275,977
Covered by Private or Public Insurance									
Number...	275,304	272,051	269,018	263,665	260,381	255,132	255,940	252,563	269,639
Percent...	95.3	95.2	96.3	96.0	96.2	95.6	97.3	97.4	97.7
Uninsured									
Number...	13,476	13,679	10,192	10,898	10,261	11,701	6,992	6,847	6,338
Percent...	4.7	4.8	3.7	4.0	3.8	4.4	2.7	2.6	2.3
Percent in the U.S. not covered	8.6	8.0	7.5	7.2	7.1	6.0	4.8	4.5	5.0

[1] 2017 data is for individuals under 19 years of age.

Table NH-7. Employment Status by Demographic Group, 2018

(Numbers in thousands, percent.)

Characteristic	Civilian noninstitutional population	Civilian labor force		Employed		Unemployed	
		Number	Percent of population	Number	Percent of population	Number	Percent of population
Total...	1,109	762	68.7	742	66.9	20	2.6
Sex							
Male..	545	404	74.1	393	72.1	11	2.6
Female..	564	358	63.5	349	61.9	9	2.6
Race, Sex, and Hispanic Origin							
White..	1,041	715	68.7	697	66.9	18	2.5
Male..	515	382	74.1	372	72.2	10	2.5
Female...	526	333	63.3	324	61.7	9	2.5
Black or African American................	NA	NA	NA	NA	NA	NA	NA
Male..	NA	NA	NA	NA	NA	NA	NA
Female...	NA	NA	NA	NA	NA	NA	NA
Hispanic or Latino ethnicity[1]	NA	NA	NA	NA	NA	NA	NA
Male..	NA	NA	NA	NA	NA	NA	NA
Female...	NA	NA	NA	NA	NA	NA	NA
Age							
16 to 19 years.................................	68	35	51.7	32	47.2	3	8.8
20 to 24 years.................................	84	63	74.7	60	70.7	3	5.3
25 to 34 years.................................	159	142	89.0	139	87.1	3	2.1
35 to 44 years.................................	163	144	88.3	140	86.0	4	2.7
45 to 54 years.................................	186	160	86.1	157	84.7	3	1.7
55 to 64 years.................................	214	162	75.8	159	74.4	3	1.8
65 years and over............................	236	57	24.2	56	23.8	1	1.8

NOTE: Data in Table 7 are from the Current Population Survey (CPS) and do not match the estimates in Table 8. See notes and definitions for further information.
[1] May be of any race.
NA = Not available.

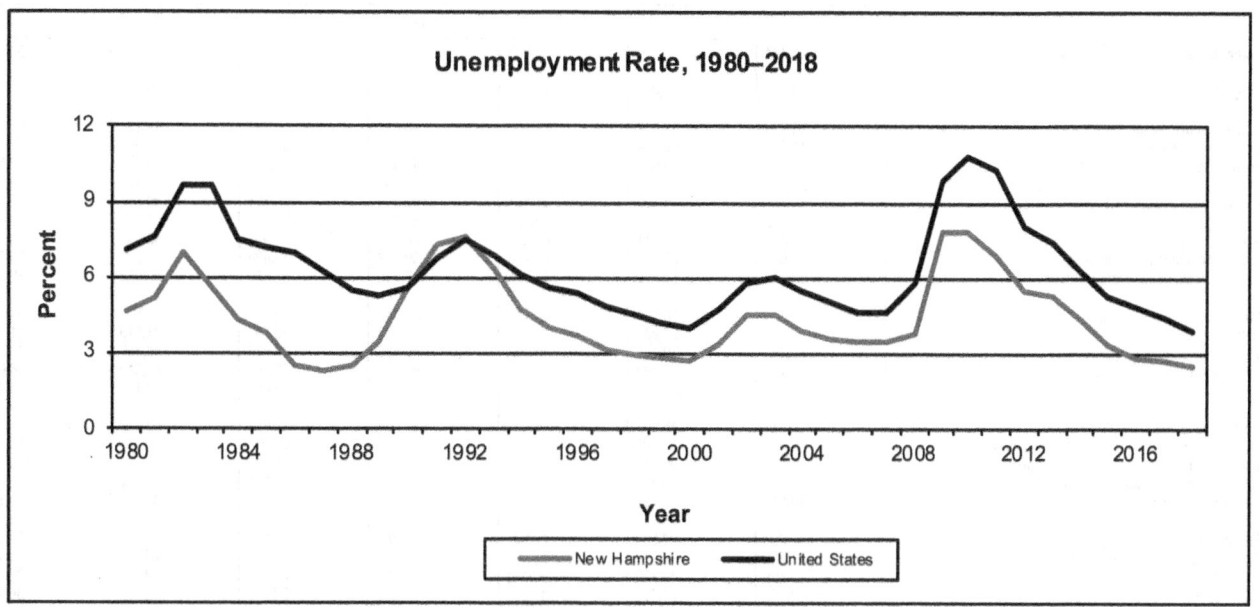

Table NH-8. Employment Status of the Civilian Noninstitutional Population Age 16 Years and Over

(Number, percent.)

Year	Civilian labor force	Civilian participation rate	Employed	Unemployed	Unemployment rate
2010..	738,257	69.9	695,135	43,122	5.8
2011..	736,302	69.6	696,532	39,770	5.4
2012..	741,097	69.5	700,371	40,726	5.5
2013..	741,285	69.2	703,534	37,751	5.1
2014..	740,667	68.7	708,977	31,690	4.3
2015..	741,937	68.5	716,874	25,063	3.4
2016..	746,452	68.4	725,154	21,298	2.9
2017..	746,549	67.9	726,607	19,942	2.7
2018..	761,752	68.4	742,512	19,240	2.5

Table NH-9. Employment and Average Wages by Industry

(Estimates are based on the 2012 *North American Industry Classification System* [NAICS].)

Industry	2011	2012	2013	2014	2015	2016	2017
	Number of jobs						
Wage and Salary Employment by Industry	633,733	640,426	647,086	655,565	666,446	676,434	682,227
Farm Wage and Salary Employment	1,229	1,450	1,658	1,664	1,658	1,548	1,544
Nonfarm Wage and Salary Employment	632,504	638,976	645,428	653,901	664,788	674,886	680,683
Private wage and salary employment	537,192	544,052	550,738	558,847	569,930	580,407	586,304
Forestry, fishing, and related activities	734	750	786	825	820	803	769
Mining	494	500	531	532	526	556	548
Utilities	2,472	2,454	2,481	2,320	2,182	2,129	2,090
Construction	22,737	22,791	23,142	23,787	24,864	26,118	27,100
Manufacturing	66,676	66,049	66,076	66,598	67,273	68,179	69,179
Durable goods manufacturing	51,169	50,195	49,886	49,950	50,169	50,801	51,455
Nondurable goods manufacturing	15,507	15,854	16,190	16,648	17,104	17,378	17,724
Wholesale trade	26,303	26,723	26,869	27,214	27,681	27,896	28,127
Retail trade	93,787	95,169	95,469	95,065	95,615	96,650	96,216
Transportation and warehousing	12,350	12,508	12,561	13,008	13,483	14,322	14,617
Information	11,175	12,093	11,927	12,044	12,285	12,532	12,579
Finance and insurance	28,047	28,772	29,174	29,418	30,159	30,841	28,467
Real estate and rental and leasing	6,951	6,717	6,921	6,932	6,809	7,021	7,164
Professional, scientific, and technical services	30,109	30,681	31,989	32,687	33,719	34,252	37,797
Management of companies and enterprises	8,096	8,151	8,187	8,191	8,646	8,906	8,956
Administrative and waste services	28,803	29,977	30,690	33,191	34,843	35,172	35,585
Educational services	21,899	22,256	22,870	23,362	24,540	25,391	25,666
Health care and social assistance	85,399	85,936	86,746	87,429	89,129	91,116	92,308
Arts, entertainment, and recreation	11,330	11,332	11,382	11,389	11,450	11,797	12,012
Accommodation and food services	52,326	53,563	55,213	56,218	57,446	58,473	59,259
Other services, except public administration	27,504	27,630	27,724	28,637	28,460	28,253	27,865
Government and government enterprises	95,312	94,924	94,690	95,054	94,858	94,479	94,379
	Dollars						
Average Wages and Salaries by Industry	46,484	47,579	48,253	50,382	51,727	52,767	54,319
Average Farm Wages and Salaries	20,333	30,607	27,287	28,806	23,616	29,029	26,413
Average Nonfarm Wages and Salaries	46,535	47,617	48,307	50,437	51,797	52,821	54,383
Average private wages and salaries	47,282	48,534	49,224	51,549	52,890	53,957	55,589
Forestry, fishing, and related activities	37,125	43,920	40,710	45,013	47,511	44,724	47,568
Mining	55,322	56,796	53,339	54,147	57,757	58,453	63,111
Utilities	96,442	94,509	94,651	102,353	103,231	103,327	111,422
Construction	50,142	51,510	52,968	54,208	57,292	58,909	61,595
Manufacturing	63,203	63,511	64,629	66,253	66,915	68,346	70,454
Durable goods manufacturing	66,682	66,794	67,986	69,827	70,096	71,524	73,725
Nondurable goods manufacturing	51,720	53,118	54,286	55,530	57,585	59,056	60,958
Wholesale trade	77,834	80,564	82,161	84,863	90,571	89,896	91,618
Retail trade	27,384	27,938	28,483	29,670	30,752	31,013	31,676
Transportation and warehousing	38,295	39,154	40,002	40,888	43,020	43,336	44,760
Information	74,493	75,489	78,946	91,493	82,669	85,312	88,097
Finance and insurance	81,375	84,500	85,901	94,523	94,655	100,186	100,414
Real estate and rental and leasing	47,282	45,037	46,136	47,654	50,873	52,139	53,369
Professional, scientific, and technical services	76,993	79,395	80,187	84,859	86,971	88,698	93,886
Management of companies and enterprises	82,356	97,910	89,768	106,453	106,548	103,648	109,439
Administrative and waste services	40,285	42,700	42,388	43,547	45,242	46,226	47,577
Educational services	40,811	41,698	42,825	44,025	45,157	45,049	44,804
Health care and social assistance	47,864	48,533	49,101	50,368	51,841	52,995	54,534
Arts, entertainment, and recreation	21,482	22,043	23,153	24,347	24,508	24,324	25,126
Accommodation and food services	19,195	19,720	20,134	20,897	21,783	22,693	23,517
Other services, except public administration	30,762	31,705	32,724	33,261	34,714	35,607	36,457
Government and government enterprises	42,327	42,364	42,971	43,902	45,227	45,843	46,890

Table NH-10. Employment Characteristics by Family Type

(Number, percent.)

Family type and labor force status	2015		2016		2017	
	Total	Families with own children under 18 years	Total	Families with own children under 18 years	Total	Families with own children under 18 years
All Families...	341,473	128,997	342,912	130,641	346,213	130,087
FAMILY TYPE AND LABOR FORCE STATUS						
Married-Couple Families.............................	268,944	91,828	271,458	92,165	275,525	92,368
Both husband and wife in labor force............................	57.5	74.1	55.9	73.4	56.6	72.4
Husband in labor force, wife not in labor force	17.3	21.3	18.2	21.0	17.3	21.8
Wife in labor force, husband not in labor force	7.3	3.1	8.2	4.0	8.5	4.5
Both husband and wife not in labor force.........................	16.8	1.1	16.4	1.3	16.5	0.8
Other Families	72,529	37,169	71,454	38,476	70,688	37,719
Female householder, no husband present........................	71.1	74.3	67.6	66.9	63.4	66.3
In labor force..	50.7	59.5	50.0	55.4	45.9	54.8
Not in labor force	20.4	14.8	17.6	11.5	17.5	11.5
Male householder, no wife present...........................	28.9	25.7	32.4	33.1	36.6	33.7
In labor force..	22.4	23.9	27.8	30.7	30.1	30.8
Not in labor force	6.4	1.8	4.6	2.5	6.5	2.9

Table NH-11. School Enrollment and Educational Attainment, 2017

(Number, percent.)

Item	State	U.S.
Enrollment		
Total population 3 years and over, enrolled in school	300,223	81,273,337
Enrolled in nursery school or preschool (percent)	5.6	6.0
Enrolled in kindergarten (percent)...................................	4.2	4.9
Enrolled in elementary school, grades 1-8 (percent)........................	38.3	40.6
Enrolled in high school, grades 9-12 (percent)	21.8	21.1
Enrolled in college or graduate school (percent).........................	30.2	27.4
Attainment		
Total population 25 years and over	958,005	221,250,083
Less than ninth grade (percent)......................................	1.9	5.1
9th to 12th grade, no diploma (percent)	5.1	6.9
High school graduate, including equivalency (percent).......................	28.0	27.1
Some college, no degree (percent)....................................	17.9	20.4
Associate's degree (percent)..	10.2	8.5
Bachelor's degree (percent)...	22.6	19.7
Graduate or professional degree (percent)...............................	14.3	12.3
High school graduate or higher (percent)................................	93.1	88.0
Bachelor's degree or higher (percent)..................................	36.9	32.0

Table NH-12. Public School Characteristics and Educational Indicators

(Number, percent; data derived from National Center of Education Statistics.)

Item	State	U.S.
Public Elementary and Secondary Schools		
Number of operational school districts, 2016-17............................	301	18,377
Number of operational schools, 2016-17.................................	490	98,330
Percent charter schools	6.3	7.1
Total public school enrollment, 2016-17.................................	180,888	50,587,859
Percent charter school enrollment	1.9	6.0
Student-teacher ratio, Fall 2015......................................	12.4	16.0
Expenditures per student (dollars), 2015-16..............................	15,535	11,841
Four-year adjusted cohort graduation rate (ACGR)[1]........................	88.9	84.6
Students eligible for free or reduced-price lunch (percent), 2015-16...............	28.3	52.1
English language learners (percent), Fall 2016............................	2.4	9.6
Students age 3 to 21 served under IDEA, part B (percent), 2017-18	16.4	13.7

Public Schools by Type, 2016-17		Percent of state public schools
Total number of schools..	490	100.0
Special education	0	-
Vocational education	0	-
Alternative education..	0	-

[1] Adjusted Cohort Graduation Rates (ACGR) differ from Averaged Freshmen Graduation Rates (AFGR).
- = Zero or rounds to zero.

Table NH-13. Reported Voting and Registration of the Voting-Age Population, November 2018

(Numbers in thousands, percent.)

Item	Total population	Total citizen population	Registered			Voted		
			Total registered	Percent registered (total population)	Percent registered (total citizen population)	Total voted	Percent voted (total population)	Percent voted (total citizen population)
U.S. Total	249,748	228,832	153,066	61.3	66.9	122,281	49.0	53.4
State Total.......................................	1,080	1,025	726	67.2	70.8	576	53.3	56.2
Sex								
Male	530	507	359	67.8	70.9	280	52.9	55.3
Female	550	519	367	66.7	70.8	296	53.8	57.1
Race								
White alone..................................	1,002	978	698	69.7	71.4	556	55.5	56.8
White, non-Hispanic alone	970	956	683	70.3	71.4	545	56.1	57.0
Black alone...................................	16	4	2	(B)	(B)	2	(B)	(B)
Asian alone	38	23	15	(B)	(B)	10	(B)	(B)
Hispanic (of any race)..........................	42	25	18	(B)	(B)	14	(B)	(B)
White alone or in combination	1,019	991	706	69.3	71.2	562	55.2	56.7
Black alone or in combination	27	12	7	(B)	(B)	6	(B)	(B)
Asian alone or in combination......................	41	26	17	(B)	(B)	13	(B)	(B)
Age								
18 to 24 years...............................	114	106	61	53.4	57.6	39	34.4	37.1
25 to 34 years...............................	153	138	84	55.3	61.1	61	39.9	44.0
35 to 44 years...............................	175	165	108	61.7	65.2	80	45.8	48.4
45 to 64 years...............................	404	387	298	73.7	76.8	241	59.6	62.1
65 years and over	234	228	175	74.9	76.8	155	66.3	68.0

B = Base is less than 75,000 and therefore too small to show the derived measure.

Table NH-14. Crime

(Number, rate per 100,000. Data are derived from the FBI Uniform Crime Reports.)

Item	State			U.S.		
	2016	2017	Percent change	2016	2017	Percent change
TOTAL POPULATION[1]	1,335,015	1,342,795	0.6	323,405,935	325,719,178	0.7
VIOLENT CRIME						
Number..	2,668	2,668	-	1,285,606	1,283,220	-0.2
Rate	199.8	198.7	-0.6	397.5	394.0	-0.9
Murder and Nonnegligent Manslaughter						
Number..	19	14	-26.3	17,413	17,284	-0.7
Rate	1.4	1.0	-26.7	5.4	5.3	-1.4
Rape[2]						
Number..	609	663	8.9	132,414	135,755	2.5
Rate	45.6	49.4	8.2	40.9	41.7	1.8
Robbery						
Number..	431	419	-2.8	332,797	319,356	-4.0
Rate	32.3	31.2	-3.3	102.9	98.0	-4.7
Aggravated Assault						
Number..	1,609	1,572	-2.3	802,982	810,825	1.0
Rate	120.5	117.1	-2.9	248.3	248.9	0.3
PROPERTY CRIME						
Number..	20,323	18,555	-8.7	7,928,530	7,694,086	-3.0
Rate	1,522.3	1,381.8	-9.2	2,451.6	2,362.2	-3.6
Burglary						
Number..	2,989	2,574	-13.9	1,516,405	1,401,840	-7.6
Rate	223.9	191.7	-14.4	468.9	430.4	-8.2
Larceny-Theft						
Number..	16,454	15,066	-8.4	5,644,835	5,519,107	-2.2
Rate	1,232.5	1,122.0	-9.0	1,745.4	1,694.4	-2.9
Motor Vehicle Theft						
Number..	880	915	4.0	767,290	773,139	0.8
Rate	65.9	68.1	3.4	237.3	237.4	-

NOTE: Although arson data are included in the trend and clearance tables, sufficient data are not available to estimate totals for this offense. Therefore, no arson data are published in this table.

- = Zero or rounds to zero.

[1] Population figures are U.S. Census Bureau provisional estimates as of July 1, 2017.

[2] The figures shown in the rape (revised definition) column were estimated using the revised Uniform Crime Reporting (UCR) definition of rape.

Table NH-15. State Government Finances, 2017

(Dollar amounts in thousands, percent distribution.)

Item	Dollars	Percent distribution
Total Revenue	9,328,812	100.0
General revenue	7,012,244	75.2
Intergovernmental revenue	2,720,430	29.2
Taxes	2,496,719	26.8
General sales	0	-
Selective sales	959,384	10.3
License taxes	329,719	3.5
Individual income tax	65,467	0.7
Corporate income tax	573,653	6.1
Other taxes	568,496	6.1
Current charges	969,753	10.4
Miscellaneous general revenue	825,342	8.8
Utility revenue	0	-
Liquor stores revenue	686,141	7.4
Insurance trust revenue[1]	1,630,427	17.5
Total Expenditure	7,882,386	100.0
Intergovernmental expenditure	831,584	10.5
Direct expenditure	7,050,802	89.5
Current operation	5,253,784	66.7
Capital outlay	493,748	6.3
Insurance benefits and repayments	791,338	10.0
Assistance and subsidies	193,058	2.4
Interest on debt	318,874	4.0
Exhibit: Salaries and wages	1,156,326	14.7
Total Expenditure	7,882,386	100.0
General expenditure	6,530,108	82.8
Intergovernmental expenditure	831,584	10.5
Direct expenditure	5,698,524	72.3
General expenditure, by function:		
Education	1,441,350	18.3
Public welfare	2,584,284	32.8
Hospitals	61,520	0.8
Health	97,799	1.2
Highways	528,633	6.7
Police protection	71,944	0.9
Correction	145,827	1.9
Natural resources	57,885	0.7
Parks and recreation	27,953	0.4
Governmental administration	304,005	3.9
Interest on general debt	318,874	4.0
Other and unallocable	890,034	11.3
Utility expenditure	14,669	0.2
Liquor stores expenditure	546,271	6.9
Insurance trust expenditure	791,338	10.0
Debt at End of Fiscal Year	7,739,447	X
Cash and Security Holdings	15,216,579	X

X = Not applicable.
- = Zero or rounds to zero.
[1] Within insurance trust revenue, net earnings of state retirement systems is a calculated statistic (the item code in the data file is X08), and thus can be positive or negative. Net earnings is the sum of earnings on investments plus gains on investments minus losses on investments. The change made in 2002 for asset valuation from book to market value in accordance with Statement 34 of the Governmental Accounting Standards Board is reflected in the calculated statistics.

Table NH-16. State Government Tax Collections, 2018

(Dollars in thousands, percent.)

Item	Dollars	Percent distribution
Total Taxes	2,920,888	100.0
Property taxes	408,769	14.0
Sales and gross receipts	1,025,902	35.1
General sales and gross receipts	X	-
Selective sales and gross receipts	1,025,902	35.1
Alcoholic beverages	12,828	0.4
Amusements	530	-
Insurance premiums	111,972	3.8
Motor fuels	183,366	6.3
Pari-mutuels	539	-
Public utilities	48,987	1.7
Tobacco products	212,698	7.3
Other selective sales	454,982	15.6
Licenses	435,544	14.9
Alcoholic beverages	17,991	0.6
Amusements	365	-
Corporations in general	67,236	2.3
Hunting and fishing	11,899	0.4
Motor vehicle	82,270	2.8
Motor vehicle operators	8,508	0.3
Public utilities	23,555	0.8
Occupation and business, NEC	216,120	7.4
Other licenses	7,600	-
Income taxes	895,770	30.7
Individual income	105,759	3.6
Corporation net income	790,011	27.0
Other taxes	154,903	5.3
Death and gift	X	-
Documentary and stock transfer	154,903	5.3
Severance	X	-
Taxes, NEC	0	-

X = Not applicable.
- = Zero or rounds to zero.

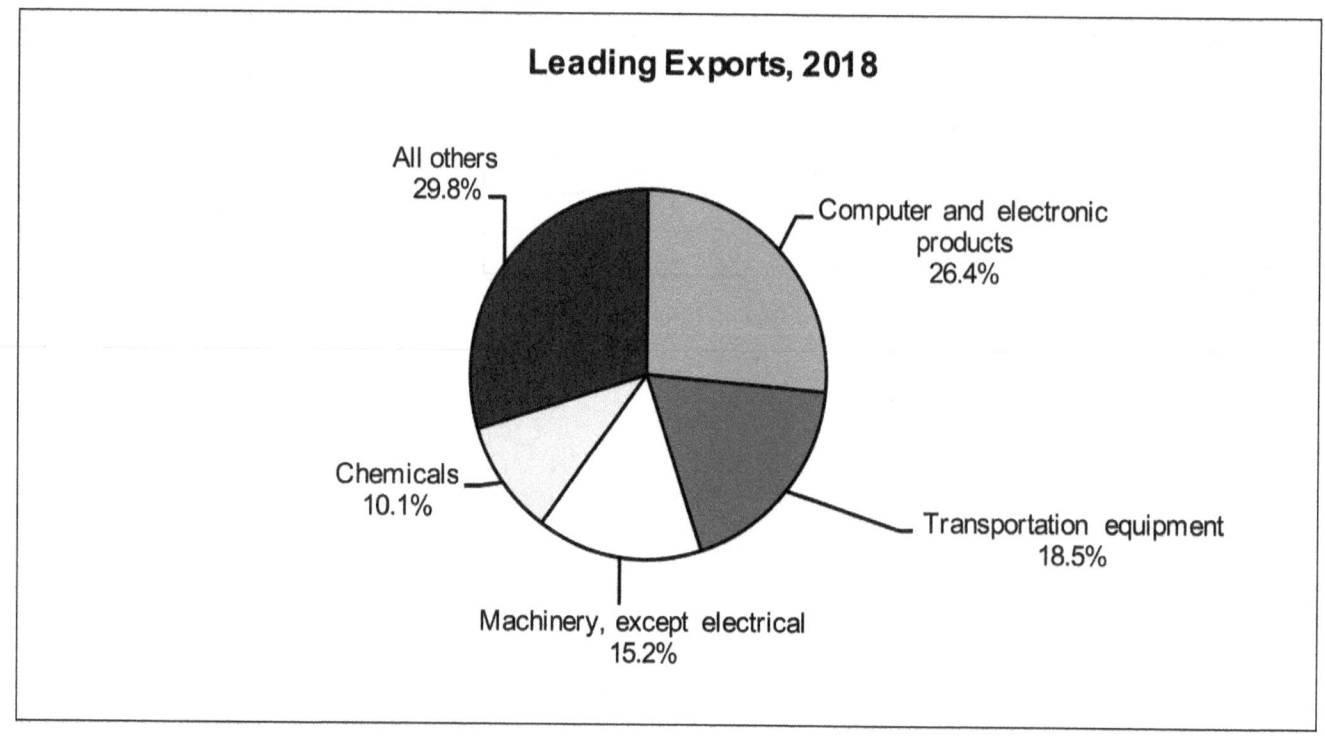

Leading Exports, 2018

All others 29.8%

Computer and electronic products 26.4%

Transportation equipment 18.5%

Machinery, except electrical 15.2%

Chemicals 10.1%

NEW JERSEY

Facts and Figures

Location: Middle Atlantic region of the United States; bordered on the N and NE by New York, on the E by the Atlantic Ocean, on the S by Delaware Bay, and on the W by Delaware and Pennsylvania

Area: 8,721 sq. mi. (22,588 sq. km.); rank—47th

Population: 8,908,520 (2018 est.); rank—11th

Principal Cities: capital—Trenton; largest—Newark

Statehood: December 18, 1787; 3rd state

U.S. Congress: 2 senators, 12 representatives

State Motto: Liberty and Prosperity

State Song: None

State Nickname: The Garden State

Abbreviations: NJ; N.J.

State Symbols: flower—common meadow violet; tree—red oak; bird—Eastern goldfinch

At a Glance

- With an increase in population of 1.3 percent, New Jersey ranked 40th among the states in growth from 2010 to 2018.

- New Jersey's median household income was $80,088 in 2017, the 3rd highest in the country.

- In 2017, 10.0 percent of the New Jersey's population lived below the poverty level, compared to 13.4 percent of the entire U.S. population.

- New Jersey's property crime rate of 1,555.5 incidents per 100,000 population, was the 6th lowest rate in the country in 2017.

- Approximately 39.7 percent of New Jersey residents had a bachelor's degree or more in 2017, the 4th highest percentage in the country.

Table NJ-1. Population by Age, Sex, Race, and Hispanic Origin

(Number, percent, except where noted.)

Sex, age, race, and Hispanic origin	2000	2010	2018 [1]	Percent change, 2010–2018
Total Population...	8,414,350	8,791,894	8,908,520	1.3
Percent of total U.S. population	3.0	2.8	2.7	X
Sex				
Male	4,082,813	4,279,600	4,352,194	1.7
Female	4,331,357	4,512,294	4,556,326	1.0
Age				
Under 5 years..	563,785	541,020	518,628	-4.1
5 to 19 years...	1,720,332	1,750,184	1,649,991	-5.7
20 to 64 years..	5,017,107	5,314,697	5,301,374	-0.3
65 years and over	1,113,136	1,185,993	1,438,527	21.3
Median age (years)	36.7	39.0	40.0	2.6
Race and Hispanic Origin				
One race				
White	6,104,705	6,546,498	6,416,347	-2.0
Black	1,141,821	1,282,005	1,337,754	4.3
American Indian and Alaska Native	19,492	49,907	54,706	9.6
Asian	480,276	746,212	889,251	19.2
Native Hawaiian or Other Pacific Islander	3,329	7,731	9,984	29.1
Two or more races	13,755	159,541	200,478	25.7
Hispanic (of any race)......................................	1,117,191	1,606,006	1,839,359	14.5

X = Not applicable.
[1] Population figures for 2018 are July 1 estimates. The 2010 estimates are taken from the 2010 Census.
- = Zero or rounds to zero.

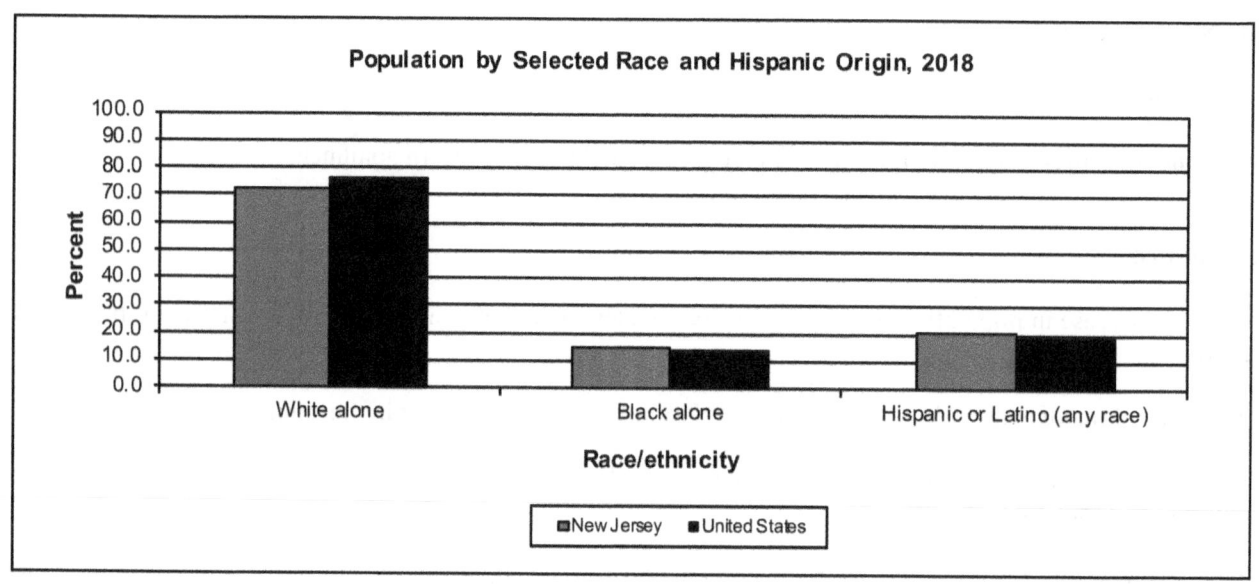

Table NJ-2. Marital Status

(Number, percent distribution.)

Sex, age, race, and Hispanic origin	2000	2010	2017
Males, 15 Years and Over.................................	3,176,413	3,419,050	3,566,444
Never married	31.1	36.4	37.7
Now married, except separated.............................	57.7	52.1	51.1
Separated...	2.0	1.8	1.5
Widowed..	2.9	2.6	2.6
Divorced..	6.2	7.1	7.2
Females, 15 Years and Over...............................	3,478,920	3,690,673	3,811,004
Never married	25.3	30.2	31.6
Now married, except separated.............................	51.8	47.6	47.3
Separated...	2.7	2.2	2.2
Widowed..	11.5	10.2	9.0
Divorced..	8.7	9.8	9.9

Table NJ-3. Households and Housing Characteristics

(Number, percent, dollars.)

Item	2000	2010	2017	Average annual percent change, 2010–2017
Total Households.................................	3,064,645	3,172,421	3,218,798	0.2
Family households	2,154,539	2,185,732	2,235,231	0.3
Married-couple family..........................	1,638,322	1,614,230	1,654,129	0.4
Other family	516,217	571,502	581,102	0.2
Male householder, no wife present.............	129,205	154,036	163,028	0.8
Female householder, no husband present........	387,012	417,466	418,074	-
Nonfamily households	910,106	986,689	983,567	-
Householder living alone......................	751,287	827,294	818,713	-0.1
Householder not living alone..................	158,819	159,395	164,854	0.5
Housing Characteristics				
Total housing units	3,310,275	3,554,909	3,615,891	0.2
Occupied housing units	3,064,645	3,172,421	3,218,798	0.2
Owner occupied	2,012,473	2,106,728	2,053,929	-0.4
Renter occupied	1,053,172	1,065,693	1,164,869	1.3
Average household size...........................	2.68	2.72	2.74	0.1
Financial Characteristics				
Median gross rent of renter-occupied housing	751	1,114	1,284	2.2
Median monthly owner costs for housing units with a mortgage	1,560	2,370	2,348	-0.1
Median value of owner-occupied housing units....	170,800	339,200	334,900	-0.2

- = Zero or rounds to zero

Table NJ-4. Migration, Origin, and Language

(Number, percent.)

Characteristic	State			U.S.		
	2016	2017	Percent change	2016	2017	Percent change
Residence 1 Year Ago						
Population 1 year and over	8,852,286	8,910,191	0.7	319,361,956	321,994,428	0.8
Same house	89.6	89.4	X	85.4	85.7	X
Different house in the U.S.	9.6	9.7	X	13.9	13.6	X
Same county	5.5	5.5	X	8.3	8.1	X
Different county	4.0	4.2	X	5.6	5.6	X
Same state	2.4	2.5	X	3.2	3.3	X
Different state	1.6	1.7	X	2.4	2.3	X
Abroad	0.8	0.9	X	0.7	0.7	X
Place of Birth						
Native born	6,928,384	6,950,582	0.3	279,388,170	281,193,323	0.6
Male	49.1	49.0	X	49.3	49.4	X
Female	50.9	51.0	X	50.7	50.6	X
Foreign born	2,016,085	2,055,062	1.9	43,739,345	44,525,855	1.8
Male	48.1	48.3	X	48.5	48.4	X
Female	51.9	51.7	X	51.5	51.6	X
Foreign born; naturalized U.S. citizen.............	1,103,588	1,136,235	3.0	21,238,372	21,948,732	3.3
Male	46.8	46.9	X	45.9	45.9	X
Female	53.2	53.1	X	54.1	54.1	X
Foreign born; not a U.S. citizen	912,497	918,827	0.7	22,500,973	22,577,123	0.3
Male	49.6	49.9	X	51.0	50.8	X
Female	50.4	50.1	X	49.0	49.2	X
Entered 2010 or later	18.5	21.6	X	18.6	21.3	X
Entered 2000 to 2009	27.3	26.1	X	26.7	25.7	X
Entered before 2000...........................	54.2	52.2	X	54.7	53.0	X
World Region of Birth, Foreign						
Foreign-born population, excluding population born at sea	2,016,085	2,055,062	1.9	43,738,901	44,525,458	1.8
Europe	15.1	13.8	X	10.9	10.8	X
Asia...	33.2	33.3	X	30.8	31.2	X
Africa	4.9	5.7	X	4.9	5.1	X
Oceania	0.1	0.1	X	0.6	0.6	X
Latin America................................	45.9	46.2	X	51	50.4	X
North America	0.8	0.8	X	1.8	1.8	X
Language Spoken at Home and Ability to Speak English						
Population 5 years and over......................	8,424,299	8,485,283	0.7	303,328,961	305,924,019	0.9
English only	68.3	68.2	X	78.4	78.2	X
Language other than English...................	31.7	31.8	X	21.6	21.8	X
Speaks English less than "very well"..........	12.6	12.3	X	8.6	8.5	X

NA = Not available.
X = Not applicable.
- = Zero or rounds to zero.

Table NJ-5. Median Income and Poverty Status, 2017

(Number, percent, except as noted.)

Characteristic	State		U.S.	
	Number	Percent	Number	Percent
Median Income				
Households (dollars)...	80,088	X	60,336	X
Families (dollars)	97,300	X	73,891	X
Below Poverty Level (All People)	882,673	10.0	42,583,651	13.4
Sex				
Male	387,129	9.0	19,004,547	12.2
Female	495,544	10.9	23,579,104	14.5
Age				
Under 18 years...	272,251	13.9	13,353,202	18.4
Related children under 18 years..	268,823	13.8	13,053,472	18.1
18 to 64 years..	494,936	9.0	24,648,677	12.6
65 years and over	115,486	8.4	4,581,772	9.3

X = Not applicable.

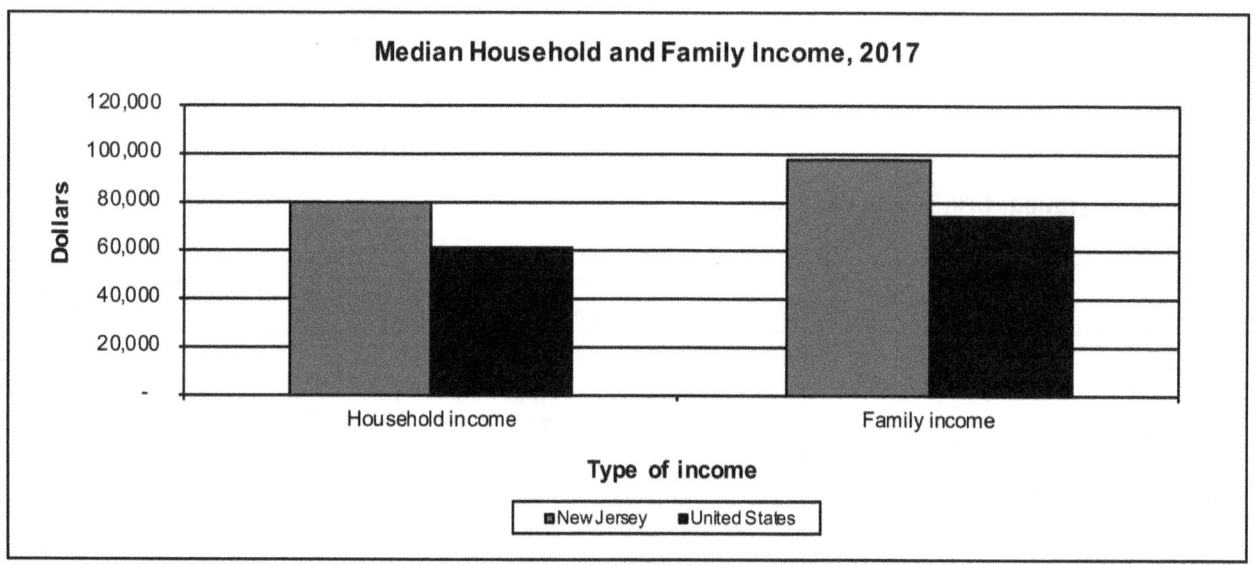

Table NJ-6. Health Insurance Coverage Status for the Civilian Noninstitutionalized Population and Children Under 18 Years of Age

(Number, percent.)

Item	2009	2010	2011	2012	2013	2014	2015	2016	2017
Civilian Noninstitutionalized Population	8,582,670	8,693,541	8,712,982	8,756,542	8,791,652	8,830,969	8,850,415	8,837,578	8,902,432
Covered by Private or Public Insurance									
Number..................................	7,498,582	7,542,383	7,573,878	7,643,733	7,631,358	7,865,558	8,079,219	8,132,608	8,214,364
Percent..................................	87.4	86.8	86.9	87.3	86.8	89.1	91.3	92.0	92.3
Uninsured									
Number..................................	1,084,088	1,151,158	1,139,104	1,112,809	1,160,294	965,411	771,196	704,970	688,068
Percent..................................	12.6	13.2	13.1	12.7	13.2	10.9	8.7	8.0	7.7
Percent in the U.S. not covered..	15.1	15.5	15.1	14.8	14.5	11.7	9.4	8.6	8.7
Children Under 18 Years of Age[1]	2,044,419	2,057,455	2,038,167	2,024,150	2,017,712	2,007,362	1,993,774	1,979,948	2,093,669
Covered by Private or Public Insurance									
Number..................................	1,914,584	1,933,999	1,933,002	1,921,334	1,905,595	1,915,520	1,919,180	1,909,909	2,015,469
Percent..................................	93.6	94.0	94.8	94.9	94.4	95.4	96.3	96.5	96.3
Uninsured									
Number..................................	129,835	123,456	105,165	102,816	112,117	91,842	74,594	70,039	78,200
Percent..................................	6.4	6.0	5.2	5.1	5.6	4.6	3.7	3.5	3.7
Percent in the U.S. not covered..	8.6	8.0	7.5	7.2	7.1	6.0	4.8	4.5	5.0

[1] 2017 data is for individuals under 19 years of age.

Table NJ-7. Employment Status by Demographic Group, 2018

(Numbers in thousands, percent.)

Characteristic	Civilian noninstitutional population	Civilian labor force		Employed		Unemployed	
		Number	Percent of population	Number	Percent of population	Number	Percent of population
Total...	7,194	4,487	62.4	4,298	59.8	189	4.2
Sex							
Male..............	3,459	2,359	68.2	2,265	65.5	94	4.0
Female	3,735	2,129	57.0	2,034	54.5	95	4.5
Race, Sex, and Hispanic Origin							
White..............	5,377	3,303	61.4	3,176	59.1	126	3.8
Male..............	2,622	1,766	67.3	1,703	64.9	63	3.6
Female..............	2,755	1,537	55.8	1,474	53.5	63	4.1
Black or African American..............	1,031	655	63.5	612	59.4	43	6.6
Male..............	470	308	65.6	286	60.8	23	7.3
Female..............	561	347	61.8	326	58.1	21	6.0
Hispanic or Latino ethnicity[1]..............	1,204	789	65.5	753	62.6	36	4.5
Male..............	578	427	73.9	412	71.2	16	3.7
Female..............	626	362	57.8	342	54.6	20	5.6
Age							
16 to 19 years..............	474	129	27.2	114	24.0	15	11.9
20 to 24 years..............	633	405	63.9	381	60.1	24	5.9
25 to 34 years..............	1,121	941	83.9	894	79.8	46	4.9
35 to 44 years..............	1,087	919	84.5	898	82.5	21	2.3
45 to 54 years..............	1,188	975	82.1	944	79.5	31	3.2
55 to 64 years..............	1,191	810	68.0	776	65.2	34	4.1
65 years and over..............	1,499	309	20.6	292	19.4	18	5.7

NOTE: Data in Table 7 are from the Current Population Survey (CPS) and do not match the estimates in Table 8. See notes and definitions for further information.
[1] May be of any race.

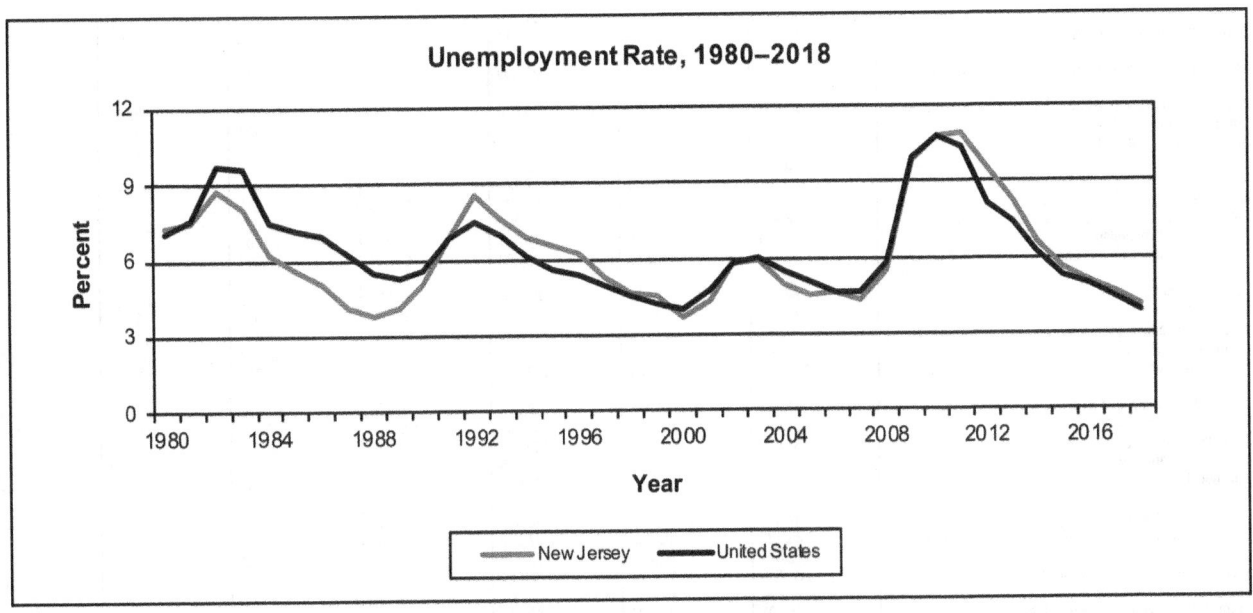

Table NJ-8. Employment Status of the Civilian Noninstitutional Population Age 16 Years and Over

(Number, percent.)

Year	Civilian labor force	Civilian participation rate	Employed	Unemployed	Unemployment rate
2010	4,555,330	66.4	4,121,455	433,875	9.5
2011	4,565,272	65.9	4,138,464	426,808	9.3
2012	4,588,033	65.7	4,159,986	428,047	9.3
2013	4,548,560	64.8	4,173,828	374,732	8.2
2014	4,527,181	64.1	4,221,267	305,914	6.8
2015	4,537,232	64.0	4,274,695	262,537	5.8
2016	4,530,784	63.6	4,305,516	225,268	5.0
2017	4,518,832	63.1	4,309,706	209,126	4.6
2018	4,422,942	62.4	4,239,567	183,375	4.1

Table NJ-9. Employment and Average Wages by Industry

(Estimates are based on the 2012 *North American Industry Classification System* [NAICS].)

Industry	2011	2012	2013	2014	2015	2016	2017
	Number of jobs						
Wage and Salary Employment by Industry..........................	3,903,364	3,937,611	3,978,040	4,010,203	4,061,862	4,123,132	4,174,996
Farm Wage and Salary Employment...............................	7,456	9,641	8,892	9,552	9,252	11,166	10,756
Nonfarm Wage and Salary Employment...........................	3,895,908	3,927,970	3,969,148	4,000,651	4,052,610	4,111,966	4,164,240
Private wage and salary employment.............................	3,271,362	3,309,962	3,350,612	3,383,679	3,439,130	3,501,160	3,553,573
Forestry, fishing, and related activities......................	3,263	3,427	2,893	3,522	3,785	4,251	4,089
Mining..	1,307	1,250	1,317	1,412	1,388	1,323	1,290
Utilities...	13,592	13,806	13,671	13,659	14,208	14,174	14,180
Construction...	133,147	134,011	141,334	144,904	151,919	157,215	159,593
Manufacturing..	253,030	245,418	242,972	242,371	238,039	242,349	244,530
Durable goods manufacturing...............................	114,369	112,031	110,875	108,906	109,329	110,017	111,336
Nondurable goods manufacturing...........................	138,661	133,387	132,097	133,465	128,710	132,332	133,194
Wholesale trade...	210,429	213,565	213,833	215,024	217,519	217,139	218,755
Retail trade..	444,424	447,418	451,587	457,378	464,351	464,953	466,095
Transportation and warehousing.............................	151,308	151,266	150,825	153,622	161,009	172,195	187,858
Information..	75,907	77,872	75,223	75,507	74,437	73,264	70,987
Finance and insurance......................................	192,136	191,456	191,144	184,597	189,520	191,194	196,766
Real estate and rental and leasing..........................	54,300	54,080	55,522	55,509	56,949	58,483	59,759
Professional, scientific, and technical services.............	278,967	280,930	285,212	289,737	297,578	303,202	301,219
Management of companies and enterprises....................	77,388	79,526	83,332	79,003	79,991	80,733	83,389
Administrative and waste services..........................	250,103	260,921	262,429	268,683	274,765	282,029	287,238
Educational services.......................................	93,328	94,771	96,875	97,744	99,396	101,924	103,260
Health care and social assistance...........................	507,341	518,161	532,091	540,275	551,789	563,699	576,097
Arts, entertainment, and recreation........................	54,054	56,511	57,866	61,268	62,579	65,376	67,672
Accommodation and food services...........................	283,463	291,240	297,127	298,823	299,157	306,793	310,914
Other services, except public administration................	193,875	194,333	195,359	200,641	200,751	200,864	199,882
Government and government enterprises......................	624,546	618,008	618,536	616,972	613,480	610,806	610,667
	Dollars						
Average Wages and Salaries by Industry	56,735	57,907	58,811	59,968	61,775	62,270	63,563
Average Farm Wages and Salaries	22,020	22,898	25,309	24,962	21,052	20,018	18,860
Average Nonfarm Wages and Salaries	56,801	57,992	58,886	60,052	61,868	62,385	63,679
Average private wages and salaries............................	56,382	57,667	58,655	59,820	61,751	62,261	63,578
Forestry, fishing, and related activities......................	24,702	24,825	27,753	27,435	28,011	31,280	32,914
Mining..	66,797	70,300	72,156	71,305	77,421	76,745	81,604
Utilities...	106,144	108,450	107,123	113,032	116,156	118,690	120,284
Construction...	61,693	62,316	63,792	64,990	67,612	68,730	71,115
Manufacturing..	74,958	75,937	77,266	79,949	77,057	78,574	78,771
Durable goods manufacturing...............................	67,954	68,942	69,681	72,136	73,705	75,390	77,739
Nondurable goods manufacturing...........................	80,735	81,812	83,632	86,323	79,904	81,221	79,635
Wholesale trade...	79,457	81,063	82,350	85,235	87,506	87,065	87,457
Retail trade..	30,376	30,586	30,964	31,707	32,929	33,262	33,914
Transportation and warehousing.............................	49,262	50,266	51,625	52,541	54,213	54,506	53,957
Information..	89,562	92,812	96,253	98,928	102,954	105,041	108,470
Finance and insurance......................................	106,897	108,764	110,969	115,946	120,813	122,880	127,795
Real estate and rental and leasing..........................	54,176	58,974	58,614	60,365	63,656	62,872	64,042
Professional, scientific, and technical services.............	91,058	95,608	97,658	100,182	106,531	106,327	108,951
Management of companies and enterprises....................	136,933	146,387	150,461	151,816	159,410	160,244	167,189
Administrative and waste services..........................	38,163	38,585	39,168	39,740	40,821	41,479	43,688
Educational services.......................................	38,260	38,897	40,078	41,313	42,341	42,787	42,811
Health care and social assistance...........................	47,494	48,309	48,534	49,511	50,971	51,576	52,245
Arts, entertainment, and recreation........................	35,482	36,852	37,077	36,288	37,064	37,444	37,360
Accommodation and food services...........................	22,674	23,099	23,733	24,517	24,651	25,262	25,681
Other services, except public administration................	31,699	32,324	32,981	33,480	34,653	35,317	36,433
Government and government enterprises......................	58,997	59,734	60,135	61,322	62,526	63,094	64,267

Table NJ-10. Employment Characteristics by Family Type

(Number, percent.)

Family type and labor force status	2015		2016		2017	
	Total	Families with own children under 18 years	Total	Families with own children under 18 years	Total	Families with own children under 18 years
All Families...	2,205,886	966,402	2,197,150	947,058	2,235,231	960,393
FAMILY TYPE AND LABOR FORCE STATUS						
Married-Couple Families............................	1,632,061	695,182	1,623,674	682,813	1,654,129	697,785
Both husband and wife in labor force..............	54.8	66.6	54.6	67.3	54.7	67.7
Husband in labor force, wife not in labor force	22.4	27.9	22.3	27.6	21.7	27.0
Wife in labor force, husband not in labor force	7.4	3.7	7.6	3.6	7.4	3.7
Both husband and wife not in labor force...........	14.6	1.4	14.7	1.1	15.3	1.3
Other Families	573,825	271,220	573,476	264,245	581,102	262,608
Female householder, no husband present..........	72.8	77.0	73.1	76.2	71.9	75.9
In labor force...	52.9	65.1	52.3	64.6	52.3	65.6
Not in labor force....................................	19.9	12.0	20.7	11.6	19.6	10.4
Male householder, no wife present.................	27.2	23.0	26.9	23.8	28.1	24.1
In labor force...	21.8	20.8	21.6	22.0	22.1	22.2
Not in labor force....................................	5.4	2.2	5.4	1.8	6.0	1.8

Table NJ-11. School Enrollment and Educational Attainment, 2017

(Number, percent.)

Item	State	U.S.
Enrollment		
Total population 3 years and over, enrolled in school	2,226,989	81,273,337
Enrolled in nursery school or preschool (percent)....................................	7.3	6.0
Enrolled in kindergarten (percent)..	4.8	4.9
Enrolled in elementary school, grades 1-8 (percent)...............................	39.6	40.6
Enrolled in high school, grades 9-12 (percent)...................................	21.5	21.1
Enrolled in college or graduate school (percent).................................	26.8	27.4
Attainment		
Total population 25 years and over	6,234,538	221,250,083
Less than ninth grade (percent)...	4.8	5.1
9th to 12th grade, no diploma (percent)......................................	5.3	6.9
High school graduate, including equivalency (percent)............................	27.2	27.1
Some college, no degree (percent)	16.3	20.4
Associate's degree (percent)...	6.7	8.5
Bachelor's degree (percent)..	24.2	19.7
Graduate or professional degree (percent).....................................	15.6	12.3
High school graduate or higher (percent)	89.9	88.0
Bachelor's degree or higher (percent)...	39.7	32.0

Table NJ-12. Public School Characteristics and Educational Indicators

(Number, percent; data derived from National Center of Education Statistics.)

Item	State	U.S.
Public Elementary and Secondary Schools		
Number of operational school districts, 2016-17...................................	678	18,377
Number of operational schools, 2016-17.......................................	2,590	98,330
Percent charter schools	3.4	7.1
Total public school enrollment, 2016-17.......................................	1,410,421	50,587,859
Percent charter school enrollment	3.4	6.0
Student-teacher ratio, Fall 2015	12.3	16.0
Expenditures per student (dollars), 2015-16....................................	19,041	11,841
Four-year adjusted cohort graduation rate (ACGR)[1]	90.5	84.6
Students eligible for free or reduced-price lunch (percent), 2015-16.................	37.6	52.1
English language learners (percent), Fall 2016	5.0	9.6
Students age 3 to 21 served under IDEA, part B (percent), 2017-18	16.9	13.7
Public Schools by Type, 2016-17		Percent of state public schools
Total number of schools..	2,590	100.0
Special education	63	2.4
Vocational education	58	2.2
Alternative education...	90	3.5

[1] Adjusted Cohort Graduation Rates (ACGR) differ from Averaged Freshmen Graduation Rates (AFGR).

Table NJ-13. Reported Voting and Registration of the Voting-Age Population, November 2018

(Numbers in thousands, percent.)

Item	Total population	Total citizen population	Registered			Voted		
			Total registered	Percent registered (total population)	Percent registered (total citizen population)	Total voted	Percent voted (total population)	Percent voted (total citizen population)
U.S. Total	249,748	228,832	153,066	61.3	66.9	122,281	49.0	53.4
State Total.....................................	7,009	6,267	4,297	61.3	68.6	3,384	48.3	54.0
Sex								
Male	3,348	2,998	2,046	61.1	68.2	1,577	47.1	52.6
Female	3,660	3,269	2,251	61.5	68.9	1,808	49.4	55.3
Race								
White alone..................................	5,227	4,788	3,349	64.1	69.9	2,678	51.2	55.9
White, non-Hispanic alone	4,081	3,944	2,847	69.7	72.2	2,283	55.9	57.9
Black alone..................................	1,013	917	611	60.3	66.6	472	46.6	51.5
Asian alone..................................	690	483	281	40.7	58.2	188	27.2	38.9
Hispanic (of any race).....................	1,259	920	578	45.9	62.9	471	37.4	51.2
White alone or in combination	5,302	4,863	3,401	64.1	69.9	2,725	51.4	56.0
Black alone or in combination..............	1,081	985	663	61.4	67.3	515	47.7	52.3
Asian alone or in combination..............	697	490	284	40.8	58.1	191	27.4	39.0
Age								
18 to 24 years...............................	811	738	350	43.1	47.4	237	29.2	32.1
25 to 34 years...............................	1,235	1,030	670	54.2	65.0	435	35.2	42.2
35 to 44 years...............................	1,076	882	661	61.4	74.9	548	50.9	62.0
45 to 64 years...............................	2,361	2,177	1,573	66.6	72.3	1,297	55.0	59.6
65 years and over...........................	1,526	1,440	1,043	68.4	72.5	868	56.8	60.3

Table NJ-14. Crime

(Number, rate per 100,000. Data are derived from the FBI Uniform Crime Reports.)

Item	State			U.S.		
	2016	2017	Percent change	2016	2017	Percent change
TOTAL POPULATION[1]	8,978,416	9,005,644	0.3	323,405,935	325,719,178	0.7
VIOLENT CRIME						
Number...	21,861	20,604	-5.7	1,285,606	1,283,220	-0.2
Rate..	243.5	228.8	-6.0	397.5	394.0	-0.9
Murder and Nonnegligent Manslaughter						
Number...	378	324	-14.3	17,413	17,284	-0.7
Rate..	4.2	3.6	-14.5	5.4	5.3	-1.4
Rape[2]						
Number...	1,454	1,505	3.5	132,414	135,755	2.5
Rate..	16.2	16.7	3.2	40.9	41.7	1.8
Robbery						
Number...	8,940	7,895	-11.7	332,797	319,356	-4.0
Rate..	99.6	87.7	-12.0	102.9	98.0	-4.7
Aggravated Assault						
Number...	11,089	10,880	-1.9	802,982	810,825	1.0
Rate..	123.5	120.8	-2.2	248.3	248.9	0.3
PROPERTY CRIME						
Number...	138,012	140,086	1.5	7,928,530	7,694,086	-3.0
Rate..	1,537.2	1,555.5	1.2	2,451.6	2,362.2	-3.6
Burglary						
Number...	25,229	23,891	-5.3	1,516,405	1,401,840	-7.6
Rate..	281.0	265.3	-5.6	468.9	430.4	-8.2
Larceny-Theft						
Number...	101,459	104,025	2.5	5,644,835	5,519,107	-2.2
Rate..	1,130.0	1,155.1	2.2	1,745.4	1,694.4	-2.9
Motor Vehicle Theft						
Number...	11,324	12,170	7.5	767,290	773,139	0.8
Rate..	126.1	135.1	7.1	237.3	237.4	-

NOTE: Although arson data are included in the trend and clearance tables, sufficient data are not available to estimate totals for this offense. Therefore, no arson data are published in this table.
- = Zero or rounds to zero.
[1] Population figures are U.S. Census Bureau provisional estimates as of July 1, 2017.
[2] The figures shown in the rape (revised definition) column were estimated using the revised Uniform Crime Reporting (UCR) definition of rape.

Table NJ-15. State Government Finances, 2017

(Dollar amounts in thousands, percent distribution.)

Item	Dollars	Percent distribution
Total Revenue	78,744,659	100.0
General revenue	62,624,120	79.5
Intergovernmental revenue	18,615,719	23.6
Taxes	32,325,850	41.1
General sales	9,591,881	12.2
Selective sales	3,796,733	4.8
License taxes	1,550,059	2.0
Individual income tax	13,958,119	17.7
Corporate income tax	2,109,930	2.7
Other taxes	1,319,128	1.7
Current charges	6,553,427	8.3
Miscellaneous general revenue	5,129,124	6.5
Utility revenue	1,122,928	1.4
Liquor stores revenue	0	-
Insurance trust revenue[1]	14,997,611	19.0
Total Expenditure	72,339,494	100.0
Intergovernmental expenditure	11,662,914	16.1
Direct expenditure	60,676,580	83.9
Current operation	38,856,499	53.7
Capital outlay	4,618,974	6.4
Insurance benefits and repayments	13,517,466	18.7
Assistance and subsidies	1,479,192	2.0
Interest on debt	2,204,449	3.0
Exhibit: Salaries and wages	10,181,242	14.1
Total Expenditure	72,339,494	100.0
General expenditure	55,739,193	77.1
Intergovernmental expenditure	11,662,914	16.1
Direct expenditure	44,076,279	60.9
General expenditure, by function:		
Education	18,497,910	25.6
Public welfare	18,558,280	25.7
Hospitals	2,223,073	3.1
Health	1,454,264	2.0
Highways	3,126,092	4.3
Police protection	715,359	1.0
Correction	1,380,091	1.9
Natural resources	474,158	0.7
Parks and recreation	194,846	0.3
Governmental administration	1,747,069	2.4
Interest on general debt	2,202,843	3.0
Other and unallocable	5,165,208	7.1
Utility expenditure	3,082,835	3.9
Liquor stores expenditure	0	-
Insurance trust expenditure	13,517,466	18.7
Debt at End of Fiscal Year	65,874,095	X
Cash and Security Holdings	115,574,492	X

X = Not applicable.
- = Zero or rounds to zero.
[1] Within insurance trust revenue, net earnings of state retirement systems is a calculated statistic (the item code in the data file is X08), and thus can be positive or negative. Net earnings is the sum of earnings on investments plus gains on investments minus losses on investments. The change made in 2002 for asset valuation from book to market value in accordance with Statement 34 of the Governmental Accounting Standards Board is reflected in the calculated statistics.

Table NJ-16. State Government Tax Collections, 2018

(Dollars in thousands, percent.)

Item	Dollars	Percent distribution
Total Taxes	35,365,046	100.0
Property taxes...........	5,016	-
Sales and gross receipts	15,424,507	43.6
General sales and gross receipts	10,459,419	29.6
Selective sales and gross receipts	4,965,088	14.0
Alcoholic beverages...........	142,459	0.4
Amusements...........	217,736	0.6
Insurance premiums...........	591,243	1.7
Motor fuels	458,892	1.3
Pari-mutuels	X	-
Public utilities	978,816	2.8
Tobacco products...........	660,315	1.9
Other selective sales	1,915,627	5.4
Licenses...........	1,542,213	4.4
Alcoholic beverages...........	4,199	-
Amusements...........	50,100	0.1
Corporations in general...........	248,405	0.7
Hunting and fishing...........	14,685	-
Motor vehicle...........	657,956	1.9
Motor vehicle operators...........	57,214	0.2
Public utilities	21,812	0.1
Occupation and business, NEC	485,902	1.4
Other licenses	1,940	-
Income taxes...........	17,273,498	48.8
Individual income...........	15,037,845	42.5
Corporation net income	2,235,653	6.3
Other taxes...........	1,119,812	3.2
Death and gift...........	605,845	1.7
Documentary and stock transfer	513,967	1.5
Severance	X	-
Taxes, NEC	0	-

X = Not applicable.
- = Zero or rounds to zero.

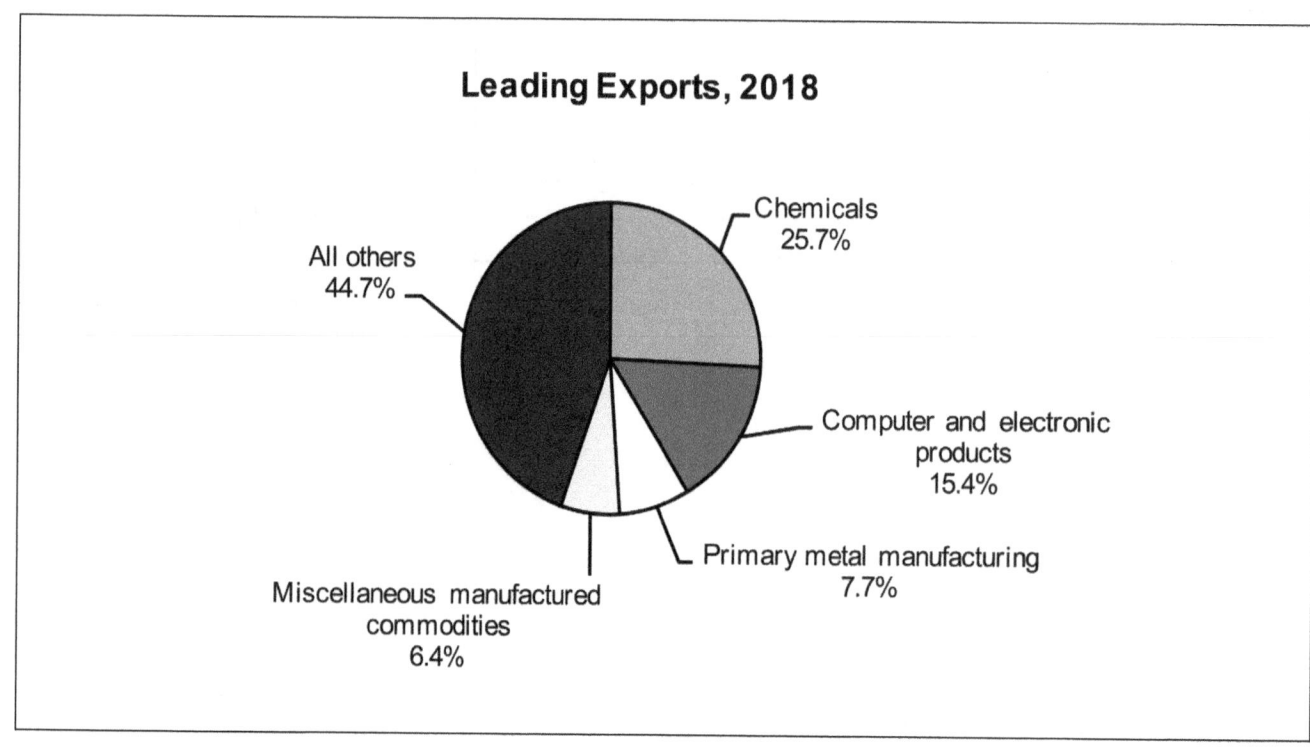

Leading Exports, 2018

Chemicals 25.7%

Computer and electronic products 15.4%

Primary metal manufacturing 7.7%

Miscellaneous manufactured commodities 6.4%

All others 44.7%

NEW MEXICO

Facts and Figures

Location: Southwestern United States; bordered on the N by Colorado, on the E by Oklahoma and Texas, on the S by Texas and Mexico, and on the W by Arizona; New Mexico is one of the Four Corner states—at its NW corner it touches Arizona, Colorado, and Utah

Area: 121,590 sq. mi. (314,915 sq. km.); rank—5th

Population: 2,095,428 (2018 est.); rank—36th

Principal Cities: capital—Santa Fe; largest—Albuquerque

Statehood: January 6, 1912; 47th state

U.S. Congress: 2 senators, 3 representatives

State Motto: *Crescit eundo* ("It grows as it goes")

State Song: "O, Fair New Mexico"

State Nickname: The Land of Enchantment

Abbreviations: NM; N. Mex.

State Symbols: flower—yucca; tree—piñon; bird—roadrunner

At a Glance

- With an increase in population of 1.8 percent, New Mexico ranked 39th among the states in growth from 2010 to 2018.

- In 2017, New Mexico's violent crime rate of 783.5 per 100,000 population was the 3rd highest rate in the country, and its property crime rate of 3,941.7 per 100,000 population, was the 2nd highest in the country.

- New Mexico (tied with Louisiana) had the 2nd highest percentage of residents living below the poverty level in 2017 (19.7 percent).

- In 2018, New Mexico had the 4th highest unemployment rate of all the states (4.9 percent). The U.S. unemployment rate was 3.9 percent.

- With approximately 49.1 percent of its residents self-identifying as "Hispanic or Latino," New Mexico was the state with the highest percentage of this population in 2018.

Table NM-1. Population by Age, Sex, Race, and Hispanic Origin

(Number, percent, except where noted.)

Sex, age, race, and Hispanic origin	2000	2010	2018[1]	Percent change, 2010–2018
Total Population....................................	1,819,046	2,059,179	2,095,428	1.8
Percent of total U.S. population	0.6	0.7	0.6	X
Sex				
Male...	894,317	1,017,421	1,037,285	2.0
Female	924,729	1,041,758	1,058,143	1.6
Age				
Under 5 years...................................	130,628	144,981	124,246	-14.3
5 to 19 years...................................	434,231	434,860	413,815	-4.8
20 to 64 years..................................	1,041,962	1,207,083	1,191,178	-1.3
65 years and over.............................	212,225	272,255	366,189	34.5
Median age (years)	34.6	36.7	38.1	3.8
Race and Hispanic origin				
One race				
White	1,214,253	1,720,992	1,718,901	-0.1
Black..	34,343	49,006	53,576	9.3
American Indian and Alaska Native	173,483	208,890	228,493	9.4
Asian..	19,255	31,253	37,256	19.2
Native Hawaiian or Other Pacific Islander	1,503	3,132	3,404	8.7
Two or more races	66,327	45,906	53,798	17.2
Hispanic (of any race)...........................	765,386	973,088	1,029,233	5.8

X = Not applicable.
- = Zero or rounds to zero.
[1] Population figures for 2018 are July 1 estimates. The 2010 estimates are taken from the 2010 Census.

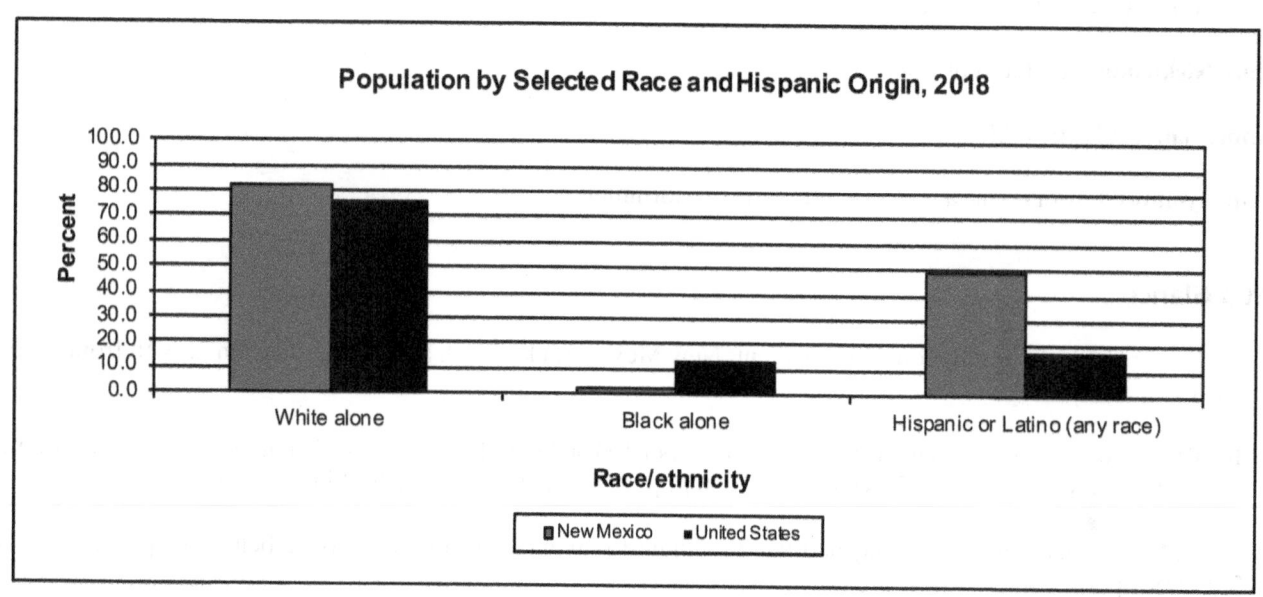

Table NM-2. Marital Status

(Number, percent distribution.)

Sex, age, race, and Hispanic origin	2000	2010	2017
Males, 15 Years and Over....................................	677,967	801,901	826,549
Never married	30.5	35.4	39.1
Now married, except separated...................................	55.0	48.4	44.4
Separated..	1.6	1.6	1.6
Widowed..	2.6	2.6	3.0
Divorced..	10.4	11.9	11.9
Females, 15 Years and Over..................................	720,529	833,357	855,417
Never married	24.7	29.9	32.0
Now married, except separated...................................	51.2	45.0	42.2
Separated..	2.0	2.6	2.1
Widowed..	9.4	8.5	9.0
Divorced..	12.8	14.1	14.7

Table NM-3. Households and Housing Characteristics

(Number, percent, dollars.)

Item	2000	2010	2017	Average annual percent change, 2010–2017
Total Households..	677,971	765,183	767,705	-
Family households..	466,515	501,092	479,092	-0.6
Married-couple family..	341,818	349,344	329,588	-0.8
Other family..	124,697	151,748	149,504	-0.2
Male householder, no wife present....................	35,075	49,041	46,606	-0.7
Female householder, no husband present...........	89,622	102,707	102,898	-
Nonfamily households..	211,456	264,091	288,613	1.3
Householder living alone......................................	172,181	216,704	245,516	1.9
Householder not living alone................................	39,275	47,387	43,097	-1.3
Housing Characteristics				
Total housing units..	780,579	902,242	937,976	0.6
Occupied housing units...	677,971	765,183	767,705	-
Owner occupied..	474,445	519,864	521,450	-
Renter occupied..	203,526	245,319	246,255	0.1
Average household size..	2.63	2.64	2.66	0.1
Financial Characteristics				
Median gross rent of renter-occupied housing..........	503	699	813	2.3
Median monthly owner costs for housing units with a mortgage..........	929	1,202	1,244	0.5
Median value of owner-occupied housing units..........	108,100	161,200	171,300	0.9

Table NM-4. Migration, Origin, and Language

(Number, percent.)

Characteristic	State			U.S.		
	2016	2017	Percent change	2016	2017	Percent change
Residence 1 Year Ago						
Population 1 year and over......................................	2,057,857	2,062,628	0.2	319,361,956	321,994,428	0.8
Same house..	85.9	87.3	X	85.4	85.7	X
Different house in the U.S...................................	13.6	12.1	X	13.9	13.6	X
Same county..	8.3	7.1	X	8.3	8.1	X
Different county..	5.3	5.0	X	5.6	5.6	X
Same state...	2.1	2.3	X	3.2	3.3	X
Different state...	3.1	2.8	X	2.4	2.3	X
Abroad...	0.5	0.5	X	0.7	0.7	X
Place of Birth						
Native born...	1,882,609	1,892,562	0.5	279,388,170	281,193,323	0.6
Male...	49.6	49.8	X	49.3	49.4	X
Female..	50.4	50.2	X	50.7	50.6	X
Foreign born..	198,406	195,508	-1.5	43,739,345	44,525,855	1.8
Male...	48.5	46.7	X	48.5	48.4	X
Female..	51.5	53.3	X	51.5	51.6	X
Foreign born; naturalized U.S. citizen......................	78,660	80,970	2.9	21,238,372	21,948,732	3.3
Male...	44.5	45.2	X	45.9	45.9	X
Female..	55.5	54.8	X	54.1	54.1	X
Foreign born; not a U.S. citizen..............................	119,746	114,538	-4.3	22,500,973	22,577,123	0.3
Male...	51.2	47.8	X	51	50.8	X
Female..	48.8	52.2	X	49	49.2	X
Entered 2010 or later..	14.1	17.9	X	18.6	21.3	X
Entered 2000 to 2009..	24.7	25.4	X	26.7	25.7	X
Entered before 2000..	61.3	56.7	X	54.7	53.0	X
World Region of Birth, Foreign						
Foreign-born population, excluding population born at sea...........	198,406	195,508	-1.5	43,738,901	44,525,458	1.8
Europe..	8.6	6.3	X	10.9	10.8	X
Asia..	13.8	13.4	X	30.8	31.2	X
Africa..	1.7	2.7	X	4.9	5.1	X
Oceania...	0.2	0.3	X	0.6	0.6	X
Latin America..	74.5	75.7	X	51	50.4	X
North America...	1.3	1.7	X	1.8	1.8	X
Language Spoken at Home and Ability to Speak English						
Population 5 years and over.....................................	1,955,889	1,961,643	0.3	303,328,961	305,924,019	0.9
English only...	65.5	67.0	X	78.4	78.2	X
Language other than English...................................	34.5	33.0	X	21.6	21.8	X
Speaks English less than "very well"......................	8.3	8.6	X	8.6	8.5	X

NA = Not available.
X = Not applicable.
- = Zero or rounds to zero.

Table NM-5. Median Income and Poverty Status, 2017

(Number, percent, except as noted.)

Characteristic	State		U.S.	
	Number	Percent	Number	Percent
Median Income				
Households (dollars)...	46,744	X	60,336	X
Families (dollars)	58,308	X	73,891	X
Below Poverty Level (All People)	401,755	19.7	42,583,651	13.4
Sex				
Male	186,027	18.5	19,004,547	12.2
Female	215,728	20.8	23,579,104	14.5
Age				
Under 18 years..	130,502	27.2	13,353,202	18.4
Related children under 18 years...	128,996	27.0	13,053,472	18.1
18 to 64 years...	229,180	18.8	24,648,677	12.6
65 years and over	42,073	12.2	4,581,772	9.3

X = Not applicable.

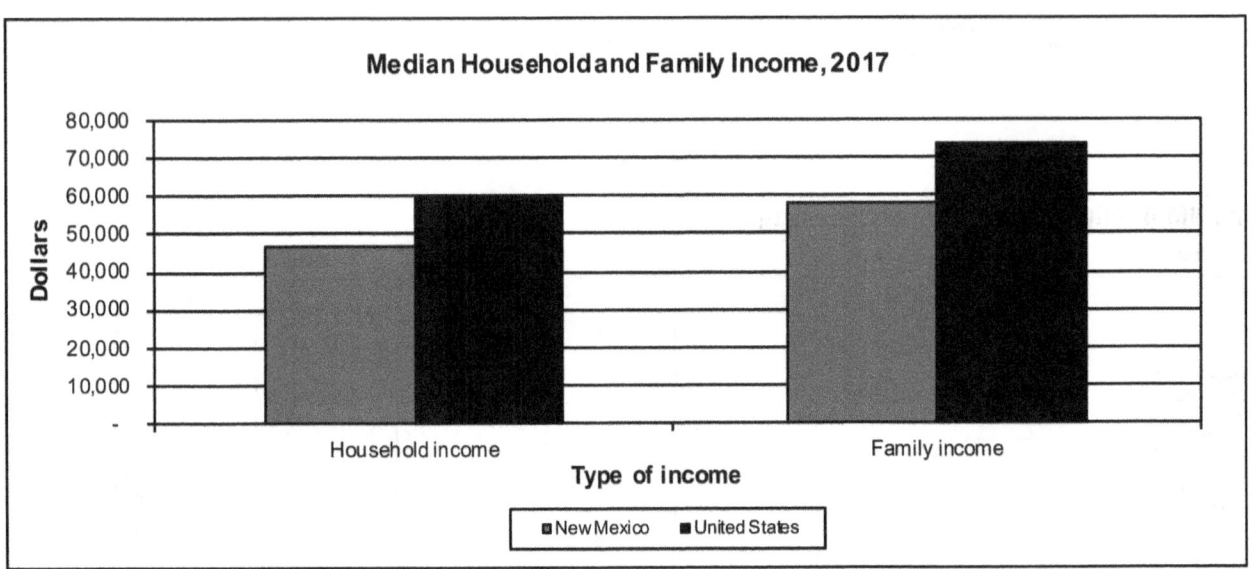

Table NM-6. Health Insurance Coverage Status for the Civilian Noninstitutionalized Population and Children Under 18 Years of Age

(Number, percent.)

Item	2009	2010	2011	2012	2013	2014	2015	2016	2017
Civilian Noninstitutionalized Population	1,975,830	2,032,699	2,047,242	2,051,805	2,051,900	2,050,369	2,050,178	2,046,001	2,054,301
Covered by Private or Public Insurance									
Number..	1,585,932	1,634,141	1,641,058	1,673,819	1,669,460	1,752,620	1,826,147	1,858,312	1,867,305
Percent...	80.3	80.4	80.2	81.6	81.4	85.5	89.1	90.8	90.9
Uninsured									
Number..	389,898	398,558	406,184	377,986	382,440	297,749	224,031	187,689	186,996
Percent...	19.7	19.6	19.8	18.4	18.6	14.5	10.9	9.2	9.1
Percent in the U.S. not covered.........................	15.1	15.5	15.1	14.8	14.5	11.7	9.4	8.6	8.7
Children Under 18 Years of Age[1]	514,098	517,658	516,787	515,341	506,951	498,680	498,415	488,598	522,820
Covered by Private or Public Insurance									
Number..	455,359	464,767	469,318	473,906	463,846	462,278	475,997	462,513	496,366
Percent...	88.6	89.8	90.8	92.0	91.5	92.7	95.5	94.7	94.9
Uninsured									
Number..	58,739	52,891	47,469	41,435	43,105	36,402	22,418	26,085	26,454
Percent...	11.4	10.2	9.2	8.0	8.5	7.3	4.5	5.3	5.1
Percent in the U.S. not covered.........................	8.6	8.0	7.5	7.2	7.1	6.0	4.8	4.5	5.0

[1] 2017 data is for individuals under 19 years of age.

Table NM-7. Employment Status by Demographic Group, 2018

(Numbers in thousands, percent.)

Characteristic	Civilian noninstitutional population	Civilian labor force		Employed		Unemployed	
		Number	Percent of population	Number	Percent of population	Number	Percent of population
Total...	1,627	946	58.1	902	55.4	44	4.7
Sex							
Male...	790	500	63.3	474	60.1	25	5.1
Female..	838	446	53.3	427	51.0	19	4.3
Race, Sex, and Hispanic Origin							
White...	1,322	776	58.6	743	56.2	33	4.2
Male...	644	416	64.6	398	61.8	18	4.3
Female..	679	360	53.0	345	50.8	15	4.0
Black or African American..................	36	25	69.4	23	63.7	2	8.0
Male...	NA	NA	NA	NA	NA	NA	NA
Female..	NA	NA	NA	NA	NA	NA	NA
Hispanic or Latino ethnicity[1]............	697	421	60.3	402	57.6	19	4.5
Male...	338	223	66.0	213	63.0	10	4.5
Female..	360	198	55.0	189	52.6	9	4.4
Age							
16 to 19 years...............................	112	38	34.0	33	29.5	5	13.2
20 to 24 years...............................	141	104	73.6	94	66.6	10	9.6
25 to 34 years...............................	269	206	76.7	196	72.8	11	5.1
35 to 44 years...............................	236	192	81.2	185	78.5	6	3.3
45 to 54 years...............................	244	183	75.2	178	72.8	6	3.2
55 to 64 years...............................	279	160	57.3	155	55.7	4	2.7
65 years and over...........................	347	64	18.3	61	17.7	2	3.8

NOTE: Data in Table 7 are from the Current Population Survey (CPS) and do not match the estimates in Table 8. See notes and definitions for further information.
[1] May be of any race.
NA = Not available.

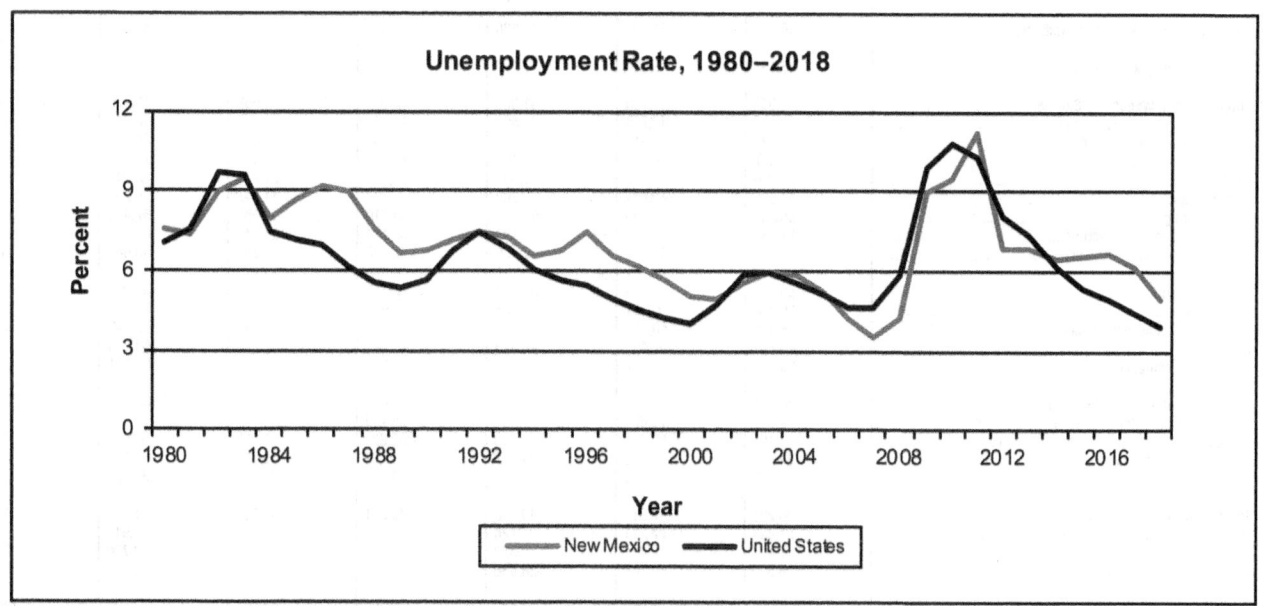

Table NM-8. Employment Status of the Civilian Noninstitutional Population Age 16 Years and Over

(Number, percent.)

Year	Civilian labor force	Civilian participation rate	Employed	Unemployed	Unemployment rate
2010..	936,088	60.0	860,154	75,934	8.1
2011..	930,356	58.8	860,305	70,051	7.5
2012..	927,795	58.4	861,617	66,178	7.1
2013..	923,899	57.9	859,804	64,095	6.9
2014..	927,142	58.0	865,229	61,913	6.7
2015..	927,999	57.8	867,387	60,612	6.5
2016..	928,732	57.6	866,704	62,028	6.7
2017..	929,567	57.4	872,382	57,185	6.2
2018..	940,359	57.6	893,823	46,536	4.9

Table NM-9. Employment and Average Wages by Industry

(Estimates are based on the 2012 *North American Industry Classification System* [NAICS].)

Industry	2011	2012	2013	2014	2015	2016	2017
	Number of jobs						
Wage and Salary Employment by Industry......................	836,180	839,254	846,495	852,348	860,023	861,222	862,272
Farm Wage and Salary Employment.............................	6,607	6,934	7,661	6,789	7,461	8,350	7,261
Nonfarm Wage and Salary Employment.......................	829,573	832,320	838,834	845,559	852,562	852,872	855,011
Private wage and salary employment..	615,758	620,409	627,979	636,207	643,993	644,350	648,726
Forestry, fishing, and related activities...............................	2,837	2,850	3,029	3,369	3,534	3,617	3,549
Mining..	21,065	23,816	25,846	27,679	25,328	19,693	20,925
Utilities..	4,367	4,386	4,446	4,418	4,384	4,441	4,353
Construction...	43,353	42,281	43,387	43,838	44,627	44,365	46,562
Manufacturing..	29,532	29,692	29,109	28,019	27,818	26,847	26,412
Durable goods manufacturing..	19,335	19,076	18,293	17,293	16,880	15,621	15,040
Nondurable goods manufacturing..	10,197	10,616	10,816	10,726	10,938	11,226	11,372
Wholesale trade	21,124	21,481	21,669	21,716	21,544	21,516	21,174
Retail trade...	90,845	91,741	92,659	93,371	94,387	93,999	91,813
Transportation and warehousing...	18,345	19,247	19,283	19,851	20,275	19,509	19,754
Information	13,513	13,584	13,085	12,564	12,735	13,063	12,421
Finance and insurance	22,084	22,065	22,277	22,870	23,173	23,476	23,978
Real estate and rental and leasing.......................................	9,866	9,867	10,112	10,159	10,267	10,224	10,145
Professional, scientific, and technical services	53,842	52,779	52,576	53,006	53,958	54,674	56,148
Management of companies and enterprises.........................	5,075	4,988	5,081	5,055	5,177	5,312	5,383
Administrative and waste services..	42,023	40,896	41,829	41,799	41,424	41,813	43,432
Educational services	10,380	10,383	10,306	10,253	10,138	10,081	10,065
Health care and social assistance...	105,122	107,026	108,216	109,707	114,570	119,340	119,784
Arts, entertainment, and recreation......................................	8,551	8,955	9,060	9,169	9,521	9,563	10,010
Accommodation and food services..	76,313	77,732	79,848	82,358	84,357	86,510	86,874
Other services, except public administration........................	37,521	36,640	36,161	37,006	36,776	36,307	35,944
Government and government enterprises.................................	213,815	211,911	210,855	209,352	208,569	208,522	206,285
	Dollars						
Average Wages and Salaries by Industry	40,871	41,695	41,828	42,950	43,538	43,653	44,725
Average Farm Wages and Salaries	33,155	35,089	35,430	38,591	29,719	30,742	35,556
Average Nonfarm Wages and Salaries	40,932	41,750	41,886	42,985	43,659	43,779	44,803
Average private wages and salaries.......................................	39,779	40,755	40,898	41,997	42,577	42,447	43,539
Forestry, fishing, and related activities...............................	22,342	22,918	23,514	23,532	24,613	26,570	27,785
Mining..	72,807	74,074	74,164	77,569	76,469	75,594	77,618
Utilities..	74,056	75,486	76,907	79,459	81,273	82,243	82,452
Construction	41,915	42,461	42,269	43,427	44,347	45,205	47,223
Manufacturing..	55,209	57,005	57,088	58,810	59,086	57,418	55,153
Durable goods manufacturing..	61,839	64,069	64,144	66,134	65,449	65,920	61,552
Nondurable goods manufacturing..	42,639	44,311	45,155	47,000	49,267	45,588	46,691
Wholesale trade	50,587	51,473	51,574	53,311	54,299	53,913	55,373
Retail trade...	26,446	26,981	27,157	27,909	28,790	29,056	29,748
Transportation and warehousing...	48,375	50,457	49,737	52,104	52,244	50,140	52,760
Information	45,771	47,457	47,519	49,723	52,678	53,210	53,172
Finance and insurance	55,076	57,347	58,651	59,661	61,931	61,721	62,793
Real estate and rental and leasing.......................................	36,131	36,287	36,786	37,863	38,619	38,090	39,900
Professional, scientific, and technical services	71,341	72,677	72,446	75,202	76,772	78,775	80,140
Management of companies and enterprises.........................	63,403	67,592	66,510	69,820	70,353	67,972	70,062
Administrative and waste services..	34,471	34,966	34,677	34,620	35,212	35,218	36,290
Educational services	31,505	32,181	32,683	32,897	33,245	34,494	34,873
Health care and social assistance...	39,223	39,917	40,160	40,641	41,234	41,353	42,132
Arts, entertainment, and recreation......................................	21,824	22,211	22,728	24,008	24,311	23,914	24,675
Accommodation and food services..	17,428	17,921	18,320	18,880	19,255	19,726	20,185
Other services, except public administration........................	26,595	27,708	28,066	28,672	29,503	30,087	31,700
Government and government enterprises.............................	44,254	44,661	44,832	45,989	47,001	47,894	48,779

Table NM-10. Employment Characteristics by Family Type

(Number, percent.)

Family type and labor force status	2015		2016		2017	
	Total	Families with own children under 18 years	Total	Families with own children under 18 years	Total	Families with own children under 18 years
All Families...	485,404	199,125	481,127	195,512	479,092	189,349
FAMILY TYPE AND LABOR FORCE STATUS						
Married-Couple Families...	341,876	122,170	334,266	119,275	329,588	111,285
Both husband and wife in labor force	43.6	58.6	43.7	60.3	40.6	58.3
Husband in labor force, wife not in labor force	24.3	32.6	23.1	31.8	23.8	32.0
Wife in labor force, husband not in labor force	9.3	4.9	9.6	4.8	8.9	5.3
Both husband and wife not in labor force........................	21.6	3.4	22.7	2.4	25.5	3.4
Other Families	143,528	76,955	146,861	76,237	149,504	78,064
Female householder, no husband present..........................	69.3	70.9	72.0	75.5	68.8	71.4
In labor force...	46.7	56.5	49.1	60.0	46.2	57.1
Not in labor force...	22.6	14.4	23.0	15.4	22.6	14.3
Male householder, no wife present..........................	30.7	29.1	28.0	24.5	31.2	28.6
In labor force...	23.3	26.7	20.3	20.4	21.9	23.4
Not in labor force...	7.3	2.4	7.6	4.1	9.2	5.2

Table NM-11. School Enrollment and Educational Attainment, 2017

(Number, percent.)

Item	State	U.S.
Enrollment		
Total population 3 years and over, enrolled in school	536,849	81,273,337
Enrolled in nursery school or preschool (percent)	5.0	6.0
Enrolled in kindergarten (percent)	5.0	4.9
Enrolled in elementary school, grades 1-8 (percent)........................	42.7	40.6
Enrolled in high school, grades 9-12 (percent)	20.8	21.1
Enrolled in college or graduate school (percent)........................	26.5	27.4
Attainment		
Total population 25 years and over	1,391,475	221,250,083
Less than ninth grade (percent)........................	5.8	5.1
9th to 12th grade, no diploma (percent)	8.1	6.9
High school graduate, including equivalency (percent)........................	26.6	27.1
Some college, no degree (percent)........................	24.0	20.4
Associate's degree (percent)........................	8.4	8.5
Bachelor's degree (percent)........................	15.2	19.7
Graduate or professional degree (percent)........................	11.8	12.3
High school graduate or higher (percent)	86.1	88.0
Bachelor's degree or higher (percent)	27.1	32.0

Table NM-12. Public School Characteristics and Educational Indicators

(Number, percent; data derived from National Center of Education Statistics.)

Item	State	U.S.
Public Elementary and Secondary Schools		
Number of operational school districts, 2016-17........................	157	18,377
Number of operational schools, 2016-17........................	869	98,330
Percent charter schools	11.4	7.1
Total public school enrollment, 2016-17........................	336,263	50,587,859
Percent charter school enrollment	7.6	6.0
Student-teacher ratio, Fall 2015........................	15.5	16.0
Expenditures per student (dollars), 2015-16........................	9,959	11,841
Four-year adjusted cohort graduation rate (ACGR)[1]	71.1	84.6
Students eligible for free or reduced-price lunch (percent), 2015-16........................	71.7	52.1
English language learners (percent), Fall 2016	13.4	9.6
Students age 3 to 21 served under IDEA, part B (percent), 2017-18........................	15.8	13.7
Public Schools by Type, 2016-17		Percent of state public schools
Total number of schools........................	869	100.0
Special education........................	5	0.6
Vocational education........................	-	-
Alternative education........................	26	3.0

[1] Adjusted Cohort Graduation Rates (ACGR) differ from Averaged Freshmen Graduation Rates (AFGR).
- = Zero or rounds to zero.

Table NM-13. Reported Voting and Registration of the Voting-Age Population, November 2018

(Numbers in thousands, percent.)

Item	Total population	Total citizen population	Registered			Voted		
			Total registered	Percent registered (total population)	Percent registered (total citizen population)	Total voted	Percent voted (total population)	Percent voted (total citizen population)
U.S. Total	249,748	228,832	153,066	61.3	66.9	122,281	49.0	53.4
State Total...................................	1,576	1,485	916	58.1	61.7	715	45.3	48.1
Sex								
Male	761	715	422	55.5	59.1	327	43.0	45.8
Female	815	770	493	60.5	64.0	387	47.5	50.3
Race								
White alone.................	1,251	1,178	764	61.1	64.9	616	49.2	52.3
White, non-Hispanic alone	644	634	465	72.2	73.4	388	60.3	61.3
Black alone	30	27	15	(B)	(B)	9	(B)	(B)
Asian alone	32	21	9	(B)	(B)	7	(B)	(B)
Hispanic (of any race)..............	666	597	322	48.3	53.9	242	36.3	40.5
White alone or in combination	1,284	1,206	777	60.5	64.5	626	48.7	51.9
Black alone or in combination	39	36	19	(B)	(B)	11	(B)	(B)
Asian alone or in combination...........	35	25	10	(B)	(B)	8	(B)	(B)
Age								
18 to 24 years..........	184	180	80	43.6	44.5	50	27.4	28.0
25 to 34 years..........	284	261	148	52.2	56.9	97	34.1	37.2
35 to 44 years..........	236	219	121	51.2	55.0	81	34.4	37.0
45 to 64 years..........	528	489	311	59.0	63.7	263	49.8	53.7
65 years and over	345	336	255	74.0	75.9	224	64.8	66.5

B = Base is less than 75,000 and therefore too small to show the derived measure.

Table NM-14. Crime

(Number, rate per 100,000. Data are derived from the FBI Uniform Crime Reports.)

Item	State			U.S.		
	2016	2017	Percent change	2016	2017	Percent change
TOTAL POPULATION[1]	2,085,432	2,088,070	0.1	323,405,935	325,719,178	0.7
VIOLENT CRIME						
Number.........................	14,585	16,359	12.2	1,285,606	1,283,220	-0.2
Rate	699.4	783.5	12.0	397.5	394.0	-0.9
Murder and Nonnegligent Manslaughter						
Number..........................	139	148	6.5	17,413	17,284	-0.7
Rate	6.7	7.1	6.3	5.4	5.3	-1.4
Rape[2]						
Number.........................	1,527	1,259	-17.6	132,414	135,755	2.5
Rate	73.2	60.3	-17.7	40.9	41.7	1.8
Robbery						
Number.........................	2,737	3,722	36.0	332,797	319,356	-4.0
Rate	131.2	178.3	35.8	102.9	98.0	-4.7
Aggravated Assault						
Number.........................	10,182	11,230	10.3	802,982	810,825	1.0
Rate	488.2	537.8	10.2	248.3	248.9	0.3
PROPERTY CRIME						
Number.........................	81,930	82,306	0.5	7,928,530	7,694,086	-3.0
Rate	3,928.7	3,941.7	0.3	2,451.6	2,362.2	-3.6
Burglary						
Number.........................	17,280	17,917	3.7	1,516,405	1,401,840	-7.6
Rate	828.6	858.1	3.6	468.9	430.4	-8.2
Larceny-Theft						
Number.........................	52,907	52,617	-0.5	5,644,835	5,519,107	-2.2
Rate	2,537.0	2,519.9	-0.7	1,745.4	1,694.4	-2.9
Motor Vehicle Theft						
Number.........................	11,743	11,772	0.2	767,290	773,139	0.8
Rate	563.1	563.8	0.1	237.3	237.4	-

NOTE: Although arson data are included in the trend and clearance tables, sufficient data are not available to estimate totals for this offense. Therefore, no arson data are published in this table.
- = Zero or rounds to zero.
[1] Population figures are U.S. Census Bureau provisional estimates as of July 1, 2017.
[2] The figures shown in the rape (revised definition) column were estimated using the revised Uniform Crime Reporting (UCR) definition of rape.

Table NM-15. State Government Finances, 2017

(Dollar amounts in thousands, percent distribution.)

Item	Dollars	Percent distribution
Total Revenue	21,523,940	100.0
General revenue	17,214,747	80.0
Intergovernmental revenue	7,226,565	33.6
Taxes	5,776,271	26.8
General sales	2,258,767	10.5
Selective sales	810,874	3.8
License taxes	307,671	1.4
Individual income tax	1,338,768	6.2
Corporate income tax	91,876	0.4
Other taxes	968,315	4.5
Current charges	1,747,179	8.1
Miscellaneous general revenue	2,464,732	11.5
Utility revenue	0	-
Liquor stores revenue	0	-
Insurance trust revenue[1]	4,309,193	20.0
Total Expenditure	20,779,257	100.0
Intergovernmental expenditure	4,878,597	23.5
Direct expenditure	15,900,660	76.5
Current operation	12,004,457	57.8
Capital outlay	829,392	4.0
Insurance benefits and repayments	2,398,282	11.5
Assistance and subsidies	277,563	1.3
Interest on debt	390,966	1.9
Exhibit: Salaries and wages	2,528,205	12.2
Total Expenditure	20,779,257	100.0
General expenditure	18,379,804	88.5
Intergovernmental expenditure	4,878,597	23.5
Direct expenditure	13,501,207	65.0
General expenditure, by function:		
Education	5,899,371	28.4
Public welfare	5,924,514	28.5
Hospitals	1,151,673	5.5
Health	412,096	2.0
Highways	651,714	3.1
Police protection	148,580	0.7
Correction	487,467	2.3
Natural resources	255,992	1.2
Parks and recreation	56,924	0.3
Governmental administration	531,362	2.6
Interest on general debt	390,966	1.9
Other and unallocable	2,469,145	11.9
Utility expenditure	1,171	-
Liquor stores expenditure	0	-
Insurance trust expenditure	2,398,282	11.5
Debt at End of Fiscal Year	7,057,656	X
Cash and Security Holdings	56,374,732	X

X = Not applicable.
- = Zero or rounds to zero.
[1] Within insurance trust revenue, net earnings of state retirement systems is a calculated statistic (the item code in the data file is X08), and thus can be positive or negative. Net earnings is the sum of earnings on investments plus gains on investments minus losses on investments. The change made in 2002 for asset valuation from book to market value in accordance with Statement 34 of the Governmental Accounting Standards Board is reflected in the calculated statistics.

Table NM-16. State Government Tax Collections, 2018

(Dollars in thousands, percent.)

Item	Dollars	Percent distribution
Total Taxes	5,671,904	100.0
Property taxes	84,224	1.5
Sales and gross receipts	2,885,892	50.9
General sales and gross receipts	2,073,118	36.6
Selective sales and gross receipts	812,774	14.3
Alcoholic beverages	45,497	0.8
Amusements	80,313	1.4
Insurance premiums	169,355	3.0
Motor fuels	230,303	4.1
Pari-mutuels	842	-
Public utilities	31,747	0.6
Tobacco products	93,862	1.7
Other selective sales	160,855	2.8
Licenses	316,690	5.6
Alcoholic beverages	0	-
Amusements	582	-
Corporations in general	32,175	0.6
Hunting and fishing	31,802	0.6
Motor vehicle	200,727	3.5
Motor vehicle operators	5,004	0.1
Public utilities	1,529	-
Occupation and business, NEC	44,871	0.8
Other licenses	0	-
Income taxes	1,344,139	23.7
Individual income	1,252,651	22.1
Corporation net income	91,488	1.6
Other taxes	1,040,959	18.4
Death and gift	1	X
Documentary and stock transfer	X	-
Severance	1,040,958	18.4
Taxes, NEC	0	-

- = Zero or rounds to zero.

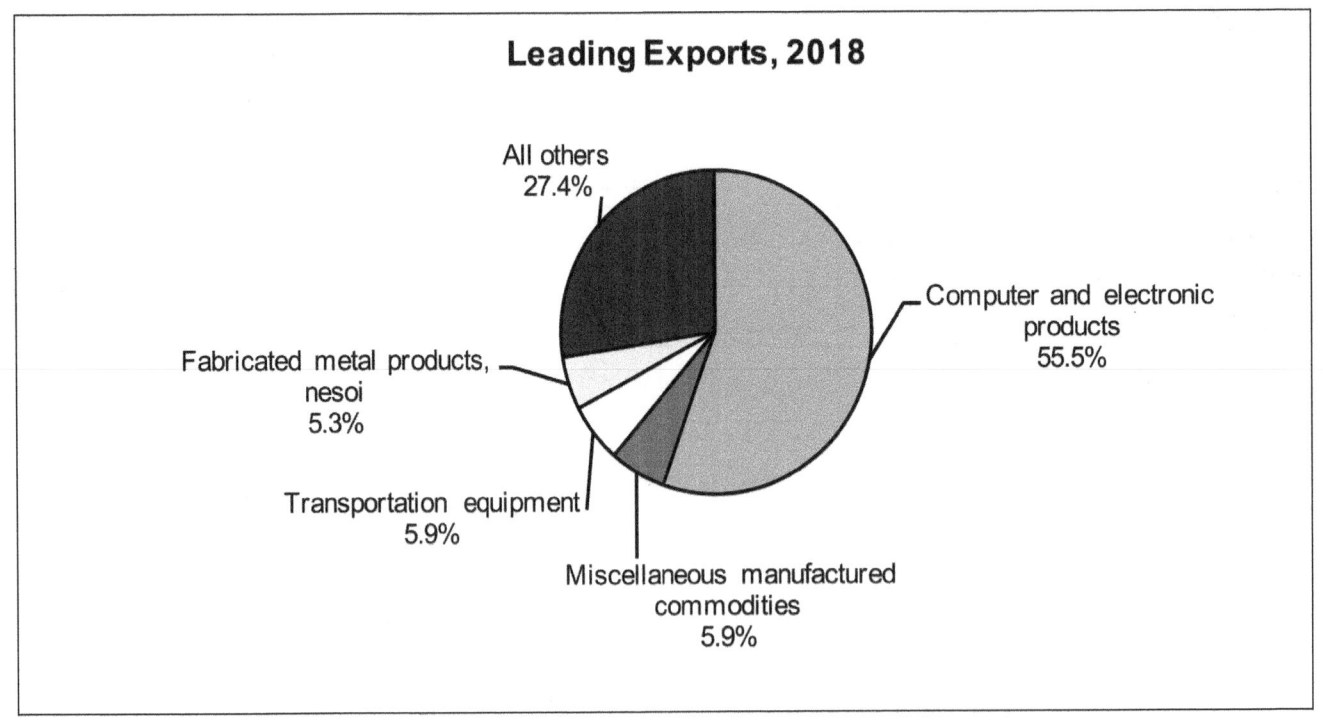

Leading Exports, 2018

All others 27.4%

Computer and electronic products 55.5%

Fabricated metal products, nesoi 5.3%

Transportation equipment 5.9%

Miscellaneous manufactured commodities 5.9%

NEW YORK

Facts and Figures

Location: Northeastern United States; bordered on the N by Canada (Ontario and Quebec) and Lake Ontario; on the E by Vermont, Massachusetts, and Connecticut; on the S by New Jersey and Pennsylvania; and on the W by Pennsylvania, Lake Erie, Canada (Ontario), and Lake Ontario

Area: 54,556 sq. mi. (141,299 sq. km.); rank—27th

Population: 19,542,209 (2018 est.); rank—4th

Principal Cities: capital—Albany; largest—New York City

Statehood: July 26, 1788; 11th state

U.S. Congress: 2 senators, 27 representatives

State Motto: *Excelsior* ("Ever upward")

State Song: "I Love New York"

State Nickname: The Empire State

Abbreviations: NY; N.Y.

State Symbols: flower—rose; tree—sugar maple; bird—bluebird

At a Glance

- With an increase in population of 0.8 percent, New York ranked 43rd among the states in growth from 2010 to 2018.

- In 2017, 5.7 percent of New Yorkers did not have health insurance, compared to 8.7 percent of the total U.S. population.

- New York had the second lowest homeownership rate in 2018, with 51.0 percent of residents owning homes.

- New York ranked 47th among the states for property crime in 2017, with 1,514.2 incidences per 100,000 population, compared to the national average of 2,362.2 incidences per 100,000 population.

- New York had the 3rd highest GDP of all states in 2018 ($1,436,957 million).

Table NY-1. Population by Age, Sex, Race, and Hispanic Origin

(Number, percent, except where noted.)

Sex, age, race, and Hispanic origin	2000	2010	2018 [1]	Percent change, 2010–2018
Total Population...	18,976,457	19,378,102	19,542,209	0.8
Percent of total U.S. population	6.7	6.3	6.0	X
Sex				
Male...	9,146,748	9,377,147	9,488,430	1.2
Female	9,829,709	10,000,955	10,053,779	0.5
Age				
Under 5 years..	1,239,417	1,155,822	1,140,442	-1.3
5 to 19 years...	3,971,834	3,741,689	3,425,488	-8.5
20 to 64 years..	11,316,854	11,862,648	11,762,745	-0.8
65 years and over	2,448,352	2,617,943	3,213,534	22.8
Median age (years)	35.9	38.0	39.0	2.6
Race and Hispanic Origin				
One race				
White	12,893,689	13,901,661	13,619,931	-2.0
Black	3,014,385	3,378,047	3,447,729	2.1
American Indian and Alaska Native	82,461	183,046	190,414	4.0
Asian	1,044,976	1,481,555	1,750,013	18.1
Native Hawaiian or Other Pacific Islander	8,818	24,000	26,745	11.4
Two or more races	590,182	409,793	507,377	23.8
Hispanic (of any race)...	2,867,583	3,564,228	3,754,130	5.3

X = Not applicable.
[1] Population figures for 2018 are July 1 estimates. The 2010 estimates are taken from the 2010 Census.
- = Zero or rounds to zero.

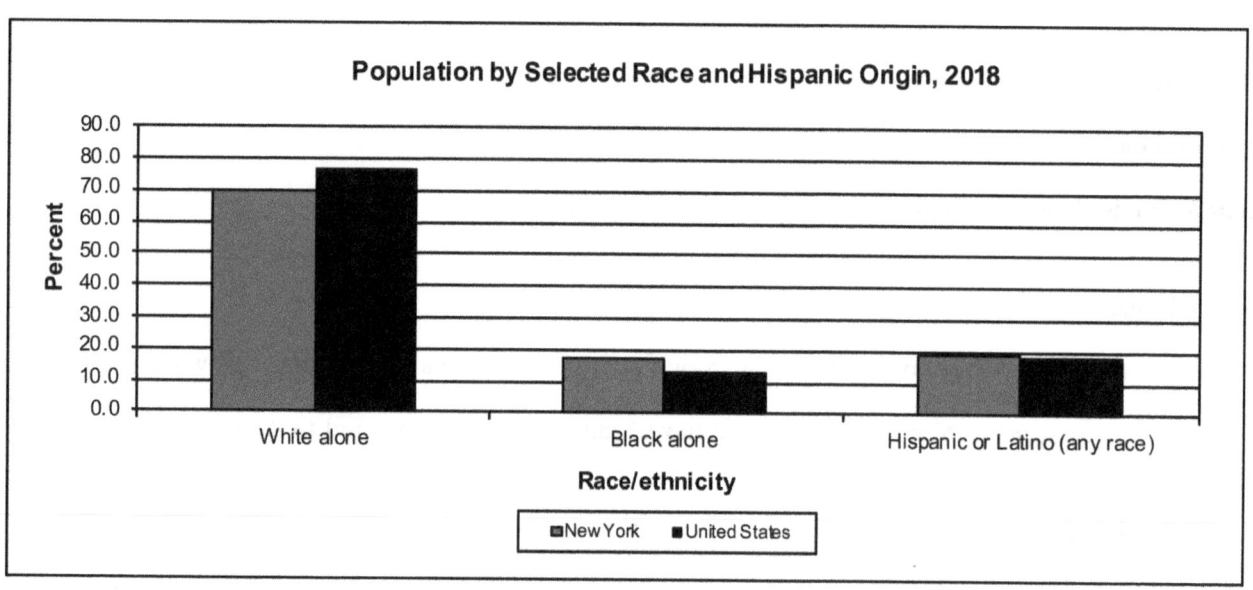

Population by Selected Race and Hispanic Origin, 2018

Table NY-2. Marital Status

(Number, percent distribution.)

Sex, age, race, and Hispanic origin	2000	2010	2017
Males, 15 Years and Over...	7,125,715	7,586,733	7,879,694
Never married	34.7	40.5	41.6
Now married, except separated...	53.3	47.6	46.6
Separated..	2.7	2.2	2.0
Widowed..	2.8	2.6	2.5
Divorced..	6.5	7.2	7.3
Females, 15 Years and Over...	7,932,161	8,283,542	8,530,853
Never married	29.0	34.8	36.0
Now married, except separated...	47.1	42.8	42.3
Separated..	3.7	3.1	2.9
Widowed..	11.2	9.6	8.8
Divorced..	8.9	9.7	10.1

Table NY-3. Households and Housing Characteristics

(Number, percent, dollars.)

Item	2000	2010	2017	Average annual percent change, 2010–2017
Total Households..	7,056,860	7,196,427	7,304,332	0.2
Family households...	4,639,387	4,632,676	4,620,008	-
Married-couple family.....................................	3,289,514	3,210,895	3,210,469	-
Other family...	1,349,873	1,421,781	1,409,539	-0.1
Male householder, no wife present..............	311,697	355,236	372,915	0.7
Female householder, no husband present.....	1,038,176	1,066,545	1,036,624	-0.4
Nonfamily households..	2,417,473	2,563,751	2,684,324	0.7
Householder living alone..................................	1,982,742	2,089,816	2,172,632	0.6
Householder not living alone............................	434,731	473,935	511,692	1.1
Housing Characteristics				
Total housing units...	7,679,301	8,108,211	8,327,621	0.4
Occupied housing units	7,056,860	7,196,427	7,304,332	0.2
Owner occupied..	3,739,166	3,904,123	3,930,033	0.1
Renter occupied..	3,317,694	3,292,304	3,374,299	0.4
Average household size.......................................	2.61	2.61	2.64	0.2
Financial Characteristics				
Median gross rent of renter-occupied housing	627	1,020	1,226	2.9
Median monthly owner costs for housing units with a mortgage	1,357	1,963	2,036	0.5
Median value of owner-occupied housing units......	148,700	296,500	314,500	0.9

- = Zero or rounds to zero.

Table NY-4. Migration, Origin, and Language

(Number, percent.)

	State			U.S.		
Characteristic	2016	2017	Percent change	2016	2017	Percent change
Residence 1 Year Ago						
Population 1 year and over	19,526,443	19,638,923	0.6	319,361,956	321,994,428	0.8
Same house	89.4	89.4	X	85.4	85.7	X
Different house in the U.S.................................	9.7	9.9	X	13.9	13.6	X
Same county	5.9	6.0	X	8.3	8.1	X
Different county	3.8	3.9	X	5.6	5.6	X
Same state	2.5	2.5	X	3.2	3.3	X
Different state	1.3	1.5	X	2.4	2.3	X
Abroad	0.9	0.7	X	0.7	0.7	X
Place of Birth						
Native born	15,209,174	15,309,018	0.7	279,388,170	281,193,323	0.6
Male	48.9	49.0	X	49.3	49.4	X
Female	51.1	51.0	X	50.7	50.6	X
Foreign born	4,536,115	4,540,381	0.1	43,739,345	44,525,855	1.8
Male	47.1	47.0	X	48.5	48.4	X
Female	52.9	53.0	X	51.5	51.6	X
Foreign born; naturalized U.S. citizen................	2,513,779	2,555,306	1.7	21,238,372	21,948,732	3.3
Male	44.6	44.4	X	45.9	45.9	X
Female	55.4	55.6	X	54.1	54.1	X
Foreign born; not a U.S. citizen........................	2,022,336	1,985,075	-1.8	22,500,973	22,577,123	0.3
Male	50.3	50.2	X	51.0	50.8	X
Female	49.7	49.8	X	49.0	49.2	X
Entered 2010 or later	17.9	19.9	X	18.6	21.3	X
Entered 2000 to 2009	25.2	24.4	X	26.7	25.7	X
Entered before 2000..	56.9	55.6	X	54.7	53.0	X
World Region of Birth, Foreign						
Foreign-born population, excluding population born at sea	4,536,115	4,540,381	0.1	43,738,901	44,525,458	1.8
Europe	15.7	15.8	X	10.9	10.8	X
Asia..	29.1	29.7	X	30.8	31.2	X
Africa	4.5	4.5	X	4.9	5.1	X
Oceania	0.3	0.3	X	0.6	0.6	X
Latin America	49.2	48.5	X	51	50.4	X
North America...	1.2	1.2	X	1.8	1.8	X
Language Spoken at Home and Ability to Speak English						
Population 5 years and over...............................	18,586,270	18,691,802	0.6	303,328,961	305,924,019	0.9
English only	69.0	69.1	X	78.4	78.2	X
Language other than English..............................	31.0	30.9	X	21.6	21.8	X
Speaks English less than "very well"..............	13.7	13.6	X	8.6	8.5	X

NA = Not available.
X = Not applicable.
- = Zero or rounds to zero.

Table NY-5. Median Income and Poverty Status, 2017

(Number, percent, except as noted.)

Characteristic	State		U.S.	
	Number	Percent	Number	Percent
Median Income				
Households (dollars)..	64,894	X	60,336	X
Families (dollars)	80,114	X	73,891	X
Below Poverty Level (All People)	2,722,257	14.1	42,583,651	13.4
Sex				
Male	1,208,091	12.9	19,004,547	12.2
Female	1,514,166	15.2	23,579,104	14.5
Age				
Under 18 years...	803,171	19.7	13,353,202	18.4
Related children under 18 years......................	785,341	19.4	13,053,472	18.1
18 to 64 years..	1,569,228	12.9	24,648,677	12.6
65 years and over	349,858	11.4	4,581,772	9.3

X = Not applicable.

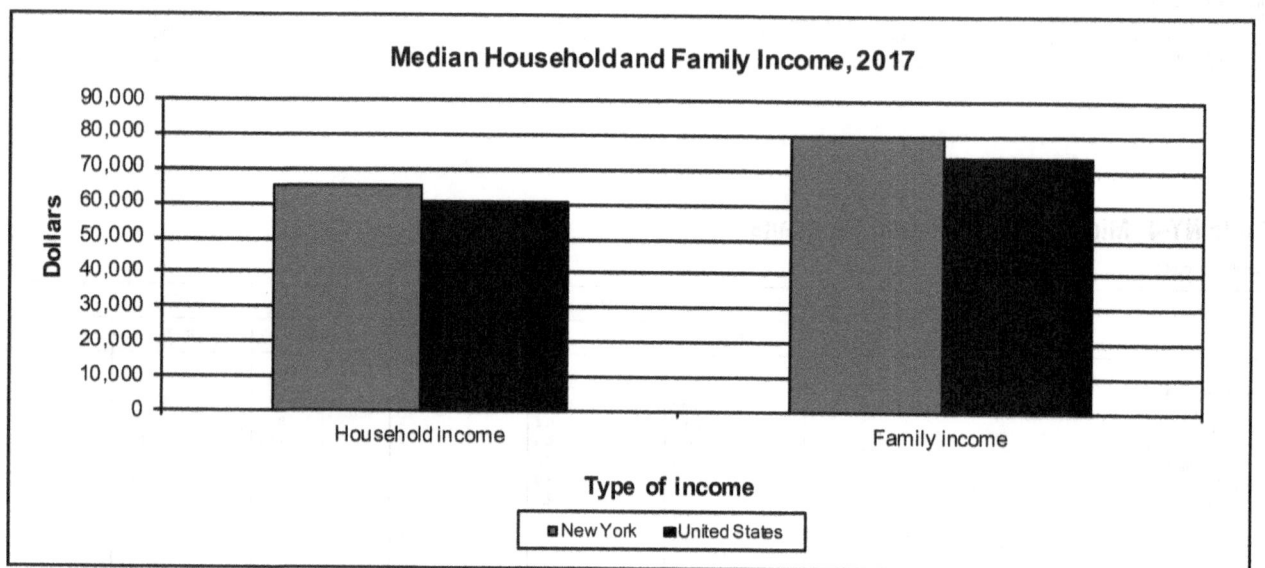

Table NY-6. Health Insurance Coverage Status for the Civilian Noninstitutionalized Population and Children Under 18 Years of Age

(Number, percent.)

Item	2009	2010	2011	2012	2013	2014	2015	2016	2017
Civilian Noninstitutionalized Population	19,264,374	19,134,281	19,208,419	19,316,728	19,400,069	19,499,548	19,556,452	19,505,596	19,608,066
Covered by Private or Public Insurance									
Number..	17,069,635	16,856,899	17,013,070	17,213,819	17,330,548	17,802,989	18,175,904	18,322,902	18,495,124
Percent..	88.6	88.1	88.6	89.1	89.3	91.3	92.9	93.9	94.3
Uninsured									
Number..	2,194,739	2,277,382	2,195,349	2,102,909	2,069,521	1,696,559	1,380,548	1,182,694	1,112,942
Percent..	11.4	11.9	11.4	10.9	10.7	8.7	7.1	6.1	5.7
Percent in the U.S. not covered............................	15.1	15.5	15.1	14.8	14.5	11.7	9.4	8.6	8.7
Children Under 18 Years of Age[1]	4,413,888	4,301,661	4,270,110	4,252,821	4,230,975	4,217,078	4,204,378	4,170,786	4,403,144
Covered by Private or Public Insurance									
Number..	4,208,891	4,093,200	4,089,276	4,085,154	4,060,192	4,079,553	4,100,735	4,069,720	4,285,641
Percent..	95.4	95.2	95.8	96.1	96.0	96.7	97.5	97.6	97.3
Uninsured									
Number..	204,997	208,461	180,834	167,667	170,783	137,525	103,643	101,066	117,503
Percent..	4.6	4.8	4.2	3.9	4.0	3.3	2.5	2.4	2.7
Percent in the U.S. not covered............................	8.6	8.0	7.5	7.2	7.1	6.0	4.8	4.5	5.0

[1] 2017 data is for individuals under 19 years of age.

Table NY-7. Employment Status by Demographic Group, 2018

(Numbers in thousands, percent.)

Characteristic	Civilian noninstitutional population	Civilian labor force		Employed		Unemployed	
		Number	Percent of population	Number	Percent of population	Number	Percent of population
Total..	15,972	9,704	60.8	9,302	58.2	402	4.1
Sex							
Male............................	7,628	5,057	66.3	4,828	63.3	229	4.5
Female..........................	8,344	4,647	55.7	4,474	53.6	173	3.7
Race, Sex, and Hispanic Origin							
White	11,309	6,962	61.6	6,703	59.3	259	3.7
Male...........................	5,501	3,707	67.4	3,555	64.6	152	4.1
Female.........................	5,809	3,255	56.0	3,148	54.2	107	3.3
Black or African American..............	2,718	1,557	57.3	1,445	53.1	113	7.2
Male...........................	1,217	723	59.4	664	54.6	59	8.1
Female.........................	1,501	834	55.6	780	52.0	54	6.5
Hispanic or Latino ethnicity[1]	2,679	1,648	61.5	1,569	58.6	79	4.8
Male...........................	1,283	891	69.5	849	66.2	43	4.8
Female.........................	1,396	757	54.2	721	51.6	36	4.8
Age							
16 to 19 years......................	970	276	28.5	248	25.5	29	10.4
20 to 24 years......................	1,307	815	62.4	753	57.6	63	7.7
25 to 34 years......................	2,903	2,375	81.8	2,278	78.5	97	4.1
35 to 44 years......................	2,470	2,008	81.3	1,931	78.2	77	3.8
45 to 54 years......................	2,364	1,877	79.4	1,814	76.8	63	3.3
55 to 64 years......................	2,669	1,686	63.1	1,639	61.4	47	2.8
65 years and over	3,289	668	20.3	640	19.5	27	4.1

NOTE: Data in Table 7 are from the Current Population Survey (CPS) and do not match the estimates in Table 8. See notes and definitions for further information.
[1] May be of any race.

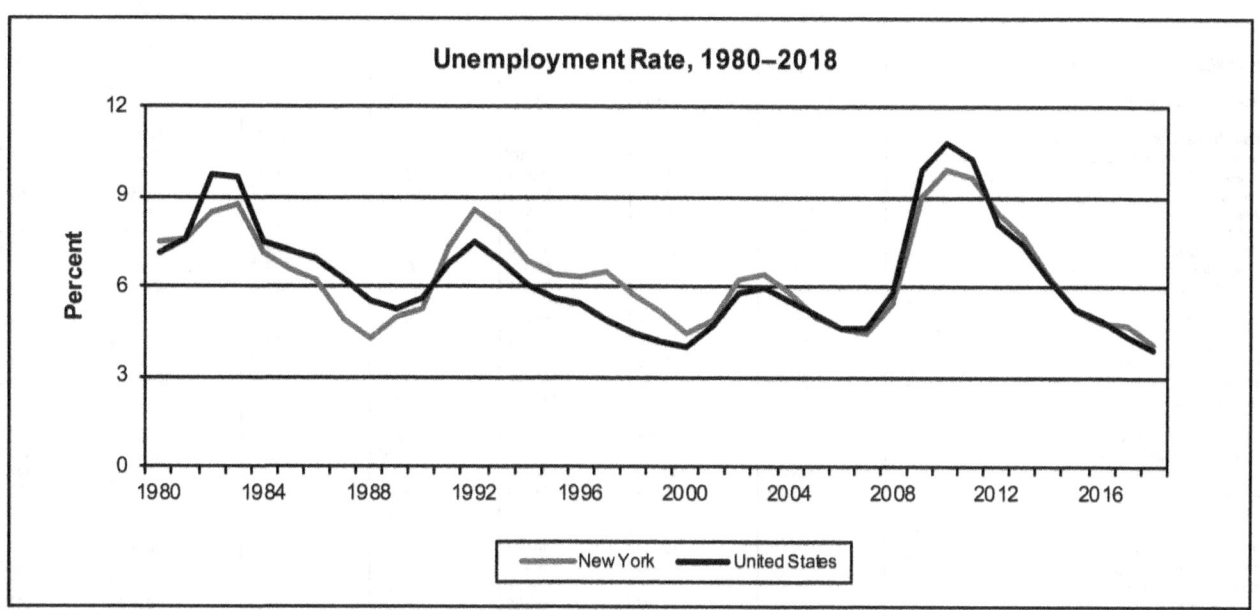

Unemployment Rate, 1980–2018

Table NY-8. Employment Status of the Civilian Noninstitutional Population Age 16 Years and Over

(Number, percent.)

Year	Civilian labor force	Civilian participation rate	Employed	Unemployed	Unemployment rate
2010..	9,595,362	62.4	8,769,723	825,639	8.6
2011..	9,517,361	61.4	8,728,057	789,304	8.3
2012..	9,612,232	61.6	8,793,385	818,847	8.5
2013..	9,659,170	61.5	8,913,788	745,382	7.7
2014..	9,591,309	60.7	8,984,074	607,235	6.3
2015..	9,644,615	60.8	9,136,151	508,464	5.3
2016..	9,668,687	60.8	9,200,266	468,421	4.8
2017..	9,704,695	60.9	9,249,225	455,470	4.7
2018..	9,574,706	61.0	9,181,058	393,648	4.1

Table NY-9. Employment and Average Wages by Industry

(Estimates are based on the 2012 *North American Industry Classification System* [NAICS].)

Industry	2011	2012	2013	2014	2015	2016	2017
	Number of jobs						
Wage and Salary Employment by Industry.....................	8,807,999	8,932,772	9,051,229	9,221,011	9,385,967	9,510,338	9,623,705
Farm Wage and Salary Employment...............................	19,821	19,707	22,515	22,608	22,524	21,022	20,976
Nonfarm Wage and Salary Employment.........................	8,788,178	8,913,065	9,028,714	9,198,403	9,363,443	9,489,316	9,602,729
Private wage and salary employment..................................	7,299,333	7,444,912	7,570,669	7,744,644	7,910,686	8,034,010	8,143,784
Forestry, fishing, and related activities............................	5,336	5,240	5,286	5,545	5,743	5,671	5,756
Mining..	4,674	4,675	4,408	4,621	4,655	4,437	4,400
Utilities...	37,267	36,035	36,174	37,697	38,330	37,643	38,082
Construction...	316,519	323,268	335,998	351,440	370,582	386,441	395,718
Manufacturing..	459,110	459,296	456,627	453,410	455,253	451,155	446,646
Durable goods manufacturing...	271,123	269,441	266,755	265,267	266,133	262,446	257,245
Nondurable goods manufacturing...................................	187,987	189,855	189,872	188,143	189,120	188,709	189,401
Wholesale trade	332,566	336,159	337,768	339,723	342,648	340,359	340,199
Retail trade...	900,223	920,821	933,745	948,836	952,897	951,509	945,365
Transportation and warehousing......................................	228,290	230,921	231,778	240,732	250,266	253,715	259,523
Information	257,100	261,262	261,361	265,665	267,490	268,216	271,047
Finance and insurance	517,414	516,507	511,596	520,750	528,371	530,540	533,040
Real estate and rental and leasing..................................	182,541	183,974	186,984	189,128	195,425	199,673	203,192
Professional, scientific, and technical services	579,119	603,605	618,757	634,744	656,986	669,050	680,032
Management of companies and enterprises.....................	133,394	134,725	138,822	142,417	143,255	142,857	144,343
Administrative and waste services...................................	431,170	442,216	454,728	461,331	475,662	490,507	502,584
Educational services	365,442	376,005	381,614	390,058	406,604	413,045	416,976
Health care and social assistance...................................	1,325,387	1,341,046	1,366,068	1,396,266	1,426,030	1,479,629	1,524,164
Arts, entertainment, and recreation.................................	143,328	150,006	157,103	165,446	165,806	170,018	174,218
Accommodation and food services...................................	628,965	658,742	687,430	714,197	737,033	754,615	778,692
Other services, except public administration...................	451,488	460,409	464,422	482,638	487,650	484,930	479,807
Government and government enterprises................................	1,488,845	1,468,153	1,458,045	1,453,759	1,452,757	1,455,306	1,458,945
	Dollars						
Average Wages and Salaries by Industry	61,035	61,979	62,417	65,173	66,820	67,348	69,947
Average Farm Wages and Salaries	20,319	30,593	26,969	28,804	23,616	29,039	26,412
Average Nonfarm Wages and Salaries	61,127	62,049	62,505	65,262	66,924	67,433	70,043
Average private wages and salaries..................................	62,525	63,418	63,762	66,683	68,318	68,716	71,491
Forestry, fishing, and related activities............................	28,683	28,899	29,643	30,350	32,417	33,621	34,478
Mining..	67,430	63,477	60,322	65,188	64,937	63,561	65,455
Utilities...	102,975	108,832	106,103	107,817	110,484	114,262	120,084
Construction...	61,462	62,353	63,422	65,249	67,511	70,104	71,465
Manufacturing..	59,971	60,928	61,176	62,072	65,497	64,161	65,874
Durable goods manufacturing...	64,384	66,019	66,333	66,870	70,323	69,343	71,240
Nondurable goods manufacturing...................................	53,607	53,704	53,931	55,309	58,706	56,953	58,586
Wholesale trade	73,732	77,724	76,834	79,573	82,993	82,573	84,342
Retail trade...	30,274	30,724	31,466	32,476	33,432	33,865	35,141
Transportation and warehousing......................................	46,112	47,235	48,279	49,219	50,011	51,322	52,371
Information	95,854	100,127	102,514	110,359	115,022	120,004	119,384
Finance and insurance	198,059	197,251	197,264	216,989	213,880	211,239	231,098
Real estate and rental and leasing..................................	56,795	59,689	60,063	63,839	66,736	69,376	71,824
Professional, scientific, and technical services	93,957	96,067	97,939	102,994	106,116	108,546	111,438
Management of companies and enterprises.....................	145,791	144,153	142,752	143,631	149,070	140,474	147,583
Administrative and waste services...................................	41,928	43,718	44,024	44,937	48,456	47,720	50,535
Educational services	42,466	43,658	44,855	46,228	49,656	51,080	52,438
Health care and social assistance...................................	45,178	45,858	46,586	47,473	48,117	48,508	49,679
Arts, entertainment, and recreation.................................	47,948	48,909	48,726	51,339	54,150	55,126	56,447
Accommodation and food services...................................	25,316	26,225	26,627	27,726	28,247	29,729	31,109
Other services, except public administration...................	33,610	34,793	35,738	36,408	37,993	39,222	41,018
Government and government enterprises................................	54,271	55,104	55,979	57,690	59,338	60,346	61,955

Table NY-10. Employment Characteristics by Family Type

(Number, percent.)

Family type and labor force status	2015		2016		2017	
	Total	Families with own children under 18 years	Total	Families with own children under 18 years	Total	Families with own children under 18 years
All Families..	4,561,118	1,918,562	4,541,583	1,876,874	4,620,008	1,885,913
FAMILY TYPE AND LABOR FORCE STATUS						
Married-Couple Families..	3,156,019	1,261,456	3,159,748	1,257,707	3,210,469	1,248,728
Both husband and wife in labor force..........................	51.9	65.5	51.5	65.6	51.7	65.9
Husband in labor force, wife not in labor force	21.3	27.4	21.4	27.5	20.9	27.2
Wife in labor force, husband not in labor force	8.7	4.7	8.6	4.5	8.6	4.5
Both husband and wife not in labor force....................	16.9	1.8	17.4	1.7	17.5	1.8
Other Families	1,405,099	657,106	1,381,835	619,167	1,409,539	637,185
Female householder, no husband present....................	74.4	77.1	73.6	77.4	73.5	77.2
In labor force..	50.4	61.2	49.4	61.4	49.7	62.0
Not in labor force	24.0	16.0	24.3	16.0	23.8	15.3
Male householder, no wife present.............................	25.6	22.9	26.4	22.6	26.5	22.8
In labor force..	19.6	20.2	19.9	19.9	20.4	20.4
Not in labor force	6.0	2.7	6.4	2.8	6.1	2.4

Table NY-11. School Enrollment and Educational Attainment, 2017

(Number, percent.)

Item	State	U.S.
Enrollment		
Total population 3 years and over, enrolled in school	4,794,761	81,273,337
Enrolled in nursery school or preschool (percent)..	6.2	6.0
Enrolled in kindergarten (percent)...	4.7	4.9
Enrolled in elementary school, grades 1-8 (percent)..	38.3	40.6
Enrolled in high school, grades 9-12 (percent)..	20.5	21.1
Enrolled in college or graduate school (percent)...	30.3	27.4
Attainment		
Total population 25 years and over	13,821,132	221,250,083
Less than ninth grade (percent)...	6.1	5.1
9th to 12th grade, no diploma (percent)...	7.3	6.9
High school graduate, including equivalency (percent)..	26.3	27.1
Some college, no degree (percent)	15.4	20.4
Associate's degree (percent)...	8.8	8.5
Bachelor's degree (percent)...	20.2	19.7
Graduate or professional degree (percent)...	15.8	12.3
High school graduate or higher (percent)..	86.6	88.0
Bachelor's degree or higher (percent)..	36.0	32.0

Table NY-12. Public School Characteristics and Educational Indicators

(Number, percent; data derived from National Center of Education Statistics.)

Item	State	U.S.
Public Elementary and Secondary Schools		
Number of operational school districts, 2016-17..	1,032	18,377
Number of operational schools, 2016-17..	4,798	98,330
Percent charter schools	5.6	7.1
Total public school enrollment, 2016-17...	2,729,776	50,587,859
Percent charter school enrollment	4.8	6.0
Student-teacher ratio, Fall 2015..	13.2	16.0
Expenditures per student (dollars), 2015-16...	22,231	11,841
Four-year adjusted cohort graduation rate (ACGR)[1]	81.8	84.6
Students eligible for free or reduced-price lunch (percent), 2015-16................................	49.5	52.1
English language learners (percent), Fall 2016	8.7	9.6
Students age 3 to 21 served under IDEA, part B (percent), 2017-18	19.2	13.7
Public Schools by Type, 2016-17		Percent of state public schools
Total number of schools..	4,798	100.0
Special education...	131	2.7
Vocational education...	21	0.4
Alternative education	56	1.2

[1] Adjusted Cohort Graduation Rates (ACGR) differ from Averaged Freshmen Graduation Rates (AFGR).

Table NY-13. Reported Voting and Registration of the Voting-Age Population, November 2018

(Numbers in thousands, percent.)

Item	Total population	Total citizen population	Registered			Voted		
			Total registered	Percent registered (total population)	Percent registered (total citizen population)	Total voted	Percent voted (total population)	Percent voted (total citizen population)
U.S. Total	249,748	228,832	153,066	61.3	66.9	122,281	49.0	53.4
State Total...	15,478	13,684	8,553	55.3	62.5	6,775	43.8	49.5
Sex								
Male	7,364	6,512	3,934	53.4	60.4	3,081	41.8	47.3
Female	8,113	7,171	4,619	56.9	64.4	3,694	45.5	51.5
Race								
White alone...	11,157	10,070	6,474	58.0	64.3	5,129	46.0	50.9
White, non-Hispanic alone	9,108	8,708	5,770	63.4	66.3	4,604	50.6	52.9
Black alone...	2,570	2,305	1,410	54.9	61.2	1,182	46.0	51.3
Asian alone...	1,443	1,061	504	34.9	47.5	344	23.8	32.4
Hispanic (of any race)	2,604	1,785	963	37.0	53.9	731	28.1	40.9
White alone or in combination	11,374	10,239	6,590	57.9	64.4	5,215	45.8	50.9
Black alone or in combination.......................	2,721	2,414	1,481	54.4	61.3	1,236	45.4	51.2
Asian alone or in combination......................	1,467	1,085	523	35.6	48.1	358	24.4	33.0
Age								
18 to 24 years...	1,762	1,518	734	41.7	48.4	505	28.6	33.3
25 to 34 years...	2,962	2,483	1,302	44.0	52.4	958	32.4	38.6
35 to 44 years...	2,421	2,005	1,301	53.8	64.9	1,005	41.5	50.1
45 to 64 years...	4,936	4,437	2,918	59.1	65.8	2,341	47.4	52.8
65 years and over	3,396	3,241	2,297	67.6	70.9	1,965	57.9	60.6

Table NY-14. Crime

(Number, rate per 100,000. Data are derived from the FBI Uniform Crime Reports.)

Item	State			U.S.		
	2016	2017	Percent change	2016	2017	Percent change
TOTAL POPULATION[1]	19,836,286	19,849,399	0.1	323,405,935	325,719,178	0.7
VIOLENT CRIME						
Number...	74,315	70,799	-4.7	1,285,606	1,283,220	-0.2
Rate	374.6	356.7	-4.8	397.5	394.0	-0.9
Murder and Nonnegligent Manslaughter						
Number...	629	548	-12.9	17,413	17,284	-0.7
Rate	3.2	2.8	-12.9	5.4	5.3	-1.4
Rape[2]						
Number...	6,281	6,324	0.7	132,414	135,755	2.5
Rate	31.7	31.9	0.6	40.9	41.7	1.8
Robbery						
Number...	22,310	20,108	-9.9	332,797	319,356	-4.0
Rate	112.5	101.3	-9.9	102.9	98.0	-4.7
Aggravated Assault						
Number...	45,095	43,819	-2.8	802,982	810,825	1.0
Rate	227.3	220.8	-2.9	248.3	248.9	0.3
PROPERTY CRIME						
Number...	305,224	300,555	-1.5	7,928,530	7,694,086	-3.0
Rate	1,538.7	1,514.2	-1.6	2,451.6	2,362.2	-3.6
Burglary						
Number...	39,850	35,002	-12.2	1,516,405	1,401,840	-7.6
Rate	200.9	176.3	-12.2	468.9	430.4	-8.2
Larceny-Theft						
Number...	250,990	252,143	0.5	5,644,835	5,519,107	-2.2
Rate	1,265.3	1,270.3	0.4	1,745.4	1,694.4	-2.9
Motor Vehicle Theft						
Number...	14,384	13,410	-6.8	767,290	773,139	0.8
Rate	72.5	67.6	-6.8	237.3	237.4	-

NOTE: Although arson data are included in the trend and clearance tables, sufficient data are not available to estimate totals for this offense. Therefore, no arson data are published in this table.
- = Zero or rounds to zero.
[1] Population figures are U.S. Census Bureau provisional estimates as of July 1, 2017.
[2] The figures shown in the rape (revised definition) column were estimated using the revised Uniform Crime Reporting (UCR) definition of rape.

Table NY-15. State Government Finances, 2017

(Dollar amounts in thousands, percent distribution.)

Item	Dollars	Percent distribution
Total Revenue	217,164,323	100.0
General revenue	164,594,240	75.8
Intergovernmental revenue	60,371,092	27.8
Taxes	79,678,037	36.7
General sales	14,132,141	6.5
Selective sales	11,230,442	5.2
License taxes	1,814,065	0.8
Individual income tax	44,631,769	20.6
Corporate income tax	4,026,353	1.9
Other taxes	3,843,267	1.8
Current charges	10,383,880	4.8
Miscellaneous general revenue	14,161,231	6.5
Utility revenue	7,716,669	3.6
Liquor stores revenue	0	-
Insurance trust revenue[1]	44,853,414	20.7
Total Expenditure	201,211,273	100.0
Intergovernmental expenditure	62,034,380	30.8
Direct expenditure	139,176,893	69.2
Current operation	99,198,791	49.3
Capital outlay	9,739,145	4.8
Insurance benefits and repayments	22,531,599	11.2
Assistance and subsidies	1,976,503	1.0
Interest on debt	5,730,855	2.8
Exhibit: Salaries and wages	18,431,443	9.2
Total Expenditure	201,211,273	100.0
General expenditure	165,472,212	82.2
Intergovernmental expenditure	62,034,380	30.8
Direct expenditure	103,437,832	51.4
General expenditure, by function:		
Education	45,766,742	22.7
Public welfare	67,311,394	33.5
Hospitals	5,325,753	2.6
Health	8,999,160	4.5
Highways	5,870,948	2.9
Police protection	1,017,705	0.5
Correction	3,403,266	1.7
Natural resources	543,360	0.3
Parks and recreation	755,001	0.4
Governmental administration	5,691,307	2.8
Interest on general debt	4,084,149	2.0
Other and unallocable	16,703,427	8.3
Utility expenditure	13,207,462	6.1
Liquor stores expenditure	0	-
Insurance trust expenditure	22,531,599	11.2
Debt at End of Fiscal Year	139,234,923	X
Cash and Security Holdings	392,826,808	X

X = Not applicable.
- = Zero or rounds to zero.
[1] Within insurance trust revenue, net earnings of state retirement systems is a calculated statistic (the item code in the data file is X08), and thus can be positive or negative. Net earnings is the sum of earnings on investments plus gains on investments minus losses on investments. The change made in 2002 for asset valuation from book to market value in accordance with Statement 34 of the Governmental Accounting Standards Board is reflected in the calculated statistics.

Table NY-16. State Government Tax Collections, 2018

(Dollars in thousands, percent.)

Item	Dollars	Percent distribution
Total Taxes	88,541,099	100.0
Property taxes	X	-
Sales and gross receipts	26,399,319	29.8
General sales and gross receipts	14,820,163	16.7
Selective sales and gross receipts	11,579,156	13.1
Alcoholic beverages	258,327	0.3
Amusements	2,848	-
Insurance premiums	1,623,191	1.8
Motor fuels	1,636,749	1.8
Pari-mutuels	21,310	-
Public utilities	877,490	1.0
Tobacco products	1,151,660	1.3
Other selective sales	6,007,581	6.8
Licenses	1,771,629	2.0
Alcoholic beverages	66,675	0.1
Amusements	X	-
Corporations in general	2,746	-
Hunting and fishing	41,964	0.0
Motor vehicle	1,411,790	1.6
Motor vehicle operators	93,205	0.1
Public utilities	28,196	-
Occupation and business, NEC	125,822	0.1
Other licenses	1,231	-
Income taxes	56,356,425	63.7
Individual income	52,738,515	59.6
Corporation net income	3,617,910	4.1
Other taxes	4,013,726	4.5
Death and gift	1,203,725	1.4
Documentary and stock transfer	1,269,623	1.4
Severance	X	-
Taxes, NEC	1,540,378	1.7

X = Not applicable.
- = Zero or rounds to zero.

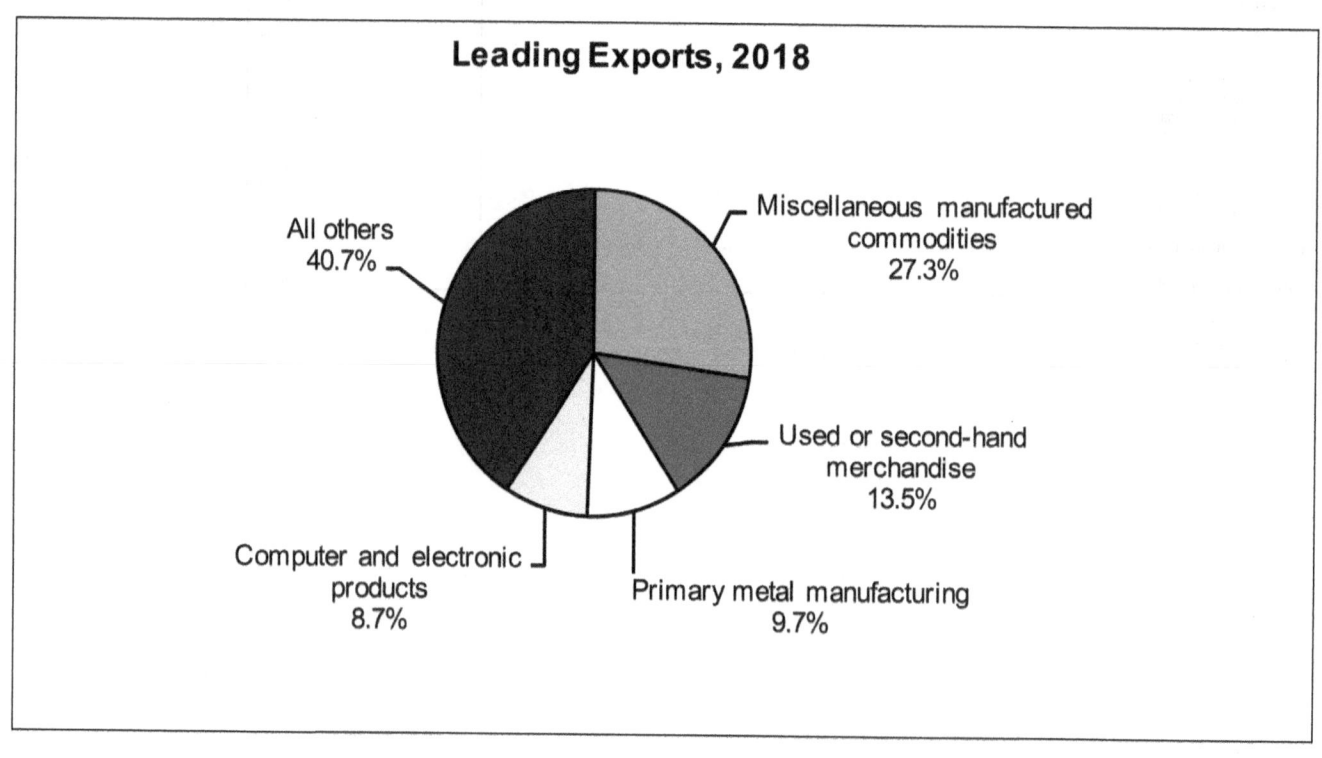

Leading Exports, 2018

All others 40.7%

Miscellaneous manufactured commodities 27.3%

Used or second-hand merchandise 13.5%

Computer and electronic products 8.7%

Primary metal manufacturing 9.7%

NORTH CAROLINA

Facts and Figures

Location: Southeastern United States; bordered on the N by Virginia, on the E by the Atlantic Ocean, on the S by South Carolina and Georgia, and on the W by Tennessee

Area: 53,819 sq. mi. (139,389 sq. km.); rank—28th

Population: 10,383,620 (2018 est.); rank—9th

Principal Cities: capital—Raleigh; largest—Charlotte

Statehood: November 21, 1789; 12th state

U.S. Congress: 2 senators, 13 representatives

State Motto: *Esse quam videri* ("To be rather than to seem")

State Song: "The Old North State"

State Nicknames: The Tar Heel State; The Old North State

Abbreviations: NC; N.C.

State Symbols: flower—flowering dogwood; tree—pine; bird—cardinal

At a Glance

- With an increase in population of 8.9 percent, North Carolina ranked 13th among the states in growth from 2010 to 2018.

- North Carolina's median household income of $52,752 ranked 39th among all states in 2017, and 14.7 percent of the population lived below the poverty level, a percent which ranked 14th.

- North Carolina's violent crime rate in 2017 was 363.7 per 100,000 population, compared to 394.0 for the entire nation.

- In 2017, 10.7 percent of North Carolinians did not have health insurance, compared to 8.7 percent of the entire U.S. population.

- North Carolina's unemployment rate of 3.9 percent ranked 22nd in the nation in 2018.

Table NC-1. Population by Age, Sex, Race, and Hispanic Origin

(Number, percent, except where noted.)

Sex, age, race, and Hispanic origin	2000	2010	2018 [1]	Percent change, 2010–2018
Total Population..	8,049,313	9,535,483	10,383,620	8.9
Percent of total U.S. population	2.9	3.1	3.2	X
Sex				
Male...	3,942,695	4,645,492	5,050,861	8.7
Female..	4,106,618	4,889,991	5,332,759	9.1
Age				
Under 5 years...	539,509	632,040	610,128	-3.5
5 to 19 years..	1,653,851	1,926,640	1,976,480	2.6
20 to 64 years..	4,886,905	5,742,724	6,107,747	6.4
65 years and over...	969,048	1,234,079	1,689,265	36.9
Median age (years)	35.3	37.4	38.9	4.0
Race and Hispanic Origin				
One race				
White..	5,804,656	6,898,296	7,334,411	6.3
Black..	1,737,545	2,088,362	2,306,797	10.5
American Indian and Alaska Native	99,551	147,566	163,078	10.5
Asian	113,689	215,952	329,284	52.5
Native Hawaiian or Other Pacific Islander	3,983	10,309	12,989	26.0
Two or more races	103,260	174,998	237,061	35.5
Hispanic (of any race)	378,963	830,172	997,349	20.1

X = Not applicable.
[1] Population figures for 2018 are July 1 estimates. The 2010 estimates are taken from the 2010 Census.

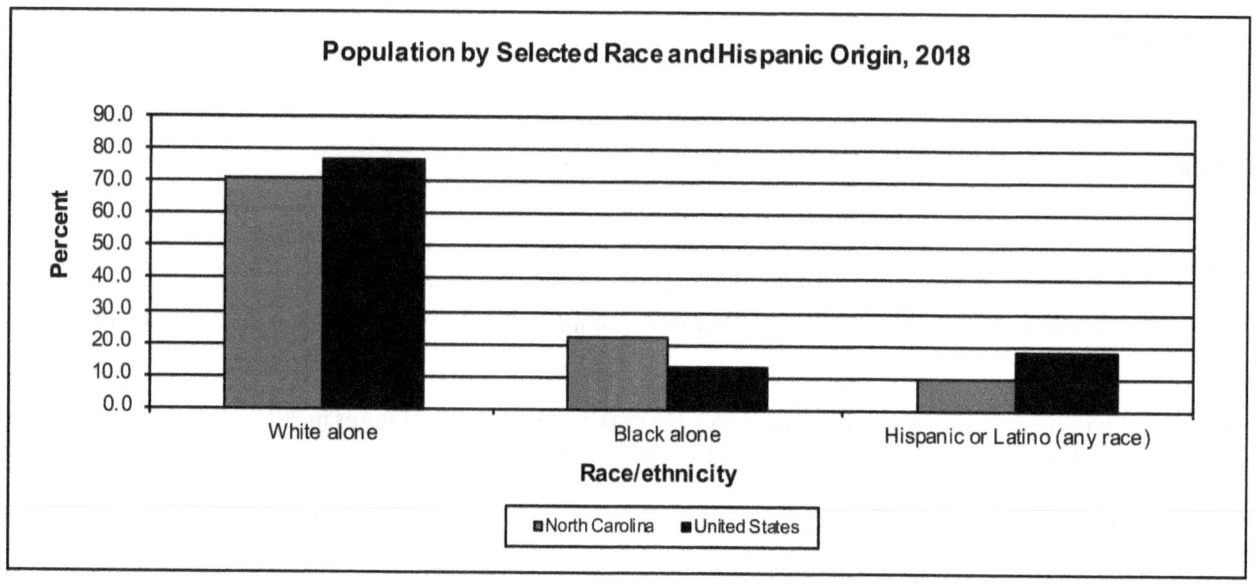

Table NC-2. Marital Status

(Number, percent distribution.)

Sex, age, race, and Hispanic origin	2000	2010	2017
Males, 15 Years and Over...	3,092,380	3,678,950	4,026,594
Never married	28.2	33.3	34.7
Now married, except separated..	58.7	51.8	50.8
Separated..	2.7	2.9	2.5
Widowed..	2.4	2.5	2.6
Divorced..	8.1	9.6	9.3
Females, 15 Years and Over...	3,301,327	3,975,748	4,350,545
Never married	22.0	27.3	29.1
Now married, except separated..	53.9	47.3	46.7
Separated..	3.3	3.5	2.9
Widowed..	10.9	9.8	9.0
Divorced..	9.9	12.1	12.4

Table NC-3. Households and Housing Characteristics

(Number, percent, dollars.)

Item	2000	2010	2017	Average annual percent change, 2010–2017
Total Households	3,132,012	3,670,859	3,955,069	1.1
Family households	2,158,869	2,441,916	2,590,180	0.9
Married-couple family	1,645,346	1,770,863	1,907,659	1.1
Other family	513,523	671,053	682,521	0.2
Male householder, no wife present	123,526	159,752	178,850	1.7
Female householder, no husband present	389,997	511,301	503,671	-0.2
Nonfamily households	973,144	1,228,943	1,364,889	1.6
Householder living alone	795,271	1,022,017	1,130,897	1.5
Householder not living alone	177,873	206,926	233,992	1.9
Housing Characteristics				
Total housing units	3,523,944	4,333,479	4,622,656	1.0
Occupied housing units	3,132,012	3,670,859	3,955,069	1.1
Owner occupied	2,172,355	2,465,551	2,586,616	0.7
Renter occupied	959,658	1,205,308	1,368,453	1.9
Average household size	2.49	2.53	2.53	-
Financial Characteristics				
Median gross rent of renter-occupied housing	548	731	861	2.5
Median monthly owner costs for housing units with a mortgage	985	1,250	1,242	-0.1
Median value of owner-occupied housing units	108,300	154,200	171,200	1.6

- = Zero or rounds to zero.

Table NC-4. Migration, Origin, and Language

(Number, percent.)

Characteristic	State			U.S.		
	2016	2017	Percent change	2016	2017	Percent change
Residence 1 Year Ago						
Population 1 year and over	10,032,407	10,158,556	1.3	319,361,956	321,994,428	0.8
Same house	84.3	85.1	X	85.4	85.7	X
Different house in the U.S.	15.2	14.3	X	13.9	13.6	X
Same county	8.0	7.7	X	8.3	8.1	X
Different county	7.1	6.6	X	5.6	5.6	X
Same state	3.8	3.5	X	3.2	3.3	X
Different state	3.3	3.1	X	2.4	2.3	X
Abroad	0.5	0.6	X	0.7	0.7	X
Place of Birth						
Native born	9,357,150	9,444,003	0.9	279,388,170	281,193,323	0.6
Male	48.4	48.6	X	49.3	49.4	X
Female	51.6	51.4	X	50.7	50.6	X
Foreign born	789,638	829,416	5.0	43,739,345	44,525,855	1.8
Male	50.6	49.2	X	48.5	48.4	X
Female	49.4	50.8	X	51.5	51.6	X
Foreign born; naturalized U.S. citizen	313,140	319,681	2.1	21,238,372	21,948,732	3.3
Male	47.5	45.3	X	45.9	45.9	X
Female	52.5	54.7	X	54.1	54.1	X
Foreign born; not a U.S. citizen	476,498	509,735	7.0	22,500,973	22,577,123	0.3
Male	52.7	51.7	X	51.0	50.8	X
Female	47.3	48.3	X	49.0	49.2	X
Entered 2010 or later	20.7	23.4	X	18.6	21.3	X
Entered 2000 to 2009	31.8	31.8	X	26.7	25.7	X
Entered before 2000	47.6	44.8	X	54.7	53.0	X
World Region of Birth, Foreign						
Foreign-born population, excluding population born at sea	789,638	829,416	5.0	43,738,901	44,525,458	1.8
Europe	10.1	10.8	X	10.9	10.8	X
Asia	27.9	27.6	X	30.8	31.2	X
Africa	6.8	7.5	X	4.9	5.1	X
Oceania	0.4	0.4	X	0.6	0.6	X
Latin America	52.5	51.0	X	51.0	50.4	X
North America	2.3	2.7	X	1.8	1.8	X
Language Spoken at Home and Ability to Speak English						
Population 5 years and over	9,552,195	9,672,238	1.3	303,328,961	305,924,019	0.9
English only	88.5	88.2	X	78.4	78.2	X
Language other than English	11.5	11.8	X	21.6	21.8	X
Speaks English less than "very well"	4.5	4.5	X	8.6	8.5	X

NA = Not available.
X = Not applicable.
- = Zero or rounds to zero.

Table NC-5. Median Income and Poverty Status, 2017

(Number, percent, except as noted.)

Characteristic	State		U.S.	
	Number	Percent	Number	Percent
Median Income				
Households (dollars)..	52,752	X	60,336	X
Families (dollars)	65,964	X	73,891	X
Below Poverty Level (All People)	1,471,339	14.7	42,583,651	13.4
Sex				
Male	643,900	13.3	19,004,547	12.2
Female	827,439	16.0	23,579,104	14.5
Age				
Under 18 years...	481,494	21.2	13,353,202	18.4
Related children under 18 years...	471,670	20.9	13,053,472	18.1
18 to 64 years..	845,190	13.7	24,648,677	12.6
65 years and over	144,655	9.1	4,581,772	9.3

X = Not applicable.

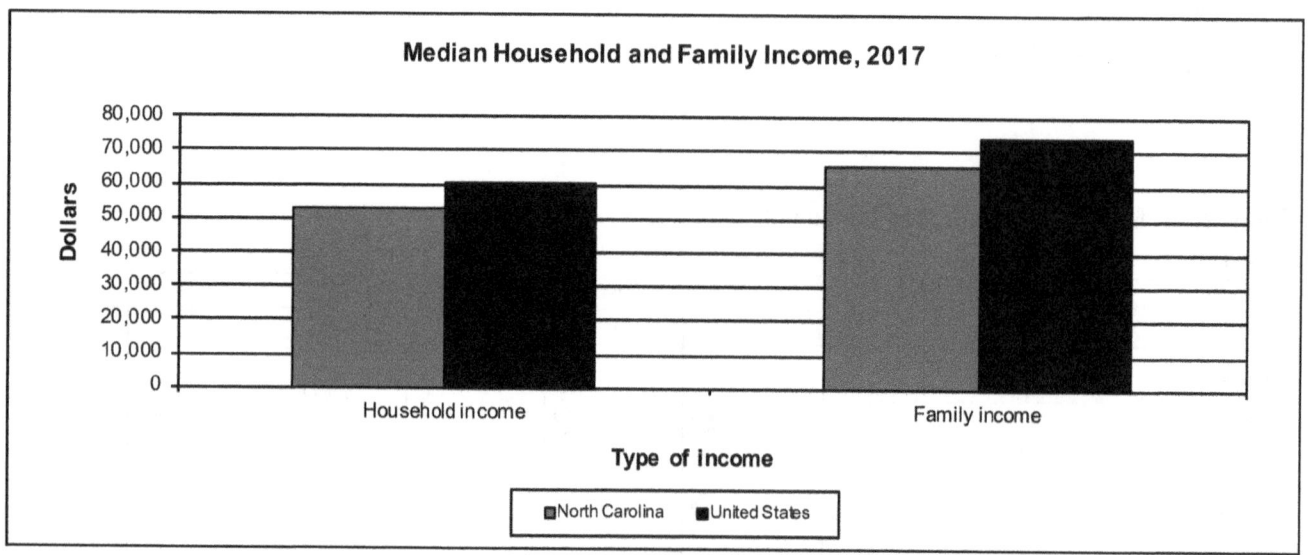

Median Household and Family Income, 2017

Table NC-6. Health Insurance Coverage Status for the Civilian Noninstitutionalized Population and Children Under 18 Years of Age

(Number, percent.)

Item	2009	2010	2011	2012	2013	2014	2015	2016	2017
Civilian Noninstitutionalized Population	9,149,289	9,360,661	9,461,018	9,552,529	9,645,320	9,752,148	9,855,612	9,957,830	10,070,781
Covered by Private or Public Insurance									
Number..	7,678,522	7,790,824	7,916,111	7,970,289	8,136,322	8,476,094	8,752,825	8,919,431	8,994,798
Percent..	83.9	83.2	83.7	83.4	84.4	86.9	88.8	89.6	89.3
Uninsured									
Number..	1,470,767	1,569,837	1,544,907	1,582,240	1,508,998	1,276,054	1,102,787	1,038,399	1,075,983
Percent..	16.1	16.8	16.3	16.6	15.6	13.1	11.2	10.4	10.7
Percent in the U.S. not covered..................	15.1	15.5	15.1	14.8	14.5	11.7	9.4	8.6	8.7
Children Under 18 Years of Age[1]	2,271,175	2,280,649	2,286,872	2,281,544	2,280,549	2,286,665	2,283,011	2,292,483	2,450,911
Covered by Private or Public Insurance									
Number..	2,085,273	2,103,949	2,112,300	2,108,583	2,136,355	2,167,587	2,183,693	2,190,251	2,332,345
Percent..	91.8	92.3	92.4	92.4	93.7	94.8	95.6	95.5	95.2
Uninsured									
Number..	185,902	176,700	174,572	172,961	144,194	119,078	99,318	102,232	118,566
Percent..	8.2	7.7	7.6	7.6	6.3	5.2	4.4	4.5	4.8
Percent in the U.S. not covered..................	8.6	8.0	7.5	7.2	7.1	6.0	4.8	4.5	5.0

[1] 2017 data is for individuals under 19 years of age.

Table NC-7. Employment Status by Demographic Group, 2018

(Numbers in thousands, percent.)

Characteristic	Civilian noninstitutional population	Civilian labor force		Employed		Unemployed	
		Number	Percent of population	Number	Percent of population	Number	Percent of population
Total..	8,144	4,991	61.3	4,801	59.0	190	3.8
Sex							
Male	3,857	2,582	66.9	2,491	64.6	91	3.5
Female	4,286	2,409	56.2	2,310	53.9	99	4.1
Race, Sex, and Hispanic Origin							
White	5,810	3,548	61.1	3,439	59.2	110	3.1
Male	2,821	1,909	67.7	1,856	65.8	53	2.8
Female	2,989	1,639	54.9	1,582	52.9	57	3.5
Black or African American...............	1,754	1,113	63.5	1,048	59.7	66	5.9
Male	786	512	65.1	480	61.1	32	6.2
Female	969	601	62.1	568	58.6	34	5.6
Hispanic or Latino ethnicity[1]	705	492	69.8	469	66.6	23	4.6
Male	353	301	85.1	293	83.0	8	2.5
Female	352	192	54.4	176	50.1	15	8.0
Age							
16 to 19 years.............................	462	149	32.2	121	26.3	27	18.4
20 to 24 years.............................	739	502	68.0	474	64.2	28	5.6
25 to 34 years.............................	1,421	1,142	80.4	1,098	77.3	44	3.8
35 to 44 years.............................	1,171	980	83.7	949	81.1	31	3.1
45 to 54 years.............................	1,382	1,102	79.7	1,068	77.3	34	3.1
55 to 64 years.............................	1,361	839	61.6	823	60.5	16	1.9
65 years and over	1,609	277	17.2	268	16.6	10	3.5

NOTE: Data in Table 7 are from the Current Population Survey (CPS) and do not match the estimates in Table 8. See notes and definitions for further information.
[1] May be of any race.

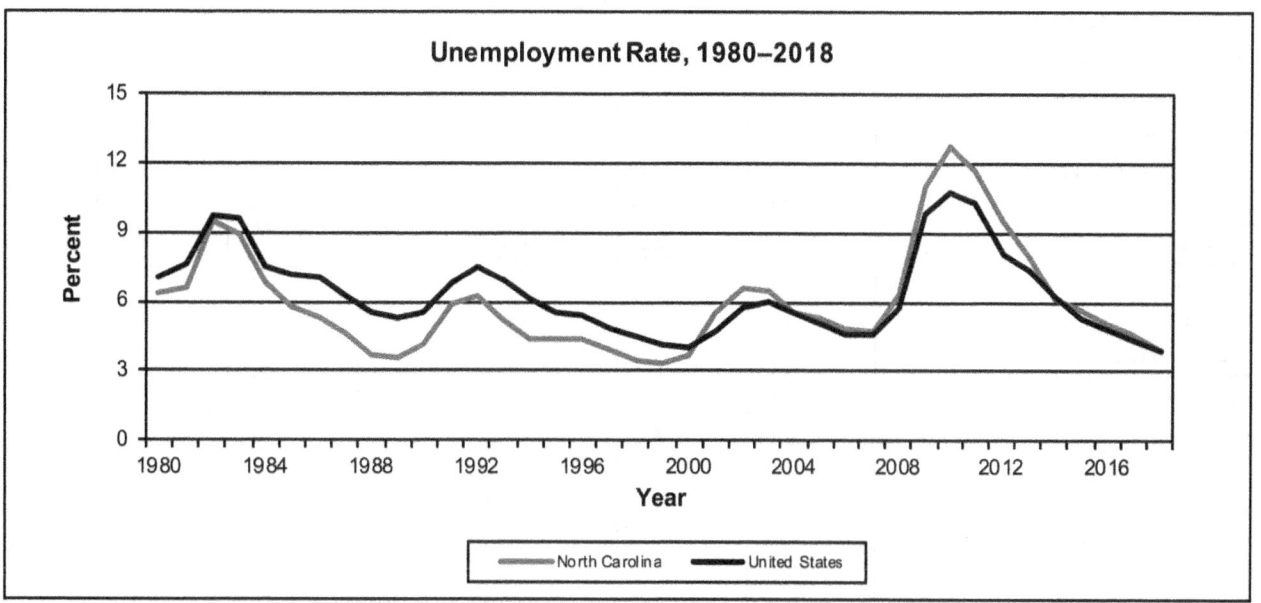

Table NC-8. Employment Status of the Civilian Noninstitutional Population Age 16 Years and Over

(Number, percent.)

Year	Civilian labor force	Civilian participation rate	Employed	Unemployed	Unemployment rate
2010..	4,616,691	63.3	4,115,629	501,062	10.9
2011..	4,633,072	62.4	4,157,543	475,529	10.3
2012..	4,680,057	62.3	4,245,675	434,382	9.3
2013..	4,692,940	61.8	4,318,114	374,826	8.0
2014..	4,699,058	61.1	4,402,450	296,608	6.3
2015..	4,768,806	61.2	4,495,190	273,616	5.7
2016..	4,854,828	61.4	4,608,229	246,599	5.1
2017..	4,941,701	61.5	4,716,832	224,869	4.6
2018..	4,981,834	61.2	4,787,320	194,514	3.9

Table NC-9. Employment and Average Wages by Industry

(Estimates are based on the 2012 *North American Industry Classification System* [NAICS].)

Industry	2011	2012	2013	2014	2015	2016	2017
	Number of jobs						
Wage and Salary Employment by Industry	4,175,842	4,241,784	4,298,323	4,380,948	4,494,854	4,588,883	4,657,504
Farm Wage and Salary Employment	22,796	20,095	22,628	24,334	27,259	27,288	24,799
Nonfarm Wage and Salary Employment	4,153,046	4,221,689	4,275,695	4,356,614	4,467,595	4,561,595	4,632,705
Private wage and salary employment	3,290,115	3,360,302	3,416,337	3,504,358	3,615,821	3,706,737	3,772,330
Forestry, fishing, and related activities	13,865	13,977	14,418	14,797	15,007	14,982	14,941
Mining	3,040	3,004	2,935	2,812	2,769	2,759	2,927
Utilities	12,304	12,273	12,460	13,645	14,045	13,947	13,908
Construction	177,546	176,511	178,220	183,470	194,223	205,634	213,525
Manufacturing	436,293	440,531	443,466	450,002	461,737	464,990	468,299
Durable goods manufacturing	226,859	234,469	236,315	240,409	248,749	251,268	253,040
Nondurable goods manufacturing	209,434	206,062	207,151	209,593	212,988	213,722	215,259
Wholesale trade	168,440	172,207	174,576	177,372	179,489	183,563	185,843
Retail trade	444,740	454,634	463,568	474,567	487,154	498,286	501,478
Transportation and warehousing	107,547	109,882	111,380	115,817	121,641	124,544	131,328
Information	68,830	69,257	69,843	72,592	76,099	78,813	78,879
Finance and insurance	153,947	155,030	156,921	161,047	166,284	171,484	177,742
Real estate and rental and leasing	48,407	49,182	51,121	53,022	55,797	57,884	59,438
Professional, scientific, and technical services	190,056	196,889	201,402	209,216	220,955	230,394	240,886
Management of companies and enterprises	76,800	80,596	77,928	80,496	81,975	83,966	82,884
Administrative and waste services	250,129	261,188	272,584	284,228	290,402	295,206	295,877
Educational services	95,829	97,996	92,330	94,565	106,701	108,158	108,113
Health care and social assistance	455,832	462,612	472,305	476,081	483,927	493,711	504,272
Arts, entertainment, and recreation	57,204	58,821	60,800	63,327	63,774	69,711	71,940
Accommodation and food services	344,742	358,990	372,376	383,833	398,078	413,711	424,934
Other services, except public administration	184,564	186,722	187,704	193,469	195,764	194,994	195,116
Government and government enterprises	862,931	861,387	859,358	852,256	851,774	854,858	860,375
	Dollars						
Average Wages and Salaries by Industry	43,097	44,107	44,731	45,865	47,351	48,252	49,867
Average Farm Wages and Salaries	19,665	27,796	25,355	22,765	20,045	24,658	27,103
Average Nonfarm Wages and Salaries	43,226	44,184	44,833	45,994	47,518	48,393	49,989
Average private wages and salaries	42,928	44,071	44,799	46,075	47,572	48,405	50,176
Forestry, fishing, and related activities	27,682	28,893	30,256	31,408	32,608	34,004	34,706
Mining	46,909	47,012	48,175	50,326	56,308	60,957	65,152
Utilities	82,979	86,360	93,365	91,011	91,068	96,026	96,315
Construction	42,257	43,793	44,768	46,445	48,536	50,959	53,273
Manufacturing	54,278	54,657	56,286	57,017	58,344	58,478	60,219
Durable goods manufacturing	58,253	59,147	61,197	61,058	62,228	62,627	64,650
Nondurable goods manufacturing	49,973	49,548	50,685	52,383	53,808	53,600	55,011
Wholesale trade	62,867	64,511	65,968	68,455	70,456	70,933	74,187
Retail trade	25,679	26,269	26,866	27,342	27,921	28,399	28,954
Transportation and warehousing	43,873	44,297	45,604	47,291	48,211	48,331	49,747
Information	66,047	69,320	72,322	76,075	78,498	80,443	82,712
Finance and insurance	77,144	79,393	82,818	86,739	90,658	91,746	96,770
Real estate and rental and leasing	39,810	42,611	43,613	45,190	47,057	48,371	49,963
Professional, scientific, and technical services	68,443	71,291	71,333	73,882	76,181	78,250	80,836
Management of companies and enterprises	92,044	95,079	97,339	102,849	108,409	106,492	111,064
Administrative and waste services	31,601	33,258	32,736	33,621	34,362	35,691	37,419
Educational services	38,025	38,337	37,250	38,039	41,100	41,409	40,792
Health care and social assistance	41,623	42,651	43,303	44,129	45,329	46,263	48,072
Arts, entertainment, and recreation	31,257	31,783	31,959	33,031	34,239	33,160	33,543
Accommodation and food services	16,856	17,444	17,630	18,068	18,565	19,138	19,828
Other services, except public administration	28,355	29,716	30,726	31,167	32,386	33,945	35,277
Government and government enterprises	44,359	44,627	44,968	45,657	47,291	48,341	49,167

Table NC-10. Employment Characteristics by Family Type

(Number, percent.)

Family type and labor force status	2015		2016		2017	
	Total	Families with own children under 18 years	Total	Families with own children under 18 years	Total	Families with own children under 18 years
All Families..	2,506,215	1,056,067	2,542,663	1,071,946	2,590,180	1,069,914
FAMILY TYPE AND LABOR FORCE STATUS						
Married-Couple Families................................	1,829,450	698,000	1,864,455	704,965	1,907,659	709,555
Both husband and wife in labor force..........................	49.4	64.4	49.2	65.4	49.8	66.2
Husband in labor force, wife not in labor force...............	22.7	29.4	22.0	28.2	21.2	27.4
Wife in labor force, husband not in labor force...............	8.1	4.2	8.6	4.4	8.5	4.2
Both husband and wife not in labor force.....................	19.2	1.7	19.5	1.6	19.6	1.8
Other Families	676,765	358,067	678,208	366,981	682,521	360,359
Female householder, no husband present...................	75.0	76.3	75.1	77.3	73.8	75.0
In labor force..	51.5	63.5	52.4	64.9	51.0	62.4
Not in labor force...	23.4	12.8	22.7	12.4	22.8	12.6
Male householder, no wife present...........................	25.0	23.7	24.9	22.7	26.2	25.0
In labor force..	18.8	21.5	18.8	20.7	19.5	22.6
Not in labor force...	6.2	2.2	6.1	2.1	6.7	2.5

Table NC-11. School Enrollment and Educational Attainment, 2017

(Number, percent.)

Item	State	U.S.
Enrollment		
Total population 3 years and over, enrolled in school	2,521,781	81,273,337
Enrolled in nursery school or preschool (percent)	5.2	6.0
Enrolled in kindergarten (percent)	4.9	4.9
Enrolled in elementary school, grades 1-8 (percent)...........................	40.9	40.6
Enrolled in high school, grades 9-12 (percent)	22.0	21.1
Enrolled in college or graduate school (percent)...........................	26.9	27.4
Attainment		
Total population 25 years and over...........................	6,991,185	221,250,083
Less than ninth grade (percent)	4.5	5.1
9th to 12th grade, no diploma (percent)	7.7	6.9
High school graduate, including equivalency (percent)...........................	25.8	27.1
Some college, no degree (percent)	21.3	20.4
Associate's degree (percent)...........................	9.4	8.5
Bachelor's degree (percent)	20.1	19.7
Graduate or professional degree (percent)...........................	11.2	12.3
High school graduate or higher (percent)	87.8	88.0
Bachelor's degree or higher (percent)	31.3	32.0

Table NC-12. Public School Characteristics and Educational Indicators

(Number, percent; data derived from National Center of Education Statistics.)

Item	State	U.S.
Public Elementary and Secondary Schools		
Number of operational school districts, 2016-17..........................	306	18,377
Number of operational schools, 2016-17..........................	2,624	98,330
Percent charter schools	6.4	7.1
Total public school enrollment, 2016-17..........................	1,550,062	50,587,859
Percent charter school enrollment	6.0	6.0
Student-teacher ratio, Fall 2015..........................	15.5	16.0
Expenditures per student (dollars), 2015-16..........................	8,717	11,841
Four-year adjusted cohort graduation rate (ACGR)[1]..........................	86.6	84.6
Students eligible for free or reduced-price lunch (percent), 2015-16..........................	57.4	52.1
English language learners (percent), Fall 2016..........................	6.0	9.6
Students age 3 to 21 served under IDEA, part B (percent), 2017-18	12.9	13.7
Public Schools by Type, 2016-17		Percent of state public schools
Total number of schools..........................	2,624	100.0
Special education	25	1.0
Vocational education	8	0.3
Alternative education	73	2.8

[1] Adjusted Cohort Graduation Rates (ACGR) differ from Averaged Freshmen Graduation Rates (AFGR).

Table NC-13. Reported Voting and Registration of the Voting-Age Population, November 2018

(Numbers in thousands, percent.)

Item	Total population	Total citizen population	Registered			Voted		
			Total registered	Percent registered (total population)	Percent registered (total citizen population)	Total voted	Percent voted (total population)	Percent voted (total citizen population)
U.S. Total	249,748	228,832	153,066	61.3	66.9	122,281	49.0	53.4
State Total...	7,911	7,444	5,160	65.2	69.3	3,899	49.3	52.4
Sex								
Male	3,748	3,495	2,384	63.6	68.2	1,822	48.6	52.1
Female	4,163	3,949	2,776	66.7	70.3	2,077	49.9	52.6
Race								
White alone...	5,775	5,400	3,830	66.3	70.9	2,903	50.3	53.8
White, non-Hispanic alone......................	5,239	5,170	3,721	71.0	72.0	2,814	53.7	54.4
Black alone...	1,685	1,646	1,110	65.9	67.4	852	50.6	51.8
Asian alone...	186	149	90	48.5	60.6	68	36.4	45.5
Hispanic (of any race).............................	588	268	131	22.3	48.9	104	17.6	38.6
White alone or in combination	5,865	5,474	3,889	66.3	71.0	2,939	50.1	53.7
Black alone or in combination..................	1,748	1,696	1,156	66.1	68.2	872	49.9	51.4
Asian alone or in combination.................	198	159	95	48.0	60.0	73	36.6	45.8
Age								
18 to 24 years...	1,002	955	468	46.7	49.0	302	30.1	31.6
25 to 34 years...	1,329	1,169	769	57.8	65.7	447	33.6	38.2
35 to 44 years...	1,200	1,071	710	59.1	66.2	526	43.9	49.1
45 to 64 years...	2,742	2,630	1,905	69.5	72.4	1,555	56.7	59.1
65 years and over....................................	1,639	1,618	1,309	79.9	80.9	1,069	65.2	66.1

Table NC-14. Crime

(Number, rate per 100,000. Data are derived from the FBI Uniform Crime Reports.)

Item	State			U.S.		
	2016	2017	Percent change	2016	2017	Percent change
TOTAL POPULATION[1]	10,156,689	10,273,419	1.1	323,405,935	325,719,178	0.7
VIOLENT CRIME						
Number..	37,767	37,364	-1.1	1,285,606	1,283,220	-0.2
Rate	371.8	363.7	-2.2	397.5	394.0	-0.9
Murder and Nonnegligent Manslaughter						
Number..	678	591	-12.8	17,413	17,284	-0.7
Rate	6.7	5.8	-13.8	5.4	5.3	-1.4
Rape[2]						
Number..	2,847	2,715	-4.6	132,414	135,755	2.5
Rate	28.0	26.4	-5.7	40.9	41.7	1.8
Robbery						
Number..	9,336	9,350	0.1	332,797	319,356	-4.0
Rate	91.9	91.0		102.9	98.0	-4.7
Aggravated Assault						
Number..	24,906	24,708	-0.8	802,982	810,825	1.0
Rate	245.2	240.5	-1.9	248.3	248.9	0.3
PROPERTY CRIME						
Number..	277,765	261,486	-5.9	7,928,530	7,694,086	-3.0
Rate	2,734.8	2,545.3	-6.9	2,451.6	2,362.2	-3.6
Burglary						
Number..	72,082	64,786	-10.1	1,516,405	1,401,840	-7.6
Rate	709.7	630.6	-11.1	468.9	430.4	-8.2
Larceny-Theft						
Number..	190,377	180,902	-5.0	5,644,835	5,519,107	-2.2
Rate	1,874.4	1,760.9	-6.1	1,745.4	1,694.4	-2.9
Motor Vehicle Theft						
Number..	15,306	15,798	3.2	767,290	773,139	0.8
Rate	150.7	153.8	2.0	237.3	237.4	-

NOTE: Although arson data are included in the trend and clearance tables, sufficient data are not available to estimate totals for this offense. Therefore, no arson data are published in this table.
- = Zero or rounds to zero.
[1] Population figures are U.S. Census Bureau provisional estimates as of July 1, 2017.
[2] This state's agencies submitted rape data according to the legacy UCR definition of rape. Use caution when comparing this data to data from states using the revised UCR definition of rape.

Table NC-15. State Government Finances, 2017

(Dollar amounts in thousands, percent distribution.)

Item	Dollars	Percent distribution
Total Revenue	67,493,557	100.0
General revenue	53,199,169	78.8
Intergovernmental revenue	16,412,180	24.3
Taxes	26,855,304	39.8
General sales	7,656,898	11.3
Selective sales	4,042,138	6.0
License taxes	2,235,904	3.3
Individual income tax	12,086,332	17.9
Corporate income tax	757,041	1.1
Other taxes	76,991	0.1
Current charges	6,137,671	9.1
Miscellaneous general revenue	3,794,014	5.6
Utility revenue	4	-
Liquor stores revenue	0	-
Insurance trust revenue[1]	14,294,384	21.2
Total Expenditure	55,570,958	100.0
Intergovernmental expenditure	13,438,382	24.2
Direct expenditure	42,132,576	75.8
Current operation	29,945,538	53.9
Capital outlay	4,170,790	7.5
Insurance benefits and repayments	6,164,825	11.1
Assistance and subsidies	1,268,690	2.3
Interest on debt	582,733	1.0
Exhibit: Salaries and wages	8,181,078	14.7
Total Expenditure	55,570,958	100.0
General expenditure	49,253,887	88.6
Intergovernmental expenditure	13,438,382	24.2
Direct expenditure	35,815,505	64.5
General expenditure, by function:		
Education	21,223,986	38.2
Public welfare	13,031,451	23.5
Hospitals	2,179,337	3.9
Health	1,265,088	2.3
Highways	4,490,147	8.1
Police protection	738,513	1.3
Correction	1,343,093	2.4
Natural resources	529,106	1.0
Parks and recreation	213,638	0.4
Governmental administration	1,636,775	2.9
Interest on general debt	582,733	1.0
Other and unallocable	2,020,020	3.6
Utility expenditure	152,246	0.2
Liquor stores expenditure	0	-
Insurance trust expenditure	6,164,825	11.1
Debt at End of Fiscal Year	16,310,177	X
Cash and Security Holdings	122,119,403	X

X = Not applicable.
- = Zero or rounds to zero.
[1] Within insurance trust revenue, net earnings of state retirement systems is a calculated statistic (the item code in the data file is X08), and thus can be positive or negative. Net earnings is the sum of earnings on investments plus gains on investments minus losses on investments. The change made in 2002 for asset valuation from book to market value in accordance with Statement 34 of the Governmental Accounting Standards Board is reflected in the calculated statistics.

Table NC-16. State Government Tax Collections, 2018

(Dollars in thousands, percent.)

Item	Dollars	Percent distribution
Total Taxes	27,855,070	100.0
Property taxes	X	-
Sales and gross receipts	12,212,671	43.8
General sales and gross receipts	8,009,850	28.8
Selective sales and gross receipts	4,202,821	15.1
Alcoholic beverages	411,971	1.5
Amusements	76	-
Insurance premiums	589,037	2.1
Motor fuels	1,974,782	7.1
Pari-mutuels	X	-
Public utilities	322	-
Tobacco products	292,143	1.0
Other selective sales	934,490	3.4
Licenses	2,197,408	7.9
Alcoholic beverages	26,757	0.1
Amusements	197	-
Corporations in general	757,429	2.7
Hunting and fishing	33,167	0.1
Motor vehicle	853,879	3.1
Motor vehicle operators	121,032	0.4
Public utilities	19,160	0.1
Occupation and business, NEC	349,981	1.3
Other licenses	35,806	0.1
Income taxes	13,352,120	47.9
Individual income	12,609,608	45.3
Corporation net income	742,512	2.7
Other taxes	92,871	0.3
Death and gift	10,735	-
Documentary and stock transfer	80,223	0.3
Severance	1,913	-
Taxes, NEC	0	-

X = Not applicable.
- = Zero or rounds to zero.

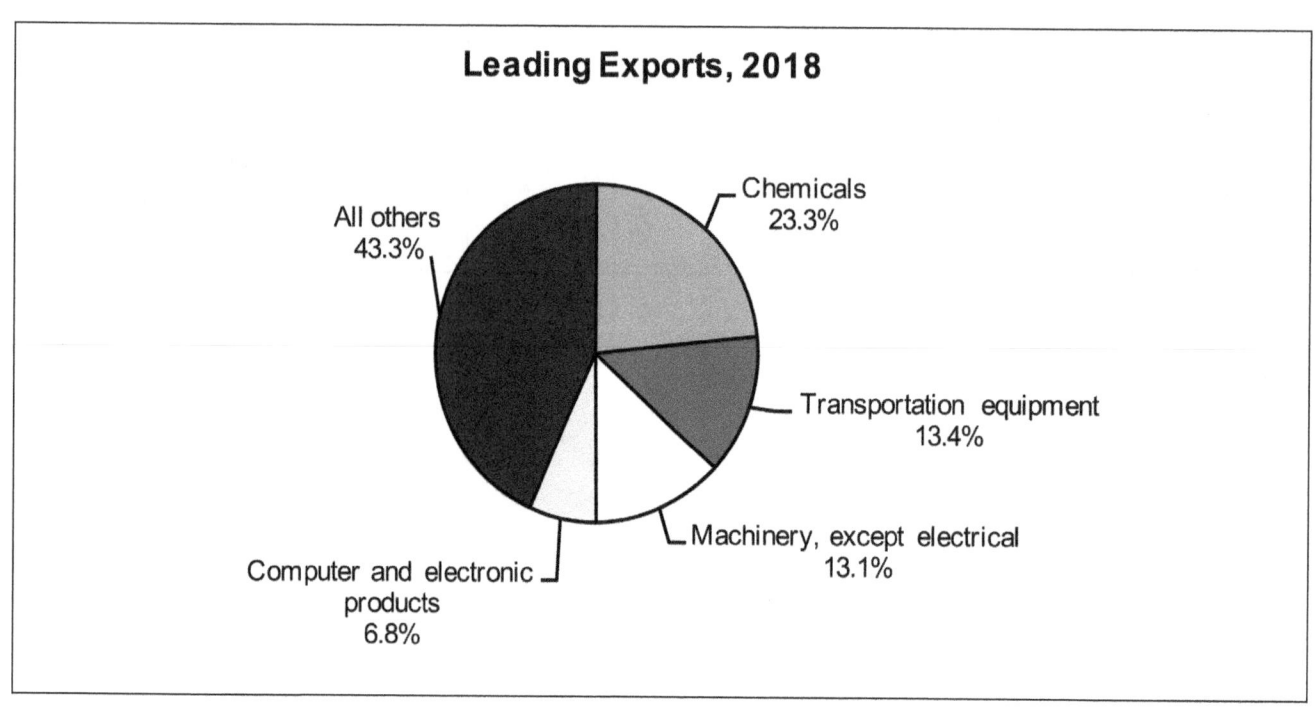

Leading Exports, 2018

Chemicals 23.3%
Transportation equipment 13.4%
Machinery, except electrical 13.1%
Computer and electronic products 6.8%
All others 43.3%

NORTH DAKOTA

Facts and Figures

Location: North central United States; bordered on the N by Canada (Manitoba and Saskatchewan), on the E by Minnesota, on the S by South Dakota, and on the W by Montana

Area: 70,700 sq. mi. (183,112 sq. km.); rank—19th

Population: 760,077 (2018 est.); rank—47th

Principal Cities: capital—Bismarck; largest—Fargo

Statehood: November 2, 1889; 39th state

U.S. Congress: 2 senators, 1 representative

State Motto: Liberty and Union, Now and Forever, One and Inseparable

State Song: "North Dakota Hymn"

State Nicknames: The Peace Garden State; The Flickertail State; The Rough Rider State

Abbreviations: ND; N.D.; N. Dak.

State Symbols: flower—wild prairie rose; tree—American elm; bird—Western meadowlark

At a Glance

- With an increase in population of 13.0 percent, North Dakota ranked 6th for population growth between 2010 and 2018.

- In 2017, 7.5 percent of North Dakotans did not have health insurance, compared to 8.7 percent of the total U.S. population.

- North Dakota had the 2nd highest birth rate in the country in 2017 (14.2 births per 1,000 population).

- In 2018, 2.6 percent of North Dakotans were unemployed, which was the 4th lowest unemployment rate in the country.

- North Dakota had the 3rd lowest childhood poverty rate in 2017, with 10.9 percent of children under 18 years old living in poverty. The national average was 18.4 percent.

Table ND-1. Population by Age, Sex, Race, and Hispanic Origin

(Number, percent, except where noted.)

Sex, age, race, and Hispanic origin	2000	2010	2018 [1]	Percent change, 2010–2018
Total Population..	642,200	672,591	760,077	13.0
Percent of total U.S. population	0.2	0.2	0.2	X
Sex				
Male..	320,524	339,864	389,350	14.6
Female...	321,676	332,727	370,727	11.4
Age				
Under 5 years..	39,400	44,595	54,695	22.6
5 to 19 years...	144,064	127,340	145,136	14.0
20 to 64 years...	364,258	403,179	443,609	10.0
65 years and over...	94,478	97,477	116,637	19.7
Median age (years)...	36.2	37.0	35.2	-4.9
Race and Hispanic Origin				
One race				
White	593,181	609,136	661,549	8.6
Black..	3,916	8,248	25,620	210.6
American Indian and Alaska Native	31,329	36,948	41,962	13.6
Asian..	3,606	7,032	13,426	90.9
Native Hawaiian or Other Pacific Islander	230	334	573	71.6
Two or more races..	7,398	10,893	16,947	55.6
Hispanic (of any race)...	7,786	14,407	29,529	105.0

X = Not applicable.
[1] Population figures for 2018 are July 1 estimates. The 2010 estimates are taken from the 2010 Census.

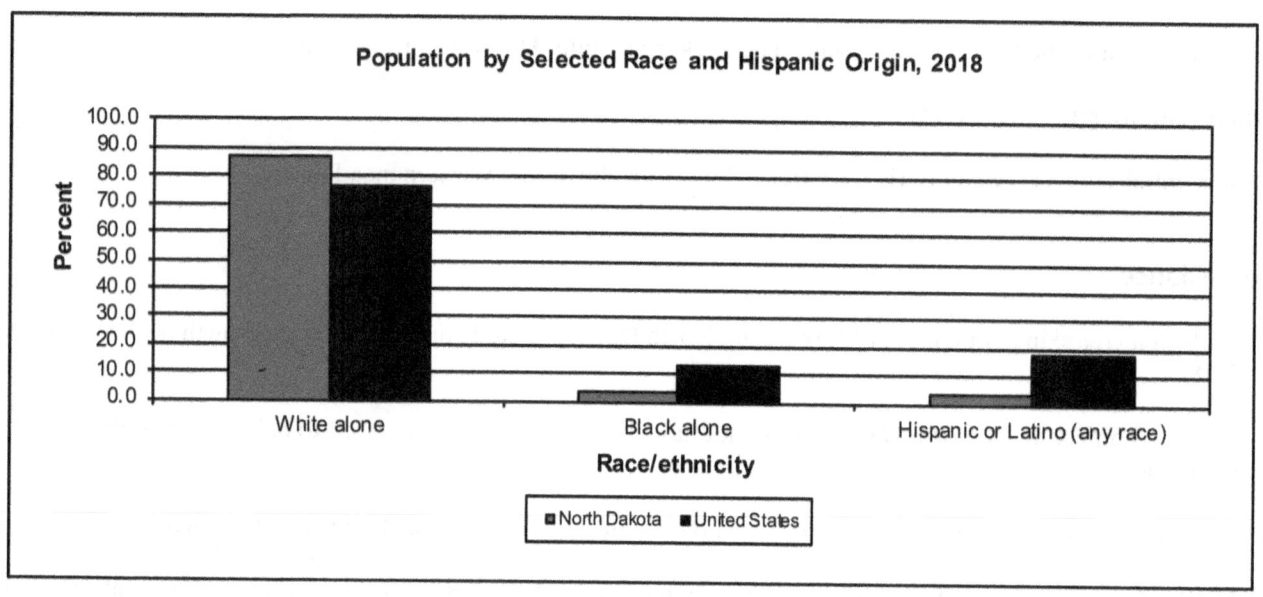

Table ND-2. Marital Status

(Number, percent distribution.)

Sex, age, race, and Hispanic origin	2000	2010	2017
Males, 15 Years and Over	253,900	278,276	311,799
Never married	32.0	35.8	37.0
Now married, except separated...	57.5	53.1	51.3
Separated...	0.6	0.6	0.7
Widowed..	2.5	2.1	2.2
Divorced..	7.3	8.4	8.8
Females, 15 Years and Over	258,381	271,462	294,917
Never married	23.2	26.6	27.0
Now married, except separated...	56.0	52.5	53.2
Separated...	0.8	0.7	0.7
Widowed..	11.7	10.1	9.4
Divorced..	8.2	10.2	9.8

Table ND-3. Households and Housing Characteristics

(Number, percent, dollars.)

Item	2000	2010	2017	Average annual percent change, 2010–2017
Total Households..	257,252	280,412	316,306	1.8
Family households	166,150	171,945	190,217	1.5
Married-couple family	137,433	140,277	152,814	1.3
Other family	28,717	31,668	37,403	2.6
Male householder, no wife present........................	8,569	8,846	13,915	8.2
Female householder, no husband present...............	20,148	22,822	23,488	0.4
Nonfamily households	91,002	108,467	126,089	2.3
Householder living alone	75,420	87,883	100,163	2.0
Householder not living alone	15,582	20,584	25,926	3.7
Housing Characteristics				
Total housing units	289,677	318,099	374,591	2.5
Occupied housing units	257,252	280,412	316,306	1.8
Owner occupied	171,299	187,673	200,554	1.0
Renter occupied	85,853	92,739	115,752	3.5
Average household size..	2.41	2.32	2.31	-0.1
Financial Characteristics				
Median gross rent of renter-occupied housing	412	583	785	4.9
Median monthly owner costs for housing units with a mortgage	818	1,133	1,356	2.8
Median value of owner-occupied housing units	74,400	123,000	194,700	8.3

- = Zero or rounds to zero.

Table ND-4. Migration, Origin, and Language

(Number, percent.)

Characteristic	State			U.S.		
	2016	2017	Percent change	2016	2017	Percent change
Residence 1 Year Ago						
Population 1 year and over	746,271	744,641	-0.2	319,361,956	321,994,428	0.8
Same house	83.2	81.8	X	85.4	85.7	X
Different house in the U.S.	16.2	17.4	X	13.9	13.6	X
Same county	9.0	8.6	X	8.3	8.1	X
Different county	7.2	8.9	X	5.6	5.6	X
Same state	3.2	3.9	X	3.2	3.3	X
Different state	4.0	5.0	X	2.4	2.3	X
Abroad	0.6	0.8	X	0.7	0.7	X
Place of Birth						
Native born	733,365	724,331	-1.2	279,388,170	281,193,323	0.6
Male	51.5	51.3	X	49.3	49.4	X
Female	48.5	48.7	X	50.7	50.6	X
Foreign born	24,588	31,062	26.3	43,739,345	44,525,855	1.8
Male	50.8	52.9	X	48.5	48.4	X
Female	49.2	47.1	X	51.5	51.6	X
Foreign born; naturalized U.S. citizen................	10,079	11,988	18.9	21,238,372	21,948,732	3.3
Male	45.6	60.0	X	45.9	45.9	X
Female	54.4	40.0	X	54.1	54.1	X
Foreign born; not a U.S. citizen........................	14,509	19,074	31.5	22,500,973	22,577,123	0.3
Male	54.3	48.5	X	51.0	50.8	X
Female	45.7	51.5	X	49.0	49.2	X
Entered 2010 or later	38.8	37.8	X	18.6	21.3	X
Entered 2000 to 2009	30.0	35.7	X	26.7	25.7	X
Entered before 2000..	31.2	26.5	X	54.7	53.0	X
World Region of Birth, Foreign						
Foreign-born population, excluding population born at sea	24,588	31,062	26.3	43,738,901	44,525,458	1.8
Europe	13.3	9.6	X	10.9	10.8	X
Asia..	35.8	32.1	X	30.8	31.2	X
Africa	21.5	26.7	X	4.9	5.1	X
Oceania	0.5	0.4	X	0.6	0.6	X
Latin America..	21.4	21.2	X	51.0	50.4	X
North America	7.5	10.0	X	1.8	1.8	X
Language Spoken at Home and Ability to Speak English						
Population 5 years and over................................	703,055	702,591	-0.1	303,328,961	305,924,019	0.9
English only	94.8	94.1	X	78.4	78.2	X
Language other than English..............................	5.2	5.9	X	21.6	21.8	X
Speaks English less than "very well"................	1.8	1.3	X	8.6	8.5	X

NA = Not available.
X = Not applicable.
- = Zero or rounds to zero.

Table ND-5. Median Income and Poverty Status, 2017

(Number, percent, except as noted.)

Characteristic	State		U.S.	
	Number	Percent	Number	Percent
Median Income				
Households (dollars)...	61,843	X	60,336	X
Families (dollars)	81,869	X	73,891	X
Below Poverty Level (All People)	75,279	10.3	42,583,651	13.4
Sex				
Male	33,158	8.9	19,004,547	12.2
Female	42,121	11.9	23,579,104	14.5
Age				
Under 18 years...	18,519	10.9	13,353,202	18.4
Related children under 18 years...	18,141	10.7	13,053,472	18.1
18 to 64 years..	46,245	10.2	24,648,677	12.6
65 years and over	10,515	9.9	4,581,772	9.3

X = Not applicable.

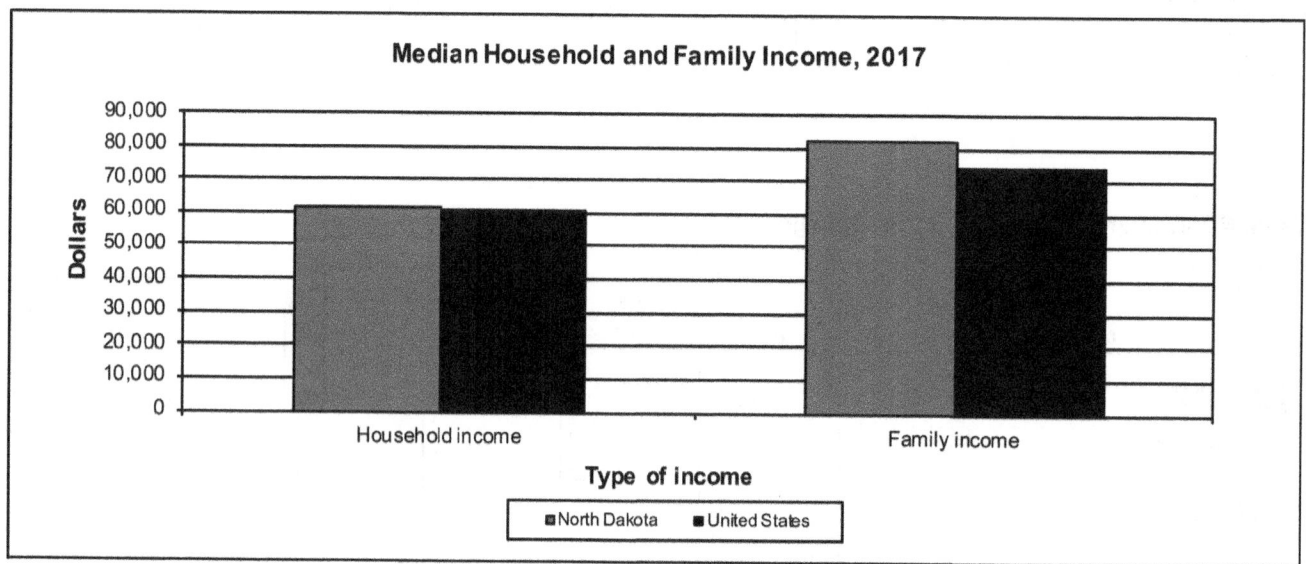

Table ND-6. Health Insurance Coverage Status for the Civilian Noninstitutionalized Population and Children Under 18 Years of Age

(Number, percent.)

Item	2009	2010	2011	2012	2013	2014	2015	2016	2017
Civilian Noninstitutionalized Population	630082	660611	669425	684776	708,181	724,451	740,547	741,486	738,177
Covered by Private or Public Insurance									
Number...	569,250	596,076	603,977	616,252	634,882	667,553	683,096	689,348	682,595
Percent..	90.3	90.2	90.2	90.0	89.6	92.1	92.2	93.0	92.5
Uninsured									
Number...	60,832	64,535	65,448	68,524	73,299	56,898	57,451	52,138	55,582
Percent..	9.7	9.8	9.8	10.0	10.4	7.9	7.8	7.0	7.5
Percent in the U.S. not covered...................	15.1	15.5	15.1	14.8	14.5	11.7	9.4	8.6	8.7
Children Under 18 Years of Age[1]	141231	150108	150853	153705	160,430	167,191	170,994	174,130	183,593
Covered by Private or Public Insurance									
Number...	133,280	140,405	141,238	143,156	147,705	155,649	157,564	160,506	169,775
Percent..	94.4	93.5	93.6	93.1	92.1	93.1	92.1	92.2	92.5
Uninsured									
Number...	7,951	9,703	9,615	10,549	12,725	11,542	13,430	13,624	13,818
Percent..	5.6	6.5	6.4	6.9	7.9	6.9	7.9	7.8	7.5
Percent in the U.S. not covered...................	8.6	8.0	7.5	7.2	7.1	6.0	4.8	4.5	5.0

[1] 2017 data is for individuals under 19 years of age.

Table ND-7. Employment Status by Demographic Group, 2018

(Numbers in thousands, percent.)

Characteristic	Civilian noninstitutional population	Civilian labor force		Employed		Unemployed	
		Number	Percent of population	Number	Percent of population	Number	Percent of population
Total.............................	579	398	68.7	387	66.8	11	2.8
Sex							
Male..................................	295	219	74.2	211	71.8	7	3.3
Female................................	284	179	63.1	175	61.6	4	2.3
Race, Sex, and Hispanic Origin							
White.................................	511	357	69.8	349	68.2	8	2.2
Male..................................	258	194	75.2	189	73.2	5	2.6
Female................................	253	163	64.3	160	63.1	3	1.8
Black or African American...............	NA	NA	NA	NA	NA	NA	NA
Male..................................	NA	NA	NA	NA	NA	NA	NA
Female................................	NA	NA	NA	NA	NA	NA	NA
Hispanic or Latino ethnicity[1].........	NA	NA	NA	NA	NA	NA	NA
Male..................................	NA	NA	NA	NA	NA	NA	NA
Female................................	NA	NA	NA	NA	NA	NA	NA
Age							
16 to 19 years.........................	NA	NA	NA	NA	NA	NA	NA
20 to 24 years.........................	54	42	77.5	41	74.9	2	3.6
25 to 34 years.........................	117	99	84.9	96	82.3	3	3.0
35 to 44 years.........................	90	79	88.4	78	86.7	2	2.0
45 to 54 years.........................	80	70	87.8	68	85.3	2	2.9
55 to 64 years.........................	96	68	71.0	66	69.2	2	2.4
65 years and over......................	109	24	22.3	24	21.8	1	2.1

NOTE: Data in Table 7 are from the Current Population Survey (CPS) and do not match the estimates in Table 8. See notes and definitions for further information.
[1] May be of any race.
NA = Not available.

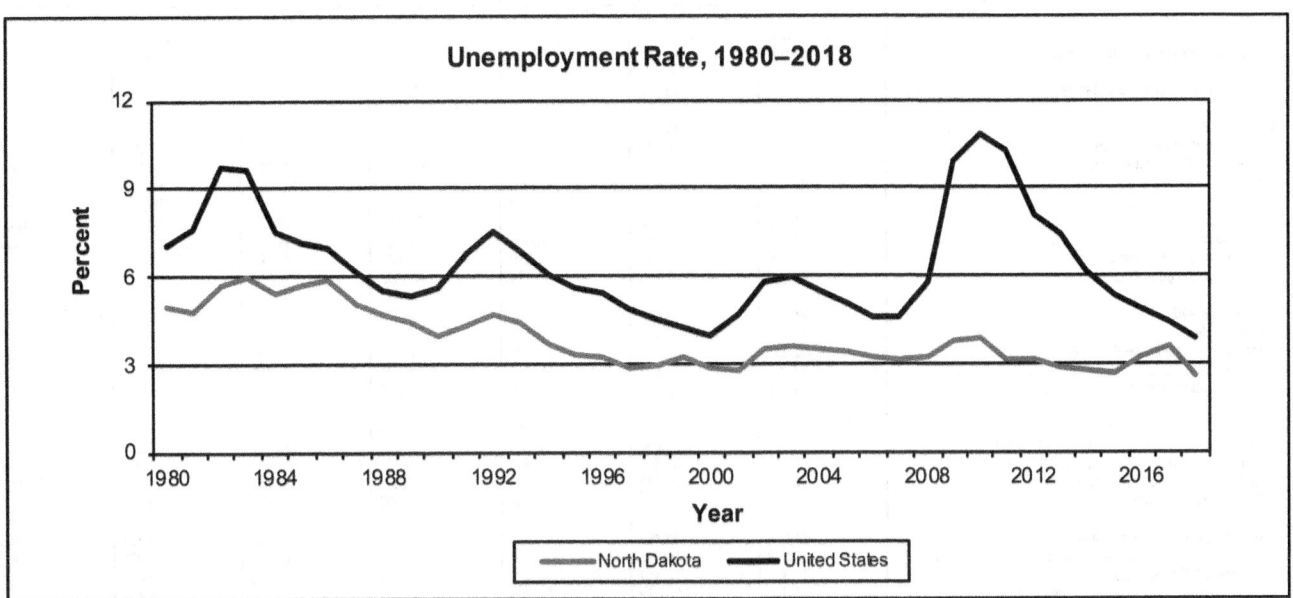

Unemployment Rate, 1980–2018

Table ND-8. Employment Status of the Civilian Noninstitutional Population Age 16 Years and Over

(Number, percent.)

Year	Civilian labor force	Civilian participation rate	Employed	Unemployed	Unemployment rate
2010..............................	378,342	72.6	364,053	14,289	3.8
2011..............................	388,634	73.0	375,153	13,481	3.5
2012..............................	397,867	73.1	385,674	12,193	3.1
2013..............................	406,193	72.7	394,392	11,801	2.9
2014..............................	414,413	72.6	403,362	11,051	2.7
2015..............................	414,210	71.4	402,667	11,543	2.8
2016..............................	414,431	71.3	401,671	12,760	3.1
2017..............................	414,399	71.5	403,610	10,789	2.6
2018..............................	404,299	69.5	393,755	10,544	2.6

Table ND-9. Employment and Average Wages by Industry

(Estimates are based on the 2012 *North American Industry Classification System* [NAICS].)

Industry	2011	2012	2013	2014	2015	2016	2017
	Number of jobs						
Wage and Salary Employment by Industry........................	412,875	447,229	463,244	480,665	471,312	450,659	447,667
Farm Wage and Salary Employment................................	5,316	6,260	6,599	7,292	5,149	4,849	5,223
Nonfarm Wage and Salary Employment............................	407,559	440,969	456,645	473,373	466,163	445,810	442,444
Private wage and salary employment............................	323,382	355,395	370,521	387,500	378,606	356,734	353,855
Forestry, fishing, and related activities........................	2,329	2,517	2,593	2,612	2,598	2,632	2,626
Mining..	16,580	24,113	25,960	29,598	23,038	15,189	17,705
Utilities..	3,418	3,506	3,593	3,702	3,831	3,843	3,781
Construction	24,908	30,238	33,205	35,617	34,940	31,876	27,381
Manufacturing..	23,777	25,181	25,429	25,968	25,449	24,574	24,704
Durable goods manufacturing..............................	15,836	16,949	17,232	17,655	17,089	16,197	16,273
Nondurable goods manufacturing..........................	7,941	8,232	8,197	8,313	8,360	8,377	8,431
Wholesale trade	22,762	25,202	26,515	27,406	26,773	24,524	24,034
Retail trade..	45,057	47,420	49,357	50,890	51,048	49,465	48,024
Transportation and warehousing..............................	16,131	21,131	22,511	24,662	22,747	18,326	18,506
Information	7,134	6,960	6,820	6,844	6,622	6,638	6,510
Finance and insurance	17,362	17,442	17,925	18,521	18,843	18,880	18,863
Real estate and rental and leasing...........................	4,103	4,723	5,203	5,821	5,732	5,194	5,296
Professional, scientific, and technical services	12,753	14,433	15,679	16,841	17,192	16,484	16,029
Management of companies and enterprises..................	4,470	4,763	5,133	5,291	5,338	5,258	5,318
Administrative and waste services	12,807	13,539	13,567	14,311	13,816	12,921	13,170
Educational services	3,952	4,027	4,184	4,129	4,303	4,451	4,540
Health care and social assistance............................	53,094	54,559	55,797	56,098	57,435	59,200	59,940
Arts, entertainment, and recreation..........................	3,770	4,003	4,176	4,399	4,354	4,545	4,651
Accommodation and food services...........................	31,847	34,263	35,227	36,365	36,292	34,988	34,913
Other services, except public administration.................	17,128	17,375	17,647	18,425	18,255	17,746	17,864
Government and government enterprises.......................	84,177	85,574	86,124	85,873	87,557	89,076	88,589
	Dollars						
Average Wages and Salaries by Industry	41,092	45,112	46,835	49,904	49,718	48,041	49,441
Average Farm Wages and Salaries	35,655	44,523	38,992	40,004	33,785	38,597	38,163
Average Nonfarm Wages and Salaries	41,163	45,120	46,948	50,057	49,894	48,144	49,574
Average private wages and salaries............................	41,950	46,671	48,582	51,953	51,522	49,258	50,780
Forestry, fishing, and related activities.......................	25,736	26,464	27,145	28,243	29,958	31,852	32,727
Mining..	89,108	95,852	97,066	103,875	100,835	95,404	100,871
Utilities..	81,945	82,092	86,453	90,554	95,223	96,277	100,355
Construction	51,167	56,416	60,161	64,853	64,917	64,240	63,000
Manufacturing..	44,728	46,680	48,063	49,760	51,187	51,039	52,601
Durable goods manufacturing..............................	45,399	47,357	48,610	49,960	50,765	50,302	51,550
Nondurable goods manufacturing..........................	43,390	45,285	46,914	49,335	52,050	52,463	54,631
Wholesale trade	57,543	63,642	65,247	68,068	66,617	62,722	65,070
Retail trade..	25,675	27,491	28,344	29,706	30,809	30,288	30,633
Transportation and warehousing..............................	56,098	62,007	64,029	68,577	66,695	61,650	64,608
Information	50,883	54,443	55,749	58,339	59,769	63,207	65,083
Finance and insurance	49,881	52,935	54,116	56,343	59,359	60,735	63,069
Real estate and rental and leasing...........................	44,237	50,418	53,425	59,749	56,583	48,343	50,454
Professional, scientific, and technical services	55,954	63,250	67,253	71,693	69,698	67,564	69,903
Management of companies and enterprises..................	65,945	69,365	69,950	76,662	81,419	77,015	80,856
Administrative and waste services	27,896	31,643	31,949	34,061	34,947	36,590	37,986
Educational services	21,706	22,534	22,498	23,699	23,625	22,600	22,835
Health care and social assistance............................	41,296	43,463	44,554	46,553	49,318	49,461	50,531
Arts, entertainment, and recreation..........................	16,278	16,825	17,346	17,591	18,437	18,079	18,366
Accommodation and food services...........................	15,307	17,314	18,478	19,564	19,773	19,660	19,801
Other services, except public administration.................	25,436	28,033	30,083	31,954	33,434	33,443	34,799
Government and government enterprises.......................	38,139	38,681	39,921	41,498	42,850	43,683	44,759

Table ND-10. Employment Characteristics by Family Type

(Number, percent.)

Family type and labor force status	2015		2016		2017	
	Total	Families with own children under 18 years	Total	Families with own children under 18 years	Total	Families with own children under 18 years
All Families..	188,210	82,326	184,904	82,171	190,217	80,754
FAMILY TYPE AND LABOR FORCE STATUS						
Married-Couple Families...................................	150,297	58,631	150,317	59,433	152,814	58,734
Both husband and wife in labor force..................	60.5	76.5	60.0	76.3	62.8	79.7
Husband in labor force, wife not in labor force..........	17.1	19.6	17.2	18.8	15.8	17.2
Wife in labor force, husband not in labor force..........	6.6	2.3	7.3	3.1	5.8	2.1
Both husband and wife not in labor force................	15.3	0.9	14.9	1.6	15.1	0.7
Other Families	37,913	23,695	34,587	22,738	37,403	22,020
Female householder, no husband present..................	64.1	66.0	65.2	65.0	62.8	65.6
In labor force...	49.8	56.1	51.2	55.1	48.9	58.0
Not in labor force.......................................	14.3	9.9	14.0	9.9	13.9	7.6
Male householder, no wife present.........................	35.9	34.0	34.8	35.0	37.2	34.4
In labor force...	30.2	31.1	30.6	33.2	33.3	33.4
Not in labor force.......................................	5.7	2.9	4.2	1.9	3.9	1.0

Table ND-11. School Enrollment and Educational Attainment, 2017

(Number, percent.)

Item	State	U.S.
Enrollment		
Total population 3 years and over, enrolled in school	179,366	81,273,337
Enrolled in nursery school or preschool (percent)..	5.0	6.0
Enrolled in kindergarten (percent)...	5.5	4.9
Enrolled in elementary school, grades 1-8 (percent).....................................	40.5	40.6
Enrolled in high school, grades 9-12 (percent)..	18.7	21.1
Enrolled in college or graduate school (percent)...	30.3	27.4
Attainment		
Total population 25 years and over	495,904	221,250,083
Less than ninth grade (percent)	2.8	5.1
9th to 12th grade, no diploma (percent)	4.3	6.9
High school graduate, including equivalency (percent)...................................	26.4	27.1
Some college, no degree (percent)	22.4	20.4
Associate's degree (percent)..	13.4	8.5
Bachelor's degree (percent)...	21.8	19.7
Graduate or professional degree (percent)..	9.0	12.3
High school graduate or higher (percent)...	92.9	88.0
Bachelor's degree or higher (percent)...	30.7	32.0

Table ND-12. Public School Characteristics and Educational Indicators

(Number, percent; data derived from National Center of Education Statistics.)

Item	State	U.S.
Public Elementary and Secondary Schools		
Number of operational school districts, 2016-17...	222	18,377
Number of operational schools, 2016-17..	518	98,330
Percent charter schools	NA	7.1
Total public school enrollment, 2016-17...	109,706	50,587,859
Percent charter school enrollment	NA	6.0
Student-teacher ratio, Fall 2015..	11.8	16.0
Expenditures per student (dollars), 2015-16..	13,358	11,841
Four-year adjusted cohort graduation rate (ACGR)[1]	87.2	84.6
Students eligible for free or reduced-price lunch (percent), 2015-16...............	29.9	52.1
English language learners (percent), Fall 2016...	2.9	9.6
Students age 3 to 21 served under IDEA, part B (percent), 2017-18................	13.9	13.7
Public Schools by Type, 2016-17		Percent of state public schools
Total number of schools..	519	100.0
Special education..	32	6.2
Vocational education..	13	2.5
Alternative education...	0	-

[1] Adjusted Cohort Graduation Rates (ACGR) differ from Averaged Freshmen Graduation Rates (AFGR).
NA = Not available.
- = Zero or rounds to zero.

Table ND-13. Reported Voting and Registration of the Voting-Age Population, November 2018

(Numbers in thousands, percent.)

Item	Total population	Total citizen population	Registered			Voted		
			Total registered	Percent registered (total population)	Percent registered (total citizen population)	Total voted	Percent voted (total population)	Percent voted (total citizen population)
U.S. Total	249,748	228,832	153,066	61.3	66.9	122,281	49.0	53.4
State Total	560	541	397	70.9	73.4	335	59.8	61.9
Sex								
Male	286	275	194	67.8	70.5	160	56.0	58.2
Female	274	266	204	74.3	76.5	175	63.8	65.7
Race								
White alone	499	494	368	73.7	74.6	315	63.1	63.8
White, non-Hispanic alone	488	483	362	74.2	74.9	311	63.7	64.3
Black alone	14	6	2	(B)	(B)	1	(B)	(B)
Asian alone	8	3	-	(B)	(B)	-	(B)	(B)
Hispanic (of any race)	16	15	10	(B)	(B)	7	(B)	(B)
White alone or in combination	507	501	374	73.7	74.6	320	63.1	63.8
Black alone or in combination	15	7	3	(B)	(B)	2	(B)	(B)
Asian alone or in combination	9	4	2	(B)	(B)	1	(B)	(B)
Age								
18 to 24 years	74	72	42	(B)	(B)	26	(B)	(B)
25 to 34 years	122	113	78	64.0	68.9	60	49.4	53.2
35 to 44 years	81	77	57	69.9	73.8	47	57.9	61.1
45 to 64 years	165	162	125	75.3	76.7	112	67.9	69.1
65 years and over	118	118	96	81.6	81.8	90	76.1	76.4

- = Zero or rounds to zero.
B = Base is less than 75,000 and therefore too small to show the derived measure.

Table ND-14. Crime

(Number, rate per 100,000. Data are derived from the FBI Uniform Crime Reports.)

Item	State			U.S.		
	2016	2017	Percent change	2016	2017	Percent change
TOTAL POPULATION[1]	755,548	755,393	-	323,405,935	325,719,178	0.7
VIOLENT CRIME						
Number	1,905	2,125	11.5	1,285,606	1,283,220	-0.2
Rate	252.1	281.3	11.6	397.5	394.0	-0.9
Murder and Nonnegligent Manslaughter						
Number	16	10	-37.5	17,413	17,284	-0.7
Rate	2.1	1.3	-37.5	5.4	5.3	-1.4
Rape[2]						
Number	356	399	12.1	132,414	135,755	2.5
Rate	47.1	52.8	12.1	40.9	41.7	1.8
Robbery						
Number	181	183	1.1	332,797	319,356	-4.0
Rate	24.0	24.2	1.1	102.9	98.0	-4.7
Aggravated Assault						
Number	1,352	1,533	13.4	802,982	810,825	1.0
Rate	178.9	202.9	13.4	248.3	248.9	0.3
PROPERTY CRIME						
Number	17,451	16,602	-4.9	7,928,530	7,694,086	-3.0
Rate	2,309.7	2,197.8	-4.8	2,451.6	2,362.2	-3.6
Burglary						
Number	3,248	2,942	-9.4	1,516,405	1,401,840	-7.6
Rate	429.9	389.5	-9.4	468.9	430.4	-8.2
Larceny-Theft						
Number	12,249	11,887	-3.0	5,644,835	5,519,107	-2.2
Rate	1,621.2	1,573.6	-2.9	1,745.4	1,694.4	-2.9
Motor Vehicle Theft						
Number	1,954	1,773	-9.3	767,290	773,139	0.8
Rate	258.6	234.7	-9.2	237.3	237.4	-

NOTE: Although arson data are included in the trend and clearance tables, sufficient data are not available to estimate totals for this offense. Therefore, no arson data are published in this table.
- = Zero or rounds to zero.
[1] Population figures are U.S. Census Bureau provisional estimates as of July 1, 2017.
[2] The figures shown in the rape (revised definition) column were estimated using the revised Uniform Crime Reporting (UCR) definition of rape.

Table ND-15. State Government Finances, 2017

(Dollar amounts in thousands, percent distribution.)

Item	Dollars	Percent distribution
Total Revenue	7,921,242	100.0
General revenue	6,648,047	83.9
Intergovernmental revenue	1,825,980	23.1
Taxes	3,465,326	43.7
General sales	872,176	11.0
Selective sales	477,252	6.0
License taxes	213,985	2.7
Individual income tax	319,507	4.0
Corporate income tax	60,871	0.8
Other taxes	1,521,535	19.2
Current charges	791,199	10.0
Miscellaneous general revenue	565,542	7.1
Utility revenue	0	-
Liquor stores revenue	0	-
Insurance trust revenue[1]	1,273,195	16.1
Total Expenditure	7,532,032	100.0
Intergovernmental expenditure	1,978,548	26.3
Direct expenditure	5,553,484	73.7
Current operation	3,824,126	50.8
Capital outlay	805,462	10.7
Insurance benefits and repayments	660,183	8.8
Assistance and subsidies	183,493	2.4
Interest on debt	80,220	1.1
Exhibit: Salaries and wages	1,097,761	14.6
Total Expenditure	7,532,032	100.0
General expenditure	6,791,284	90.2
Intergovernmental expenditure	1,978,548	26.3
Direct expenditure	4,812,736	63.9
General expenditure, by function:		
Education	2,356,128	31.3
Public welfare	1,287,765	17.1
Hospitals	27,100	0.4
Health	375,497	5.0
Highways	970,114	12.9
Police protection	31,401	0.4
Correction	105,537	1.4
Natural resources	142,237	1.9
Parks and recreation	40,661	0.5
Governmental administration	204,538	2.7
Interest on general debt	80,220	1.1
Other and unallocable	1,170,085	15.5
Utility expenditure	80,565	1.0
Liquor stores expenditure	0	-
Insurance trust expenditure	660,183	8.8
Debt at End of Fiscal Year	2,885,664	X
Cash and Security Holdings	28,614,819	X

X = Not applicable.
- = Zero or rounds to zero.
[1] Within insurance trust revenue, net earnings of state retirement systems is a calculated statistic (the item code in the data file is X08), and thus can be positive or negative. Net earnings is the sum of earnings on investments plus gains on investments minus losses on investments. The change made in 2002 for asset valuation from book to market value in accordance with Statement 34 of the Governmental Accounting Standards Board is reflected in the calculated statistics.

Table ND-16. State Government Tax Collections, 2018

(Dollars in thousands, percent.)

Item	Dollars	Percent distribution
Total Taxes	4,205,184	100.0
Property taxes	4,549	0.1
Sales and gross receipts	1,395,503	33.2
General sales and gross receipts	912,532	21.7
Selective sales and gross receipts	482,971	11.5
Alcoholic beverages	8,819	0.2
Amusements	3,139	0.1
Insurance premiums	63,274	1.5
Motor fuels	196,649	4.7
Pari-mutuels	1,498	-
Public utilities	49,663	1.2
Tobacco products	28,001	0.7
Other selective sales	131,928	3.1
Licenses	214,463	5.1
Alcoholic beverages	395	-
Amusements	1,088	-
Corporations in general	X	-
Hunting and fishing	15,286	0.4
Motor vehicle	118,080	2.8
Motor vehicle operators	5,049	0.1
Public utilities	3	-
Occupation and business, NEC	74,562	1.8
Other licenses	0	-
Income taxes	474,912	11.3
Individual income	367,635	8.7
Corporation net income	107,277	2.6
Other taxes	2,115,757	50.3
Death and gift	X	-
Documentary and stock transfer	X	-
Severance	2,115,757	50.3
Taxes, NEC	0	-

- = Zero or rounds to zero.
X = Not applicable.

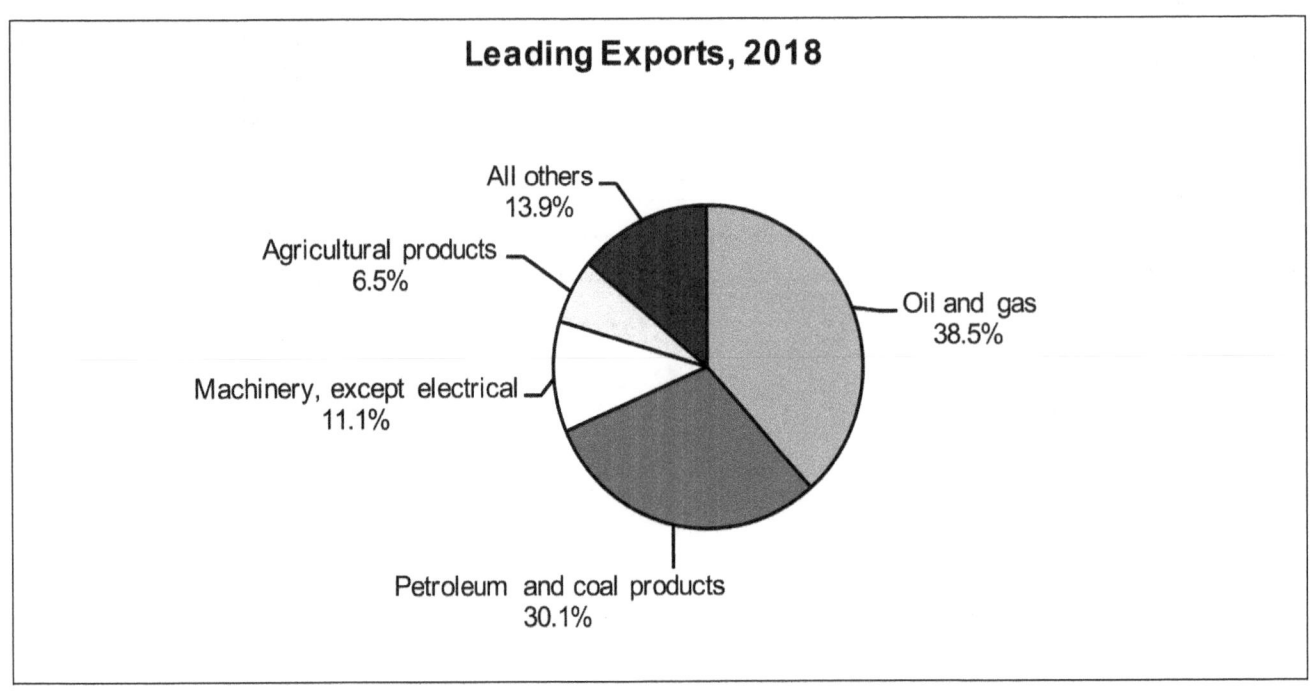

Leading Exports, 2018

All others 13.9%
Agricultural products 6.5%
Machinery, except electrical 11.1%
Petroleum and coal products 30.1%
Oil and gas 38.5%

OHIO

Facts and Figures

Location: East north central United States; bordered on the N by Michigan and Lake Erie, on the E by Pennsylvania and West Virginia, on the S by West Virginia and Kentucky, and on the W by Indiana

Area: 44,825 sq. mi. (116,096 sq. km.); rank—34th

Population: 11,689,442 (2018 est.); rank—7th

Principal Cities: capital—Columbus; largest—Columbus

Statehood: March 1, 1803; 17th state

U.S. Congress: 2 senators, 16 representatives

State Motto: With God, All Things Are Possible

State Song: "Beautiful Ohio"

State Nickname: The Buckeye State

Abbreviations: OH

State Symbols: flower—scarlet carnation; tree—Ohio buckeye; bird—cardinal

At a Glance

- With an increase in population of 1.3 percent, Ohio ranked 40th among the states in growth from 2010 to 2018.

- Ohio's violent crime rate in 2017 was 297.5 per 100,000 population, compared to 394.0 for the entire nation.

- In 2017, 6.0 percent of Ohioans did not have health insurance, compared to 8.7 percent of the entire U.S. population.

- Ohio had the 2nd highest drug overdose death rate in 2017, with 46.3 deaths per 100,000 population.

- Ohio had 50.4 full-time equivalent state and local government employees per 1,000 residents in 2018, which was close to the national average of 50.9 employees per 1,000 residents.

Table OH-1. Population by Age, Sex, Race, and Hispanic Origin

(Number, percent, except where noted.)

Sex, age, race, and Hispanic origin	2000	2010	2018 [1]	Percent change, 2010–2018
Total Population..	11,353,140	11,536,504	11,689,442	1.3
Percent of total U.S. population	4.0	3.7	3.6	X
Sex				
Male..	5,512,262	5,632,156	5,730,718	1.7
Female	5,840,878	5,904,348	5,958,724	0.9
Age				
Under 5 years..	754,930	720,856	694,789	-3.6
5 to 19 years..	2,461,025	2,346,270	2,207,832	-5.9
20 to 64 years..	6,629,428	6,847,363	6,791,799	-0.8
65 years and over..	1,507,757	1,622,015	1,995,022	23.0
Median age (years)	36.2	38.8	39.4	1.5
Race and Hispanic Origin				
One race				
White	9,645,453	9,664,524	9,571,522	-1.0
Black	1,301,307	1,426,861	1,517,999	6.4
American Indian and Alaska Native	24,486	29,674	33,566	13.1
Asian	132,633	196,693	287,222	46.0
Native Hawaiian or Other Pacific Islander	2,749	5,336	6,994	31.1
Two or more races	157,885	213,416	272,139	27.5
Hispanic (of any race)..	217,123	375,004	460,877	22.9

X = Not applicable.
- = Zero or rounds to zero.
[1] Population figures for 2018 are July 1 estimates. The 2010 estimates are taken from the 2010 Census.

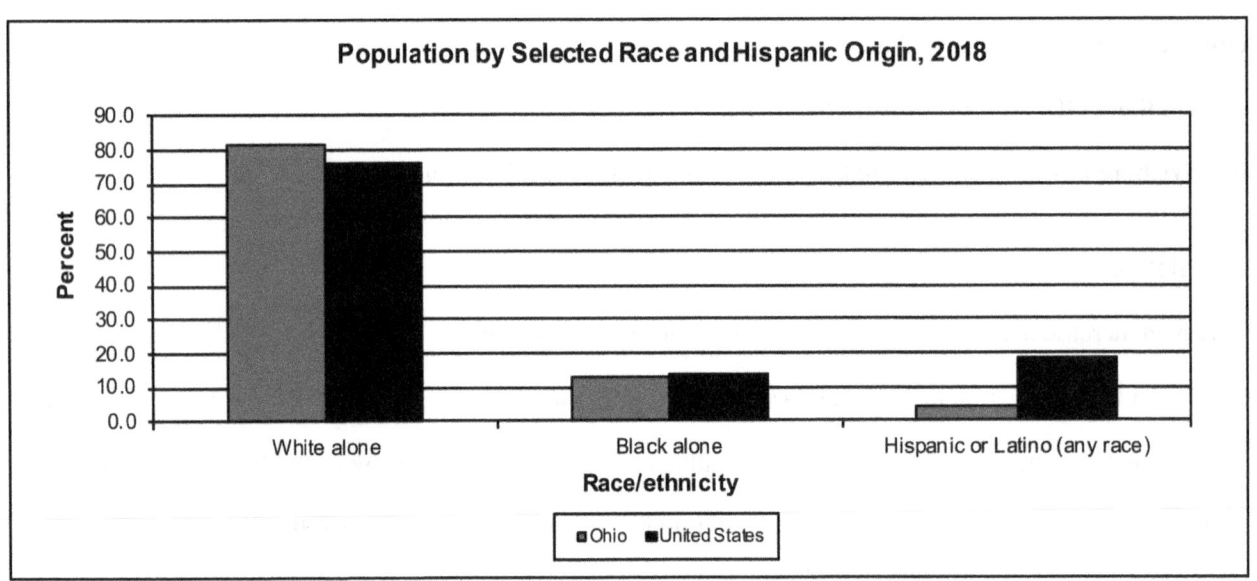

Table OH-2. Marital Status

(Number, percent distribution.)

Sex, age, race, and Hispanic origin	2000	2010	2017
Males, 15 Years and Over	4,281,736	4,487,900	4,613,739
Never married	29.2	33.5	35.7
Now married, except separated..	57.0	51.2	48.9
Separated..	1.4	1.7	1.6
Widowed..	2.7	2.9	3.0
Divorced..	9.7	10.8	10.8
Females, 15 Years and Over	4,670,985	4,809,613	4,902,084
Never married	23.5	27.9	29.7
Now married, except separated..	52.1	46.9	46.1
Separated..	1.7	2.1	1.8
Widowed..	11.1	10.1	9.4
Divorced..	11.5	12.9	13.1

Table OH-3. Households and Housing Characteristics

(Number, percent, dollars.)

Item	2000	2010	2017	Average annual percent change, 2010–2017
Total Households...................................	4,445,773	4,525,066	4,667,192	0.4
Family households	2,993,023	2,960,107	2,951,170	-
Married-couple family	2,285,798	2,169,003	2,136,801	-0.2
Other family	707,225	791,104	814,369	0.4
Male householder, no wife present........	170,347	196,130	228,915	2.4
Female householder, no husband present..	536,878	594,974	585,454	-0.2
Nonfamily households	1,452,750	1,564,959	1,716,022	1.4
Householder living alone	1,215,614	1,315,321	1,415,180	1.1
Householder not living alone.................	237,136	249,638	300,842	2.9
Housing Characteristics				
Total housing units................................	4,783,051	5,128,113	5,201,701	0.2
Occupied housing units	4,445,773	4,525,066	4,667,192	0.4
Owner occupied	3,072,522	3,095,197	3,070,181	-0.1
Renter occupied	1,373,251	1,429,869	1,597,011	1.7
Average household size..........................	2.49	2.48	2.43	-0.3
Financial Characteristics				
Median gross rent of renter-occupied housing	515	685	772	1.8
Median monthly owner costs for housing units with a mortgage	983	1,246	1,214	-0.4
Median value of owner-occupied housing units..........	103,700	134,400	144,200	1.0

- = Zero or rounds to zero.

Table OH-4. Migration, Origin, and Language

(Number, percent.)

Characteristic	State			U.S.		
	2016	2017	Percent change	2016	2017	Percent change
Residence 1 Year Ago						
Population 1 year and over	11,481,752	11,520,109	0.3	319,361,956	321,994,428	0.8
Same house	85.0	85.3	X	85.4	85.7	X
Different house in the U.S......................	14.6	14.3	X	13.9	13.6	X
Same county	9.4	9.1	X	8.3	8.1	X
Different county	5.2	5.3	X	5.6	5.6	X
Same state	3.5	3.5	X	3.2	3.3	X
Different state	1.7	1.7	X	2.4	2.3	X
Abroad	0.4	0.4	X	0.7	0.7	X
Place of Birth						
Native born	11,100,781	11,130,318	0.3	279,388,170	281,193,323	0.6
Male	49.0	49.0	X	49.3	49.4	X
Female	51.0	51.0	X	50.7	50.6	X
Foreign born	513,592	528,291	2.9	43,739,345	44,525,855	1.8
Male	50.1	48.9	X	48.5	48.4	X
Female	49.9	51.1	X	51.5	51.6	X
Foreign born; naturalized U.S. citizen........	270,314	270,333	-	21,238,372	21,948,732	3.3
Male	47.5	46.6	X	45.9	45.9	X
Female	52.5	53.4	X	54.1	54.1	X
Foreign born; not a U.S. citizen..............	243,278	257,958	6.0	22,500,973	22,577,123	0.3
Male	53.0	51.3	X	51.0	50.8	X
Female	47.0	48.7	X	49.0	49.2	X
Entered 2010 or later	26.9	32.9	X	18.6	21.3	X
Entered 2000 to 2009	29.7	26.4	X	26.7	25.7	X
Entered before 2000............................	43.4	40.7	X	54.7	53.0	X
World Region of Birth, Foreign						
Foreign-born population, excluding population born at sea	513,592	528,291	2.9	43,738,901	44,525,458	1.8
Europe	21.7	20.2	X	10.9	10.8	X
Asia	43.2	42.7	X	30.8	31.2	X
Africa	13.4	13.4	X	4.9	5.1	X
Oceania	0.5	0.4	X	0.6	0.6	X
Latin America....................................	18.3	20.1	X	51.0	50.4	X
North America....................................	2.9	3.2	X	1.8	1.8	X
Language Spoken at Home and Ability to Speak English						
Population 5 years and over.....................	10,921,628	10,963,479	0.4	303,328,961	305,924,019	0.9
English only	93.0	92.8	X	78.4	78.2	X
Language other than English..................	7.0	7.2	X	21.6	21.8	X
Speaks English less than "very well"........	2.5	2.4	X	8.6	8.5	X

NA = Not available.
X = Not applicable.
- = Zero or rounds to zero.

Table OH-5. Median Income and Poverty Status, 2017

(Number, percent, except as noted.)

Characteristic	State		U.S.	
	Number	Percent	Number	Percent
Median Income				
Households (dollars)...	54,021	X	60,336	X
Families (dollars)	69,632	X	73,891	X
Below Poverty Level (All People)	1,582,931	14.0	42,583,651	13.4
Sex				
Male	708,021	12.8	19,004,547	12.2
Female	874,910	15.1	23,579,104	14.5
Age				
Under 18 years..	513,238	20.1	13,353,202	18.4
Related children under 18 years..................................	501,013	19.7	13,053,472	18.1
18 to 64 years	925,669	13.4	24,648,677	12.6
65 years and over	144,024	7.7	4,581,772	9.3

X = Not applicable.

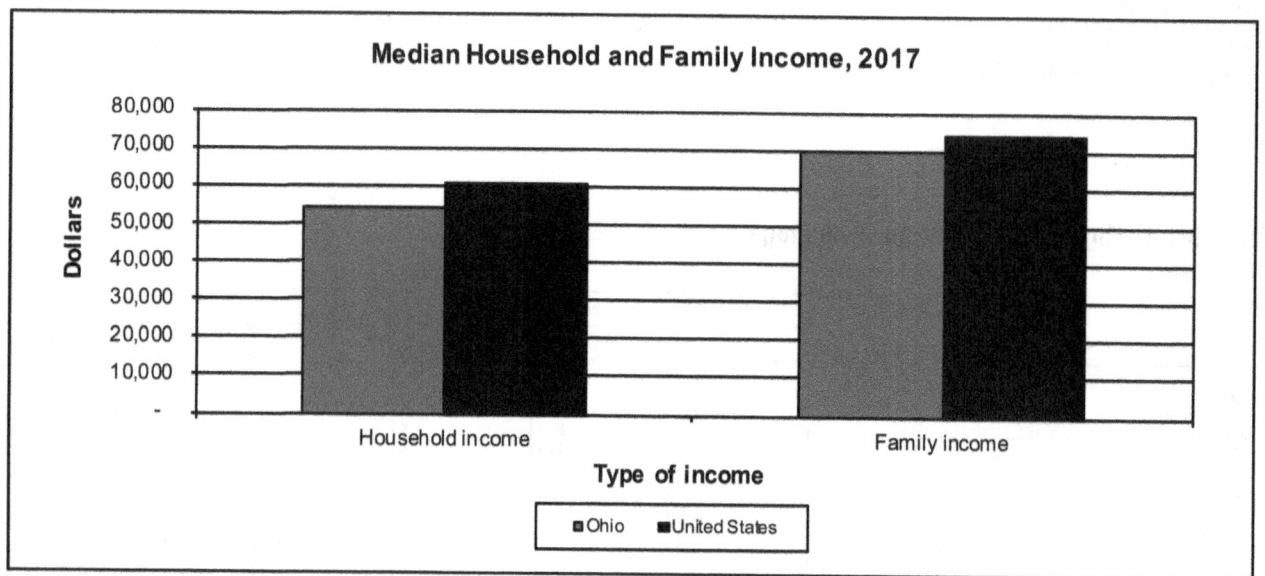

Table OH-6. Health Insurance Coverage Status for the Civilian Noninstitutionalized Population and Children Under 18 Years of Age

(Number, percent.)

Item	2009	2010	2011	2012	2013	2014	2015	2016	2017
Civilian Noninstitutionalized Population	11,351,905	11,358,640	11,369,102	11,371,766	11,398,298	11,420,809	11,442,029	11,439,848	11,485,078
Covered by Private or Public Insurance									
Number...	9,969,267	9,959,697	10,014,671	10,067,519	10,140,742	10,465,604	10,695,753	10,796,120	10,799,064
Percent..	87.8	87.7	88.1	88.5	89.0	91.6	93.5	94.4	94.0
Uninsured									
Number...	1,382,638	1,398,943	1,354,431	1,304,247	1,257,556	955,205	746,276	643,728	686,014
Percent..	12.2	12.3	11.9	11.5	11.0	8.4	6.5	5.6	6.0
Percent in the U.S. not covered................................	15.1	15.5	15.1	14.8	14.5	11.7	9.4	8.6	8.7
Children Under 18 Years of Age[1]	2,710,364	2,715,122	2,688,340	2,656,700	2,644,952	2,631,481	2,626,771	2,605,997	2,759,296
Covered by Private or Public Insurance									
Number...	2,538,017	2,553,168	2,531,138	2,516,034	2,503,584	2,505,342	2,511,790	2,511,444	2,633,901
Percent..	93.6	94.0	94.2	94.7	94.7	95.2	95.6	96.4	95.5
Uninsured									
Number...	172,347	161,954	157,202	140,666	141,368	126,139	114,981	94,553	125,395
Percent..	6.4	6.0	5.8	5.3	5.3	4.8	4.4	3.6	4.5
Percent in the U.S. not covered................................	8.6	8.0	7.5	7.2	7.1	6.0	4.8	4.5	5.0

[1] 2017 data is for individuals under 19 years of age.

Table OH-7. Employment Status by Demographic Group, 2018

(Numbers in thousands, percent.)

Characteristic	Civilian noninstitutional population	Civilian labor force		Employed		Unemployed	
		Number	Percent of population	Number	Percent of population	Number	Percent of population
Total..	9,227	5,755	62.4	5,494	59.5	261	4.5
Sex							
Male..	4,453	3,025	67.9	2,869	64.4	156	5.2
Female...	4,774	2,730	57.2	2,625	55.0	105	3.8
Race, Sex, and Hispanic Origin							
White...	7,710	4,847	62.9	4,644	60.2	202	4.2
Male..	3,746	2,588	69.1	2,470	66.0	118	4.6
Female.......................................	3,964	2,258	57.0	2,174	54.8	85	3.7
Black or African American..................	1,106	647	58.5	606	54.8	41	6.4
Male..	506	292	57.8	267	52.8	25	8.7
Female.......................................	600	355	59.2	339	56.5	16	4.5
Hispanic or Latino ethnicity[1]...............	274	185	67.5	173	63.3	11	6.2
Male..	140	110	78.5	100	71.6	10	8.8
Female.......................................	NA	NA	NA	NA	NA	NA	NA
Age							
16 to 19 years................................	633	262	41.3	223	35.3	38	14.6
20 to 24 years................................	753	587	77.9	541	71.8	45	7.7
25 to 34 years................................	1,521	1,268	83.4	1,218	80.0	51	4.0
35 to 44 years................................	1,322	1,106	83.7	1,065	80.5	41	3.7
45 to 54 years................................	1,500	1,190	79.3	1,146	76.4	44	3.7
55 to 64 years................................	1,559	1,013	65.0	984	63.2	29	2.9
65 years and over	1,939	330	17.0	317	16.4	13	3.8

NOTE: Data in Table 7 are from the Current Population Survey (CPS) and do not match the estimates in Table 8. See notes and definitions for further information.
[1] May be of any race.

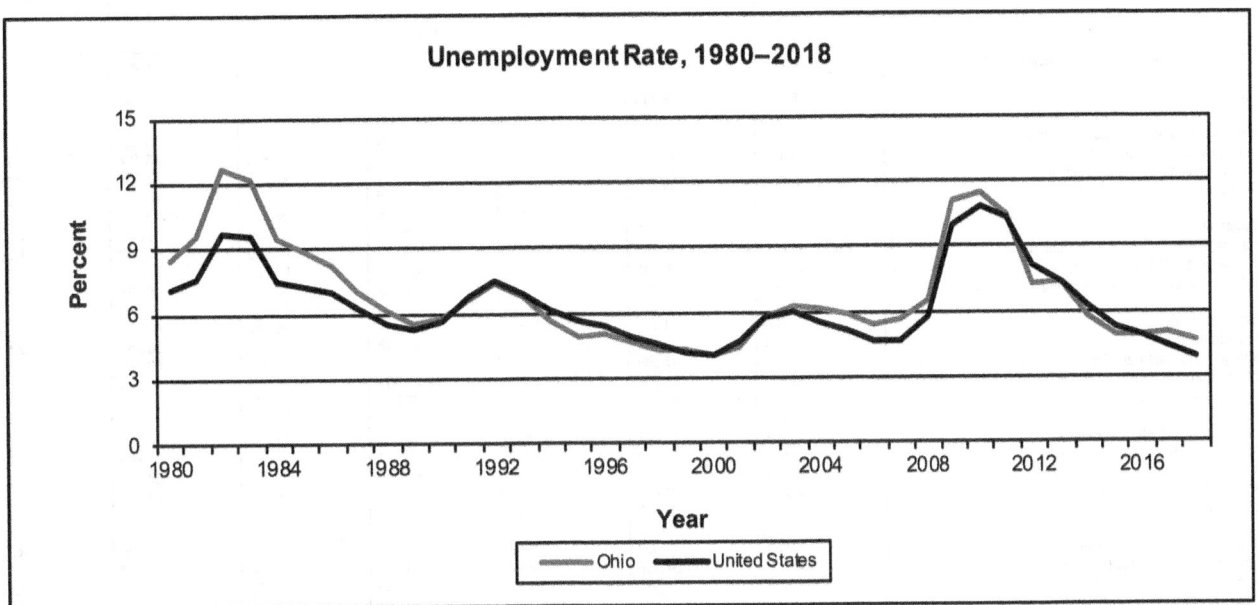

Unemployment Rate, 1980–2018

Table OH-8. Employment Status of the Civilian Noninstitutional Population Age 16 Years and Over

(Number, percent.)

Year	Civilian labor force	Civilian participation rate	Employed	Unemployed	Unemployment rate
2010...	5,846,886	65.2	5,247,050	599,836	10.3
2011...	5,771,469	64.2	5,261,238	510,231	8.8
2012...	5,705,591	63.3	5,284,001	421,590	7.4
2013...	5,716,730	63.2	5,290,609	426,121	7.5
2014...	5,701,477	62.7	5,370,560	330,917	5.8
2015...	5,694,303	62.5	5,414,872	279,431	4.9
2016...	5,739,296	62.7	5,451,315	287,981	5.0
2017...	5,780,021	62.9	5,491,174	288,847	5.0
2018...	5,754,931	62.4	5,491,585	263,346	4.6

Table OH-9. Employment and Average Wages by Industry

(Estimates are based on the 2012 *North American Industry Classification System* [NAICS].)

Industry	2011	2012	2013	2014	2015	2016	2017
	Number of jobs						
Wage and Salary Employment by Industry........................	5,221,997	5,316,428	5,369,126	5,442,337	5,521,571	5,583,348	5,625,472
Farm Wage and Salary Employment...............................	13,254	19,593	16,061	12,576	18,013	20,092	17,618
Nonfarm Wage and Salary Employment...........................	5,208,743	5,296,835	5,353,065	5,429,761	5,503,558	5,563,256	5,607,854
Private wage and salary employment.............................	4,401,187	4,497,544	4,557,727	4,635,030	4,709,574	4,762,380	4,801,924
Forestry, fishing, and related activities.....................	4,570	4,875	5,090	5,236	5,411	5,425	5,394
Mining..	11,370	12,209	12,142	14,398	13,722	11,019	11,100
Utilities..	19,308	19,109	18,799	18,217	19,208	19,228	19,112
Construction...	180,932	186,095	190,957	200,442	205,508	211,088	222,156
Manufacturing...	638,824	657,464	663,411	675,230	686,582	685,684	687,099
Durable goods manufacturing..............................	428,883	444,728	449,332	459,947	467,557	462,738	462,182
Nondurable goods manufacturing........................	209,941	212,736	214,079	215,283	219,025	222,946	224,917
Wholesale trade..	219,503	225,244	228,843	233,781	237,114	236,645	237,338
Retail trade..	559,078	563,903	566,414	569,189	574,164	579,110	580,148
Transportation and warehousing..............................	168,664	173,096	175,879	181,930	191,299	193,718	196,132
Information...	76,207	74,741	75,412	72,722	71,803	71,809	71,652
Finance and insurance	217,229	219,515	220,295	220,267	224,716	230,399	237,204
Real estate and rental and leasing...........................	59,211	59,335	60,785	61,905	63,623	64,309	64,798
Professional, scientific, and technical services...........	247,338	244,036	246,344	250,318	252,930	259,046	260,183
Management of companies and enterprises.................	112,862	127,184	132,404	137,524	138,957	138,015	141,689
Administrative and waste services............................	294,808	306,027	313,758	324,531	328,336	330,050	326,695
Educational services..	116,836	115,633	113,618	114,519	115,911	117,368	119,075
Health care and social assistance............................	746,764	759,491	770,026	775,945	790,032	806,728	812,228
Arts, entertainment, and recreation..........................	63,879	68,610	74,169	77,706	78,010	79,434	81,053
Accommodation and food services............................	422,377	434,823	446,771	453,318	464,355	475,727	482,971
Other services, except public administration...............	241,427	246,154	242,610	247,852	247,893	247,578	245,897
Government and government enterprises........................	807,556	799,291	795,338	794,731	793,984	800,876	805,930
	Dollars						
Average Wages and Salaries by Industry	43,701	44,997	45,523	46,865	47,936	48,494	49,988
Average Farm Wages and Salaries	28,886	26,740	30,162	34,633	31,486	32,229	27,750
Average Nonfarm Wages and Salaries	43,738	45,064	45,569	46,893	47,990	48,553	50,058
Average private wages and salaries.............................	43,445	44,846	45,411	46,849	47,895	48,437	49,971
Forestry, fishing, and related activities.....................	26,253	27,005	27,839	29,101	29,728	31,554	33,020
Mining..	71,367	73,311	65,213	71,149	69,419	69,963	72,797
Utilities..	86,813	88,798	90,582	93,300	96,641	96,947	100,997
Construction...	49,703	51,539	52,933	54,960	56,790	57,951	61,761
Manufacturing...	57,147	57,355	57,644	59,483	60,150	60,692	61,994
Durable goods manufacturing..............................	58,322	58,491	58,735	60,535	60,776	61,260	62,760
Nondurable goods manufacturing........................	54,745	54,981	55,353	57,237	58,813	59,514	60,420
Wholesale trade..	62,483	64,089	64,668	66,543	68,357	68,783	71,094
Retail trade..	25,750	26,424	26,671	27,348	28,094	28,287	29,061
Transportation and warehousing..............................	46,307	47,589	47,838	49,270	50,337	50,348	52,012
Information...	60,319	61,953	63,631	64,904	66,919	68,299	70,192
Finance and insurance	65,070	66,650	69,375	72,291	74,433	75,574	78,797
Real estate and rental and leasing...........................	39,534	41,311	42,401	44,426	45,920	46,855	48,418
Professional, scientific, and technical services...........	66,054	67,424	68,714	70,598	72,618	73,905	74,954
Management of companies and enterprises.................	96,476	108,082	104,995	108,850	106,428	108,894	109,831
Administrative and waste services............................	30,621	31,650	32,301	33,125	34,287	34,111	35,617
Educational services..	30,074	30,555	30,892	31,175	31,544	31,868	32,054
Health care and social assistance............................	41,651	42,933	43,656	44,722	45,995	46,520	47,825
Arts, entertainment, and recreation..........................	30,583	32,106	32,078	34,110	35,066	35,583	37,444
Accommodation and food services............................	15,703	16,372	16,727	17,289	17,867	18,351	18,844
Other services, except public administration...............	27,557	28,604	29,115	30,080	31,320	32,394	34,299
Government and government enterprises........................	45,335	46,289	46,480	47,153	48,553	49,242	50,576

Table OH-10. Employment Characteristics by Family Type

(Number, percent.)

Family type and labor force status	2015 Total	2015 Families with own children under 18 years	2016 Total	2016 Families with own children under 18 years	2017 Total	2017 Families with own children under 18 years
All Families..............................	2,922,095	1,218,342	2,929,661	1,212,345	2,951,170	1,200,698
FAMILY TYPE AND LABOR FORCE STATUS						
Married-Couple Families....................	2,123,886	781,230	2,121,616	769,547	2,136,801	766,939
Both husband and wife in labor force....	52.0	69.8	51.9	69.8	51.6	70.4
Husband in labor force, wife not in labor force........	20.0	24.1	20.0	24.4	19.9	23.8
Wife in labor force, husband not in labor force............	8.6	4.0	8.2	3.9	8.3	3.9
Both husband and wife not in labor force........	19.0	1.8	19.3	1.5	19.5	1.6
Other Families	798,209	437,112	808,045	442,798	814,369	433,759
Female householder, no husband present............	73.6	75.6	72.6	74.0	71.9	74.5
In labor force............	50.9	62.2	50.1	61.3	50.2	62.2
Not in labor force............	22.7	13.3	22.5	12.7	21.7	12.3
Male householder, no wife present..........	26.4	24.4	27.4	26.0	28.1	25.5
In labor force............	20.2	21.7	21.1	23.3	21.5	23.3
Not in labor force............	6.2	2.7	6.4	2.7	6.6	2.2

Table OH-11. School Enrollment and Educational Attainment, 2017

(Number, percent.)

Item	State	U.S.
Enrollment		
Total population 3 years and over, enrolled in school ...	2,812,859	81,273,337
Enrolled in nursery school or preschool (percent) ...	6.0	6.0
Enrolled in kindergarten (percent)...	4.7	4.9
Enrolled in elementary school, grades 1-8 (percent)...	41.4	40.6
Enrolled in high school, grades 9-12 (percent)...	21.8	21.1
Enrolled in college or graduate school (percent)...	26.1	27.4
Attainment		
Total population 25 years and over ...	7,981,885	221,250,083
Less than ninth grade (percent) ...	2.7	5.1
9th to 12th grade, no diploma (percent) ...	7.0	6.9
High school graduate, including equivalency (percent)...	33.3	27.1
Some college, no degree (percent) ...	20.2	20.4
Associate's degree (percent) ...	8.8	8.5
Bachelor's degree (percent) ...	17.3	19.7
Graduate or professional degree (percent)...	10.6	12.3
High school graduate or higher (percent) ...	90.3	88.0
Bachelor's degree or higher (percent)...	28.0	32.0

Table OH-12. Public School Characteristics and Educational Indicators

(Number, percent; data derived from National Center of Education Statistics.)

Item	State	U.S.
Public Elementary and Secondary Schools		
Number of operational school districts, 2016-17...	1,088	18,377
Number of operational schools, 2016-17...	3,591	98,330
Percent charter schools ...	10.1	7.1
Total public school enrollment, 2016-17...	1,710,143	50,587,859
Percent charter school enrollment ...	6.8	6.0
Student-teacher ratio, Fall 2015 ...	16.9	16.0
Expenditures per student (dollars), 2015-16...	11,933	11,841
Four-year adjusted cohort graduation rate (ACGR)[1] ...	84.2	84.6
Students eligible for free or reduced-price lunch (percent), 2015-16...	44.9	52.1
English language learners (percent), Fall 2016 ...	3.3	9.6
Students age 3 to 21 served under IDEA, part B (percent), 2017-18...	15.7	13.7

Public Schools by Type, 2016-17		Percent of state public schools
Total number of schools...	3,591	100.0
Special education...	51	6.2
Vocational education...	74	2.5
Alternative education...	0	-

[1] Adjusted Cohort Graduation Rates (ACGR) differ from Averaged Freshmen Graduation Rates (AFGR).
- = Zero or rounds to zero.

Table OH-13. Reported Voting and Registration of the Voting-Age Population, November 2018

(Numbers in thousands, percent.)

Item	Total population	Total citizen population	Registered			Voted		
			Total registered	Percent registered (total population)	Percent registered (total citizen population)	Total voted	Percent voted (total population)	Percent voted (total citizen population)
U.S. Total	249,748	228,832	153,066	61.3	66.9	122,281	49.0	53.4
State Total..	8,873	8,640	6,062	68.3	70.2	4,538	51.1	52.5
Sex								
Male	4,294	4,158	2,840	66.1	68.3	2,035	47.4	48.9
Female	4,579	4,482	3,222	70.4	71.9	2,503	54.7	55.9
Race								
White alone.......................................	7,372	7,280	5,152	69.9	70.8	3,889	52.8	53.4
White, non-Hispanic alone	7,203	7,142	5,058	70.2	70.8	3,849	53.4	53.9
Black alone.......................................	1,054	1,010	707	67.1	70.0	519	49.2	51.4
Asian alone	207	129	93	45.1	72.4	65	31.3	50.1
Hispanic (of any race).......................	235	185	121	51.5	65.4	60	25.7	32.6
White alone or in combination	7,519	7,420	5,215	69.4	70.3	3,920	52.1	52.8
Black alone or in combination............	1,171	1,120	761	65.0	68.0	544	46.5	48.6
Asian alone or in combination............	223	145	98	43.9	67.4	69	31.0	47.7
Age								
18 to 24 years	1,033	1,007	503	48.7	49.9	226	21.9	22.5
25 to 34 years	1,472	1,399	882	59.9	63.0	601	40.8	42.9
35 to 44 years	1,365	1,322	956	70.1	72.3	706	51.8	53.4
45 to 64 years	3,127	3,043	2,238	71.6	73.6	1,750	56.0	57.5
65 years and over	1,876	1,869	1,482	79.0	79.3	1,254	66.9	67.1

Table OH-14. Crime

(Number, rate per 100,000. Data are derived from the FBI Uniform Crime Reports.)

Item	State			U.S.		
	2016	2017	Percent change	2016	2017	Percent change
TOTAL POPULATION[1]	11,622,554	11,658,609	0.3	323,405,935	325,719,178	0.7
VIOLENT CRIME						
Number..	35,759	34,683	-3.0	1,285,606	1,283,220	-0.2
Rate	307.7	297.5	-3.3	397.5	394.0	-0.9
Murder and Nonnegligent Manslaughter						
Number..	683	710	4.0	17,413	17,284	-0.7
Rate	5.9	6.1	3.6	5.4	5.3	-1.4
Rape[2]						
Number..	5,754	5,859	1.8	132,414	135,755	2.5
Rate	49.5	50.3	1.5	40.9	41.7	1.8
Robbery						
Number..	12,574	11,605	-7.7	332,797	319,356	-4.0
Rate	108.2	99.5	-8.0	102.9	98.0	-4.7
Aggravated Assault						
Number..	16,748	16,509	-1.4	802,982	810,825	1.0
Rate	144.1	141.6	-1.7	248.3	248.9	0.3
PROPERTY CRIME						
Number..	300,945	282,034	-6.3	7,928,530	7,694,086	-3.0
Rate	2,589.3	2,419.1	-6.6	2,451.6	2,362.2	-3.6
Burglary						
Number..	67,081	58,573	-12.7	1,516,405	1,401,840	-7.6
Rate	577.2	502.4	-13.0	468.9	430.4	-8.2
Larceny-Theft						
Number..	214,102	203,208	-5.1	5,644,835	5,519,107	-2.2
Rate	1,842.1	1,743.0	-5.4	1,745.4	1,694.4	-2.9
Motor Vehicle Theft						
Number..	19,762	20,253	2.5	767,290	773,139	0.8
Rate	170.0	173.7	2.2	237.3	237.4	-

NOTE: Although arson data are included in the trend and clearance tables, sufficient data are not available to estimate totals for this offense. Therefore, no arson data are published in this table.
- = Zero or rounds to zero.
[1] Population figures are U.S. Census Bureau provisional estimates as of July 1, 2017.
[2] The figures shown in the rape (revised definition) column were estimated using the revised Uniform Crime Reporting (UCR) definition of rape.

Table OH-15. State Government Finances, 2017

(Dollar amounts in thousands, percent distribution.)

Item	Dollars	Percent distribution
Total Revenue	100,598,743	100.0
General revenue	69,775,759	69.4
Intergovernmental revenue	24,305,702	24.2
Taxes	30,306,468	30.1
General sales	13,343,149	13.3
Selective sales	6,230,259	6.2
License taxes	2,300,778	2.3
Individual income tax	8,377,450	8.3
Corporate income tax	8,833	-
Other taxes	45,999	-
Current charges	9,518,654	9.5
Miscellaneous general revenue	5,644,935	5.6
Utility revenue	0	-
Liquor stores revenue	1,154,329	1.1
Insurance trust revenue[1]	29,668,655	29.5
Total Expenditure	88,232,183	100.0
Intergovernmental expenditure	18,796,046	21.3
Direct expenditure	69,436,137	78.7
Current operation	44,386,728	50.3
Capital outlay	4,605,675	5.2
Insurance benefits and repayments	17,323,549	19.6
Assistance and subsidies	1,803,259	2.0
Interest on debt	1,316,926	1.5
Exhibit: Salaries and wages	8,301,530	9.4
Total Expenditure	88,232,183	100.0
General expenditure	70,094,702	79.4
Intergovernmental expenditure	18,796,046	21.3
Direct expenditure	51,298,656	58.1
General expenditure, by function:		
Education	23,187,805	26.3
Public welfare	25,824,087	29.3
Hospitals	4,351,948	4.9
Health	2,459,852	2.8
Highways	4,044,349	4.6
Police protection	390,158	0.4
Correction	1,815,411	2.1
Natural resources	442,609	0.5
Parks and recreation	191,652	0.2
Governmental administration	2,149,592	2.4
Interest on general debt	1,316,926	1.5
Other and unallocable	3,920,313	4.4
Utility expenditure	0	-
Liquor stores expenditure	813,932	0.9
Insurance trust expenditure	17,323,549	19.6
Debt at End of Fiscal Year	33,493,235	X
Cash and Security Holdings	224,628,316	X

X = Not applicable.
- = Zero or rounds to zero.
[1] Within insurance trust revenue, net earnings of state retirement systems is a calculated statistic (the item code in the data file is X08), and thus can be positive or negative. Net earnings is the sum of earnings on investments plus gains on investments minus losses on investments. The change made in 2002 for asset valuation from book to market value in accordance with Statement 34 of the Governmental Accounting Standards Board is reflected in the calculated statistics.

Table OH-16. State Government Tax Collections, 2018

(Dollars in thousands, percent.)

Item	Dollars	Percent distribution
Total Taxes	29,130,040	100.0
Property taxes	X	-
Sales and gross receipts	18,086,156	62.1
General sales and gross receipts	12,148,485	41.7
Selective sales and gross receipts	5,937,671	20.4
Alcoholic beverages	104,977	0.4
Amusements	270,480	0.9
Insurance premiums	582,794	2.0
Motor fuels	1,912,191	6.6
Pari-mutuels	5,185	-
Public utilities	927,171	3.2
Tobacco products	941,105	3.2
Other selective sales	1,193,768	4.1
Licenses	2,269,604	7.8
Alcoholic beverages	43,804	0.2
Amusements	34,850	0.1
Corporations in general	297,490	1.0
Hunting and fishing	36,260	0.1
Motor vehicle	787,276	2.7
Motor vehicle operators	80,227	0.3
Public utilities	34,222	0.1
Occupation and business, NEC	907,882	3.1
Other licenses	47,593	0.2
Income taxes	8,707,947	29.9
Individual income	8,698,901	29.9
Corporation net income	9,046	-
Other taxes	66,333	0.2
Death and gift	213	-
Documentary and stock transfer	X	-
Severance	66,120	0.2
Taxes, NEC	0	-

X = Not applicable.
- = Zero or rounds to zero.

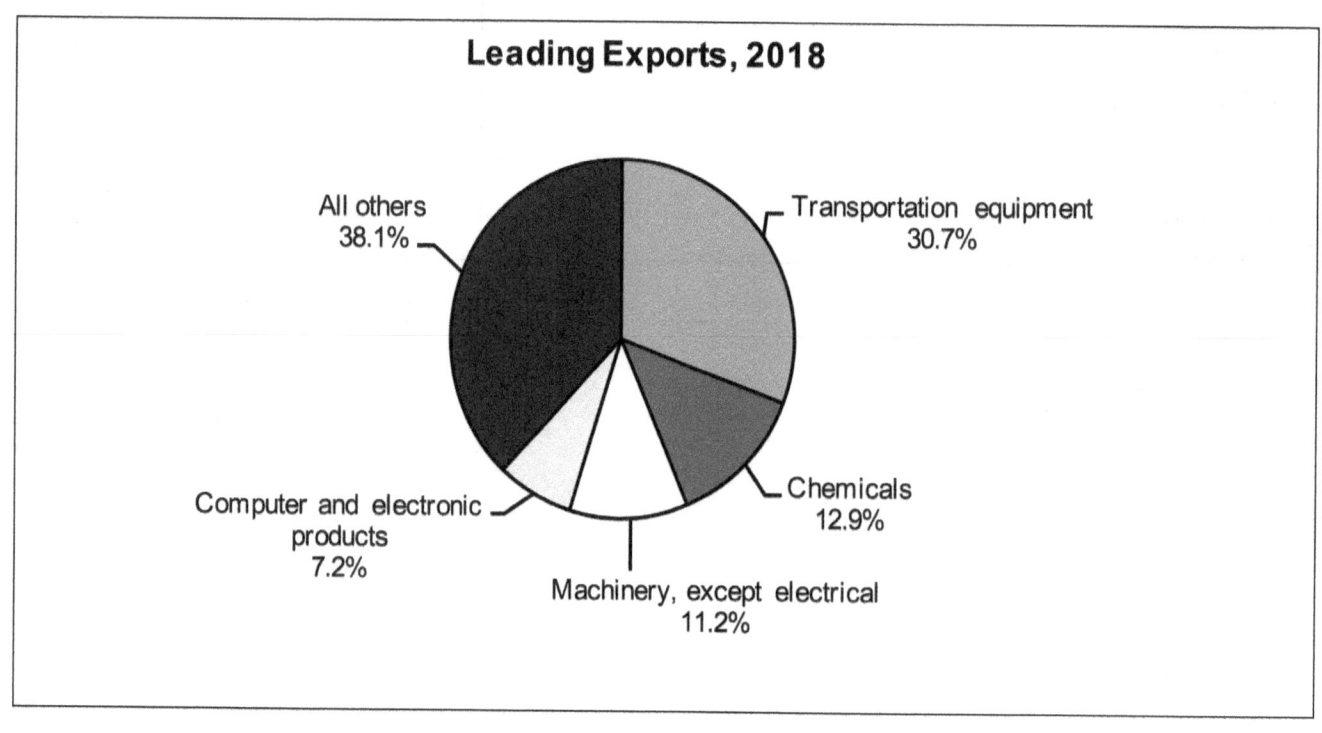

Leading Exports, 2018

All others 38.1%

Transportation equipment 30.7%

Chemicals 12.9%

Machinery, except electrical 11.2%

Computer and electronic products 7.2%

OKLAHOMA

Facts and Figures

Location: West south central United States; bordered on the N by Colorado and Kansas, on the E by Missouri and Arkansas, on the S by Texas, and on the W by Texas and New Mexico

Area: 69,898 sq. mi. (181,036 sq. km.); rank—20th

Population: 3,943,079 (2018 est.); rank—28th

Principal Cities: capital—Oklahoma City; largest—Oklahoma City

Statehood: November 16, 1907; 46th state

U.S. Congress: 2 senators, 5 representatives

State Motto: *Labor omnia vincit* ("Labor conquers all things")

State Song: "Oklahoma!"

State Nickname: The Sooner State

Abbreviations: OK; Okla.

State Symbols: flower—mistletoe; tree—redbud; bird—scissor-tailed flycatcher

At a Glance

- With an increase in population of 5.1 percent, Oklahoma ranked 24th among the states in growth from 2010 to 2018.

- Oklahoma's median household income in 2017 was $50,051, and 15.8 percent of the population lived below the poverty level.

- In 2017, 14.2 percent of Oklahomans did not have health insurance, making it the state with the 2nd highest percent of uninsured residents.

- Oklahoma's violent crime rate in 2017 was 456.2 per 100,000 population, compared to 394.0 for the entire nation.

- Its 2017 property crime rate of 2,876.4 incidences per 100,000 residents made Oklahoma the state with the 12th highest property crime rate in the country.

Table OK-1. Population by Age, Sex, Race, and Hispanic Origin

(Number, percent, except where noted.)

Sex, age, race, and Hispanic origin	2000	2010	2018 [1]	Percent change, 2010–2018
Total Population..	3,450,654	3,751,351	3,943,079	5.1
Percent of total U.S. population	1.2	1.2	1.2	X
Sex				
Male..	1,695,895	1,856,977	1,953,046	5.2
Female	1,754,759	1,894,374	1,990,033	5.0
Age				
Under 5 years..	236,353	264,126	260,429	-1.4
5 to 19 years...	765,927	777,484	802,047	3.2
20 to 64 years...	1,992,424	2,203,027	2,261,050	2.6
65 years and over..	455,950	506,714	619,553	22.3
Median age (years)	35.5	36.2	36.7	1.4
Race and Hispanic Origin				
One race				
White	2,628,434	2,851,510	2,924,365	2.6
Black	260,968	284,332	306,890	7.9
American Indian and Alaska Native	273,230	335,664	367,043	9.3
Asian	46,767	67,126	92,179	37.3
Native Hawaiian or Other Pacific Islander	2,372	5,354	7,568	41.4
Two or more races	155,985	207,365	245,034	18.2
Hispanic (of any race)...	179,304	351,542	429,078	22.1

X = Not applicable.
- = Zero or rounds to zero.
[1] Population figures for 2018 are July 1 estimates. The 2010 estimates are taken from the 2010 Census.

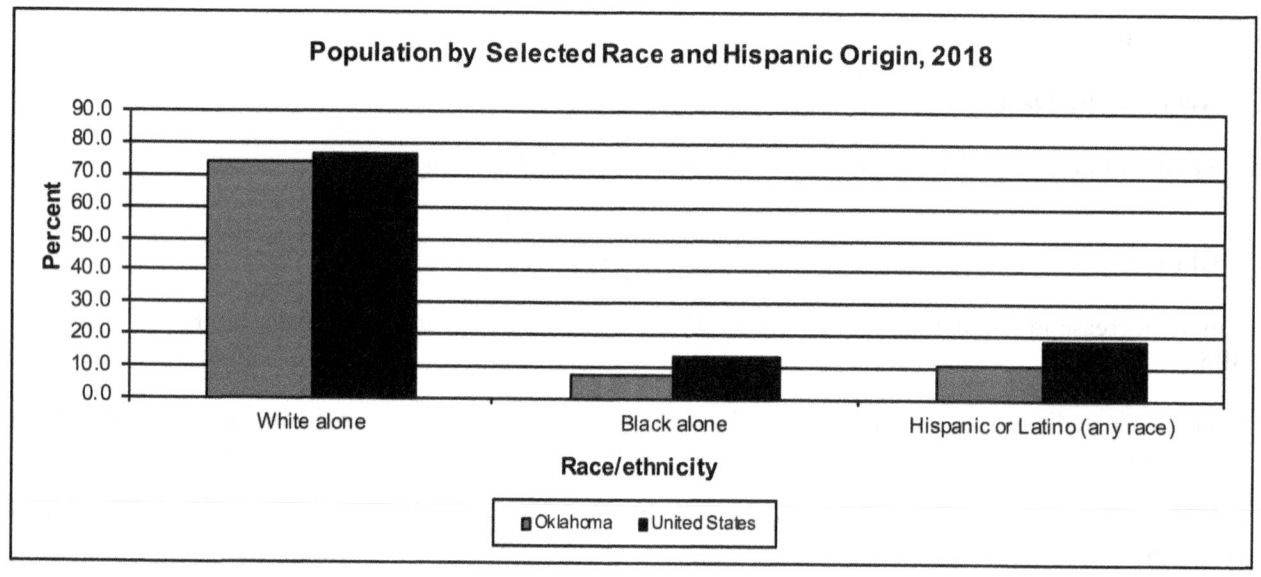

Population by Selected Race and Hispanic Origin, 2018

Oklahoma ▪ United States

Table OK-2. Marital Status

(Number, percent distribution.)

Sex, age, race, and Hispanic origin	2000	2010	2017
Males, 15 Years and Over..	1,318,729	1,457,860	1,536,080
Never married	25.8	30.7	32.6
Now married, except separated..	59.5	52.2	50.2
Separated..	1.6	1.8	1.9
Widowed..	2.5	3.0	3.1
Divorced..	10.6	12.3	12.2
Females, 15 Years and Over	1,398,823	1,521,546	1,593,249
Never married	19.1	23.8	25.5
Now married, except separated..	55.3	49.7	47.7
Separated..	1.9	2.7	2.4
Widowed..	11.1	10.1	10.0
Divorced..	12.5	13.7	14.4

Table OK-3. Households and Housing Characteristics

(Number, percent, dollars.)

Item	2000	2010	2017	Average annual percent change, 2010–2017
Total Households..	1,342,293	1,432,959	1,470,364	0.4
Family households	921,750	954,622	964,144	0.1
Married-couple family................................	717,611	709,256	705,584	-0.1
Other family	204,139	245,366	258,560	0.8
Male householder, no wife present..................	51,564	62,855	74,945	2.7
Female householder, no husband present..........	152,575	182,511	183,615	0.1
Nonfamily households	420,543	478,337	506,220	0.8
Householder living alone...........................	358,560	400,840	418,593	0.6
Householder not living alone......................	61,983	77,497	87,627	1.9
Housing Characteristics				
Total housing units.....................................	1,514,400	1,666,205	1,734,074	0.6
Occupied housing units	1,342,293	1,432,959	1,470,364	0.4
Owner occupied	918,259	971,378	962,483	-0.1
Renter occupied	424,034	461,581	507,881	1.4
Average household size................................	2.49	2.55	2.60	0.3
Financial Characteristics				
Median gross rent of renter-occupied housing	456	659	780	2.6
Median monthly owner costs for housing units with a mortgage	764	1,089	1,183	1.2
Median value of owner-occupied housing units........	70,700	111,400	137,400	3.3

Table OK-4. Migration, Origin, and Language

(Number, percent.)

Characteristic	State 2016	State 2017	State Percent change	U.S. 2016	U.S. 2017	U.S. Percent change
Residence 1 Year Ago						
Population 1 year and over	3,873,232	3,875,922	0.1	319,361,956	321,994,428	0.8
Same house	83.3	83.0	X	85.4	85.7	X
Different house in the U.S.	16.3	16.6	X	13.9	13.6	X
Same county	9.6	9.7	X	8.3	8.1	X
Different county	6.7	6.9	X	5.6	5.6	X
Same state	4.1	4.3	X	3.2	3.3	X
Different state	2.6	2.6	X	2.4	2.3	X
Abroad	0.4	0.4	X	0.7	0.7	X
Place of Birth						
Native born	3,695,147	3,706,981	0.3	279,388,170	281,193,323	0.6
Male	49.4	49.4	X	49.3	49.4	X
Female	50.6	50.6	X	50.7	50.6	X
Foreign born	228,414	223,883	-2.0	43,739,345	44,525,855	1.8
Male	51.0	52.8	X	48.5	48.4	X
Female	49.0	47.2	X	51.5	51.6	X
Foreign born; naturalized U.S. citizen.................	77,757	79,635	2.4	21,238,372	21,948,732	3.3
Male..	47.1	49.1	X	45.9	45.9	X
Female	52.9	50.9	X	54.1	54.1	X
Foreign born; not a U.S. citizen......................	150,657	144,248	-4.3	22,500,973	22,577,123	0.3
Male..	53.1	54.7	X	51.0	50.8	X
Female	46.9	45.3	X	49.0	49.2	X
Entered 2010 or later	21.8	26.8	X	18.6	21.3	X
Entered 2000 to 2009	34.1	27.2	X	26.7	25.7	X
Entered before 2000...................................	44.2	46.0	X	54.7	53.0	X
World Region of Birth, Foreign						
Foreign-born population, excluding population born at sea	228,414	223,883	-2.0	43,738,901	44,525,458	1.8
Europe	7.6	7.0	X	10.9	10.8	X
Asia	27.7	29.1	X	30.8	31.2	X
Africa	3.6	4.1	X	4.9	5.1	X
Oceania	1.5	2.1	X	0.6	0.6	X
Latin America	58.1	56.6	X	51.0	50.4	X
North America	1.4	1.2	X	1.8	1.8	X
Language Spoken at Home and Ability to Speak English						
Population 5 years and over	3,659,465	3,668,303	0.2	303,328,961	305,924,019	0.9
English only	89.7	89.8	X	78.4	78.2	X
Language other than English........................	10.3	10.2	X	21.6	21.8	X
Speaks English less than "very well".............	4.0	3.7	X	8.6	8.5	X

NA = Not available.
X = Not applicable.
- = Zero or rounds to zero.

Table OK-5. Median Income and Poverty Status, 2017

(Number, percent, except as noted.)

Characteristic	State Number	State Percent	U.S. Number	U.S. Percent
Median Income				
Households (dollars)..	50,051	X	60,336	X
Families (dollars)	61,471	X	73,891	X
Below Poverty Level (All People)	603,864	15.8	42,583,651	13.4
Sex				
Male	272,340	14.5	19,004,547	12.2
Female	331,524	17.1	23,579,104	14.5
Age				
Under 18 years...	202,674	21.5	13,353,202	18.4
Related children under 18 years......................................	199,326	21.2	13,053,472	18.1
18 to 64 years..	348,125	15.2	24,648,677	12.6
65 years and over	53,065	9.1	4,581,772	9.3

X = Not applicable.

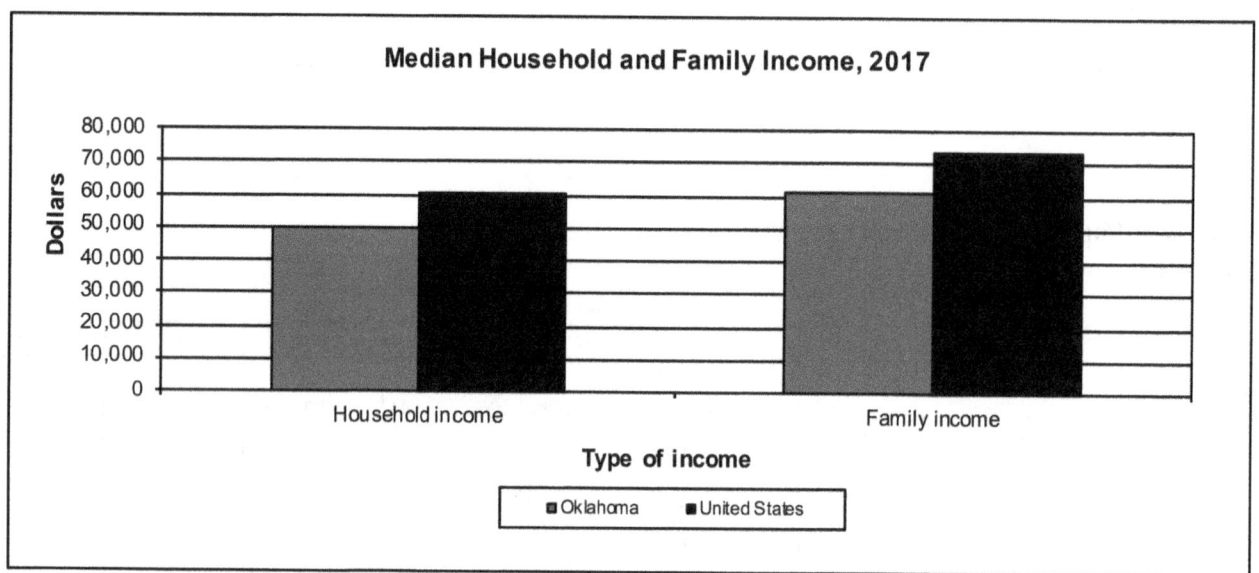

Table OK-6. Health Insurance Coverage Status for the Civilian Noninstitutionalized Population and Children Under 18 Years of Age

(Number, percent.)

Item	2009	2010	2011	2012	2013	2014	2015	2016	2017
Civilian Noninstitutionalized Population	3,590,307	3,677,206	3,710,368	3,733,058	3,770,254	3,797,966	3,830,329	3,845,697	3,851,302
Covered by Private or Public Insurance									
Number..	2,918,644	2,983,655	3,016,823	3,047,982	3,104,481	3,214,454	3,297,820	3,316,039	3,305,819
Percent...	81.3	81.1	81.3	81.6	82.3	84.6	86.1	86.2	85.8
Uninsured									
Number..	671,663	693,551	693,545	685,076	665,773	583,512	532,509	529,658	545,483
Percent...	18.7	18.9	18.7	18.4	17.7	15.4	13.9	13.8	14.2
Percent in the U.S. not covered......................	15.1	15.5	15.1	14.8	14.5	11.7	9.4	8.6	8.7
Children Under 18 Years of Age[1]	918,593	929,349	933,893	934,617	946,133	950,123	958,418	959,850	1,018,753
Covered by Private or Public Insurance									
Number..	815,915	836,828	834,509	840,408	851,091	867,872	887,310	889,761	936,357
Percent...	88.8	90.0	89.4	89.9	90.0	91.3	92.6	92.7	91.9
Uninsured									
Number..	102,678	92,521	99,384	94,209	95,042	82,251	71,108	70,089	82,396
Percent...	11.2	10.0	10.6	10.1	10.0	8.7	7.4	7.3	8.1
Percent in the U.S. not covered......................	8.6	8.0	7.5	7.2	7.1	6.0	4.8	4.5	5.0

[1] 2017 data is for individuals under 19 years of age.

Table OK-7. Employment Status by Demographic Group, 2018

(Numbers in thousands, percent.)

Characteristic	Civilian noninstitutional population	Civilian labor force		Employed		Unemployed	
		Number	Percent of population	Number	Percent of population	Number	Percent of population
Total...	3,009	1,844	61.3	1,781	59.2	63	3.4
Sex							
Male...	1,460	1,016	69.6	982	67.2	34	3.4
Female..	1,549	828	53.5	799	51.6	29	3.5
Race, Sex, and Hispanic Origin							
White...	2,325	1,427	61.4	1,389	59.8	38	2.7
Male...	1,133	797	70.3	776	68.4	21	2.7
Female..	1,191	631	52.9	614	51.5	17	2.7
Black or African American.................	205	125	61.0	116	56.6	9	7.2
Male...	99	66	67.2	61	61.9	5	7.9
Female..	NA	NA	NA	NA	NA	NA	NA
Hispanic or Latino ethnicity[1].............	323	222	68.8	215	66.4	8	3.4
Male...	168	142	84.5	138	82.3	4	2.6
Female..	155	81	51.8	77	49.4	4	4.8
Age							
16 to 19 years................................	206	76	36.8	68	32.8	8	10.9
20 to 24 years................................	240	170	71.1	160	66.8	10	6.0
25 to 34 years................................	548	426	77.7	411	75.0	15	3.5
35 to 44 years................................	479	387	80.9	376	78.5	11	2.9
45 to 54 years................................	441	343	77.8	334	75.8	9	2.5
55 to 64 years................................	487	317	65.0	312	64.0	5	1.6
65 years and over...........................	609	125	20.5	121	19.8	4	3.3

NOTE: Data in Table 7 are from the Current Population Survey (CPS) and do not match the estimates in Table 8. See notes and definitions for further information.
[1] May be of any race.

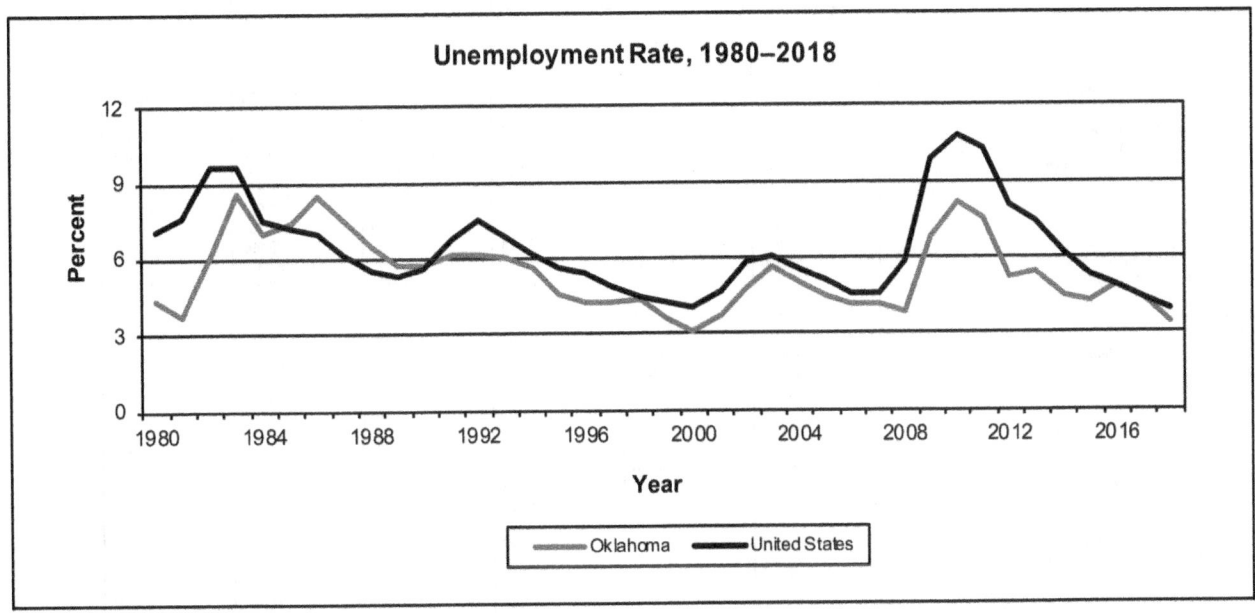

Table OK-8. Employment Status of the Civilian Noninstitutional Population Age 16 Years and Over

(Number, percent.)

Year	Civilian labor force	Civilian participation rate	Employed	Unemployed	Unemployment rate
2010...	1,768,284	62.4	1,648,138	120,146	6.8
2011...	1,772,666	61.9	1,668,418	104,248	5.9
2012...	1,803,863	62.4	1,709,258	94,605	5.2
2013...	1,802,073	61.8	1,706,861	95,212	5.3
2014...	1,796,183	61.0	1,715,600	80,583	4.5
2015...	1,830,358	61.7	1,749,626	80,732	4.4
2016...	1,829,413	61.3	1,741,277	88,136	4.8
2017...	1,834,312	61.2	1,755,604	78,708	4.3
2018...	1,841,872	61.2	1,779,370	62,502	3.4

Table OK-9. Employment and Average Wages by Industry

(Estimates are based on the 2012 *North American Industry Classification System* [NAICS].)

Industry	2011	2012	2013	2014	2015	2016	2017
	Number of jobs						
Wage and Salary Employment by Industry..........................	1,624,865	1,657,282	1,679,717	1,699,657	1,705,980	1,688,995	1,693,826
Farm Wage and Salary Employment.................................	8,747	10,448	11,398	9,773	5,799	7,400	6,980
Nonfarm Wage and Salary Employment.............................	1,616,118	1,646,834	1,668,319	1,689,884	1,700,181	1,681,595	1,686,846
Private wage and salary employment..........................	1,244,038	1,278,735	1,297,705	1,320,453	1,328,465	1,310,569	1,317,325
Forestry, fishing, and related activities	4,115	4,157	4,329	4,451	4,554	4,675	4,688
Mining...	50,867	57,761	59,645	61,379	53,544	43,902	47,518
Utilities...	11,189	11,729	11,722	12,021	12,094	11,495	10,717
Construction...	70,103	72,255	76,914	77,541	79,330	79,335	79,109
Manufacturing...	132,105	137,796	139,052	142,097	139,486	131,205	130,697
Durable goods manufacturing...........................	87,901	94,760	96,163	98,877	96,557	87,858	87,629
Nondurable goods manufacturing......................	44,204	43,036	42,889	43,220	42,929	43,347	43,068
Wholesale trade	58,433	60,675	62,252	63,623	60,478	58,589	58,546
Retail trade..	171,715	174,724	176,169	179,677	184,473	184,893	180,201
Transportation and warehousing...........................	43,166	45,220	46,603	47,723	52,146	52,916	55,285
Information	24,131	22,697	21,846	21,733	21,142	21,130	20,449
Finance and insurance	57,840	59,148	58,798	59,776	60,256	60,074	60,371
Real estate and rental and leasing......................	22,009	21,977	22,561	20,971	21,015	20,693	20,899
Professional, scientific, and technical services..........	65,161	66,513	67,529	68,275	69,874	69,739	70,392
Management of companies and enterprises..............	14,927	16,052	16,599	18,678	18,689	18,096	18,744
Administrative and waste services........................	94,830	96,585	96,232	98,508	98,290	94,569	97,596
Educational services	20,537	21,251	21,509	21,887	22,086	22,581	22,122
Health care and social assistance........................	184,403	186,329	188,054	188,083	191,840	194,774	195,501
Arts, entertainment, and recreation......................	14,116	14,450	14,760	15,353	16,159	17,216	17,517
Accommodation and food services.......................	129,240	133,479	137,499	141,445	146,142	148,705	151,052
Other services, except public administration..............	75,151	75,937	75,632	77,232	76,867	75,982	75,921
Government and government enterprises...................	372,080	368,099	370,614	369,431	371,716	371,026	369,521
	Dollars						
Average Wages and Salaries by Industry	40,722	42,328	43,044	44,454	45,083	44,716	45,997
Average Farm Wages and Salaries	32,127	33,284	24,925	32,314	33,121	28,820	32,319
Average Nonfarm Wages and Salaries	40,769	42,386	43,168	44,524	45,124	44,785	46,054
Average private wages and salaries........................	40,950	42,744	43,660	45,118	45,652	45,026	46,476
Forestry, fishing, and related activities	23,220	23,878	24,693	26,285	27,597	29,672	31,600
Mining...	95,018	92,283	94,831	96,610	103,110	97,233	102,268
Utilities...	82,911	92,089	96,380	114,337	99,909	98,566	101,112
Construction...	42,412	44,695	46,824	47,990	49,707	50,617	51,569
Manufacturing...	49,516	51,901	53,174	55,245	55,690	55,496	57,433
Durable goods manufacturing...........................	51,580	53,987	55,321	57,406	57,313	57,033	59,098
Nondurable goods manufacturing......................	45,412	47,308	48,359	50,301	52,041	52,381	54,045
Wholesale trade	52,463	54,919	55,673	58,056	59,204	58,784	60,973
Retail trade..	25,928	26,941	27,354	27,905	28,383	28,633	29,245
Transportation and warehousing...........................	53,011	54,450	55,642	57,678	56,858	54,282	57,628
Information	51,796	53,052	55,031	56,547	57,110	58,111	60,274
Finance and insurance	52,467	55,161	56,767	60,089	60,659	61,995	64,273
Real estate and rental and leasing......................	39,366	47,062	42,098	42,818	43,248	42,238	43,685
Professional, scientific, and technical services	55,813	59,354	60,954	62,141	63,030	63,172	64,447
Management of companies and enterprises..............	96,089	88,150	88,731	82,009	88,985	86,988	86,885
Administrative and waste services........................	31,746	33,131	33,411	34,634	35,925	35,762	36,986
Educational services	30,106	30,577	31,270	32,413	31,178	31,981	32,160
Health care and social assistance........................	40,072	41,359	42,020	43,465	45,045	45,546	46,175
Arts, entertainment, and recreation......................	28,674	31,207	31,302	33,707	35,225	36,303	35,955
Accommodation and food services.......................	15,980	16,708	16,989	17,538	17,873	18,173	18,558
Other services, except public administration..........	27,355	28,506	29,422	30,243	31,461	32,294	33,563
Government and government enterprises...................	40,163	41,141	41,445	42,402	43,236	43,934	44,552

Table OK-10. Employment Characteristics by Family Type

(Number, percent.)

Family type and labor force status	2015 Total	2015 Families with own children under 18 years	2016 Total	2016 Families with own children under 18 years	2017 Total	2017 Families with own children under 18 years
All Families....................	969,588	417,301	961,731	412,764	964,144	415,329
FAMILY TYPE AND LABOR FORCE STATUS						
Married-Couple Families....................	713,308	274,692	710,097	275,619	705,584	272,320
Both husband and wife in labor force....................	48.5	62.7	48.5	63.1	48.7	63.5
Husband in labor force, wife not in labor force....................	23.9	30.2	24.0	29.6	23.3	28.9
Wife in labor force, husband not in labor force....................	8.2	4.2	8.0	4.5	8.0	4.6
Both husband and wife not in labor force....................	18.7	2.3	18.8	2.5	19.2	2.2
Other Families	256,280	142,609	251,634	137,145	258,560	143,009
Female householder, no husband present....................	69.7	71.8	69.8	70.1	71.0	73.0
In labor force....................	47.6	57.5	46.5	56.2	47.6	58.6
Not in labor force....................	22.0	14.3	23.3	13.9	23.4	14.4
Male householder, no wife present....................	30.3	28.2	30.2	29.9	29.0	27.0
In labor force....................	23.6	25.1	23.2	26.8	22.2	23.9
Not in labor force....................	6.7	3.1	7.0	3.1	6.8	3.2

Table OK-11. School Enrollment and Educational Attainment, 2017

(Number, percent.)

Item	State	U.S.
Enrollment		
Total population 3 years and over, enrolled in school	1,011,241	81,273,337
Enrolled in nursery school or preschool (percent)....................	6.6	6.0
Enrolled in kindergarten (percent)....................	5.4	4.9
Enrolled in elementary school, grades 1-8 (percent)....................	43.0	40.6
Enrolled in high school, grades 9-12 (percent)....................	21.1	21.1
Enrolled in college or graduate school (percent)....................	23.9	27.4
Attainment		
Total population 25 years and over	2,586,414	221,250,083
Less than ninth grade (percent)....................	4.1	5.1
9th to 12th grade, no diploma (percent)....................	7.9	6.9
High school graduate, including equivalency (percent)....................	31.1	27.1
Some college, no degree (percent)....................	23.3	20.4
Associate's degree (percent)....................	8.1	8.5
Bachelor's degree (percent)....................	16.9	19.7
Graduate or professional degree (percent)....................	8.6	12.3
High school graduate or higher (percent)....................	88.1	88.0
Bachelor's degree or higher (percent)....................	25.5	32.0

Table OK-12. Public School Characteristics and Educational Indicators

(Number, percent; data derived from National Center of Education Statistics.)

Item	State	U.S.
Public Elementary and Secondary Schools		
Number of operational school districts, 2016-17....................	600	18,377
Number of operational schools, 2016-17....................	1,792	98,330
Percent charter schools	2.7	7.1
Total public school enrollment, 2016-17....................	693,903	50,587,859
Percent charter school enrollment	3.5	6.0
Student-teacher ratio, Fall 2015....................	16.3	16.0
Expenditures per student (dollars), 2015-16....................	8,091	11,841
Four-year adjusted cohort graduation rate (ACGR)[1]....................	82.6	84.6
Students eligible for free or reduced-price lunch (percent), 2015-16....................	62.2	52.1
English language learners (percent), Fall 2016	6.7	9.6
Students age 3 to 21 served under IDEA, part B (percent), 2017-18....................	16.1	13.7

Public Schools by Type, 2016-17		Percent of state public schools
Total number of schools....................	1,792	100.0
Special education....................	4	0.2
Vocational education....................	0	-
Alternative education....................	5	0.3

[1] Adjusted Cohort Graduation Rates (ACGR) differ from Averaged Freshmen Graduation Rates (AFGR).
- = Zero or rounds to zero.

Table OK-13. Reported Voting and Registration of the Voting-Age Population, November 2018

(Numbers in thousands, percent.)

Item	Total population	Total citizen population	Registered			Voted		
			Total registered	Percent registered (total population)	Percent registered (total citizen population)	Total voted	Percent voted (total population)	Percent voted (total citizen population)
U.S. Total	249,748	228,832	153,066	61.3	66.9	122,281	49.0	53.4
State Total...................................	2,868	2,732	1,777	62.0	65.1	1,350	47.1	49.4
Sex								
Male	1,388	1,330	824	59.4	62.0	626	45.1	47.1
Female	1,480	1,402	953	64.4	68.0	724	48.9	51.6
Race								
White alone................................	2,254	2,148	1,422	63.1	66.2	1,098	48.7	51.1
White, non-Hispanic alone................	1,957	1,951	1,341	68.5	68.7	1,035	52.9	53.0
Black alone.................................	195	184	90	46.1	48.8	61	31.2	33.0
Asian alone.................................	70	50	23	(B)	(B)	15	(B)	(B)
Hispanic (of any race).....................	310	210	88	28.5	42.1	71	22.8	33.7
White alone or in combination	2,370	2,264	1,510	63.7	66.7	1,162	49.0	51.3
Black alone or in combination.............	212	201	103	48.7	51.2	72	34.1	35.9
Asian alone or in combination.............	73	53	26	(B)	(B)	18	(B)	(B)
Age								
18 to 24 years	309	287	110	35.6	38.2	65	21.1	22.6
25 to 34 years	507	471	275	54.2	58.3	191	37.6	40.5
35 to 44 years	509	469	305	59.8	64.9	202	39.7	43.1
45 to 64 years	912	876	600	65.8	68.5	486	53.2	55.4
65 years and over	631	628	487	77.2	77.6	406	64.4	64.7

B = Base is less than 75,000 and therefore too small to show the derived measure.

Table OK-14. Crime

(Number, rate per 100,000. Data are derived from the FBI Uniform Crime Reports.)

Item	State			U.S.		
	2016	2017	Percent change	2016	2017	Percent change
TOTAL POPULATION[1]	3,921,207	3,930,864	0.2	323,405,935	325,719,178	0.7
VIOLENT CRIME						
Number..	17,855	17,934	0.4	1,285,606	1,283,220	-0.2
Rate	455.3	456.2	0.2	397.5	394.0	-0.9
Murder and Nonnegligent Manslaughter						
Number..	247	242	-2.0	17,413	17,284	-0.7
Rate	6.3	6.2	-2.3	5.4	5.3	-1.4
Rape[2]						
Number..	2,100	2,142	2.0	132,414	135,755	2.5
Rate	53.6	54.5	1.7	40.9	41.7	1.8
Robbery						
Number..	3,174	3,000	-5.5	332,797	319,356	-4.0
Rate	80.9	76.3	-5.7	102.9	98.0	-4.7
Aggravated Assault						
Number..	12,334	12,550	1.8	802,982	810,825	1.0
Rate	314.5	319.3	1.5	248.3	248.9	0.3
PROPERTY CRIME						
Number..	118,010	113,066	-4.2	7,928,530	7,694,086	-3.0
Rate	3,009.5	2,876.4	-4.4	2,451.6	2,362.2	-3.6
Burglary						
Number..	29,376	28,608	-2.6	1,516,405	1,401,840	-7.6
Rate	749.2	727.8	-2.9	468.9	430.4	-8.2
Larceny-Theft						
Number..	76,358	72,207	-5.4	5,644,835	5,519,107	-2.2
Rate	1,947.3	1,836.9	-5.7	1,745.4	1,694.4	-2.9
Motor Vehicle Theft						
Number..	12,276	12,251	-0.2	767,290	773,139	0.8
Rate	313.1	311.7	-0.4	237.3	237.4	-

NOTE: Although arson data are included in the trend and clearance tables, sufficient data are not available to estimate totals for this offense. Therefore, no arson data are published in this table.
- = Zero or rounds to zero.
[1] Population figures are U.S. Census Bureau provisional estimates as of July 1, 2017.
[2] The figures shown in the rape (revised definition) column were estimated using the revised Uniform Crime Reporting (UCR) definition of rape.

Table OK-15. State Government Finances, 2017

(Dollar amounts in thousands, percent distribution.)

Item	Dollars	Percent distribution
Total Revenue	27,168,522	100.0
General revenue	21,102,389	77.7
Intergovernmental revenue	7,280,359	26.8
Taxes	8,569,402	31.5
General sales	2,465,383	9.1
Selective sales	1,299,512	4.8
License taxes	1,062,358	3.9
Individual income tax	3,122,602	11.5
Corporate income tax	157,894	0.6
Other taxes	461,653	1.7
Current charges	2,890,003	10.6
Miscellaneous general revenue	2,362,625	8.7
Utility revenue	620,922	2.3
Liquor stores revenue	0	-
Insurance trust revenue[1]	5,445,211	20.0
Total Expenditure	25,252,040	100.0
Intergovernmental expenditure	4,446,655	17.6
Direct expenditure	20,805,385	82.4
Current operation	14,433,262	57.2
Capital outlay	2,509,741	9.9
Insurance benefits and repayments	2,852,310	11.3
Assistance and subsidies	597,283	2.4
Interest on debt	412,789	1.6
Exhibit: Salaries and wages	3,300,913	13.1
Total Expenditure	25,252,040	100.0
General expenditure	21,342,494	84.5
Intergovernmental expenditure	4,446,655	17.6
Direct expenditure	16,895,839	66.9
General expenditure, by function:		
Education	8,323,116	33.0
Public welfare	6,747,383	26.7
Hospitals	262,911	1.0
Health	1,037,585	4.1
Highways	2,168,570	8.6
Police protection	230,799	0.9
Correction	575,015	2.3
Natural resources	160,437	0.6
Parks and recreation	83,468	0.3
Governmental administration	716,346	2.8
Interest on general debt	330,852	1.3
Other and unallocable	706,012	2.8
Utility expenditure	1,057,236	3.9
Liquor stores expenditure	0	-
Insurance trust expenditure	2,852,310	11.3
Debt at End of Fiscal Year	8,457,322	X
Cash and Security Holdings	45,207,967	X

X = Not applicable.
- = Zero or rounds to zero.
[1] Within insurance trust revenue, net earnings of state retirement systems is a calculated statistic (the item code in the data file is X08), and thus can be positive or negative. Net earnings is the sum of earnings on investments plus gains on investments minus losses on investments. The change made in 2002 for asset valuation from book to market value in accordance with Statement 34 of the Governmental Accounting Standards Board is reflected in the calculated statistics.

Table OK-16. State Government Tax Collections, 2018

(Dollars in thousands, percent.)

Item	Dollars	Percent distribution
Total Taxes	9,563,830	100.0
Property taxes	X	-
Sales and gross receipts	4,062,259	42.5
General sales and gross receipts	2,724,367	28.5
Selective sales and gross receipts	1,337,892	14.0
Alcoholic beverages	122,247	1.3
Amusements	26,428	0.3
Insurance premiums	328,756	3.4
Motor fuels	485,376	5.1
Pari-mutuels	1,085	-
Public utilities	43,755	0.5
Tobacco products	313,411	3.3
Other selective sales	16,834	0.2
Licenses	1,050,390	11.0
Alcoholic beverages	1,037	-
Amusements	168,006	1.8
Corporations in general	58,897	0.6
Hunting and fishing	20,494	0.2
Motor vehicle	768,712	8.0
Motor vehicle operators	31,733	0.3
Public utilities	5	-
Occupation and business, NEC	727	-
Other licenses	779	-
Income taxes	3,730,132	39.0
Individual income	3,495,264	36.5
Corporation net income	234,868	2.5
Other taxes	721,049	7.5
Death and gift	0	-
Documentary and stock transfer	21,112	0.2
Severance	699,937	7.3
Taxes, NEC	0	-

X = Not applicable.
- = Zero or rounds to zero.

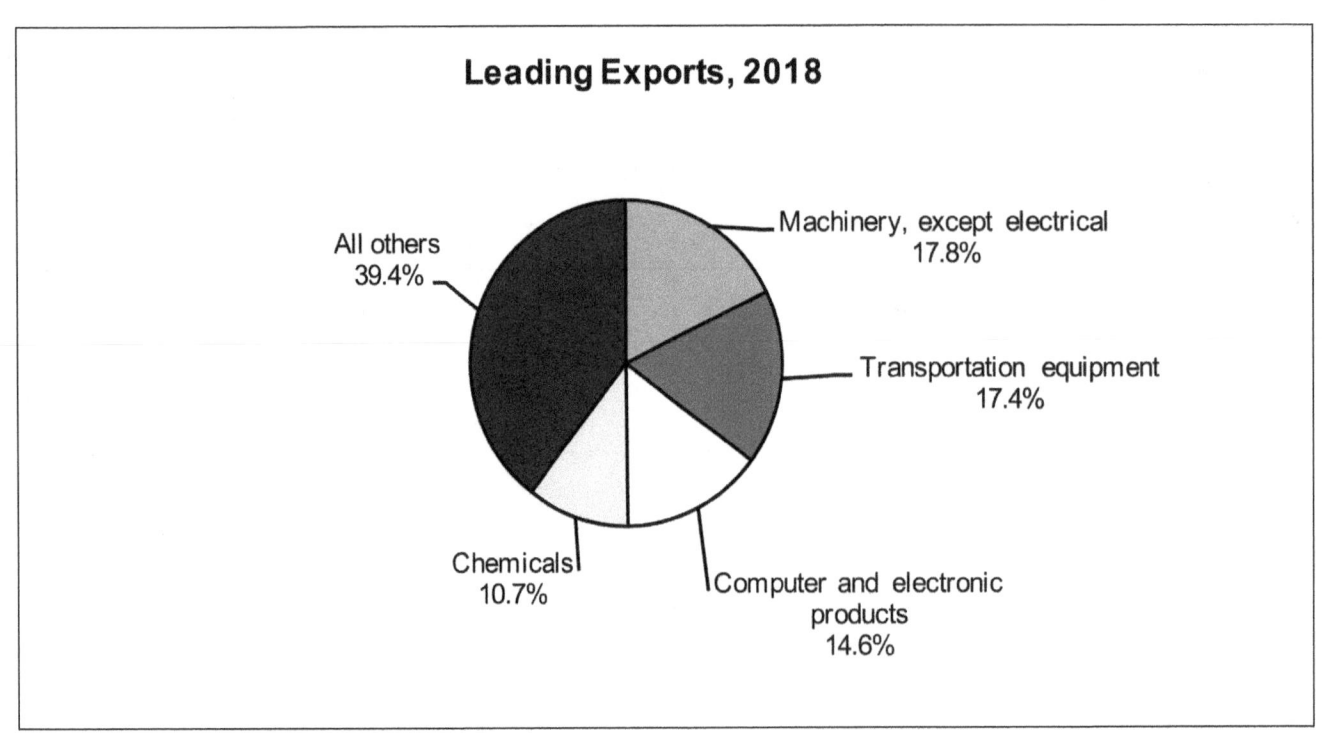

Leading Exports, 2018

- Machinery, except electrical 17.8%
- Transportation equipment 17.4%
- Computer and electronic products 14.6%
- Chemicals 10.7%
- All others 39.4%

OREGON

Facts and Figures

Location: Northwestern United States; bordered on the N by Washington, on the E by Idaho, on the S by Nevada and California, and on the W by the Pacific Ocean

Area: 98,381 sq. mi. (254,805 sq. km.); rank—9th

Population: 4,190,713 (2018 est.); rank—27th

Principal Cities: capital—Salem; largest—Portland

Statehood: February 14, 1859; 33rd state

U.S. Congress: 2 senators, 5 representatives

State Motto: She Flies With Her Own Wings

State Song: "Oregon, My Oregon"

State Nickname: The Beaver State

Abbreviations: OR; Oreg.

State Symbols: flower—Oregon grape; tree—Douglas fir; bird—Western meadowlark

At a Glance

- With an increase in population of 9.4 percent, Oregon ranked 12th among the states in growth from 2010 to 2018.

- In 2017, 6.8 percent of Oregonians did not have health insurance, compared to 8.7 percent of the total U.S. population.

- Oregon's violent crime rate in 2017 was 281.8 per 100,000 population, compared to 394.0 for the entire nation.

- The homeownership rate in Oregon in 2018 was 62.0 percent, compared to the national homeownership rate of 64.4 percent.

- The median household income in Oregon was $60,212 in 2017, and the poverty rate was 13.2 percent.

Table OR-1. Population by Age, Sex, Race, and Hispanic Origin

(Number, percent, except where noted.)

Sex, age, race, and Hispanic origin	2000	2010	2018 [1]	Percent change, 2010–2018
Total Population...	3,421,399	3,831,074	4,190,713	9.4
Percent of total U.S. population	1.2	1.2	1.3	X
Sex				
Male..	1,696,550	1,896,002	2,077,494	9.6
Female	1,724,849	1,935,072	2,113,219	9.2
Age				
Under 5 years..	223,005	237,556	234,214	-1.4
5 to 19 years...	720,999	734,627	738,624	0.5
20 to 64 years..	2,039,218	2,325,358	2,479,184	6.6
65 years and over	438,177	533,533	738,691	38.5
Median age (years)	36.3	38.4	39.4	2.6
Race and Hispanic Origin				
One race				
White	2,961,623	3,403,252	3,635,926	6.8
Black...	55,662	74,414	92,958	24.9
American Indian and Alaska Native	45,211	66,784	76,023	13.8
Asian	101,350	145,009	202,394	39.6
Native Hawaiian or Other Pacific Islander	7,976	14,649	18,999	29.7
Two or more races	104,745	126,966	164,413	29.5
Hispanic (of any race)..	275,314	467,030	556,396	19.1

X = Not applicable.
[1] Population figures for 2018 are July 1 estimates. The 2010 estimates are taken from the 2010 Census.

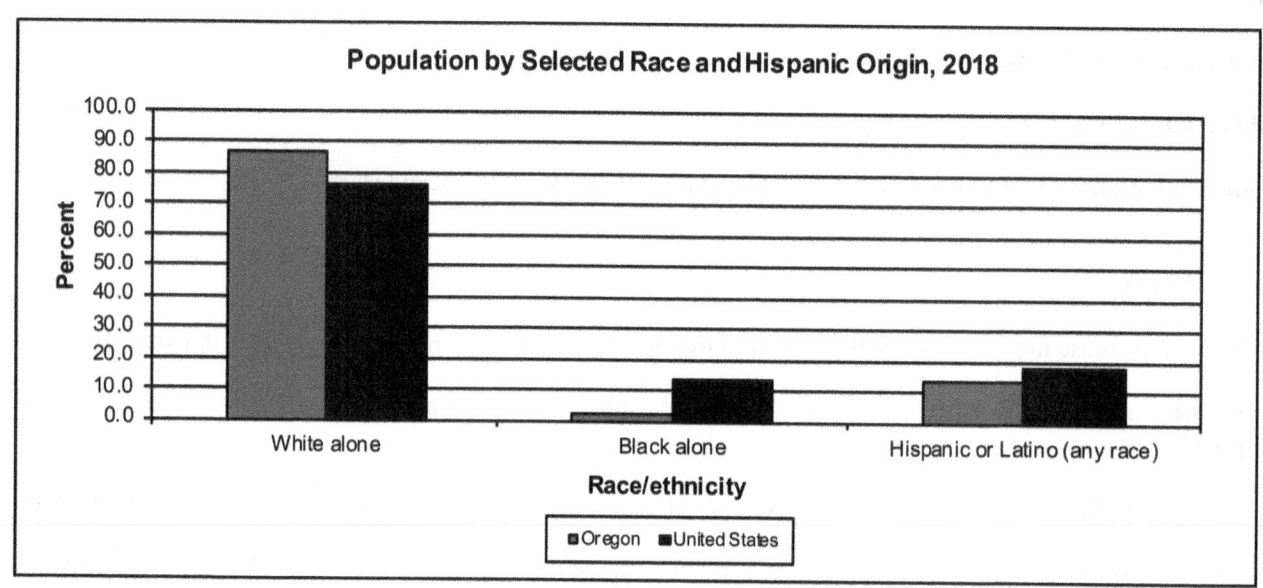

Population by Selected Race and Hispanic Origin, 2018

(Chart: Percent by Race/ethnicity — White alone, Black alone, Hispanic or Latino (any race); Oregon and United States)

Table OR-2. Marital Status

(Number, percent distribution.)

Sex, age, race, and Hispanic origin	2000	2010	2017
Males, 15 Years and Over	1,336,805	1,533,177	1,681,085
Never married	28.5	32.6	35.0
Now married, except separated...	57.1	51.4	49.9
Separated..	1.5	1.6	1.4
Widowed..	2.4	2.7	2.4
Divorced..	10.6	11.8	11.2
Females, 15 Years and Over	1,385,329	1,588,428	1,735,831
Never married	21.9	25.8	27.7
Now married, except separated...	53.9	48.9	48.5
Separated..	1.9	1.9	1.9
Widowed..	9.6	8.5	7.6
Divorced..	12.7	14.9	14.3

Table OR-3. Households and Housing Characteristics

(Number, percent, dollars.)

Item	2000	2010	2017	Average annual percent change, 2010–2017
Total Households...	1,333,723	1,507,137	1,603,635	0.9
Family households.....................................	877,671	963,362	1,010,975	0.7
Married-couple family.............................	692,532	733,095	780,758	0.9
Other family..	185,139	230,267	230,217	-
Male householder, no wife present.........	54,357	65,972	71,983	1.3
Female householder, no husband present...	130,782	164,295	158,234	-0.5
Nonfamily households................................	456,032	543,775	592,660	1.3
Householder living alone..........................	347,624	416,500	444,167	0.9
Householder not living alone....................	108,428	127,275	148,493	2.4
Housing Characteristics				
Total housing units.....................................	1,452,709	1,676,476	1,768,582	0.8
Occupied housing units................................	1,333,723	1,507,137	1,603,635	0.9
Owner occupied......................................	856,951	942,674	1,007,015	1.0
Renter occupied......................................	476,772	564,463	596,620	0.8
Average household size................................	2.51	2.49	2.53	0.2
Financial Characteristics				
Median gross rent of renter-occupied housing	620	816	1079	4.6
Median monthly owner costs for housing units with a mortgage ...	1,125	1,577	1,629	0.5
Median value of owner-occupied housing units........	152,100	244,500	319,200	4.4

- = Zero or rounds to zero.

Table OR-4. Migration, Origin, and Language

(Number, percent.)

Characteristic	State			U.S.		
	2016	2017	Percent change	2016	2017	Percent change
Residence 1 Year Ago						
Population 1 year and over	4,052,221	4,102,048	1.2	319,361,956	321,994,428	0.8
Same house..	81.6	83.0	X	85.4	85.7	X
Different house in the U.S.	17.7	16.3	X	13.9	13.6	X
Same county..	10.4	9.3	X	8.3	8.1	X
Different county	7.3	7.1	X	5.6	5.6	X
Same state	3.9	3.4	X	3.2	3.3	X
Different state	3.4	3.6	X	2.4	2.3	X
Abroad	0.7	0.6	X	0.7	0.7	X
Place of Birth						
Native born	3,699,248	3,734,058	0.9	279,388,170	281,193,323	0.6
Male	49.6	49.6	X	49.3	49.4	X
Female	50.4	50.4	X	50.7	50.6	X
Foreign born	394,217	408,718	3.7	43,739,345	44,525,855	1.8
Male	48.6	49.1	X	48.5	48.4	X
Female	51.4	50.9	X	51.5	51.6	X
Foreign born; naturalized U.S. citizen...........	174,922	185,646	6.1	21,238,372	21,948,732	3.3
Male	45.3	46.4	X	45.9	45.9	X
Female	54.7	53.6	X	54.1	54.1	X
Foreign born; not a U.S. citizen...................	219,295	223,072	1.7	22,500,973	22,577,123	0.3
Male	51.2	51.3	X	51.0	50.8	X
Female	48.8	48.7	X	49.0	49.2	X
Entered 2010 or later	18.7	21.1	X	18.6	21.3	X
Entered 2000 to 2009	25.4	24.2	X	26.7	25.7	X
Entered before 2000.................................	55.9	54.6	X	54.7	53.0	X
World Region of Birth, Foreign						
Foreign-born population, excluding population born at sea	394,217	408,718	3.7	43,738,901	44,525,458	1.8
Europe	16.1	15.5	X	10.9	10.8	X
Asia...	32.2	33.1	X	30.8	31.2	X
Africa	3.1	4.4	X	4.9	5.1	X
Oceania	1.8	1.8	X	0.6	0.6	X
Latin America..	42.9	42.0	X	51.0	50.4	X
North America.......................................	4.0	3.2	X	1.8	1.8	X
Language Spoken at Home and Ability to Speak English						
Population 5 years and over......................	3,858,883	3,910,523	1.3	303,328,961	305,924,019	0.9
English only	84.8	84.7	X	78.4	78.2	X
Language other than English....................	15.2	15.3	X	21.6	21.8	X
Speaks English less than "very well"........	5.9	5.5	X	8.6	8.5	X

NA = Not available.
X = Not applicable.
- = Zero or rounds to zero.

Table OR-5. Median Income and Poverty Status, 2017

(Number, percent, except as noted.)

Characteristic	State		U.S.	
	Number	Percent	Number	Percent
Median Income				
Households (dollars)...	60,212	X	60,336	X
Families (dollars)	73,202	X	73,891	X
Below Poverty Level (All People)	537,974	13.2	42,583,651	13.4
Sex				
Male	247,360	12.3	19,004,547	12.2
Female	290,614	14.1	23,579,104	14.5
Age				
Under 18 years...	141,151	16.5	13,353,202	18.4
Related children under 18 years..	134,574	15.9	13,053,472	18.1
18 to 64 years..	335,916	13.4	24,648,677	12.6
65 years and over..	60,907	8.7	4,581,772	9.3

X = Not applicable.

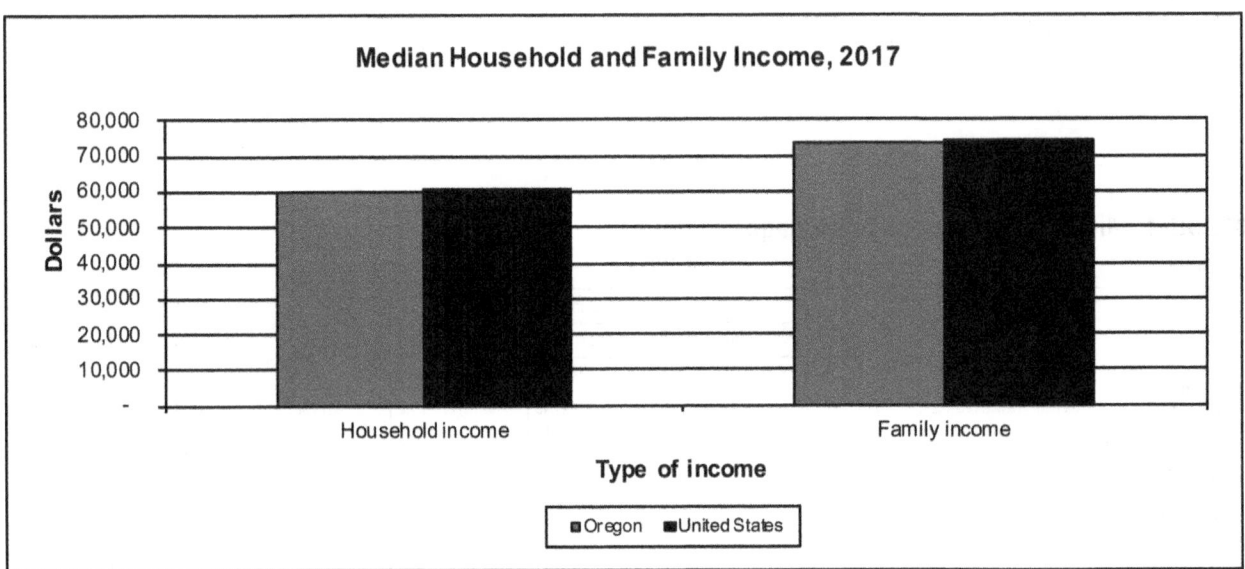

Table OR-6. Health Insurance Coverage Status for the Civilian Noninstitutionalized Population and Children Under 18 Years of Age

(Number, percent.)

Item	2009	2010	2011	2012	2013	2014	2015	2016	2017
Civilian Noninstitutionalized Population	3,779,860	3,799,107	3,832,640	3,860,452	3,893,092	3,931,306	3,991,133	4,054,353	4,102,901
Covered by Private or Public Insurance									
Number..	3,136,858	3,147,603	3,230,263	3,284,443	3,322,210	3,548,645	3,710,870	3,801,587	3,822,085
Percent..	83.0	82.9	84.3	85.1	85.3	90.3	93.0	93.8	93.2
Uninsured									
Number..	643,002	651,504	602,377	576,009	570,882	382,661	280,263	252,766	280,816
Percent..	17.0	17.1	15.7	14.9	14.7	9.7	7.0	6.2	6.8
Percent in the U.S. not covered..	15.1	15.5	15.1	14.8	14.5	11.7	9.4	8.6	8.7
Children Under 18 Years of Age[1]	871,362	865,362	861,059	859,846	858,259	857,084	859,408	866,585	928,115
Covered by Private or Public Insurance									
Number..	780,835	789,611	798,172	805,216	808,087	818,051	828,340	837,985	895,141
Percent..	89.6	91.2	92.7	93.6	94.2	95.4	96.4	96.7	96.4
Uninsured									
Number..	90,527	75,751	62,887	54,630	50,172	39,033	31,068	28,600	32,974
Percent..	10.4	8.8	7.3	6.4	5.8	4.6	3.6	3.3	3.6
Percent in the U.S. not covered..	8.6	8.0	7.5	7.2	7.1	6.0	4.8	4.5	5.0

[1] 2017 data is for individuals under 19 years of age.

Table OR-7. Employment Status by Demographic Group, 2018

(Numbers in thousands, percent.)

Characteristic	Civilian noninstitutional population	Civilian labor force		Employed		Unemployed	
		Number	Percent of population	Number	Percent of population	Number	Percent of population
Total...	3,381	2,089	61.8	2,002	59.2	87	4.1
Sex							
Male...	1,654	1,097	66.3	1,049	63.4	49	4.4
Female..	1,727	991	57.4	953	55.2	38	3.8
Race, Sex, and Hispanic Origin							
White..	2,952	1,814	61.4	1,739	58.9	75	4.1
Male...	1,445	959	66.4	916	63.4	43	4.5
Female..	1,507	855	56.7	823	54.6	32	3.7
Black or African American.................................	NA	NA	NA	NA	NA	NA	NA
Male...	NA	NA	NA	NA	NA	NA	NA
Female..	NA	NA	NA	NA	NA	NA	NA
Hispanic or Latino ethnicity[1]...........................	387	286	73.9	270	69.8	16	5.6
Male...	199	156	78.4	147	74.1	9	5.5
Female..	188	130	69.2	123	65.3	7	5.6
Age							
16 to 19 years..	190	67	35.3	59	30.9	8	12.5
20 to 24 years..	238	179	75.3	167	70.4	12	6.4
25 to 34 years..	600	488	81.4	466	77.8	22	4.5
35 to 44 years..	570	482	84.5	465	81.5	17	3.6
45 to 54 years..	496	409	82.4	395	79.6	14	3.4
55 to 64 years..	539	334	61.9	325	60.2	9	2.7
65 years and over	750	131	17.4	126	16.8	5	3.7

NOTE: Data in Table 7 are from the Current Population Survey (CPS) and do not match the estimates in Table 8. See notes and definitions for further information.
[1] May be of any race.
NA = Not available.

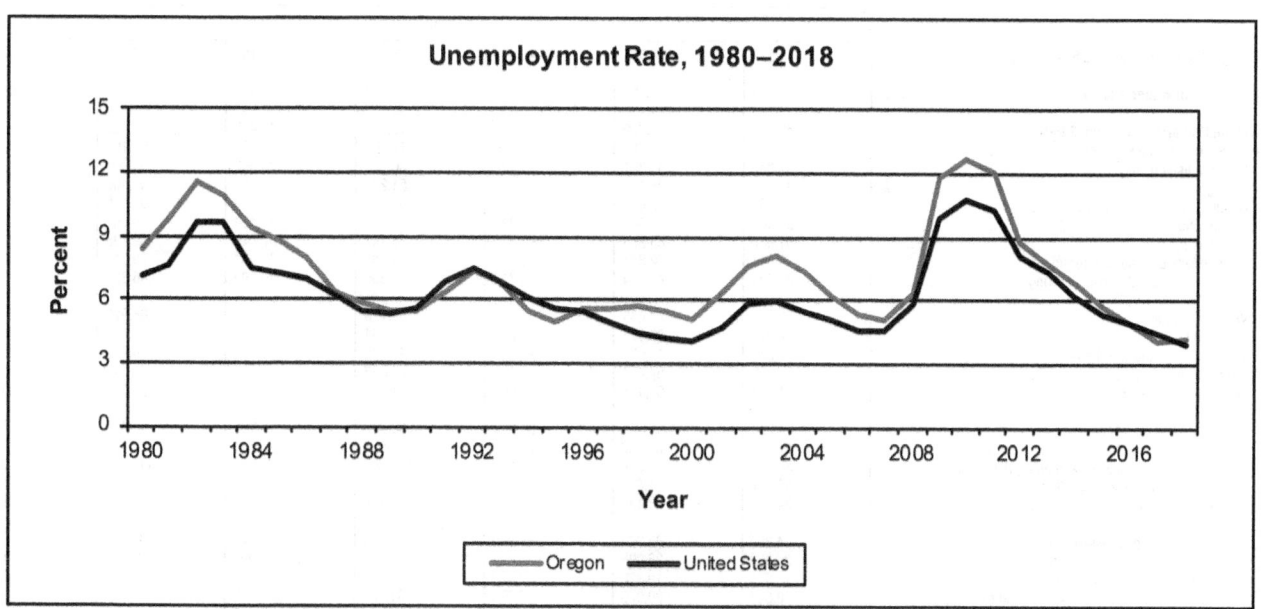

Table OR-8. Employment Status of the Civilian Noninstitutional Population Age 16 Years and Over

(Number, percent.)

Year	Civilian labor force	Civilian participation rate	Employed	Unemployed	Unemployment rate
2010..	1,984,039	65.4	1,773,076	210,963	10.6
2011..	1,993,889	65.1	1,804,320	189,569	9.5
2012..	1,953,439	63.1	1,780,790	172,649	8.8
2013..	1,910,702	61.2	1,760,302	150,400	7.9
2014..	1,935,884	61.2	1,804,417	131,467	6.8
2015..	1,978,226	61.6	1,867,407	110,819	5.6
2016..	2,049,480	62.6	1,951,218	98,262	4.8
2017..	2,104,078	63.2	2,017,292	86,786	4.1
2018..	2,104,516	62.3	2,017,155	87,361	4.2

Table OR-9. Employment and Average Wages by Industry

(Estimates are based on the 2012 *North American Industry Classification System* [NAICS].)

Industry	2011	2012	2013	2014	2015	2016	2017
	Number of jobs						
Wage and Salary Employment by Industry..........................	1,696,317	1,717,522	1,750,628	1,799,533	1,851,480	1,901,515	1,945,586
Farm Wage and Salary Employment...............................	34,088	29,669	30,183	29,615	24,152	24,674	30,223
Nonfarm Wage and Salary Employment..........................	1,662,229	1,687,853	1,720,445	1,769,918	1,827,328	1,876,841	1,915,363
Private wage and salary employment...............................	1,378,523	1,408,430	1,444,962	1,492,363	1,544,909	1,590,073	1,627,274
Forestry, fishing, and related activities............................	20,156	21,182	22,253	22,400	22,938	22,334	22,169
Mining..	1,599	1,593	1,527	1,546	1,701	1,748	1,832
Utilities..	4,493	4,562	4,497	4,512	4,485	4,563	4,666
Construction...	69,071	70,960	75,365	81,274	84,610	91,724	99,193
Manufacturing...	167,907	171,641	174,834	179,225	185,655	187,821	189,475
Durable goods manufacturing............................	118,507	121,542	123,115	125,982	130,082	131,012	131,309
Nondurable goods manufacturing........................	49,400	50,099	51,719	53,243	55,573	56,809	58,166
Wholesale trade	74,225	75,465	71,646	72,583	73,997	75,611	76,785
Retail trade..	185,557	188,203	192,499	197,116	203,335	206,266	211,664
Transportation and warehousing.............................	49,288	50,079	50,942	53,195	55,346	56,580	59,008
Information..	32,201	32,685	32,343	32,179	33,224	33,370	34,258
Finance and insurance	58,384	58,507	58,928	59,178	59,596	59,574	61,115
Real estate and rental and leasing............................	23,900	23,849	24,258	24,584	25,558	26,266	27,099
Professional, scientific, and technical services......................	73,911	77,257	80,477	84,603	88,052	92,517	94,974
Management of companies and enterprises......................	30,416	30,456	37,980	40,220	42,951	45,352	47,108
Administrative and waste services...........................	83,819	88,466	91,246	95,308	98,635	101,534	101,967
Educational services	43,162	44,276	45,139	45,548	45,784	45,379	45,952
Health care and social assistance............................	214,884	218,270	222,966	229,829	240,739	250,851	256,215
Arts, entertainment, and recreation...........................	22,082	21,904	22,627	23,993	24,055	25,974	27,322
Accommodation and food services...........................	144,174	148,914	154,504	159,980	168,344	174,556	179,765
Other services, except public administration........................	79,294	80,161	80,931	85,090	85,904	88,053	86,707
Government and government enterprises............................	283,706	279,423	275,483	277,555	282,419	286,768	288,089
	Dollars						
Average Wages and Salaries by Industry	43,572	44,897	45,773	47,258	49,154	50,383	51,951
Average Farm Wages and Salaries	24,070	27,156	29,778	29,294	30,400	34,450	28,287
Average Nonfarm Wages and Salaries	43,972	45,209	46,053	47,559	49,402	50,592	52,325
Average private wages and salaries...............................	43,453	44,786	45,546	47,068	48,985	50,101	51,776
Forestry, fishing, and related activities............................	31,867	33,321	34,431	36,363	38,506	38,901	39,760
Mining..	48,462	48,140	50,620	51,229	53,831	57,496	59,248
Utilities..	86,863	88,619	89,592	93,693	96,245	98,575	103,211
Construction	50,063	51,506	52,431	54,158	54,434	56,667	58,795
Manufacturing...	61,887	63,865	63,520	65,742	67,445	69,136	69,853
Durable goods manufacturing............................	70,044	72,377	71,840	74,781	76,524	79,015	79,361
Nondurable goods manufacturing........................	42,321	43,214	43,713	44,355	46,192	46,354	48,386
Wholesale trade	69,528	71,485	63,124	65,118	67,518	68,925	72,026
Retail trade..	27,248	27,843	28,276	29,054	29,890	30,671	31,533
Transportation and warehousing.............................	44,070	45,001	45,414	47,122	47,990	48,429	50,192
Information..	67,660	67,707	69,173	72,606	75,381	77,148	82,084
Finance and insurance	64,008	67,428	69,661	71,420	76,212	79,047	80,609
Real estate and rental and leasing............................	34,236	35,534	36,268	38,275	40,309	42,517	44,844
Professional, scientific, and technical services	63,573	66,379	67,699	70,558	73,715	75,580	78,992
Management of companies and enterprises......................	80,986	84,388	107,059	112,297	121,932	117,284	119,523
Administrative and waste services...........................	30,707	31,633	32,053	33,351	34,852	35,780	37,070
Educational services	24,354	25,137	25,735	26,176	26,726	27,866	28,259
Health care and social assistance............................	44,259	45,240	45,950	47,043	49,070	49,986	51,529
Arts, entertainment, and recreation...........................	25,368	28,096	27,225	27,511	28,905	29,038	31,107
Accommodation and food services...........................	18,551	19,326	19,829	20,551	21,364	22,123	23,373
Other services, except public administration........................	28,826	29,976	30,676	31,283	33,102	34,297	36,085
Government and government enterprises............................	46,498	47,343	48,712	50,195	51,679	53,316	55,425

Table OR-10. Employment Characteristics by Family Type

(Number, percent.)

Family type and labor force status	2015		2016		2017	
	Total	Families with own children under 18 years	Total	Families with own children under 18 years	Total	Families with own children under 18 years
All Families.........................	978,396	396,731	995,749	402,585	1,010,975	410,152
FAMILY TYPE AND LABOR FORCE STATUS						
Married-Couple Families...............	749,945	272,127	766,154	278,913	780,758	286,919
Both husband and wife in labor force............	48.8	65.6	48.1	64.3	48.5	65.6
Husband in labor force, wife not in labor force	20.0	27.0	21.4	29.0	19.9	26.9
Wife in labor force, husband not in labor force	8.2	4.9	8.3	4.6	8.9	5.1
Both husband and wife not in labor force..........	21.8	1.8	21.2	1.6	21.5	1.7
Other Families	228,451	124,604	229,595	123,672	230,217	123,233
Female householder, no husband present..................	70.2	73.2	69.4	69.2	68.7	71.4
In labor force.................	49.7	61.0	49.7	58.3	48.7	60.0
Not in labor force................	20.5	12.1	19.7	10.9	20.0	11.4
Male householder, no wife present................	29.8	26.8	30.6	30.8	31.3	28.6
In labor force.................	23.5	24.5	25.1	28.2	25.3	26.5
Not in labor force	6.2	2.4	5.5	2.6	6.0	2.1

Table OR-11. School Enrollment and Educational Attainment, 2017

(Number, percent.)

Item	State	U.S.
Enrollment		
Total population 3 years and over, enrolled in school	953,051	81,273,337
Enrolled in nursery school or preschool (percent).........	6.0	6.0
Enrolled in kindergarten (percent).........	4.6	4.9
Enrolled in elementary school, grades 1-8 (percent).........	41.1	40.6
Enrolled in high school, grades 9-12 (percent).........	21.5	21.1
Enrolled in college or graduate school (percent).........	26.8	27.4
Attainment		
Total population 25 years and over	2,901,195	221,250,083
Less than ninth grade (percent).........	3.5	5.1
9th to 12th grade, no diploma (percent).........	5.5	6.9
High school graduate, including equivalency (percent).........	23.2	27.1
Some college, no degree (percent).........	25.2	20.4
Associate's degree (percent).........	8.8	8.5
Bachelor's degree (percent).........	21.0	19.7
Graduate or professional degree (percent).........	12.7	12.3
High school graduate or higher (percent).........	91.0	88.0
Bachelor's degree or higher (percent).........	33.7	32.0

Table OR-12. Public School Characteristics and Educational Indicators

(Number, percent; data derived from National Center of Education Statistics.)

Item	State	U.S.
Public Elementary and Secondary Schools		
Number of operational school districts, 2016-17.........	221	18,377
Number of operational schools, 2016-17.........	1,243	98,330
Percent charter schools	10.0	7.1
Total public school enrollment, 2016-17.........	578,947	50,587,859
Percent charter school enrollment	5.7	6.0
Student-teacher ratio, Fall 2015	20.9	16.0
Expenditures per student (dollars), 2015-16.........	10,823	11,841
Four-year adjusted cohort graduation rate (ACGR)[1]	76.7	84.6
Students eligible for free or reduced-price lunch (percent), 2015-16.........	51.4	52.1
English language learners (percent), Fall 2016	9.8	9.6
Students age 3 to 21 served under IDEA, part B (percent), 2017-18	14.3	13.7

Public Schools by Type, 2016-17		Percent of state public schools
Total number of schools.........	1,243	100.0
Special education	1	0.1
Vocational education	0	-
Alternative education.........	32	2.6

[1] Adjusted Cohort Graduation Rates (ACGR) differ from Averaged Freshmen Graduation Rates (AFGR).
- = Zero or rounds to zero.

Table OR-13. Reported Voting and Registration of the Voting-Age Population, November 2018

(Numbers in thousands, percent.)

Item	Total population	Total citizen population	Registered			Voted		
			Total registered	Percent registered (total population)	Percent registered (total citizen population)	Total voted	Percent voted (total population)	Percent voted (total citizen population)
U.S. Total	249,748	228,832	153,066	61.3	66.9	122,281	49.0	53.4
State Total	3,293	3,138	2,274	69.1	72.5	1,918	58.2	61.1
Sex								
Male	1,612	1,542	1,078	66.9	69.9	912	56.6	59.2
Female	1,681	1,596	1,197	71.2	75.0	1,006	59.8	63.0
Race								
White alone..........................	2,874	2,781	2,059	71.6	74.0	1,769	61.5	63.6
White, non-Hispanic alone	2,584	2,569	1,956	75.7	76.1	1,694	65.6	65.9
Black alone..........................	78	71	43	55.5	(B)	41	52.1	(B)
Asian alone	172	138	71	41.1	51.3	36	21.0	26.2
Hispanic (of any race).............	365	267	140	38.3	52.3	93	25.4	34.8
White alone or in combination	3,005	2,892	2,138	71.1	73.9	1,826	60.8	63.2
Black alone or in combination..........	97	90	59	60.5	65.4	52	53.4	57.7
Asian alone or in combination.........	189	155	83	44.0	53.7	41	21.6	26.4
Age								
18 to 24 years.......................	336	331	205	61.1	62.0	128	38.2	38.8
25 to 34 years.......................	626	585	403	64.4	68.9	334	53.3	57.1
35 to 44 years.......................	539	493	336	62.4	68.1	259	48.1	52.5
45 to 64 years.......................	976	929	708	72.6	76.2	633	64.9	68.1
65 years and over	816	799	622	76.2	77.8	564	69.1	70.6

B = Base is less than 75,000 and therefore too small to show the derived measure.

Table OR-14. Crime

(Number, rate per 100,000. Data are derived from the FBI Uniform Crime Reports.)

Item	State			U.S.		
	2016	2017	Percent change	2016	2017	Percent change
TOTAL POPULATION[1]	4,085,989	4,142,776	1.4	323,405,935	325,719,178	0.7
VIOLENT CRIME						
Number	10,983	11,674	6.3	1,285,606	1,283,220	-0.2
Rate	268.8	281.8	4.8	397.5	394.0	-0.9
Murder and Nonnegligent Manslaughter						
Number...........................	116	104	-10.3	17,413	17,284	-0.7
Rate	2.8	2.5	-11.6	5.4	5.3	-1.4
Rape[2]						
Number...........................	1,784	1,999	12.1	132,414	135,755	2.5
Rate	43.7	48.3	10.5	40.9	41.7	1.8
Robbery						
Number...........................	2,307	2,432	5.4	332,797	319,356	-4.0
Rate	56.5	58.7	4.0	102.9	98.0	-4.7
Aggravated Assault						
Number...........................	6,776	7,139	5.4	802,982	810,825	1.0
Rate	165.8	172.3	3.9	248.3	248.9	0.3
PROPERTY CRIME						
Number...........................	121,716	123,722	1.6	7,928,530	7,694,086	-3.0
Rate	2,978.9	2,986.5	0.3	2,451.6	2,362.2	-3.6
Burglary						
Number...........................	16,919	17,705	4.6	1,516,405	1,401,840	-7.6
Rate	414.1	427.4	3.2	468.9	430.4	-8.2
Larceny-Theft						
Number...........................	91,507	88,877	-2.9	5,644,835	5,519,107	-2.2
Rate	2,239.5	2,145.3	-4.2	1,745.4	1,694.4	-2.9
Motor Vehicle Theft						
Number...........................	13,290	17,140	29.0	767,290	773,139	0.8
Rate	325.3	413.7	27.2	237.3	237.4	-

NOTE: Although arson data are included in the trend and clearance tables, sufficient data are not available to estimate totals for this offense. Therefore, no arson data are published in this table.
- = Zero or rounds to zero.
[1] Population figures are U.S. Census Bureau provisional estimates as of July 1, 2017.
[2] The figures shown in the rape (revised definition) column were estimated using the revised Uniform Crime Reporting (UCR) definition of rape.

Table OR-15. State Government Finances, 2017

(Dollar amounts in thousands, percent distribution.)

Item	Dollars	Percent distribution
Total Revenue	43,033,559	100.0
General revenue	30,351,031	70.5
Intergovernmental revenue	9,988,321	23.2
Taxes	11,914,567	27.7
General sales	0	-
Selective sales	1,598,677	3.7
License taxes	1,067,836	2.5
Individual income tax	8,379,225	19.5
Corporate income tax	633,046	1.5
Other taxes	235,783	0.5
Current charges	5,711,806	13.3
Miscellaneous general revenue	2,736,337	6.4
Utility revenue	404	-
Liquor stores revenue	595,077	1.4
Insurance trust revenue[1]	12,087,047	28.1
Total Expenditure	36,975,575	100.0
Intergovernmental expenditure	5,732,009	15.5
Direct expenditure	31,243,566	84.5
Current operation	23,902,443	64.6
Capital outlay	914,421	2.5
Insurance benefits and repayments	5,580,577	15.1
Assistance and subsidies	492,836	1.3
Interest on debt	353,289	1.0
Exhibit: Salaries and wages	4,882,807	13.2
Total Expenditure	36,975,575	100.0
General expenditure	30,971,476	83.8
Intergovernmental expenditure	5,732,009	15.5
Direct expenditure	25,239,467	68.3
General expenditure, by function:		
Education	9,744,277	26.4
Public welfare	10,591,348	28.6
Hospitals	2,332,476	6.3
Health	902,075	2.4
Highways	1,195,771	3.2
Police protection	201,595	0.5
Correction	897,609	2.4
Natural resources	422,795	1.1
Parks and recreation	101,855	0.3
Governmental administration	1,688,171	4.6
Interest on general debt	353,289	1.0
Other and unallocable	2,540,215	6.9
Utility expenditure	33,123	0.1
Liquor stores expenditure	390,399	1.1
Insurance trust expenditure	5,580,577	15.1
Debt at End of Fiscal Year	12,656,643	X
Cash and Security Holdings	91,921,084	X

X = Not applicable.
- = Zero or rounds to zero.
[1] Within insurance trust revenue, net earnings of state retirement systems is a calculated statistic (the item code in the data file is X08), and thus can be positive or negative. Net earnings is the sum of earnings on investments plus gains on investments minus losses on investments. The change made in 2002 for asset valuation from book to market value in accordance with Statement 34 of the Governmental Accounting Standards Board is reflected in the calculated statistics.

Table OR-16. State Government Tax Collections, 2018

(Dollars in thousands, percent.)

Item	Dollars	Percent distribution
Total Taxes	12,644,869	100.0
Property taxes	20,116	0.2
Sales and gross receipts	1,659,392	13.1
General sales and gross receipts	X	-
Selective sales and gross receipts	1,659,392	13.1
Alcoholic beverages	19,216	0.2
Amusements	X	-
Insurance premiums	70,903	0.6
Motor fuels	538,539	4.3
Pari-mutuels	1,876	-
Public utilities	8,757	0.1
Tobacco products	263,860	2.1
Other selective sales	756,241	6.0
Licenses	1,087,449	8.6
Alcoholic beverages	4,868	-
Amusements	2,799	-
Corporations in general	40,017	0.3
Hunting and fishing	57,598	0.5
Motor vehicle	539,474	4.3
Motor vehicle operators	39,758	0.3
Public utilities	14,577	0.1
Occupation and business, NEC	381,707	3.0
Other licenses	6,651	0.1
Income taxes	9,684,005	76.6
Individual income	8,879,552	70.2
Corporation net income	804,453	6.4
Other taxes	193,907	1.5
Death and gift	176,453	1.4
Documentary and stock transfer	1,772	-
Severance	15,682	0.1
Taxes, NEC	0	-

X = Not applicable.
- = Zero or rounds to zero.

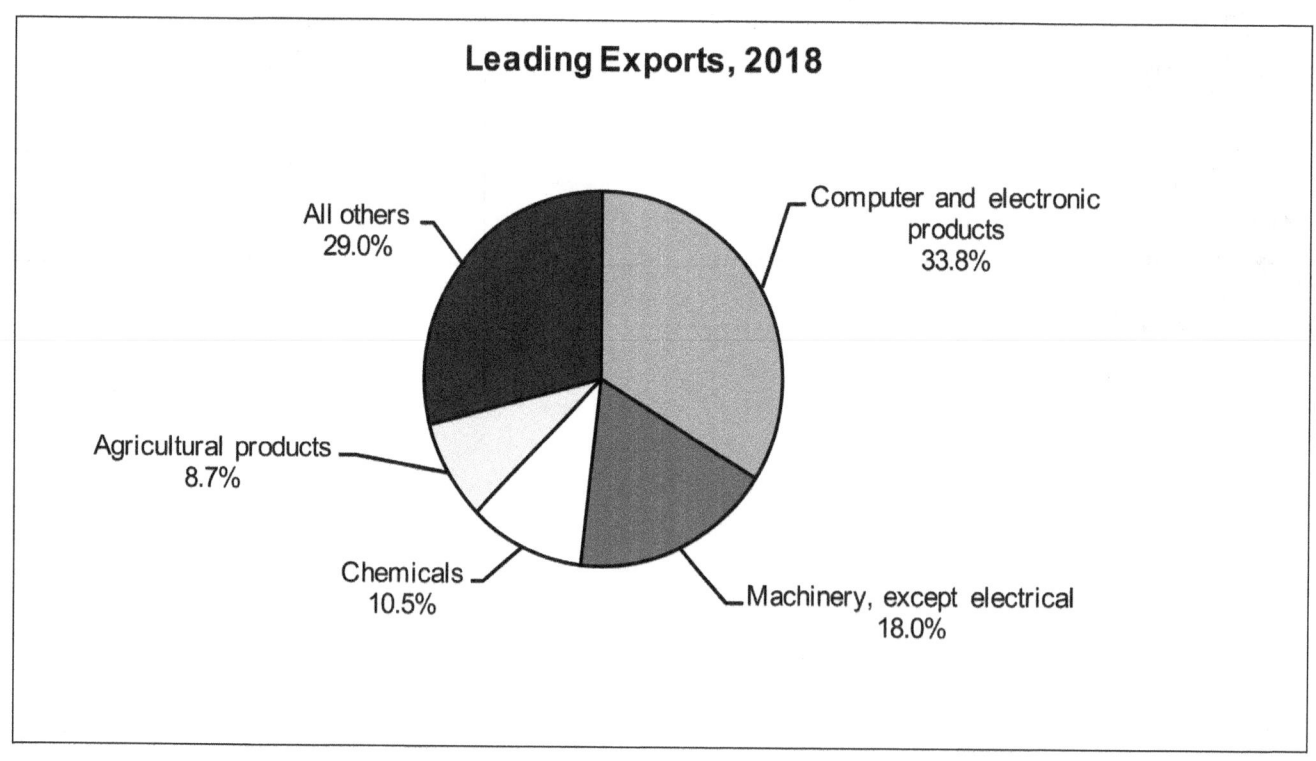

Leading Exports, 2018

Computer and electronic products 33.8%

All others 29.0%

Agricultural products 8.7%

Chemicals 10.5%

Machinery, except electrical 18.0%

PENNSYLVANIA

Facts and Figures

Location: Northeastern United States; bordered on the N by Lake Erie and New York, on the E by New York and New Jersey, on the S by Delaware, Maryland, and West Virginia, and on the W by West Virginia and Ohio

Area: 46,055 sq. mi. (119,283 sq. km.); rank—33rd

Population: 12,807,060 (2018 est.); rank—5th

Principal Cities: capital—Harrisburg; largest—Philadelphia

Statehood: December 12, 1787; 2nd state

U.S. Congress: 2 senators, 18 representatives

State Motto: Virtue, Liberty, and Independence

State Song: "Pennsylvania"

State Nicknames: The Keystone State; The Quaker State

Abbreviations: PA; Penn.

State Symbols: flower—mountain laurel; tree—Eastern hemlock; bird—ruffed grouse

At a Glance

- With an increase in population of 0.8 percent, Pennsylvania ranked 43rd among the states in growth from 2010 to 2018.

- Pennsylvania's median household income in 2017 was $59,195, and 12.5 percent of the population lived below the poverty level.

- Approximately 5.5 percent of Pennsylvanians did not have health insurance in 2017, compared to the national rate of 8.7 percent.

- Pennsylvania's violent crime rate in 2017 was 313.3 per 100,000 population, compared to 394.0 for the entire nation.

- The unemployment rate in Pennsylvania was 4.3 percent in 2018, compared to the national unemployment rate of 3.9 percent.

Table PA-1. Population by Age, Sex, Race, and Hispanic Origin

(Number, percent, except where noted.)

Sex, age, race, and Hispanic origin	2000	2010	2018 [1]	Percent change, 2010–2018
Total Population..	12,281,054	12,702,379	12,807,060	0.8
Percent of total U.S. population	4.4	4.1	3.9	X
Sex				
Male..	5,929,663	6,190,363	6,274,660	1.4
Female	6,351,391	6,512,016	6,532,400	0.3
Age				
Under 5 years..	727,804	729,538	702,997	-3.6
5 to 19 years...	2,542,780	2,449,852	2,291,147	-6.5
20 to 64 years...	7,091,305	7,563,682	7,477,286	-1.1
65 years and over	1,919,165	1,959,307	2,335,630	19.2
Median age (years)	38.0	40.1	40.8	1.7
Race and Hispanic Origin				
One race				
White	10,484,203	10,663,774	10,476,085	-1.8
Black	1,224,612	1,431,826	1,531,457	7.0
American Indian and Alaska Native	18,348	39,735	49,563	24.7
Asian	219,813	358,195	474,071	32.3
Native Hawaiian or Other Pacific Islander	3,417	7,115	10,056	41.3
Two or more races	142,224	201,734	265,828	31.8
Hispanic (of any race)	394,088	758,058	976,143	28.8

X = Not applicable.
[1] Population figures for 2018 are July 1 estimates. The 2010 estimates are taken from the 2010 Census.
- = Zero or rounds to zero.

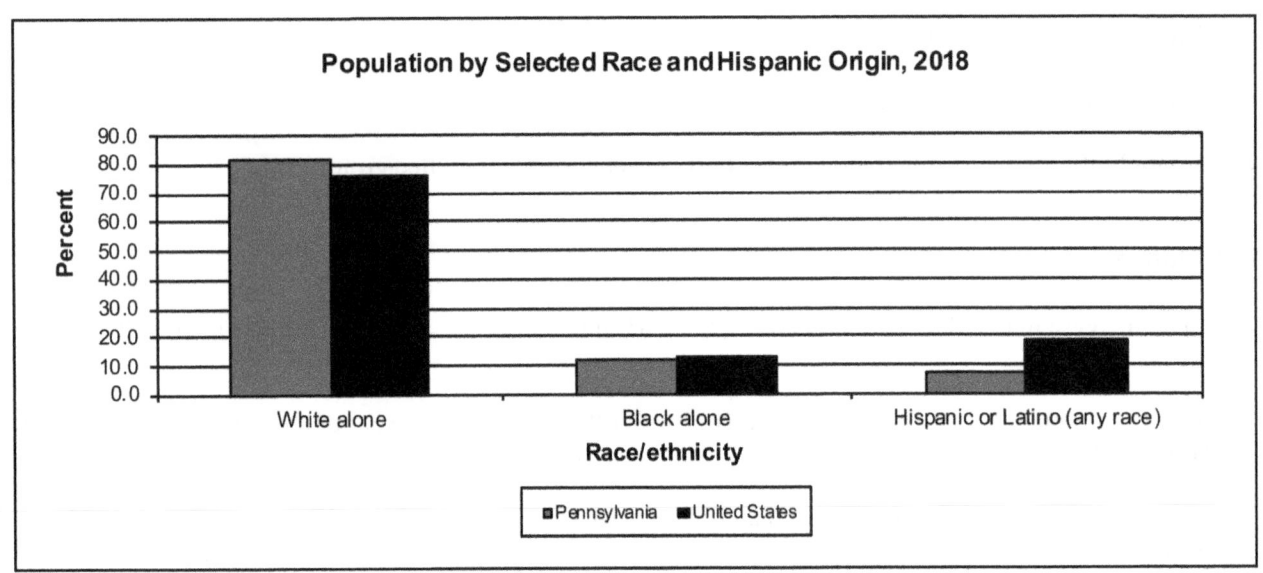

Table PA-2. Marital Status

(Number, percent distribution.)

Sex, age, race, and Hispanic origin	2000	2010	2017
Males, 15 Years and Over	4,686,277	5,031,761	5,148,815
Never married	30.1	35.9	37.1
Now married, except separated...	57.4	50.6	49.3
Separated...	1.9	2.0	1.8
Widowed...	3.3	3.1	3.1
Divorced...	7.3	8.5	8.8
Females, 15 Years and Over	5,175,436	5,406,494	5,462,622
Never married	24.6	29.8	31.2
Now married, except separated...	51.5	46.2	45.8
Separated...	2.4	2.7	2.2
Widowed...	12.7	11.2	10.1
Divorced...	8.8	10.2	10.7

Table PA-3. Households and Housing Characteristics

(Number, percent, dollars.)

Item	2000	2010	2017	Average annual percent change, 2010–2017
Total Households..	4,777,003	4,936,030	5,008,751	0.2
Family households	3,208,388	3,197,710	3,177,289	-0.1
Married-couple family	2,467,673	2,381,094	2,377,086	-
Other family	740,715	816,616	800,203	-0.3
Male householder, no wife present..........................	186,022	215,082	229,197	0.9
Female householder, no husband present................	554,693	601,534	571,006	-0.7
Nonfamily households	1,568,615	1,738,320	1,831,462	0.8
Householder living alone..	1,320,941	1,458,055	1,521,688	0.6
Householder not living alone...................................	247,674	280,265	309,774	1.5
Housing Characteristics				
Total housing units..	5,249,750	5,568,820	5,694,402	0.3
Occupied housing units	4,777,003	4,936,030	5,008,751	0.2
Owner occupied	3,406,337	3,461,678	3,421,017	-0.2
Renter occupied	1,370,666	1,474,352	1,587,734	1.1
Average household size..	2.48	2.49	2.47	-0.1
Financial Characteristics				
Median gross rent of renter-occupied housing	531	763	893	2.4
Median monthly owner costs for housing units with a mortgage	1,010	1,390	1,438	0.5
Median value of owner-occupied housing units	97,000	165,500	181,200	1.4

- = Zero or rounds to zero

Table PA-4. Migration, Origin, and Language

(Number, percent.)

Characteristic	State			U.S.		
	2016	2017	Percent change	2016	2017	Percent change
Residence 1 Year Ago						
Population 1 year and over	12,645,493	12,674,642	0.2	319,361,956	321,994,428	0.8
Same house	87.1	87.4	X	85.4	85.7	X
Different house in the U.S..	12.3	12.2	X	13.9	13.6	X
Same county	7.6	7.4	X	8.3	8.1	X
Different county	4.8	4.8	X	5.6	5.6	X
Same state	2.8	2.8	X	3.2	3.3	X
Different state	2.0	2.0	X	2.4	2.3	X
Abroad	0.5	0.5	X	0.7	0.7	X
Place of Birth						
Native born	11,913,314	11,911,768	-	279,388,170	281,193,323	0.6
Male	49.0	49.0	X	49.3	49.4	X
Female	51.0	51.0	X	50.7	50.6	X
Foreign born	870,913	893,769	2.6	43,739,345	44,525,855	1.8
Male	48.7	48.9	X	48.5	48.4	X
Female	51.3	51.1	X	51.5	51.6	X
Foreign born; naturalized U.S. citizen.................................	454,730	470,412	3.4	21,238,372	21,948,732	3.3
Male	46.9	46.6	X	45.9	45.9	X
Female	53.1	53.4	X	54.1	54.1	X
Foreign born; not a U.S. citizen	416,183	423,357	1.7	22,500,973	22,577,123	0.3
Male	50.8	51.4	X	51.0	50.8	X
Female	49.2	48.6	X	49.0	49.2	X
Entered 2010 or later	24.5	26.2	X	18.6	21.3	X
Entered 2000 to 2009	28.9	27.8	X	26.7	25.7	X
Entered before 2000..	46.6	46.0	X	54.7	53.0	X
World Region of Birth, Foreign						
Foreign-born population, excluding population born at sea	870,913	893,769	2.6	43,738,901	44,525,458	1.8
Europe	19.0	18.8	X	10.9	10.8	X
Asia..	38.7	39.2	X	30.8	31.2	X
Africa..	9.3	8.2	X	4.9	5.1	X
Oceania	0.3	0.3	X	0.6	0.6	X
Latin America..	30.8	31.6	X	51.0	50.4	X
North America	2.0	1.8	X	1.8	1.8	X
Language Spoken at Home and Ability to Speak English						
Population 5 years and over...	12,074,484	12,100,519	0.2	303,328,961	305,924,019	0.9
English only	88.7	88.5	X	78.4	78.2	X
Language other than English..	11.3	11.5	X	21.6	21.8	X
Speaks English less than "very well"...............................	4.3	4.4	X	8.6	8.5	X

NA = Not available.
X = Not applicable.
- = Zero or rounds to zero.

Table PA-5. Median Income and Poverty Status, 2017

(Number, percent, except as noted.)

Characteristic	State		U.S.	
	Number	Percent	Number	Percent
Median Income				
Households (dollars)..	59,195	X	60,336	X
Families (dollars)	75,949	X	73,891	X
Below Poverty Level (All People)	1,548,720	12.5	42,583,651	13.4
Sex				
Male	675,818	11.2	19,004,547	12.2
Female	872,902	13.7	23,579,104	14.5
Age				
Under 18 years...	444,486	17.0	13,353,202	18.4
Related children under 18 years...	435,266	16.7	13,053,472	18.1
18 to 64 years	918,379	12.1	24,648,677	12.6
65 years and over	185,855	8.5	4,581,772	9.3

X = Not applicable.

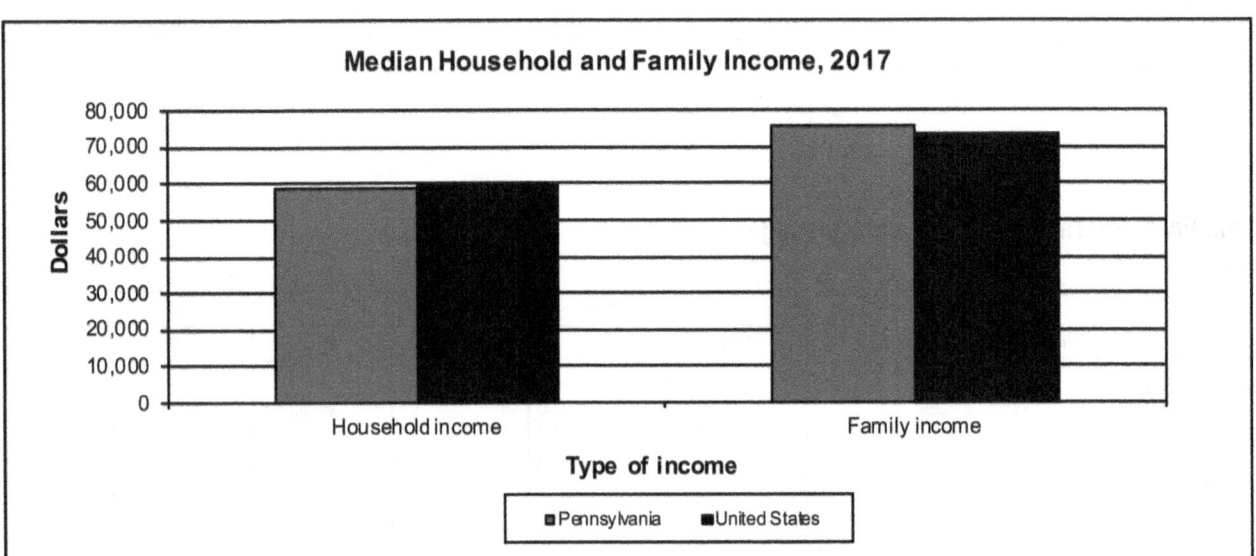

Table PA-6. Health Insurance Coverage Status for the Civilian Noninstitutionalized Population and Children Under 18 Years of Age

(Number, percent.)

Item	2009	2010	2011	2012	2013	2014	2015	2016	2017
Civilian Noninstitutionalized Population	12,365,826	12,506,000	12,539,757	12,559,315	12,569,375	12,582,815	12,599,417	12,579,422	12,602,472
Covered by Private or Public Insurance									
Number...	11,145,510	11,234,820	11,275,209	11,334,666	11,346,970	11,518,238	11,797,490	11,870,945	11,910,269
Percent..	90.1	89.8	89.9	90.2	90.3	91.5	93.6	94.4	94.5
Uninsured									
Number...	1,220,316	1,271,180	1,264,548	1,224,649	1,222,405	1,064,577	801,927	708,477	692,203
Percent..	9.9	10.2	10.1	9.8	9.7	8.5	6.4	5.6	5.5
Percent in the U.S. not covered...	15.1	15.5	15.1	14.8	14.5	11.7	9.4	8.6	8.7
Children Under 18 Years of Age[1]	2,765,748	2,778,233	2,754,741	2,730,989	2,708,843	2,693,074	2,685,304	2,666,701	2,834,916
Covered by Private or Public Insurance									
Number...	2,618,320	2,634,049	2,605,514	2,592,035	2,561,540	2,553,957	2,573,940	2,550,327	2,709,999
Percent..	94.7	94.8	94.6	94.9	94.6	94.8	95.9	95.6	95.6
Uninsured									
Number...	147,428	144,184	149,227	138,954	147,303	139,117	111,364	116,374	124,917
Percent..	5.3	5.2	5.4	5.1	5.4	5.2	4.1	4.4	4.4
Percent in the U.S. not covered...	8.6	8.0	7.5	7.2	7.1	6.0	4.8	4.5	5.0

[1] 2017 data is for individuals under 19 years of age.

Table PA-7. Employment Status by Demographic Group, 2018

(Numbers in thousands, percent.)

Characteristic	Civilian noninstitutional population	Civilian labor force		Employed		Unemployed	
		Number	Percent of population	Number	Percent of population	Number	Percent of population
Total..	10,286	6,441	62.6	6,165	59.9	276	4.3
Sex							
Male..	4,957	3,387	68.3	3,236	65.3	151	4.5
Female.......................................	5,329	3,055	57.3	2,929	55.0	126	4.1
Race, Sex, and Hispanic Origin							
White...	8,490	5,307	62.5	5,097	60.0	209	3.9
Male......................................	4,132	2,838	68.7	2,723	65.9	115	4.0
Female...................................	4,358	2,469	56.7	2,375	54.5	94	3.8
Black or African American...................	1,119	693	62.0	645	57.6	49	7.0
Male......................................	509	330	64.8	304	59.9	25	7.7
Female...................................	610	364	59.6	340	55.8	24	6.5
Hispanic or Latino ethnicity[1]...............	646	404	62.6	379	58.6	26	6.3
Male......................................	311	221	70.9	207	66.7	13	6.0
Female...................................	335	184	54.8	171	51.1	12	6.7
Age							
16 to 19 years...............................	664	282	42.5	250	37.7	32	11.5
20 to 24 years...............................	794	569	71.7	530	66.8	40	7.0
25 to 34 years...............................	1,631	1,369	83.9	1,302	79.8	66	4.9
35 to 44 years...............................	1,495	1,266	84.7	1,222	81.7	44	3.5
45 to 54 years...............................	1,571	1,310	83.4	1,272	81.0	38	2.9
55 to 64 years...............................	1,782	1,182	66.3	1,143	64.2	38	3.3
65 years and over............................	2,349	463	19.7	445	18.9	18	3.9

NOTE: Data in Table 7 are from the Current Population Survey (CPS) and do not match the estimates in Table 8. See notes and definitions for further information.
[1] May be of any race.

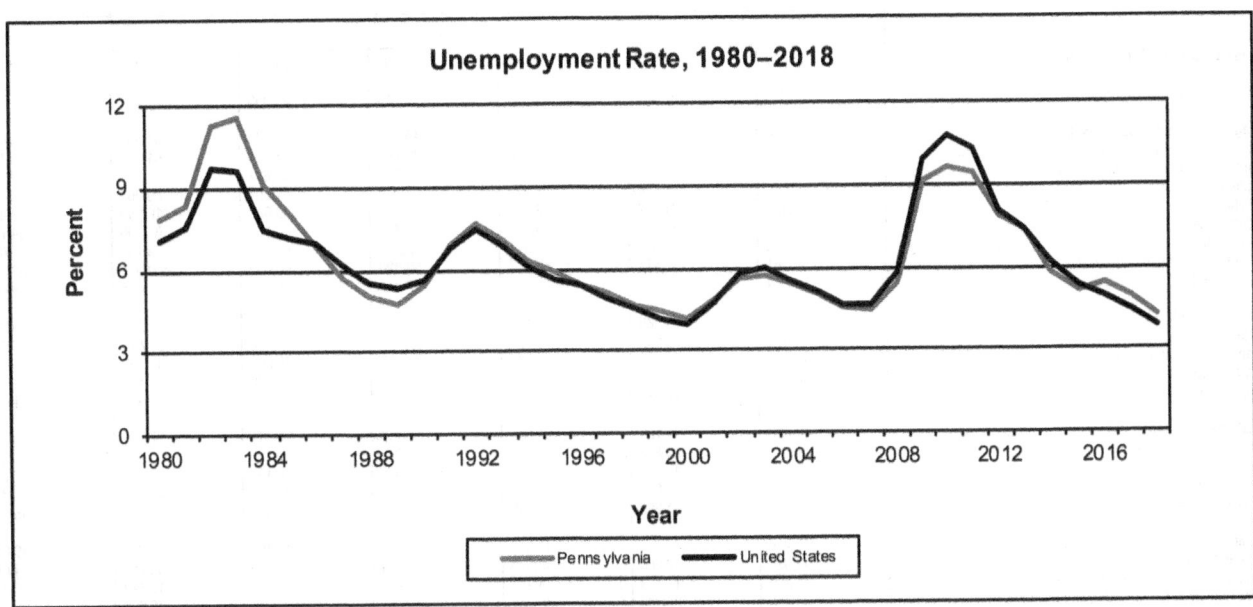

Unemployment Rate, 1980–2018

Table PA-8. Employment Status of the Civilian Noninstitutional Population Age 16 Years and Over

(Number, percent.)

Year	Civilian labor force	Civilian participation rate	Employed	Unemployed	Unemployment rate
2010..	6,380,949	63.5	5,840,887	540,062	8.5
2011..	6,395,506	63.2	5,888,745	506,761	7.9
2012..	6,462,939	63.6	5,957,314	505,625	7.8
2013..	6,442,411	63.3	5,967,811	474,600	7.4
2014..	6,396,041	62.7	6,021,005	375,036	5.9
2015..	6,420,702	62.8	6,080,219	340,483	5.3
2016..	6,452,812	63.0	6,105,223	347,589	5.4
2017..	6,427,370	62.6	6,111,633	315,737	4.9
2018..	6,424,421	62.6	6,148,635	275,786	4.3

Table PA-9. Employment and Average Wages by Industry

(Estimates are based on the 2012 *North American Industry Classification System* [NAICS].)

Industry	2011	2012	2013	2014	2015	2016	2017
	Number of jobs						
Wage and Salary Employment by Industry......................	5,852,406	5,907,982	5,933,931	5,987,610	6,037,780	6,086,529	6,144,339
Farm Wage and Salary Employment.............................	18,537	24,202	22,320	21,096	23,223	28,025	27,002
Nonfarm Wage and Salary Employment.........................	5,833,869	5,883,780	5,911,611	5,966,514	6,014,557	6,058,504	6,117,337
Private wage and salary employment......................................	5,028,333	5,096,115	5,122,503	5,184,742	5,239,185	5,284,777	5,344,216
Forestry, fishing, and related activities..........................	7,529	7,698	7,983	8,024	7,826	7,953	7,900
Mining...	32,316	35,896	35,017	36,747	32,872	24,196	25,676
Utilities..	22,294	22,301	22,007	21,466	24,200	23,961	23,749
Construction...	228,582	232,098	231,742	236,823	241,359	245,041	254,827
Manufacturing..	565,647	567,719	564,247	567,886	567,973	559,081	562,315
Durable goods manufacturing.................................	342,253	347,810	346,410	346,580	346,136	335,559	335,999
Nondurable goods manufacturing............................	223,394	219,909	217,837	221,306	221,837	223,522	226,316
Wholesale trade...	228,711	228,764	226,462	226,870	225,646	220,519	219,699
Retail trade..	634,058	638,908	636,957	637,105	637,471	637,434	629,364
Transportation and warehousing..................................	216,992	220,216	223,734	231,137	242,041	251,164	259,495
Information..	91,409	90,627	88,568	85,327	85,144	84,513	83,462
Finance and insurance...	260,679	262,070	263,434	266,776	266,531	264,978	270,081
Real estate and rental and leasing...............................	59,648	59,797	60,217	61,758	63,333	63,907	64,526
Professional, scientific, and technical services........................	310,499	319,350	326,834	331,310	338,512	350,700	353,765
Management of companies and enterprises........................	123,139	129,597	133,362	132,872	132,518	135,026	136,171
Administrative and waste services................................	285,720	288,029	294,086	300,887	311,803	313,640	314,754
Educational services...	243,056	244,165	245,970	249,647	252,468	259,240	263,081
Health care and social assistance................................	915,575	930,661	936,745	952,147	964,511	988,061	1,011,187
Arts, entertainment, and recreation..............................	93,146	94,376	93,038	94,463	93,504	96,401	99,026
Accommodation and food services...............................	420,184	432,034	442,440	447,976	455,122	464,703	471,716
Other services, except public administration...................	289,149	291,809	289,660	295,521	296,351	294,259	293,422
Government and government enterprises.....................	805,536	787,665	789,108	781,772	775,372	773,727	773,121
	Dollars						
Average Wages and Salaries by Industry	46,084	47,390	48,064	49,495	51,062	51,337	52,865
Average Farm Wages and Salaries	22,019	22,897	25,011	26,710	21,053	20,021	18,858
Average Nonfarm Wages and Salaries	46,160	47,491	48,151	49,576	51,178	51,482	53,015
Average private wages and salaries...............................	46,177	47,661	48,312	49,789	51,351	51,616	53,193
Forestry, fishing, and related activities..........................	26,125	27,163	28,146	29,173	30,631	32,097	32,815
Mining...	72,652	75,524	77,728	82,934	81,304	80,062	89,379
Utilities..	100,357	101,827	103,325	109,277	109,587	110,850	113,855
Construction...	54,648	56,068	56,823	58,765	60,153	61,596	64,759
Manufacturing..	55,206	56,374	56,671	58,546	59,552	59,789	61,084
Durable goods manufacturing.................................	56,161	56,871	57,293	59,320	60,099	60,042	62,072
Nondurable goods manufacturing............................	53,744	55,586	55,682	57,335	58,698	59,408	59,618
Wholesale trade...	68,687	70,826	72,471	76,288	77,303	77,528	79,577
Retail trade..	25,315	25,691	25,797	26,242	27,322	27,810	28,281
Transportation and warehousing..................................	41,481	42,313	42,942	44,447	45,863	45,493	47,070
Information..	65,695	67,450	69,087	70,632	73,526	75,193	78,915
Finance and insurance...	74,983	78,989	80,538	84,384	87,424	87,911	91,652
Real estate and rental and leasing...............................	48,626	51,138	51,230	54,089	56,581	57,730	58,280
Professional, scientific, and technical services........................	79,028	82,333	82,781	84,902	87,760	89,048	92,312
Management of companies and enterprises........................	106,938	114,501	115,056	120,870	130,137	122,988	127,088
Administrative and waste services................................	31,322	31,963	32,324	32,854	33,735	34,241	35,472
Educational services...	40,166	41,252	42,235	42,842	43,982	44,613	45,166
Health care and social assistance................................	43,226	44,218	44,916	45,846	47,487	47,958	49,031
Arts, entertainment, and recreation..............................	31,990	32,265	32,573	33,314	34,629	34,798	34,043
Accommodation and food services...............................	17,156	17,729	18,274	18,783	19,401	19,874	20,411
Other services, except public administration...................	28,689	29,490	30,231	31,094	32,331	32,977	34,013
Government and government enterprises.....................	46,057	46,390	47,107	48,162	50,006	50,568	51,783

Table PA-10. Employment Characteristics by Family Type

(Number, percent.)

Family type and labor force status	2015		2016		2017	
	Total	Families with own children under 18 years	Total	Families with own children under 18 years	Total	Families with own children under 18 years
All Families..	3,204,295	1,252,169	3,150,563	1,229,437	3,177,289	1,247,427
FAMILY TYPE AND LABOR FORCE STATUS						
Married-Couple Families...........................	2,366,755	830,337	2,341,561	828,926	2,377,086	841,903
Both husband and wife in labor force....................	52.1	69.7	51.7	70.0	52.8	70.9
Husband in labor force, wife not in labor force...........	20.0	24.8	19.4	24.0	19.2	23.2
Wife in labor force, husband not in labor force...........	8.3	3.7	8.4	4.0	7.9	3.8
Both husband and wife not in labor force.................	19.0	1.6	19.7	1.6	19.3	1.5
Other Families	837,540	421,832	809,002	400,511	800,203	405,524
Female householder, no husband present.................	72.8	75.0	71.7	74.2	71.4	73.6
In labor force...................................	48.6	60.0	49.6	62.2	48.9	60.1
Not in labor force...............................	24.2	15.0	22.0	12.0	22.5	13.5
Male householder, no wife present......................	27.2	25.0	28.3	25.8	28.6	26.4
In labor force...................................	20.7	22.6	21.3	23.0	22.1	24.1
Not in labor force...............................	6.5	2.4	7.0	2.8	6.5	2.4

Table PA-11. School Enrollment and Educational Attainment, 2017

(Number, percent.)

Item	State	U.S.
Enrollment		
Total population 3 years and over, enrolled in school	2,941,997	81,273,337
Enrolled in nursery school or preschool (percent)...................	6.2	6.0
Enrolled in kindergarten (percent)................................	4.5	4.9
Enrolled in elementary school, grades 1-8 (percent).................	40.6	40.6
Enrolled in high school, grades 9-12 (percent).....................	21.1	21.1
Enrolled in college or graduate school (percent)...................	27.6	27.4
Attainment		
Total population 25 years and over	8,960,842	221,250,083
Less than ninth grade (percent)...................................	3.2	5.1
9th to 12th grade, no diploma (percent)...........................	6.3	6.9
High school graduate, including equivalency (percent)..............	35.0	27.1
Some college, no degree (percent).................................	15.8	20.4
Associate's degree (percent)......................................	8.3	8.5
Bachelor's degree (percent)	18.9	19.7
Graduate or professional degree (percent).........................	12.5	12.3
High school graduate or higher (percent)..........................	90.6	88.0
Bachelor's degree or higher (percent).............................	31.4	32.0

Table PA-12. Public School Characteristics and Educational Indicators

(Number, percent; data derived from National Center of Education Statistics.)

Item	State	U.S.
Public Elementary and Secondary Schools		
Number of operational school districts, 2016-17........................	789	18,377
Number of operational schools, 2016-17................................	3,004	98,330
Percent charter schools	6.0	7.1
Total public school enrollment, 2016-17...............................	1,727,497	50,587,859
Percent charter school enrollment	7.8	6.0
Student-teacher ratio, Fall 2015......................................	14.2	16.0
Expenditures per student (dollars), 2015-16...........................	15,165	11,841
Four-year adjusted cohort graduation rate (ACGR)[1]	86.6	84.6
Students eligible for free or reduced-price lunch (percent), 2015-16....	48.2	52.1
English language learners (percent), Fall 2016	3.3	9.6
Students age 3 to 21 served under IDEA, part B (percent), 2017-18	18.6	13.7
Public Schools by Type, 2016-17		Percent of state public schools
Total number of schools..	3,004	100.0
Special education..	4	0.1
Vocational education...	84	2.8
Alternative education..	6	0.2

[1] Adjusted Cohort Graduation Rates (ACGR) differ from Averaged Freshmen Graduation Rates (AFGR).
- = Zero or rounds to zero.

Table PA-13. Reported Voting and Registration of the Voting-Age Population, November 2018

(Numbers in thousands, percent.)

Item	Total population	Total citizen population	Registered			Voted		
			Total registered	Percent registered (total population)	Percent registered (total citizen population)	Total voted	Percent voted (total population)	Percent voted (total citizen population)
U.S. Total	249,748	228,832	153,066	61.3	66.9	122,281	49.0	53.4
State Total.................................	9,928	9,475	6,469	65.2	68.3	5,173	52.1	54.6
Sex								
Male	4,736	4,532	3,056	64.5	67.4	2,445	51.6	53.9
Female	5,192	4,943	3,414	65.7	69.1	2,728	52.5	55.2
Race								
White alone................................	8,277	8,073	5,628	68.0	69.7	4,461	53.9	55.3
White, non-Hispanic alone	7,712	7,635	5,434	70.5	71.2	4,323	56.1	56.6
Black alone................................	1,059	1,028	653	61.7	63.5	562	53.1	54.7
Asian alone	423	230	106	25.1	46.0	87	20.6	37.9
Hispanic (of any race).....................	657	529	218	33.2	41.2	154	23.4	29.1
White alone or in combination	8,418	8,189	5,693	67.6	69.5	4,510	53.6	55.1
Black alone or in combination	1,169	1,113	700	59.8	62.9	589	50.4	52.9
Asian alone or in combination..............	440	247	123	28.0	49.8	104	23.8	42.2
Age								
18 to 24 years	1,144	1,109	546	47.7	49.2	365	31.9	33.0
25 to 34 years	1,622	1,457	883	54.4	60.6	603	37.2	41.4
35 to 44 years	1,464	1,326	903	61.6	68.1	705	48.1	53.2
45 to 64 years	3,381	3,292	2,437	72.1	74.0	2,034	60.2	61.8
65 years and over	2,317	2,291	1,702	73.5	74.3	1,465	63.2	63.9

Table PA-14. Crime

(Number, rate per 100,000. Data are derived from the FBI Uniform Crime Reports.)

Item	State			U.S.		
	2016	2017	Percent change	2016	2017	Percent change
TOTAL POPULATION[1]	12,787,085	12,805,537	0.1	323,405,935	325,719,178	0.7
VIOLENT CRIME						
Number....................................	40,389	40,120	-0.7	1,285,606	1,283,220	-0.2
Rate.......................................	315.9	313.3	-0.8	397.5	394.0	-0.9
Murder and Nonnegligent Manslaughter						
Number....................................	674	739	9.6	17,413	17,284	-0.7
Rate.......................................	5.3	5.8	9.5	5.4	5.3	-1.4
Rape[2]						
Number....................................	4,459	4,201	-5.8	132,414	135,755	2.5
Rate.......................................	34.9	32.8	-5.9	40.9	41.7	1.8
Robbery						
Number....................................	12,314	11,793	-4.2	332,797	319,356	-4.0
Rate.......................................	96.3	92.1	-4.4	102.9	98.0	-4.7
Aggravated Assault						
Number....................................	22,942	23,387	1.9	802,982	810,825	1.0
Rate.......................................	179.4	182.6	1.8	248.3	248.9	0.3
PROPERTY CRIME						
Number....................................	222,394	211,220	-5.0	7,928,530	7,694,086	-3.0
Rate.......................................	1,739.2	1,649.4	-5.2	2,451.6	2,362.2	-3.6
Burglary						
Number....................................	35,178	32,057	-8.9	1,516,405	1,401,840	-7.6
Rate.......................................	275.1	250.3	-9.0	468.9	430.4	-8.2
Larceny-Theft						
Number....................................	174,147	166,178	-4.6	5,644,835	5,519,107	-2.2
Rate.......................................	1,361.9	1,297.7	-4.7	1,745.4	1,694.4	-2.9
Motor Vehicle Theft						
Number....................................	13,069	12,985	-0.6	767,290	773,139	0.8
Rate.......................................	102.2	101.4	-0.8	237.3	237.4	-

NOTE: Although arson data are included in the trend and clearance tables, sufficient data are not available to estimate totals for this offense. Therefore, no arson data are published in this table.
- = Zero or rounds to zero.
[1] Population figures are U.S. Census Bureau provisional estimates as of July 1, 2017.
[2] The figures shown in the rape (revised definition) column were estimated using the revised Uniform Crime Reporting (UCR) definition of rape.

Table PA-15. State Government Finances, 2017

(Dollar amounts in thousands, percent distribution.)

Item	Dollars	Percent distribution
Total Revenue	102,872,955	100.0
General revenue	83,569,986	81.2
Intergovernmental revenue	29,475,131	28.7
Taxes	37,853,091	36.8
General sales	10,509,734	10.2
Selective sales	9,119,703	8.9
License taxes	2,240,809	2.2
Individual income tax	12,063,782	11.7
Corporate income tax	2,344,344	2.3
Other taxes	1,574,719	1.5
Current charges	11,498,190	11.2
Miscellaneous general revenue	4,743,574	4.6
Utility revenue	0	-
Liquor stores revenue	2,012,789	2.0
Insurance trust revenue[1]	17,290,180	16.8
Total Expenditure	103,525,142	100.0
Intergovernmental expenditure	22,256,314	21.5
Direct expenditure	81,268,828	78.5
Current operation	56,147,568	54.2
Capital outlay	7,955,848	7.7
Insurance benefits and repayments	12,734,112	12.3
Assistance and subsidies	2,929,398	2.8
Interest on debt	1,501,902	1.5
Exhibit: Salaries and wages	10,490,084	10.1
Total Expenditure	103,525,142	100.0
General expenditure	88,868,535	85.8
Intergovernmental expenditure	22,256,314	21.5
Direct expenditure	66,612,221	64.3
General expenditure, by function:		
Education	27,912,815	27.0
Public welfare	31,373,090	30.3
Hospitals	5,132,420	5.0
Health	3,428,716	3.3
Highways	8,159,034	7.9
Police protection	1,093,448	1.1
Correction	2,183,012	2.1
Natural resources	733,442	0.7
Parks and recreation	339,885	0.3
Governmental administration	2,633,479	2.5
Interest on general debt	1,501,902	1.5
Other and unallocable	4,377,292	4.2
Utility expenditure	1,760	-
Liquor stores expenditure	1,920,735	1.9
Insurance trust expenditure	12,734,112	12.3
Debt at End of Fiscal Year	47,519,575	X
Cash and Security Holdings	118,258,436	X

X = Not applicable.
- = Zero or rounds to zero.
[1] Within insurance trust revenue, net earnings of state retirement systems is a calculated statistic (the item code in the data file is X08), and thus can be positive or negative. Net earnings is the sum of earnings on investments plus gains on investments minus losses on investments. The change made in 2002 for asset valuation from book to market value in accordance with Statement 34 of the Governmental Accounting Standards Board is reflected in the calculated statistics.

Table PA-16. State Government Tax Collections, 2018

(Dollars in thousands, percent.)

Item	Dollars	Percent distribution
Total Taxes	40,709,545	100.0
Property taxes	34,399	0.1
Sales and gross receipts	21,034,252	51.7
General sales and gross receipts	10,920,832	26.8
Selective sales and gross receipts	10,113,420	24.8
Alcoholic beverages	397,092	1.0
Amusements	1,429,632	3.5
Insurance premiums	836,186	2.1
Motor fuels	3,375,429	8.3
Pari-mutuels	10,182	-
Public utilities	1,155,009	2.8
Tobacco products	1,372,695	3.4
Other selective sales	1,537,195	3.8
Licenses	2,721,979	6.7
Alcoholic beverages	51,644	0.1
Amusements	215,406	0.5
Corporations in general	5,717	-
Hunting and fishing	76,245	0.2
Motor vehicle	1,183,964	2.9
Motor vehicle operators	72,896	0.2
Public utilities	56,798	0.1
Occupation and business, NEC	1,038,215	2.6
Other licenses	21,094	0.1
Income taxes	15,287,269	37.6
Individual income	12,800,890	31.4
Corporation net income	2,486,379	6.1
Other taxes	1,631,646	4.0
Death and gift	982,470	2.4
Documentary and stock transfer	625,056	1.5
Severance	X	-
Taxes, NEC	24,120	0.1

X = Not applicable.
- = Zero or rounds to zero.

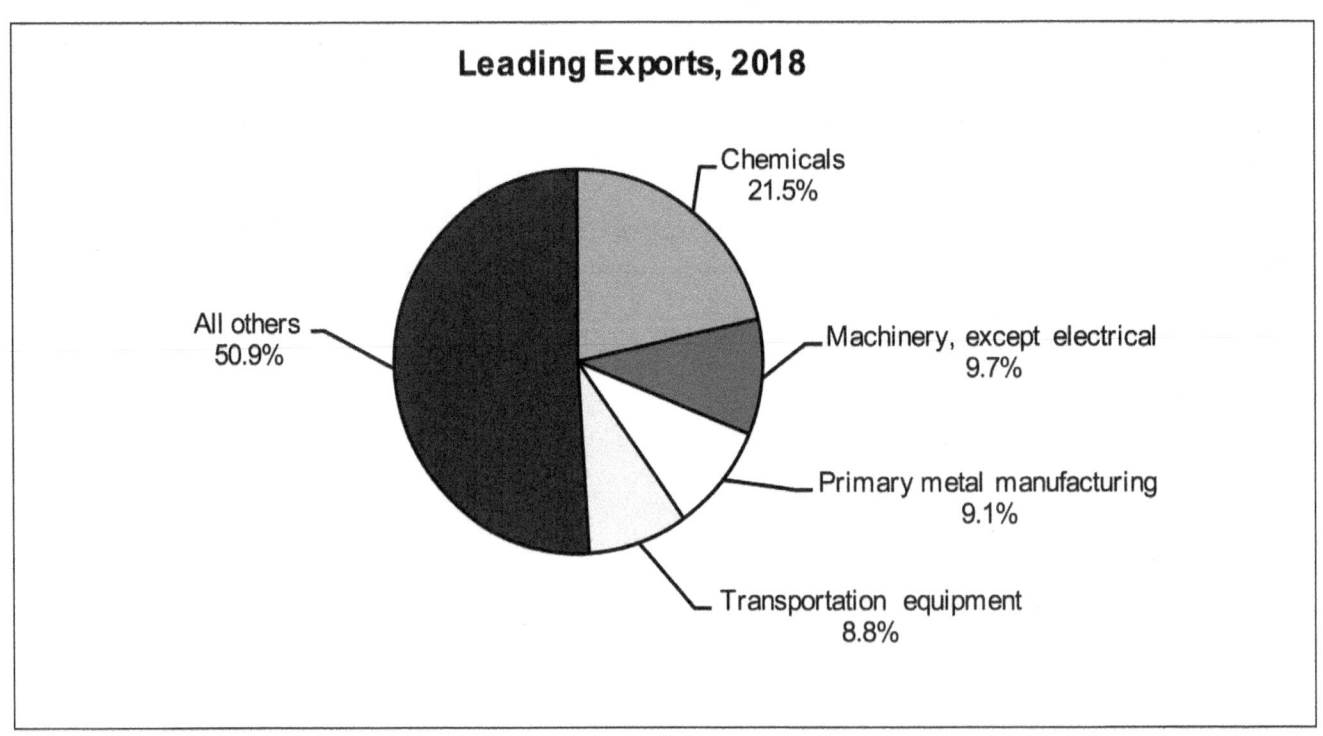

Leading Exports, 2018

Chemicals 21.5%
Machinery, except electrical 9.7%
Primary metal manufacturing 9.1%
Transportation equipment 8.8%
All others 50.9%

RHODE ISLAND

Facts and Figures

Location: Eastern United States; bordered on the N by Massachusetts, on the E by Massachusetts and the Atlantic Ocean, on the S by Block Island Sound and the Atlantic Ocean, and on the W by Connecticut

Area: 1,545 sq. mi. (4,002 sq. km.); rank—50th

Population: 1,057,315 (2018 est.); rank—44th

Principal Cities: capital—Providence; largest—Providence

Statehood: May 29, 1790; 13th state

U.S. Congress: 2 senators, 2 representatives

State Motto: Hope

State Song: "Rhode Island"

State Nickname: The Ocean State

Abbreviations: RI; R.I.

State Symbols: flower—violet; tree—red maple; bird—Rhode Island red

At a Glance

- With an increase in population of 0.5 percent, Rhode Island ranked 47th among the states in growth from 2010 to 2018.

- In 2017, 4.6 percent of Rhode Islanders did not have health insurance, compared to 8.7 percent of the total U.S. population.

- Rhode Island's violent crime rate in 2017 was 232.2 per 100,000 population, compared to 394.0 for the entire nation.

- The state's median income in 2017 was $63,870, and 11.6 percent of its residents lived below the poverty level.

- In 2018, 19.4 percent of Rhode Island's population was under 18 years old, and 17.2 percent of its population was 65 years or older, compared to the national averages of 22.4 percent and 16.0 percent respectively.

Table RI-1. Population by Age, Sex, Race, and Hispanic Origin

(Number, percent, except where noted.)

Sex, age, race, and Hispanic origin	2000	2010	2018 [1]	Percent change, 2010–2018
Total Population..	1,048,319	1,052,567	1,057,315	0.5
Percent of total U.S. population	0.4	0.3	0.3	X
Sex				
Male...	503,635	508,400	514,332	1.2
Female	544,684	544,167	542,983	-0.2
Age				
Under 5 years..	63,896	57,448	54,413	-5.3
5 to 19 years..	218,720	204,310	185,087	-9.4
20 to 64 years...	613,301	638,928	635,561	-0.5
65 years and over	152,402	151,881	182,254	20.0
Median age (years)	36.7	39.4	40.1	1.8
Race and Hispanic Origin				
One race				
White	891,191	910,253	887,259	-2.5
Black	46,908	75,073	88,411	17.8
American Indian and Alaska Native	5,121	9,173	11,308	23.3
Asian	23,665	31,768	38,419	20.9
Native Hawaiian or Other Pacific Islander	567	1,602	2,135	33.3
Two or more races	28,251	24,698	29,783	20.6
Hispanic (of any race)..	90,820	137,169	168,342	22.7

X = Not applicable.
- = Zero or rounds to zero.
[1] Population figures for 2018 are July 1 estimates. The 2010 estimates are taken from the 2010 Census.

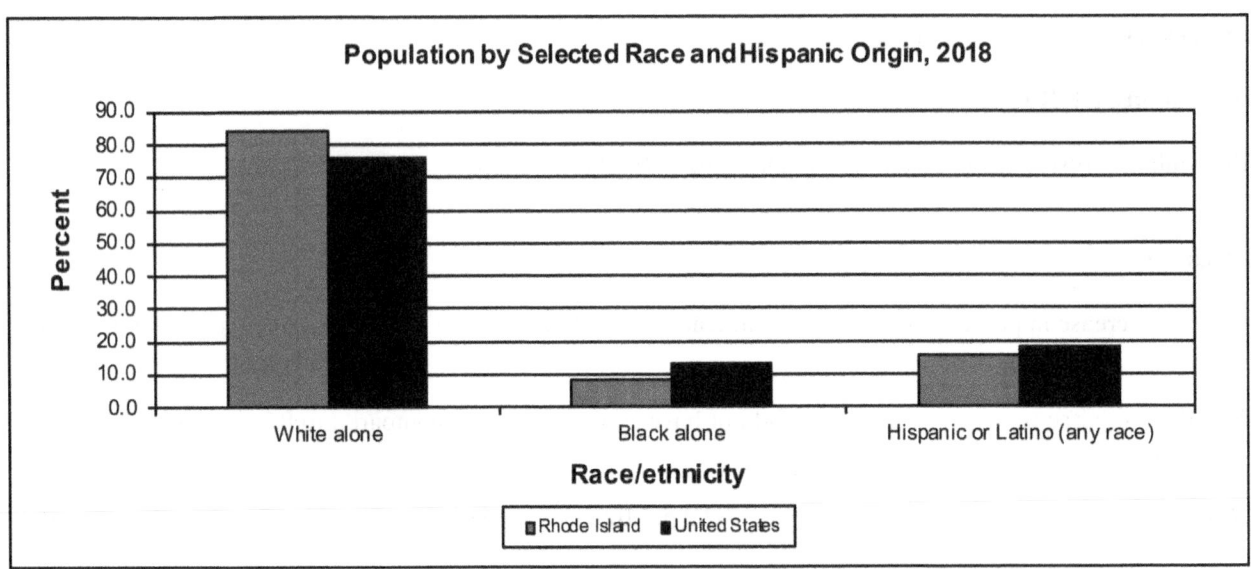

Population by Selected Race and Hispanic Origin, 2018

Table RI-2. Marital Status

(Number, percent distribution.)

Sex, age, race, and Hispanic origin	2000	2010	2017
Males, 15 Years and Over..	396,396	414,628	426,468
Never married	32.5	39.8	39.1
Now married, except separated.....................................	54.9	45.2	48.5
Separated..	1.5	1.6	1.2
Widowed...	3.0	3.1	2.7
Divorced...	8.0	10.3	8.5
Females, 15 Years and Over	445,107	456,425	463,865
Never married	27.1	32.4	35.1
Now married, except separated.....................................	48.5	41.8	42.3
Separated..	2.3	2.4	1.3
Widowed...	11.5	10.4	8.9
Divorced...	10.7	13.0	12.4

Table RI-3. Households and Housing Characteristics

(Number, percent, dollars.)

Item	2000	2010	2017	Average annual percent change, 2010–2017
Total Households...	408,424	402,295	408,748	0.2
Family households	265,398	246,028	251,811	0.3
Married-couple family	196,757	173,848	186,052	1.0
Other family	68,641	72,180	65,759	-1.3
Male householder, no wife present..................	16,032	17,525	16,342	-1.0
Female householder, no husband present........	52,609	54,655	49,417	-1.4
Nonfamily households	143,026	156,267	156,937	0.1
Householder living alone...................................	116,678	125,371	132,122	0.8
Householder not living alone............................	26,348	30,896	24,815	-2.8
Housing Characteristics				
Total housing units...	439,837	463,416	468,266	0.1
Occupied housing units	408,424	402,295	408,748	0.2
Owner occupied	245,156	244,516	248,723	0.2
Renter occupied	163,268	157,779	160,025	0.2
Average household size..	2.47	2.51	2.49	-0.1
Financial Characteristics				
Median gross rent of renter-occupied housing	553	868	941	1.2
Median monthly owner costs for housing units with a mortgage	1,205	1,837	1,782	-0.4
Median value of owner-occupied housing units........	133,000	254,500	257,800	0.2

- = Zero or rounds to zero.

Table RI-4. Migration, Origin, and Language

(Number, percent.)

Characteristic	State			U.S.		
	2016	2017	Percent change	2016	2017	Percent change
Residence 1 Year Ago						
Population 1 year and over	1,045,691	1,048,549	0.3	319,361,956	321,994,428	0.8
Same house	85.9	88.0	X	85.4	85.7	X
Different house in the U.S.	13.3	11.5	X	13.9	13.6	X
Same county	8.4	6.4	X	8.3	8.1	X
Different county	4.9	5.1	X	5.6	5.6	X
Same state	1.8	1.6	X	3.2	3.3	X
Different state	3.1	3.5	X	2.4	2.3	X
Abroad	0.7	0.6	X	0.7	0.7	X
Place of Birth						
Native born	907,946	912,622	0.5	279,388,170	281,193,323	0.6
Male	48.3	48.3	X	49.3	49.4	X
Female	51.7	51.7	X	50.7	50.6	X
Foreign born	148,480	147,017	-1.0	43,739,345	44,525,855	1.8
Male	49.2	49.3	X	48.5	48.4	X
Female	50.8	50.7	X	51.5	51.6	X
Foreign born; naturalized U.S. citizen...............	81,710	79,049	-3.3	21,238,372	21,948,732	3.3
Male	46.1	47.7	X	45.9	45.9	X
Female	53.9	52.3	X	54.1	54.1	X
Foreign born; not a U.S. citizen........................	66,770	67,968	1.8	22,500,973	22,577,123	0.3
Male	53.1	51.1	X	51.0	50.8	X
Female	46.9	48.9	X	49.0	49.2	X
Entered 2010 or later	19.6	24.9	X	18.6	21.3	X
Entered 2000 to 2009	23.5	23.3	X	26.7	25.7	X
Entered before 2000..	56.9	51.8	X	54.7	53.0	X
World Region of Birth, Foreign						
Foreign-born population, excluding population born at sea	148,480	147,017	-1.0	43,738,901	44,525,458	1.8
Europe	24.3	20.6	X	10.9	10.8	X
Asia	18.2	20.8	X	30.8	31.2	X
Africa	12.9	11.0	X	4.9	5.1	X
Oceania	0.5	0.1	X	0.6	0.6	X
Latin America	42.2	46.0	X	51.0	50.4	X
North America	2.0	1.4	X	1.8	1.8	X
Language Spoken at Home and Ability to Speak English						
Population 5 years and over...................................	1,002,282	1,004,620	0.2	303,328,961	305,924,019	0.9
English only	77.2	77.1	X	78.4	78.2	X
Language other than English............................	22.8	22.9	X	21.6	21.8	X
Speaks English less than "very well".................	8.4	9.0	X	8.6	8.5	X

NA = Not available.
X = Not applicable.
- = Zero or rounds to zero.

Table RI-5. Median Income and Poverty Status, 2017

(Number, percent, except as noted.)

Characteristic	State		U.S.	
	Number	Percent	Number	Percent
Median Income				
Households (dollars)...	63,870	X	60,336	X
Families (dollars)	84,557	X	73,891	X
Below Poverty Level (All People)	118,367	11.6	42,583,651	13.4
Sex				
Male	50,039	10.1	19,004,547	12.2
Female	68,328	13.1	23,579,104	14.5
Age				
Under 18 years...	33,858	16.6	13,353,202	18.4
Related children under 18 years...	33,334	16.4	13,053,472	18.1
18 to 64 years..	69,228	10.7	24,648,677	12.6
65 years and over	15,281	9.0	4,581,772	9.3

X = Not applicable.

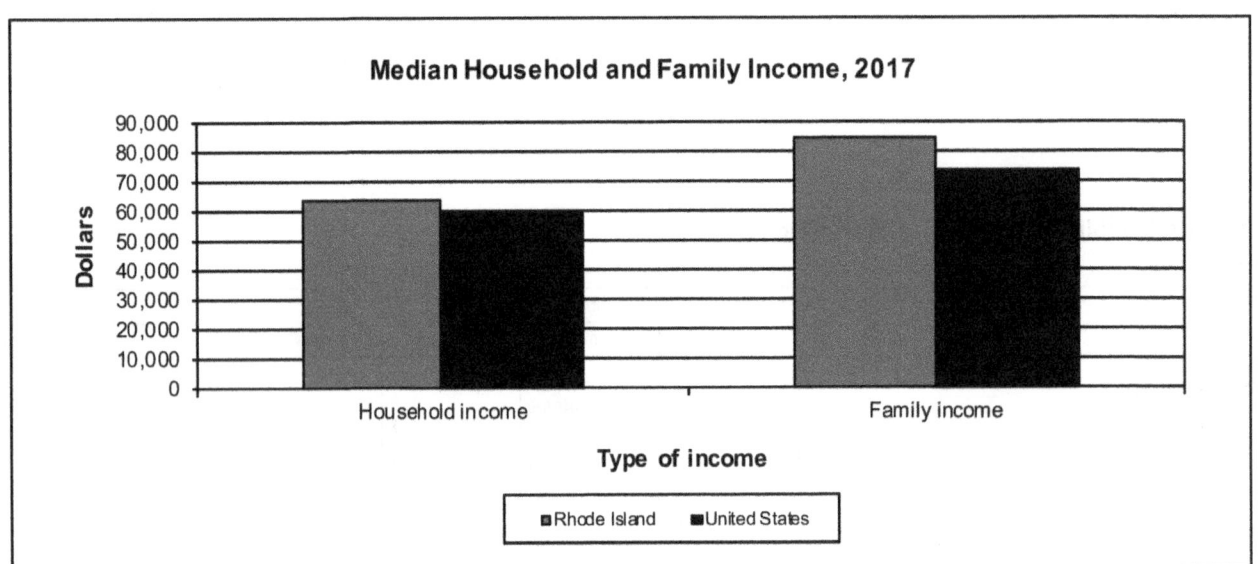

Median Household and Family Income, 2017

Table RI-6. Health Insurance Coverage Status for the Civilian Noninstitutionalized Population and Children Under 18 Years of Age

(Number, percent.)

Item	2009	2010	2011	2012	2013	2014	2015	2016	2017
Civilian Noninstitutionalized Population	1,035,366	1,036,743	1,035,117	1,034,895	1,036,046	1,039,789	1,041,268	1,040,259	1,044,111
Covered by Private or Public Insurance									
Number...	918,668	910,559	923,283	920,030	915,586	962,670	981,858	995,293	995,921
Percent..	88.7	87.8	89.2	88.9	88.4	92.6	94.3	95.7	95.4
Uninsured									
Number...	116,698	126,184	111,834	114,865	120,460	77,119	59,410	44,966	48,190
Percent..	11.3	12.2	10.8	11.1	11.6	7.4	5.7	4.3	4.6
Percent in the U.S. not covered............................	15.1	15.5	15.1	14.8	14.5	11.7	9.4	8.6	8.7
Children Under 18 Years of Age[1]	226,681	223,970	218,624	216,675	212,430	212,271	211,397	208,268	224,008
Covered by Private or Public Insurance									
Number...	214,388	211,480	209,952	206,885	200,866	205,164	204,137	204,269	219,375
Percent..	94.6	94.4	96.0	95.5	94.6	96.7	96.6	98.1	97.9
Uninsured									
Number...	12,293	12,490	8,672	9,790	11,564	7,107	7,260	3,999	4,633
Percent..	5.4	5.6	4.0	4.5	5.4	3.3	3.4	1.9	2.1
Percent in the U.S. not covered............................	8.6	8.0	7.5	7.2	7.1	6.0	4.8	4.5	5.0

[1] 2017 data is for individuals under 19 years of age.

Table RI-7. Employment Status by Demographic Group, 2018

(Numbers in thousands, percent.)

Characteristic	Civilian noninstitutional population	Civilian labor force		Employed		Unemployed	
		Number	Percent of population	Number	Percent of population	Number	Percent of population
Total...	866	559	64.6	537	62.0	23	4.1
Sex							
Male..	415	290	69.9	278	66.9	12	4.2
Female..	451	270	59.8	259	57.4	11	4.0
Race, Sex, and Hispanic Origin							
White...	761	488	64.1	470	61.7	18	3.7
Male..	365	252	69.0	242	66.3	10	3.8
Female..	396	236	59.6	227	57.4	9	3.6
Black or African American....................	59	41	69.7	38	65.3	3	6.3
Male..	NA	NA	NA	NA	NA	NA	NA
Female..	NA	NA	NA	NA	NA	NA	NA
Hispanic or Latino ethnicity[1]...............	120	80	67.1	75	62.3	6	7.2
Male..	53	40	75.2	37	69.3	3	7.9
Female..	67	41	60.6	38	56.7	3	6.5
Age							
16 to 19 years..................................	NA	NA	NA	NA	NA	NA	NA
20 to 24 years..................................	65	49	76.1	46	71.2	3	6.5
25 to 34 years..................................	147	124	84.4	120	81.5	5	3.6
35 to 44 years..................................	134	115	85.7	112	83.5	3	2.5
45 to 54 years..................................	131	108	82.5	105	79.6	4	3.5
55 to 64 years..................................	155	104	66.9	100	64.5	4	3.6
65 years and over	178	37	20.7	36	20.2	1	2.2

NOTE: Data in Table 7 are from the Current Population Survey (CPS) and do not match the estimates in Table 8. See notes and definitions for further information.
[1] May be of any race.

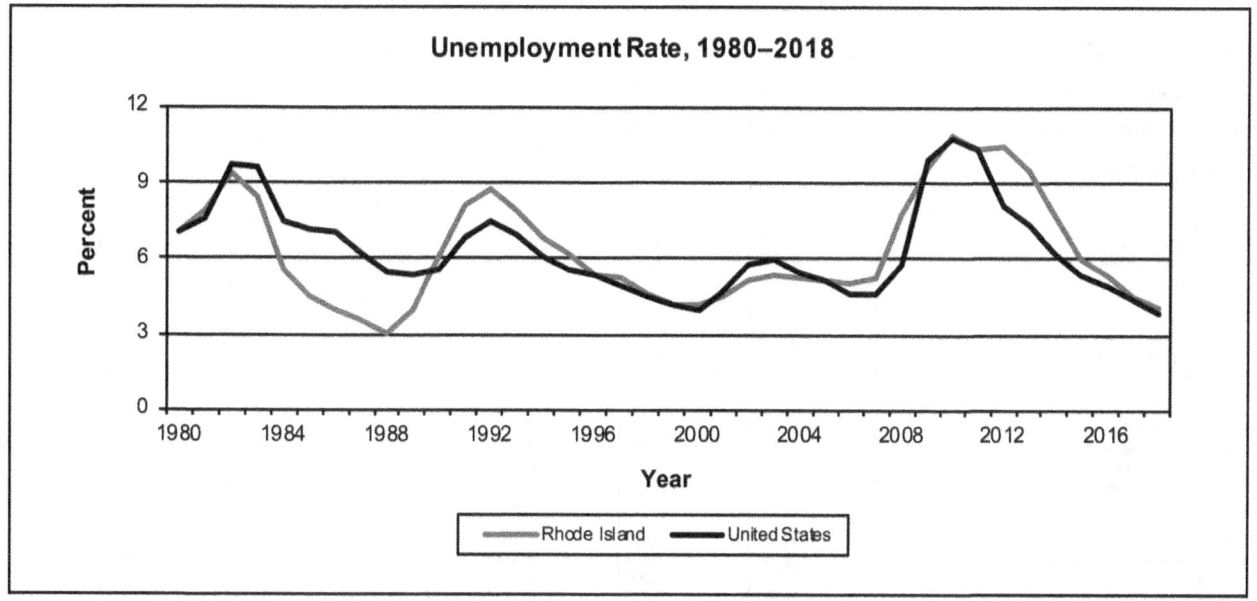

Unemployment Rate, 1980–2018

Table RI-8. Employment Status of the Civilian Noninstitutional Population Age 16 Years and Over

(Number, percent.)

Year	Civilian labor force	Civilian participation rate	Employed	Unemployed	Unemployment rate
2010..	566,704	67.3	503,216	63,488	11.2
2011..	560,056	66.4	498,248	61,808	11.0
2012..	558,487	66.0	500,434	58,053	10.4
2013..	556,926	65.6	505,370	51,556	9.3
2014..	555,909	65.2	513,121	42,788	7.7
2015..	554,486	64.8	521,255	33,231	6.0
2016..	553,555	64.5	524,745	28,810	5.2
2017..	554,658	64.3	529,867	24,791	4.5
2018..	555,807	64.5	533,171	22,636	4.1

Table RI-9. Employment and Average Wages by Industry

(Estimates are based on the 2012 *North American Industry Classification System* [NAICS].)

Industry	2011	2012	2013	2014	2015	2016	2017
	Number of jobs						
Wage and Salary Employment by Industry........................	475,367	477,449	483,908	491,596	499,350	502,469	506,216
Farm Wage and Salary Employment..............................	550	537	613	615	614	572	571
Nonfarm Wage and Salary Employment...........................	474,817	476,912	483,295	490,981	498,736	501,897	505,645
Private wage and salary employment..........................	402,555	405,473	411,564	419,162	426,862	429,804	433,213
Forestry, fishing, and related activities	(D)	554	(D)	(D)	(D)	(D)	(D)
Mining	(D)	188	(D)	(D)	(D)	(D)	(D)
Utilities	1,077	1,058	1,060	1,057	1,082	1,080	1,093
Construction	16,088	16,467	16,545	16,898	17,441	18,578	(D)
Manufacturing	40,421	39,705	40,130	40,940	41,195	40,449	40,419
Durable goods manufacturing	25,853	25,340	25,597	26,138	26,015	25,228	25,133
Nondurable goods manufacturing	14,568	14,365	14,533	14,802	15,180	15,221	15,286
Wholesale trade	16,223	16,889	16,763	16,900	17,025	16,730	16,615
Retail trade	47,246	47,289	46,892	47,480	48,376	48,511	48,852
Transportation and warehousing	9,553	9,720	9,727	9,934	10,255	10,350	10,587
Information	10,167	9,597	9,096	8,867	8,644	8,075	6,136
Finance and insurance	23,882	24,194	24,717	25,060	25,568	25,531	27,640
Real estate and rental and leasing	5,791	5,910	6,038	6,024	6,129	6,219	6,309
Professional, scientific, and technical services	21,121	21,658	22,162	23,001	24,074	24,568	25,256
Management of companies and enterprises	9,858	10,531	11,343	12,013	12,572	13,394	13,509
Administrative and waste services	23,649	24,319	25,550	26,262	27,347	28,055	28,980
Educational services	25,615	24,317	24,341	25,402	26,690	26,558	26,866
Health care and social assistance	79,162	79,586	81,417	81,178	81,252	81,141	80,921
Arts, entertainment, and recreation	7,600	7,716	8,481	9,098	9,040	9,463	9,557
Accommodation and food services	42,791	44,345	45,401	46,572	47,514	48,458	49,150
Other services, except public administration	21,605	21,430	21,189	21,718	21,838	21,839	21,739
Government and government enterprises	72,262	71,439	71,731	71,819	71,874	72,093	72,432
	Dollars						
Average Wages and Salaries by Industry	46,309	47,465	48,459	49,989	51,271	51,962	53,408
Average Farm Wages and Salaries	20,302	30,561	27,290	28,821	23,581	29,051	26,410
Average Nonfarm Wages and Salaries	46,339	47,484	48,485	50,016	51,306	51,989	53,438
Average private wages and salaries..........................	44,692	45,922	47,065	48,768	50,019	50,767	52,210
Forestry, fishing, and related activities	(D)	41,386	(D)	(D)	(D)	(D)	(D)
Mining	(D)	51,404	(D)	(D)	(D)	(D)	(D)
Utilities	93,868	92,192	96,739	97,868	98,678	104,545	109,432
Construction	53,812	54,493	55,199	56,100	57,771	59,346	(D)
Manufacturing	52,627	53,621	55,330	56,772	57,995	58,276	59,848
Durable goods manufacturing	54,277	55,214	56,989	58,117	59,026	59,576	61,935
Nondurable goods manufacturing	49,698	50,811	52,407	54,397	56,228	56,122	56,416
Wholesale trade	65,432	67,086	69,412	70,479	70,989	72,725	76,171
Retail trade	27,724	28,213	28,639	29,840	31,142	31,663	32,297
Transportation and warehousing	39,954	40,650	41,352	42,414	43,100	43,608	43,781
Information	65,794	68,731	67,771	70,540	71,966	74,904	73,152
Finance and insurance	80,318	84,167	86,567	93,725	93,749	96,726	101,774
Real estate and rental and leasing	40,020	41,605	42,636	44,268	46,486	47,093	48,113
Professional, scientific, and technical services	66,465	67,386	69,314	72,371	74,492	75,048	77,387
Management of companies and enterprises	106,264	114,538	116,746	122,500	124,259	122,815	124,079
Administrative and waste services	32,215	33,172	34,539	35,370	36,138	36,604	37,603
Educational services	39,444	40,683	42,356	42,729	42,446	41,207	42,624
Health care and social assistance	43,285	43,687	44,108	45,198	46,935	47,374	48,182
Arts, entertainment, and recreation	28,053	28,818	29,438	31,215	33,989	35,686	37,031
Accommodation and food services	18,764	19,366	19,985	20,673	21,570	22,672	23,529
Other services, except public administration	29,024	29,857	31,010	32,009	33,320	34,205	35,062
Government and government enterprises	55,518	56,350	56,635	57,301	58,947	59,271	60,785

D = Not shown to avoid disclosure of confidential information, but the estimates for this item are included in the total.

Table RI-10. Employment Characteristics by Family Type

(Number, percent.)

Family type and labor force status	2015		2016		2017	
	Total	Families with own children under 18 years	Total	Families with own children under 18 years	Total	Families with own children under 18 years
All Families...	250,262	105,051	247,448	99,442	251,811	103,757
FAMILY TYPE AND LABOR FORCE STATUS						
Married-Couple Families..............................	174,967	65,193	172,506	61,174	186,052	70,544
Both husband and wife in labor force................	56.7	74.9	54.0	71.2	56.4	73.6
Husband in labor force, wife not in labor force	17.2	18.2	17.8	21.0	19.8	22.8
Wife in labor force, husband not in labor force	7.8	4.3	8.9	5.3	8.4	2.9
Both husband and wife not in labor force..............	17.2	2.2	17.8	1.6	14.2	0.4
Other Families	75,295	39,858	74,942	38,268	65,759	33,213
Female householder, no husband present..............	75.7	80.1	75.9	77.4	75.1	78.1
In labor force..	54.9	67.1	55.1	65.3	53.1	62.5
Not in labor force	20.8	13.0	20.9	12.1	22.0	15.6
Male householder, no wife present...................	24.3	19.9	24.1	22.6	24.9	21.9
In labor force..	19.9	18.6	19.2	20.0	19.1	19.7
Not in labor force	4.4	1.3	4.9	2.6	5.7	2.2

Table RI-11. School Enrollment and Educational Attainment, 2017

(Number, percent.)

Item	State	U.S.
Enrollment		
Total population 3 years and over, enrolled in school	260,894	81,273,337
Enrolled in nursery school or preschool (percent)	4.9	6.0
Enrolled in kindergarten (percent)..	3.6	4.9
Enrolled in elementary school, grades 1-8 (percent)............................	36.3	40.6
Enrolled in high school, grades 9-12 (percent).................................	18.0	21.1
Enrolled in college or graduate school (percent)..............................	37.3	27.4
Attainment		
Total population 25 years and over	736,969	221,250,083
Less than ninth grade (percent)...	5.1	5.1
9th to 12th grade, no diploma (percent).......................................	6.6	6.9
High school graduate, including equivalency (percent).........................	29.9	27.1
Some college, no degree (percent)..	16.9	20.4
Associate's degree (percent)...	8.0	8.5
Bachelor's degree (percent)	20.3	19.7
Graduate or professional degree (percent)....................................	13.1	12.3
High school graduate or higher (percent).....................................	88.3	88.0
Bachelor's degree or higher (percent)..	33.5	32.0

Table RI-12. Public School Characteristics and Educational Indicators

(Number, percent; data derived from National Center of Education Statistics.)

Item	State	U.S.
Public Elementary and Secondary Schools		
Number of operational school districts, 2016-17...............................	63	18,377
Number of operational schools, 2016-17.......................................	315	98,330
Percent charter schools	9.5	7.1
Total public school enrollment, 2016-17......................................	142,150	50,587,859
Percent charter school enrollment	5.8	6.0
Student-teacher ratio, Fall 2015..	13.4	16.0
Expenditures per student (dollars), 2015-16..................................	16,082	11,841
Four-year adjusted cohort graduation rate (ACGR)[1]..........................	84.1	84.6
Students eligible for free or reduced-price lunch (percent), 2015-16.........	47.0	52.1
English language learners (percent), Fall 2016...............................	7.8	9.6
Students age 3 to 21 served under IDEA, part B (percent), 2017-18............	16.7	13.7
Public Schools by Type, 2016-17		Percent of state public schools
Total number of schools...	315	100.0
Special education...	1	0.3
Vocational education..	10	3.2
Alternative education...	2	0.6

[1] Adjusted Cohort Graduation Rates (ACGR) differ from Averaged Freshmen Graduation Rates (AFGR).

Table RI-13. Reported Voting and Registration of the Voting-Age Population, November 2018

(Numbers in thousands, percent.)

Item	Total population	Total citizen population	Registered			Voted		
			Total registered	Percent registered (total population)	Percent registered (total citizen population)	Total voted	Percent voted (total population)	Percent voted (total citizen population)
U.S. Total	249,748	228,832	153,066	61.3	66.9	122,281	49.0	53.4
State Total....................................	828	782	532	64.2	68.0	403	48.7	51.6
Sex								
Male ...	394	373	238	60.5	63.8	186	47.4	49.9
Female	435	408	293	67.5	71.9	217	49.9	53.1
Race								
White alone.............................	724	699	488	67.4	69.8	374	51.6	53.4
White, non-Hispanic alone	642	633	447	69.8	70.7	345	53.8	54.5
Black alone............................	53	45	26	(B)	(B)	16	(B)	(B)
Asian alone	26	16	7	(B)	(B)	5	(B)	(B)
Hispanic (of any race)	98	79	44	45.0	55.8	30	30.5	37.8
White alone or in combination	746	718	498	66.7	69.3	382	51.2	53.2
Black alone or in combination................	71	60	34	(B)	(B)	23	(B)	(B)
Asian alone or in combination..............	30	19	7	(B)	(B)	5	(B)	(B)
Age								
18 to 24 years	90	82	50	55.5	61.5	34	37.8	41.8
25 to 34 years	145	136	72	49.6	52.9	45	31.0	33.1
35 to 44 years	129	122	79	60.8	64.5	57	44.2	46.9
45 to 64 years	304	287	210	69.2	73.2	172	56.4	59.7
65 years and over	159	155	121	75.7	78.0	95	59.8	61.6

B = Base is less than 75,000 and therefore too small to show the derived measure.

Table RI-14. Crime

(Number, rate per 100,000. Data are derived from the FBI Uniform Crime Reports.)

Item	State			U.S.		
	2016	2017	Percent change	2016	2017	Percent change
TOTAL POPULATION[1]	1,057,566	1,059,639	0.2	323,405,935	325,719,178	0.7
VIOLENT CRIME						
Number................................	2,529	2,460	-2.7	1,285,606	1,283,220	-0.2
Rate	239.1	232.2	-2.9	397.5	394.0	-0.9
Murder and Nonnegligent Manslaughter						
Number................................	29	20	-31.0	17,413	17,284	-0.7
Rate	2.7	1.9	-31.2	5.4	5.3	-1.4
Rape[2]						
Number................................	445	445	-	132,414	135,755	2.5
Rate	42.1	42.0	-0.2	40.9	41.7	1.8
Robbery						
Number................................	541	474	-12.4	332,797	319,356	-4.0
Rate	51.2	44.7	-12.6	102.9	98.0	-4.7
Aggravated Assault						
Number................................	1,514	1,521	0.5	802,982	810,825	1.0
Rate	143.2	143.5	0.3	248.3	248.9	0.3
PROPERTY CRIME						
Number................................	18,910	18,561	-1.8	7,928,530	7,694,086	-3.0
Rate	1,788.1	1,751.6	-2.0	2,451.6	2,362.2	-3.6
Burglary						
Number................................	3,650	3,217	-11.9	1,516,405	1,401,840	-7.6
Rate	345.1	303.6	-12.0	468.9	430.4	-8.2
Larceny-Theft						
Number................................	14,157	13,861	-2.1	5,644,835	5,519,107	-2.2
Rate	1,338.6	1,308.1	-2.3	1,745.4	1,694.4	-2.9
Motor Vehicle Theft						
Number................................	1,103	1,483	34.5	767,290	773,139	0.8
Rate	104.3	140.0	34.2	237.3	237.4	-

NOTE: Although arson data are included in the trend and clearance tables, sufficient data are not available to estimate totals for this offense. Therefore, no arson data are published in this table.
- = Zero or rounds to zero.
[1] Population figures are U.S. Census Bureau provisional estimates as of July 1, 2017.
[2] The figures shown in the rape (revised definition) column were estimated using the revised Uniform Crime Reporting (UCR) definition of rape.

Table RI-15. State Government Finances, 2017

(Dollar amounts in thousands, percent distribution.)

Item	Dollars	Percent distribution
Total Revenue	9,261,892	100.0
General revenue	7,506,405	81.0
Intergovernmental revenue	2,519,225	27.2
Taxes	3,266,663	35.3
General sales	996,390	10.8
Selective sales	695,392	7.5
License taxes	110,461	1.2
Individual income tax	1,238,928	13.4
Corporate income tax	129,732	1.4
Other taxes	95,760	1.0
Current charges	837,896	9.0
Miscellaneous general revenue	882,621	9.5
Utility revenue	24,931	0.3
Liquor stores revenue	0	-
Insurance trust revenue[1]	1,730,556	18.7
Total Expenditure	8,780,280	100.0
Intergovernmental expenditure	1,277,277	14.5
Direct expenditure	7,503,003	85.5
Current operation	5,153,303	58.7
Capital outlay	442,114	5.0
Insurance benefits and repayments	1,288,574	14.7
Assistance and subsidies	169,679	1.9
Interest on debt	449,333	5.1
Exhibit: Salaries and wages	1,325,482	15.1
Total Expenditure	8,780,280	100.0
General expenditure	7,319,018	83.4
Intergovernmental expenditure	1,277,277	14.5
Direct expenditure	6,041,741	68.8
General expenditure, by function:		
Education	2,168,254	24.7
Public welfare	2,770,134	31.5
Hospitals	66,227	0.8
Health	186,540	2.1
Highways	320,743	3.7
Police protection	87,077	1.0
Correction	199,314	2.3
Natural resources	49,743	0.6
Parks and recreation	60,176	0.7
Governmental administration	406,932	4.6
Interest on general debt	448,794	5.1
Other and unallocable	555,084	6.3
Utility expenditure	172,688	2.0
Liquor stores expenditure	0	-
Insurance trust expenditure	1,288,574	14.7
Debt at End of Fiscal Year	8,932,377	X
Cash and Security Holdings	15,786,466	X

X = Not applicable.
- = Zero or rounds to zero.
[1] Within insurance trust revenue, net earnings of state retirement systems is a calculated statistic (the item code in the data file is X08), and thus can be positive or negative. Net earnings is the sum of earnings on investments plus gains on investments minus losses on investments. The change made in 2002 for asset valuation from book to market value in accordance with Statement 34 of the Governmental Accounting Standards Board is reflected in the calculated statistics.

Table RI-16. State Government Tax Collections, 2018

(Dollars in thousands, percent.)

Item	Dollars	Percent distribution
Total Taxes	3,483,100	100.0
Property taxes	2,704	0.1
Sales and gross receipts	1,682,021	48.3
General sales and gross receipts	1,048,957	30.1
Selective sales and gross receipts	633,064	18.2
Alcoholic beverages	19,918	0.6
Amusements	X	-
Insurance premiums	81,519	2.3
Motor fuels	79,858	2.3
Pari-mutuels	1,074	-
Public utilities	59,651	1.7
Tobacco products	146,691	4.2
Other selective sales	244,353	7.0
Licenses	102,202	2.9
Alcoholic beverages	92	-
Amusements	202	-
Corporations in general	4,910	0.1
Hunting and fishing	1,844	0.1
Motor vehicle	20,755	0.6
Motor vehicle operators	4,865	0.1
Public utilities	2,070	0.1
Occupation and business, NEC	61,959	1.8
Other licenses	5,505	0.2
Income taxes	1,447,270	41.6
Individual income	1,329,152	38.2
Corporation net income	118,118	3.4
Other taxes	248,903	7.1
Death and gift	133,103	3.8
Documentary and stock transfer	115,800	3.3
Severance	X	-
Taxes, NEC	0	-

X = Not applicable.
- = Zero or rounds to zero.

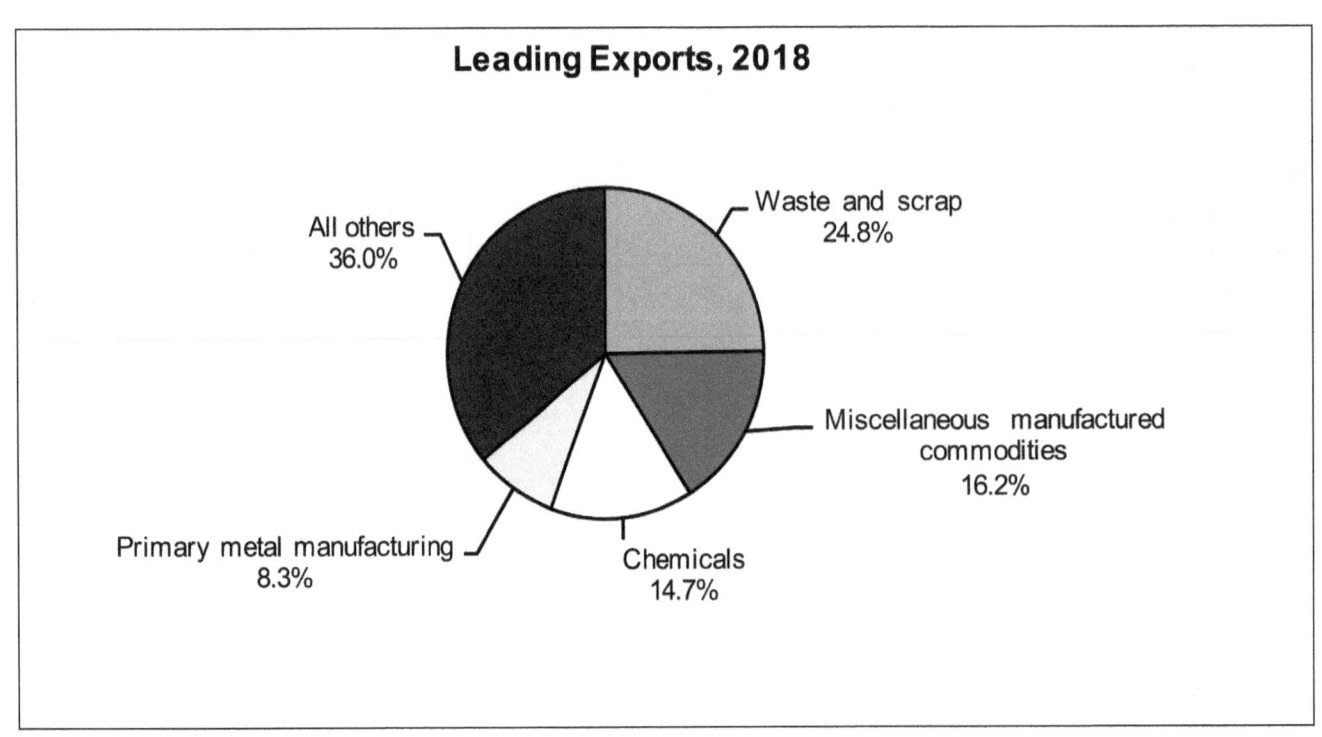

Leading Exports, 2018

- Waste and scrap 24.8%
- Miscellaneous manufactured commodities 16.2%
- Chemicals 14.7%
- Primary metal manufacturing 8.3%
- All others 36.0%

Facts and Figures

Location: Southeastern United States; bordered on the N by North Carolina, on the E by the Atlantic Ocean, on the S by the Atlantic Ocean and Georgia, and on the W by Georgia

Area: 32,020 sq. mi. (82,932 sq. km.); rank—40th

Population: 5,084,127 (2018 est.); rank—23rd

Principal Cities: capital—Columbia; largest—Columbia

Statehood: May 23, 1788; 8th state

U.S. Congress: 2 senators, 7 representatives

State Mottoes: *Animis opibusque parati* ("Prepared in mind and resources"); *Dum spiro, spero* ("While I breathe, I hope")

State Songs: "Carolina"; "South Carolina on My Mind"

State Nickname: The Palmetto State

Abbreviations: SC; S.C.

State Symbols: flower—yellow jessamine; tree—cabbage palmetto; bird—Carolina wren

At a Glance

- With an increase in population of 9.9 percent, South Carolina ranked 11th among the states in growth from 2010 to 2018.

- South Carolina's median household income in 2017 was $50,570, and 15.4 percent of the population lived below the poverty level.

- South Carolina's violent crime rate in 2017 was 506.2 incidents per 100,000 population, which ranked 11th in the nation.

- In 2017, 11.0 percent of South Carolinians did not have health insurance, compared to 8.7 percent of the total U.S. population.

- South Carolina once again had the highest rate of traffic fatalities in the U.S. in 2017, with 1.80 deaths per 100 million vehicle miles driven.

Table SC-1. Population by Age, Sex, Race, and Hispanic Origin

(Number, percent, except where noted.)

Sex, age, race, and Hispanic origin	2000	2010	2018 [1]	Percent change, 2010–2018
Total Population..	4,012,013	4,625,364	5,084,127	9.9
Percent of total U.S. population	1.4	1.5	1.6	X
Sex				
Male...	1,948,929	2,250,101	2,463,326	9.5
Female	2,063,083	2,375,263	2,620,801	10.3
Age				
Under 5 years..	264,679	302,297	292,391	-3.3
5 to 19 years...	871,099	922,128	949,703	3.0
20 to 64 years..	2,390,901	2,769,065	2,942,118	6.2
65 years and over......................................	485,333	631,874	899,915	42.4
Median age (years)	35.4	37.9	39.6	4.5
Race and Hispanic Origin				
One race				
White	2,695,560	3,164,143	3,483,455	10.1
Black	1,185,216	1,302,865	1,380,145	5.9
American Indian and Alaska Native	13,718	24,665	27,694	12.3
Asian	36,014	61,247	89,962	46.9
Native Hawaiian or Other Pacific Islander	1,628	3,957	5,153	30.2
Two or more races.....................................	39,950	68,487	97,718	42.7
Hispanic (of any race).................................	95,076	243,923	296,046	21.4

X = Not applicable.
[1] Population figures for 2018 are July 1 estimates. The 2010 estimates are taken from the 2010 Census.

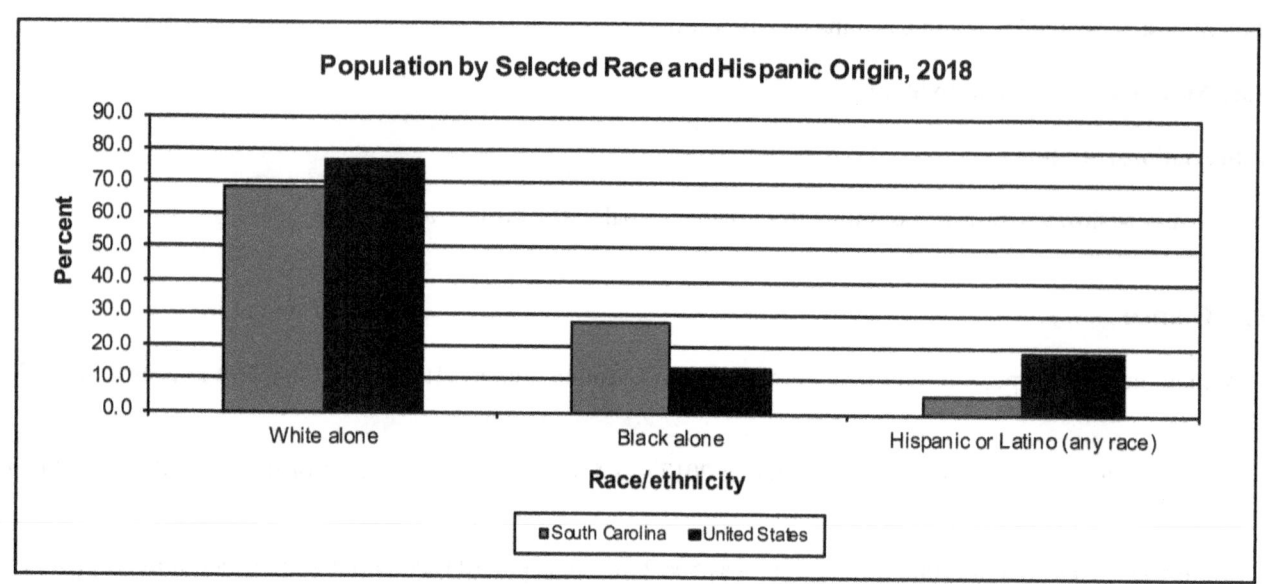

Table SC-2. Marital Status

(Number, percent distribution.)

Sex, age, race, and Hispanic origin	2000	2010	2017
Males, 15 Years and Over	1,516,125	1,797,441	1,971,172
Never married	28.8	35.2	36.7
Now married, except separated...........................	57.3	49.4	48.9
Separated..	2.8	3.0	2.4
Widowed...	2.7	2.8	3.0
Divorced...	8.3	9.5	9.1
Females, 15 Years and Over	1,652,793	1,939,054	2,138,926
Never married	23.4	29.1	30.2
Now married, except separated...........................	51.4	45.2	45.2
Separated..	3.8	3.9	3.2
Widowed...	11.5	10.6	9.6
Divorced...	9.9	11.2	11.7

Table SC-3. Households and Housing Characteristics

(Number, percent, dollars.)

Item	2000	2010	2017	Average annual percent change, 2010–2017
Total Households..	1,533,854	1,761,393	1,905,100	1.2
Family households	1,072,822	1,180,687	1,253,260	0.9
Married-couple family	783,142	827,387	901,707	1.3
Other family	289,680	353,300	351,553	-0.1
Male householder, no wife present............................	62,722	77,062	79,210	0.4
Female householder, no husband present....................	226,958	276,238	272,343	-0.2
Nonfamily households	461,032	580,706	651,840	1.7
Householder living alone..	383,142	489,995	551,198	1.8
Householder not living alone..	77,890	90,711	100,642	1.6
Housing Characteristics				
Total housing units..	1,753,670	2,140,337	2,284,820	1.0
Occupied housing units	1,533,854	1,761,393	1,905,100	1.2
Owner occupied	1,107,617	1,210,160	1,309,670	1.2
Renter occupied	426,237	551,233	595,430	1.1
Average household size..	2.53	2.55	2.57	0.1
Financial Characteristics				
Median gross rent of renter-occupied housing	510	728	848	2.4
Median monthly owner costs for housing units with a mortgage	894	1,177	1,195	0.2
Median value of owner-occupied housing units	94,900	138,100	161,800	2.5

Table SC-4. Migration, Origin, and Language

(Number, percent.)

Characteristic	State 2016	State 2017	State Percent change	U.S. 2016	U.S. 2017	U.S. Percent change
Residence 1 Year Ago						
Population 1 year and over	4,903,788	4,966,211	1.3	319,361,956	321,994,428	0.8
Same house	85.2	85.5	X	85.4	85.7	X
Different house in the U.S.	14.4	14.1	X	13.9	13.6	X
Same county	7.7	7.4	X	8.3	8.1	X
Different county	6.8	6.6	X	5.6	5.6	X
Same state	3.4	3.3	X	3.2	3.3	X
Different state	3.4	3.4	X	2.4	2.3	X
Abroad	0.4	0.4	X	0.7	0.7	X
Place of Birth						
Native born	4,723,155	4,780,075	1.2	279,388,170	281,193,323	0.6
Male	48.4	48.4	X	49.3	49.4	X
Female	51.6	51.6	X	50.7	50.6	X
Foreign born	237,964	244,294	2.7	43,739,345	44,525,855	1.8
Male	49.6	50.7	X	48.5	48.4	X
Female	50.4	49.3	X	51.5	51.6	X
Foreign born; naturalized U.S. citizen.........................	94,759	106,194	12.1	21,238,372	21,948,732	3.3
Male	45.5	45.6	X	45.9	45.9	X
Female	54.5	54.4	X	54.1	54.1	X
Foreign born; not a U.S. citizen.................................	143,205	138,100	-3.6	22,500,973	22,577,123	0.3
Male	52.4	54.6	X	51.0	50.8	X
Female	47.6	45.4	X	49.0	49.2	X
Entered 2010 or later	20.2	23.6	X	18.6	21.3	X
Entered 2000 to 2009	31.7	32.1	X	26.7	25.7	X
Entered before 2000..	48.1	44.3	X	54.7	53.0	X
World Region of Birth, Foreign						
Foreign-born population, excluding population born at sea	237,964	244,294	2.7	43,738,901	44,525,458	1.8
Europe	18.7	16.8	X	10.9	10.8	X
Asia	24.2	25.5	X	30.8	31.2	X
Africa	3.1	4.1	X	4.9	5.1	X
Oceania	0.3	0.8	X	0.6	0.6	X
Latin America..	50.2	49.5	X	51.0	50.4	X
North America	3.5	3.2	X	1.8	1.8	X
Language Spoken at Home and Ability to Speak English						
Population 5 years and over.......................................	4,671,107	4,734,830	1.4	303,328,961	305,924,019	0.9
English only	93.2	92.8	X	78.4	78.2	X
Language other than English......................................	6.8	7.2	X	21.6	21.8	X
Speaks English less than "very well"..........................	2.7	2.7	X	8.6	8.5	X

NA = Not available.
X = Not applicable.
- = Zero or rounds to zero.

Table SC-5. Median Income and Poverty Status, 2017

(Number, percent, except as noted.)

Characteristic	State		U.S.	
	Number	Percent	Number	Percent
Median Income				
Households (dollars)...	50,570	X	60,336	X
Families (dollars)	62,432	X	73,891	X
Below Poverty Level (All People)	751,907	15.4	42,583,651	13.4
Sex				
Male	326,969	13.9	19,004,547	12.2
Female	424,938	16.8	23,579,104	14.5
Age				
Under 18 years..	245,023	22.6	13,353,202	18.4
Related children under 18 years...........................	241,143	22.3	13,053,472	18.1
18 to 64 years...	429,037	14.5	24,648,677	12.6
65 years and over	77,847	9.2	4,581,772	9.3

X = Not applicable.

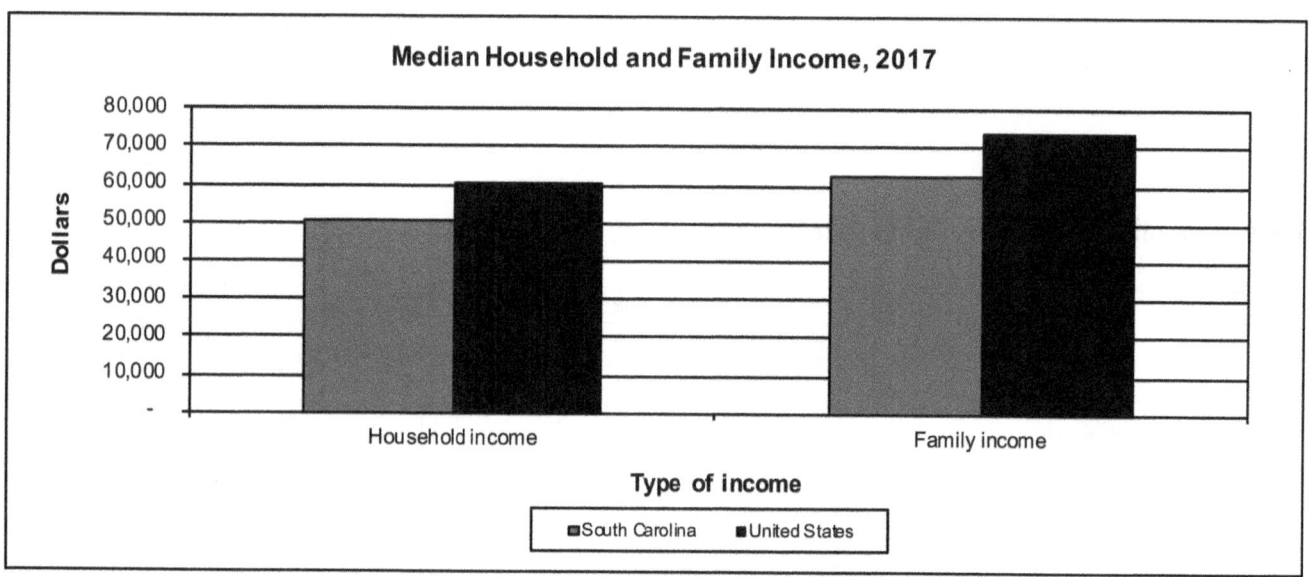

Median Household and Family Income, 2017

Table SC-6. Health Insurance Coverage Status for the Civilian Noninstitutionalized Population and Children Under 18 Years of Age

(Number, percent.)

Item	2009	2010	2011	2012	2013	2014	2015	2016	2017
Civilian Noninstitutionalized Population	4,454,344	4,536,835	4,579,231	4,623,171	4,678,122	4,733,742	4,801,301	4,861,188	4,928,260
Covered by Private or Public Insurance									
Number...	3,704,507	3,741,560	3,812,927	3,844,990	3,939,270	4,092,185	4,278,073	4,375,282	4,386,727
Percent...	83.2	82.5	83.3	83.2	84.2	86.4	89.1	90.0	89.0
Uninsured									
Number...	749,837	795,275	766,304	778,181	738,852	641,557	523,228	485,906	541,533
Percent...	16.8	17.5	16.7	16.8	15.8	13.6	10.9	10.0	11.0
Percent in the U.S. not covered..................................	15.1	15.5	15.1	14.8	14.5	11.7	9.4	8.6	8.7
Children Under 18 Years of Age[1]	1,078,199	1,078,477	1,079,476	1,078,022	1,076,621	1,080,779	1,086,607	1,097,385	1,169,363
Covered by Private or Public Insurance									
Number...	970,760	976,620	988,285	988,908	1,004,026	1,020,796	1,042,427	1,053,682	1,109,164
Percent...	90.0	90.6	91.6	91.7	93.3	94.5	95.9	96.0	94.9
Uninsured									
Number...	107,439	101,857	91,191	89,114	72,595	59,983	44,180	43,703	60,199
Percent...	10.0	9.4	8.4	8.3	6.7	5.5	4.1	4.0	5.1
Percent in the U.S. not covered..................................	8.6	8.0	7.5	7.2	7.1	6.0	4.8	4.5	5.0

[1] 2017 data is for individuals under 19 years of age.

Table SC-7. Employment Status by Demographic Group, 2018

(Numbers in thousands, percent.)

Characteristic	Civilian noninstitutional population	Civilian labor force		Employed		Unemployed	
		Number	Percent of population	Number	Percent of population	Number	Percent of population
Total...	4,009	2,320	57.9	2,238	55.8	82	3.5
Sex							
Male..	1,891	1,224	64.7	1,182	62.5	42	3.4
Female...	2,118	1,096	51.7	1,056	49.9	40	3.6
Race, Sex, and Hispanic Origin							
White...	2,850	1,637	57.5	1,596	56.0	41	2.5
Male..	1,374	899	65.4	879	64.0	20	2.3
Female...	1,476	738	50.0	717	48.6	21	2.8
Black or African American..........................	1,040	602	57.9	564	54.2	38	6.3
Male..	462	286	62.0	267	57.8	19	6.7
Female...	578	316	54.6	297	51.4	19	6.0
Hispanic or Latino ethnicity[1]...................	184	129	69.9	123	66.8	6	4.5
Male..	104	88	85	85	82	3	3.1
Female...	NA	NA	NA	NA	NA	NA	NA
Age							
16 to 19 years..	254	85	33.3	74	29.1	11	12.7
20 to 24 years..	291	207	71.1	192	66.1	15	7.2
25 to 34 years..	651	525	80.7	502	77.1	24	4.5
35 to 44 years..	611	497	81.4	487	79.7	11	2.1
45 to 54 years..	604	462	76.6	450	74.5	13	2.7
55 to 64 years..	669	385	57.5	379	56.6	6	1.6
65 years and over	929	158	17.0	155	16.6	3	2.1

NOTE: Data in Table 7 are from the Current Population Survey (CPS) and do not match the estimates in Table 8. See notes and definitions for further information.
[1] May be of any race.

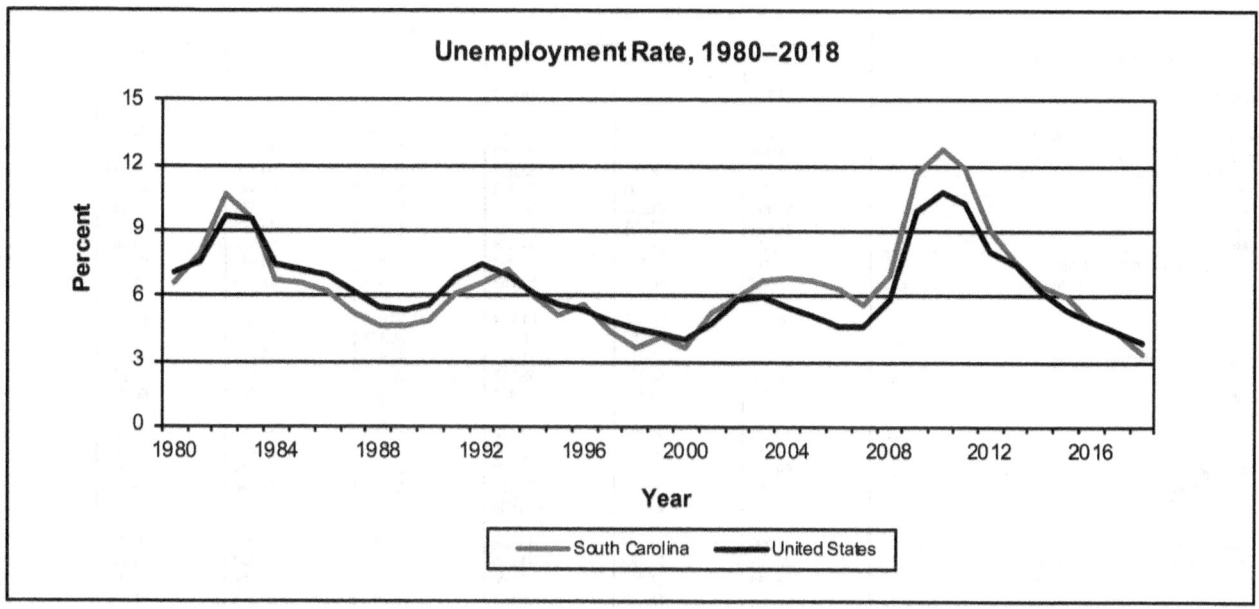

Table SC-8. Employment Status of the Civilian Noninstitutional Population Age 16 Years and Over

(Number, percent.)

Year	Civilian labor force	Civilian participation rate	Employed	Unemployed	Unemployment rate
2010..	2,155,668	60.5	1,915,045	240,623	11.2
2011..	2,175,523	60.2	1,945,900	229,623	10.6
2012..	2,186,878	59.8	1,985,618	201,260	9.2
2013..	2,190,968	59.2	2,023,642	167,326	7.6
2014..	2,222,978	59.2	2,079,565	143,413	6.5
2015..	2,269,339	59.4	2,134,244	135,095	6.0
2016..	2,293,666	59.0	2,179,521	114,145	5.0
2017..	2,312,651	58.6	2,213,894	98,757	4.3
2018..	2,323,209	58.0	2,243,656	79,553	3.4

Table SC-9. Employment and Average Wages by Industry

(Estimates are based on the 2012 *North American Industry Classification System* [NAICS].)

Industry	2011	2012	2013	2014	2015	2016	2017
	Number of jobs						
Wage and Salary Employment by Industry.........................	1,913,077	1,947,212	1,985,126	2,032,855	2,090,400	2,133,752	2,173,815
Farm Wage and Salary Employment...............................	6,817	6,839	7,775	6,085	7,511	7,270	9,290
Nonfarm Wage and Salary Employment...........................	1,906,260	1,940,373	1,977,351	2,026,770	2,082,889	2,126,482	2,164,525
Private wage and salary employment.................................	1,514,253	1,544,843	1,578,018	1,626,266	1,676,940	1,719,909	1,754,938
Forestry, fishing, and related activities................................	6,915	6,778	6,963	7,073	7,269	7,296	7,231
Mining..	1,233	1,194	1,141	1,157	1,236	1,467	1,684
Utilities..	11,919	12,134	12,212	12,349	12,347	12,370	12,356
Construction...	78,773	79,761	82,074	84,712	89,164	96,912	103,350
Manufacturing...	216,463	221,519	225,172	230,774	236,121	238,259	240,799
Durable goods manufacturing.................................	121,011	126,047	129,356	133,704	137,653	139,580	139,909
Nondurable goods manufacturing............................	95,452	95,472	95,816	97,070	98,468	98,679	100,890
Wholesale trade	64,778	65,939	66,719	68,411	71,193	72,027	72,740
Retail trade..	227,146	228,066	232,665	238,473	243,263	248,285	248,446
Transportation and warehousing..................................	47,932	50,151	52,595	56,594	60,728	63,234	66,165
Information..	25,893	25,782	26,431	26,472	27,057	27,045	27,471
Finance and insurance	68,620	69,502	70,580	70,386	70,804	72,039	73,543
Real estate and rental and leasing................................	26,141	25,930	26,757	27,629	28,691	29,800	30,250
Professional, scientific, and technical services	79,607	80,339	82,461	85,612	89,242	94,241	97,522
Management of companies and enterprises........................	15,060	15,882	16,489	17,039	16,699	17,946	20,250
Administrative and waste services................................	136,671	141,871	144,898	153,318	158,396	159,475	162,543
Educational services	29,758	30,409	30,855	32,184	33,170	33,487	33,254
Health care and social assistance..................................	174,365	177,713	181,077	185,814	192,677	198,671	203,217
Arts, entertainment, and recreation................................	26,510	26,900	27,442	28,739	29,145	29,861	30,772
Accommodation and food services.................................	185,166	191,062	196,678	201,982	210,983	218,999	224,939
Other services, except public administration........................	91,303	93,911	94,809	97,548	98,755	98,495	98,406
Government and government enterprises	392,007	395,530	399,333	400,504	405,949	406,573	409,587
	Dollars						
Average Wages and Salaries by Industry	39,672	40,576	41,033	42,033	43,277	44,189	45,499
Average Farm Wages and Salaries	18,287	27,521	19,034	23,408	22,974	19,459	14,836
Average Nonfarm Wages and Salaries	39,748	40,622	41,119	42,089	43,351	44,273	45,630
Average private wages and salaries................................	38,916	39,864	40,332	41,361	42,638	43,575	45,045
Forestry, fishing, and related activities............................	31,331	32,768	33,395	35,127	36,259	37,588	39,874
Mining..	50,690	53,295	55,275	57,682	69,443	66,378	66,306
Utilities..	80,466	81,356	84,784	87,453	92,420	95,116	97,384
Construction	42,934	44,651	45,392	47,210	48,886	51,066	54,422
Manufacturing...	52,827	54,018	54,938	56,963	58,534	59,583	60,831
Durable goods manufacturing.................................	55,307	56,385	57,298	59,814	60,997	62,306	63,452
Nondurable goods manufacturing............................	49,683	50,893	51,752	53,035	55,089	55,733	57,195
Wholesale trade	58,181	60,478	61,244	63,914	65,509	66,490	68,936
Retail trade..	25,492	25,933	26,209	26,478	27,267	27,855	28,497
Transportation and warehousing..................................	41,149	42,013	41,924	42,431	43,757	43,476	44,851
Information..	52,167	53,760	55,517	57,901	59,157	60,341	63,639
Finance and insurance	57,390	59,417	60,478	61,840	65,044	66,814	69,284
Real estate and rental and leasing................................	36,202	37,772	39,112	40,796	42,450	43,302	45,502
Professional, scientific, and technical services	61,312	63,755	64,092	65,683	67,653	69,305	71,343
Management of companies and enterprises........................	69,611	72,763	71,579	71,921	74,614	77,309	81,919
Administrative and waste services................................	33,762	33,425	32,873	33,520	34,140	34,698	35,755
Educational services	28,712	29,361	30,038	30,636	31,100	32,161	32,303
Health care and social assistance..................................	42,290	43,255	43,665	44,826	46,284	46,855	48,142
Arts, entertainment, and recreation................................	20,967	21,169	21,030	21,323	22,522	22,773	23,018
Accommodation and food services.................................	17,368	18,006	18,290	18,572	19,138	19,794	20,350
Other services, except public administration........................	28,065	28,427	29,631	30,313	31,571	32,583	33,753
Government and government enterprises	42,963	43,584	44,230	45,041	46,296	47,227	48,139

Table SC-10. Employment Characteristics by Family Type

(Number, percent.)

Family type and labor force status	2015 Total	2015 Families with own children under 18 years	2016 Total	2016 Families with own children under 18 years	2017 Total	2017 Families with own children under 18 years
All Families................................	1,220,885	475,168	1,224,695	473,087	1,253,260	479,160
FAMILY TYPE AND LABOR FORCE STATUS						
Married-Couple Families............................	867,390	299,238	872,181	297,386	901,707	298,299
Both husband and wife in labor force..................	47.1	66.4	47.4	67.2	46.3	68.0
Husband in labor force, wife not in labor force........	21.7	27.6	21.4	26.8	21.3	26.4
Wife in labor force, husband not in labor force........	8.4	3.7	8.7	3.9	8.5	3.6
Both husband and wife not in labor force...............	22.3	2.1	21.8	1.7	23.1	1.8
Other Families	353,495	175,930	352,514	175,701	351,553	180,861
Female householder, no husband present................	76.8	79.5	75.9	78.6	77.5	79.6
In labor force.............	52.3	65.8	52.0	66.4	52.3	67.1
Not in labor force........	24.5	13.8	23.9	12.2	25.1	12.5
Male householder, no wife present....................	23.2	20.5	24.1	21.4	22.5	20.4
In labor force..................	17.2	18.6	16.7	18.0	16.3	17.5
Not in labor force	5.9	1.8	7.4	3.4	6.2	2.9

Table SC-11. School Enrollment and Educational Attainment, 2017

(Number, percent.)

Item	State	U.S.
Enrollment		
Total population 3 years and over, enrolled in school	1,183,515	81,273,337
Enrolled in nursery school or preschool (percent)........	5.0	6.0
Enrolled in kindergarten (percent)........	5.9	4.9
Enrolled in elementary school, grades 1-8 (percent)........	42.5	40.6
Enrolled in high school, grades 9-12 (percent)	21.1	21.1
Enrolled in college or graduate school (percent)........	25.6	27.4
Attainment		
Total population 25 years and over	3,443,851	221,250,083
Less than ninth grade (percent)........	4.0	5.1
9th to 12th grade, no diploma (percent)........	8.6	6.9
High school graduate, including equivalency (percent)........	29.5	27.1
Some college, no degree (percent)........	20.3	20.4
Associate's degree (percent)........	9.6	8.5
Bachelor's degree (percent)	17.6	19.7
Graduate or professional degree (percent)........	10.4	12.3
High school graduate or higher (percent)........	87.4	88.0
Bachelor's degree or higher (percent)........	28.0	32.0

Table SC-12. Public School Characteristics and Educational Indicators

(Number, percent; data derived from National Center of Education Statistics.)

Item	State	U.S.
Public Elementary and Secondary Schools		
Number of operational school districts, 2016-17	101	18,377
Number of operational schools, 2016-17........	1,252	98,330
Percent charter schools	5.6	7.1
Total public school enrollment, 2016-17........	771,250	50,587,859
Percent charter school enrollment	4.2	6.0
Student-teacher ratio, Fall 2015........	15.2	16.0
Expenditures per student (dollars), 2015-16........	10,045	11,841
Four-year adjusted cohort graduation rate (ACGR)[1]........	83.6	84.6
Students eligible for free or reduced-price lunch (percent), 2015-16........	60.0	52.1
English language learners (percent), Fall 2016	5.7	9.6
Students age 3 to 21 served under IDEA, part B (percent), 2017-18	13.5	13.7

Public Schools by Type, 2016-17		Percent of state public schools
Total number of schools........	1,252	100.0
Special education	8	0.6
Vocational education	42	3.4
Alternative education........	12	1.0

[1] Adjusted Cohort Graduation Rates (ACGR) differ from Averaged Freshmen Graduation Rates (AFGR).

Table SC-13. Reported Voting and Registration of the Voting-Age Population, November 2018

(Numbers in thousands, percent.)

Item	Total population	Total citizen population	Registered			Voted		
			Total registered	Percent registered (total population)	Percent registered (total citizen population)	Total voted	Percent voted (total population)	Percent voted (total citizen population)
U.S. Total	249,748	228,832	153,066	61.3	66.9	122,281	49.0	53.4
State Total....................................	3,914	3,769	2,430	62.1	64.5	1,836	46.9	48.7
Sex								
Male	1,849	1,767	1,121	60.6	63.5	828	44.8	46.9
Female	2,066	2,002	1,309	63.4	65.4	1,007	48.8	50.3
Race								
White alone................................	2,790	2,677	1,727	61.9	64.5	1,276	45.7	47.7
White, non-Hispanic alone....................	2,610	2,588	1,690	64.8	65.3	1,257	48.1	48.6
Black alone.................................	1,000	996	646	64.6	64.9	519	51.9	52.1
Asian alone.................................	54	29	19	(B)	(B)	9	(B)	(B)
Hispanic (of any race)......................	207	110	36	17.7	33.3	19	9.3	17.6
White alone or in combination	2,836	2,722	1,756	61.9	64.5	1,298	45.8	47.7
Black alone or in combination...............	1,041	1,036	672	64.6	64.9	539	51.8	52.0
Asian alone or in combination..............	56	32	19	(B)	(B)	9	(B)	(B)
Age								
18 to 24 years.............................	391	378	176	44.9	46.4	91	23.3	24.1
25 to 34 years.............................	752	720	407	54.1	56.6	228	30.3	31.7
35 to 44 years.............................	556	500	323	58.1	64.6	265	47.7	53.1
45 to 64 years.............................	1,249	1,215	802	64.2	66.1	638	51.1	52.5
65 years and over	965	956	721	74.8	75.5	613	63.6	64.2

B = Base is less than 75,000 and therefore too small to show the derived measure.

Table SC-14. Crime

(Number, rate per 100,000. Data are derived from the FBI Uniform Crime Reports.)

Item	State			U.S.		
	2016	2017	Percent change	2016	2017	Percent change
TOTAL POPULATION[1]	4,959,822	5,024,369	1.3	323,405,935	325,719,178	0.7
VIOLENT CRIME						
Number..	25,137	25,432	1.2	1,285,606	1,283,220	-0.2
Rate	506.8	506.2	-0.1	397.5	394.0	-0.9
Murder and Nonnegligent Manslaughter						
Number..	358	390	8.9	17,413	17,284	-0.7
Rate	7.2	7.8	7.5	5.4	5.3	-1.4
Rape[2]						
Number..	2,491	2,504	0.5	132,414	135,755	2.5
Rate	50.2	49.8	-0.8	40.9	41.7	1.8
Robbery						
Number..	4,071	3,870	-4.9	332,797	319,356	-4.0
Rate	82.1	77.0	-6.2	102.9	98.0	-4.7
Aggravated Assault						
Number..	18,217	18,668	2.5	802,982	810,825	1.0
Rate	367.3	371.5	1.2	248.3	248.9	0.3
PROPERTY CRIME						
Number..	161,534	160,575	-0.6	7,928,530	7,694,086	-3.0
Rate	3,256.9	3,195.9	-1.9	2,451.6	2,362.2	-3.6
Burglary						
Number..	33,149	31,306	-5.6	1,516,405	1,401,840	-7.6
Rate	668.4	623.1	-6.8	468.9	430.4	-8.2
Larceny-Theft						
Number..	114,455	115,012	0.5	5,644,835	5,519,107	-2.2
Rate	2,307.6	2,289.1	-0.8	1,745.4	1,694.4	-2.9
Motor Vehicle Theft						
Number..	13,930	14,257	2.3	767,290	773,139	0.8
Rate	280.9	283.8	1.0	237.3	237.4	-

NOTE: Although arson data are included in the trend and clearance tables, sufficient data are not available to estimate totals for this offense. Therefore, no arson data are published in this table.
- = Zero or rounds to zero.
[1] Population figures are U.S. Census Bureau provisional estimates as of July 1, 2017.
[2] The figures shown in the rape (revised definition) column were estimated using the revised Uniform Crime Reporting (UCR) definition of rape.

Table SC-15. State Government Finances, 2017

(Dollar amounts in thousands, percent distribution.)

Item	Dollars	Percent distribution
Total Revenue	34,340,032	100.0
General revenue	26,188,283	76.3
Intergovernmental revenue	9,007,621	26.2
Taxes	9,828,825	28.6
General sales	3,285,007	9.6
Selective sales	1,352,342	3.9
License taxes	518,886	1.5
Individual income tax	4,142,276	12.1
Corporate income tax	375,655	1.1
Other taxes	154,659	0.5
Current charges	5,243,200	15.3
Miscellaneous general revenue	2,108,637	6.1
Utility revenue	1,729,338	5.0
Liquor stores revenue	0	-
Insurance trust revenue[1]	6,422,411	18.7
Total Expenditure	33,880,302	100.0
Intergovernmental expenditure	6,735,297	19.9
Direct expenditure	27,145,005	80.1
Current operation	19,325,690	57.0
Capital outlay	2,338,303	6.9
Insurance benefits and repayments	3,683,587	10.9
Assistance and subsidies	1,198,414	3.5
Interest on debt	599,011	1.8
Exhibit: Salaries and wages	4,031,756	11.9
Total Expenditure	33,880,302	100.0
General expenditure	28,580,071	84.4
Intergovernmental expenditure	6,735,297	19.9
Direct expenditure	21,844,774	64.5
General expenditure, by function:		
Education	10,274,900	30.3
Public welfare	7,811,767	23.1
Hospitals	1,871,970	5.5
Health	1,264,559	3.7
Highways	2,068,516	6.1
Police protection	205,857	0.6
Correction	520,001	1.5
Natural resources	281,506	0.8
Parks and recreation	148,364	0.4
Governmental administration	630,300	1.9
Interest on general debt	355,443	1.0
Other and unallocable	3,146,888	9.3
Utility expenditure	1,616,644	4.7
Liquor stores expenditure	0	-
Insurance trust expenditure	3,683,587	10.9
Debt at End of Fiscal Year	15,744,638	X
Cash and Security Holdings	41,526,844	X

X = Not applicable.
- = Zero or rounds to zero.
[1] Within insurance trust revenue, net earnings of state retirement systems is a calculated statistic (the item code in the data file is X08), and thus can be positive or negative. Net earnings is the sum of earnings on investments plus gains on investments minus losses on investments. The change made in 2002 for asset valuation from book to market value in accordance with Statement 34 of the Governmental Accounting Standards Board is reflected in the calculated statistics.

Table SC-16. State Government Tax Collections, 2018

(Dollars in thousands, percent.)

Item	Dollars	Percent distribution
Total Taxes	10,550,096	100.0
Property taxes	37,298	0.4
Sales and gross receipts	4,948,178	46.9
General sales and gross receipts	3,303,220	31.3
Selective sales and gross receipts	1,644,958	15.6
Alcoholic beverages	179,115	1.7
Amusements	39,774	0.4
Insurance premiums	239,215	2.3
Motor fuels	646,581	6.1
Pari-mutuels	X	-
Public utilities	29,003	0.3
Tobacco products	27,199	0.3
Other selective sales	484,071	4.6
Licenses	582,294	5.5
Alcoholic beverages	12,600	0.1
Amusements	6,389	0.1
Corporations in general	110,199	1.0
Hunting and fishing	18,898	0.2
Motor vehicle	274,093	2.6
Motor vehicle operators	4,486	-
Public utilities	10,670	0.1
Occupation and business, NEC	126,871	1.2
Other licenses	18,088	0.2
Income taxes	4,856,152	46.0
Individual income	4,432,104	42.0
Corporation net income	424,048	4.0
Other taxes	126,174	1.2
Death and gift	X	-
Documentary and stock transfer	126,174	1.2
Severance	X	-
Taxes, NEC	0	-

X = Not applicable.
- = Zero or rounds to zero.

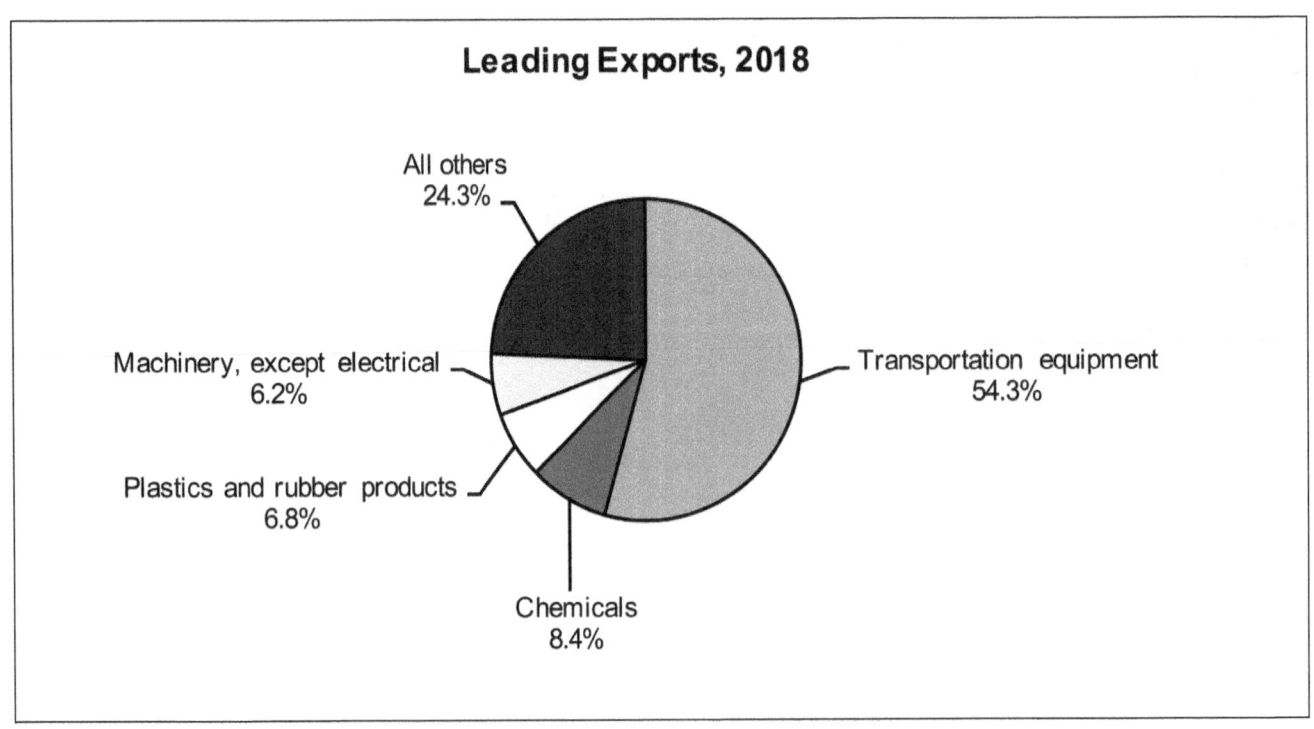

Leading Exports, 2018

All others
24.3%

Machinery, except electrical
6.2%

Plastics and rubber products
6.8%

Chemicals
8.4%

Transportation equipment
54.3%

SOUTH DAKOTA

Facts and Figures

Location: North central United States; bordered on the N by North Dakota, on the E by Minnesota and Iowa, on the S by Nebraska, and on the W by Wyoming and Montana

Area: 77,117 sq. mi. (199,731 sq. km.); rank—17th

Population: 882,235 (2018 est.); rank—46th

Principal Cities: capital—Pierre; largest—Sioux Falls

Statehood: November 2, 1889; 40th state

U.S. Congress: 2 senators, 1 representative

State Motto: Under God the People Rule

State Song: "Hail, South Dakota"

State Nickname: The Mount Rushmore State

Abbreviations: SD; S.D.; S. Dak.

State Symbols: flower—pasqueflower; tree—Black Hills spruce; bird—ring-necked pheasant

At a Glance

- With an increase in population of 8.4 percent, South Dakota ranked 15th among the states in growth from 2010 to 2018.

- In 2017, 9.1 percent of South Dakotans did not have health insurance, compared to 8.7 percent of the total U.S. population.

- South Dakota's violent crime rate in 2017 was 433.6 incidents per 100,000 population, compared to 394.0 for the entire nation.

- South Dakota's median income in 2017 was $56,521, and 13.0 percent of its residents lived below the poverty level.

- In 2018, South Dakota's unemployment rate was 3.0 percent, compared to the national unemployment rate of 3.9 percent.

Table SD-1. Population by Age, Sex, Race, and Hispanic Origin

(Number, percent, except where noted.)

Sex, age, race, and Hispanic origin	2000	2010	2018 [1]	Percent change, 2010–2018
Total Population...	754,844	814,180	882,235	8.4
Percent of total U.S. population	0.4	0.3	0.3	X
Sex				
Male..	374,558	407,381	445,531	9.4
Female..	380,286	406,799	436,704	7.4
Age				
Under 5 years..	51,069	59,621	62,132	4.2
5 to 19 years..	176,412	167,119	179,318	7.3
20 to 64 years...	419,232	470,859	493,931	4.9
65 years and over	108,131	116,581	146,854	26.0
Median age (years)..	35.6	36.9	37.1	0.5
Race and Hispanic Origin				
One race				
White	669,404	706,690	744,733	5.4
Black..	4,685	10,533	21,000	99.4
American Indian and Alaska Native	62,283	72,782	79,412	9.1
Asian..	4,378	7,775	15,093	94.1
Native Hawaiian or Other Pacific Islander	261	517	747	44.5
Two or more races	10,156	15,883	21,250	33.8
Hispanic (of any race).......................................	10,903	23,699	36,402	53.6

X = Not applicable.
[1] Population figures for 2018 are July 1 estimates. The 2010 estimates are taken from the 2010 Census.
- = Zero or rounds to zero.

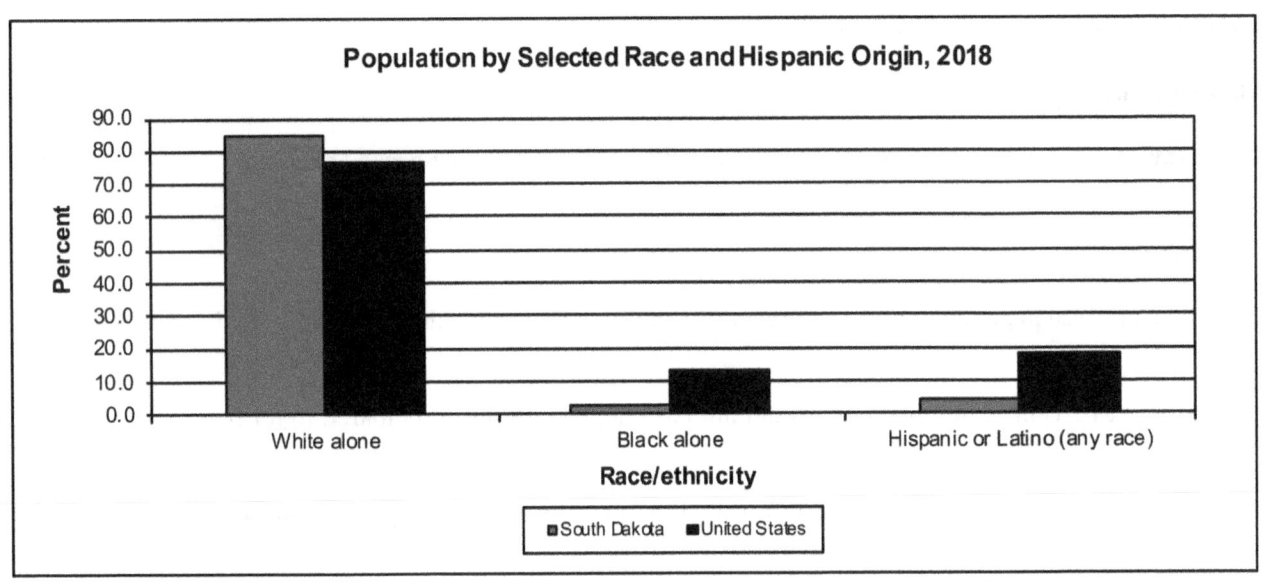

Table SD-2. Marital Status

(Number, percent distribution.)

Sex, age, race, and Hispanic origin	2000	2010	2017
Males, 15 Years and Over	289,858	322,689	347,676
Never married	29.8	33.5	34.1
Now married, except separated.................................	58.2	52.5	50.2
Separated...	1.0	0.9	1.2
Widowed...	2.4	2.8	2.8
Divorced..	8.5	10.3	11.9
Females, 15 Years and Over	299,754	325,640	342,606
Never married	22.5	26.0	26.9
Now married, except separated.................................	55.9	52.1	51.9
Separated...	1.1	1.0	1.4
Widowed...	11.4	9.5	9.2
Divorced..	9.0	11.4	10.5

Table SD-3. Households and Housing Characteristics

(Number, percent, dollars.)

Item	2000	2010	2017	Average annual percent change, 2010–2017
Total Households	290,245	318,955	344,260	1.1
Family households	194,330	204,029	213,402	0.7
Married-couple family	157,391	161,534	167,651	0.5
Other family	36,939	42,495	45,751	1.1
Male householder, no wife present	10,734	12,526	15,376	3.3
Female householder, no husband present	26,205	29,969	30,375	0.2
Nonfamily households	95,915	114,926	130,858	2.0
Householder living alone	80,040	95,610	108,566	1.9
Householder not living alone	15,875	19,316	22,292	2.2
Housing Characteristics				
Total housing units	323,208	364,031	392,650	1.1
Occupied housing units	290,245	318,955	344,260	1.1
Owner occupied	197,940	216,821	233,092	1.1
Renter occupied	92,305	102,134	111,168	1.3
Average household size	2.50	2.45	2.43	-0.1
Financial Characteristics				
Median gross rent of renter-occupied housing	426	591	722	3.2
Median monthly owner costs for housing units with a mortgage	828	1,151	1,283	1.6
Median value of owner-occupied housing units	79,600	129,700	167,600	4.2

Table SD-4. Migration, Origin, and Language

(Number, percent.)

Characteristic	State			U.S.		
	2016	2017	Percent change	2016	2017	Percent change
Residence 1 Year Ago						
Population 1 year and over	853,832	856,726	0.3	319,361,956	321,994,428	0.8
Same house	84.4	84.5	X	85.4	85.7	X
Different house in the U.S.	15.2	14.7	X	13.9	13.6	X
Same county	7.8	7.2	X	8.3	8.1	X
Different county	7.3	7.5	X	5.6	5.6	X
Same state	3.6	4.4	X	3.2	3.3	X
Different state	3.7	3.0	X	2.4	2.3	X
Abroad	0.5	0.8	X	0.7	0.7	X
Place of Birth						
Native born	834,528	840,265	0.7	279,388,170	281,193,323	0.6
Male	50.3	50.4	X	49.3	49.4	X
Female	49.7	49.6	X	50.7	50.6	X
Foreign born	30,926	29,401	-4.9	43,739,345	44,525,855	1.8
Male	51.7	51.5	X	48.5	48.4	X
Female	48.3	48.5	X	51.5	51.6	X
Foreign born; naturalized U.S. citizen	10,982	12,589	14.6	21,238,372	21,948,732	3.3
Male	48.0	47.0	X	45.9	45.9	X
Female	52.0	53.0	X	54.1	54.1	X
Foreign born; not a U.S. citizen	19,944	16,812	-15.7	22,500,973	22,577,123	0.3
Male	53.8	54.8	X	51.0	50.8	X
Female	46.2	45.2	X	49.0	49.2	X
Entered 2010 or later	42.1	36.2	X	18.6	21.3	X
Entered 2000 to 2009	30.1	33.2	X	26.7	25.7	X
Entered before 2000	27.8	30.6	X	54.7	53.0	X
World Region of Birth, Foreign						
Foreign-born population, excluding population born at sea	30,926	29,401	-4.9	43,738,901	44,525,458	1.8
Europe	13.7	16.2	X	10.9	10.8	X
Asia	33.2	27.2	X	30.8	31.2	X
Africa	21.6	21.8	X	4.9	5.1	X
Oceania	0.2	0.7	X	0.6	0.6	X
Latin America	25.8	29.3	X	51.0	50.4	X
North America	5.5	4.8	X	1.8	1.8	X
Language Spoken at Home and Ability to Speak English						
Population 5 years and over	804,562	809,206	0.6	303,328,961	305,924,019	0.9
English only	93.5	93.6	X	78.4	78.2	X
Language other than English	6.5	6.4	X	21.6	21.8	X
Speaks English less than "very well"	2.3	2.1	X	8.6	8.5	X

NA = Not available.
X = Not applicable.
- = Zero or rounds to zero.

Table SD-5. Median Income and Poverty Status, 2017

(Number, percent, except as noted.)

Characteristic	State		U.S.	
	Number	Percent	Number	Percent
Median Income				
Households (dollars)..	56,521	X	60,336	X
Families (dollars)	73,236	X	73,891	X
Below Poverty Level (All People)	109,099	13.0	42,583,651	13.4
Sex				
Male	50,655	12.0	19,004,547	12.2
Female	58,444	14.0	23,579,104	14.5
Age				
Under 18 years...	34,442	16.6	13,353,202	18.4
Related children under 18 years..	33,620	16.3	13,053,472	18.1
18 to 64 years..	63,803	12.9	24,648,677	12.6
65 years and over	10,854	8.0	4,581,772	9.3

X = Not applicable.

Median Household and Family Income, 2017

■ South Dakota   ■ United States

Table SD-6. Health Insurance Coverage Status for the Civilian Noninstitutionalized Population and Children Under 18 Years of Age

(Number, percent.)

Item	2009	2010	2011	2012	2013	2014	2015	2016	2017
Civilian Noninstitutionalized Population	792,969	798,141	805,505	816,425	827,039	835,403	841,363	848,774	851,826
Covered by Private or Public Insurance									
Number..	689,058	699,255	709,597	722,292	733,713	753,472	755,448	774,556	774,488
Percent...	86.9	87.6	88.1	88.5	88.7	90.2	89.8	91.3	90.9
Uninsured									
Number..	103,911	98,886	95,908	94,133	93,326	81,931	85,915	74,218	77,338
Percent...	13.1	12.4	11.9	11.5	11.3	9.8	10.2	8.7	9.1
Percent in the U.S. not covered..	15.1	15.5	15.1	14.8	14.5	11.7	9.4	8.6	8.7
Children Under 18 Years of Age[1]	194,825	200,893	200,704	203,033	207,264	209,586	208,580	212,981	224,414
Covered by Private or Public Insurance									
Number..	180,074	184,198	188,665	191,198	194,142	197,674	194,544	203,436	210,566
Percent...	92.4	91.7	94.0	94.2	93.7	94.3	93.3	95.5	93.8
Uninsured									
Number..	14,751	16,695	12,039	11,835	13,122	11,912	14,036	9,545	13,848
Percent...	7.6	8.3	6.0	5.8	6.3	5.7	6.7	4.5	6.2
Percent in the U.S. not covered..	8.6	8.0	7.5	7.2	7.1	6.0	4.8	4.5	5.0

[1] 2017 data is for individuals under 19 years of age.

Table SD-7. Employment Status by Demographic Group, 2018

(Numbers in thousands, percent.)

Characteristic	Civilian noninstitutional population	Civilian labor force		Employed		Unemployed	
		Number	Percent of population	Number	Percent of population	Number	Percent of population
Total......................................	666	458	68.8	445	66.8	14	2.9
Sex							
Male..	333	245	73.7	238	71.6	7	2.9
Female.......................................	333	213	63.9	207	62.0	7	3.0
Race, Sex, and Hispanic Origin							
White	579	407	70.4	399	69.0	8	1.9
Male......................................	293	220	75.1	215	73.6	4	2.0
Female...................................	286	187	65.5	184	64.3	4	1.9
Black or African American...................	NA	NA	NA	NA	NA	NA	NA
Male......................................	NA	NA	NA	NA	NA	NA	NA
Female...................................	NA	NA	NA	NA	NA	NA	NA
Hispanic or Latino ethnicity[1]	NA	NA	NA	NA	NA	NA	NA
Male......................................	NA	NA	NA	NA	NA	NA	NA
Female...................................	NA	NA	NA	NA	NA	NA	NA
Age							
16 to 19 years...............................	NA	NA	NA	NA	NA	NA	NA
20 to 24 years...............................	60	47	78.3	44	72.7	3	7.2
25 to 34 years...............................	106	92	87.1	89	83.9	3	3.6
35 to 44 years...............................	99	88	88.6	86	86.9	2	1.8
45 to 54 years...............................	97	85	87.9	83	85.8	2	2.4
55 to 64 years...............................	117	90	77.1	89	75.9	1	1.3
65 years and over	54	50	93.1	48	90.1	2	3.1

NOTE: Data in Table 7 are from the Current Population Survey (CPS) and do not match the estimates in Table 8. See notes and definitions for further information.
[1] May be of any race.
NA = Not available.
... = Fewer than 500 persons

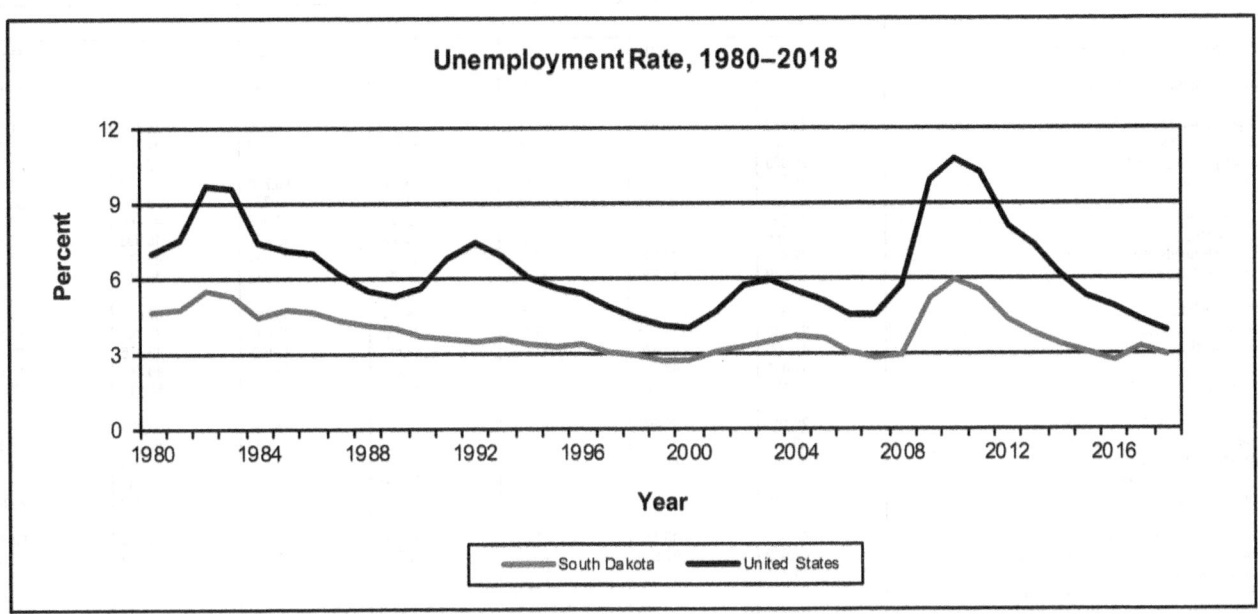

Table SD-8. Employment Status of the Civilian Noninstitutional Population Age 16 Years and Over

(Number, percent.)

Year	Civilian labor force	Civilian participation rate	Employed	Unemployed	Unemployment rate
2010..	441,339	71.3	419,355	21,984	5.0
2011..	440,934	70.7	420,054	20,880	4.7
2012..	442,442	70.1	423,501	18,941	4.3
2013..	443,079	69.4	426,284	16,795	3.8
2014..	446,475	69.4	431,139	15,336	3.4
2015..	449,408	69.4	435,450	13,958	3.1
2016..	451,934	69.2	438,377	13,557	3.0
2017..	455,175	69.0	440,028	15,147	3.3
2018..	459,459	68.7	445,599	13,860	3.0

Table SD-9. Employment and Average Wages by Industry

(Estimates are based on the 2012 *North American Industry Classification System* [NAICS].)

Industry	2011	2012	2013	2014	2015	2016	2017
	Number of jobs						
Wage and Salary Employment by Industry........................	427,213	435,054	438,191	444,468	447,390	450,749	453,399
Farm Wage and Salary Employment............................	5,557	6,844	6,290	6,366	4,908	4,622	4,979
Nonfarm Wage and Salary Employment.........................	421,656	428,210	431,901	438,102	442,482	446,127	448,420
Private wage and salary employment................................	336,574	344,185	347,829	353,666	358,339	361,171	362,636
Forestry, fishing, and related activities..........................	2,258	2,394	2,466	2,426	2,442	2,463	2,458
Mining..	833	850	846	816	837	849	872
Utilities..	2,071	1,969	1,950	1,967	1,996	2,019	1,994
Construction	20,672	20,709	21,039	21,790	22,773	23,381	22,894
Manufacturing..	39,260	41,225	41,573	42,466	42,641	42,196	43,137
Durable goods manufacturing....................................	25,879	27,209	27,514	28,506	28,528	27,569	27,597
Nondurable goods manufacturing..............................	13,381	14,016	14,059	13,960	14,113	14,627	15,540
Wholesale trade	19,039	19,579	19,971	20,877	21,209	21,267	21,082
Retail trade..	50,555	51,449	51,594	52,151	53,247	54,108	53,333
Transportation and warehousing..................................	10,380	10,437	10,480	11,221	11,500	11,260	11,276
Information	6,396	6,208	6,025	6,063	5,895	5,771	5,724
Finance and insurance	25,489	26,142	27,131	27,131	26,920	26,482	26,582
Real estate and rental and leasing...............................	3,502	3,537	3,619	3,700	3,805	3,855	3,859
Professional, scientific, and technical services	11,237	11,642	12,537	12,477	12,623	13,001	13,454
Management of companies and enterprises..................	3,768	4,144	4,235	4,572	4,936	5,079	4,907
Administrative and waste services	13,796	13,618	13,092	13,371	13,330	13,378	13,107
Educational services	7,994	8,104	8,072	8,081	8,131	8,020	8,079
Health care and social assistance................................	57,480	59,090	59,928	60,004	60,849	62,349	63,848
Arts, entertainment, and recreation..............................	6,404	6,335	6,184	6,526	6,604	6,614	6,830
Accommodation and food services	37,268	38,223	38,687	39,253	39,793	40,408	40,455
Other services, except public administration...............	18,172	18,530	18,400	18,774	18,808	18,671	18,745
Government and government enterprises	85,082	84,025	84,072	84,436	84,143	84,956	85,784
	Dollars						
Average Wages and Salaries by Industry	34,994	36,211	36,824	38,249	39,630	40,695	41,912
Average Farm Wages and Salaries	35,419	43,868	38,995	40,036	33,787	38,756	38,114
Average Nonfarm Wages and Salaries	34,988	36,088	36,792	38,223	39,695	40,715	41,954
Average private wages and salaries................................	34,929	36,133	36,969	38,521	40,069	41,043	42,276
Forestry, fishing, and related activities..........................	25,035	25,289	26,659	25,863	27,417	29,010	29,831
Mining..	55,681	57,315	55,962	58,757	60,718	58,178	60,280
Utilities..	67,051	69,447	73,253	74,705	76,281	78,359	80,303
Construction	38,990	39,926	40,943	42,883	44,987	47,666	47,374
Manufacturing..	41,465	42,179	42,444	44,506	45,447	45,993	47,888
Durable goods manufacturing....................................	42,404	42,844	43,532	45,245	45,994	46,511	48,724
Nondurable goods manufacturing..............................	39,649	40,889	40,314	42,997	44,343	45,018	46,402
Wholesale trade	48,915	51,358	52,920	54,998	56,251	57,027	58,393
Retail trade..	23,730	24,553	25,168	26,194	27,036	27,349	27,803
Transportation and warehousing..................................	41,060	42,026	42,816	43,893	44,983	45,476	46,137
Information	41,831	42,778	43,366	44,812	45,729	46,647	47,159
Finance and insurance	48,160	49,773	50,335	52,973	56,369	58,717	60,904
Real estate and rental and leasing...............................	28,107	29,603	30,640	32,335	34,794	33,888	35,580
Professional, scientific, and technical services	49,153	51,623	49,917	52,696	56,409	57,467	59,363
Management of companies and enterprises..................	88,044	89,115	91,577	92,717	93,532	96,695	102,847
Administrative and waste services	25,533	26,956	27,163	29,191	29,978	31,147	33,208
Educational services	24,245	24,518	24,891	25,068	25,598	26,422	25,859
Health care and social assistance................................	41,622	43,118	44,284	45,830	47,788	48,943	50,473
Arts, entertainment, and recreation..............................	17,939	17,956	18,294	18,802	19,711	19,414	19,851
Accommodation and food services	14,398	14,985	15,533	16,083	17,171	17,874	18,341
Other services, except public administration...............	25,074	25,658	27,010	28,123	29,445	30,037	31,284
Government and government enterprises............................	35,224	35,906	36,063	36,973	38,099	39,319	40,593

Table SD-10. Employment Characteristics by Family Type

(Number, percent.)

Family type and labor force status	2015		2016		2017	
	Total	Families with own children under 18 years	Total	Families with own children under 18 years	Total	Families with own children under 18 years
All Families...	217,013	94,326	209,986	92,357	213,402	91,048
FAMILY TYPE AND LABOR FORCE STATUS						
Married-Couple Families.................................	170,511	64,388	164,515	64,612	167,651	63,888
Both husband and wife in labor force..................................	61.1	78.4	61.4	79.8	59.2	78.3
Husband in labor force, wife not in labor force	16.2	18.3	15.7	15.8	16.1	17.8
Wife in labor force, husband not in labor force	6.5	1.9	6.7	2.8	6.7	2.5
Both husband and wife not in labor force...........................	15.8	1.3	15.8	1.1	17.2	1.2
Other Families	46,502	29,938	45,471	27,745	45,751	27,160
Female householder, no husband present........................	69.5	70.4	68.3	69.1	66.4	70.7
In labor force...	53.7	62.3	48.2	55.6	51.1	61.7
Not in labor force	15.8	8.1	20.1	13.5	15.3	9.1
Male householder, no wife present...........................	30.5	29.6	31.7	30.9	33.6	29.3
In labor force...	26.2	27.6	25.1	28.2	27.7	26.2
Not in labor force	4.3	2.0	6.7	2.7	6.0	3.1

Table SD-11. School Enrollment and Educational Attainment, 2017

(Number, percent.)

Item	State	U.S.
Enrollment		
Total population 3 years and over, enrolled in school	214,085	81,273,337
Enrolled in nursery school or preschool (percent)	7.5	6.0
Enrolled in kindergarten (percent)	5.5	4.9
Enrolled in elementary school, grades 1-8 (percent)...	43.2	40.6
Enrolled in high school, grades 9-12 (percent)	21.0	21.1
Enrolled in college or graduate school (percent)...	22.8	27.4
Attainment		
Total population 25 years and over	574,559	221,250,083
Less than ninth grade (percent)	2.9	5.1
9th to 12th grade, no diploma (percent)	5.4	6.9
High school graduate, including equivalency (percent)..	30.8	27.1
Some college, no degree (percent)	22.0	20.4
Associate's degree (percent)...	10.8	8.5
Bachelor's degree (percent)	19.1	19.7
Graduate or professional degree (percent)...	9.0	12.3
High school graduate or higher (percent)..	91.7	88.0
Bachelor's degree or higher (percent)...	28.1	32.0

Table SD-12. Public School Characteristics and Educational Indicators

(Number, percent; data derived from National Center of Education Statistics.)

Item	State	U.S.
Public Elementary and Secondary Schools		
Number of operational school districts, 2016-17..	167	18,377
Number of operational schools, 2016-17..	697	98,330
Percent charter schools	NA	7.1
Total public school enrollment, 2016-17..	136,302	50,587,859
Percent charter school enrollment	NA	6.0
Student-teacher ratio, Fall 2015...	13.9	16.0
Expenditures per student (dollars), 2015-16..	9,335	11,841
Four-year adjusted cohort graduation rate (ACGR)[1]	83.7	84.6
Students eligible for free or reduced-price lunch (percent), 2015-16..	41.7	52.1
English language learners (percent), Fall 2016..	3.4	9.6
Students age 3 to 21 served under IDEA, part B (percent), 2017-18	15.4	13.7

Public Schools by Type, 2016-17		Percent of state public schools
Total number of schools..	697	100.0
Special education...	12	1.7
Vocational education..	3	0.4
Alternative education...	33	4.7

[1] Adjusted Cohort Graduation Rates (ACGR) differ from Averaged Freshmen Graduation Rates (AFGR).
NA = Not available.

Table SD-13. Reported Voting and Registration of the Voting-Age Population, November 2018

(Numbers in thousands, percent.)

Item	Total population	Total citizen population	Registered			Voted		
			Total registered	Percent registered (total population)	Percent registered (total citizen population)	Total voted	Percent voted (total population)	Percent voted (total citizen population)
U.S. Total	249,748	228,832	153,066	61.3	66.9	122,281	49.0	53.4
State Total......................................	648	637	429	66.2	67.3	331	51.0	51.9
Sex								
Male	325	319	207	63.8	65.0	160	49.4	50.3
Female	323	318	222	68.6	69.7	170	52.7	53.5
Race								
White alone....................................	573	568	392	68.5	69.1	305	53.3	53.8
White, non-Hispanic alone	561	559	389	69.4	69.6	303	54.1	54.3
Black alone....................................	12	7	2	(B)	(B)	1	(B)	(B)
Asian alone	5	3	1	(B)	(B)	1	(B)	(B)
Hispanic (of any race)......................	15	13	5	(B)	(B)	4	(B)	(B)
White alone or in combination	579	575	395	68.1	68.7	308	53.1	53.5
Black alone or in combination..............	14	9	2	(B)	(B)	1	(B)	(B)
Asian alone or in combination...............	6	4	2	(B)	(B)	2	(B)	(B)
Age								
18 to 24 years.................................	91	90	42	46.2	47.1	24	25.8	26.3
25 to 34 years.................................	109	105	57	52.5	54.2	33	30.3	31.3
35 to 44 years.................................	95	93	61	64.4	65.8	40	42.5	43.4
45 to 64 years.................................	204	202	155	76.1	76.8	136	66.7	67.3
65 years and over	150	148	114	75.9	77.0	98	65.5	66.4

B = Base is less than 75,000 and therefore too small to show the derived measure.

Table SD-14. Crime

(Number, rate per 100,000. Data are derived from the FBI Uniform Crime Reports.)

Item	State			U.S.		
	2016	2017	Percent change	2016	2017	Percent change
TOTAL POPULATION[1]	861,542	869,666	0.9	323,405,935	325,719,178	0.7
VIOLENT CRIME						
Number..	3,636	3,771	3.7	1,285,606	1,283,220	-0.2
Rate	422.0	433.6	2.7	397.5	394.0	-0.9
Murder and Nonnegligent Manslaughter						
Number..	28	25	-10.7	17,413	17,284	-0.7
Rate	3.2	2.9	-11.5	5.4	5.3	-1.4
Rape[2]						
Number..	526	595	13.1	132,414	135,755	2.5
Rate	61.1	68.4	12.1	40.9	41.7	1.8
Robbery						
Number..	274	238	-13.1	332,797	319,356	-4.0
Rate	31.8	27.4	-14.0	102.9	98.0	-4.7
Aggravated Assault						
Number..	2,808	2,913	3.7	802,982	810,825	1.0
Rate	325.9	335.0	2.8	248.3	248.9	0.3
PROPERTY CRIME						
Number..	17,207	16,317	-5.2	7,928,530	7,694,086	-3.0
Rate	1,997.2	1,876.2	-6.1	2,451.6	2,362.2	-3.6
Burglary						
Number..	3,002	2,707	-9.8	1,516,405	1,401,840	-7.6
Rate	348.4	311.3	-10.7	468.9	430.4	-8.2
Larceny-Theft						
Number..	12,705	12,227	-3.8	5,644,835	5,519,107	-2.2
Rate	1,474.7	1,405.9	-4.7	1,745.4	1,694.4	-2.9
Motor Vehicle Theft						
Number..	1,500	1,383	-7.8	767,290	773,139	0.8
Rate	174.1	159.0	-8.7	237.3	237.4	-

NOTE: Although arson data are included in the trend and clearance tables, sufficient data are not available to estimate totals for this offense. Therefore, no arson data are published in this table.
- = Zero or rounds to zero.
[1] Population figures are U.S. Census Bureau provisional estimates as of July 1, 2017.
[2] The figures shown in the rape (revised definition) column were estimated using the revised Uniform Crime Reporting (UCR) definition of rape.

Table SD-15. State Government Finances, 2017

(Dollar amounts in thousands, percent distribution.)

Item	Dollars	Percent distribution
Total Revenue	6,106,444	100.0
General revenue	4,400,106	72.1
Intergovernmental revenue	1,567,365	25.7
Taxes	1,828,543	29.9
General sales	1,065,361	17.4
Selective sales	452,612	7.4
License taxes	269,481	4.4
Individual income tax	0	-
Corporate income tax	30,728	0.5
Other taxes	10,361	0.2
Current charges	399,283	6.5
Miscellaneous general revenue	604,915	9.9
Utility revenue	0	-
Liquor stores revenue	0	-
Insurance trust revenue[1]	1,706,338	27.9
Total Expenditure	5,265,167	100.0
Intergovernmental expenditure	863,182	16.4
Direct expenditure	4,401,985	83.6
Current operation	2,998,573	57.0
Capital outlay	587,919	11.2
Insurance benefits and repayments	572,221	10.9
Assistance and subsidies	134,712	2.6
Interest on debt	108,560	2.1
Exhibit: Salaries and wages	788,555	15.0
Total Expenditure	5,265,167	100.0
General expenditure	4,692,946	89.1
Intergovernmental expenditure	863,182	16.4
Direct expenditure	3,829,764	72.7
General expenditure, by function:		
Education	1,519,557	28.9
Public welfare	1,154,441	21.9
Hospitals	23,579	0.4
Health	165,103	3.1
Highways	664,095	12.6
Police protection	47,261	0.9
Correction	120,790	2.3
Natural resources	187,574	3.6
Parks and recreation	42,070	0.8
Governmental administration	203,930	3.9
Interest on general debt	108,560	2.1
Other and unallocable	455,986	8.7
Utility expenditure	0	-
Liquor stores expenditure	0	-
Insurance trust expenditure	572,221	10.9
Debt at End of Fiscal Year	3,527,703	X
Cash and Security Holdings	17,051,254	X

X = Not applicable.
- = Zero or rounds to zero.
[1] Within insurance trust revenue, net earnings of state retirement systems is a calculated statistic (the item code in the data file is X08), and thus can be positive or negative. Net earnings is the sum of earnings on investments plus gains on investments minus losses on investments. The change made in 2002 for asset valuation from book to market value in accordance with Statement 34 of the Governmental Accounting Standards Board is reflected in the calculated statistics.

Table SD-16. State Government Tax Collections, 2018

(Dollars in thousands, percent.)

Item	Dollars	Percent distribution
Total Taxes	1,917,548	100.0
Property taxes	X	-
Sales and gross receipts	1,585,089	82.7
General sales and gross receipts	1,103,624	57.6
Selective sales and gross receipts	481,465	25.1
Alcoholic beverages	18,939	1.0
Amusements	9,135	0.5
Insurance premiums	92,488	4.8
Motor fuels	187,424	9.8
Pari-mutuels	177	-
Public utilities	3,510	0.2
Tobacco products	59,158	3.1
Other selective sales	110,634	5.8
Licenses	291,896	15.2
Alcoholic beverages	1,222	0.1
Amusements	6,353	0.3
Corporations in general	5,984	0.3
Hunting and fishing	28,690	1.5
Motor vehicle	83,369	4.3
Motor vehicle operators	5,676	0.3
Public utilities	X	-
Occupation and business, NEC	135,433	7.1
Other licenses	25,169	1.3
Income taxes	32,376	1.7
Individual income	X	-
Corporation net income	32,376	1.7
Other taxes	8,187	0.4
Death and gift	X	-
Documentary and stock transfer	187	-
Severance	8,000	0.4
Taxes, NEC	0	-

X = Not applicable.
- = Zero or rounds to zero.

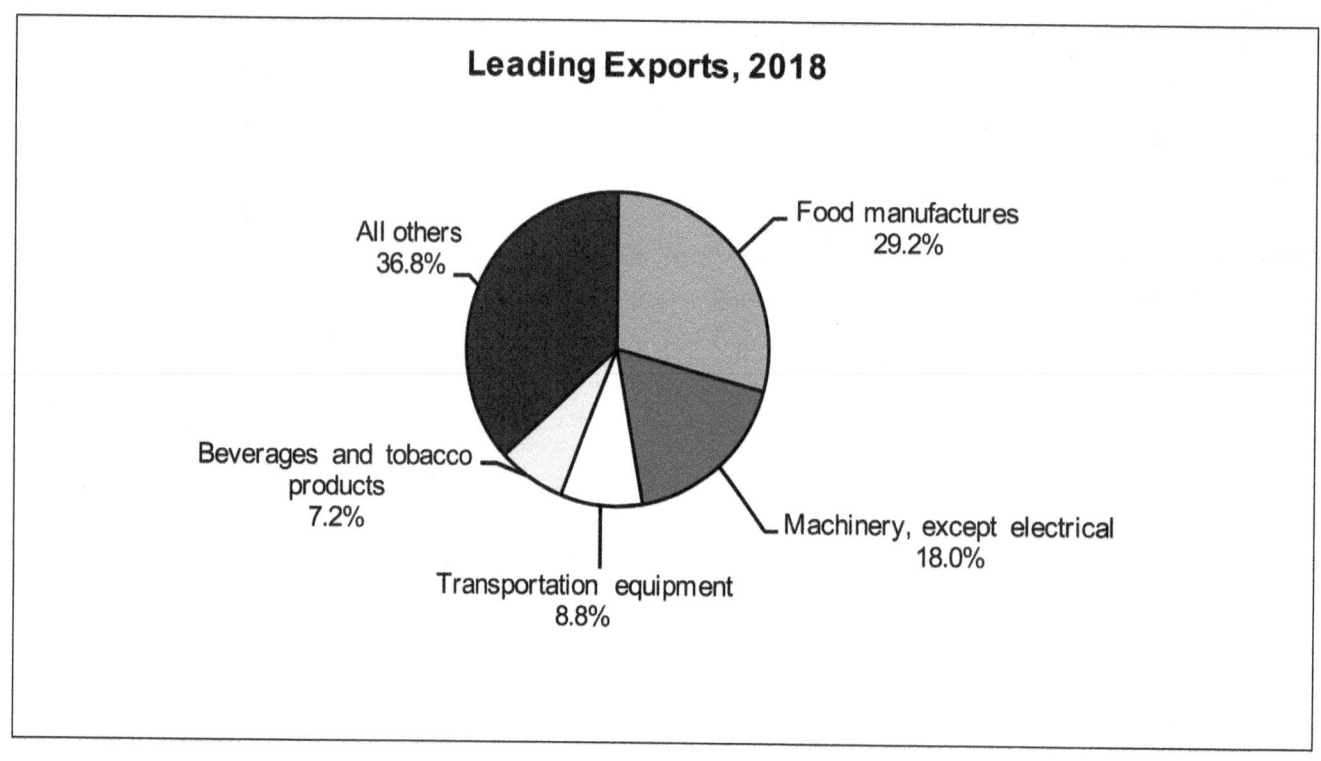

Leading Exports, 2018

- All others 36.8%
- Food manufactures 29.2%
- Machinery, except electrical 18.0%
- Transportation equipment 8.8%
- Beverages and tobacco products 7.2%

TENNESSEE

Facts and Figures

Location: South central United States; bordered on the N by Kentucky and Virginia, on the E by North Carolina, on the S by Georgia, Alabama, and Mississippi, and on the W by Arkansas and Missouri

Area: 42,143 sq. mi. (109,151 sq. km.); rank—36th

Population: 6,770,010 (2018 est.); rank—16th

Principal Cities: capital—Nashville; largest—Nashville

Statehood: June 1, 1796; 16th state

U.S. Congress: 2 senators, 9 representatives

State Motto: Agriculture and Commerce

State Song: "The Tennessee Waltz"

State Nickname: The Volunteer State

Abbreviations: TN; Tenn.

State Symbols: flower—iris; tree—yellow poplar (tulip poplar); bird—mockingbird

At a Glance

- With an increase in population of 6.7 percent, Tennessee ranked 18th among the states in growth from 2010 to 2018.

- Tennessee's median household income in 2017 was $51,340, and 15.0 percent of the population lived below the poverty level.

- In 2017, 9.5 percent of Tennesseans did not have health insurance, compared to 8.7 percent of the total U.S. population.

- Tennessee's violent crime rate in 2017 was 651.5 per 100,000 population, compared to 394.0 for the entire nation; this was the 4th highest rate in the country.

- Tennessee's unemployment rate of 3.5 percent ranked 31st among the states in 2018 and was slightly below the national rate of 3.9 percent.

Table TN-1. Population by Age, Sex, Race, and Hispanic Origin

(Number, percent, except where noted.)

Sex, age, race, and Hispanic origin	2000	2010	2018 [1]	Percent change, 2010–2018
Total Population..	5,689,283	6,346,105	6,770,010	6.7
Percent of total U.S. population	2.0	2.1	2.1	X
Sex				
Male..	2,770,275	3,093,504	3,302,924	6.8
Female	2,919,008	3,252,601	3,467,086	6.6
Age				
Under 5 years...	374,880	407,813	406,574	-0.3
5 to 19 years..	1,186,152	1,268,308	1,267,779	-0.0
20 to 64 years..	3,424,940	3,816,522	3,985,960	4.4
65 years and over	703,311	853,462	1,109,697	30.0
Median age (years)	35.9	38.0	38.8	2.1
Race and Hispanic Origin				
One race				
White	4,563,310	5,056,311	5,315,272	5.1
Black	932,809	1,068,010	1,155,631	8.2
American Indian and Alaska Native	15,152	26,256	31,826	21.2
Asian	56,662	93,897	128,526	36.9
Native Hawaiian or Other Pacific Islander	2,205	5,426	6,496	19.7
Two or more races	63,109	96,205	132,259	37.5
Hispanic (of any race)..	123,838	301,090	380,772	26.5

X = Not applicable.

[1] Population figures for 2018 are July 1 estimates. The 2010 estimates are taken from the 2010 Census.

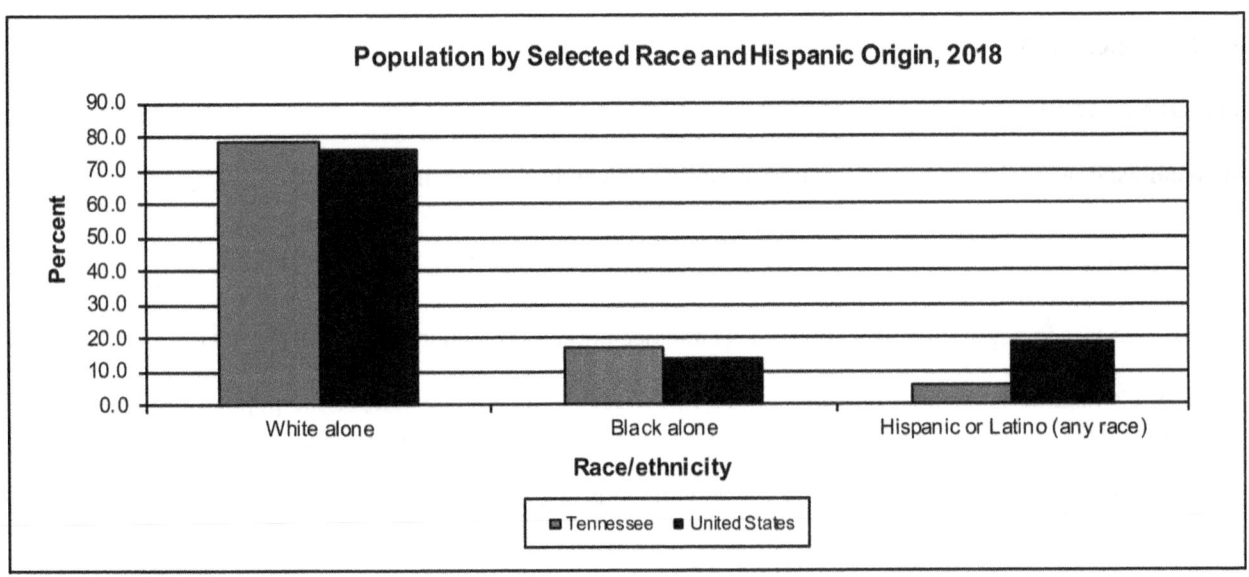

Table TN-2. Marital Status

(Number, percent distribution.)

Sex, age, race, and Hispanic origin	2000	2010	2017
Males, 15 Years and Over	2,169,327	2,461,573	2,637,308
Never married	26.6	31.4	33.2
Now married, except separated..	58.9	52.2	51.0
Separated..	1.7	2.1	2.0
Widowed..	2.5	2.7	2.9
Divorced..	10.4	11.7	11.0
Females, 15 Years and Over	2,353,303	2,652,823	2,829,679
Never married	20.7	25.3	27.8
Now married, except separated..	53.6	47.9	47.5
Separated..	2.3	2.7	2.2
Widowed..	11.2	10.3	9.4
Divorced..	12.2	13.7	13.2

Table TN-3. Households and Housing Characteristics

(Number, percent, dollars.)

Item	2000	2010	2017	Average annual percent change, 2010–2017
Total Households...	2,232,905	2,440,663	2,588,655	0.9
Family households	1,547,835	1,644,896	1,707,488	0.5
Married-couple family	1,173,960	1,195,406	1,255,384	0.7
Other family	373,875	449,490	452,104	0.1
Male householder, no wife present................................	85,976	106,616	120,332	1.8
Female householder, no husband present........................	287,899	342,874	331,772	-0.5
Nonfamily households	685,070	795,767	881,167	1.5
Householder living alone...	576,401	675,565	733,758	1.2
Householder not living alone..	108,669	120,202	147,409	3.2
Housing Characteristics				
Total housing units	2,439,443	2,815,087	2,958,799	0.7
Occupied housing units	2,232,905	2,440,663	2,588,655	0.9
Owner occupied	1,561,363	1,662,768	1,693,790	0.3
Renter occupied	671,542	777,895	894,865	2.1
Average household size..	2.48	2.54	2.53	-0.1
Financial Characteristics				
Median gross rent of renter-occupied housing	505	697	833	2.8
Median monthly owner costs for housing units with a mortgage	882	1,161	1,184	0.3
Median value of owner-occupied housing units...................	93,000	139,000	167,500	2.9

- = Zero or rounds to zero.

Table TN-4. Migration, Origin, and Language

(Number, percent.)

Characteristic	State			U.S.		
	2016	2017	Percent change	2016	2017	Percent change
Residence 1 Year Ago						
Population 1 year and over	6,580,953	6,642,072	0.9	319,361,956	321,994,428	0.8
Same house	85.8	85.5	X	85.4	85.7	X
Different house in the U.S.	13.9	14.2	X	13.9	13.6	X
Same county	8.3	8.1	X	8.3	8.1	X
Different county	5.6	6.0	X	5.6	5.6	X
Same state	3.0	3.1	X	3.2	3.3	X
Different state	2.6	2.9	X	2.4	2.3	X
Abroad	0.4	0.4	X	0.7	0.7	X
Place of Birth						
Native born	6,331,173	6,368,230	0.6	279,388,170	281,193,323	0.6
Male	48.7	48.6	X	49.3	49.4	X
Female	51.3	51.4	X	50.7	50.6	X
Foreign born	320,021	347,754	8.7	43,739,345	44,525,855	1.8
Male	50.7	50.5	X	48.5	48.4	X
Female	49.3	49.5	X	51.5	51.6	X
Foreign born; naturalized U.S. citizen..............................	117,924	129,798	10.1	21,238,372	21,948,732	3.3
Male	45.8	47.2	X	45.9	45.9	X
Female	54.2	52.8	X	54.1	54.1	X
Foreign born; not a U.S. citizen.....................................	202,097	217,956	7.8	22,500,973	22,577,123	0.3
Male	53.6	52.5	X	51.0	50.8	X
Female	46.4	47.5	X	49.0	49.2	X
Entered 2010 or later	25.1	28.5	X	18.6	21.3	X
Entered 2000 to 2009	34.3	35.0	X	26.7	25.7	X
Entered before 2000..	40.5	36.5	X	54.7	53.0	X
World Region of Birth, Foreign						
Foreign-born population, excluding population born at sea	320,021	347,357	8.5	43,738,901	44,525,458	1.8
Europe	11.1	10.4	X	10.9	10.8	X
Asia	30.7	32.0	X	30.8	31.2	X
Africa	8.4	10.7	X	4.9	5.1	X
Oceania	0.6	0.4	X	0.6	0.6	X
Latin America	46.7	44.6	X	51.0	50.4	X
North America	2.6	1.9	X	1.8	1.8	X
Language Spoken at Home and Ability to Speak English						
Population 5 years and over...	6,247,026	6,310,856	1.0	303,328,961	305,924,019	0.9
English only	93.0	92.9	X	78.4	78.2	X
Language other than English..	7.0	7.1	X	21.6	21.8	X
Speaks English less than "very well"............................	2.9	3.1	X	8.6	8.5	X

NA = Not available.
X = Not applicable.
- = Zero or rounds to zero.

Table TN-5. Median Income and Poverty Status, 2017

(Number, percent, except as noted.)

Characteristic	State		U.S.	
	Number	Percent	Number	Percent
Median Income				
Households (dollars)...	51,340	X	60,336	X
Families (dollars)	62,926	X	73,891	X
Below Poverty Level (All People)	980,284	15.0	42,583,651	13.4
Sex				
Male	428,432	13.5	19,004,547	12.2
Female	551,852	16.3	23,579,104	14.5
Age				
Under 18 years..	314,781	21.2	13,353,202	18.4
Related children under 18 years..	309,848	20.9	13,053,472	18.1
18 to 64 years...	570,196	14.2	24,648,677	12.6
65 years and over	95,307	9.2	4,581,772	9.3

X = Not applicable.

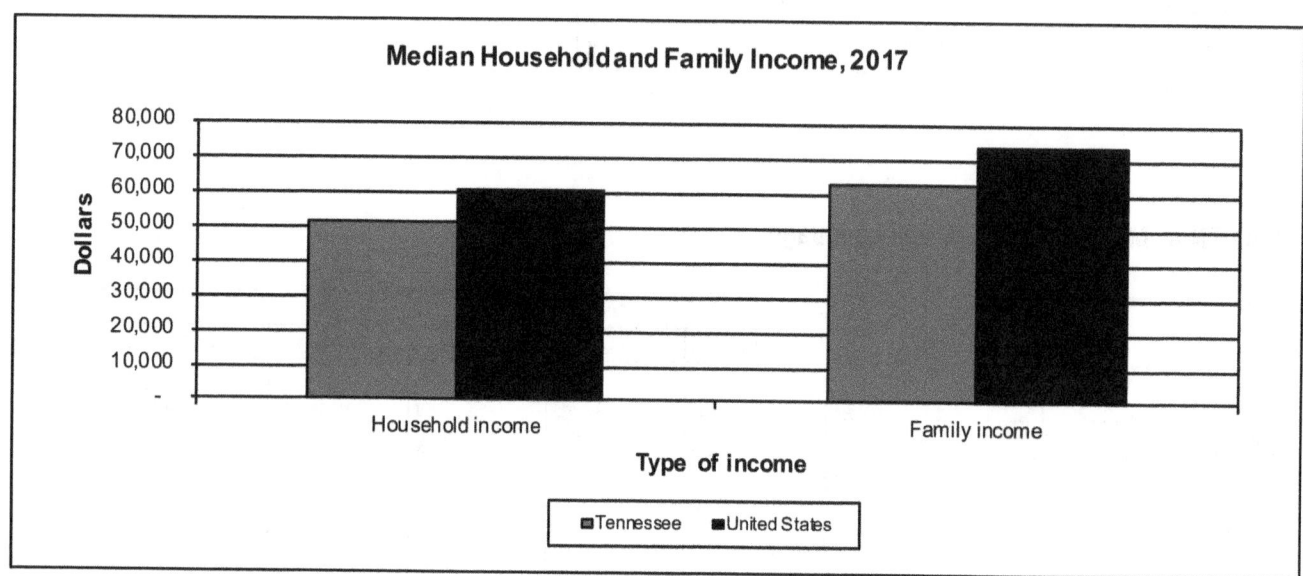

Table TN-6. Health Insurance Coverage Status for the Civilian Noninstitutionalized Population and Children Under 18 Years of Age

(Number, percent.)

Item	2009	2010	2011	2012	2013	2014	2015	2016	2017
Civilian Noninstitutionalized Population	6,188,118	6,259,546	6,302,351	6,354,629	6,394,644	6,448,737	6,496,300	6,546,914	6,612,552
Covered by Private or Public Insurance									
Number..	5,304,803	5,360,985	5,379,701	5,472,509	5,507,982	5,672,418	5,828,883	5,954,604	5,983,410
Percent..	85.7	85.6	85.4	86.1	86.1	88.0	89.7	91.0	90.5
Uninsured									
Number..	883,315	898,561	922,650	882,120	886,662	776,319	667,417	592,310	629,142
Percent..	14.3	14.4	14.6	13.9	13.9	12.0	10.3	9.0	9.5
Percent in the U.S. not covered.............................	15.1	15.5	15.1	14.8	14.5	11.7	9.4	8.6	8.7
Children Under 18 Years of Age[1]	1,487,977	1,493,097	1,487,779	1,490,249	1,489,574	1,489,620	1,490,949	1,500,902	1,600,422
Covered by Private or Public Insurance									
Number..	1,400,671	1,413,853	1,402,852	1,405,719	1,404,287	1,412,007	1,428,845	1,447,865	1,529,643
Percent..	94.1	94.7	94.3	94.3	94.3	94.8	95.8	96.5	95.6
Uninsured									
Number..	87,306	79,244	84,927	84,530	85,287	77,613	62,104	53,037	70,779
Percent..	5.9	5.3	5.7	5.7	5.7	5.2	4.2	3.5	4.4
Percent in the U.S. not covered.............................	8.6	8.0	7.5	7.2	7.1	6.0	4.8	4.5	5.0

[1] 2017 data is for individuals under 19 years of age.

Table TN-7. Employment Status by Demographic Group, 2018

(Numbers in thousands, percent.)

Characteristic	Civilian noninstitutional population	Civilian labor force		Employed		Unemployed	
		Number	Percent of population	Number	Percent of population	Number	Percent of population
Total...	5,339	3,248	60.8	3,133	58.7	114	3.5
Sex							
Male..	2,553	1,729	67.7	1,674	65.6	55	3.2
Female...	2,786	1,518	54.5	1,459	52.4	59	3.9
Race, Sex, and Hispanic Origin							
White..	4,218	2,544	60.3	2,464	58.4	81	3.2
Male..	2,045	1,389	67.9	1,351	66.1	38	2.8
Female...	2,173	1,155	53.1	1,113	51.2	42	3.6
Black or African American.........................	865	539	62.3	510	58.9	29	5.4
Male..	390	257	65.8	244	62.4	13	5.1
Female...	475	282	59.5	266	56.1	16	5.7
Hispanic or Latino ethnicity[1]...................	250	175	70.0	169	67.5	6	3.6
Male..	134	116	86.7	113	84.6	3	2.4
Female...	NA	NA	NA	NA	NA	NA	NA
Age							
16 to 19 years..	325	123	37.8	109	33.5	14	11.2
20 to 24 years..	465	341	73.2	314	67.5	27	7.8
25 to 34 years..	929	777	83.7	755	81.2	22	2.9
35 to 44 years..	780	608	78.0	591	75.8	17	2.8
45 to 54 years..	848	648	76.4	633	74.7	15	2.3
55 to 64 years..	896	548	61.1	533	59.5	15	2.6
65 years and over....................................	1,096	203	18.5	198	18.1	5	2.6

NOTE: Data in Table 7 are from the Current Population Survey (CPS) and do not match the estimates in Table 8. See notes and definitions for further information.
[1] May be of any race.

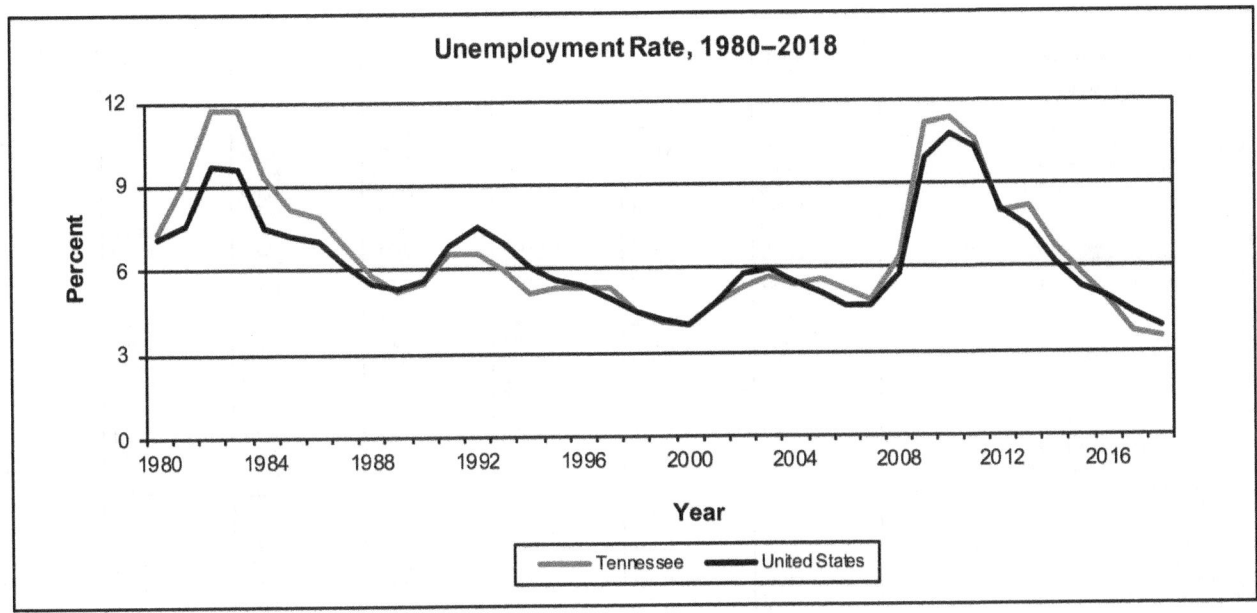

Table TN-8. Employment Status of the Civilian Noninstitutional Population Age 16 Years and Over

(Number, percent.)

Year	Civilian labor force	Civilian participation rate	Employed	Unemployed	Unemployment rate
2010..	3,090,795	62.8	2,792,063	298,732	9.7
2011..	3,125,307	62.9	2,844,662	280,645	9.0
2012..	3,100,671	61.8	2,857,945	242,726	7.8
2013..	3,067,431	60.6	2,828,479	238,952	7.8
2014..	3,022,927	59.2	2,824,016	198,911	6.6
2015..	3,062,706	59.4	2,890,640	172,066	5.6
2016..	3,134,725	60.1	2,987,074	147,651	4.7
2017..	3,198,767	60.6	3,080,210	118,557	3.7
2018..	3,244,921	60.9	3,131,660	113,261	3.5

Table TN-9. Employment and Average Wages by Industry

(Estimates are based on the 2012 *North American Industry Classification System* [NAICS].)

Industry	2011	2012	2013	2014	2015	2016	2017
	Number of jobs						
Wage and Salary Employment by Industry.........................	2,754,090	2,806,427	2,846,413	2,903,868	2,974,822	3,039,254	3,081,388
Farm Wage and Salary Employment...............................	9,323	9,902	9,138	9,927	11,141	9,177	10,626
Nonfarm Wage and Salary Employment..........................	2,744,767	2,796,525	2,837,275	2,893,941	2,963,681	3,030,077	3,070,762
Private wage and salary employment.............................	2,290,228	2,346,643	2,389,213	2,448,513	2,521,355	2,585,872	2,624,991
Forestry, fishing, and related activities..........................	4,584	4,720	4,865	5,030	5,112	4,999	4,971
Mining...	3,593	3,426	3,425	3,430	3,457	3,061	3,276
Utilities..	3,317	3,356	3,342	3,380	3,366	3,395	3,577
Construction..	107,382	107,699	106,545	109,155	115,688	117,844	123,092
Manufacturing..	304,232	313,900	318,901	325,377	332,659	343,890	348,777
Durable goods manufacturing................................	183,591	194,324	198,982	205,524	210,630	219,138	221,877
Nondurable goods manufacturing............................	120,641	119,576	119,919	119,853	122,029	124,752	126,900
Wholesale trade...	117,921	121,103	122,839	123,636	121,540	120,376	121,808
Retail trade...	312,224	315,337	317,119	322,890	327,928	335,900	337,984
Transportation and warehousing................................	134,493	140,470	143,839	147,365	155,367	162,474	163,404
Information...	43,244	42,797	43,474	43,349	43,622	44,961	45,507
Finance and insurance	107,224	108,395	106,827	109,194	111,288	113,290	116,054
Real estate and rental and leasing.............................	31,692	32,333	33,547	34,943	37,129	38,776	40,319
Professional, scientific, and technical services................	110,198	111,883	114,996	120,908	129,122	132,943	137,237
Management of companies and enterprises.....................	28,992	31,547	35,228	37,306	41,468	44,066	44,796
Administrative and waste services..............................	185,824	195,498	204,851	216,801	224,740	229,108	226,877
Educational services..	53,922	55,172	56,458	57,792	59,145	61,407	62,058
Health care and social assistance..............................	336,090	343,718	347,800	350,288	360,644	367,745	372,876
Arts, entertainment, and recreation.............................	30,149	30,671	31,634	33,449	34,795	36,235	38,471
Accommodation and food services..............................	238,636	248,009	255,997	265,117	274,868	285,354	292,753
Other services, except public administration...................	136,511	136,609	137,526	139,103	139,417	140,048	141,154
Government and government enterprises........................	454,539	449,882	448,062	445,428	442,326	444,205	445,771
	Dollars						
Average Wages and Salaries by Industry	41,883	43,412	43,575	44,706	46,191	46,929	48,322
Average Farm Wages and Salaries	15,891	21,052	23,255	22,681	16,509	23,000	18,027
Average Nonfarm Wages and Salaries	41,972	43,491	43,640	44,782	46,303	47,002	48,427
Average private wages and salaries.............................	42,366	44,058	44,117	45,222	46,852	47,538	48,935
Forestry, fishing, and related activities	23,838	24,657	24,946	25,861	26,648	28,616	29,113
Mining...	61,498	64,442	63,465	67,845	68,194	67,512	67,586
Utilities..	63,006	63,791	65,515	67,995	70,785	71,788	72,503
Construction	45,589	47,132	47,569	49,910	52,845	54,488	56,584
Manufacturing..	52,866	54,740	54,664	56,296	57,344	58,104	59,531
Durable goods manufacturing................................	51,750	54,279	53,199	55,124	56,268	57,331	58,767
Nondurable goods manufacturing............................	54,565	55,488	57,094	58,307	59,201	59,463	60,865
Wholesale trade...	59,673	62,076	61,563	64,271	67,297	70,120	70,828
Retail trade...	27,721	28,108	27,881	28,629	29,532	29,994	30,746
Transportation and warehousing................................	49,473	50,079	50,677	51,231	52,646	53,035	54,950
Information	57,060	59,034	58,955	61,755	62,689	64,380	68,480
Finance and insurance	68,069	72,412	72,250	74,945	75,997	77,912	79,722
Real estate and rental and leasing.............................	39,883	42,137	42,656	44,661	46,732	48,664	48,975
Professional, scientific, and technical services	66,061	70,914	70,548	72,042	75,858	75,701	75,515
Management of companies and enterprises.....................	83,136	99,458	98,318	97,031	100,547	98,574	101,866
Administrative and waste services..............................	31,169	32,672	33,172	32,317	33,088	33,827	35,421
Educational services..	34,282	35,333	35,986	36,349	36,903	37,476	38,365
Health care and social assistance..............................	45,551	46,394	46,673	47,796	49,708	49,865	51,450
Arts, entertainment, and recreation.............................	41,537	44,184	44,134	47,047	53,613	50,397	53,822
Accommodation and food services..............................	18,053	18,454	18,345	18,869	19,417	20,214	20,947
Other services, except public administration...................	28,813	30,284	30,633	32,008	33,331	34,266	35,619
Government and government enterprises.............................	39,986	40,536	41,097	42,358	43,173	43,882	45,437

Table TN-10. Employment Characteristics by Family Type

(Number, percent.)

Family type and labor force status	2015		2016		2017	
	Total	Families with own children under 18 years	Total	Families with own children under 18 years	Total	Families with own children under 18 years
All Families....................	1,675,678	675,024	1,670,605	668,357	1,707,488	675,153
FAMILY TYPE AND LABOR FORCE STATUS						
Married-Couple Families........................	1,213,001	438,614	1,223,193	437,507	1,255,384	440,939
Both husband and wife in labor force.............	48.6	65.9	47.6	64.4	48.7	66.4
Husband in labor force, wife not in labor force	22.8	27.3	22.7	28.8	21.8	27.1
Wife in labor force, husband not in labor force	8.5	4.5	8.3	4.3	8.7	4.1
Both husband and wife not in labor force..........	19.6	2.2	20.8	2.2	20.1	2.0
Other Families	462,677	236,410	447,412	230,850	452,104	234,214
Female householder, no husband present..........	74.2	75.9	74.4	76.0	73.4	74.3
In labor force.......................	49.6	61.5	49.3	61.2	48.6	60.0
Not in labor force.......................	24.5	14.4	25.0	14.8	24.8	14.3
Male householder, no wife present................	25.8	24.1	25.6	24.0	26.6	25.7
In labor force.......................	18.7	20.8	18.4	20.6	20.2	23.7
Not in labor force.......................	7.1	3.3	7.3	3.3	6.4	2.0

Table TN-11. School Enrollment and Educational Attainment, 2017

(Number, percent.)

Item	State	U.S.
Enrollment		
Total population 3 years and over, enrolled in school	1,573,379	81,273,337
Enrolled in nursery school or preschool (percent).......................................	5.3	6.0
Enrolled in kindergarten (percent)..	5.2	4.9
Enrolled in elementary school, grades 1-8 (percent).......................................	42.7	40.6
Enrolled in high school, grades 9-12 (percent).......................................	22.2	21.1
Enrolled in college or graduate school (percent)..................................	24.6	27.4
Attainment		
Total population 25 years and over	4,588,453	221,250,083
Less than ninth grade (percent)..	4.4	5.1
9th to 12th grade, no diploma (percent)....................................	7.8	6.9
High school graduate, including equivalency (percent).......................	32.4	27.1
Some college, no degree (percent)..................................	20.8	20.4
Associate's degree (percent)..	7.2	8.5
Bachelor's degree (percent)	17.2	19.7
Graduate or professional degree (percent)................................	10.1	12.3
High school graduate or higher (percent)..	87.8	88.0
Bachelor's degree or higher (percent)..	27.3	32.0

Table TN-12. Public School Characteristics and Educational Indicators

(Number, percent; data derived from National Center of Education Statistics.)

Item	State	U.S.
Public Elementary and Secondary Schools		
Number of operational school districts, 2016-17..	146	18,377
Number of operational schools, 2016-17..	1,774	98,330
Percent charter schools	5.9	7.1
Total public school enrollment, 2016-17..	1,001,562	50,587,859
Percent charter school enrollment	3.5	6.0
Student-teacher ratio, Fall 2015	15.1	16.0
Expenditures per student (dollars), 2015-16..	8,876	11,841
Four-year adjusted cohort graduation rate (ACGR)[1]	89.8	84.6
Students eligible for free or reduced-price lunch (percent), 2015-16........................	58.8	52.1
English language learners (percent), Fall 2016	4.3	9.6
Students age 3 to 21 served under IDEA, part B (percent), 2017-18	12.9	13.7
Public Schools by Type, 2016-17		Percent of state public schools
Total number of schools..	1,774	100.0
Special education..	16	0.9
Vocational education..	4	0.2
Alternative education..	18	1.0

[1] Adjusted Cohort Graduation Rates (ACGR) differ from Averaged Freshmen Graduation Rates (AFGR).

Table TN-13. Reported Voting and Registration of the Voting-Age Population, November 2018

(Numbers in thousands, percent.)

Item	Total population	Total citizen population	Registered			Voted		
			Total registered	Percent registered (total population)	Percent registered (total citizen population)	Total voted	Percent voted (total population)	Percent voted (total citizen population)
U.S. Total	249,748	228,832	153,066	61.3	66.9	122,281	49.0	53.4
State Total.......................................	5,202	5,016	3,183	61.2	63.5	2,487	47.8	49.6
Sex								
Male	2,501	2,386	1,476	59.0	61.9	1,174	46.9	49.2
Female	2,701	2,630	1,707	63.2	64.9	1,313	48.6	49.9
Race								
White alone	4,156	4,015	2,606	62.7	64.9	2,039	49.1	50.8
White, non-Hispanic alone	3,879	3,852	2,536	65.4	65.9	1,991	51.3	51.7
Black alone	830	801	484	58.3	60.4	368	44.3	45.9
Asian alone	109	97	32	29.4	33.0	29	26.8	30.2
Hispanic (of any race)...........................	282	167	69	24.5	41.3	48	17.0	28.7
White alone or in combination	4,244	4,099	2,660	62.7	64.9	2,087	49.2	50.9
Black alone or in combination	866	837	496	57.3	59.3	376	43.5	45.0
Asian alone or in combination..................	124	109	36	29.2	33.4	34	27.0	30.9
Age								
18 to 24 years....................................	601	593	265	44.1	44.7	184	30.7	31.1
25 to 34 years....................................	917	833	466	50.8	55.9	338	36.8	40.5
35 to 44 years....................................	832	784	533	64.1	68.1	388	46.6	49.5
45 to 64 years....................................	1,738	1,695	1,143	65.8	67.4	916	52.7	54.0
65 years and over	1,114	1,111	776	69.6	69.8	661	59.4	59.5

Table TN-14. Crime

(Number, rate per 100,000. Data are derived from the FBI Uniform Crime Reports.)

Item	State			U.S.		
	2016	2017	Percent change	2016	2017	Percent change
TOTAL POPULATION [1]	6,649,404	6,715,984	1.0	323,405,935	325,719,178	0.7
VIOLENT CRIME						
Number...	42,459	43,755	3.1	1,285,606	1,283,220	-0.2
Rate	638.5	651.5	2.0	397.5	394.0	-0.9
Murder and Nonnegligent Manslaughter						
Number...	495	527	6.5	17,413	17,284	-0.7
Rate	7.4	7.8	5.4	5.4	5.3	-1.4
Rape [2]						
Number...	2,803	2,934	4.7	132,414	135,755	2.5
Rate	42.2	43.7	3.6	40.9	41.7	1.8
Robbery						
Number...	7,829	7,862	0.4	332,797	319,356	-4.0
Rate	117.7	117.1	-0.6	102.9	98.0	-4.7
Aggravated Assault						
Number...	31,332	32,432	3.5	802,982	810,825	1.0
Rate	471.2	482.9	2.5	248.3	248.9	0.3
PROPERTY CRIME						
Number...	191,199	197,488	3.3	7,928,530	7,694,086	-3.0
Rate	2,875.4	2,940.6	2.3	2,451.6	2,362.2	-3.6
Burglary						
Number...	40,607	38,716	-4.7	1,516,405	1,401,840	-7.6
Rate	610.7	576.5	-5.6	468.9	430.4	-8.2
Larceny-Theft						
Number...	135,353	140,248	3.6	5,644,835	5,519,107	-2.2
Rate	2,035.6	2,088.3	2.6	1,745.4	1,694.4	-2.9
Motor Vehicle Theft						
Number...	15,239	18,524	21.6	767,290	773,139	0.8
Rate	229.2	275.8	20.4	237.3	237.4	-

NOTE: Although arson data are included in the trend and clearance tables, sufficient data are not available to estimate totals for this offense. Therefore, no arson data are published in this table.
- = Zero or rounds to zero.
[1] Population figures are U.S. Census Bureau provisional estimates as of July 1, 2017.
[2] The figures shown in the rape (revised definition) column were estimated using the revised Uniform Crime Reporting (UCR) definition of rape.

Table TN-15. State Government Finances, 2017

(Dollar amounts in thousands, percent distribution.)

Item	Dollars	Percent distribution
Total Revenue	35,414,548	100.0
General revenue	29,405,724	83.0
Intergovernmental revenue	11,161,689	31.5
Taxes	13,893,728	39.2
General sales	7,260,193	20.5
Selective sales	2,750,772	7.8
License taxes	1,635,495	4.6
Individual income tax	249,977	0.7
Corporate income tax	1,726,223	4.9
Other taxes	271,068	0.8
Current charges	2,292,033	6.5
Miscellaneous general revenue	2,058,274	5.8
Utility revenue	0	-
Liquor stores revenue	0	-
Insurance trust revenue[1]	6,008,824	17.0
Total Expenditure	33,218,749	100.0
Intergovernmental expenditure	7,882,887	23.7
Direct expenditure	25,335,862	76.3
Current operation	19,566,883	58.9
Capital outlay	1,530,839	4.6
Insurance benefits and repayments	2,654,456	8.0
Assistance and subsidies	1,327,944	4.0
Interest on debt	255,740	0.8
Exhibit: Salaries and wages	4,100,046	12.3
Total Expenditure	33,218,749	100.0
General expenditure	30,562,884	92.0
Intergovernmental expenditure	7,882,887	23.7
Direct expenditure	22,679,997	68.3
General expenditure, by function:		
Education	10,574,305	31.8
Public welfare	12,447,574	37.5
Hospitals	409,713	1.2
Health	738,464	2.2
Highways	1,641,757	4.9
Police protection	277,908	0.8
Correction	972,601	2.9
Natural resources	352,507	1.1
Parks and recreation	109,297	0.3
Governmental administration	966,453	2.9
Interest on general debt	255,740	0.8
Other and unallocable	1,816,565	5.5
Utility expenditure	1,409	-
Liquor stores expenditure	0	-
Insurance trust expenditure	2,654,456	8.0
Debt at End of Fiscal Year	6,127,422	X
Cash and Security Holdings	64,259,479	X

X = Not applicable.
- = Zero or rounds to zero.
[1] Within insurance trust revenue, net earnings of state retirement systems is a calculated statistic (the item code in the data file is X08), and thus can be positive or negative. Net earnings is the sum of earnings on investments plus gains on investments minus losses on investments. The change made in 2002 for asset valuation from book to market value in accordance with Statement 34 of the Governmental Accounting Standards Board is reflected in the calculated statistics.

Table TN-16. State Government Tax Collections, 2018

(Dollars in thousands, percent.)

Item	Dollars	Percent distribution
Total Taxes	14,269,061	100.0
Property taxes	X	-
Sales and gross receipts	10,343,084	72.5
General sales and gross receipts	7,469,547	52.3
Selective sales and gross receipts	2,873,537	20.1
Alcoholic beverages	201,713	1.4
Amusements	X	-
Insurance premiums	970,831	6.8
Motor fuels	1,086,693	7.6
Pari-mutuels	X	-
Public utilities	8,520	0.1
Tobacco products	248,673	1.7
Other selective sales	357,107	2.5
Licenses	1,763,747	12.4
Alcoholic beverages	1,862	-
Amusements	283	-
Corporations in general	920,053	6.4
Hunting and fishing	36,730	0.3
Motor vehicle	357,692	2.5
Motor vehicle operators	59,648	0.4
Public utilities	6,039	-
Occupation and business, NEC	372,981	2.6
Other licenses	8,459	0.1
Income taxes	1,890,667	13.3
Individual income	246,508	1.7
Corporation net income	1,644,159	11.5
Other taxes	271,563	1.9
Death and gift	0	-
Documentary and stock transfer	251,574	1.8
Severance	1,025	-
Taxes, NEC	18,964	0.1

X = Not applicable.
- = Zero or rounds to zero.

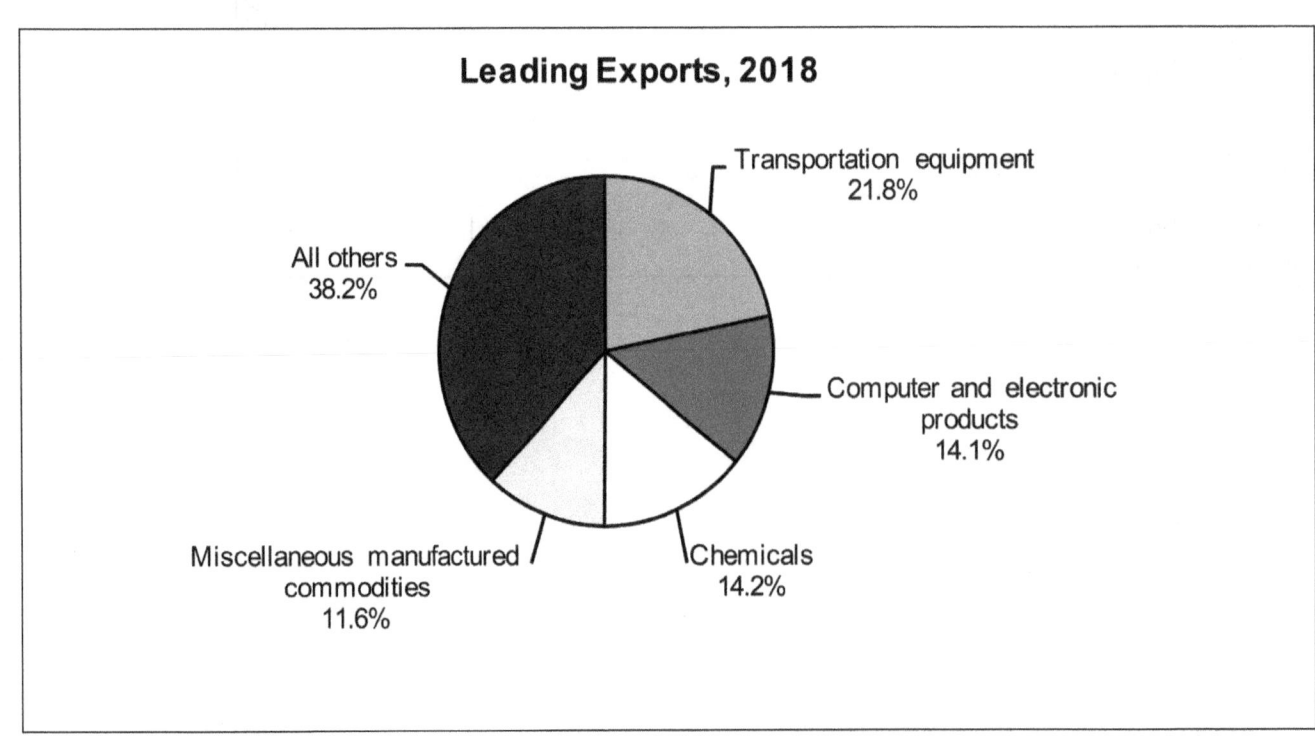

Leading Exports, 2018

Transportation equipment 21.8%

All others 38.2%

Computer and electronic products 14.1%

Chemicals 14.2%

Miscellaneous manufactured commodities 11.6%

Facts and Figures

Location: West South Central United States; bordered on the N by Oklahoma, on the E by Arkansas and Louisiana, on the S by Mexico and the Gulf of Mexico, and on the W by Mexico and New Mexico

Area: 268,581 sq. mi. (695,621 sq. km.); rank—2nd

Population: 28,701,845 (2018 est.); rank—2nd

Principal Cities: capital—Austin; largest—Houston

Statehood: December 29, 1845; 28th state

U.S. Congress: 2 senators, 36 representatives

State Motto: Friendship

State Song: "Texas, Our Texas"

State Nickname: The Lone Star State

Abbreviations: TX; Tex.

State Symbols: flower—bluebonnet; tree—pecan; bird—mockingbird

At a Glance

- With an increase in population of 14.1 percent, Texas ranked 3rd among the states in growth from 2010 to 2018.

- In 2018, Texas ranked 2nd for the highest percent of its population under 18 years old (25.8 percent).

- Texas's median household income in 2017 was $59,206, and 14.7 percent of the population lived below the poverty level.

- In 2017, 17.3 percent of Texans did not have health insurance, making it the state with the highest percent of uninsured residents.

- Texas ranked 17th among states for its violent crime rate and 22nd for its property crime rate in 2017, which were 438.9 and 2,562.6 per 100,000 population respectively.

Table TX-1. Population by Age, Sex, Race, and Hispanic Origin

(Number, percent, except where noted.)

Sex, age, race, and Hispanic origin	2000	2010	2018 [1]	Percent change, 2010–2018
Total Population..	20,851,820	25,145,561	28,701,845	14.1
Percent of total U.S. population	7.4	8.1	8.8	X
Sex				
Male..	10,352,910	12,472,280	14,260,106	14.3
Female	10,498,910	12,673,281	14,441,739	14.0
Age				
Under 5 years...	1,625,628	1,928,473	2,024,126	5.0
5 to 19 years...	4,291,608	5,693,241	6,171,509	8.4
20 to 64 years..	12,233,052	14,921,961	16,903,890	13.3
65 years and over	2,072,532	2,601,886	3,602,320	38.5
Median age (years)	32.3	33.6	34.8	3.6
Race and Hispanic Origin				
One race				
White	14,799,505	20,389,793	22,624,867	11.0
Black	2,404,566	3,070,440	3,673,855	19.7
American Indian and Alaska Native	118,362	251,209	290,961	15.8
Asian	562,319	1,000,473	1,486,266	48.6
Native Hawaiian or Other Pacific Islander	14,434	31,242	42,333	35.5
Two or more races	514,633	402,404	583,563	45.0
Hispanic (of any race)..	6,699,666	9,578,505	11,368,849	18.7

X = Not applicable.

[1] Population figures for 2018 are July 1 estimates. The 2010 estimates are taken from the 2010 Census.

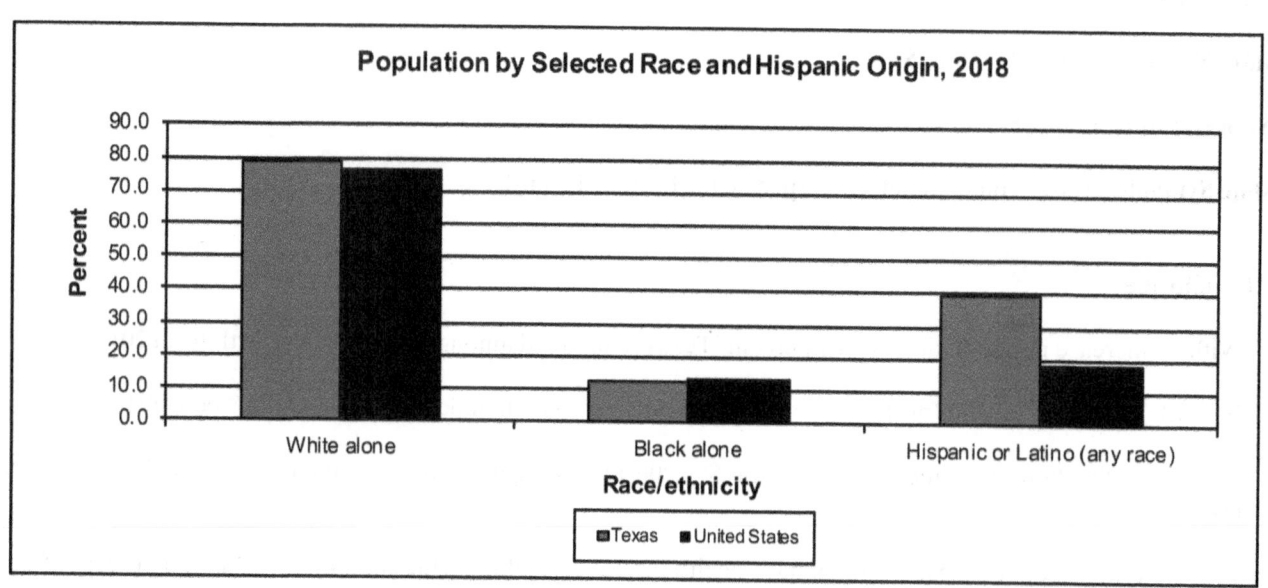

Population by Selected Race and Hispanic Origin, 2018

Table TX-2. Marital Status

(Number, percent distribution.)

Sex, age, race, and Hispanic origin	2000	2010	2017
Males, 15 Years and Over	7,820,248	9,587,343	10,923,789
Never married	28.6	34.6	36.2
Now married, except separated...	58.8	51.6	50.4
Separated..	2.0	2.3	1.9
Widowed..	2.1	2.2	2.3
Divorced...	8.5	9.4	9.3
Females, 15 Years and Over	8,117,395	9,903,147	11,240,818
Never married	22.6	27.6	30.0
Now married, except separated...	54.3	48.5	47.6
Separated..	2.9	3.3	2.9
Widowed..	9.1	8.1	7.6
Divorced...	11.0	12.5	12.0

Table TX-3. Households and Housing Characteristics

(Number, percent, dollars.)

Item	2000	2010	2017	Average annual percent change, 2010–2017
Total Households...	7,393,354	8,738,664	9,623,874	1.4
Family households	5,247,794	6,091,590	6,696,061	1.4
Married-couple family...	3,989,741	4,386,996	4,879,009	1.6
Other family..	1,258,053	1,704,594	1,817,052	0.9
Male householder, no wife present.......................	320,464	436,727	494,678	1.9
Female householder, no husband present	937,489	1,267,867	1,322,374	0.6
Nonfamily households	2,145,560	2,647,074	2,927,813	1.5
Householder living alone...	1,752,141	2,166,469	2,401,909	1.6
Householder not living alone...................................	393,419	480,605	525,904	1.3
Housing Characteristics				
Total housing units..	8,157,575	9,996,209	10,933,375	1.3
Occupied housing units	7,393,354	8,738,664	9,623,874	1.4
Owner occupied	4,716,959	5,555,903	5,964,183	1.0
Renter occupied	2,676,395	3,182,761	3,659,691	2.1
Average household size..	2.74	2.82	2.88	0.3
Financial Characteristics				
Median gross rent of renter-occupied housing	574	801	987	3.3
Median monthly owner costs for housing units with a mortgage	986	1,402	1,513	1.1
Median value of owner-occupied housing units	82,500	128,100	172,200	4.9

Table TX-4. Migration, Origin, and Language

(Number, percent.)

Characteristic	State			U.S.		
	2016	2017	Percent change	2016	2017	Percent change
Residence 1 Year Ago						
Population 1 year and over	27,472,626	27,924,632	1.6	319,361,956	321,994,428	0.8
Same house	84.1	84.3	X	85.4	85.7	X
Different house in the U.S.	15.0	14.9	X	13.9	13.6	X
Same county..	9.2	9.1	X	8.3	8.1	X
Different county	5.8	5.8	X	5.6	5.6	X
Same state	3.9	3.9	X	3.2	3.3	X
Different state	1.9	1.9	X	2.4	2.3	X
Abroad	0.9	0.8	X	0.7	0.7	X
Place of Birth						
Native born	23,132,676	23,450,456	1.4	279,388,170	281,193,323	0.6
Male	49.5	49.6	X	49.3	49.4	X
Female	50.5	50.4	X	50.7	50.6	X
Foreign born	4,729,920	4,854,140	2.6	43,739,345	44,525,855	1.8
Male	50.3	49.9	X	48.5	48.4	X
Female	49.7	50.1	X	51.5	51.6	X
Foreign born; naturalized U.S. citizen............	1,748,614	1,812,428	3.6	21,238,372	21,948,732	3.3
Male	48.1	47.6	X	45.9	45.9	X
Female	51.9	52.4	X	54.1	54.1	X
Foreign born; not a U.S. citizen	2,981,306	3,041,712	2.0	22,500,973	22,577,123	0.3
Male	51.5	51.2	X	51.0	50.8	X
Female	48.5	48.8	X	49.0	49.2	X
Entered 2010 or later	19.4	22.9	X	18.6	21.3	X
Entered 2000 to 2009	28.3	26.9	X	26.7	25.7	X
Entered before 2000....................................	52.3	50.2	X	54.7	53.0	X
World Region of Birth, Foreign						
Foreign-born population, excluding population born at sea	4,729,920	4,854,140	2.6	43,738,901	44,525,458	1.8
Europe	4.1	4.1	X	10.9	10.8	X
Asia	21.1	22.0	X	30.8	31.2	X
Africa	5.0	5.2	X	4.9	5.1	X
Oceania	0.3	0.3	X	0.6	0.6	X
Latin America	68.6	67.5	X	51.0	50.4	X
North America	0.9	1.0	X	1.8	1.8	X
Language Spoken at Home and Ability to Speak English						
Population 5 years and over	25,855,685	26,284,432	1.7	303,328,961	305,924,019	0.9
English only...	64.4	64.4	X	78.4	78.2	X
Language other than English.........................	35.6	35.6	X	21.6	21.8	X
Speaks English less than "very well"	14.0	13.8	X	8.6	8.5	X

NA = Not available.
X = Not applicable.
- = Zero or rounds to zero.

Table TX-5. Median Income and Poverty Status, 2017

(Number, percent, except as noted.)

Characteristic	State		U.S.	
	Number	Percent	Number	Percent
Median Income				
Households (dollars)	59,206	X	60,336	X
Families (dollars)	70,136	X	73,891	X
Below Poverty Level (All People)	4,076,905	14.7	42,583,651	13.4
Sex				
Male	1,821,917	13.3	19,004,547	12.2
Female	2,254,988	16.1	23,579,104	14.5
Age				
Under 18 years	1,524,712	20.9	13,353,202	18.4
Related children under 18 years	1,501,179	20.7	13,053,472	18.1
18 to 64 years	2,188,328	12.9	24,648,677	12.6
65 years and over	363,865	10.8	4,581,772	9.3

X = Not applicable.

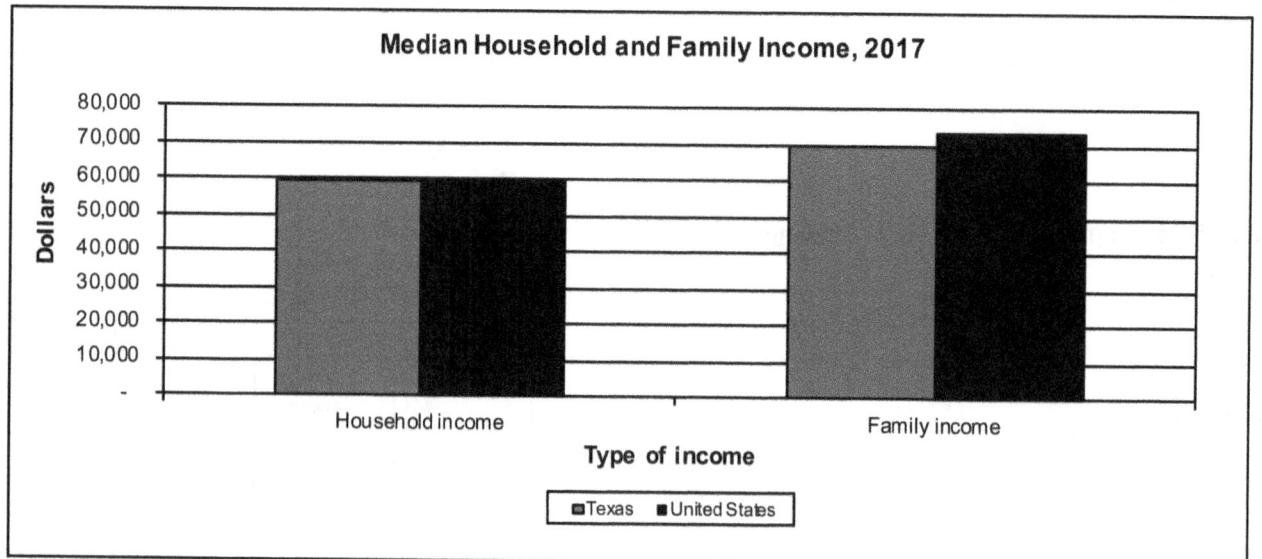

Median Household and Family Income, 2017

Table TX-6. Health Insurance Coverage Status for the Civilian Noninstitutionalized Population and Children Under 18 Years of Age

(Number, percent.)

Item	2009	2010	2011	2012	2013	2014	2015	2016	2017
Civilian Noninstitutionalized Population	24,291,561	24,779,450	25,197,453	25,584,499	25,976,562	26,485,838	26,990,435	27,386,023	27,836,924
Covered by Private or Public Insurance									
Number	18,508,305	18,903,976	19,407,607	19,822,141	20,228,395	21,438,361	22,375,210	22,840,643	23,019,956
Percent	76.2	76.3	77.0	77.5	77.9	80.9	82.9	83.4	82.7
Uninsured									
Number	5,783,256	5,875,474	5,789,846	5,762,358	5,748,167	5,047,477	4,615,225	4,545,380	4,816,968
Percent	23.8	23.7	23.0	22.5	22.1	19.1	17.1	16.6	17.3
Percent in the U.S. not covered	15.1	15.5	15.1	14.8	14.5	11.7	9.4	8.6	8.7
Children Under 18 Years of Age[1]	6,877,730	6,876,022	6,946,969	6,971,878	7,028,782	7,106,727	7,197,853	7,282,033	7,781,845
Covered by Private or Public Insurance									
Number	5,758,045	5,879,529	6,030,447	6,108,588	6,140,477	6,322,789	6,515,730	6,611,211	6,947,175
Percent	83.7	85.5	86.8	87.6	87.4	89.0	90.5	90.8	89.3
Uninsured									
Number	1,119,685	996,493	916,522	863,290	888,305	783,938	682,123	670,822	834,670
Percent	16.3	14.5	13.2	12.4	12.6	11.0	9.5	9.2	10.7
Percent in the U.S. not covered	8.6	8.0	7.5	7.2	7.1	6.0	4.8	4.5	5.0

[1] 2017 data is for individuals under 19 years of age.

Table TX-7. Employment Status by Demographic Group, 2018

(Numbers in thousands, percent.)

Characteristic	Civilian noninstitutional population	Civilian labor force		Employed		Unemployed	
		Number	Percent of population	Number	Percent of population	Number	Percent of population
Total...	21,617	13,876	64.2	13,342	61.7	534	3.8
Sex							
Male	10,525	7,639	72.6	7,358	69.9	282	3.7
Female	11,092	6,237	56.2	5,985	54.0	253	4.1
Race, Sex, and Hispanic Origin							
White	17,023	10,839	63.7	10,450	61.4	389	3.6
Male	8,342	6,103	73.2	5,897	70.7	205	3.4
Female	8,681	4,737	54.6	4,553	52.4	184	3.9
Black or African American...................	2,700	1,807	66.9	1,705	63.1	103	5.7
Male	1,245	852	68.4	796	63.9	56	6.6
Female	1,454	955	65.7	909	62.5	47	4.9
Hispanic or Latino ethnicity[1]	7,896	5,132	65.0	4,908	62.2	224	4.4
Male	3,952	3,012	76.2	2,888	73.1	124	4.1
Female	3,943	2,120	53.8	2,021	51.2	100	4.7
Age							
16 to 19 years..................................	1,568	504	32.1	440	28.1	64	12.6
20 to 24 years..................................	2,024	1,426	70.4	1,330	65.7	96	6.7
25 to 34 years..................................	4,083	3,285	80.5	3,168	77.6	118	3.6
35 to 44 years..................................	3,711	3,055	82.3	2,960	79.8	95	3.1
45 to 54 years..................................	3,440	2,775	80.7	2,701	78.5	75	2.7
55 to 64 years..................................	3,151	2,071	65.7	2,005	63.6	66	3.2
65 years and over	3,639	760	20.9	739	20.3	21	2.8

NOTE: Data in Table 7 are from the Current Population Survey (CPS) and do not match the estimates in Table 8. See notes and definitions for further information.
[1] May be of any race.

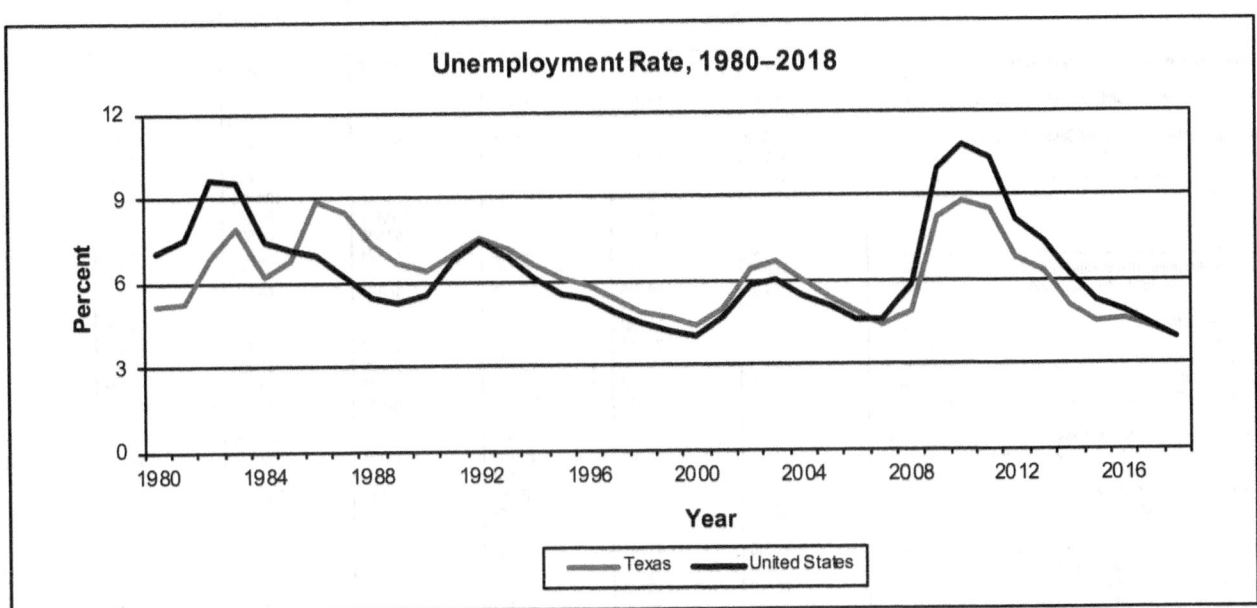

Table TX-8. Employment Status of the Civilian Noninstitutional Population Age 16 Years and Over

(Number, percent.)

Year	Civilian labor force	Civilian participation rate	Employed	Unemployed	Unemployment rate
2010..	12,241,970	65.9	11,244,632	997,338	8.1
2011..	12,504,498	65.9	11,535,095	969,403	7.8
2012..	12,670,455	65.6	11,818,675	851,780	6.7
2013..	12,857,595	65.3	12,052,646	804,949	6.3
2014..	13,024,701	64.9	12,360,368	664,333	5.1
2015..	13,074,570	63.8	12,493,197	581,373	4.4
2016..	13,317,176	63.7	12,702,122	615,054	4.6
2017..	13,538,385	63.7	12,960,595	577,790	4.3
2018..	13,848,080	64.0	13,314,203	533,877	3.9

Table TX-9. Employment and Average Wages by Industry

(Estimates are based on the 2012 *North American Industry Classification System* [NAICS].)

Industry	2011	2012	2013	2014	2015	2016	2017
	Number of jobs						
Wage and Salary Employment by Industry......................	11,026,067	11,358,574	11,664,195	12,019,579	12,306,014	12,448,418	12,644,682
Farm Wage and Salary Employment................................	41,977	43,719	47,444	47,110	49,030	50,698	47,860
Nonfarm Wage and Salary Employment...........................	10,984,090	11,314,855	11,616,751	11,972,469	12,256,984	12,397,720	12,596,822
Private wage and salary employment..................................	8,993,107	9,344,849	9,641,641	9,987,530	10,245,568	10,357,353	10,538,306
Forestry, fishing, and related activities.............................	31,410	32,040	32,238	32,901	33,700	33,794	33,672
Mining..	234,254	268,671	288,452	307,690	271,697	218,710	219,594
Utilities..	49,010	48,693	48,981	49,026	49,508	49,806	50,333
Construction..	579,968	601,482	630,241	668,106	701,741	718,755	728,768
Manufacturing..	837,441	864,113	875,085	888,655	879,061	846,192	853,261
Durable goods manufacturing..	543,685	569,020	578,574	590,171	577,587	541,233	542,591
Nondurable goods manufacturing......................................	293,756	295,093	296,511	298,484	301,474	304,959	310,670
Wholesale trade..	517,194	542,711	564,503	576,387	590,924	583,155	590,939
Retail trade..	1,169,749	1,197,059	1,226,715	1,261,716	1,305,301	1,330,491	1,334,880
Transportation and warehousing.......................................	388,404	405,397	416,151	436,143	458,604	470,286	491,252
Information...	195,842	197,235	201,252	203,226	201,364	202,421	202,359
Finance and insurance	476,119	492,734	507,022	517,251	534,354	545,239	561,632
Real estate and rental and leasing...................................	178,238	183,681	192,042	199,652	205,198	208,164	217,434
Professional, scientific, and technical services..............	591,959	627,258	652,772	683,593	714,562	732,190	749,697
Management of companies and enterprises......................	83,406	89,931	93,917	111,922	116,858	119,357	128,420
Administrative and waste services....................................	674,593	707,309	727,401	760,783	775,344	786,004	800,972
Educational services..	158,961	162,975	166,288	170,156	176,442	185,294	188,601
Health care and social assistance....................................	1,224,855	1,262,746	1,294,699	1,324,471	1,377,347	1,426,207	1,457,934
Arts, entertainment, and recreation.................................	111,300	112,981	118,518	128,047	131,235	137,691	142,018
Accommodation and food services...................................	937,629	981,179	1,027,754	1,069,189	1,117,193	1,159,908	1,185,162
Other services, except public administration...................	552,775	566,654	577,610	598,616	605,135	603,689	601,378
Government and government enterprises............................	1,990,983	1,970,006	1,975,110	1,984,939	2,011,416	2,040,367	2,058,516
	Dollars						
Average Wages and Salaries by Industry	48,299	50,090	50,668	52,666	53,751	53,847	55,374
Average Farm Wages and Salaries	31,574	31,452	25,688	30,935	33,207	27,607	30,452
Average Nonfarm Wages and Salaries	48,363	50,162	50,770	52,751	53,833	53,955	55,468
Average private wages and salaries..................................	49,086	51,136	51,706	53,784	54,792	54,750	56,314
Forestry, fishing, and related activities.............................	25,144	26,025	26,238	27,553	28,642	30,331	31,860
Mining..	121,994	120,595	119,583	126,238	128,051	131,123	127,017
Utilities..	90,248	98,758	97,638	100,433	104,041	105,098	111,521
Construction..	50,929	54,211	55,705	58,586	60,509	61,677	63,176
Manufacturing..	65,902	68,258	68,520	71,104	72,813	73,125	75,746
Durable goods manufacturing..	68,324	70,130	70,288	73,097	74,119	75,480	78,583
Nondurable goods manufacturing......................................	61,419	64,648	65,069	67,163	70,312	68,945	70,791
Wholesale trade..	71,421	74,580	74,138	75,833	77,269	78,022	79,901
Retail trade..	27,893	28,852	29,083	29,987	30,702	30,891	31,608
Transportation and warehousing.......................................	55,381	58,780	58,338	59,899	61,336	59,605	61,249
Information...	70,675	73,392	75,296	76,634	79,628	81,189	84,286
Finance and insurance	71,444	74,514	75,762	79,588	82,456	83,654	87,273
Real estate and rental and leasing...................................	49,455	52,881	53,967	57,272	58,248	58,868	61,355
Professional, scientific, and technical services..............	79,565	81,908	83,822	86,534	88,389	89,313	91,117
Management of companies and enterprises......................	106,973	114,417	113,568	123,337	123,876	123,032	131,917
Administrative and waste services....................................	36,957	38,350	38,962	40,649	41,809	42,169	43,380
Educational services..	36,899	37,510	38,766	39,125	39,983	40,761	41,227
Health care and social assistance....................................	41,710	42,348	42,568	43,925	45,415	45,964	46,991
Arts, entertainment, and recreation.................................	32,455	33,894	32,988	33,555	35,508	36,479	37,484
Accommodation and food services...................................	18,879	19,571	19,896	20,546	21,055	21,497	22,115
Other services, except public administration...................	28,858	30,130	31,108	32,316	33,461	34,291	35,718
Government and government enterprises............................	45,097	45,541	46,196	47,553	48,947	49,918	51,138

Table TX-10. Employment Characteristics by Family Type

(Number, percent.)

Family type and labor force status	2015 Total	2015 Families with own children under 18 years	2016 Total	2016 Families with own children under 18 years	2017 Total	2017 Families with own children under 18 years
All Families..	6,520,909	3,076,309	6,602,215	3,112,730	6,696,061	3,120,193
FAMILY TYPE AND LABOR FORCE STATUS						
Married-Couple Families..............................	4,709,478	2,092,503	4,757,297	2,118,877	4,879,009	2,158,191
Both husband and wife in labor force........................	49.3	58.6	49.9	60.0	49.4	59.5
Husband in labor force, wife not in labor force	28.5	36.0	28.0	35.0	27.9	35.2
Wife in labor force, husband not in labor force	6.9	3.5	6.6	3.2	6.9	3.4
Both husband and wife not in labor force.....................	14.7	1.5	14.8	1.5	15.0	1.5
Other Families	1,811,431	983,806	1,844,918	993,853	1,817,052	962,002
Female householder, no husband present......................	73.0	76.6	73.0	76.9	72.8	76.9
In labor force...	52.9	63.4	52.8	64.1	53.0	64.5
Not in labor force	20.1	13.2	20.2	12.8	19.7	12.4
Male householder, no wife present...........................	27.0	23.4	27.0	23.1	27.2	23.1
In labor force...	22.2	21.7	22.1	21.5	21.8	21.1
Not in labor force	4.8	1.8	4.9	1.6	5.4	2.0

Table TX-11. School Enrollment and Educational Attainment, 2017

(Number, percent.)

Item	State	U.S.
Enrollment		
Total population 3 years and over, enrolled in school	7,679,163	81,273,337
Enrolled in nursery school or preschool (percent)	5.9	6.0
Enrolled in kindergarten (percent)...	5.1	4.9
Enrolled in elementary school, grades 1-8 (percent)...	43.3	40.6
Enrolled in high school, grades 9-12 (percent)...	21.6	21.1
Enrolled in college or graduate school (percent)...	24.1	27.4
Attainment		
Total population 25 years and over	18,149,346	221,250,083
Less than ninth grade (percent)	8.1	5.1
9th to 12th grade, no diploma (percent)	8.2	6.9
High school graduate, including equivalency (percent)...	25.1	27.1
Some college, no degree (percent)	21.7	20.4
Associate's degree (percent)...	7.3	8.5
Bachelor's degree (percent)...	19.3	19.7
Graduate or professional degree (percent)...	10.3	12.3
High school graduate or higher (percent)	83.6	88.0
Bachelor's degree or higher (percent)...	29.6	32.0

Table TX-12. Public School Characteristics and Educational Indicators

(Number, percent; data derived from National Center of Education Statistics.)

Item	State	U.S.
Public Elementary and Secondary Schools		
Number of operational school districts, 2016-17	1,228	18,377
Number of operational schools, 2016-17...	8,912	98,330
Percent charter schools	8.4	7.1
Total public school enrollment, 2016-17...	5,360,849	50,587,859
Percent charter school enrollment	5.8	6.0
Student-teacher ratio, Fall 2015	15.3	16.0
Expenditures per student (dollars), 2015-16...	9,352	11,841
Four-year adjusted cohort graduation rate (ACGR)[1]	89.7	84.6
Students eligible for free or reduced-price lunch (percent), 2015-16...	58.9	52.1
English language learners (percent), Fall 2016	17.2	9.6
Students age 3 to 21 served under IDEA, part B (percent), 2017-18	9.2	13.7

Public Schools by Type, 2016-17		Percent of state public schools
Total number of schools...	8,909	100.0
Special education	11	0.1
Vocational education	0	-
Alternative education...	932	10.5

[1] Adjusted Cohort Graduation Rates (ACGR) differ from Averaged Freshmen Graduation Rates (AFGR).
- = Zero or rounds to zero.

Table TX-13. Reported Voting and Registration of the Voting-Age Population, November 2018

(Numbers in thousands, percent.)

Item	Total population	Total citizen population	Registered			Voted		
			Total registered	Percent registered (total population)	Percent registered (total citizen population)	Total voted	Percent voted (total population)	Percent voted (total citizen population)
U.S. Total	249,748	228,832	153,066	61.3	66.9	122,281	49.0	53.4
State Total............................	21,064	18,374	11,634	55.2	63.3	8,886	42.2	48.4
Sex								
Male	10,274	8,812	5,361	52.2	60.8	4,064	39.6	46.1
Female	10,790	9,562	6,273	58.1	65.6	4,822	44.7	50.4
Race								
White alone............................	16,689	14,555	9,331	55.9	64.1	7,158	42.9	49.2
White, non-Hispanic alone............	9,492	9,345	6,686	70.4	71.5	5,394	56.8	57.7
Black alone.............................	2,625	2,490	1,580	60.2	63.4	1,203	45.8	48.3
Asian alone.............................	1,097	736	397	36.2	54.0	288	26.3	39.1
Hispanic (of any race)...............	7,658	5,594	2,843	37.1	50.8	1,918	25.0	34.3
White alone or in combination........	16,991	14,838	9,496	55.9	64.0	7,276	42.8	49.0
Black alone or in combination........	2,722	2,583	1,629	59.8	63.1	1,231	45.2	47.6
Asian alone or in combination........	1,192	831	471	39.5	56.7	354	29.7	42.6
Age								
18 to 24 years........................	2,875	2,664	1,217	42.3	45.7	718	25.0	27.0
25 to 34 years........................	4,189	3,527	1,835	43.8	52.0	1,297	31.0	36.8
35 to 44 years........................	3,690	3,053	1,895	51.3	62.1	1,388	37.6	45.5
45 to 64 years........................	6,564	5,681	4,061	61.9	71.5	3,223	49.1	56.7
65 years and over.....................	3,746	3,448	2,627	70.1	76.2	2,259	60.3	65.5

Table TX-14. Crime

(Number, rate per 100,000. Data are derived from the FBI Uniform Crime Reports.)

Item	State			U.S.		
	2016	2017	Percent change	2016	2017	Percent change
TOTAL POPULATION[1]	27,904,862	28,304,596	1.4	323,405,935	325,719,178	0.7
VIOLENT CRIME						
Number..	121,064	124,238	2.6	1,285,606	1,283,220	-0.2
Rate	433.8	438.9	1.2	397.5	394.0	-0.9
Murder and Nonnegligent Manslaughter						
Number..	1,478	1,412	-4.5	17,413	17,284	-0.7
Rate	5.3	5.0	-5.8	5.4	5.3	-1.4
Rape[2]						
Number..	13,446	14,470	7.6	132,414	135,755	2.5
Rate	48.2	51.1	6.1	40.9	41.7	1.8
Robbery						
Number..	33,298	32,267	-3.1	332,797	319,356	-4.0
Rate	119.3	114.0	-4.5	102.9	98.0	-4.7
Aggravated Assault						
Number..	72,842	76,089	4.5	802,982	810,825	1.0
Rate	261.0	268.8	3.0	248.3	248.9	0.3
PROPERTY CRIME						
Number..	769,892	725,328	-5.8	7,928,530	7,694,086	-3.0
Rate	2,759.0	2,562.6	-7.1	2,451.6	2,362.2	-3.6
Burglary						
Number..	148,796	134,066	-9.9	1,516,405	1,401,840	-7.6
Rate	533.2	473.7	-11.2	468.9	430.4	-8.2
Larceny-Theft						
Number..	552,106	523,221	-5.2	5,644,835	5,519,107	-2.2
Rate	1,978.5	1,848.5	-6.6	1,745.4	1,694.4	-2.9
Motor Vehicle Theft						
Number..	68,990	68,041	-1.4	767,290	773,139	0.8
Rate	247.2	240.4	-2.8	237.3	237.4	-

NOTE: Although arson data are included in the trend and clearance tables, sufficient data are not available to estimate totals for this offense. Therefore, no arson data are published in this table.
- = Zero or rounds to zero.
[1] Population figures are U.S. Census Bureau provisional estimates as of July 1, 2017.
[2] The figures shown in the rape (revised definition) column were estimated using the revised Uniform Crime Reporting (UCR) definition of rape.

Table TX-15. State Government Finances, 2017

(Dollar amounts in thousands, percent distribution.)

Item	Dollars	Percent distribution
Total Revenue	163,975,910	100.0
General revenue	128,756,803	78.5
Intergovernmental revenue	44,657,763	27.2
Taxes	53,612,926	32.7
General sales	32,490,144	19.8
Selective sales	14,407,208	8.8
License taxes	3,432,901	2.1
Individual income tax	0	-
Corporate income tax	0	-
Other taxes	3,282,673	2.0
Current charges	15,915,730	9.7
Miscellaneous general revenue	14,570,384	8.9
Utility revenue	0	-
Liquor stores revenue	0	-
Insurance trust revenue[1]	35,219,107	21.5
Total Expenditure	147,926,154	100.0
Intergovernmental expenditure	30,619,865	20.7
Direct expenditure	117,306,289	79.3
Current operation	83,891,069	56.7
Capital outlay	11,054,783	7.5
Insurance benefits and repayments	18,228,620	12.3
Assistance and subsidies	2,826,829	1.9
Interest on debt	1,304,988	0.9
Exhibit: Salaries and wages	18,986,791	12.8
Total Expenditure	147,926,154	100.0
General expenditure	129,693,879	87.7
Intergovernmental expenditure	30,619,865	20.7
Direct expenditure	99,074,014	67.0
General expenditure, by function:		
Education	55,466,634	37.5
Public welfare	38,496,187	26.0
Hospitals	7,134,155	4.8
Health	2,943,615	2.0
Highways	10,039,223	6.8
Police protection	1,183,713	0.8
Correction	4,219,031	2.9
Natural resources	836,608	0.6
Parks and recreation	256,743	0.2
Governmental administration	2,367,314	1.6
Interest on general debt	1,304,988	0.9
Other and unallocable	5,445,668	3.7
Utility expenditure	3,655	-
Liquor stores expenditure	0	-
Insurance trust expenditure	18,228,620	12.3
Debt at End of Fiscal Year	50,963,262	X
Cash and Security Holdings	338,343,392	X

X = Not applicable.
- = Zero or rounds to zero.
[1] Within insurance trust revenue, net earnings of state retirement systems is a calculated statistic (the item code in the data file is X08), and thus can be positive or negative. Net earnings is the sum of earnings on investments plus gains on investments minus losses on investments. The change made in 2002 for asset valuation from book to market value in accordance with Statement 34 of the Governmental Accounting Standards Board is reflected in the calculated statistics.

Table TX-16. State Government Tax Collections, 2018

(Dollars in thousands, percent.)

Item	Dollars	Percent distribution
Total Taxes	60,328,843	100.0
Property taxes	X	-
Sales and gross receipts	51,462,209	85.3
General sales and gross receipts	36,129,876	59.9
Selective sales and gross receipts	15,332,333	25.4
Alcoholic beverages	1,321,516	2.2
Amusements	30,023	-
Insurance premiums	2,445,005	4.1
Motor fuels	3,710,307	6.2
Pari-mutuels	6,510	-
Public utilities	630,057	1.0
Tobacco products	1,440,336	2.4
Other selective sales	5,748,579	9.5
Licenses	3,635,024	6.0
Alcoholic beverages	78,742	0.1
Amusements	16,387	-
Corporations in general	152,899	0.3
Hunting and fishing	110,770	0.2
Motor vehicle	2,358,248	3.9
Motor vehicle operators	141,892	0.2
Public utilities	22,456	-
Occupation and business, NEC	609,900	1.0
Other licenses	143,730	0.2
Income taxes	X	-
Individual income	X	-
Corporation net income	X	-
Other taxes	5,231,610	8.7
Death and gift	X	-
Documentary and stock transfer	X	-
Severance	5,231,610	8.7
Taxes, NEC	0	-

X = Not applicable.
- = Zero or rounds to zero.

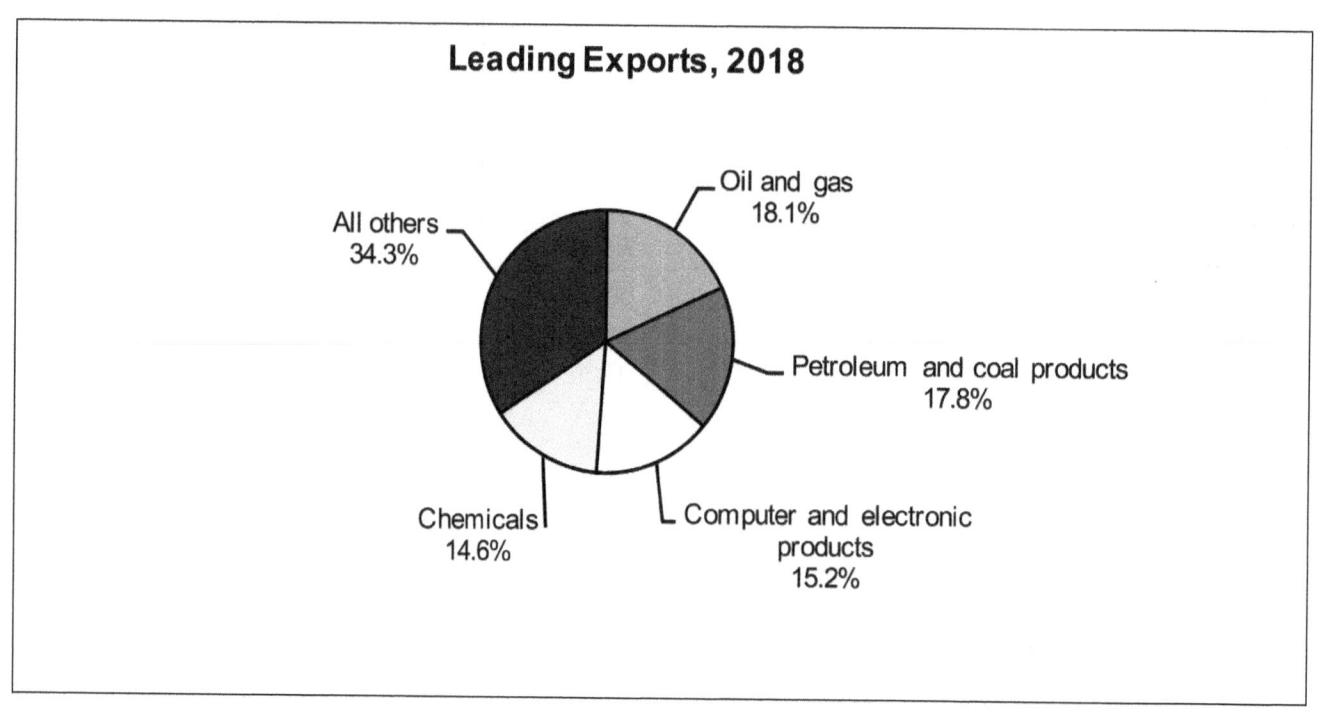

Leading Exports, 2018

Oil and gas 18.1%

Petroleum and coal products 17.8%

Computer and electronic products 15.2%

Chemicals 14.6%

All others 34.3%

Facts and Figures

Location: Western United States; bordered on the N by Idaho and Wyoming, on the E by Colorado, on the S by Arizona, and on the W by Nevada; Utah is one of the Four Corner states—at its SE corner it touches Arizona, Colorado, and New Mexico

Area: 84,899 sq. mi. (219,887 sq. km.); rank—13th

Population: 3,161,105 (2018 est.); rank—30th

Principal Cities: capital—Salt Lake City; largest—Salt Lake City

Statehood: January 4, 1896; 45th state

U.S. Congress: 2 senators, 4 representatives

State Motto: Industry

State Song: "Utah, We Love Thee"

State Nickname: The Beehive State

Abbreviations: UT

State Symbols: flower—sego lily; tree—blue spruce; bird—California seagull

At a Glance

- With an increase in population of 14.4 percent, Utah ranked 2nd among the states in growth from 2010 to 2018.

- Utah's violent crime rate in 2017 was 238.9 per 100,000 population, compared to 394.0 for the entire nation.

- Of all the states, Utah had the highest percent of children in 2018, with 29.5 percent of its population under age 18.

- Utah also has the highest birth rate among states in 2017, at a rate of 15.7 births per 1,000 population.

- In 2017, 9.2 percent of Utahns did not have health insurance, compared to 8.7 percent of the total U.S. population.

Table UT-1. Population by Age, Sex, Race, and Hispanic Origin

(Number, percent, except where noted.)

Sex, age, race, and Hispanic origin	2000	2010	2018 [1]	Percent change, 2010–2018
Total Population..	2,233,169	2,763,885	3,161,105	14.4
Percent of total U.S. population	0.8	0.9	1.0	X
Sex				
Male..	1,119,031	1,388,317	1,592,143	14.7
Female..	1,114,138	1,375,568	1,568,962	14.1
Age				
Under 5 years..	209,378	263,924	253,004	-4.1
5 to 19 years...	601,599	698,613	774,862	10.9
20 to 64 years..	1,231,970	1,551,886	1,782,761	14.9
65 years and over	190,222	249,462	350,478	40.5
Median age (years)...	27.1	29.2	31.0	6.2
Race and Hispanic Origin				
One race				
White	1,992,975	2,547,328	2,865,634	12.5
Black..	17,657	33,864	45,700	35.0
American Indian and Alaska Native	29,684	40,729	48,628	19.4
Asian..	37,108	57,800	85,389	47.7
Native Hawaiian or Other Pacific Islander	15,145	26,049	33,495	28.6
Two or more races	47,185	58,114	82,259	41.5
Hispanic (of any race)...	201,559	370,870	450,218	21.4

X = Not applicable.
[1] Population figures for 2018 are July 1 estimates. The 2010 estimates are taken from the 2010 Census.

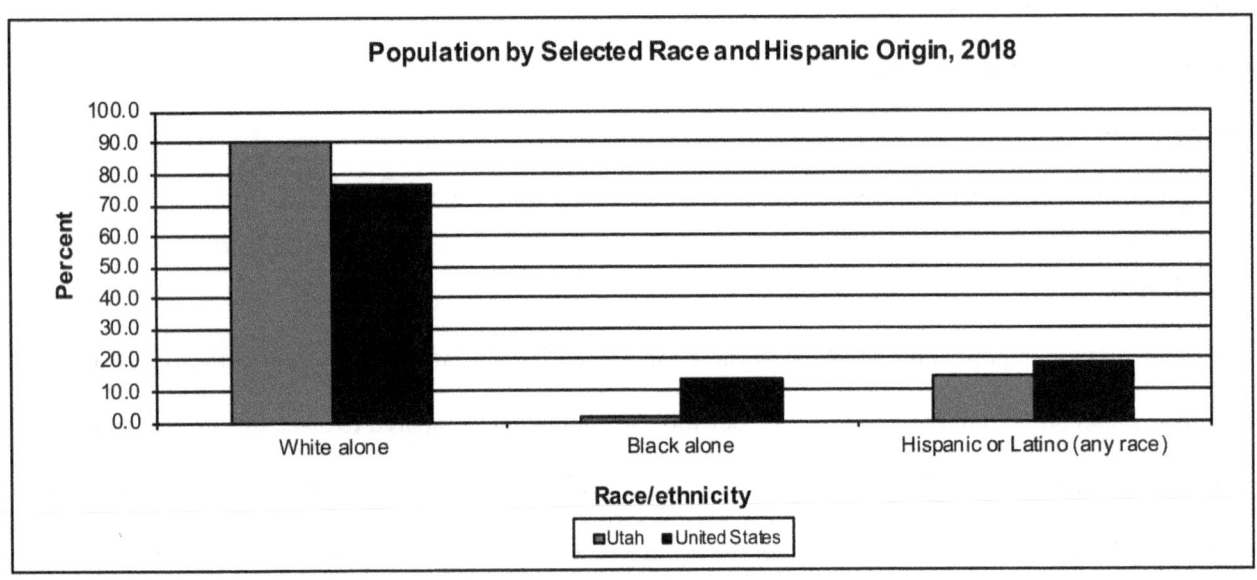

Table UT-2. Marital Status

(Number, percent distribution.)

Sex, age, race, and Hispanic origin	2000	2010	2017
Males, 15 Years and Over	813,693	1,014,706	1,164,596
Never married	30.6	31.3	33.4
Now married, except separated...	59.5	58.0	55.8
Separated...	1.1	1.3	0.9
Widowed...	1.6	1.8	1.8
Divorced...	7.3	7.6	8.2
Females, 15 Years and Over	852,995	1,019,010	1,163,337
Never married	25.2	25.8	27.3
Now married, except separated...	58.0	56.6	55.3
Separated...	1.4	1.6	1.6
Widowed...	6.6	5.8	5.6
Divorced...	8.8	10.1	10.2

Table UT-3. Households and Housing Characteristics

(Number, percent, dollars.)

Item	2000	2010	2017	Average annual percent change, 2010–2017
Total Households...	701,281	880,025	975,448	1.5
Family households	535,294	665,964	723,175	1.2
Married-couple family	442,931	543,212	592,208	1.3
Other family	92,363	122,752	130,967	1.0
Male householder, no wife present........................	26,422	37,258	42,979	2.2
Female householder, no husband present..............	65,941	85,494	87,988	0.4
Nonfamily households	165,987	214,061	252,273	2.6
Householder living alone...	124,756	164,863	191,331	2.3
Householder not living alone.....................................	41,231	49,198	60,942	3.4
Housing Characteristics				
Total housing units..	768,594	981,821	1,084,685	1.5
Occupied housing units	701,281	880,025	975,448	1.5
Owner occupied	501,547	615,142	681,563	1.5
Renter occupied	188,734	264,883	293,885	1.6
Average household size..	3.13	3.10	3.13	0.1
Financial Characteristics				
Median gross rent of renter-occupied housing	597	796	986	3.4
Median monthly owner costs for housing units with a mortgage	1,102	1,433	1,467	0.3
Median value of owner-occupied housing units............	146,100	217,200	275,100	3.8

- = Zero or rounds to zero.

Table UT-4. Migration, Origin, and Language

(Number, percent.)

Characteristic	State 2016	State 2017	State Percent change	U.S. 2016	U.S. 2017	U.S. Percent change
Residence 1 Year Ago						
Population 1 year and over	3,002,244	3,056,193	1.8	319,361,956	321,994,428	0.8
Same house	82.4	82.9	X	85.4	85.7	X
Different house in the U.S..	16.8	16.3	X	13.9	13.6	X
Same county	9.7	9.6	X	8.3	8.1	X
Different county	7.1	6.7	X	5.6	5.6	X
Same state	3.5	3.5	X	3.2	3.3	X
Different state	3.6	3.3	X	2.4	2.3	X
Abroad	0.8	0.8	X	0.7	0.7	X
Place of Birth						
Native born	2,798,884	2,832,594	1.2	279,388,170	281,193,323	0.6
Male	50.5	50.5	X	49.3	49.4	X
Female	49.5	49.5	X	50.7	50.6	X
Foreign born	252,333	269,239	6.7	43,739,345	44,525,855	1.8
Male	49.5	49.0	X	48.5	48.4	X
Female	50.5	51.0	X	51.5	51.6	X
Foreign born; naturalized U.S. citizen.........................	93,582	105,056	12.3	21,238,372	21,948,732	3.3
Male	46.7	46.0	X	45.9	45.9	X
Female	53.3	54.0	X	54.1	54.1	X
Foreign born; not a U.S. citizen..................................	158,751	164,183	3.4	22,500,973	22,577,123	0.3
Male	51.2	50.8	X	51.0	50.8	X
Female	48.8	49.2	X	49.0	49.2	X
Entered 2010 or later	21.5	24.3	X	18.6	21.3	X
Entered 2000 to 2009	31.3	28.3	X	26.7	25.7	X
Entered before 2000..	47.2	47.4	X	54.7	53.0	X
World Region of Birth, Foreign						
Foreign-born population, excluding population born at sea	252,333	269,239	6.7	43,738,901	44,525,458	1.8
Europe	10.3	10.3	X	10.9	10.8	X
Asia..	21.0	21.8	X	30.8	31.2	X
Africa	3.1	4.0	X	4.9	5.1	X
Oceania	3.6	2.8	X	0.6	0.6	X
Latin America	58.9	57.5	X	51.0	50.4	X
North America	3.0	3.6	X	1.8	1.8	X
Language Spoken at Home and Ability to Speak English						
Population 5 years and over...	2,797,795	2,848,744	1.8	303,328,961	305,924,019	0.9
English only	84.7	84.4	X	78.4	78.2	X
Language other than English.....................................	15.3	15.6	X	21.6	21.8	X
Speaks English less than "very well"....................	4.9	4.9	X	8.6	8.5	X

NA = Not available.
X = Not applicable.
- = Zero or rounds to zero.

Table UT-5. Median Income and Poverty Status, 2017

(Number, percent, except as noted.)

Characteristic	State		U.S.	
	Number	Percent	Number	Percent
Median Income				
Households (dollars)	68,358	X	60,336	X
Families (dollars)	77,940	X	73,891	X
Below Poverty Level (All People)	296,557	9.7	42,583,651	13.4
Sex				
Male	138,333	9.0	19,004,547	12.2
Female	158,224	10.4	23,579,104	14.5
Age				
Under 18 years	97,832	10.7	13,353,202	18.4
Related children under 18 years	94,273	10.4	13,053,472	18.1
18 to 64 years	177,435	9.8	24,648,677	12.6
65 years and over	21,290	6.4	4,581,772	9.3

X = Not applicable.

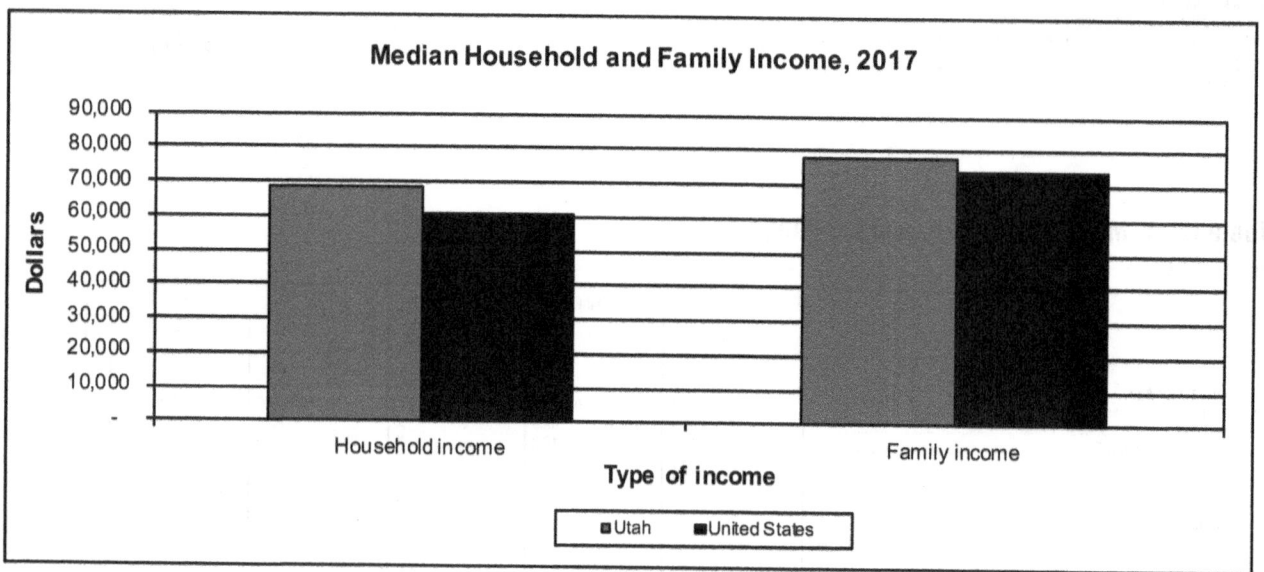

Table UT-6. Health Insurance Coverage Status for the Civilian Noninstitutionalized Population and Children Under 18 Years of Age

(Number, percent.)

Item	2009	2010	2011	2012	2013	2014	2015	2016	2017
Civilian Noninstitutionalized Population	2,755,284	2,750,354	2,789,648	2,829,001	2,874,213	2,916,303	2,971,003	3,024,767	3,076,318
Covered by Private or Public Insurance									
Number	2,354,207	2,328,430	2,363,584	2,419,830	2,472,089	2,550,780	2,659,662	2,759,960	2,794,565
Percent	85.4	84.7	84.7	85.5	86.0	87.5	89.5	91.2	90.8
Uninsured									
Number	401,077	421,924	426,064	409,171	402,124	365,523	311,341	264,807	281,753
Percent	14.6	15.3	15.3	14.5	14.0	12.5	10.5	8.8	9.2
Percent in the U.S. not covered	15.1	15.5	15.1	14.8	14.5	11.7	9.4	8.6	8.7
Children Under 18 Years of Age[1]	868,873	870,383	877,812	884,012	893,685	902,311	909,285	918,971	972,601
Covered by Private or Public Insurance									
Number	779,741	775,692	780,570	794,321	808,794	817,543	844,090	865,371	901,414
Percent	89.7	89.1	88.9	89.9	90.5	90.6	92.8	94.2	92.7
Uninsured									
Number	89,132	94,691	97,242	89,691	84,891	84,768	65,195	53,600	71,187
Percent	10.3	10.9	11.1	10.1	9.5	9.4	7.2	5.8	7.3
Percent in the U.S. not covered	8.6	8.0	7.5	7.2	7.1	6.0	4.8	4.5	5.0

[1] 2017 data is for individuals under 19 years of age.

Table UT-7. Employment Status by Demographic Group, 2018

(Numbers in thousands, percent.)

Characteristic	Civilian noninstitutional population	Civilian labor force		Employed		Unemployed	
		Number	Percent of population	Number	Percent of population	Number	Percent of population
Total...................................	2,300	1,553	67.5	1,503	65.3	51	3.3
Sex							
Male..	1,143	870	76.1	844	73.8	26	2.9
Female.....................................	1,157	684	59.1	659	56.9	25	3.7
Race, Sex, and Hispanic Origin							
White......................................	2,136	1,439	67.4	1,394	65.3	46	3.2
Male.....................................	1,059	807	76.2	783	73.9	24	3.0
Female..................................	1,077	633	58.8	611	56.7	22	3.5
Black or African American............	NA	NA	NA	NA	NA	NA	NA
Male.....................................	NA	NA	NA	NA	NA	NA	NA
Female..................................	NA	NA	NA	NA	NA	NA	NA
Hispanic or Latino ethnicity[1]	304	214	70.5	206	67.8	8	3.8
Male.....................................	155	124	79.9	119	76.9	5	3.8
Female..................................	148	90	60.6	86	58.3	4	3.9
Age							
16 to 19 years...........................	189	97	51.3	87	45.9	10	10.4
20 to 24 years...........................	260	208	80.1	198	76.2	10	4.9
25 to 34 years...........................	433	344	79.6	335	77.3	10	2.8
35 to 44 years...........................	453	375	82.9	367	81.0	8	2.2
45 to 54 years...........................	288	239	82.9	234	81.3	5	1.9
55 to 64 years...........................	299	217	72.6	213	71.2	4	1.9
65 years and over.......................	378	72	19.0	69	18.2	3	4.3

NOTE: Data in Table 7 are from the Current Population Survey (CPS) and do not match the estimates in Table 8. See notes and definitions for further information.
[1] May be of any race.
NA = Not available.

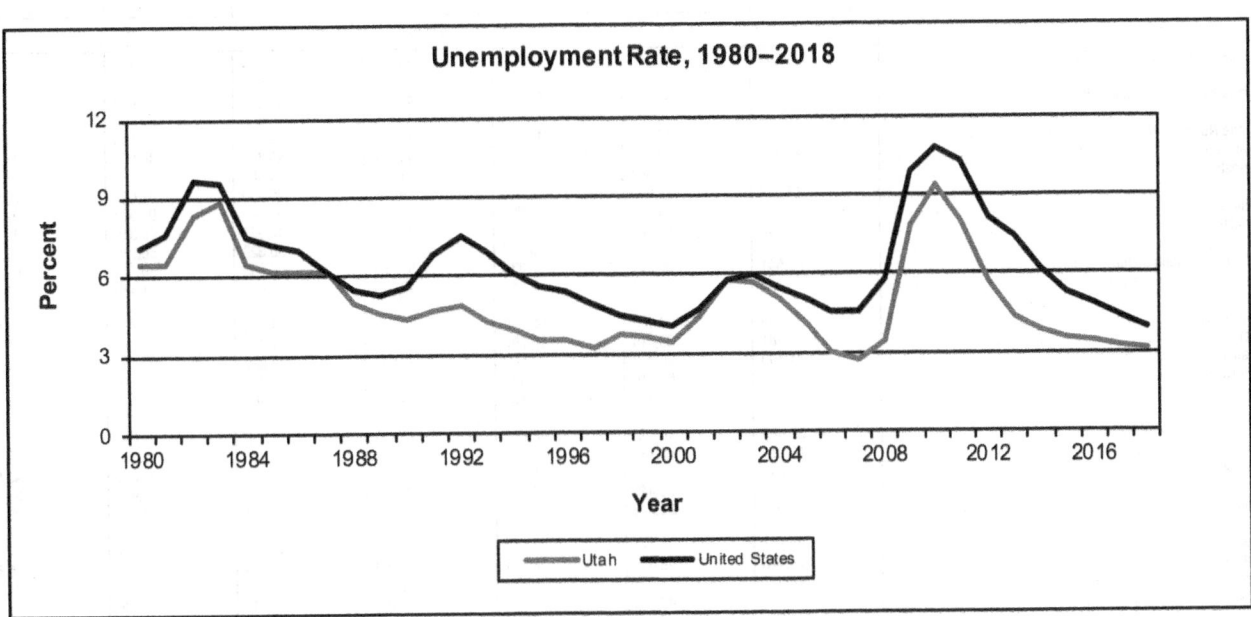

Table UT-8. Employment Status of the Civilian Noninstitutional Population Age 16 Years and Over

(Number, percent.)

Year	Civilian labor force	Civilian participation rate	Employed	Unemployed	Unemployment rate
2010...	1,356,097	68.8	1,249,814	106,283	7.8
2011...	1,350,444	67.8	1,259,337	91,107	6.7
2012...	1,372,971	67.8	1,298,807	74,164	5.4
2013...	1,405,630	68.1	1,341,192	64,438	4.6
2014...	1,428,293	68.0	1,373,801	54,492	3.8
2015...	1,464,173	68.3	1,411,194	52,979	3.6
2016...	1,511,279	68.8	1,459,309	51,970	3.4
2017...	1,560,846	69.4	1,510,208	50,638	3.2
2018...	1,572,136	68.3	1,523,158	48,978	3.1

Table UT-9. Employment and Average Wages by Industry

(Estimates are based on the 2012 *North American Industry Classification System* [NAICS].)

Industry	2011	2012	2013	2014	2015	2016	2017
	Number of jobs						
Wage and Salary Employment by Industry......................	1,262,617	1,303,995	1,342,353	1,381,561	1,428,802	1,480,533	1,524,228
Farm Wage and Salary Employment.............................	4,477	4,495	4,792	4,501	4,373	4,619	5,557
Nonfarm Wage and Salary Employment..........................	1,258,140	1,299,500	1,337,561	1,377,060	1,424,429	1,475,914	1,518,671
Private wage and salary employment...........................	1,018,724	1,058,148	1,096,532	1,134,425	1,179,882	1,225,591	1,263,387
Forestry, fishing, and related activities..............	1,390	1,396	1,451	1,513	1,573	1,621	1,582
Mining...	11,582	12,483	12,138	12,183	10,321	8,461	8,595
Utilities..	4,019	4,019	3,908	3,888	3,915	3,857	3,917
Construction...	66,910	71,176	75,452	80,601	86,833	93,815	99,788
Manufacturing..	113,007	115,975	118,061	120,068	122,991	125,143	128,499
Durable goods manufacturing........................	74,010	76,613	77,827	79,085	81,595	82,418	84,489
Nondurable goods manufacturing.....................	38,997	39,362	40,234	40,983	41,396	42,725	44,010
Wholesale trade..	46,205	47,973	48,464	48,816	50,198	50,087	51,017
Retail trade...	139,557	144,820	148,790	152,529	159,094	165,764	169,104
Transportation and warehousing.........................	44,697	46,465	47,119	48,755	51,413	53,183	55,984
Information..	28,406	30,228	31,306	32,163	33,343	35,708	37,287
Finance and insurance	54,074	55,207	57,632	59,435	63,203	65,413	67,606
Real estate and rental and leasing....................	16,947	17,141	18,028	18,486	18,987	19,493	20,019
Professional, scientific, and technical services	68,577	72,955	78,975	83,585	88,787	92,619	96,767
Management of companies and enterprises................	16,750	17,274	17,408	18,134	18,334	18,469	18,192
Administrative and waste services.....................	73,366	76,478	80,315	82,572	86,584	90,535	91,474
Educational services..................................	40,803	41,898	42,911	44,232	46,313	49,619	52,075
Health care and social assistance.....................	121,373	124,264	130,113	132,587	138,703	145,168	149,665
Arts, entertainment, and recreation...................	18,068	19,318	19,664	20,624	21,322	23,333	24,651
Accommodation and food services.......................	96,056	99,958	104,575	108,525	113,088	115,991	119,395
Other services, except public administration..........	56,937	59,120	60,222	65,729	64,880	67,312	67,770
Government and government enterprises.....................	239,416	241,352	241,029	242,635	244,547	250,323	255,284
	Dollars						
Average Wages and Salaries by Industry	41,142	42,243	42,723	43,839	45,234	46,124	47,447
Average Farm Wages and Salaries	33,012	37,998	39,762	40,861	35,594	39,013	32,614
Average Nonfarm Wages and Salaries	41,171	42,258	42,734	43,849	45,263	46,146	47,502
Average private wages and salaries...........................	41,415	42,730	43,180	44,377	45,804	46,662	48,062
Forestry, fishing, and related activities..............	27,224	28,304	30,164	31,914	31,907	33,722	35,690
Mining...	74,024	77,063	77,998	79,239	80,530	81,677	77,946
Utilities..	87,887	86,755	88,992	90,935	93,348	94,582	99,443
Construction...	43,835	44,923	44,269	45,693	47,341	48,319	49,962
Manufacturing..	51,691	52,680	53,216	54,549	56,323	56,929	58,471
Durable goods manufacturing........................	55,541	56,044	56,336	57,764	59,238	59,770	62,236
Nondurable goods manufacturing.....................	44,385	46,132	47,181	48,344	50,576	51,450	51,242
Wholesale trade..	58,756	60,129	62,389	62,847	64,068	65,730	67,940
Retail trade...	27,281	28,415	28,797	29,770	31,252	32,223	33,030
Transportation and warehousing.........................	44,609	45,279	46,509	47,501	48,822	50,465	51,170
Information..	58,044	60,616	61,447	65,095	69,302	72,179	73,134
Finance and insurance	58,676	62,949	63,491	66,148	69,967	70,161	71,762
Real estate and rental and leasing....................	38,879	40,302	40,692	42,836	46,302	47,182	49,825
Professional, scientific, and technical services	62,950	63,742	63,515	66,889	67,988	68,578	71,711
Management of companies and enterprises................	78,819	86,228	85,400	84,988	86,742	90,523	93,593
Administrative and waste services.....................	29,671	30,445	31,384	32,155	33,000	34,958	36,761
Educational services..................................	28,028	28,343	28,997	29,904	30,281	29,741	30,410
Health care and social assistance.....................	39,334	40,174	40,560	41,403	42,042	43,537	44,204
Arts, entertainment, and recreation...................	25,146	25,042	26,531	26,754	27,719	28,667	30,691
Accommodation and food services.......................	16,972	17,599	17,752	18,387	19,258	19,873	20,597
Other services, except public administration..........	41,350	43,388	43,959	43,432	45,644	45,436	47,132
Government and government enterprises.....................	40,135	40,187	40,705	41,377	42,655	43,621	44,728

Table UT-10. Employment Characteristics by Family Type

(Number, percent.)

Family type and labor force status	2015		2016		2017	
	Total	Families with own children under 18 years	Total	Families with own children under 18 years	Total	Families with own children under 18 years
All Families...	693,181	346,662	711,124	357,341	723,175	360,393
FAMILY TYPE AND LABOR FORCE STATUS						
Married-Couple Families................................	564,803	278,527	578,132	286,278	592,208	289,186
Both husband and wife in labor force........................	50.3	56.3	50.9	57.5	51.9	58.9
Husband in labor force, wife not in labor force	30.3	40.0	29.3	38.8	28.2	37.3
Wife in labor force, husband not in labor force	5.0	2.0	5.1	2.4	5.1	2.1
Both husband and wife not in labor force......................	13.9	1.4	14.1	0.8	13.9	1.1
Other Families	128,378	68,135	132,992	71,063	130,967	71,207
Female householder, no husband present......................	69.0	71.4	67.8	69.8	67.2	68.4
In labor force..	49.3	60.7	49.8	59.8	50.4	57.9
Not in labor force	19.7	10.6	18.0	10.1	16.8	10.4
Male householder, no wife present...........................	31.0	28.6	32.2	30.2	32.8	31.6
In labor force..	25.7	26.4	27.2	28.6	28.1	30.0
Not in labor force	5.3	2.2	5.0	1.6	4.7	1.6

Table UT-11. School Enrollment and Educational Attainment, 2017

(Number, percent.)

Item	State	U.S.
Enrollment		
Total population 3 years and over, enrolled in school	984,783	81,273,337
Enrolled in nursery school or preschool (percent)................	5.9	6.0
Enrolled in kindergarten (percent)................................	5.0	4.9
Enrolled in elementary school, grades 1-8 (percent)..............	42.3	40.6
Enrolled in high school, grades 9-12 (percent)..................	20.7	21.1
Enrolled in college or graduate school (percent)................	26.1	27.4
Attainment		
Total population 25 years and over	1,827,035	221,250,083
Less than ninth grade (percent)	2.7	5.1
9th to 12th grade, no diploma (percent).........................	5.1	6.9
High school graduate, including equivalency (percent)...........	22.3	27.1
Some college, no degree (percent)	25.7	20.4
Associate's degree (percent)....................................	9.5	8.5
Bachelor's degree (percent)	22.8	19.7
Graduate or professional degree (percent).......................	11.8	12.3
High school graduate or higher (percent)	92.1	88.0
Bachelor's degree or higher (percent)...........................	34.6	32.0

Table UT-12. Public School Characteristics and Educational Indicators

(Number, percent; data derived from National Center of Education Statistics.)

Item	State	U.S.
Public Elementary and Secondary Schools		
Number of operational school districts, 2016-17..................	156	18,377
Number of operational schools, 2016-17...........................	1,037	98,330
Percent charter schools	12.0	7.1
Total public school enrollment, 2016-17..........................	659,801	50,587,859
Percent charter school enrollment	10.8	6.0
Student-teacher ratio, Fall 2015................................	22.9	16.0
Expenditures per student (dollars), 2015-16......................	7,006	11,841
Four-year adjusted cohort graduation rate (ACGR)[1]	86.0	84.6
Students eligible for free or reduced-price lunch (percent), 2015-16...	36.4	52.1
English language learners (percent), Fall 2016..................	6.3	9.6
Students age 3 to 21 served under IDEA, part B (percent), 2017-18	12.6	13.7

Public Schools by Type, 2016-17		Percent of state public schools
Total number of schools...	1,037	100.0
Special education...	59	5.7
Vocational education..	6	0.6
Alternative education...	28	2.7

[1] Adjusted Cohort Graduation Rates (ACGR) differ from Averaged Freshmen Graduation Rates (AFGR).

Table UT-13. Reported Voting and Registration of the Voting-Age Population, November 2018

(Numbers in thousands, percent.)

Item	Total population	Total citizen population	Registered			Voted		
			Total registered	Percent registered (total population)	Percent registered (total citizen population)	Total voted	Percent voted (total population)	Percent voted (total citizen population)
U.S. Total	249,748	228,832	153,066	61.3	66.9	122,281	49.0	53.4
State Total.................................	2,247	2,109	1,443	64.2	68.4	1,214	54.0	57.6
Sex								
Male	1,109	1,040	691	62.3	66.4	568	51.2	54.6
Female	1,138	1,068	752	66.1	70.4	646	56.8	60.5
Race								
White alone................................	2,080	1,969	1,385	66.6	70.4	1,171	56.3	59.5
White, non-Hispanic alone	1,799	1,785	1,293	71.9	72.4	1,092	60.7	61.2
Black alone.................................	31	29	8	(B)	(B)	5	(B)	(B)
Asian alone................................	63	44	26	(B)	(B)	22	(B)	(B)
Hispanic (of any race)..................	291	189	96	32.8	50.5	82	28.3	43.6
White alone or in combination	2,091	1,979	1,392	66.6	70.3	1,175	56.2	59.4
Black alone or in combination........	35	33	12	(B)	(B)	10	(B)	(B)
Asian alone or in combination........	67	48	26	(B)	(B)	22	(B)	(B)
Age								
18 to 24 years............................	323	305	142	44.0	46.6	107	33.1	35.1
25 to 34 years............................	477	423	248	52.0	58.5	181	37.9	42.6
35 to 44 years............................	471	439	315	66.8	71.8	263	55.8	59.9
45 to 64 years............................	606	581	456	75.3	78.5	399	65.8	68.6
65 years and over	370	361	282	76.3	78.2	265	71.8	73.5

B = Base is less than 75,000 and therefore too small to show the derived measure.

Table UT-14. Crime

(Number, rate per 100,000. Data are derived from the FBI Uniform Crime Reports.)

Item	State			U.S.		
	2016	2017	Percent change	2016	2017	Percent change
TOTAL POPULATION[1]	3,044,321	3,101,833	1.9	323,405,935	325,719,178	0.7
VIOLENT CRIME						
Number..	7,406	7,410	0.1	1,285,606	1,283,220	-0.2
Rate..	243.3	238.9	-1.8	397.5	394.0	-0.9
Murder and Nonnegligent Manslaughter						
Number..	74	73	-1.4	17,413	17,284	-0.7
Rate..	2.4	2.4	-3.2	5.4	5.3	-1.4
Rape[2]						
Number..	1,560	1,697	8.8	132,414	135,755	2.5
Rate..	51.2	54.7	6.8	40.9	41.7	1.8
Robbery						
Number..	1,528	1,468	-3.9	332,797	319,356	-4.0
Rate..	50.2	47.3	-5.7	102.9	98.0	-4.7
Aggravated Assault						
Number..	4,244	4,172	-1.7	802,982	810,825	1.0
Rate..	139.4	134.5	-3.5	248.3	248.9	0.3
PROPERTY CRIME						
Number..	90,561	86,238	-4.8	7,928,530	7,694,086	-3.0
Rate..	2,974.8	2,780.2	-6.5	2,451.6	2,362.2	-3.6
Burglary						
Number..	12,938	11,817	-8.7	1,516,405	1,401,840	-7.6
Rate..	425.0	381.0	-10.4	468.9	430.4	-8.2
Larceny-Theft						
Number..	68,261	64,892	-4.9	5,644,835	5,519,107	-2.2
Rate..	2,242.2	2,092.1	-6.7	1,745.4	1,694.4	-2.9
Motor Vehicle Theft						
Number..	9,362	9,529	1.8	767,290	773,139	0.8
Rate..	307.5	307.2	-0.1	237.3	237.4	-

NOTE: Although arson data are included in the trend and clearance tables, sufficient data are not available to estimate totals for this offense. Therefore, no arson data are published in this table.
- = Zero or rounds to zero.
[1] Population figures are U.S. Census Bureau provisional estimates as of July 1, 2017.
[2] The figures shown in the rape (revised definition) column were estimated using the revised Uniform Crime Reporting (UCR) definition of rape.

Table UT-15. State Government Finances, 2017

(Dollar amounts in thousands, percent distribution.)

Item	Dollars	Percent distribution
Total Revenue	22,642,916	100.0
General revenue	18,699,738	82.6
Intergovernmental revenue	4,524,182	20.0
Taxes	7,832,889	34.6
General sales	2,533,961	11.2
Selective sales	996,848	4.4
License taxes	321,715	1.4
Individual income tax	3,621,199	16.0
Corporate income tax	329,577	1.5
Other taxes	29,589	0.1
Current charges	5,154,042	22.8
Miscellaneous general revenue	1,188,625	5.2
Utility revenue	0	-
Liquor stores revenue	380,544	1.7
Insurance trust revenue[1]	3,562,634	15.7
Total Expenditure	20,595,842	100.0
Intergovernmental expenditure	3,767,592	18.3
Direct expenditure	16,828,250	81.7
Current operation	12,151,372	59.0
Capital outlay	1,739,728	8.4
Insurance benefits and repayments	1,871,857	9.1
Assistance and subsidies	828,978	4.0
Interest on debt	236,315	1.1
Exhibit: Salaries and wages	3,560,494	17.3
Total Expenditure	20,595,842	100.0
General expenditure	18,449,015	89.6
Intergovernmental expenditure	3,767,592	18.3
Direct expenditure	14,681,423	71.3
General expenditure, by function:		
Education	8,444,264	41.0
Public welfare	3,769,434	18.3
Hospitals	1,970,170	9.6
Health	335,385	1.6
Highways	1,211,388	5.9
Police protection	150,315	0.7
Correction	372,616	1.8
Natural resources	213,338	1.0
Parks and recreation	53,370	0.3
Governmental administration	999,727	4.9
Interest on general debt	236,315	1.1
Other and unallocable	692,693	3.4
Utility expenditure	0	-
Liquor stores expenditure	274,970	1.3
Insurance trust expenditure	1,871,857	9.1
Debt at End of Fiscal Year	7,453,346	X
Cash and Security Holdings	36,227,909	X

X = Not applicable.
- = Zero or rounds to zero.
[1] Within insurance trust revenue, net earnings of state retirement systems is a calculated statistic (the item code in the data file is X08), and thus can be positive or negative. Net earnings is the sum of earnings on investments plus gains on investments minus losses on investments. The change made in 2002 for asset valuation from book to market value in accordance with Statement 34 of the Governmental Accounting Standards Board is reflected in the calculated statistics.

Table UT-16. State Government Tax Collections, 2018

(Dollars in thousands, percent.)

Item	Dollars	Percent distribution
Total Taxes	8,038,709	100.0
Property taxes	X	-
Sales and gross receipts	3,268,914	40.7
General sales and gross receipts	2,248,774	28.0
Selective sales and gross receipts	1,020,140	12.7
Alcoholic beverages	51,420	0.6
Amusements	X	-
Insurance premiums	135,180	1.7
Motor fuels	496,789	6.2
Pari-mutuels	X	-
Public utilities	24,351	0.3
Tobacco products	114,492	1.4
Other selective sales	197,908	2.5
Licenses	336,255	4.2
Alcoholic beverages	6,315	0.1
Amusements	X	-
Corporations in general	465	-
Hunting and fishing	31,299	0.4
Motor vehicle	218,386	2.7
Motor vehicle operators	16,772	0.2
Public utilities	X	-
Occupation and business, NEC	56,433	0.7
Other licenses	6,585	0.1
Income taxes	4,392,285	54.6
Individual income	3,991,400	49.7
Corporation net income	400,885	5.0
Other taxes	41,255	0.5
Death and gift	X	-
Documentary and stock transfer	X	-
Severance	41,236	0.5
Taxes, NEC	19	-

X = Not applicable.
- = Zero or rounds to zero.

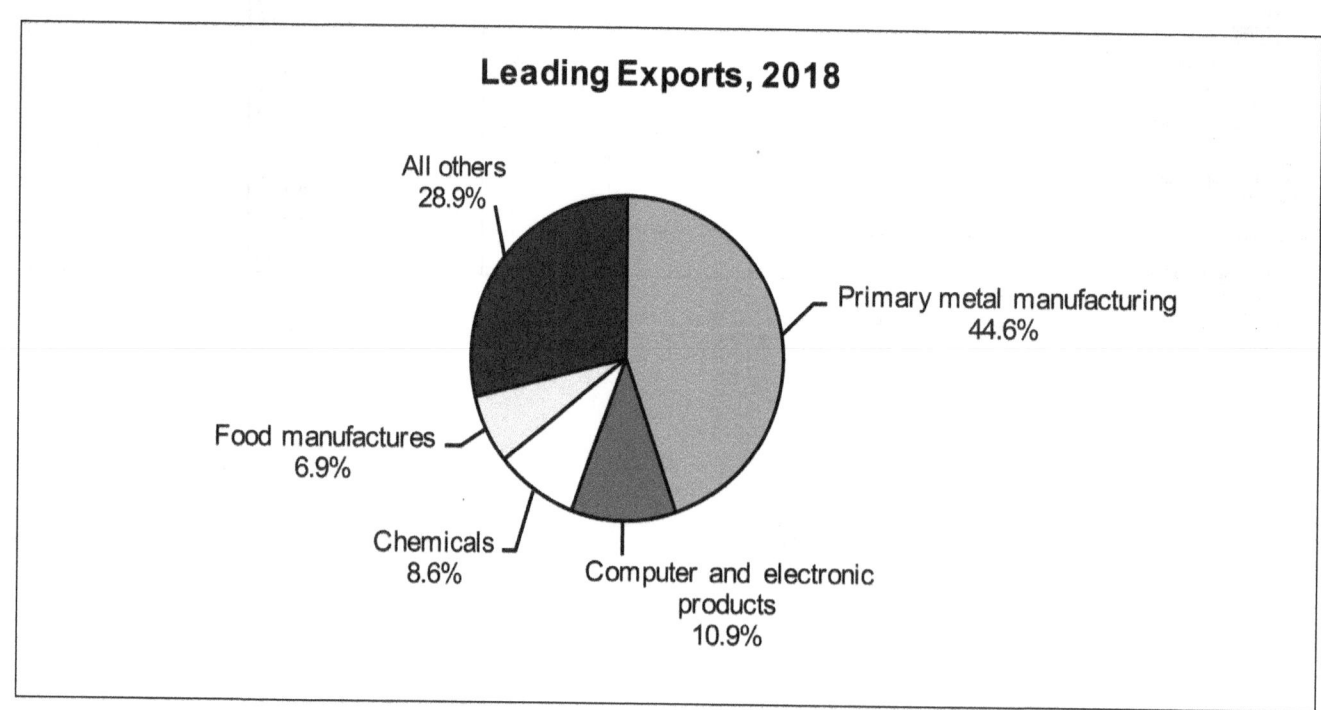

Leading Exports, 2018

- All others 28.9%
- Primary metal manufacturing 44.6%
- Computer and electronic products 10.9%
- Chemicals 8.6%
- Food manufactures 6.9%

VERMONT

Facts and Figures

Location: Northeastern United States; bordered on the N by Canada (Quebec), on the E by New Hampshire, on the S by Massachusetts, and on the W by New York

Area: 9,614 sq. mi. (24,901 sq. km.); rank—45th

Population: 626,299 (2018 est.); rank—50th

Principal Cities: capital—Montpelier; largest—Burlington

Statehood: March 4, 1791; the 14th state

U.S. Congress: 2 senators, 1 representative

State Motto: Freedom and Unity

State Song: "These Green Mountains"

State Nickname: The Green Mountain State

Abbreviations: VT; Vt.

State Symbols: flower—red clover; tree—sugar maple; bird—hermit thrush

At a Glance

- Vermont experienced a slight increase in population of just 0.1 percent between 2010 and 2018.

- Vermont's median household income in 2017 was $57,513, and 11.3 percent of the population lived below the poverty level.

- Vermont's violent crime rate in 2017 was the 2nd lowest in the nation at 165.8 per 100,000 population.

- In 2017, 4.6 percent of Vermonters did not have health insurance, which was the 5th lowest percent in the country.

- Vermont had the 2nd lowest percent of its population under age 18 in 2018, with 18.5 percent of its residents in this age group. It also had the 2nd lowest birth rate in 2017, with 9.1 births per 100,000 population.

Table VT-1. Population by Age, Sex, Race, and Hispanic Origin

(Number, percent, except where noted.)

Sex, age, race, and Hispanic origin	2000	2010	2018 [1]	Percent change, 2010–2018
Total Population...	608,827	625,741	626,299	0.1
Percent of total U.S. population	0.2	0.2	0.2	X
Sex				
Male..	298,337	308,206	309,252	-
Female..	310,490	317,535	317,047	-0.2
Age				
Under 5 years...	33,989	31,952	29,681	-7.1
5 to 19 years...	132,268	118,323	107,318	-9.3
20 to 64 years..	365,060	384,388	368,093	-4.2
65 years and over	77,510	91,078	121,207	33.1
Median age (years)...	37.7	41.5	42.8	3.1
Race and Hispanic Origin				
One race				
White	589,208	598,592	589,986	-1.4
Black	3,063	6,456	8,753	35.6
American Indian and Alaska Native	2,420	2,308	2,457	6.5
Asian	5,217	8,069	12,581	55.9
Native Hawaiian or Other Pacific Islander	141	175	247	41.1
Two or more races	7,335	10,141	12,275	21.0
Hispanic (of any race).....................................	5,504	9,962	12,534	25.8

X = Not applicable.
- = Zero or rounds to zero.
[1] Population figures for 2018 are July 1 estimates. The 2010 estimates are taken from the 2010 Census.

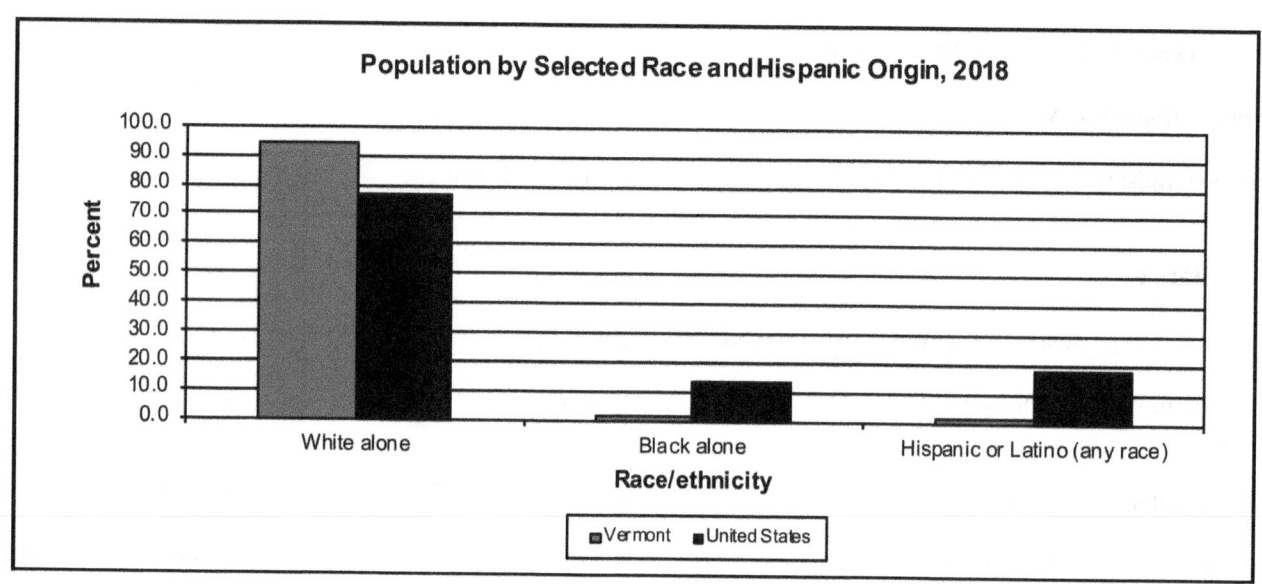

Population by Selected Race and Hispanic Origin, 2018

Table VT-2. Marital Status

(Number, percent distribution.)

Sex, age, race, and Hispanic origin	2000	2010	2017
Males, 15 Years and Over	236,517	254,288	257,783
Never married	29.7	34.2	35.5
Now married, except separated..	57.1	51.3	48.7
Separated..	1.2	1.3	1.2
Widowed...	2.4	2.5	3.0
Divorced...	9.6	10.7	11.6
Females, 15 Years and Over	251,764	266,860	268,968
Never married	23.9	27.7	28.6
Now married, except separated..	53.3	49.7	47.4
Separated..	1.4	1.4	1.2
Widowed...	10.0	8.2	8.4
Divorced...	11.5	13.0	14.3

Table VT-3. Households and Housing Characteristics

(Number, percent, dollars.)

Item	2000	2010	2017	Average annual percent change, 2010–2017
Total Households..	240,634	256,922	256,629	-
Family households	157,763	159,846	153,648	-0.6
Married-couple family.................................	126,413	125,678	119,775	-0.7
Other family	31,350	34,168	33,873	-0.1
Male householder, no wife present................	9,078	10,887	10,379	-0.7
Female householder, no husband present........	22,272	23,281	23,494	0.1
Nonfamily households	82,871	97,076	102,981	0.9
Householder living alone.............................	63,112	75,243	79,584	0.8
Householder not living alone........................	19,759	21,833	23,397	1.0
Housing Characteristics				
Total housing units...	294,382	322,698	335,248	0.6
Occupied housing units	240,634	256,922	256,629	-
Owner occupied	169,784	180,847	178,405	-0.2
Renter occupied	70,850	76,075	78,224	0.4
Average household size....................................	2.44	2.34	2.33	-0.1
Financial Characteristics				
Median gross rent of renter-occupied housing	553	823	950	2.2
Median monthly owner costs for housing units with a mortgage	1,021	1,445	1,527	0.8
Median value of owner-occupied housing units........	111,500	216,800	226,300	0.6

- = Zero or rounds to zero

Table VT-4. Migration, Origin, and Language

(Number, percent.)

Characteristic	State			U.S.		
	2016	2017	Percent change	2016	2017	Percent change
Residence 1 Year Ago						
Population 1 year and over	619,387	619,089	-	319,361,956	321,994,428	0.8
Same house	86.4	86.6	X	85.4	85.7	X
Different house in the U.S.	13.2	12.8	X	13.9	13.6	X
Same county	7.6	7.0	X	8.3	8.1	X
Different county	5.7	5.9	X	5.6	5.6	X
Same state	2.2	2.3	X	3.2	3.3	X
Different state	3.4	3.5	X	2.4	2.3	X
Abroad	0.3	0.5	X	0.7	0.7	X
Place of Birth						
Native born	596,371	595,574	-0.1	279,388,170	281,193,323	0.6
Male	49.7	49.7	X	49.3	49.4	X
Female	50.3	50.3	X	50.7	50.6	X
Foreign born	28,223	28,083	-0.5	43,739,345	44,525,855	1.8
Male	41.5	42.0	X	48.5	48.4	X
Female	58.5	58.0	X	51.5	51.6	X
Foreign born; naturalized U.S. citizen.............	16,364	15,426	-5.7	21,238,372	21,948,732	3.3
Male	42.5	42.2	X	45.9	45.9	X
Female	57.5	57.8	X	54.1	54.1	X
Foreign born; not a U.S. citizen	11,859	12,657	6.7	22,500,973	22,577,123	0.3
Male	40.0	41.8	X	51.0	50.8	X
Female	60.0	58.2	X	49.0	49.2	X
Entered 2010 or later	22.0	27.0	X	18.6	21.3	X
Entered 2000 to 2009	18.4	22.6	X	26.7	25.7	X
Entered before 2000..	59.5	50.4	X	54.7	53.0	X
World Region of Birth, Foreign						
Foreign-born population, excluding population born at sea	28,223	28,083	-0.5	43,738,901	44,525,458	1.8
Europe	29.7	30.5	X	10.9	10.8	X
Asia	29.4	34.0	X	30.8	31.2	X
Africa	10.3	8.6	X	4.9	5.1	X
Oceania	1.1	1.1	X	0.6	0.6	X
Latin America	9.4	9.9	X	51.0	50.4	X
North America	20.1	15.9	X	1.8	1.8	X
Language Spoken at Home and Ability to Speak English						
Population 5 years and over	594,130	593,561	-0.1	303,328,961	305,924,019	0.9
English only	94.5	94.4	X	78.4	78.2	X
Language other than English............................	5.5	5.6	X	21.6	21.8	X
Speaks English less than "very well".............	1.3	1.3	X	8.6	8.5	X

NA = Not available.
X = Not applicable.
- = Zero or rounds to zero.

Table VT-5. Median Income and Poverty Status, 2017

(Number, percent, except as noted.)

Characteristic	State		U.S.	
	Number	Percent	Number	Percent
Median Income				
Households (dollars)..	57,513	X	60,336	X
Families (dollars)	74,426	X	73,891	X
Below Poverty Level (All People)	67,841	11.3	42,583,651	13.4
Sex				
Male	31,257	10.6	19,004,547	12.2
Female	36,584	12.0	23,579,104	14.5
Age				
Under 18 years..	15,946	13.8	13,353,202	18.4
Related children under 18 years...	15,435	13.4	13,053,472	18.1
18 to 64 years...	43,774	11.8	24,648,677	12.6
65 years and over	8,121	7.1	4,581,772	9.3

X = Not applicable.

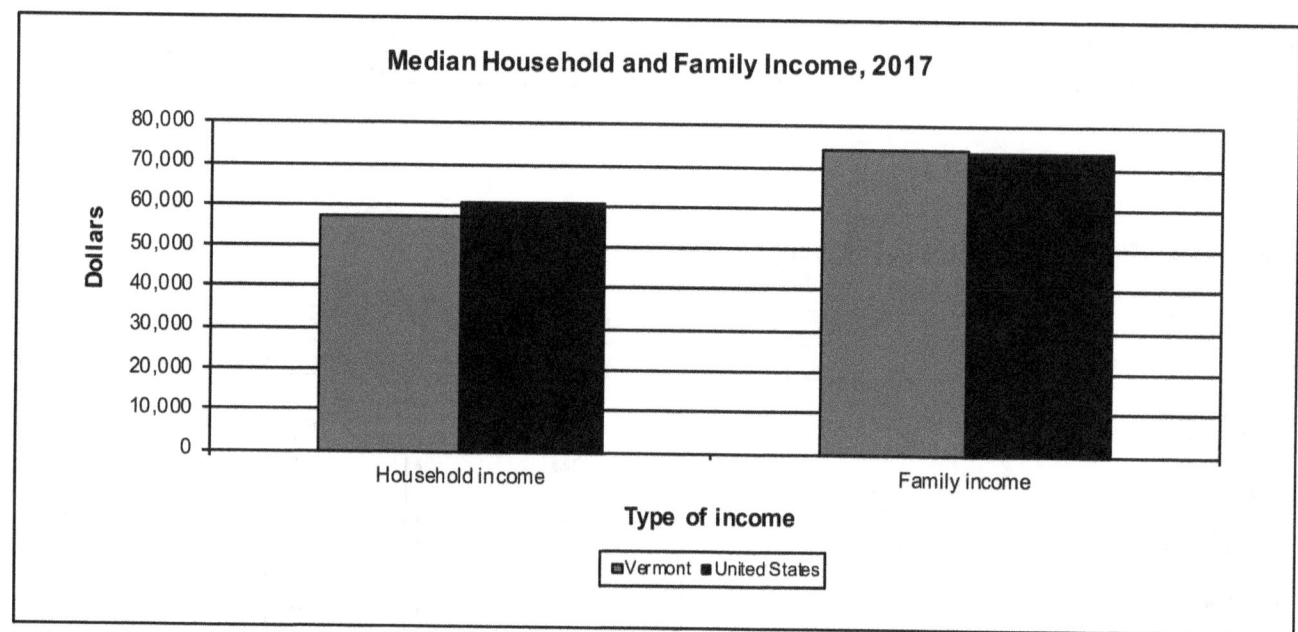

Median Household and Family Income, 2017

Table VT-6. Health Insurance Coverage Status for the Civilian Noninstitutionalized Population and Children Under 18 Years of Age

(Number, percent.)

Item	2009	2010	2011	2012	2013	2014	2015	2016	2017
Civilian Noninstitutionalized Population	615,376	619,886	620,159	619,928	620,896	620,453	620,107	618,622	617,556
Covered by Private or Public Insurance									
Number..	562,184	570,006	578,950	579,875	575,992	589,737	596,431	595,628	589,445
Percent..	91.4	92.0	93.4	93.5	92.8	95.0	96.2	96.3	95.4
Uninsured									
Number..	53,192	49,880	41,209	40,053	44,904	30,716	23,676	22,994	28,111
Percent..	8.6	8.0	6.6	6.5	7.2	5.0	3.8	3.7	4.6
Percent in the U.S. not covered...............................	15.1	15.5	15.1	14.8	14.5	11.7	9.4	8.6	8.7
Children Under 18 Years of Age[1]	126,482	129,661	125,599	123,563	123,812	121,472	119,828	118,351	127,105
Covered by Private or Public Insurance									
Number..	122,493	127,034	122,580	120,072	119,930	118,832	118,577	116,493	125,077
Percent..	96.8	98.0	97.6	97.2	96.9	97.8	99.0	98.4	98.4
Uninsured									
Number..	3,989	2,627	3,019	3,491	3,882	2,640	1,251	1,858	2,028
Percent..	3.2	2.0	2.4	2.8	3.1	2.2	1.0	1.6	1.6
Percent in the U.S. not covered...............................	8.6	8.0	7.5	7.2	7.1	6.0	4.8	4.5	5.0

[1] 2017 data is for individuals under 19 years of age.

Table VT-7. Employment Status by Demographic Group, 2018

(Numbers in thousands, percent.)

Characteristic	Civilian noninstitutional population	Civilian labor force		Employed		Unemployed	
		Number	Percent of population	Number	Percent of population	Number	Percent of population
Total..........................	517	346	66.9	337	65.1	9	2.7
Sex							
Male..........................	253	180	70.9	175	69.2	4	2.4
Female........................	263	166	63.2	161	61.3	5	3.0
Race, Sex, and Hispanic Origin							
White.........................	490	328	66.8	319	65.1	9	2.6
Male........................	239	169	70.6	165	68.9	4	2.4
Female......................	251	159	63.2	154	61.4	5	2.9
Black or African American...........	NA	NA	NA	NA	NA	NA	NA
Male........................	NA	NA	NA	NA	NA	NA	NA
Female......................	NA	NA	NA	NA	NA	NA	NA
Hispanic or Latino ethnicity[1].......	NA	NA	NA	NA	NA	NA	NA
Male........................	NA	NA	NA	NA	NA	NA	NA
Female......................	NA	NA	NA	NA	NA	NA	NA
Age							
16 to 19 years................	NA	NA	NA	NA	NA	NA	NA
20 to 24 years................	37	28	75.3	27	72.1	1	4.6
25 to 34 years................	78	68	87.4	66	85.7	1	1.9
35 to 44 years................	78	69	88.1	67	85.6	2	2.8
45 to 54 years................	82	69	84.0	67	82.1	2	2.5
55 to 64 years................	88	66	75.7	65	74.0	1	2.1
65 years and over	125	33	26.5	32	25.9	1	2.4

NOTE: Data in Table 7 are from the Current Population Survey (CPS) and do not match the estimates in Table 8. See notes and definitions for further information.
[1] May be of any race.
NA = Not available.

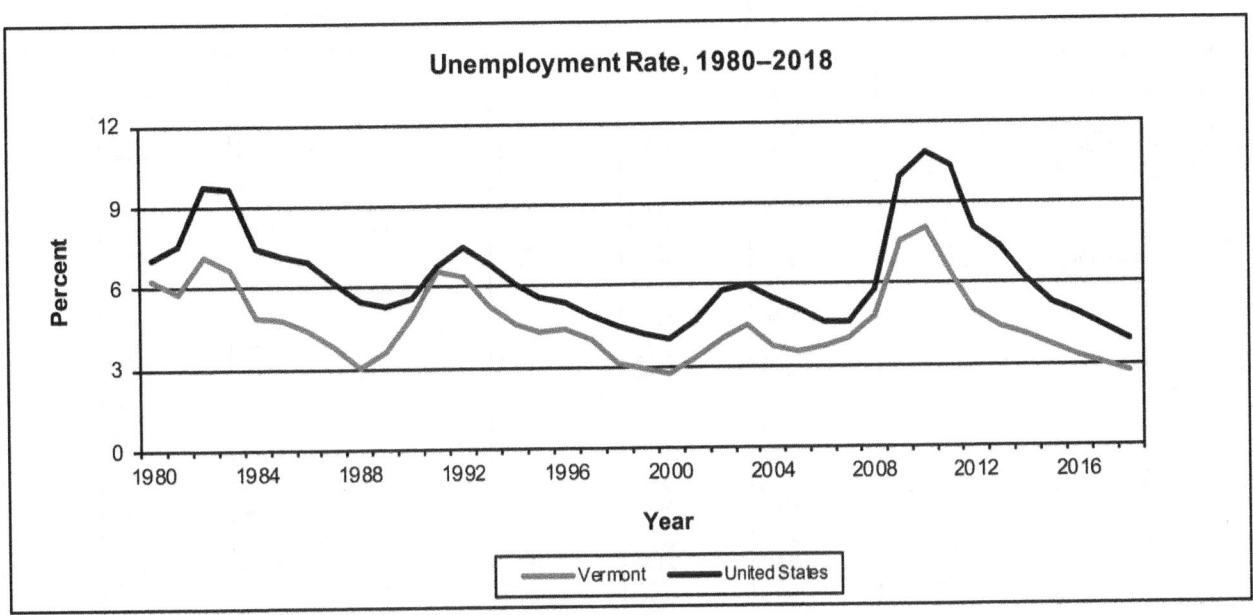

Table VT-8. Employment Status of the Civilian Noninstitutional Population Age 16 Years and Over

(Number, percent.)

Year	Civilian labor force	Civilian participation rate	Employed	Unemployed	Unemployment rate
2010....................................	359,402	70.8	337,488	21,914	6.1
2011....................................	358,108	70.3	338,463	19,645	5.5
2012....................................	354,857	69.5	337,284	17,573	5.0
2013....................................	350,447	68.4	334,964	15,483	4.4
2014....................................	347,172	67.6	333,438	13,734	4.0
2015....................................	344,520	67.0	332,199	12,321	3.6
2016....................................	344,572	67.0	333,399	11,173	3.2
2017....................................	344,760	66.9	334,378	10,382	3.0
2018....................................	346,061	66.7	336,838	9,223	2.7

Table VT-9. Employment and Average Wages by Industry

(Estimates are based on the 2012 *North American Industry Classification System* [NAICS].)

Industry	2011	2012	2013	2014	2015	2016	2017
	Number of jobs						
Wage and Salary Employment by Industry........................	313,167	318,183	320,076	323,339	325,842	326,845	327,624
Farm Wage and Salary Employment...............................	2,459	2,581	2,949	2,961	2,951	2,754	2,748
Nonfarm Wage and Salary Employment...........................	310,708	315,602	317,127	320,378	322,891	324,091	324,876
Private wage and salary employment...............................	253,449	257,934	259,316	261,972	264,746	266,002	266,990
Forestry, fishing, and related activities............................	909	859	880	921	931	902	900
Mining..	611	648	621	600	646	639	616
Utilities..	1,801	1,828	1,790	1,727	1,548	1,342	1,261
Construction	14,445	14,596	14,475	15,145	15,562	15,659	15,541
Manufacturing...	30,935	31,964	31,747	31,238	30,967	30,008	29,569
Durable goods manufacturing....................................	21,614	21,749	21,225	20,392	19,699	18,771	18,294
Nondurable goods manufacturing..............................	9,321	10,215	10,522	10,846	11,268	11,237	11,275
Wholesale trade	9,635	9,239	9,254	9,279	9,339	9,518	9,336
Retail trade..	38,280	37,915	38,011	38,200	38,180	38,400	38,139
Transportation and warehousing....................................	7,111	7,057	6,918	6,949	6,834	6,767	6,820
Information	4,961	4,671	4,680	4,769	4,643	4,646	4,485
Finance and insurance	9,355	9,292	9,185	9,247	9,246	9,192	9,296
Real estate and rental and leasing................................	3,019	3,061	3,132	3,124	3,016	3,023	3,055
Professional, scientific, and technical services	13,747	14,170	14,181	13,965	14,334	14,438	14,626
Management of companies and enterprises....................	1,418	1,961	1,949	2,081	2,219	2,086	2,026
Administrative and waste services.................................	9,671	10,241	10,477	10,742	11,073	11,440	11,987
Educational services	14,041	14,245	14,239	14,571	14,980	15,819	15,811
Health care and social assistance.................................	47,739	48,881	49,580	49,980	50,794	51,663	52,564
Arts, entertainment, and recreation...............................	3,928	4,033	4,079	4,341	4,181	4,325	4,483
Accommodation and food services................................	28,878	29,574	30,452	31,060	32,087	32,126	33,007
Other services, except public administration..................	12,965	13,699	13,666	14,033	14,166	14,009	13,468
Government and government enterprises.........................	57,259	57,668	57,811	58,406	58,145	58,089	57,886
	Dollars						
Average Wages and Salaries by Industry	39,487	40,201	41,237	42,190	43,289	44,173	45,314
Average Farm Wages and Salaries	20,314	30,596	27,297	28,805	23,609	29,033	26,405
Average Nonfarm Wages and Salaries	39,639	40,279	41,366	42,314	43,469	44,302	45,474
Average private wages and salaries...............................	39,043	39,773	40,831	41,774	42,909	43,693	44,810
Forestry, fishing, and related activities............................	28,987	29,049	29,727	31,160	32,096	33,373	33,358
Mining..	54,214	52,637	54,473	55,833	57,243	59,197	59,641
Utilities..	92,686	95,708	98,061	104,380	123,169	105,244	103,795
Construction	43,305	43,669	45,394	46,235	46,929	48,621	50,118
Manufacturing...	53,794	54,258	54,653	55,287	55,949	55,797	57,967
Durable goods manufacturing....................................	58,380	58,810	59,085	59,214	59,890	59,465	62,039
Nondurable goods manufacturing..............................	43,159	44,566	45,712	47,903	49,061	49,669	51,360
Wholesale trade	54,640	56,330	56,573	56,473	59,043	62,971	61,460
Retail trade..	26,738	26,586	27,460	28,382	29,432	29,640	30,539
Transportation and warehousing....................................	37,658	38,050	38,343	40,032	40,267	40,607	41,505
Information	49,248	48,892	51,416	53,754	56,141	56,070	58,287
Finance and insurance	64,153	66,042	67,666	69,803	73,163	74,453	80,400
Real estate and rental and leasing................................	34,473	36,116	37,860	38,498	39,636	41,108	41,977
Professional, scientific, and technical services	64,707	65,977	68,808	70,921	73,622	75,514	77,731
Management of companies and enterprises....................	78,310	77,965	81,898	87,230	86,148	92,751	92,827
Administrative and waste services.................................	29,239	31,718	34,529	36,630	36,129	37,980	40,942
Educational services	30,785	31,163	32,442	33,323	32,994	36,115	37,356
Health care and social assistance.................................	39,206	40,073	41,165	42,055	43,519	44,286	44,433
Arts, entertainment, and recreation...............................	23,541	23,932	25,264	25,641	25,125	26,246	26,449
Accommodation and food services................................	20,622	21,094	21,824	22,636	23,629	24,190	25,142
Other services, except public administration..................	26,046	26,859	27,768	28,376	29,506	30,551	31,493
Government and government enterprises.........................	42,280	42,543	43,768	44,733	46,021	47,088	48,540

Table VT-10. Employment Characteristics by Family Type

(Number, percent.)

Family type and labor force status	2015 Total	2015 Families with own children under 18 years	2016 Total	2016 Families with own children under 18 years	2017 Total	2017 Families with own children under 18 years
All Families..............................	152,379	58,593	154,421	58,887	153,648	56,689
FAMILY TYPE AND LABOR FORCE STATUS						
Married-Couple Families..............................	123,509	41,961	120,302	39,099	119,775	38,353
Both husband and wife in labor force...........................	57.1	75.8	56.4	75.7	54.9	74.3
Husband in labor force, wife not in labor force............	15.2	17.7	15.6	18.0	15.6	17.7
Wife in labor force, husband not in labor force...........	9.1	4.2	8.9	4.7	9.3	5.4
Both husband and wife not in labor force.......................	16.6	1.5	17.7	0.9	18.4	2.0
Other Families	28,870	16,632	34,119	19,788	33,873	18,336
Female householder, no husband present........................	70.1	68.6	67.5	70.5	69.4	69.2
In labor force..	50.8	57.8	46.8	53.9	50.9	58.0
Not in labor force...	19.2	10.9	20.7	16.6	18.4	11.2
Male householder, no wife present..........................	29.9	31.4	32.5	29.5	30.6	30.8
In labor force..	21.9	25.3	26.2	24.8	24.7	28.8
Not in labor force...	8.1	6.0	6.3	4.7	6.0	2.1

Table VT-11. School Enrollment and Educational Attainment, 2017

(Number, percent.)

Item	State	U.S.
Enrollment		
Total population 3 years and over, enrolled in school	144,025	81,273,337
Enrolled in nursery school or preschool (percent)...........................	6.9	6.0
Enrolled in kindergarten (percent)...........................	4.1	4.9
Enrolled in elementary school, grades 1-8 (percent)...........................	37.0	40.6
Enrolled in high school, grades 9-12 (percent)...........................	19.8	21.1
Enrolled in college or graduate school (percent)...........................	32.0	27.4
Attainment		
Total population 25 years and over	439,267	221,250,083
Less than ninth grade (percent)...........................	2.2	5.1
9th to 12th grade, no diploma (percent)...........................	5.2	6.9
High school graduate, including equivalency (percent)...........................	29.0	27.1
Some college, no degree (percent)...........................	16.8	20.4
Associate's degree (percent)...........................	8.5	8.5
Bachelor's degree (percent)...........................	22.5	19.7
Graduate or professional degree (percent)...........................	15.8	12.3
High school graduate or higher (percent)...........................	92.6	88.0
Bachelor's degree or higher (percent)...........................	38.3	32.0

Table VT-12. Public School Characteristics and Educational Indicators

(Number, percent; data derived from National Center of Education Statistics.)

Item	State	U.S.
Public Elementary and Secondary Schools		
Number of operational school districts, 2016-17...........................	343	18,377
Number of operational schools, 2016-17...........................	312	98,330
Percent charter schools...........................	NA	7.1
Total public school enrollment, 2016-17...........................	88,428	50,587,859
Percent charter school enrollment...........................	NA	6.0
Student-teacher ratio, Fall 2015...........................	10.5	16.0
Expenditures per student (dollars), 2015-16...........................	19,023	11,841
Four-year adjusted cohort graduation rate (ACGR)[1]...........................	89.1	84.6
Students eligible for free or reduced-price lunch (percent), 2015-16...........................	38.4	52.1
English language learners (percent), Fall 2016...........................	1.7	9.6
Students age 3 to 21 served under IDEA, part B (percent), 2017-18...........................	16.7	13.7

Public Schools by Type, 2016-17		Percent of state public schools
Total number of schools...........................	312	100.0
Special education...........................	0	-
Vocational education...........................	15	4.8
Alternative education...........................	1	0.3

[1] Adjusted Cohort Graduation Rates (ACGR) differ from Averaged Freshmen Graduation Rates (AFGR).
NA = Not available.
- = Zero or rounds to zero.

Table VT-13. Reported Voting and Registration of the Voting-Age Population, November 2018

(Numbers in thousands, percent.)

Item	Total population	Total citizen population	Registered			Voted		
			Total registered	Percent registered (total population)	Percent registered (total citizen population)	Total voted	Percent voted (total population)	Percent voted (total citizen population)
U.S. Total	249,748	228,832	153,066	61.3	66.9	122,281	49.0	53.4
State Total..	503	497	343	68.1	69.0	273	54.2	54.9
Sex								
Male	247	243	168	68.2	69.1	132	53.6	54.3
Female	257	253	175	68.0	69.0	141	54.7	55.5
Race								
White alone..	478	473	330	68.9	69.7	263	55.0	55.6
White, non-Hispanic alone...............	472	466	323	68.6	69.4	258	54.6	55.3
Black alone...	4	4	2	(B)	(B)	1	(B)	(B)
Asian alone..	5	4	3	(B)	(B)	3	(B)	(B)
Hispanic (of any race).........................	8	8	7	(B)	(B)	6	(B)	(B)
White alone or in combination	493	486	338	68.7	69.6	268	54.5	55.2
Black alone or in combination..............	7	7	3	(B)	(B)	2	(B)	(B)
Asian alone or in combination..............	8	7	5	(B)	(B)	3	(B)	(B)
Age								
18 to 24 years	46	45	22	(B)	(B)	16	(B)	(B)
25 to 34 years	86	84	50	57.8	59.0	34	39.6	40.4
35 to 44 years	77	75	47	60.9	62.2	37	48.7	49.7
45 to 64 years	164	163	121	73.5	74.1	98	59.5	60.0
65 years and over	130	129	104	80.0	80.8	88	67.5	68.2

B = Base is less than 75,000 and therefore too small to show the derived measure.
- = Zero or rounds to zero.

Table VT-14. Crime

(Number, rate per 100,000. Data are derived from the FBI Uniform Crime Reports.)

Item	State			U.S.		
	2016	2017	Percent change	2016	2017	Percent change
TOTAL POPULATION[1]	623,354	623,657	-	323,405,935	325,719,178	0.7
VIOLENT CRIME						
Number..	851	1,034	21.5	1,285,606	1,283,220	-0.2
Rate	136.5	165.8	21.4	397.5	394.0	-0.9
Murder and Nonnegligent Manslaughter						
Number..	14	14	-	17,413	17,284	-0.7
Rate	2.2	2.2	-	5.4	5.3	-1.4
Rape[2]						
Number..	170	218	28.2	132,414	135,755	2.5
Rate	27.3	35.0	28.2	40.9	41.7	1.8
Robbery						
Number..	78	92	17.9	332,797	319,356	-4.0
Rate	12.5	14.8	17.9	102.9	98.0	-4.7
Aggravated Assault						
Number..	589	710	20.5	802,982	810,825	1.0
Rate	94.5	113.8	20.5	248.3	248.9	0.3
PROPERTY CRIME						
Number..	9,705	8,960	-7.7	7,928,530	7,694,086	-3.0
Rate	1,556.9	1,436.7	-7.7	2,451.6	2,362.2	-3.6
Burglary						
Number..	1,884	1,854	-1.6	1,516,405	1,401,840	-7.6
Rate	302.2	297.3	-1.6	468.9	430.4	-8.2
Larceny-Theft						
Number..	7,637	6,912	-9.5	5,644,835	5,519,107	-2.2
Rate	1,225.1	1,108.3	-9.5	1,745.4	1,694.4	-2.9
Motor Vehicle Theft						
Number..	184	194	5.4	767,290	773,139	0.8
Rate	29.5	31.1	5.4	237.3	237.4	-

NOTE: Although arson data are included in the trend and clearance tables, sufficient data are not available to estimate totals for this offense. Therefore, no arson data are published in this table.
- = Zero or rounds to zero.
[1] Population figures are U.S. Census Bureau provisional estimates as of July 1, 2017.
[2] The figures shown in the rape (revised definition) column were estimated using the revised Uniform Crime Reporting (UCR) definition of rape.

Table VT-15. State Government Finances, 2017

(Dollar amounts in thousands, percent distribution.)

Item	Dollars	Percent distribution
Total Revenue	6,883,953	100.0
General revenue	6,025,734	87.5
Intergovernmental revenue	1,991,516	28.9
Taxes	3,127,523	45.4
General sales	375,870	5.5
Selective sales	682,699	9.9
License taxes	127,049	1.8
Individual income tax	743,630	10.8
Corporate income tax	81,395	1.2
Other taxes	1,116,880	16.2
Current charges	660,970	9.6
Miscellaneous general revenue	245,725	3.6
Utility revenue	0	-
Liquor stores revenue	64,126	0.9
Insurance trust revenue[1]	794,093	11.5
Total Expenditure	7,007,463	100.0
Intergovernmental expenditure	1,800,627	25.7
Direct expenditure	5,206,836	74.3
Current operation	4,189,825	59.8
Capital outlay	336,308	4.8
Insurance benefits and repayments	396,364	5.7
Assistance and subsidies	183,266	2.6
Interest on debt	101,073	1.4
Exhibit: Salaries and wages	959,299	13.7
Total Expenditure	7,007,463	100.0
General expenditure	6,550,330	93.5
Intergovernmental expenditure	1,800,627	25.7
Direct expenditure	4,749,703	67.8
General expenditure, by function:		
Education	2,844,714	40.6
Public welfare	1,843,184	26.3
Hospitals	23827	0.3
Health	364,778	5.2
Highways	437,888	6.2
Police protection	110,600	1.6
Correction	154,553	2.2
Natural resources	111,555	1.6
Parks and recreation	21,426	0.3
Governmental administration	194,190	2.8
Interest on general debt	101,073	1.4
Other and unallocable	342,542	4.9
Utility expenditure	21	-
Liquor stores expenditure	60,748	0.9
Insurance trust expenditure	396,364	5.7
Debt at End of Fiscal Year	3,502,960	X
Cash and Security Holdings	6,455,448	X

X = Not applicable.
- = Zero or rounds to zero.
[1] Within insurance trust revenue, net earnings of state retirement systems is a calculated statistic (the item code in the data file is X08), and thus can be positive or negative. Net earnings is the sum of earnings on investments plus gains on investments minus losses on investments. The change made in 2002 for asset valuation from book to market value in accordance with Statement 34 of the Governmental Accounting Standards Board is reflected in the calculated statistics.

Table VT-16. State Government Tax Collections, 2018

(Dollars in thousands, percent.)

Item	Dollars	Percent distribution
Total Taxes	3,284,231	100.0
Property taxes	1,065,767	32.5
Sales and gross receipts	1,095,321	33.4
General sales and gross receipts	397,691	12.1
Selective sales and gross receipts	697,630	21.2
Alcoholic beverages	26,892	0.8
Amusements	X	-
Insurance premiums	59,370	1.8
Motor fuels	82,953	2.5
Pari-mutuels	X	-
Public utilities	8,878	0.3
Tobacco products	71,078	2.2
Other selective sales	448,459	13.7
Licenses	126,404	3.8
Alcoholic beverages	469	-
Amusements	23	-
Corporations in general	3,686	0.1
Hunting and fishing	7,294	0.2
Motor vehicle	72,957	2.2
Motor vehicle operators	11,972	0.4
Public utilities	X	-
Occupation and business, NEC	25,674	0.8
Other licenses	4,329	0.1
Income taxes	930,149	28.3
Individual income	819,330	24.9
Corporation net income	110,819	3.4
Other taxes	66,590	2.0
Death and gift	22,935	0.7
Documentary and stock transfer	38,366	1.2
Severance	X	-
Taxes, NEC	5,289	0.2

X = Not applicable.
- = Zero or rounds to zero.

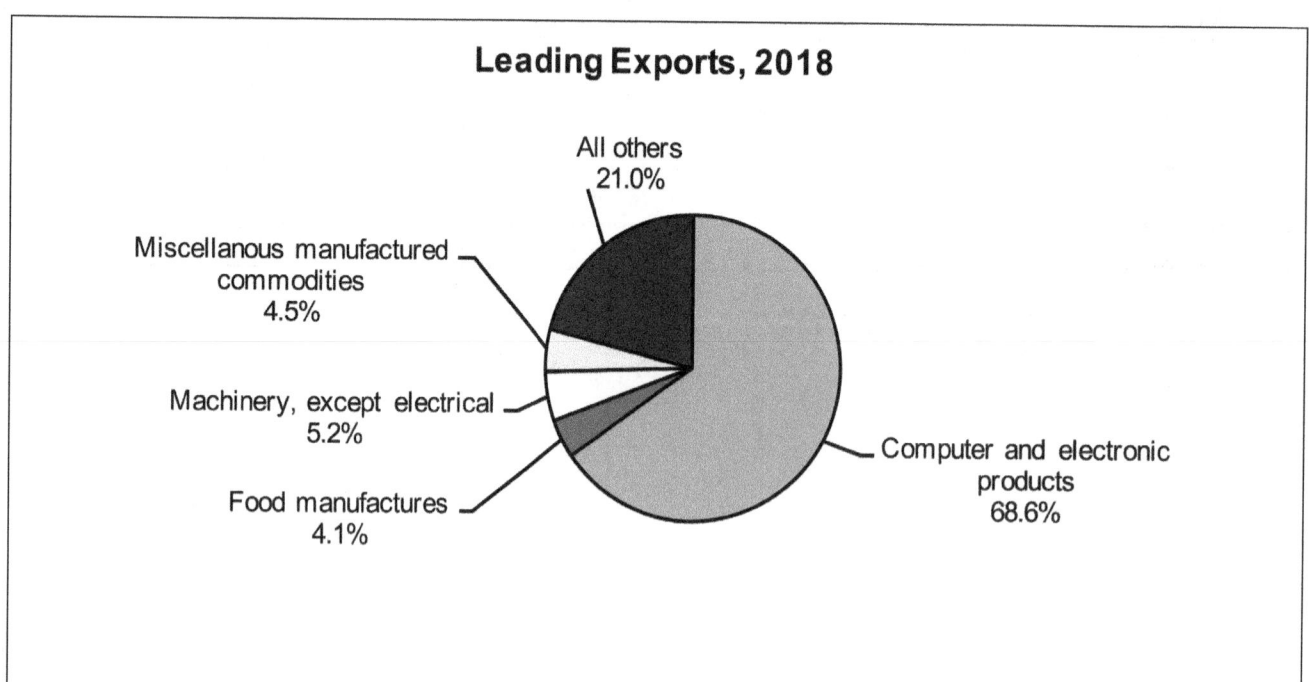

Leading Exports, 2018

All others 21.0%

Miscellanous manufactured commodities 4.5%

Machinery, except electrical 5.2%

Food manufactures 4.1%

Computer and electronic products 68.6%

VIRGINIA

Facts and Figures

Location: Eastern United States; bordered on the N and NE by Maryland and the District of Columbia, on the E by the Atlantic Ocean, on the S by North Carolina and Tennessee, and on the W by Kentucky and West Virginia

Area: 42,774 sq. mi. (110,785 sq. km.); rank—35th

Population: 8,517,685 (2018 est.); rank—12th

Principal Cities: capital—Richmond; largest—Virginia Beach

Statehood: June 25, 1788; 10th state

U.S. Congress: 2 senators, 11 representatives

State Motto: *Sic semper tyrannis* ("Thus always to tyrants")

State Song: "Our Great Virginia" and "Sweet Virginia Breeze"

State Nickname: The Old Dominion State

Abbreviations: VA; Va.

State Symbols: flower—flowering dogwood; tree—flowering dogwood; bird—cardinal

At a Glance

- With an increase in population of 6.5 percent, Virginia ranked 19th among the states in growth from 2010 to 2018.

- Virginia's violent crime rate (208.2 incidents per 100,000 population) was the 4th lowest in the country in 2017.

- In 2018, 3.0 percent of Virginians were unemployed, compared to 3.9 percent of the total U.S. population.

- Virginia's median household income in 2017 was $71,535, and 10.6 percent of the population lived below the poverty level, a percent that ranked 41st among all states.

- In 2018, 6.9 percent of Virginians identified as "Asian alone," ranking it 8th among the states in this category.

Table VA-1. Population by Age, Sex, Race, and Hispanic Origin

(Number, percent, except where noted.)

Sex, age, race, and Hispanic origin	2000	2010	2018 [1]	Percent change, 2010–2018
Total Population....................................	7,078,515	8,001,024	8,517,685	6.5
Percent of total U.S. population	2.5	2.6	2.6	X
Sex				
Male....................................	3,471,895	3,925,983	4,190,648	6.7
Female	3,606,620	4,075,041	4,327,037	6.2
Age				
Under 5 years....................................	461,982	509,625	510,924	0.3
5 to 19 years....................................	1,475,104	1,574,060	1,585,103	0.7
20 to 64 years....................................	4,349,096	4,940,402	5,106,257	3.4
65 years and over	79,233	976,937	1,315,401	34.6
Median age (years)	35.7	37.5	38.4	2.4
Race and Hispanic Origin				
One race				
White	5,120,110	5,725,432	5,918,670	3.4
Black	1,390,293	1,579,414	1,691,267	7.1
American Indian and Alaska Native	21,172	41,525	46,409	11.8
Asian	261,025	449,149	589,046	31.1
Native Hawaiian or Other Pacific Islander	3,946	8,201	9,998	21.9
Two or more races	143,069	197,303	262,295	32.9
Hispanic (of any race)	329,540	660,501	820,874	24.3

X = Not applicable.
[1] Population figures for 2018 are July 1 estimates. The 2010 estimates are taken from the 2010 Census.
- = Zero or rounds to zero.

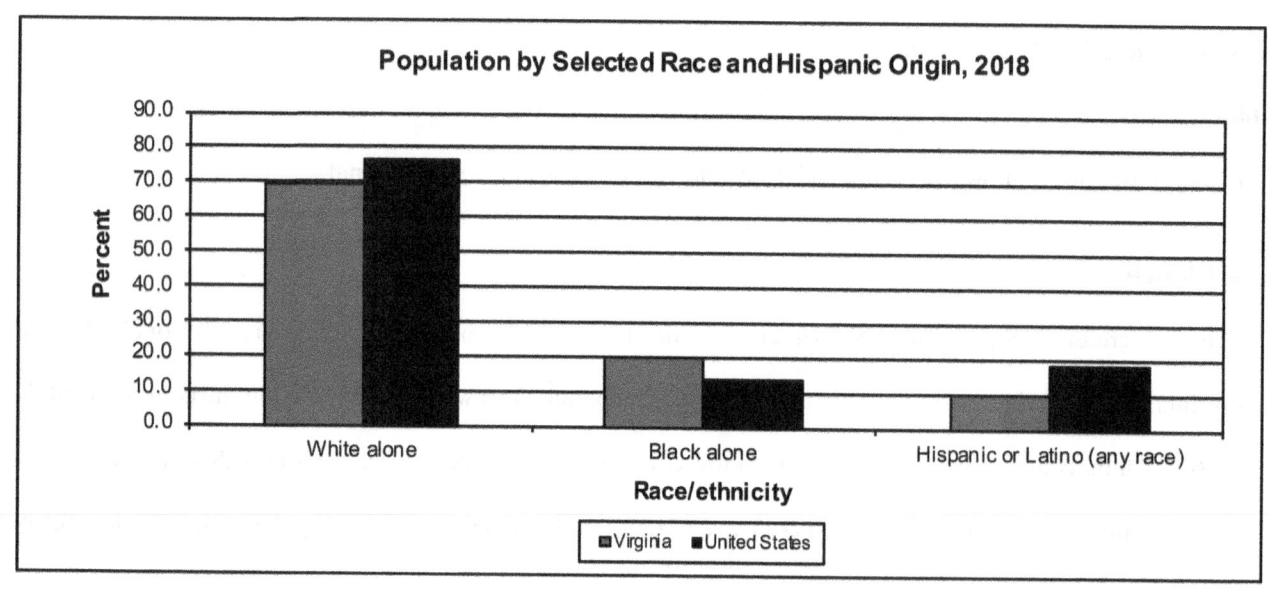

Table VA-2. Marital Status

(Number, percent distribution.)

Sex, age, race, and Hispanic origin	2000	2010	2017
Males, 15 Years and Over	2,724,334	3,156,115	3,370,061
Never married	29.1	34.2	35.0
Now married, except separated....................................	58.2	52.6	52.0
Separated....................................	2.6	2.3	2.0
Widowed....................................	2.3	2.3	2.4
Divorced....................................	7.9	8.5	8.7
Females, 15 Years and Over	2,899,294	3,331,264	3,549,559
Never married	23.5	28.0	29.9
Now married, except separated....................................	53.4	49.0	48.1
Separated....................................	3.2	2.9	2.5
Widowed....................................	9.9	8.7	8.3
Divorced....................................	10.0	11.4	11.2

Table VA-3. Households and Housing Characteristics

(Number, percent, dollars.)

Item	2000	2010	2017	Average annual percent change, 2010–2017
Total Households..	2,699,173	2,992,732	3,120,880	0.6
Family households...	1,847,796	2,013,520	2,091,237	0.6
Married-couple family.....................................	1,426,044	1,517,627	1,588,086	0.7
Other family..	421,752	495,893	503,151	0.2
Male householder, no wife present..................	101,462	124,273	136,384	1.4
Female householder, no husband present.........	320,290	371,620	366,767	-0.2
Nonfamily households.....................................	851,377	979,212	1,029,643	0.7
Householder living alone.................................	676,907	794,535	831,439	0.7
Householder not living alone...........................	174,470	184,677	198,204	1.0
Housing Characteristics				
Total housing units..	2,904,192	3,368,674	3,512,917	0.6
Occupied housing units	2,699,173	2,992,732	3,120,880	0.6
Owner occupied..	1,837,939	2,025,240	2,077,417	0.4
Renter occupied...	861,234	967,492	1,043,463	1.1
Average household size...................................	2.54	2.60	2.64	0.2
Financial Characteristics				
Median gross rent of renter-occupied housing	650	1,019	1,179	2.2
Median monthly owner costs for housing units with a mortgage	1,144	1,728	1,718	-0.1
Median value of owner-occupied housing units	125,400	249,100	273,400	1.4

Table VA-4. Migration, Origin, and Language

(Number, percent.)

Characteristic	State 2016	State 2017	State Percent change	U.S. 2016	U.S. 2017	U.S. Percent change
Residence 1 Year Ago						
Population 1 year and over	8,312,297	8,372,522	0.7	319,361,956	321,994,428	0.8
Same house	84.3	84.7	X	85.4	85.7	X
Different house in the U.S.	14.7	14.4	X	13.9	13.6	X
Same county	6.5	6.6	X	8.3	8.1	X
Different county	8.2	7.9	X	5.6	5.6	X
Same state	5.0	4.9	X	3.2	3.3	X
Different state	3.2	3.0	X	2.4	2.3	X
Abroad	0.9	0.9	X	0.7	0.7	X
Place of Birth						
Native born	7,380,639	7,407,650	0.4	279,388,170	281,193,323	0.6
Male	49.3	49.3	X	49.3	49.4	X
Female	50.7	50.7	X	50.7	50.6	X
Foreign born	1,031,169	1,062,370	3.0	43,739,345	44,525,855	1.8
Male	48.3	47.9	X	48.5	48.4	X
Female	51.7	52.1	X	51.5	51.6	X
Foreign born; naturalized U.S. citizen................	530,624	554,602	4.5	21,238,372	21,948,732	3.3
Male	46.8	47.1	X	45.9	45.9	X
Female	53.2	52.9	X	54.1	54.1	X
Foreign born; not a U.S. citizen........................	500,545	507,768	1.4	22,500,973	22,577,123	0.3
Male	49.9	48.8	X	51.0	50.8	X
Female	50.1	51.2	X	49.0	49.2	X
Entered 2010 or later	20.7	24.5	X	18.6	21.3	X
Entered 2000 to 2009.....................................	31.9	29.3	X	26.7	25.7	X
Entered before 2000..	47.5	46.2	X	54.7	53.0	X
World Region of Birth, Foreign						
Foreign-born population, excluding population born at sea	1,031,169	1,062,370	3.0	43,738,901	44,525,458	1.8
Europe	9.8	9.9	X	10.9	10.8	X
Asia..	43.2	42.7	X	30.8	31.2	X
Africa	10.4	11.0	X	4.9	5.1	X
Oceania	0.3	0.2	X	0.6	0.6	X
Latin America	35.2	35.0	X	51.0	50.4	X
North America..	1.2	1.2	X	1.8	1.8	X
Language Spoken at Home and Ability to Speak English						
Population 5 years and over..............................	7,908,026	7,968,048	0.8	303,328,961	305,924,019	0.9
English only	83.8	83.5	X	78.4	78.2	X
Language other than English............................	16.2	16.5	X	21.6	21.8	X
Speaks English less than "very well"..............	6.0	5.9	X	8.6	8.5	X

NA = Not available.
X = Not applicable.
- = Zero or rounds to zero.

Table VA-5. Median Income and Poverty Status, 2017

(Number, percent, except as noted.)

Characteristic	State		U.S.	
	Number	Percent	Number	Percent
Median Income				
Households (dollars)..	71,535	X	60,336	X
Families (dollars)	86,279	X	73,891	X
Below Poverty Level (All People)	874,483	10.6	42,583,651	13.4
Sex				
Male	385,003	9.6	19,004,547	12.2
Female	489,480	11.6	23,579,104	14.5
Age				
Under 18 years...	258,133	14.0	13,353,202	18.4
Related children under 18 years..	251,407	13.7	13,053,472	18.1
18 to 64 years..	528,123	10.3	24,648,677	12.6
65 years and over	88,227	7.1	4,581,772	9.3

X = Not applicable.

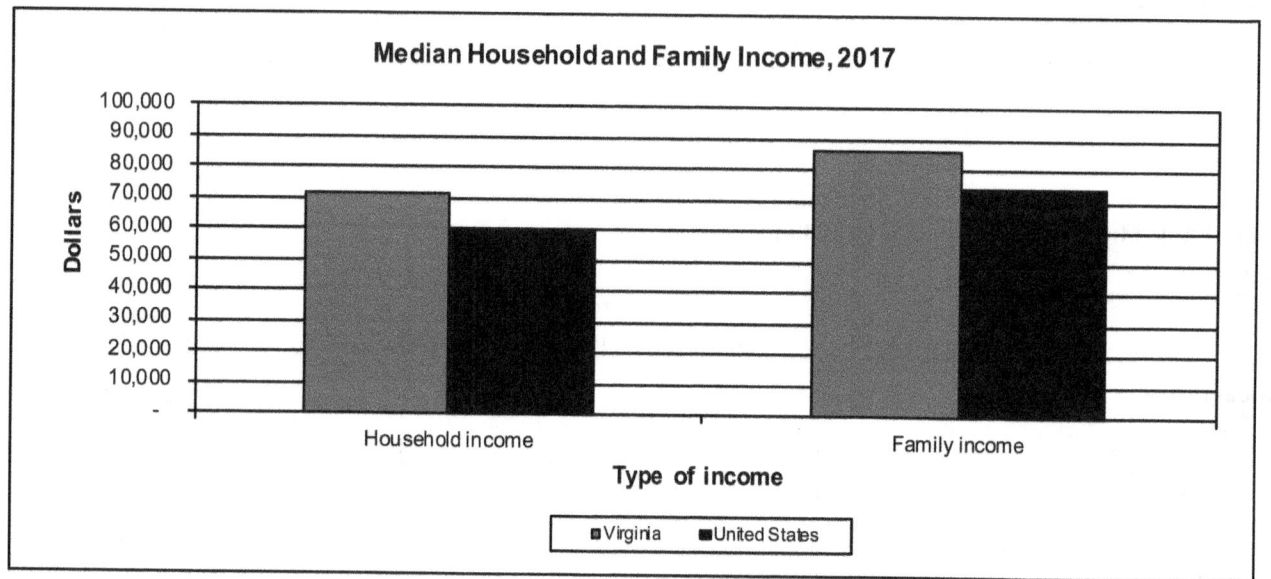

Table VA-6. Health Insurance Coverage Status for the Civilian Noninstitutionalized Population and Children Under 18 Years of Age

(Number, percent.)

Item	2009	2010	2011	2012	2013	2014	2015	2016	2017
Civilian Noninstitutionalized Population	7,643,783	7,807,416	7,887,164	7,973,466	8,054,191	8,114,884	8,162,517	8,199,576	8,256,810
Covered by Private or Public Insurance									
Number..	6,736,026	6,787,286	6,904,303	6,973,731	7,063,565	7,231,248	7,416,224	7,484,692	7,527,631
Percent..	88.1	86.9	87.5	87.5	87.7	89.1	90.9	91.3	91.2
Uninsured									
Number..	907,757	1,020,130	982,861	999,735	990,626	883,636	746,293	714,884	729,179
Percent..	11.9	13.1	12.5	12.5	12.3	10.9	9.1	8.7	8.8
Percent in the U.S. not covered..	15.1	15.5	15.1	14.8	14.5	11.7	9.4	8.6	8.7
Children Under 18 Years of Age[1]	1,842,559	1,849,665	1,849,081	1,851,845	1,861,658	1,864,738	1,867,092	1,864,852	1,983,006
Covered by Private or Public Insurance									
Number..	1,720,976	1,728,285	1,740,598	1,747,907	1,760,407	1,757,636	1,776,406	1,775,840	1,881,588
Percent..	93.4	93.4	94.1	94.4	94.6	94.3	95.1	95.2	94.9
Uninsured									
Number..	121,583	121,380	108,483	103,938	101,251	107,102	90,686	89,012	101,418
Percent..	6.6	6.6	5.9	5.6	5.4	5.7	4.9	4.8	5.1
Percent in the U.S. not covered..	8.6	8.0	7.5	7.2	7.1	6.0	4.8	4.5	5.0

[1] 2017 data is for individuals under 19 years of age.

Table VA-7. Employment Status by Demographic Group, 2018

(Numbers in thousands, percent.)

Characteristic	Civilian noninstitutional population	Civilian labor force		Employed		Unemployed	
		Number	Percent of population	Number	Percent of population	Number	Percent of population
Total..................................	6,661	4,362	65.5	4,235	63.6	128	2.9
Sex							
Male..................................	3,194	2,297	71.9	2,228	69.7	70	3.0
Female...............................	3,467	2,065	59.6	2,007	57.9	58	2.8
Race, Sex, and Hispanic Origin							
White.................................	4,749	3,080	64.9	3,003	63.2	77	2.5
Male..............................	2,300	1,665	72.4	1,623	70.6	42	2.5
Female............................	2,450	1,416	57.8	1,381	56.4	35	2.5
Black or African American...............	1,269	861	67.8	823	64.9	38	4.4
Male..............................	576	397	68.8	377	65.4	20	5.0
Female............................	694	465	67.0	447	64.4	18	3.9
Hispanic or Latino ethnicity[1]...........	702	525	74.9	505	72.0	20	3.8
Male..............................	359	297	82.6	286	79.6	11	3.6
Female............................	343	229	66.7	219	64.0	9	4.1
Age							
16 to 19 years.........................	440	156	35.4	138	31.3	18	11.6
20 to 24 years.........................	471	357	75.8	338	71.7	19	5.4
25 to 34 years.........................	1,181	989	83.7	960	81.3	29	2.9
35 to 44 years.........................	1,073	895	83.4	876	81.6	20	2.2
45 to 54 years.........................	1,137	938	82.5	918	80.7	20	2.2
55 to 64 years.........................	1,138	781	68.7	766	67.4	15	1.9
65 years and over......................	1,221	246	20.1	239	19.5	7	2.8

NOTE: Data in Table 7 are from the Current Population Survey (CPS) and do not match the estimates in Table 8. See notes and definitions for further information.
[1] May be of any race.

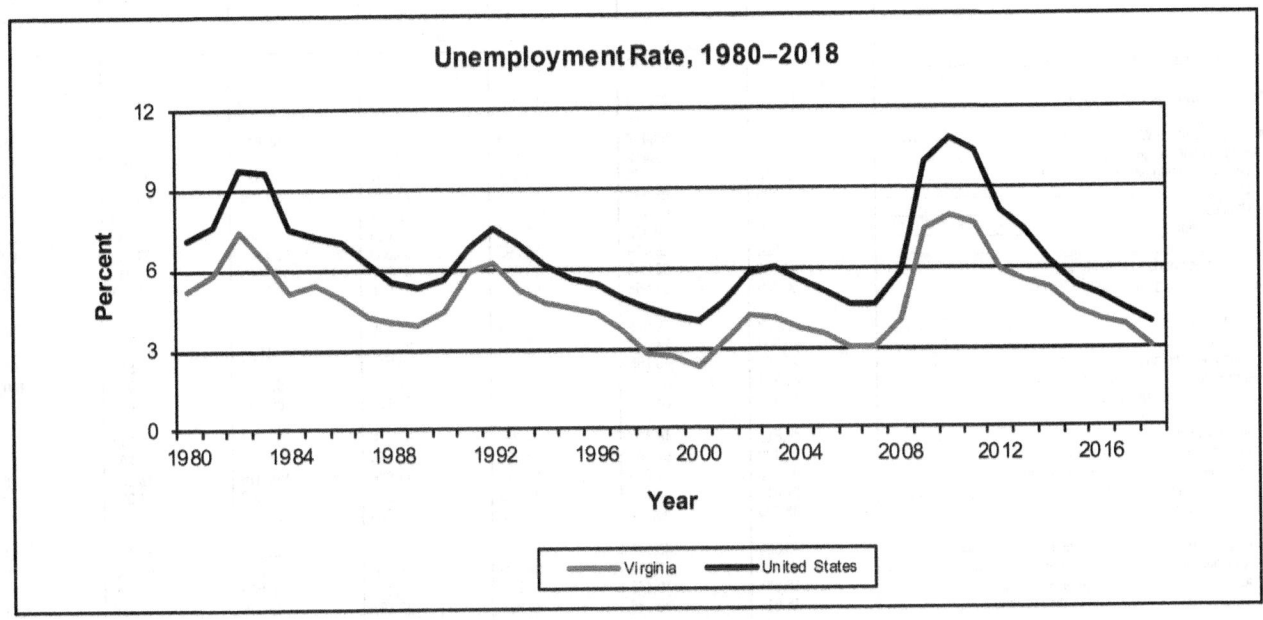

Table VA-8. Employment Status of the Civilian Noninstitutional Population Age 16 Years and Over

(Number, percent.)

Year	Civilian labor force	Civilian participation rate	Employed	Unemployed	Unemployment rate
2010..................................	4,157,658	67.7	3,860,386	297,272	7.1
2011..................................	4,211,802	67.4	3,934,326	277,476	6.6
2012..................................	4,223,844	66.8	3,967,987	255,857	6.1
2013..................................	4,237,277	66.3	3,995,182	242,095	5.7
2014..................................	4,244,109	65.9	4,022,160	221,949	5.2
2015..................................	4,216,974	64.9	4,029,043	187,931	4.5
2016..................................	4,242,650	64.8	4,069,139	173,511	4.1
2017..................................	4,307,753	65.2	4,146,134	161,619	3.8
2018..................................	4,331,380	65.2	4,202,801	128,579	3.0

Table VA-9. Employment and Average Wages by Industry

(Estimates are based on the 2012 *North American Industry Classification System* [NAICS].)

Industry	2011	2012	2013	2014	2015	2016	2017
	Number of jobs						
Wage and Salary Employment by Industry......................	3,881,669	3,926,526	3,947,829	3,972,994	4,049,013	4,100,137	4,138,213
Farm Wage and Salary Employment..............................	10,307	10,499	11,663	14,301	12,948	11,967	9,671
Nonfarm Wage and Salary Employment..........................	3,871,362	3,916,027	3,936,166	3,958,693	4,036,065	4,088,170	4,128,542
Private wage and salary employment............................	3,000,893	3,043,911	3,066,711	3,088,877	3,162,460	3,210,985	3,249,618
Forestry, fishing, and related activities........................	5,547	5,726	5,950	6,073	6,797	7,001	7,063
Mining..	9,053	9,033	8,073	7,465	6,840	5,771	5,976
Utilities..	10,889	10,636	10,536	10,646	10,784	10,857	10,761
Construction..	183,086	181,725	181,745	182,886	189,681	193,073	198,104
Manufacturing..	230,763	231,751	231,376	232,106	233,595	232,335	234,535
Durable goods manufacturing...................................	134,294	136,451	136,594	137,574	138,392	135,300	136,353
Nondurable goods manufacturing..............................	96,469	95,300	94,782	94,532	95,203	97,035	98,182
Wholesale trade...	112,616	111,774	111,792	111,311	111,346	111,529	111,738
Retail trade...	405,371	409,199	413,745	416,581	421,521	422,544	420,641
Transportation and warehousing.................................	103,840	104,924	105,692	108,481	115,418	119,078	121,844
Information..	74,401	71,794	71,229	71,686	69,890	68,241	67,993
Finance and insurance	128,435	131,498	134,028	135,832	139,224	141,973	146,413
Real estate and rental and leasing.............................	52,019	52,669	52,982	52,364	53,838	53,873	55,121
Professional, scientific, and technical services	393,924	398,819	397,401	392,536	403,041	413,335	421,166
Management of companies and enterprises.........................	73,350	76,389	75,619	73,973	74,196	73,355	73,939
Administrative and waste services..............................	203,375	207,837	210,242	216,546	227,201	232,924	238,538
Educational services...	72,839	73,095	73,806	72,542	73,979	75,481	76,626
Health care and social assistance..............................	387,999	397,500	406,114	410,403	423,026	434,626	439,581
Arts, entertainment, and recreation.............................	47,914	49,135	50,357	51,158	53,503	55,948	55,943
Accommodation and food services.............................	303,057	311,878	318,053	323,323	334,632	345,633	351,255
Other services, except public administration.................	202,415	208,529	207,971	212,965	213,948	213,408	212,381
Government and government enterprises.....................	870,469	872,116	869,455	869,816	873,605	877,185	878,924
	Dollars						
Average Wages and Salaries by Industry	52,064	53,019	53,307	54,334	55,696	56,253	58,022
Average Farm Wages and Salaries	19,703	27,900	25,271	22,123	19,960	24,784	27,832
Average Nonfarm Wages and Salaries	52,150	53,087	53,390	54,451	55,810	56,345	58,093
Average private wages and salaries............................	51,367	52,442	52,820	53,784	55,172	55,613	57,458
Forestry, fishing, and related activities........................	28,518	29,273	30,011	31,634	33,137	34,691	35,588
Mining..	70,605	68,541	69,165	71,032	69,121	68,091	70,475
Utilities..	100,698	101,453	101,262	105,902	105,707	105,738	109,278
Construction..	48,605	49,020	49,650	51,003	52,584	54,339	57,182
Manufacturing..	54,524	55,479	56,293	58,535	59,981	58,740	60,126
Durable goods manufacturing...................................	57,131	58,009	59,089	61,942	63,605	61,914	64,098
Nondurable goods manufacturing..............................	50,896	51,858	52,264	53,578	54,712	54,313	54,609
Wholesale trade...	72,279	72,585	73,645	75,536	78,168	78,724	81,411
Retail trade...	26,800	27,385	27,696	28,233	29,041	29,466	30,127
Transportation and warehousing.................................	47,770	49,705	51,128	52,041	52,004	51,807	53,341
Information..	81,828	84,352	88,031	92,735	97,572	99,388	100,649
Finance and insurance	78,472	83,272	83,606	86,107	89,737	90,627	95,093
Real estate and rental and leasing.............................	46,810	48,772	49,594	51,425	53,944	54,540	56,639
Professional, scientific, and technical services	96,133	97,705	98,127	99,143	100,973	102,208	104,474
Management of companies and enterprises.........................	107,476	112,233	112,749	114,626	121,816	118,025	125,683
Administrative and waste services..............................	37,812	38,664	38,575	39,273	40,563	41,355	43,100
Educational services...	38,190	38,447	38,935	39,260	39,432	40,035	40,317
Health care and social assistance..............................	45,826	46,640	47,041	48,040	48,964	49,618	51,001
Arts, entertainment, and recreation.............................	26,471	27,256	27,179	28,178	28,877	28,592	29,859
Accommodation and food services.............................	18,887	19,448	19,753	20,292	20,889	21,384	22,008
Other services, except public administration.................	35,616	36,248	36,894	37,793	39,155	40,056	41,424
Government and government enterprises.....................	54,848	55,337	55,400	56,820	58,119	59,023	60,441

Table VA-10. Employment Characteristics by Family Type

(Number, percent.)

Family type and labor force status	2015		2016		2017	
	Total	Families with own children under 18 years	Total	Families with own children under 18 years	Total	Families with own children under 18 years
All Families...	2,054,857	882,330	2,063,049	880,662	2,091,237	876,654
FAMILY TYPE AND LABOR FORCE STATUS						
Married-Couple Families..............................	1,549,808	620,930	1,557,536	620,079	1,588,086	629,664
Both husband and wife in labor force..........................	54.0	67.4	53.6	67.7	53.9	69.6
Husband in labor force, wife not in labor force............	22.1	27.5	21.7	26.6	21.2	25.7
Wife in labor force, husband not in labor force............	7.5	3.5	7.7	4.1	7.3	3.0
Both husband and wife not in labor force....................	15.7	1.3	16.3	1.2	16.8	1.3
Other Families	505,049	261,400	505,513	260,583	503,151	246,990
Female householder, no husband present.....................	73.2	76.5	73.1	75.8	72.9	75.5
In labor force...	53.2	64.9	52.4	62.8	52.4	64.3
Not in labor force	20.0	11.6	20.7	13.0	20.5	11.2
Male householder, no wife present.............................	26.8	23.5	26.9	24.2	27.1	24.5
In labor force...	21.6	21.6	21.3	22.4	21.2	22.9
Not in labor force	5.2	1.9	5.6	1.8	5.9	1.5

Table VA-11. School Enrollment and Educational Attainment, 2017

(Number, percent.)

Item	State	U.S.
Enrollment		
Total population 3 years and over, enrolled in school	2,138,155	81,273,337
Enrolled in nursery school or preschool (percent)...	5.8	6.0
Enrolled in kindergarten (percent)...	4.9	4.9
Enrolled in elementary school, grades 1-8 (percent)..	38.9	40.6
Enrolled in high school, grades 9-12 (percent)...	20.2	21.1
Enrolled in college or graduate school (percent)...	30.2	27.4
Attainment		
Total population 25 years and over	5,779,221	221,250,083
Less than ninth grade (percent)..	4.2	5.1
9th to 12th grade, no diploma (percent)..	6.1	6.9
High school graduate, including equivalency (percent).....................................	24.2	27.1
Some college, no degree (percent)	19.0	20.4
Associate's degree (percent)...	7.9	8.5
Bachelor's degree (percent)...	22.0	19.7
Graduate or professional degree (percent)...	16.7	12.3
High school graduate or higher (percent)..	89.7	88.0
Bachelor's degree or higher (percent)...	38.7	32.0

Table VA-12. Public School Characteristics and Educational Indicators

(Number, percent; data derived from National Center of Education Statistics.)

Item	State	U.S.
Public Elementary and Secondary Schools		
Number of operational school districts, 2016-17...	222	18,377
Number of operational schools, 2016-17..	2,134	98,330
Percent charter schools...	0.4	7.1
Total public school enrollment, 2016-17...	1,287,026	50,587,859
Percent charter school enrollment...	0.1	6.0
Student-teacher ratio, Fall 2015...	14.2	16.0
Expenditures per student (dollars), 2015-16..	11,435	11,841
Four-year adjusted cohort graduation rate (ACGR)[1]	86.9	84.6
Students eligible for free or reduced-price lunch (percent), 2015-16......................	41.2	52.1
English language learners (percent), Fall 2016...	7.8	9.6
Students age 3 to 21 served under IDEA, part B (percent), 2017-18	13.4	13.7
Public Schools by Type, 2016-17		Percent of state public schools
Total number of schools...	2,134	100.0
Special education..	53	2.5
Vocational education..	89	4.2
Alternative education..	125	5.9

[1] Adjusted Cohort Graduation Rates (ACGR) differ from Averaged Freshmen Graduation Rates (AFGR).

Table VA-13. Reported Voting and Registration of the Voting-Age Population, November 2018

(Numbers in thousands, percent.)

Item	Total population	Total citizen population	Registered			Voted		
			Total registered	Percent registered (total population)	Percent registered (total citizen population)	Total voted	Percent voted (total population)	Percent voted (total citizen population)
U.S. Total	249,748	228,832	153,066	61.3	66.9	122,281	49.0	53.4
State Total.....................	6,386	5,773	4,159	65.1	72.0	3,319	52.0	57.5
Sex								
Male	3,051	2,724	1,958	64.2	71.9	1,578	51.7	57.9
Female	3,335	3,049	2,201	66.0	72.2	1,742	52.2	57.1
Race								
White alone............	4,496	4,094	3,065	68.2	74.9	2,412	53.7	58.9
White, non-Hispanic alone.......................	3,874	3,808	2,924	75.5	76.8	2,314	59.7	60.8
Black alone....................	1,198	1,130	754	63.0	66.8	637	53.2	56.4
Asian alone	510	368	226	44.3	61.4	169	33.2	46.0
Hispanic (of any race)......	669	324	159	23.8	49.0	112	16.8	34.6
White alone or in combination	4,617	4,215	3,156	68.4	74.9	2,490	53.9	59.1
Black alone or in combination...................	1,258	1,190	786	62.5	66.1	664	52.8	55.8
Asian alone or in combination...............	587	445	286	48.7	64.3	224	38.2	50.4
Age								
18 to 24 years	618	558	313	50.6	56.1	221	35.8	39.7
25 to 34 years	1,191	1,023	674	56.6	65.9	514	43.1	50.2
35 to 44 years	1,063	874	605	56.9	69.2	411	38.6	47.0
45 to 64 years	2,223	2,070	1,539	69.2	74.3	1,298	58.4	62.7
65 years and over	1,291	1,249	1,029	79.7	82.4	875	67.8	70.1

Table VA-14. Crime

(Number, rate per 100,000. Data are derived from the FBI Uniform Crime Reports.)

Item	State			U.S.		
	2016	2017	Percent change	2016	2017	Percent change
TOTAL POPULATION[1]	8,414,380	8,470,020	0.7	323,405,935	325,719,178	0.7
VIOLENT CRIME						
Number..........	18,495	17,632	-4.7	1,285,606	1,283,220	-0.2
Rate	219.8	208.2	-5.3	397.5	394.0	-0.9
Murder and Nonnegligent Manslaughter						
Number..........	482	453	-6.0	17,413	17,284	-0.7
Rate	5.7	5.3	-6.6	5.4	5.3	-1.4
Rape[2]						
Number..........	2,830	2,862	1.1	132,414	135,755	2.5
Rate	33.6	33.8	0.5	40.9	41.7	1.8
Robbery						
Number..........	4,826	4,332	-10.2	332,797	319,356	-4.0
Rate	57.4	51.1	-10.8	102.9	98.0	-4.7
Aggravated Assault						
Number..........	10,357	9,985	-3.6	802,982	810,825	1.0
Rate	123.1	117.9	-4.2	248.3	248.9	0.3
PROPERTY CRIME						
Number..........	157,292	151,855	-3.5	7,928,530	7,694,086	-3.0
Rate	1,869.3	1,792.9	-4.1	2,451.6	2,362.2	-3.6
Burglary						
Number..........	20,159	18,468	-8.4	1,516,405	1,401,840	-7.6
Rate	239.6	218.0	-9.0	468.9	430.4	-8.2
Larceny-Theft						
Number..........	127,285	123,215	-3.2	5,644,835	5,519,107	-2.2
Rate	1,512.7	1,454.7	-3.8	1,745.4	1,694.4	-2.9
Motor Vehicle Theft						
Number..........	9,848	10,172	3.3	767,290	773,139	0.8
Rate	117.0	120.1	2.6	237.3	237.4	-

NOTE: Although arson data are included in the trend and clearance tables, sufficient data are not available to estimate totals for this offense. Therefore, no arson data are published in this table.
- = Zero or rounds to zero.
[1] Population figures are U.S. Census Bureau provisional estimates as of July 1, 2017.
[2] The figures shown in the rape (revised definition) column were estimated using the revised Uniform Crime Reporting (UCR) definition of rape.

Table VA-15. State Government Finances, 2017

(Dollar amounts in thousands, percent distribution.)

Item	Dollars	Percent distribution
Total Revenue	61,398,238	100.0
General revenue	47,186,364	76.9
Intergovernmental revenue	10,699,877	17.4
Taxes	22,213,025	36.2
General sales	3,970,133	6.5
Selective sales	2,945,964	4.8
License taxes	856,649	1.4
Individual income tax	13,052,887	21.3
Corporate income tax	826,961	1.3
Other taxes	560,431	0.9
Current charges	10,188,344	16.6
Miscellaneous general revenue	4,085,118	6.7
Utility revenue	0	-
Liquor stores revenue	779,038	1.3
Insurance trust revenue[1]	13,432,836	21.9
Total Expenditure	53,436,948	100.0
Intergovernmental expenditure	11,927,574	22.3
Direct expenditure	41,509,374	77.7
Current operation	30,985,866	58.0
Capital outlay	3,231,529	6.0
Insurance benefits and repayments	5,008,883	9.4
Assistance and subsidies	1,168,612	2.2
Interest on debt	1,114,484	2.1
Exhibit: Salaries and wages	7,751,506	14.5
Total Expenditure	53,436,948	100.0
General expenditure	47,653,847	89.2
Intergovernmental expenditure	11,927,574	22.3
Direct expenditure	35,726,273	66.9
General expenditure, by function:		
Education	16,598,849	31.1
Public welfare	11,120,056	20.8
Hospitals	4,954,417	9.3
Health	1,547,918	2.9
Highways	4,837,855	9.1
Police protection	670,451	1.3
Correction	1,538,611	2.9
Natural resources	315,847	0.6
Parks and recreation	165,607	0.3
Governmental administration	1,467,779	2.7
Interest on general debt	1,114,484	2.1
Other and unallocable	3,321,973	6.2
Utility expenditure	151,169	0.2
Liquor stores expenditure	623,049	1.2
Insurance trust expenditure	5,008,883	9.4
Debt at End of Fiscal Year	27,825,929	X
Cash and Security Holdings	103,445,108	X

X = Not applicable.
- = Zero or rounds to zero.
[1] Within insurance trust revenue, net earnings of state retirement systems is a calculated statistic (the item code in the data file is X08), and thus can be positive or negative. Net earnings is the sum of earnings on investments plus gains on investments minus losses on investments. The change made in 2002 for asset valuation from book to market value in accordance with Statement 34 of the Governmental Accounting Standards Board is reflected in the calculated statistics.

Table VA-16. State Government Tax Collections, 2018

(Dollars in thousands, percent.)

Item	Dollars	Percent distribution
Total Taxes	23,489,398	100.0
Property taxes	31,890	0.1
Sales and gross receipts	7,087,195	30.2
General sales and gross receipts	4,076,636	17.4
Selective sales and gross receipts	3,010,559	12.8
Alcoholic beverages	231,250	1.0
Amusements	84	-
Insurance premiums	516,743	2.2
Motor fuels	1,031,034	4.4
Pari-mutuels	X	-
Public utilities	116,584	0.5
Tobacco products	160,383	0.7
Other selective sales	954,481	4.1
Licenses	878,751	3.7
Alcoholic beverages	14,591	0.1
Amusements	107	-
Corporations in general	64,102	0.3
Hunting and fishing	29,393	0.1
Motor vehicle	492,825	2.1
Motor vehicle operators	41,288	0.2
Public utilities	X	-
Occupation and business, NEC	231,791	1.0
Other licenses	4,654	-
Income taxes	14,967,663	63.7
Individual income	14,105,766	60.1
Corporation net income	861,897	3.7
Other taxes	523,899	2.2
Death and gift	932	-
Documentary and stock transfer	386,598	1.6
Severance	2,695	-
Taxes, NEC	133,674	0.6

- = Zero or rounds to zero.

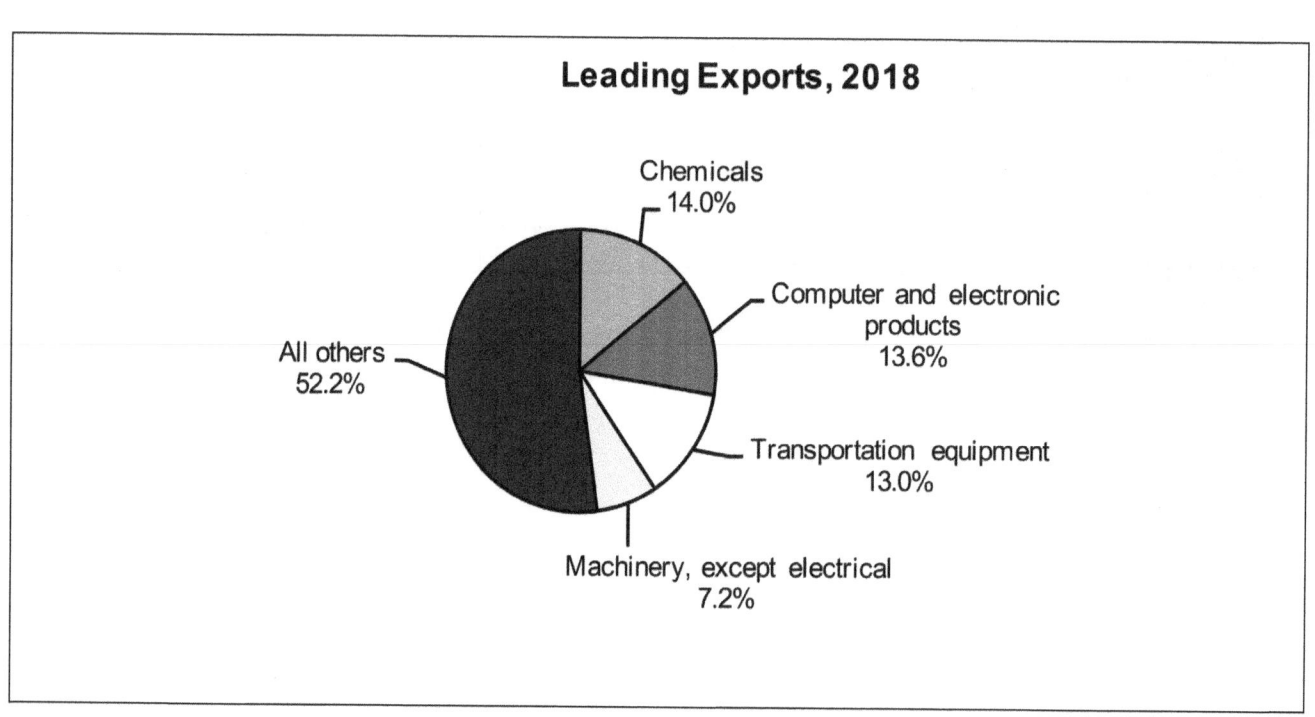

Leading Exports, 2018

Chemicals 14.0%

Computer and electronic products 13.6%

Transportation equipment 13.0%

Machinery, except electrical 7.2%

All others 52.2%

WASHINGTON

Facts and Figures

Location: Northwestern United States; bordered on the N by Canada (British Columbia), on the E by Idaho, on the S by Oregon, and on the W by the Pacific Ocean

Area: 71,300 sq. mi. (184,665 sq. km.); rank—18th

Population: 7,535,591 (2018 est.); rank—13th

Principal Cities: capital—Olympia; largest—Seattle

Statehood: November 11, 1889; 42nd state

U.S. Congress: 2 senators, 10 representatives

State Motto: *Alki* ("By and by")

State Song: "Washington, My Home"

State Nickname: The Evergreen State

Abbreviations: WA; Wash.

State Symbols: flower—coast rhododendron; tree—Western hemlock; bird—willow goldfinch

At a Glance

- With an increase in population of 12.1 percent, Washington ranked 9th among the states in growth from 2010 to 2018.

- Washington's median household income in 2017 was $70,979, and 11.0 percent of the population lived below the poverty level.

- In 2017, 6.1 percent of Washingtonians did not have health insurance, compared to 8.7 percent of the total U.S. population.

- Washington had the 6th highest property crime rate in the country in 2017 (3,173.6 incidences per 100,000 population).

- Approximately 35.5 percent of Washingtonians had a bachelor's degree or more in 2017, compared to 32.0 percent of all U.S. residents.

Table WA-1. Population by Age, Sex, Race, and Hispanic Origin

(Number, percent, except where noted.)

Sex, age, race, and Hispanic origin	2000	2010	2018 [1]	Percent change, 2010–2018
Total population...	5,894,121	6,724,540	7,535,591	12.1
Percent of total U.S. population	2.1	2.2	2.3	X
Sex				
Male..	2,934,300	3,349,707	3,769,911	12.5
Female	2,959,821	3,374,833	3,765,680	11.6
Age				
Under 5 years..	394,306	439,657	462,701	5.2
5 to 19 years...	1,288,713	1,330,238	1,376,767	3.5
20 to 64 years...	3,548,954	4,126,968	4,531,891	9.8
65 years and over	662,148	827,677	1,164,232	40.7
Median age (years)	35.9	37.3	37.7	1.1
Race and Hispanic origin				
One race				
White	4,821,823	5,535,262	5,944,924	7.4
Black	190,267	252,333	322,826	27.9
American Indian and Alaska Native	93,301	122,649	144,450	17.8
Asian	322,335	491,685	703,455	43.1
Native Hawaiian or Other Pacific Islander	23,953	43,505	59,001	35.6
Two or more races	213,519	279,106	360,935	29.3
Hispanic (of any race)..	441,509	776,539	970,358	25.0

X = Not applicable.
[1] Population figures for 2018 are July 1 estimates. The 2010 estimates are taken from the 2010 Census.

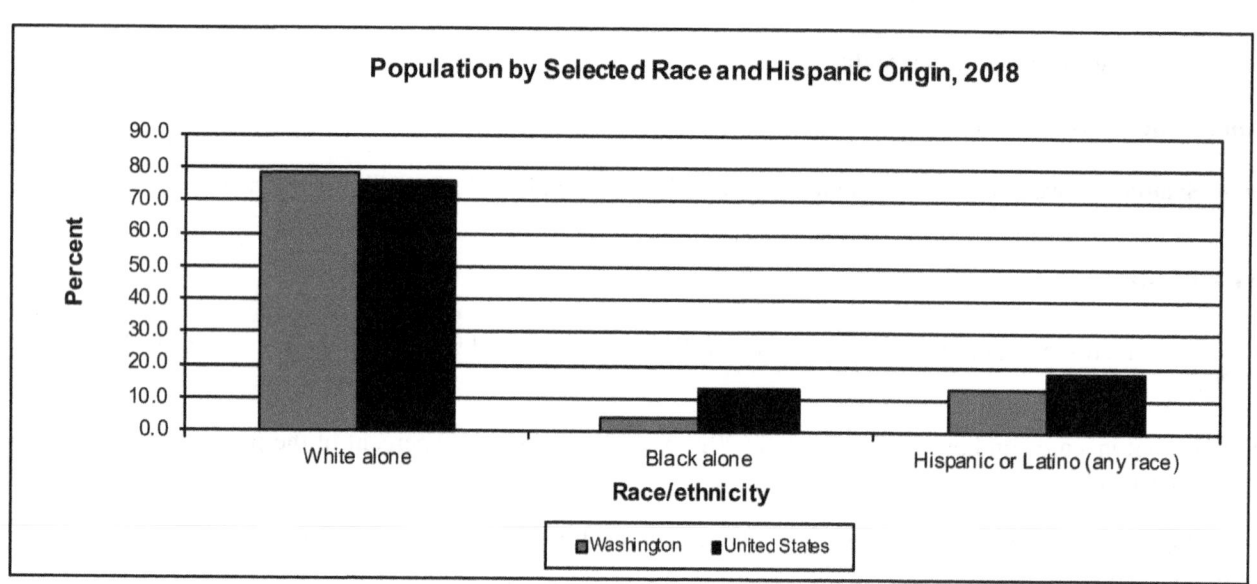

Table WA-2. Marital Status

(Number, percent distribution.)

Sex, age, race, and Hispanic origin	2000	2010	2017
Males, 15 Years and Over	2,287,431	2,686,801	2,996,661
Never married	29.8	33.8	34.9
Now married, except separated..	56.6	52.0	51.3
Separated..	1.4	1.6	1.2
Widowed..	2.1	2.1	2.2
Divorced..	10.1	10.5	10.4
Females, 15 Years and Over	2,352,091	2,746,158	3,032,141
Never married	22.8	26.4	27.3
Now married, except separated..	54.1	50.6	50.0
Separated..	1.8	2.1	1.7
Widowed..	8.6	7.8	7.6
Divorced..	12.7	13.2	13.4

Table WA-3. Households and Housing Characteristics

(Number, percent, dollars.)

Item	2000	2010	2017	Average annual percent change, 2010–2017
Total Households..	2,271,398	2,606,863	2,840,377	1.3
Family households	1,499,127	1,681,386	1,833,793	1.3
Married-couple family	1,181,995	1,297,240	1,418,536	1.3
Other family	317,132	384,146	415,257	1.2
Male householder, no wife present............................	92,514	114,187	135,946	2.7
Female householder, no husband present...................	224,618	269,959	279,311	0.5
Nonfamily households	772,271	925,477	1,006,584	1.3
Householder living alone	594,325	731,452	754,085	0.4
Householder not living alone	117,946	194,025	252,499	4.3
Housing Characteristics				
Total housing units..	2,451,075	2,888,594	3,103,263	1.1
Occupied housing units	2,271,398	2,606,863	2,840,377	1.3
Owner occupied	1,467,009	1,644,939	1,783,549	1.2
Renter occupied	804,389	961,924	1,056,828	1.4
Average household size..	2.53	2.53	2.56	0.2
Financial Characteristics				
Median gross rent of renter-occupied housing	663	908	1,216	4.8
Median monthly owner costs for housing units with a mortgage	1,268	1,736	1,806	0.6
Median value of owner-occupied housing units	168,300	271,800	339,000	3.5

Table WA-4. Migration, Origin, and Language

(Number, percent.)

Characteristic	State 2016	State 2017	State Percent change	U.S. 2016	U.S. 2017	U.S. Percent change
Residence 1 Year Ago						
Population 1 year and over	7,202,119	7,318,811	1.6	319,361,956	321,994,428	0.8
Same house	82.3	82.2	X	85.4	85.7	X
Different house in the U.S.	16.9	16.9	X	13.9	13.6	X
Same county...	10.2	10.0	X	8.3	8.1	X
Different county	6.7	7.0	X	5.6	5.6	X
Same state	3.1	3.4	X	3.2	3.3	X
Different state	3.6	3.6	X	2.4	2.3	X
Abroad	0.9	0.9	X	0.7	0.7	X
Place of Birth						
Native born	6,267,606	6,345,590	1.2	279,388,170	281,193,323	0.6
Male	50.3	50.2	X	49.3	49.4	X
Female	49.7	49.8	X	50.7	50.6	X
Foreign born	1,020,394	1,060,153	3.9	43,739,345	44,525,855	1.8
Male	47.6	48.1	X	48.5	48.4	X
Female	52.4	51.9	X	51.5	51.6	X
Foreign born; naturalized U.S. citizen............................	482,135	507,513	5.3	21,238,372	21,948,732	3.3
Male	44.9	44.6	X	45.9	45.9	X
Female	55.1	55.4	X	54.1	54.1	X
Foreign born; not a U.S. citizen....................................	538,259	552,640	2.7	22,500,973	22,577,123	0.3
Male	50.0	51.4	X	51.0	50.8	X
Female	50.0	48.6	X	49.0	49.2	X
Entered 2010 or later	20.9	24.5	X	18.6	21.3	X
Entered 2000 to 2009	28.6	27.8	X	26.7	25.7	X
Entered before 2000..	50.5	47.7	X	54.7	53.0	X
World Region of Birth, Foreign						
Foreign-born population, excluding population born at sea	1,020,359	1,060,153	3.9	43,738,901	44,525,458	1.8
Europe	14.4	14.5	X	10.9	10.8	X
Asia	42.5	44.5	X	30.8	31.2	X
Africa	6.2	6.0	X	4.9	5.1	X
Oceania	2.1	1.3	X	0.6	0.6	X
Latin America	30.2	29.5	X	51.0	50.4	X
North America	4.6	4.3	X	1.8	1.8	X
Language Spoken at Home and Ability to Speak English						
Population 5 years and over...	6,838,056	6,950,728	1.6	303,328,961	305,924,019	0.9
English only	80.7	80.4	X	78.4	78.2	X
Language other than English......................................	19.3	19.6	X	21.6	21.8	X
Speaks English less than "very well"........................	7.7	7.7	X	8.6	8.5	X

NA = Not available.
X = Not applicable.
- = Zero or rounds to zero.

Table WA-5. Median Income and Poverty Status, 2017

(Number, percent, except as noted.)

Characteristic	State		U.S.	
	Number	Percent	Number	Percent
Median Income				
Households (dollars)..	70,979	X	60,336	X
Families (dollars)	84,594	X	73,891	X
Below Poverty Level (All People)	802,159	11.0	42,583,651	13.4
Sex				
Male	370,838	10.2	19,004,547	12.2
Female	431,321	11.8	23,579,104	14.5
Age				
Under 18 years..	232,452	14.3	13,353,202	18.4
Related children under 18 years........................	222,667	13.8	13,053,472	18.1
18 to 64 years...	481,468	10.6	24,648,677	12.6
65 years and over	88,239	8.0	4,581,772	9.3

X = Not applicable.

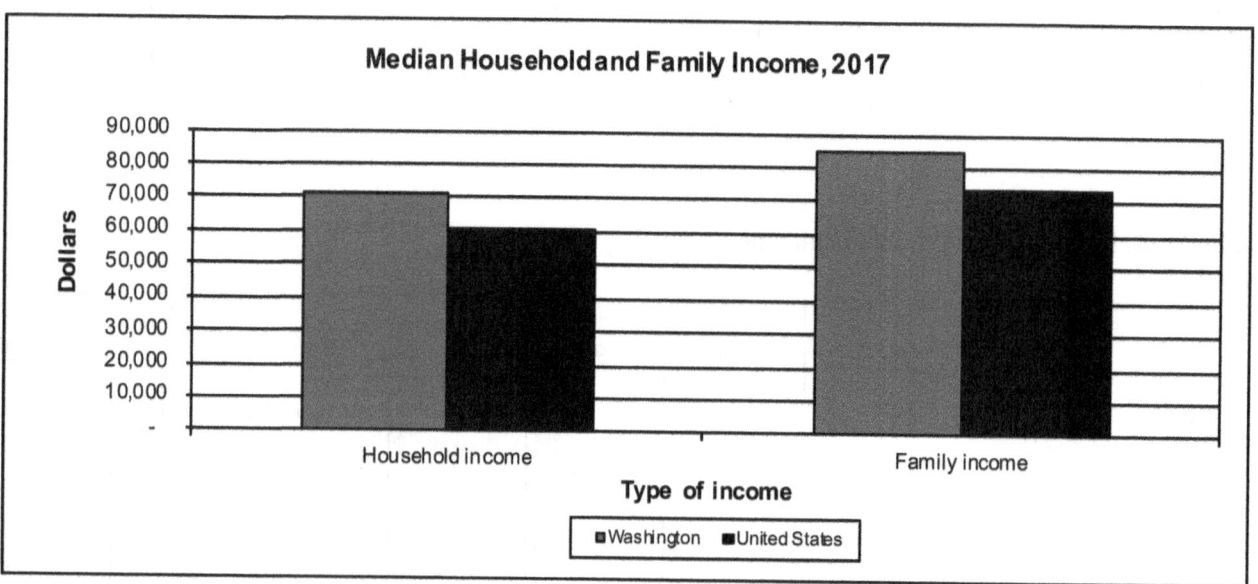

Table WA-6. Health Insurance Coverage Status for the Civilian Noninstitutionalized Population and Children Under 18 Years of Age

(Number, percent.)

Item	2009	2010	2011	2012	2013	2014	2015	2016	2017
Civilian Noninstitutionalized Population	6,546,149	6,638,081	6,716,822	6,793,078	6,864,149	6,954,806	7,066,812	7,184,110	7,299,812
Covered by Private or Public Insurance									
Number..	5,668,541	5,692,492	5,764,192	5,848,307	5,904,158	6,312,152	6,598,845	6,756,018	6,853,706
Percent..	86.6	85.8	85.8	86.1	86.0	90.8	93.4	94.0	93.9
Uninsured									
Number..	877,608	945,589	952,630	944,771	959,991	642,654	467,967	428,092	446,106
Percent..	13.4	14.2	14.2	13.9	14.0	9.2	6.6	6.0	6.1
Percent in the U.S. not covered...........................	15.1	15.5	15.1	14.8	14.5	11.7	9.4	8.6	8.7
Children Under 18 Years of Age[1]	1,569,540	1,582,936	1,578,179	1,583,595	1,594,503	1,601,029	1,610,562	1,627,304	1,739,832
Covered by Private or Public Insurance									
Number..	1,462,000	1,481,322	1,480,971	1,492,516	1,499,708	1,526,102	1,568,043	1,585,868	1,693,734
Percent..	93.1	93.6	93.8	94.2	94.1	95.3	97.4	97.5	97.4
Uninsured									
Number..	107,540	101,614	97,208	91,079	94,795	74,927	42,519	41,436	46,098
Percent..	6.9	6.4	6.2	5.8	5.9	4.7	2.6	2.5	2.6
Percent in the U.S. not covered...........................	8.6	8.0	7.5	7.2	7.1	6.0	4.8	4.5	5.0

[1] 2017 data is for individuals under 19 years of age.

Table WA-7. Employment Status by Demographic Group, 2018

(Numbers in thousands, percent.)

Characteristic	Civilian noninstitutional population	Civilian labor force		Employed		Unemployed	
		Number	Percent of population	Number	Percent of population	Number	Percent of population
Total...............................	5,937	3,779	63.6	3,611	60.8	168	4.4
Sex							
Male....................................	2,928	2,075	70.9	1,977	67.5	98	4.7
Female.................................	3,009	1,704	56.6	1,634	54.3	69	4.1
Race, Sex, and Hispanic Origin							
White...................................	4,758	2,997	63.0	2,868	60.3	129	4.3
Male....................................	2,354	1,661	70.5	1,585	67.3	75	4.5
Female.................................	2,403	1,336	55.6	1,282	53.4	54	4.0
Black or African American............	224	145	64.7	139	62.0	6	4.3
Male....................................	118	86	73.3	83	71.0	3	3.3
Female.................................	NA	NA	NA	NA	NA	NA	NA
Hispanic or Latino ethnicity[1]........	749	517	69.1	481	64.2	36	7.0
Male....................................	380	299	78.6	279	73.5	19	6.5
Female.................................	369	218	59.2	202	54.7	17	7.7
Age							
16 to 19 years.........................	380	128	33.7	108	28.5	20	15.3
20 to 24 years.........................	473	325	68.7	294	62.1	31	9.6
25 to 34 years.........................	1,084	906	83.5	867	79.9	39	4.3
35 to 44 years.........................	972	791	81.4	766	78.8	26	3.2
45 to 54 years.........................	967	790	81.8	767	79.3	23	2.9
55 to 64 years.........................	997	655	65.7	634	63.6	21	3.2
65 years and over.....................	1,065	184	17.3	177	16.6	8	4.3

NOTE: Data in Table 7 are from the Current Population Survey (CPS) and do not match the estimates in Table 8. See notes and definitions for further information.
[1] May be of any race.

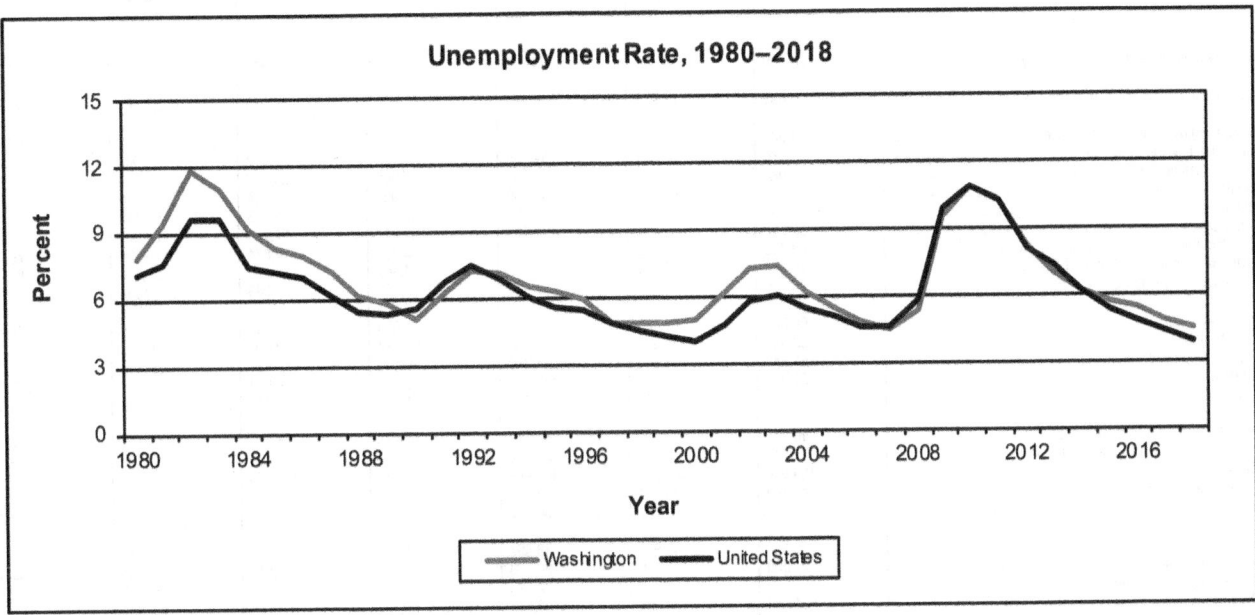

Table WA-8. Employment Status of the Civilian Noninstitutional Population Age 16 Years and Over

(Number, percent.)

Year	Civilian labor force	Civilian participation rate	Employed	Unemployed	Unemployment rate
2010..	3,511,326	67.0	3,160,544	350,782	10.0
2011..	3,461,428	65.2	3,140,190	321,238	9.3
2012..	3,471,282	64.6	3,189,271	282,011	8.1
2013..	3,463,869	63.7	3,219,842	244,027	7.0
2014..	3,489,666	63.3	3,275,753	213,913	6.1
2015..	3,545,904	63.2	3,345,496	200,408	5.7
2016..	3,635,200	63.6	3,444,126	191,074	5.3
2017..	3,724,722	63.9	3,547,430	177,292	4.8
2018..	3,793,095	63.9	3,622,299	170,796	4.5

Table WA-9. Employment and Average Wages by Industry

(Estimates are based on the 2012 *North American Industry Classification System* [NAICS].)

Industry	2011	2012	2013	2014	2015	2016	2017
	Number of jobs						
Wage and Salary Employment by Industry......................	3,028,900	3,129,397	3,196,913	3,281,417	3,361,935	3,448,656	3,523,477
Farm Wage and Salary Employment.............................	47,194	56,396	53,313	53,511	51,723	52,493	53,491
Nonfarm Wage and Salary Employment..........................	2,981,706	3,073,001	3,143,600	3,227,906	3,310,212	3,396,163	3,469,986
Private wage and salary employment..............................	2,356,257	2,452,382	2,524,370	2,606,842	2,680,960	2,756,713	2,821,787
Forestry, fishing, and related activities..........................	28,222	29,991	30,682	31,300	32,341	31,742	31,891
Mining..	2,203	2,157	2,162	2,245	2,400	2,435	2,562
Utilities..	4,869	4,913	4,823	4,838	4,943	4,646	4,823
Construction..	139,529	142,641	153,034	164,788	179,299	191,759	204,557
Manufacturing..	269,040	280,468	286,568	288,634	291,161	289,695	283,889
Durable goods manufacturing..............................	193,073	204,353	209,185	209,565	211,198	207,338	200,185
Nondurable goods manufacturing.........................	75,967	76,115	77,383	79,069	79,963	82,357	83,704
Wholesale trade	122,102	124,382	127,601	130,909	133,520	133,481	134,739
Retail trade...	314,823	321,787	331,791	345,122	358,633	372,116	387,173
Transportation and warehousing...............................	86,612	88,927	89,979	94,264	98,304	100,601	103,145
Information..	104,466	105,441	106,435	109,682	114,614	120,859	126,574
Finance and insurance	93,610	94,450	96,336	98,130	99,063	99,959	102,082
Real estate and rental and leasing............................	45,403	45,710	47,171	48,215	50,404	51,412	53,315
Professional, scientific, and technical services	168,888	172,892	176,836	184,546	190,534	197,459	202,313
Management of companies and enterprises....................	33,264	36,300	38,894	39,992	41,939	43,177	44,300
Administrative and waste services............................	139,641	142,768	147,472	152,139	160,239	164,876	170,082
Educational services...	51,637	52,466	53,694	55,123	55,986	55,722	56,724
Health care and social assistance............................	336,814	379,915	392,978	402,147	398,408	411,309	419,621
Arts, entertainment, and recreation..........................	45,967	46,313	46,917	48,749	48,645	51,180	52,754
Accommodation and food services............................	226,343	232,609	242,201	252,062	264,141	274,954	280,824
Other services, except public administration..................	142,824	148,252	148,796	153,957	156,386	159,331	160,419
Government and government enterprises	625,449	620,619	619,230	621,064	629,252	639,450	648,199
	Dollars						
Average Wages and Salaries by Industry	51,099	52,433	53,347	55,329	56,997	58,950	61,893
Average Farm Wages and Salaries	23,691	26,611	28,769	27,985	29,479	32,384	27,430
Average Nonfarm Wages and Salaries	51,533	52,907	53,763	55,783	57,427	59,361	62,424
Average private wages and salaries.............................	51,776	53,274	54,106	56,229	57,892	59,906	63,159
Forestry, fishing, and related activities.......................	33,928	35,248	34,999	35,368	35,427	37,589	38,643
Mining..	59,749	60,992	63,150	63,998	68,064	67,940	71,680
Utilities..	81,832	83,770	85,780	87,775	93,335	91,146	94,130
Construction	52,852	53,661	54,402	55,717	57,726	59,871	62,232
Manufacturing...	68,425	69,795	71,728	75,435	74,874	75,007	76,408
Durable goods manufacturing..............................	75,730	76,901	79,332	84,307	83,290	83,516	85,322
Nondurable goods manufacturing.........................	49,859	50,718	51,173	51,921	52,645	53,584	55,091
Wholesale trade	66,800	69,468	69,078	71,040	73,204	74,439	77,499
Retail trade...	32,563	34,569	36,200	38,844	42,090	46,320	52,829
Transportation and warehousing...............................	51,843	53,503	54,340	55,148	56,551	58,115	60,274
Information..	121,685	135,531	137,008	150,237	150,574	159,038	172,239
Finance and insurance	73,178	77,449	79,405	81,936	85,411	87,599	90,555
Real estate and rental and leasing............................	40,355	42,762	44,177	46,141	48,009	50,193	52,468
Professional, scientific, and technical services	77,900	80,677	82,596	85,691	86,061	89,155	92,941
Management of companies and enterprises....................	104,036	107,213	106,965	109,039	108,964	109,700	112,746
Administrative and waste services............................	43,184	43,621	43,538	44,639	46,249	47,357	48,797
Educational services...	28,924	29,727	30,579	30,918	31,780	31,883	32,222
Health care and social assistance............................	46,542	43,929	43,897	44,888	48,251	49,419	51,378
Arts, entertainment, and recreation..........................	27,550	27,856	30,573	32,607	33,513	33,826	35,023
Accommodation and food services............................	21,136	22,730	22,723	23,035	23,739	24,570	26,874
Other services, except public administration..................	31,982	32,658	33,818	33,679	34,756	36,634	38,004
Government and government enterprises........................	50,617	51,455	52,366	53,909	55,447	57,010	59,222

Table WA-10. Employment Characteristics by Family Type

(Number, percent.)

Family type and labor force status	2015		2016		2017	
	Total	Families with own children under 18 years	Total	Families with own children under 18 years	Total	Families with own children under 18 years
All Families...	1,760,593	760,914	1,784,043	761,244	1,833,793	776,767
FAMILY TYPE AND LABOR FORCE STATUS						
Married-Couple Families............................	1,363,817	539,460	1,388,872	552,273	1,418,536	562,987
Both husband and wife in labor force.................	50.0	61.8	49.6	61.6	50.6	63.6
Husband in labor force, wife not in labor force	23.2	31.9	23.2	31.5	22.3	30.6
Wife in labor force, husband not in labor force	7.7	4.3	8.0	4.7	7.3	3.7
Both husband and wife not in labor force..................	18.0	1.6	17.9	1.8	18.4	1.6
Other Families..	396,776	221,454	395,171	208,971	415,257	213,780
Female householder, no husband present...............	69.1	70.6	68.4	69.0	67.3	69.1
In labor force..	48.7	57.0	47.8	56.1	48.5	57.9
Not in labor force	20.4	13.7	20.5	12.9	18.8	11.2
Male householder, no wife present.......................	30.9	29.4	31.6	31.0	32.7	30.9
In labor force..	24.8	26.9	25.8	28.1	25.5	27.8
Not in labor force	6.1	2.5	5.8	2.9	7.2	3.0

Table WA-11. School Enrollment and Educational Attainment, 2017

(Number, percent.)

Item	State	U.S.
Enrollment		
Total population 3 years and over, enrolled in school	1,750,825	81,273,337
Enrolled in nursery school or preschool (percent)	6.3	6.0
Enrolled in kindergarten (percent)..	5.3	4.9
Enrolled in elementary school, grades 1-8 (percent).......................	41.6	40.6
Enrolled in high school, grades 9-12 (percent)...........................	20.8	21.1
Enrolled in college or graduate school (percent)........................	25.9	27.4
Attainment		
Total population 25 years and over	5,101,968	221,250,083
Less than ninth grade (percent)	3.7	5.1
9th to 12th grade, no diploma (percent)	5.0	6.9
High school graduate, including equivalency (percent).....................	22.1	27.1
Some college, no degree (percent)	23.6	20.4
Associate's degree (percent)	10.1	8.5
Bachelor's degree (percent)	22.2	19.7
Graduate or professional degree (percent)...............................	13.3	12.3
High school graduate or higher (percent)	91.3	88.0
Bachelor's degree or higher (percent)	35.5	32.0

Table WA-12. Public School Characteristics and Educational Indicators

(Number, percent; data derived from National Center of Education Statistics.)

Item	State	U.S.
Public Elementary and Secondary Schools		
Number of operational school districts, 2016-17..........................	332	18,377
Number of operational schools, 2016-17.................................	2,436	98,330
Percent charter schools	0.3	7.1
Total public school enrollment, 2016-17.................................	1,101,711	50,587,859
Percent charter school enrollment	0.2	6.0
Student-teacher ratio, Fall 2015..	18.8	16.0
Expenditures per student (dollars), 2015-16.............................	11,484	11,841
Four-year adjusted cohort graduation rate (ACGR)[1]	79.4	84.6
Students eligible for free or reduced-price lunch (percent), 2015-16.......	45.4	52.1
English language learners (percent), Fall 2016..........................	11.1	9.6
Students age 3 to 21 served under IDEA, part B (percent), 2017-18	12.9	13.7
Public Schools by Type, 2016-17		Percent of state public schools
Total number of schools...	2,436	100.0
Special education..	95	3.9
Vocational education...	19	0.8
Alternative education..	314	12.9

[1] Adjusted Cohort Graduation Rates (ACGR) differ from Averaged Freshmen Graduation Rates (AFGR).

Table WA-13. Reported Voting and Registration of the Voting-Age Population, November 2018

(Numbers in thousands, percent.)

Item	Total population	Total citizen population	Registered			Voted		
			Total registered	Percent registered (total population)	Percent registered (total citizen population)	Total voted	Percent voted (total population)	Percent voted (total citizen population)
U.S. Total	249,748	228,832	153,066	61.3	66.9	122,281	49.0	53.4
State Total.........................	5,775	5,228	3,852	66.7	73.7	3,234	56.0	61.9
Sex								
Male	2,869	2,590	1,861	64.9	71.9	1,541	53.7	59.5
Female	2,906	2,638	1,991	68.5	75.5	1,693	58.2	64.2
Race								
White alone...............	4,663	4,314	3,219	69.0	74.6	2,736	58.7	63.4
White, non-Hispanic alone	3,995	3,905	2,983	74.7	76.4	2,558	64.0	65.5
Black alone...............	232	232	155	66.8	66.8	103	44.2	44.2
Asian alone	530	356	262	49.4	73.4	224	42.2	62.8
Hispanic (of any race)	736	468	267	36.3	57.2	204	27.8	43.7
White alone or in combination	4,792	4,434	3,321	69.3	74.9	2,816	58.8	63.5
Black alone or in combination	255	255	175	68.4	68.4	117	45.7	45.7
Asian alone or in combination.........	559	386	287	51.4	74.5	237	42.4	61.6
Age								
18 to 24 years	624	577	315	50.4	54.5	201	32.2	34.8
25 to 34 years	1,067	914	637	59.7	69.7	455	42.6	49.8
35 to 44 years	1,034	897	672	65.0	74.8	591	57.1	65.8
45 to 64 years	1,972	1,798	1,365	69.2	75.9	1,185	60.1	65.9
65 years and over	1,079	1,041	864	80.1	83.0	802	74.3	77.0

Table WA-14. Crime

(Number, rate per 100,000. Data are derived from the FBI Uniform Crime Reports.)

Item	State			U.S.		
	2016	2017	Percent change	2016	2017	Percent change
TOTAL POPULATION[1]	7,280,934	7,405,743	1.7	323,405,935	325,719,178	0.7
VIOLENT CRIME						
Number........................	22,101	22,548	2.0	1,285,606	1,283,220	-0.2
Rate	303.5	304.5	0.3	397.5	394.0	-0.9
Murder and Nonnegligent Manslaughter						
Number........................	195	230	17.9	17,413	17,284	-0.7
Rate	2.7	3.1	16.0	5.4	5.3	-1.4
Rape[2]						
Number........................	3,133	3,255	3.9	132,414	135,755	2.5
Rate	43.0	44.0	2.1	40.9	41.7	1.8
Robbery						
Number........................	5,649	5,390	-4.6	332,797	319,356	-4.0
Rate	77.6	72.8	-6.2	102.9	98.0	-4.7
Aggravated Assault						
Number........................	13,124	13,673	4.2	802,982	810,825	1.0
Rate	180.3	184.6	2.4	248.3	248.9	0.3
PROPERTY CRIME						
Number........................	254,994	235,027	-7.8	7,928,530	7,694,086	-3.0
Rate	3,502.2	3,173.6	-9.4	2,451.6	2,362.2	-3.6
Burglary						
Number........................	49,249	43,720	-11.2	1,516,405	1,401,840	-7.6
Rate	676.4	590.4	-12.7	468.9	430.4	-8.2
Larceny-Theft						
Number........................	173,423	162,511	-6.3	5,644,835	5,519,107	-2.2
Rate	2,381.9	2,194.4	-7.9	1,745.4	1,694.4	-2.9
Motor Vehicle Theft						
Number........................	32,322	28,796	-10.9	767,290	773,139	0.8
Rate	443.9	388.8	-12.4	237.3	237.4	-

NOTE: Although arson data are included in the trend and clearance tables, sufficient data are not available to estimate totals for this offense. Therefore, no arson data are published in this table.
- = Zero or rounds to zero.
[1] Population figures are U.S. Census Bureau provisional estimates as of July 1, 2017.
[2] The figures shown in the rape (revised definition) column were estimated using the revised Uniform Crime Reporting (UCR) definition of rape.

Table WA-15. State Government Finances, 2017

(Dollar amounts in thousands, percent distribution.)

Item	Dollars	Percent distribution
Total Revenue	63,099,690	100.0
General revenue	47,201,281	74.8
Intergovernmental revenue	14,228,084	22.5
Taxes	23,997,592	38.0
General sales	14,509,841	23.0
Selective sales	4,660,927	7.4
License taxes	1,453,628	2.3
Individual income tax	0	-
Corporate income tax	0	-
Other taxes	3,373,196	5.3
Current charges	5,981,097	9.5
Miscellaneous general revenue	2,994,508	4.7
Utility revenue	221	-
Liquor stores revenue	0	-
Insurance trust revenue[1]	15,898,188	25.2
Total Expenditure	55,159,390	100.0
Intergovernmental expenditure	12,690,612	23.0
Direct expenditure	42,468,778	77.0
Current operation	29,506,720	53.5
Capital outlay	2,943,348	5.3
Insurance benefits and repayments	7,190,780	13.0
Assistance and subsidies	1,322,879	2.4
Interest on debt	1,505,051	2.7
Exhibit: Salaries and wages	8,302,069	15.1
Total Expenditure	55,159,390	100.0
General expenditure	47,717,753	86.5
Intergovernmental expenditure	12,690,612	23.0
Direct expenditure	35,027,141	63.5
General expenditure, by function:		
Education	19,541,468	35.4
Public welfare	12,291,087	22.3
Hospitals	4,401,811	8.0
Health	1,907,677	3.5
Highways	2,825,558	5.1
Police protection	429,369	0.8
Correction	998,831	1.8
Natural resources	902,741	1.6
Parks and recreation	142,693	0.3
Governmental administration	1,241,385	2.3
Interest on general debt	1,505,051	2.7
Other and unallocable	1,530,082	2.8
Utility expenditure	250,857	0.4
Liquor stores expenditure	0	-
Insurance trust expenditure	7,190,780	13.0
Debt at End of Fiscal Year	33,427,752	X
Cash and Security Holdings	112,997,143	X

X = Not applicable.

- = Zero or rounds to zero.

[1] Within insurance trust revenue, net earnings of state retirement systems is a calculated statistic (the item code in the data file is X08), and thus can be positive or negative. Net earnings is the sum of earnings on investments plus gains on investments minus losses on investments. The change made in 2002 for asset valuation from book to market value in accordance with Statement 34 of the Governmental Accounting Standards Board is reflected in the calculated statistics.

Table WA-16. State Government Tax Collections, 2018

(Dollars in thousands, percent.)

Item	Dollars	Percent distribution
Total Taxes	26,574,889	100.0
Property taxes	2,769,520	10.4
Sales and gross receipts	20,323,086	76.5
General sales and gross receipts	15,643,017	58.9
Selective sales and gross receipts	4,680,069	17.6
Alcoholic beverages	370,738	1.4
Amusements	X	-
Insurance premiums	630,657	2.4
Motor fuels	1,713,782	6.4
Pari-mutuels	1,724	-
Public utilities	500,703	1.9
Tobacco products	422,264	1.6
Other selective sales	1,040,201	3.9
Licenses	2,070,930	7.8
Alcoholic beverages	152,625	0.6
Amusements	5,920	-
Corporations in general	41,834	0.2
Hunting and fishing	42,450	0.2
Motor vehicle	1,129,671	4.3
Motor vehicle operators	135,270	0.5
Public utilities	21,148	0.1
Occupation and business, NEC	365,363	1.4
Other licenses	176,649	0.7
Income taxes	X	-
Individual income	X	-
Corporation net income	X	-
Other taxes	1,411,353	5.3
Death and gift	208,610	0.8
Documentary and stock transfer	1,161,436	4.4
Severance	41,307	0.2
Taxes, NEC	0	-

X = Not applicable.
- = Zero or rounds to zero.

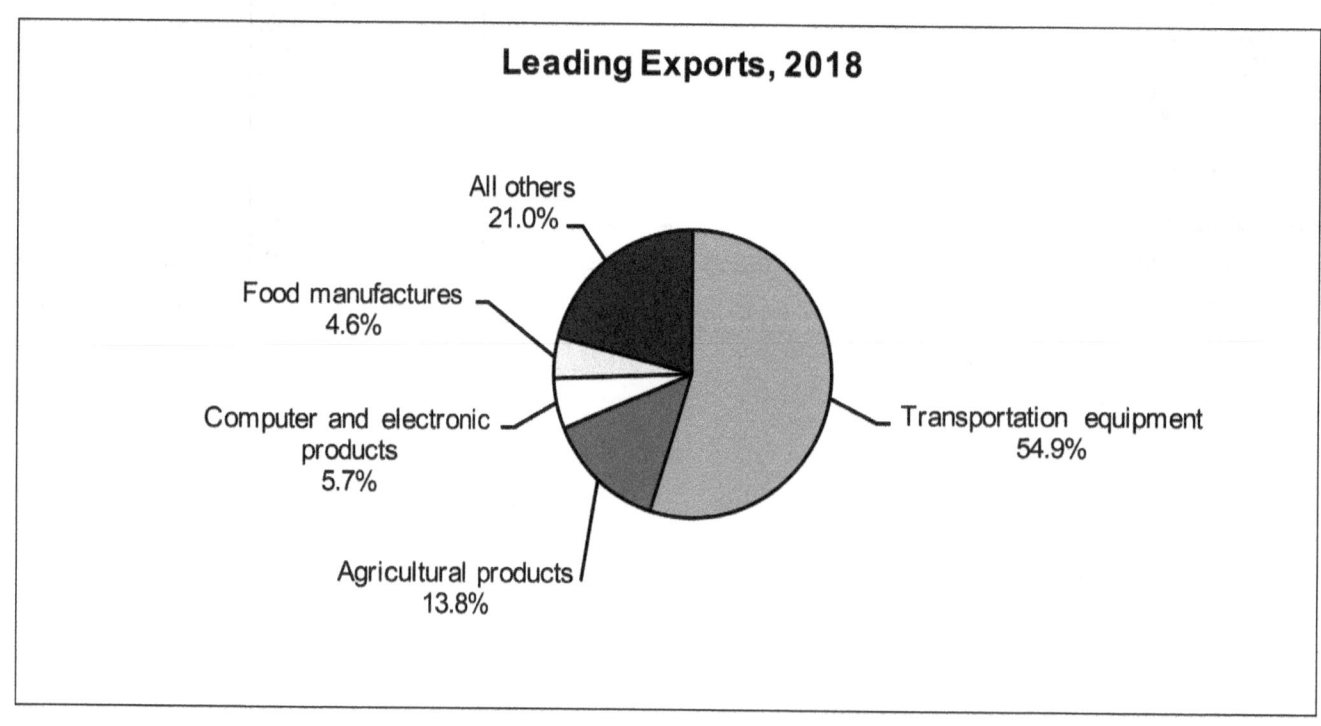

Leading Exports, 2018

All others 21.0%

Food manufactures 4.6%

Computer and electronic products 5.7%

Agricultural products 13.8%

Transportation equipment 54.9%

WEST VIRGINIA

Facts and Figures

Location: East central United States; bordered on the N by Ohio and Pennsylvania, on the E by Pennsylvania, Maryland, and Virginia, on the S by Virginia and Kentucky, and on the W by Kentucky and Ohio

Area: 24,230 sq. mi. (62,755 sq. km.); rank—41st

Population: 1,805,832 (2018 est.); rank—38th

Principal Cities: capital—Charleston; largest—Charleston

Statehood: June 20, 1863; 35th state

U.S. Congress: 2 senators, 3 representatives

State Motto: *Montani semper liberi* (Mountaineers are always free)

State Songs: "West Virginia Hills"; "This Is My West Virginia"; "West Virginia, My Home Sweet Home"

State Nickname: The Mountain State

Abbreviations: WV; W. Va.

State Symbols: flower—rhododendron (great laurel); tree—sugar maple; bird—cardinal

At a Glance

- West Virginia experienced the largest population decline among the states from 2010 to 2018, with its population falling 2.5 percent.

- West Virginia's median household income was $43,469 in 2017, the lowest among the states, and 19.1 percent of the state's population lived below the poverty level.

- At a rate more than twice the national average, West Virginia once again had the highest rate of drug overdose deaths in 2017 (57.8 deaths per 100,000 residents).

- West Virginia tied with Maine for the lowest percent of residents that self-identified as "Hispanic or Latino" in 2018, with 1.7 percent of its population in this category.

- West Virginia had the highest homeownership rate of all the states in 2018, with 74.7 percent of residents owning homes.

Table WV-1. Population by Age, Sex, Race, and Hispanic Origin

(Number, percent, except where noted.)

Sex, age, race, and Hispanic origin	2000	2010	2018 [1]	Percent change, 2010–2018
Total Population..	1,808,344	1,852,994	1,805,832	-2.5
Percent of total U.S. population	0.6	0.6	0.6	X
Sex				
Male..	879,170	913,586	894,340	-2.1
Female	929,174	939,408	911,492	-3.0
Age				
Under 5 years..	101,805	104,060	95,257	-8.5
5 to 19 years..	352,910	335,153	312,658	-6.7
20 to 64 years..	1,076,734	1,116,377	1,038,039	-7.0
65 years and over	276,895	297,404	359,878	21.0
Median age (years)	38.9	41.3	42.7	3.4
Race and Hispanic Origin				
One race				
White	1,718,777	1,746,513	1,687,993	-3.4
Black	57,232	63,885	65,231	2.1
American Indian and Alaska Native	3,606	3,975	4,526	13.9
Asian	9,434	12,637	15,338	21.4
Native Hawaiian or Other Pacific Islander	400	485	528	8.9
Two or more races	15,788	25,499	32,216	26.3
Hispanic (of any race)	12,279	23,679	30,201	27.5

X = Not applicable.
- = Zero or rounds to zero.
[1] Population figures for 2018 are July 1 estimates. The 2010 estimates are taken from the 2010 Census.

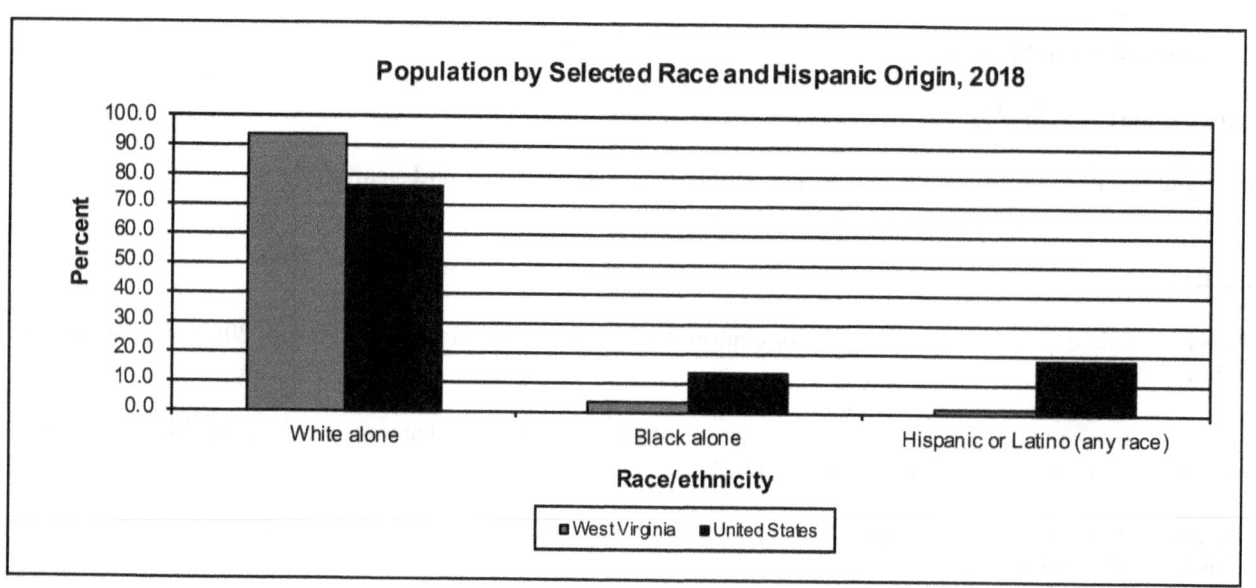

Population by Selected Race and Hispanic Origin, 2018

Table WV-2. Marital Status

(Number, percent distribution.)

Sex, age, race, and Hispanic origin	2000	2010	2017
Males, 15 Years and Over	710,443	750,542	736,517
Never married	25.4	30.3	31.9
Now married, except separated..	59.9	52.1	49.7
Separated..	1.3	1.6	1.3
Widowed..	3.2	3.4	4.0
Divorced..	10.1	12.6	13.1
Females, 15 Years and Over	768,858	785,182	769,314
Never married	19.1	22.6	24.8
Now married, except separated..	54.7	49.7	48.2
Separated..	1.6	1.7	1.5
Widowed..	13.9	12.8	12.0
Divorced..	10.8	13.2	13.5

Table WV-3. Households and Housing Characteristics

(Number, percent, dollars.)

Item	2000	2010	2017	Average annual percent change, 2010–2017
Total Households..	736,481	741,940	715,308	-0.5
Family households..	504,055	485,652	461,542	-0.7
Married-couple family..	397,499	372,301	346,532	-1.0
Other family..	106,556	113,351	115,010	0.2
Male householder, no wife present.........................	27,436	28,515	37,110	4.3
Female householder, no husband present.................	79,120	84,836	77,900	-1.2
Nonfamily households	232,426	256,288	253,766	-0.1
Householder living alone..	199,587	219,848	213,676	-0.4
Householder not living alone..................................	32,839	36,440	40,090	1.4
Housing Characteristics				
Total housing units..	844,623	882,213	892,240	0.2
Occupied housing units	736,481	741,940	715,308	-0.5
Owner occupied...	553,699	553,429	518,882	-0.9
Renter occupied..	182,782	188,511	196,426	0.6
Average household size...	2.40	2.43	2.47	0.2
Financial Characteristics				
Median gross rent of renter-occupied housing	401	571	690	3.0
Median monthly owner costs for housing units with a mortgage	713	918	984	1.0
Median value of owner-occupied housing units.........	72,800	95,100	119,800	3.7

Table WV-4. Migration, Origin, and Language

(Number, percent.)

Characteristic	State 2016	State 2017	State Percent change	U.S. 2016	U.S. 2017	U.S. Percent change
Residence 1 Year Ago						
Population 1 year and over	1,810,709	1,798,306	-0.7	319,361,956	321,994,428	0.8
Same house	87.4	88.4	X	85.4	85.7	X
Different house in the U.S.....................................	12.4	11.4	X	13.9	13.6	X
Same county..	7.0	6.6	X	8.3	8.1	X
Different county...	5.4	4.8	X	5.6	5.6	X
Same state..	2.7	2.6	X	3.2	3.3	X
Different state...	2.6	2.2	X	2.4	2.3	X
Abroad	0.2	0.2	X	0.7	0.7	X
Place of Birth						
Native born	1,799,332	1,785,903	-0.7	279,388,170	281,193,323	0.6
Male..	49.2	49.4	X	49.3	49.4	X
Female...	50.8	50.6	X	50.7	50.6	X
Foreign born	31,770	29,954	-5.7	43,739,345	44,525,855	1.8
Male..	47.0	47.0	X	48.5	48.4	X
Female...	53.0	53.0	X	51.5	51.6	X
Foreign born; naturalized U.S. citizen....................	15,066	15,690	4.1	21,238,372	21,948,732	3.3
Male..	38.0	45.3	X	45.9	45.9	X
Female...	62.0	54.7	X	54.1	54.1	X
Foreign born; not a U.S. citizen............................	16,704	14,264	-14.6	22,500,973	22,577,123	0.3
Male..	55.1	48.9	X	51.0	50.8	X
Female...	44.9	51.1	X	49.0	49.2	X
Entered 2010 or later..	26.3	24.7	X	18.6	21.3	X
Entered 2000 to 2009..	21.5	27.8	X	26.7	25.7	X
Entered before 2000..	52.2	47.4	X	54.7	53.0	X
World Region of Birth, Foreign						
Foreign-born population, excluding population born at sea	31,770	29,954	-5.7	43,738,901	44,525,458	1.8
Europe	18.9	19.7	X	10.9	10.8	X
Asia	41.1	41.3	X	30.8	31.2	X
Africa	10.1	12.7	X	4.9	5.1	X
Oceania	1.8	1.2	X	0.6	0.6	X
Latin America	24.2	19.6	X	51.0	50.4	X
North America	3.8	5.5	X	1.8	1.8	X
Language Spoken at Home and Ability to Speak English						
Population 5 years and over	1,729,434	1,717,970	-0.7	303,328,961	305,924,019	0.9
English only	97.5	97.6	X	78.4	78.2	X
Language other than English..................................	2.5	2.4	X	21.6	21.8	X
Speaks English less than "very well"......................	0.8	0.7	X	8.6	8.5	X

NA = Not available.
X = Not applicable.
- = Zero or rounds to zero.

Table WV-5. Median Income and Poverty Status, 2017

(Number, percent, except as noted.)

Characteristic	State		U.S.	
	Number	Percent	Number	Percent
Median Income				
Households (dollars)...	43,469	X	60,336	X
Families (dollars)	56,086	X	73,891	X
Below Poverty Level (All People)	336,301	19.1	42,583,651	13.4
Sex				
Male	148,846	17.2	19,004,547	12.2
Female	187,455	20.9	23,579,104	14.5
Age				
Under 18 years...	93,758	25.9	13,353,202	18.4
Related children under 18 years........................	91,734	25.5	13,053,472	18.1
18 to 64 years...	207,751	19.6	24,648,677	12.6
65 years and over	34,792	10.2	4,581,772	9.3

X = Not applicable.

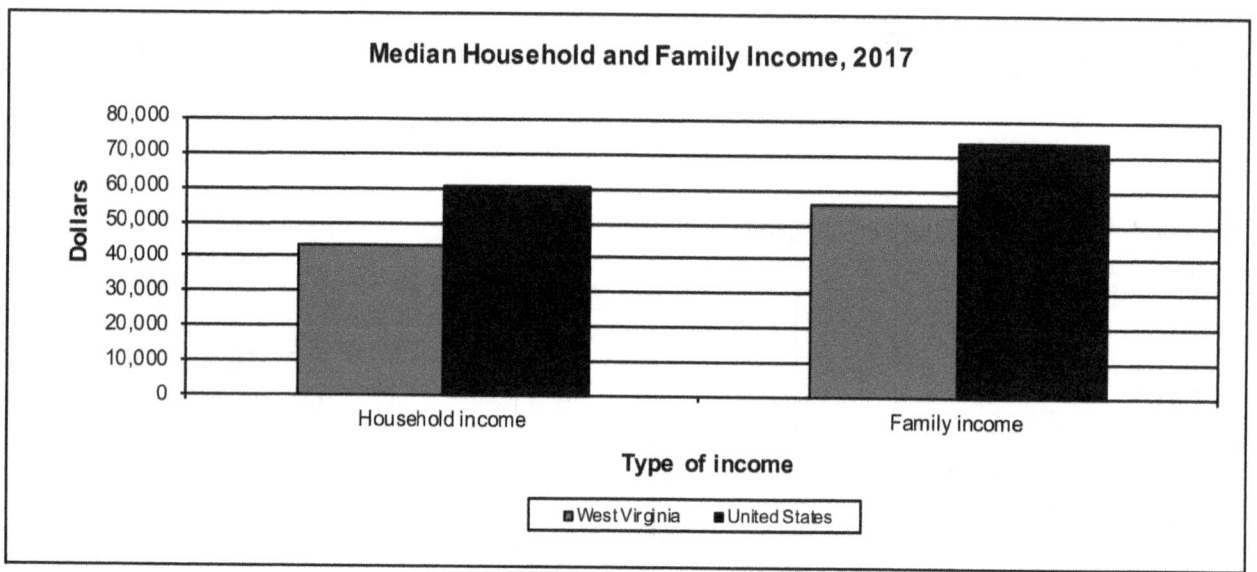

Median Household and Family Income, 2017

Table WV-6. Health Insurance Coverage Status for the Civilian Noninstitutionalized Population and Children Under 18 Years of Age

(Number, percent.)

Item	2009	2010	2011	2012	2013	2014	2015	2016	2017
Civilian Noninstitutionalized Population	1,793,105	1,823,372	1,826,485	1,826,512	1,824,821	1,820,836	1,815,505	1,802,572	1,787,126
Covered by Private or Public Insurance									
Number..	1,539,190	1,557,211	1,554,198	1,562,703	1,569,752	1,664,746	1,707,423	1,706,690	1,678,237
Percent..	85.8	85.4	85.1	85.6	86.0	91.4	94.0	94.7	93.9
Uninsured									
Number..	253,915	266,161	272,287	263,809	255,069	156,090	108,082	95,882	108,889
Percent..	14.2	14.6	14.9	14.4	14.0	8.6	6.0	5.3	6.1
Percent in the U.S. not covered............................	15.1	15.5	15.1	14.8	14.5	11.7	9.4	8.6	8.7
Children Under 18 Years of Age[1]	382,883	385,274	385,302	382,980	381,156	382,225	378,396	375,790	399,352
Covered by Private or Public Insurance									
Number..	361,750	367,756	368,308	367,957	360,851	370,788	367,613	368,007	388,819
Percent..	94.5	95.5	95.6	96.1	94.7	97.0	97.2	97.9	97.4
Uninsured									
Number..	21,133	17,518	16,994	15,023	20,305	11,437	10,783	7,783	10,533
Percent..	5.5	4.5	4.4	3.9	5.3	3.0	2.8	2.1	2.6
Percent in the U.S. not covered............................	8.6	8.0	7.5	7.2	7.1	6.0	4.8	4.5	5.0

[1] 2017 data is for individuals under 19 years of age.

Table WV-7. Employment Status by Demographic Group, 2018

(Numbers in thousands, percent.)

Characteristic	Civilian noninstitutional population	Civilian labor force		Employed		Unemployed	
		Number	Percent of population	Number	Percent of population	Number	Percent of population
Total...	1,453	782	53.8	741	51.0	41	5.3
Sex							
Male...	709	420	59.1	395	55.6	25	5.9
Female...	744	363	48.8	347	46.6	16	4.5
Race, Sex, and Hispanic Origin							
White...	1,367	729	53.3	693	50.7	37	5.0
Male...	666	390	58.6	369	55.3	22	5.6
Female.....................................	701	339	48.3	324	46.2	15	4.4
Black or African American................	45	27	59.4	25	54.0	2	8.9
Male...	NA	NA	NA	NA	NA	NA	NA
Female.....................................	NA	NA	NA	NA	NA	NA	NA
Hispanic or Latino ethnicity[1]............	NA	NA	NA	NA	NA	NA	NA
Male...	NA	NA	NA	NA	NA	NA	NA
Female.....................................	NA	NA	NA	NA	NA	NA	NA
Age							
16 to 19 years..............................	88	28	31.8	23	25.8	5	18.8
20 to 24 years..............................	112	75	67.2	68	60.8	7	9.3
25 to 34 years..............................	213	163	76.4	151	71.0	11	7.0
35 to 44 years..............................	202	154	76.3	146	72.2	8	5.3
45 to 54 years..............................	237	173	73.1	168	71.0	5	2.7
55 to 64 years..............................	256	137	53.4	133	52.1	4	2.6
65 years and over.........................	345	52	15.2	52	15.0	1	1.5

NOTE: Data in Table 7 are from the Current Population Survey (CPS) and do not match the estimates in Table 8. See notes and definitions for further information.
[1] May be of any race.
NA = Not available.

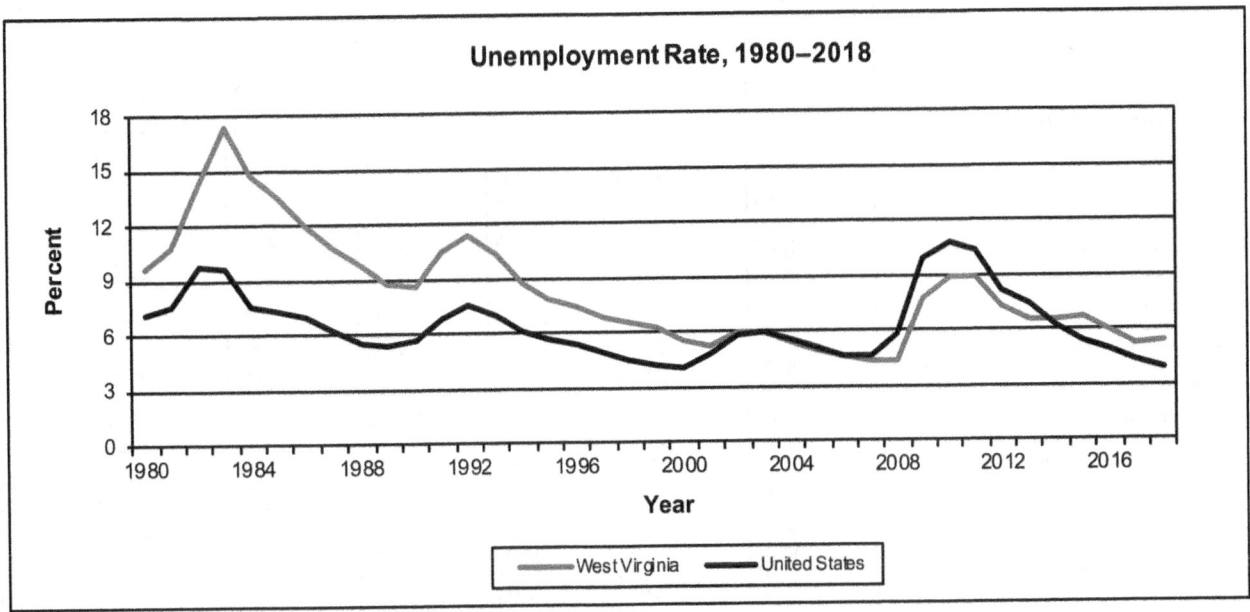

Table WV-8. Employment Status of the Civilian Noninstitutional Population Age 16 Years and Over

(Number, percent.)

Year	Civilian labor force	Civilian participation rate	Employed	Unemployed	Unemployment rate
2010...	811,125	54.9	740,910	70,215	8.7
2011...	807,021	54.3	741,972	65,049	8.1
2012...	807,917	54.4	747,384	60,533	7.5
2013...	798,530	53.8	744,410	54,120	6.8
2014...	787,845	53.1	735,511	52,334	6.6
2015...	780,428	52.8	727,758	52,670	6.7
2016...	781,600	53.1	733,980	47,620	6.1
2017...	778,821	53.3	738,309	40,512	5.2
2018...	783,344	53.8	742,179	41,165	5.3

Table WV-9. Employment and Average Wages by Industry

(Estimates are based on the 2012 *North American Industry Classification System* [NAICS].)

Industry	2011	2012	2013	2014	2015	2016	2017
	Number of jobs						
Wage and Salary Employment by Industry........................	741,944	751,073	743,403	740,039	733,992	721,162	720,173
Farm Wage and Salary Employment...............................	1,425	1,698	1,567	1,703	1,912	1,575	1,823
Nonfarm Wage and Salary Employment...........................	740,519	749,375	741,836	738,336	732,080	719,587	718,350
Private wage and salary employment.............................	579,235	586,870	583,486	581,584	576,322	563,322	563,483
Forestry, fishing, and related activities.........................	1,273	1,370	1,366	1,412	1,481	1,512	1,486
Mining..	32,875	32,719	30,889	29,202	25,012	19,344	20,909
Utilities..	5,438	5,307	5,178	5,204	5,051	5,167	5,299
Construction...	33,867	36,642	35,305	34,632	33,267	30,806	32,334
Manufacturing...	49,577	49,199	48,468	47,885	47,756	46,878	46,603
Durable goods manufacturing..............................	29,962	29,624	29,149	28,942	28,696	28,067	27,999
Nondurable goods manufacturing..........................	19,615	19,575	19,319	18,943	19,060	18,811	18,604
Wholesale trade	23,363	23,600	23,015	22,721	22,356	21,225	20,803
Retail trade...	87,724	88,309	88,212	87,324	87,340	87,425	85,311
Transportation and warehousing...............................	19,649	19,247	20,163	20,862	21,468	20,253	20,602
Information..	10,384	9,633	9,515	9,591	9,646	9,667	8,619
Finance and insurance	20,396	20,231	19,943	19,646	19,304	19,083	18,974
Real estate and rental and leasing.............................	6,861	6,834	6,800	6,924	6,951	6,749	6,573
Professional, scientific, and technical services	25,215	25,729	26,131	26,359	26,116	25,174	25,625
Management of companies and enterprises.....................	5,696	6,684	6,490	6,381	6,406	6,247	6,469
Administrative and waste services.............................	32,235	32,712	32,744	34,625	35,067	34,578	34,688
Educational services	8,926	9,135	8,966	8,912	8,962	9,491	9,461
Health care and social assistance.............................	110,417	113,190	114,079	113,942	114,846	115,653	115,937
Arts, entertainment, and recreation............................	7,272	7,636	7,711	7,919	7,673	7,659	7,933
Accommodation and food services	65,900	67,054	67,287	66,900	67,331	66,974	66,908
Other services, except public administration..................	32,167	31,639	31,224	31,143	30,289	29,437	28,949
Government and government enterprises	161,284	162,505	158,350	156,752	155,758	156,265	154,867
	Dollars						
Average Wages and Salaries by Industry	38,530	39,193	39,656	40,634	41,195	41,158	42,871
Average Farm Wages and Salaries	15,897	21,062	23,267	22,682	16,503	22,992	18,027
Average Nonfarm Wages and Salaries	38,573	39,234	39,690	40,676	41,260	41,198	42,934
Average private wages and salaries.............................	38,530	39,317	39,587	40,594	41,134	40,952	43,012
Forestry, fishing, and related activities.........................	26,622	27,748	27,758	28,929	29,738	30,026	30,334
Mining..	78,893	79,287	80,113	80,803	78,790	75,296	80,779
Utilities..	80,483	80,678	81,296	85,132	88,951	89,160	91,707
Construction	46,997	50,852	51,957	53,522	53,331	52,550	57,999
Manufacturing	51,704	52,790	53,076	55,058	55,910	56,523	58,657
Durable goods manufacturing..............................	48,408	50,015	49,675	51,405	51,693	52,289	54,373
Nondurable goods manufacturing..........................	56,739	56,989	58,209	60,638	62,259	62,840	65,106
Wholesale trade	51,249	51,742	52,197	54,980	55,982	56,166	58,694
Retail trade..	23,726	24,127	24,387	24,633	25,612	26,022	26,583
Transportation and warehousing...............................	48,416	50,113	48,752	50,045	50,354	49,873	51,742
Information	48,485	48,640	47,609	48,738	51,247	50,706	50,441
Finance and insurance	46,735	46,083	47,645	49,393	50,858	52,058	54,909
Real estate and rental and leasing.............................	34,991	36,327	36,538	37,839	37,967	37,454	38,818
Professional, scientific, and technical services	50,692	53,054	53,746	55,173	56,153	56,925	59,814
Management of companies and enterprises.....................	81,772	70,905	69,869	72,396	73,968	72,210	77,409
Administrative and waste services.............................	28,496	29,060	29,576	31,294	31,921	32,173	34,222
Educational services	24,333	24,579	24,801	24,749	25,205	24,596	25,505
Health care and social assistance.............................	37,840	38,803	39,623	41,005	42,735	43,911	45,604
Arts, entertainment, and recreation............................	19,386	19,345	19,105	19,271	19,999	19,987	19,793
Accommodation and food services	17,207	17,658	17,678	18,047	18,729	19,151	19,582
Other services, except public administration..................	26,053	26,860	27,723	28,221	29,082	29,892	31,243
Government and government enterprises	38,729	38,933	40,069	40,978	41,723	42,086	42,653

Table WV-10. Employment Characteristics by Family Type

(Number, percent.)

Family type and labor force status	2015		2016		2017	
	Total	Families with own children under 18 years	Total	Families with own children under 18 years	Total	Families with own children under 18 years
All Families...	471,947	172,703	467,396	171,163	461,542	163,039
FAMILY TYPE AND LABOR FORCE STATUS						
Married-Couple Families............................	351,328	112,219	347,095	111,119	346,532	108,893
Both husband and wife in labor force................	39.5	60.7	41.4	62.1	41.1	64.5
Husband in labor force, wife not in labor force	22.1	30.0	20.1	26.4	20.4	26.1
Wife in labor force, husband not in labor force	10.7	5.3	10.5	6.1	9.9	5.3
Both husband and wife not in labor force.............	27.1	3.6	27.6	5.0	28.1	3.8
Other Families	120,619	60,484	120,301	60,044	115,010	54,146
Female householder, no husband present.............	70.3	70.5	72.4	73.7	67.7	67.4
In labor force..	40.9	52.1	43.1	55.4	37.4	50.0
Not in labor force.....................................	29.4	18.4	29.3	18.3	30.3	17.3
Male householder, no wife present......................	29.7	29.5	27.6	26.3	32.3	32.6
In labor force..	18.2	23.8	17.6	23.3	20.0	25.5
Not in labor force.....................................	11.5	5.7	9.9	3.0	12.3	7.1

Table WV-11. School Enrollment and Educational Attainment, 2017

(Number, percent.)

Item	State	U.S.
Enrollment		
Total population 3 years and over, enrolled in school	397,036	81,273,337
Enrolled in nursery school or preschool (percent)..	5.4	6.0
Enrolled in kindergarten (percent)...	5.2	4.9
Enrolled in elementary school, grades 1-8 (percent)...	43.1	40.6
Enrolled in high school, grades 9-12 (percent)...	21.1	21.1
Enrolled in college or graduate school (percent)..	25.3	27.4
Attainment		
Total population 25 years and over	1,279,350	221,250,083
Less than ninth grade (percent)..	4.5	5.1
9th to 12th grade, no diploma (percent)..	8.4	6.9
High school graduate, including equivalency (percent)..	41.2	27.1
Some college, no degree (percent)	18.6	20.4
Associate's degree (percent)..	7.1	8.5
Bachelor's degree (percent)..	12.2	19.7
Graduate or professional degree (percent)...	8.0	12.3
High school graduate or higher (percent)...	87.1	88.0
Bachelor's degree or higher (percent)...	20.2	32.0

Table WV-12. Public School Characteristics and Educational Indicators

(Number, percent; data derived from National Center of Education Statistics.)

Item	State	U.S.
Public Elementary and Secondary Schools		
Number of operational school districts, 2016-17	57	18,377
Number of operational schools, 2016-17	739	98,330
Percent charter schools	NA	7.1
Total public school enrollment, 2016-17	273,855	50,587,859
Percent charter school enrollment	NA	6.0
Student-teacher ratio, Fall 2015	14.1	16.0
Expenditures per student (dollars), 2015-16..	11,424	11,841
Four-year adjusted cohort graduation rate (ACGR)[1]	89.4	84.6
Students eligible for free or reduced-price lunch (percent), 2015-16..........................	49.4	52.1
English language learners (percent), Fall 2016	0.9	9.6
Students age 3 to 21 served under IDEA, part B (percent), 2017-18.............................	17.3	13.7

Public Schools by Type, 2016-17		Percent of state public schools
Total number of schools...	739	100.0
Special education...	3	0.4
Vocational education..	33	4.5
Alternative education...	33	4.5

[1] Adjusted Cohort Graduation Rates (ACGR) differ from Averaged Freshmen Graduation Rates (AFGR).
NA = Not available.

Table WV-13. Reported Voting and Registration of the Voting-Age Population, November 2018

(Numbers in thousands, percent.)

Item	Total population	Total citizen population	Registered			Voted		
			Total registered	Percent registered (total population)	Percent registered (total citizen population)	Total voted	Percent voted (total population)	Percent voted (total citizen population)
U.S. Total	249,748	228,832	153,066	61.3	66.9	122,281	49.0	53.4
State Total.......................................	1,406	1,384	892	63.4	64.5	610	43.4	44.1
Sex								
Male	685	674	423	61.7	62.7	294	43.0	43.7
Female	721	710	470	65.1	66.1	316	43.8	44.5
Race								
White alone.......................................	1,312	1,303	856	65.2	65.7	585	44.6	44.9
White, non-Hispanic alone	1,291	1,286	847	65.6	65.9	582	45.1	45.2
Black alone.......................................	49	47	19	(B)	(B)	12	(B)	(B)
Asian alone	17	6	4	(B)	(B)	3	(B)	(B)
Hispanic (of any race)	24	20	10	(B)	(B)	4	(B)	(B)
White alone or in combination	1,334	1,324	867	65.0	65.5	594	44.5	44.8
Black alone or in combination............	64	63	29	(B)	(B)	19	(B)	(B)
Asian alone or in combination............	19	7	5	(B)	(B)	4	(B)	(B)
Age								
18 to 24 years	169	159	79	47.0	49.8	36	21.3	22.6
25 to 34 years	201	194	98	48.7	50.6	50	24.8	25.8
35 to 44 years	199	197	120	59.9	60.6	73	36.7	37.1
45 to 64 years	478	476	320	67.0	67.3	229	47.9	48.1
65 years and over	358	358	275	76.7	76.8	222	62.0	62.1

B = Base is less than 75,000 and therefore too small to show the derived measure.

Table WV-14. Crime

(Number, rate per 100,000. Data are derived from the FBI Uniform Crime Reports.)

Item	State			U.S.		
	2016	2017	Percent change	2016	2017	Percent change
TOTAL POPULATION[1]	1,828,637	1,815,857	-0.7	323,405,935	325,719,178	0.7
VIOLENT CRIME						
Number	6,633	6,368	-4.0	1,285,606	1,283,220	-0.2
Rate	362.7	350.7	-3.3	397.5	394.0	-0.9
Murder and Nonnegligent Manslaughter						
Number..	85	85	0.0	17,413	17,284	-0.7
Rate	4.6	4.7	0.7	5.4	5.3	-1.4
Rape[2]						
Number..	684	795	16.2	132,414	135,755	2.5
Rate	37.4	43.8	17.0	40.9	41.7	1.8
Robbery						
Number..	720	524	-27.2	332,797	319,356	-4.0
Rate	39.4	28.9	-26.7	102.9	98.0	-4.7
Aggravated Assault						
Number..	5,144	4,964	-3.5	802,982	810,825	1.0
Rate	281.3	273.4	-2.8	248.3	248.9	0.3
PROPERTY CRIME						
Number..	37,282	33,630	-9.8	7,928,530	7,694,086	-3.0
Rate	2,038.8	1,852.0	-9.2	2,451.6	2,362.2	-3.6
Burglary						
Number..	9,127	7,628	-16.4	1,516,405	1,401,840	-7.6
Rate	499.1	420.1	-15.8	468.9	430.4	-8.2
Larceny-Theft						
Number..	25,657	23,000	-10.4	5,644,835	5,519,107	-2.2
Rate	1,403.1	1,266.6	-9.7	1,745.4	1,694.4	-2.9
Motor Vehicle Theft						
Number..	2,498	3,002	20.2	767,290	773,139	0.8
Rate	136.6	165.3	21.0	237.3	237.4	-

NOTE: Although arson data are included in the trend and clearance tables, sufficient data are not available to estimate totals for this offense. Therefore, no arson data are published in this table.

- = Zero or rounds to zero.

[1] Population figures are U.S. Census Bureau provisional estimates as of July 1, 2017.

[2] The figures shown in the rape (revised definition) column were estimated using the revised Uniform Crime Reporting (UCR) definition of rape.

Table WV-15. State Government Finances, 2017

(Dollar amounts in thousands, percent distribution.)

Item	Dollars	Percent distribution
Total Revenue	16,383,096	100.0
General revenue	13,182,692	80.5
Intergovernmental revenue	5,109,431	31.2
Taxes	5,092,275	31.1
General sales	1,334,168	8.1
Selective sales	1,338,719	8.2
License taxes	148,951	0.9
Individual income tax	1,813,866	11.1
Corporate income tax	116,305	0.7
Other taxes	340,266	2.1
Current charges	1,805,124	11.0
Miscellaneous general revenue	1,175,862	7.2
Utility revenue	2,732	-
Liquor stores revenue	93,039	0.6
Insurance trust revenue[1]	3,104,633	19.0
Total Expenditure	14,686,179	100.0
Intergovernmental expenditure	2,457,100	16.7
Direct expenditure	12,229,079	83.3
Current operation	9,226,052	62.8
Capital outlay	906,260	6.2
Insurance benefits and repayments	1,571,731	10.7
Assistance and subsidies	318,476	2.2
Interest on debt	206,560	1.4
Exhibit: Salaries and wages	1,816,508	12.4
Total Expenditure	14,686,179	100.0
General expenditure	13,028,758	88.7
Intergovernmental expenditure	2,457,100	16.7
Direct expenditure	10,571,658	72.0
General expenditure, by function:		
Education	4,285,354	29.2
Public welfare	4,732,909	32.2
Hospitals	149,541	1.0
Health	298,684	2.0
Highways	1,148,911	7.8
Police protection	81,031	0.6
Correction	301,041	2.0
Natural resources	272,671	1.9
Parks and recreation	53,902	0.4
Governmental administration	483,631	3.3
Interest on general debt	206,560	1.4
Other and unallocable	1,014,523	6.9
Utility expenditure	10,001	0.1
Liquor stores expenditure	75,689	0.5
Insurance trust expenditure	1,571,731	10.7
Debt at End of Fiscal Year	7,547,010	X
Cash and Security Holdings	21,743,103	X

X = Not applicable.
- = Zero or rounds to zero.
[1] Within insurance trust revenue, net earnings of state retirement systems is a calculated statistic (the item code in the data file is X08), and thus can be positive or negative. Net earnings is the sum of earnings on investments plus gains on investments minus losses on investments. The change made in 2002 for asset valuation from book to market value in accordance with Statement 34 of the Governmental Accounting Standards Board is reflected in the calculated statistics.

Table WV-16. State Government Tax Collections, 2018

(Dollars in thousands, percent.)

Item	Dollars	Percent distribution
Total Taxes	5,417,673	100.0
Property taxes	7,316	0.1
Sales and gross receipts	2,731,739	50.4
General sales and gross receipts	1,311,930	24.2
Selective sales and gross receipts	1,419,809	26.2
Alcoholic beverages	17,576	0.3
Amusements	35,152	0.6
Insurance premiums	169,607	3.1
Motor fuels	419,528	7.7
Pari-mutuels	2,704	-
Public utilities	119,736	2.2
Tobacco products	177,840	3.3
Other selective sales	477,666	8.8
Licenses	194,048	3.6
Alcoholic beverages	1,927	-
Amusements	3,672	0.1
Corporations in general	737	-
Hunting and fishing	12,325	0.2
Motor vehicle	4,498	0.1
Motor vehicle operators	160,076	3.0
Public utilities	449	-
Occupation and business, NEC	8,144	0.2
Other licenses	2,220	-
Income taxes	2,060,639	38.0
Individual income	1,950,571	36.0
Corporation net income	110,068	2.0
Other taxes	423,931	7.8
Death and gift	X	-
Documentary and stock transfer	12,036	0.2
Severance	411,895	7.6
Taxes, NEC	0	-

- = Zero or rounds to zero.
X = Not applicable.

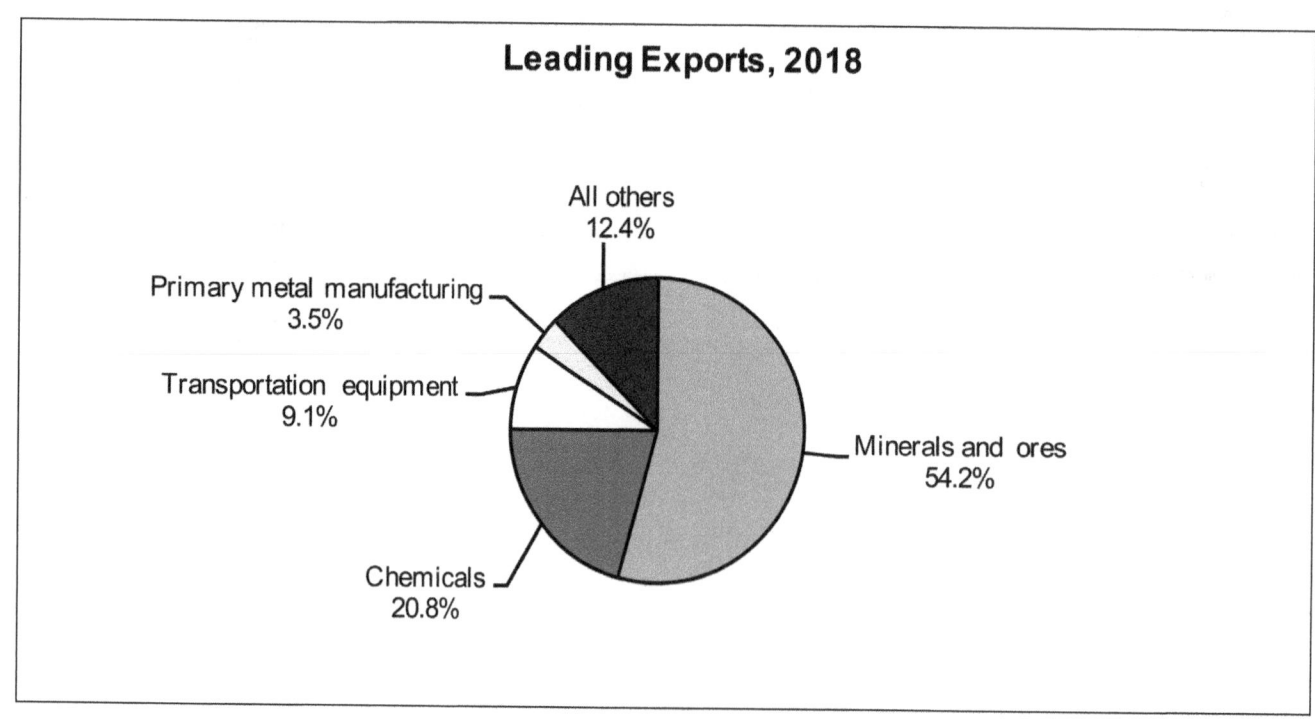

Leading Exports, 2018

All others 12.4%

Primary metal manufacturing 3.5%

Transportation equipment 9.1%

Minerals and ores 54.2%

Chemicals 20.8%

WISCONSIN

Facts and Figures

Location: North central United States; bordered on the N by Michigan and Lake Superior, on the E by Lake Michigan, on the S by Illinois, and on the W by Iowa and Minnesota

Area: 65,498 sq. mi. (169,639 sq. km.); rank—23rd

Population: 5,813,568 (2018 est.); rank—20th

Principal Cities: capital—Madison; largest—Milwaukee

Statehood: May 29, 1848; 30th state

U.S. Congress: 2 senators, 8 representatives

State Motto: Forward

State Song: "On, Wisconsin!"

State Nickname: The Badger State

Abbreviations: WI; Wis.; Wisc.

State Symbols: flower—wood violet; tree—sugar maple; bird—robin

At a Glance

- With an increase in population of 2.2 percent, Wisconsin ranked 37th among the states in growth from 2010 to 2018.

- Wisconsin's violent crime rate in 2017 was 319.9 per 100,000 population, compared to 394.0 for the entire nation.

- Wisconsin's median household income in 2017 was $59,305, and 11.3 percent of the population lived below the poverty level.

- In the November 2018 election, 62.2 percent of Wisconsin's eligible voters cast ballots, making it 3rd in the nation for voter turnout.

- The unemployment rate in Wisconsin in 2018 was 3.0 percent, compared to the national rate of 3.9 percent.

Table WI-1. Population by Age, Sex, Race, and Hispanic Origin

(Number, percent, except where noted.)

Sex, age, race, and Hispanic origin	2000	2010	2018 [1]	Percent change, 2010–2018
Total Population...	5,363,675	5,686,986	5,813,568	2.2
Percent of total U.S. population	1.9	1.8	1.8	X
Sex				
Male...	2,649,041	2,822,400	2,892,273	2.5
Female	2,714,634	2,864,586	2,921,295	2.0
Age				
Under 5 years..	342,340	358,443	334,382	-6.7
5 to 19 years...	1,189,753	1,143,753	1,097,565	-4.0
20 to 64 years...	3,129,029	3,407,476	3,396,148	-0.3
65 years and over	702,553	777,314	985,473	26.8
Median age (years)	36.0	38.5	39.6	2.9
Race and Hispanic Origin				
One race				
White	4,769,857	5,036,923	5,063,526	0.5
Black	304,460	367,021	389,047	6.0
American Indian and Alaska Native	47,228	60,100	67,571	12.4
Asian..	88,763	131,828	176,147	33.6
Native Hawaiian or Other Pacific Islander	1,630	2,505	3,243	29.5
Two or more races	66,895	88,609	114,034	28.7
Hispanic (of any race).....................................	192,291	349,366	403,955	15.6

X = Not applicable.
[1] Population figures for 2018 are July 1 estimates. The 2010 estimates are taken from the 2010 Census.

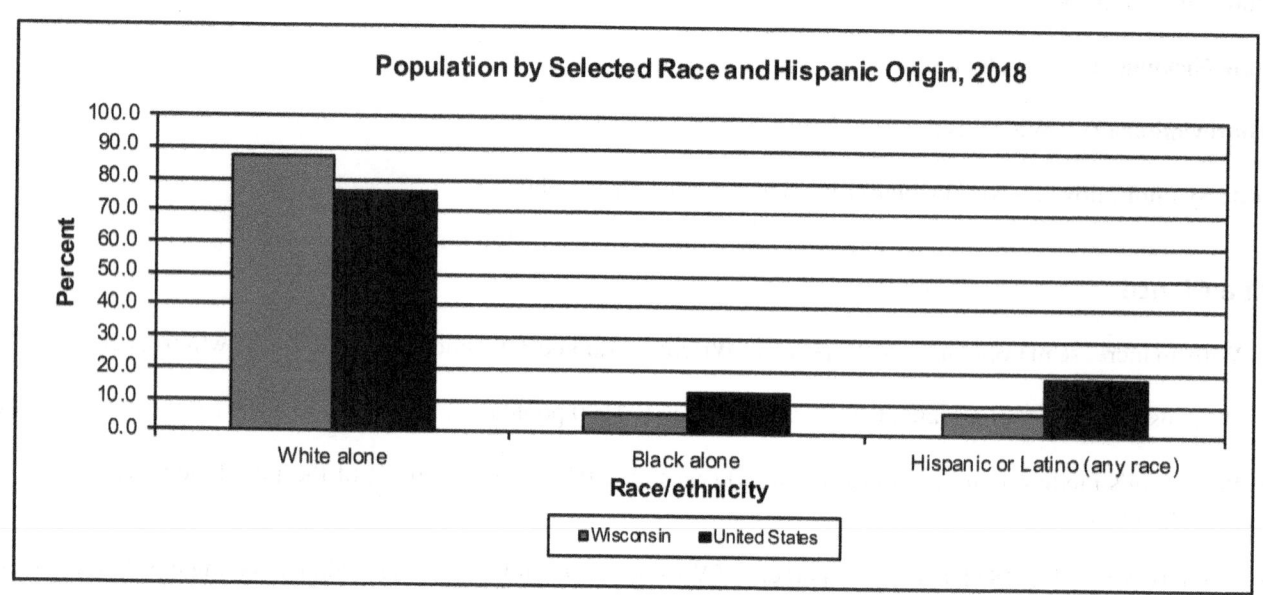

Table WI-2. Marital Status

(Number, percent distribution.)

Sex, age, race, and Hispanic origin	2000	2010	2017
Males, 15 Years and Over	2,072,397	2,261,022	2,341,660
Never married	30.2	34.1	35.5
Now married, except separated..	57.9	52.1	51.0
Separated..	1.1	1.0	0.8
Widowed..	2.4	2.6	2.6
Divorced..	8.4	10.2	10.1
Females, 15 Years and Over	2,167,164	2,328,733	2,398,001
Never married	24.3	28.1	29.3
Now married, except separated..	54.6	50.1	49.5
Separated..	1.3	1.2	1.1
Widowed..	10.2	9.2	8.4
Divorced..	9.7	11.4	11.7

Table WI-3. Households and Housing Characteristics

(Number, percent, dollars.)

Item	2000	2010	2017	Average annual percent change, 2010–2017
Total Households..	2,084,544	2,279,532	2,350,293	0.4
Family households...	1,386,815	1,453,332	1,478,375	0.2
Married-couple family..	1,108,597	1,125,314	1,139,307	0.2
Other family..	278,218	328,018	339,068	0.5
Male householder, no wife present...............................	77,918	96,237	105,880	1.4
Female householder, no husband present.......................	200,300	231,781	233,188	0.1
Nonfamily households...	697,729	826,200	871,918	0.8
Householder living alone...	557,875	669,106	692,937	0.5
Householder not living alone..	139,854	157,094	178,981	2.0
Housing Characteristics				
Total housing units..	2,321,144	2,625,477	2,695,303	0.4
Occupied housing units	2,084,544	2,279,532	2,350,293	0.4
Owner occupied...	1,426,361	1,566,039	1,565,599	-
Renter occupied..	658,183	713,493	784,694	1.4
Average household size...	2.50	2.43	2.40	-0.2
Financial Characteristics				
Median gross rent of renter-occupied housing	540	715	819	2.1
Median monthly owner costs for housing units with a mortgage	1,024	1,404	1,358	-0.5
Median value of owner-occupied housing units...................	112,200	169,400	178,900	0.8

- = Zero or rounds to zero.

Table WI-4. Migration, Origin, and Language

(Number, percent.)

Characteristic	State 2016	State 2017	State Percent change	U.S. 2016	U.S. 2017	U.S. Percent change
Residence 1 Year Ago						
Population 1 year and over	5,712,104	5,731,549	0.3	319,361,956	321,994,428	0.8
Same house	85.4	85.6	X	85.4	85.7	X
Different house in the U.S.	14.3	14.0	X	13.9	13.6	X
Same county	8.5	8.5	X	8.3	8.1	X
Different county	5.8	5.4	X	5.6	5.6	X
Same state	3.7	3.5	X	3.2	3.3	X
Different state	2.1	2.0	X	2.4	2.3	X
Abroad	0.3	0.4	X	0.7	0.7	X
Place of Birth						
Native born	5,490,165	5,507,431	0.3	279,388,170	281,193,323	0.6
Male	49.7	49.7	X	49.3	49.4	X
Female	50.3	50.3	X	50.7	50.6	X
Foreign born	288,544	288,052	-0.2	43,739,345	44,525,855	1.8
Male	50.7	49.3	X	48.5	48.4	X
Female	49.3	50.7	X	51.5	51.6	X
Foreign born; naturalized U.S. citizen..............................	131,355	134,202	2.2	21,238,372	21,948,732	3.3
Male	47.0	46.1	X	45.9	45.9	X
Female	53.0	53.9	X	54.1	54.1	X
Foreign born; not a U.S. citizen.....................................	157,189	153,850	-2.1	22,500,973	22,577,123	0.3
Male	53.9	52.0	X	51.0	50.8	X
Female	46.1	48.0	X	49.0	49.2	X
Entered 2010 or later	21.8	23.6	X	18.6	21.3	X
Entered 2000 to 2009	29.1	28.5	X	26.7	25.7	X
Entered before 2000..	49.1	47.9	X	54.7	53.0	X
World Region of Birth, Foreign						
Foreign-born population, excluding population born at sea	288,544	288,052	-0.2	43,738,901	44,525,458	1.8
Europe	16.3	17.0	X	10.9	10.8	X
Asia	37.0	39.0	X	30.8	31.2	X
Africa	5.4	4.6	X	4.9	5.1	X
Oceania	0.2	0.8	X	0.6	0.6	X
Latin America	38.4	36.0	X	51.0	50.4	X
North America	2.6	2.6	X	1.8	1.8	X
Language Spoken at Home and Ability to Speak English						
Population 5 years and over	5,444,618	5,461,498	0.3	303,328,961	305,924,019	0.9
English only	91.2	91.4	X	78.4	78.2	X
Language other than English..	8.8	8.6	X	21.6	21.8	X
Speaks English less than "very well"...............................	3.2	3.1	X	8.6	8.5	X

NA = Not available.
X = Not applicable.
- = Zero or rounds to zero.

Table WI-5. Median Income and Poverty Status, 2017

(Number, percent, except as noted.)

Characteristic	State		U.S.	
	Number	Percent	Number	Percent
Median Income				
Households (dollars)...	59,305	X	60,336	X
Families (dollars)	75,413	X	73,891	X
Below Poverty Level (All People)	639,564	11.3	42,583,651	13.4
Sex				
Male	281,601	10.1	19,004,547	12.2
Female	357,963	12.6	23,579,104	14.5
Age				
Under 18 years..	181,828	14.5	13,353,202	18.4
Related children under 18 years..........................	174,921	14.0	13,053,472	18.1
18 to 64 years..	385,263	11.1	24,648,677	12.6
65 years and over	72,473	7.8	4,581,772	9.3

X = Not applicable.

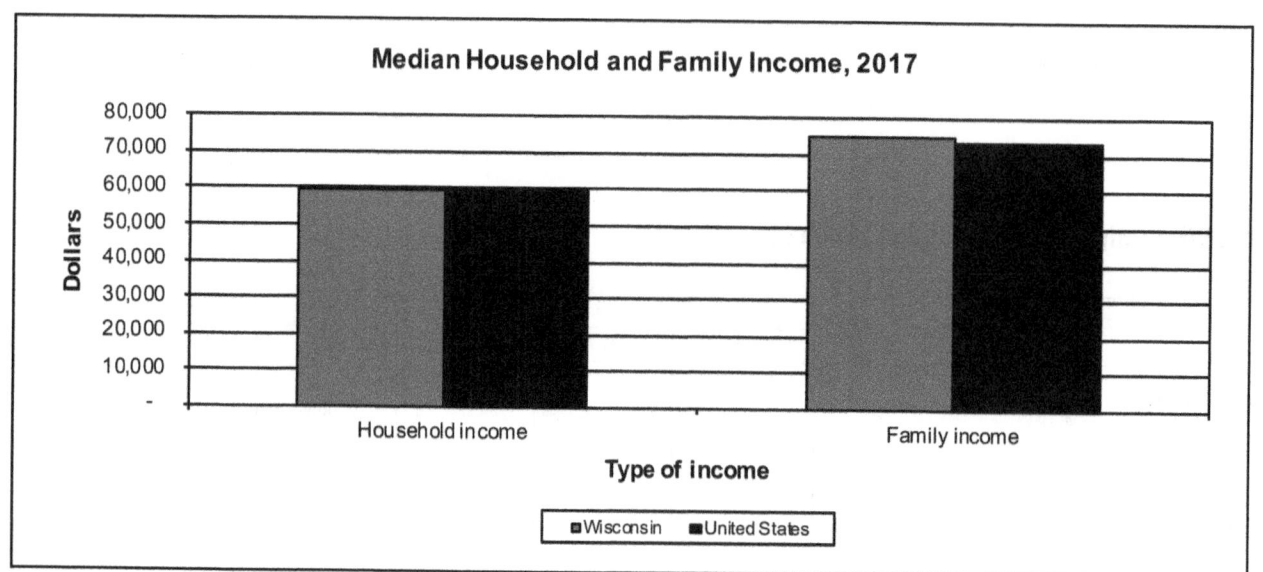

Median Household and Family Income, 2017

Table WI-6. Health Insurance Coverage Status for the Civilian Noninstitutionalized Population and Children Under 18 Years of Age

(Number, percent.)

Item	2009	2010	2011	2012	2013	2014	2015	2016	2017
Civilian Noninstitutionalized Population	5,566,055	5,613,402	5,634,063	5,652,085	5,669,266	5,684,725	5,698,995	5,706,681	5,723,963
Covered by Private or Public Insurance									
Number..	5,045,182	5,084,202	5,127,389	5,146,087	5,151,470	5,267,002	5,376,379	5,406,475	5,414,559
Percent..	90.6	90.6	91.0	91.0	90.9	92.7	94.3	94.7	94.6
Uninsured									
Number..	520,873	529,200	506,674	505,998	517,796	417,723	322,616	300,206	309,404
Percent..	9.4	9.4	9.0	9.0	9.1	7.3	5.7	5.3	5.4
Percent in the U.S. not covered...........................	15.1	15.5	15.1	14.8	14.5	11.7	9.4	8.6	8.7
Children Under 18 Years of Age[1]	1,302,837	1,334,158	1,322,921	1,315,276	1,304,781	1,297,792	1,290,350	1,283,539	1,361,508
Covered by Private or Public Insurance									
Number..	1,237,430	1,267,048	1,264,685	1,253,719	1,243,493	1,240,181	1,244,122	1,238,131	1,308,778
Percent..	95.0	95.0	95.6	95.3	95.3	95.6	96.4	96.5	96.1
Uninsured									
Number..	65,407	67,110	58,236	61,557	61,288	57,611	46,228	45,408	52,730
Percent..	5.0	5.0	4.4	4.7	4.7	4.4	3.6	3.5	3.9
Percent in the U.S. not covered...........................	8.6	8.0	7.5	7.2	7.1	6.0	4.8	4.5	5.0

[1] 2017 data is for individuals under 19 years of age.

Table WI-7. Employment Status by Demographic Group, 2018

(Numbers in thousands, percent.)

Characteristic	Civilian noninstitutional population	Civilian labor force		Employed		Unemployed	
		Number	Percent of population	Number	Percent of population	Number	Percent of population
Total..	4,619	3,123	67.6	3,031	65.6	92	3.0
Sex							
Male.......................	2,273	1,612	70.9	1,563	68.8	49	3.0
Female.....................	2,346	1,512	64.4	1,468	62.6	44	2.9
Race, Sex, and Hispanic Origin							
White.........................	4,151	2,807	67.6	2,732	65.8	75	2.7
Male.......................	2,051	1,466	71.5	1,425	69.5	41	2.8
Female.....................	2,100	1,342	63.9	1,307	62.2	35	2.6
Black or African American...........	252	158	62.7	146	57.9	12	7.7
Male.......................	NA	NA	NA	NA	NA	NA	NA
Female.....................	NA	NA	NA	NA	NA	NA	NA
Hispanic or Latino ethnicity[1]...........	248	184	74.1	177	71.5	6	3.5
Male.......................	NA	NA	NA	NA	NA	NA	NA
Female.....................	NA	NA	NA	NA	NA	NA	NA
Age							
16 to 19 years..................	291	164	56.5	150	51.6	14	8.6
20 to 24 years..................	365	293	80.4	279	76.6	14	4.8
25 to 34 years..................	740	648	87.6	626	84.7	22	3.3
35 to 44 years..................	716	647	90.3	640	89.4	7	1.0
45 to 54 years..................	706	604	85.5	587	83.2	16	2.7
55 to 64 years..................	831	582	70.0	566	68.1	16	2.8
65 years and over................	970	186	19.1	182	18.7	4	2.0

NOTE: Data in Table 7 are from the Current Population Survey (CPS) and do not match the estimates in Table 8. See notes and definitions for further information.
[1] May be of any race.
NA = Not available.

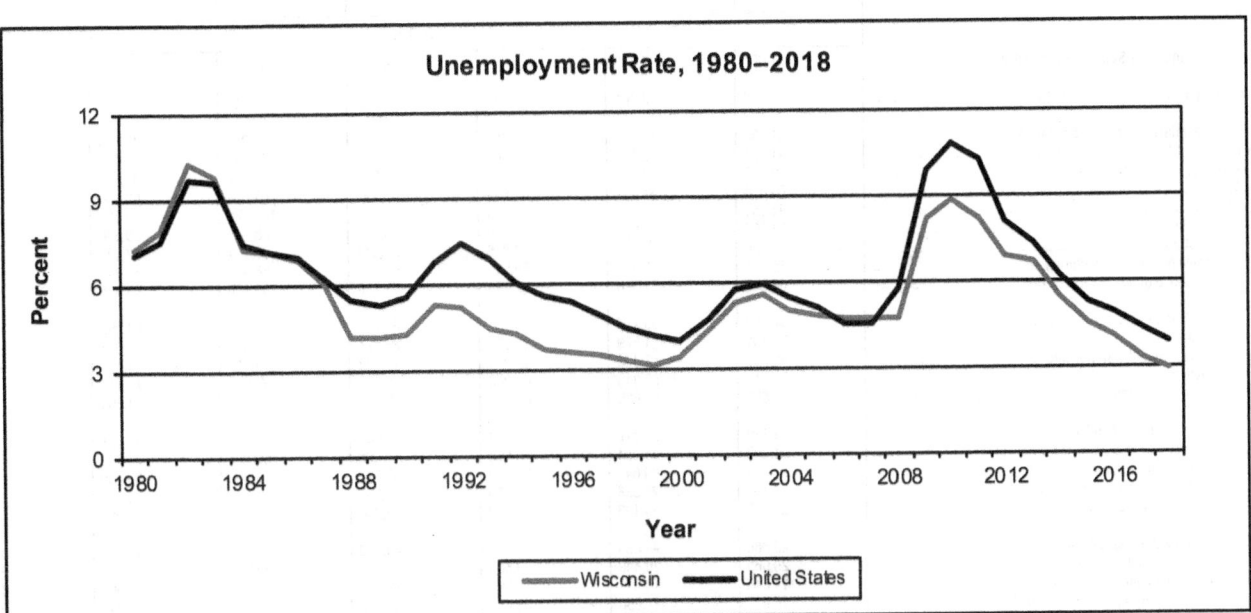

Unemployment Rate, 1980–2018

Wisconsin — United States

Table WI-8. Employment Status of the Civilian Noninstitutional Population Age 16 Years and Over

(Number, percent.)

Year	Civilian labor force	Civilian participation rate	Employed	Unemployed	Unemployment rate
2010..	3,081,512	69.5	2,814,393	267,119	8.7
2011..	3,079,759	69.1	2,840,996	238,763	7.8
2012..	3,073,981	68.6	2,857,418	216,563	7.0
2013..	3,079,305	68.4	2,871,997	207,308	6.7
2014..	3,082,564	68.1	2,915,848	166,716	5.4
2015..	3,094,351	68.1	2,953,622	140,729	4.5
2016..	3,130,520	68.6	3,005,478	125,042	4.0
2017..	3,151,909	68.6	3,048,242	103,667	3.3
2018..	3,133,294	67.9	3,039,295	93,999	3.0

Table WI-9. Employment and Average Wages by Industry

(Estimates are based on the 2012 *North American Industry Classification System* [NAICS].)

Industry	2011	2012	2013	2014	2015	2016	2017
	Number of jobs						
Wage and Salary Employment by Industry........................	2,809,126	2,840,826	2,874,503	2,912,213	2,945,464	2,980,084	3,000,006
Farm Wage and Salary Employment..............................	24,276	21,306	25,213	24,495	22,635	22,731	21,672
Nonfarm Wage and Salary Employment..........................	2,784,850	2,819,520	2,849,290	2,887,718	2,922,829	2,957,353	2,978,334
Private wage and salary employment..........................	2,351,539	2,385,612	2,415,066	2,451,523	2,488,641	2,518,437	2,542,669
Forestry, fishing, and related activities....................	5,525	5,697	5,822	5,890	6,209	6,560	6,568
Mining..	2,304	2,752	3,009	3,407	3,448	2,999	3,623
Utilities...	10,915	10,898	10,707	10,418	10,536	9,701	9,549
Construction	95,263	96,192	101,212	106,118	112,456	115,418	120,186
Manufacturing..	445,394	456,323	458,070	465,362	467,976	464,773	467,973
Durable goods manufacturing..............................	270,531	279,549	279,719	283,764	284,907	280,088	281,024
Nondurable goods manufacturing.........................	174,863	176,774	178,351	181,598	183,069	184,685	186,949
Wholesale trade	114,915	117,308	119,553	120,908	122,828	124,192	126,488
Retail trade..	297,335	297,749	300,748	304,680	307,242	311,206	310,405
Transportation and warehousing..............................	90,986	91,602	91,623	93,660	96,967	99,425	101,178
Information	47,118	46,684	47,297	48,073	49,100	49,077	47,808
Finance and insurance	129,912	130,550	129,009	126,681	127,472	127,522	128,684
Real estate and rental and leasing...........................	24,866	24,803	25,030	24,852	25,478	25,964	26,831
Professional, scientific, and technical services	96,735	99,329	100,565	102,141	105,705	108,325	109,993
Management of companies and enterprises.................	50,751	53,014	55,773	59,397	62,454	68,686	69,129
Administrative and waste services............................	138,686	140,686	144,443	147,916	147,260	147,568	147,343
Educational services..	54,592	54,901	55,865	56,059	55,936	55,958	56,554
Health care and social assistance............................	362,738	368,513	374,338	379,312	384,882	393,796	398,377
Arts, entertainment, and recreation..........................	35,419	36,195	36,448	37,833	38,317	40,351	41,393
Accommodation and food services............................	218,427	222,224	226,296	228,394	234,048	237,281	240,818
Other services, except public administration................	129,658	130,192	129,258	130,422	130,327	129,635	129,769
Government and government enterprises	433,311	433,908	434,224	436,195	434,188	438,916	435,665
	Dollars						
Average Wages and Salaries by Industry	41,607	42,668	43,376	44,431	45,878	46,532	47,804
Average Farm Wages and Salaries	24,908	36,861	31,548	35,368	32,312	39,052	38,048
Average Nonfarm Wages and Salaries	41,753	42,712	43,480	44,507	45,983	46,589	47,875
Average private wages and salaries...........................	41,961	43,133	43,907	44,972	46,501	47,200	48,534
Forestry, fishing, and related activities.....................	30,787	32,035	33,130	34,352	36,377	37,456	38,835
Mining..	60,078	61,402	61,603	67,095	63,674	63,308	64,713
Utilities...	95,980	98,018	103,594	101,383	103,025	100,327	105,613
Construction	51,190	52,693	54,210	56,152	58,031	59,588	60,990
Manufacturing..	53,190	54,188	54,818	56,035	57,114	57,030	58,779
Durable goods manufacturing..............................	55,208	55,996	56,505	57,766	58,403	58,418	60,534
Nondurable goods manufacturing.........................	50,067	51,328	52,174	53,330	55,107	54,925	56,141
Wholesale trade	57,429	59,277	60,131	61,723	63,602	64,908	67,229
Retail trade..	24,191	24,579	24,931	25,527	26,651	26,985	27,754
Transportation and warehousing..............................	40,780	42,475	42,945	44,622	45,017	44,439	45,565
Information	56,211	58,843	61,288	65,528	69,571	71,176	73,947
Finance and insurance	62,559	65,835	67,041	69,262	72,880	74,665	76,788
Real estate and rental and leasing...........................	34,180	34,947	35,706	37,087	39,293	41,301	42,187
Professional, scientific, and technical services	61,757	64,054	64,976	67,288	69,966	71,179	72,513
Management of companies and enterprises.................	87,344	89,640	91,843	93,747	96,956	98,489	96,710
Administrative and waste services............................	27,199	27,338	28,125	28,566	29,805	30,724	32,067
Educational services..	34,248	35,103	35,800	36,096	37,047	38,952	39,066
Health care and social assistance............................	43,886	44,689	45,325	45,290	46,685	47,161	48,602
Arts, entertainment, and recreation..........................	29,065	28,449	29,863	30,649	29,953	30,155	31,408
Accommodation and food services............................	14,316	14,946	15,199	15,750	16,416	17,004	17,687
Other services, except public administration................	26,977	27,686	28,442	29,402	30,664	31,647	32,956
Government and government enterprises.....................	40,620	40,398	41,106	41,899	43,011	43,081	44,029

Table WI-10. Employment Characteristics by Family Type

(Number, percent.)

Family type and labor force status	2015		2016		2017	
	Total	Families with own children under 18 years	Total	Families with own children under 18 years	Total	Families with own children under 18 years
All Families..	1,469,666	618,822	1,460,922	608,206	1,478,375	613,930
FAMILY TYPE AND LABOR FORCE STATUS						
Married-Couple Families................................	1,137,483	422,095	1,129,359	412,090	1,139,307	410,247
Both husband and wife in labor force................	56.8	75.1	56.3	76.3	56.2	76.6
Husband in labor force, wife not in labor force...........	16.1	19.2	16.1	18.7	16.4	18.9
Wife in labor force, husband not in labor force...........	8.2	4.0	8.1	3.6	7.6	3.3
Both husband and wife not in labor force..............	18.4	1.4	18.9	1.1	19.1	0.9
Other Families	332,183	196,727	331,563	196,116	339,068	203,683
Female householder, no husband present................	68.8	69.6	68.3	69.4	68.8	70.2
In labor force..	51.1	59.2	51.6	59.5	51.4	60.3
Not in labor force..	17.6	10.3	16.7	9.9	17.4	9.9
Male householder, no wife present....................	31.2	30.4	31.7	30.6	31.2	29.8
In labor force..	25.5	27.9	26.2	28.8	25.4	27.8
Not in labor force	5.7	2.5	5.6	1.8	5.9	2.0

Table WI-11. School Enrollment and Educational Attainment, 2017

(Number, percent.)

Item	State	U.S.
Enrollment		
Total population 3 years and over, enrolled in school	1,411,349	81,273,337
Enrolled in nursery school or preschool (percent)..............................	5.2	6.0
Enrolled in kindergarten (percent)...	5.6	4.9
Enrolled in elementary school, grades 1-8 (percent)...........................	40.9	40.6
Enrolled in high school, grades 9-12 (percent)	21.2	21.1
Enrolled in college or graduate school (percent)...............................	27.1	27.4
Attainment		
Total population 25 years and over	3,958,231	221,250,083
Less than ninth grade (percent)...	2.6	5.1
9th to 12th grade, no diploma (percent)...	5.1	6.9
High school graduate, including equivalency (percent).........................	30.7	27.1
Some college, no degree (percent)	20.3	20.4
Associate's degree (percent)..	10.9	8.5
Bachelor's degree (percent)	19.8	19.7
Graduate or professional degree (percent).......................................	10.6	12.3
High school graduate or higher (percent)...	92.4	88.0
Bachelor's degree or higher (percent)...	30.4	32.0

Table WI-12. Public School Characteristics and Educational Indicators

(Number, percent; data derived from National Center of Education Statistics.)

Item	State	U.S.
Public Elementary and Secondary Schools		
Number of operational school districts, 2016-17	461	18,377
Number of operational schools, 2016-17..	2,256	98,330
Percent charter schools	10.5	7.1
Total public school enrollment, 2016-17..	864,432	50,587,859
Percent charter school enrollment	5.1	6.0
Student-teacher ratio, Fall 2015...	14.9	16.0
Expenditures per student (dollars), 2015-16.......................................	11,664	11,841
Four-year adjusted cohort graduation rate (ACGR)[1]	88.6	84.6
Students eligible for free or reduced-price lunch (percent), 2015-16.............	39.9	52.1
English language learners (percent), Fall 2016	5.4	9.6
Students age 3 to 21 served under IDEA, part B (percent), 2017-18...............	14.0	13.7
Public Schools by Type, 2016-17		Percent of state public schools
Total number of schools..	2,256	100.0
Special education	11	0.5
Vocational education	6	0.3
Alternative education..	91	4.0

[1] Adjusted Cohort Graduation Rates (ACGR) differ from Averaged Freshmen Graduation Rates (AFGR).
NA = Not available.

Table WI-13. Reported Voting and Registration of the Voting-Age Population, November 2018

(Numbers in thousands, percent.)

Item	Total population	Total citizen population	Registered			Voted		
			Total registered	Percent registered (total population)	Percent registered (total citizen population)	Total voted	Percent voted (total population)	Percent voted (total citizen population)
U.S. Total	249,748	228,832	153,066	61.3	66.9	122,281	49.0	53.4
State Total....................................	4,436	4,296	3,129	70.5	72.8	2,776	62.6	64.6
Sex								
Male	2,186	2,105	1,519	69.5	72.2	1,328	60.7	63.1
Female	2,250	2,191	1,610	71.6	73.5	1,448	64.4	66.1
Race								
White alone..............................	3,948	3,865	2,883	73.0	74.6	2,574	65.2	66.6
White, non-Hispanic alone	3,782	3,759	2,815	74.5	74.9	2,514	66.5	66.9
Black alone..............................	264	239	137	51.7	57.1	110	41.7	46.0
Asian alone	89	79	52	58.6	66.0	52	58.6	66.0
Hispanic (of any race)...............	232	142	91	39.3	64.2	84	36.3	59.4
White alone or in combination	4,015	3,932	2,923	72.8	74.4	2,599	64.7	66.1
Black alone or in combination......	313	266	159	50.7	59.6	123	39.1	46.1
Asian alone or in combination......	94	84	57	60.5	67.8	57	60.5	67.8
Age								
18 to 24 years............................	471	462	254	54.0	55.0	221	46.9	47.7
25 to 34 years............................	747	689	424	56.8	61.6	339	45.5	49.3
35 to 44 years............................	703	663	438	62.3	66.1	388	55.2	58.5
45 to 64 years............................	1,490	1,467	1,189	79.8	81.0	1,056	70.9	72.0
65 years and over	1,026	1,015	824	80.3	81.2	772	75.2	76.0

Table WI-14. Crime

(Number, rate per 100,000. Data are derived from the FBI Uniform Crime Reports.)

Item	State			U.S.		
	2016	2017	Percent change	2016	2017	Percent change
TOTAL POPULATION[1]	5,772,917	5,795,483	0.4	323,405,935	325,719,178	0.7
VIOLENT CRIME						
Number..	17,716	18,539	4.6	1,285,606	1,283,220	-0.2
Rate	306.9	319.9	4.2	397.5	394.0	-0.9
Murder and Nonnegligent Manslaughter						
Number..	232	186	-19.8	17,413	17,284	-0.7
Rate	4.0	3.2	-20.1	5.4	5.3	-1.4
Rape[2]						
Number..	2,005	2,139	6.7	132,414	135,755	2.5
Rate	34.7	36.9	6.3	40.9	41.7	1.8
Robbery						
Number..	4,707	4,345	-7.7	332,797	319,356	-4.0
Rate	81.5	75.0	-8.1	102.9	98.0	-4.7
Aggravated Assault						
Number..	10,772	11,869	10.2	802,982	810,825	1.0
Rate	186.6	204.8	9.8	248.3	248.9	0.3
PROPERTY CRIME						
Number..	111,911	104,802	-6.4	7,928,530	7,694,086	-3.0
Rate	1,938.6	1,808.3	-6.7	2,451.6	2,362.2	-3.6
Burglary						
Number..	19,498	17,599	-9.7	1,516,405	1,401,840	-7.6
Rate	337.7	303.7	-10.1	468.9	430.4	-8.2
Larceny-Theft						
Number..	82,455	77,735	-5.7	5,644,835	5,519,107	-2.2
Rate	1,428.3	1,341.3	-6.1	1,745.4	1,694.4	-2.9
Motor Vehicle Theft						
Number..	9,958	9,468	-4.9	767,290	773,139	0.8
Rate	172.5	163.4	-5.3	237.3	237.4	-

NOTE: Although arson data are included in the trend and clearance tables, sufficient data are not available to estimate totals for this offense. Therefore, no arson data are published in this table.
- = Zero or rounds to zero.
[1] Population figures are U.S. Census Bureau provisional estimates as of July 1, 2017.
[2] The figures shown in the rape (revised definition) column were estimated using the revised Uniform Crime Reporting (UCR) definition of rape.

Table WI-15. State Government Finances, 2017

(Dollar amounts in thousands, percent distribution.)

Item	Dollars	Percent distribution
Total Revenue	46,800,615	100.0
General revenue	35,545,520	76.0
Intergovernmental revenue	9,583,175	20.5
Taxes	18,133,496	38.7
General sales	5,223,935	11.2
Selective sales	2,749,024	5.9
License taxes	1,179,054	2.5
Individual income tax	7,792,543	16.7
Corporate income tax	959,699	2.1
Other taxes	229,241	0.5
Current charges	4,643,405	9.9
Miscellaneous general revenue	3,185,444	6.8
Utility revenue	0	-
Liquor stores revenue	0	-
Insurance trust revenue[1]	11,255,095	24.0
Total Expenditure	39,873,101	100.0
Intergovernmental expenditure	8,826,031	22.1
Direct expenditure	31,047,070	77.9
Current operation	21,277,727	53.4
Capital outlay	2,991,683	7.5
Insurance benefits and repayments	5,459,008	13.7
Assistance and subsidies	665,198	1.7
Interest on debt	653,454	1.6
Exhibit: Salaries and wages	4,351,591	10.9
Total Expenditure	39,873,101	100.0
General expenditure	34,332,896	86.1
Intergovernmental expenditure	8,826,031	22.1
Direct expenditure	25,506,865	64.0
General expenditure, by function:		
Education	12,363,945	31.0
Public welfare	10,691,615	26.8
Hospitals	2,356,650	5.9
Health	562,177	1.4
Highways	3,844,589	9.6
Police protection	51,250	0.1
Correction	1,069,838	2.7
Natural resources	526,931	1.3
Parks and recreation	21,261	0.1
Governmental administration	1,001,273	2.5
Interest on general debt	653,454	1.6
Other and unallocable	1,189,913	3.0
Utility expenditure	81,197	0.2
Liquor stores expenditure	0	-
Insurance trust expenditure	5,459,008	13.7
Debt at End of Fiscal Year	23,252,381	X
Cash and Security Holdings	112,614,203	X

X = Not applicable.
- = Zero or rounds to zero.
[1] Within insurance trust revenue, net earnings of state retirement systems is a calculated statistic (the item code in the data file is X08), and thus can be positive or negative. Net earnings is the sum of earnings on investments plus gains on investments minus losses on investments. The change made in 2002 for asset valuation from book to market value in accordance with Statement 34 of the Governmental Accounting Standards Board is reflected in the calculated statistics.

Table WI-16. State Government Tax Collections, 2018

(Dollars in thousands, percent.)

Item	Dollars	Percent distribution
Total Taxes	18,742,929	100.0
Property taxes	163,446	0.9
Sales and gross receipts	8,232,896	43.9
General sales and gross receipts	5,484,375	29.3
Selective sales and gross receipts	2,748,521	14.7
Alcoholic beverages	62,498	0.3
Amusements	214	-
Insurance premiums	207,729	1.1
Motor fuels	1,051,479	5.6
Pari-mutuels	239	-
Public utilities	361,696	1.9
Tobacco products	617,415	3.3
Other selective sales	447,251	2.4
Licenses	1,182,001	6.3
Alcoholic beverages	1,958	-
Amusements	482	-
Corporations in general	22,225	0.1
Hunting and fishing	67,571	0.4
Motor vehicle	518,115	2.8
Motor vehicle operators	40,398	0.2
Public utilities	65,805	0.4
Occupation and business, NEC	464,571	2.5
Other licenses	876	-
Income taxes	9,061,928	48.3
Individual income	8,151,462	43.5
Corporation net income	910,466	4.9
Other taxes	102,658	0.5
Death and gift	1,733	-
Documentary and stock transfer	76,138	0.4
Severance	10,667	0.1
Taxes, NEC	14,120	0.1

- = Zero or rounds to zero.

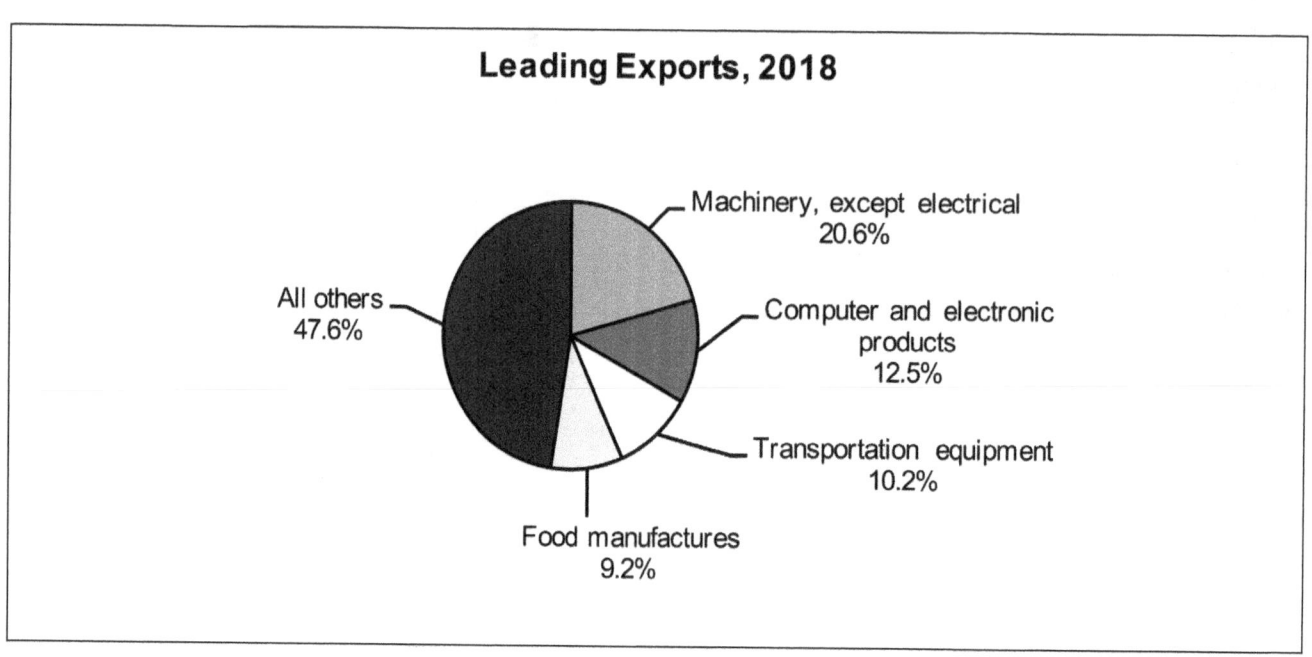

Leading Exports, 2018

Machinery, except electrical 20.6%

Computer and electronic products 12.5%

Transportation equipment 10.2%

Food manufactures 9.2%

All others 47.6%

WYOMING

Facts and Figures

Location: Western United States; bordered on the N by Montana, on the E by South Dakota and Nebraska, on the S by Colorado and Utah, and on the W by Utah and Idaho

Area: 97,814 sq. mi. (253,336 sq. km.); rank—10th

Population: 577,737 (2018 est.); rank—51st

Principal Cities: capital—Cheyenne; largest—Cheyenne

Statehood: July 10, 1890; 44th state

U.S. Congress: 2 senators, 1 representative

State Motto: Equal Rights

State Song: "Wyoming"

State Nicknames: The Equality State; The Cowboy State

Abbreviations: WY; Wyo.

State Symbols: flower—Indian paintbrush; tree—cottonwood; bird—Western meadowlark

At a Glance

- With an increase in population of 2.5 percent, Wyoming ranked 34th among the states in growth from 2010 to 2018.

- Wyoming's violent crime rate in 2017 was 237.5 per 100,000 population, compared to the U.S. rate of 394.0 per 100,000 population.

- Wyoming's median household income in 2017 was $60,434, and 11.3 percent of the population lived below the poverty level.

- In 2017, 11.3 percent of Wyoming residents and 13.3 percent of Wyoming's children lived below the poverty level, compared to the national poverty rates of 13.4 percent and 18.4 percent respectively.

- In 2017, 12.3 percent of Wyoming residents did not have health insurance, compared to 8.7 percent of total U.S. residents.

Table WY-1. Population by Age, Sex, Race, and Hispanic Origin

(Number, percent, except where noted.)

Sex, age, race, and Hispanic origin	2000	2010	2018 [1]	Percent change, 2010–2018
Total Population..	493,782	563,626	577,737	2.5
Percent of total U.S. population	0.2	0.2	0.2	X
Sex				
Male..	248,374	287,437	294,534	2.5
Female	245,408	276,189	283,203	2.5
Age				
Under 5 years..	30,940	40,203	35,912	-10.7
5 to 19 years...	114,406	111,310	113,264	1.8
20 to 64 years...	290,743	342,023	333,186	-2.6
65 years and over	57,693	70,090	95,375	36.1
Median age (years)	36.2	36.8	38.0	3.3
Race and Hispanic Origin				
One race				
White	454,670	529,110	534,943	1.1
Black	3,722	5,135	7,557	47.2
American Indian and Alaska Native	11,133	14,457	15,860	9.7
Asian	2,771	4,649	6,213	33.6
Native Hawaiian or Other Pacific Islander	302	521	572	9.8
Two or more races..	8,883	9,754	12,592	29.1
Hispanic (of any race).......................................	31,669	52,112	58,227	11.7

X = Not applicable.
- = Zero or rounds to zero.
[1] Population figures for 2018 are July 1 estimates. The 2010 estimates are taken from the 2010 Census.

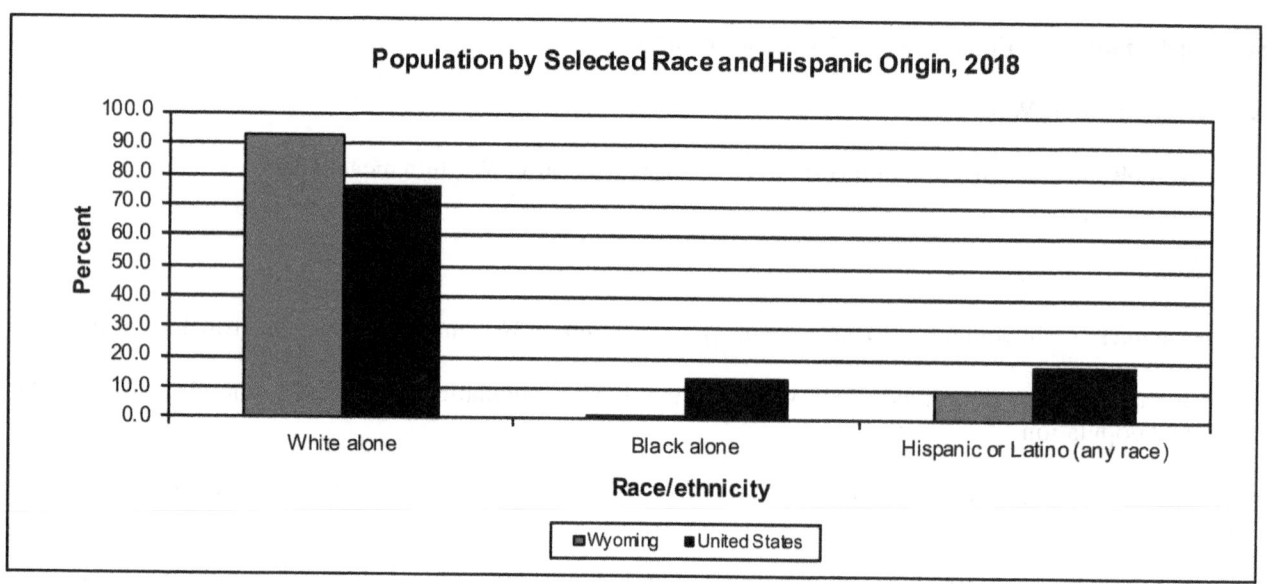

Population by Selected Race and Hispanic Origin, 2018

Table WY-2. Marital Status

(Number, percent distribution.)

Sex, age, race, and Hispanic origin	2000	2010	2017
Males, 15 Years and Over..	195,412	228,725	235,576
Never married	26.6	29.0	31.4
Now married, except separated..	58.8	56.2	52.6
Separated..	1.0	1.3	1.0
Widowed..	2.3	2.4	2.6
Divorced..	11.3	11.2	12.4
Females, 15 Years and Over..	195,433	220,169	227,038
Never married	20.0	20.7	23.3
Now married, except separated..	57.5	55.1	52.8
Separated..	1.3	2.0	1.4
Widowed..	9.2	8.6	8.4
Divorced..	12.0	13.6	14.2

Table WY-3. Households and Housing Characteristics

(Number, percent, dollars.)

Item	2000	2010	2017	Average annual percent change, 2010–2017
Total Households...	193,608	222,803	225,796	0.2
Family households	130,497	147,394	145,719	-0.2
Married-couple family	106,179	119,756	116,508	-0.4
Other family	24,318	27,638	29,211	0.8
Male householder, no wife present..............	7,481	7,804	9,950	3.9
Female householder, no husband present......	16,837	19,834	19,261	-0.4
Nonfamily households	63,111	75,409	80,077	0.9
Householder living alone..............................	50,980	61,775	64,313	0.6
Householder not living alone.........................	12,131	13,634	15,764	2.2
Housing Characteristics				
Total housing units..	223,854	262,286	276,733	0.8
Occupied housing units	193,608	222,803	225,796	0.2
Owner occupied	135,514	155,278	159,792	0.4
Renter occupied	58,094	67,525	66,004	-0.3
Average household size..................................	2.48	2.47	2.50	0.2
Financial Characteristics				
Median gross rent of renter-occupied housing	437	693	832	2.9
Median monthly owner costs for housing units with a mortgage	825	1,300	1,386	0.9
Median value of owner-occupied housing units.........	96,600	180,100	214,300	2.7

Table WY-4. Migration, Origin, and Language

(Number, percent.)

Characteristic	State 2016	State 2017	State Percent change	U.S. 2016	U.S. 2017	U.S. Percent change
Residence 1 Year Ago						
Population 1 year and over	577,567	573,483	-0.7	319,361,956	321,994,428	0.8
Same house	81.9	83.9	X	85.4	85.7	X
Different house in the U.S..........................	17.7	15.7	X	13.9	13.6	X
Same county	10.7	10.0	X	8.3	8.1	X
Different county	7.1	5.6	X	5.6	5.6	X
Same state	2.5	2.4	X	3.2	3.3	X
Different state	4.6	3.2	X	2.4	2.3	X
Abroad	0.4	0.4	X	0.7	0.7	X
Place of Birth						
Native born	566,645	558,795	-1.4	279,388,170	281,193,323	0.6
Male	51.1	51.1	X	49.3	49.4	X
Female	48.9	48.9	X	50.7	50.6	X
Foreign born	18,856	20,520	8.8	43,739,345	44,525,855	1.8
Male	46.5	51.1	X	48.5	48.4	X
Female	53.5	48.9	X	51.5	51.6	X
Foreign born; naturalized U.S. citizen............	7,396	7,228	-2.3	21,238,372	21,948,732	3.3
Male..	44.9	52.0	X	45.9	45.9	X
Female	55.1	48.0	X	54.1	54.1	X
Foreign born; not a U.S. citizen....................	11,460	13,292	16.0	22,500,973	22,577,123	0.3
Male..	47.6	50.6	X	51.0	50.8	X
Female	52.4	49.4	X	49.0	49.2	X
Entered 2010 or later	21.0	19.5	X	18.6	21.3	X
Entered 2000 to 2009	34.3	34.1	X	26.7	25.7	X
Entered before 2000	44.7	46.4	X	54.7	53.0	X
World Region of Birth, Foreign						
Foreign-born population, excluding population born at sea	18,856	20,520	8.8	43,738,901	44,525,458	1.8
Europe	18.2	16.6	X	10.9	10.8	X
Asia	24.2	20.8	X	30.8	31.2	X
Africa	6.8	2.0	X	4.9	5.1	X
Oceania	0.5	1.0	X	0.6	0.6	X
Latin America	46.9	53.6	X	51.0	50.4	X
North America..	3.5	6.0	X	1.8	1.8	X
Language Spoken at Home and Ability to Speak English						
Population 5 years and over	547,628	541,405	-1.1	303,328,961	305,924,019	0.9
English only	92.4	91.8	X	78.4	78.2	X
Language other than English..........................	7.6	8.2	X	21.6	21.8	X
Speaks English less than "very well"..........	2.0	2.3	X	8.6	8.5	X

NA = Not available.
X = Not applicable.
- = Zero or rounds to zero.

Table WY-5. Median Income and Poverty Status, 2017

(Number, percent, except as noted.)

Characteristic	State		U.S.	
	Number	Percent	Number	Percent
Median Income				
Households (dollars)..	60,434	X	60,336	X
Families (dollars)	74,868	X	73,891	X
Below Poverty Level (All People)	64,054	11.3	42,583,651	13.4
Sex				
Male	30,054	10.5	19,004,547	12.2
Female	34,000	12.2	23,579,104	14.5
Age				
Under 18 years...	18,013	13.3	13,353,202	18.4
Related children under 18 years..	17,528	13.0	13,053,472	18.1
18 to 64 years..	38,610	11.3	24,648,677	12.6
65 years and over	7,431	8.4	4,581,772	9.3

X = Not applicable.

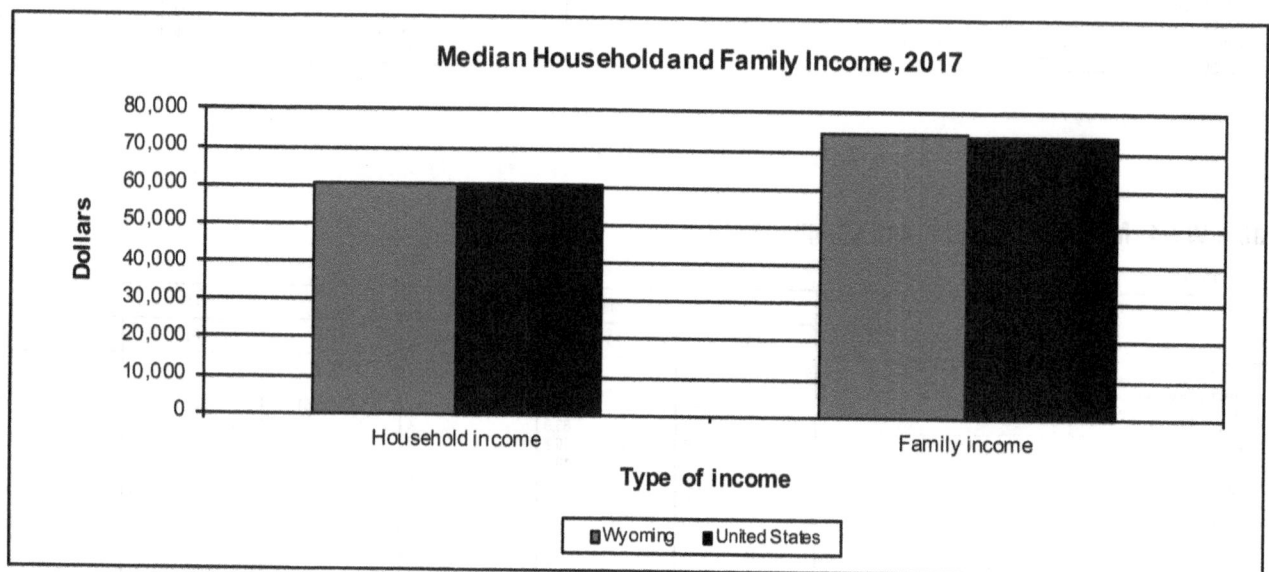

Table WY-6. Health Insurance Coverage Status for the Civilian Noninstitutionalized Population and Children Under 18 Years of Age

(Number, percent.)

Item	2009	2010	2011	2012	2013	2014	2015	2016	2017
Civilian Noninstitutionalized Population	533,716	555,010	558,832	567,082	573,210	574,798	576,557	576,027	568,891
Covered by Private or Public Insurance									
Number..	452,788	472,174	473,001	479,998	496,182	506,050	510,063	509,514	499,176
Percent..	84.8	85.1	84.6	84.6	86.6	88.0	88.5	88.5	87.7
Uninsured									
Number..	80,928	82,836	85,831	87,084	77,028	68,748	66,494	66,513	69,715
Percent..	15.2	14.9	15.4	15.4	13.4	12.0	11.5	11.5	12.3
Percent in the U.S. not covered......................................	15.1	15.5	15.1	14.8	14.5	11.7	9.4	8.6	8.7
Children Under 18 Years of Age[1]	128,421	136,229	134,594	136,132	139,291	137,296	138,953	140,464	145,904
Covered by Private or Public Insurance									
Number..	116,924	125,461	122,956	123,417	131,357	129,159	128,097	128,136	131,974
Percent..	91.0	92.1	91.4	90.7	94.3	94.1	92.2	91.2	90.5
Uninsured									
Number..	11,497	10,768	11,638	12,715	7,934	8,137	10,856	12,328	13,930
Percent..	9.0	7.9	8.6	9.3	5.7	5.9	7.8	8.8	9.5
Percent in the U.S. not covered......................................	8.6	8.0	7.5	7.2	7.1	6.0	4.8	4.5	5.0

[1] 2017 data is for individuals under 19 years of age.

Table WY-7. Employment Status by Demographic Group, 2018

(Numbers in thousands, percent.)

Characteristic	Civilian noninstitutional population	Civilian labor force		Employed		Unemployed	
		Number	Percent of population	Number	Percent of population	Number	Percent of population
Total...	445	287	64.7	275	62.0	12	4.2
Sex							
Male...	224	158	70.4	151	67.5	6	4.0
Female...	221	130	58.8	124	56.3	6	4.3
Race, Sex, and Hispanic Origin							
White..	416	268	64.5	258	62.1	10	3.8
Male..	210	148	70.5	143	68.1	5	3.5
Female...	206	120	58.4	115	56.0	5	4.1
Black or African American...................	NA	NA	NA	NA	NA	NA	NA
Male..	NA	NA	NA	NA	NA	NA	NA
Female...	NA	NA	NA	NA	NA	NA	NA
Hispanic or Latino ethnicity[1]	39	26	67.1	25	63.1	2	5.9
Male..	19	14	74.3	13	69.7	1	6.1
Female...	20	12	60.3	11	57.0	1	5.5
Age							
16 to 19 years...................................	31	15	48.0	13	42.5	2	11.2
20 to 24 years...................................	33	25	77.0	24	71.8	2	6.7
25 to 34 years...................................	78	63	81.3	60	77.5	3	4.6
35 to 44 years...................................	68	60	89.5	59	87.4	1	2.3
45 to 54 years...................................	62	52	83.5	50	80.1	2	4.2
55 to 64 years...................................	78	50	64.5	49	62.8	1	2.4
65 years and over..............................	96	22	22.7	21	21.6	1	4.6

NOTE: Data in Table 7 are from the Current Population Survey (CPS) and do not match the estimates in Table 8. See notes and definitions for further information.
[1] May be of any race.
NA = Not available.

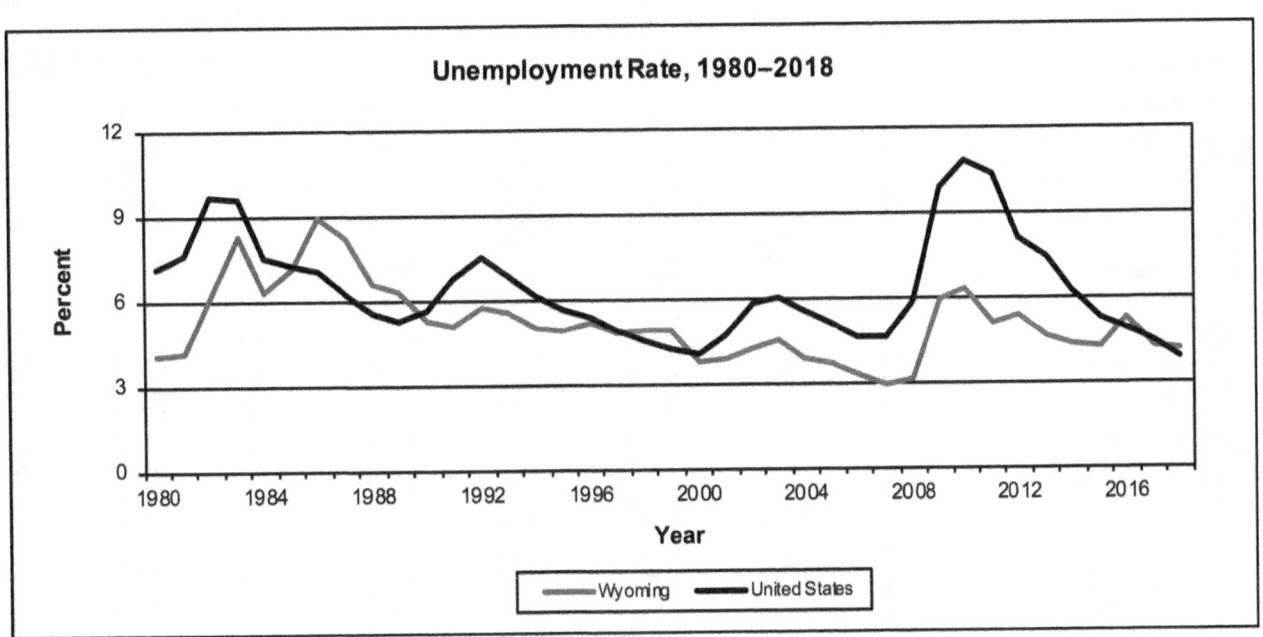

Unemployment Rate, 1980–2018

Table WY-8. Employment Status of the Civilian Noninstitutional Population Age 16 Years and Over

(Number, percent.)

Year	Civilian labor force	Civilian participation rate	Employed	Unemployed	Unemployment rate
2010...	303,297	70.4	283,744	19,553	6.4
2011...	306,815	70.2	289,019	17,796	5.8
2012...	307,267	69.2	290,932	16,335	5.3
2013...	306,608	68.4	292,131	14,477	4.7
2014...	306,331	68.1	293,657	12,674	4.1
2015...	304,775	67.5	291,686	13,089	4.3
2016...	300,922	66.7	285,052	15,870	5.3
2017...	293,347	65.5	281,017	12,330	4.2
2018...	289,574	64.7	277,820	11,754	4.1

Table WY-9. Employment and Average Wages by Industry

(Estimates are based on the 2012 *North American Industry Classification System* [NAICS].)

Industry	2011	2012	2013	2014	2015	2016	2017
	Number of jobs						
Wage and Salary Employment by Industry......................	293,811	298,289	299,508	303,951	302,522	291,463	289,601
Farm Wage and Salary Employment................................	3,272	3,710	3,683	3,566	3,822	3,871	4,480
Nonfarm Wage and Salary Employment............................	290,539	294,579	295,825	300,385	298,700	287,592	285,121
Private wage and salary employment...............................	215,480	218,894	220,058	225,017	222,859	211,367	209,803
Forestry, fishing, and related activities............................	1,055	1,099	1,134	1,168	1,170	1,171	(D)
Mining..	27,183	27,531	26,482	27,130	23,740	18,703	19,566
Utilities..	2,488	2,471	2,484	2,489	2,535	2,541	2,476
Construction..	21,610	22,128	22,416	24,377	23,865	21,649	20,056
Manufacturing..	9,184	9,361	9,475	9,819	9,767	9,229	(D)
Durable goods manufacturing..................................	4,614	4,733	4,705	4,875	4,713	4,145	(D)
Nondurable goods manufacturing..............................	4,570	4,628	4,770	4,944	5,054	5,084	(D)
Wholesale trade..	8,858	9,194	9,288	9,532	9,541	8,532	8,156
Retail trade..	29,409	29,675	29,999	29,979	30,979	30,858	29,871
Transportation and warehousing.................................	12,133	12,248	12,410	13,238	13,158	11,749	11,648
Information..	3,858	3,916	3,801	3,780	3,782	3,747	3,687
Finance and insurance	7,102	7,094	7,179	7,195	7,240	7,240	7,306
Real estate and rental and leasing..............................	4,065	4,148	4,420	4,505	4,366	4,066	4,160
Professional, scientific, and technical services..............	9,141	9,304	9,324	9,600	9,465	8,935	8,996
Management of companies and enterprises.....................	866	956	1,032	1,014	1,025	901	868
Administrative and waste services..............................	7,900	7,907	7,911	7,948	8,158	8,090	8,301
Educational services..	2,083	2,030	2,130	2,139	2,208	2,274	2,263
Health care and social assistance..............................	24,021	24,102	24,382	24,436	24,617	25,161	25,093
Arts, entertainment, and recreation.............................	2,797	2,849	2,920	3,092	3,174	3,341	3,694
Accommodation and food services..............................	30,414	31,229	31,856	32,458	33,145	32,703	32,808
Other services, except public administration...................	11,313	11,652	11,415	11,118	10,924	10,477	10,320
Government and government enterprises.......................	75,059	75,685	75,767	75,368	75,841	76,225	75,318
	Dollars						
Average Wages and Salaries by Industry	44,038	45,401	45,853	47,400	47,182	46,006	47,285
Average Farm Wages and Salaries	30,014	34,596	38,877	38,757	30,603	34,981	30,400
Average Nonfarm Wages and Salaries	44,196	45,537	45,940	47,503	47,394	46,154	47,551
Average private wages and salaries...............................	44,345	45,870	46,263	48,043	47,558	45,696	47,307
Forestry, fishing, and related activities...........................	23,613	23,835	24,594	25,927	26,729	28,324	(D)
Mining..	80,883	83,401	85,509	88,868	88,770	85,792	89,302
Utilities..	84,345	84,531	85,594	88,876	92,338	92,152	94,797
Construction..	48,426	50,106	51,138	52,318	51,927	51,253	51,753
Manufacturing..	56,164	57,211	58,894	62,391	64,758	66,016	(D)
Durable goods manufacturing..................................	48,595	50,156	50,898	53,721	54,105	53,216	(D)
Nondurable goods manufacturing..............................	63,806	64,425	66,782	70,939	74,692	76,452	(D)
Wholesale trade..	57,558	59,045	59,482	64,232	61,196	59,071	62,818
Retail trade..	26,737	28,026	27,857	28,581	29,011	28,766	29,651
Transportation and warehousing.................................	55,821	57,524	57,008	59,073	58,805	56,770	59,921
Information..	41,847	43,084	44,290	45,939	47,473	47,614	48,615
Finance and insurance	51,120	54,102	55,109	57,977	60,080	60,113	62,237
Real estate and rental and leasing..............................	43,100	45,364	46,648	49,020	47,499	44,354	47,083
Professional, scientific, and technical services..............	56,025	58,642	59,356	62,523	61,921	60,076	62,164
Management of companies and enterprises.....................	105,248	114,437	113,451	100,183	103,816	102,041	101,373
Administrative and waste services..............................	32,106	31,824	31,902	32,613	33,508	33,041	35,175
Educational services..	29,038	29,982	29,581	29,832	28,337	28,521	29,093
Health care and social assistance..............................	40,532	42,030	41,546	42,603	43,820	43,511	44,141
Arts, entertainment, and recreation.............................	21,491	21,442	22,100	23,780	23,962	24,498	24,767
Accommodation and food services..............................	18,995	19,884	20,724	21,224	21,735	22,220	22,844
Other services, except public administration...................	31,630	32,866	33,458	33,198	34,095	33,509	34,397
Government and government enterprises.......................	43,766	44,572	45,000	45,890	46,913	47,426	48,231

Table WY-10. Employment Characteristics by Family Type

(Number, percent.)

Family type and labor force status	2015		2016		2017	
	Total	Families with own children under 18 years	Total	Families with own children under 18 years	Total	Families with own children under 18 years
All Families...	145,470	63,698	145,524	59,042	145,719	62,720
FAMILY TYPE AND LABOR FORCE STATUS						
Married-Couple Families................................	117,245	45,664	117,038	41,342	116,508	44,501
Both husband and wife in labor force.................................	56.4	68.9	52.9	70.2	55.0	73.2
Husband in labor force, wife not in labor force	20.3	26.3	20.0	25.6	19.4	22.8
Wife in labor force, husband not in labor force	6.7	3.5	8.3	3.7	7.9	3.0
Both husband and wife not in labor force...............................	16.3	1.1	18.2	0.4	17.0	0.7
Other Families	28,225	18,034	28,486	17,700	29,211	18,219
Female householder, no husband present.............................	58.1	56.7	61.5	61.3	65.9	71.4
In labor force	45.0	49.4	47.2	56.7	49.6	58.2
Not in labor force	13.1	7.3	14.4	4.6	16.3	13.3
Male householder, no wife present.............................	41.9	43.3	38.5	38.7	34.1	28.6
In labor force...	35.8	40.4	34.3	37.5	28.7	28.3
Not in labor force	6.1	3.0	4.1	1.2	5.3	0.3

Table WY-11. School Enrollment and Educational Attainment, 2017

(Number, percent.)

Item	State	U.S.
Enrollment		
Total population 3 years and over, enrolled in school	147,108	81,273,337
Enrolled in nursery school or preschool (percent)	5.9	6.0
Enrolled in kindergarten (percent).......................................	4.6	4.9
Enrolled in elementary school, grades 1–8 (percent)	44.0	40.6
Enrolled in high school, grades 9–12 (percent)	20.5	21.1
Enrolled in college or graduate school (percent).......................................	25.1	27.4
Attainment		
Total population 25 years and over	387,700	221,250,083
Less than ninth grade (percent)	2.0	5.1
9th to 12th grade, no diploma (percent)	5.1	6.9
High school graduate, including equivalency (percent).......................................	29.6	27.1
Some college, no degree (percent)	25.3	20.4
Associate's degree (percent)	10.4	8.5
Bachelor's degree (percent)	17.4	19.7
Graduate or professional degree (percent).......................................	10.3	12.3
High school graduate or higher (percent)	92.9	88.0
Bachelor's degree or higher (percent).......................................	27.6	32.0

Table WY-12. Public School Characteristics and Educational Indicators

(Number, percent; data derived from National Center of Education Statistics.)

Item	State	U.S.
Public Elementary and Secondary Schools		
Number of operational school districts, 2016-17.......................................	60	18,377
Number of operational schools, 2016-17.......................................	371	98,330
Percent charter schools	1.3	7.1
Total public school enrollment, 2016-17.......................................	94,170	50,587,859
Percent charter school enrollment	0.5	6.0
Student-teacher ratio, Fall 2015.......................................	12.4	16.0
Expenditures per student (dollars), 2015-16.......................................	16,431	11,841
Four-year adjusted cohort graduation rate (ACGR)[1]	86.2	84.6
Students eligible for free or reduced-price lunch (percent), 2015-16.......................................	37.5	52.1
English language learners (percent), Fall 2016	3.0	9.6
Students age 3 to 21 served under IDEA, part B (percent), 2017-18.......................................	16.6	13.7
Public Schools by Type, 2016-17		Percent of state public schools
Total number of schools.......................................	371	100.0
Special education.......................................	3	0.5
Vocational education.......................................	0	-
Alternative education.......................................	6	4.0

[1] Adjusted Cohort Graduation Rates (ACGR) differ from Averaged Freshmen Graduation Rates (AFGR).
- = Zero or rounds to zero.

Table WY-13. Reported Voting and Registration of the Voting-Age Population, November 2018

(Numbers in thousands, percent.)

Item	Total population	Total citizen population	Registered			Voted		
			Total registered	Percent registered (total population)	Percent registered (total citizen population)	Total voted	Percent voted (total population)	Percent voted (total citizen population)
U.S. Total	249,748	228,832	153,066	61.3	66.9	122,281	49.0	53.4
State Total...	430	422	268	62.4	63.5	220	51.2	52.1
Sex								
Male	216	212	134	61.8	62.9	107	49.7	50.6
Female	214	210	135	62.9	64.1	113	52.7	53.6
Race								
White alone..	408	402	259	63.6	64.5	214	52.5	53.2
White, non-Hispanic alone...............	369	368	244	66.0	66.3	202	54.7	54.9
Black alone..	5	4	3	(B)	(B)	2	(B)	(B)
Asian alone	3	1	-	(B)	(B)	-	(B)	(B)
Hispanic (of any race).......................	41	37	16	(B)	(B)	13	(B)	(B)
White alone or in combination	410	405	261	63.6	64.4	216	52.5	53.2
Black alone or in combination............	6	5	3	(B)	(B)	2	(B)	(B)
Asian alone or in combination............	3	1	-	(B)	(B)	-	(B)	(B)
Age								
18 to 24 years	44	44	15	(B)	(B)	9	(B)	(B)
25 to 34 years	84	80	42	50.1	52.4	28	33.6	35.2
35 to 44 years	67	65	40	(B)	(B)	28	(B)	(B)
45 to 64 years	142	141	98	69.3	69.8	88	62.0	62.5
65 years and over	94	93	73	77.3	78.1	67	71.1	71.8

- = Zero or rounds to zero.
B = Base is less than 75,000 and therefore too small to show the derived measure.

Table WY-14. Crime

(Number, rate per 100,000. Data are derived from the FBI Uniform Crime Reports.)

Item	State			U.S.		
	2016	2017	Percent change	2016	2017	Percent change
TOTAL POPULATION[1]	584,910	579,315	-1.0	323,405,935	325,719,178	0.7
VIOLENT CRIME						
Number...	1,431	1,376	-3.8	1,285,606	1,283,220	-0.2
Rate..	244.7	237.5	-2.9	397.5	394.0	-0.9
Murder and Nonnegligent Manslaughter						
Number...	20	15	-25.0	17,413	17,284	-0.7
Rate..	3.4	2.6	-24.3	5.4	5.3	-1.4
Rape[2]						
Number...	206	263	27.7	132,414	135,755	2.5
Rate..	35.2	45.4	28.9	40.9	41.7	1.8
Robbery						
Number...	59	76	28.8	332,797	319,356	-4.0
Rate..	10.1	13.1	30.1	102.9	98.0	-4.7
Aggravated Assault						
Number...	1,146	1,022	-10.8	802,982	810,825	1.0
Rate..	195.9	176.4	-10.0	248.3	248.9	0.3
PROPERTY CRIME						
Number...	11,460	10,604	-7.5	7,928,530	7,694,086	-3.0
Rate..	1,959.3	1,830.4	-6.6	2,451.6	2,362.2	-3.6
Burglary						
Number...	1,771	1,593	-10.1	1,516,405	1,401,840	-7.6
Rate..	302.8	275.0	-9.2	468.9	430.4	-8.2
Larceny-Theft						
Number...	8,889	8,232	-7.4	5,644,835	5,519,107	-2.2
Rate..	1,519.7	1,421.0	-6.5	1,745.4	1,694.4	-2.9
Motor Vehicle Theft						
Number...	800	779	-2.6	767,290	773,139	0.8
Rate..	136.8	134.5	-1.7	237.3	237.4	-

NOTE: Although arson data are included in the trend and clearance tables, sufficient data are not available to estimate totals for this offense. Therefore, no arson data are published in this table.
- = Zero or rounds to zero.
[1] Population figures are U.S. Census Bureau provisional estimates as of July 1, 2017.
[2] The figures shown in the rape (revised definition) column were estimated using the revised Uniform Crime Reporting (UCR) definition of rape.

Table WY-15. State Government Finances, 2017

(Dollar amounts in thousands, percent distribution.)

Item	Dollars	Percent distribution
Total Revenue	6,785,544	100.0
General revenue	5,519,043	81.3
Intergovernmental revenue	2,566,761	37.8
Taxes	1,649,550	24.3
General sales	588,866	8.7
Selective sales	173,722	2.6
License taxes	161,973	2.4
Individual income tax	0	-
Corporate income tax	0	-
Other taxes	724,989	10.7
Current charges	220,442	3.2
Miscellaneous general revenue	1,082,290	15.9
Utility revenue	431	-
Liquor stores revenue	111,231	1.6
Insurance trust revenue[1]	1,154,839	17.0
Total Expenditure	8,205,985	100.0
Intergovernmental expenditure	3,083,277	37.6
Direct expenditure	5,122,708	62.4
Current operation	3,504,853	42.7
Capital outlay	708,810	8.6
Insurance benefits and repayments	837,909	10.2
Assistance and subsidies	49,220	0.6
Interest on debt	21,916	.0.3
Exhibit: Salaries and wages	703,571	8.6
Total Expenditure	8,205,985	100.0
General expenditure	7,214,813	87.9
Intergovernmental expenditure	3,083,277	37.6
Direct expenditure	4,131,536	50.3
General expenditure, by function:		
Education	2,278,896	27.8
Public welfare	824,371	10.0
Hospitals	3,559	0.0
Health	416,965	5.1
Highways	738,379	9.0
Police protection	39,435	0.5
Correction	126,045	1.5
Natural resources	242,614	3.0
Parks and recreation	24,242	0.3
Governmental administration	370,556	4.5
Interest on general debt	21,916	0.3
Other and unallocable	2,127,835	25.9
Utility expenditure	56,639	0.8
Liquor stores expenditure	96,624	1.2
Insurance trust expenditure	837,909	10.2
Debt at End of Fiscal Year	769,721	X
Cash and Security Holdings	27,240,867	X

X = Not applicable.
- = Zero or rounds to zero.
[1] Within insurance trust revenue, net earnings of state retirement systems is a calculated statistic (the item code in the data file is X08), and thus can be positive or negative. Net earnings is the sum of earnings on investments plus gains on investments minus losses on investments. The change made in 2002 for asset valuation from book to market value in accordance with Statement 34 of the Governmental Accounting Standards Board is reflected in the calculated statistics.

Table WY-16. State Government Tax Collections, 2018

(Dollars in thousands, percent.)

Item	Dollars	Percent distribution
Total Taxes	1,837,401	100.0
Property taxes	250,153	13.6
Sales and gross receipts	862,797	47.0
General sales and gross receipts	689,207	37.5
Selective sales and gross receipts	173,590	9.4
Alcoholic beverages	1,920	0.1
Amusements	X	-
Insurance premiums	23,481	1.3
Motor fuels	113,622	6.2
Pari-mutuels	4,698	0.3
Public utilities	4,893	0.3
Tobacco products	22,076	1.2
Other selective sales	2,900	0.2
Licenses	187,522	10.2
Alcoholic beverages	X	-
Amusements	X	-
Corporations in general	14,205	0.8
Hunting and fishing	37,187	2.0
Motor vehicle	91,663	5.0
Motor vehicle operators	4,158	0.2
Public utilities	X	-
Occupation and business, NEC	40,309	2.2
Other licenses	0	-
Income taxes	X	-
Individual income	X	-
Corporation net income	X	-
Other taxes	536,929	29.2
Death and gift	0	-
Documentary and stock transfer	X	-
Severance	531,659	28.9
Taxes, NEC	5,270	0.3

X = Not applicable.
- = Zero or rounds to zero.

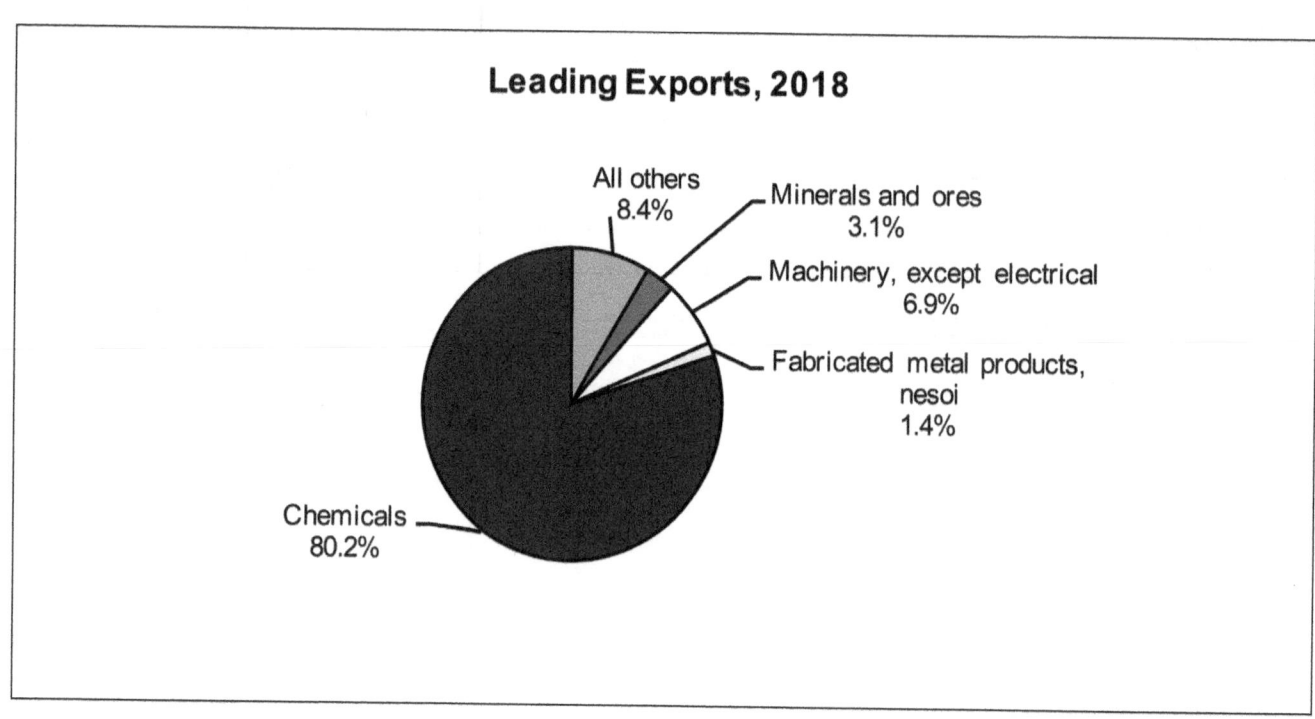

Leading Exports, 2018

All others 8.4%
Minerals and ores 3.1%
Machinery, except electrical 6.9%
Fabricated metal products, nesoi 1.4%
Chemicals 80.2%

The state chapters in this book follow a standard plan of organization, and the same data sources are used for the tables and figures found in each chapter. These notes describe the standard data sources, which are presented by topic in the order in which they appear in each chapter. Definitions, brief descriptions of methodology, and sources of additional information are also provided.

Symbols used are included in the footnotes of the tables.

Table 1.
Source: U.S. Department of Commerce. U.S Census Bureau. 2000 and 2010 Decennial Census. Census statistics, 2018.
<http://factfinder.census.gov/>.

Population estimates data are accessed through American FactFinder from the U.S. Census Bureau, as well as from the Census Bureau itself. The data for percent change, 2010–2018, were calculated by the editor.

Population estimates and the decennial census. Population data are estimates produced by the Census Bureau. The Bureau's Population Estimates Program (PEP) produces estimates of the population as of July 1 for each year following the most recently published decennial census (the actual physical count of the population made every ten years, which is described below). Existing data on births, deaths, and domestic and international immigration are used to update the decennial census base. PEP estimates are used to set federal funding allocations, update national surveys, and monitor recent demographic changes.

Noncitizens residing in the United States are included, regardless of their immigration status.

Persons temporarily away from their usual residence on Census Day (April 1), for reasons such as vacation or business trips, were counted as being at their usual residence. People who live at more than one residence during the week, month, or year were counted as being at the place in which they lived most of the year. However, people without a usual residence were counted as being where they were staying on Census Day.

Age, sex, race, and ethnicity. While estimates of the age and sex of the population are straightforward, estimates of race and ethnicity are not. Decennial census data on race and ethnicity are based on self-identification by the respondent, and the same respondent may answer differently on separate occasions. On the 2000 decennial census, respondents could report more than one race; in previous censuses, respondents had to identify themselves as belonging to only one race.

The Census Bureau treats Hispanic or Latino origin as a separate and distinct concept from race. Beginning with the 2000 census, a separate self-identification question was asked regarding Hispanic or Latino origin. Persons of Hispanic or Latino origin are those who classified themselves as belonging to one of the specific categories listed on the questionnaire—Mexican, Puerto Rican, Cuban, or Other Spanish/Hispanic origin (including those whose origins are from Spain, the Spanish-speaking countries of Central and South America, or the Dominican Republic). People who are Hispanic may be of any race, and people in each race group may be Hispanic. The overlap of race and Hispanic origin is a major comparability issue, because Hispanics may be of any race. For a further discussion of this issue, see: U.S. Census Bureau. *U.S. Census Bureau Guidance on the Presentation and Comparison of Race and Hispanic Origin Data.* (June 12, 2003.) <http://www.census.gov/population/www/socdemo/compraceho.html>.

Table 2.
Source: U.S. Department of Commerce. U.S Census Bureau. 2000 Decennial Census. American Community Survey, 2000, 2010, and 2017.
<http://factfinder.census.gov/>.

Data on marital status were tabulated for persons 15 years and over. Marital status was reported for each person as either "now married," "widowed," "divorced," "separated," or "never married." Individuals who were living together (unmarried people, people in commonlaw marriages) reported the marital status they considered most appropriate.

Now Married, Except Separated. Includes people whose current marriage has not ended through widowhood, divorce, or separation (regardless of previous marital history). The category may also include couples who live together or people in common-law marriages if they consider this category the most appropriate. In certain tabulations, currently married people are further classified as "spouse present" or "spouse absent."

Separated. Refers to people who were not living with their spouse due to marital discord.

Divorced. Indicates people who reported being divorced and had not remarried.

Widowed. Refers to people whose last marriage ended with the death of their spouse and who had not remarried.

Never married. The term applies to those who had never been legally married or people whose only marriage ended in an annulment.

Table 3.
Source: U.S. Department of Commerce. U.S Census Bureau. 2000 Decennial Census. American Community Survey, 2000, 2010, and 2017.
<http://factfinder.census.gov/>.

The annual data were obtained from the Census Bureau. The data for average annual percent change, 2010–2017, were calculated by the editor.

Households. A household comprises one or more persons occupying a single housing unit, such as a house, apartment, or a room occupied as separate living quarters. A household may consist of a person living alone, a single family, two or more families living together, or any other group of unrelated individuals sharing a housing unit.

Householder. The person, or one of the people, in whose name the home is owned, being bought, or rented. If there is no such person present, any household member 15 years old and over can serve as the householder for the purposes of the census.

Two types of householders are distinguished: a family householder and a nonfamily householder. A family householder is a householder living with one or more people related to him or her by birth, marriage, or adoption. The householder and all people in the household related to him are family members. A nonfamily householder is a householder living alone or with nonrelatives only.

Housing unit. A house, an apartment, a mobile home or trailer, a group of rooms, or a single room occupied as separate living quarters, or if vacant, intended for occupancy as separate living quarters.

Median gross rent. The monthly amount of contract rent plus the estimated average monthly cost of utilities (electricity, gas, water, and sewer) and fuels (oil, coal, kerosene, wood, etc.).

Median monthly owner costs for housing units with a mortgage. The sum of payments for mortgages, deeds of trust, contracts to purchase, or similar debts on the property (including payments for the first mortgage, second mortgages, home equity loans, and other junior mortgages); real estate taxes; fire, hazard, and flood insurance on the property; utilities (electricity, gas, water, and sewer); and fuels (oil, coal, kerosene, wood, etc.). It also includes, where appropriate, the monthly condominium fee for condominiums and mobile home costs (installment loan payments, personal property taxes, site rent, registration fees, and license fees). Selected monthly owner costs were tabulated for all owner-occupied units, and usually are shown separately for units "with a mortgage" and for units "not mortgaged.

Median value of owner-occupied housing units. Data for the median value of owner-occupied housing units are respondents' estimates of how much their property would sell for if it was currently on the market.

Table 4.
Source: U.S. Department of Commerce. U.S Census Bureau. American Community Survey, 2016 and 2017.
<http://factfinder.census.gov/>.

The annual data derives from Census estimates. The data for percent change were calculated by the editor.

Residence 1 year ago. The data on residence 1 year ago were derived from answers to Question 15, which were asked of the population 1 year and older. For the American Community Survey, people who had moved from another residence in the United States or Puerto Rico 1 year earlier were asked to report the exact address (number and street name); the name of the city, town, or post office; the name of the U.S. county; and the ZIP Code where they lived 1 year ago. People living outside the United States and Puerto Rico were asked to report the name of the foreign country or U.S. Island Area where they were living 1 year ago.

Native born. The native population includes anyone who was a U.S. citizen or a U.S. national at birth. This includes respondents who indicated they were born in the United States, Puerto Rico, a U.S. Island Area (such as Guam), or abroad of an American (U.S. citizen) parent or parents.

Foreign born. The foreign-born population includes anyone who was not a U.S. citizen or a U.S. national at birth. This includes respondents who indicated they were a U.S. citizen by naturalization or not a U.S. citizen.

Respondent's ability to speak English. Respondents who reported speaking a language other than English were asked to indicate their English-speaking ability based on one of the following categories: "Very well," "Well," "Not well," or "Not at all." Those who answered "Well," "Not well," or "Not at all" are sometimes referred as "Less than 'very well.'" Respondents were not instructed on how to interpret the response categories in this question. Households in which no one 14 and over speaks English only or speaks a language other than English at home and speaks English "very well" identifies households that may need English language assistance. This arises when no one 14 and over meets either of two conditions: (1) they speak English at home or (2) even though they speak another language, they also report that they speak English "very well".

Table 5.
Source: U.S. Department of Commerce. U.S Census Bureau. American Community Survey.
<http://factfinder.census.gov/>.

Median household income. Includes the income of the householder and all other individuals 15 years old and over in the household, whether they are related to the householder or not. Because many households consist of only one person, average household income is usually less than average family income. Total income is the sum of the amounts reported separately for wage or salary income; net self-employment income; interest, dividends, or net rental or royalty income or income from estates and trusts; Social Security or railroad retirement income; Supplemental Security Income (SSI); public assistance or welfare payments; retirement, survivor, or disability pensions; and all other income. Receipts from the following sources are not included as income: capital gains, money received from the sale of property (unless the recipient was engaged in the business of selling such property); the value of income "in kind" from food stamps, public housing subsidies, medical care, employer contributions for individuals, etc.; withdrawal of bank deposits; money borrowed; tax refunds; exchange of money between relatives living in the same household; gifts; and lump-sum inheritances, insurance payments, and other types of lump-sum receipts.

Median family income. The incomes of all members 15 years old and over related to the householder are summed and treated as a single amount.

Poverty. Following the Office of Management and Budget standards that have been in use since the late 1960s, the Census Bureau uses a set of money income thresholds that vary by family size and composition to determine the proportion of Americans in poverty. If a household's total income is less than the threshold for the applicable family size, age of householder, and number of children present

in the family under 18 years of age, every individual in that household is considered to be living in poverty.

Table 6.
Source: U.S. Department of Commerce. U.S. Census Bureau. American Community Survey.
<http://factfinder.census.gov/>.

The data on health insurance coverage were derived from answers to Question 16 in the American Community Survey (ACS), which was asked of all respondents. Respondents were instructed to report their current coverage and to mark "yes" or "no" for each of the eight types of private and public insurance listed. Health insurance coverage in the ACS and other Census Bureau surveys define coverage to include plans and programs that provide comprehensive health coverage. Plans that provide insurance for specific conditions or situations such as cancer and long-term care policies are not considered coverage. Likewise, other types of insurance like dental, vision, life, and disability insurance are not considered health insurance coverage.

Private health insurance. Coverage through an employer or union, a plan purchased by an individual from a private company, or TRICARE or other military health care.

Public health insurance. Coverage includes the federal programs Medicare, Medicaid, and VA Health Care (provided through the Department of Veterans Affairs); the Children's Health Insurance Program (CHIP); and individual state health plans.

Table 7.
Source: U.S. Department of Labor. Bureau of Labor Statistics. Current Population Survey.
<http://www.bls.gov/cps/>.

Annual data on the labor force, employment, and unemployment for state and local areas are available from two major sources: the Current Population Survey (CPS) and the Local Area Unemployment Statistics (LAUS) program. In Table 7, the data are obtained from the CPS. The CPS is a monthly survey of approximately 60,000 households conducted by the Census Bureau for the Bureau of Labor Statistics. It provides comprehensive data on topics such as the labor force, employment, unemployment, and persons not in the labor force. The data for 2018 in Table 7 are preliminary, so the data may differ slightly from the final table when it is released, but it should be little changed.

Civilian noninstitutional population. Includes persons 16 years of age and older residing in the 50 States and the District of Columbia who are not inmates of institutions (for example, penal and mental facilities, homes for the aged), and who are not on active duty in the Armed Forces.

Civilian labor force. Includes all persons classified as employed or unemployed who are not inmates of institutions (for example, penal and mental facilities, homes for the aged), and who are not on active duty in the Armed Forces. Civilians 16 years of age and over in the noninstitutional population who are not classified as employed or unemployed are defined as not in the labor force.

Employment. Includes persons 16 years and over in the civilian noninstitutional population who, during the reference week, (a) did any work at all (at least 1 hour) as paid employees; worked in their own business, profession, or on their own farm, or worked 15 hours or more as unpaid workers in an enterprise operated by a member of the family; and (b) all those who were not working but who had jobs or businesses from which they were temporarily absent because of vacation, illness, bad weather, childcare problems, maternity or paternity leave, labor-management dispute, job training, or other family or personal reasons, whether or not they were paid for the time off or were seeking other jobs.

Unemployed persons. All civilians who were not employed (according to the above definition) during the reference week, but who were available for work—except for temporary illness—and who had made specific efforts to find employment sometime during the previous four weeks. Persons who did not look for work because they were on layoff are also counted as unemployed.

Unemployment rate. The number of unemployed as a percentage of the civilian labor force.

Table 8.
Source: U.S. Department of Labor. Bureau of Labor Statistics. Local Area Unemployment Statistics. <http://www.bls.gov/lau/home.htm>.

The Local Area Unemployment Statistics (LAUS) program is a Federal-State cooperative effort in which monthly estimates of total employment and unemployment are prepared for approximately 7,300 areas.

The concepts and definitions underlying LAUS data come from the Current Population Survey (CPS), the household survey that is the official measure of the labor force for the nation. State monthly model estimates are controlled in "real time" to sum to national monthly labor force estimates from the CPS. These models combine

current and historical data from the CPS, the Current Employment Statistics (CES) program, and State unemployment insurance (UI) systems. Estimates for seven large areas and their respective balances of State are also model-based. Estimates for the remainder of the substate labor market areas are produced through a building-block approach known as the "Handbook method." This procedure also uses data from several sources, including the CPS, the CES program, State UI systems, and the decennial census, to create estimates that are adjusted to the statewide measures of employment and unemployment. Below the labor market area level, estimates are prepared using disaggregation techniques based on inputs from the decennial census, annual population estimates, and current UI data.

Table 9.
Source: U.S. Department of Commerce. Bureau of Economic Analysis. <http://www.bea.gov/regional>.

In this table, the data by industry reflect the North American Industry Classification System (NAICS), a supply- or production-based system that replaced the Standard Industrial Classification (SIC) system in January 2003. Estimates of state employment and earnings by industry use NAICS. NAICS was adopted to more fully reflect the current composition of U.S. businesses and to establish a standard measure of industry classification throughout the United States, Canada, and Mexico, in accordance with the North American Free Trade Agreement, to enhance cross-border comparisons among these trading partners.

Wage and salary employment. Also referred to as wage and salary jobs, measures the average annual number of full-time and part-time jobs in each area by place-of-work. All jobs for which wages and salaries are paid are counted. Full-time and part-time jobs are counted with equal weight. Jury and witness service, as well as paid employment of prisoners, are not counted as wage and salary employment; the payments for these activities are classified as "other labor income" in the personal income measure. Corporate directorships are counted as self-employment. This concept of employment differs from that in the Current Population Survey (CPS), which is the source of the employment data in the table on population and labor force. The CPS is a household survey. It counts each individual only once, no matter how many jobs the person holds, and it includes only civilian employment.

Wages and salaries. Consist of the monetary remuneration of employees, including corporate officer salaries and bonuses, commissions, pay-in-kind, incentive payments, and tips. It reflects the amount of payments disbursed, but not necessarily earned during the year. Wage and salary disbursements are measured before deductions, such as social security contributions and union dues. In recent years, stock options have become a point of discussion. Wage and salary disbursements include stock options of nonqualified plans at the time that they have been exercised by the individual. Stock options are reported in wage and salary disbursements. The value that is included in wages is the difference between the exercise price and the price that the stock options were granted. Average annual wages and salaries were calculated by the editor by dividing total wages and salaries paid during the year in each sector by total wage and salary employment in that sector.

Table 10.
Source: U.S. Department of Commerce. U.S. Census Bureau. American Community Survey, 2015, 2016, 2017. <http://factfinder.census.gov/>.

Civilian labor force. (See definition under Table 7.)

Employment. (See definition under Table 7.)

Family. A family consists of a householder and one or more other people living in the same household who are related to the householder by birth, marriage, or adoption. All people in a household who are related to the householder are regarded as members of his or her family. A family household may contain people not related to the householder, but those people are not included as part of the householder's family in tabulations. Thus, the number of family households is equal to the number of families, but family households may include more members than do families. A household can contain only one family for purposes of tabulations. Not all households contain families since a household may be comprised of a group of unrelated people or of one person living alone – these are called nonfamily households. Families are classified by type as either a "married-couple family" or "other family" according to the sex of the householder and the presence of relatives. The data on family type are based on answers to questions on sex and relationship that were asked of all people.

Married-couple family. A family in which the householder and his or her spouse are listed as members of the same household.

Other family:

Male householder, no wife present. A family with a male householder and no spouse of householder present.

Female householder, no husband present. A family with a female householder and no spouse of householder present.

Table 11.
Source: U.S. Department of Commerce. U.S. Census Bureau. American Community Survey, 2017. <http://www.census.gov/programs-surveys/acs.html>.

Data on school enrollment and educational attainment were derived from a sample of the population. Persons were classified as enrolled in school if they reported attending a "regular" public or private school (or college) during the year. The instructions were to "include only nursery school, kindergarten, elementary school, and schooling which would lead to a high school diploma or a college degree" as regular school. The Census Bureau defines a public school as "any school or college controlled and supported by a local, county, state, or federal government." Schools primarily supported and controlled by religious organizations or other private groups are defined as private schools.

Data on educational attainment are tabulated for the population 25 years old and over. The data were derived from a question that asked respondents for the highest level of school completed or the highest degree received. Persons who had passed a high school equivalency examination were considered high school graduates. Schooling received in foreign schools was to be reported as the equivalent grade or years in the regular American school system.

Vocational and technical training, such as barber school training; business, trade, technical, and vocational schools; or other training for a specific trade are specifically excluded.

High school graduate or more. This category includes persons whose highest degree was a high school diploma or its equivalent, and those who reported any level higher than a high school diploma.

Bachelor's degree or more. This category includes persons who have received bachelor's degrees, master's degrees, professional school degrees (such as law school or medical school degrees), and doctoral degrees.

Graduate degree or more. This category includes persons who have a master's degree, including the traditional MA and MS degrees and field-specific degrees, such as MSW, MEd, MBA, MLS, and MEng., or a professional school degree: medicine, dentistry, chiropractic, optometry, osteopathic medicine, pharmacy, podiatry, veterinary medicine, law, and theology.

Table 12.
Source: U.S. Department of Education, National Center for Education Statistics. *Common Core of Data.*
<http://nces.ed.gov/ccd/>.

The data are from the Common Core of Data (CCD), which is made up of a set of five surveys sent to state education departments. Most of the data are obtained from administrative records maintained by the state education agencies (SEAs). Statistical information is collected annually from approximately 100,000 public elementary and secondary schools and approximately 18,000 public school districts (including supervisory unions and regional education service agencies) in the 50 states, the District of Columbia, Department of Defense Schools, and the outlying areas. The SEAs compile CCD requested data into prescribed formats and transmit the information to NCES.

A **school district** or Local Education Agency (LEA) is the agency at the local level whose primary responsibility is to operate public schools or to contract for public school services.

The primary grades include pre-kindergarten through grade 4. Middle school grades included grades 5 through 8. High school grades include grades 9 through 12. Ungraded students are included in the total but are not separately listed. Some states have no ungraded students.

The **student-teacher ratio** is calculated by dividing the number of students in all schools by the number of full-time equivalent teachers employed by all schools and agencies.

Current expenditures per student are derived by dividing total current expenditures by the fall student membership count from the CCD. Current expenditures are comprised of expenditures for the day-to-day operation of schools and school districts for public elementary and secondary education, including expenditures for staff salaries and benefits, supplies, and purchased services. They exclude expenditures for construction, equipment, property, debt services, and programs outside of public elementary and secondary education, such as adult education and community services. Student membership consists of the count of students enrolled on or about October 1 and is comparable across all states. Data are for FY 2013; please see the NCES Web site for the exact beginning and ending dates of fiscal years for each state.

The **4-year adjusted cohort graduation rate (ACGR)** is the number of students who graduate in 4 years with a regular high school diploma divided by the number of students who form the adjusted cohort for the graduating class. From the beginning of 9th grade (or the earliest high school grade), students who are entering that grade for the first time form a cohort that is "adjusted" by adding any students who subsequently transfer into the cohort and subtracting any students who subsequently transfer out, emigrate to another country, or die.

Students are eligible for **free and reduced-price lunch** under the National School Lunch Program, which was established by President Truman in 1946. The program is a federally assisted meal program operated in public and private nonprofit schools and residential child care centers and provides cash subsidies for free or reduced-price meals to students based on family size and income criteria. Participation in the National School Lunch Program depends on income, and eligibility is often used to estimate student needs.

An **English language learner** is an individual who, due to any of the reasons listed below, has enough difficulty speaking, reading, writing, or understanding the English language that it affects their ability to learn in an English-speaking classroom. Such an individual (1) was not born in the United States or has a native language other than English; (2) comes from environments where a language other than English is dominant; or (3) is an American Indian or Alaska Native and comes from environments where a language other than English has had a significant impact on the individual's level of English language proficiency.

Individuals with Disabilities Education Act (IDEA) is a federal law requiring services to children with disabilities throughout the nation. IDEA governs how states and public agencies provide early intervention, special education, and related services to eligible infants, toddlers, children, and youth with disabilities. Infants and toddlers with disabilities (birth–age 2) and their families receive early intervention services under IDEA, Part C. Children and youth (ages 3–21) receive special education and related services under IDEA, Part B.

Public School Types

A **special education school** focuses primarily on special education—including instruction for students with any of the following conditions: autism, deaf-blindness, developmental delay, hearing impairment, mental retardation, multiple disabilities, orthopedic impairment, serious emotional disturbance, specific learning disability, speech or language impairment, traumatic brain injury, visual impairment, and other health impairments—and that adapts curriculum, materials, or instruction for students served.

A **vocational education school** focuses primarily on providing formal preparation for semiskilled, skilled, technical, or professional occupations for high school-age students who have opted to develop or expand their employment opportunities, often in lieu of preparing for college entry.

An **alternative education school** is an elementary/secondary school that (1) addresses needs of students that typically cannot be met in a regular school, (2) provides nontraditional education, (3) serves as an adjunct to a regular school, or (4) falls outside the categories of regular, special education, or vocational education.

Table 13.
Source: U.S. Department of Commerce. U.S. Census Bureau. November Supplement to the Current Population Survey (CPS). *Voting and Registration in the Election of November 2018.*
<https://www.census.gov/topics/public-sector/voting/data/tables.html>

Voter participation data are obtained from additional questions regarding voting and voter registration, which are added to the Current Population Survey each November. Because these data are from a sample of the noninstitutional population, they differ from the "official" tally of voter participation reported by the Clerk of the U.S. House of Representatives.

Voting, people eligible to register. The population of voting age includes a considerable number of people who meet the age requirement but cannot register and vote. People who are not citizens are not eligible to vote. Among citizens of voting age, some people are not permitted to vote because they have been committed to penal institutions, mental hospitals, or other institutions, or because they fail to meet state and local resident requirements for various reasons. The eligibility to register is governed by state laws, which differ in many respects.

Registration is the act of qualifying to vote by formally enrolling on a list of voters. People who have moved to another election district must take steps to have their names placed on the voting rolls in their new place of residence.

In a few states or parts of states, no formal registration is required. Voters merely present themselves at the polling place on Election Day with proof that they are of age and have met the appropriate residence requirements. Therefore, in these areas people who are citizens and of voting age, and who meet the residence requirement, would be considered as being registered.

Voter, reported participation. Voter participation data are derived from replies to the following question asked of people (excluding noncitizens) of voting age: "In any election some people are not able to vote because they are sick or busy, or have some other reason, and others do not want to vote. Did (this person) vote in the election held on November (date varies)?"

Those of voting age were classified as "voted" or "did not vote." In most tables, this "did not vote" class includes those reported as "did not vote," "do not know," noncitizens, and nonrespondents. Nonrespondents and people who reported that they did not know if they voted were included in the "did not vote" class because of the general over-reporting by respondents in the sample.

Voter, reported registration. The data on registration were obtained by tabulating replies to the following question for those people included in the category "did not vote." "Was (this person) registered to vote in the November (date varies) election?"

All people reported as having voted were assumed to have been registered. Therefore, the total registered population is obtained by combining the number of people who voted and people included in the category "did not vote," but who had registered.

Table 14.
Source: U.S. Department of Justice. Federal Bureau of Investigation. Uniform Crime Reports. *Crime in the United States, 2017.*
<https://ucr.fbi.gov/crime-in-the-u.s/2017/crime-in-the-u.s.-2017>

The Uniform Crime Reports (UCR) Program, administered by the Federal Bureau of Investigation (FBI), was created in 1929 and collects information on the following crimes reported to law enforcement authorities: murder and nonnegligent manslaughter, rape, robbery, aggravated assault, burglary, larceny-theft, motor vehicle theft, and arson. Law enforcement agencies also report arrest data for 21 additional crime categories.

The UCR Program compiles data from monthly law enforcement reports and from individual crime incident records transmitted directly to the FBI or to centralized state agencies that report to the FBI. The program thoroughly examines each report it receives for reasonableness, accuracy, and deviations that may indicate errors. Large variations in crime levels may indicate modified records procedures, incomplete reporting, or changes in a jurisdiction's boundaries. To identify any unusual fluctuations in an agency's crime counts, the program compares monthly reports to previous submissions of the agency and to those for similar agencies.

The FBI annually publishes its findings in a preliminary release in the spring of the following calendar year, followed by a detailed annual report, *Crime in the United States*, issued in the fall. (The printed copy of *Crime in the United States* is published by Bernan Press.) In addition to crime counts and trends, this report includes data on crimes cleared, persons arrested (age, sex, and race), law enforcement personnel (including the number of sworn officers killed or assaulted), and the characteristics of homicides (including age, sex, and race of victims and offenders; victim-offender relationships; weapons used; and circumstances surrounding the homicides). Other periodic reports are also available from the UCR Program. Any deviations from UCR standard data are noted in the table.

Note for Users

Since crime is a sociological phenomenon influenced by a variety of factors, the FBI discourages data users from ranking agencies and using the data as a measurement of the effectiveness of law enforcement. Until data users examine all the variables that affect crime in a town, city, county, state, region, or college or university, they can make no meaningful comparisons.

Violent crime is composed of four offenses: murder and nonnegligent manslaughter, rape, robbery, and aggravated assault. According to the UCR Program's definition, violent crimes involve force or threat of force.

Murder and nonnegligent manslaughter is the willful (nonnegligent) killing of one human being by another. Deaths caused by negligence, attempts to kill, assaults to kill, suicides, and accidental deaths are excluded. The program classifies justifiable homicides separately and limits the definition to (1) the killing of a felon by a law enforcement officer in the line of duty; or (2) the killing of a felon, during the commission of a felony, by a private citizen.

Rape is defined as: penetration, no matter how slight, of the vagina or anus with any body part or object, or oral penetration by a sex organ of another person, without the consent of the victim. The FBI UCR Program's definition of rape, formerly "forcible rape," was revised in 2013. Attempts or assaults to commit rape are also included; however, statutory rape (no force used—victim is under the age of consent) and incest are excluded. Due to the revised definition, figures for rape in 2013 and later are not comparable to data from previous years. North

Carolina's agencies submitted rape data according to the legacy definition of rape. Use caution when comparing the rape data for North Carolina in this volume to that of other states.

Robbery is the taking or attempted taking of anything of value from the care, custody, or control of a person or persons by force or threat of force or violence and/or by putting the victim in fear.

Aggravated assault is an unlawful attack by one person upon another for the purpose of inflicting severe or aggravated bodily injury. This type of assault usually is accompanied by the use of a weapon or by means likely to produce death or great bodily harm. Attempted aggravated assaults that involve the display of—or threat to use—a gun, knife, or other weapon is included in this crime category because serious personal injury would likely result if the assault were completed. When aggravated assault and larceny-theft occur together, the offense falls under the category of robbery. Simple assaults are excluded.

Property crime includes the offenses of burglary, larceny-theft, motor vehicle theft, and arson. The object of the theft-type offenses is the taking of money or property, but there is no force or threat of force against the victims. The property crime category includes arson because the offense involves the destruction of property; however, arson victims may be subjected to force.

Burglary (breaking or entering) is the unlawful entry of a structure to commit a felony or a theft. The use of force to gain entry need not have occurred. The Program has three subclassifications for burglary: forcible entry, unlawful entry where no force is used, and attempted forcible entry. The UCR definition of "structure" includes, for example, apartment, barn, house trailer or houseboat when used as a permanent dwelling, office, railroad car (but not automobile), stable, and vessel (i.e., ship).

Larceny-theft (except motor vehicle theft) is the unlawful taking, carrying, leading, or riding away of property from the possession or constructive possession of another. Examples are thefts of bicycles or automobile accessories, shoplifting, pocket-picking, or the stealing of any property or article that is not taken by force and violence or by fraud. Attempted larcenies are included. Embezzlement, confidence games, forgery, worthless checks, and the like, are excluded.

Motor vehicle theft is the theft or attempted theft of a motor vehicle. It includes the stealing of automobiles, trucks, buses, motorcycles, snowmobiles, and the like. The taking of a motor vehicle for temporary use by persons having lawful access is excluded from this definition. A motor vehicle is self-propelled and runs on land surface and not on rails. Motorboats, construction equipment, airplanes, and farming equipment are specifically excluded from this category.

Table 15.
Source: U.S. Department of Commerce. U.S Census Bureau.
<http://www.census.gov/govs/index.html>.

The Census Bureau conducts an annual survey covering a range of government finance activities carried out by all state and local governments in the United States, including revenue, expenditures, debt, and assets. The data in this volume relate to state revenues and expenditures only, with the exception of the District of Columbia, for which local government data was used. Data generally reference state government fiscal year 2017, but data for the District of Columbia is for fiscal year 2016. General revenue comprises all revenue except utilities, liquor store, and insurance trust revenue. Intergovernmental revenue is funds from other governments (mainly the federal government), including general support, grants, shared taxes, and loans or advances. Other data on government finance by state, not shown in this volume, include federal government expenditures, obligations, contract awards, and insurance programs.

Table 16.
Source: U.S. Department of Commerce. U.S. Census Bureau.
<http://www.census.gov/govs/statetax/>.

State tax data include all required taxes taken by government for public purposes, except for employer and employee assessments for Social Security and unemployment compensation. The data are shown in this volume are for each state's and the District of Columbia's fiscal year 2018.

INDEX